MW00783282

PRENTICE HALL

WORLD
HISTORY

VOLUME 1

Elisabeth Gaynor Ellis
Anthony Esler

PEARSON
Prentice
Hall

Boston, Massachusetts
Upper Saddle River, New Jersey

Authors

Elisabeth Gaynor Ellis

Elisabeth Gaynor Ellis holds a BS from Smith College and an MA and MS from Columbia University. Before she began writing textbooks, Ms. Ellis taught World Cultures, European History, and Russian Studies in Ardsley, New York. Ms. Ellis co-authored Prentice Hall's *World Cultures: A Global Mosaic*, and *World History: Connections to Today* with Dr. Anthony Esler. Ms. Ellis has also written other social studies materials, including *America's Holidays*, individual state histories, and a variety of Teacher's Edition materials. Ms. Ellis is currently working on a middle grades curriculum on Korea as well as a historical novel.

Anthony Esler

Anthony Esler is an emeritus professor of history at the College of William and Mary in Williamsburg, Virginia. His books include several studies of the conflict of generations in world history, half a dozen historical novels, and two other surveys of world and Western history besides this one. He is a member of the American Historical Association, the World History Association, and the Authors Guild. He has received Fulbright, Social Science Research Council, and other research grants, and is listed in the *Directory of American Scholars*, the *Directory of Poets and Fiction Writers*, and *Who's Who in America*. Books by Dr. Esler include *Bombs, Beards, and Barricades*, *Forbidden City*, and *The Human Venture*.

Senior Consultant

Burton F. Beers

Burton F. Beers is a retired professor of History from North Carolina State University. He has taught European history, Asian history, and American history. Dr. Beers has published numerous articles in historical journals and several books, including *The Far East: A History of Western Impacts and Eastern Responses*, with Paul H. Clyde, and *World History: Patterns of Civilization*.

Senior Reading Consultants

Kate Kinsella

Kate Kinsella, EdD, a specialist in second-language and adolescent literacy, is a faculty member in the Department of Secondary Education at San Francisco State University. Her teaching addresses language and literacy development across the secondary curricula. Dr. Kinsella earned her MA in TESOL from San Francisco State University, and her EdD in Second Language Acquisition from the University of San Francisco.

Kevin Feldman

Kevin Feldman, EdD, is the Director of Reading and Early Intervention with the Sonoma County Office of Education (SCOE) and an independent educational consultant. At the SCOE, he develops, organizes, and monitors programs related to K-12 literacy. Dr. Feldman has an MA in Special Education, Learning Disabilities and Instructional Design from the University of California, Riverside. He earned his EdD in Curriculum and Instruction from the University of San Francisco.

Cover and title page image: Terracotta sculpture of Ife king, c. 12th century

Acknowledgments appear on page 751, which constitutes an extension of this copyright page.

Copyright © 2008 by Pearson Education, Inc., publishing as Pearson Prentice Hall, Boston, Massachusetts 02116. All rights reserved. Printed in the United States of America. This publication is protected by copyright, and permission should be obtained from the publisher prior to any prohibited reproduction, storage in a retrieval system, or transmission in any form or by any means, electronic, mechanical, photocopying, recording, or likewise. For information regarding permission(s), write to: Rights and Permissions Department, One Lake Street, Upper Saddle River, New Jersey 07458.

Discovery School® is a registered trademark of Discovery Communications, Inc. Use of the trademark implies no relationship, sponsorship, endorsement, sale, or promotion on the part of Pearson Prentice Hall.

Pearson Prentice Hall™ is a trademark of Pearson Education, Inc.

Pearson® is a registered trademark of Pearson plc.

Prentice Hall® is a registered trademark of Pearson Education, Inc.

ISBN 0-13-360050-5

2 3 4 5 6 7 8 9 10   10 09 08 07

Academic Reviewers

Africa
Barbara B. Brown, PhD
African Studies Center
Boston University
Boston, Massachusetts

Ancient World
Maud W. Gleason
Department of Classics
Stanford University
Stanford, California

Evelyn DeLong Mangie, PhD
Department of History
University of South Florida
Tampa, Florida

David Pilbeam
Biological Anthropology
Harvard University
Cambridge, Massachusetts

Chicano/a Studies
Shirlene Soto
Chicano/a Studies
California State University,
    Northridge
Northridge, California

East Asia
Mark Arlen Peterson
Coordinator of Asian Studies
Brigham Young University
Provo, Utah

Economics
Mark V. Siegler
Department of Economics
California State University,
    Sacramento
Sacramento, California

Medieval Europe
Kathryn Reyerson
Department of History
University of Minnesota
Minneapolis, Minnesota

Modern Europe
Douglas R. Skopp, PhD
Distinguished University Teaching
    Professor, History Department
State University of New York at
    Plattsburgh
Plattsburgh, New York

Religion
Susan Douglass
Education Consultant
Falls Church, Virginia

Shabbir Mansuri
Founding Director
Council on Islamic Education
Fountain Valley, California

Gordon D. Newby
Middle Eastern and South Asian
    Studies
Emory University
Atlanta, Georgia

William L. Pitts, Jr.
Religion Department
Baylor University
Waco, Texas

Benjamin Ravid
Near Eastern and Judaic Studies
Brandeis University
Waltham, Massachusetts

Russia and Eastern Europe
Bradley F. Abrams
Department of History
Columbia University
New York, New York

South Asia
Susan S. Wadley
Anthropology Department
Syracuse University
Syracuse, New York

Southeast Asia and the Pacific Rim
Barbara S. Gaerlan
Center for Southeast Asian Studies
University of California, Los Angeles
Los Angeles, California

Southwest Asia
Palmira Brummett
Department of History
University of Tennessee
Knoxville, Tennessee

Women's History
Lyn Reese
Women in World History Curriculum
Berkeley, California

Teacher Reviewers

Jonathan Barnett
John Adams High School
Ozone Park, New York

Stephen Bullick
Mt. Lebanon School District
Pittsburgh, Pennsylvania

Elizabeth DeFreitas
East Islip HS 1
Islip Terrace, New York

Todd E. Gibson
Muncie Central High School
Muncie, Indiana

Mayrene A. Graef
Heritage High School
Newport News, Virginia

Sheila Hanley
James Madison High School
Brooklyn, New York

Geraldine L. Hayes
Louis D. Brandeis High School
New York, New York

Jennifer Herman
Winters Mill High School
Westminster, Maryland

Aimee Horowitz, JD
College of Staten Island High School
    for International Studies
Staten Island, New York

David Kenewell
California Community Schools
Sterling Heights, Michigan

Mary Oppegard
Oklahoma Baptist University
Shawnee, Oklahoma

Richard Renyer
Eleanor Roosevelt High School
Greenbelt, Maryland

James A. Weidemoyer
School District of Lancaster
Lancaster, Pennsylvania

Social Studies Master Teacher Board

Peggy Althof
District 11 Colorado Springs
Colorado Springs, Colorado

Kathy Deforge
Marcellus Central Schools
Marcellus, New York

Roceal Duke
District of Columbia Public Schools
Washington, D.C.

Pam Gothart
Sparkman High School
Harvest, Alabama

Tom Gray
De Ruyter Central School
De Ruyter, New York

Maureen Mackin
Downsville Central School
Downsville, New York

Barbara McCarry
Chicago Public Schools
Chicago, Illinois

Deborah Miller
Detroit Public Schools
Detroit, Michigan

Steve Missal
Plainfield Public Schools
Plainfield, New Jersey

Jeanne Salvado
Bethesda-Chevy Chase High School
Bethesda, Maryland

Deborah Washington
Boston Public Schools Unified Student
   Services
Dorchester, Massachusetts

Reading Consultants

Kate Kinsella
Department of Secondary Education
San Francisco State University
San Francisco, California

Kevin Feldman
Director of Reading and Early
   Intervention
Sonoma County Office of Education
Santa Rosa, California

Differentiated Instruction Writers

Colleen Blankenship
Brookwood High School
Snellville, Georgia

Kerry Dunne
Framingham High School
Framingham, Massachusetts

Grant Miller
Boston College
Newton, Massachusetts

Adam Steiner
Westborough High School
Westborough, Massachusetts

Matthew Underwood
Francis W. Parker Charter
   Essential School
Devens, Massachusetts

Differentiated Instruction Advisory Board

Don Deshler
Professor of Special Education
   (Learning Disabilities)
University of Kansas
Lawrence, Kansas

Anthony Bashir
Associate Professor of Language
   and Speech
Emerson College
Boston, Massachusetts

Cathy Collins Block
Professor of Curriculum and
   Instruction
Texas Christian University
Fort Worth, Texas

Anna Uhl Chamot
Professor of Secondary Education
   (ESL)
George Washington University
Washington, D.C.

John Guthrie
Professor of Human Development
University of Maryland
College Park, Maryland

Susan Miller
Professor of Education
University of Nevada, Las Vegas
Las Vegas, Nevada

Jennifer Platt
Associate Dean of the College of
   Education
University of Central Florida
Orlando, Florida

Teacher's Edition Consultants

Steven Goldberg
New Rochelle High School
New Rochelle, New York

Diane Hart
Social Studies Author and Assessment
   Consultant
Menlo Park, California

Sam Intrator
Smith College
Northampton, Massachusetts

John Poggio
Professor, Department of Educational
   Psychology and Research
University of Kansas
Lawrence, Kansas

Program Advisors

Michal Howden
Social Studies Consultant
Zionsville, Indiana

Kathy Lewis
Social Studies Consultant
Fort Worth, Texas

Joe Wieczorek
Social Studies Consultant
Baltimore, Maryland

TABLE OF CONTENTS

Before you begin your study of World History, use the pages listed below to help you prepare for success.

Skills Handbook   SH1

Your success in this World History course depends on your ability to read and think critically and to demonstrate your knowledge through writing and speaking. Use this series of skills handbooks as a reference throughout the course.

Concept Connector Handbooks   664

The Concept Connector handbooks provide you with reference information that will make it easier for you to compare key concepts across time.

▼ A young archaeologist takes measurements.

UNIT 1

EARLY CIVILIZATIONS

(Prehistory–A.D. 1570)

▲ Phoenician vase

◀ Spartan woman athlete

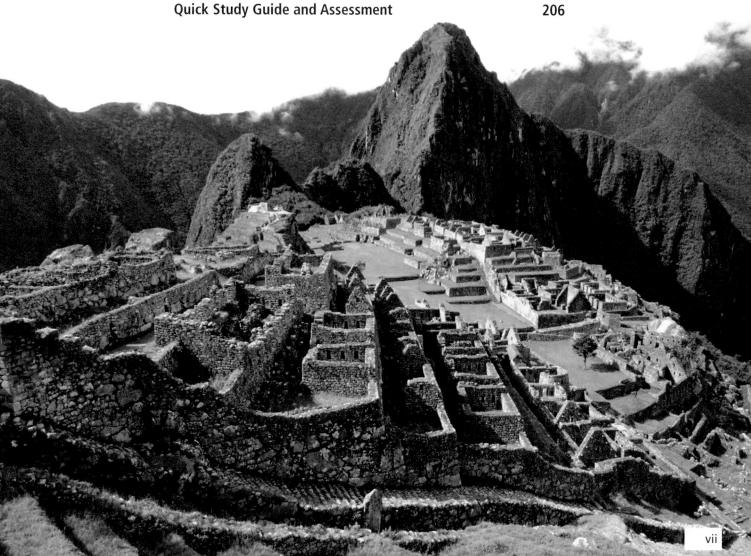

▼ Ruins of Machu Picchu, Peru

▲ Mehmet II

▼ Bayeux Tapestry,
c. 1000s

▲ Copernican (top) and Ptolemaic (bottom) solar systems

UNIT 4

ENLIGHTENMENT AND REVOLUTION

(1700–1850)

▲ Catherine the Great

SPECIAL FEATURES AND MULTIMEDIA

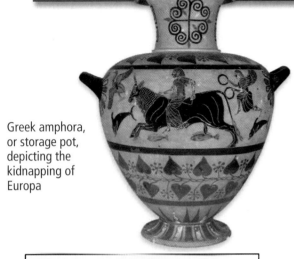

Greek amphora, or storage pot, depicting the kidnapping of Europa

Zeus Kidnaps Europa

"Europa, the beautiful daughter of the king of Phoenicia, was gathering flowers when she saw a bull quietly grazing with her father's herds. The bull was actually Zeus, king of all the Greek gods, who had fallen in love with her. When Europa reached up to place flowers on his horns, he suddenly bounded into the air and carried the weeping princess far across the Mediterranean Sea to the island of Crete. Eventually, Europa married the king of Crete and gave her name to a new continent—Europe."

 AUDIO

WITNESS HISTORY AUDIO

Primary source audio accounts throughout the text bring the voices and sounds of history to life.*

*Available on Witness History Audio CD and online at PHSchool.com

WITNESS HISTORY VIDEO

Witness History Discovery School™ videos for each chapter bring
the events you read about in the text to life.

Ruins of Great
Zimbabwe

History Interactive   Events That Changed the World

Audio, video, and animation-filled features help you explore
major turning points in history.

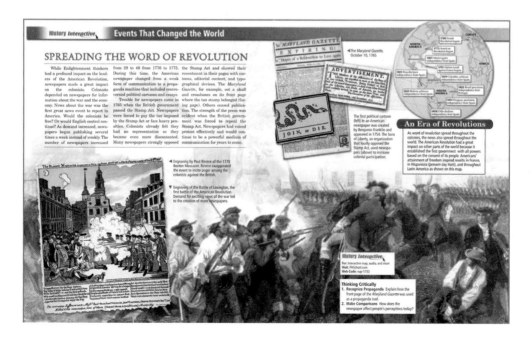

Primary Sources

Full page excerpts allow you to relive history through eyewitness accounts and documents.

In-text Primary Sources

Gain insights as you read by reading the words of people who were there.

Traveler's Tales

View historic places through the eyes of those who traveled there.

COMPARING VIEWPOINTS

Explore issues by analyzing two opposing viewpoints.

HUMANITIES

Experience great literature and arts from around the world.

Make Connections

SPECIAL FEATURES AND MULTIMEDIA

BIOGRAPHIES

Meet fascinating history makers.

INFOGRAPHICS

Photographs, maps, charts, illustrations, audio, and text help you understand the significance of important historical events and developments.

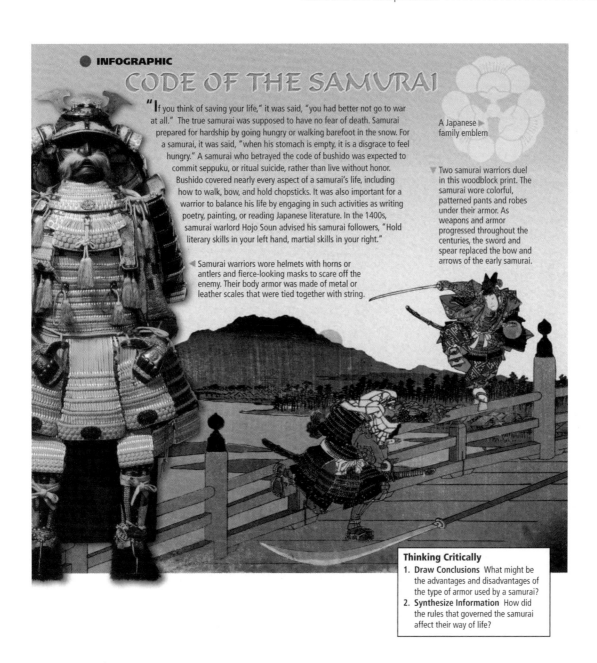

● **INFOGRAPHIC**

CODE OF THE SAMURAI

"If you think of saving your life," it was said, "you had better not go to war at all." The true samurai was supposed to have no fear of death. Samurai prepared for hardship by going hungry or walking barefoot in the snow. For a samurai, it was said, "when his stomach is empty, it is a disgrace to feel hungry." A samurai who betrayed the code of bushido was expected to commit seppuku, or ritual suicide, rather than live without honor. Bushido covered nearly every aspect of a samurai's life, including how to walk, bow, and hold chopsticks. It was also important for a warrior to balance his life by engaging in such activities as writing poetry, painting, or reading Japanese literature. In the 1400s, samurai warlord Hojo Soun advised his samurai followers, "Hold literary skills in your left hand, martial skills in your right."

A Japanese ▶ family emblem

▼ Two samurai warriors duel in this woodblock print. The samurai wore colorful, patterned pants and robes under their armor. As weapons and armor progressed throughout the centuries, the sword and spear replaced the bow and arrows of the early samurai.

◀ Samurai warriors wore helmets with horns or antlers and fierce-looking masks to scare off the enemy. Their body armor was made of metal or leather scales that were tied together with string.

Thinking Critically
1. **Draw Conclusions** What might be the advantages and disadvantages of the type of armor used by a samurai?
2. **Synthesize Information** How did the rules that governed the samurai affect their way of life?

Document Based Assessment

Practice the art and science of a historian by analyzing an event by examining multiple historical documents, data, and images.

Cause and Effect

Diagrams help you see the short- and long-term causes and effects of history's most important events.

Charts and Graphs

Diagrams and data help you understand history through visuals.

Charts and Graphs

Maps Geography Interactive

Interactive maps and Audio Guided Tours for each map with a Web code help you understand where history happened.

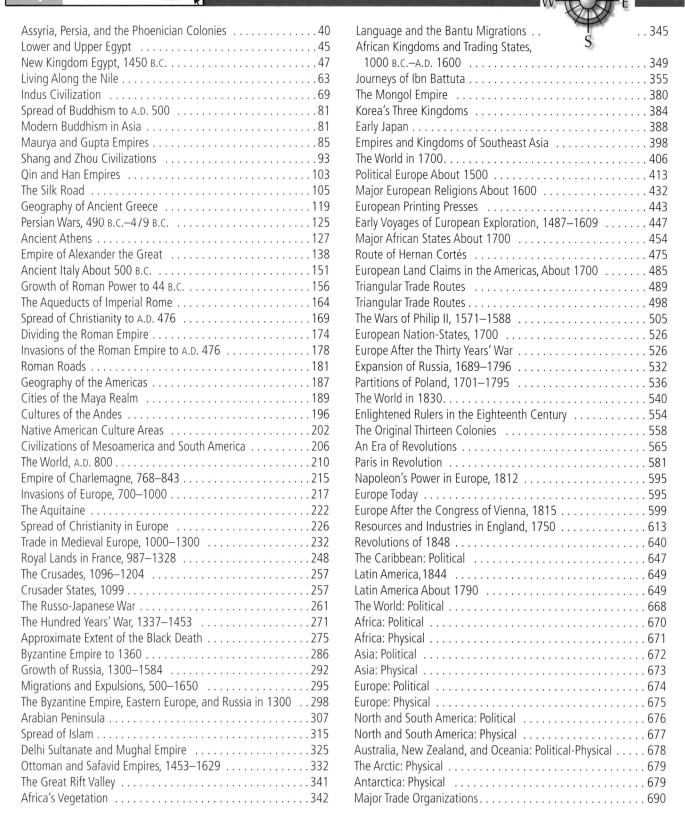

Maps Geography *Interactive*

Keys to Unlocking
WORLD HISTORY

Learning about the entire span of World History is no small task. Luckily, your text and its companion Web site—PHSchool.com—come with a number of important tools to make your study of World History easier and more worthwhile.

Experience the Drama of History

WITNESS HISTORY

- **Witness History Audio**
  Throughout your text, you'll notice audio symbols like this 🔊 AUDIO that indicate sound clips that you can listen to to make the history on the page come alive. These clips are available on the Witness History Audio CD.

- **Witness History Video**
  What did it feel like to live during the Middle Ages? **Witness History Discovery School™** video program brings the sights and sounds of times like this to life in every chapter.

History *Interactive*

Some events in history are so dramatic that words alone cannot convey their impact. For these events we've created online interactive Web sites where you'll hear audio clips of people who were there; see photos, maps, and timelines; and view animations to help you experience the full drama of history. Use the Web Codes in your text to go directly to the action.

History *Interactive*
Go Online at PHSchool.com
For: Interactive map, audio, and more
Visit: PHSchool.com
Web Code: nap-0852
Use the Web Codes that appear throughout this book to access additional information and activities.
1. Go to PHSchool.com.
2. Enter the Web code.
3. Click Go.

Key Concepts

■ **History**
Empire
Cooperation
Conflict
Revolution
Nationalism
Genocide

■ **Government**
Democracy
Political Systems
Dictatorship

■ **Geography**
Migration
Geography's Impact
People and the
   Environment

■ **Economics**
Trade
Economic Systems

■ **Culture**
Cultural Diffusion
Belief Systems

■ **Science and
Technology**
Advances in
   Science
Advances in
   Technology

Make Connections

Concept Connector

The job of a historian requires more than studying events as they unfolded chronologically. Historians must also look for patterns across time and place. We've created a set of tools to help you do just that. The Concept Connector system was designed to help you connect 18 key concepts across time.

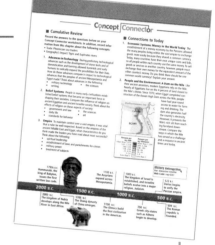

◀ Concept Connector Features

Each of the 18 concepts that you'll be tracking during the course is defined and described in features throughout the text.

Cumulative Review and Connections to Today ▶

Cumulative Review and Connections to Today appear on the Concept Connector page at the end of each chapter. Cumulative Review questions will help you make connections between chapter events and earlier events. Connections to Today will help you make connections between chapter events and more current events.

◀ Concept Connector Worksheets

Complete these worksheets over the course of the year to help you see patterns across time. There are 18 worksheets in all, one for each of the key concepts listed on this page. You can access and print the Concept Connector Worksheets at PHSchool.com. At the end of each chapter, Cumulative Review questions will direct you to record information on your worksheets. At the end of the course, you can use the completed worksheets to prepare for thematic essays that may appear on your tests.

Concept Connector Handbooks ▶

A series of six handbooks at the end of your text provides you with important reference materials to help you see patterns across time and compare and contrast concepts over time.

Develop Key Skills

Geography *Interactive*

Historical maps are important for understanding where events took place, so we've created easy-to-read maps for your exploration. To make sure you get the most out of each map, we've also provided you with your own historian to take you on an audio-guided tour of each map. You can access these audio tours through the Web Codes provided in your text.

Some of the maps in your text are interactive. Online versions of the map will allow you to see how events shown on the map unfolded over time or will give you additional images and information to make the places shown on the map come alive.

Go Online at PHSchool.com

Geography *Interactive*

For: Audio guided tour
Visit: PHSchool.com
Web Code: nap-1041
Use the Web Codes that appear throughout this book to access additional information and activities.
1. Go to PHSchool.com.
2. Enter the Web code.
3. Click Go.

SKILLS
Handbook

The Skills Handbook at the front of this text allows you to brush up on important skills at the beginning of the course or at any time you need help.

- ## Reading Informational Texts
  Reading a text is not the same as reading a novel. Make the most of the time you spend reading your text and improve your reading comprehension by looking at some proven reading strategies to use before you read, while you read, and after you read.

- ## Writing Handbook
  Learning to be a good writer is key to your success in this class, on tests, and in life. Use this part of the Skills Handbook to study models of good writing and to learn hints for writing various types of essays, including expository and persuasive essays.

- ## Geography Skills Handbook
  Maps cover core information in a visual format and expand on concepts taught in the text. Improving your ability to read and understand maps will help you succeed in this course and in other history classes.

- ## Critical Thinking About Texts, Visuals, and Media Sources
  As a practicing historian, you need to train yourself to think critically about everything you read, see, and hear. Is what you're reading accurate? Biased? Use this part of the Skills Handbook to practice your critical thinking skills.

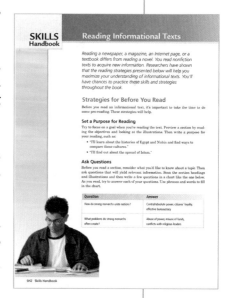

- ## Speaking and Listening
  Speaking is another way to demonstrate what you've learned. Good listening is another key to success in every classroom. Look for key tips on how to prepare a presentation and how to listen actively in this part of the Skills Handbook.

Prepare for Tests

Note Taking

Throughout most of this course, you'll be reading and studying information as it occurred chronologically. In each section of the text, you'll find suggestions for how to take notes using graphic organizers, timelines, and outlines. Complete these graphic organizers in your own notebook, in your Reading and Note Taking Study Guide, or on the Note Taking Worksheets for each section, which you can download at PHSchool.com. If you complete all of the suggested note taking strategies, you'll be able to use your notes to prepare for chapter, midterm, and high stakes end-of-course tests.

Progress Monitoring *Online*

Web Codes at the end of every section take you to an online quiz with multiple-choice questions on section content and vocabulary. At the end of every chapter, you'll find an online self-test on chapter content and a crossword puzzle to test your vocabulary mastery. Both quizzes and tests provide you with instant help to prepare you for in-class exams.

Go Online at PHSchool.com

Progress Monitoring *Online*
For: Self-test with vocabulary practice
Web Code: naa-0861

Quick Study Guide

In addition to the note taking graphics that you create yourself, we've provided some for each chapter on the end-of-chapter Quick Study pages. Use these pages to review for tests and to make sure you've mastered the content in the chapter. The Quick Study pages also include a timeline of key events discussed in the chapter. Interactive versions of these timelines are available online at PHSchool.com.

Document-Based Assessment

To prepare you for document-based questions on in-class and high-stakes tests, each chapter ends with a page of Document-Based Assessment. Each of these pages contains several documents followed by multiple-choice questions that help you analyze documents and practice your map, graph, visual learning, and critical reading skills. A writing task helps you compare, contrast, and draw conclusions about the various documents.

SKILLS Handbook

Contents

A series of handbooks provide skills instruction to help you read, learn, and demonstrate your knowledge of world history.

Reading Informational Texts

Writing Handbook

Geography Skills Handbook

Critical Thinking About Texts, Visuals, and Media Sources

Speaking and Listening

Reading Informational Texts

Reading a newspaper, a magazine, an Internet page, or a textbook differs from reading a novel. You read nonfiction texts to acquire new information. Researchers have shown that the reading strategies presented below will help you maximize your understanding of informational texts. You'll have chances to practice these skills and strategies throughout the book.

Strategies for Before You Read

Before you read an informational text, it's important to take the time to do some pre-reading. These strategies will help.

Set a Purpose for Reading

Try to focus on a goal when you're reading the text. Preview a section by reading the objectives and looking at the illustrations. Then write a purpose for your reading, such as:

- "I'll learn about the histories of Egypt and Nubia and find ways to compare these cultures."
- "I'll find out about the spread of Islam."

Ask Questions

Before you read a section, consider what you'd like to know about a topic. Then ask questions that will yield relevant information. Scan the section headings and illustrations and then write a few questions in a chart like the one below. As you read, try to answer each of your questions. Use phrases and words to fill in the chart.

Question	Answer
How do strong monarchs unite nations?	Central/absolute power, citizens' loyalty, effective bureaucracy
What problems do strong monarchs often create?	Abuse of power, misuse of funds, conflicts with religious leaders

Predict

Engage in the reading process by making predictions about what you are preparing to learn. Scan the section headings and the visuals. Then write a prediction, such as:

- "I will find out what caused feudalism in Europe to develop and later to disappear."

Keep your predictions in mind as you read—do they turn out to be accurate or do you need to revise them?

Use Prior Knowledge

Research shows that if you connect the new information in your reading to your prior knowledge, you'll be more likely to remember the new information. You'll also see the value of studying history if you see how it connects to the present. After previewing a section, create a chart like this one. Complete the chart as you read the section.

What I Know	What I Want to Know	What I Learned
Many people today are Calvinists or Lutherans.	How and when did these religions begin?	John Calvin and Martin Luther led people to start new Protestant churches during the sixteenth-century Reformation.

Strategies for During Reading

It's important to be an active reader. Use these strategies as you read an informational text.

Reread or Read Ahead

If you don't understand a certain passage, reread it to look for connections among the words and sentences. For example, look for cause-and-effect words that link ideas, or sequence words that show when events took place. Or, try reading ahead to see if the ideas are clarified later on. Once you find new clarifying information, return to the confusing text and read it again with the new information in mind.

Paraphrase

To paraphrase is to restate information in your own words, as in the example below. Paraphrasing is a good way to check your understanding of the reading. Think of it this way—if you can explain it to someone else, you understand it.

Original Paragraph	Paraphrase
When Ireland won independence in 1922, Britain retained control of six northern counties where there was a Protestant majority. Faced with widespread discrimination, Catholics demanded civil rights and the reunification of Ireland. Protestants wanted to remain part of Britain.	After Irish independence in 1922, Britain controlled six Protestant-dominated counties in the north. People in these counties divided along religious lines: Catholics called for both civil rights and reunification of the Irish nation; Protestants supported British control.

Summarize

Summarizing—a version of paraphrasing—can also help you confirm your understanding of the text. Summarizing focuses on restating the main ideas of a passage, as you can see in the example below. Include a few important details, such as the time period, to orient yourself or other readers to the text.

Original Paragraph	Summary
Ottoman expansion threatened the crumbling Byzantine empire. After several failed attempts to capture Constantinople, Muhammad II finally succeeded in 1453. Over the next 200 years, the Ottoman empire continued to expand.	The Byzantine empire gave way to the Ottoman empire around 1453, resulting in 200 years of Ottoman rule.

Identify Main Ideas and Details

A main idea is the most important point in a paragraph or section of text. Some main ideas are stated directly, but others are implied. You must determine these yourself by reading carefully. Pause occasionally to make sure you can identify the main idea.

Main idea

Europeans continued to seek new routes around or through the Americas. In 1513, the Spanish adventurer Vasco Núñez de Balboa, with the help of Native Americans, hacked a passage through the tropical forests of Panama to reach what he called the South Sea. In November 1529, Spanish nobleman Ferdinand Magellan sailed through a passage at the tip of South America. After a difficult journey filled with brutal storms, rushing tides, and unpredictable winds, Magellan's ships emerged into Balboa's South Sea, which Magellan renamed the Pacific—that is, peaceful—Ocean.

Main ideas are supported by details. Record main ideas and details in an outline format like the one shown here.

Main idea

Details

European Exploration in the Americas
I. Continued as Europeans sought new routes around or through the Americas
   A. Balboa and Native Americans found a passage across Panama.
   B. Balboa named the South Sea.
   C. Magellan found passage around tip of South America.
   D. Magellan reached the South Sea and renamed it the Pacific Ocean.

Vocabulary

Here are several strategies to help you understand the meaning of a word you do not recognize.

Use Context Clues You can often define an unfamiliar word with clues from the surrounding text. For example, in the sentence "Crusaders fought on and off for more than 200 years, and many died for their cause," the words *fought* and *died* are clues indicating that a Crusader was someone who fought wars. Context clues can be in the same sentence as the unfamiliar word or in nearby sentences or paragraphs.

Analyze Word Parts Use your knowledge of word parts to help you define unfamiliar words. Break the word into its parts—root, prefix, suffix. What do you know about these parts? For example, the suffixes *–ify* and *–ation* mean "make into" and "action or process." The word *desertify* means "turn into a desert." *Desertification* means "the process of turning into a desert."

Recognize Word Origins Another way to figure out the meaning of an unfamiliar word is to understand the word's origins. Use your knowledge of Greek or Latin roots, for example, to build meaning. The words *formation* and *reformation* contain the Latin root *form,* which means "shape." *Formation* is the shape in which something is arranged. *Reformation* is a change in the shape of an idea or institution.

Analyze the Text's Structure

Just as you organize a story about your weekend to highlight the most important parts, authors will organize their writing to stress their key ideas. Analyzing text structure can help you tap into this organization. In a social studies text, the author frequently uses one of the structures listed in the chart at right to organize information. Learn to identify structures in texts and you'll remember text information more effectively.

Analyze the Author's Purpose

Different reading materials are written with different goals, or purposes. For example, this book is written to teach you about world history. The technical manual that accompanies computer software is written to teach readers how to use the product. In a newspaper, some articles will be written to inform readers about news events, while editorials will be written to persuade readers to accept a particular view about those events.

> ### Structures for Organizing Information
>
> **Compare and Contrast** Here, an author highlights similarities and differences between two or more ideas, cultures, processes, people, etc. Look for clue words such as *on the other hand* or *similarly.*
>
> **Sequence** Here, an author recounts the order in which events occurred or steps were taken. History is often told in chronological sequence but can also involve flashbacks from later times to earlier times. Look for sequence words such as *initially, later,* and *ultimately.*
>
> **Cause and Effect** Here, an author highlights the impact of one event on another or the effects of key events. Cause and effect is critical to understanding history because events in one time often strongly influence those in later times. Look for clue words such as *because, so,* or *as a result.*

An author's purpose influences not only how the material is presented but also how you read it. Thus you must identify the purpose, whether it is stated directly or merely suggested. If it is not directly stated, use clues in the text—such as opinion words in an editorial—to identify the author's purpose.

Distinguish Between Facts and Opinions/Recognize Bias

It's important to read actively, especially when reading informational texts. Decide whether information is factual—which means it can be proven—or if it includes opinions or bias—that is, people's views or evaluations.

Anytime you read material that conveys opinions, such as an editorial, keep an eye out for author bias. This bias might be revealed in the use of emotionally charged words or faulty logic. For example, the newspaper editorial below includes factual statements (in blue) and opinion statements (in red). Underlined words are emotionally charged words—they'll get a rise out of people. Faulty logic (in green) may include circular reasoning that returns to its beginning and either/or arguments that ignore other possibilities.

Editorial

In 1993, the people of Brazil voted to keep their government a republic rather than revert to a monarchy. Voters chose between the two options in a special election. Clearly, anyone who favored monarchy was a reactionary dinosaur who maliciously wanted to undermine Brazil's progress. The republican format allows Brazilians to vote for their leaders directly. As a result, our brilliant leader Fernando Henrique Carlosa spearheaded life-saving reforms to Brazil's dying and antiquated economic system. In a monarchy, this would be impossible.

Identify Evidence

Read critically. Don't accept an author's conclusion automatically. Identify and evaluate the author's evidence. Does it justify the conclusion in quantity and content? An author may present facts to support a claim, but there may be more to the story than facts. For example, what evidence does the writer of the editorial above present to support the claim that a monarch could not help Brazil's economy? Perhaps a monarch would use his or her more centralized authority to achieve more sweeping and rapid reforms.

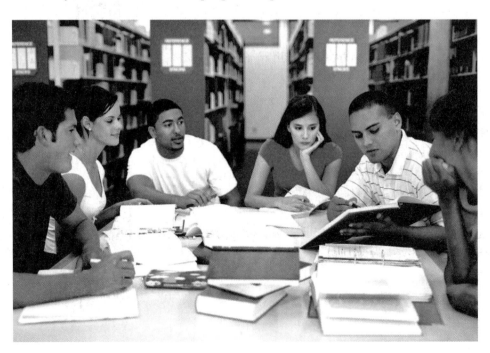

Evaluate Credibility

After you evaluate evidence, check an author's credentials. Consider his or her level of experience and expertise about the topic. Is he or she likely to be knowledgeable *and* objective about the topic? Evaluating credibility is especially important with sites you may visit on the Internet. Ask the following questions to determine if a site and its author are reliable.

- Who sponsors the Web site? Is it a respected organization, a discussion group of individuals, or a single person?

- What is the source of the Web site's information? Does the site list sources for facts and statements?

- Does the Web site creator include his or her name and credentials?

- Is the information on the Web site balanced and objective or biased to reflect only one point of view?

- Can you verify the Web site's information using two other sources, such as an encyclopedia or news agency?

- Is the information current? Is there a date on the Web site to show when it was created or last updated?

Strategies for After Reading

Evaluate Understanding

Evaluate how well you understand what you've read.

- Go back to the questions you asked yourself before reading. Try to answer each of them.
- Check the predictions you made and revise them if appropriate.
- Draw a conclusion about the author's evidence and credibility.
- Check meanings of unfamiliar words in the dictionary to confirm your definitions.

Recall Information

Before moving on to new material, you should be able to answer the following questions fully:

- What is the text about?
- What is the purpose of the text?
- How is the text structured?

You should also be able to place the new information in the context of your prior knowledge of the topic.

Writing Handbook

Writing is one of the most powerful communication tools you will use for the rest of your life. Research shows that writing about what you read actually helps you learn new information and ideas. A systematic approach to writing—including prewriting, drafting, revising, and proofing—can help you write better, whether you're writing an essay or a research paper.

Narrative Essay

Narrative writing tells a story, often about a personal experience. In social studies, this story might be a narrative essay that recounts how a recent or historical event affected you or your family.

❶ Prewriting

Choose a topic. The focus of your essay should be an experience of significance to you. Use these ideas as a guide.

- **Look at photos** that show you and/or your family. Perhaps you attended a political rally or visited an important historical monument.
- **Scan the news** in print or through electronic media. Consider how current events relate to you and your family.
- **Brainstorm** with family or friends about recent events. How did you respond to these events? Jot down ideas like the ones below.

> Connections to History This Year
> — trip to art museum: Renaissance painters
> — historical books: World War II Africa
> — mock debate: Vietnam War

Consider audience and purpose.

- Keep your **audience's** knowledge and experience level in mind. Make sure you provide any necessary background information.
- Choose a **purpose** as well. If you want to entertain, include humorous details. To convey how the experience changed you, you might share more serious insights.

Gather details. Collect the facts and details you need to tell your story.

- **Research** any background about the historical event that readers might need to know about.
- **List details** about your own experience as it relates to the event.

② Drafting

Identify the climax, or most interesting part of your story. Then logically organize your story into a beginning, middle, and end. Narratives are usually told in chronological order.

Open strongly with an engaging sentence, such as the one below, that will catch your reader's attention.

Use sensory details, such as sights, sounds, or smells, to make the story vivid for readers. Describe people's actions and gestures. Pinpoint and describe locations

Write a conclusion that sums up the significance of the event or situation you have experienced.

> I never expected to find myself arguing to support America's role in Vietnam. Our recent mock debate on the Vietnam War gave me new insight about this complex time in my nation's history. **Research took me inside the perspective of those who supported the War and its goals.** On the day of the debate, my hands were covered in sweat and my heart pounded as I stood to explain this currently unpopular position.

Strong opening engages the reader.

Insight or significance tells the reader what this event means to you.

Sensory details help the reader envision the experience.

③ Revising

Add dialogue or description. Dialogue, or conveying a person's thoughts or feelings in his or her own words, can make a narrative more effective. Look for places where the emotions are especially intense. In the model, this might be when the writer's opponents respond to the debate position.

First Draft	Revised Original
At the debate, my hands were wet and my heart beat fast.	On the day of the debate, my hands were covered in sweat and my heart pounded.

Revise word choice. Replace general words with more specific, colorful ones. Choose vivid action verbs, precise adjectives, and specific nouns to convey your meaning. Look at the examples above. Notice how much more effective the revised version is at conveying the experience.

Read your draft aloud. Listen for grammatical errors and statements that are unclear. Revise your sentences as necessary.

④ Publishing and Presenting

Share by reading aloud. Highlight text you want to emphasize and then read your essay aloud to the class. Invite and respond to questions.

Expository Writing

Expository writing explains ideas or information in detail. The strategies on these pages examine each of several expository writing styles.

1 Prewriting

Choose a topic. In social studies, the focus of your writing might be explaining a historical process, comparing and contrasting cultural trends, explaining causes and effects of current events, or exploring problems societies have faced and the solutions they have sought. These ideas are a guide.

- **Ask questions.** For process writing, consider the question *how*. Think about *how* people in history have accomplished their goals, such as building a giant monument. Identify the steps and procedures involved.

> Question: How did great thinkers of the 1600s change people's view of the world?
>
> Answer: They developed the scientific method.

- **Create a compare/contrast grab bag.** With a small group, write on separate slips of paper examples from each category: ideas, cultures, or time periods. Mix the slips in a bag and choose two. Compare and contrast the two ideas, cultures, or time periods.

- **Interview** someone who made a major change in lifestyle, such as moving from one culture to another. Find out how and why the person did this. Understanding *why* is the basis of any cause and effect essay.

- **Take a mental walk.** Study a map and envision taking a tour of the region. Think about problems each area you visit might face, such as armed conflict, natural disaster, or governmental change. Choose a problem and suggest solutions for it.

Consider audience and purpose. Consider how much your readers know about the problem, comparison, event, or process you will address. Suit your writing to your audience's knowledge or plan to give explanations of unfamiliar terms and concepts.

Gather details. Collect the facts and details you need to write your essay.

Research the topic. Use books, the Internet, or interviews of local experts. List facts, details, and other evidence related to your topic. Also consider your personal experience. For example, you might know about a process from personal experience or have witnessed the effects of a historic legal decision.

Create a graphic organizer. For cause-and-effect or problem-solution essays, use a two-column chart. Process writing can be listed as a bulleted list of steps. A Venn diagram can help you compare and contrast.

World War I
- new weapons used: machine guns, poison gas, submarines
- 8.5 million military deaths

- fought by two powerful alliances
- began in Europe, then spread

World War II
- new weapon used: atomic bomb
- 20 million military deaths

Identify causes and effects. List possible explanations for events. Remember that many events result from multiple causes. Identify effects both large and small. Note that some events may have effects that in turn cause other events. Look for causes and effects in all your expository essays. For example, in a process explanation, one step often causes the next.

Fine-tune your ideas. For a problem-solution essay, decide what you will suggest as a solution. Keep your solution narrow to be achievable in cost, effort, and timing. Make sure no one has tried it before, or if it has been tried and it failed, address the failure.

➋ Drafting

Match structure to purpose. Typically, process writing and cause-and-effect writing are written in sequence order. Problem-solution essays benefit from block organization, which presents the entire problem and proposes a solution. For compare/contrast essays, you can organize by subject or by point.

> By subject: Discuss the events and outcomes of World War I, and then compare and contrast these with those of World War II.
>
> By point: Introduce a category, such as use of new weapons. Relate both wars to this category, comparing or contrasting them along the way.

Give background. To discuss events from history, first orient the reader to time and place. Choose the important facts but don't overwhelm the reader with detail. If you need to, return to prewriting to narrow your topic further.

Elaborate for interest and emphasis. Give details about each point in your essay. For example, add facts that make the link between events so that a cause-and-effect relationship is clear. Also, readers will support proposed solutions more if your details clearly show how these solutions will solve the stated problem. Use facts and human experiences to make your essay vivid.

Connect to today. Even when you write about historical events, you may find links to today. Explore these links in your essay.

> Mexico's population underwent great change during the mid–twentieth century. Population shifted from rural areas to urban areas. The nation's society went from largely agricultural to largely industrial and urban. Urban populations exploded, with Mexico City alone growing from 1.5 million people in 1940 to nearly 20 million later in the century. These changes resulted from several causes.
>
> First, land reform begun in the 1930s failed. The millions of acres redistributed by then–President Lázaro Cárdenas proved arid and unproductive. Second, the rural population was growing rapidly. This placed increased demands on the land. The land became even more depleted and unproductive. Finally, several Mexican governments in turn shifted their attention from the small rural peasant farmer toward larger scale farming operations.
>
> Mexico's shifting population and changing economic patterns yielded new problems for its leaders by late in the twentieth century.

— Identify the topic to orient readers.

— Chronological order walks readers through the cause-effect sequence.

— Elaboration supports the relationship you are highlighting.

— Connection to today tells readers why this matters to them.

Revising

Add transition words. Make cause-and-effect relationships clear with words such as *because, as a result,* and *so.* To compare or contrast ideas, use linking words, such as *similarly, both, equally* or *in contrast, instead, yet.* Use words such as *first, second, next,* and *finally* to help readers follow steps in a process. Look at the following examples. In the revised version, a reader knows the correct order in which to perform the steps.

First Draft	Revised
Scientists form an educated guess called a hypothesis. They test that hypothesis with an experiment.	<u>Next,</u> scientists form an educated guess called a hypothesis. <u>Then,</u> they test that hypothesis with an experiment.

Remember purpose. Shape your draft so that it answers the question or thesis you began with. For a problem-solution essay—in which your purpose is to sell your solution—that means anticipating opposing arguments and responding to them. For cause-and-effect, you want to stress the way one event leads to the next. Always tell readers *why* they should care about your topic.

Review organization. Confirm that your ideas flow in a logical order. Write main points on index cards. Reorganize these until you are satisfied that the order best strengthens your essay.

Add details. Make sure you haven't left out any steps in your essay, and don't assume readers will make the connections. For example, you might forget to state explicitly that a process must be repeated in order to produce accurate results. Add more background if necessary for clarity.

Revise sentences and words. Look at your sentence length. Vary it to include both short and long sentences. Then scan for vague words, such as *good.* Replace them with specific and vibrant words, such as *effective.* Use technical terms only when necessary, and then define them.

Peer review. Ask a peer to read your draft. Is it clear? Can he or she follow your ideas? Revise areas of confusion.

④ Publishing and Presenting

Collect in a class manual. Contribute your process explanation to a class manual of *History How-To's.*

Submit to a library. Find a specialized library, such as a presidential library. Mail your essay to the library's publications or public relations department.

Seek publication. If your historical events or issues are local, seek publication in a local historical magazine or contact a historical society. You might speak to their members.

Mail to an advocacy group. Find a local, national, or international organization that is concerned with your topic. Send them your essay and ask for comments on its ideas. Make sure to include a self-addressed stamped envelope and a note explaining your essay and offering thanks for its review.

Research Writing

❶ Prewriting

Choose a topic. Often, a teacher will assign your research topic. You may have flexibility in choosing your focus or you may have the opportunity to completely define your topic. These ideas are a guide.

- **Catalog scan.** Using a card or electronic catalog, search for topics that interest you. When a title looks promising, find the book on the shelves. Libraries usually use the Dewey Decimal Classification system to group research materials by subject, so you should find other books on similar subjects nearby. You can use them all to decide on your final topic.

- **Notes review.** Review your social studies notes from the last month or so. Jot down topics that you found interesting. Then repeat the process with your other classes. For example, you might find a starting point for research into the Scientific Revolution from a math theorem.

- **Social studies categories game.** With a group, brainstorm categories in social studies. For example, you might list key world leaders or important wars. Within each category, take turns adding subtopics. The chart below looks at different transportation topics.

You can use sources such as newspapers to get ideas.

Analyze the audience. Your research and your paper should be strongly influenced by the audience. How much will readers know about this topic and how much will you have to teach them?

Gather details. Collect the facts and details you need to write your paper. Use resources beyond the typical history books. Look at nonfiction books such as memoirs or collections of letters. Also look at magazine and newspaper articles. Consider news magazines, as well as those focused on topics such as history or travel. You may find interviews with experts on your topic or travel articles about a region that interests you. Search the Internet, starting with online encyclopedias, news organizations, and history Web sites.

Organize evidence and ideas. Use note cards to record information and to help you organize your thoughts. Start with a general thesis statement in mind. Then begin reading and taking notes. Write a heading at the top of each note card to group it under a subtopic. Note a number or title to identify the information source. In the examples below, the number 3 is used. Use the same number for an additional source card containing the bibliographic information you will need.

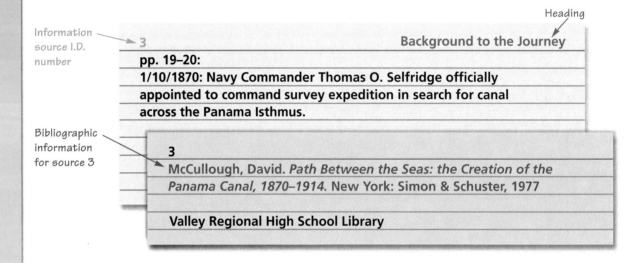

Heading

Information source I.D. number

3   **Background to the Journey**

pp. 19–20:
1/10/1870: Navy Commander Thomas O. Selfridge officially
appointed to command survey expedition in search for canal
across the Panama Isthmus.

Bibliographic information for source 3

3
McCullough, David. *Path Between the Seas: the Creation of the Panama Canal, 1870–1914.* New York: Simon & Schuster, 1977

Valley Regional High School Library

❷ Drafting

Fine-tune your thesis. Review your notes to find relationships between ideas. Shape a thesis that is supported by the majority of your information, then check that it is narrow enough to address thoroughly in the allotted time and space. Remember, you can fine-tune your thesis further as you draft or even when you revise.

Organize to fit your purpose. Do you want to persuade readers of a particular position about your topic, compare and contrast aspects of the topic, or show a cause-and-effect relationship? Organize appropriately—for example, by looking at parts of a whole to examine events leading to building and completing the Panama Canal.

Make an outline. Create an outline in which you identify each topic and subtopic in a single phrase. You can then turn these phrases into sentences and later into the topic sentences of your draft paragraphs. Study the example at the top of the next page to see how to do this well.

Write by paragraph. Write an introduction, at least three body paragraphs, and a conclusion. Address a subtopic of your main topic in each body paragraph. Support all your statements with the facts and details you gathered.

Building the Panama Canal

Outline
I. Introduction
II. Why the Canal Was Built
III. How the Canal Was Built
  A. Physical Challenges
  B. Medical Challenges
IV. Conclusion

Introduction
Ever since Christopher Columbus first explored the Isthmus of Panama, the Spanish had been looking for a water route through it. They wanted to be able to sail west from Spain to Asia without sailing around South America. However, it was not until 1914 that the dream became a reality.

Conclusion
It took eight years and more than 70,000 workers to build the Panama Canal. It remains one of the greatest engineering feats of modern times.

An outline helps you structure your information.

Each body paragraph looks at a part of the whole topic.

The introduction puts the topic in a context of time and place. The entire paragraph conveys the thesis: Building the Panama Canal was a dream that took centuries to achieve.

The conclusion recaps key points and leaves readers with a final statement to remember.

❸ Revising

Add detail. Mark points where more details would strengthen your statements. Look at the following examples. Notice the added details in the revised version. When adding facts, make certain that they are accurate.

First Draft	Revised
The Navy excursion was a huge undertaking. Supplies were gathered to support the team for many months.	The Navy excursion was a huge undertaking. Supplies were gathered to support the team for many months, including more than 600 pairs of shoes, 100 miles of telegraph wire, 2,500 pounds of coffee, and 10,000 pounds of bread! (McCullough 20).

Make the connection for readers. Help readers find their way through your ideas. First, check that your body paragraphs and the information within them flow in a logical sequence. If they do not, revise to correct this. Then add transition words to link ideas and paragraphs.

Give credit. Check that you have used your own words or given proper credit for borrowed words. You can give credit easily with parenthetical notes. These include the author's last name and the relevant page number from the source. For example, you could cite the note card here as (McCullough 19–20).

❹ Publishing and Presenting

Plan a conference. Gather a group of classmates and present your research projects. You may each wish to create visual materials to accompany your presentations. After you share your papers, hold a question and answer session.

Persuasive Essay

Persuasive writing supports an opinion or position. In social studies, persuasive essays often argue for or against positions on historical or current issues.

1 Prewriting

Choose a topic. Choose a topic that provokes an argument and has at least two sides. Use these ideas as a guide.

- **Round-table discussion.** Talk with classmates about issues you have studied recently. Outline pro and con positions about these issues.
- **Textbook flip.** Scan the table of contents or flip through the pages of your textbook. Focus on historical issues that engage your feelings.
- **Make connections.** Relate current events to history. Develop a position for or against a situation of importance today using historical evidence.

Narrow your topic.

- **Cover part of the topic** if you find too many pros and cons for a straightforward argument.
- **Use looping.** Write for five minutes on the general topic. Circle the most important idea. Then write for five minutes on that idea. Continue looping until the topic is manageable.

Consider your audience. Choose arguments that will appeal to the audience for your writing and that are likely to persuade them to agree with your views.

Gather evidence. Collect the evidence to support your position convincingly.

- **Identify pros and cons.** Use a graphic organizer like the one below to list points on both sides of the issue.

Position: Education is key to improving life in developing nations.	
Pro ⟵	⟶ **Con**
• Education allows people to get higher-paying jobs. • With more money, people can help boost the economy. • With education, people can better handle disease and disaster.	• Building new schools may cost more than the government has available for education. • Some countries have other large problems to handle, such as serious diseases.

- **Interview** adults who have lived or worked in developing nations. What do they think? Ask them for reasons to support their views.
- **Research** to get your facts straight. Read articles or books about life in developing nations.

2 Drafting

State your thesis. Clearly state your position, as in this example:

> Education is the key to revitalizing developing nations. Once many people are educated, many other problems can be solved.

Use your introduction to provide a context for the issue. Tell your readers when and why the issue arose, and identify the important people involved.

Sequence your arguments. Open or close with your strongest argument. If you close with the strongest argument, open with the second-best argument.

Acknowledge opposition. State, and then refute, opposing arguments.

Use facts and details. Include quotations, statistics, or comparisons to build your case. Include personal experiences or reactions to the topic, such as those a family member might have shared when interviewed.

Write a conclusion that restates your thesis and closes with a strong, compelling argument.

Many people living in developing nations want to improve life in their countries. They want the people to have everything they need, such as food and clean water, electricity, medicines, and even fun items like televisions and bicycles. Education is the key to revitalizing developing nations. Once many people are educated, many other problems can be solved.

Education allows people to get higher-paying jobs. With more money, people can help boost the economy. As well, education is an added tool people can use to deal with other problems. It's true that building new schools costs a lot. And in some places, people face many other major problems such as serious diseases. But education will only help them handle these issues....

Background orients readers.

Thesis identifies your main argument.

Supporting argument clarifies your thesis.

Opposing argument, noted and refuted, adds to your position.

③ Revising

Add information. Extra details can generate interest in your topic. For example, add a quotation from a news article that assesses the role of education in a developing nation or a poor area.

Review arguments. Make sure your arguments are logically sound and clearly developed. Avoid faulty logic such as circular reasoning (arguing a point by merely restating it differently). Evidence is the best way to support your points. Look at the following examples. Notice how much more effectively the revised version supports the argument.

First Draft	Revised
Education allows people to make more money, which is helpful.	Education allows people to get higher-paying jobs. With more money, people can help boost the economy.

Use transition words to guide readers through your ideas.

- To show contrast: *however, although, despite*
- To point out a reason: *since, because, if*
- To signal conclusion: *therefore, consequently, so, then*

④ Publishing and Presenting

Persuasive Speech. Many persuasive essays are delivered orally. Prepare your essay as a speech, highlighting words for emphasis and adding changes in tone, volume, or speed.

Biographical Writing

Prewriting

Choose a topic. Biographical writing tells the story of a real person's life. For social studies, you should focus on the life of an important historical or current figure. The following ideas are a guide.

- **Find a hero.** Think about a person from history whom you admire—for example, a world leader, a great thinker, or an inventor. Remember to choose someone about whom information is easily available.

- **Name game.** On an index card, write the name of a person in the news today. Write a sentence or phrase explaining what makes this person interesting to you, as on the examples below. With a group, shuffle all the cards and then take turns drawing topics. If you like, trade your topic with a friend.

Martin Luther
He thought the Bible—not the pope—should guide a person's actions.

Wangari Maathai
She thinks preserving the environment can improve people's lives.

- **Table of Contents scan.** Your history book lists the short biographies that are included in the text. Scan this listing in the book's Table of Contents for three possible subjects. Read the biography of each subject before you make a final choice.

Focus your approach. Decide how you want to approach your subject. For example, you could emphasize the person's influence on historical events, or you could show how personal experiences affected his or her achievements.

Gather details. Collect the facts and details you need to write your paper. Use the research methods for gathering information explained on page SH14. In particular, check biographical source materials in the reference section of the library.

Isolate episodes. As you learn about your subject, focus on the particular episodes that seem to be most important. Then learn more about the events surrounding these episodes and take notes on them, as in the example below.

Model: Isolate an Episode

Martin Luther

Appeared at the Diet of Worms to defend his religious views ——→ What was the Diet of Worms? Meeting of church leaders in Worms, Germany, 1521

Focus your fact-gathering. Your goal is to bring this person's life to readers—to share facts and opinions relating to that life and respond to them with your own conclusions. As you determine the main points you wish to make about this person, find facts to support your assertions. Make sure to give enough factual background for readers to appreciate your points.

2 Drafting

Focus your essay. In a single paper, you will probably need to focus on an aspect of your subject's life or on a quick overview of major events in that life.

Organize important events. Choose the events you will discuss, and then order them in a logical way. Biographies are usually organized chronologically.

Reveal your subject. Include direct description of your subject, which allows you to convey information quickly. Balance this with quotations or examples of the person's actions, which lend color and authenticity to your essay.

Open strongly. Get readers' attention immediately with an engaging quotation, an interesting fact about your subject, or an anecdote that sets the tone.

"Here I stand, I cannot do otherwise." Martin Luther spoke these words at the Diet of Worms in 1521. The Diet, a conference of religious leaders, had summoned Luther to explain his controversial religious views.

Martin Luther was born in 1483 into a German family. Raised a Catholic, Luther entered a monastery after experiencing a religious calling. He became both devout and committed to strict observance. Over time, this approach brought him into conflict with the Church. For example, Luther felt that the Catholic Church should not sell indulgences, or guarantees of good grace after death.

Luther developed new ideas about the Church and its leadership. At the core were his beliefs that people should have a direct relationship to the Bible and that the Church and the pope stood in the way of this. In his 95 Theses, Luther called for widespread reforms in the Catholic Church and later in the German government. Because his views were contrary to accepted beliefs, Luther was called in front of the Diet of Worms. He refused to back down, so the Church expelled him in 1521.

A quote gets the readers attention and quickly establishes the subject's personality.

The biography will focus on this aspect of Luther's life.

Chronological organization helps readers see the development of Luther's ideas.

The conclusion brings the biography back to its initial anecdote.

3 Revising

Examine word choice. Bring your subject to life with vivid adjectives, specific verbs, and precise nouns. Then link your chronological organization with words that show sequence. The draft above uses dates as well as phrases such as *over time* to show the sequence of Luther's life and religious growth.

Make connections for readers. For example, the sentence below connects Luther's life to current times by linking it to the modern Lutheran Church.

Although Luther himself never called for a new church, today the Protestant branch named for him claims more than 5 million members in America alone.

Give credit. Cite sources for any facts, statistics, or quotations you include. If several pieces of information in a paragraph come from a single source, you may cite the source once at the end of the paragraph. Always check with your teacher for specific bibliographic requirements.

4 Publishing and Presenting

Create a biographical character. Use what you've learned about this person's life to appear as that person. If you wish, wear a costume. Explain who you are and what is most important to you. Ask and answer questions.

Writing for Assessment

Assessment writing differs from all other writing that you do. You have many fewer choices as a writer, and you almost always face a time limit. In social studies, you'll need to write both short answers and extended responses for tests. While these contrast in some ways, they share many requirements.

① Prewriting

Choose a topic. Short-answer questions seldom offer a topic choice. For extended response, however, you may have a choice of more than one question. Use the following strategies to help you navigate that choice.

- **Examine the question.** To choose a question you can answer effectively, analyze what each question is asking. Use key words such as those listed below to help you choose topics and respond to short-answer questions in which the topic is given.

Key Words	What You Need in an Answer
Explain	Give a clear, complete account of how something works or why something happened.
Compare/Contrast	Show how two or more things are alike and different.
Define	Give examples to explain meaning.
Argue, Convince, Support, Persuade	Take a position on an issue and present strong reasons to support your side of the issue.
Summarize	Provide the most important elements of a subject.
Evaluate/Judge	Assign a value or explain an opinion.
Interpret	Support a thesis with examples from the text.

Notice in the examples below that the key words are underlined:

Short answer: <u>Describe</u> one way that Chief Joseph showed his <u>military expertise</u>.

Extended response: According to the author of this article, Chief Joseph was both a <u>peace chief</u> and a <u>military genius</u>. Use information from the article to <u>support this conclusion</u>.

- **Plot your answer.** After choosing a question, quickly plot the answer in your mind. Do you have the information to answer this question? If the answer is *no*, try another question.

Measure your time. Your goal is to show the instructor that you've mastered the material. To stay focused on this goal, divide your time: one-quarter on prewriting; half on drafting; one-quarter on revising. For short-answer questions, determine how much of the overall test time you can spend on each question. Don't spend more than that.

Gather details. Organize the facts and details you need to write your answer. For short-answer questions, this usually involves identifying exactly what information is required.

Use a graphic organizer. For extended response, divide your topic into subtopics that fit the type of question. Jot down facts and details for each. For the question on Chief Joseph, the following organizer would be effective:

Chief Joseph of the Nez Percé
Peace Chief
- traded peacefully with white settlers (1)
- reluctantly went to war (2)
- famous speech, "I will fight no more forever." (3)

Military Genius
- won battles with fewer warriors than opposing troops had (a)
- avoided capture for many months (b)
- led his people more than 1,000 miles (c)
- knew when to surrender for the good of his people (c)

② Drafting

Choose an organization that fits the question. With a short-answer question, write one to three complete sentences. With extended response, you'll need more elaborate organization. For the question on Chief Joseph, organize your points by importance within each subtopic. For a summary or explanation, use chronological order. For compare/contrast, present similarities first, then differences.

Open and close strongly. Start your answer by restating the question or using its language to state your position. This helps you focus and shows the instructor that you understand the question. Finish with a strong conclusion that restates your position. For short answer, include some language from the question in your response.

One way that Chief Joseph showed his military expertise was by defeating U.S. Army troops despite having fewer warriors than they had.

Support your ideas. Each paragraph should directly or indirectly support your main idea. Choose facts that build a cohesive argument. The numbered sentences in the draft below show how this writer organized support.

Chief Joseph was both a peace chief and a military genius. He was a peace chief because he traded peacefully with white settlers for many years. (1) He went to war reluctantly after the government ordered his people to move to a reservation. (2) When he finally surrendered, he said in a famous speech, "I will fight no more forever." (3) Chief Joseph was also a military genius. He fought off U.S. Army forces with fewer warriors than they had, (a) and he avoided capture for many months. (b) He led his people more than 1,000 miles (c) before he made the decision to surrender. Chief Joseph will long be remembered for his dual roles as peace chief and military genius.

The opening restates the question and presents the main idea.

The writer uses information from the graphic organizer, in order of importance.

The writer supports the second subtopic.

The conclusion recaps the main idea and again uses the question's language.

③ Revising

Examine word choice. Replace general words with specific words. Add transitions where these improve clarity. Read the following examples. The revised version shows the relative importance of the writer's supporting evidence.

First Draft	Revised
Chief Joseph was both a peace chief and a military genius. He was a peace chief because he traded peacefully with white settlers for many years. He went to war reluctantly...	Chief Joseph was both a peace chief and a military genius. He was a peace chief for several reasons. First, he traded peacefully with white settlers for many years. Second, he went to war reluctantly...

Check organization. Make sure your introduction includes a main idea and defines subtopics. Review each paragraph for a single main idea. Check that your conclusion summarizes the information you've presented.

④ Publishing and Presenting

Edit and proof. Check spelling, grammar, and mechanics. Make sure that tenses match, that subjects agree with verbs, and that sentences are not too long. Finally, confirm that you have responded to all the questions you were asked to answer.

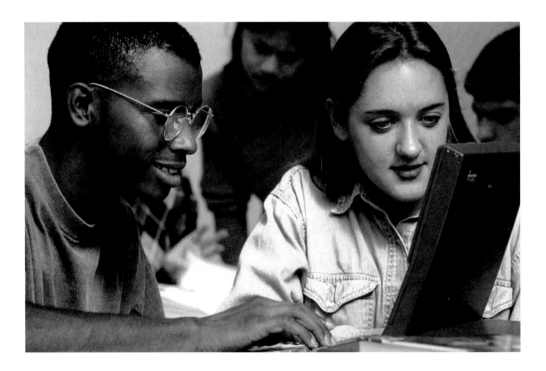

Writing Rubrics

SAT PREP ACT

Use these charts, or rubrics, to evaluate your writing.

SAT

SCORE OF 6
An essay in this category is **outstanding**, demonstrating **clear and consistent mastery**, although it may have a few minor errors. A typical essay

- effectively and insightfully develops a point of view on the issue and demonstrates outstanding critical thinking, using clearly appropriate examples, reasons, and other evidence to support its position
- is well organized and clearly focused, demonstrating clear coherence and smooth progression of ideas
- exhibits skillful use of language, using a varied, accurate, and apt vocabulary
- demonstrates meaningful variety in sentence structure
- is free of most errors in grammar, usage, and mechanics

SCORE OF 5
An essay in this category is **effective**, demonstrating **reasonably consistent mastery**, although it will have occasional errors or lapses in quality. A typical essay

- effectively develops a point of view on the issue and demonstrates strong critical thinking, generally using appropriate examples, reasons, and other evidence to support its position
- is well organized and focused, demonstrating coherence and progression of ideas
- exhibits facility in the use of language, using appropriate vocabulary
- demonstrates variety in sentence structure
- is generally free of most errors in grammar, usage, and mechanics

SCORE OF 4
An essay in this category is **competent**, demonstrating **adequate mastery**, although it will have lapses in quality. A typical essay

- develops a point of view on the issue and demonstrates competent critical thinking, using adequate examples, reasons, and other evidence to support its position
- is generally organized and focused, demonstrating some coherence and progression of ideas
- exhibits adequate but inconsistent facility in the use of language, using generally appropriate vocabulary
- demonstrates some variety in sentence structure
- has some errors in grammar, usage, and mechanics

SCORE OF 3
An essay in this category is **inadequate**, but demonstrates **developing mastery**, and is marked by **one or more** of the following weaknesses:

- develops a point of view on the issue, demonstrating some critical thinking, but may do so inconsistently or use inadequate examples, reasons, or other evidence to support its position
- is limited in its organization or focus, but may demonstrate some lapses in coherence or progression of ideas
- displays developing facility in the use of language, but sometimes uses weak vocabulary or inappropriate word choice
- lacks variety or demonstrates problems in sentence structure
- contains an accumulation of errors in grammar, usage, and mechanics

SCORE OF 2
An essay in this category is **seriously limited**, demonstrating **little mastery**, and is flawed by **one or more** of the following weaknesses:

- develops a point of view on the issue that is vague or seriously limited, demonstrating weak critical thinking, providing inappropriate or insufficient examples, reasons, or other evidence to support its position
- is poorly organized and/or focused, or demonstrates serious problems with coherence or progression of ideas
- displays very little facility in the use of language, using very limited vocabulary or incorrect word choice
- demonstrates frequent problems in sentence structure
- contains errors in grammar, usage, and mechanics so serious that meaning is somewhat obscured

SCORE OF 1
An essay in this category is **fundamentally lacking**, demonstrating **very little** or **no mastery**, and is severely flawed by one or more of the following weaknesses:

- develops no viable point of view on the issue, or provides little or no evidence to support its position
- is disorganized or unfocused, resulting in a disjointed or incoherent essay
- displays fundamental errors in vocabulary
- demonstrates severe flaws in sentence structure
- contains pervasive errors in grammar, usage, or mechanics that persistently interfere with meaning

SCORE OF 0
Essays not written on the essay assignment will receive a score of zero.

ACT	Scores of 4–6	Scores of 1–3
Purpose	Shows a clear understanding of the essay's purpose by articulating a perspective and developing ideas	Does not clearly articulate a perspective
Support	Most generalizations developed with specific examples to support the perspective	Demonstrates some development of ideas but may be overly general or repetitious
Focus	Clear focus maintained throughout	Focus maintained on general prompt topic but is not sufficiently specific
Language	Shows competent use of language	Language is mostly understandable, organization is clear but simple
Mechanics	Minimal errors that only occasionally distract and do not interfere with meaning	Errors frequently distract and interfere with meaning

Analyze the Five Themes of Geography

The five themes of geography are tools you can use to analyze geographic information given in photographs, charts, maps, and text.

- **Location** answers the question "Where is it?" The answer might be an absolute location, such as 167 River Lane, or a relative location, such as six miles west of Mill City.
- **Regions** are areas that share at least one common feature. Climate, culture, and government are features that can be used to define a region.
- **Place** identifies natural and human features that make a place different from other places. Landforms, climate, plants, animals, people, culture, and languages are features that can be used to identify a specific place.
- **Movement** answers the question "How do people, goods, and ideas move from place to place?"
- **Human-Environment Interaction** focuses on the relationship between people and the environment. Humans often make changes to the environment, and the environment often affects how humans live.

Use the photograph and steps that follow to analyze the five themes of geography.

The Nile River in Egypt

Read supporting information such as a caption or key. Use this information and your own knowledge of the world to determine location and region.

Analyze the content. Consider the elements of the visual or text to develop ideas about region, place, movement, and human-environment interaction.

Practice and Apply the Skill

Use the photograph above to answer the following questions:

1. How might you describe the relative location of the fields of crops?
2. What is the climate region shown here? How do you know?
3. What elements in the scene identify this specific place?
4. How do you think people, goods, and ideas move to and from this place?
5. How have the people of this area changed their environment?

Understand Latitude and Longitude

Geographers divide the globe along imaginary horizontal lines called parallels of latitude. They measure these parallels in degrees (°) north or south of the Equator, which itself is a line of latitude. Geographers also divide the globe along imaginary vertical lines called meridians of longitude. They measure these meridians in degrees east or west of the Prime Meridian, a line of longitude running through Greenwich, England. All meridians intersect at the North Pole and the South Pole. Together, the lines of latitude and longitude form a grid that gives an absolute location for every place on Earth. Use the globes and the steps that follow to understand latitude and longitude.

Study purpose. Study the two main globes to understand why geographers divide the globe into parallels and meridians. Study the two smaller globes to understand the role of the Equator and the Prime Meridian as starting points for measuring parallels and meridians.

Read labels and captions. Read the labels and captions to understand how to determine the latitude and longitude of a given location, as well as to identify which hemispheres it sits in.

Identify absolute location. You can use lines of latitude and longitude together to identify the absolute location of any spot on Earth.

Practice and Apply the Skill

Use the text and globes above to answer the following questions:

1. Which part of the location 67° N, 55° E represents the longitude?
2. What line of latitude lies halfway from the Equator to the North Pole?
3. Do lines of latitude ever intersect one another? Explain.
4. If you followed the 70° W line of longitude north to the North Pole and then continued on the same line south, what line of longitude would you be on? (Hint: The globe, like a circle, has a total of 360 degrees.)

Understand Movements of Earth

Earth revolves around the sun in a path called an orbit. One revolution, or complete orbit, takes a year. As Earth revolves, it also rotates on its axis—an invisible line from the North Pole to the South Pole. Every 24 hours, Earth completes one full rotation. As Earth rotates, it is day on the side facing the sun and night on the side away from the sun. Earth's axis is tilted at an angle. Because of this tilt, sunlight strikes different parts of Earth more or less directly at different times of year, creating seasons. Use the diagram below and the steps that follow to understand Earth's movements.

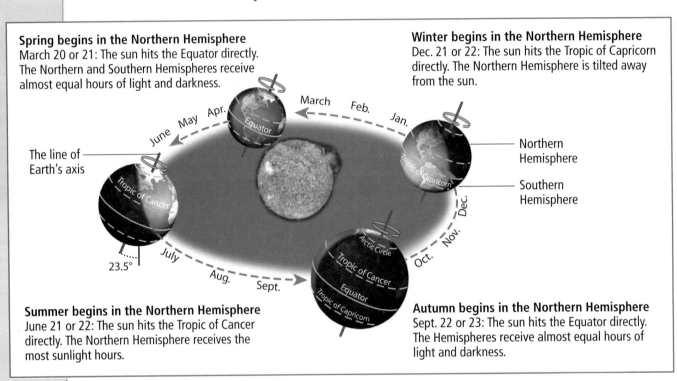

Spring begins in the Northern Hemisphere
March 20 or 21: The sun hits the Equator directly. The Northern and Southern Hemispheres receive almost equal hours of light and darkness.

Winter begins in the Northern Hemisphere
Dec. 21 or 22: The sun hits the Tropic of Capricorn directly. The Northern Hemisphere is tilted away from the sun.

The line of Earth's axis

Northern Hemisphere

Southern Hemisphere

23.5°

Summer begins in the Northern Hemisphere
June 21 or 22: The sun hits the Tropic of Cancer directly. The Northern Hemisphere receives the most sunlight hours.

Autumn begins in the Northern Hemisphere
Sept. 22 or 23: The sun hits the Equator directly. The Hemispheres receive almost equal hours of light and darkness.

Focus on the main ideas. The diagram shows why the seasons change and how seasons differ north and south of the Equator. It also shows how night changes into day. Focus on these ideas one at a time.

Identify the content. Look at each element of the diagram. You see Earth in four different positions around the sun.

Read labels and captions. The caption and labels on each position of Earth describe a different season.

Restate the main points. In your own words, describe to yourself why the seasons change, how seasons differ in the Southern and Northern Hemispheres, and how night changes into day.

Practice and Apply the Skill

Use the diagram above to answer the following questions:

1. At the beginning of winter in the Northern Hemisphere, which of Earth's poles receives more sunlight?

2. How are the Tropic of Capricorn and the Tropic of Cancer related?

3. The term *equinox* means "equal night" and refers to the hours of darkness and sunlight. Which two seasons begin on an equinox?

4. Which hemisphere, Northern or Southern, receives more hours of sunlight on April 1? Explain.

Analyze Map Projections

Because maps are flat, they cannot show the correct size and shape of every feature on Earth's curved surface. Mapmakers must shrink some places and stretch others. Different types of map projections distort Earth's surface in different ways. Mapmakers choose the projection that has the least distortion for the information they are presenting.

Same-shape map projections such as the Mercator projection accurately show the shapes of landmasses. However, they distort sizes and distances. Equal-area map projections show the correct size of landmasses but distort shapes, especially at the edges of a map. The Robinson projection keeps the size and shape relationships of most continents and oceans but distorts the size of the polar regions. Use the maps below and the steps that follow to help you learn how to analyze map projections.

Equal-area projection
The sizes of landmasses are accurate relative to one another.

Mercator projection

The greatest distortion is at the far northern and southern latitudes.

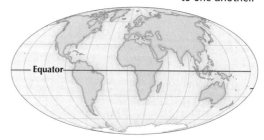

Robinson projection
The entire top edge of the map is the North Pole.

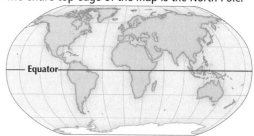

The entire bottom edge of the map is the South Pole.

Identify each projection. Study the appearance of each type of projection.

Read labels and captions. Read the labels and captions to understand the important details of each projection.

Compare the maps. Compare the shape of the maps and then the shapes of landmasses on them. Last, compare the amount of curvature of the lines of latitude and longitude on the maps.

Practice and Apply the Skill

Use the maps above to answer the following questions:

1. If you wanted to plot a course to sail from one port to another on the most direct route, which map projection would work best? Why?

2. Which map shows the most accurate relative size of Antarctica, the white region on each map? Why?

3. How do the grid lines on the Mercator projection vary from a globe's?

4. Why do you think many maps in this book use the Robinson projection?

Read Maps

Mapmakers provide clues to help you read maps, such as a title, compass rose, key, and locator globe. Another helpful feature is a scale bar. Like the two shown here, maps are often drawn to different scales, depending on their purpose. Use the maps below and the steps that follow to learn how to analyze maps.

Read the title. The title tells you the subject of the map.

Study the locator globe. The locator globe shows where in the world the area shown on the map is located.

Read the key. The key explains the symbols, lines, and colors on the map.

Use the scale bar and compass rose. Use the scale bar to determine distances between places on the map. Use the compass rose to determine the relative directions of places on the map.

Compare maps of different scale. Since the smaller map zooms in on an area of the main map, it is at a larger scale than the main map. Notice the different features shown on these two maps of different scales.

Practice and Apply the Skill

Use the maps above to answer the following questions:

1. Which body of water borders Japan on the west?
2. On what body of water is Tokyo located?
3. What is the distance between Tokyo and Hiroshima?
4. What is the purpose of the main map? Of the smaller map?
5. Which map could help you get from Tokyo International Airport to downtown Tokyo? How could it help?

Analyze Special-Purpose Maps

Maps can show many different types of information. A physical map represents what a region looks like by showing its major physical features, such as mountains and plains. A political map focuses on elements related to government, such as nations, borders, and cities.

A special-purpose map provides information on a specific subject—for example, land use, population distribution, natural resources, or trade routes. Road maps are special-purpose maps, as are weather maps. These maps often use a variety of colors and symbols to show different pieces of information, so the key is very important. Use the map below and the steps that follow to practice analyzing a special-purpose map.

Trade Routes Across the Pacific Ocean

Study the title, locator globe, scale bar, and compass rose. Together, these features tell you the map's context—what part of the world it shows and why.

Read the key. Use the key to learn the specific details shown on the map.

Apply the key and labels to the map. Locate the symbols, lines, or colors from the key on the map. Also read any labels on the map. Then use the information given in the key and labels to understand what the map shows.

Practice and Apply the Skill

Use the map above to answer the following questions:

1. What is the purpose of this map? What part of the world does it show?
2. What do the blue lines on the map represent?
3. How many trade routes go through Panama? Through New Zealand?
4. If trade goods arrive in Hawaii from the northeast, where could they have come from?
5. Name three countries that exchange goods with the continental United States along the trade routes shown on the map.

Analyze Graphic Data

The study of history requires that you think critically about the text you're reading as well as any visuals or media sources. This section of the Skills Handbook will allow you to practice and apply some important skills for critical thinking.

Graphs show numerical facts in picture form. Bar graphs and line graphs compare things at different times or places, such as changes in school enrollment. Circle graphs show how a whole is divided into parts. To interpret a graph, look closely at its features. Use the graphs below and the steps that follow to practice analyzing graphic data.

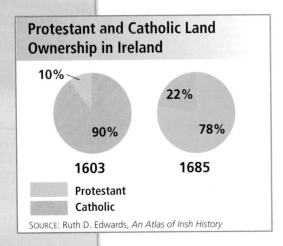

Protestant and Catholic Land Ownership in Ireland

SOURCE: Ruth D. Edwards, *An Atlas of Irish History*

Travel Times to London

SOURCE: E. J. Hobsbaum, *Industry and Empire*

Read the title to learn the main topic of the graph.

Use labels and the key to read the data given in the graph. The bar graph is labeled in hours, with intervals of 10 hours. The keys on all three graphs assign different colors to different groups or dates.

Interpret the graph. Look for interesting patterns in the data. Look at changes over time or compare information for different groups.

Practice and Apply the Skill

Use the graphs above to answer the following questions:

1. What is the title of the bar graph? What is its topic?
2. Which cities show the longest travel times to London, and in which years? What does this tell you about changes in transportation?
3. What color on the circle graphs shows Catholic land ownership? How did Irish land ownership change over time? What might explain this change?
4. Could the information in the circle graph be shown as a bar graph? Explain.

Analyze Images

Television, film, the Internet, and print media all carry images that seek to convey information or influence attitudes. To respond, you must develop the ability to understand and interpret visuals. Use the photograph below and the steps that follow to practice analyzing images.

In the 1950s, people everywhere worried about nuclear attack. This 1954 image advertised a bogus "radiation-resistant" blanket.

Identify the content. Look at all parts of the image and determine which are most important.

Note emotions. Study facial expressions and body positions. Consider the emotions they may suggest.

Read captions/credits. Gather information about the image, such as when it was produced.

Study purpose. Consider who might have created this image. Decide if the purpose was to entertain, inform, or persuade.

Consider context. Determine the context in which the image was created—in this case, the Cold War between the United States and the Soviet Union.

Respond. Decide if a visual's impact achieves its purpose—to inform, to entertain, or to persuade.

Practice and Apply the Skill

Use the photograph above to answer the following questions:

1. What are the three main images in this photograph?
2. What feelings are conveyed by the boy's facial expression?
3. What do you think the photograph's purpose is?
4. When was this image produced? How did historical context influence its production?

Analyze Timelines

Timelines show the order in which events occur as well as the amount of time that passes between events. To understand a timeline, study its labels and captions carefully. Use the timeline below and the steps that follow to practice analyzing timelines

■ **Key Events of the Industrial Revolution**

Early 1800s Romanticism begins to shape Western art and literature.

1807 First factories open in Belgium, setting off the Industrial Revolution on the European continent.

1839 French inventor Louis Daguerre perfects an effective method of photography.

1859 Charles Darwin publishes *On the Origin of Species.* Many religious leaders denounce his theory of evolution.

Chapter Events Global Events

1800   **1815**   **1830**   **1845**   **1860**

1819 Simón Bolívar establishes Gran Colombia.

1842 The Treaty of Nanjing gives Britain trading rights in China.

1861 Tsar Alexander II emancipates Russian serfs.

Identify time units. Find the main time units of the timeline. Determine how much time is represented by the entire timeline.

Read each entry. Read each of the entries on the timeline. Connect each entry to the events before and after it.

Look for patterns among the events shown. Determine if any of the entries fall into a common category. Think about whether the events might be causes and/or effects.

Practice and Apply the Skill

Use the timeline above to answer the following questions.

1. What is the most recent event on the timeline? When did it take place?

2. When did the first factories open in Belgium?

3. How many years after the first factories opened did Louis Daguerre perfect his method of photography?

4. What happened in 1859?

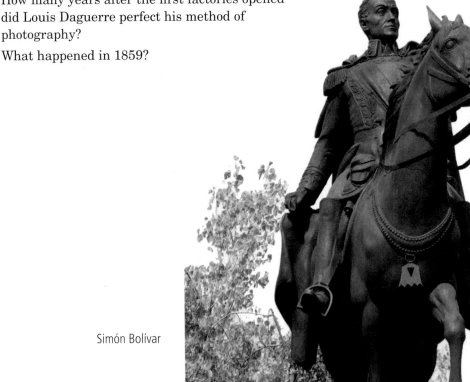

Simón Bolívar

Analyze Primary Sources

Primary sources include official documents and firsthand accounts of events or visual evidence such as photographs, paintings, and political cartoons. Such sources provide valuable information about the past. Use the excerpt below and the steps that follow to learn to analyze primary sources.

The following excerpt is a translation from *The Satires*, a series of poems written in Latin by Juvenal about life in Rome in the first century A.D. In this excerpt, Juvenal recounts a friend's reasons for moving away from Rome.

> **Primary Source**
>
> 66 Since at Rome there is no place for honest pursuits, no profit to be got by honest toil—my fortune is less to-day than it was yesterday. . . .
>
> What shall *I* do at Rome? I can not lie; if a book is bad, I can not praise it and beg a copy. I know not the motions of the stars. . . . no one shall be a thief by my co-operation. . . .
>
> Who, now-a-days, is beloved except the confidant of crime. . .? 99
>
> —Juvenal, *The Satires of Juvenal, Persius, Sulpicia, and Lucilius*

Read the headnote, caption, or attribution line. Determine the source's historical context—who wrote it, when, and why.

Read the primary source. Identify and define unfamiliar words. Then look for the writer's main point.

Identify facts and opinions. Facts can be proven. Opinions reflect a person's views or feelings. Use opinion clues to help: exaggeration, phrases such as "I think," or descriptive words such as "gorgeous."

Identify bias and evaluate credibility. Consider whether the author's opinions suggest bias. Evaluate other factors that might lead to author bias, such as his or her previous experiences. Decide if the author knows enough to be credible and was objective enough to be reliable. Determine whether the source might be propaganda, that is, material published to promote a policy, idea, or cause.

Practice and Apply the Skill

Political cartoons reflect an artist's observations about events of the time. They often use symbols to represent things or exaggeration to make a point. Use the cartoon at right to answer the following questions.

1. Who is the author of this primary source?
2. What does the bulldozer represent?
3. What is exaggerated in this cartoon?
4. What opinion is the cartoonist expressing?
5. Do you think the cartoonist's opinion is valid? Why or why not?

This cartoon by Arcadio Esquivel of Costa Rica comments on environmental destruction.

Compare Viewpoints

A person's viewpoint is shaped by subjective influences such as feelings, prejudices, and past experiences. Two politicians will recommend different policies to address the same problem. Comparing such viewpoints will help you understand issues and form your own views. The excerpts below offer two different views on the purpose of education. Use the excerpts and the steps that follow to learn about comparing viewpoints.

King Henri Christophe of Haiti set up schools for outstanding students. He believed these schools would secure Haiti's new and hard-won freedom. In 1817, he wrote:

Primary Source

66To form good citizens we must educate our children. From our national institutions will proceed a race of men capable of defending by their knowledge and talents those rights so long denied by tyrants. It is from these sources that light will be diffused among the whole mass of the population.99

—Henri Christophe, 1817

Leo Tolstoy, a Russian aristocrat of the late 1800s, became a famous novelist as a young man. As he grew older, he increasingly focused on social issues in his writing. In 1902, he wrote:

Primary Source

66You can take a puppy and feed him, and teach him to carry something, and enjoy the sight of him; but it is not enough to rear and bring up a man, and teach him Greek: he has to be taught to live, that is, to take less from others, and give more.99

—Leo Tolstoy, 1902

Identify the authors. Determine when and where the authors lived.

Examine the viewpoints. Identify the author's main idea and evaluate his or her supporting arguments. Determine whether the arguments are logical and the evidence is sufficient to support the main idea. Confirm that the evidence is valid by doing research if necessary.

Determine the author's frame of reference. Consider how the author's attitudes, beliefs, and past experiences might affect his or her viewpoint.

Recognize facts and opinions. Identify which statements are opinions and which are facts. Opinions represent the author's viewpoint.

Evaluate each viewpoint's validity. Decide whether the viewpoints are based on facts and/or reasonable arguments. Consider whether or not you agree with the viewpoints.

Practice and Apply the Skill

Use the excerpts above to answer the following questions.

1. Who are the authors of these two documents? Where and when did each one live?
2. What is each man's main argument about education? What evidence or supporting arguments does each provide?
3. How might each man's frame of reference affect his viewpoint?
4. How does Tolstoy's phrase "he has to be taught to live" signal an opinion?
5. Are these two viewpoints based on reasonable arguments? Explain.

Synthesize Information

Just as you might ask several friends about a movie before deciding to see it, you can combine information from different sources to develop a fuller understanding of any topic. This process, called synthesizing, will help you become better informed. Study the documents below about developments in the 1400s and 1500s. Then use the steps that follow to learn to synthesize information.

Document A

This caravel helped Europeans sail across and into the wind.

Document B

Improved Technology

Several improvements in technology helped Europeans navigate the vast oceans of the world. Cartographers, or mapmakers, created more accurate maps and sea charts. European sailors learned to use the astrolabe, an instrument developed by the ancient Greeks and perfected by the Arabs, to determine their latitude at sea.

Europeans also designed larger and better ships. The Portuguese developed the caravel, which combined the square sails of European ships with Arab lateen, or triangular, sails. Caravels also adapted the sternpost rudder and numerous masts used on Chinese ships. The new rigging made it easier to sail across or even into the wind.

Document C

Hardships on the Uncharted Sea

In his journal, Italian sailor Antonio Pigafetta detailed the desperate conditions Magellan's sailors experienced as they crossed the Pacific Ocean:

> **Primary Source**
>
> 66We remained three months and twenty days without taking in provisions or other refreshments, and we only ate old biscuit reduced to powder, and full of grubs, and stinking from the dirt which the rats had made on it. . . . we drank water that was yellow and stinking. We also ate the ox hides which were under the main-yard [and] were very hard on account of the sun, rain, and wind. . . .99
>
> —Journal of Antonio Pigafetta

Identify thesis statements. Before you can synthesize, you must understand the thesis, or main idea, of each source.

Compare and contrast. Analyze how the information and ideas in the sources are the same or different. When several sources agree, the information is more reliable and thus more significant.

Draw conclusions and generalize. Look at all the information. Use it to draw conclusions that form a single picture of the topic. Make a generalization, or statement that applies to all the sources.

Practice and Apply the Skill

Use the documents above to answer the following questions.

1. What is the main idea of each source?
2. Which sources support the idea that European sailors became better equipped to sail the seas?
3. What view does Antonio Pigafetta contribute to the topic?
4. Draw a conclusion about European ocean exploration in the early 1500s.

Analyze Cause and Effect

One of a historian's main tasks is to understand the causes and effects of the event he or she is studying. Study the facts below, which are listed in random order. Then use the steps that follow to learn how to analyze cause and effect.

> In the 1980s and 1990s, the Soviet Union underwent a major change in its economy and government. As a result, the Soviet Union ceased to exist. This list shows key elements in that change.
>
> - Low output of crops and consumer goods
> - Soviets want to ensure influence in neighboring Afghanistan, so they invade that nation in 1979
> - Soviet Union breaks up into 15 republics after its central government collapses
> - Changeover to market economy in Russia
> - Ethnic and nationalist movements to achieve independence from Soviet Union
> - Cold War with United States leads to high military spending
> - Food and fuel shortages
> - Rise to power of Mikhail Gorbachev in 1985
> - Russian republic approves a new constitution
> - Baltic states of Estonia, Latvia, and Lithuania demonstrate for independence
> - Cold War ends

Identify the central event. Determine to what event or issue all the facts listed relate.

Locate clue words. Use words such as *because, so,* and *due to* to spot causes and effects.

Identify causes and effects. Causes precede the central event and contribute to its occurrence. Effects come after the central event. They occur or emerge as a result of it.

Consider timeframe. Decide if causes have existed for a long period of time or emerged just prior to the central event. Short-term causes are usually single or narrowly defined events. Long-term causes usually arise from ongoing conditions.

Make recommendations. Use what you've learned to suggest actions or make predictions.

Practice and Apply the Skill

Use the list above to answer the following questions:

1. Which item on the list describes the central event whose causes and effects can be determined?
2. Name three facts that are long-term causes.
3. Name three facts that are probably short-term causes.
4. Name three facts that were most likely effects of the central event.

Problem Solving and Decision Making

You will face many problems in your life, from disputes with friends to how to vote on issues facing your nation. You will be most likely to find solutions if you make decisions in a logical way. Study the situation outlined below. Then use the steps that follow to learn the skills of problem solving and decision making.

A Problem for Japan and China

In the 1800s, Japan and China faced a problem. Industrialized nations had developed machinery and weapons that were superior to those that the Japanese and Chinese had. Some industrialized nations used their new power to demand special trading privileges in Asia.

Options for Japan and China

Option	Advantages	Disadvantages
1. Give in to demands of the industrialized powers.	• Avoid conflict. •	• Native merchants lose profits to foreigners.
2. Give in to demands, but also build modern machines and weapons.	• •	• •
3. Refuse the demands and reject much of the new technology.	• •	• •

The Decisions
- The Japanese government decided to follow option 2.
- The Chinese government decided to follow option 3.

Effects of the Decisions
- Japan quickly became a modern industrial and military power. Although it demilitarized after suffering defeat in World War II, it remains one of the world's leading industrial powers.
- China was weakened by a century of conflict with Great Britain and other major powers, and was invaded and occupied by Japan. Foreign nations gained special privileges in China. Today, China is still struggling to become a leading industrial power.

Identify the problem. You cannot solve a problem until you examine it and understand it.

Gather information and identify options. Most problems have many solutions. Identify as many solution options as possible.

Consider advantages and disadvantages. Analyze each option by predicting benefits and drawbacks.

Decide on and implement the solution. Pick the option with the most desirable benefits and least important drawbacks.

Evaluate the decision. After time, reexamine your solution. If necessary, make a new decision.

Practice and Apply the Skill

Use information from the box above to answer the following questions:

1. What problem did China and Japan face? What caused this problem?
2. Describe an option that Japan or China could have chosen other than those in the list.
3. Identify two advantages and two disadvantages for options 2 and 3.
4. Why do you think China and Japan chose the options they did?

Draw Inferences and Conclusions

Text and artwork may not contain all the facts and ideas you need to understand a topic. You may need to add information from your own experience or knowledge, or use information that is implied but not directly stated in the text or artwork. Study the biography below. Then use the steps that follow to learn how to draw inferences and conclusions.

BIOGRAPHY

James Watt

How did a clever Scottish engineer become the "Father of the Industrial Revolution"? After repairing a Newcomen steam engine, James Watt (1736–1819) had become fascinated with the idea of improving the device. Within a few months, he knew he had a product that would sell. Still, Watt lacked the money needed to produce and market it.

Fortunately, he was able to form a partnership with the shrewd manufacturer Matthew Boulton. They then founded Soho Engineering Works in Birmingham, England, to manufacture steam engines. Watt's version of the steam engine shown here had a separate condensing chamber and was patented in 1769. Eventually, a measure of mechanical and electrical power, the watt, would be named for James Watt. **How might the Industrial Revolution have been different if Watt had not found a business partner?**

Study the facts. Determine what facts and information the text states.

Summarize information. Confirm your understanding of the text by briefly summarizing it.

Ask questions. Use *who, what, when, where, why,* and *how* questions to analyze the text and learn more. For example, you might compare and contrast, or look for causes or effects.

Add your own knowledge. Consider what you know about the topic. Use this knowledge to evaluate the information.

Draw inferences and conclusions. Use what you learned from the text and your own knowledge to draw inferences and conclusions about the topic.

Practice and Apply the Skill

Use the biography above to answer these questions.

1. Who is discussed in the biography? When did he live?
2. Briefly summarize the text.
3. How do Watt's accomplishments still have an impact on our lives today?
4. Why do you think Watt wanted to improve a technology that already existed?

Use the Internet for Research

The Internet is a valuable research tool that provides links to millions of sources of information created by businesses, governments, schools, organizations, and individuals all over the world. Follow the steps to learn how you could use the Internet to research the European Renaissance.

Sample search engine

Begin a search. Use search engines on the Internet to help you find useful Web sites. Type in key words that briefly summarize your topic. Use *and* between words to find documents containing all your keywords. Use *or* between words to find documents containing any one of several keywords.

Find reliable information. Universities, museums, libraries, and government agencies are usually the most reliable and useful for social studies research. The URLs for education sites end in *.edu,* government sites in *.gov,* and not-for-profit organization sites in *.org.* Read each site summary and choose those most likely to be reliable. Click on links to access individual sites.

Evaluate Web sites. Explore each Web site. Note its sponsor and when it was last updated.

Use advanced searches. Try advanced search options. Limit by date or type of site, such as educational institutions. Try new or different key words if you still don't get what you need.

Practice and Apply the Skill

Use a computer connected to the Internet to answer the following questions:

1. What key words might you use to learn about the European Renaissance? Type them into a search engine Web site and see what results you get.

2. Which of the first ten sites that came up in your search is most likely to be reliable? Why?

3. Who is the sponsor of the site you chose? What does this suggest about its quality or its possible bias?

Speaking and listening are forms of communication you use every day. In certain situations, however, specific skills and strategies can increase the effectiveness of your communication. The strategies offered in this section will help you improve both your speaking and listening skills.

Participating in Group Discussions

A group discussion is an informal meeting of people that is used to openly discuss ideas and topics. You can express your views and hear those of others.

Identify Issues

Before you speak, identify the issues and main points you want to address. Incorporate what you already know about these issues into your views. Then find the best words to convey your ideas effectively.

Interact With the Group

As with persuasive writing, in a discussion it helps to accept the validity of opposing views, then argue your position. Always acknowledge the views of others respectfully, but ask questions that challenge the accuracy, logic, or relevance of those views.

Debating

A debate is a formal argument about a specific issue. Explicit rules govern the procedure of a debate, with each debater or team given an allotted time to make arguments and respond to opposing positions. You may also find yourself arguing a position you don't personally hold.

Prepare Your Arguments

If you support a position, use your existing knowledge of it to direct your research. If you personally oppose an assigned position, use that knowledge to identify likely opposing arguments. Generate an outline and then number note cards to highlight key information for each of you main points.

Avoid Common Pitfalls

Stay focused on your arguments. Be aware of words that may reveal bias, such as *unpatriotic*. Speak assertively, but avoid getting overly emotional. Vary the pitch and tone of your voice to keep listeners engaged. Try to speak actively, rather than just reading aloud, and use eye contact and gestures to emphasize your message.

Giving an Oral or Multimedia Presentation

An oral or multimedia presentation provides an audience with information through a variety of media.

Choose Media

If you are limited to speaking only, focus your time on developing a presentation that engages listeners. If you can include other media, consider what kind of information each form of media conveys most effectively.

Maps	Graphs/charts	Pictures	Diagrams	Audio/video
Clarify historical or geographical information	Show complicated information in an accessible format	Illustrate objects, scenes, or other details	Show link between parts and a whole or a process	Brings the subject to life and engages audience

Generate Text

Gather information using library and online sources. Develop your most important ideas in the body of your presentation. Back up assertions with solid facts and use multimedia examples to illustrate key points.

Present With Authority

Practice your presentation to gain comfort with the text and the presentation sequence. Experiment with the timing of how to include multimedia elements. Make sure you have the necessary equipment and know how to use it.

Active Listening

Active listening is a key component of the communication process. Like all communication, it requires your engaged participation.

Focus Your Attention on Ideas

Look at and listen to the speaker. Think about what you hear and see. Which ideas are emphasized or repeated? What gestures or expressions suggest strong feelings? Can you connect the speaker's ideas to your own experiences?

Listen to Fit the Situation

Active listening involves matching your listening to the situation. Listen critically to a speech given by a candidate for office. Listen empathetically to the feelings of a friend. Listen appreciatively to a musical performance.

Ask Questions

Try to think of questions while you're listening. Look at these examples:

Open-ended	Closed	Fact
Why do you think it is so important for young people to vote?	Do you support the current voting age of 18?	How many people aged 18–25 voted in the most recent election?

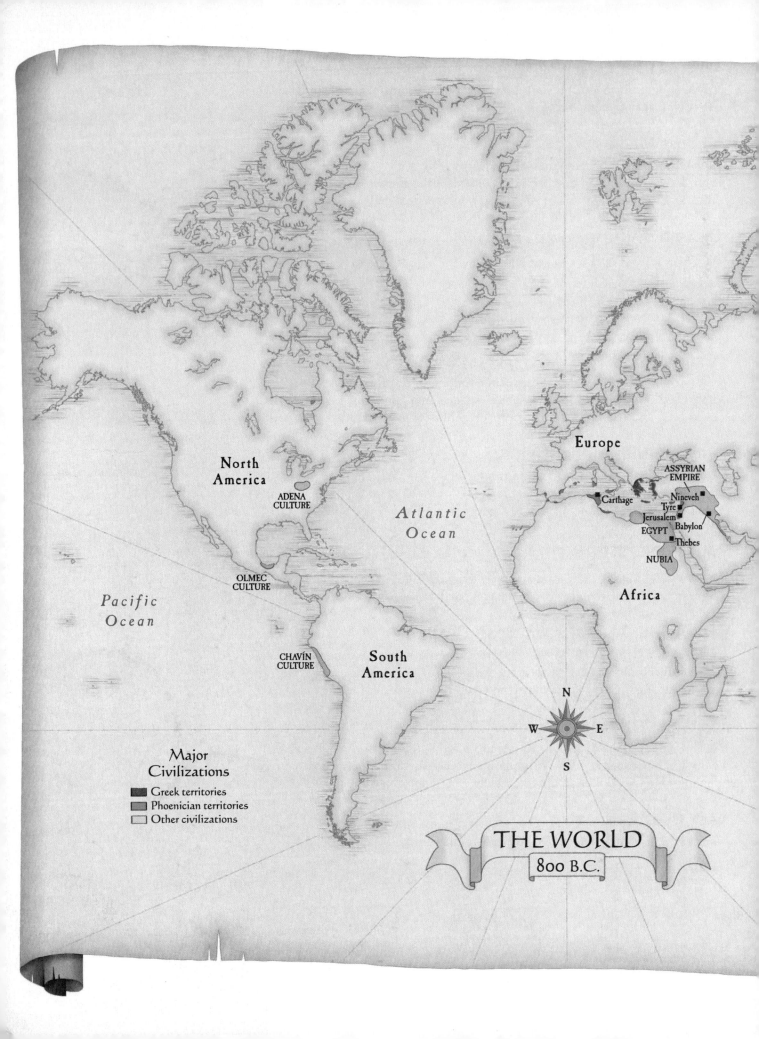

North
America

ADENA
CULTURE

OLMEC
CULTURE

*Atlantic
Ocean*

*Pacific
Ocean*

CHAVÍN
CULTURE

South
America

Europe

ASSYRIAN
EMPIRE

Carthage   Nineveh
Tyre
Jerusalem   Babylon
EGYPT
Thebes
NUBIA

Africa

N

W   E

S

Major
Civilizations

Greek territories
Phoenician territories
Other civilizations

THE WORLD
800 B.C.

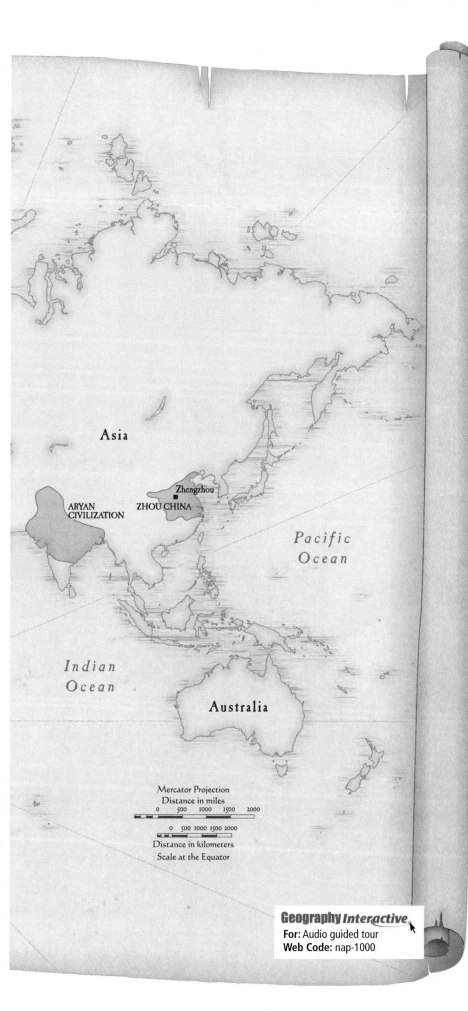

Asia

Zhengzhou

ARYAN
CIVILIZATION

ZHOU CHINA

Pacific
Ocean

Indian
Ocean

Australia

Mercator Projection
Distance in miles
0   500   1000   1500   2000

0   500 1000 1500 2000
Distance in kilometers
Scale at the Equator

Geography *Interactive*
For: Audio guided tour
Web Code: nap-1000

Foundations of Civilization
Prehistory–300 B.C.

Discovering the Ancient Past

British archaeologist Howard Carter described his discovery of the tomb of ancient Egypt's King Tutankhamen like this:

> 66 Three thousand, four thousand years maybe, have passed and gone since human feet last trod [walked on] the floor on which you stand, and yet . . . you feel it might have been but yesterday. . . . [You feel] the exhilaration of discovery, the fever of suspense, the almost overmastering impulse, born of curiosity, to break down seals and lift the lids of boxes, the thought—pure joy to the investigator—that you are about to add a page to history. 99

Listen to the Witness History audio to hear more about Carter's discovery.

◄ **Howard Carter (left) carefully cleans the golden coffin of King Tutankhamen soon after discovering it in 1922.**

King Tutankhamen's funeral mask

Chapter Preview

Chapter Focus Question What was life like in early times, and how did it change as civilizations began to develop?

Ancient cave painting from Altamira, Spain

Section 1
Understanding Our Past

Section 2
Turning Point:
The Neolithic Revolution

Section 3
Beginnings of Civilization

Ancient Mesopotamian dog statue

Note Taking Study Guide *Online*
For: Note Taking and Concept Connector worksheets
Web Code: nad-1010

An anthropologist studying the Laetoli footprints (at left); a 2-million-year-old skull (top right)

WITNESS HISTORY ◄)) AUDIO

A Clue From the Past

Mary Leakey spent her career studying the earliest ancestors of humans. In 1978, in Laetoli, Tanzania, she uncovered a remarkable and unique remnant of the early ancestors of humans—their footprints, preserved over time in volcanic ash. As Leakey studied the pattern of the footprints, she imagined how they might have been created:

66 At one point, . . . the traveler stops, pauses, turns to the left to glance at some possible threat or irregularity, then continues to the north. This motion, so intensely human, transcends time. Three million seven hundred thousand years ago, a remote ancestor— just as you or I—experienced a moment of doubt. 99

Focus Question What have scholars learned about the ancestors of humans, and how have they done so?

Understanding Our Past

Objectives

- Learn how scholars study the historical past.
- Find out how anthropologists investigate the period of prehistory.
- Understand how discoveries in Africa and beyond have influenced anthropologists' views about early humans and their ancestors.

Terms, People, and Places

prehistory	Mary Leakey
historian	Louis Leakey
artifact	Olduvai Gorge
anthropology	technology
culture	Donald Johanson
archaeology	

Note Taking

Reading Skill: Summarize As you read, use a concept web like the one below to identify the types of scholars who study the past and summarize what each type does.

By about 5,000 years ago, groups of people in different parts of the world had begun to keep written records. The invention and use of writing marked the beginning of recorded history. However, humans and their ancestors had lived on Earth for thousands upon thousands of years before the recording of history began. We call the long period of time before people invented writing **prehistory.**

Studying the Historical Past

Historians are scholars who study and write about the historical past. Historians often learn details of the past from **artifacts,** or objects made by humans. Clothing, coins, artwork, and tombstones are all types of artifacts. However, historians rely even more on written evidence, such as letters or tax records. Although it is often hard to find thorough written records from early times, those that exist offer us a narrative of events, as well as names and dates. Historians of the recent past also study such evidence as photographs or films.

Like a detective, a historian must evaluate all evidence to determine if it is reliable. Do records of a meeting between two officials tell us exactly what was said? Who was taking notes? Was a letter writer really giving an eyewitness report or just passing on rumors? Could the letter be a forgery? Historians try to find the answers to questions like these. They then interpret the evidence, or explain what it means. Often, a historian's goal is to determine the causes of a certain development or event, such as a war or an economic collapse. By explaining why things occurred in the past, historians can help us understand what happens today and what may happen in the future.

Generally, historians try to give a straightforward account of events. However, sometimes their personal experiences, cultural backgrounds, or political opinions bias their interpretations. Other times, historians disagree with one another about what the evidence proves. Such differences can lead to lively debates.

 Checkpoint What kinds of evidence do historians use to study the past?

Investigating Prehistory

About 150 years ago, scholars began studying the period of prehistory. They hoped to learn about the origins and development of people and their societies. Today, we call this field of study **anthropology.**

Anthropology Modern anthropologists specialize in certain areas of their field. For example, some study the bones of our ancestors to understand how human physical traits have changed over time. Other anthropologists focus on the characteristics of human cultures from both the past and present. In anthropology, **culture** refers to the way of life of a society, which includes its beliefs, values, and practices. Culture is handed down from one generation to the next through learning and experience.

Archaeology Within the field of anthropology, a specialized branch exists called archaeology (ahr kee AHL uh jee). **Archaeology** is the study of past people and cultures through their material remains. These remains include buildings and artifacts such as tools, weapons, pottery, clothing, and jewelry. Archaeologists find and analyze artifacts to learn about life during prehistory as well as during historical times. This helps them draw conclusions about the beliefs, values, and activities of our ancestors. However, most archaeologists agree that the story of the past is never fully known. Since archaeologists make new discoveries frequently, at times they must revise their theories in light of the new evidence.

Mycenaean pottery from about 1350 B.C.

Dating Material Remains

Relative Dating Methods

For artifacts such as pottery that change in style over time, archaeologists can group similar artifacts and then order the groups in a series from earliest style to latest style.	Archaeologists can create a chronology of artifacts based on the fact that, in general, older artifacts are found in lower levels of the site than newer ones.	When the ages of geological features at the site are known, archaeologists can use these dates to help determine the ages of material remains found near them.

Absolute Dating Methods

Because scientists know that bones lose chemical elements at a certain rate, archaeologists can determine whether or not bones found near each other were buried at the same time.	Because the age of a tree can be determined by studying the inside of its trunk, archaeologists can determine fairly accurate ages for structures built from wood.	All living things contain carbon-14, a radioactive element that decays at a set rate. Archaeologists can use carbon-14 levels to date the remains of once-living items such as bones, wood, and ash.

Chart Skills Relative dating means determining whether material remains are older or newer than one another. Absolute dating means determining exact ages. *How might you determine the ages of ten pots found buried under the floor of a wooden structure?*

Archaeologists at Work Finding ancient artifacts can be difficult, but archaeologists have devised many useful means of doing so. In the 1800s and early 1900s, archaeologists would pick a likely place, called a site, and begin digging. The farther down they dug, the older the artifacts they found. Some of the objects, which had been buried for very long periods of time, crumbled as soon as they were removed from the ground. Today, archaeologists and others who work with them take great care to preserve such fragile artifacts.

Once archaeologists have found artifacts, they analyze them. One technique is to mark the location of each type of artifact found on a map of the site. After studying the map, an archaeologist may be able to tell what activities people took part in at different locations within the site. An area full of rabbit bones, for example, might suggest the workplace of a cook. Archaeologists also need to find out how old the artifacts are.

Vocabulary Builder

technique—(tek NEEK) *n.* procedure, skill, or art used in a particular task

● **INFOGRAPHIC**

Piecing the Past Together

Many objects, monuments, or structures that archaeologists find have fallen apart over the course of time. To understand what the remains represent, an archaeologist must figure out how to piece them together correctly and then analyze their form and location. Sometimes this means fitting a building back together brick by brick; other times, it means carefully digging a skeleton out of the ground and studying the items found directly around it. The possibilities of what archaeologists might find and where they will find them are quite numerous, so they use careful procedures and their well-trained eyes to solve as best they can whatever puzzles they encounter.

Perched atop a newly found building, an archaeologist studies blocks of ancient Maya writing that have fallen from the wall they once supported.

Geologists, or experts on earth science, can help with this task by determining the age of rocks located near archaeological sites. In addition, botanists and zoologists—experts on plants and on animals—examine seeds and animal bones to learn about the diets of our ancestors. Experts on climate determine what conditions our ancestors faced on the plains of Africa or in ice-covered parts of Europe. Biologists analyze human bones as well as bloodstains found on old stone tools and weapons.

In addition to working with experts in various fields, archaeologists today use many modern innovations to study their findings. Computers help them store and sort data or develop accurate maps of archaeological sites. Aerial photographs help archaeologists to better see the layout of land and structures once lived in by past people. Techniques for measuring radioactivity aid scientists in determining the age of objects.

✓ **Checkpoint** What types of evidence do anthropologists and archaeologists study to learn about prehistory?

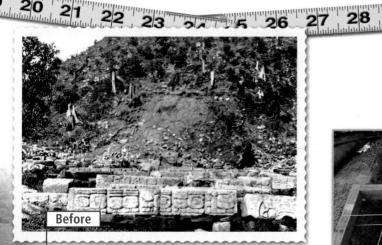

Before

In the late 1800s, archaeologists began excavating this hillside in Copán, Honduras, across which lay scattered building stones inscribed with Maya writing.

Inside a neatly dug pit with a measuring grid laid over it, an archaeologist uses a paintbrush to carefully remove dirt from a fragile skeleton. ▼

After

Today, instead of seeing a hillside, visitors to Copán marvel at a 63-step stairway reconstructed by archaeologists to look as it did when used by the ancient Maya.

Thinking Critically
1. **Analyze Information** Which of the various aspects of archaeological work do these images represent?
2. **Draw Conclusions** What challenges do you think archaeologists faced in piecing together the stairway in Copán?

Note Taking

Reading Skill: Summarize As you read, keep track of the key details scholars have learned about different hominid groups by completing a summary table like the one below. Look for dates, innovations, and other details about each hominid group.

Hominids	
Group	**Summary**
Australopithecines	

Discoveries in Africa and Beyond

Before the 1950s, anthropologists knew little about early humans and their ancestors. Prehistoric groups did not have cities, countries, organized central governments, or complex inventions, so clues about them were hard to find. However, archaeologists in East Africa started uncovering ancient footprints, bones, and tools. With these first key discoveries, scholars began to form a picture of life during prehistory.

Ancient Clues Found in East Africa In the 1930s, anthropologists Mary Leakey and Louis Leakey started searching for clues to the human past in a deep canyon in Tanzania called Olduvai Gorge (OHL duh vy). Geologists have dated the bottom layers of Olduvai Gorge to an age of 1.7 to 2.1 million years. As the Leakeys searched the sides of the gorge, they found very ancient tools chipped from stone. Although these tools looked simple, with jagged edges and rough surfaces, they showed that whoever had made them had learned to develop technologies to help them survive. Technology refers to the skills and tools people use to meet their basic needs and wants. More recent stone tools proved more sophisticated—both smooth and polished—but the older ones were exciting to the Leakeys. They felt there must be evidence of the makers of those tools in Olduvai Gorge as well.

BIOGRAPHY

Mary Leakey

Mary Leakey (1913–1996) was born in London, England. During her childhood, she traveled throughout Europe and visited numerous prehistoric sites, which increased her interest in the fields of archaeology and geology. Because of her natural artistic talent, Leakey began working as an illustrator at archaeological sites during her teenage years. In particular, she focused on drawing Stone Age tools. Through this work, she met Louis Leakey, whom she married in 1936. Together they spent 30 years digging for early humans in East Africa. Mary Leakey found many remains that have become key to our understanding of early hominids. **How did Mary Leakey become interested in studying the ancient past?**

Louis Leakey

Louis Leakey (1903–1972) was born in Kenya, where his English parents lived with the Kikuyu people. Leakey was initiated as a Kikuyu warrior at age 13 and continued to speak the Kikuyu language for many years after leaving Kenya. Leakey moved to England to attend Cambridge University, where he studied anthropology. Afterward, he returned to East Africa to search for the remains of early humans. He and his wife, Mary, found many tools, bones, and other artifacts. In later life, he traveled all over the world, lecturing and raising funds for new research projects. Leakey's enthusiasm inspired a generation of anthropologists. **Why might someone devote his or her life to studying early humans?**

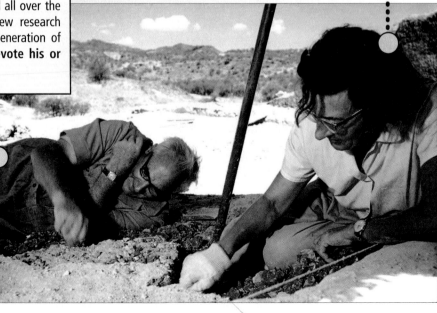

In 1959, after more than two decades of searching, Mary Leakey found a skull embedded in ancient rock at Olduvai Gorge. After careful testing, the Leakeys concluded that the skull belonged to an early hominid. Hominids, a group that includes humans and their closest relatives, all walk upright on two feet. Humans are the only hominids that live today.

Additional evidence of early hominids was found in 1974 by anthropologist **Donald Johanson.** In Ethiopia, Johanson found many pieces of a single hominid skeleton, which was dated to at least 3 million years ago. For the first time, archaeologists had enough of one skeleton to piece together and really look at an early hominid. Johanson named his historic find "Lucy" after a Beatles' song. Studying Lucy's skeleton, Johanson could see that she was an upright walker who was about 4 feet (1.2 meters) tall.

Donald Johanson was with another researcher, Tom Gray, when he began finding pieces of Lucy's skeleton. How would you describe Johanson's reaction to their discovery?

Primary Source

66 [Gray] picked it up. It was the back of a small skull. A few feet away was part of a femur: a thighbone. . . . We stood up, and began to see other bits of bone on the slope: a couple of vertebrae, part of a pelvis—all of them hominid. An unbelievable, impermissible thought flickered through my mind. Suppose all these fitted together? Could they be parts of a single, extremely primitive skeleton? No such skeleton had ever been found—anywhere.
'Look at that,' said Gray. 'Ribs.'
A single individual?
'I can't believe it,' I said. 'I just can't believe it.'99
—Donald Johanson AUDIO

Donald Johanson at work in Ethiopia

Evidence of Early Hominid Groups As of today, scientists and anthropologists have discovered and studied numerous remains and artifacts of hominids. From this work, they have established that a number of different groups of hominids lived over the course of several million years. They call the earliest group of hominids australopithecines (aw stray loh PITH uh synz). Lucy and the hominids who left their footprints in Laetoli were australopithecines. All the australopithecines lived in Africa. Anthropologists think that they may have lived there as early as 7 million years ago.

About 2 million years ago, a group of hominids emerged that anthropologists call *Homo habilis*. Scholars gave the group this name, which means "handy man," because they thought these were the first hominids to make stone tools. Since the discovery of *Homo habilis*, anthropologists have uncovered even older stone tools—2.6 million years in age—but they have not determined which hominids created them. By studying many stone tools, anthropologists have concluded that *Homo habilis* used their tools for purposes such as cutting, scraping, chopping, or sawing plants, animals, and wood.

Another group of hominids, called *Homo erectus*, also appeared around 2 million years ago. They were given their name, which means "upright man," because their skeletons show that they were fully upright walkers. *Homo erectus* were notable for having larger brains and bones and smaller teeth than other hominids. They also showed a greater range of capabilities. For example, *Homo erectus* are thought to be the first hominids to learn how to use fire. They also pioneered a new form of stone tool, called a hand ax, that could be used as the earlier tools were but also worked for digging, shattering stone or bone, and boring holes into hard surfaces. *Homo erectus* remains have been found in Asia and Europe, making scholars think they were the first hominids to migrate out of Africa.

Migrations of *Homo sapiens*
Once *Homo sapiens* had emerged, they migrated along the various routes shown on the map. Many of these routes followed the paths of large herd animals such as bison. *What do you think was the benefit to* Homo sapiens *of following large herd animals?*

First Finds of Humans Around the World Scientists think that between 250,000 and 100,000 years ago, *Homo erectus* disappeared and a new group of hominids emerged. This new group, called *Homo sapiens*, is the group to which modern humans belong. There is some dispute over where *Homo sapiens* first lived. Many scholars think the archaeological and scientific evidence supports the "Out of Africa" theory, which says that *Homo sapiens* first lived in Africa and then migrated into other areas of the world. Other scientists think that *Homo erectus* developed into *Homo sapiens* around the same time in different parts of the world.

Either way, scholars think that two groups of *Homo sapiens* soon arose—Neanderthals and the earliest modern humans. Early modern humans eventually spread all over the world, while Neanderthals lived mostly in Europe and western Asia. Sometime between 50,000 and 30,000 years ago, the Neanderthals disappeared, leaving early modern humans as the only hominids on Earth.

✓ **Checkpoint** What have anthropologists learned about the use of tools during prehistory?

Assessment

Progress Monitoring *Online*
For: Self-quiz with vocabulary practice
Web Code: naa-0111

Terms, People, and Places

1. For each term, person, or place listed at the beginning of the section, write a sentence explaining its significance.

Note Taking

2. **Reading Skill: Summarize** Use your completed concept web and table to answer the Focus Question: What have scholars learned about the ancestors of humans, and how have they done so?

Comprehension and Critical Thinking

3. **Express Problems Clearly** What types of obstacles do historians have to overcome to give a straightforward account of events? How do you think they might do this?

4. **Analyze Information** In what ways do archaeologists work with new technologies and other scholars in their work?

5. **Synthesize Information** Describe the story that anthropologists think the bones and tools they have discovered reveal about prehistory.

● **Writing About History**

Quick Write: Explore a Topic Choose a specific topic from this section and write a series of questions that you could use to direct your research for a report on it. For example, on the topic of Olduvai Gorge, you could ask the following:
- Why did the Leakeys decide to investigate this particular site?
- Have any discoveries other than the ones described in the text been made at Olduvai Gorge?

Egyptian wooden model of an agricultural scene from about 2000 B.C.

WITNESS HISTORY ◀)) AUDIO

The World's First Revolution

66 For hundreds of thousands of years, [man] had lived on wild foods, as a hunter and gatherer. . . . The revolutionary step forward was the discovery that wild grains could be cultivated and made more productive, and wild animals herded and their products made constantly available. With this discovery, the growth of fixed settlements became possible. . . . From this, all civilisation is derived.99
—Kathleen Kenyon, archaeologist

Focus Question How was the introduction of agriculture a turning point in prehistory?

Turning Point: The Neolithic Revolution

Objectives

- Describe the skills and beliefs that early modern humans developed during the Old Stone Age.
- Analyze why the beginning of farming is considered the start of the New Stone Age and the Neolithic Revolution.
- Explain how the Neolithic Revolution dramatically changed the way people lived.

Terms, People, and Places

Old Stone Age
Paleolithic Period
New Stone Age
Neolithic Period
nomad

animism
Neolithic Revolution
domesticate
Çatalhüyük
Jericho

Note Taking

Reading Skill: Summarize Use the chart below to summarize the eras of prehistory before and after the introduction of agriculture.

Eras of Prehistory	
Life Before Farming	Life After Farming
•	•
•	•
•	•

Based on the evidence gathered by anthropologists over many years, scholars have divided prehistory into different eras. They call the long period from at least 2 million B.C. to about 10,000 B.C. the **Old Stone Age**, or **Paleolithic Period**. They refer to the period from about 10,000 B.C. until the end of prehistory as the **New Stone Age**, or **Neolithic Period**. During both eras, people created and used various types of stone tools. However, during the New Stone Age, people began to develop new skills and technologies that led to dramatic changes in their everyday lives.

Skills and Beliefs of the Old Stone Age

Early modern humans lived toward the end of the Old Stone Age. Researchers have pieced together evidence left by early modern humans to paint a picture of what daily life was like for them. Early modern people were **nomads,** or people who move from place to place to find food. Typically, about 20 or 30 people lived together in small bands, or groups. They survived by hunting and by gathering food. In general, men hunted or fished. Women and children gathered berries, fruits, nuts, grains, roots, or shellfish. This food kept the band alive when game animals were scarce.

Humans Develop Strategies for Survival Early people depended heavily on their environment for food and shelter. They also found ways to adapt their surroundings to their needs. As hominids had throughout the Stone Age, early humans made tools

Techniques for Making Stone Tools

Archaeologists have discovered vast quantities of stone tools and artifacts related to their creation. Hominids made many early tools from stones such as flint that are relatively easy to shape by chipping off flakes of the stone. Once chipped, these stones have very sharp edges. Even stone tools from locations very far apart were made in similar sizes and shapes and with similar techniques.

Chopper

Flake

Oldowan Choppers and Flakes*

2.6–1.2 million years ago
Toolmakers chipped a few flakes off a stone to create a sharp-edged chopper. They often also used the flakes for scraping and cutting.

Acheulian Hand Axes

1.5 million–200,000 years ago Toolmakers chipped flakes off both sides of a stone and then shaped it into an oval with two straight, sharp edges.

Flake

Levallois Axes*

200,000–35,000 years ago
Toolmakers chipped sharp edges all around a stone. Then they knocked off one large flake that was thick in the center and sharp all around.

*Images are about 60 percent of actual size.

Creating any type of stone tool required patience, skill, strength, and a number of other tools.

Using a hard stone, the toolmaker strikes flakes off another stone to create the rough shape of an Acheulian ax.

The toolmaker uses a piece of bone to carefully refine the tool's shape.

Using a small chisel, the toolmaker chips the final flakes off the stone.

Thinking Critically

1. **Make Comparisons** How were the Acheulian hand axes and the Levallois axes similar? How were they different?
2. **Make Inferences** What can we infer about hominids communication skills from the stone tools they made?

and weapons out of the materials at hand—stone, bone, or wood. They built fires for cooking and used animal skins for clothing. At some point, early modern humans developed spoken language, which allowed them to cooperate during the hunt and perhaps discuss plans for the future.

Some Old Stone Age people also learned to travel across water, which helped them spread into new places. For example, people boated from Southeast Asia to Australia at least 40,000 years ago, most likely using rafts or canoes. They may have stopped for years at islands along the way, but in between they would have had to boat across as much as 40 miles (64 kilometers) of open ocean.

Clues About Early Religious Beliefs Toward the end of the Old Stone Age, people began to leave evidence of their belief in a spiritual world. About 100,000 years ago, some people began burying their dead with great care. Some anthropologists think that this practice suggests a belief in life after death. Old Stone Age people may have believed the afterlife would be similar to life in this world and thus provided the dead with tools, weapons, and other needed goods to take with them.

Many scholars think that our ancestors believed the world was full of spirits and forces that might reside in animals, objects, or dreams. Such beliefs are known as **animism.** In Europe, Australia, and Africa, cave or rock paintings vividly portray animals such as deer, horses, and buffaloes. Some cave paintings show people, too. The paintings often lie deep in caves, far from a band's living quarters. Some scholars think cave paintings were created as part of animist religious rituals.

 Checkpoint What skills did Old Stone Age people develop in order to adapt their surroundings to their needs?

The New Stone Age Begins With Farming

The New Stone Age began about 12,000 years ago (or about 10,000 B.C.), when nomadic people made a breakthrough that had far-reaching effects—they learned to farm.

The Neolithic Revolution By producing their own food, people no longer needed to roam in search of animals, fish, or plants. For the first time, they could remain in one place throughout the year. As a result, early farmers settled the first permanent villages. They also developed entirely new skills and technologies. This <u>transition</u> from nomadic life to settled farming brought about such dramatic changes in way of life that it is often called the **Neolithic Revolution.**

People Domesticate Plants and Animals These early farmers were the first humans to **domesticate** plants and animals—that is, to raise them in a controlled way that makes them best suited to human use. Plant domestication may have begun with food gatherers realizing that seeds scattered on the ground would produce new plants the next year. Animal domestication may have begun with people deciding to round up the animals they usually hunted. They could then use the animals as they always had—for food and skins—as well as to provide other benefits, such as milk or eggs.

Evidence shows that people began to farm in different parts of the world at different times, and that they did not domesticate all the same plants or animals in each place. For example, domestication seems to have begun in China about 13,000 B.C., when people domesticated the dog. From about 8000 B.C. to 6000 B.C., people in western Asia domesticated goats, sheep, and pigs, while people in Turkey and western Africa domesticated cattle, and people in South America domesticated llamas and alpacas. Around the same time—from about 10,000 B.C. to 6000 B.C.—people in Africa and Southeast Asia domesticated yams, in China millet and rice, in Central America and Mexico squash and gourds, and in the Middle East barley, chickpeas, peas, lentils, and wheat.

 Checkpoint What major lifestyle changes did farming allow people to make?

Vocabulary Builder

<u>transition</u>—(tran ZISH un) *n.* process of undergoing a change from one stage to another

World's First Domesticated Animal
About 10,000 years after people first domesticated dogs, people in some cultures began depicting dogs in their artwork. Around 2000 B.C., an artist from Mesopotamia created this stone sculpture of a dog, which is covered in ancient writing.

The inhabitants might use the upper floor to store crops such as wheat and apples.

Many houses included a shrine. It was decorated with bulls' horns and sometimes wall paintings. A burial often lay sheltered beneath the shrine floor.

Food was prepared in a small clay oven or over a hearth.

History Interactive
For: Interactive illustration
Web Code: nap-0121

At Home in Çatalhüyük
Archaeologists have studied the ruins of Çatalhüyük to learn about the village's houses. They think people entered a house through a hole in its roof. *Based on the illustration, what evidence do you think archaeologists used to learn about the interior of the houses?*

The Neolithic Revolution Brings Dramatic Change

Once the Neolithic Revolution had begun, no greater change in the way people lived took place until the Industrial Revolution of the late 1700s. Settled farming led to the establishment of the first villages and to significant advances in technology and culture. As you will read in the next section, these advances eventually led to a new stage of development—the emergence of cities and civilizations.

Earliest Villages Established Archaeologists have unearthed the remains of some of the first Neolithic villages, including Çatalhüyük (chah TAHL hyoo YOOK) in modern-day Turkey and Jericho (JEHR ih koh), which still exists today as an Israeli-controlled city. Jericho was built between 10,000 and 9000 B.C. Although the village was tiny—about the size of a few soccer fields—a few thousand people lived in it. The village was surrounded by a huge wall, which suggests that it had a government or leader who was able to organize a large construction project. Çatalhüyük seems to have developed around 7000 B.C. and may have had a population as large as 6,500 people. The village covered about three times more land than Jericho and included hundreds of rectangular mud-brick houses, all connected and all about the same size.

Settled People Change Their Ways of Life Like their Paleolithic ancestors, early farmers probably divided up the work by gender and age. Still, important differences began to emerge. In settled farming communities, men came to dominate family, economic, and political life. Heads of families, probably older men, formed a council of elders and made decisions about when to plant and harvest. When food was scarce, warfare increased, and some men gained prestige as warriors. These elite warriors asserted power over others in society.

Settled people had more personal property than nomadic people. In addition, some settled people accumulated more possessions than their neighbors, so differences in wealth began to appear.

Villagers Invent New Technologies To farm successfully, people had to develop new technologies. Like farmers today, they had to find ways to protect their crops and measure out enough seed for the next year's harvest. They also needed to measure time accurately to know when to plant and harvest. Eventually, people would use such measurements to create the first calendars. As well, many farmers learned to use animals such as oxen or water buffalo to plow the fields.

Archaeological evidence shows that some villages had separate workshops where villagers made tools, including smooth, polished ax heads and chipped arrowheads. In some parts of the world, Neolithic people learned to weave cloth from animal hair or vegetable fibers. Many Neolithic people began using clay to create pottery for cooking and storage. Archaeologists have learned about life during this period from finds such as "the Iceman"—the body of a Neolithic man found preserved in snow in the European Alps alongside various tools and belongings.

Technologies were not invented everywhere at the same time. Knowledge of some traveled slowly from one area to another, perhaps taking thousands of years to spread across continents. Other technologies were invented separately in different parts of the world and showed varying degrees of similarity.

✔ **Checkpoint** What new technologies did people invent as a result of agriculture?

WITNESS HISTORY VIDEO

Watch *Secrets of the Iceman* on the **Witness History Discovery School**™ video program to learn more about the discovery of the Iceman.

Discovery SCHOOL

SECTION 2 Assessment

Progress Monitoring *Online*
For: Self-quiz with vocabulary practice
Web Code: naa-0121

Terms, People, and Places

1. What do many of the key terms listed at the beginning of the section have in common? Explain.

Note Taking

2. **Reading Skill: Summarize** Use your completed chart to answer the Focus Question: How was the introduction of agriculture a turning point in prehistory?

Comprehension and Critical Thinking

3. **Predict Consequences** How do you think the development of spoken language influenced people's development of skills and religious beliefs?

4. **Determine Relevance** How are our lives today affected by the Neolithic Revolution that occurred 11,000 years ago?

5. **Make Comparisons** How was settled village life different from nomadic life? Consider population size, social status, and technology in your answer.

● **Writing About History**

Quick Write: Gather Information Choose a topic from this section to write a research report about and gather sources related to it. Your sources may include books, magazines, and the Internet. For example, on the topic of cave paintings, you might locate the following:

- a magazine article that describes and shows photographs of the paintings in a particular cave
- a book that compares Stone Age cave paintings from different regions

Paleolithic Cave Art

The surviving examples of the first human art date from the end of the Paleolithic Period, from roughly 30,000 to 12,000 B.C. Examples have been discovered in about 250 caves in southern France and northern Spain. A few caves containing art have also been found in Italy, Siberia, southern and eastern Africa, and Australia. Cave paintings, which often cover entire walls, are a common form of Paleolithic cave art. Paleolithic people also engraved drawings on cave walls and carved the stone when it was soft enough.

Sculpture
Paleolithic carved sculpture such as this clay bison has only been found in caves in France. On some of the sculptures, traces of pigment can still be found, indicating that they were once painted.

Wall Paintings
Many of the Paleolithic cave paintings found so far show large animals such as horses, bison, bulls, and deer. Lions, bears, seals, and owls appear occasionally. The animals are usually painted in pigments made from minerals such as hematite, kaolin, and charcoal.

Cave Lamp
Paleolithic artists created light in the caves by burning animal fat in lamps like this one.

Kaolin

Charcoal

Hematite

Thinking Critically

1. **Make Generalizations** What might the fact that Paleolithic people created art on cave walls tell you about their skills and experiences?
2. **Express Problems Clearly** What challenges do you think people face today when trying to locate Paleolithic cave art?

Ancient Mesopotamian carving of a carpenter at work

The Daily Grind Begins

The development of the first civilizations brought about a major change in daily life. Instead of everyone working on a few major tasks necessary for day-to-day survival, such as farming and hunting, people in early civilizations developed and perfected many new trades. A carpenter like the one shown at left might spend his day shaping wooden furniture, while his wife might weave fabrics and sell them in a local market.

Focus Question How did the world's first civilizations arise and develop?

Beginnings of Civilization

Objectives
- Analyze the conditions under which the first cities and civilizations arose.
- Outline the basic features that define civilization.
- Understand the ways in which civilizations have changed over time.

Terms, People, and Places

surplus	pictograph
traditional economy	scribe
civilization	cultural diffusion
steppe	city-state
polytheistic	empire
artisan	

Note Taking

Reading Skill: Summarize As you read, create a chart showing the different phases of the development of civilizations. Summarize each phase using details from the text.

The Development of Civilizations		
Rise of Cities and Civilizations	**Features of Civilizations**	**Changes Over Time**
•	•	•
•	•	•

The establishment of villages such as Çatalhüyük and Jericho symbolized a huge step in human development. Societies were becoming more organized, and people's technological innovations were becoming increasingly complex. Soon would follow a momentous change in human existence—the development of civilizations.

First Cities and Civilizations Arise

The earliest civilizations to develop were all situated near major rivers. These rivers provided a regular water supply and a means of transportation. The animals that flocked to the rivers to drink were a source of food. Perhaps most important, conditions in the river valleys favored farming. Floodwaters spread silt—tiny bits of rock and dirt from the river bottom—across the valleys, renewing the soil and keeping it fertile.

In such rich conditions, farmers were able to produce **surpluses** of food, or more than was necessary. These surpluses allowed them to feed growing populations and to store food for the future. Thus they were able to produce enough food to support increasingly large populations. As populations expanded, some villages swelled into the world's first cities. In these cities, some of the people were able to work at jobs other than farming. This was a radical departure from the traditional economies of the Stone Age. A **traditional economy** relies on habit, custom, or ritual and tends not to change over time. As you will read, in cities, many aspects of life were dramatically different than they had been before.

River Valley Civilizations

Geography *Interactive*
For: Audio guided tour
Web Code: nap-0131

EUROPE

ASIA

Egypt

Sumer

Shang China

Indus civilization

AFRICA

Atlantic Ocean

Indian Ocean

Equator

Miller Projection

0   500   1000   1500 mi

0   500   1000   1500 km

Egypt, 2575–2130 B.C.
Indus civilization, 2600–1900 B.C.
Shang China, 1766–1122 B.C.
Sumer, 3300–1900 B.C.

Tropic of Capricorn

AUSTRALIA

0°

30°S

0°

60°E

90°E

Egypt

Mediterranean Sea

Nile Delta

Giza

Memphis

Libyan Desert

Nile River

Thebes

Red Sea

Nubian Desert

Miller Projection

0   200 mi

0   200 km

Sumer

Tigris River

Euphrates River

Uruk

Ur

Arabian Desert

Persian Gulf

Miller Projection

0   200 mi

0   200 km

Indus civilization

Hindu Kush

Indus River

Harappa

Mohenjo-Daro

Thar Desert

HIMALAYAS

Northern Plain

Ganges R.

Vindhya Mts.

Narmada River

Arabian Sea

Miller Projection

0   250 mi

0   250 km

Shang China

Huang River

Anyang

Huang River

Wei River

Luoyang

Zhengzhou

Yellow Sea

Chang River

East China Sea

Miller Projection

0   300 mi

0   300 km

Map Skills The world's earliest civilizations arose in fertile river valleys in Africa and Asia.

1. **Locate** (a) Sumer (b) Mohenjo-Daro (c) Chang River (d) Giza

2. **Region** Locate the Indus civilization. What types of natural features surround the region? Name one feature of each type.

3. **Make Comparisons** How did the four River Valley Civilizations compare to one another in size? In time frame? How might you explain Sumer's small size based on the comparison of time frames?

River Valley Civilizations The rise of cities was the main feature of civilization. A civilization is a complex, highly organized social order. The world's first civilizations arose independently in a number of river valleys. These River Valley Civilizations include Sumer, between the Tigris and Euphrates rivers in the Middle East; Egypt, along the Nile River; the Indus civilization, along the Indus River in India; and the Shang civilization, along the Huang (hwahng) River, or Yellow River, in China. You will read in depth about each of these River Valley Civilizations in later chapters.

First Civilizations in the Americas Unlike the first civilizations in Asia and Africa, the first civilizations in the Americas arose away from river valleys. Major civilizations emerged in the highlands of Peru, Mexico, and Central America, where people learned to farm on the sides of mountains or to fill in swamps with land for farming. You will read about the achievements of civilizations such as the Inca, the Olmec, and the Maya in a later chapter.

Life Away From Cities Away from the first cities, many people continued to hunt, gather food, or live in farming villages. On some less fertile lands or on sparse, dry grasslands called steppes, nomadic herders tended cattle, sheep, goats, or other animals. Because the lands did not have abundant water or grass, these nomads had to keep moving to find new pasture.

 Checkpoint In what ways were river valleys ideal locations for civilizations to develop?

Basic Features That Define Civilization

What did the early civilizations that arose in different parts of the world have in common? While cities are the main feature of civilization, historians distinguish several other basic features of most early civilizations. Seven of the major features are (1) organized governments, (2) complex religions, (3) job specialization, (4) social classes, (5) arts and architecture, (6) public works, and (7) writing.

Organized Governments Councils of elders or chiefs ruled many of the world's farming villages. However, in cities, more powerful organized governments arose to oversee large-scale efforts that benefited the people. For example, as cities grew, their residents required a steady supply of food. A central government could coordinate the production of large amounts of food. In addition, farmers near rivers needed to control flooding and channel waters to the fields. A well-organized government could bring people together for projects such as building dikes, digging canals, and carving out irrigation ditches.

Many rulers also relied on royal officials to help them govern by issuing laws, collecting taxes, and organizing systems of defense. Over time, governments became more complex, and separate departments often evolved to oversee different functions of government. In many early cases, priests probably had the greatest power in government. In others, warrior kings emerged as the main political leaders. Often, they claimed that their right to rule came from the gods, and they passed their power on from father to son. Thus, many political rulers gained religious power as well.

Vocabulary Builder

complex—(kahm PLEKS) *adj.* made up of many interrelated parts

Complex Religions Most ancient people were **polytheistic,** which means they believed in many gods. People appealed to sun gods, river goddesses, and other gods that they believed controlled natural forces or human activities such as birth or war.

In early religions, priests and worshipers sought to gain the favor of the gods through complex rituals such as ceremonies, dances, prayers, and hymns. To ensure divine help, people built temples and sacrificed animals, crops, or sometimes other humans to the gods. Sacrifices and other ceremonies required the full-time attention of priests, who had special training and knowledge.

Job Specialization The lives of city dwellers differed from those of nomads. Urban people developed so many new crafts that a single individual could not master all the skills needed to make tools, weapons, or other goods. For the first time, individuals began to specialize in certain jobs. Some became **artisans,** or skilled craftspeople, and made pottery or finely carved or woven goods. Among the crafts developed in cities, metalworking was particularly important. People learned to make tools and weapons, first out of copper and later out of bronze, a more durable mixture of copper and tin.

Cities had other specialists, too. Bricklayers built city walls. Soldiers defended these walls. Merchants sold goods in the marketplace. Singers, dancers, and storytellers entertained on public occasions. Such specialization made people dependent on others for their various needs.

Social Classes In cities, social organization became more complex. People were ranked according to their jobs. Such ranking led to the growth of social classes. Priests and nobles usually occupied the top level of an ancient society. Next came a small class of wealthy merchants, followed by artisans. Below them came the vast majority of people—peasant farmers who lived in the surrounding villages and produced food for the city.

In many civilizations, slaves occupied the lowest social level. Slaves sometimes came from poor families who sold family members into slavery to pay their debts. Others became slaves as punishment for crimes or were prisoners captured in war. Because male captives were often killed, women and children made up the largest number of slaves in some societies.

Arts and Architecture The arts and architecture of ancient civilizations expressed the talents, beliefs, and values of the people who created them. Temples and palaces often dominated the city landscape. Many rulers may have ordered such buildings to be constructed in order to remind people of the strength and power of their government and religion. The skilled workers who built these massive buildings decorated them with wall paintings, statues of gods, goddesses, or rulers, and other stunning pieces of design work.

Basic Features of Civilizations

Feature	Description
Cities	Population centers that are notably larger and more organized than towns or villages and that support the other features of civilizations
Organized Governments	Structured governments that coordinate large-scale projects such as food production or construction, establish laws, and organize defense systems
Complex Religions	Systems of religious beliefs that usually include rituals and worship of one or more gods and/or goddesses
Job Specialization	System in which there are different types of jobs and each worker focuses on one particular type
Social Classes	Ranked groups within society that are determined by job or economic standing
Arts and Architecture	Various types of artwork and buildings that express the talents, beliefs, and values of people in a society
Public Works	Large-scale and often costly projects that benefit the city and its people
Writing	Structured writing systems used initially by governments or religious leaders to record important information

Chart Skills The basic features of civilizations help show how early civilizations differed from smaller farming societies and nomadic lifestyles. *Which features of civilizations do you think most affected the daily lives of average people?*

INFOGRAPHIC
Bridges: Then and Now

Today, bridges span countless waterways, ravines, highways, and other areas around the world that people need to pass over. Their construction requires solid leadership, thorough planning, and often immense resources. In ancient times, such public works projects could only be undertaken once civilizations had established organized governments and developed the mathematical and engineering knowledge needed to construct bridges that would remain standing over time.

▲ **600 B.C.** The oldest stone bridge still standing today was constructed under the rule of Assyrian King Sennacherib. It spans a small river in Jerwan, Iraq.

▲ **A.D. 600** Chinese Emperor Yang Ti oversaw the construction of the An Ji Bridge. It was the first of its kind, called an open-spandrel arched bridge.

◄ **1992** Like the dramatic Alamillo Bridge built in Seville, Spain, many modern-day bridges are suspension bridges supported by strong cables.

Thinking Critically
1. **Draw Conclusions** Why would ancient societies have valued bridges?
2. **Recognize Sufficient Evidence** What evidence would archaeologists need to learn how ancient bridges were built?

Public Works Strong rulers also ordered vast public works to be built. Such projects included irrigation systems, roads, bridges, and defensive walls. These public works projects were meant to benefit the city by protecting it from attack, ensuring its food supply, or enhancing the reputation of its ruler. The projects were often quite costly, requiring a great deal of human labor and sometimes resulting in the loss of lives during construction.

Writing Of the earliest civilizations, some but not all developed a critical skill—writing. The first writing systems were established in different places and at different times, in many cases with no contact among the different groups who created them. Thus the earliest writing systems varied in appearance, structure, and purpose. Some were first used in temples, where priests needed to record amounts of grain collected, accurate information about the seasons, and precise rituals and prayers. Other writing systems were first used on public monuments, where rulers spelled out their greatest achievements as a means of advertising their power to the people. Archaeologists have found masses of ancient writings, some on clay tablets or vases, others on stone statues, and yet others on the walls of buildings.

The first step people made toward developing writing was to use **pictographs** (also called pictograms), or simple drawings that look like the objects they represent. Later, they developed complex writing systems including symbols that represent words, syllables, or letters. As writing grew more complex, only specially trained people called **scribes** could read and write. Scribes kept records for priests, rulers, and merchants. Only a few societies permitted women to become scribes, an occupation that could lead to political power.

Cause and Effect

Causes

- Neolithic people learn to farm.➤ Hunters and gatherers settle into farming communities.➤ Some farmers settle in river valleys, where the soil is very fertile.➤ New technologies improve farming.➤ Food surpluses support growing populations.➤ The first cities are built in fertile valleys.

Rise of River Valley Civilizations

Effects

- Complex forms of government develop.
- Arts become more elaborate.
- Job specialization leads to social classes.
- People invent writing.
- Early civilizations conquer neighboring lands.

Connections to Today

- Archaeologists continue to discover rich stores of information about Neolithic people and early civilizations.
- In the modern day, people continue to live along rivers, in both villages and large cities.

Analyze Cause and Effect A series of different factors caused the rise of River Valley Civilizations. *Which cause do you think led most directly to job specialization? Why?*

Comparing Nomadic Life and Civilizations Nomadic cultures differed from civilizations in their social organization—that is, they did not exhibit many of the characteristics of civilization. The people did not build cities, and their governments were simpler than those of civilizations. However, nomadic peoples often excelled in arts and sciences. For example, many groups developed sophisticated traditions in oral poetry, music, weaving, jewelry making, and animal raising.

 Checkpoint What roles did governments play in early civilizations?

Civilizations Change Over Time

Ancient civilizations changed in many ways over the centuries. Among the chief causes of change were shifts in the physical environment and interactions among people. Among the major results was the expansion of cities into larger political entities.

Environment Affects People's Lives Like their Stone Age ancestors, people living in early civilizations depended heavily on the physical environment. They needed ample rain and fertile soil to be able to produce crops. Resources such as stone, timber, or metals were also essential. Significant changes in the environment could have an immediate impact on people's lives.

At times, a sudden, drastic event would devastate a community. An earthquake or the eruption of a volcano could wipe out an entire civilization. Farming the same land too much could destroy soil fertility, and rivers could become too salty. Cities would then suffer famine, and survivors would be forced to move away.

If people used up nearby timber or ran out of other building resources, they would have to find ways to adapt to this scarcity. They might, for example, trade with people in areas where such resources were readily available. Or they might use alternate building materials such as reeds.

Culture Changes Hands and Changes Shape Another major source of change for people living in ancient times was **cultural diffusion,** the spread of ideas, customs, and technologies from one people to another. Cultural diffusion occurred through migration, trade, and warfare.

As famine, drought, or other disasters led people to migrate, they interacted with others whose lives differed from their own. As a result, people often shared and adapted the customs of others. Trade, too, introduced people to new goods or better methods of producing them. In ancient times, skills such as working with bronze and writing, as well as religious beliefs, passed from one society to another. Warfare also brought change. Often, victorious armies forced their way of life upon the people they defeated. On other occasions, the victors incorporated the ways of a conquered people into their society.

Cities Grow Into City-States As ancient rulers gained more power, they conquered territories beyond the boundaries of their cities. This expansion led to the rise of the **city-state,** a political unit that included a city and its surrounding lands and villages. Rulers, nobles, and priests often controlled the land outside the city and forced peasants to give them some of the crops they grew on it. In some places, a <u>significant</u> portion of each harvest went to support the government and temples.

First Empires Are Established Rival leaders often battled for power. Sometimes, ambitious rulers conquered many cities and villages, creating the first empires. An **empire** is a group of states or territories controlled by one ruler. For the conquered people, defeat was painful and often cruel. At the same time, empire building also brought benefits. It helped end war between neighboring communities and created common bonds among people. As you will soon read, many impressive civilizations and powerful empires developed all over the world and left a lasting legacy behind them.

☑ **Checkpoint** How have different types of challenges encouraged peoples and civilizations to change over time?

With Empires Come Warfare
One of the most powerful empires of ancient history was that of Alexander the Great. Here, Darius III of Persia leads his troops into a ferocious—but losing—battle against Alexander.

Vocabulary Builder
<u>significant</u>—(sig NIF uh kint) *adj.* relatively large in amount

SECTION **3** Assessment

Progress Monitoring *Online*
For: Self-quiz with vocabulary practice
Web Code: naa-0131

Terms, People, and Places

1. Place each of the terms listed at the beginning of the section into one of the following categories: government, culture, economy, geography, or technology. Write a sentence for each term explaining your choice.

Note Taking

2. **Reading Skill: Summarize** Use your completed chart to answer the Focus Question: How did the world's first civilizations arise and develop?

Comprehension and Critical Thinking

3. **Make Comparisons** How were the conditions under which early civilizations developed in Asia and Africa different from those of the Americas?

4. **Synthesize Information** In early civilizations, how did religion influence government and social classes?

5. **Identify Central Issues** (a) Give three examples of cultural change in early civilizations. (b) Give two examples of cultural diffusion today.

● **Writing About History**
Quick Write: Make an Outline Choose a topic from this section and make an outline of a research report about it. In your outline, include main ideas and details that support them. For example, on the topic of the invention of writing, you might include these main ideas in your outline:

- Writing was a major achievement of early civilizations.
- The first known writing system was developed in Mesopotamia.
- Writing was first used for different reasons in different civilizations.

CHAPTER 1

Quick Study Guide

Progress Monitoring *Online*
For: Self-test with vocabulary practice
Web Code: naa-0141

■ Scholars Who Study the Past

Historians	Anthropologists/Archaeologists
Study and write about the people and events of history	Study the origins and developments of people and their societies during prehistory and history; study physical and cultural traits of people
Primarily analyze written records; also analyze artifacts	Primarily analyze artifacts and material remains; also analyze written records
Evaluate the evidence using reasonable judgments and the work of other scholars	Evaluate the evidence using reasonable judgments, modern innovations, and the work of other types of scholars
Interpret and explain the evidence	Interpret and explain the evidence
Sort out disagreements over the evidence and change theories in light of new evidence	Sort out disagreements over the evidence and change theories in light of new evidence

■ Hominid Groups Over Time

Hominid Group	Earliest Known Evidence
Australopithecines	7 million years ago
Homo habilis	2 million years ago
Homo erectus	2 million years ago
Homo sapiens • Neanderthals • Early modern humans	250,000–100,000 years ago

■ Key Stages of Human Development

Old Stone Age
- creation of stone, bone, and wood tools and weapons
- use of fire
- spoken language
- ability to travel across water in boats
- belief in a spiritual world
- creation of cave paintings
- burial of the dead

New Stone Age
- farming and domestication of plants and animals
- settling of permanent villages
- dominance of family, economic, and political life by men
- gaining of prestige by warriors
- appearance of differences in wealth
- creation of first calendars
- more elaborate tools and new technologies

Rise of Civilizations
- production of surpluses of food
- expansion of populations
- development of cities, civilizations, and governments
- government oversight of large-scale projects
- belief in polytheistic religions
- job specialization
- development of social classes
- development of arts and architecture
- invention of writing systems
- expansion of some cities into city-states and empires
- cultural diffusion

■ Key Events of Prehistory

2 million B.C.
Early human ancestors have begun making and using simple stone tools.

| **7 million B.C.** | **2 million B.C.** | **100,000 B.C.** |

7 million B.C.
By this time, the earliest ancestors of modern humans may live in Africa.

100,000 B.C.
The earliest modern humans, called *Homo sapiens*, begin to spread throughout the world.

Concept Connector

Cumulative Review

Record the answers to the questions below on your Concept Connector worksheets. In addition, record information from this chapter about the following concepts:

- Advances in Technology: Paleolithic stone tools
- Belief Systems: animism
- Geography's Impact: rivers and the rise of civilization

1. **Migration** Populations of both *Homo erectus* and *Homo sapiens* eventually migrated into various parts of the world. Additionally, migration was a regular part of life for nomads during the periods of prehistory and history. What factors do you think contributed to the migrations of early people? Think about the following:
   - sources of food
   - climate changes
   - environmental events
   - competition among groups of people

2. **People and the Environment** Compare the ways that Stone Age hominids adapted the environment to their needs to the ways that Neolithic farmers adapted the environment to their needs.

3. **Cultural Diffusion** Cultural diffusion has long been a key source of change in society. Do you think that all changes that took place during the Old Stone Age, the New Stone Age, and the time of early civilizations were the result of cultural diffusion? Think about the following:
   - the use of fire
   - the creation of stone tools
   - the painting of caves
   - the domestication of plants and animals
   - the locations of early civilizations

Connections to Today

1. **Civilization: The History of Cities** Just as the first cities were built in river valleys because of the benefits they offered, many of today's major cities were also built in advantageous locations. Some cities—such as St. Louis, Missouri; London, England; and Delhi, India—do lie along rivers. Other cities—such as New York, New York; Cape Town, South Africa; Rio de Janeiro, Brazil; and Lisbon, Portugal—sit alongside the open ocean. Yet others rise up from the rare low ground amidst mountain ranges. Conduct research on three major world cities to find out why they were built in their particular locations. Write a few paragraphs explaining your findings.

2. **Technology: The Computer Revolution** The introduction of farming during the New Stone Age is considered the world's first technological revolution. During the twentieth century, the computer revolutionized life as well. Early computers were enormous machines, but by the 1970s, they began to be built smaller, and by the 1990s, many households owned at least one personal computer. In addition, the Internet and numerous small electronic devices soon made personal computing a basic part of life for many people. Computers also revolutionized work life, as many industries have come to rely on computers to power their operations. Considering the various ways in which computers have changed daily life, what similarities and differences do you see between the impact of the Neolithic Revolution and that of the computer revolution?

40,000 B.C.
By this time, people have traveled across the ocean by boat from Southeast Asia to Australia.

9000 B.C.
People learn to grow their own crops and begin settling in permanent farming villages.

History Interactive
For: Interactive timeline
Web Code: nap-0141

40,000 B.C.   9000 B.C.   3000 B.C.

30,000 B.C.
Early people begin painting animals on the walls of caves.

3200 B.C.
The world's first civilizations begin to develop in river valleys.

Chapter Assessment

Terms, People, and Places

Choose the italicized term in parentheses that best completes each sentence.

1. The way of life of a society is its *(technology/culture)*.
2. *(Mary Leakey/Donald Johanson)* gave the name Lucy to an australopithecine skeleton.
3. The *(Paleolithic Period/Neolithic Period)* lasted from at least 2 million B.C. to about 10,000 B.C.
4. *(Çatalhüyük/Jericho)* was a tiny Neolithic village surrounded by a huge wall.
5. A highly organized social order is a *(steppe/civilization)*.
6. People who believe in many gods are *(scribes/polytheistic)*.
7. A group of states or territories controlled by one ruler is a(n) *(empire/city-state)*.

Main Ideas

Section 1 (pp. 4–10)
8. In what part of the world did the earliest hominids live?
9. For what purposes did hominids create stone tools?

Section 2 (pp. 11–16)
10. How did Old Stone Age people find food?
11. What change marked the beginning of the New Stone Age? In what ways did this change alter people's way of life?

Section 3 (pp. 17–23)
12. In which four river valleys did early civilizations emerge?
13. List the eight basic features of most early civilizations.

Chapter Focus Question
14. What was life like in early times, and how did it change as civilizations began to develop?

Critical Thinking

15. **Analyze Cartoons** How does this cartoon reflect the challenges that archaeologists face when interpreting the evidence that they find?

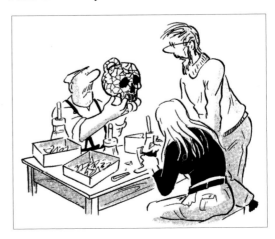

16. **Draw Inferences** Many scholars interpret evidence such as cave paintings and burials as indications of early people's beliefs. How do you think material remains help show people's feelings and thoughts?
17. **Make Comparisons** Think about the ways of life of both early nomads and early farmers. How do you think geography affected each group in both positive and negative ways?
18. **Predict Consequences** Before writing systems were invented, people had to share and remember ideas, customs, and technology by word of mouth. How do you think writing eventually changed this?
19. **Recognize Cause and Effect** Which feature(s) of civilization do you think most allowed empires to develop?

● Writing About History

Writing a Research Report The period of prehistory includes many fascinating topics related to the development of early humans and civilizations. Write a research report on one of the following topics: discoveries at Olduvai Gorge, cave painting, the Neolithic Revolution, early writing systems. Be sure to describe some of the evidence that anthropologists and archaeologists have gathered and explain what it tells us about the topic. Consult page SH13 of the Writing Handbook for additional help.

Prewriting
- Choose the topic that interests you most and take notes about the evidence scholars have found and what they think it means.
- Create a set of questions about the topic and gather additional resources that will help you answer those questions.

Drafting
- Develop a working thesis and choose information to support it.
- Make an outline organizing the report.
- Write an introduction explaining why the topic is interesting. Then write the body of the text and a conclusion.

Revising
- Use the guidelines for revising your report on page SH15 of the Writing Handbook.

Document-Based Assessment

Who Were These Tiny Hominids?

When anthropologists make new finds, they are not always sure exactly what they have discovered. As you study the reports below of researchers finding the remains of tiny hominids, consider the challenges of determining the meaning of ancient evidence.

Document A

"Scientists have discovered a new species of ancient human that lived 18,000 years ago on an island east of the Java Sea—a pre-historic hunter. . . . These "little people" stood about three feet tall and had heads the size of grapefruit. . . . The research team . . . described the remains—a fairly complete skull, the jawbone and much of the skeleton—as those of a 30-year-old woman. . . . The team also found . . . the remains of between five and seven people in all."

—Guy Gugliotta, **washingtonpost.com,** October 28, 2004

Document B

"So what was this strange creature, and what was it doing on [the island of] Flores? The [researchers] have had to make difficult choices in deciding how to classify the creature, although it is clear that this person was definitely not a modern human. The small brain size and the hip-bone shape might favour classification as an australopithecine, whereas the size and shape of the skull might suggest a primitive form of *H. erectus.* Given the unique combination of features, the [researchers] have decided to give the specimen a new name: *Homo floresiensis.*"

—Chris Stringer, **news@nature.com,** October 27, 2004

Document C

"The researchers estimate that the tiny people lived on [the island of] Flores from about 95,000 years ago until at least 13,000 years ago. The scientists base their theory on charred bones and stone tools found on the island. The [tools] were apparently used to hunt big game. . . . The Flores people used fire in hearths for cooking and hunted stegodon, a primitive dwarf elephant found on the island. . . . Almost all of the stegodon bones associated with the human artifacts are of juveniles [youths], suggesting the tiny humans selectively hunted the smallest stegodons."

—Hillary Mayell, **nationalgeographic.com,** October 27, 2004

Document D

An adult *Homo floresiensis* skull (left) beside an adult modern human skull (right)

Analyzing Documents

Use your knowledge of prehistory and Documents A, B, C, and D to answer questions 1–4.

1. Documents B and C describe the discovery of
   A modern human remains.
   B australopithecine remains.
   C *Homo erectus* remains.
   D *Homo floresiensis* remains.

2. Which is NOT a theory that researchers have expressed about the tiny hominids whose remains were found on Flores?
   A The tiny hominids lived at least 13,000 years ago.
   B The tiny hominids were juveniles.
   C The tiny hominids had small heads and brains.
   D The tiny hominids hunted dwarf elephants.

3. Which is the most accurate conclusion that can be drawn from Document D about the relative sizes of *Homo floresiensis* and modern human adults?
   A Modern human adults have larger bodies than *Homo floresiensis* adults.
   B Modern human adults have larger skulls than *Homo floresiensis* adults.
   C The modern human skull pictured is larger than the *Homo floresiensis* skull pictured.
   D The *Homo floresiensis* skull pictured is older than the modern human skull pictured.

4. **Writing Task** Which information given in Documents A, B, C, and D seems the most reliable to you? Which seems the least reliable? Use your knowledge and specific information from these documents to support your opinion.

2 Ancient Middle East and Egypt

3200 B.C.–500 B.C.

Expanding Empires, Elite Troops

As the world's first civilizations and empires arose, military power became one of the defining aspects of success. The Persian rulers who controlled a vast empire relied on a large army that included a famous and elite branch of troops. The Greek historian Herodotus described these troops as follows:

❝This corps was known as the Immortals, because it was invariably kept up to strength; if a man was killed or fell sick, the vacancy he left was filled at once, so that the total strength of the corps was never less—and never more— than 10,000.❞

Listen to the Witness History audio to hear more about ancient Persia.

◀ The brightly colored archers that emerge from the walls of the palace of Persian ruler Darius I in Susa are thought to represent the Immortals.

An ancient coin from the Persian empire

A musical instrument called a lyre from ancient Sumer

Chapter Preview

Chapter Focus Question What distinct characteristics did the early civilizations and empires of the Middle East and Egypt develop?

The blue glass drinking vessel of an ancient Egyptian king

Note Taking Study Guide *Online*
For: Note Taking and Concept Connector worksheets
Web Code: nad-0201

Sumerian depiction of a man playing a lyre (above); Sumerian lyre (right)

WITNESS HISTORY 🔊 AUDIO

Ancient Times, Ancient Tunes

Music may be one of the most difficult artistic forms of early civilizations for us to find evidence of because the songs themselves leave no physical trace. But in the ruins of Sumer, the world's first civilization, archaeologists have turned up both musical instruments and artwork showing musicians playing them. Although we may never know how Sumerian music sounded, we do know that even in the world's first cities, musicians filled the air with song.

Focus Question What were the characteristics of the world's first civilization?

City-States of Ancient Sumer

Objectives

- Understand how geography influenced the development of civilization in the Fertile Crescent.
- Outline the main features of Sumerian civilization.
- Explain how the advances in learning made by the Sumerians left a lasting legacy for later peoples to build on.

Terms, People, and Places

Fertile Crescent	hierarchy
Mesopotamia	ziggurat
Sumer	cuneiform
The Epic of Gilgamesh	

N͟ote Taking

Reading Skill: Identify Main Ideas Use this concept web to record the main idea of each section of text that follows a red heading.

A number of early civilizations arose in the Fertile Crescent, a region of the Middle East named for its rich soils and golden wheat fields. Over time, nomadic herders, ambitious invaders, and traders easily overcame the region's few natural barriers. As a result, the region became a crossroads where people and ideas met and mingled. Each new group that arrived made its own contributions to the history of the region.

Geography Influences Fertile Crescent Civilization

The Fertile Crescent curves from the Persian Gulf to the eastern coast of the Mediterranean Sea. Within the Fertile Crescent lies a region that the ancient Greeks later named Mesopotamia, which means "between the rivers." Mesopotamia is the area of land between the Tigris and Euphrates rivers, which flow from the highlands of modern-day Turkey through Iraq into the Persian Gulf. Around 3300 B.C., the world's first civilization developed in southeastern Mesopotamia, in a region called Sumer.

Organizing for Floods and Irrigation Control of the Tigris and Euphrates was key to developments in Mesopotamia. The rivers frequently rose in terrifying floods that washed away topsoil and destroyed mud-brick villages. The Mesopotamian narrative poem *The Epic of Gilgamesh,* which was first told orally in Sumer, describes a great flood that destroys the world. Archaeologists have indeed found evidence that catastrophic floods occurred regularly in the ancient days of the Fertile Crescent.

To survive and to protect their farmland, villagers along the river-banks had to work together. Even during the dry season, the rivers had to be controlled in order to channel water to the fields. Temple priests or royal officials provided the leadership that was necessary to <u>ensure</u> cooperation. They organized villagers to work together on projects such as building dikes to hold back floodwaters and irrigation ditches to carry water to their fields.

Sumerians Build Thriving Cities The Sumerians had few natural resources, but they made the most of what they did have. They lacked building materials such as timber or stone, so they built with clay and water. They used the clay to make bricks, which they shaped in wooden molds and dried in the sun. These bricks were the building blocks for some of the world's first great cities, such as Ur and Uruk.

Trade brought riches to Sumerian cities. Traders sailed along the rivers or risked the dangers of desert travel to carry goods to distant regions. Although it is unclear where and when the wheel was invented, the Sumerians may have made the first wheeled vehicles. Archaeologists have found goods from as far away as Egypt and India in the rubble of Sumerian cities.

✔ **Checkpoint** What geographic characteristics made the Fertile Crescent a good place for civilization to develop?

Vocabulary Builder

<u>ensure</u>—(en SHOOR) *v.* to make sure that something will happen

Sumer and the Fertile Crescent

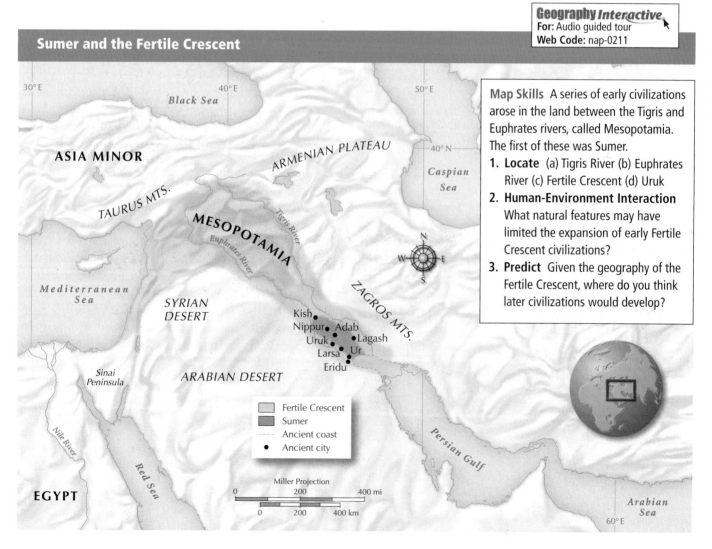

Geography *Interactive*
For: Audio guided tour
Web Code: nap-0211

Map Skills A series of early civilizations arose in the land between the Tigris and Euphrates rivers, called Mesopotamia. The first of these was Sumer.
1. **Locate** (a) Tigris River (b) Euphrates River (c) Fertile Crescent (d) Uruk
2. **Human-Environment Interaction** What natural features may have limited the expansion of early Fertile Crescent civilizations?
3. **Predict** Given the geography of the Fertile Crescent, where do you think later civilizations would develop?

Sumerian Civilization Takes Shape

Within a few hundred years of its beginning, Sumer included at least 12 separate city-states. Rival city-states often battled for control of land and water. For protection, people turned to war leaders. Over time, the practice of rule by war leaders <u>evolved</u> into hereditary rule.

Vocabulary Builder
<u>evolved</u>—(ee VAHLVD) *vt.* developed gradually into something

Complex Government Unfolds In each city-state, the ruler was responsible for maintaining the city walls and the irrigation systems. He led its armies in war, enforced the laws, and employed scribes to carry out functions such as collecting taxes and keeping records. The ruler was seen as the chief servant of the gods and led ceremonies meant to please them.

Sumerians Structure Their Society Each Sumerian city-state had a distinct social **hierarchy** (HY ur ahr kee), or system of ranking groups. The highest class included the ruling family, leading officials, and high priests. A small middle class was made up of lesser priests, scribes, merchants, and artisans. Artisans who practiced the same trade, such as weavers or carpenters, often lived and worked on the same street.

The majority of people were peasant farmers, and they formed the lowest level of society. Some had their own land, but most worked land belonging to the king or to temples. Sumerians also owned slaves. Most slaves had been captured in war. Some, though, had sold themselves into slavery to pay their debts.

The role of women in Mesopotamian society changed over time. In Sumer, goddesses were highly honored in religious practice. Perhaps because of the importance of female deities, women held a higher social standing in Sumer than in later civilizations of the region. However, Sumerian women never held legal rights equal to those of men. But some rulers' wives had supervisory powers, and a number wrote songs about their husbands, revealing to later scholars that they had learned writing and music. On rare occasion, a woman may have inherited property.

Sumerians Practice Religion Like most ancient peoples, the Sumerians were polytheistic, worshiping many gods. These gods were thought to control every aspect of life, especially the forces of nature. Sumerians believed that gods and goddesses behaved like ordinary people—they ate, drank, married, and raised families. Although the gods favored truth and justice, they were also responsible for causing violence and suffering.

Sumerians believed their highest duty was to keep these divine beings happy and, by doing so, ensure the safety of their city-state. Each city built a **ziggurat** (ZIG oo rat), a large, stepped platform thought to have been topped by a temple dedicated to the city's chief god or goddess. As well, Sumerians celebrated holy days with ceremonies and processions. In one ritual, the king went through a symbolic wedding to Inanna, the life-giving goddess of love. This rite was meant to ensure a prosperous new year.

The Sumerians believed in an afterlife. In their view, all people lived after death in a grim underworld from which there was no release. One character in *The Epic of Gilgamesh* describes the underworld as "the place where they live on dust, their food is mud, / . . . and they see no light, living in blackness / on the door and door-bolt, deeply settled dust."

Temple to the Gods
Priests and priestesses could climb stairs to the top of the ziggurat to perform rituals and prayers. The people watched from below. They also prayed and offered sacrifices of animals, grain, and wine to win the favor of the gods.

1 The Sumerians sometimes pressed tokens into the surface of a clay envelope before placing them within it, perhaps to indicate its contents.

2 A scribe listed quantities of various commodities on this clay tablet using both token impressions and a stylus.

3 Scribes wrote cuneiform on both sides of a tablet, which was small enough to hold in one hand.

Cuneiform Develops in Stages

Around 8000 B.C., Sumerians began using differently shaped clay tokens to represent various items of exchange, such as sheep, bread, or oil. To record economic transactions, they placed the tokens inside clay envelopes often shaped like balls. Around 3500 B.C., Sumerians began to press the tokens into clay tablets to make signs. They also started marking the clay using a sharp tool called a stylus. Around 3200 B.C., they created a true writing system that included symbols that represented words or syllables.

Cuneiform Symbol			
Meaning	Mountain	Orchard	Fish

SOURCE: Stephen Bertman, *Handbook to Life in Ancient Mesopotamia*

Using a stylus, a Sumerian scribe wrote in columns beginning at the top left corner of the tablet and working to the right.

Thinking Critically
1. **Draw Inferences** How do you think the use of clay shaped the writing system the Sumerians developed?
2. **Make Comparisons** How did cuneiform writing allow Sumerians to communicate more effectively than they could using tokens and clay envelopes?

Sumerians Invent Writing By 3200 B.C., Sumerians had invented the earliest known writing. It was later called **cuneiform** (kyoo NEE uh fawrm), from the Latin word *cuneus* for "wedge," because scribes wrote by making wedge-shaped marks on clay tablets. Cuneiform grew out of a system of pictographs used to record goods brought to temple storehouses. Later, the Sumerians developed symbols to represent more complicated thoughts. As their writing evolved, the Sumerians used it to record not only economic exchanges but also myths, prayers, laws, and business contracts.

Sumerian scribes had to go through years of difficult schooling to acquire their skills. Discipline was strict. Untidy copying or talking in class could be punished by caning. Students who did well often learned about religion, mathematics, and literature as well.

✓ **Checkpoint** How was Sumerian society structured?

The Story of the Stars

Mesopotamian astronomers were the first to associate many constellations with the shapes we know them for today. It was they who saw the lion in the stars we now call Leo and the scorpion in those we call Scorpio. *How do you think ancient notions of the night sky were passed on over so much time?*

▲ Leo

▲ Scorpio

Lasting Legacy of Sumer

Beginning around 2500 B.C., armies of conquering peoples swept across Mesopotamia and overwhelmed the Sumerian city-states. By 1900 B.C., the Sumerian civilization had been replaced by other civilizations and empires that you will read about in the next section.

However, Sumer left behind a lasting legacy. Newcomers to the region adopted many ideas and innovations from the Sumerians. For example, the Akkadians, Babylonians, and Assyrians adapted cuneiform so it could be used with their own languages. These peoples then helped spread Sumerian learning across the Middle East.

Over the centuries, Sumerian scholars had begun to develop astronomy and mathematics. They studied the skies and recorded the movements of planets and stars. They also established a number system based on six, dividing the hour into 60 minutes and the circle into 360 degrees, as we still do today. The Babylonians later built on this Sumerian learning to develop basic algebra and geometry, to create accurate calendars, and to predict eclipses of the sun and moon. Later peoples also elaborated on Sumerian oral narratives, such as *The Epic of Gilgamesh*, which was written down in cuneiform by both the Akkadians and the Babylonians.

In addition, by means of the various peoples who conquered the Middle East, Sumerian knowledge passed on to the Greeks and Romans. As you will read in later chapters, they, in turn, had a powerful impact on the development of the Western world.

 Checkpoint What advances did the Sumerians make in mathematics and astronomy?

Progress Monitoring *Online*
For: Self-quiz with vocabulary practice
Web Code: naa-0211

SECTION 1 Assessment

Terms, People, and Places

1. For each term, person, or place listed at the beginning of the section, write a sentence explaining its significance.

Note Taking

2. **Reading Skill: Identify Main Ideas** Use your completed concept web to answer the Focus Question: What were the characteristics of the world's first civilization?

Comprehension and Critical Thinking

3. **Draw Inferences** Sumerians faced significant geographic challenges, such as floods. How do you think facing these challenges played a role in the formation of a strong government?

4. **Determine Relevance** How might the invention of cuneiform writing have strengthened Sumerian government and religious practices?

5. **Analyze Information** Describe ways in which later peoples built on Sumerian learning. Would this have been possible without the invention of writing?

● Writing About History

Quick Write: Determine the Purpose When you write a biographical essay, start by determining its purpose. For example, your purpose might be to bring attention to someone who is not well known. Another purpose might be to describe the achievements that made someone very famous. Make a list of people about whom you could write an essay for either of these purposes, or for another purpose you may want to explore.

The Epic of Gilgamesh

The Epic of Gilgamesh may date from about 2000 B.C. Many different versions of it have been found, but all are missing many lines. Thus a "standard version" has been compiled from the many versions. The result is a collection of tales about a hero named Gilgamesh, who may have been a real-life king of the Sumerian city of Uruk. In this excerpt, Gilgamesh listens to Utnapishtim (ut nuh PISH tim), a man given immortality by the gods, and is tempted to believe in eternal life. However, he comes to realize that death is the fate of all people.

Artists have depicted scenes from *The Epic of Gilgamesh* for thousands of years. About 2,500 years ago, a Persian artist created this gold plate (above) showing Gilgamesh fighting two lions. A modern-day American artist created this print (below) revealing the snake carrying away Gilgamesh's plant.

Utnapishtim said to him, to Gilgamesh: . . .
"A secret of the gods let me tell you.
There is a plant. Its roots go deep, like the boxthorn;
its spike [thorn] will prick your hand like a bramble.
If you get your hands on that plant, you'll have everlasting life."

Gilgamesh, on hearing this, . . . bound heavy stones to his feet;
they dragged him down into the abyss[1] and he saw the plant.
He seized the plant, though it cut into his hand;
he cut the heavy stones from his feet;
the sea cast him up onto its shore.

Gilgamesh said to Urshanabi the Boatman:
"Urshanabi, this is the plant . . . by which a man can get
   life within. . . .
Its name is The-Old-Man-Will-Be-Made-Young.
I too will eat it, and I will return to what I was in my youth." . . .

Gilgamesh saw a pool of cool water.
He went down into it and bathed in the water.
A snake smelled the fragrance of the plant.
It came up through the water and carried the plant away.
As it turned it threw off its skin.

That day Gilgamesh sat down weeping.
Over his face the tears flowed.
He took the hand of Urshanabi the Boatman.
"For whom, Urshanabi, do my arms toil[2]?
For whom has the blood of my heart dried up?
I have not won any good for myself;
it's the lion-of-the ground [snake] that has won good fortune."

1. **abyss** (uh BIS) *n.* something that is immeasurably deep
2. **toil** (toyl) *vi.* to work long and hard

Thinking Critically

1. **Summarize** Why does Gilgamesh pick the plant that Utnapishtim has described? What does he want it to do for him?
2. **Analyze Literature** Which physical characteristic of a snake makes it work well as the character who ends up benefiting from the plant?

Hammurabi (front); Hammurabi's Code (back)

WITNESS HISTORY 🔊 AUDIO

Establishing the Law

To establish the law of the land, Babylonian king Hammurabi set the law in stone and placed it in public view. He began the law code with a statement of his authority:

❝ Then [the gods] Anu and Bel called by name me, Hammurabi, the exalted prince, who feared God, to bring about the rule of righteousness in the land . . . so that the strong should not harm the weak; so that I should rule over the [people] and enlighten the land, to further the well-being of mankind. ❞

Focus Question How did various strong rulers unite the lands of the Fertile Crescent into well-organized empires?

Invaders, Traders, and Empire Builders

Objectives

- Outline the achievements of the first empires that arose in Mesopotamia.
- Understand how conquests brought new empires and ideas into the Middle East.
- Describe how the Persians established a huge empire.
- Summarize the contributions the Phoenicians made to the ancient Middle East.

Terms, People, and Places

Sargon	barter economy
Hammurabi	money economy
codify	Zoroaster
civil law	colony
criminal law	alphabet
Nebuchadnezzar	

Note Taking

Reading Skill: Identify Main Ideas Use a table like this one to record the main idea of each section of text that follows a red heading.

Red Heading	Main Idea
First Empires Arise in Mesopotamia	
Conquests Bring New Empires and Ideas	

Through thousands of years of war and peace, the peoples of the Middle East built great empires and made long-lasting innovations. The region became a vital crossroads where warriors and traders met, clashed, and mingled. Many of the beliefs and ideas of the ancient Middle East survived to shape our modern world.

First Empires Arise in Mesopotamia

Again and again through time, nomadic peoples or ambitious warriors descended on the rich cities of the Fertile Crescent. While many invaders simply looted and burned, some stayed to rule. Powerful leaders created large, well-organized empires, bringing peace and prosperity to the region.

Sargon Builds the First Empire About 2300 B.C., **Sargon,** the ruler of Akkad, invaded and conquered the neighboring city-states of Sumer. He continued to expand his territory, building the first empire known to history. He appointed local rulers, each of whom served as king of the land he oversaw. However, the world's first empire did not last long. After Sargon's death, other invaders swept into the wide valley between the rivers, tumbling his empire into ruin.

Hammurabi Brings Babylon to Power In time, the Sumerian city-states revived, and they resumed their power struggles. Eventually, however, new conquerors followed in Sargon's footsteps and imposed unity over the Fertile Crescent. About

1790 B.C., **Hammurabi** (hah muh RAH bee), king of Babylon, brought much of Mesopotamia under the control of his empire.

Hammurabi's most ambitious and lasting contribution was his publication of a set of laws known as Hammurabi's Code. Most of the laws had been around since Sumerian times, but Hammurabi wanted to ensure that everyone in his empire knew the legal principles his government would follow. He had artisans carve nearly 300 laws on a stone pillar for all to see. Hammurabi's Code was the first important attempt by a ruler to codify, or arrange and set down in writing, all the laws that would govern a state.

Establishing Civil Law One section of Hammurabi's Code codified civil law. This branch of law deals with private rights and matters, such as business contracts, property inheritance, taxes, marriage, and divorce. Much of Hammurabi's civil code was designed to protect the powerless, such as slaves or women. Some laws, for example, allowed a woman to own property and pass it on to her children. Another law spelled out the rights of a married woman, saying that if she was found to be blameless for the problems between herself and her husband, she could leave the marriage. If she were found to be at fault, however, the law instructed that she be thrown in the river.

In general, Babylonian civil law gave a husband both legal authority over his wife and a legal duty to support her. The code also gave a father nearly unlimited authority over his children. The Babylonians believed that an orderly household was necessary for a stable empire.

Defining Crime and Punishment Hammurabi's Code also addressed criminal law. This branch of law deals with offenses against others, such as robbery, assault, or murder. Earlier traditions often permitted victims of crimes or their families to take the law into their own hands. By setting out specific punishments for specific offenses, Hammurabi's Code limited personal vengeance and encouraged social order.

By today's standards, the punishments in Hammurabi's Code often seem cruel, following the principle of "an eye for an eye and a life for a life." For example, if a house collapsed because of poor construction and the owner died as a result, the house's builder could be put to death. Still, such a legal code imposed more social order than existed when individuals sought their own justice.

Other Accomplishments Made by Hammurabi Although most famous for his code of laws, Hammurabi took other steps to successfully unite his empire. He improved the system of irrigation, organized a well-trained army, and ordered many temples to be repaired. To encourage religious unity across his empire, he promoted Marduk, the patron god of Babylon, over older Sumerian gods. In time, Marduk became the chief god of Babylonian worship.

Civilizations Expand
As new civilizations took control of Fertile Crescent lands, their empires expanded but stayed near the two large rivers. Many elements of shared culture existed among these civilizations, including worship of Marduk (above), who became the region's chief god.

✔ **Checkpoint** How do civil law and criminal law differ?

Conquests Bring New Empires and Ideas

Later empires shaped the Middle East in different ways. Some conquerors, such as the Hittites, brought new skills to the region's people. Other conquerors uprooted the peoples they defeated, which had the side effect of spreading to new regions the ideas of those forced to move.

Hittites Learn the Secret of Ironworking

The Hittites pushed out of Asia Minor into Mesopotamia in about 1400 B.C. They brought with them a major advancement—the knowledge of how to extract iron from ore. The tools and weapons they made with iron were harder and had sharper edges than those made out of bronze or copper. Because iron was plentiful, the Hittites were able to arm more people at less expense.

The Hittites tried to keep this valuable technology secret. But as their empire collapsed in about 1200 B.C., Hittite ironsmiths migrated to serve customers elsewhere. The new knowledge thus spread across Asia, Africa, and Europe, ushering in the Iron Age.

Assyrian Warriors Expand Ancient Knowledge

The Assyrians, who lived on the upper Tigris, also learned to forge iron weapons. They had established an empire by about 1350 B.C., and by 1100 B.C., they began expanding their empire across Mesopotamia. Over the course of 500 years, they earned a reputation for being among the most feared warriors in history.

Historians are unsure why warfare was so central to Assyrian culture. Was it to keep others from attacking, or to please their god Assur by bringing wealth to the region? Whatever the reason, Assyrian rulers boasted of their conquests. One told of capturing Babylon. He proclaimed, "The city and its houses, from top to bottom, I destroyed and burned with fire."

Despite their fierce reputation, Assyrian rulers encouraged a well-ordered society. They used riches from trade and war loot to pay for splendid palaces in their well-planned cities. They were also the first rulers to develop extensive laws regulating life within the royal household. For example, women of the palace were confined to secluded quarters and had to wear veils when they appeared in public.

At Nineveh (NIN uh vuh), King Assurbanipal (ahs ur BAH nee pahl) founded one of the world's first libraries. There, he kept cuneiform tablets that he ordered scribes to collect from all over the Fertile Crescent. Those tablets have offered modern scholars a wealth of information about the ancient Middle East.

Nebuchadnezzar Revives Babylon

In 612 B.C., shortly after Assurbanipal's death, neighboring peoples joined forces to crush the once-dreaded Assyrian armies. In their absence, Babylon—which a king named Nabopolassar had reestablished as a power in 625 B.C.—quickly revived under its aggressive and ruthless second king, **Nebuchadnezzar** (neb yuh kud NEZ ur). The new Babylonian empire stretched from the Persian Gulf to the Mediterranean Sea.

Rebuilding Babylon
When Nebuchadnezzar became king, he had much of Babylon rebuilt in glorious fashion. The Ishtar Gate (below) is famous for its now faded blue bricks and animals depicting various gods. *Why might Nebuchadnezzar have erected such a substantial gateway to the city and in honor of the gods?*

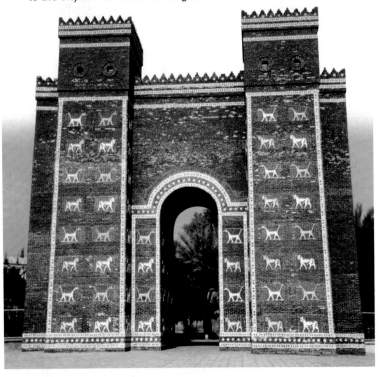

HITTITES REFINE THE HORSE-DRAWN CHARIOT

Technological advances such as the use of iron to build powerful weapons were key to the success of conquering empires. From the Hittites, other peoples picked up the use of iron and began building new tools and weapons. In the same manner, the Hittites modified a military technology invented by others—the horse-drawn chariot—to increase their own firepower capabilities.

▲ A Hittite warrior

Three men could fit in each chariot. One drove while the other two fought the approaching enemy.

The axle connecting the wheels ran across the middle of the chariot rather than at its back. This allowed the chariot to support an additional man.

Hittite charioteers swept across the battlefield in thick lines, wielding lances, axes, and bows and arrows.

◄ Iron spearhead from near Jerusalem, 900s B.C.

▲ Iron axe blade from Syria, 1300s B.C.

Thinking Critically

1. **Synthesize Information** How did Hittite modifications to the chariot increase their firepower capabilities?
2. **Draw Conclusions** How do you think the addition of a third man might have hindered a chariot?

After nearly a thousand years of the city facing decline and destruction, Nebuchadnezzar oversaw the rebuilding of the canals, temples, walls, and palaces of Babylon. During his reign, the city became one of the largest and most highly regarded in the history of ancient Mesopotamia.

Nebuchadnezzar surrounded Babylon with a defensive moat and a brick wall that was 85 feet (26 meters) thick. Nine solid gateways dedicated to important gods allowed people to pass through the wall. The most famous one today, the Ishtar Gate, was made of bricks glazed bright blue and covered in lions representing the goddess Ishtar, dragons representing the god Marduk, and bulls representing the god Hadad. At the center of the city, Nebuchadnezzar enlarged and decorated the city's ziggurat to the gods and restored the temple honoring the city's chief god, Marduk.

Although their remains have not yet been found, Nebuchadnezzar may have built the famous Hanging Gardens—known as one of the "seven wonders of the ancient world"—near his main palace. The gardens were probably made by planting trees and flowering plants on the steps of a huge ziggurat. According to legend, Nebuchadnezzar had the gardens built to please his wife, who was homesick for the hills where she had grown up.

 Checkpoint   Name a significant contribution made by the Hittites, Assyrians, and Babylonians after each group's conquest in the Middle East.

Assyria, Persia, and the Phoenician Colonies

Map Skills The Assyrians and Persians built huge empires in the ancient Middle East. The Phoenicians, on the other hand, had a relatively small homeland but established trade and colonies throughout the Mediterranean world.

1. **Locate** (a) Assyrian empire (b) Persepolis (c) Phoenicia (d) Carthage
2. **Movement** What information on the map supports the claim that the Phoenicians were skilled sailors?
3. **Analyze Information** Study the locations of the Persian capitals. Were they well placed for rule over the entire empire?

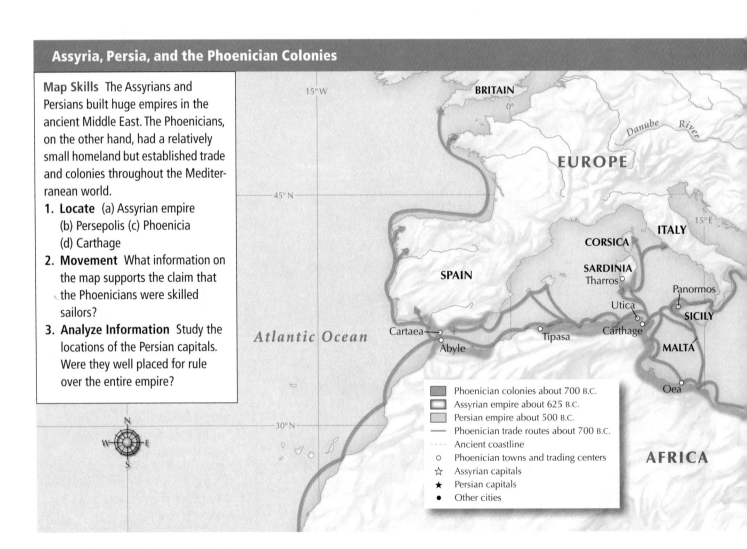

Phoenician colonies about 700 B.C.
Assyrian empire about 625 B.C.
Persian empire about 500 B.C.
—— Phoenician trade routes about 700 B.C.
---- Ancient coastline
○ Phoenician towns and trading centers
☆ Assyrian capitals
★ Persian capitals
● Other cities

The Persians Establish a Huge Empire

The thick walls built by Nebuchadnezzar failed to hold back new conquerors. In 539 B.C., Babylon fell to the Persian armies of Cyrus the Great. Cyrus and his <u>successors</u> went on to build the largest empire yet seen. The Persians eventually controlled a wide sweep of territory that stretched from Asia Minor to India, including present-day Turkey, Iran, Egypt, Afghanistan, and Pakistan. In general, Persian kings pursued a policy of tolerance, or acceptance, of the people they conquered. The Persians respected the customs of the diverse groups in their empire.

Darius Unites Many Peoples The real unification of the Persian empire was accomplished under the emperor Darius I, who ruled from 522 B.C. to 486 B.C. A skilled organizer, Darius set up a government that became a model for later rulers. He divided the empire into provinces, each called a satrapy and headed by a governor called a satrap. Each satrapy had to pay taxes based on its resources and wealth. Special officials visited each satrapy to check on the satraps.

Darius adapted laws from the peoples he conquered and, like Hammurabi, drew up a single code of laws for the empire. To encourage unity, he had hundreds of miles of roads built or repaired. Roads made it easier to communicate with different parts of the empire. Darius himself kept moving from one royal capital to another. In each, he celebrated important festivals and was seen by the people.

Vocabulary Builder

<u>successor</u>—(suk SES ur)
n. somebody or something that follows another and takes up the same position

Geography *Interactive*
For: Audio guided tour
Web Code: nap-0221

Money and Economics

Benefits of a Money Economy

- Exchanges are simplified because only one party is purchasing items rather than two.

- Comparison of items being considered for purchase is simplified because all items are given exact values.

- Money can be kept for use at a later time, whereas barter items such as live animals may not last.

Chart Skills Barter economies, in which Phoenician glassware might be traded for Israeli figs, continued to exist throughout the world. But money economies developed quickly as well, thanks to the benefits they offered to the exchange process. **What advantages did a money economy offer?**

Fresh figs ▲

Persian coin ▶

◀ Greek coin

◀ Phoenician glass vessel

Lydian coin ▶

Improving Economic Life To improve trade, Darius set up a common set of weights and measures. He also encouraged the use of coins, which the Lydians of Asia Minor had first introduced. Most people continued to be part of the barter economy, which means they exchanged one set of goods or services for another. Coins, however, brought merchants and traders into an early form of a money economy. In this system, goods and services are paid for through the exchange of some token of an agreed value, such as a coin or a bill. By setting up a single Persian coinage, Darius created economic links among his far-flung subjects.

A New Religion Takes Hold Religious beliefs put forward by the Persian thinker Zoroaster (ZOH ruh as tur) also helped to unite the empire. Zoroaster lived about 600 B.C. He rejected the old Persian gods and taught that a single wise god, Ahura Mazda (AH hoo ruh MAHZ duh), ruled the world. Ahura Mazda, however, was in constant battle against Ahriman (AH rih mun), the prince of lies and evil. Each individual would have to choose which side to support.

In the end, taught Zoroaster, Ahura Mazda would triumph over the forces of evil. On a final judgment day, all individuals would be judged for their actions, as described below:

Primary Source

66 Then the assembly . . . will meet , that is, all men of this earth will stand. In that assembly, every person will see his own good deeds and evil deeds. The righteous will be as conspicuous [obvious] amongst the wicked as a white sheep among the black. . . . They will then [carry] the righteous to the abode of harmony [heaven], and cast the wicked back to the wicked existence [hell]. . . . Then [the last savior] Soshyant by order of the Creator will give reward and recompense to all men in conformity with their deeds. 99
—*Bundahishn*, Zoroastrian scripture

Vocabulary Builder

emerged—(ee MURJD) *vi.* arose, appeared, or occurred

Two later religions that emerged in the Middle East, Christianity and Islam, also stressed ideas of heaven, hell, and a final judgment day.

✔ **Checkpoint** What are two steps that Darius took to unite the Persian Empire?

Contributions of Phoenician Sea Traders

While powerful rulers subdued large empires, many small states of the ancient Middle East made their own contributions to civilization. The Phoenicians (fuh NISH unz), for example, gained fame as both sailors and traders. They occupied a string of cities along the eastern Mediterranean coast, in the area that today is Lebanon and Syria.

Expanding Manufacturing and Trade The coastal land, though narrow, was fertile and supported farming. Still, because of their location near the sea, the resourceful Phoenicians became best known for manufacturing and trade. They made glass from coastal sand. From a tiny sea snail, they produced a widely admired purple dye, called "Tyrian purple" after the city of Tyre.

Phoenicians traded with people all around the Mediterranean Sea. To promote trade, they set up colonies from North Africa to Sicily and Spain. A colony is a territory settled and ruled by people from another land. A few Phoenician traders braved the stormy Atlantic and sailed as far as Britain. There, they exchanged goods from the Mediterranean for tin.

Sculpture of a Phoenician trading ship from about 100 B.C.

Establishing an Alphabet Historians have called the Phoenicians "carriers of civilization" because they spread Middle Eastern civilization around the Mediterranean. One of the most significant Phoenician contributions to culture was their alphabet. Unlike cuneiform, in which symbols represent syllables or whole words, an alphabet is a writing system in which each symbol represents a single basic sound, such as a consonant or vowel.

Phoenician traders developed an alphabetic system of 22 symbols that stood for consonant sounds. Later, the Greeks adapted the Phoenician alphabet and added symbols for the vowel sounds. From this Greek alphabet came the letters in which this book is written—that is, the alphabet we use today.

✔ **Checkpoint** How has the Phoenician development of an alphabet been a lasting contribution to civilization?

SECTION 2 Assessment

Progress Monitoring *Online*
For: Self-quiz with vocabulary practice
Web Code: naa-0221

Terms, People, and Places

1. For each term, person, or place listed at the beginning of the section, write a sentence explaining its significance.

Note Taking

2. **Reading Skill: Identify Main Ideas** Use your completed table to answer the Focus Question: How did various strong rulers unite the lands of the Fertile Crescent into well-organized empires?

Comprehension and Critical Thinking

3. **Demonstrate Reasoned Judgment** What do you think was the most important achievement of Sargon? Of Hammurabi? Why?

4. **Draw Inferences** How do you think the Persian policy of tolerance helped the empire grow so large?

5. **Draw Conclusions** One effect of warfare and conquest was that knowledge and beliefs spread among different peoples. How else did people of the ancient Middle East spread their ideas?

● **Writing About History**

Quick Write: Gather Information Choose a person from this section about whom you want to write a biographical essay and list important facts about him. You may want to use the Internet or the library to gather information about the person. Include details such as when and where he was born, what he did in his life, and what he did that most interests you.

Ancient Egyptian wall painting of a man hunting birds in the marshes of the Nile

WITNESS HISTORY 🔊 AUDIO

The Gift of the Nile

Every year, as the Nile River flooded its banks, the people of ancient Egypt sang a hymn of praise. They honored the river for nourishing the land and filling their storehouses with food:

66 But all is changed for mankind when [the Nile] comes. . . .
If [the Nile] shines, the earth is joyous, every stomach is full of rejoicing, every spine is happy, every jaw-bone crushes [its food]. 99
—Hymn to the Nile

Focus Question How did the Nile influence the rise of the powerful civilization of Egypt?

Kingdom on the Nile

Objectives

- Understand the ways in which geography helped shape ancient Egypt.
- Analyze the achievements of the Old Kingdom in Egypt.
- Describe the events that brought turbulence to Egypt's Middle Kingdom.
- Explain how Egypt grew strong during the New Kingdom.

Terms, People, and Places

cataract	vizier
delta	Hatshepsut
dynasty	Thutmose III
pharaoh	Ramses II
bureaucracy	

Note Taking

Reading Skill: Identify Supporting Details
Use an outline like this one to record the main idea of each section of the text that follows a red heading. Include at least two supporting details for each main idea.

```
I.
  A.
  B.
II.
  A.
  B.
```

The fertile lands of the Nile Valley attracted Stone Age farmers. People migrated there from the Mediterranean area, from hills and deserts near the Nile, and from other parts of Africa. In time, a powerful civilization emerged that depended heavily on the control of river waters.

Geography Helps Shape Egypt

"Egypt," said the ancient Greek historian Herodotus, "is wholly the gift of the Nile." Without the Nile, Egypt would be just the barren desert that surrounds the river. But while the desert protected Egypt from invasion, it also limited where people could settle.

In ancient times, as today, farming villages dotted the narrow band of land watered by the Nile. Beyond the rich, irrigated "Black Land," generally no more than 10 miles wide, lay the "Red Land," a sun-baked desert that stretches across North Africa. Farmers took advantage of the fertile soil of the Nile Valley to grow wheat and flax, a plant whose fibers were used for clothing.

Yearly Floods Bring Benefits The Nile rises in the highlands of Ethiopia and the lakes of central Africa. Every spring, the rains in this interior region send water racing down streams that feed the Nile River. In ancient times, Egyptians eagerly awaited the annual flood. It soaked the land with life-giving water and deposited a layer of rich silt.

People had to cooperate to control the Nile's floods. Under the direction of early governments, they built dikes, reservoirs, and irrigation ditches to channel the rising river and store water for the dry season.

Uniting Two Regions Ancient Egypt had two distinct regions, Upper Egypt in the south and Lower Egypt in the north. Upper Egypt stretched from the Nile's first cataract, or waterfall, to within 100 miles of the Mediterranean Sea. Lower Egypt covered the delta region where the Nile empties into the Mediterranean. A delta is a triangular area of marshland formed by deposits of silt at the mouth of some rivers.

About 3100 B.C., Menes, the king of Upper Egypt, united the two regions. He founded Egypt's first capital at Memphis, a site near where the Nile empties into its delta. Menes and his successors used the Nile as a highway linking north and south. They could send officials or armies to towns along the river. The Nile thus helped make Egypt one of the world's first unified states.

The river also served as a trade route. Egyptian merchants traveled up and down the Nile in sailboats and barges, exchanging the products of Africa, the Middle East, and the Mediterranean region.

✔ **Checkpoint** How did the yearly floods of the Nile influence life in ancient Egypt?

World's Longest River
As the world's longest river, the Nile extends about another 3,600 miles south of its first cataract, which you can see on the map. Egyptians today continue to rely on the river (above) to provide water for agriculture as well as for transportation. *Do you think Egypt was the only civilization to arise along the Nile? Why or why not?*

The Old Kingdom Forms

Scholars divide the history of ancient Egypt into three main periods: the Old Kingdom (about 2575 B.C.–2130 B.C.), the Middle Kingdom (about 1938 B.C.–1630 B.C.), and the New Kingdom (about 1539 B.C.–1075 B.C.). Although power passed from one dynasty, or ruling family, to another, the land generally remained united.

A Strong Government Takes Hold During the Old Kingdom, Egyptian kings, later called pharaohs (FEHR ohz), organized a strong, centralized state. Pharaohs played key roles in government and religion. Egyptians believed each pharaoh was a god. He held absolute power, owning and ruling all the land in the kingdom. However, the pharaohs were seen as human as well as divine. The people expected their pharaohs to behave morally and judged the pharaohs for their deeds.

Pharaohs of the Old Kingdom took pride in preserving justice and order. They did so by means of a bureaucracy—a system of government that includes different job functions and levels of authority. In the Egyptian bureaucracy, a pharaoh depended on a vizier (vih ZEER), or chief minister, to supervise the business of government. Under the vizier, various departments looked after such matters as tax collection, farming, and the all-important irrigation system. Thousands of scribes carried out the vizier's instructions.

Ptah-hotep (ptah HOH tep), who lived around 2450 B.C. in Egypt, was a vizier to a pharaoh who took an interest in training young officials. Based on his vast experience of government, he wrote a book, *Instructions of the Vizier Ptah-hotep,* in which he emphasized the importance of being humble and honest, obedient to one's father and superiors, and fair in dealing with other officials of all ranks.

The Great Pyramids Are Built During the Old Kingdom, Egyptian pharoahs built many necropolises (neh KRAHP uh lis iz), or cemeteries, containing majestic pyramids in the areas surrounding Memphis. Today, the best known are the Great Pyramids that still stand at Giza. Tombs within the pyramids were considered homes in which the deceased would live for eternity. Because Egyptians believed in an afterlife, they preserved the bodies of their dead rulers and provided them with everything they would need in their new lives. Building each of the pyramids took so long that often a pharaoh would begin to build his tomb as soon as he came to power.

 Checkpoint How was Egyptian government structured during the Old Kingdom?

The Turbulent Middle Kingdom

Power struggles, crop failures, and the cost of building the pyramids all contributed to the collapse of the Old Kingdom. Then, after more than a century of disunity, new pharaohs reunited the land, ushering in a new era, the Middle Kingdom.

The Middle Kingdom was a turbulent period. The Nile did not rise as regularly as it had in the past. Corruption and rebellions were common. Still, strong rulers did organize a large drainage project, creating vast new stretches of arable, or farmable, land. In addition, Egyptian armies occupied part of Nubia (also known as Kush), a gold-rich land to the south about which you will read more in a later chapter. Traders also had greater contacts with the peoples of the Middle East and the Mediterranean island of Crete.

About 1700 B.C., foreign invaders called the Hyksos (HIK sohs) occupied the Nile delta region. Although the Hyksos took over the governance of Egypt, there was little conflict between the new rulers and the Egyptian people. The Hyksos awed the Egyptians with their horse-drawn war chariots. In time, the Egyptians mastered this new military technology. The Hyksos, in turn, were impressed by Egyptian civilization. They soon adopted Egyptian customs, beliefs, and even names. Finally, after more than 100 years of Hyksos rule, new Egyptian leaders arose and established the New Kingdom.

 Checkpoint In what ways was the Middle Kingdom turbulent?

New Kingdom Egypt Grows Strong

During the years of New Kingdom, a number of powerful and ambitious pharaohs created a large empire. At its height around 1450 B.C., the Egyptian empire reached as far north as Syria and the Euphrates River. The New Kingdom proved to be an age of conquest that brought Egyptians into greater contact with peoples in southwestern Asia as well as other parts of Africa.

WITNESS HISTORY VIDEO

Watch *The Nile: Where Egypt Began* on the **Witness History Discovery School**™ video program to learn more about the Nile's role in early Egypt.

DISCOVERY
SCHOOL

Geography *Interactive*
For: Audio guided tour
Web Code: nap-0231

Map Skills Under the control of Thutmose III (below), Egypt's borders expanded into the eastern Mediterranean region.

1. **Locate** (a) Nile River (b) Nubia (c) Giza (d) Syria
2. **Movement** What were the northernmost areas reached by Egyptian traders?
3. **Make Comparisons** How did the Hittite empire compare in size to the Egyptian empire around 1450 B.C.? Which do you think was more advantageously situated?

Map legend:
- Egyptian empire
- Hittite empire
- Egyptian trade routes
- Cataract

Miller Projection
0   200   400 mi
0   200   400 km

Powerful Rulers Control Egypt During the New Kingdom, Egypt's first female ruler took charge. Her name was **Hatshepsut** (haht SHEP soot), and she exercised all the rights of a pharaoh. From about 1472 B.C. to 1458 B.C., she encouraged trade with eastern Mediterranean lands and along the Red Sea coast of Africa. Her stepson, **Thutmose III** (thoot MOH suh), took over as pharaoh once he reached adulthood. A great military general, Thutmose III stretched Egypt's borders to their greatest extent ever.

Much later, **Ramses II** (RAM seez) became pharaoh of the New Kingdom. He ruled for 66 years, from 1279 B.C. to 1213 B.C., and during that time pushed Egyptian control northward again as far as Syria. He may be the best known of the Egyptian rulers because he boasted of his conquests on numerous temples and monuments, although his greatest reported victory may not actually have taken place.

Egypt Battles With Its Neighbors During the reign of Ramses II, Egypt fought a number of fierce battles against the Hittites of Asia Minor. After years of fighting, the Egyptians and the Hittites signed a peace treaty, the first such document in history known to have survived. It declared that Egypt and the Hittites "shall be at peace and in brotherhood forever."

New Kingdom pharaoh Thutmose III

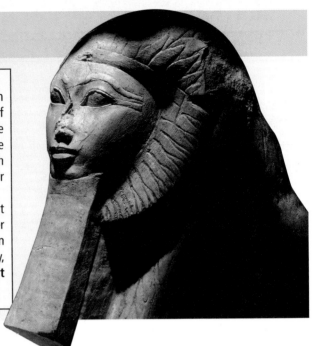

Hatshepsut

Hatshepsut (?1540 B.C.–?1457 B.C.) was the daughter of the pharaoh Thutmose I, the wife and widow of Thutmose II, and the stepmother of Thutmose III. Like some earlier Egyptian queens, she began ruling in the name of a male heir—her stepson—who was too young to take the throne. However, she later took the bold step of declaring herself pharaoh and won the support of key officials. Because Egyptians thought of their rulers as male, she wore a false beard as a sign of authority.

For herself and her father, Hatshepsut had constructed a magnificent funeral temple on the walls of which she left behind a record of her reign. Carvings depict a construction project as well as an expedition she sent down the Red Sea coast of Africa, which brought back ivory, spices, and incense. **For what reasons do you think Hatshepsut wanted to leave a record of her accomplishments?**

Vocabulary Builder

<u>displaced</u>—(dis PLAYSD) *vt.* took the place of somebody or something

To the south of Egypt, Nubia had developed along the Nile. For centuries, Egyptians traded or fought with their southern neighbor. From Nubia, they acquired ivory, cattle, and slaves. During the New Kingdom, Egypt conquered Nubia. Ramses II used gold from Nubia to pay charioteers in his army. Nubians served in Egyptian armies and left their mark on Egyptian culture. Much Egyptian art of this period shows Nubian soldiers, musicians, or prisoners.

Egypt Declines After 1100 B.C., Egyptian power slowly declined. Invaders, such as the Assyrians and the Persians, conquered the Nile region. In 332 B.C., the last Egyptian dynasty ended as the Greeks took control. In 30 B.C., Roman armies <u>displaced</u> the Greeks. Each new conqueror was eager to add the fertile Nile Valley to a growing empire.

✔ **Checkpoint** What role did Egyptian conquest of others play during Egypt's New Kingdom?

SECTION 3 Assessment

Progress Monitoring Online
For: Self-quiz with vocabulary practice
Web Code: naa-0231

Terms, People, and Places

1. What do the key people listed at the beginning of the section have in common? Explain.

Note Taking

2. **Reading Skill: Identify Supporting Details** Use your completed outline to answer the Focus Question: How did the Nile influence the rise of the powerful civilization of Egypt?

Comprehension and Critical Thinking

3. **Summarize** How did the Nile play a crucial role in uniting Egypt?
4. **Analyze Information** What knowledge did Egyptians gain from their conquerors the Hyksos? How do you think this helped them later on?
5. **Draw Conclusions** What types of information about ancient Egypt can we learn from colossal monuments such as the Great Pyramids or the building projects of Hatshepsut and Ramses II?

Writing About History

Quick Write: Draw Conclusions Choose a person from this section about whom you want to write a biographical essay and draw conclusions about his or her personality traits. Consider the person's actions and what they tell you about his or her personality. You may want to use the Internet or the library to gather more information about the person.

Building the Pyramids

Building an Egyptian pyramid was costly and required great planning. For example, the pharaoh Khufu built the first and largest of the pyramids at Giza. Thousands of farmers worked on the pyramid (shown below) when not planting or harvesting crops. They had no iron tools or wheeled vehicles. To complete the pyramid, workers quarried millions of huge limestone blocks. They transported the cut stones on barges along the Nile and then pulled them on sleds up a long ramp to and around the pyramid.

Broken remain of an ancient Egyptian A-frame, used to ensure that walls being constructed were level

Great Pyramid of Khufu: Fascinating Facts*

Height	481 feet (146.5 meters)
Type of stone	Mostly limestone and some granite
Distance from limestone quarry to Great Pyramid	500 yards
Number of cut stones used	2.3 million
Average weight of one cut stone	2.5 tons
Average weight of largest cut stone	40 tons
Total weight of Great Pyramid	6 million tons
Length of construction	20–30 years
Size of workforce	20,000–30,000 workers, skilled and unskilled
Types of workers	Construction workers, carpenters, water carriers, toolmakers, potters, overseers, scribes, cooks, bakers, butchers, physicians, priests

* All figures except the Great Pyramid's height are estimated values.
SOURCES: Encyclopedia Britannica Online; NOVA Online; Kevin Jackson and Jonathan Stamp, *Building the Great Pyramid*; Tim McNeese, *The Pyramids of Giza*

Thinking Critically

1. **Identify Ideologies** What Egyptian beliefs made it seem reasonable to spend so many resources and years building pyramids?

2. **Draw Conclusions** Based on the information given here, why do you think the Giza pyramids built after Khufu's were not as large as his?

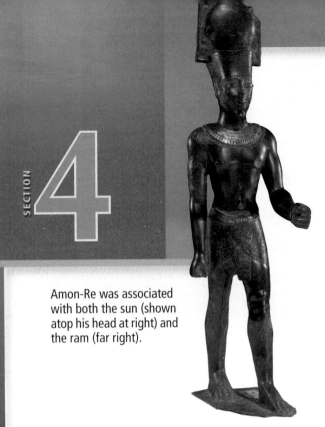

Amon-Re was associated with both the sun (shown atop his head at right) and the ram (far right).

WITNESS HISTORY 🔊 AUDIO

The Greatest of Gods

In ancient Egypt, the people of each city tended to worship one god in particular over all others. In time, however, the god Amon-Re became revered as the greatest of the gods. Most importantly, people believed the pharaohs received their right to rule from Amon-Re. They said of him, "Far away he is as one who sees, near he is as one who hears." Therefore even the pharaohs had to be careful of their actions, for Amon-Re's judgment could not only alter their lives but also put their leadership in jeopardy.

Focus Question How did religion and learning play important roles in ancient Egyptian civilization?

Egyptian Civilization

Objectives

- Describe the ways in which religious beliefs shaped the lives of ancient Egyptians.
- Understand how Egyptians viewed the afterlife.
- Explain how the Egyptians organized their society.
- Outline the advances that the Egyptians made in learning, the arts, science, and literature.

Terms, People, and Places

Amon-Re	hieroglyphics
Osiris	papyrus
Isis	decipher
Akhenaton	Rosetta Stone
mummification	

Note Taking

Reading Skill: Identify Supporting Details Use a chart to record the main idea of each section of text that follows a red heading. Include at least two supporting details for each main idea.

Egyptian Civilization			
Red Heading	Main Idea	Supporting Detail	Supporting Detail

Religious beliefs about gods, values, and life after death affected the daily lives of ancient Egyptians. In addition, scribes used one of the world's earliest forms of writing to record information, and scholars and artists made advances in science, art, and literature.

Religion Shapes Life in Ancient Egypt

Today, much of what we know about Egyptian religion comes from inscriptions on monuments and wall paintings in tombs. These inscriptions describe Egyptians appealing to the divine forces that they believed ruled this world and the afterlife.

Chief Gods and Goddesses In the sun-drenched land of Egypt, the chief god was the sun god. During the Old Kingdom, Egyptians worshipped a sun god named Re (ray). By the Middle Kingdom, Egyptians associated Re with another god, Amon (AH mun), and called this great lord of the gods **Amon-Re.** The pharaohs, whom Egyptians viewed as gods as well as kings, were believed to receive their right to rule from Amon-Re.

Most Egyptians related more to the god **Osiris** (oh SY ris) and the goddess **Isis** (EYE sis), whose story touched human emotions such as love and jealousy. According to mythology, Osiris ruled Egypt until his jealous brother, Set, killed him. Set then cut Osiris into pieces, which he tossed all over Egypt. Osiris' wife, Isis, saved him. She reassembled his body and brought him back to life. Because Osiris could no longer rule over the living, he became god of the dead and judge of souls seeking admission to the afterlife.

To Egyptians, Osiris was especially important because, in addition to ruling over the underworld, he was also god of the Nile. In that role, he controlled the annual flood that made the land fertile. Isis had special appeal for women, who believed that she had first taught women to grind corn, spin flax, weave cloth, and care for children. Like Osiris, Isis promised the faithful that they would have life after death.

A Pharaoh Tries to Reshape Religion About 1380 B.C., a young pharaoh named Amenhotep IV (ah mun HOH tep) challenged the powerful priests of Amon-Re. He devoted his life to the worship of Aton, a minor god. The pharaoh took the name **Akhenaton** (ah keh NAH tun), meaning "he who serves Aton." He ordered priests to worship only Aton and to remove the names of other gods from their temples.

Akhenaton's radical ideas had little success. Priests of Amon-Re and of other gods resisted such revolutionary changes. The people, too, were afraid to abandon their old gods in favor of Aton. Nobles also deserted the pharaoh because he neglected his duty of defending the empire. After Akhenaton's death, priests of the old gods reasserted their power.

✔ **Checkpoint** Which details about the Egyptian gods show the importance of agriculture to Egyptian society?

Vocabulary Builder

radical—(RAD ih kul) *adj.* favoring or making economic, political, or social changes of a sweeping or extreme nature

How Egyptians Viewed the Afterlife

As you have read, Egyptians believed that Osiris and Isis had promised them eternal life after death. Belief in the afterlife affected all Egyptians, from the highest noble to the lowest peasant.

Proving Oneself to Osiris The Egyptians believed that each soul had to pass a test to win eternal life. First, the dead soul would be ferried across a lake of fire to the hall of Osiris. Then, the dead person's heart would be weighed against the feather of truth. Those Osiris judged to be sinners would be fed to the crocodile-shaped Eater of the Dead. Worthy souls would enter the Happy Field of Food, where they would live forever in bliss. To survive the dangerous journey through the underworld, Egyptians relied on the *Book of the Dead*. It contained spells, charms, and formulas for the dead to use in the afterlife.

The *Book of the Dead* (page shown at left) includes the Negative Confession below, which the dead could use to prove his or her worthiness to Osiris. *What sorts of crimes does the confession say one has not committed?*

Primary Source

❝I have caused none to feel pain. I have made [no man] to weep. I have not committed murder. . . . I have not stolen from the orchards; nor have I trampled down the fields. . . . I have not turned back water at its springtide. . . . I am pure. I am pure. I am pure.❞
—*Book of the Dead*

🔊 AUDIO

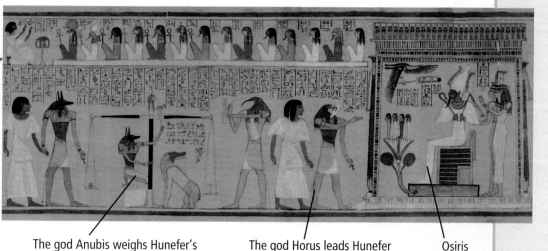

The god Anubis weighs Hunefer's heart against a feather.

The god Horus leads Hunefer to Osiris for judgment.

Osiris

History *Interactive*
For: Interactive infographic
Web Code: nap-0241

Mummification

The ancient Egyptians made a science out of mummifying the dead. Skilled embalmers extracted the brain of the dead person through the nostrils and removed most of the internal organs. They then filled the body cavity with linen and a drying powder, sprinkled spices on the body, and rubbed a mixture that kept out moisture into the skin. Later they wrapped the body in strips of linen. This costly process took months to complete.

Mummies were often laid to rest ▼ inside a nest of coffins. King Tutankhamen's coffins, shown here, were made of gold and wood and highly decorated.

◄ Mummification preserves bodies so well that even thousands of years later, they look lifelike when unwrapped.

Thinking Critically

1. **Determine Relevance** What does mummification tell us about ancient Egyptian religious views?
2. **Predict Consequences** Which fields of science do you think mummification helped the Egyptians learn about?

▲ Once removed from the body, the internal organs were also mummified. They were then stored in jars and placed within the tomb of the deceased.

Preparing the Dead for the Afterlife Egyptians believed that the afterlife would be much like life on Earth. As a result, they buried their dead with everything they would need for eternity. To give a soul use of its body in the afterlife, Egyptians perfected skills in mummification (mum uh fih KAY shun), the preservation of dead bodies by embalming them and wrapping them in cloth. At first, mummification was a privilege reserved for rulers and nobles. Eventually, ordinary Egyptians also won the right to mummify their dead, including beloved pets.

Evidence Found in the Tomb of Tutankhamen During the New Kingdom, many pharaohs were buried in a desolate valley known as the Valley of the Kings. Their tombs, known to be filled with fantastic riches, were a temptation to robbers in ancient times. As a result, most royal tombs were stripped of their treasures long ago. In 1922, however, British archaeologist Howard Carter unearthed the tomb of the young pharaoh Tutankhamen (toot ahng KAH mun), who was the son-in-law of Akhenaton. The tomb had remained almost untouched for more than 3,000 years. Its treasures have provided scholars a wealth of evidence about Egyptian civilization.

Portrait of Tutankhamen as a boy

The body of the 18-year-old "King Tut" had been placed in a solid-gold coffin, nested within richly decorated outer coffins. Today, the dazzling array of objects found in the tomb fills several rooms in the Egyptian Museum in Cairo. The treasures include chariots, weapons, furniture, jewelry, toys, and games. Tutankhamen was only a minor king. We can only imagine what treasures must have filled the tombs of great pharaohs like Thutmose III or Ramses II.

 Checkpoint How did mummification reflect Egyptian beliefs about the afterlife?

Egyptians Organize Their Society

Like other early civilizations, Egypt had its own class system. As both a god and an earthly leader, the pharaoh stood at the top of society, along with the royal family. Directly under the pharaoh were government officials and the high priests and priestesses, who served the gods and goddesses. Next came a tiny class of merchants, scribes, and artisans. They provided for the needs of the rich and powerful. The bottom layer of society was the largest—made up of peasants who worked the land.

Most People Were Farmers Most Egyptians were peasant farmers. Many were slaves. Men and women spent their days working the soil and repairing the dikes. One ancient record describes the life of a typical Egyptian peasant. "When the water is full he irrigates [the fields] and repairs his equipment. He spends the day cutting tools for cultivating barley, and the night twisting ropes."

In the off-season, peasant men were expected to serve the pharaoh, laboring to build palaces, temples, and tombs. Besides working in the fields, women also spent much time raising children, collecting water, and preparing food.

Changes to Social Structure During the New Kingdom, social classes became more fluid as trade and warfare increased. Trade offered new opportunities to the growing merchant class. Foreign conquests brought riches to Egypt, which in turn meant more business for artisans.

These skilled craftworkers made fine jewelry, furniture, and fabrics for the palaces and tombs of pharaohs and nobles.

Egyptian Women Enjoyed Higher Status Egyptian women generally enjoyed a higher status and greater independence than women elsewhere in the ancient world. For example, Ramses II declared, "The foot of an Egyptian woman may walk where it pleases her and no one may deny her." Under Egyptian law, women could inherit property, enter business deals, buy and sell goods, go to court, and obtain a divorce.

Although there were often clear distinctions between the occupations of women and men, women's work was not confined to the home. Women manufactured perfume and textiles, managed farming estates, and served as doctors. Women could also enter the priesthood, especially in the service of goddesses. Despite their many rights and opportunities, few women learned to read and write. Even if they did, they were excluded from becoming scribes or holding government jobs.

✔ **Checkpoint** Which social class grew in size as a result of trade and warfare?

Egyptians Make Advances in Learning

Learned scribes played a central role in Egyptian society. Some kept records of ceremonies, taxes, and gifts. Others served government officials or the pharaoh. Scribes also acquired skills in mathematics, medicine, and engineering. With skill and luck, a scribe from a poor family might become rich and powerful.

Keeping Written Records Like people in other early civilizations, the ancient Egyptians developed writing. In fact, they developed multiple writing systems. The first was **hieroglyphics** (hy ur oh GLIF iks), a system in which symbols or pictures called hieroglyphs represent objects, concepts, or sounds. The Egyptians used hieroglyphs to record important economic, administrative, and royal information. Often, priests and scribes carved hieroglyphs in stone. Such inscriptions on temples and other monuments are records of Egyptian culture that have endured for thousands of years.

Around the time that hieroglyphics came into use, scribes also developed hieratic (hy ur AT ik) writing, a simpler script for everyday use. The hieratic script was a cursive form of writing created by simplifying the shapes of the hieroglyphs. Over time, hieratic script was replaced by a similar one called demotic. The Egyptians also learned to make a paperlike writing material from **papyrus** (puh PY rus), a plant that grows along the banks of the Nile. (Paper would

Simplified Writing
Because hieroglyphs took a lot of time and care to write, Egyptian scribes also developed the cursive hieratic and demotic scripts for quicker use. *How much do the cursive forms of each symbol resemble their equivalent hieroglyphs?*

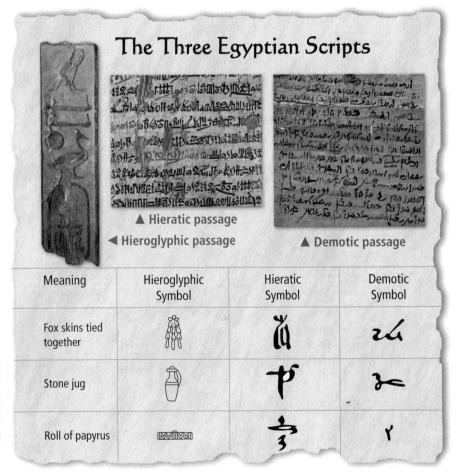

The Three Egyptian Scripts

▲ Hieratic passage
◄ Hieroglyphic passage
▲ Demotic passage

Meaning	Hieroglyphic Symbol	Hieratic Symbol	Demotic Symbol
Fox skins tied together			
Stone jug			
Roll of papyrus			

not be invented until about A.D. 100, in China.) Writing cursive scripts with reed pens and ink on the smooth surface of papyrus strips was much easier than chiseling words onto stone. When writing official histories, however, scribes continued to carve hieroglyphs.

The Clues of the Rosetta Stone After ancient Egypt declined, the meanings of ancient hieroglyphs were lost. Not until the early 1800s did a French scholar, Jean Champollion (zhahn shahm poh LYOHN), unravel the then mysterious writings on Egypt's great monuments. Champollion did so by **deciphering,** or figuring out the meaning of, passages written on the **Rosetta Stone.** This flat, black stone presents the same passage carved in hieroglyphics, demotic script, and Greek. By comparing the three versions, Champollion worked out the meanings of many hieroglyphs. As a result of that breakthrough, scholars could begin to read the thousands of surviving records from ancient Egypt.

Furthering Science and Mathematics The ancient Egyptians accumulated a vast store of knowledge in fields such as medicine, astronomy, and mathematics. Like most doctors until recent times, Egyptian physicians believed in various kinds of magic. However, they learned a great deal about the human body through their knowledge of mummification. They also became skilled at observing symptoms, diagnosing illnesses, and finding cures.

Doctors also performed complex surgical operations, which we know about today because they are described on papyrus scrolls that survived through time. Many plant parts that Egyptian doctors prescribed as medicines—such as anise, castor beans, and saffron—are still used today for various purposes.

Egyptian priest-astronomers studied the heavens, mapping constellations and charting the movements of the planets. With this knowledge, they developed a calendar that included 12 months of 30 days each as well as 5 days added at the end of each year. With a few changes, this ancient Egyptian calendar became the basis for our modern calendar.

Egyptians developed mathematics partly in response to practical problems that they faced. Flooding Nile waters forced Egyptians to redraw the boundaries of their fields each year. To do this, scholars developed geometry in order to survey the land. Egyptian engineers also used geometry to calculate the exact size and location of each block of stone to be used in construction of a pyramid or temple. Huge projects such as building pyramids required considerable skills in design and engineering.

✔ **Checkpoint** Describe three advances in learning made by the ancient Egyptians.

Ancient Medicine
Art and artifacts like the ones below have also given us clues about the medical knowledge of the ancient Egyptians. An Old Kingdom wall carving (below top) shows a wounded man walking on crutches to meet a doctor. The skillfully shaped artificial toe (below bottom) was discovered on a mummy from the New Kingdom. *What medical skills do these pieces reveal?*

Egyptians Develop Arts and Literature

The Egyptians left behind them a rich legacy of art and literature. Statues, paintings, poems, and tales have given us a wealth of information about ancient Egyptian viewpoints and values.

Egyptian Arts The arts of ancient Egypt included statues, wall paintings in tombs, and carvings on temples. Some show everyday scenes of trade, farming, family life, or religious ceremonies. Others boast of victories in battle.

Painting and sculpture styles remained almost unchanged for thousands of years. Artists always presented gods and pharaohs as much larger than other figures—size indicated the subject's importance, not his or her real size. Also, artists usually depicted people with their heads and limbs in profile but their eyes and shoulders facing the viewer.

Statues often showed people in stiff, standard poses. Some human figures have animal heads that represent special qualities. The Sphinx that crouches near the Great Pyramids at Giza portrays an early pharaoh as a powerful lion-man. Egyptians also erected many stone buildings and monuments, mostly tombs and temples.

Colorful Variety of Art
Ancient Egyptian artists created a great variety of colorful and intricate pieces of art, such as Thutmose III's blue glass drinking vessel (above right), the lifelike bust of Akhenaton's wife Nefertiti (above left), and Tutankhamen's decorative pectoral jewelry (right).

Egyptian Literature The oldest Egyptian literature includes hymns and prayers to gods, proverbs, and love poems. Other writings tell of royal victories in battle or, like Ptah-hotep's book, give practical advice.

In Egypt, as in other early societies, folk tales were popular, especially *The Tale of Sinuhe*. It relates the wanderings of Sinuhe (SIN oo hay), an Egyptian official forced to flee into what is now Syria. He fights his way to fame among the desert people, whom the Egyptians consider uncivilized. As he gets older, Sinuhe longs to return home. The story ends happily when the pharaoh welcomes him back to court. *The Tale of Sinuhe* helps us see how Egyptians viewed both themselves and the people of the surrounding desert.

✓ **Checkpoint** What art forms were common in ancient Egypt?

SECTION **4** Assessment

Progress Monitoring *Online*
For: Self-quiz with vocabulary practice
Web Code: naa-0241

Terms, People, and Places
1. What do three of the key names listed at the beginning of the section have in common? Explain.

Note Taking
2. **Reading Skill: Identify Supporting Details** Use your completed chart to answer the Focus Question: How did religion and learning play important roles in ancient Egyptian civilization?

Comprehension and Critical Thinking
3. **Predict Consequences** Egyptians believed that their pharaohs received the right to rule from Amon-Re. How do you think replacing him with the god Aton would have affected the authority of the pharaohs?
4. **Make Comparisons** How do the Book of the Dead and the tomb of Tutankhamen offer different types of information about Egyptian views of the afterlife?
5. **Summarize** What jobs were Egyptian women allowed to hold? What jobs were they not allowed to hold?
6. **Analyze Information** Considering the materials that ancient Egyptians used to create their writing and art, what do you think are the challenges of locating examples of them today?

● **Writing About History**
Quick Write: Write an Introduction
Choose a person from ancient Egypt about whom you want to write a biographical essay and write an introduction. Be sure to include a thesis statement that explains who the person was and why he or she is worth learning about. Try to find an anecdote or quotation to use to set the tone for your essay.

Moses

WITNESS HISTORY 🔊 AUDIO

The One God of Judaism

❝I am the LORD your God, who brought you out of the land of Egypt, out of the house of bondage. You shall have no other gods before Me.❞
—Exodus 20:2–3

In the Hebrew Bible, God speaks these words to Moses to explain a belief that set the Israelites apart from all other people of the ancient world at that time. Instead of worshiping many gods, the Israelites prayed to just one god for guidance and protection.

Focus Question How did the worship of only one god shape Judaism?

Roots of Judaism

Objectives

- Understand what made the ancient Israelites' belief system unique from others at the time.
- Outline the main events in the early history of the Israelites.
- Analyze the moral and ethical ideas of Judaism.

Terms, People, and Places

monotheistic   Solomon
Torah   patriarchal
Abraham   Sabbath
covenant   prophet
Moses   ethics
David   Diaspora

Note Taking

Reading Skill: Identify Supporting Details Use a chart to record the main idea of each section of text that follows a red heading. Include at least two supporting details for each main idea.

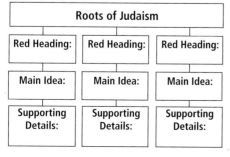

Roots of Judaism		
Red Heading:	Red Heading:	Red Heading:
Main Idea:	Main Idea:	Main Idea:
Supporting Details:	Supporting Details:	Supporting Details:

The present-day nation of Israel lies at the far western end of the Fertile Crescent, on the eastern coast of the Mediterranean Sea. About 4,000 years ago, the ancient Israelites developed the religion of Judaism, which became a defining feature of their culture. Today, Judaism is one of the world's major faiths.

The Ancient Israelites Shape a Unique Belief System

The beliefs of the ancient Israelites, also called the Hebrews, differed in basic ways from those of nearby peoples. The Israelites were **monotheistic,** believing that there was only one god. At the time, all other peoples worshiped many gods. A few religious leaders, such as the Egyptian pharaoh Akhenaton, spoke of a single powerful god. However, such ideas did not have the lasting impact that Israelite beliefs did.

The Israelites believed in an all-knowing, all-powerful god who was present everywhere. In their views, history and faith were interconnected. Each event reflected God's plan for the people of Israel. As a result, they recorded events and laws in the **Torah** (TOH ruh), their most sacred text. The Torah includes the first five books of the Hebrew Bible—that is, the books of Genesis, Exodus, Leviticus, Numbers, and Deuteronomy. The Hebrew Bible includes a total of 24 books. Additional laws and customs written down much later make up another important text, the Talmud.

✓ **Checkpoint** How did the beliefs of ancient Israelites differ from those of other nearby peoples?

The Dead Sea Scrolls

The oldest known texts of the Hebrew Bible were discovered in 1947 in a region along the northwest shore of the Dead Sea. They were written about 2,000 years ago on papyrus scrolls and bound in leather and copper. At some point, the Dead Sea Scrolls were stored carefully in clay jars and tucked away in a series of caves near Qumran, where an unsuspecting young shepherd happened upon them one day.

The caves of Qumran (above); a clay storage jar (top left); and one of the aged scrolls (bottom left)

◄ Many of the scrolls were so worn by time and weather that they had broken into many fragments, which had to be pieced back together carefully to be read.

Thinking Critically
1. **Determine Relevance** Why do you think the Dead Sea Scrolls were considered an important find?
2. **Draw Conclusions** Why might someone have decided to store these scrolls in a cave?

The Ancient Israelites

According to the Torah, a man named **Abraham** lived near Ur in Mesopotamia. About 2000 B.C., he and his family migrated, herding their sheep and goats into a region called Canaan (KAY nun). (Centuries later, under Roman rule, this land became known as Palestine.) Abraham is considered the father of the Israelite people.

God Makes a Covenant With the Israelites The Israelites believed that God had made the following **covenant,** or binding agreement, with Abraham:

66 You shall be the father of a multitude of nations. . . . I will make nations of you, and kings shall come forth from you. And I will establish my covenant between me and you and your descendants after you throughout their generations for an everlasting covenant, to be God to you and to your descendants after you. And I will give to you, and to your descendants after you, the land of your sojournings [short stay], all the land of Canaan. . . . 99
—Genesis 17:4–8

God's covenant with Abraham included two declarations that became the basis of two key beliefs of Judaism. First, God declared that He would have a special relationship with Abraham and his descendants. Because of this, the Israelites viewed themselves as God's "chosen people." Second, God declared that Canaan would one day belong to the Israelites. As a result, the Israelites viewed Canaan as their "promised land."

An Israelite named Moses later renewed God's covenant with the Israelites. Genesis tells that a famine forced many Israelites to migrate to Egypt. There, they were eventually enslaved. In the book of Exodus, Moses tells the Israelites that in return for faithful obedience to God, God will lead them out of bondage and into the promised land. In time, Moses led the Israelites in their exodus, or departure, from Egypt. After 40 years, they reached Canaan, although Moses died just before they arrived.

The Kingdom of Israel Established By 1000 B.C., the Israelites had set up the kingdom of Israel. The Torah tells of twelve separate tribes of Israel that had feuded up until this time. Then David, the strong and wise second king of Israel, united these tribes into a single nation.

According to the Torah, David's son Solomon followed him as king. Solomon undertook the task of turning the city of Jerusalem into an impressive capital. Jerusalem was praised for its splendid temple dedicated to God, which David had begun constructing and Solomon completed. Solomon also won fame for his wisdom and understanding. Additionally, he tried to increase Israel's influence around the region by negotiating with powerful empires in Egypt and Mesopotamia.

Israel Suffers Division and Conquest Israel paid a heavy price for Solomon's ambitions. His building projects required such high taxes and so much forced labor that revolts erupted after he died about 922 B.C. The kingdom then split into Israel in the north and Judah in the south.

The Israelites remained independent for 200 years but eventually fell to more powerful peoples. In 722 B.C., the Assyrians conquered Israel. In 586 B.C., Babylonian armies captured Judah. Nebuchadnezzar destroyed the great temple and forced many of those he defeated into exile in Babylon. This period of exile, called the Babylonian Captivity, lasted about 50 years.

In 539 B.C., the Persian ruler Cyrus the Great conquered Babylon and soon freed the Israelites. Since most of them had come from the kingdom of Judah, they became known as Jews. Many Jews returned to their homeland, where they rebuilt a smaller version of Solomon's temple. However, like other groups in the region, they lived under Persian rule.

✔ **Checkpoint** According to the Torah, where did the Israelites go once they left Egypt? What was special to them about this place?

Judaism Teaches About Law and Morality

From early times, the concept of law was central to the Israelites. The Torah includes many laws and is thus often referred to as the Books of the Law. Some of the laws deal with everyday matters such as cleanliness and food preparation. Others deal with criminal behavior.

Israelite society was patriarchal, which means that men held the greatest legal and moral authority. A family's oldest male relative was the head of the household and arranged marriages for his daughters. Women had few legal rights. Still, in early times, a few outstanding women, such as the judge Deborah, won great honor.

Two Key Beliefs of Judaism Derived From God's Covenant

Chosen People: God established a special relationship with the Israelites, promising to be their God and the God of their descendants.

Promised Land: God promised to give the land of Canaan to the Israelites and their descendants.

Vocabulary Builder

undertook—(un dur TOOK) *vt.* began to do something

The Ten Commandments as a Guide At the heart of Judaism are the Ten Commandments, a set of laws that Jews believe God gave to them through Moses. The first four commandments stress religious duties toward God, such as keeping the Sabbath, a holy day for rest and worship. The rest address conduct toward others. They include "Honor your father and mother," "You shall not kill," and "You shall not steal."

Teaching an Ethical Worldview Often in Jewish history, spiritual leaders emerged to interpret God's will. These prophets, such as Isaiah and Jeremiah, warned that failure to obey God's law would lead their people to disaster.

The prophets also taught a strong code of ethics, or moral standards of behavior. They urged both personal morality and social justice, calling on the rich and powerful to protect the poor and weak. All people, they said, were equal before God. Unlike many ancient societies in which the ruler was seen as a god, Jews saw their leaders as fully human and bound to obey God's law.

Jews Maintain Their Beliefs Over Time and Place For a 500-year period that began with the Babylonian Captivity, many Jews left their homeland and moved to different parts of the world. This spreading out of the Jewish people was called the Diaspora (dy AS pur uh). Some Jews were exiled, others moved to farther reaches of the empires that controlled their land, and yet others moved because of discontent with political rulers. Wherever Jews settled, many maintained their identity as a people by living in close-knit communities and obeying their religious laws and traditions. These traditions helped them survive centuries of persecution, or unfair treatment inflicted on a particular group of people, which you will read about in later chapters.

Today, Judaism is considered a major world religion for its unique contribution to religious thought. It influenced both Christianity and Islam, two other monotheistic faiths that also arose in the Middle East. Jews, Christians, and Muslims alike honor Abraham, Moses, and the prophets, and they all teach the ethical worldview developed by the Israelites. In the West, this shared heritage of Jews and Christians is known as the Judeo-Christian tradition.

✔ **Checkpoint** How did the prophets help Jews uphold the law?

SECTION 5 Assessment

Progress Monitoring *Online*
For: Self-quiz with vocabulary practice
Web Code: naa-0251

Terms, People, and Places

1. What do many of the key terms and people listed at the beginning of the section have in common? Explain.

Note Taking

2. **Reading Skill: Identify Supporting Details** Use your completed chart to answer the Focus Question: How did the worship of only one god shape Judaism?

Comprehension and Critical Thinking

3. **Recognize Ideologies** Which events recorded in the Torah reflect the Israelite belief that God had a plan for the people of Israel?

4. **Summarize** At which points in its early history was Israel unified, divided, or ruled by outsiders?

5. **Categorize** What types of laws does Judaism uphold?

● **Writing About History**

Quick Write: Present Evidence Choose a person from ancient Israel about whom you want to write a biographical essay and present interesting biographical evidence about him or her. Start by writing a thesis statement that explains why you think this person is important. Then write a paragraph summarizing facts, details, and examples from the person's life that support the thesis statement.

Psalm 23

The Psalms are a collection of 150 religious hymns. These songs reflect the Israelites' belief in God as the powerful savior of Israel. Many of the psalms praise the faithfulness of God to each of his people. In Psalm 23, the speaker describes his faith in God's protection and celebrates the Israelites' sense of a special relationship with a loving God.

The LORD is my shepherd,
 I shall not want;

he makes me lie down in green pastures.
He leads me beside still waters;

he restores my soul.
He leads me in paths of righteousness for his name's sake.

Even though I walk through the valley of the shadow of death,
I fear no evil;
for thou art with me;
thy rod and thy staff,
they comfort me.

Thou preparest a table before me in the presence of my enemies;
thou anointest[1] my head with oil, my cup overflows.

Surely goodness and mercy shall follow me all the days of my life;
and I shall dwell in the house of the LORD for ever.

1. anointest (uh NOYNT ist) *v.* to rub into a part of the body as part of a religious ceremony

Scribes hand-wrote Hebrew Bibles from right to left on long scrolls of parchment. Medieval scribes copied religious texts and decorated the pages, as in this version of Psalm 23 from about A.D. 1280.

Scribes still hand-write scriptures today.

Thinking Critically

1. **Analyze Information** How does the speaker feel as a result of his relationship with God?
2. **Analyze Literature** Based on what you know about God's covenant with the Israelites, do you think the comparison of God to a shepherd makes sense?

CHAPTER 2

Quick Study Guide

Progress Monitoring *Online*
For: Self-test with vocabulary practice
Web Code: naa-0261

■ Key Civilizations

Civilization	Time Period	Notable Rulers
Sumer	3200 B.C.–1900 B.C.	
Egypt	Old Kingdom 2575 B.C.–2130 B.C. Middle Kingdom 1938 B.C.–1630 B.C. New Kingdom 1539 B.C.–1075 B.C.	Hatshepsut Thutmose III Ramses II
Akkad	2300 B.C.–2150 B.C.	Sargon
Babylon	Old 1790 B.C.–1595 B.C. New 626 B.C.–539 B.C.	Hammurabi Nebuchadnezzar
Hittite	1650 B.C.–1200 B.C.	
Assyria	1350 B.C.–609 B.C.	Assurbanipal
Israel	1000 B.C.–586 B.C.	David Solomon
Persia	539 B.C.–323 B.C.	Cyrus the Great Darius I

■ Key Innovations

Sumer: social hierarchy; cuneiform writing; advances in astronomy and mathematics
Egypt: bureaucracy; pyramids; peace treaty; mummification; social hierarchy; hieroglyphic, hieratic, and demotic writing; papyrus; advances in medicine, astronomy, and mathematics; 365-day calendar
Babylon: legal code; advances in astronomy and mathematics
Hittites: iron working
Assyrians: legal regulation of royal household; libraries
Israel: monotheistic religion, Judaism
Persians: government organized into provinces with governors; roads; common set of weights and measures; use of coins and money economy; new religion of Zoroaster
Phoenicians: Tyrian purple dye; alphabet

■ Key Causes of Rise and Fall of Civilization

- Leadership able to coordinate control of rivers (Sumer, Egypt)
- Wealth gained from economic pursuits such as trade (Sumer, Persia, Phoenicia, Egypt)
- Conquest of existing states (Akkad, Babylon, Assyria, Persia)
- Unification of existing regions (Persia, Egypt, Israel)

→ **Rise of Civilization**

- Conquest by others (Sumer, Akkad, Assyria, Babylon, Egypt, Israel)

→ **Fall of Civilization**

■ The Rise of Civilization

3300 B.C.
City-states flourish in Sumer.

2575 B.C.
Egypt's Old Kingdom begins.

2300 B.C.
Sargon, the ruler of Akkad, conquers Sumer.

Chapter Events
World Events

3500 B.C.   **3000 B.C.**   **2500 B.C.**

2600 B.C.
Cities are built in the Indus Valley of South Asia.

Concept Connector

■ Cumulative Review

Record the answers to the questions below on your Concept Connector worksheets. In addition, record information from this chapter about the following concepts:

• Trade: Phoenician sea traders
• Geography's Impact: Tigris and Euphrates rivers

1. **Advances in Technology** During prehistory, technological advances such as the development of stone tools and of domestication and farming allowed hominids and early humans to radically expand the possibilities for their lives. How do those advances compare in impact to technological advances that the peoples of ancient Mesopotamia and Egypt made? Think about advances in the following:
   • military technology   • the sciences
   • writing

2. **Belief Systems** People in many early civilizations established belief systems that became an important force in shaping their societies. Compare the influence of religion on ancient Egyptian and ancient Israelite society. Think about the effects of religion on these aspects of society:
   • government and law   • the sciences
   • daily life   • art
   • standards for behavior

3. **Empire** To maintain control over a vast empire, it was vital that a ruler be well-respected. Based on the empires of the ancient Middle East and Egypt, what characteristics do you think made the leaders you have read about most successful? Think about the following:
   • spiritual leadership
   • establishment of laws and punishments for crimes
   • military power
   • treatment of subjects

■ Connections to Today

1. **Economic Systems: Money in the World Today** The establishment of a money economy by the Persians allowed the many peoples living within the vast empire to exchange goods more easily because they shared a common currency. Today, many countries have their own unique coins and bills, so all people within each country use the same money. To sell goods or services in another country, however, people must exchange their own money for the equivalent amount of the other country's money. Do you think there should be one common world currency? Explain your answer.

2. **People and the Environment: A Dam on the Nile** Like their ancient ancestors, modern Egyptians rely on the Nile. Nearly all Egyptians live on the 4 percent of land closest to the Nile's shores. Since 1970, when Egypt completed construction of the Aswan High Dam across the Nile, people have had year-round access to water for farming and drinking. The dam also generates half the country's electricity. However, it prevents the Nile's rich silt from reaching farmland downstream. Compare the ways in which the Nile has served as a challenge and a resource in ancient times and today.

Persons per sq. mile	Persons per sq. kilometer
More than 3,119	More than 1,204
520–3,119	200–1,204
260–519	100–199
130–259	50–99
25–129	10–49
1–24	1–9
Less than 1	Less than 1

History Interactive
For: Interactive timeline
Web Code: nap-0261

1790s B.C.
Hammurabi, the king of Babylon, issues the first written law code.

1100 B.C.
The Assyrians expand across Mesopotamia.

1000 B.C.
The kingdom of Israel is established, and Israelite beliefs evolve into a major religion, Judaism.

522 B.C.
Darius begins to unify the Persian empire.

2000 B.C.   1500 B.C.   1000 B.C.   500 B.C.

2000 B.C.
The kingdom of Nubia develops along the Nile River in East Africa.

1766 B.C.
The Shang dynasty of China emerges.

1150 B.C.
The Olmecs build the first civilization in the Americas.

750 B.C.
Greek city-states such as Athens begin to develop.

509 B.C.
The Roman republic is founded.

Chapter Assessment

Terms, People, and Places

Match the following terms with the definitions below.

ziggurat	Hatshepsut
Torah	Osiris
prophet	colony
Zoroaster	codify
delta	dynasty
Fertile Crescent	ethics

1. moral standards of behavior
2. Egyptian god of the underworld
3. a territory ruled by outsiders
4. to arrange and set down in writing
5. the most sacred text in Judaism
6. triangular area of marshland at the mouth of some rivers
7. large, stepped platform
8. ruling family
9. Egypt's first female ruler
10. a region of the Middle East with rich soil and wheat fields
11. spiritual leader who interprets God's will
12. Persian founder of a new religion

Main Ideas

Section 1 (pp. 30–35)
13. Describe Sumer's social hierarchy.
14. How was the development of writing in Sumer influenced by economic needs?

Section 2 (pp. 36–43)
15. Explain the significance of Hammurabi's Code.
16. How did the knowledge of iron working help both the Hittites and the Assyrians to expand?

Section 3 (pp. 44–49)
17. Describe the government bureaucracy of Old Kingdom Egypt.

Section 4 (pp. 50–56)
18. Describe three gods or goddesses who were important to ancient Egyptians. How did Akhenaton try to change their roles?
19. Name an achievement the ancient Egyptians made in each of the following fields: medicine, astronomy, and mathematics.

Section 5 (pp. 57–61)
20. Why did the Israelites consider themselves to be God's "chosen people"?
21. How does the Torah reflect the Israelites' respect for the law?

Chapter Focus Question
22. What distinct characteristics did the early civilizations and empires of the Middle East and Egypt develop?

Critical Thinking

23. **Make Comparisons** Compare the views about the afterlife of the Sumerians, the ancient Egyptians, and Zoroaster. Point out similarities and differences.
24. **Recognize Cause and Effect** How did an Egyptian religious practice—mummification—affect the field of medicine?
25. **Analyze Information** Consider the separate inventions of writing in Sumer and in Egypt. Why do you think that, in both cases, writing continued to change in form and in use over time?
26. **Demonstrate Reasoned Judgment** Many ancient peoples, including the Babylonians, Assyrians, and Israelites, lived in societies guided by well-established laws. Do you think that having a code of laws is an essential aspect of civilization? Why or why not?
27. **Synthesize Information** Conquest by different leaders was a constant theme of life in the lands of the ancient Middle East and Egypt. In what ways did leaders unite the often distant and culturally different lands that they ruled?

● Writing About History

Writing a Biographical Essay As civilizations developed in the ancient Middle East and Egypt, many important and interesting people played a role. Write a biographical essay on one of the following people: Nebuchadnezzar, Darius I, Hatshepsut, Solomon, or any other person mentioned in the chapter. Consult page SH18 of the Writing Handbook for additional help.

Prewriting
• Decide which person from the chapter interests you most. You may choose someone whose actions you admire or someone who seems particularly unique and interesting to you.

• Decide whether you want to focus more on the historical events the person took part in or on details of the person's life.
• Do research to gather facts and details about the actions or life of the person.

Drafting
• Develop a focus for your essay and choose information to support that focus.
• Make an outline organizing the events or details in a logical way, such as chronologically.
• Write an introduction, a body, and a conclusion. Be sure to use direct descriptions, quotations, and anecdotes.

Revising
• Use the guidelines for revising your report on page SH19 of the Writing Handbook.

Document-Based Assessment

War in the Ancient Middle East

Military campaigns were conducted frequently in the ancient Middle East. Scribes and artists often recorded their leaders' victories on monuments. The following documents reveal that these early wars were both devastating and widespread.

Document A

"... [My troops] were like lions roaring upon the mountaintops. The chariotry consisted of runners, of picked men, of every good and capable chariot-warrior. The horses were quivering in every part of their bodies, prepared to crush the foreign countries under their hoofs. ... Those who reached my frontier, ... their heart and their soul are finished forever and ever. Those who came forward together on the sea, the full flame was in front of them at the river-mouths, while a stockade of lances surrounded them on the shore. ... I have made the lands turn back from (even) mentioning Egypt; for when they pronounce my name in their land, then they are burned up."

—From Pharaoh Ramses III of Egypt

Document B

"In the eighteenth year of my rule I crossed the Euphrates for the sixteenth time. [King] Hazael of Damascus put his trust upon his numerous army and called up his troops in great number. ... I fought with him and inflicted a defeat upon him, killing with the sword 16,000 of his experienced soldiers. I took away from him 1,121 chariots, 470 riding horses as well as his camp. ... I followed him and besieged him in Damascus, his royal residence. I cut down his gardens. ... I marched as far as the mountains of Hauran, destroying, tearing down and burning innumerable towns, carrying booty away from them which was beyond counting. I marched as far as the mountains of Ba'li-ra'si ... and erected there a stela [stone pillar] with my image as king."

—From King Shalmaneser III of Assyria

Document C
Soldiers of Ramses III in Battle

Document D
Soldiers of Shalmaneser III in Battle

Analyzing Documents

Use your knowledge of ancient warfare and Documents A, B, C, and D to answer questions 1–4.

1. Documents A and B are told from the point of view of
   A a victim of an ambush.
   B the ally of a conquering ruler.
   C the enemy of a conquering ruler.
   D the leader of a successful campaign.

2. What did the narrator of Document B do in the mountains of Ba'li-ra'si after he conquered the king of Damascus?
   A conquer a great city
   B set up a monument showing his image
   C chase the enemies' leader
   D receive tribute from the conquered people

3. Which can you learn from Documents C and D?
   A who won each battle shown
   B how many men fought in each battle
   C where each battle took place
   D what weapons the soldiers used in battle

4. **Writing Task** Consider that inscriptions and artwork were two different means for rulers to tell their people about their conquests. What motives would have led the rulers to have such documents created? Do you think such documents serve as reliable records of historical events? Use your knowledge and specific information from these documents to support your opinion.

3
Ancient India and China
2600 B.C.–A.D. 550

A Life-Size Legacy

China's first emperor, who took power in 221 B.C., later built a tomb that astonished archaeologists when they uncovered it more than 2,000 years later. He had buried himself with a life-size clay army of 6,000 soldiers and horses. The Chinese historian Sima Qian described the construction of the tomb:

66 The labourers . . . built models of palaces, pavilions, and offices and filled the tomb with fine vessels, precious stones, and rarities. . . . With quicksilver [mercury] the various waterways of the empire . . . were created and made to flow and circulate mechanically. With shining pearls the heavenly constellations were depicted above, and with figures of birds in gold and silver and of pine trees carved of jade the earth was laid out below. 99

Listen to the Witness History audio to hear more about this remarkable tomb.

◄ Artists constructed each soldier by hand, so that no two are identical.

Chapter Preview

Chapter Focus Question In what ways did the civilizations and empires of ancient India and China lay long-lasting social and political foundations?

Section 1
Early Civilizations of India and Pakistan

Section 2
Hinduism and Buddhism

Section 3
Powerful Empires of India

Section 4
Rise of Civilization in China

Section 5
Strong Rulers Unite China

China's first emperor, Shi Huangdi

The Hindu god Shiva

India's first emperor, Chandragupta Maurya

Note Taking Study Guide *Online*
For: Note Taking and Concept Connector worksheets
Web Code: nad-0301

Indus stone bust, possibly of a priest or ruler

Indus clay figurine

WITNESS HISTORY 🔊 AUDIO

Forgotten Civilization Discovered

❝Not often has it been given to archaeologists . . . to light upon the remains of a long-forgotten civilisation. It looks, however, at this moment, as if we were on the threshold of such a discovery in the plains of the Indus.

Up to the present our knowledge of Indian antiquities [ancient history] has carried us back hardly further than the third century [B.C.]. Of the long ages before the coming of the Greeks and the rise of the Maurya dynasty; of the birth and growth of civilisation in the great river basins . . . archaeology has given us but the faintest glimmerings.❞
—Sir John Marshall, Director General
of Archaeology in India, 1924

Focus Question How have scholars learned about India's first two civilizations, the Indus and the Aryan?

Early Civilizations of India and Pakistan

Objectives
- Describe the Indian subcontinent's geography.
- Understand the clues archaeology has provided about the rise and fall of the Indus civilization.
- Analyze the main characteristics of the Aryan civilization and the Vedic Age.
- Explain what ancient Indian epics reveal about Aryan life.

Terms, People, and Places

subcontinent	Mohenjo-Daro	Indra
plateau	veneration	brahman
monsoon	Vedas	mystic
Harappa	rajah	acculturation

Note Taking

Reading Skill: Recognize Sequence Keep track of the sequence of important events in early India by recording them in the order they occurred.

Date	Event

In the early 1900s, archaeologists digging in the Indus River valley of Pakistan made some startling discoveries. They unearthed bricks, small clay seals, figurines, and other artifacts dissimilar in style to any they had seen before. The archaeologists soon realized they had uncovered a civilization that had flourished 4,500 years earlier. It had been unknown to the world ever since.

Geography of the Indian Subcontinent

The Indus Valley is located in the region known as South Asia, or the Indian subcontinent. A **subcontinent** is a large landmass that juts out from a continent. The Indian subcontinent is a huge peninsula extending into the Indian Ocean. Today, it includes three of the world's ten most populous countries—India, Pakistan, and Bangladesh—as well as the island nation of Sri Lanka (sree LAHNG kuh) and the mountain nations of Nepal and Bhutan.

Towering, snow-covered mountain ranges mark the northern border of the subcontinent, including the Hindu Kush and the Himalayas. These mountains limited contacts with other lands, leaving India's distinct culture to develop on its own. However, the mountains were not a complete barrier. Steep passes through the Hindu Kush served as gateways to migrating and invading peoples for thousands of years.

Natural Features Define Regions The Indian subcontinent is divided into three major zones: the fertile Gangetic Plain in the north, the dry Deccan plateau, and the coastal plains on either side of the Deccan.

The Gangetic Plain lies just south of the Himalayas. This fertile region is watered by mighty rivers: the Indus, which gives India its name, the Ganges (GAN jeez), and the Brahmaputra (brah muh POO truh). These rivers and their tributaries carry melting snow from the mountains to the plains, making agriculture possible.

The Deccan is a plateau, or raised area of level land, that juts into the Indian Ocean. Much of it lacks the melting snows that feed the rivers of the north and provide water for irrigation. As a result, parts are arid, agriculturally unproductive, and sparsely populated.

The coastal plains are separated from the Deccan by low-lying mountain ranges, the Eastern and Western Ghats. Rivers and heavy seasonal rains provide water for farmers. Also, from very early times, people in this region used the seas for fishing and as highways for trade.

Monsoons Affect Climate A defining feature of life in the Indian subcontinent is the monsoons, or seasonal winds that regularly blow from a certain direction for part of the year. In October, the winter monsoons blow from the northeast, bringing hot, dry air that withers crops. In mid-June, the summer monsoons blow from the southwest. They pick up moisture over the Indian Ocean and drench the land with downpours.

The monsoons have shaped Indian life. Each year, people welcome the rains that are desperately needed to water the crops. If the rains are late, famine and starvation may occur. However, if the rains are too heavy, rushing rivers will unleash deadly floods.

✓ **Checkpoint** How has geography affected where people live in the Indian subcontinent?

Geography *Interactive*
For: Audio guided tour
Web Code: nap-0311

Indus Civilization

Indus civilization, 2600 B.C.–1900 B.C.

Map Skills The earliest civilization in the Indian subcontinent developed in the Indus Valley.
1. **Locate** (a) Himalayas (b) Deccan (c) Indus River (d) Ganges River (e) Harappa
2. **Place** What natural features did people benefit from by living in the Indus River valley?
3. **Make Comparisons** How do you think the Narmada River valley would have compared to the Indus River valley as a site for a civilization to develop?

Mortimer Wheeler

Much of what we know about Indus civilization comes from the work of Sir Mortimer Wheeler (1890–1976), who directed the excavations of Harappa and Mohenjo-Daro in the 1940s. Previously, Wheeler had led one of England's first university archaeology departments, run a museum, and headed the first archaeological excavation to use trained volunteers rather than untrained laborers.

As well, through publications and frequent appearances on popular radio and television shows, Wheeler inspired thousands of people to visit his research sites. Indeed, Wheeler succeeded in fascinating the public with the work of archaeologists. **What did Wheeler contribute to archaeology?**

Indus Civilization Rises and Falls

About 2600 B.C., the earliest South Asian civilization emerged in the Indus River valley, in present-day Pakistan. The Indus civilization flourished for about 700 years. However, only since the 1920s have its once-prosperous cities emerged beneath the archaeologists' picks and shovels.

Archaeologists have investigated numerous Indus sites. Unfortunately, they have not yet turned up any names of kings or queens, tax records, literature, or accounts of famous victories. The written remains of Indus civilization are found only rarely, usually on small clay seals that do not include any long passages. Still, we do know that the Indus Valley civilization covered the largest area of any civilization until the rise of Persia more than 1,000 years later. We know, too, that its cities rivaled those of Sumer.

Well-Planned Cities Reveal Organized Government Archaeologists' investigations in recent years have led them to believe that at least five large cities may have been prominent during the course of the civilization's history. A few hundred smaller sites have also been studied. Since their discovery in the 1920s, the Indus cities of **Harappa** and **Mohenjo-Daro** (moh HEN joh DAH roh) have been considered possible twin capitals of the civilization or cities that ruled the area one after the other. Both were large, some three miles in circumference. Each was dominated by a massive hilltop structure whose exact purpose is unknown. Each city also included a huge warehouse used for storage.

A notable feature of Mohenjo-Daro and a few smaller sites is how carefully planned they were. Mohenjo-Daro was laid out in an organized pattern, with long, wide main streets and large rectangular blocks. Most of its houses were built with baked clay bricks of a standard size. At Harappa and other Indus sites, mud and unbaked bricks were also common building materials. In addition, Indus houses had complex plumbing systems, with baths, drains, and water chutes that led into sewers beneath the streets. Indus merchants used a uniform system of weights and measures. From such evidence, archaeologists have concluded that these Indus cities had a well-organized government.

Making a Living by Farming and Trading As in other early civilizations, most people living in the Indus civilization were farmers. They grew a wide variety of crops, including wheat, barley, melons, and dates. They also may have been the first people to cultivate cotton and weave its fibers into cloth.

Some people were merchants and traders. Their ships carried cargoes of cotton cloth, grain, copper, pearls, and ivory combs to distant lands. By hugging the coast of the Arabian Sea and sailing up the Persian Gulf, Indus vessels reached the cities of Sumer. Scholars think that this contact with Sumer may have prompted the people of the Indus Valley to develop their own system of writing; however, the Indus writing system is unique, showing no relationship to Sumerian cuneiform.

Religious Beliefs Develop From clues such as statues and images on small clay seals, archaeologists have speculated about the religious beliefs of Indus Valley people. Many think that, like other ancient peoples, the people of the Indus were polytheistic. A mother goddess, the source of creation, seems to have been widely honored, as perhaps was a leading male god. Indus people also seem to have viewed certain animals as sacred, including the buffalo and the bull. Some scholars think these early practices influenced later Indian beliefs, especially the **veneration** of, or special regard for, cattle.

Indus Civilization Declines By 1900 B.C., the quality of life in the Indus Valley was declining. Crude pottery replaced the finer works of earlier days. The use of writing halted. Mohenjo-Daro was entirely abandoned. The populations of the other Indus cities and towns also dwindled to small numbers.

Scholars do not know for sure what happened to the Indus civilization, but they have offered several explanations for its decline. They once thought that invaders attacked and overran the cities of the Indus, but this now seems unlikely. Some suggest that damage to the local environment was a factor. Possibly too many trees were cut down to fuel the ovens of brick makers. Tons of river mud found in the streets of Mohenjo-Daro suggest a major flood. Other evidence points to a devastating earthquake. Today scholars think that some of these events may have worked together to bring an end to Indus civilization.

 Checkpoint What evidence shows that Indus civilization included a well-organized government?

The Remnants of Indus Civilization

Archaeologists have considered numerous explanations for how the Indus civilization ended, but most agree that there was likely not one single cause. While people did continue to live in the Indus Valley, the basic features of civilization dwindled away as they returned to simpler ways of life. Read the primary source at right. *What types of evidence did archaeologists stop finding after the Indus civilization's decline?*

▲ The Indus people carved seals with writing and depictions of animals.

The ruins of Mohenjo-Daro still stand today. ▼

▲ The Indus people developed standardized cubic weights to measure the masses of various objects.

Primary Source

❝ The Indus Civilization remains an historical enigma [puzzle]. A remarkably uniform [culture], distributed over a vast geographical area, utterly disappears without an apparent successor. Cities, writing, the high achievement of their crafts, the use of standardized weights, long distance trade with the Gulf, and their exceptional system of urban sanitation simply disappear from the South Asian social landscape. [These were] replaced by what had existed before: regionally distinctive cultures inhabiting small villages with a limited scattering of modest sized towns that [were] wholly distinctive from that of the Indus Civilization. ❞
—Carl Lamberg-Karlovsky, archaeologist

Aryan Civilization Develops During the Vedic Age

Possibly before 2000 B.C. and certainly by 1500 B.C., a nomadic people called the Aryans arrived in the Indian subcontinent. Over many centuries, waves of Aryans had been migrating slowly with their herds of cattle and horses from what is now southern Russia. They traveled through the mountain passes into northwestern India and became the founders of a new civilization.

Aryans Migrate Into India The Aryans were one of many groups of speakers of Indo-European languages who migrated across Europe and Asia. The early Aryans who settled in India built no cities and left behind very little archaeological evidence. Most of what we know about them comes from the Vedas, a collection of hymns, chants, ritual instructions, and other religious teachings. Aryan priests memorized and recited the Vedas for a thousand years before they ever wrote down these sacred teachings. As a result, the period from 1500 B.C. to 500 B.C. is often called the Vedic Age.

In the Vedas, the Aryans appear as warriors who fought in chariots with bows and arrows. They loved food, drink, music, chariot races, and dice games. These nomadic herders valued cattle, which provided them with food and clothing. Later, when they became settled farmers, families continued to measure their wealth in cows and bulls.

From Nomadic Life to Farming As time passed, the Aryans mingled with the people they conquered. Gradually, they gave up their nomadic ways and settled into villages to cultivate crops and breed cattle. From the local people, the Aryans learned farming and other skills as well as new crafts.

In time, the Aryans spread eastward to colonize the heavily forested Ganges basin. By about 800 B.C., they learned to make tools out of iron. Equipped with iron axes and weapons, restless pioneers carved farms and villages out of the rain forests of the northeast.

Aryan tribes were led by chiefs who were called rajahs. A rajah, who was often the most skilled war leader, had been elected to his position by an assembly of warriors. As he ruled, he considered the advice of a council of elders made up of the heads of families. Rajahs often fought with one another to control trade and territory across the Gangetic Plain. Some rajahs became powerful hereditary rulers, extending their influence over many villages.

Aryans Structure Society From the Vedas, we learn that the Aryans divided their society into ranked groups based on occupation. The highest group was made up of the Brahmins, or priests. Next came the Kshatriyas (kuh SHAT ree yuhz), or warriors. The third group, the Vaisyas (VYS yuz), included herders, farmers, artisans, and merchants. The Aryans separated people who had little or no Aryan heritage into a fourth group, the Sudras (SOO druz). This group included farmworkers, servants, and other laborers who occupied the lowest level of society. Many of them were Dravidians, the Indian people whom the Aryans had conquered.

The gods' creation of the universe is described in the *Rig Veda*. It says they divided the body of Purusha, the first man, into four parts to create the four social groups of ancient India. Which parts of the body became the warriors?

Primary Source

66 When they divided Purusha, in how many different portions did they arrange him? What became of his mouth, what of his two arms? What were his two thighs and his two feet called?

His mouth became the Brahmin; his two arms were made into the Rajanya [Kshatriya]; his two thighs the Vaisya; from his two feet the Sudra was born. 99
—*Rig Veda*, "Hymn of Man"

Aryan Religious Beliefs Develop The Aryans were polytheistic. They worshiped gods and goddesses who <u>embodied</u> natural forces such as sky, sun, storm, and fire. The chief Aryan deity was fierce **Indra,** the god of war. Indra's weapon was the thunderbolt, which he used not only to destroy demons but also to announce the arrival of rain, so vital to Indian life. Other major gods included Varuna, the god of order and creation, and Agni, the god of fire and the messenger who communicated human wishes to the gods. The Aryans also honored animal deities, such as monkey and snake gods.

Brahmins offered sacrifices of food and drink to the gods. Through the correct rituals and prayers, the Aryans believed, they could call on the gods for health, wealth, and victory in war.

As the lives of the Aryans changed, so, too, did their beliefs. Some religious thinkers were moving toward the notion of **brahman,** a single spiritual power that existed beyond the many gods of the Vedas and that resided in all things. There was also a move toward mysticism. **Mystics** are people who seek direct communion with divine forces. Aryan mystics practiced meditation and yoga, spiritual and bodily disciplines designed to enhance the attempt to achieve direct contact with the divine. The religions that emerged in India after the Vedic Age were influenced by both mysticism and the notion of brahman.

✓ **Checkpoint**   How were Aryan society and government structured?

Vocabulary Builder

<u>embodied</u>—(em BAH deed) *vt.* gave a visible form to something abstract

Communing With the Divine
Below, a young woman in China practices yoga, which is popular around the world today. At left, a 1,500-year-old Indian sculpture shows a Hindu man seated in a traditional meditation pose. Meditation, too, is still practiced by many people. *Why do you think these disciplines have appealed to people for so long?*

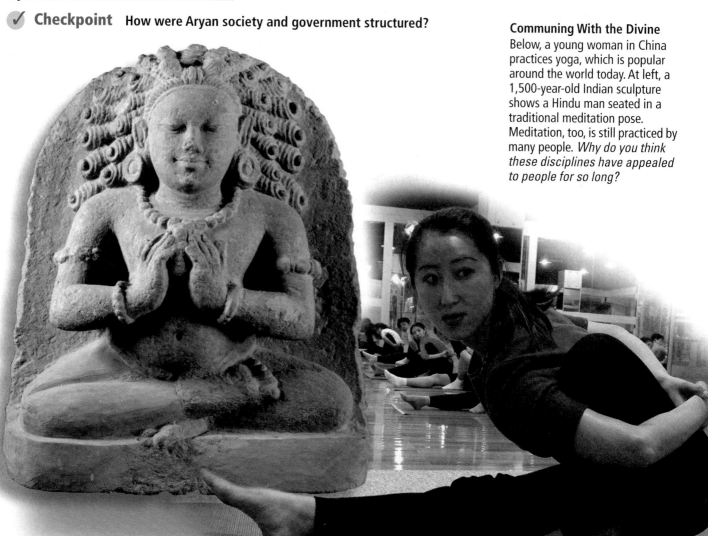

Epic Literature Tells About Aryan Life

By 500 B.C., Indian civilization consisted of many rival kingdoms. However, through **acculturation,** or the blending of two or more cultures, a common culture rooted in both Aryan and Dravidian traditions emerged. By this time, too, the written language, Sanskrit, that priests had used to write sacred texts began to flourish in literary usage.

The Aryans maintained a strong oral tradition as well. They continued to memorize and recite ancient hymns, as well as two long epic poems, the *Mahabharata* (muh hah BAH rah tuh) and the *Ramayana* (rah MAH yuh nuh). Like the Sumerian *Epic of Gilgamesh*, the Indian epics mix history, mythology, adventure, and religion.

***Mahabharata* Tells of Warfare and Religion** The *Mahabharata* is India's greatest epic. Through its nearly 100,000 verses, we hear echoes of the battles that rival Aryan tribes fought to gain control of the Ganges region. Five royal brothers, the Pandavas, lose their kingdom to their cousins. After a great battle that lasts 18 days, the Pandavas regain their kingdom and restore peace to India. One episode, a lengthy poem known as the *Bhagavad-Gita* (BUG uh vud GEE tuh), reflects important Indian religious beliefs about the immortality of the soul and the value of performing one's duty. In its verses, the god Krishna instructs Prince Arjuna on the importance of duty over personal desires and ambitions.

***Ramayana* Teaches Values of Behavior** The *Ramayana* is much shorter but equally memorable. It recounts the fantastic deeds of the daring hero Rama and his beautiful bride Sita. Early on, Sita is kidnapped by the demon-king Ravana. The rest of the story tells how Rama finally rescues Sita with the aid of the monkey general Hanuman.

Like the Aryan religion, these epics evolved over thousands of years. Priest-poets added new morals to the tales to teach different lessons. For example, they pointed to Rama as a model of virtue or as an ideal king. Likewise, Sita came to be honored as an ideal woman who remained loyal and obedient to her husband through many hardships.

 Checkpoint What types of values are revealed in Indian epics?

SECTION 1 Assessment

Progress Monitoring *Online*
For: Self-quiz with vocabulary practice
Web Code: naa-0311

Terms, People, and Places

1. Place each of the key terms at the beginning of the section into one of the following categories: politics, culture, or geography. Write a sentence for each term explaining your choice.

Note Taking

2. **Reading Skill: Recognize Sequence** Use your completed chart to answer the Focus Question: How have scholars learned about India's first two civilizations, the Indus and the Aryan?

Comprehension and Critical Thinking

3. **Analyze Information** Describe two ways in which geography and climate have influenced the people of the Indian subcontinent.

4. **Recognize Sufficient Evidence** What types of evidence do you think archaeologists should look for to explain how the Indus civilization declined and became unknown to the world for 4,000 years?

5. **Draw Conclusions** How reliably do you think epic literature tells us about Aryan life?

● Writing About History

Quick Write: Draft a Main Idea On some essay tests, you may be asked to choose one of several topics to write about. You may find it easiest to select the topic for which you can most quickly develop a main idea statement. Choose one of the following topics and draft a main idea statement for it:

- the decline of the Indus civilization
- the role(s) of the Vedas in Aryan history
- the nature of Aryan religious beliefs

The *Mahabharata*

An epic of the ancient Aryans, the *Mahabharata* has served as a major source of social and religious doctrine for India for many hundreds of years. Indian storytellers still recite segments of the 100,000 stanzas to entertain and instruct village audiences. This excerpt tells of the rewards the god Indra bestows upon a dutiful king, Vasu, who upholds the law of the gods.

▲ A central theme of the *Mahabharata* is battle between feuding families. Here we see two of the victors, Arjuna and Krishna, preparing to fight.

Indra said:

May never on earth, O lord of this earth, the Law be confused! Protect it, for the upheld Law holds up all the world. Guard the this-worldly Law, forever on guard and attentive; if yoked[1] to the Law, you shall win the blessed worlds of eternity. You standing on earth have become the dear friend of me standing in heaven—now possess . . . a country that is the udder of earth, abounding in cattle and holy, of stable [climate], with wealth and rice aplenty, protected by the skies. . . . It is a country beyond all others, with riches and jewels and all good things. . . .

The country people are accustomed to the Law, quite content and upright. No lies are spoken there even in jest, let alone in earnest. Sons are devoted to their elders there; they do not divide off from their fathers. Cows are never yoked to the cart, and even lean cows yield plenty. All the classes abide by[2] their own Law, in this land. . . .

This large celestial[3] crystalline chariot in the sky, which it is the God's privilege to enjoy, this airborne chariot will come to you as my gift. Among all mortals you alone shall stand upon a grand and sky-going chariot, and indeed, you will ride there above, like a God come to flesh! And I give you this garland Vaijayanti, woven of lotuses that never fade, which shall sustain you in battle, never hurt by swords. That shall be your mark of distinction here, sovereign of men—grand, rich, unmatched, and renowned[4] as "Indra's Garland"!

▲ Indra

1. **yoked** (yohkd) *vt.* joined or linked forcibly
2. **abide by** (uh BYD by) *vi.* to accept and submit to
3. **celestial** (suh LES chul) *adj.* belonging to, suitable for, in, or typical of heaven
4. **renowned** (rih NOWND) *adj.* well known or famous

Thinking Critically

1. **Identify Central Issues** What seems to be the king's most important function, and why do you think it is so significant?
2. **Synthesize Information** What rewards does Indra say Vasu will receive for pleasing the gods?

A woman prays in the Ganges (right). The colors of marigolds floating in the water (left) have symbolic meaning.

WITNESS HISTORY 🔊 AUDIO

River Waters Bring Salvation

❝ Thus said the God of Fire:—Now I shall describe the sanctity of the river Ganges, which imparts to men enjoyment of earthly cheers in this life and salvation in the next. The countries which the Ganges meanders through should be deemed as hallowed [holy] grounds. The river Ganges is the earthly door to salvation to men who long for emancipation [freedom] from this prison house of life. . . . Hundreds, nay thousands, of impious [immoral] persons become sinless and pure, by seeing, touching, or drinking of the river Ganges. ❞
—*Agni Puranam*, a Hindu sacred text

Focus Question In what ways were religion and society intertwined in ancient India?

Hinduism and Buddhism

Objectives
- Outline the essential beliefs of Hinduism.
- Analyze how the caste system shaped India.
- Understand the key teachings of the Buddha.
- Explore how Buddhism grew and changed as it spread beyond India.

Terms, People, and Places

atman	caste
moksha	Siddhartha Gautama
reincarnation	Four Noble Truths
karma	Eightfold Path
dharma	nirvana
ahimsa	sect

Note Taking

Reading Skill: Recognize Sequence Keep track of the development of Hinduism and Buddhism by filling in a flowchart like the one below with important stages, in the order they occurred.

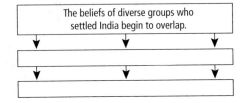

Thousands of years ago, two major religions—Hinduism and Buddhism—emerged in ancient India. The ethical and spiritual messages of both religions profoundly shaped Indian civilization.

The Beliefs of Hinduism Develop

Unlike most major religions, Hinduism has no single founder and no single sacred text. Instead, it grew out of the overlapping beliefs of the diverse groups who settled India. The process probably began when the Aryans added the gods of the Indus civilization to their own. Later people brought other gods, beliefs, and practices. As a result, Hinduism became one of the world's most complex religions, with countless gods and goddesses and many forms of worship existing side by side. Despite this diversity, all Hindus share certain basic beliefs.

One Force Underlies Everything "God is one, but wise people know it by many names." This ancient proverb reflects the Hindu belief that everything is part of the unchanging, all-powerful spiritual force called brahman. Hindus worship a variety of gods who give concrete form to brahman. The most important Hindu gods are Brahma, the Creator; Vishnu, the Preserver; and Shiva, the Destroyer. Each can take many forms, human or animal, to represent the various aspects of brahman with which he is associated. Some Hindus also worship various forms of the powerful goddess Shakti. She is both kind and cruel, a creator and a destroyer.

Sacred Texts Reveal Hindu Beliefs Over many hundreds of years, Hindu teachings were recorded in the sacred texts of the Vedas. The Upanishads (oo PAN ih shadz) are a section of the Vedas that address mystical questions related to Hinduism. These sacred texts use vivid images to examine complex ideas about the human soul and the connectedness of all life. In addition, literary works such as the *Bhagavad-Gita* were also revered for their representations of Hindu beliefs.

Achieving Moksha Is the Goal of Life To Hindus, every person has an essential self, or **atman** (AHT mun). Some view it as the same as brahman and others as a form of brahman. The ultimate goal of existence, Hindus believe, is achieving **moksha** (MAHK shuh), or union with brahman. To do that, individuals must free themselves from selfish desires that separate them from brahman. Most people cannot achieve moksha in one lifetime, but Hindus believe in **reincarnation,** or the rebirth of the soul in another bodily form. Reincarnation allows people to continue working toward moksha through several lifetimes.

In each existence, Hindus believe, a person can come closer to achieving moksha by obeying the law of karma. **Karma** refers to all the actions of a person's life that affect his or her fate in the next life. To Hindus, all existence is ranked. Humans are closest to brahman. Then come animals, plants, and objects like rocks or water. People who live virtuously earn good karma and are reborn at a higher level of existence. Those who do evil acquire bad karma and are reborn into suffering at a lower level of existence. In Indian art, this cycle of death and rebirth is symbolized by the image of the wheel.

To escape the wheel of fate, Hinduism stresses the importance of **dharma** (DAHR muh), the religious and moral duties of an individual. These duties vary according to class, occupation, gender, and age. Another key moral principle of Hinduism is **ahimsa** (uh HIM sah), or nonviolence. To Hindus, all people and things are aspects of brahman and therefore deserve to be respected. Many Hindus try to follow the path of ahimsa.

Key Hindu Gods

▲ Brahma, the Creator

▲ Vishnu, the Preserver

▲ Shiva, the Destroyer

Artisans covered each Hindu temple with masterful carvings, including depictions of the various forms of the god to whom a temple was dedicated. This temple at Somnathpur honors Vishnu.

Jainism Develops From Hinduism About 500 B.C., the teacher Mahavira (mah hah VEE ruh) founded Jainism (JY niz um), a religion that grew out of Hindu traditions and that is still practiced today. Mahavira rejected the idea that Brahmin priests alone could perform certain sacred rites. Jain teachings emphasize meditation, self-denial, and an extreme form of ahimsa. To avoid accidentally killing a living thing, even an insect, Jains carry brooms to sweep the ground in front of their feet.

✓ **Checkpoint** How do the Hindu gods relate to brahman?

The Caste System Shapes India

As you read in Section 1, the Aryans divided society into four groups. Non-Aryans held the lowest jobs. During the Vedic Age, class divisions moved more toward reflecting social and economic roles than ethnic differences between Aryans and non-Aryans. As these changes occurred, they led to a more complex system of **castes,** or social groups into which people are born and which can rarely be changed.

Complex Rules Uphold the Caste System Caste was closely linked to Hindu beliefs. To Hindus, people in different castes were different species of beings. A high-caste Brahmin, for example, was purer and therefore closer to moksha than someone from a lower caste. To ensure spiritual purity, a web of complex caste rules governed every aspect of life—for example, where people lived, what they ate, how they dressed, and how they earned a living. Rules forbade marrying outside one's caste or eating with members of another caste. High-caste people had the strictest rules to protect them from the spiritually polluted, or impure, lower castes. Because they had jobs such as digging graves, cleaning streets, or turning animal hides into leather, some people were considered so impure that they were called "untouchables."

For the untouchables, today called dalits, life was harsh and restricted. Other castes feared that contact with an untouchable could spread pollution. Untouchables had to live apart and to sound a wooden instrument called a clapper to warn of their approach.

Caste Affects the Social Order Despite its inequalities, caste ensured a stable social order. People believed that the law of karma determined their caste. While they could not change their status in this life, they could reach a higher state in a future life by faithfully fulfilling the duties of their present caste.

The caste system gave many people a sense of identity and interdependence. Each caste had its own occupation and its own leaders. Caste members cooperated to help one another. In addition, each caste had its own special role in Indian society as a whole. Although strictly separated, different castes depended on one another for their basic needs. A lower-caste carpenter, for example, built the home of a higher-caste scholar. The caste system also adapted to changing conditions.

Over time, many additional castes and subcastes evolved. As people migrated into the subcontinent, they formed new castes. Other castes grew out of new occupations and religions. This flexibility allowed people with diverse customs to live side by side in relative harmony. By modern times, there were thousands of major castes and subcastes.

✓ **Checkpoint** How did caste provide a sense of order in society?

THE LIFE OF THE BUDDHA

Central to Buddhism is the idea that one must live a moral life. Over the centuries, as many Buddhists have strived to do this, they have taken lessons from the life and actions of the Buddha, Siddhartha Gautama. Reminders of the Buddha's traits and actions abound in Asia and throughout the world in the form of sculpture both colossal and small, paintings, and literature. A few climactic scenes from the Buddha's life are repeated consistently in this art.

▲ **Gaining Awareness** In this illustration, Prince Gautama sees a dead man for the first time. From this and other journeys out of the palace, Gautama was inspired to abandon his life of privilege—a model many Buddhists attempt to follow.

Meditating This large bronze Buddha sits in a classic meditation pose—with legs crossed and hands resting face up in his lap. Buddhists believe that like Gautama, they can achieve enlightenment through meditation. ▶

◀ **Achieving Nirvana** Artwork of the Buddha lying down depicts his death—and final nirvana. In it he usually has a look of peace on his face.

Thinking Critically
1. **Make Generalizations** Why do you think Buddhists find it important to tell the story of the Buddha's life in art?
2. **Recognize Ideologies** Which of the basic beliefs of Buddhism are revealed in the Buddha sculptures shown here?

Key Teachings of the Buddha

In the foothills of the Himalayas, a reformer appeared named **Siddhartha Gautama** (sih DAHR tuh gow TUH muh). His teachings eventually spread across Asia to become the core beliefs of one of the world's most influential religions, Buddhism.

From Boy to Buddha Gautama's early life is known mostly through various religious writings and literature. He was born a prince about 563 B.C. According to tradition, his mother dreamed that a radiant white elephant descended to her from heaven. Signs such as this led a prophet to predict that the boy would someday become a wandering holy man. To prevent that—in hopes of his son one day becoming a ruler—Gautama's father kept him in the family's palaces, surrounded by comfort and luxury. At age 16, Gautama married a beautiful woman and enjoyed a happy life.

At age 29, Gautama's life changed. One day he took a ride beyond the palace gardens and saw an old man. On following rides, he also saw a sick person and a dead body. For the first time, Gautama became aware of human suffering. Deeply disturbed, he bade farewell to his family and left the palace, never to return. He set out to discover "the realm of life where there is neither suffering nor death."

Gautama wandered for years, seeking answers from Hindu scholars and holy men whose ideas failed to satisfy him. He fasted and meditated. At some point, he took a seat under a large tree, determined to stay there until he understood the mystery of life. Throughout the night, legend tells, evil spirits tempted Gautama to give up his meditations, but he fended them off. When he rose, he believed he understood the cause of and cure for suffering and sorrow. He was no longer Gautama; he had become the Buddha, or "Enlightened One."

Following the Four Noble Truths The Buddha spent the rest of his life teaching others what he had learned. In his first sermon after reaching enlightenment, he explained the **Four Noble Truths** that lie at the heart of Buddhism:

1. All life is full of suffering, pain, and sorrow.
2. The cause of suffering is nonvirtue, or negative deeds and mindsets such as hatred and desire.
3. The only cure for suffering is to overcome nonvirtue.
4. The way to overcome nonvirtue is to follow the Eightfold Path.

Vocabulary Builder
aspiration—(as puh RAY shun) n. desire or ambition to achieve something

The Buddha described the **Eightfold Path** as "right views, right aspirations, right speech, right conduct, right livelihood, right effort, right mindfulness, and right contemplation." The first two steps involved understanding the Four Noble Truths and committing oneself to the Eightfold Path. Next, a person had to live a moral life, avoiding evil words and actions. Through meditation, a person might at last achieve enlightenment. For the Buddhist, the final goal is **nirvana,** or union with the universe and release from the cycle of rebirth.

The Buddha saw the Eightfold Path as a middle way between a life devoted to pleasure and one based on harsh self-denial. He stressed moral principles such as honesty, charity, and kindness to all living creatures.

Comparing Buddhism and Hinduism Buddhism grew from the same traditions as Hinduism. Both Hindus and Buddhists stressed nonviolence and believed in karma, dharma, and a cycle of rebirth. Yet the religions differed in several ways. Instead of focusing on the priests, formal rituals, and many gods of Hinduism, the Buddha urged each person to seek enlightenment through meditation. Buddhists also rejected the caste system, offering the hope of nirvana to all regardless of birth.

✔ **Checkpoint**   What did Gautama hope to learn when he left home?

Buddhism Spreads Beyond India

The Buddha attracted many disciples, or followers, who accompanied him as he preached across northern India. Many men and women who accepted the Buddha's teachings set up monasteries and convents for meditation and study. Some Buddhist monasteries grew into major centers of learning.

Spread of Buddhism to A.D. 500

Geography *Interactive*
For: Audio guided tour
Web Code: nap 0321

Map Skills Missionaries and merchants spread Buddhism to many parts of Asia. It still thrives there today—though it is not practiced much in India.

1. **Locate** (a) India (b) China (c) Sri Lanka (d) Korea

2. **Movement** How did Buddhism spread to Japan?

3. **Synthesize Information** Looking at both maps, which arrows on the large map do you think represent the spread of Theravada Buddhism?

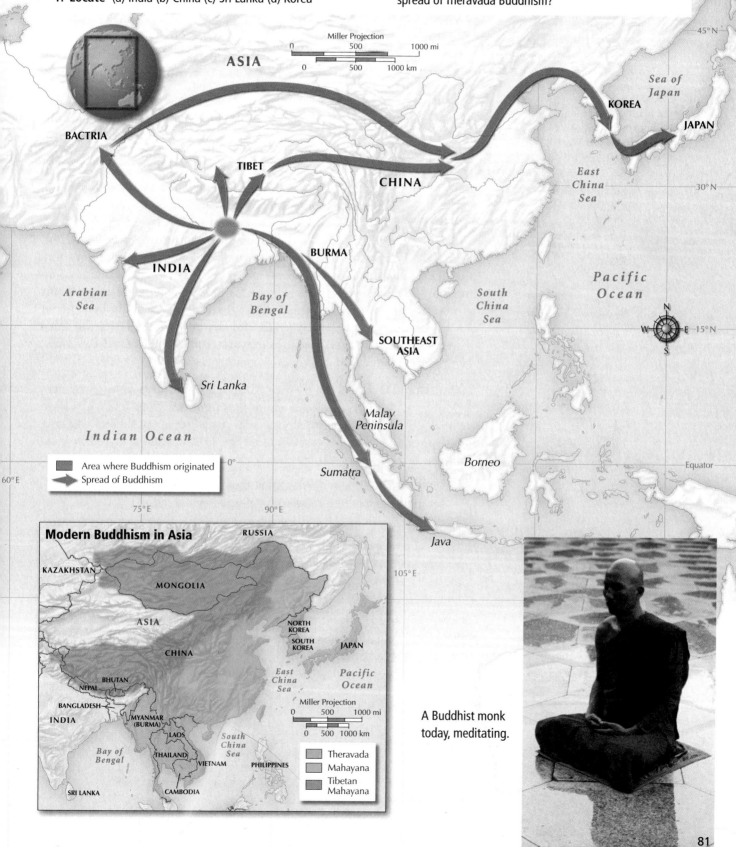

A Buddhist monk today, meditating.

81

Buddhist Stupas
Relics of the Buddha and other holy people are housed in Buddhist stupas, or large dome-shaped shrines like the Great Stupa at Sanchi, above. While stupas are quite plain, their gateways feature elaborate carvings that tell stories of the Buddha's life.

Collecting the Buddha's Teachings Legend holds that at age 80, the Buddha ate spoiled food. As he lay dying, he told his disciples, "Decay is inherent in all things. Work out your own salvation with diligence." After the Buddha's death, his followers collected his teachings into the *Tripitaka*, or "Three Baskets of Wisdom." One of the "baskets" includes sayings like this one, which echoes the Hindu emphasis on duty: "Let a man, after he has discerned his own duty, be always attentive to his duty. " Other sayings give the Buddha's version of the golden rule: "Overcome anger by not growing angry. Overcome evil with good. Overcome the liar by truth."

Buddhism Spreads and Divides Missionaries and traders spread Buddhism across India to many parts of Asia. Gradually, Buddhism split into two major **sects,** or subgroups. These were Theravada (thehr uh VAH duh) Buddhism and Mahayana (mah huh YAH nuh) Buddhism.

Theravada Buddhism closely followed the Buddha's original teachings. It required a life devoted to hard spiritual work. Only the most dedicated seekers, such as monks and nuns, could hope to reach nirvana. The Theravada sect spread to Sri Lanka and Southeast Asia.

The Mahayana sect made Buddhism easier for ordinary people to follow. Even though the Buddha had forbidden followers to worship him, Mahayana Buddhists pictured him and other holy beings as compassionate gods. People turned to these gods for help in solving daily problems as well as in achieving salvation. While the Buddha had said little about the nature of nirvana, Mahayana Buddhists described an afterlife filled with many heavens and hells. Mahayana Buddhism spread to China, Tibet, Korea, and Japan.

Buddhism Declines in India Although Buddhism took firm root across Asia, it slowly declined in India. Hinduism eventually absorbed some Buddhist ideas and made room for Buddha as another Hindu god. A few Buddhist centers survived until the 1100s, when they fell to Muslim armies that invaded India.

 Checkpoint How do you think the collecting of the Buddha's teachings helped the religion to spread beyond India?

SECTION **2** Assessment

Progress Monitoring *Online*
For: Self-quiz with vocabulary practice
Web Code: naa-0321

Terms, People, and Places

1. For each term, person, or place listed at the beginning of the section, write a sentence explaining its significance.

Note Taking

2. **Reading Skill: Recognize Sequence** Use your completed flowchart to answer the Focus Question: In what ways were religion and society intertwined in ancient India?

Comprehension and Critical Thinking

3. **Summarize** Explain the roles of karma, dharma, and reincarnation in the process of achieving moksha.

4. **Analyze Information** What aspects of the caste system relate to basic Hindu beliefs?

5. **Recognize Ideologies** According to the Buddha, how can people escape worldly suffering?

6. **Draw Conclusions** What about Mahayana teachings do you think appealed to many people?

● **Writing About History**

Quick Write: Gather Details On some essay tests, you may be asked to compare and contrast two topics that you have studied. Before you write a response, you may find it useful to gather details related to the two topics and create a graphic organizer to compare and contrast those details. Gather details about Hinduism and Buddhism and create a graphic organizer to compare and contrast them.

Belief Systems

▲ The Greek god Hermes is shown here as a messenger.

What major belief systems have emerged over time?

Hinduism, Buddhism, Confucianism, and Daoism are all belief systems that originated in ancient India or China and that still attract many followers. Today, thousands of different belief systems exist around the world. Most of them share certain characteristics—for example, belief in the existence of spiritual powers such as gods and respectful worship by followers, often through prayer. Belief systems vary in whether their followers worship gods and if so, how many, as the following examples show:

▲ Many Daoists painted peaceful nature scenes like this one.

Many Gods

The earliest belief systems focused on the idea that a powerful spirit inhabited every element of nature. In later belief systems, followers often worshiped gods associated with natural forces—such as sun, rain, or fire—or forces related to life and death. Of the many Hindu gods, the three most important are a creator, a preserver, and a destroyer. Other belief systems, such as those of the Greeks and Romans, identified each god with human characteristics and behaviors. For example, the Greek god Hermes was known as a trickster and a thief.

One God

Judaism, Christianity, and Islam share the belief that one god created the universe and rules over it. Jews believe that God's law is clear—"You shall have no other gods before me." Jesus, among whose followers Christianity developed, was a Jew. For that reason, much of the Jewish belief system was incorporated into Christianity, including its monotheism. Muslims, or followers of Islam, believe they should serve God by accepting five basic duties. The first is the daily declaration of faith that "there is no God but Allah."

No Gods

Other major belief systems have no gods. Buddhism, Confucianism, and Daoism, for example, all arose in response to the inspiring ideas of wise, human teachers. Siddhartha Gautama, the Buddha, stressed moral principles that would lead people to a state of enlightenment. Confucius offered guidelines about how to live virtuously, his goal being to ensure social order and good government. Laozi, who was believed to be Daoism's founder, taught his followers how to live in harmony with nature.

An Italian artist depicted the Christian God as a father in this painting. ▶

Thinking Critically

1. **Analyze Information** Do you think there is at least one element that all belief systems have in common? If so, what is it?
2. **Connections to Today** Do research to learn more about one of the belief systems described above. Write a summary telling how many people follow this belief system today, and in which countries.

The *Arthashastra* was written for India's first emperor, Chandragupta Maurya, who is still honored today.

WITNESS HISTORY ◀)) AUDIO

Behavior Fit For a King

❝In the happiness of his subjects lies [a king's] happiness, in their welfare his welfare. He shall not consider as good that which pleases him but treat as beneficial to him whatever pleases his subjects.❞
—*Arthashastra*, a Maurya handbook on governance

According to Hindu teachings, a ruler's duties included maintaining peace and order by enforcing laws, resisting invaders, and encouraging economic growth. Those who successfully achieved those goals became some of India's great rulers.

Focus Question In what ways did Maurya and Gupta rulers achieve peace and order for ancient India?

Powerful Empires of India

Objectives
- Analyze how Maurya rulers created a strong central government for their empire.
- Explore the kingdoms that arose across the Deccan.
- Explain why the period of Gupta rule in India is considered a golden age.
- Understand how family and village life shaped Indian society.

Terms, People, and Places

Chandragupta Maurya	golden age
dissent	decimal system
Asoka	joint family
missionary	dowry

Note Taking

Reading Skill: Recognize Sequence Use a timeline to record the sequence of important events that occurred during the Maurya and Gupta periods.

321 B.C.

Northern India was often a battleground where rival rajahs fought for control of the rich Ganges valley. But in 321 B.C., a young adventurer, **Chandragupta Maurya** (chun druh GUP tuh MOWR yuh), forged the first Indian empire.

The Maurya Empire Creates a Strong Government

We know about Chandragupta largely from reports written by Megasthenes (muh GAS thuh neez), a Greek ambassador to the Maurya court. He described the great Maurya capital at Pataliputra. It boasted schools and a library as well as splendid palaces and temples. An awed Megasthenes reported that the wall around the city "was crowned with 530 towers and had 64 gates."

Chandragupta Forges an Empire Chandragupta first gained power in the Ganges valley. He then conquered northern India. His son and grandson later pushed south, adding much of the Deccan to their empire. From 321 B.C. to 185 B.C., the Maurya dynasty ruled over a vast, united empire.

Chandragupta maintained order through a well-organized bureaucracy. Royal officials supervised the building of roads and harbors to benefit trade. Other officials collected taxes and managed state-owned factories and shipyards. People sought justice in royal courts. Chandragupta's rule was effective but harsh. A brutal secret police force reported on corruption, crime, and **dissent**—that is, ideas that opposed those of the government. Fearful of his many enemies, Chandragupta had specially trained women warriors guard his palace.

Asoka Rules by Moral Example The most honored Maurya emperor was Chandragupta's grandson, Asoka (uh SOH kuh). A few years after becoming emperor in 268 B.C., Asoka fought a long, bloody war to conquer the Deccan region of Kalinga. Then, horrified at the slaughter—more than 100,000 people are said to have died—Asoka turned his back on further conquests. He converted to Buddhism, rejected violence, and resolved to rule by moral example.

True to the Buddhist principle of respect for all life, Asoka stopped eating most meats and limited Hindu animal sacrifices. He sent missionaries, or people sent on a religious mission, to spread Buddhism across India and to Sri Lanka. By doing so, he paved the way for the spread of Buddhism throughout Asia. Although Asoka promoted Buddhism, he also preached tolerance for other religions.

Asoka had stone pillars set up across India, offering moral advice and promising a just government. Asoka's rule brought peace and prosperity and helped unite the diverse peoples within his empire. He built hospitals and Buddhist shrines. To aid transportation, he built roads and rest houses for travelers. "I have had banyan trees planted on the roads to give shade to people and animals," he noted. "I have planted mango groves, and I have had [wells] dug and shelters erected along the roads."

Division and Disunity Set In
After Asoka's death, Maurya power declined. By 185 B.C., the unity of the Maurya empire was shattered as rival princes again battled for power across the Gangetic Plain.

In fact, during its long history, India has seldom remained united for long. In ancient times, as today, the subcontinent was home to many peoples. Although the Aryan north shared a common civilization, fierce local rivalries kept it divided. Meanwhile, distance and cultural differences separated the peoples of the north and the peoples of the Deccan in the south. Adding to the turmoil, foreigners frequently pushed through mountain passes into northern India. The divided northern kingdoms often proved incapable of resisting these conquerors.

✔ **Checkpoint** How did Chandragupta organize Maurya government?

WITNESS HISTORY VIDEO

Watch *Asoka's Elephant Warriors* on the **Witness History Discovery School**™ video program to learn more about Asoka's conquests and his conversion to Buddhism.

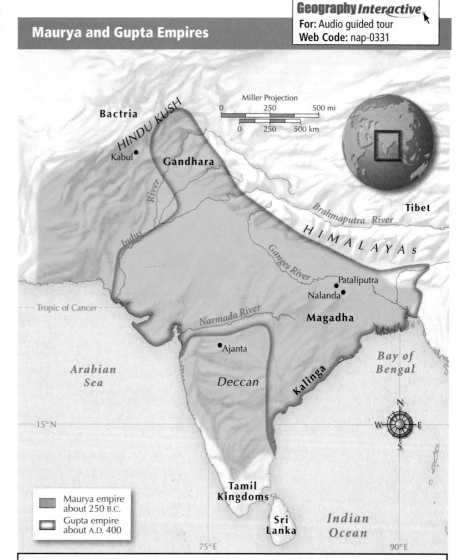

Maurya and Gupta Empires

Geography *Interactive*
For: Audio guided tour
Web Code: nap-0331

Bactria · Kabul · Gandhara · HINDU KUSH · Indus River · Tibet · Brahmaputra River · HIMALAYAS · Ganges River · Pataliputra · Nalanda · Magadha · Tropic of Cancer · Narmada River · Ajanta · Arabian Sea · Deccan · Kalinga · Bay of Bengal · Tamil Kingdoms · Sri Lanka · Indian Ocean · 15°N · 75°E · 90°E

Miller Projection
0   250   500 mi
0   250   500 km

Maurya empire about 250 B.C.
Gupta empire about A.D. 400

Map Skills Maurya and Gupta emperors were able to unite much of India under their rule.
1. **Locate** (a) Ganges River (b) Indus River (c) Tamil Kingdoms (d) Hindu Kush (e) Nalanda
2. **Movement** How did geography limit the northward expansion of both empires?
3. **Analyze Information** What region of the Indian subcontinent remained separate from both the Maurya and the Gupta empires?

Kingdoms Arise Across the Deccan

Like the Gangetic Plain, the Deccan was divided into many kingdoms after the decline of Maurya power. Each kingdom had its own capital with magnificent temples and bustling workshops. The peoples of the Deccan were Dravidians with very different languages and traditions from the peoples of the Aryan north. Over the centuries, Hindu and Buddhist traditions and Sanskrit writings drifted south and blended with local cultures. Deccan rulers generally tolerated all religions as well as the many foreigners who settled in their busy ports.

In the Tamil kingdoms, which occupied much of the southernmost part of India, trade was important. Tamil rulers improved harbors to support overseas trade. Tamil merchants sent spices, fine textiles, and other luxuries westward to eager buyers in the Roman empire. And as the Roman empire declined, Tamil trade with China increased.

The Tamil kingdoms left a rich and diverse literature. Tamil poets described fierce wars, heroic deeds, and festive occasions, along with the ordinary routines of peasant and city life.

 Checkpoint How do you think trade helped link the separate kingdoms of the Deccan?

The Guptas Bring About a Golden Age

Although many kingdoms flourished in the Deccan, the most powerful Indian states rose to its north. About 500 years after the Mauryas, the Gupta dynasty again united much of India. Gupta emperors organized a strong central government that promoted peace and prosperity. Under the Guptas, who ruled from A.D. 320 to about 540, India enjoyed a golden age, or period of great cultural achievement.

Peace and Prosperity Abound Gupta rule was probably looser than that of the Mauryas. Much power was left in the hands of individual villages and city governments elected by merchants and artisans. Faxian (FAH shyahn), a Chinese Buddhist monk who visited India in the 400s, reported on the mild nature of Gupta rule:

> **Primary Source**
>
> 66 The people are numerous and happy; . . . only those who cultivate the royal land have to pay [a portion of] the grain from it. . . . The king governs without . . . corporal punishments. Criminals are simply fined, lightly or heavily, according to the circumstances [of each case]. 99
> —Faxian, *A Record of Buddhistic Kingdoms*

Trade and farming flourished across the Gupta empire. Farmers harvested crops of wheat, rice, and sugar cane. In cities, artisans produced cotton cloth, pottery, and metalware for local markets and for export to East Africa, the Middle East, and Southeast Asia. The prosperity of Gupta India contributed to a flowering in the arts and learning.

Indians Make Advances in Learning Under Gupta rule, students were educated in religious schools. However, in Hindu and Buddhist centers, learning was not limited to religion and philosophy. The large Buddhist monastery-university at Nalanda, which attracted students from many parts of Asia, taught mathematics, medicine, physics, languages, literature, and other subjects.

GOLDEN AGE IN THE ARTS

Gupta artists may be best known for the magnificent sculpture that they carved on stone temples for the rajahs who sponsored an immense flowering in the arts. Such buildings were literally covered with carvings of mostly religious subjects. In addition, the golden age of the Gupta dynasty encompassed other arts, including painting, music, dance, and literature. Regarded as highly now as they were when created, the Gupta arts influenced artistic styles in later Indian societies as well as in many other parts of Asia.

▲ **Music** Musicians often entertained in Gupta courts. This terracotta tile shows a musician playing a lyre.

◄ **Sculpture** Scenes from Indian religious myths abound in Gupta sculpture. This one depicts the Hindu god Vishnu (center top) rescuing from a serpent a man who was cursed into the form of an elephant.

▼ **Painting** Famous Gupta murals decorate a series of cave temples carved into rock cliffs at Ajanta, in western India. The vibrant paintings, such as this one showing divine musicians, recall Buddhist stories and legends.

Dance Dancers have performed Indian classical dances since a few centuries before the Gupta era up through the present day. Each movement of the arms, hands, and eyes carries particular meaning. ▶

Thinking Critically
1. **Synthesize Information** What role did religion play in the arts of Gupta India? What role do you think the arts played in religion?
2. **Make Comparisons** Compare the subject matter of the three pieces of art shown here. What is similar? What is different?

Performed for Centuries
The Indian play *Shakuntala* has been re-enacted for centuries. In this scene from a modern-day performance, Shakuntala, her husband, and her son reunite at the end of the play, with gods watching over them. *What about this play might appeal to people throughout time?*

Indian advances in mathematics had a wide impact on the rest of the world. Gupta mathematicians devised the system of writing numbers that we use today. (However, these numerals are now called "Arabic" numerals because Arabs carried them from India to the Middle East and Europe.) Indian mathematicians also originated the concept of zero and developed the **decimal system** of numbers based on ten digits, which we still use today.

By Gupta times, Indian physicians were using herbs and other remedies to treat illness. Surgeons were skilled in setting bones and in simple surgery to repair injuries. It seems that doctors also began vaccinating people against smallpox about 1,000 years before this practice was used in Europe.

Expanding India's Literature During Gupta times, many fine writers added to the rich heritage of Indian literature. They collected and recorded fables and folk tales in the Sanskrit language. In time, Indian fables were carried west to Persia, Egypt, and Greece.

The greatest Gupta poet and playwright was Kalidasa. His most famous play, *Shakuntala* (shahk oon TAH luh), tells the story of a king who marries the lovely orphan Shakuntala. Under an evil spell, the king forgets his bride. After many plot twists, he finally recovers his memory and is reunited with her.

The Gupta Empire Declines Eventually, Gupta India declined under the pressure of weak rulers, civil war, and foreign invaders. From central Asia came the White Huns, a nomadic people who overran the weakened Gupta empire, destroying its cities and trade. Once again, India split into many kingdoms. It would see no other great empire like those of the Mauryas or Guptas for almost 1,000 years.

✅ **Checkpoint** How did religion influence learning and the arts in Gupta India?

Family and Village Life Shape Indian Society

Most Indians knew nothing of the dazzling courts of the Mauryas or Guptas. The vast majority were peasants who lived in the villages that dotted the Indian landscape. In Indian society, everyday life revolved around the rules and duties associated with caste, family, and village.

Joint Family Structure The ideal family was a joint family, in which parents, children, and their offspring shared a common dwelling. Indian families were patriarchal—the father or oldest male in a family headed the household. Adult sons continued to live with their parents even after they married and had children. (A daughter would go to live with her husband and his family.) Often only the wealthy could afford such large households. Still, even when they did not share the same house, close ties linked brothers, uncles, cousins, and nephews.

A father was thought to have wisdom and experience, and he enjoyed great authority. Even so, his power was limited by sacred laws and tradition. Usually, he made decisions after consulting his wife and other family members. Property belonged to the whole family.

The Family Performs Certain Duties The family performed the essential function of training children in the traditions and duties of their castes. Thus family interests came before individual wishes. Children worked with older relatives in the fields or at a family trade. While still young, a daughter learned that as a wife she would be expected to serve and obey her husband and his family. A son learned the rituals to honor the family's ancestors. Such rites linked the living and the dead, deepening family bonds across the generations.

For parents, an important duty was arranging good marriages for their children, based on caste and family interests. Marriage customs varied. In northern India, for example, a bride's family commonly provided a dowry, or payment to the bridegroom, and financed the costly wedding festivities. After marriage, the daughter left her home and became part of her husband's family.

Role of Women Changes Over Time In early Aryan society, women seem to have enjoyed a higher <u>status</u> than in later times. Aryan women even composed a few Vedic hymns. However, attitudes and customs affecting women varied across India and changed over time. By late Gupta times, upper-class women were increasingly restricted to the home. When they went outside the home, they were supposed to cover themselves from head to foot. Lower-class women, however, labored in the fields or worked at spinning and weaving.

Women were thought to have shakti, a creative energy that men lacked. In marriage, a woman's shakti helped to make the husband complete. Still, shakti might also be a destructive force. A husband's duty was to channel his wife's energy in the proper direction. Women had few rights within the family and society. Their primary duties were to marry and raise children.

For a woman, rebirth into a higher existence was gained through devotion to her husband. Often, a widow was expected to join her dead husband on his funeral fire. In this way, a widow became a sati, or "virtuous woman." Some widows accepted this painful death as a noble duty that wiped out their own and their husbands' sins. Other women bitterly resisted the custom.

Vocabulary Builder

status—(STAT us) *n.* social standing or prestige

Primary Source

❝With the monsoon, the tempo of life and death increases. Almost overnight grass begins to grow and leafless trees turn green. . . . While the monsoon lasts, the showers start and stop without warning. The clouds fly across, dropping their rain on the plains as it pleases them, till they reach the Himalayas. . . . Lightning and thunder never cease.❞
—Khushwant Singh,
Train to Pakistan   ◀))) AUDIO

A family escapes the floodwaters caused by the monsoons, which still bring both hardship and needed rain to people in India today.

Typical Village Structure

Typical Village Structure Throughout India's history, the village was at the heart of daily life. The size of villages varied, from a handful of people to hundreds of families. A typical village included a cluster of homes made of earth or stone. Beyond these dwellings stretched the fields, where farmers grew wheat, rice, cotton, sugar cane, or other crops according to region.

Each village included people of different castes who performed the necessary tasks of daily life. It ran its own affairs based on caste rules and traditions and faced little outside interference as long as it paid its share of taxes. A village headman and council made decisions. The council included the most respected people of the village. In early times, women served on the council. As Hindu law began to place greater restrictions on women, they were later excluded. The headman and council organized villagers to cooperate on vital local projects such as building irrigation systems and larger regional projects like building roads and temples.

Agriculture and Trade Shape Life In most of India, farming depended on the rains brought by the summer monsoons. Too much or too little rain meant famine. Landlords owned much of the land. Farmers who worked the land had to give the owner part of the harvest. Often, what remained was hardly enough to feed the farmers and their families.

Villages usually produced most of the food and goods that they needed. However, they relied on trade for some essentials, such as salt and spices, as well as various manufactured goods. People regularly interacted with others from nearby villages while attending weddings, visiting relatives, or shopping at marketplaces. This continual interchange was crucial in the establishment of common ideas across the subcontinent.

 Checkpoint Describe the structure of a typical Indian family.

SECTION 3 **Assessment**

Progress Monitoring *Online*
For: Self-quiz with vocabulary practice
Web Code: naa-0331

Terms, People, and Places

1. For each term, person, or place listed at the beginning of the section, write a sentence explaining its significance.

Note Taking

2. **Reading Skill: Recognize Sequence** Use your completed timeline to answer the Focus Question: In what ways did Maurya and Gupta rulers achieve peace and order for ancient India?

Comprehension and Critical Thinking

3. **Make Comparisons** Compare the approaches of Chandragupta and Asoka to ruling the Maurya empire.
4. **Analyze Information** Describe three achievements of the Gupta period that made it a golden age.
5. **Recognize Ideologies** How did the roles played by family and village in Indian life reveal the value of placing the needs of the community or group above those of the individual?

● **Writing About History**

Quick Write: Gather Details On some essay tests, you may be asked to defend a position about a topic that you have studied. Before you write a response, you may find it useful to gather details that support your position and organize them in an outline. Gather details and write an outline defending your position on the following topic: What was the most important way in which religion influenced life in ancient India?

Asoka's Edicts

During his rule of Maurya India, Asoka converted to Buddhism, rejected violence, and resolved to rule by moral example. The messages he published on stone pillars across India pronounced moral edicts, or commands, and described the just actions of his government. The following are excerpts from several of the pillars.

▲ Asoka

All men are my children. Just as I seek the welfare and happiness of my own children in this world and the next, I seek the same things for all men.

It is difficult to achieve happiness, either in this world or in the next, except by intense love of Dharma, intense self-examination, intense obedience, intense fear [of sin], and intense enthusiasm. Yet as a result of my instruction, regard for Dharma and love of Dharma have increased day by day and will continue to increase.... For these are the rules: to govern according to Dharma, to administer justice according to Dharma, to advance the people's happiness according to Dharma, and to protect them according to Dharma.

The faiths of others all deserve to be honored for one reason or another. By honoring them, one exalts[1] one's own faith and at the same time performs a service to the faith of others. By acting otherwise, one injures one's own faith and also does disservice to that of others.... Therefore concord[2] alone is commendable.

Whatever good deeds I have done the people have imitated, and they have followed them as a model. In doing so, they have progressed and will progress in obedience to parents and teachers, in respect for elders, in courtesy to priests and ascetics[3], to the poor and distressed, and even to slaves and servants.

There is no gift that can equal the gift of Dharma.... If one acts in this way, one achieves ... happiness in this world and infinite merit in the world to come.

I have commanded this edict on Dharma to be inscribed so that it may last forever and so that my descendants may conform to it.

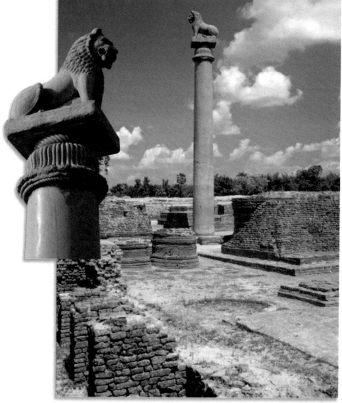

▲ Many of Asoka's pillars, such as this one in Vaishali, India, were erected in places where people often congregated.

1. **exalt** (eg ZAWLT) *vt.* raise up
2. **concord** (KAHN kawrd) *n.* friendly relations or peace
3. **ascetic** (uh SET ik) *n.* someone who chooses a life of self-denial

Thinking Critically
1. **Identify Central Issues** What are the major themes in these edicts?
2. **Predict Consequences** In what ways do you think Asoka's edicts may have contributed to the peace and prosperity of the Maurya empire?

Emperor Yu

WITNESS HISTORY 🔊 AUDIO

The Rewards of Devotion

In very ancient times, relates a Chinese legend, floodwaters rose to the top of the highest hills. Yu, a hard-working official, labored for a decade to drain the waters, not going home once to see his family. As a reward for his selfless efforts, the emperor appointed Yu the next ruler of China.

66 The emperor said, 'Come, Yu. The inundating [flooding] waters filled me with dread, [but then] you realized all that you represented, and accomplished your task— thus showing your superiority to other men. . . . I see how great is your virtue, how admirable your vast achievements.' 99
—Books of Yu

Focus Question What characteristics defined the civilization that developed in China under its early rulers?

Rise of Civilization in China

Objectives
- Understand how geography influenced early Chinese civilization.
- Analyze how Chinese culture took shape under the Shang and Zhou dynasties.
- Describe the religions and belief systems that developed in early China.
- List some achievements made in early China.

Terms, People, and Places

loess
clan
dynastic cycle
feudalism
Confucius
Laozi

philosophy
filial piety
oracle bone
character
calligraphy

Note Taking

Reading Skill: Recognize Sequence Keep track of the sequence of events in early China by making an outline of the events in the order they occurred.

```
I.
   A.
   B.
II.
   A.
   B.
```

The legend of Yu offers insights into early China. The Chinese depended so much on rivers for irrigation and transportation that they highly valued the ability to control floodwaters and to develop irrigation systems. The legend also shows how much the Chinese prized devotion to duty. Both themes played a key role in the development of Chinese civilization.

Geography Influences Civilization

Long distances and physical barriers separated China from Egypt, the Middle East, and India. This isolation contributed to the Chinese belief that China was the center of the earth and the sole source of civilization. These beliefs in turn led the ancient Chinese to call their land Zhongguo (jahng gwoh), or the Middle Kingdom.

Geographic Barriers Set China Apart To the west and southwest of China, brutal deserts and high mountain ranges—the Tian Shan (tyen shahn) and the Himalayas—blocked the easy movement of people. To the southeast, thick rainforests divided China from Southeast Asia. To the north awaited a forbidding desert, the Gobi. To the east lay the vast Pacific Ocean.

Despite these formidable barriers, the Chinese did have contact with the outside world. They traded with neighboring people and, in time, Chinese goods reached the Middle East and beyond. More often, the outsiders whom the Chinese encountered were nomadic invaders. Such conquerors, however, were usually absorbed into the advanced Chinese civilization.

China Includes Varied Regions As the Chinese expanded over an enormous area, their empire came to include many regions. The Chinese heartland lay along the east coast and the valleys of the Huang, or Yellow, River and the Chang River. In ancient times, as today, these fertile farming regions supported the largest populations. Then, as now, the rivers provided water for irrigation and served as transportation routes.

Beyond the heartland are the outlying regions of Xinjiang (shin jyahng) and Mongolia. These regions have harsh climates and rugged terrain. Until recent times, they were mostly occupied by nomads and subsistence farmers. Nomads repeatedly attacked and plundered Chinese cities. At times, however, powerful Chinese rulers conquered or made alliances with the people of these regions and another outlying region, Manchuria. China also extended its influence over the Himalayan region of Tibet, which the Chinese called Xizang (shih dzahng).

Settling Along the "River of Sorrows" Chinese history began in the Huang River valley, where Neolithic people learned to farm. As in other places, the need to control the flow of the river through large water projects probably led to the rise of a strong central government and the founding of what is sometimes called the Yellow River civilization.

The Huang River got its name from the **loess,** or fine windblown yellow soil, that it carries eastward from Siberia and Mongolia. Long ago, the Huang River earned a bitter nickname, "River of Sorrows." As loess settles to the river bottom, it raises the water level. Chinese peasants labored constantly to build and repair dikes to prevent the river from overflowing. If the dikes broke, floodwaters burst over the land. Such disasters destroyed crops and brought mass starvation.

✓ **Checkpoint** In what different ways did people live in ancient China?

Geography *Interactive*
For: Audio guided tour
Web Code: nap-0341

Shang and Zhou Civilizations

Map Skills Today, China extends west from the Pacific Ocean deep into central Asia. Its first civilizations existed in the eastern part of the modern-day country.

1. **Locate** (a) Chang River (b) Gobi (c) Huang River (d) Anyang
2. **Place** What physical features acted as obstacles to contact outside China?

3. **Draw Inferences** In which directions from China do you think it was easiest for the Chinese to make contact with other people? Why?

93

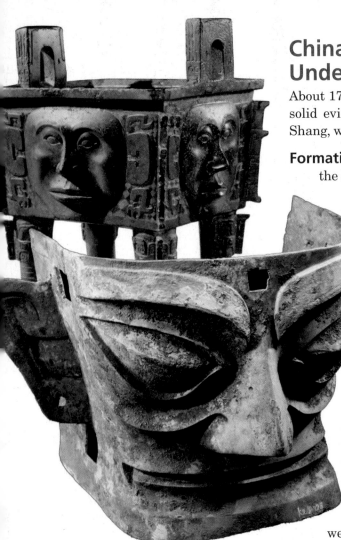

Shang artists were famous for their bronze works, such as the mask and vessel shown here.

China Begins to Take Shape Under the Shang Dynasty

About 1766 B.C., the first Chinese dynasty for which scholars have found solid evidence arose in a corner of northern China. This dynasty, the Shang, would dominate the region until about 1122 B.C.

Formation of Government Archaeologists have uncovered some of the large palaces and rich tombs of Shang rulers. The evidence indicates that from their walled capital city at Anyang, the Shang emerged to drive off nomads from the northern steppes and deserts. Shang kings probably controlled only a small area. Loyal princes and local nobles governed most of the land. They were likely the heads of important **clans,** or groups of families who claim a common ancestor.

In one Shang tomb, archaeologists discovered the burial place of Fu Hao (foo how), wife of the Shang king Wu Ding. Artifacts show that she owned land and helped to lead a large army against invaders. This evidence suggests that noblewomen may have had considerable status during the Shang period.

Social Classes Develop As in other early civilizations, the top level of Shang society included the royal family and a class of noble warriors. Shang warriors used leather armor, bronze weapons, and horse-drawn chariots. They may have learned of chariots from other Asian peoples with whom they <u>interacted</u>.

Early Chinese cities supported a class of artisans and merchants. Artisans produced goods for nobles, including bronze weapons, silk robes, and jade jewelry. Merchants exchanged food and crafts made by local artisans for salt, certain types of shells, and other goods not found in northeastern China.

The majority of people in Shang China were peasants. They clustered together in farming villages. Many lived in thatch-roofed pit houses whose earthen floors were dug several feet below the surrounding ground. Peasants led grueling lives. All family members worked in the fields, using stone tools to prepare the ground for planting or to harvest grain. When they were not in the fields, peasants had to repair the dikes. If war broke out between noble families, the men had to fight alongside their lords.

✓ **Checkpoint** How was China governed during the Shang dynasty?

The Zhou Dynasty Further Defines China

In 1122 B.C., the battle-hardened Zhou (joh) people marched out of their kingdom on the western frontier to overthrow the Shang. They set up the Zhou dynasty, which lasted until 256 B.C.

Receiving the Mandate of Heaven To justify their rebellion against the Shang, the Zhou promoted the idea of the Mandate of Heaven, or the divine right to rule. The cruelty of the last Shang king, they declared, had so outraged the gods that they had sent ruin on him. The gods then passed the Mandate of Heaven to the Zhou, who "treated the multitudes of the people well."

Vocabulary Builder

<u>interacted</u>—(in tur AKT ed) *vi.* was involved in communication, work, or social activity with someone else

The Chinese later expanded the idea of the Mandate of Heaven to explain the **dynastic cycle,** or the rise and fall of dynasties. As long as a dynasty provided good government, it enjoyed the Mandate of Heaven. If the rulers became weak or corrupt, the Chinese believed that heaven would withdraw its support. Floods, famine, or other catastrophes were signs that a dynasty had lost the favor of heaven. In the resulting chaos, an ambitious leader might seize power and set up a new dynasty. His success and strong government showed the people that the new dynasty had won the Mandate of Heaven. The dynastic cycle would then begin again.

Establishing a Feudal State The Zhou rewarded their supporters by granting them control over different regions. Thus, under the Zhou, China developed into a feudal state. **Feudalism** (FYOOD ul iz um) was a system of government in which local lords governed their own lands but owed military service and other forms of support to the ruler.

In theory, Zhou kings ruled China for more than 850 years. For about 250 of those years, they actually did enjoy great power and prestige. After the 800s B.C., however, feudal lords exercised the real power and profited from the lands worked by peasants within their domains.

Spurring Economic Growth During the Zhou period, China's economy grew. Knowledge of ironworking reached China in the 600s B.C. As iron axes and ox-drawn iron plows replaced stone, wood, and bronze tools, farmers produced more food. Peasants also began to grow new crops, such as soybeans. Some feudal lords organized large-scale irrigation works, making farming even more productive.

WITNESS HISTORY VIDEO

Watch *Discovering Ancient Shang China* on the **Witness History Discovery School**™ video program to learn more about archaeologists' investigations of Shang China.

DISCOVERY SCHOOL

History *Interactive*

For: Interactive diagram
Web Code: nap-0342

Dynastic Rule in China

Dynasties ruled China for most of its history until 1912. The Chinese believed that dynasties could gain or lose the Mandate of Heaven, depending on how wisely an emperor ruled. A Zhou emperor is shown here in his chariot. *According to the diagram, how did a new dynasty try to repair the problems left by an aging dynasty?*

Dynasties of China	
Dynasty	**Dates**
Shang	1766 B.C.–1122 B.C.
Zhou	1122 B.C.–256 B.C.
Qin	221 B.C.–206 B.C.
Han	202 B.C.–A.D. 220
Sui	A.D. 581–A.D. 618
Tang	A.D. 618–A.D. 907
Song	A.D. 960–A.D. 1279
Ming	A.D. 1368–A.D. 1644
Qing	A.D. 1644–A.D. 1911

The Dynastic Cycle

The New Dynasty
- Restores peace
- Appoints loyal officials
- Redistributes land to peasants
- Builds canals, irrigation systems, and roads
- Repairs defensive walls

After several generations, the new dynasty becomes an aging dynasty.

The Aging Dynasty
- Neglects government duties
- Ignores corrupt officials
- Loses control of the provinces
- Imposes heavy taxes to pay for luxuries
- Allows defensive walls to decay

New dynasty claims the Mandate of Heaven.

Aging dynasty loses the Mandate of Heaven.

Problems
- Floods, famine, earthquakes
- Invasions
- Armed bandits in the provinces
- Peasant revolts

Commerce expanded, too. The Chinese began to use money for the first time. Chinese copper coins were made with holes in the center so that they could be strung on cords. This early form of a money economy made trade easier. Merchants also benefited from new roads and canals that feudal lords constructed.

Economic expansion led to an increase in China's population. People from the Huang River heartland advanced into central China and soon began to farm the immense Chang River basin. As well, feudal nobles expanded their territories and encouraged peasants to settle in the conquered territories.

Zhou Dynasty Ends By 256 B.C., China was a large, wealthy, and highly developed center of civilization. Yet the Zhou dynasty was too weak to control feudal lords who ignored the emperor and battled one another in savage wars. Out of these wars rose a ruthless leader who was determined to impose political unity. His triumphs brought an end to the Zhou dynasty and ushered in the Qin (chin) dynasty, which you will read about in the next section.

 Checkpoint Explain three ways that China expanded during the Zhou dynasty.

Religious Beliefs Develop in Early China

By Shang times, the Chinese had developed complex religious beliefs, many of which continued to be practiced for thousands of years. The early Chinese prayed to many gods and nature spirits. Chief among them was the supreme god, Shang Di (shahng dee). The king was seen as the link between the people and Shang Di.

Gods as great as Shang Di, the Chinese believed, would not respond to the pleas of mere mortals. Only the spirits of the greatest people, such as the ancestors of the king, could possibly get the ear of the gods. Thus, the prayers of rulers and nobles to their ancestors were thought to serve the community as a whole, ensuring such benefits as good harvests or victory in war.

At first, only the royal family and other nobles had ancestors important enough to influence the gods. Gradually, other classes shared in these rituals. The Chinese called on the spirits of their ancestors to bring good fortune to the family. To honor their ancestors' spirits, they offered them sacrifices of food and other necessities. When westerners reached China, they mistakenly called this practice "ancestor worship."

 Checkpoint What did early Chinese communities do to ensure good harvests?

Two Major Belief Systems Take Root in Zhou China

During the late Zhou period, when war and social changes were disrupting old ways of life, new belief systems developed that would form the basis of China's culture and government for centuries to come. Thinkers such as **Confucius** (known by the Chinese as Kong Fuzi) and **Laozi** (LOW dzuh) put forward ideas on how to restore social order and maintain harmony with nature.

Confucius

Confucius (551 B.C.–479 B.C.) decided at an early age to dedicate himself to education and public service. He felt that educated people had a responsibility to serve in government so that they could translate their good ideas into action.

As a teacher, Confucius spread education to both rich and poor. He inspired thousands of followers with his guidelines about the proper way to live. As a public servant, he did not fare so well, however. His high standards of conduct often brought him into conflict with corrupt officials. According to Confucius, "The superior man understands righteousness. The inferior man understands profit." **Why do you think people were inspired by Confucius' teachings?**

The Master said, If out of the three hundred *Songs* I had to take one phrase to cover all my teaching, I would say 'Let there be no evil in your thoughts.'

Tzu-kung asked about the true gentleman. The Master said, He does not preach what he practices till he has practiced what he preaches.

The Master said, Yu, shall I teach you what knowledge is? When you know a thing, to recognize that you know it, and when you do not know a thing, to recognize that you do not know it. That is knowledge.

—*Analects*

Confucius Spreads His Wisdom Confucius was born in 551 B.C. to a noble but poor family. A brilliant scholar, Confucius hoped to become an adviser to a local ruler. He studied ancient texts to learn the rules of conduct that had guided the ancestors. For years, he wandered from court to court talking to rulers about how to govern. Unable to find a permanent government position, he turned to teaching. As his reputation for wisdom grew, he attracted many students. Like two other influential thinkers who lived about the same time—Siddhartha Gautama in India and Socrates in Greece—Confucius never wrote down his ideas. Rather, his students collected many of his sayings in the *Analects*.

Unlike the Buddha, Confucius took little interest in spiritual matters such as salvation. Instead, he developed a **philosophy,** or system of ideas, that was concerned with worldly goals, especially those of ensuring social order and good government.

Five Relationships Shape Behavior Confucius taught that harmony resulted when people accepted their place in society. He stressed five key relationships: ruler to subject, parent to child, husband to wife, elder brother to younger brother, and friend to friend. Confucius believed that, except for friendship, none of these relationships were equal. For example, he felt that older people were superior to younger ones and men were superior to women.

According to Confucius, everyone had duties and responsibilities. Superiors should care for their inferiors and set a good example, while inferiors owed loyalty and obedience to their superiors. Correct behavior, Confucius believed, would bring order and stability. Confucius put **filial piety,** or respect for parents, above all other duties. Other Confucian values included honesty, hard work, and concern for others. "Do not do to others," he declared, "what you do not wish yourself."

Confucius also taught that it was a ruler's responsibility to provide good government. In return, the people would be respectful and loyal subjects. Confucius said the best ruler was a virtuous one who led people by good example. In addition, Confucius believed that government leaders and officials should be well educated. "By nature, men are pretty much alike," he said. "It is learning and practice that set them apart." He urged rulers to take the advice of wise, educated men.

Confucianism Has Great Influence In the centuries after Confucius died, his ideas influenced many aspects of Chinese life. Chinese rulers relied on Confucian ideas and chose Confucian scholars as officials. The Confucian emphasis on filial piety bolstered traditional customs such as reverence for ancestors. Confucianism also introduced a long-lasting Chinese belief that the universe reflected a delicate balance between two forces, yin and yang. Yin was linked to Earth, darkness, and female forces, while yang stood for heaven, light, and male forces. To the Chinese, the well-being of the universe depended on maintaining balance between yin and yang. For example, the king should make the proper sacrifices to heaven while also taking practical steps to rule well.

As Chinese civilization spread, hundreds of millions of people in Korea, Japan, and Vietnam accepted Confucian beliefs. Nearly one third of the world's population came under the influence of these ideas.

Daoism Teaches Harmony With Nature Laozi, or "Old Master," is said to have lived at the time of Confucius and to have founded a philosophy called Daoism (DOW iz um). Although little is known about Laozi, he has been credited with writing the *Dao De Jing* (dow duh jing), or *The Way of Virtue*, a book that had enormous influence on Chinese life.

Unlike Confucianism, Daoism was not concerned with bringing order to human affairs. Instead, Daoists sought to live in harmony with nature. Laozi stressed that people should look beyond everyday cares to focus on the Dao, or "the way" of the universe. The Dao, he explained, was hard to understand fully or put into words. Thus he taught, "Those who know the Dao do not speak of it. Those who speak of it do not know it." To know the Dao, one should reject conflict and strife. Daoists stressed the simple ways of nature and the virtue of yielding. Water, they pointed out, does not resist, but rather yields to outside pressure—yet it is an unstoppable force.

Many Daoists turned from the "unnatural" ways of society. Some became hermits, artists, or poets. Daoists viewed government as unnatural and, therefore, the cause of many problems. "If the people are difficult to govern," Laozi declared, "it is because those in authority are too fond of action." To Daoists, the best government was one that governed the least.

Confucianism and Daoism Change and Blend Although scholars kept to Daoism's original teachings, the philosophy also evolved into a popular religion with gods, goddesses, and magical practices. Chinese peasants turned to Daoist priests for charms to protect them from unseen forces. In addition, people gradually blended Confucian and Daoist teachings. Although the two belief systems differed, people took beliefs and practices from each. Confucianism showed them how to behave. Daoism influenced their view of the natural world.

✓ **Checkpoint** Explain the different ways in which Confucianism and Daoism taught that people should live their lives.

To show the harmony of yin and yang, the Chinese have traditionally depicted them as two halves of a circle, one dark and one light.

Achievements Abound in Early China

The people of Shang and Zhou China are known for numerous cultural achievements. For example, Shang astronomers studied the movement of planets and recorded eclipses of the sun. Their findings helped them develop an accurate calendar with $365\frac{1}{4}$ days. In addition, the Chinese also improved the art and technology of bronze-making, producing stunning bronze weapons and ritual vessels covered with intricate decorations.

Discovering the Secret of Silk-making By 2640 B.C., the Chinese had made a discovery with extremely long-lasting impact: they had learned how to make silk thread from the cocoons of silkworms. Soon, the Chinese were cultivating both silkworms and the mulberry trees on which they fed. Women did the laborious work of tending the silkworms and processing the cocoons into thread. They then wove silk threads into a smooth cloth that was colored with brilliant dyes.

Only royalty and nobles could afford robes made from this luxurious silk. In time, silk became China's most valuable export. To protect their control of this profitable trade item, the Chinese kept the process of silk-making a secret for many hundreds of years.

● **INFOGRAPHIC** # The Secrets of Making Silk

Long viewed as a luxurious fabric, silk was a special commodity manufactured only in China for many hundreds of years. The ancient Chinese could not have begun to produce the fine fabric had they not discovered the special relationship between a tiny creature—the silkworm—and a small tree—the mulberry. Silkworms were so important to the Chinese that they used jade, a precious stone, to carve their likeness (above).

▲ This Chinese painting shows women combing out the silk threads (at left) after unwinding them from the cocoon and then inspecting the silk cloth (at right).

▼ Swath of silk fabric, about 2,000 years old

The silkworm is actually a caterpillar. As it spins a cocoon (below), it produces a thin fiber—silk. But it won't produce any silk if it hasn't feasted on the leaves of a mulberry tree (at left). ▼

Thinking Critically
1. **Determine Relevance** Why do you think the Chinese kept the technology of making silk secret for so long?
2. **Draw Inferences** How does silk-making show that even highly developed civilizations can be reliant on the environment?

99

The Chinese have written with characters such as these (at top) since the time of their invention through to today. A calligrapher might use a brush like this one (above).

Establishing a Complex System of Writing Written Chinese took shape at least 4,000 years ago, if not earlier. Some of the oldest examples are found on **oracle bones.** These are animal bones or turtle shells on which Shang priests wrote questions addressed to the gods or to the spirit of an ancestor. Priests then heated each bone or shell until it cracked. They believed that by interpreting the pattern of cracks, they could provide answers or advice from the ancestors.

Over time, a writing system evolved that includes tens of thousands of **characters,** or written symbols. Each character represents a whole word or idea. To write a character requires a number of different brush or pen strokes. In the past century, the Chinese have simplified their characters, but Chinese remains one of the most difficult languages to learn to read and write. A person must memorize several thousand characters to read a newspaper. By contrast, languages such as English or Arabic, which are based on an alphabet, contain only about two dozen symbols that represent basic sounds.

Although it was complex, this written language fostered unity in early China. People in different parts of China often could not understand one another's spoken language, but they all used the same system of writing. Not surprisingly, in earlier times, only the well-to-do could afford the years of study needed to master the skills of reading and writing. Working with brush and ink, Chinese scholars later turned writing into an elegant art form called **calligraphy.**

Creating the First Books Under the Zhou, the Chinese made the first books. They bound thin strips of wood or bamboo together and then carefully drew characters on the flat surface with a brush and ink. Among the greatest Zhou works is the lovely *Book of Songs.* Many of its poems describe such events in the lives of farming people as planting and harvesting. Others praise kings or describe court ceremonies. The book also includes tender or sad love songs.

✓ **Checkpoint** For what purpose did writing begin in China?

SECTION **4** Assessment

Progress Monitoring *Online*
For: Self-quiz with vocabulary practice
Web Code: naa-0341

Terms, People, and Places

1. Place each of the key terms at the beginning of the section into one of the following categories: politics, culture, or geography. Write a sentence for each term explaining your choice.

Note Taking

2. **Reading Skill: Recognize Sequence** Use your completed chart to answer the Focus Question: What characteristics defined the civilization that developed in China under its early rulers?

Comprehension and Critical Thinking

3. **Summarize** What geographic challenges did China's early rulers face when trying to unite China or make alliances with peoples outside of China?

4. **Synthesize Information** What were the characteristics of the Shang and Zhou government and social structure?

5. **Analyze Information** What aspects of Confucianism and Daoism do you think contributed to their long-lasting influence?

6. **Draw Inferences** How do the various cultural developments of early China still affect the lives of people today?

● **Writing About History**

Quick Write: Gather Details On some essay tests, you may be asked to show causes and effects. Before you write a response, you may find it useful to gather details about the topic, and then create a graphic organizer to sort out the causes and related effects. Gather details about China's isolation during its early history. Then create a graphic organizer that presents the causes of the isolation and predicts its effects.

Shi Huangdi

Records of the
Grand Historian

WITNESS HISTORY 🔊 AUDIO

A New Age In China

Sima Qian (sih MAH chen), who served later Chinese emperors as Grand Historian, recounted an inscription on a monument built by the first Qin emperor to praise his own deeds:

66 The Emperor . . . rectified [put right] the laws, by which all things are regulated, human affairs are clarified, and fathers and sons united.

Being sagacious [wise], intelligent, benevolent, and righteous, he manifested [made clear to see] the Way [the Dao] and reason . . .

All things receive his favor, and live peacefully in their own abode [house]. 99
—*Records of the Grand Historian*

Focus Question How did powerful emperors unite much of China and bring about a golden age of cultural achievements?

Strong Rulers Unite China

Objectives

- Understand how Shi Huangdi unified China and established a Legalist government.
- Describe how Han rulers strengthened the economy and government of China.
- Outline why the Han period is considered a golden age of Chinese civilization.
- Analyze why many Chinese people accepted Buddhist ideas.

Terms, People, and Places

Shi Huangdi	civil servant
Wudi	warlord
monopoly	acupuncture
expansionism	

Note Taking

Reading Skill: Recognize Sequence Keep track of the sequence of important events in the Qin and Han periods by recording them in a chart like this one in the order they occurred.

Date	Event

From his base in western China, the powerful ruler of the state of Qin rose to unify all of China. An ancient Chinese poet and historian described how Zheng (jeng) crushed all his rivals: "Cracking his long whip, he drove the universe before him, swallowing up the eastern and the western Zhou and overthrowing the feudal lords."

In 221 B.C., Zheng proclaimed himself **Shi Huangdi** (shur hwahng dee), or "First Emperor." Although his methods were brutal, he ushered in China's classical age—a term historians use when a civilization sets patterns in government, philosophy, religion, science, and the arts that serve as a framework for later cultures.

Shi Huangdi Unifies China

Shi Huangdi was determined to end the divisions that had splintered Zhou China. He spent nearly 20 years conquering most of the warring states. Then, imposing punishments for failure, he built the strong, authoritarian Qin government.

Legalism Establishes Harsh Rule Shi Huangdi centralized power with the help of Legalist advisers. Legalism was based on the teachings of Hanfeizi (hahn fay dzuh), who had died in 233 B.C. According to Hanfeizi, "the nature of man is evil. His goodness is acquired." Greed, he declared, was the motive for most actions and the cause of most conflicts. Hanfeizi insisted that the only way to achieve order was to pass strict laws and impose harsh punishments for crimes.

A Chinese artist captured Shi Huangdi's harsh approach in this painting, in which Legalists execute scholars as books burn in the foreground.

To Legalists, strength, not goodness, was a ruler's greatest virtue. "The ruler alone possesses power," declared Hanfeizi, "wielding it like lightning or like thunder." Many feudal rulers chose Legalism as the most effective way to keep order. Shi Huangdi made it the official policy of the Qin government. He then moved harshly against his critics. He tortured, killed, or enslaved many who opposed his rule. Hardest hit were the feudal nobles and Confucian scholars who loathed his laws.

To end dissent, Shi Huangdi approved a ruthless campaign of book burning, ordering the destruction of all writings other than manuals on topics such as medicine and agriculture. Laws such as these were so cruel that later generations despised Legalism. Yet Legalist ideas survived for hundreds of years in laws that forced people to work on government projects and punished those who shirked their duties. Indeed, the policy of enslaving people as punishment for crimes lasted through most of the following dynasty, though only a very small percentage of Chinese were enslaved.

Unity Imposed Shi Huangdi also abolished feudalism, which required little allegiance from local rulers to the central government. He replaced the feudal states with 36 military districts and appointed loyal officials to administer them. Shi Huangdi forced noble families to live in his capital at Xianyang (shyahn yahng), where he could monitor them. He distributed the lands of the displaced nobles to peasants. Still, peasants had to pay high taxes to support Shi Huangdi's armies and building projects.

To promote unity, the First Emperor standardized weights and measures and replaced the diverse coins of the Zhou states with Qin coins. He also had scholars create uniformity in Chinese writing. Workers repaired and extended roads and canals to strengthen the transportation system. A new law even required cart axles to be the same width so that wheels could run in the same ruts on all Chinese roads.

Constructing the Great Wall Shi Huangdi's most remarkable and costly achievement was the Great Wall. In the past, individual feudal states had built walls to defend their lands against raiders. Shi Huangdi ordered the walls to be joined. Hundreds of thousands of laborers worked for years through bitter cold and burning heat. They pounded earth and stone into a mountainous wall almost 25 feet high and topped with a wide brick road. Many workers died in the harsh conditions.

Over the centuries, the wall was extended and rebuilt many times. Eventually, it snaked for thousands of miles across northern China. While the wall did not keep invaders out of China, it did demonstrate the emperors' ability to mobilize China's vast resources. The Great Wall became an important symbol to the Chinese people, dividing and protecting their civilized world from the nomadic bands north of the wall.

Qin Dynasty Collapses When Shi Huangdi died in 210 B.C., anger over heavy taxes, forced labor, and cruel policies exploded into revolts. As Qin power officially collapsed in 206 B.C., Gao Zu (gow dzoo), an illiterate peasant leader, defeated rival armies and founded the new Han dynasty four years later.

 Checkpoint What kind of government did Legalists favor?

Map Skills Under the Qin and Han dynasties, Chinese rule expanded significantly, as did the Great Wall (pictured below).

1. **Locate** (a) Great Wall (b) Qin empire (c) Han empire (d) Chengdu (e) Takla Makan Desert
2. **Place** What natural barriers helped protect China from invaders?
3. **Draw Conclusions** How did the Great Wall's placement relate to the extent of the empires? What does this tell you about where invaders came from?

Qin empire, 221 B.C.–206 B.C.
Han empire, 202 B.C.–A.D. 220
Han protectorate
Great Wall

The Han Dynasty Strengthens China

As emperor, Gao Zu set about restoring order and justice to his empire. Although he continued earlier efforts to unify China, he lowered taxes and eased Legalist policies. In a key move, he appointed Confucian scholars as advisors. His policies created strong foundations for the Han dynasty, which lasted from 202 B.C. until A.D. 220.

Emperor Wudi Makes Improvements The most famous Han emperor, **Wudi** (woo dee), took China to new heights. During his long reign from about 141 B.C. to 87 B.C., he strengthened the government and economy. Like Gao Zu, he chose officials from Confucian "men of wisdom and virtue." To train scholars, he set up an imperial university at Xian (shyahn).

Wudi furthered economic growth by improving canals and roads. He had granaries set up across the empire so the government could buy grain when it was abundant and sell it at stable prices when it was scarce. He reorganized finances and imposed a government monopoly on iron and salt. A **monopoly** is the complete control of a product or business by one person or group. The sale of iron and salt gave the government a source of income other than taxes on peasants.

Zhang Qian Explores Outside China

Sima Qian's *Records of the Grand Historian* includes the accounts of Zhang Qian, a diplomat whom Emperor Wudi sent on various journeys to establish contact with peoples outside the Han empire. Zhang traveled as far as India and the eastern edge of the Roman empire. The information he brought back about the rich kingdoms he had seen led to the founding of the Silk Road, the legendary trade network that connected China and the western empires.

> "Southeast of Ta-hsia [Bactria] is the kingdom of Shen-tu [India]. 'When I was in Ta-hsia, Chang Ch'ien [Zhang Qian] reported, 'I saw bamboo canes from Ch'iung and cloth made in the [Chinese] province of Shu. When I asked the people how they had gotten such articles, they replied, 'Our merchants go to buy them in the markets of Shen-tu.' Shen-tu, they told me, lies several thousand *li*[1] southeast of Ta-hsia. The people cultivate the land and live much like the people of Ta-shia. The region is said to be hot and damp. The inhabitants ride elephants when they go into battle. The kingdom is situated on a great river. . . .
>
> Thus the emperor learned of . . . great states rich in unusual products whose people cultivated the land and made their living in much the same way as the Chinese."
>
> —*Records of the Grand Historian*

1 A *li* is an ancient Chinese measurement equal to about one third of a mile.

Wudi followed a policy of **expansionism,** or expanding a country's territory, by increasing the amount of land under Chinese rule. He fought many battles to expand China's borders and to drive nomadic peoples beyond the Great Wall. Chinese armies added outposts in Manchuria, Korea, northern Vietnam, Tibet, and Central Asia. Soldiers, traders, and settlers slowly spread Chinese influence across these areas.

Silk Road Links China to the West The emperor Wudi opened up a network of trade routes, later called the Silk Road, that would link China and the West for centuries. During the Han period, new foods such as grapes, figs, cucumbers, and walnuts flowed into China from western Asia. Lucky traders might return to China bearing furs from Central Asia, muslin from India, or glass from Rome. At the same time, the Chinese sent large quantities of silk westward to fill a growing demand for the prized fabric.

Eventually, the Silk Road stretched for 4,000 miles, linking China to the Fertile Crescent in the Middle East. Few traders covered the entire distance, however; instead, goods were relayed in stages from one set of traders to another. At the western end, trade was controlled by various peoples, including the Persians.

China Selects Scholar-Officials Han emperors made Confucianism the official belief system of the state. They relied on well-educated scholars to run the bureaucratic government. A scholar-official was expected to match the Confucian ideal of a gentleman. He would be courteous and dignified and possess a thorough knowledge of history, music, poetry, and Confucian teachings.

Founding the Civil Service System Han emperors adopted the idea that **civil servants**—that is, officials in the government—should win their positions by merit, rather than through family ties as had occurred

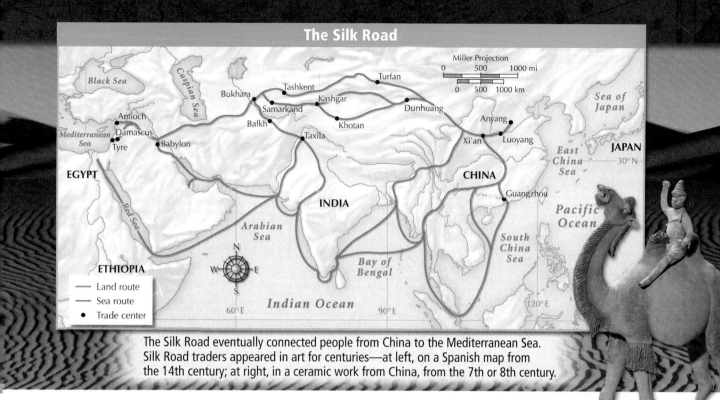

The Silk Road

The Silk Road eventually connected people from China to the Mediterranean Sea. Silk Road traders appeared in art for centuries—at left, on a Spanish map from the 14th century; at right, in a ceramic work from China, from the 7th or 8th century.

in the past. In the Han civil service system, a young man would start in a clerical job. Once he proved his abilities, he would move up in local government. If he continued to excel, he would eventually be recruited into the civil service and might be tested on his knowledge of government policy. Essential to his studies were the Five Classics, a collection of histories, poems, and handbooks compiled by Confucius and others that served as a guide to conduct for about 2,000 years.

Much later, in the 580s, the Sui dynasty set up a formal system of civil service exams, which were given at the local, provincial, and national levels. In theory, any man could take the exams. In practice, only those who could afford years of study, such as the sons of wealthy landowners or officials, could hope to succeed. Occasionally, a village or wealthy family might pay for the education of a brilliant peasant boy. If he passed the exams and obtained a government job, he, his family, and his clan all enjoyed immense prestige and moved up in society. Confucian teachings about filial piety and the superiority of men prevented women from taking the civil service exam. As a result, women were excluded from government jobs.

The civil service system remained in use until 1912. It put men trained in Confucian thought at every level of government and created an enduring system of values. Dynasties rose and fell, but Confucian influence survived.

Han Empire Overthrown

As the Han dynasty aged, signs of decay appeared. Court intrigues undermined emperors who could no longer control powerful **warlords,** or local military rulers. Weak emperors let canals and roads fall into disrepair. Burdened by heavy taxes and crushing debt, many peasants revolted. Thousands of rebellious peasants abandoned their villages and fled to the mountains. There they joined secret groups of bandits known by colorful names like the "Red Eyebrows" and the "Green Woodsmen."

Thinking Critically
1. **Synthesize Information** How were people in Ta-hsia able to buy goods from the Chinese province of Shu?
2. **Analyze Information** How do you think the knowledge Zheng gained helped establish the Silk Road?

Vocabulary Builder
compiled—(kum PYLD) *vt.* created by gathering things together

In A.D. 220, ambitious warlords overthrew the last Han emperor. After 400 years of unity, China broke up into several kingdoms. Adding to the disorder, invaders poured over the Great Wall and set up their own states. In time, many of these newcomers were absorbed into Chinese civilization.

✓ **Checkpoint**   How did Han emperors further economic growth?

Achievements of the Han Golden Age

The Han period was one of the golden ages of Chinese civilization. Han China made such tremendous advances in so many fields that the Chinese later called themselves "the people of Han."

Advancing Science and Medicine Han scientists wrote texts on chemistry, zoology, botany, and other subjects. Han astronomers carefully observed and measured movements of the stars and planets, which enabled them to improve earlier calendars and invent better timekeeping devices. One scientist invented a simple seismograph to detect and measure earthquakes.

The scientist Wang Chong disagreed with the widely held belief that comets and eclipses showed heaven's anger. "On the average, there is one moon eclipse about every 180 days," he wrote, "and a solar eclipse about every 41 or 42 months. Eclipses . . . are not caused by political action." Wang Chong argued that no scientific theories should be accepted unless they were supported by proof.

Chinese physicians diagnosed diseases, developed anesthetics, and experimented with herbal remedies and other drugs. Many doctors promoted the use of **acupuncture.** In this medical treatment, developed about 2500 B.C., the doctor inserts needles into the skin at specific points to relieve pain or treat various illnesses.

Forging Ahead With Technology and Engineering In its time, Han China was the most technologically advanced civilization in the world. Cai Lun (ky loon), an official of the Han court, invented a method for making paper out of wood pulp. His basic method is still used to manufacture paper today. The Chinese also pioneered advanced methods of shipbuilding and invented the rudder to steer. Other practical inventions included bronze and iron stirrups, fishing reels, wheelbarrows, and suspension bridges. Some of these ideas moved west slowly, reaching Europe hundreds of years later.

Expanding the Arts The walled cities of Han China boasted splendid temples and palaces amid elegant parks. Although these wooden buildings have not survived, Han poets and historians have described their grandeur. In addition, artisans produced delicate jade and ivory carvings and fine ceramic figures. Bronze-workers and silk-makers improved on earlier techniques and set high standards for future generations.

Lessons for Women, a handbook of behavior written by Ban Zhao (bahn jow) around A.D. 100, carefully spells out the proper behavior for women and men. Ban Zhao favored equal education for boys and girls. However, she stressed that women should be obedient, respectful, and submissive. "Let a woman modestly yield to others," she advised. "Let her respect others."

✓ **Checkpoint**   What sorts of achievements made the Han period a golden age?

Acupuncturists like this woman place needles in specific spots on the body to treat each ailment.

The Chinese Accept Buddhism

By A.D. 100, missionaries and merchants had spread Mahayana Buddhism from India into China. At first, the Chinese had trouble with the new faith. For example, Chinese tradition valued family loyalty, while Buddhism honored monks and nuns who gave up the benefits of family life for a life of solitary meditation.

Despite obstacles such as this, Buddhism became increasingly popular, especially in times of crisis. Its great appeal was the promise of escape from suffering. Mahayana Buddhism offered the hope of eternal happiness and presented the Buddha as a compassionate, merciful god. Through prayer, good works, and devotion, anyone could hope to gain salvation. Neither Daoism nor Confucianism emphasized this idea of personal salvation.

By A.D. 400, Buddhism had spread throughout China. Buddhist monasteries became important centers of learning and the arts. Buddhism absorbed many Confucian and Daoist traditions. Chinese Buddhist monks stressed filial piety and honored Confucius.

✔ **Checkpoint** Why did Buddhism appeal to many people in China?

Looking Ahead

Shi Huangdi, Gao Zu, Wudi, and later Han rulers forged a vast and varied land into a united China. Han rulers created an empire roughly the size of the continental United States. During this period, Chinese officials established the system of administration that would survive until 1912. In coming centuries, China would undergo great changes. It would break up and be painfully reassembled over and over. On the whole, however, Chinese civilization would flourish. After periods of disunity, in A.D. 581 a new dynasty, the Sui, would turn to Confucian scholars to revive the days of Han greatness.

In Mahayana Buddhism, people hope to become *bodhisattvas*, or enlightened people, who help others gain salvation. The *bodhisattva* of compassion and mercy (above), called Kuan-yin in China, is one of the most popular.

SECTION 5 Assessment

Progress Monitoring *Online*
For: Self-quiz with vocabulary practice
Web Code: naa-0351

Terms, People, and Places

1. For each term, person, or place listed at the beginning of the section, write a sentence explaining its significance.

Note Taking

2. **Reading Skill: Recognize Sequence** Use your completed chart to answer the Focus Question: How did powerful emperors unite much of China and bring about a golden age of cultural achievements?

Comprehension and Critical Thinking

3. **Summarize** What were three steps Shi Huangdi took to unify China?
4. **Demonstrate Reasoned Judgment** What aspects of the civil service system do you think allowed it to last for such a great length of time?
5. **Determine Relevance** Select three achievements made during the Han period and describe why you think they were significant advancements.

● Writing About History

Quick Write: Draft a Quick Outline On some essay tests, you will not be given much time to write an essay. Drafting a quick outline can help you save time as you write your response. Write a quick outline of a response to one of the following essay topics:

- the role of Legalism in Qin government
- the importance of the Silk Road
- the greatest cultural achievements of the Han

CHAPTER 3

Quick Study Guide

Progress Monitoring *Online*
For: Self-test with vocabulary practice
Web Code: naa-0361

■ Eras of Civilization

India		China	
Indus civilization	2600 B.C. to 1900 B.C.	Shang dynasty	1766 B.C. to 1122 B.C.
Aryan civilization	1500 B.C. to ?	Zhou dynasty	1122 B.C. to 256 B.C.
Maurya empire	321 B.C. to 185 B.C.	Qin dynasty	221 B.C. to 206 B.C.
Gupta empire	A.D. 320 to A.D. 550	Han dynasty	202 B.C. to A.D. 220

■ Unification of China

Cause and Effect

Long-Term Causes	Immediate Causes
• Confucian ideas dominate education. • China's isolation permits development without much outside interference. • A common system of writing evolves.	• Zheng conquers the eastern and western Zhou and overthrows the feudal lords. • Zheng proclaims himself Shi Huangdi ("First Emperor").

Unification of China

Immediate Effects	Long-Term Effects
• Shi Huangdi abolishes feudalism. • Shi Huangdi standardizes weights and measures and money. • The government cracks down on dissenters. • Shi Huangdi supervises work on the Great Wall.	• China makes advances in government and trade. • Confucian-educated officials hold most government jobs. • Its common culture helps China survive upheavals.

■ Religions Founded in India

Hinduism
• Originated with the Aryans
• Ultimate goal: moksha, or union with brahman
• Achieve moksha by following laws of karma and dharma through various cycles of life

• Karma
• Dharma
• Reincarnation

Buddhism
• Founded by Siddhartha Gautama, the Buddha
• Ultimate goal: nirvana, or union with the universe
• Achieve nirvana by following the Four Noble Truths and the Eightfold Path; follow karma and dharma along the way

■ Philosophies Founded in China

Confucianism	Daoism
• Founded by Confucius • Focuses on worldly goals of ensuring social order and good government • Stresses accepting one's place in society and behaving correctly • Views government as responsible for setting a good example for people and for being run by well-educated people	• Possibly founded by Laozi • Focuses on living in harmony with nature • Stresses simple ways of nature and the virtue of yielding • Views government as unnatural and as a body that should govern the people as little as possible

■ Expansion of Civilization

2600 B.C. Civilization arises on the Indian subcontinent in the Indus River valley.

2000 B.C. Civilization emerges along China's river valleys.

Chapter Events
World Events

3500 B.C.

2500 B.C.

3200 B.C. Civilization begins in Sumer.

2700 B.C. Egypt's Old Kingdom is established.

108

Concept Connector

■ Cumulative Review

Record the answers to the questions below on your Concept Connector worksheets. In addition, record information from the chapter about the following concepts:

- Cultural Diffusion: Arabic numerals, decimal system, Hinduism, and Buddhism
- Migration: Indo-European migrations

1. **Empire** Consider the history of empire-building in India, China, Egypt, and the Middle East. In which cases did the civilization endure even as power changed hands? In which did the end of power lead to the end of the civilization?

2. **Belief Systems** Compare the views of ancient Egyptians and ancient Indians about the results of a persons actions during his or her lifetime. Think about the following:
   - the role of the god Osiris
   - the concepts of karma, dharma, and reincarnation
   - the Eightfold Path

   How do you think each of these views helped establish a set of morals by which people could lead their daily lives?

3. **Trade** How was the trade network of the Phoenicians similar to the Silk Road in its impact on economics and culture? For each trade network, think about the following:
   - its geographic extent
   - the various civilizations it involved
   - the trade items exchanged along it
   - instances of cultural diffusion that occurred because of it

■ Connections to Today

1. **Economic Systems: The Use of Monopolies** When Han emperor Wudi established the first monopolies in China's history, he hoped the resulting lack of competition would ensure the government a reliable new source of income. In many economic systems today, however, monopolies are banned or carefully controlled so that competition is always possible. Both the United States and Great Britain have passed laws to severely limit monopolies. What do you think are the advantages and the disadvantages of monopolies? Why might monopolies have been viewed differently in ancient times than in the world today? Study the political cartoon below to start generating ideas.

History Interactive
For: Interactive timeline
Web Code: nap-0361

| 1650 B.C.
China's first known dynasty, the Shang, is established. | 1500 B.C.
The Aryans establish a civilization and Hinduism in India. | 566 B.C.
Siddhartha Gautama, the founder of Buddhism, is born. | 321 B.C.
India's first empire, the Maurya, begins. | A.D. 320
The Gupta empire begins a golden age in India. |

1500 B.C.   500 B.C.   A.D. 500

| | 1500 B.C.
The Olmecs build the first civilization in the Americas. | 509 B.C.
The Roman republic is founded. | 460 B.C.
The Age of Pericles begins in Greece. | A.D. 250
Maya city-states flourish in Mexico and Central America. | A.D. 476
The western Roman empire collapses. |

Chapter Assessment

Terms, People, and Places

Complete each sentence by choosing the correct answer from the terms below. You will not use all the terms.

brahman
monopoly
rajah
filial piety
dynastic cycle
feudalism

golden age
warlord
reincarnation
dowry
karma
atman

1. The chiefs who led Aryan tribes were called _____.
2. In Hinduism, the essential self is called _____.
3. A _____ is a period of great cultural achievements.
4. _____ means respect for one's parents.
5. The rise and fall of Chinese dynasties is called the _____.
6. The complete control of a product or business by one person or group is a _____.

Main Ideas

Section 1 (pp. 68–75)
7. What documents from the Aryan written tradition tell us about Aryan society?

Section 2 (pp. 76–83)
8. In Hinduism, what is a person's ultimate goal? What is it in Buddhism?

Section 3 (pp. 84–91)
9. How did caste rules affect the daily lives of Indians during Maurya and Gupta times?

Section 4 (pp. 92–100)
10. Summarize the roles of the Mandate of Heaven and the dynastic cycle in China.
11. Describe two cultural achievements made in early China.

Section 5 (pp. 101–107)
12. How did Shi Huangdi centralize power in China? How did Wudi then expand China's power?

Chapter Focus Question
13. In what ways did the civilizations and empires of ancient India and China lay long-lasting social and political foundations?

Critical Thinking

14. **Synthesize Information** Describe two aspects of Indian society that began in Aryan times and have lasted until the present day.
15. **Make Comparisons** What similarities and differences exist between Hindu and Buddhist teachings about the way that a person should live?
16. **Geography and History** Monsoons greatly affected life in India in early times. How might their effect be similar or different today?
17. **Analyze Information** Consider two major achievements made in ancient China—Shi Huangdi's expansion of the Great Wall and Wudi's opening up of the Silk Road. How did each affect China's relationship with the outside world?
18. **Draw Inferences** Compare the initial intention of feudalism with its resulting effect on the Zhou dynasty. Under what circumstances might feudalism have been more successful?
19. **Demonstrate Reasoned Judgment** Confucianism lay at the foundations of the Chinese civil service system, which lasted for 2,000 years. What about Confucianism do you think led to such a stable administrative structure?
20. **Analyzing Visuals** What types of information can scholars learn from studying Indus artifacts such as the seal and cubic weights shown on page 71?

● Writing About History

Writing for Assessment To prepare for a test about ancient India and China, write an essay responding to one of the following topics.

(1) Explain two key cultural achievements of ancient India or China.
(2) Compare the belief systems developed in ancient India to those developed in ancient China.
(3) Argue which approach to governing taught in ancient India or ancient China is the best.

Consult page SH20 of the Writing Handbook for additional help.

Prewriting
• Choose a topic by examining each question and determining which you are best able to answer.
• Decide how to divide your time between prewriting, drafting, and revising.
• Gather details related to the topic and use a graphic organizer to organize them.

Drafting
• Choose a logical strategy for organizing the points you will make, such as chronologically.
• Write an opening for the essay that restates the question and a conclusion that recaps your points.
• Select facts that support the main idea of your essay.

Revising
• Use the guidelines for revising your essay on page SH22 of the Writing Handbook.

Document-Based Assessment

Three Paths in Chinese Philosophy

The Chinese philosophies established in ancient times laid out varied approaches to living and governing. The documents below illustrate some of the differences among Daoist, Confucian, and Legalist advice on governance.

Document A

"Refrain from exalting [praising] the worthy,
　　So that the people will not scheme and contend;
Refrain from prizing rare possessions,
　　So that the people will not steal;
Refrain from displaying objects of desire,
　　So that the people's hearts will not be disturbed.

Therefore a sage [wise one] rules his people thus:
　　He empties their minds,
　　　　And fills their bellies;
　　He weakens their ambitions,
　　　　And strengthens their bones.

He strives always to keep the people innocent of knowledge and desires, and to keep the knowing ones from meddling."

—From the **Dao De Jing**

Document B

"Behave when away from home as though you were in the presence of an important guest. Deal with the common people as though you were officiating [presiding] at an important sacrifice. Do not do to others what you would not want others to do to you, then there will be no dissatisfaction either in the state or at home. . . .

　　Lead the people by laws and regulate them by penalties, and the people will try to keep out of jail, but will have no sense of shame. Lead the people by virtue and restrain them by the rules of decorum [social expectations], and the people will have a sense of shame, and moreover will become good."

—From the **Analects** of Confucius

Document C

". . . rewards should be rich and certain so that the people will be attracted by them; punishments should be severe and definite so that the people will fear them; and laws should be uniform and steadfast so that the people will be familiar with them. Consequently, the sovereign [ruler] should show no wavering in bestowing reward and grant no pardon in administering punishments, and he should add honor to rewards and disgrace to punishments—when this is done, then both the worthy and the unworthy will want to exert themselves. . ."

—From the writings of Hanfeizi

Document D
Chinese Imperial Dragon

The dragon was the symbol of the Chinese emperor.

Analyzing Documents

Use your knowledge of history and Documents A, B, C, and D to answer questions 1–4.

1. According to the *Dao De Jing*, a wise ruler governs well by
   A displaying power and wealth.
   B promoting education.
   C holding up some people as most worthy.
   D feeding and supporting the people.

2. How does Confucius say rulers should treat common people?
   A with harsh but just punishments and occasional rewards
   B with the same respect they would show at an important ceremony
   C with the same distrust and fear they feel toward rivals
   D with disinterest

3. Which words best describe Hanfeizi's approach to governance?
   A kind, compassionate, fair
   B decent, modest, unassuming
   C direct, strict, unwavering
   D sly, methodical, devious

4. **Writing Task** Suppose you had to advise an ancient Chinese ruler. What advice would you give, and which philosophy would you base it on? Use Documents A, B, and C along with information from the chapter to write your answer.

111

The Highest Good

The independent sovereignty of the city-state was the basic political structure of ancient Greece. Although the governments that ruled the city-states were varied and numerous, the goals these communities strived to attain were similar as described in *Politics* by the great philosopher Aristotle.

66Every State is a community of some kind, and every community is established with a view to some good; for mankind always act in order to obtain that which they think good. But, if all communities aim at some good, the state or political community, which is the highest of all, and which embraces all the rest, aims at good in a greater degree than any other, and at the highest good.99

Listen to the Witness History audio to hear more about Greek government and philosophy.

◀ **Men voting under the watchful eye of the Greek goddess Athena**

The Greek philosopher Aristotle

Sixth century B.C. bronze helmet

Chapter Preview

Chapter Focus Question What enduring traditions and institutions did Greek culture extend to most of the Western world?

Relief tile depicting Plato and his student Aristotle

Note Taking Study Guide *Online*
For: Note Taking and Concept Connector worksheets
Web Code: nad-0401

Greek amphora, or storage pot, depicting the kidnapping of Europa

WITNESS HISTORY 🔊 AUDIO

Zeus Kidnaps Europa

Europa, the beautiful daughter of the king of Phoenicia, was gathering flowers when she saw a bull quietly grazing with her father's herds. The bull was actually Zeus, king of all the Greek gods, who had fallen in love with her. When Europa reached up to place flowers on his horns, he suddenly bounded into the air and carried the weeping princess far across the Mediterranean Sea to the island of Crete. Eventually, Europa married the king of Crete and gave her name to a new continent—Europe.

Focus Question How did the Minoans and Mycenaeans shape early Greek civilizations?

Early People of the Aegean

Objectives
- Identify the influences on Minoan culture and how the civilization prospered.
- Summarize how Mycenaeans ruled the sea trade and started the Trojan War.
- Describe the works of Homer and their influence on Greek culture.

Terms, People, and Places

Knossos	Trojan War
shrine	strait
fresco	Homer

Note Taking

Reading Skill: Identify Main Ideas Create a table like the one below. Then, use the table to record the main ideas relating to the groups of people discussed in the section.

Minoans	Mycenaeans	Dorians
•	•	•
•	•	•

The island of Crete (kreet) was the cradle of an early civilization that later influenced Greeks living on the European mainland. The people of Crete, however, had absorbed many ideas from the older civilizations of Egypt and Mesopotamia. Europa's mythic journey from Phoenicia to Crete suggests this movement of ideas from east to west.

Minoans Trade and Prosper

Washed by the warm waters of the Aegean (ee JEE un) Sea, Crete was home to a brilliant early civilization. We do not actually know what the people who built this civilization called themselves. However, the British archaeologist who unearthed its ruins called them Minoans after Minos, a legendary king of Crete. Minoan civilization reached its height, or greatest success, between 1600 B.C. and 1500 B.C.

The success of the Minoans was based on trade, not conquest. Minoan traders set up outposts throughout the Aegean world. From their island home in the eastern Mediterranean, they crossed the seas to the Nile Valley and the Middle East. Through contact with Egypt and Mesopotamia, they acquired ideas and technology in fields such as writing and architecture that they adapted to their own culture.

Minoan Art at Knossos The rulers of this trading empire lived in a vast palace at **Knossos** (NAHS us). It housed rooms for the royal family, banquet halls, and working areas for artisans. It also included religious **shrines,** areas dedicated to the honor of gods and goddesses.

The walls of the palace at Knossos were covered with colorful **frescoes,** watercolor paintings done on wet plaster. These frescoes tell us much about Minoan society. Leaping dolphins reflect the importance of the sea to the Minoan people. Religious images indicate that the Minoans worshiped the bull as well as a mother goddess. Other frescoes show young men and women strolling through gardens or jumping through the horns of a charging bull. The paintings also suggest that women appeared freely in public and may have enjoyed more rights than women in most other ancient civilizations.

Minoan Civilization Disappears By about 1400 B.C., Minoan civilization had vanished. Archaeologists are not sure of the reasons for its disappearance. A sudden volcanic eruption on a nearby island may have rained flaming death on Knossos. Or perhaps an earthquake may have destroyed the palace, followed by an immense wave that drowned the inhabitants of the island. However, it is certain that invaders played some role in the destruction of Minoan civilization. These intruders were the Mycenaeans (my suh NEE unz), the first Greek-speaking people of whom we have a written record.

✔ **Checkpoint** How does the art at Knossos reflect Minoan culture?

Trade and War in Mycenae

Like the Aryans who swept into India, the Mycenaeans were an Indo-European people. They conquered the Greek mainland before overrunning the island of Crete.

Sea Trade Brings Wealth Mycenaean civilization dominated the Aegean world from about 1400 B.C. to 1200 B.C. Like the Minoans, the Mycenaeans were sea traders. They reached out beyond the Aegean to Sicily, Italy, Egypt, and Mesopotamia. The Mycenaeans learned many skills from the Minoans, including the art of writing. They, too, absorbed Egyptian and Mesopotamian customs, many of which they passed on to later Greeks.

The Mycenaeans lived in separate city-states on the mainland. In each, a warrior-king built a thick-walled fortress from which he ruled the surrounding villages. Wealthy rulers amassed treasure, including fine gold ornaments that archaeologists have unearthed from their tombs.

Life Near the Sea
This detail from an ancient Minoan fresco decorates the wall of a house located on the Greek island of Thera. *How do the scene depicted above and the daggers below reflect the importance of the sea to the Minoan and Mycenaean civilizations?*

A Mycenaean dagger and sheath with inlaid depictions of sea creatures, *c.* 1200 B.C.

The Trojan Horse
The story of the Trojan horse had great significance to ancient Greeks. The image of the horse was often used by Greek artisans to decorate their work, such as this relief on the neck of a seventh-century B.C. amphora. *Why do you think the ancient Greeks would memorialize the Trojan War in their art?*

The Trojan War The Mycenaeans are best remembered for their part in the **Trojan War,** which took place around 1250 B.C. The conflict may have had its origins in economic rivalry between Mycenae and Troy, a rich trading city in present-day Turkey, that controlled the vital **straits,** or narrow water passages, connecting the Mediterranean and Black seas.

In Greek legend, however, the war had a more romantic cause. When the Trojan prince, Paris, kidnaps Helen, the beautiful wife of a Greek king, the Mycenaeans sail to Troy to rescue her. For the next 10 years, the two sides battle until the Greeks finally seize Troy and burn the city to the ground.

For centuries, most people regarded the Trojan War as pure legend. Then, in the 1870s, a wealthy German businessman, Heinrich Schliemann (HYN rik SCHLEE mahn), set out to prove that the legend was rooted in fact. As Schliemann excavated the site of ancient Troy, he found evidence of fire and war dating to about 1250 B.C. Though most of the details remain lost in legend, modern scholars now agree that the Trojan War was an actual event.

✔ **Checkpoint**   How did trade shape Mycenaean society?

Homer and the Great Legends of Greece

Not long after their victory over Troy, the Mycenaens themselves came under attack from sea raiders and also from another Greek-speaking people, the Dorians, invading from the north. As Mycenaean power faded, their people abandoned the cities and trade declined. People forgot many skills, including the art of writing. From the end of the Mycenaean civilization in about 1100 B.C. until about 900 B.C., Greek civilization seemed to step backward.

Much of what we know about the Trojan War and life during this period comes from two great epic poems, the *Iliad* and the *Odyssey*. These epics may have been the work of many people, but they are credited to the poet **Homer,** who probably lived about 750 B.C. According to tradition, Homer was a blind poet who wandered from village to village, singing of heroic deeds. Like the great Indian epics, Homer's tales were passed on orally for generations before they were finally written down.

The *Iliad,* full as it is of gods, goddesses, and even a talking horse, is our chief source of information about the Trojan War. At the start of the poem, Achilles (uh KIL eez), the mightiest Greek warrior, has withdrawn from battle because he has been unfairly treated and insulted by his commander. The war soon turns against the Greeks, but Achilles stubbornly refuses to listen to pleas that he rejoin the fighting. Only after his best friend is killed does Achilles return to battle.

The *Odyssey* tells of the many struggles of the Greek hero Odysseus (oh DIS ee us) on his return home to his faithful wife, Penelope, after the fall of Troy. On his long voyage, Odysseus encounters a sea monster, a race of one-eyed giants, and a beautiful sorceress who turns men into swine.

The *Iliad* and *Odyssey* reveal much about the values of the ancient Greeks. The heroes display honor, courage, and eloquence, as when Achilles rallies his troops:

Vocabulary Builder
eloquence—(EL uh kwens) *n.* a manner of speech that is vivid and persuasive

66 Every man make up his mind to fight
And move on his enemy! Strong as I am,
It's hard for me to face so many men
And fight with all at once. . . .
And yet I will!**99**
—Homer, *Iliad*

For almost 3,000 years, the epics of Homer have inspired European writers and artists.

✓ **Checkpoint** What do Homer's epics reveal about Greek culture?

Looking Ahead

After the Dorian invasions, the land of Greece passed several centuries in obscurity. The people lived in small isolated villages and had few contacts with the outside world. Over time they made the stories about Crete and Mycenae a part of their heritage, and they built upon the legacy of those and other civilizations to forge a new, Greek civilization. When it emerged, this Greek civilization would not only dominate the region, it would ultimately extend the influence of Greek culture over most of the Western world.

Hero of the *Odyssey*
Odysseus was admired for his cleverness. Here, he outwits the siren, whose song lures sailors to their doom. In order to hear their song and yet survive, Odysseus fills his crew's ears with beeswax. Then, he has himself tied to the ship's mast so he can hear the siren's song without endangering the ship or his crew.

SECTION 1 Assessment

Progress Monitoring *Online*
For: Self-quiz with vocabulary practice
Web Code: naa-0411

Terms, People, and Places

1. For each term, person, or place listed at the beginning of the section, write a sentence explaining its significance.

Note Taking

2. **Reading Skill: Identify Main Ideas** Use your completed table to answer the Focus Question: How did the Minoans and Mycenaens shape early Greek civilizations?

Comprehension and Critical Thinking

3. **Determine Relevance** How did trade contribute to the development of the Minoan and Mycenaean cultures?

4. **Draw Inferences** What values of the ancient Greeks are found in the poems of Homer?

5. **Demonstrate Reasoned Judgment** Do you think the epics of Homer are a reliable source of information about the history of the ancient Greeks? Why or why not?

● Writing About History

Quick Write: Write a Thesis Statement Review the section and think of how early people of the Aegean contributed to Greek civilization. Write a thesis statement that expresses your thought. Remember that a thesis statement should provide the main idea for an essay.

A bronze Corinthian helmet, *c.* 500s B.C.

WITNESS HISTORY 🔊 AUDIO

For the People's Good

Tyrtaeus, a Spartan poet in the 600s B.C., wrote elegies that praised and encouraged bravery and honor on the Spartan battlefields. Here, while championing courage in the phalanx, Tyrtaeus captures the essence of how the Greeks held the city-state, or *polis,* above all else.

“ This is the common good, for the *polis* and the whole *demos* [the people], when a man stands firm in the front ranks without flinching and puts disgraceful flight completely from his mind, making his soul and spirit endure and with his words encourages the man stationed next to him. ”

Focus Question How did government and culture develop as Greek city-states grew?

Battling soldiers in phalanx formation

The Rise of Greek City-States

Objectives

- Understand how geography influenced the Greek city-states.
- Define the three types of government that developed in the Greek city-states.
- Explain how Sparta and Athens differed.
- Identify the culture and values shared by Greeks.

Terms, People, and Places

polis	phalanx
acropolis	Sparta
citizen	Athens
monarchy	democracy
aristocracy	tyrant
oligarchy	legislature

Note Taking

Reading Skill: Identify Supporting Details
Create an outline to record the main ideas and supporting details described in this section.

I. Geography Shapes Greece
   A. Landscape defines political boundaries
     1.
     2.
   B. Life by the sea
     1.
     2.

The Mediterranean and Aegean seas were as central to the development of Greek civilization as the Nile was to the Egyptians. The ancient Greeks absorbed many ideas and beliefs from the older civilizations of Mesopotamia and Egypt. At the same time, they developed their own unique ways. In particular, the Greeks developed new ideas about how best to govern each individual Greek *polis* (POH lis), or city-state.

Geography Shapes Greece

As you have read, the earliest civilizations rose in fertile river valleys. There, strong rulers organized irrigation works that helped farmers produce food surpluses needed to support large cities. A very different set of geographic conditions influenced the rise of Greek civilization.

Landscape Defines Political Boundaries Greece is part of the Balkan peninsula, which extends southward into the eastern Mediterranean Sea. Mountains divide the peninsula into isolated valleys. Beyond the rugged coast, hundreds of rocky islands spread toward the horizon.

The Greeks who farmed the valleys or settled on the scattered islands did not create a large empire such as that of the Egyptians or Persians. Instead, they built many small city-states, cut off from one another by mountains or water. Each included a city and its surrounding countryside. Greeks fiercely defended the independence of their small city-states, and endless rivalry frequently led to war.

Life by the Sea While mountains divided Greeks from one another, the seas provided a vital link to the world outside. With its hundreds of bays, the Greek coastline offered safe harbors for ships. The Greeks became skilled sailors and carried cargoes of olive oil, wine, and marble to parts throughout the eastern Mediterranean. They returned not only with grains and metals but also with ideas, which they adapted to their own needs. For example, the Greeks adapted the Phoenician alphabet to meet their needs. The resulting alphabet in turn became the basis for all later Western alphabets.

By 750 B.C., rapid population growth forced many Greeks to leave their own overcrowded valleys. With fertile land limited, the Greeks expanded overseas. Gradually, a scattering of Greek colonies took root all around the Mediterranean from Spain to Egypt. Wherever they traveled, Greek settlers and traders carried their ideas and culture.

✔ **Checkpoint** How did the sea contribute to Greek commerce?

Governing the City-States

As their world expanded after 750 B.C., the Greeks evolved a unique version of the city-state, which they called the polis. The polis was made up of a major city or town and its surrounding countryside. Typically, the city itself was built on two levels. On the top of a hill stood the **acropolis** (uh KRAH puh lis), or high city, with its great marble temples dedicated to different gods and goddesses. On flatter ground below lay the walled main city with its marketplace, theater, public buildings, and homes.

The population of each city-state was fairly small, which helped the **citizens,** or free residents, share a sense of responsibility for its triumphs and defeats. In the warm climate of Greece, free men spent much time outdoors in the marketplace, debating issues that affected their lives. The whole community joined in festivals honoring the city's special god or goddess. The rights of citizens were unequal, however; and male landowners held all the political power.

Development of the Alphabet

Phoenician	Greek	Roman
∢	A	A
⊿	B	B
◁	△	D
⋊	K	K
∟	∧	L
⌇	N	N

Chart Skills Our alphabet comes to us from the Phoenicians by way of the Greeks. The word *alphabet* itself comes from the first two Greek letters, *alpha* and *beta*. *Describe how the modern letter* L *has changed over time.*

Geography of Ancient Greece

Geography Interactive
For: Audio guided tour
Web Code: nap-0421

Mycenaen world about 1300 B.C.
Centers of ancient Greek civilization
Gold
Silver
Iron
Marble
Timber

Axiós River
Mt. Olympus
40°N
PINDUS MTS.
Piniós River
Miller Projection
0 50 100 mi
0 50 100 km
Delphi
GREECE
Corinth
Olympia Mycenae
Peloponnesus
Sparta
Athens
Aegean Sea
ASIA MINOR
Ephesus
Milos
Rhodes
36°N
Mediterranean Sea
Crete
20°E 24°E 28°E

Map Skills Ancient Greek civilization was shaped by rugged mountainous terrain and the surrounding seas. These geographic features worked as both a barrier and a link.
1. **Locate** (a) Greece (b) Crete (c) Mycenae (d) Athens (e) Sparta (f) Aegean Sea (g) Peloponnesus
2. **Region** How did the geography of Greece present obstacles to unity?
3. **Analyze Information** How did the geography of Greece differ from that of other ancient civilizations?

Types of Government Evolve Between 750 B.C. and 500 B.C., different forms of government evolved in Greece. At first, the ruler of the polis, like those in the river valley empires, was a king. A government in which a hereditary ruler exercises central power is a **monarchy.** Slowly, however, power shifted to a class of noble landowners. Because only they could afford bronze weapons and chariots, these nobles were also the military defenders of the city-states. At first these landowners defended the king. In time, however, they won power for themselves. The result was an **aristocracy,** or rule by a hereditary landholding elite.

As trade expanded, a new middle class of wealthy merchants, farmers, and artisans emerged in some cities. They challenged the landowning nobles for power and came to dominate some city-states. The result was a form of government called an **oligarchy.** In an oligarchy, power is in the hands of a small, wealthy elite.

New Warfare Methods Shape Greece Changes in military technology increased the power of the middle class. By about 650 B.C., iron weapons replaced bronze ones. Since iron was cheaper, ordinary citizens could afford iron helmets, shields, and swords. Meanwhile, a new method of fighting emerged—the **phalanx,** a massive tactical formation of heavily armed foot soldiers. It required long hours of drill to master. Shared training created a strong sense of unity among the citizen-soldiers.

By putting the defense of the city-state in the hands of ordinary citizens, the phalanx reduced class differences. The new type of warfare, however, led the two most influential city-states—Athens and Sparta—to develop very different ways of life. While Sparta stressed military virtues and stern discipline, Athens glorified the individual and extended political rights to more citizens.

✓ **Checkpoint** How was a city-state shaped by its citizenry?

Sparta: A Warrior Society

Dorian invaders from the north conquered Laconia, in the southern part of the Peloponnesus (pel uh puh NEE sus). The Dorians settled here and built the city-state of **Sparta.** The invaders turned the conquered people into state-owned slaves, called helots, and made them work the land. Because the helots greatly outnumbered their rulers, the Spartans set up a brutal system of strict control.

The Spartan government included two kings and a council of elders who advised the monarchs. An assembly made up of all citizens approved major decisions. Citizens were male, native-born Spartans over the age of 30. The assembly also elected five ephors, or officials, who ran day-to-day affairs.

Daily Life Ruled by Discipline From childhood, a Spartan prepared to be part of a military state. Officials examined every newborn, and sickly children were abandoned to die. Spartans wanted future soldiers and the future mothers of soldiers to be healthy.

At the age of seven, boys began training for a lifetime in the military. They moved into barracks, where they were toughened by a coarse diet, hard exercise, and rigid discipline. This strict and harsh discipline made Spartan youths excellent soldiers. To develop cunning and supplement their diet, boys were even encouraged to steal food. If caught, though, they were beaten severely.

Spartan Education

An Athenian historian explains the system of education set up by Lycurgus, the Spartan lawgiver:

Primary Source

❝Instead of softening the boys' feet with sandals, he required them to harden their feet by going without shoes. He believed that if this habit were cultivated, it would enable them to climb hills more easily and descend steep inclines with less danger, and that a youth who had accustomed himself to go barefoot would leap and jump and run more nimbly than a boy in sandals. And instead of letting them be pampered in the matter of clothing, he introduced the custom of wearing one garment throughout the year, believing that they would thus be better prepared to face changes of heat and cold.❞

—Xenophon, *Constitution of the Lacedaemonians*

Describe the Spartan student dress code. What was its purpose?)) AUDIO

At the age of 20, a man could marry, but he continued to live in the barracks for another 10 years and to eat there for another 40 years. At the age of 30, after further training, he took his place in the assembly.

Women of Sparta Girls, too, had a rigorous upbringing. As part of a warrior society, they were expected to produce healthy sons for the army. They therefore were required to exercise and strengthen their bodies.

Like other Greek women, Spartan women had to obey their fathers or husbands. Yet under Spartan law, they had the right to inherit property. Because men were occupied with war, some women took on responsibilities such as running the family's estate.

Sparta Stands Alone The Spartans isolated themselves from other Greeks. They looked down on trade and wealth, forbade their own citizens to travel, and had little use for new ideas or the arts. While other Greeks admired the Spartans' military skills, no other city-state imitated their rigorous way of life. "Spartans are willing to die for their city," some suggested, "because they have no reason to live."

 Checkpoint Why was discipline important to Spartans?

Athens Evolves Into a Democracy

Athens was located in Attica, just north of the Peloponnesus. As in many Greek city-states, Athenian government evolved from a monarchy into an aristocracy. By 700 B.C., landowners held power. They chose the chief officials, judged major court cases, and dominated the assembly.

Demands for Change Under the aristocracy, Athenian wealth and power grew. Yet discontent spread among ordinary people. Merchants and soldiers resented the power of the nobles. They argued that their service to Athens entitled them to more rights. Foreign artisans, who produced many of the goods that Athens traded abroad, were resentful that foreigners were barred from becoming citizens. Farmers, too, demanded change. During hard times, many farmers were forced to sell their land to nobles. A growing number even sold themselves and their families into slavery to pay their debts.

As discontent spread, Athens moved slowly toward democracy, or government by the people. As you will see, the term had a different meaning for the ancient Greeks than it has for us today.

Solon Reforms Government Solon, a wise and trusted leader, was appointed archon (AHR kahn), or chief official, in 594 B.C. Athenians gave Solon a free hand to make needed reforms. He outlawed debt slavery and freed those who had already been sold into slavery for debt. He opened high offices to more citizens, granted citizenship to some foreigners, and gave the Athenian assembly more say in important decisions.

Solon introduced economic reforms as well. He encouraged the export of wine and olive oil. This policy helped merchants and farmers by increasing demand for their products.

Despite Solon's reforms, citizenship remained limited, and many positions were open only to the wealthy. Continued and widespread unrest

Spartan Fitness
The Spartans put great emphasis on the strength and agility of the human body. The sculpture above shows a Spartan woman exercising, a task rarely expected of other Greek women.

led to the rise of **tyrants,** or people who gained power by force. Tyrants often won support from the merchant class and the poor by <u>imposing</u> reforms to help these groups. Although Greek tyrants often governed well, the word *tyrant* has come to mean a vicious and brutal ruler.

Citizens Share Power and Wealth The Athenian tyrant Pisistratus (py SIS truh tus) seized power in 546 B.C. He helped farmers by giving them loans and land taken from nobles. New building projects gave jobs to the poor. By giving poor citizens a greater voice, he further weakened the aristocracy.

In 507 B.C., another reformer, Cleisthenes (KLYS thuh neez), broadened the role of ordinary citizens in government. He set up the Council of 500, whose members were chosen by lot from among all citizens over the age of 30. The council prepared laws considered by the assembly and supervised the day-to-day work of government. Cleisthenes made the assembly a genuine **legislature,** or lawmaking body, that debated laws before deciding to approve or reject them. All male citizens were members of the assembly and were expected to participate.

A Limited Democracy By modern standards, Athenian democracy was quite limited. Only citizens could participate in government, and citizenship was restricted to landowning men. Women were excluded along with merchants and foreigners. So were the tens of thousands of Athenian slaves who lacked political rights as well as personal freedom, although it was their labor that gave citizens the time to participate in government. Still, Athens gave more people a say in decision making than any other ancient civilization.

Women in Athens As in other Greek city-states, women in Athens had no share in political life. According to Aristotle, "the man is by nature fitter for command than the female just as an older person is superior to a younger, more immature person." Although some men disagreed, most Greeks accepted the view that women must be guided by men.

Women played their most significant public role in religion. Their participation in sacred processions and ceremonies was considered essential for the city's well-being. In well-to-do Athenian homes, women managed the entire household. They spun and wove, cared for their children, and prepared food, but lived a secluded existence and were rarely seen in public. Their slaves or children were sent to buy food and to fetch water from the public well. Poorer women worked outside the home, tending sheep or working as spinners, weavers, or potters.

Educating the Youth Unlike girls, who received little or no formal education, boys attended school if their families could afford it. Besides learning to read and write, they studied music, memorized poetry, and studied public speaking because, as citizens in a democracy, they would have to voice their views. Although they received military training and participated in athletic contests, unlike Sparta, which put military training above all else, Athens encouraged young men to explore many areas of knowledge.

Athenian Education

This drinking cup from 480 B.C. illustrates some of the subjects studied by Athenian boys, including instruction in speech and playing the lyre. *How does this image demonstrate the differences between the Athenian and Spartan systems of education?*

✓ **Checkpoint** How was democracy limited in Athens?

Forces for Unity

Strong local identification, an independent spirit, and economic rivalry led to fighting among the Greek city-states. Despite these divisions, Greeks shared a common culture. They spoke the same language, honored the same ancient heroes, participated in common festivals, and prayed to the same gods.

Religion Like most other ancient people, the Greeks were polytheistic, believing in more than one deity. They believed that the gods lived on Mount Olympus in northern Greece. The most powerful Olympian was Zeus (zoos), who presided over the affairs of gods and humans. His children included Ares (EHR eez), god of war, and, Aphrodite (af ruh DY tee), goddess of love. His daughter Athena (uh THEE nuh), goddess of wisdom, gave her name to Athens.

Greeks honored their gods with temples and festivals, which included processions, sacrifices, feasts, dramatic performances, choral singing, and athletic competitions. To discover the will of the gods, Greeks consulted the oracles, priests or priestesses through whom the gods were thought to speak. Although religion was important, some Greek thinkers came to believe that the universe was regulated not by the will of gods but by natural laws.

Greek View of Foreigners As trade and colonies expanded, the Greeks came in contact with people from foreign lands with different languages and customs. Greeks called them *barbaroi*, people who did not speak Greek, and felt superior to them. The English word *barbarian* comes from this Greek term. These "barbarians" even included the Phoenicians and Egyptians, from whom the Greeks borrowed important ideas and inventions. This sense of uniqueness and superiority would help the Greeks when they were threatened by the mightiest power in the Mediterranean world—the Persian empire.

✓ **Checkpoint** What factors united the city-states of Greece?

Ruins of the Sanctuary of Athena at the Tholos Temple in Delphi

Progress Monitoring *Online*
For: Self-quiz with vocabulary practice
Web Code: naa-0421

SECTION 2 Assessment

Terms, People, and Places

1. What do each of the key terms listed at the beginning of the section have in common? Explain.

Note Taking

2. **Reading Skill: Identify Supporting Details** Use your completed outline to answer the Focus Question: How did government and culture develop as Greek city-states grew?

Comprehension and Critical Thinking

3. **Summarize** How did geography influence the development of Greece?

4. **Synthesize Information** Why do you think the three different forms of government evolved over time?

5. **Draw Conclusions** (a) In what ways was Athenian democracy limited? (b) Despite such limits, Athens is still admired as an early model of democracy. Why do you think this is the case?

● **Writing About History**

Quick Write: Choose a Topic A persuasive essay supports an opinion or position. Suppose you are given the assignment to write a persuasive essay about ancient Greece. Review this section and select three possible topics for your essay. Your topics might be about democracy, the rights of citizens, or political systems. Then write a brief summary for each topic and describe what arguments you could make to support it in a persuasive essay.

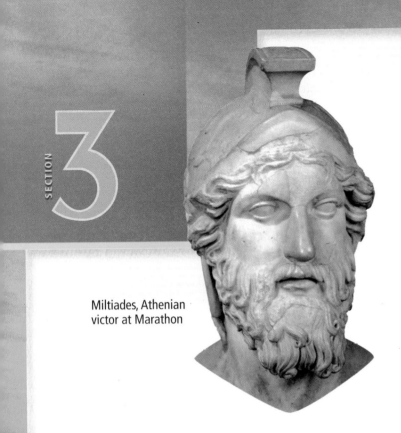

Miltiades, Athenian victor at Marathon

WITNESS HISTORY ◀)) AUDIO

Athens Demands Action

As the Persian invaders grew dangerously close, the Athenian generals were split between going into battle or waiting for Spartan reinforcements. To break the deadlock, the Athenian general Miltiades approached Callimachus, the commander-in-chief, and pleaded that a decision must be made.

❝Callimachus, it is up to you, *right now*, to enslave Athens or to make her free. . . . Athens is in the most perilous moment of her history. . . . If we fight now, why then we can survive this battle. . . . It hangs on your decision—*now*. If you vote with me, your fatherland will be free . . . , but if you choose . . . not to fight, then the opposite of all good . . . will fall to you.❞

Focus Question How did war with invaders and conflict among Greeks affect the city-states?

Conflict in the Greek World

Objectives

- Summarize how the Persian Wars affected Greece.
- Explain how Pericles instituted a direct democracy in Athens.
- Understand the causes and effects of the Peloponnesian War.

Terms, People, and Places

alliance	stipend
Pericles	jury
direct democracy	ostracism

Note Taking

Reading Skill: Identify Supporting Details
Make a table like the one below. Then, use the table to record the supporting details as they relate to the main ideas discussed in the section.

Persian Wars	Athenian Democracy	Peloponnesian War
• Athens is victorious at Marathon.	•	• Greeks resent Athenian domination.
•	•	•

Like the Athenian generals, divided on whether or not to go into battle, the Greek city-states were often at odds with one another. Yet, when the Persians threatened them, the Greeks briefly put aside their differences to defend their freedom.

The Persian Wars

As you have read, the Persians conquered a huge empire stretching from Asia Minor to the border of India. Their subjects included the Greek city-states of Ionia in Asia Minor. Though under Persian rule, these Ionian city-states were largely self-governing. Still, they resented their situation.

In 499 B.C., Ionian Greeks rebelled against Persian rule. Athens sent ships to help them. As the historian Herodotus wrote some years later, "These ships were the beginning of mischief both to the Greeks and to the barbarians."

Athenians Win at Marathon The Persians soon crushed the rebel cities. However, Darius I was furious at the role Athens played in the uprising. In time, Darius sent a huge force across the Aegean to punish Athens for its interference. The mighty Persian army landed near Marathon, a plain north of Athens, in 490 B.C. The Athenians asked for help from neighboring Greek city-states, but received little support.

Geography *Interactive*
For: Audio guided tour
Web Code: nap-0431

Black Sea

MACEDONIA

40°N

20°E

Aegean Sea

PERSIAN EMPIRE

Thermopylae

Thebes

Marathon

IONIA

Sardis

Salamis   Athens

Delos

Peloponnesus   ATTICA

Sparta

LACONIA

Rhodes

36°N   24°E

Miller Projection
0   50   100 mi

Crete

0   50   100 km

Mediterranean Sea   28°E

Areas settled by Greeks
Athenian Empire about 450 B.C.
Route of Xerxes' fleet
Route of Persian army
Battle sites

Map Skills When the Persian empire attacked Greece, the Greek city-states briefly joined forces to defend their independence.
1. **Locate** (a) Athens (b) Sparta (c) Marathon (d) Thermopylae (e) Salamis
2. **Movement** Describe the routes of the Persian army and navy toward the city-state of Athens.
3. **Making Inferences** Why do you think Xerxes' fleet hugged the Greek coastline instead of sailing directly across the Aegean Sea?

The Persians greatly outnumbered Athenian forces. Yet the invaders were amazed to see "a mere handful of men coming on at a run without either horsemen or archers." The Persians responded with a rain of arrows, but the Greeks rushed onward. They broke through the Persian line and engaged in fierce hand-to-hand combat. Overwhelmed by the fury of the assault, the Persians hastily retreated to their ships.

The Athenians celebrated their triumph. Still, the Athenian leader, Themistocles (thuh MIS tuh kleez), knew the victory at Marathon had bought only a temporary lull in the fighting. He urged Athenians to build a fleet of warships and prepare other defenses.

Greek City-States Unite Darius died before he could mass his troops for another attack. But in 480 B.C., his son Xerxes (ZURK seez) sent a much larger force to conquer Greece. By this time, Athens had persuaded Sparta and other city-states to join in the fight against Persia.

Once again, the Persians landed in northern Greece. A small Spartan force guarded the narrow mountain pass at Thermopylae (thur MAHP uh lee). Led by the great warrior-king Leonidas (lee AHN ih dus), the Spartans held out heroically against the enormous Persian force, but were defeated in the end. The Persians marched south and burned Athens. The city was empty, however. The Athenians had already withdrawn to safety.

The Greeks now put their faith in the fleet of ships that Themistocles had urged them to build. The Athenians lured the Persian navy into the narrow strait of Salamis (SAHL uh mis). Then, Athenian warships, powered by rowers, drove into the Persian boats with underwater battering rams. On the shore, Xerxes watched helplessly as his mighty fleet sank.

A relief illustrating the Athenian battle with the Persians at Marathon

The next year, the Greeks defeated the Persians on land in Asia Minor. This victory marked the end of the Persian invasions. In a brief moment of unity, the Greek city-states had saved themselves from the Persian threat.

Athens Leads the Delian League Victory in the Persian Wars increased the Greeks' sense of their own uniqueness. The gods, they felt, had protected their superior form of government—the city-state—against invaders from Asia.

Vocabulary Builder
uniqueness—(yoo NEEK ness) *n.* the quality of being without equal; individuality

Athens emerged from the war as the most powerful city-state in Greece. To continue to defend against Persia, it organized with other Greek city-states an **alliance,** or a formal agreement between two or more nations or powers to cooperate and come to one another's defense. Modern scholars call this alliance the Delian League after Delos, the location where the league held meetings.

From the start, Athens dominated the Delian League. It slowly used its position of leadership to create an Athenian empire. It moved the league treasury from the island of Delos to Athens, using money contributed by other city-states to rebuild its own city. When its allies protested and tried to withdraw from the league, Athens used force to make them remain. Yet, while Athens was enforcing its will abroad, Athenian leaders were championing political freedom at home.

✔ **Checkpoint** What factors led to the Persian defeat?

The Age of Pericles and Direct Democracy

The years after the Persian Wars from 460 B.C. to 429 B.C. were a golden age for Athens under the able statesman **Pericles** (PEHR uh kleez). Because of his wise and skillful leadership, the economy thrived and the government became more democratic.

Athenian Democracy Periclean Athens was a **direct democracy.** Under this system, citizens take part directly in the day-to-day affairs of government. By contrast, in most democratic countries today, citizens participate in government indirectly through elected representatives.

By the time of Pericles, the Athenian assembly met several times a month. A Council of 500, selected by lot, conducted daily government business. Pericles believed that all citizens, regardless of wealth or social class, should take part in government. Athens therefore began to pay a **stipend,** or fixed salary, to men who participated in the Assembly and its governing Council. This reform enabled poor men to serve in government.

In addition, Athenians also served on juries. A **jury** is a panel of citizens who have the authority to make the final judgment in a trial. Unlike a modern American trial jury, which is usually made up of 12 members, an Athenian jury might include hundreds or even thousands of jurors. Citizens over 30 years of age were chosen by lot to serve on the jury for a year.

Athenian citizens could also vote to banish, or send away, a public figure whom they saw as a threat to their democracy. This process was called **ostracism** (AHS truh siz um). The person with the largest number of votes cast against him was ostracized, meaning that that individual would have to live outside the city, usually for a period of 10 years.

Culture Thrives in Athens Athens prospered during the Age of Pericles. With the empire's riches, Pericles directed the rebuilding of the Acropolis, which the Persians had destroyed. With the help of an

ATHENIAN DEMOCRACY

The Athenians called their political system *demokratia*, which means "rule by the people." In a democracy, the people hold supreme political authority and government is conducted only by and with the consent of the people. By the 6th century B.C., ordinary citizens of Athens could participate fully in government. Some of the most basic principles of modern democracies originated in Athens—including majority rule, civic debate, impartial juries, and the rule of law.

1-PARTHENON
2-ERECHTHEION
3-PROPYLAIA
4-TEMPLE OF ATHENA NIKE
5-THEATER OF DIONYSOS

▶ **The Courts and Juries**
Athenian courts enforced and interpreted the laws passed by the ecclesia. Juries were large to prevent corruption. A solid disc was a vote for innocence. A disk with a hole was a vote for guilt.

The Boule, or Council of 500
Day-to-day decisions and the agenda for the ecclesia were made by a Council of 500 known as the boule. The boule met at the bouleuterion (see map above) and members slept nearby in the Tholos in order to be able to respond to emergencies. Members of the council were chosen by lot from the entire citizenry and served for one year.

▼ **The Ecclesia**
The assembly of all citizens of Athens, the ecclesia met about three times a month outside the city on Pnyx hill (below). Here, citizens would gather to debate important issues (left) and would vote on laws. Once a year, citizens could vote to ostracize, or exile, someone by writing their name on an ostrakon (above left).

Geography *Interactive*
For: Interactive map skills
Web Code: nap-0432

Thinking Critically

1. **Identify Main Ideas** Why is Athens's system of government described as a "direct democracy" as opposed to an "indirect democracy"?
2. **Make Comparisons** How does Athenian democracy compare to the democratic system of the United States?

educated foreign-born woman named Aspasia (as PAY shuh), Pericles turned Athens into the cultural center of Greece. They encouraged the arts through public festivals, dramatic competitions, and building programs. Such building projects increased Athenians' prosperity by creating jobs for artisans and workers.

✓ **Checkpoint** Describe Pericles's influence on Athens.

The Peloponnesian War

Many Greeks outside Athens resented Athenian domination. Before long, the Greek world was split into rival camps. To counter the Delian League, Sparta and other enemies of Athens formed the Peloponnesian League. In 431 B.C., warfare broke out between Athens and Sparta. This conflict, which became known as the Peloponnesian War, soon engulfed all of Greece. The fighting would last for 27 years.

Sparta Defeats Athens Despite its riches and powerful navy, Athens faced a serious geographic disadvantage. Because Sparta was inland, Athens could not use its navy to attack. Sparta's powerful army, however, had only to march north to attack Athens. When the Spartan troops came near, Pericles allowed people from the countryside to move inside the city walls. The overcrowded conditions led to a terrible plague that killed many Athenians, including Pericles himself.

As the war dragged on, each side committed savage acts against the other. Sparta even allied itself with Persia, the longtime enemy of the Greeks. Finally, in 404 B.C., with the help of the Persian navy, the Spartans captured Athens. The victors stripped the Athenians of their fleet and empire. However, Sparta rejected calls from its allies to destroy Athens.

Greek Dominion Declines The Peloponnesian War ended Athenian domination of the Greek world. The Athenian economy eventually revived and Athens remained the cultural center of Greece. However, its spirit and vitality declined. Meanwhile, as Greeks battled among themselves, a new power rose in Macedonia (mas uh DOH nee uh), a kingdom to the north of Greece. By 359 B.C., its ambitious ruler stood poised to conquer the quarrelsome Greek city-states.

✓ **Checkpoint** How did conflict lead to the decline of Athens?

Armor of the Hoplites
The Greek hoplite was named after his unique shield, the *hoplon*. These heavily armored soldiers were usually men from the middle class who could afford to purchase the armor and weapons.

SECTION 3 Assessment

Progress Monitoring *Online*
For: Self-quiz with vocabulary practice
Web Code: naa-0431

Terms, People, and Places

1. For each term, person, or place listed at the beginning of the section, write a sentence explaining its significance.

Note Taking

2. **Reading Skill: Identify Supporting Details** Use your completed table to answer the Focus Question: How did war with invaders and conflict among Greeks affect the city-states?

Comprehension and Critical Thinking

3. **Summarize** How did the Persian Wars affect the Greek city-states?
4. **Analyze Information** How did Pericles contribute to Athenian greatness?
5. **Demonstrate Reasoned Judgement** Do you think the process of ostracism is fair or unfair? Explain.
6. **Recognize Cause and Effect** How did the growth of Athenian power lead to war?

● **Writing About History**

Quick Write: Organize Evidence Write an opening paragraph that introduces a persuasive essay arguing for or against Athenian direct democracy. The paragraph should include a thesis statement reflecting the position you will prove and should indicate what the essay will discuss. Remember that an opening paragraph should grab the reader's attention and make the topic sound interesting.

The Funeral Oration of Pericles

This excerpt from Thucydides' *History of the Peloponnesian War* records a speech made by the Athenian leader Pericles in honor of those who died fighting Sparta in the first year of the war (431 B.C.). In the speech, Pericles describes the superior qualities of Athenian democracy as compared with life in Sparta. This speech is one of the most famous defenses of democracy of all time.

Marble bust of the great Athenian statesman Pericles

For our government is not copied from those of our neighbors; we are an example to them rather than they to us. Our constitution is named a democracy because it is in the hands not of the few but of the many. But our laws secure equal justice for all in their private disputes, and our public opinion welcomes and honors talent in every branch of achievement, not for any sectional reason but on grounds of excellence alone. And as we give free play to all in our public life, so we carry the same spirit into our daily relations with one another. . . .

We are lovers of beauty without extravagance[1], and lovers of wisdom without unmanliness. Wealth to us is not mere material for vainglory[2] but an opportunity for achievement; and poverty we think it no disgrace to acknowledge but a real degradation[3] to make no effort to overcome. Our citizens attend both to public and private duties, and do not allow absorption[4] in their own various affairs to interfere with their knowledge of the city's. We differ from other states in regarding the man who holds aloof[5] from public life not as 'quiet' but as useless; we decide or debate, carefully and in person, all matters of policy, holding not that words and deeds go ill together but that acts are foredoomed to failure when undertaken undiscussed. For we are noted for being at once adventurous in action and most reflective beforehand. Other men are bold in ignorance, while reflection will stop their onset. But the bravest are surely those who have the clearest vision of what is before them, glory and danger alike, and yet notwithstanding[6] go out to meet it. . . . In a word I claim that our city as a whole is an education to Greece, and that her members yield to none, man by man, for independence of spirit, many-sidedness of attainment[7], and complete self-reliance in limbs and brain.

1. **extravagance** (ek STRAV uh guns) *n.* excess
2. **vainglory** (VAYN glawr ee) *n.* vanity, excessive pride
3. **degradation** (deg ruh DAY shun) *n.* decline to a low or demoralized state
4. **absorption** (ab SAWRP shun) *n.* entire occupation of the mind
5. **aloof** (uh LOOF) *adj.* removed, distant
6. **notwithstanding** (naht with STAND ing) *adv.* nevertheless, however
7. **attainment** (uh TAYN munt) *n.* accomplishment

Thinking Critically

1. **Analyze Information** How does Pericles define *democracy*?
2. **Synthesize Information** What does Pericles say it takes for a person to be a good citizen?

The great philosopher Aristotle

WITNESS HISTORY ◀))) AUDIO

Aristotle Meditates on Thought

Aristotle is considered one of the greatest philosophers of all time. After studying under Plato for twenty years, Aristotle eventually became a teacher himself. His interests varied greatly and he studied numerous subjects including biology, political theory, and logic. In *Metaphysics,* Aristotle theorized on the nature of divine thinking:

66 It is of itself that the divine thought thinks (since it is the most excellent of things), and its thinking is a thinking on thinking.**99**

Focus Question How did Greek thinkers, artists, and writers explore the nature of the universe and people's place in it?

The Glory That Was Greece

Objectives
- Analyze the political and ethical ideas developed by Greek philosophers.
- Understand how balance and order governed Greek art and architecture.
- Identify the themes explored by Greek writers and historians.

Terms, People, and Places

philosopher	Aristotle
logic	Parthenon
rhetoric	tragedy
Socrates	comedy
Plato	Herodotus

Note Taking

Reading Skill: Identify Supporting Details
Make a concept web similar to the one below. Then use the diagram to record the supporting details of the Greek achievements discussed in the section. Add circles as necessary.

Even in the midst of wars and political turmoil, Greeks had confidence in the power of the human mind. Driven by curiosity and a belief in reason, Greek thinkers, artists, and writers explored the nature of the universe and the place of people in it. To later admirers, Greek achievements in the arts represented the height of human development in the Western world. They looked back with deep respect on what one poet called "the glory that was Greece."

Philosophers: Lovers of Wisdom

As you have read, some Greek thinkers challenged the belief that events were caused by the whims of gods. Instead, they used observation and reason to find causes for events. The Greeks called these thinkers **philosophers,** meaning "lovers of wisdom."

Greek philosophers explored many subjects, from mathematics and music to **logic,** or rational thinking. Through reason and observation, they believed, they could discover laws that governed the universe. Much modern science traces its roots to the Greek search for such principles.

Debating Morality and Ethics Some Greek philosophers were interested in ethics and morality. They debated such questions as what was the best kind of government and what standards should rule human behavior.

In Athens, the Sophists questioned accepted ideas. To them, success was more important than moral truth. They developed skills in **rhetoric,** the art of skillful speaking. Ambitious men could use clever and persuasive rhetoric to advance their careers. The turmoil of the Peloponnesian War led many young Athenians to follow the Sophists. Older citizens, however, accused the Sophists of undermining traditional Greek values.

Socrates Questions Tradition

One outspoken critic of the Sophists was Socrates, an Athenian stonemason and philosopher. Most of what we know about Socrates comes from his student Plato. Socrates himself wrote no books. Instead, he passed his days in the town square asking people about their beliefs. Using a process we now call the Socratic method, he would pose a series of questions to a student or passing citizen, and challenge them to examine the implications of their answers. To Socrates, this patient examination was a way to help others seek truth and self-knowledge. To many Athenians, however, such questioning was a threat to accepted values and traditions.

When he was about 70 years old, Socrates was put on trial. His enemies accused him of corrupting the city's youth and failing to respect the gods. Standing before a jury of 501 citizens, Socrates offered a calm and reasoned defense. But the jurors condemned him to death. Loyal to the laws of Athens, Socrates accepted the death penalty. He drank a cup of hemlock, a deadly poison.

Plato Envisions A Perfect Society

The execution of Socrates left Plato with a lifelong distrust of democracy. He fled Athens for 10 years. When he returned, he set up a school called the Academy. There, he taught and wrote about his own ideas. Like Socrates, Plato emphasized the importance of reason. Through rational thought, he argued, people could discover unchanging ethical values, recognize perfect beauty, and learn how best to organize society.

In his book *The Republic*, Plato described his vision of an ideal state. He rejected Athenian democracy because it had condemned Socrates just as it tended to other excesses. Instead, Plato argued that the state should regulate every aspect of its citizens' lives in order to provide for their best interests. He divided his ideal society into three classes: workers to produce the necessities of life, soldiers to defend the state, and philosophers to rule. This elite class of leaders would be specially trained to ensure order and justice. The wisest of them, a philosopher-king, would have the ultimate authority.

Plato thought that, in general, men surpassed women in mental and physical tasks, but that some women were superior to some men. Talented women, he said, should be educated to serve the state. The ruling elite, both men and women, would take military training together and raise their children in communal centers for the good of the republic.

Aristotle Pursues the Golden Mean

Plato's most famous student, Aristotle, developed his own ideas about government. He analyzed all forms of government, from monarchy to democracy, and found good and bad examples of each. Like Plato, he was suspicious of democracy, which he thought could lead to mob rule. In the end, he favored rule by a single strong and virtuous leader.

Aristotle also addressed the question of how people ought to live. In his view, good conduct meant pursuing the "golden mean," a moderate course between the extremes. He promoted reason as the guiding force for learning. He set up a school, the Lyceum, for the study of all branches

BIOGRAPHY

Socrates

Contrasting with his glorified image in Jacques-Louis David's painting *The Death of Socrates* (above), to most Athenians, Socrates (469 B.C.–399 B.C.) was not an impressive figure. Tradition tells us that his clothes were untidy and he made a poor living. But young men loved to watch him as he questioned citizens and led them to contradict themselves.

Many Athenians felt that Socrates was annoying, but Plato had a different view of his teacher. He called Socrates "the wisest, justest, and best of all I have ever known." As for Socrates himself, he knew what he was doing. When he was put on trial, he told the jury, "All day long and in all places I am always fastening upon you, stirring you and persuading you and reproaching you. You will not easily find another like me."

Socrates said, "The unexamined life is not worth living." How did his actions support this idea?

of knowledge. He left writings on politics, ethics, logic, biology, literature, and many other subjects. When the first European universities evolved some 1,500 years later, their courses were based largely on the works and ideas of Aristotle.

✔ **Checkpoint** Why might some of the philosophers' ideas be a threat to Greek tradition?

Idealism in Architecture and Art

Plato argued that every object on Earth had an ideal form. The work of Greek artists and architects reflected a similar concern with balance, order, and beauty.

Monumental Architecture Greek architects sought to convey a sense of perfect balance to reflect the harmony and order of the universe. The most famous example of Greek architecture is the **Parthenon,** a temple dedicated to the goddess Athena. The basic plan of the Parthenon is a

INFOGRAPHIC

ART AND ARCHITECTURE OF ANCIENT GREECE

▲ A sphinx made of bone illustrates the influence of Egyptian culture on early Greece.

The art of early Greece was similar in style to that of ancient Egypt—stylized and static. Images and statues were stiff and lifeless. By the fifth century B.C., however, the Greeks had developed an important and radical artistic skill. They were able to represent a more realistic human form both at rest and, most significantly, in motion. In their idealized representations of the human form, Greek artists expressed their love of beauty, balance, and harmony. Over time, these ideals were reflected in all Greek art forms including architecture, ceramics, and jewelry. Today, the art and architecture of ancient Greece is considered "classic"—a standard of excellence against which other art forms are compared.

Thousands of surviving ▲ painted vases provide us with most of what we know about daily life in ancient Greece.

The Dying Gaul portrays a mortally wounded warrior gasping for his last breath. ▼

simple rectangle, with tall columns supporting a gently sloping roof. The delicate curves and placement of the columns add dignity and grace.

Greek architecture has been widely admired for centuries. Today, many public buildings throughout the world have incorporated Greek architectural elements, such as columns, in their designs.

Artists Craft Lifelike Human Forms Early Greek sculptors carved figures in <u>rigid</u> poses, perhaps imitating Egyptian styles. By 450 B.C., Greek sculptors had developed a new style that emphasized more natural forms. While their work was lifelike, it was also idealistic. That is, sculptors carved gods, goddesses, athletes, and famous men in a way that showed human beings in their most perfect, graceful form.

The only Greek paintings to survive are on pottery. They offer intriguing views of every day Greek life. Women carry water from wells, warriors race into battle, and athletes compete in javelin contests. Each scene is designed to fit the shape of the pottery.

Vocabulary Builder

<u>rigid</u>—(RIJ id) *adj.* stiff; unbending; severe

✓ **Checkpoint** How did Greek art reflect the idea of an ideal form?

Nike of Samothrace, also ▶ known as *Winged Victory*, reflects the artist's amazing ability to create a sense of power, movement, and grace in a work of stone.

The Greek ideals ▲ of balance and beauty are even apparent in this gold sprig of leaves and flowers.

Built over a fifteen-year period at the direction of Pericles, the Parthenon epitomizes the Greek ideals of balance and order. ▼

Thinking Critically
1. **Synthesize Information** Study the photograph of the Parthenon. What kinds of modern buildings were influenced by its architecture? Why do you think this is so?
2. **Draw Conclusions** Why do you think the ability to portray movement was important in the development of Greek art?

133

A Roman fresco believed to be the Greek poetess, Sappho ▶

Greek Literature

In literature, as in art, the ancient Greeks developed their own style. To later Europeans, Greek styles were a model of perfection. They admired what they called the "classical style," referring to the elegant and balanced forms of traditional Greek works of art.

Greek literature began with the epic poems of Homer, whose stirring tales inspired later writers. In later times, the poet Sappho sang of love and of the beauty of her island home, while the poetry of Pindar celebrated the victors in athletic contests.

Tragic Drama Perhaps the most important Greek contribution to literature was in the field of drama. The first Greek plays evolved out of religious festivals, especially those held in Athens to honor the god of fertility and wine, Dionysus (dy uh NY sus). Plays were performed in large outdoor theaters with little or no scenery. Actors wore elaborate costumes and stylized masks. A chorus sang or chanted comments on the action taking place on stage. Greek dramas were often based on popular myths and legends. Through these familiar stories, playwrights discussed moral and social issues or explored the relationship between people and the gods.

The greatest Athenian playwrights were Aeschylus (ES kih lus), Sophocles (SAH fuh kleez), and Euripides (yoo RIP ih deez). All three wrote **tragedies,** plays that told stories of human suffering that usually ended in disaster. The purpose of tragedy, the Greeks felt, was to stir up and then relieve the emotions of pity and fear. For example in his play *Oresteia* (aw res TEE uh), Aeschylus showed a powerful family torn apart by betrayal, murder, and revenge. Audiences saw how even the powerful could be subject to horrifying misfortune and how the wrath of the gods could bring down even the greatest heroes.

In *Antigone* (an TIG uh nee), Sophocles explored what happens when an individual's moral duty conflicts with the laws of the state. Antigone is a young woman whose brother has been killed leading a rebellion. King Creon forbids anyone to bury the traitor's body. When Antigone buries her brother anyway, she is sentenced to death. She defiantly tells Creon that duty to the gods is greater than human law:

Primary Source

66 For me, it was not Zeus who made that order. . . .
Nor did I think your orders were so strong
that you, a mortal man, could overrun
the gods' unwritten and unfailing laws. 99
—Sophocles, *Antigone*

Like Sophocles, Euripides survived the horrors of the Peloponnesian War. That experience probably led him to question many accepted ideas of his day. His plays suggested that people, not the gods, were the cause of human misfortune and suffering. In *The Trojan Women,* he stripped war of its glamour by showing the suffering of women who were victims of the war.

Theatrical Masks
Greek masks, with their exaggerated facial features, enabled those sitting far from the stage to recognize the characters. A small mouthpiece inside the mask helped project the actor's voice.

Greek Comedy Some Greek playwrights wrote comedies, humorous plays that mocked people or customs. Almost all the surviving Greek comedies were written by Aristophanes (a rih STAHF uh neez). In *Lysistrata,* he shows the women of Athens banding together to force their husbands to end a war against Sparta. Unlike tragedy which focused on events of the past, comedies ridiculed individuals of the day, including political figures, philosophers, and prominent members of society. Through ridicule, comic playwrights sharply criticized society, much as political cartoonists do today.

✓ **Checkpoint** How was drama used to influence Greek society?

Vocabulary Builder
bias—(BI uhs) *n.* a mental leaning; prejudice; slant

Recording Events as History

The Greeks also applied observation, reason, and logic to the study of history. Herodotus is often called the "Father of History" in the Western world because he went beyond listing names of rulers or the retelling of ancient legends. Before writing *The Persian Wars,* Herodotus visited many lands, collecting information from people who remembered the actual events he chronicled. In fact, Herodotus used the Greek term *historie,* which means inquiry, to define his work. Our *history* comes from this word, but its definition has evolved today to simply mean the recording and study of past events.

Herodotus cast a critical eye on his sources, noting bias and conflicting accounts. However, despite this special care for detail and accuracy, his writings reflected his own view that the war was a clear moral victory of Greek love of freedom over Persian tyranny. He even invented conversations and speeches for historical figures.

Another historian Thucydides, who was a few years younger than Herodotus, wrote about the Peloponnesian War, a much less happy subject for the Greeks. He had lived through the war and vividly described the war's savagery and corrupting influence on all those involved. Although he was an Athenian, he tried to be fair to both sides.

Both writers set standards for future historians. Herodotus stressed the importance of research. Thucydides showed the need to avoid bias.

✓ **Checkpoint** Why is Herodotus considered the "Father of History"?

Herodotus, the "Father of History"

Progress Monitoring Online
For: Self-quiz with vocabulary practice
Web Code: naa-0441

SECTION 4 Assessment

Terms, People, and Places

1. For each term, person, or place listed at the beginning of the section, write a sentence explaining its significance.

Note Taking

2. **Reading Skill: Identify Supporting Details** Use your completed concept web to answer the Focus Question: How did Greek thinkers, artists, and writers explore the nature of the universe and people's place in it?

Comprehension and Critical Thinking

3. **Make Generalizations** (a) Why did Plato reject democracy? (b) Describe the ideal form of government set forth in Plato's *Republic.*

4. **Summarize** What standards of beauty did Greek artists follow?

5. **Analyze Information** (a) How were Greek plays performed? (b) What were the topics of Greek poetry and plays?

6. **Identify Central Issues** Why do you think research and avoiding bias is important to the writing of history?

● **Writing About History**

Quick Write: Write a Thesis Statement Suppose you are writing a persuasive essay using Plato's ideas about what constitutes a perfect society to persuade the reader that Athenian democracy was imperfect. Based on what you have read, write a thesis statement for your essay.

Aristotle: *Politics*

The Greek philosopher Aristotle (384 B.C.–322 B.C.) was suspicious of democracy, which he thought could lead to mob rule. Instead, Aristotle favored rule by a single strong and virtuous leader. In this excerpt from his *Politics,* Aristotle outlines the forms of government and discusses the strengths and weaknesses of each form. Besides describing the ideal state, Aristotle also writes about practical matters relating to the preservation and improvement of government.

The Greek philosopher Aristotle

Thinking Critically

1. **Summarize** How does Aristotle describe constitutional government?
2. **Analyze Information** What do you think Aristotle means when he states that "man is by nature a political animal"?

First, let us consider what is the purpose of a state, and how many forms of government there are by which human society is regulated. We have already said, in the first part of this treatise[1]...that man is by nature a political animal. And therefore, men, even when they do not require one another's help, desire to live together . . . and are also brought together by their common interests . . . well-being . . . is certainly the chief end, both of individuals and of states. . . .

The conclusion is evident: that governments which have a regard to the common interest are constituted[2] in accordance with strict principles of justice, and are therefore true forms; but those which regard only the interest of the rulers are all defective and perverted forms, for they are despotic[3], whereas a state is a community of freemen. . . .

Of forms of government in which one rules, we call that which regards the common interests kingship or royalty; that in which more than one, but not many, rule, aristocracy; and it is so called, either because the rulers are the best men, or because they have at heart the best interests of the state and of the citizens. But when the citizens at large administer the state for the common interest, the government is called by the generic[4] name—a constitution. . . .

Of the above-mentioned forms, the perversions are as follows: of royalty, tyranny; of aristocracy, oligarchy; of constitutional government, democracy. For tyranny is a kind of monarchy which has in view the interest of the monarch only; oligarchy has in view the interest of the wealthy; democracy, of the needy; none of them the common good of all.

1. **treatise** (TREET is) *n.* a written argument
2. **constituted** (KAHN stuh too ted) *vt.* made or composed of
3. **despotic** (des PAHT ik) *adj.* characteristic of a tyrant or absolute ruler
4. **generic** (juh NEHR ik) *adj.* relating to a group, general

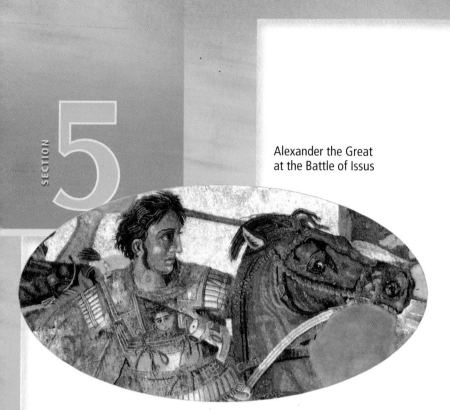

Alexander the Great
at the Battle of Issus

WITNESS HISTORY ◀)) AUDIO

Alexander Shares the Rewards

A young man named Alexander inherited the Macedonian empire from his father, Philip II. Alexander proceeded to extend the empire to epic proportions. However, he did not do it alone. Here, in a speech attributed to him, Alexander rallies his troops to continue the quest of expanding the empire.

66 I could not have blamed you for being the first to lose heart if I . . . had not shared in your exhausting marches and your perilous campaigns. . . . You and I . . . have shared the labor and shared the danger, and the rewards are for us all. . . . whoever wishes to return home will be allowed to go. . . . I will make those who stay the envy of those who return. 99

Focus Question How did Alexander the Great expand his empire and spread Greek culture throughout the realm?

Alexander and the Hellenistic Age

Objectives
- Explain how Alexander the Great built an extensive empire.
- Describe the empire's cultural impact.
- Identify individuals who contributed to Hellenistic civilization.

Terms, People, and Places

Alexander the Great	Pythagoras
Philip II	heliocentric
assassination	Archimedes
assimilate	Hippocrates
Alexandria	

Note Taking

Reading Skill: Identify Supporting Details As you read this section, make an outline to keep track of the important main ideas and supporting details of the empire of Alexander the Great.

I. The Empire of Alexander the Great
  A. Philip II conquers Greece
    1.
    2.
  B. Alexander takes Persia
    1.
    2.

In 338 B.C., Athens fell to the Macedonian army. Athens and the other Greek city-states lost their independence. Yet the disaster ushered in a new age in which Greek culture spread from the Mediterranean to the borders of India. The architect of this new era was the man who would eventually become known to history as **Alexander the Great.**

The Empire of Alexander the Great

To the Greeks, the rugged, mountainous kingdom of Macedonia was a backward, half-civilized land. The rulers of this frontier land, in fact, were of Greek origin and kept ties to their Greek neighbors. As a youth, **Philip II** had lived in Thebes and had come to admire Greek culture. Later, he hired Aristotle as a tutor to his young son Alexander.

Philip II Conquers Greece When Philip II gained the throne in 359 B.C., he dreamed of conquering the prosperous city-states to the south. He built a superb and powerful army. Through threats, bribery, and diplomacy, he formed alliances with many Greek city-states. Others he conquered. In 338 B.C., when Athens and Thebes joined forces against him, Philip II defeated them at the battle of Chaeronea (kehr uh NEE uh). He then brought all of Greece under his control.

Philip had a still grander dream—to conquer the Persian empire. Before he could achieve that plan, though, he was assassinated at

Empire of Alexander the Great

Geography *Interactive*
For: Audio guided tour
Web Code: nap-0451

Map Legend

- Macedonia, 336 B.C.
- Alexander's empire at its height, 323 B.C.
- → Route of Alexander, 334 B.C.–323 B.C.
- ○ Towns founded by Alexander and his followers
- • Other cities

Miller Projection
0 200 400 mi
0 200 400 km

Alexander's death, 323 B.C.

Although eventually stopped short from achieving his goal, Alexander once described the limitless size he envisioned his empire would one day reach:

Primary Source

❝Our ships will sail round from the Persian Gulf to Libya as far as the Pillars of Hercules, whence all Libya to the eastward will soon be ours, and all Asia too, and to this empire there will be no boundaries but what God Himself has made for the whole world.❞

A youthful image of the powerful Alexander the Great (top) and the revered leader's profile on a gold coin minted in Macedonia (bottom)

Map Skills The ambitions of Alexander the Great led him to conquer lands across an expansive area.
1. **Locate** (a) Mediterranean Sea (b) Arabian Sea (c) Indus River (d) Nile River (e) Euphrates River (f) Babylon
2. **Region** Locate the map entitled *Assyria, Persia, and the Phoenician Colonies,* which appears in an earlier chapter. (a) Which of the empires was largest? (b) Which parts of Alexander's empire had not been part of the Persian empire?
3. **Predicting Consequences** Judging from this map, do you think Alexander's empire would be difficult to keep united? Explain your reasoning.

his daughter's wedding. **Assassination** is the murder of a public figure, usually for political reasons. Philip's queen, Olympias, then outmaneuvered his other wives and children to put her own son, Alexander, on the throne.

Alexander Takes Persia Alexander was only 20 years old. Yet he was already an experienced soldier who shared his father's ambitions. With Greece subdued, he began organizing the forces needed to conquer Persia. By 334 B.C., he had enough ships to cross the Dardanelles, the strait separating Europe from Asia Minor.

Persia was no longer the great power it had once been. The emperor Darius III was weak, and the provinces were often in rebellion against him. Still, the Persian empire stretched more than 2,000 miles from Egypt to India.

Alexander won his first victory against the Persians at the Granicus River. He then moved from victory to victory, marching through Asia Minor into Palestine and south to Egypt before turning east again to take Babylon in 331 B.C. Other cities followed. But before Alexander could capture Darius, the Persian emperor was murdered.

Advance Into India With much of the Persian empire under his control, the restless Alexander headed farther east. He crossed the Hindu Kush into northern India. There, in 326 B.C., his troops for the first time faced soldiers mounted on war elephants. Although Alexander never lost a battle, his soldiers were tired of the long campaign and refused to go farther east. Reluctantly, Alexander agreed to turn back. After a long and difficult march, they reached Babylon, where Alexander began planning a new campaign.

Alexander's Early Death Before he could set out again, the thirty-two-year-old fell victim to a sudden fever. As Alexander lay dying, his commanders asked to whom he left his immense empire. "To the strongest," he is said to have whispered.

In fact, no one leader proved strong enough to succeed Alexander. Instead, after years of disorder, three generals divided up the empire. Macedonia and Greece went to one general, Egypt to another, and most of Persia to a third. For the next 300 years, their descendants competed for power over the lands Alexander had conquered.

✔ **Checkpoint** Why was Alexander the Great able to conquer the Persian empire?

The Legacy of Alexander

Although Alexander's empire soon crumbled following his premature death, he had unleashed changes that would ripple across the Mediterranean world and the Middle East for centuries. His most lasting achievement was the spread of Greek culture.

Cultures Combine Across his far-flung empire, Alexander founded many new cities, most of them named after him. The generals who succeeded him founded still more. Greek soldiers, traders, and artisans settled these new cities. From Egypt to the borders of India, they built Greek temples, filled them with Greek statues, and held athletic contests as they had in Greece. Local people **assimilated,** or absorbed, Greek ideas. In turn, Greek settlers adopted local customs.

WITNESS HISTORY VIDEO

Watch *Alexander the Great* on the **Witness History Discovery School**™ video program to learn more about the powerful empire created by Alexander's conquests.

Discovery SCHOOL

Greek Artistic Influence
Alexander's conquests helped spread Greek culture throughout the empire. The influence of the assimilated culture is frequently found in art such as this sitting Buddha who is portrayed here with a typical Greek topknot and flowing robes.

Scientific Advances in the Hellenistic Age

The vast size of Alexander's empire and his encouragement of scholarship brought many advances in science and mathematics. Throughout Alexander's empire, ideas and theories were exchanged and improved upon. A great research institute and library were built in the Egyptian city of Alexandria. Scholars from all regions converged on the city to conduct research and discuss their theories with the best minds of the day. The city became the largest center of learning and scholarship during the Hellenistic Age, which lasted from the death of Alexander to about A.D. 100.

► An engraver's depiction of the Library of Alexandria (top), which is estimated to have had up to 700,000 scrolls, perhaps including the works of Euclid (bottom right).

Alexander had encouraged a blending of eastern and western cultures when he had married a Persian woman and urged his soldiers to follow his example. He had also adopted many Persian customs, including Persian dress. Gradually, after his death, a vital new culture emerged that blended Greek, Persian, Egyptian, and Indian influences. This Hellenistic civilization would flourish for several centuries.

Alexandria: The Cultural Capital At the very heart of the Hellenistic world stood the city of **Alexandria,** Egypt. Located on the sea lanes between Europe and Asia, its markets boasted a wide range of goods, from Greek marble to Arabian spices to East African ivory. A Greek architect had drawn up plans for the city, which would become home to almost a million people. Among the city's marvelous sights was the Pharos, an enormous lighthouse that soared 440 feet into the air.

Alexander and his successors encouraged the work of scholars. The rulers of Alexandria built the great Museum as a center of learning. The Museum boasted laboratories, lecture halls, and a zoo. Its library had thousands of scrolls representing the <u>accumulated</u> knowledge of the ancient world. Unfortunately, the library was later destroyed in a fire.

New Roles for Women Paintings, statues, and legal codes show that women were no longer restricted to their homes during the Hellenistic period. More women learned to read and write. Some became philosophers

Vocabulary Builder

accumulate—(uh KYOOM yoo layt) *vt.* to gather together or collect over a period of time

Thinking Critically
1. **Determine Relevance** How did the vast expanse of Alexander's empire help promote advances in science and mathematics?
2. **Draw Conclusions** Why do you think there were so many advances made during the Hellenistic Age?

▲ Medicine reached a new level with the innovative theory that illnesses occurred by natural and identifiable causes and were not due to the will of the gods. Patients were observed to help determine the cause and cure for an illness.

The Egyptian astronomer, Ptolemy, developed ▶ a model of his theory of the geocentric, or Earth-centered, structure of the universe. The brass sphere at right demonstrates his theory, which remained the accepted model of planetary movement until it was disproved in the sixteenth century.

▲ One of the innovations of the great Greek mathematician and inventor, Archimedes, was the Archimedean screw. This simple machine transferred water from a low level to a higher level. Powered by a windmill or animal labor, this invention simplified the process of field irrigation.

or poets. Royal women held considerable power, working alongside husbands and sons who were the actual rulers. In Egypt, the able and clever queen Cleopatra VII came to rule in her own right.

✓ **Checkpoint** How did Alexander encourage the blending of cultures?

Hellenistic Arts and Sciences

The cities of the Hellenistic world employed armies of architects and artists. Temples, palaces, and other public buildings were much larger and grander than the buildings of classical Greece. The <u>elaborate</u> new style reflected the desire of Hellenistic rulers to glorify themselves as godlike.

New Philosophies Political turmoil during the Hellenistic age contributed to the rise of new schools of philosophy. The most influential was Stoicism. Its founder, Zeno, urged people to avoid desires and disappointments by accepting calmly whatever life brought. Stoics preached high moral standards, such as the idea of protecting the rights of fellow humans. They taught that all people, including women and slaves, though unequal in society, were morally equal because all had the power of reason. Stoicism later influenced many Roman and Christian thinkers.

Advances in Math and Astronomy During the Hellenistic age, scholars built on earlier Greek, Babylonian, and Egyptian knowledge. In

Vocabulary Builder
elaborate—(ee LAB uh rit) *adj.* developed in great detail; highly ornamented

The methods ancient Greek doctors used to diagnose disease are so unlike those of today that scholars find many ancient Greek medical writings difficult to decipher. However, the ancient Greek code of ethics—the Hippocratic oath—is still used by medical professionals today.

Primary Source

❝I will use my power to help the sick to the best of my ability and judgment; I will abstain from harming or wronging any man by it. . . .

Whatever I see or hear, professionally, or privately, which ought not to be divulged, I will keep secret . . .

If, therefore, I observe this oath and do not violate it, may I prosper both in my life and in my profession, earning good repute among all men for all time.❞

Why do you think the Hippocratic oath has continued through the centuries as a guide to doctors?

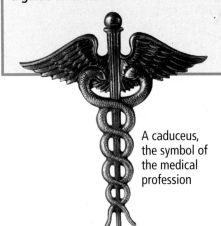

A caduceus, the symbol of the medical profession

mathematics, **Pythagoras** (pih THAG uh rus) derived a formula to calculate the relationship between the sides of a right triangle. Euclid (YOO klid) wrote *The Elements,* a textbook that became the basis for modern geometry.

Using mathematics and careful observation, the astronomer Aristarchus (a ris TAHR kus) argued that the Earth rotated on its axis and orbited the sun. This theory of a **heliocentric,** or sun-centered, solar system was not accepted by most scientists until almost 2,000 years later. Another Hellenistic astronomer, Eratosthenes, (eh ruh TAHS thuh neez), showed that the Earth was round and accurately calculated its circumference.

The most famous Hellenistic scientist, **Archimedes** (ahr kuh MEE deez), applied principles of physics to make practical inventions. He mastered the use of the lever and pulley and boasted, "Give me a lever long enough and a place to stand on, and I will move the world." Then, to demonstrate the power of his invention, Archimedes used it to draw a ship over the land before a crowd of awed spectators.

Improving Medical Practice About 400 B.C., the Greek physician **Hippocrates** (hih PAH kruh teez) studied the causes of illnesses and looked for cures. The Hippocratic oath attributed to him set ethical standards for doctors. Greek physicians swore to "help the sick according to my ability and judgment but never with a view to injury and wrong." Doctors today still take a similar oath.

 Checkpoint In what fields did Hellenistic civilization make advancements?

Looking Ahead

With its conquest of Asia Minor in 133 B.C., Rome replaced Greece as the dominant power in the Mediterranean world. However, the Greek legacy remains. Greek works in the arts and sciences set a standard for later people of Europe. Greek ideas about law, freedom, justice, and government continue to influence political thinking to the present day. These achievements were especially remarkable because they were produced by a scattering of tiny city-states whose rivalries left them too weak to defend themselves from conquest. Later, you will learn how the Greek legacy influenced the civilizations of Rome and of Western Europe.

SECTION **5** Assessment

Progress Monitoring Online
For: Self-quiz with vocabulary practice
Web Code: naa-0451

Terms, People, and Places

1. For each term, person, or place listed at the beginning of the section, write a sentence explaining its significance.

Note Taking

2. **Reading Skill: Identify Supporting Details** Use your completed outline to answer the Focus Question: How did Alexander the Great expand his empire and spread Greek culture throughout the realm?

Comprehension and Critical Thinking

3. **Summarize** What was the extent of Alexander's vast empire and how did he acquire it?

4. **Synthesize Information** How did Alexander's conquests lead to a new civilization?

5. **Recognize Ideologies** What new ideas did the Stoics introduce?

6. **Draw Conclusions** Why do you think the Hippocratic oath is considered a medical advance?

● **Writing About History**

Quick Write: Organize Evidence In organizing a persuasive essay, one should often save the strongest argument for last. For practice, write a concluding paragraph for a persuasive essay from the perspective of a conquered person who either supports or opposes the assimilation of Greek ideas and culture.

Golden Age of Greek Drama

The ancient Greeks loved going to plays. During the golden age of Greek drama—the 400s B.C.—almost every Greek city had an open-air theater. Enthusiastic audiences filled the stone benches to watch comedies and tragedies performed by two or three actors and a chorus. Many of the techniques developed in these Greek theaters have influenced dramatic productions from ancient times though Shakespeare's era to our own day.

◄ The papyrus at left shows the text of Aeschylus's 400s B.C. drama *The Net-Pullers*; the papyrus was probably copied by a scribe about A.D. 200.

▲ In this modern production of Aeschylus's tragedy *The Persians*, the actors wear character masks like the ones Greek actors would have worn.

The actors performed on the **stage** and on the **skene** (skay NAY), a building directly behind the stage. The roof of the skene could represent the heavens.

The audience sat in the **theatron** (THAY ah tran), or "viewing place." The ruins of this Greek theater are in Sicily.

The **orchestra**, or "dancing place," was a round, level place where the chorus performed. There was often an altar in the center.

Thinking Critically

1. **Draw Inferences** How do you think wearing masks affected the way actors showed their characters emotions?
2. **Connect to Today** Which Greek theater terms and techniques are still used today?

143

Quick Study Guide

Progress Monitoring *Online*
For: Self-test with vocabulary practice
Web Code: naa-0461

■ Major Conflicts in Ancient Greece

Conflict	Participants	Reason	Victor
Trojan War	Mycenae and Troy	Economic rivalry	Mycenaeans
Persian War	Greek city-states and Persia	Halt the spread of the Persian empire	Greek city-states
Peloponnesian War	Athens and Sparta (spread to all of Greece)	Resentment of Athenian domination and disagreement on form of government	Sparta and allies

■ Key Political Leaders

Leader	Accomplishments
Solon	Athenian archon who introduced reforms making the government more democratic and the economy more profitable
Pisistratus	Athenian tyrant who gave poor citizens a voice in government and weakened the aristocracy
Cleisthenes	Athenian leader who created the Council of 500 and made the assembly a legislature
Pericles	Athenian statesman who instituted direct democracy in Athens, increased participation in government, provided salaries for government employees, and encouraged the cultural development of Athens
Philip II	Macedonian king who conquered Greece
Alexander the Great	Macedonian leader who conquered an empire stretching from Greece to India and encouraged the spread of Greek culture throughout his empire

■ Important Cultural Figures of Greece

Individual	Achievement
Philosophy	
Socrates	Sought truth and self-knowledge; Socratic method
Plato	Favored the rule of a philosopher-king; wrote *The Republic*
Aristotle	Promoted the idea of the ¡golden mean "; wrote *Politics*
Zeno	Founder of Stoicism
Literature	
Homer	Poet; wrote the *Iliad* and the *Odyssey*
Aeschylus	Tragic playwright; wrote the *Oresteia*
Sophocles	Tragic playwright; wrote *Antigone*
Euripides	Tragic playwright; wrote *The Trojan Women*
Aristophanes	Comic playwright; wrote *Lysistrata*
History	
Herodotus	Historian; encouraged research in histories; wrote *The Persian Wars*
Thucydides	Historian; promoted unbiased writing of histories
Mathematics and Science	
Pythagoras	Developed the formula for the relationship among the sides of a right triangle known as the Pythagorean theorem
Euclid	Developed the basis for modern geometry; wrote *The Elements*
Aristarchus	Theorized that the solar system is heliocentric
Eratosthenes	Determined that the Earth is round and calculated its circumference
Archimedes	Mastered the lever and pulley
Hippocrates	Developed a code of ethics for medical practitioners

■ Key Events in Ancient Greece

1600 B.C.
Minoan civilization at its height

594 B.C.
Solon appointed archon.

460 B.C.
Age of Pericles marks the height of democracy in Athens.

Chapter Events
World Events

1600 B.C. — **600 B.C.** — **500 B.C.**

800 B.C.
Olmec civilization disappearing in present-day Mexico

539 B.C.
Persian empire is founded.

500 B.C.
Nok civilization in West Africa is on the rise.

Concept Connector

Cumulative Review

Record the answers to the questions below on your Concept Connector worksheets. In addition, record information from this chapter about the following concepts:

- Geography's Impact: the Aegean and Mediterranean seas
- Conflict: the Persian War
- Political Systems: Oligarchy

1. **Trade** The culture and economy of ancient Greece were greatly influenced by trade. However, Greece was not the first civilization to be defined by its trade with others. Compare and contrast the system of trade in ancient Greece and Phoenicia. For each group, think about the following:
   - the form of travel used and the routes taken
   - the range of territory reached by each group
   - the building and settlement of towns
   - contact with other groups and cultural diffusion

2. **Science and Technology** Make a chart comparing the advancement in mathematics and science of the ancient Greeks with those of the ancient Indian and Chinese civilizations. Summarize how these advances still affect us today. Think about the following:
   - the factors that contribute to the development of major advances in science and mathematics
   - the exchange of theories and knowledge
   - the impact of scientific advances on our own times

3. **Cultural Diffusion** As you have read, the Phoenician alphabet was borrowed and modified by the Greeks. That alphabet was then borrowed and adapted by the Romans. This evolution of the alphabet led to the version we use today. How do you think the alphabet spread among these cultures? Why do you think this alphabet more than any other form of ancient writing is still used in most Western cultures today?

Connections To Today

1. **Cooperation: Alliances of the 21st Century** Throughout history, nations have joined together to form alliances like the Delian League in Greece. Conduct research on one of the following organizations: the League of Nations, the European Union, the North Atlantic Treaty Organization, the United Nations, the African Union, the Association of Southeast Asian Nations, the Organization for Economic Cooperation and Development, or the League of Arab States. Then write a summary about it. Be sure to include the original reason for the creation of the group, the year it was created, the organization's main purpose or goals, and the number and names of the member nations.

2. **Culture: Architecture** The style of architecture developed by the ancient Greeks has influenced architecture for over 2,000 years. During the Renaissance, the Greek style, called the "classical" style, was revived and was perceived as the perfect form of architecture. The style is still frequently used today. Recently, the Ronald Reagan Building (below) in Washington, D.C., was built in this style. Conduct research to identify three additional buildings that have been influenced by the classical Greek style. Create a poster with images of the buildings, include a brief description of its location and purpose, and explain why you think the classical Greek style of architecture was used.

431 B.C. Peloponnesian War begins.	331 B.C. Alexander the Great conquers the Persian empire.	323 B.C. The Hellenistic Age begins.	133 B.C. Dominance in the Mediterranean passes from Greece to Rome.

400 B.C.   **300 B.C.**   **200 B.C.**

450 B.C. Roman Republic publishes its legal code.	321 B.C. The Maurya dynasty begins in India.	221 B.C. Shi Huangdi unites China.

History Interactive
For: Interactive timeline
Web Code: nap-0461

Chapter Assessment

Terms, People, and Places

Complete each sentence by choosing the correct answer from the list of terms below. You will not use all of the terms listed.

fresco	rhetoric
aristocracy	Aristotle
tyrant	tragedy
alliance	logic
direct democracy	Plato
Pericles	strait

1. A system of government in which a large number of citizens take part in the day-to-day affairs is called a(n) _____.
2. _____ set up the Lyceum, a school for the study of all branches of knowledge.
3. The art of skillful speaking is known as _____.
4. _____ believed that all men should take part in government regardless of wealth or class.
5. A play that tells a story of human suffering is known as a(n) _____.
6. A(n) _____ is a watercolor painting done on wet plaster.
7. A government ruled by a hereditary landholding elite is known as a(n) _____.
8. In ancient Greece, someone who gained power by force was known as a(n) _____.

Main Ideas

Section 1 (pp. 114–117)

9. How did trade affect the development of early Greek civilizations?

Section 2 (pp. 118–123)

10. How did the systems of government and education differ between Athens and Sparta?

Section 3 (pp. 124–129)

11. What were the results of the Persian Wars?
12. How did the leadership of Pericles affect the government and culture of Athens?

Section 4 (pp. 130–136)

13. Why were some of the ideas of ancient Greek philosophers considered a threat to Greek society and tradition?
14. What was the design objective of the art and architecture of ancient Greece?

Section 5 (pp. 137–143)

15. What was the extent of Alexander's empire, and why was he able to conquer such an extended area?
16. What were some of the cultural achievements of the Hellenistic period?

Chapter Focus Question

17. What enduring traditions and institutions did Greek culture extend to most of the Western world?

Critical Thinking

18. **Geography and History** What role did the Mediterranean and Aegean seas play in the development of the culture of ancient Greece?
19. **Recognize Cause and Effect** Identify two immediate and two long-term causes of the Peloponnesian War. Why might it be said that all Greeks lost the Peloponnesian War?
20. **Make Comparisons** How was the form of government outlined in Plato's *Republic* similar to and different from the government of Sparta?
21. **Draw Inferences** How did Athenian culture stress the importance of the individual?
22. **Recognize Ideologies** Why do you think many Greeks condemned the ideas of the Sophists?
23. **Draw Conclusions** Would you agree that Alexander deserved to be called "the Great"? Why or why not?

● **Writing About History**

Writing a Persuasive Essay The cultures of ancient Athens and Sparta were quite different from each other. Their rivalry frequently led to conflict between the two city-states. Although they joined forces to defeat the Persians, their differences eventually led to the Peloponnesian War. Write a persuasive essay from the point of view of an Athenian statesmen in which you try to prevent war by persuading the Spartan leadership of the benefits of direct democracy. Consult page SH16 of the Writing Handbook for additional help.

Prewriting
- Make a list of what you believe to be the strongest arguments of the Athenian statesman.
- Organize the arguments on your list from weakest to strongest.

Drafting
- Write a thesis statement clearly stating the position that you will prove.
- Sequence your arguments so that you open or close with your strongest argument.
- Write a conclusion that restates your thesis and closes with a strong argument.

Revising
- Review your arguments to make sure that you have explained them logically and clearly.
- Use the guidelines for revising your essay on page SH17 of the Writing Handbook.

Document-Based Assessment

Politics and Philosophy in Ancient Greece

Philosophy flourished under Athenian democracy. In their search for the best form of government, the best leaders, and the perfect society, Greek philosophers created works that have influenced thinkers for ages. These "lovers of wisdom" used reason to guide their quest for truth, as the documents below show.

Document A

"[Justice] is not a matter of external behavior, but of the inward self and of attending to all that is, in the fullest sense, a man's proper concern. The just man does not allow the several elements in his soul to usurp one another's functions; he is indeed one who sets his house in order, by self-mastery and discipline coming to be at peace with himself, and bringing into tune those . . . parts. . . . Only when he has linked these parts together in well-tempered harmony . . . will he be ready to go about whatever he may have to do, whether it be making money . . . or business transactions, or the affairs of state. In all these fields when he speaks of just and honorable conduct, he will mean the behavior that helps to produce and to preserve this habit of mind; and by wisdom he will mean the knowledge which presides over such conduct. Any action which tends to break down this habit will be for him unjust: and the notions governing it he will call ignorance and folly.

That is perfectly true, Socrates.

Good, said I. I believe we should not be thought altogether mistaken, if we claimed to have discovered the just man and the just state, and wherein their justice consists."

—Plato's ***Republic***, quoting Socrates

Document B

"The legislator should always include the middle class in his government; if he makes laws oligarchical, to the middle class let him look; if he makes them democratical, he should equally by his laws try to attach this class to the state. There only can the government ever be stable where the middle class exceeds one or both of the others, and in that case there will be no fear that the rich will unite with the poor against the rulers. . . . There comes a time when out of a false good there arises a true evil, since the encroachments of the rich are more destructive to the constitution than those of the people."

—***Politics,*** Aristotle

▲ Plato and Aristotle in a detail from the sixteenth century "School of Athens" fresco by Raphael

Document C

"[F]or the truth is that you can have a well-governed society only if you can discover for your future rulers a better way of life than being in office; then only will power be in the hands of men who are rich, not in gold, but in the wealth that brings happiness, a good and wise life. All goes wrong when, starved for lack of anything good in their own lives, men turn to public affairs hoping to snatch from thence the happiness they hunger for. They set about fighting for power and this internecine [mutually destructive] conflict ruins them and their country. The life of true philosophy is the only one that looks down upon offices of state; and access to power must be confined to men who are not in love with it."

—***Republic,*** Plato

Analyzing Documents

Use your knowledge of Greek philosophy and Documents A, B, and C to answer the questions below.

1. According to Socrates (Document A), a just state depends on
   A scientific truth and reason.
   B the harmony and discipline of the individual.
   C the stability of the elected government.
   D wisdom, education, and wealth.

2. According to Plato (Document C), which group of people would make the best rulers?
   A artists
   B rich aristocrats
   C philosophers
   D soldiers

3. According to Aristotle (Document B), why is the middle class necessary for a stable government?
   A to give rich people allies
   B to offer hope to poor people
   C to contribute a reasonable tax base
   D to balance the rich and the poor

4. **Writing Task** Greek philosophers held a deep interest in politics. What does this reflect about Greek society? Base your response on these documents and information provided in the chapter.

147

5 Ancient Rome and the Rise of Christianity

509 B.C.–A.D. 476

The Glory That Would Be Rome

Of the many accomplished artists and writers who lived in ancient Rome, the poet Virgil may be most beloved. His epic poem, the *Aeneid,* describes the history of Rome from the city's founding through the establishment of one of the world's great empires.

> ❝Come, I shall tell of the glory to come . . .
> My son, noble Rome shall equal her power with earth,
> Her might with Olympus [home of the Greek gods],
> . . . Now turn your eyes this way to see . . . This man,
> This is he whom again and again you have heard in the promise
> Of prophecy, Caesar Augustus [first Roman emperor], son of a god.
> He shall found once again an era of gold in the land
> Of Latium [the land surrounding Rome] . . .❞

Listen to the Witness History audio to hear more of the *Aeneid.*

◀ Roman artists are famous for colorful wall paintings like this one that features the lives of everyday Romans.

Roman dictator Julius Caesar

Roman chariot racers

Chapter Preview

Chapter Focus Question How did Rome grow from a single city to a huge, diverse empire?

Roman emperor Constantine

Note Taking Study Guide *Online*
For: Note Taking and Concept Connector worksheets
Web Code: nad-0501

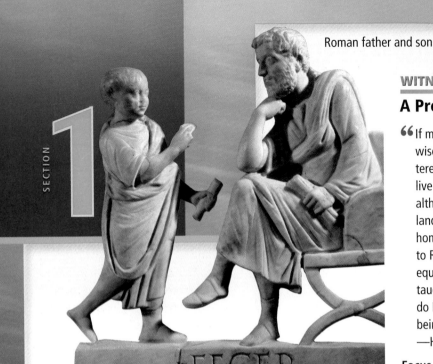

Roman father and son

WITNESS HISTORY 🔊 AUDIO

A Proud Son Speaks of His Father

❝ If my character is flawed by a few minor faults, but is otherwise decent and moral, if you can point out only a few scattered blemishes on an otherwise immaculate surface, . . . if I live a virtuous life, . . . my father deserves all the credit. For although he was a poor man, with only an infertile plot of land, he was not content to send me to [the school in his home town]. . . . My father had the courage to take his boy to Rome, to have him taught the same skills which any equestrian [rider of horses] or senator would have his sons taught. . . . I could never be ashamed of such a father, nor do I feel any need, as many people do, to apologize for being a freedman's [former slave's] son. ❞
—Horace, Roman poet

Focus Question What values formed the basis of Roman society and government?

The Roman World Takes Shape

Objectives
- Describe the physical and cultural settings in which Roman civilization arose.
- Outline how the Roman republic was structured and governed.
- Understand the rights and religious practices that characterized Roman society.
- Explain how the Roman republic grew and maintained its conquests.

Terms, People, and Places

Etruscans	plebeian
republic	tribune
patrician	veto
consul	legion
dictator	

Note Taking

Reading Skill: Identify Causes and Effects For each red heading, fill in a cause-and-effect chart like the one below to identify the cause(s) and the effect(s) of an important event that you read about.

Rome began as a small city in Italy and became a ruler of the Mediterranean and beyond. The story of the Romans and how they built a world empire begins with the land in which they lived.

Roman Civilization Arises in Italy

The Italian peninsula is centrally located in the Mediterranean Sea, and the city of Rome sits toward the center of Italy. This location would benefit the Romans as they expanded—first within Italy and then into the lands bordering the Mediterranean.

Unifying the Lands of Italy Because of its geography, Italy proved much easier to unify than Greece. Unlike Greece, Italy is not broken up into small, isolated valleys. In addition, the Apennine Mountains, which run down the length of the Italian peninsula, are less rugged than the mountains of Greece. Finally, Italy has broad, fertile plains in the north and the west. These plains supported the growing population.

Early Peoples Settle Italy By about 800 B.C., the ancestors of the Romans, called the Latins, migrated into Italy. The Latins settled along the Tiber River in small villages scattered over seven low-lying hills. There, they herded and farmed. Their villages would in time grow together into Rome, the city on seven hills. Legend held that twin brothers, Romulus and Remus, had founded the city. Romans regarded this tale highly because the twins were said to be sons of a Latin woman and the war god Mars, lending the Romans a divine origin.

ALPS
Po River
45° N
Genoa
Rubicon River
Arno River
APENNINE MTS.
Adriatic Sea
Corsica
Alalia
Rome
Sardinia
40° N
Tyrrhenian Sea
20° E
Mediterranean Sea
10° E
Ionian Sea
Sicily
Syracuse
Conic Projection
0   50   100 mi
0   50 100 km
Carthage
AFRICA
35° N

■	Carthaginians
■	Etruscans
■	Greeks
■	Italic-speaking peoples

15° E

Map Skills At the time the state of Rome was founded, the Romans' many neighbors on the Italian peninsula included other speakers of Italic languages such as Latin.

1. **Locate** (a) Rome (b) Apennine Mountains (c) Mediterranean Sea (d) Carthage (e) Tiber River
2. **Region** Based on this map, which group would you think most influenced the Romans? Explain.
3. **Make Generalizations** What do you think are some advantages and disadvantages of living near a variety of different peoples?

The Roman god Jupiter, whose traits resembled those of Tinia, an important Etruscan god

The Romans shared the Italian peninsula with other peoples. Among them were Greek colonists whose city-states dotted southern Italy and the **Etruscans,** who lived mostly north of Rome. The origins of the Etruscan civilization are uncertain. One theory says they migrated from Asia Minor, while another suggests they came from the Alps. What is certain is that, for a time, the Etruscans ruled much of central Italy, including Rome itself.

The Romans learned much from Etruscan civilization. They adapted the alphabet that the Etruscans had earlier acquired from the Greeks. The Romans also learned from the Etruscans to use the arch in construction, and they adapted Etruscan engineering techniques to drain the marshy lands along the Tiber. As well, the Romans adopted some Etruscan gods and goddesses and merged them with Roman deities.

✔ **Checkpoint** How did geography influence the origins and expansion of Rome?

The Romans Establish a Republic

The Romans drove out their Etruscan ruler in 509 B.C. This date is traditionally considered to mark the founding of the Roman state, which would last for 500 years. The Romans established their state with a form of government called in Latin a *res publica,* or "that which belongs to the people." In this form of government, which today we call a **republic,** the people chose some of the officials. A republic, Romans thought, would prevent any individual from gaining too much power.

INFOGRAPHIC
THE ROMAN *CURSUS HONORUM*

In 180 B.C., the Romans enacted a law that formalized the career path of Roman officials. Called the *cursus honorum*, this path dictated that men hold particular offices in a certain order and assigned age requirements to these offices. Previously, Roman men could fill the offices in any order and do so at any age, as long as they had already completed a period of military service. The *cursus honorum* became the foundation of a Roman political system in which politicians advanced based on merit and experience rather than popularity, influence, or class.

Censor (2)
- Patricians only originally; as of 339 B.C., one had to be plebeian; must have held consulship first
- Maintained the official list of Roman citizens; held much authority
- No minimum age

Consul (2)
- Patricians only originally; as of 367 B.C., one had to be plebeian; must have held praetorship first
- Served as joint head of state; could veto other consul
- Minimum age of 42 for plebeians and 40 for patricians

Praetor (8 by 100 B.C.)
- Patricians only originally; as of 337 B.C., plebeians eligible; must have held quaestorship first
- Served as legal officers with broad authority in government; stood in for consuls when they were away
- Minimum age set at 39

Tribune of the Plebs (10)
- Plebeians only; usually held quaestorship first
- Presided over plebeian assembly and advocated for plebeian demands
- No minimum age

Aedile (4 by 366 B.C.)
- Plebeians only originally; as of 366 B.C., 2 new offices open to plebeians and patricians; must have held quaestorship first
- Oversaw care of the city, distribution of grain, public games
- Minimum age 36

Quaestor (20 by 82 B.C.)
- Patricians only originally; as of 421 B.C., plebeians eligible
- Oversaw finances in treasury and military
- Minimum age set at 30 in 82 B.C.

Thinking Critically
1. **Draw Conclusions** Why do you think at least one of the censors had to be a plebeian?
2. **Predict Consequences** In what ways might the *cursus honorum* have changed politics in Rome?

Structuring the Republic
In the early republic, the most powerful governing body was the senate. Originally, its 300 members were all **patricians,** or members of the landholding upper class. Senators, who served for life, strongly influenced the republic's laws.

Each year, the senators nominated two **consuls** from the patrician class. Their job was to supervise the business of government and command the armies. Consuls, however, could serve only one term. They were also expected to approve each other's decisions. By limiting their time in office and making them responsible to each other, Rome had a system of checks on the power of government.

In the event of war, the senate might choose a **dictator,** or ruler who has complete control over a government. Each Roman dictator was granted power to rule for six months. After that time, he had to give up power. Romans particularly admired Cincinnatus as a model dictator. Cincinnatus organized an army, led the Romans to victory over the attacking enemy, attended victory celebrations, and returned to his farmlands—all within 15 days.

Plebeians Fight for Their Rights
At first, all government officials were patricians. **Plebeians** (plih BEE unz), the farmers, merchants, artisans, and traders who made up the bulk of the population, had little influence. The efforts of the plebeians to gain power shaped politics in the early republic.

In time, the plebeians gained the right to elect their own officials, called **tribunes,** to protect their interests. The tribunes could **veto,** or block, those laws that they felt were harmful to plebeians. Little by little, plebeians forced the senate to choose plebeians as consuls, appoint plebeians to other high offices, and finally to open the senate itself to plebeians.

Another breakthrough for the plebeians came in 450 B.C., when the government oversaw the inscription of the laws of Rome on 12 tablets, which were set up in the Forum, Rome's marketplace. Plebeians had protested that citizens could not know what the laws were because they were not written down. The Laws of the Twelve Tables made it possible for the first time for plebeians to appeal a judgment handed down by a patrician judge.

Romans Leave a Lasting Legacy Although the senate still <u>dominated</u> the government, the common people had gained access to power and won safeguards for their rights without having to resort to war or revolution. More than 2,000 years later, the framers of the United States Constitution would adapt such Roman ideas as the senate, the veto, and checks on political power.

✓ **Checkpoint**   How did the membership of the senate change over time?

Vocabulary Builder
<u>dominated</u>—(DAHM uh nayt id) *vt.* had authority over

Characterizing Roman Society

The family was the basic unit of Roman society. Under Roman law, the male head of the household—usually the father—had absolute power in the family. He enforced strict discipline and demanded total respect for his authority. His wife was subject to his authority and was not allowed to administer her own affairs. The ideal Roman woman was loving, dutiful, dignified, and strong.

The Role of Women Changes Over Time Roman women played a larger role in society than did Greek women. They could own property, and, in later Roman times, women from all classes ran a variety of businesses, from small shops to major shipyards. Those who made their fortunes earned respect by supporting the arts or paying for public festivals. However, most women worked at home, raising their families, spinning, and weaving.

Over the centuries, Roman women gained greater freedom and influence. Patrician women went to the public baths, dined out, and attended the theater or other forms of public entertainment with their husbands. Some women, such as Livia and Agrippina the Younger, had highly visible public roles and exercised significant political influence.

Romans Educate all Children Both girls and boys from the upper and lower classes learned to read and write. By the later years of the republic, many wealthy Romans would hire private tutors, often Greeks, to supervise the education of their children. Under their guidance, children memorized major events and developments in Roman history. Rhetoric was an important subject for boys who wanted to pursue political careers.

Roman Religious Practices The Romans believed in numerous gods and goddesses, many of whom they adapted from Greek religion. Like the Greek god Zeus, the Roman god Jupiter ruled over the sky and the other gods. His wife Juno, like the Greek goddess Hera, protected marriage. Romans also prayed to Neptune, god of the sea, whose powers were the same as those of the Greek god Poseidon. On the battlefield, they turned to Mars, the god of war.

The Roman calendar was full of feasts and other celebrations to honor the gods and goddesses and to ensure divine favor for the city. As loyal citizens, most Romans joined in these festivals, which inspired a sense of community. Throughout Rome, dozens of temples housed statues of the gods. In front of these temples, Romans took part in ritual activities such as worshipping the gods and asking for divine assistance.

✓ **Checkpoint**   What social rights did Roman women have?

The Roman Republic Grows

As Rome's political and social systems evolved at home, its armies expanded Roman power across Italy. Roman armies conquered first the Etruscans and then the Greek city-states in the south. By about 270 B.C., Rome controlled most of the Italian peninsula.

Citizen-Soldiers Make Up the Roman Army Rome's success was due to skillful diplomacy and to its loyal, well-trained army. The basic military unit was the **legion,** each of which included about 5,000 men. As in Greece, Roman armies consisted of citizen-soldiers who originally fought without being paid and had to supply their own weapons. Eventually, they received a small stipend, or payment, but their main compensation was always a share of the spoils of victory. Roman citizens often made good soldiers because they were brought up to value loyalty, courage, and respect for authority.

To ensure success, Roman commanders mixed rewards with harsh punishment. Young soldiers who showed courage in action won praise and gifts. If a unit fled from battle, however, one out of every ten men from the disgraced unit was put to death.

Rome Is Just With Conquered Lands Rome generally treated its defeated enemies with justice. Conquered peoples had to acknowledge Roman leadership, pay taxes, and supply soldiers for the Roman army. In return, Rome let them keep their own customs, money, and local government.

To a few privileged groups among the conquered people, Rome gave the highly prized right of full citizenship. Others became partial citizens, who were allowed to marry Romans and carry on trade in Rome. As a result of such generous policies, most conquered lands remained loyal to Rome even in troubled times.

Maintaining the State To protect its conquests, Rome posted soldiers throughout the land. It also built a network of all-weather military roads to link distant territories to Rome. As trade and travel increased, local peoples incorporated Latin into their languages and adopted many Roman customs and beliefs. Slowly, Italy began to unite under Roman rule.

✓ **Checkpoint** How did the Romans treat the people they conquered?

During the time of the late republic, praetorians (above), or bodyguards, began protecting army generals. Later, they would become an elite guard for Roman emperors.

SECTION 1 Assessment

Progress Monitoring *Online*
For: Self-quiz with vocabulary practice
Web Code: naa-0511

Terms, People, and Places

1. What do many of the key terms listed at the beginning of the section have in common? Explain.

Note Taking

2. **Reading Skill: Identify Causes and Effects** Use your completed cause-and-effect chart to answer the Focus Question: What values formed the basis of Roman society and government?

Comprehension and Critical Thinking

3. **Summarize** Describe the cultural setting in which Rome developed.

4. **Identify Central Issues** In both Roman politics and Roman society, equality was prized. Describe an example of Romans achieving political or social equality.

5. **Recognize Cause and Effect** What were two reasons for Rome's success in expanding its power across Italy?

● **Writing About History**

Quick Write: Take Notes for Comparison Take notes on the government of the Roman republic, including details about its structure and functions. Then make a list of other governments in history to which you could compare the Roman republic.

Golden bracelet of
a wealthy Roman

Roman laborers hard at
work crushing grapes

WITNESS HISTORY ◀)) AUDIO

A Plea for Reform

While the republic grew in size, everyone did not benefit
from the new wealth. Addressing a group of plebeians, the
Roman tribune Tiberius Gracchus described an injustice he
saw in Roman society:

66 The wild beasts that roam over Italy . . . have every one of
them a cave or lair to lurk in; but the men who fight and
die for Italy enjoy the common air and light, indeed, but
nothing else; . . . they fight and die to support others in
wealth and luxury, and though they are styled [referred to
as] masters of the world, they have not a single clod of
earth that is their own.99
—*Plutarch's Lives*

Focus Question What factors led to the decline of the
Roman republic and the rise of the Roman empire?

From Republic to Empire

Objectives
- Understand how the Roman republic grew
  through a series of conquests.
- Identify the events leading to the decline of the
  Roman republic.
- Describe the nature of the new age that dawned
  with the Roman empire.

Terms, People, and Places

imperialism	Julius Caesar
latifundia	Augustus
Tiberius Gracchus	census
Gaius Gracchus	Hadrian

Note Taking

Reading Skill: Recognize Multiple Causes As
you read, fill in a chart like the one below with
factors that led to the decline of the Roman
republic and the rise of the Roman empire.

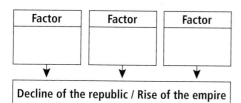

Factor	Factor	Factor

↓ ↓ ↓

Decline of the republic / Rise of the empire

After gaining control of the Italian peninsula, Rome began to build
an empire around the Mediterranean Sea. This expansion created
conflicts in Roman society that weakened and finally crushed the
republic. Out of the rubble, however, rose the Roman empire and a
new chapter in Rome's long history.

Rome Grows Through Conquest

Rome's conquest of the Italian peninsula brought it into contact
with Carthage, a city-state on the northern coast of Africa. Settled
by North Africans and Phoenician traders, Carthage ruled over an
empire that stretched across North Africa and the western Mediterranean, including parts of Spain. As Rome expanded westward,
conflict between these two powers became inevitable.

Rome Fights Carthage in the Punic Wars Between 264 B.C.
and 146 B.C., Rome fought three wars against Carthage. They are
called the Punic Wars, from *Punicus*, the Latin word for Phoenician. In the First Punic War, Rome defeated Carthage and won the
islands of Sicily, Corsica, and Sardinia.

The Carthaginians sought revenge in the Second Punic War. In
218 B.C., the Carthaginian general Hannibal led his army, including dozens of war elephants, on an epic march across the Pyrenees,
through France, and over the Alps into Italy. The trek cost Hannibal one third of his army. But with it he surprised the Romans,
who had expected an invasion from the south. For 15 years, Hannibal and his army moved across Italy, winning battle after battle.

Geography *Interactive*
For: Audio guided tour
Web Code: nap-0521

Map Legend:
- 500 B.C.
- to 264 B.C.
- to 146 B.C.
- to 44 B.C.
- Territory gained from Carthage
- → Hannibal's invasion route

Conic Projection
0   200   400 mi
0   200   400 km

Map Skills Although Hannibal (below) posed a challenge, the Roman republic gradually gained control of lands around the Mediterranean Sea through conquest and diplomacy.

1. **Locate** (a) Spain (b) Gaul (c) Asia Minor (d) Macedonia (e) Pyrenees Mountains
2. **Region** During what period did Asia Minor come under Roman control?
3. **Synthesize Information** What does this map tell you about the outcome of the Punic Wars with Carthage, which lasted from 264 B.C. to 146 B.C.?

The Carthaginians failed to capture Rome itself, however. In the end, the Romans outflanked Hannibal by sending an army to attack Carthage. Hannibal returned to defend his homeland, where the Romans defeated him at last. Carthage gave up all its lands outside of Africa. Nevertheless, many Romans still saw Carthage as a rival and wanted revenge for the terrible destruction that Hannibal's army had brought to Italy. For years, the senator Cato ended every speech he made with the words "Carthage must be destroyed."

Finally, in the Third Punic War, Rome completely destroyed Carthage. Survivors were killed or sold into slavery. The Romans poured salt over the earth so that nothing would grow there again. The Romans were now masters of the western Mediterranean.

Ruling the Mediterranean "The Carthaginians fought for their own preservation and the sovereignty of Africa," observed a Greek witness to the fall of Carthage; "the Romans, for supremacy and world domination." The Romans were committed to a policy of **imperialism,** or establishing control over foreign lands and peoples. While Rome fought Carthage in the west, it was also expanding into the eastern Mediterranean. There, Romans confronted the Hellenistic rulers who had divided up the empire of Alexander the Great.

Sometimes to defend Roman interests, sometimes simply for plunder, Rome launched a series of wars in the area. One by one, Macedonia, Greece, and parts of Asia Minor surrendered and became Roman provinces. Other regions, such as Egypt, allied with Rome. By 133 B.C., Roman power extended from Spain to Egypt. Truly, the Romans were justified in calling the Mediterranean *Mare Nostrum*, or "Our Sea."

The Impact at Home Conquests and control of busy trade routes brought incredible riches into Rome. Generals, officials, and traders amassed fortunes from loot, taxes, and commerce. A new class of wealthy Romans emerged. They built lavish mansions and filled them with luxuries imported from the east. Wealthy families bought up huge estates, called latifundia. As the Romans conquered more and more lands, they forced people captured in war to work as slaves on the latifundia.

The widespread use of slave labor hurt small farmers, who were unable to produce food as cheaply as the latifundia could. The farmers' problems were compounded when huge quantities of grain pouring in from the conquered lands drove down grain prices. Many farmers fell into debt and had to sell their land.

In despair, landless farmers flocked to Rome and other cities looking for jobs. There, they joined an already restless class of unemployed people. As the gap between rich and poor widened, angry mobs began to riot. In addition, the new wealth led to increased corruption. Greed and self-interest replaced virtues such as simplicity, hard work, and devotion to duty, which had been so prized in the time of the early republic.

Making Attempts at Reforms Two young plebeians, brothers named Tiberius and Gaius Gracchus (GAY us GRAK us), were among the first to attempt reform. Tiberius, elected a tribune in 133 B.C., called on the state to distribute land to poor farmers. Gaius, elected a tribune ten years later, sought a wider range of reforms, including the use of public funds to buy grain to feed the poor. The reforms of the Gracchus brothers angered the senate, which saw them as a threat to its power. The brothers and thousands of their followers were killed in waves of street violence set off by senators and their hired thugs.

✔ **Checkpoint** What challenges did Rome face while building an empire around the Mediterranean Sea?

Slavery in Ancient Rome
Rome relied heavily on the labor of slaves, especially for public works projects and agriculture. Many people, like the two here wearing chains (above), were enslaved after being taken captive in combat. For identification, slaves often had to wear a collar (inset) with the master's name and address inscribed on it.

The Roman Republic Declines

Unable to resolve its problems peacefully, Rome plunged into a series of civil wars. At issue was who should hold power—the senate, which wanted to govern as it had in the past, or popular political leaders, who wanted to weaken the senate and enact reforms.

The turmoil sparked slave uprisings at home and revolts among Rome's allies. Meanwhile, the old legions of Roman citizen-soldiers became professional armies whose first loyalty was to their commanders. This often

BIOGRAPHY

Julius Caesar

The bold rise to power of Julius Caesar (100 B.C. [?]–44 B.C.) echoed his boldness on the battlefield (at left). His brilliant conquest of Gaul made him enormously popular. Romans were thrilled by reports of his many victories, which added great riches and huge territories to the empire. In nine years of campaigning, Caesar lost only two battles. His tactics in Gaul are still studied at military academies today.

When Caesar, in defiance of Pompey's orders, crossed the Rubicon River from Gaul back into Italy, he said, "iacta alea est," or "the die is cast," meaning there was no turning back. Today, people use the phrase "crossing the Rubicon" to mean making a decision from which there is no turning back. Painters and writers such as William Shakespeare have also immortalized Caesar in their works. **In what different ways did Caesar leave a lasting impact on the world?**

happened because commanders provided them with more benefits—such as parcels of captured land—than the state did. Once rival commanders had their own armies, they could march into Rome to advance their ambitions.

Julius Caesar the Dictator Out of this chaos emerged Julius Caesar, an ambitious military commander. For a time, Caesar and another brilliant general, Pompey, dominated Roman politics.

In 58 B.C., Caesar set out with his army to make new conquests. After nine years of fighting, he completed the conquest of Gaul—the area that is now France and Belgium. Fearful of Caesar's rising fame, Pompey persuaded the senate to order Caesar to disband his army and return to Rome. Caesar defied the order. Swiftly and secretly, he led his army across the Rubicon River into northern Italy and headed toward Rome. Once again, civil war erupted across the Roman world.

Caesar crushed Pompey and his supporters. He then swept around the Mediterranean, suppressing rebellions. "Veni, vidi, vici"—"I came, I saw, I conquered"—he announced after one victory. Later, returning to Rome, he forced the senate to make him dictator. Although he maintained the senate and other features of the republic, he was in fact the absolute ruler of Rome.

Caesar Makes Reforms Between 48 B.C. and 44 B.C., Caesar pushed through a number of reforms intended to deal with Rome's many problems. He launched a program of public works to employ the jobless and gave public land to the poor. He also reorganized the government of the provinces and granted Roman citizenship to more people. Caesar's most lasting reform was the introduction of a new calendar based on that of the Egyptians. The Roman calendar, later named the Julian calendar, was used in western Europe for more than 1,600 years. With minor changes, it is still our calendar today.

Caesar Killed, War Follows Caesar's enemies worried that he planned to make himself king of Rome. To save the republic, they plotted against him. In March of 44 B.C., as Caesar arrived in the senate, his enemies stabbed him to death.

The death of Julius Caesar plunged Rome into a new round of civil wars. Mark Antony, Caesar's chief general, and Octavian, Caesar's grandnephew,

Vocabulary Builder

suppressing—(suh PRES ing) *vt.* using force to put an end to something joined forces to hunt down the murderers. The two men soon quarreled, however, setting off a bitter struggle for power. In 31 B.C., Octavian finally defeated Antony and his powerful ally, Queen Cleopatra of Egypt.

 Checkpoint What central issue sparked the warfare that eventually led to the decline of Rome?

The Age of the Roman Empire Dawns

The senate gave the triumphant Octavian the title of **Augustus,** or Exalted One, and declared him princeps, or first citizen. Although he was careful not to call himself king, a title that Romans had hated since Etruscan times, Augustus exercised absolute power and named his successor, just as a king would do.

Under Augustus, who ruled until A.D. 14, the 500-year-old republic came to an end. Romans did not know it at the time, but a new age had dawned—the age of the Roman empire.

Augustus Builds a Stable Government Through firm but moderate policies, Augustus laid the foundation for a stable government. He left the senate in place and created an efficient, well-trained civil service to enforce its laws. High-level jobs were open to men of talent, regardless of their class. In addition, he cemented the allegiance of cities and provinces to Rome by allowing them a large amount of self-government.

Augustus also undertook economic reforms. To make the tax system more fair, he ordered a **census,** or population count, of the empire so there would be records of all who should be taxed. He set up a postal service and issued new coins to make trade easier. He put the jobless to work building roads and temples and sent others to farm the land.

The government that Augustus organized functioned well for 200 years. Still, a serious problem kept arising: Who would rule after an emperor died? Romans did not accept the idea of power passing automatically from father to son. As a result, the death of an emperor often led to intrigue and violence.

Emperors Vary Not all Augustus' successors were great rulers. Some were weak and incompetent. Two early emperors, Caligula and Nero, were considered evil and perhaps insane. Caligula, for example, appointed his favorite horse as consul. Nero viciously persecuted Christians and was even blamed for setting a great fire that destroyed much of Rome.

Between A.D. 96 and A.D. 180, the empire benefited from the rule of a series of "good emperors." **Hadrian,** for example, codified Roman law, making it the same for all provinces. He also had soldiers build a wall across Britain to hold back attackers from the non-Roman north.

Marcus Aurelius, who read philosophy while leading wars, was close to being Plato's ideal of a philosopher-king. His *Meditations* show his commitment to duty: "Hour by hour resolve firmly . . . to do what comes to hand with correct and natural dignity."

Comparing Structures of Government	
Roman Republic	**Roman Empire**
Highest Official(s)	
Two consuls • annually elected • held equal power **Dictator** • appointed in times of emergency • held office for 6 months only	**Emperor** • inherited power • served for life • if served well, was worshipped as a god after death
Governing Bodies	
Senate • issued advisory decrees to magistrates and people • in practice, held enormous power • had about 300 members **Popular Assemblies** • two assemblies: centuriate (military), tribal (nonmilitary) • elected magistrates, held legislative power, made key decisions	**Senate** • issued binding decrees, acted as a high court, elected magistrates • in practice, held little power as compared to the emperor • had about 600 members

Chart Skills Given the differences in these two structures of government, why do you think the senate held less power in the empire than it did in the republic?

WITNESS HISTORY VIDEO

Watch *Rome: The Rise of Empire* on the **Witness History Discovery School**™ video program to learn more about the growth of Rome and the Pax Romana.

The Pax Romana Brings Prosperity The 200-year span that began with Augustus and ended with Marcus Aurelius is known as the period of the *Pax Romana*, or "Roman Peace." During that time, Roman rule brought peace, order, unity, and prosperity to lands stretching from the Euphrates River in the east to Britain in the west, an area roughly equal in size to the continental United States.

During the Pax Romana, Roman legions maintained and protected the roads, and Roman fleets chased pirates from the seas. Trade flowed freely to and from distant lands. Egyptian farmers supplied Romans with grain. From other parts of Africa came ivory and gold, as well as lions and other wild animals to be used for public entertainment. From India came spices, cotton, and precious stones. Trade caravans traveled along the great Silk Road, bringing silk and other goods from China. People, too, moved easily within the Roman empire, spreading ideas and knowledge, especially the advances of the Hellenistic east.

The Distraction of Entertainment Throughout the empire, rich and poor alike loved spectacular forms of entertainment. At the Circus Maximus, Rome's largest racecourse, chariots thundered around an oval course, making dangerously tight turns at either end. Fans bet feverishly on their favorite teams—the Reds, Greens, Blues, or Whites—and successful charioteers were hailed as heroes.

Gladiator contests were even more popular. Many gladiators were slaves who had been trained to fight. In the arena, they battled one another, either singly or in groups. Crowds cheered a skilled gladiator, and a good fighter might even win his freedom. But if a gladiator made a poor showing, sometimes the crowd turned thumbs down, a signal that he should be killed.

During the Pax Romana, the general prosperity hid underlying social and economic problems. To the emperors who paid for them with taxes they collected from the empire, these amusements were a way to pacify the city's restless mobs. In much the same spirit, the government provided free grain to feed the poor. Critics warned against this policy of "bread and circuses," but few listened.

This Roman mosaic shows charioteers ready to race at the Circus Maximus.

✓ **Checkpoint** How did Augustus lay the foundation for stable government in the Roman empire?

SECTION 2 Assessment

Progress Monitoring *Online*
For: Self-quiz with vocabulary practice
Web Code: naa-0521

Terms, People, and Places

1. For each term, person, or place listed at the beginning of the section, write a sentence explaining its significance.

Note Taking

2. **Reading Skill: Recognize Multiple Causes** Use your completed chart to answer the Focus Question: What factors led to the decline of the Roman republic and the rise of the Roman empire?

Comprehension and Critical Thinking

3. **Make Comparisons** Compare the positive and negative results of conquest for Rome. Which do you think had the most impact?

4. **Predict Consequences** Do you think the reforms Caesar enacted would have been enough to maintain the Roman republic, had he not been killed?

5. **Analyze Information** How do you think the founders of the Roman republic would have viewed the government of the Roman empire?

● **Writing About History**

Quick Write: Make a Venn Diagram Use what you have read in this section and the previous one to make a Venn diagram comparing the Roman republic and the Roman empire. Consider different aspects of their structures such as who held the most power and who could take part in government.

Cicero launches an attack in the Senate.

Safety Under the Law

Marcus Tullius Cicero was a philosopher, politician, and passionate defender of law. As the republic declined, he often attacked ambitious men such as Julius Caesar. When Caesar came to power by force, one might have expected Cicero to be in danger. But Caesar forgave Cicero, noting that it was "more glorious to have enlarged the limits of the Roman mind than the boundaries of Roman rule."

Focus Question How did advances in arts, learning, and the law show the Romans' high regard for cultural and political achievements?

The Roman Achievement

Objectives

- Summarize the works of Roman literary figures, historians, and philosophers.
- Describe the art and architecture developed by the Romans.
- Understand how the Romans applied science and mathematics for practical use.
- Explain how Rome's legal codes protected everyone in the empire.

Terms, People, and Places

Virgil	engineering
satirize	aqueduct
mosaic	Ptolemy

Note Taking

Reading Skill: Understand Effects The Romans prized cultural and political achievement. As you read, use a concept web like the one below to list developments that show the effects of achievements like these.

Effects

Through war and conquest, Roman generals carried the achievements of Roman civilization to distant lands. Yet the civilization that developed was not simply Roman. Rather, it blended Greek, Hellenistic, and Roman achievements.

Romans Write Literature, History, and Philosophy

In its early days, Rome absorbed ideas from Greek colonists in southern Italy, and it continued to borrow heavily from Greek culture after it conquered Greece. To the Romans, Greek art, literature, philosophy, and scientific genius represented the height of cultural achievement. Their admiration never wavered, leading the Roman poet Horace to note, "Greece has conquered her rude conqueror."

The Romans adapted Greek and Hellenistic achievements, just as the Greeks had once absorbed ideas from Egypt and the Fertile Crescent. The blending of Greek, Hellenistic, and Roman traditions produced what is known as Greco-Roman civilization. Trade and travel during the Pax Romana helped spread this vital new civilization.

Poets Write With Respect and Humor In the field of literature, the Romans owed a great debt to the Greeks. Many Romans spoke Greek and imitated Greek styles in prose and poetry. Still, the greatest Roman writers used Latin to create their own literature.

In his epic poem the *Aeneid,* **Virgil** tried to show that Rome's past was as heroic as that of Greece. He linked his epic to Homer's work by telling how Aeneas escaped from Troy to found Rome. Virgil wrote the *Aeneid* soon after Augustus came to power. He hoped it would arouse patriotism and help unite Rome after years of civil wars.

Other poets used verse to **satirize,** or make fun of, Roman society. Horace's satires were gentle, using playful wit to attack human folly. Those of Juvenal and Martial were more biting. Martial's poems, for example, were so harsh that he had to use fictitious names to protect himself from retribution.

Historians Tell the Story of Rome Roman historians pursued their own theme—the rise and fall of Roman power. Like the poet Virgil, the historian Livy sought to arouse patriotic feeling and restore traditional Roman virtues by recalling images of Rome's heroic past. In his history of Rome, Livy recounted tales of great heroes such as Horatius and Cincinnatus.

Another historian, Tacitus, wrote bitterly about Augustus and his successors, who, he felt, had destroyed Roman liberty. He admired the simple culture of the Germans who lived on Rome's northern frontier and would later invade the empire.

Romans Adapt Greek Philosophy Romans borrowed much of their philosophy from the Greeks. The Hellenistic philosophy of Stoicism impressed Roman thinkers such as the emperor Marcus Aurelius. Stoics stressed the importance of duty and acceptance of one's fate. They also showed concern for the well-being of all people, an idea that would be reflected in the Christian teachings you will read about in Section 4.

✔ **Checkpoint** How did Roman writers promote patriotism?

Roman Art and Architecture Develops

To a large degree, Roman art and architecture were based on Greek and Etruscan models. However, as with literature, the Romans made adaptations to develop their own style.

Creating Expressive Art Like the Greeks before them, Roman sculptors stressed realism, portraying their subjects with every wart and vein in place. The Romans also broke new ground by focusing on revealing an individual's character. A statue of a soldier, a writer, or an emperor might capture an expression of smugness, discontent, or haughty pride.

Some Roman sculpture, however, was idealistic. For example, sculptors transformed Augustus, who was neither handsome nor imposing, into a symbol of power and leadership.

Romans used works of art to beautify their homes. Examples of these works were preserved in Pompeii, a city buried by the volcanic eruption of Mount Vesuvius in A.D. 79. Artists depicted scenes from Roman literature and daily life in splendid frescoes and mosaics. A **mosaic** is a picture made from chips of colored stone or glass.

Advancing Architecture While the Greeks aimed for simple elegance in architecture, the Romans emphasized grandeur. Immense palaces, temples, and stadiums stood as mighty monuments to Roman power and dignity.

The Romans also improved on existing structural devices such as columns and arches. Utilizing concrete as a building material, they developed the rounded dome as a roof for large spaces. The most famous domed structure is the Pantheon, a temple that honors the many Roman gods. It still stands in Rome today.

✔ **Checkpoint** How did Roman architecture differ from Greek architecture?

In this passage, Livy (shown below) comments on the importance of studying history. In what ways does he say we can learn from history?

Primary Source

❝ . . . in history you have a record of the infinite variety of human experience plainly set out for all to see; and in that record you can find for yourself and your country both examples and warnings: fine things to take as models, base things, rotten through and through, to avoid.❞

—Livy, *The History of Rome*

Vocabulary Builder

<u>utilizing</u>—(YOOT ul lyz ing) *vt.* making use of something

REMNANTS OF ROMAN DAILY LIFE

Many Romans played music at home. This fresco shows a woman playing the cithara, or lyre. ▼

When trying to learn about everyday people in ancient times, scholars often face two challenges. First, time has worn away at the remnants of the past, leaving investigators much less to study than once existed. Second, usually those most able to commission texts or art were the political and social elite; often little remains to shed light on the lives of other classes. In ancient Rome, however, a traumatic event—the eruption of Mount Vesuvius in A.D. 79—perfectly preserved many artifacts. In the ash and mud that buried cities such as Herculaneum and Pompeii, archaeologists have found records of all aspects of Roman daily life.

◄ Theater was popular in ancient Rome. In this mosaic, actors begin to don costumes and masks before a play.

As Mount Vesuvius erupted, some 18 feet of volcanic debris fell on Pompeii. Many people died trying to escape. In the mid-1800s, archaeologist Guiseppe Fiorelli poured plaster into cavities in the ash that were left behind once bodies decayed. Like this one, the plaster casts he created show vividly the desperate struggle to flee the eruption. ▼

▼ Pompeii's remains tell us about a variety of Roman professions. The oven and grain mills of a bakery still stand in Pompeii (below), and a petrified loaf of bread (left) was found nearby.

Thinking Critically

1. **Synthesize Information** What are some aspects of Roman daily life that these artifacts reveal to us?

2. **Determine Relevance** Why do you think Fiorelli thought it important to create plaster casts of the victims?

THE AQUEDUCTS OF IMPERIAL ROME

Eleven separate aqueducts like the one below covered more than 260 miles of land to supply the city of Rome with clean water from mountain springs outside the city. Once in the city, the water was piped into public buildings and baths, some houses, and gardens. Much of the water ended up in public fountains, where many people gathered it for cooking and drinking.

CAMP OF THE PRAETORIAN GUARD

MAUSOLEUM OF AUGUSTUS

AQUA VIRGO

TEMPLE OF HADRIAN

PANTHEON

AQUA MARCIA TEPULA

ANIO VETUS

AQUA MARCIA

TEMPLE OF TRAJAN

FORUMS OF THE EMPERORS

ROMAN FORUM

Tiber River

COLOSSEUM

ARCH OF CONSTANTINE

AQUA ALSIETINA

CIRCUS MAXIMUS

AQUA CLAUDIA

AQUA APPIA

AQUA ANTONINIANA

AQUEDUCT
CITY WALL, 300s B.C.
CITY WALL, A.D. 271
ROAD

Mercator Projection

| 0 | Meters | 1000 |
| 0 | Yards | 1000 |

Romans Apply Science and Mathematics for Practical Use

The Romans excelled in **engineering**, which is the application of science and mathematics to develop useful structures and machines. Roman engineers built roads, bridges, and harbors throughout the empire. Roman roads were so solidly built that many of them were still used long after the fall of the empire. Roman engineers also built many immense **aqueducts**, or bridgelike stone structures that carried water from the hills into Roman cities. The wealthy had water piped in, and almost every city boasted public baths. Here, people gathered not only to wash themselves but also to hear the latest news and exchange gossip.

The Romans generally left scientific research to the Greeks, who were by that time citizens of the empire. In Alexandria, Egypt, Hellenistic scientists exchanged ideas freely. It was there that astronomer-mathematician **Ptolemy** (TAHL uh mee) proposed his theory that the Earth was the center of the universe, a mistaken idea that was accepted in the Western world for nearly 1,500 years.

The Greek doctor Galen advanced the frontiers of medical science by insisting on experiments to prove a conclusion. Galen compiled a medical encyclopedia summarizing what was known in the field at the time. It remained a standard text for more than 1,000 years.

Although the Romans did little original research, they did put science to practical use. They applied geography to make maps and medical knowledge to help doctors improve public health. Like Galen, they collected knowledge into encyclopedias. Pliny the Elder, a Roman scientist, compiled volumes on geography, zoology, botany, and other topics, all based on other people's works.

✔ **Checkpoint** Who in the Roman empire engaged in scientific research? Who put science to practical use?

New Law Codes Protect the Empire

"Let justice be done," proclaimed a Roman saying, "though the heavens fall!" Probably the greatest legacy of Rome was its commitment to the rule of law and to justice. During the Roman empire, the rule of law fostered unity and stability. Many centuries later, the principles of Roman law would become the basis for legal systems throughout the world, including that of the United States.

Two Codes Become One During the republic, Rome developed a system of law, known as the civil law, that applied to its citizens. As Rome expanded, however, it ruled many foreigners who were not covered under the civil law. Gradually, a second system of law, known as the law of nations, emerged. It applied to all people under Roman rule, both citizens and non-citizens. Later, when Rome extended citizenship across the empire, the two systems merged.

Leaving a Legal Legacy As Roman law developed, certain basic principles evolved. Many of these principles are familiar to Americans today. An accused person was presumed innocent until proven guilty. The accused was allowed to face the accuser and offer a defense against the charge. Guilt had to be established "clearer than daylight," using solid evidence. Judges were allowed to interpret the laws and were expected to make fair decisions. Penalties, however, varied according to social class, and lower-class defendants could be treated more harshly.

✔ **Checkpoint** What were the basic principles of Roman law?

Progress Monitoring *Online*
For: Self-quiz with vocabulary practice
Web Code: naa-0531

Terms, People, and Places

1. For each term, person, or place listed at the beginning of the section, write a sentence explaining its significance.

Note Taking

2. **Reading Skill: Understand Effects** Use your completed concept web to answer the Focus Question: How did advances in arts, learning, and the law show the Romans' high regard for cultural and political achievements?

Comprehension and Critical Thinking

3. **Make Generalizations** How did Greek culture influence the development of Roman civilization?

4. **Synthesize Information** How did Romans use science and mathematics to improve life in the empire?

5. **Determine Relevance** Give two examples of how Roman principles of law affect life in the United States today.

● **Writing About History**

Quick Write: Write an Introduction
Prepare for a compare-and-contrast essay about Roman writers and artists by writing an introductory paragraph. Include brief mention of the different types of writing and arts the Romans practiced as well as the overall focus of each type.

Renaissance painter Raphael depicted the cross appearing above Constantine (right); the fish and the cross (far right) were early Christian symbols.

WITNESS HISTORY ◀)) AUDIO

Roman Emperor Accepts Christianity

The Roman empire was tolerant of different religions, but it was almost 300 years before a Roman emperor fully supported the new religion of Christianity. Legend has it that the emperor Constantine—just before battle—saw a cross in the sky along with the words "By this you shall conquer." He had his troops mark their shields with a Christian symbol. After winning the battle, he fully embraced Christianity.

Focus Question How did Christianity emerge and then spread to become the official religion of the Roman empire?

The Rise of Christianity

Objectives
- Understand the diverse religions included in the early Roman empire.
- Summarize the teachings of Jesus and how they were spread.
- Outline the development of the early Christian Church.

Terms, People, and Places

messiah	bishop
apostle	patriarch
Paul	pope
martyr	heresy
Constantine	Augustine
clergy	

Note Taking

Reading Skill: Understand Effects As you read, fill in a chart like the one below with factors that allowed the rise of Christianity and its establishment as the official religion of the Roman empire.

Causes	Effects
• • •	• Rise of Christianity • Establishment of Christianity as empire's official religion

Early in the Pax Romana, a new religion, Christianity, arose in a distant corner of the Roman empire. At first, Christianity was one of many religions practiced in the empire. But the new faith grew rapidly, and throughout the A.D. 380s and 390s it was gradually made the official religion of the Roman empire. As it gained strength and spread through the empire, Christianity reshaped Roman beliefs. When the Roman empire fell, the Christian Church took over much of its role, becoming the central institution of Western civilization for nearly 1,000 years.

Early Empire Includes Diverse Religions

Within the culturally diverse Roman empire, various religious beliefs coexisted. Jupiter, Mars, Juno, and other traditional Roman gods remained important. However, a growing number of people looked elsewhere for spiritual fulfillment.

Rome Tolerates Diversity Some people turned to the so-called mystery religions, which emphasized secret rituals and promised special rewards. One of the most popular of these was the cult of Isis, which started in Egypt and offered women equal status with men. Roman soldiers favored the cult of the Persian god Mithras, who championed good over evil and offered life after death.

Generally, Rome tolerated the varied religious traditions of its subjects. As long as citizens showed loyalty by honoring Roman gods and acknowledging the divine spirit of the emperor, the government allowed them to worship other gods as they pleased. Because most people were polytheistic, they were content to worship the Roman gods along with their own.

The Limits of Toleration
The Romans' destruction of Jerusalem's temple in A.D. 70 (above left) was a massive assault against revolt. Three years later, rebellion against Rome ended with the siege of Masada (above right), a mountaintop fortress at which nearly 1,000 Jews may have taken their own lives to avoid being killed by Romans. *Why would a government only believe in toleration to a certain point?*

Divisions Arise in Judea By 63 B.C., the Romans had conquered Judea, the southern part of Palestine where most Jews of the time lived. To avoid violating the Jewish belief in one god, the Romans excused Jews from worshiping Roman gods. Among the Jewish people themselves, however, religious ferment was creating deep divisions. During the Hellenistic age, many Jews absorbed Greek customs and ideas. Concerned about the weakening of their religion, Jewish conservatives rejected these influences and called for strict obedience to Jewish laws and traditions.

While most Jews were reluctantly willing to live under Roman rule, others, called Zealots, were not. They called on Jews to revolt against Rome and reestablish an independent state. Some Jews believed that a **messiah,** or anointed king sent by God, would soon appear to lead their people to freedom.

A Jewish Rebellion Is Defeated In A.D. 66, discontent flared into rebellion. Four years later, Roman forces crushed the rebels, captured Jerusalem, and destroyed the Jewish temple. When revolts broke out again in the next century, Roman armies leveled Jerusalem. Thousands of Jews were killed in the fighting, and many others were enslaved and transported to various parts of the empire. Faced with the destruction that resulted from the rebellions, growing numbers of Jews decided to leave Judea.

Although the Jewish people were defeated in their efforts to regain political independence, they survived in scattered communities around the Mediterranean. Over the centuries, Jewish religious teachers called rabbis extended and preserved the Jewish law, and Judaism survived.

✓ **Checkpoint** What was Rome's policy toward most of the religions in the empire?

Jesus Proclaims His Teachings

As turmoil engulfed the Jews in Palestine, a new religion, Christianity, arose among them. It began among the followers of a Jew named Jesus. Almost all the information we have about the life of Jesus comes from the Gospels, the first four books of the New Testament of the Christian Bible. Early Christians attributed the writing of these accounts to four followers of Jesus—Matthew, Mark, Luke, and John.

In the Sermon on the Mount, Jesus (below) summarized his ethical message, which echoed Jewish ideas of mercy and sympathy for the poor and helpless. What does he say is the reward for being merciful?

Primary Source

66 Blessed are the meek, for they shall inherit the earth.
Blessed are those who hunger and thirst for righteousness, for they shall be satisfied.
Blessed are the merciful, for they shall obtain mercy.
Blessed are the pure in heart, for they shall see God.
Blessed are the peacemakers, for they will be called sons of God.99

—Matthew 5:5–9

🔊 AUDIO

Jesus Begins Preaching Jesus was born about 4 B.C. in Bethlehem, near Jerusalem. According to the Gospels, he was a descendant of King David of Israel. The Gospels say an angel told Jesus' mother, Mary, that she would give birth to the messiah. "He will be great," said the angel, "and will be called the Son of the Most High God."

Growing up in the small town of Nazareth, Jesus worshiped God and followed Jewish law. As a young man, he may have worked as a carpenter. At the age of 30, the Gospels relate, he began preaching to villagers near the Sea of Galilee. Large crowds gathered to hear his teachings, especially when word spread that he had performed miracles of healing. Jesus often used parables, or short stories with simple moral lessons, to communicate his ideas. He recruited 12 of his disciples, or close followers, to help him in his mission. He called these 12 the **apostles,** a name that in Greek means "a person sent forth." After three years, Jesus and his disciples went to Jerusalem to spread his message there.

Jesus Teaches New Beliefs Jesus' teachings were firmly rooted in Jewish tradition. Jesus believed in one God and accepted the Ten Commandments. He preached obedience to the laws of Moses and defended the teachings of the Jewish prophets. However, Jesus also preached new beliefs. According to his followers, he called himself the Son of God. Many people believed he was the long-anticipated messiah. Jesus proclaimed that his mission was to bring spiritual salvation and eternal life to anyone who believed in him.

Echoing the teachings of Judaism, Jesus emphasized God's love and taught the need for justice, morality, and service to others. According to Jesus, a person's major duties were to observe the Jewish command to "love the Lord your God with all your heart" and to "love your neighbor as yourself." Jesus also emphasized the importance of forgiveness.

Condemned to Death According to the Gospels, Jesus traveled to Jerusalem near the time of the Jewish festival of Passover, a celebration of the exodus from Egypt. To the Roman authorities, Jesus was a threat because his speeches could inflame those eager to end Roman rule.

The Gospels state that Jesus was betrayed by one of his disciples. He was then arrested by the Romans, tried, and condemned to death by crucifixion. In this method of execution, which the Romans often used, a person was nailed or bound to a cross and left to die. Jesus' crucifixion threw his disciples into confusion. But then rumors spread through Jerusalem that Jesus was not dead at all. The Gospels report that his disciples saw and talked with Jesus, who had risen from death. The Gospels go on to say that Jesus, after commanding his disciples to spread his teachings to all people, ascended into heaven.

✔ **Checkpoint** What aspects of Jesus' message were unique?

The Message of Christianity Spreads

After Jesus' death, the apostles and other disciples did spread his message. At first, they preached only among the Jews of Judea. Some Jews accepted the teaching that Jesus was the messiah, or the Christ, from the Greek word for "anointed one." Soon, they were called Christians.

Geography *Interactive*
For: Interactive map
Web Code: nap-0541

Christian areas, A.D. 325
Christian areas added by A.D. 476
Boundary of Roman empire, A.D. 476
→ Paul's first journey
→ Paul's second journey
→ Paul's third journey
→ Paul's journey to Rome

Conic Projection
0   200   400 mi
0   200   400 km

Gradually, these disciples went to preach in Jewish communities throughout the Roman world. According to tradition, the apostle Peter established Christianity in the city of Rome itself. But **Paul,** a Jew from Asia Minor, played the most influential role in spreading Christianity.

Paul Spreads Christianity Paul had never met Jesus. In fact, he had been among those who persecuted Jesus' followers. But one day Paul had a vision of Jesus speaking to him. He immediately joined the Christians and decided to spread Jesus' teachings to gentiles, or non-Jews.

Until this time, Christianity had remained a sect within Judaism. The work of missionaries like Paul set Christianity on the road to becoming a world religion. A tireless traveler, Paul journeyed around the Mediterranean and set up churches in Asia Minor and Greece. In letters to the Christian communities, he explained difficult doctrines, judged disputes, and expanded Christian teachings, emphasizing that Jesus had sacrificed his life out of love for humankind. Paul asserted that those who believed Jesus was the son of God and <u>complied</u> with his teachings would achieve salvation, or eternal life. His letters became part of the New Testament.

Christians Are Oppressed Rome's tolerant attitude toward religion was not extended to Christianity. Roman officials found the Christians disloyal to Rome because they refused to honor the emperor with sacrifices or ask the traditional gods to protect the Roman state. When Christians met in secret to avoid persecution, rumors spread that they were engaged in evil practices.

Map Skills Aided by the work of Paul and other missionaries, Christianity gradually spread across the Roman empire.
1. **Locate** (a) Jerusalem (b) Ephesus (c) Antioch (d) Constantinople (e) Alexandria
2. **Movement** In what areas did Paul travel on his first journey?
3. **Analyze Information** How did the extent of Christianity in A.D. 325 compare to that in A.D. 476? Was there a significant difference?

Vocabulary Builder
<u>complied</u>—(kum PLYD) *vi.* obeyed or conformed to something

Peter

As the chief apostle, Peter (d. A.D. 64[?]) devoted his life to spreading the teachings of Jesus. He had been born with the name Simon, but according to the New Testament Jesus changed his name, saying, "Thou art Peter, and upon this rock I will build my church."

Peter became a missionary and is said to have later become the first bishop of both Antioch and Rome. However, his devotion to Jesus and Christianity cost him his life. Tradition tells of Peter's persecution under the Roman emperor Nero. In one account, when Peter learns he is to be crucified, he insists on being turned upside down, saying he is not worthy of dying in the same way that Jesus had. **What does Peter's behavior indicate about his devotion to his faith?**

In times of trouble, persecution increased. Some Roman rulers, such as Nero, used Christians as scapegoats, blaming them for social or economic ills. Over the centuries, those Christians who were killed in periods of persecution became known as **martyrs,** or people who suffer or die for their beliefs. According to tradition, both Peter and Paul were martyred in Rome during the reign of Nero.

The Message Appeals to Many Despite the attacks, Christianity continued to spread throughout the Roman world. Jesus had welcomed all people, especially the lowly, the poor, and the oppressed. These people found comfort in his message of love, as well as in his teachings of equality, dignity, and the promise of a better life beyond the grave.

As they did their work, Christian missionaries like Paul used ideas from Plato, the Stoics, and other Greek thinkers to explain Jesus' message. A religion that incorporated the discipline and moderation of Greek philosophy appealed in particular to educated Romans. The unity of the Roman empire also eased the work of missionaries. Christians traveled along Roman roads and across the Mediterranean Sea, which was protected by Roman fleets. Early Christian documents were usually written in Greek or Latin, languages that many people across the empire understood.

Even persecution brought new converts. Observing the willingness of Christians to die for their religion, people were impressed by the strength of Christians' belief. "The blood of the martyrs is the seed of the [Christian] Church," noted one Roman.

Rome Accepts Christianity The persecution of Christians finally ended in A.D. 313, when the emperor **Constantine** issued the Edict of Milan. It granted freedom of worship to all citizens of the Roman empire. By the end of century, the emperor Theodosius (thee uh DOH shus) had made Christianity the official religion of the Roman empire and repressed the practice of other faiths.

✔ **Checkpoint** What factors enabled Christianity to spread throughout the Roman empire?

The Early Christian Church Develops

Early Christian communities shared a common faith in the teachings of Jesus and a common way of worship. Only gradually, however, did these scattered communities come together as a structured Church.

Joining the Church To join the Christian community, a person had to be baptized, or blessed with holy water. Christians believed that through the rite of baptism their sins were forgiven by the grace of God. Members of the community were considered equals, and they addressed each other as "brother" or "sister." Each Sunday, Christians gathered for a ceremony of thanksgiving to God. The baptized ate bread and drank wine in a sacred rite called the Eucharist. They did this in memory of Jesus, whose last supper was described in the Gospels.

Many women welcomed Christianity's promise that in the Church "there is neither Jew nor Greek . . . neither slave nor free . . . neither male nor female." In early Christian communities, women served as teachers and administrators. Later, women were barred from any official role in the Church. Like men, however, they continued to work as missionaries sent out by the Church to convert people to Christianity both within the Roman empire and beyond.

Structuring the Clergy Only men were eligible to become members of the Christian **clergy,** or the group of people who conduct Christian services. Each Christian community and its clergy were grouped together as a diocese. Every diocese had its own priest. Over the priest presided a **bishop,** a high Church official responsible for everyone in his diocese. Bishops traced their spiritual authority to the apostles, and through the apostles, to Jesus himself. In the early Christian Church, all bishops were considered equal successors of the apostles.

Gradually, the bishops of the most important cities in the Roman empire—Rome, Antioch, Alexandria, Jerusalem, and Constantinople—gained greater authority. These bishops took on the honorary title of **patriarch** and exercised authority over other bishops in their area. The Christian Church thus developed into a hierarchy, or organization in which officials are arranged according to rank.

Differences Arise Within the Church As the rituals and structure of the Church became more defined, rivalry among the patriarchs developed. In the Latin-speaking west, bishops of Rome, who came to be called **popes,** began to claim authority over all other bishops. In the Greek-speaking east, where the other four patriarchs lived, the patriarchs felt that the five should share spiritual authority as equals.

The emergence of **heresies,** or beliefs said to be contrary to official Church teachings, also caused division. To end disputes over questions of faith, councils of Church leaders met to decide official Christian teachings.

Scholars Further Define Christianity Early Christians produced an abundance of works defining Christian theology. The word *theology* is Greek and means "talk or discourse about God." Two leading scholars of the early Church were Clement and Origen. Both worked as teachers in Egypt, in Alexandria, a major center of learning in the Roman world. Perhaps the greatest of the early Church scholars was **Augustine,** bishop of Hippo in North Africa. He combined Christian doctrine with Greco-Roman learning, especially the philosophy of Plato.

✔ **Checkpoint** How was the early Christian clergy organized?

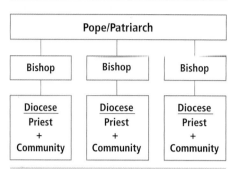

The Christian Clergy

Pope/Patriarch

Bishop | Bishop | Bishop

Diocese Priest + Community | Diocese Priest + Community | Diocese Priest + Community

Chart Skills Over time the structure of the Christian church developed into a hierarchy. *What are some positive and negative elements that may arise from this type of organizational structure?*

SECTION 4 Assessment

Progress Monitoring *Online*
For: Self-quiz with vocabulary practice
Web Code: naa-0541

Terms, People, and Places

1. What do each of the key people listed at the beginning of the section have in common? Explain.

Note Taking

2. **Reading Skill: Understand Effects** Use your completed chart to answer the Focus Question: How did Christianity emerge and then spread to become the official religion of the Roman empire?

Comprehension and Critical Thinking

3. **Identify Central Issues** Why were many Jews unhappy under Roman rule even though the Romans were tolerant of their religion?

4. **Synthesize Information** What were three basic teachings of Jesus?

5. **Summarize** What practices and organizational structures helped establish the early Christian Church?

● **Writing About History**

Quick Write: Make an Outline To prepare for an essay comparing the experiences of Jews and of Christians in the Roman empire, make an outline identifying key points of comparison. Include details under each key point.

First Letter to the Corinthians

Around A.D. 51, Paul founded a Christian community in the thriving commercial city of Corinth. After his departure, he wrote two letters to the newly converted Christians to encourage and guide them in their faith. In this excerpt from Paul's First Letter to the Corinthians, Paul declares that, for a Christian, love is more important than any other quality.

Paul writing one of his epistles, or letters

If I speak in the tongues of men and of angels, but have not love, I am a noisy gong or a clanging cymbal. And if I have prophetic[1] powers and understand all mysteries and all knowledge, and if I have all faith, so as to remove mountains, but have no love, I am nothing. If I give away all I have, and if I deliver my body to be burned, but have not love, I gain nothing.

Love is patient and kind; love is not jealous or boastful; it is not arrogant or rude. Love does not insist on its own way; it is not irritable or resentful; it does not rejoice at wrong, but rejoices in the right. Love bears all things, believes all things, hopes all things, endures all things.

Love never ends; as for prophecies, they will pass away; as for tongues, they will cease; as for knowledge, it will pass away. For our knowledge is imperfect and our prophecy is imperfect; but when the perfect comes, the imperfect will pass away. When I was a child, I spoke like a child, I thought like a child, I reasoned like a child; when I became a man, I gave up childish ways. For now we see in a mirror dimly, but then face to face. Now I know in part; then I shall understand fully, even as I have been fully understood. So faith, hope, love abide, these three; but the greatest of these is love.

Thinking Critically

1. **Analyze Literature** Paul uses repetition of words and phrases throughout this letter. What purpose does this serve?
2. **Draw Conclusions** What does Paul mean when he says that love "endures all things"?

1. **prophetic** (pruh FET ik) *adj.* able to predict events

The western Roman empire came to an end in 476, when the emperor gave up his crown.

A plaque from an invader's shield

WITNESS HISTORY 🔊 AUDIO

The Exhausted Empire

After 300 years of empire, Rome was weakening due to various causes. The oppressive government and corrupt upper class generated hostility among those who suffered in the weak economy. When invaders came from the north and east, the empire's days were numbered. The Roman writer Salvian noted the mood of the Roman people:

❝ In the districts taken over by the barbarians, there is one desire among all the Romans, that they should never again find it necessary to pass under Roman jurisdiction [authority]. **❞**
—Salvian, *On the Governance of God*

Focus Question How did military, political, social, and economic factors combine to cause the fall of the western Roman empire?

The Long Decline

Objectives
- Explain how and why the Roman empire divided.
- Describe how waves of invaders contributed to the decline of the Roman empire.
- Identify the various types of problems that led to the fall of Rome.

Terms, People, and Places

Diocletian
inflation
Constantinople
Huns
mercenary

Note Taking

Reading Skill: Recognize Multiple Causes As you read, complete a chart like the one below by filling in the causes of the fall of the western Roman empire.

Causes of the Fall of the Western Roman Empire			
Military:	Social:	Political:	Economic:
•	•	•	•
•	•	•	•

After ruling the Mediterranean for hundreds of years, the Roman empire faced threats from inside and outside. Economic problems, foreign invasions, and a decline in traditional values were undermining stability and security.

The Roman Empire Divides

After the death of the emperor Marcus Aurelius in 180, the golden age of the Pax Romana ended. For the next 100 years, political and economic turmoil rocked the Roman empire.

Political Violence Becomes Common During this period, a disruptive political pattern emerged. Again and again, emperors were overthrown by political intriguers or ambitious generals who seized power with the support of their troops. Those who rose to the imperial throne in this way ruled for just a few months or years until they, too, were overthrown or assassinated. In one 50-year period, at least 26 emperors reigned. Only one died of natural causes. Political violence and instability had become the rule.

Social and Economic Problems Arise At the same time, the empire was shaken by disturbing social and economic trends. High taxes to support the army and the bureaucracy placed heavy burdens on business people and small farmers. Farmland that had been over-cultivated for too long lost its productivity.

Many poor farmers left their land and sought protection from wealthy landowners. Living on large estates, they worked for the landowners and farmed small plots for themselves. Although technically free, they were not allowed to leave the land.

Emperor Diocletian Shares Power In 284, the emperor **Diocletian** (dy uh KLEE shun) set out to restore order. To better handle the challenge of governing the huge empire, he divided it into two parts. He kept control of the wealthier eastern part for himself and appointed a co-emperor, Maximian, to rule the western provinces.

Diocletian also took steps to end the empire's economic decay. To slow **inflation,** or the rapid rise of prices, he fixed the prices of many goods and services. Other laws forced farmers to remain on the land. In cities, sons were required to follow their fathers' occupations. These rules were meant to ensure steady production of food and other goods.

Emperor Constantine Makes Further Reforms In 312, the talented general Constantine gained the throne. As emperor, Constantine continued Diocletian's reforms. In addition, he took two steps that changed the course of European history. First, as you have read, Constantine granted toleration to Christians. Second, he established a new capital at the centuries-old city of Byzantium, which he renamed **Constantinople.** With this "New Rome," Constantine made the eastern empire the center of power.

Improvements Prove Temporary The reforms of Diocletian and Constantine had mixed results. They revived the economy, and by increasing the power of government, they helped hold the empire together for another century. Still, the reforms failed to stop the long-term decline. In the end, internal problems combined with attacks from outside to bring the empire down.

✔ **Checkpoint** How do you think Rome's unstable government affected the economy?

● **INFOGRAPHIC**

Redefining the Empire

By the 200s, the days of the empire were numbered. Diocletian and Constantine undertook numerous reforms to help keep it alive. Although they could not stop the decline, Diocletian and Constantine redefined the empire both politically and religiously. The effects of their changes would last well beyond the official "fall of Rome." While the western empire would face failure, the eastern empire would maintain power for another thousand years as the Byzantine empire.

�◄ Diocletian and Maximian, the co-emperors

Political Reforms
Diocletian's division of the empire into eastern and western halves (at left) made the huge territory more manageable to oversee. When Constantine later moved the capital from Rome to Constantinople (background image), he set the eastern empire on a path to long-lasting power. Previously called Byzantium, Constantinople would thrive as the capital of the Byzantine empire until 1453.

Map labels: North Sea, BRITAIN, GAUL, Atlantic Ocean, SPAIN, Tagus River, ITALY, Rome, Carthage, GREECE, Mediterranean Sea, Black Sea, Constantinople, ASIA MINOR, Dnieper River, Caspian Sea, Tigris River, Euphrates River, EGYPT, Red Sea, AFRICA

Conic Projection
0   400 mi
0   400 km

☐ Western Roman empire
■ Eastern Roman empire

Invaders Threaten the Roman Empire

For centuries, Rome had faced attacks from the Germanic peoples who lived east of the Rhine and north of the Danube rivers. When Rome was powerful, the legions on the frontiers were successful in holding back the invaders. Some of the Germanic peoples who lived along the borders learned Roman ways and became allies of the Romans.

Migrating Nomads Attack As early as 200, wars in East Asia set off a chain of events that would eventually overwhelm Rome, thousands of miles to the west. Those wars sent a nomadic people, the **Huns,** migrating from central Asia toward eastern Europe, which they reached by 370. These skilled riders fought fierce battles to dislodge the Germanic peoples in their path. The Visigoths, Ostrogoths, and other Germanic peoples crossed into Roman territory seeking safety.

With the empire in decline, Roman legions were hard pressed to halt the invaders. Under pressure from attacks, the Roman empire surrendered first Britain, then France and Spain. It was only a matter of time before foreign invaders marched into Italy and took over Rome itself.

Rome Is Sacked In 378, when a Roman army tried to turn back the Visigoths at Adrianople, it suffered a stunning defeat. Roman power was fading. New waves of invaders were soon hammering at Rome's borders, especially in the west. In 410, the Visigoth general Alaric overran Italy and plundered the city of Rome. Meanwhile, a Germanic people called the Vandals moved through Gaul and Spain into North Africa. Gradually, Germanic groups occupied more and more of the western Roman empire.

Religious Reforms

Before Constantine came to power, many Roman emperors had persecuted Christians, arresting or executing them. Diocletian had been among the most brutal persecutors. This painting shows the Christian martyr Lucy being burned under his reign (an ordeal she is said to have survived).

Growth of Christianity in the Roman Empire

Year	Number of Christians*
0	0
50	1,400
100	7,530
150	40,496
200	217,795
250	1,171,356
300	6,299,832
350	33,882,008

*Numbers are estimates.
SOURCE: Rodney Stark, *The Rise of Christianity*

Whether Constantine (above) fueled Christianity's growth or its growth fueled his acceptance is not known. What is clear is that in the 300s, Christianity was thriving in the empire. It would underlie social and cultural developments for centuries onward.

Thinking Critically
1. **Make Comparisons** Compare the short-term and long-term effects of Diocletian's division of the empire.
2. **Synthesize Information** How do you think the acceptance of Christianity changed life in the empire?

What Kind of Downfall?

Historians have long held that the "fall of Rome" was an important historical event, but they argue over many details. **Critical Thinking** *What about Rome's end most surprises Gibbons? How does Brown differ with him on this point?*

Argument for an Enduring Rome

The Roman empire lasted a lot longer than its supposed date of collapse.... Things don't change overnight in a big, lazy empire. The life of the cities remained much more vigorous than was thought; the classics continued to be taught with great intensity and a real feeling that they were still relevant. Even after the official end of the empire, as late as 476 A.D., many of the social structures we associate with the empire endured.

—Historian Peter Brown

Argument for a Ruined Rome

[T]he decline of Rome was the natural and inevitable effect of immoderate [excessive] greatness. Prosperity ripened the ... decay; the causes of destruction multiplied with the extent of conquest; and as soon as time or accident had removed the artificial supports, the stupendous fabric yielded to the pressure of its own weight. The story of its ruin is simple and obvious; and instead of inquiring *why* the Roman empire was destroyed, we should rather be surprised that it had subsisted so long.

—Historian Edward Gibbons

For Rome, the worst was yet to come. Starting in 434, the Hun leader Attila embarked on a savage campaign of conquest across much of Europe. Christians called Attila the "scourge of God" because they believed his attacks were a punishment for the sins of humankind. The Hun invasion sent still more Germanic peoples fleeing into the lands of Roman empire.

Finally, in 476, Odoacer (oh doh AY sur), a Germanic leader, ousted the emperor in Rome. Later, historians referred to that event as the "fall" of Rome. By then, however, the Roman empire had already lost many of its territories, and Roman power in the west had ended.

✓ **Checkpoint**   How did the Hun invasion weaken the Roman empire?

Many Problems Cause Rome to Fall

The passing of Rome's power and greatness was a major turning point in the history of Western civilization. Why did Rome "fall"? Modern historians identify a number of interrelated causes.

Military Attacks Perhaps the most obvious cause of Rome's fall was the invasions. Still, these attacks were successful partly because Roman legions of the late empire lacked the discipline and training from which earlier Roman armies had benefited. To meet its need for soldiers, Rome hired **mercenaries,** or foreign soldiers serving for pay, to defend its borders. Many were Germanic warriors who, according to some historians, felt little loyalty to Rome.

Political Turmoil Political problems also contributed to Rome's decline. First, as the government became more oppressive and authoritarian, it lost the support of the people. Growing numbers of corrupt officials undermined loyalty, too. So did frequent civil wars over succession to the imperial throne. Again and again, rival armies battled to have their commanders chosen as emperor. Perhaps most important, dividing the empire at a time when it was under attack may have weakened it beyond repair. The richer eastern Roman empire did little to help the west.

Economic Weakness Economic problems were widespread in the empire. Heavier and heavier taxes were required to support the vast government bureaucracy and huge military establishment. At the same time, reliance on slave labor discouraged Romans from exploring new technology. The wealth of the empire dwindled as farmers abandoned their land and the middle classes sank into poverty. Some scholars have suggested that climate change was yet another reason for reduced agricultural productivity. In addition, the population itself declined as war and epidemic diseases swept the empire.

Social Decay For centuries, worried Romans pointed to the decline in values such as patriotism, discipline, and devotion to duty on which the empire was built. The need to replace citizen-soldiers with mercenaries testified to the decline of patriotism. The upper class, which had once provided leaders, devoted itself to luxury and <u>prestige</u>. Besides being costly, providing "bread and circuses" may have undermined the self-reliance of the masses.

Did Rome Fall? Although we talk of the "fall" of Rome, the Roman empire did not disappear from the map in 476. An emperor still ruled the eastern Roman empire, which continued to exist for another 1,000 years under the name of the Byzantine empire.

The phrase "the fall of Rome" is, in fact, shorthand for a long, slow change from one way of life to another. Roman civilization survived the events of 476. In Italy, people continued to live much as they had before, though under new rulers. Many still spoke Latin and obeyed Roman laws.

Over the following centuries, however, Germanic customs and languages replaced much of Roman culture. Old Roman cities crumbled, and Roman roads disappeared. Still, the Christian Church preserved elements of Roman civilization. In later chapters, you will read how Roman and Christian traditions gave rise to medieval civilization in western Europe.

 Checkpoint What social problems contributed to the decline of the Roman empire?

Vocabulary Builder

<u>prestige</u>—(pres TEEZH) *n.* the power to impress or influence because of success or wealth

---

SECTION 5 Assessment

Progress Monitoring *Online*
For: Self-quiz with vocabulary practice
Web Code: naa-0551

Terms, People, and Places

1. For each term, person, or place listed at the beginning of the section, write a sentence explaining its significance.

Note Taking

2. **Reading Skill: Recognize Multiple Causes** Use your completed chart to answer the Focus Question: How did military, political, social, and economic factors combine to cause the fall of the western Roman empire?

Comprehension and Critical Thinking

3. **Summarize** Describe the crisis that afflicted the Roman empire after the Pax Romana ended. How did Diocletian try to resolve the crisis?

4. **Express Problems Clearly** How did the successes of invaders such as the Huns reveal the fading power of the Roman empire?

5. **Identify Central Issues** What features of the western Roman empire survived after the year 476?

● **Writing About History**

Quick Write: Write a Conclusion Compare the various factors that led to the "fall" of Rome. Write a conclusion paragraph for an essay explaining which factors you think played the greatest role.

THE FALL OF ROME

Many factors contributed to the fall of Rome, but perhaps none is as vivid and dramatic as the military plundering of the capital and its surrounding territory by invading groups. Although the Roman armies fought hard to defend their lands, aggressive leaders and fierce warriors wreaked havoc on all regions of the western Roman empire and parts of the east.

North Sea

JUTES

SAXONS

ANGLES

BRITAIN

Saxons

VISIGOTHS

Atlantic Ocean

Rhine

LOMBARDS

Dnieper River

HUNS

FRANKS

Troyes

HUNS

River

GAUL

HUNS

VISIGOTHS

HUNS

VANDALS

VISIGOTHS

Danube River

Black Sea

SPAIN

VISIGOTHS

VISIGOTHS

Adrianople

Constantinople

Rome

ITALY

ASIA MINOR

VANDALS

VANDALS

VANDALS

Carthage

GREECE

VANDALS

Mediterranean Sea

EGYPT

AFRICA

INVASIONS OF THE ROMAN EMPIRE TO A.D. 476

◼ WESTERN ROMAN EMPIRE
◼ EASTERN ROMAN EMPIRE
✗ MAJOR BATTLE SITES

Conic Projection
Miles
0   400
0   Kilometers   400

History *Interactive*

For: Interactive map, audio, and more
Web Code: nap-0551

378
At Adrianople, the Visigoths slay the Roman emperor Valens and much of his army.

441
Attila, king of the Huns, begins assaults along the northeastern borders of the Roman empire.

451
The Romans and Visigoths push back Attila and his troops.

476
The German king Odoacer overthrows the Roman emperor Romulus Augustulus and becomes king of Italy, thus finalizing the "fall of Rome."

400
425
450
500

375
475

The Roman general Stilicho defeats the Visigoths and their leader, Alaric.

402

420
Gunderic, king of the Vandals and the Alanis, defeats the Romans and the Goths.

455
The Vandals and Alani, led by Gaiseric, capture and ransack Rome.

410
Alaric plunders Rome. Roman troops withdraw from Britain and Gaul.

406
The Vandals pillage Gaul.

Ostrogothic helmet ▶

HUNS

Caspian Sea

Tigris River

Euphrates River

Of all the invaders, the Huns may have most terrified the Romans. Roman scholar Jerome wrote of them as follows: "They filled the whole earth with slaughter and panic as they flitted here and there on their swift horses. . . . They were at hand everywhere before they were expected: by their speed they outstripped rumour, and they took pity on neither religion nor rank nor age nor wailing childhood."

AREA ENLARGED

Red Sea

Thinking Critically
1. **Map Skills** Through which parts of the Roman empire did the invaders spread? Which parts did they not enter?
2. **Timeline Skills** At what point did the Romans begin to pull out of the western territory of the empire?
3. **Synthesize Information** In what ways does the information above suggest that the eastern empire would fare better than the western empire over time?

CHAPTER 5

Quick Study Guide

Progress Monitoring *Online*
For: Self-test with vocabulary practice
Web Code: naa-0561

■ Roman Rulers Who Made History

Ruler	Dates	Key Accomplishments
Julius Caesar	100 B.C.(?)–44 B.C.	• Attempted to make reforms to help save the ailing republic • Made himself absolute ruler
Octavian/ Augustus	63 B.C.–A.D. 14	• Declared Exalted One and first citizen by the Senate • First ruler of the Pax Romana
Marcus Aurelius	A.D. 121–A.D. 180	• Last great emperor of the Pax Romana
Diocletian	A.D. 245–A.D. 316	• Divided the empire into two parts, eastern and western
Constantine	A.D. 280(?)–A.D. 337	• Moved Roman power eastward by building a new capital at Constantinople • Granted toleration to Christians through the Edict of Milan

■ Key Roles in Early Christianity

Individual/Function	Role
Jesus	Jesus taught a new faith, which came to be called Christianity. He recruited followers and spread his message widely.
Apostles	These 12 men were close followers of Jesus. They spread Christianity after his death.
Paul	Through his teachings and writings, Paul spread Christianity throughout the Roman empire.
Missionaries	These religious teachers traveled with the sole purpose of spreading Christianity.
Priests	These leaders of Christian communities formed the majority of the church clergy.
Bishops	These church officials ranked over the priests. Each served an area called a diocese. They were considered the successors of the apostles.
Patriarchs	These men were bishops of major cities and exercised authority over other bishops in their area.

■ Governors of the Republic

Senate—patricians, served for life and made laws for Rome
Consuls—patricians, elected by Senate to supervise the running of Rome
Dictators—patricians, elected by Senate on occasions of war
Tribunes—plebeians, elected by plebeians to guard the interests of plebeians
Citizen-soldiers—citizens, served in the Roman military

■ Pressures Leading to Decline

Military
• Germanic invasions
• Weakened Roman army

Economic
• Heavy taxes
• Population decline

Political
• Oppressive government
• Corrupt officals
• Divided empire

Social
• Erosion of traditional values
• Weakened Roman army
• iBread and circuses"

ROMAN EMPIRE

■ The Rise of Rome

509 B.C.
The Romans establish a republic.

218 B.C.
The Carthaginian general Hannibal invades Italy during the Punic Wars.

Chapter Events
World Events

500 B.C.

250 B.C.

460 B.C.
The Age of Pericles begins in Athens.

321 B.C.
The Maurya dynasty begins in India.

221 B.C.
Shi Huangdi unites China.

Concept Connector

■ Cumulative Review

Record the answers to the questions below on your Concept Connector worksheets. In addition, record information from this chapter about the following concepts:

- Cultural Diffusion: Spread of Roman culture
- Belief Systems: Christianity
- Democracy: Roman citizenship

1. **Empire** The Roman empire and the Han dynasty in China each exerted control over a wide area and a variety of people. Compare the ways the two empires maintained control over such large areas. Provide specific examples of the methods of control. Think about the following:
   - use of military force
   - methods of communication
   - structure of government
   - sharing of culture

2. **Conflict** Roman settlements spread throughout the Mediterranean just as Greek city-states did around the Aegean. Both groups came into conflict with powers on the other side of the sea. What did the Roman conflict in the Punic Wars and the Greek conflict in the Persian Wars have in common? Think about these areas of comparison:
   - overseas trade
   - Greek and Roman culture

3. **Cultural Diffusion** The spread of religions depends on a variety of factors, including the religion's message and its acceptance by the government. Compare the spread of Christianity and of Buddhism. Think about the following:
   - pre-existing religions
   - missionaries
   - the popularity or appeal of the founder

4. **Political Systems** Political systems vary widely in their power structures. Compare the Roman republic to the oligarchies of ancient Greece. Consider how people relate to their government in each system. Think about the following:
   - democracy versus aristocracy
   - the rights of citizens

■ Connections to Today

1. **Dictatorship** During the Roman republic, the Senate was given the power to establish a dictator who could rule for just six months at a time. The need for such absolute leadership was seen as a solution to the problem of war or internal crisis—that is, it was seen as a temporary solution to a dire situation. Through the course of history, however, dictators have often seized power, rather than been given it, and many of them have ruled their countries for years or even decades on end. In the past few decades, dictators have controlled countries such as North Korea, Chile, and Iraq. Conduct research on a recent dictator of a country anywhere in the world and write a summary of how and why he or she took power.

2. **Advances in Technology: Communication** The sprawling system of Roman roads (see below) was crucial in unifying the Roman empire. New technologies often shape communication and, therefore, society. Today, communication is being revolutionized by the Internet. How are the effects of the Internet similar to those of Rome's well-built system of roads? How might the Internet and Roman roads be similar in their impact on culture and trade?

Conic Projection
0   300   600 mi
0   300 600 km

Roman empire
Major road

A.D. 27	A.D. 286	A.D. 330	A.D. 380	A.D. 476
The Roman republic ends. Augustus founds the Roman empire.	Diocletian divides the Roman empire into two parts.	The capital of the Roman empire moves eastward to Constantinople.	Christianity becomes the official Roman religion.	Odoacer, a Germanic leader, unseats the last Roman emperor.

A.D. 1   **A.D. 250**   **A.D. 500**

A.D. 300	A.D. 320	A.D. 350s	
The Maya golden age begins in Mexico and Central America.	The Gupta empire begins a golden age in India.	Axum, located in Ethiopia, conquers Meroë.	**History Interactive** For: Interactive timeline Web Code: nap-0561

Chapter Assessment

Terms, People, and Places

Choose the italicized term in parentheses that best completes each sentence.

1. The application of science and mathematics to develop useful structures is called *(aqueducts/engineering)*.
2. A person who dies or suffers for his or her beliefs is a *(martyr/apostle)*.
3. The senate gave *(Octavian/Julius Caesar)* the title of Augustus, or "Exalted One."
4. Men elected by the senate to supervise the business of the government were called *(consuls/plebeians)*.
5. *(Patricians/Mercenaries)* were foreign soldiers serving in the Roman army for pay.
6. A *(legion/mosaic)* is a picture made from chips of colored stone or glass.
7. Beliefs that were contrary to official Church teachings were called *(heresies/latifundia)*.
8. The rapid rise of prices is called *(inflation/census)*.

Main Ideas

Section 1 (pp. 150–154)
9. What values of the Roman republic were revealed in the establishment of the role of tribune?

Section 2 (pp. 155–160)
10. How did Augustus' rise to power mark a significant change in Rome's form of government?

Section 3 (pp. 161–165)
11. How did the concept of Greco-Roman civilization come into existence?
12. What were three important principles of Roman law?

Section 4 (pp. 166–171)
13. How did Christianity spread through the Roman empire?

Section 5 (pp. 173–177)
14. Describe three reasons for the fall of the Roman empire.

Chapter Focus Question
15. How did Rome grow from a single city to a huge, diverse empire?

Critical Thinking

16. **Geography and History** How did both Greece and Rome benefit from their location on the Mediterranean Sea?
17. **Identify Point of View** "History," said Cicero, "illuminates reality, vitalizes memory, provides guidance in daily life, and brings us tidings of antiquity." How do you think the works of Roman historians like Livy and Tacitus illustrate Cicero's point of view?
18. **Draw Conclusions** What were some possible negative consequences of following the Roman policy of "bread and circuses"?
19. **Analyze Information** Give two examples of how the principles of law developed by Rome affect life in the United States today.
20. **Analyze Visuals** Look back at the photograph of a Roman aqueduct on page 164. Why do you think the construction of aqueducts can be called a major accomplishment of Roman civilization?
21. **Recognize Cause and Effect** What were the causes and effects of the division of the Roman empire into two parts?
22. **Draw Conclusions** Some emperors persecuted Christians for their refusal to make sacrifices to the emperor or to honor Roman gods. Why do you think emperors considered this refusal a threat to the empire?

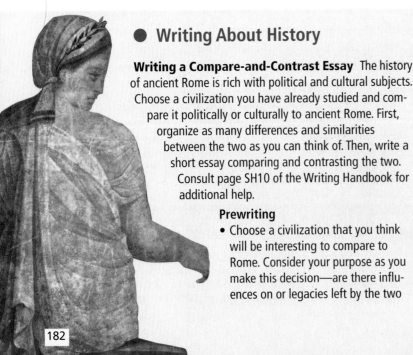

● Writing About History

Writing a Compare-and-Contrast Essay The history of ancient Rome is rich with political and cultural subjects. Choose a civilization you have already studied and compare it politically or culturally to ancient Rome. First, organize as many differences and similarities between the two as you can think of. Then, write a short essay comparing and contrasting the two. Consult page SH10 of the Writing Handbook for additional help.

Prewriting
- Choose a civilization that you think will be interesting to compare to Rome. Consider your purpose as you make this decision—are there influences on or legacies left by the two

civilizations that make them particularly interesting to compare and contrast?
- Gather details of the similarities and differences between Rome and the other civilization. Create a graphic organizer to organize these details.

Drafting
- Write an attention-grabbing introduction that defines how and why you are comparing and contrasting the two civilizations.
- Give details about each point of comparison/contrast and use parallel structure to cover similar points for the two cases.

Revising
- Use the guidelines for revising your report on page SH12 of the Writing Handbook.

Document-Based Assessment

Julius Caesar: Father of the Roman Empire

Julius Caesar has been called the father of the Roman empire and the most influential man in European history. After Caesar's assassination, his nephew Octavian declared him a god. The documents below are just a few of many impressions of him that writers, historians, and artists have left behind for centuries.

Document A

"There is a story that while he was crossing the Alps he came to a small village with hardly any inhabitants and altogether a miserable-looking place. His friends were laughing and joking about it, saying: 'No doubt here too one would find people trying hard to gain office, and here too there are struggles to get the first place [in government] and jealous rivalries among the great men.' Caesar then said to them in all seriousness: 'As far as I am concerned, I would rather be the first man here than the second in Rome.'"

—From *Life of Caesar* by Plutarch

Document B

"O mighty Caesar, dost thou lie so low?
Are all thy conquests, glories, triumphs, spoils,
Shrunk to this little measure? Fare thee well.
I know not, gentlemen, what you intend,
Who else must be let blood, who else is rank.
If I myself, there is no hour so fit
As Caesar's death's hour, nor no instrument
Of half that worth as those your swords, made rich
With the most noble blood of all this world."

—Mark Antony, upon discovering Caesar's murder;
From *The Tragedy of Julius Caesar*
by William Shakespeare

Document C

"In eloquence and warlike achievements, he equaled at least, if he did not surpass, the greatest of men. . . . Cicero, in recounting to Brutus the famous orators, declares, 'that he does not see that Caesar was inferior to any one of them'; and says, 'that he had an elegant, splendid, noble, and magnificent vein of eloquence.'"

—From *The Lives of the Twelve Caesars*
by Suetonius

Document D
Julius Caesar

Analyzing Documents

Use your knowledge of history and Documents A, B, C, and D to answer questions 1–4.

1. Which side of Caesar does Plutarch's anecdote reveal?
   A his drive to be the best
   B his desire to serve Rome
   C his wish to reach high spiritual levels
   D his interest in having many areas of achievement

2. According to Shakespeare's Mark Antony, Caesar was
   A cunning, cruel, and ambitious.
   B weak, foolish, and condescending.
   C honorable, noble, and great.
   D humble, kind, and compassionate.

3. What about Caesar did Cicero admire?
   A that he was a cunning strategist
   B that he was a practical and realistic leader
   C that he was a humble and kind man
   D that he was an engaging and talented speaker

4. **Writing Task** Julius Caesar was murdered more than 2,000 years ago. Why has he continued to be a figure of interest through modern times?

6 Civilizations of the Americas
Prehistory–A.D. 1570

Rediscovering the Ancient Maya

From 1830 to 1842, British diplomat and lawyer John Lloyd Stephens traveled across Mesoamerica. His tales of Maya ruins sparked immense interest in the ancient civilization. Here he marvels at Palenque, the first Maya city to be re-discovered in the modern era.

66What we had before our eyes was grand, curious, and remarkable enough. Here were the remains of a cultivated, polished . . . people, who had passed through all the stages incident to [accompanying] the rise and fall of nations; reached their golden age, and perished, . . . and these [ruins] were the only memorials of their footsteps upon earth. . . . Wherever we moved we saw the evidences of their taste, their skill in arts, their wealth and power. In the midst of desolation and ruin . . . we called back into life the strange people who gazed at us . . . from the walls. **99**

Listen to the Witness History audio to hear more about the ancient Maya world.

◀ **The 1946 discovery of Bonampak, an ancient Maya site, revealed spectacular murals of warriors and nobles. Here, musicians perform at a large celebration.**

Burial mask of Pakal, ruler of Palenque

Golden Inca llama

Inuit snow goggles

Chapter Preview

Chapter Focus Question What circumstances helped the civilizations and diverse cultures of the Americas to develop in ways both common and unique?

Section 1
Civilizations of Mesoamerica

Section 2
Andean Cultures of South America

Section 3
Peoples of North America

Note Taking Study Guide *Online*
For: Note Taking and Concept Connector worksheets
Web Code: nad-0601

Aztec eagle warrior

South American
bird warrior

WITNESS HISTORY 🔊 AUDIO

Elite Warriors Uphold an Empire

Among the Aztecs, a force of fierce soldiers emerged to aid the ruler in maintaining an empire. The most highly regarded fighters were eagle and jaguar warriors, who wore costumes resembling the honored animals for whom they were named (a tradition in other cultures of the Americas as well). Indeed, Aztec warfare served both a political purpose—defending the empire—and a ritual one. It was the gods whom the Aztec rulers believed granted them the right to rule. Sacrificing humans—the captives of battle—was the leading way to appeal to the gods.

Focus Question What factors encouraged the rise of powerful civilizations in Mesoamerica?

Civilizations of Mesoamerica

Objectives
- Describe when and where people first settled the Americas.
- Analyze the main characteristics of the Olmec and Maya civilizations.
- Outline how the Aztec empire and Aztec society took shape.

Terms, People, and Places

Mesoamerica	Tenochtitlán
maize	chinampas
Olmecs	tribute
stela	Teotihuacán
Valley of Mexico	

Note Taking

Reading Skill: Compare and Contrast Use a chart like the one below to take notes on similarities and differences in how early people adapted to climate and geography in different parts of the Americas.

Adapting to the Americas	
Climate	**Geography**
•	•
•	•

The Americas include two continents, North America and South America. Within these two geographic regions lies a cultural region called **Mesoamerica,** which is made up of Mexico and Central America. Some of the earliest civilizations in the Americas developed in Mesoamerica.

People Settle in the Americas

Sometime between 12,000 and 10,000 years ago, most scholars believe, people first arrived in the Americas. Scholars are still trying to understand the details of how this great migration occurred. Originally, it was believed that people came from Asia and entered through Alaska. This migration is thought to have taken place near the end of the last Ice Age, which lasted from about 100,000 years ago to about 10,000 years ago. During the ice age, so much water froze into thick ice sheets that the sea level dropped, exposing a land bridge between Siberia and Alaska in the area that is now the Bering Strait. About 10,000 B.C., Earth's climate warmed and the ice melted. As a result, water levels rose and covered the Bering land bridge.

The earliest evidence supported the theory that hunters followed herds of bison and mammoths across the land bridge and then south through North America, Central America, and South America. Recent data suggest something different—that people migrated to parts of the Americas much earlier and along coastal routes, perhaps paddling small boats. Although neither theory has been proved, researchers now base the dates of migration into the Americas mostly on evidence found at prehistoric sites.

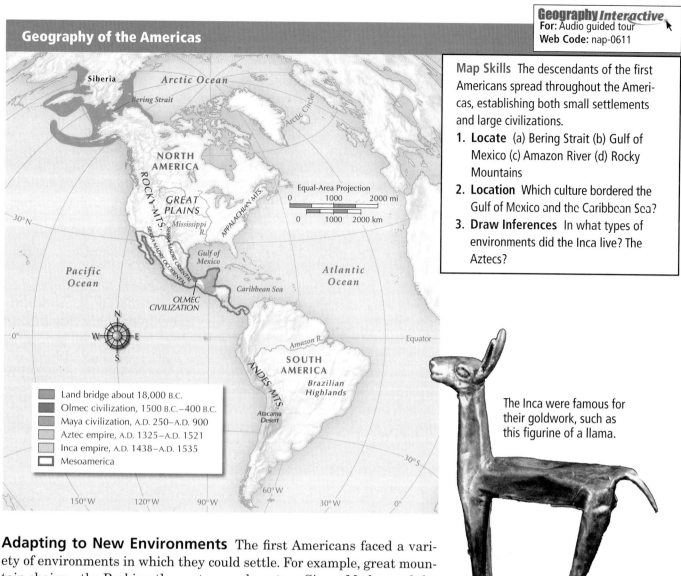

Geography *Interactive*
For: Audio guided tour
Web Code: nap-0611

Map Skills The descendants of the first Americans spread throughout the Americas, establishing both small settlements and large civilizations.
1. **Locate** (a) Bering Strait (b) Gulf of Mexico (c) Amazon River (d) Rocky Mountains
2. **Location** Which culture bordered the Gulf of Mexico and the Caribbean Sea?
3. **Draw Inferences** In what types of environments did the Inca live? The Aztecs?

Map legend:
- Land bridge about 18,000 B.C.
- Olmec civilization, 1500 B.C.–400 B.C.
- Maya civilization, A.D. 250–A.D. 900
- Aztec empire, A.D. 1325–A.D. 1521
- Inca empire, A.D. 1438–A.D. 1535
- Mesoamerica

The Inca were famous for their goldwork, such as this figurine of a llama.

Adapting to New Environments The first Americans faced a variety of environments in which they could settle. For example, great mountain chains—the Rockies, the eastern and western Sierra Madre, and the Andes—dominate the western Americas. In addition, through the continents flow two of the world's four longest rivers, the Amazon of South America and the Mississippi of North America. Far to the north and south of the continents, people learned to survive in icy, treeless lands. Closer to the Equator, people settled in the hot, wet climate and dense vegetation of the Amazon rain forest. Elsewhere, hunters adapted to deserts like the Atacama of Chile, woodlands like those in eastern North America, and the fertile plains of both continents.

People Begin to Farm and Build Villages In the Americas, as elsewhere, the greatest adaptation occurred when people learned to domesticate plants and animals. These changes took place slowly between about 8500 B.C. and 2000 B.C. In Mesoamerica, Neolithic people cultivated a range of crops, including beans, sweet potatoes, peppers, tomatoes, squash, and **maize**—the Native American name for corn. People in South America cultivated crops such as maize and cassava and domesticated llamas and other animals valued for their wool. By 3000 B.C. in parts of South America and 1500 B.C. in parts of Mesoamerica, farmers had settled in villages. Populations then expanded, and some villages eventually grew into the great early cities of the Americas.

✔ **Checkpoint** How did early Americans adapt to different environments?

Civilization Arises With the Olmecs

The earliest American civilization, that of the **Olmecs,** emerged in the tropical forests along the Gulf Coast of Mexico. The civilization lasted from about 1500 B.C. to 400 B.C. Compared to other civilizations, archaeologists know little about the Olmecs. They do not know where the Olmecs came from or what they called themselves. But evidence in the form of temples and large and small pieces of art suggests that a powerful class of priests and nobles stood at the top of society. These elite groups may have lived in ceremonial centers, while the common people lived in surrounding farming villages.

Much of Olmec art is carved stone. The smallest examples include jade figurines of people and gods. The most dramatic remains are 14 giant stone heads found at the major ceremonial centers of San Lorenzo and La Venta. Scholars believe that these colossal heads, which the Olmecs carved from 40-ton stones, are portraits of rulers. No one knows exactly how the Olmecs moved these stones from distant quarries without wheeled vehicles or draft animals.

The Olmecs also engaged in trade, through which they influenced a wide area. The grinning jaguars and serpents that decorate many Olmec carvings appear in the arts of later Mesoamerican peoples. The Olmecs also invented a calendar, and they carved hieroglyphic writing into stone. Because later Mesoamerican peoples adopted such advances, many scholars consider the Olmecs the "mother culture" of Mesoamerica.

✓ **Checkpoint**   **What aspects of Olmec culture have archaeologists uncovered?**

The Maya Build Widespread Civilization

Among the peoples the Olmecs influenced were the Maya. By 300 B.C., the Maya were building large cities, such as El Mirador in Guatemala. By about A.D. 250, the Maya golden age—known as the Classic Period—began, with city-states flourishing from the Yucatán Peninsula in southern Mexico through much of Central America.

Agriculture Thrives Before the Maya developed large population centers, they lived scattered across the land. They developed two farming methods that allowed them to thrive in the tropical environment. In many areas, farmers burned down forests and then cleared the land in order to plant on it. After a few years, the fields were no longer fertile. The Maya would then abandon these lands until they could be used once again. In the meantime, farmers would burn and clear new lands for farming. In addition, along the banks of rivers, Maya farmers built raised fields to lift crops up above the annual floodwaters. These methods allowed the Maya to produce enough maize and other crops to support rapidly growing cities.

Powerful City-States Emerge The Maya cities that developed before and during the Classic Period never formed an empire. Instead, individual and powerful city-states evolved. The smaller city-states ruled over the people living directly within and near their borders. The largest ones reigned over neighboring areas as well—often requiring nearby cities to show allegiance to their kings and to participate in their ritual activities. Over the course of hundreds of years, many different city-states held

Colossal Olmec head from La Venta

Note Taking

Reading Skill: Compare and Contrast
Use a Venn diagram to keep track of key similarities and differences among the cultures of Mesoamerica.

Cities of the Maya Realm

Gulf of Mexico

Dzibilchaltun
Chichén Itzá • Coba
Uxmal • Kabah
Jaina • Sayil • Labna
Santa Rosa Xtampak'
Etzna

20° N

Comalcalco
Becan • Xpuhil
Río Bec • Cerros •
Calakmul • El Palmar
El Mirador • Nakbe
Palenque • Uaxactun • Nak'um
Piedras • El Perú • Tikal
Tonina • Negras • Yaxchilan • Yaxha • Naranjo
Bonampak • Seibal • Caracol
Altar de Sacrificios •
Dos Pilas • Pusilha
88° W

16° N

Miller Projection
0   50   100 mi
0   50   100 km

Izapa
Copán •
Kaminaljuyu

Pacific Ocean

Monte Alto

96° W   92° W

Quirigua

Caribbean Sea

☐ Extent of Maya civilization
• Key Maya city, 300 B.C.–A.D. 250
○ Key Maya city, A.D. 250–A.D. 900

Geography *Interactive*
For: Interactive map
Web Code: nap-0612

Map Skills Many Maya cities were hidden for centuries beneath tropical overgrowth. The archaeologists who uncovered them have learned that numerous powerful governments once ruled the area.

1. **Locate** (a) Tikal (b) Calakmul (c) Copán (d) Palenque (e) Piedras Negras
2. **Region** How did the geography of the Maya region differ from north to south?
3. **Make Generalizations** Some Maya cities existed only in the earlier era shown on the map, some only in the later era, and some in both. Why might the lifespan of a Maya city have varied?

power, with warfare and trade a constant theme of life among them. Cities such as Palenque, Copán, and Piedras Negras all carried great influence in their time, but the largest and most supreme power resided in the rulers of Tikal and Calakmul.

While the Maya were not united politically, city-states maintained regular contact through a system of economic exchange, which generated much wealth. Traders carried valuable cargoes long distances by sea and along roads made of packed earth. Trade goods included items of daily use—such as honey, salt, and cotton—and nonessential but prized items such as feathers, jade, and jaguar pelts. These goods might have been used in ceremonies or to show status.

Structuring Society Each Maya city had its own ruler, who was usually male. Maya records and carvings show that women occasionally governed on their own or in the name of young sons. Nobles served many functions in support of the ruler. Some were military leaders, while others managed public works, collected taxes, and enforced laws. Scribes, painters, and sculptors were also very highly respected. Merchants may have formed a middle class in society, though the wealthiest and most powerful merchants were certainly nobles.

The majority of the Maya were farmers. They grew maize, beans, and squash—the basic food crops of Mesoamerica—as well as fruit trees, cotton, and brilliant tropical flowers. To support the cities, farmers paid taxes in food and worked on construction projects. Some cities also included a population of slaves, who generally were commoners who had been captured in war.

Powerful Maya rulers included Yax Pac of Copán (above, receiving the staff of leadership from the city's first ruler) and Pakal of Palenque (who wore the jade burial mask at left).

✓ **Checkpoint** How did the Maya political structure differ from an empire?

Cultural Life of the Maya

The cultural life of the Maya included impressive advances in learning and the arts. In addition, the Maya developed a complex polytheistic religion that influenced their cultural life as well as their spiritual beliefs. Many Maya today maintain elements of the traditional religion established by the ancient Maya, such as the belief that each person's spirit is associated with a particular animal.

Sculptors Leave a Legacy in Stone The cities of the Maya are known today for their towering temples and palaces built from stone. Temples rested on pyramid-shaped platforms that were often quite large. Atop the temples, priests performed rites and sacrifices, while the people watched from the plazas below. Some temples also served as burial places for rulers, nobles, and priests. Palaces may have been used as royal residences as well as locations for meetings, courts, and other governmental activities.

The Maya placed elaborately carved sculpture on many of their buildings. They also sculpted tall stone monuments, each of which is called a **stela** (STEE luh). These carvings preserve striking images of nobles, warriors in plumed headdresses, and powerful rulers. They also represent the Maya gods, including the creator god Itzamna (et SAHM nah), the rain god Chac (chakh), and the sun god K'inich Ajaw (keen EECH ah HOW).

Scribes Record Historical Events The Maya also developed a hieroglyphic writing system, which scholars did not decipher until recent decades. Maya scribes carved inscriptions on stelae that include names of rulers, mentions of neighboring city-states, and dates and descriptions of events. They also wrote about astronomy, rituals, and other religious matters in books made of bark paper. Spanish conquerors later burned most of these books, considering any works that were written by non-Christians to be unacceptable. Three books, however, were taken to Europe and have survived into the present.

Priests Develop Astronomy and Mathematics Maya priests needed to measure time accurately in order to hold ceremonies at the correct moment. As a result, many priests became expert mathematicians and astronomers. They developed an accurate 365-day solar calendar as well as a 260-day ritual calendar. Maya priests also invented a numbering system that included place values and the concept of zero.

Maya Civilization Declines About A.D. 900, the Maya abandoned many of their cities. In the Yucatán Peninsula, cities flourished for a few more centuries, but there, too, the Maya eventually stopped building them. By the time the Spanish arrived in the 1500s, the Maya mostly lived in farming villages. Archaeologists do not know for sure why Maya civilization declined, although theories abound. For example, frequent warfare may have taken its toll on society, or overpopulation could have led to over-farming and exhaustion of the soil.

Throughout the region, however, the remoteness of their jungle and mountain locations allowed many Maya to survive the encounter with the Spanish. Today, more than two million Maya people live in Guatemala and southern Mexico.

✓ **Checkpoint** What do Maya arts and writing tell us about their religion and history?

Photographs From the Past
British archaeologist Alfred P. Maudslay won fame in the late 1800s for his sharp and stunning photographs of Maya ruins, such as this stela showing a ruler from the city of Quirigua.

The Common Culture of Mesoamerica

In addition to the societies you are reading about in this section, numerous others arose in Mesoamerica between the time of the Olmecs and the arrival of Spanish explorers in the 1500s. While each developed individual traits that set it apart from the other groups, they all shared various cultural elements. For example, both the Maya and the Aztecs used the complicated "calendar round," which combined days from a 260-ritual calendar and a 365-solar calendar to form 52-year cycles similar in cultural importance to our centuries.

Writing
All Mesoamerican societies that developed writing used a hieroglyphic system. The level of complexity varied from group to group, however. The Zapotec (back) and the Maya (front) systems were the most advanced.

Architecture
Throughout the region, architecture varied in style and decoration. However, the stepped pyramid prevailed as a basic shape of buildings in all cultures, from the small temple at the Toltec capital at Tula (above) to this enormous structure (right) at the Maya city of Tikal.

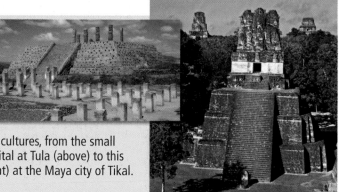

Sport and Ritual Although rules varied in the famous Mesoamerican ballgame, the basic format stayed the same. Players competed on an I-shaped ballcourt with sloped walls, like the Zapotec court below. They wore thick padding (as on the Maya ballplayer figurine above) to avoid injury as they tried to knock a solid rubber ball down the court and through a small hoop. The challenging game carried great ritual importance, representing the movements of the moon and sun. Sometimes, the losing team would be sacrificed to keep these heavenly bodies in motion (as shown at right).

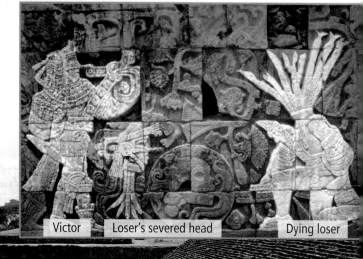

Victor Loser's severed head Dying loser

Thinking Critically
1. **Draw Inferences** In what ways do you think these societies passed elements of culture to one another?
2. **Determine Relevance** How might learning about the shared elements of culture help scholars understand each Mesoamerican society?

The Aztec Empire Forms in Mexico

Sometime shortly after about A.D. 1200, bands of nomadic people from the north migrated into the Valley of Mexico, which lies in the high plateau of central Mexico. These people identified themselves as separate tribes, such as the Mexica (may SHEE kah), from whom Mexico gets it name. All the tribes spoke one language—Nahuatl (NAH hwaht el)—and believed their origins began in the same legendary birthplace, Aztlan. Together, these tribes are known as the Aztecs.

The Aztecs Settle in the Valley of Mexico In A.D. 1325, the Aztecs founded their capital city, Tenochtitlán (teh nawch tee TLAHN). According to Aztec legend, the gods had told the Aztecs to search for an eagle holding a snake in its beak and perching atop a cactus. When they saw this sign, they would know where to build their capital. Indeed, they finally saw the sign on a swampy island in Lake Texcoco (tesh KOH koh), and there they built their city. Today, Mexico City sits atop this same site.

As their population grew, the Aztecs found ingenious ways to create more farmland in their lake environment. They built **chinampas**, artificial islands made of mud piled atop reed mats that were anchored to the shallow lake-bed with willow trees. On these "floating gardens," the Aztecs raised maize, squash, and beans. They gradually filled in parts of the lake and created canals for transportation. Wide stone causeways linked Tenochtitlán to the mainland.

Vocabulary Builder

ingenious—(in JEEN yus) *adj.* clever, original, and effective

Tenochtitlán: Building an Island City

The Aztecs built causeways to connect Tenochtitlán to the rural settlements of the mainland. After the Spanish invaded in the 1500s, they drew a map of the city (at left). Although not to scale, it shows the causeways and dense buildings of the large capital. The diagram (below) shows how the chinampas were built. *What engineering skills must the Aztecs have used to build the city?*

Causeway

Maize

Willow tree

Mud-and-reed mat

Woven reed wall

Mud and manure

The Empire Expands In the 1400s, the Aztecs greatly expanded their territory. Through a combination of fierce conquests and shrewd alliances, they spread their rule across most of Mexico, from the Gulf of Mexico in the east to the Pacific Ocean in the west. By 1517, the Aztec empire numbered an estimated five to six million people.

✓ **Checkpoint** What are some advantages and disadvantages of building a city on an island in a lake?

Aztec Society Takes Shape

War brought immense wealth as well as power to the Aztec empire. Tribute, or payment from conquered peoples, helped the Aztecs turn their capital into a magnificent city. From its temples and royal palaces to its zoos and floating gardens, Tenochtitlán seemed a city of wonders. It was also the center of a complex, well-ordered empire.

Structuring Government and Society Unlike the Maya city-states, each of which had its own king, the Aztec empire had a single ruler. A council of nobles, priests, and military leaders elected the emperor, whose primary function was to lead in war. Below him, nobles served as officials, judges, and governors of conquered provinces. Next came the warriors, who could rise to noble status by performing well on the battlefield. The priests were a class apart. They performed rituals to please the gods and prevent droughts or other disasters.

A powerful middle class included long-distance traders, who ferried goods across the empire and beyond. With goods from the highlands such as weapons, tools, and rope, they bartered for tropical products such as jaguar skins and cocoa beans.

The majority of people were commoners who farmed the land. At the bottom of society were serfs and slaves, who were mostly prisoners of war or debtors. Despite their low status, slaves' rights were clearly established by law. For example, slaves could own land and buy their freedom.

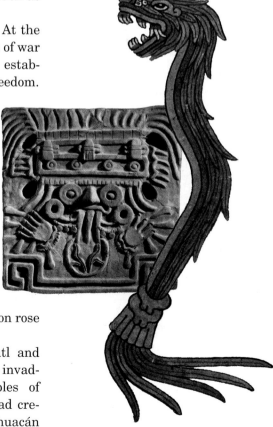

Representations of Tlaloc (left) and Quetzalcoatl (right)

Religion and Mythology Influence Culture The Aztecs believed in many gods, including Huitzilopochtli (weets ee loh POHCH tlee), whom they revered as the patron god of their people. His temple towered above central Tenochtitlán. The Aztecs also worshipped Quetzalcoatl (ket sahl koh AHT el), the feathered serpent who reigned over earth and water, plus the other powerful gods of an earlier culture that had been centered at the city of Teotihuacán (tay oh tee wah KAHN).

Teotihuacán had dominated life in the Valley of Mexico from about A.D. 200 to A.D. 750. The city was well planned, with wide roads, massive temples, and large apartment buildings to house its population of perhaps 200,000. Along the main avenue, the enormous Pyramid of the Sun and the Pyramid of the Moon rose majestically toward the sky.

Citizens of Teotihuacán worshiped gods such as Quetzalcoatl and Tlaloc (TLAH lohk), the rain god. After Teotihuacán fell, possibly to invaders, its culture survived and greatly influenced later peoples of Mesoamerica. The Aztecs, for example, believed that the gods had created the world multiple times. In their mythology, it was in Teotihuacán that the gods created the world in which the Aztecs lived.

In this translation from an Aztec text, Nanahuatzin's bravery is underscored as he proves willing to sacrifice himself where another god, the moon, was not.

Primary Source

66 It is said that when the [sun] was made, . . . there was fasting for four days. It is said that the moon would be the sun. And when four days were completed, it is said, the [sun] was made during the night. . . . a very great fire was laid . . . into which was to leap, was to fall the moon—where he was to gain renown, glory: by which he would become the sun. And the moon thereupon went in order to leap into the fire. But he did not dare do it; he feared the fire. Then all the gods shouted, they said: "When [is this to be], O gods? Let the sun stop!" But little [Nanahuatzin] had already dared; he thereupon had leaped into the fire. Thus he became the sun.

And the moon, when he was deprived of the renown, the glory, was much shamed.99
—Fray Bernardino de Sahagún, *General History of the Things of New Spain*

In Aztec mythology, the gods frequently sacrificed themselves for the good of the people. They believed a god named Nanahuatzin (nah nah WAHTS een) had sacrificed himself to become the sun. To give the sun strength to rise each day, the Aztecs offered human sacrifices. Most of the victims were prisoners of war, who were plentiful because the Aztecs carried on almost continuous warfare.

Aztec Knowledge Expands Priests were the keepers of Aztec knowledge. They recorded laws and historical events in the Aztec hieroglyphic writing system. Some priests ran schools. Others used their knowledge of astronomy and mathematics to foretell the future. The Aztecs, like the Maya, developed a 260-day ritual calendar and a 365-day solar calendar.

Like many other ancient peoples, the Aztecs believed that illness was a punishment from the gods. Still, Aztec priests used herbs and other medicines to treat fevers and wounds. Aztec physicians could set broken bones and treat dental cavities. They also prescribed steam baths as cures for various ills, a therapy still in use today.

 Checkpoint How was Aztec society structured?

Looking Ahead

The Aztecs developed a sophisticated and complex culture. But among many of the peoples they conquered, discontent festered and rebellion often flared up. At the height of Aztec power, word reached Tenochtitlán that pale-skinned, bearded men had landed on the east coast. When the armies from Spain arrived, they found ready allies among peoples who were ruled by the Aztec empire. In a later chapter, you will read about the results of the encounter between the Aztecs and the newcomers from far-off Spain.

SECTION 1 **Assessment**

Progress Monitoring Online
For: Self-quiz with vocabulary practice
Web Code: naa-0611

Terms, People, and Places

1. For each term, person, or place listed at the beginning of the section, write a sentence explaining its significance.

Note Taking

2. **Reading Skill: Compare and Contrast** Use your completed chart and Venn diagram to answer the Focus Question: What factors encouraged the rise of powerful civilizations in Mesoamerica?

Comprehension and Critical Thinking

3. **Recognize Sufficient Evidence** What types of evidence do you think archaeologists need in order to know for certain when people populated the Americas?

4. **Analyze Information** How do you think archaeologists use public buildings, monuments, and artwork to trace the influence of earlier civilizations, such as the Olmecs, on later people?

5. **Make Comparisons** Compare the Aztec and Maya civilizations. What characteristics do they share the most? In what way(s) do they differ the most?

● **Writing About History**

Quick Write: Choose a Topic When you write a narrative essay, start by choosing a topic. Suppose you want to write a narrative from the perspective of an ancient Maya person. Make a list of topics that interest you, such as a day in the life of a Maya sculptor or an account of a battle between two rival Maya city-states. You may want to do research in books and on the Internet before you settle on a topic.

On Inca roads, couriers (right) often carried quipus (far right), or recording devices.

WITNESS HISTORY 🔊 AUDIO

Impressive Inca Roads

❝In human memory, I believe that there is no account of a road as great as this, running through deep valleys, high mountains, banks of snow, torrents of water, living rock, and wild rivers. . . . In all places it was clean and swept free of refuse, with lodgings, storehouses, Sun temples, and posts along the route. Oh! Can anything similar be claimed for Alexander [the Great] or any of the [other] powerful kings who ruled the world. . . ?❞
—Pedro Cieza de León, Spanish explorer admiring the Inca road system in the 1500s

Focus Question What characterized the cultures and civilizations that developed in the Andes?

Andean Cultures of South America

Objectives
- Examine the early cultures of the Andes.
- Understand how Inca emperors extended and maintained their empire.
- Describe the daily life of the Inca.

Terms, People, and Places

Chavín	Pachacuti Inca Yupanqui
Moche	Sapa Inca
adobe	Cuzco
Nazca	quipu
Huari	ayllu
Tiahuanaco	Inti

Note Taking

Reading Skill: Contrast Contrast the cultures of the early peoples of the Andes with that of the Inca. Use a chart like the one below to organize relevant details about each culture as you read.

Chavín	
Location	
Unique achievements	

The first cultures of South America developed in the Andean region along the western edge of the continent. This region includes a variety of climates and terrains. The narrow coastal plain is a dry, lifeless desert crossed by occasional rivers. Further inland, the snow-capped Andes Mountains rise steeply, leveling off into high plateaus that bake by day and freeze at night. East of the Andes, dense jungles stretch from Peru into Brazil.

Cultures Develop in the Andes

Thousands of years ago, people settled in fishing villages along the desert coast of Peru and Chile. Gradually they expanded inland, farming the river valleys that run up into the highland plateaus. Using careful irrigation, they grew maize, cotton, squash, and beans. On mountain slopes, they cultivated potatoes, eventually producing 700 varieties. On high plateaus, they domesticated the llama and the alpaca. Eventually, they built large ceremonial centers and developed skills in pottery and weaving.

Chavín Culture Unifies a Region Archaeologists have pieced together a chronology of various cultures that left their mark on the Andean region over the course of 2,000 years. The earliest of these was the Chavín (chah VEEN) culture, named for ruins at Chavín de Huantar (chah VEEN day WAHN tahr). There, in about 900 B.C., people built a huge temple complex. Archaeologists are not sure of the Chavín political structure, but they think the culture's religion unified people throughout northern and central Peru. Chavín arts and religion continued to influence later peoples of Peru as well.

The Moche Build a Culture Between A.D. 100 and A.D. 700, the Moche (MOH chay) people—named after their most famous city—forged a civilization along the arid north coast of Peru. Skilled Moche farmers developed methods for fertilizing the soil and used canals to irrigate the land. Their leaders built roads and organized networks of relay runners to carry messages, ideas that another Andean civilization, the Inca, would later adopt.

At the city of Moche, builders constructed the largest adobe structure in the ancient Americas. Adobe is a mixture of clay and plant fibers that becomes hard as it dries in the sun. Moche artisans perfected skills in textile production, goldworking, and woodcarving and produced ceramic vessels in lifelike imitation of people and animals.

Cultures of the Southern Andes Many other Andean cultures emerged, and some left behind intriguing clues about their lives and beliefs. Between about 200 B.C. and A.D. 600 along the southern coast of Peru, the Nazca (NAHS kah) people etched geoglyphs in the desert. A geoglyph is a figure or line made on Earth's surface by clearing away rocks and soil. The Nazca geoglyphs include straight lines that run for miles as well as giant birds, whales, and other animals. Most researchers think that the geoglyphs carried some sort of spiritual meaning.

The city of Huari (WAH ree) developed east of the Nazca culture. It controlled much of Peru's mountain and coastal areas. At the same time, a powerful city, Tiahuanaco (tee ah wah NAH koh), developed on the southern shores of Lake Titicaca, in modern-day Bolivia. It reigned over parts of modern-day Argentina, Chile, and Peru. Many of the same artistic styles appear at Huari and Tiahuanaco, leading scholars to think that these two southern powers shared religious or trade affiliations.

✓ **Checkpoint** What was unique about the Nazca culture of the Andes?

Cultures of the Andes
For more than 2,000 years, cultures of varying sizes developed in the Andean region. Although not all as powerful as the Inca, most left behind fascinating clues to their skills and interests—such as this Moche laughing-man vessel (top right) and Nazca spider geoglyph (bottom right). *In the region of which earlier culture did the Inca build Cuzco?*

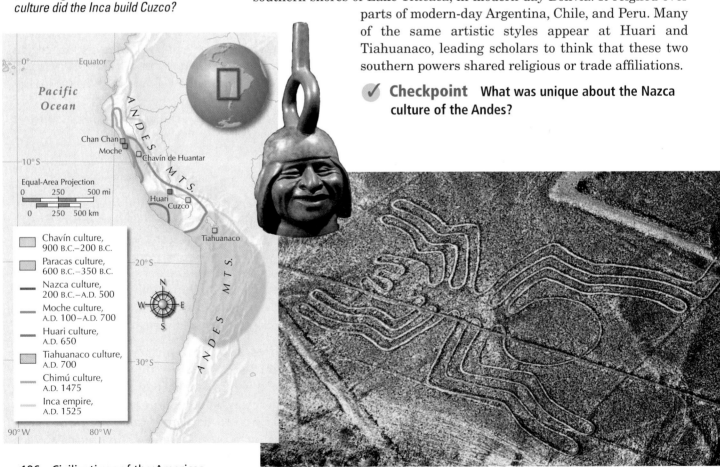

Pacific Ocean

Equator

0°

Chan Chan
Moche
Chavín de Huantar

10°S

Equal-Area Projection
0   250   500 mi
0   250   500 km

Huari
Cuzco

Tiahuanaco

ANDES MTS.

20°S

N
W   E
S

30°S

Chavín culture,
900 B.C.–200 B.C.

Paracas culture,
600 B.C.–350 B.C.

Nazca culture,
200 B.C.–A.D. 500

Moche culture,
A.D. 100–A.D. 700

Huari culture,
A.D. 650

Tiahuanaco culture,
A.D. 700

Chimú culture,
A.D. 1475

Inca empire,
A.D. 1525

90°W   80°W

Inca Rulers Maintain a Large Empire

The most powerful of the Andean civilizations—the Inca civilization—came into being in the 1100s with the founding of its first dynasty. For the next three centuries, the Inca civilization stood out no more than any other. But in 1438, a historic change occurred. Pachacuti Inca Yupanqui (pahch ah KOO tee ING kuh yoo PANG kee), a skilled warrior and leader, proclaimed himself Sapa Inca, or emperor.

From his small kingdom at Cuzco in a high mountain valley, Pachacuti set out on a campaign of conquest. Once he subdued neighboring peoples, he enlisted them in his armies. His son, emperor Topa Inca Yupanqui, continued the expansion. With Cuzco as its capital, the resulting empire stretched more than 2,500 miles along the Andes, from Ecuador in the north to Chile in the south.

The Emperor Rules Over All The Sapa Inca held absolute power. Claiming to be divine, the son of the sun itself, he was also the empire's religious leader. Gold, considered the "sweat of the sun," served as his symbol. His queen, the Coya, carried out important religious duties and sometimes governed in his absence.

The Sapa Inca laid claim over all the land, herds, mines, and people of his empire. Thus the people had no personal property, so there was little demand for items for barter or sale. As a result, trade did not play a major role in the Inca economy. Instead, the Sapa Inca kept the people fed and public works projects staffed using a labor tax. Periodically, he would call upon men of a certain age to serve as laborers for short periods, perhaps a few months. By so doing, he could access millions of laborers at once.

Inca rulers ran an efficient government. Nobles ruled the provinces along with local chieftains whom the Inca armies had conquered. Below them, officials carried out the day-to-day business of enforcing laws and organizing labor. Specially trained officials kept records on a quipu, a collection of colored strings that were knotted in different ways to represent various numbers. Scholars think that the Inca, who never invented a writing system, may have used quipus to record economic, bureaucratic, religious, and other information.

Uniting the Empire To unite their empire, the Inca imposed their language, Quechua (KECH wuh), and their religion on the people they conquered. They also created one of history's great road <u>networks</u>. At its greatest extent, it wound about 14,000 miles through mountains and deserts, passing through an area inhabited by almost 10 million people. Hundreds of bridges spanned rivers and deep gorges. Steps were cut into steep slopes and tunnels dug through hillsides. The expanse of the Inca road system was unmatched in the early Americas.

The roads allowed armies and news to move rapidly throughout the empire. At stations set regular distances apart, runners waited to carry messages. Relays of runners could carry news of a revolt swiftly from a distant province to the capital. Inca soldiers stood guard at outposts throughout the empire. Within days of an uprising, they would be on the move to crush the rebels. Ordinary people were restricted from using the roads at all.

BIOGRAPHY

Pachacuti

Growing up, Pachacuti Inca Yupanqui (1391?–1473?) did not seem destined to rule the Inca people. True, his father, Viracocha, was their king. But Viracocha had chosen another son—Urcon—as his successor.

According to Inca sagas, one day the army of a powerful neighboring people, the Chanca, threatened to sweep down on Cuzco. With the Chanca army quickly approaching, Viracocha and Urcon withdrew from Cuzco to a nearby fort. Pachacuti remained to defend the city, commanding the army and inspiring his warriors on to a stunning victory. Pachacuti then set himself up as king of Cuzco, eventually reuniting the entire Inca state under his rule. **What traits and skills must Pachacuti have needed to become emperor?**

Vocabulary Builder

<u>network</u>—(NET wurk) *n.* a widely distributed group of things that work together as a unit or system

Cuzco as Capital All roads led through Cuzco. People from all the culture groups ruled by the empire lived in the city. Members of a given group lived in a particular part of the city and wore the traditional clothing and practiced the traditional crafts of their region of origin. In the heart of the city stood the great Temple of the Sun, its interior walls lined with gold. Like Inca palaces and forts, the temple was made of enormous stone blocks, each polished and carved to fit exactly in place without mortar used to secure it. Inca engineers were so precise that many of their buildings have survived severe earthquakes.

✔ **Checkpoint** Describe three ways that the Inca united their empire.

Daily Life of the Inca

The Inca strictly regulated the lives of millions of people within their empire. The leaders of each Inca village, called an **ayllu** (EYE loo), carried out government orders. They assigned jobs to each family and organizing the community to work the land. Government officials arranged marriages to ensure that men and women were settled at a certain age.

Farming the Land Inca farmers expanded step terraces built by earlier Andean peoples. They carved out flat strips of land on steep hillsides and built stone walls to hold the land in place. The terraces the Inca created kept rains from washing away the soil and made farming possible in places where naturally flat land was scarce.

Farmers spent part of each year working land for their community, and part working land for the emperor and the temples. The government allotted part of each harvest to specific groups of people or for particular purposes. It stored the rest in case of disasters such as famine.

Mastering Metalwork and Weaving The Inca were some of the most skilled metalworkers in the Americas. They learned to work and alloy, or blend, copper, tin, bronze, silver, and gold. While they employed copper

The Heights of Inca Stonework

Machu Picchu is the most impressive example of Inca stonework. Built high in the Andes, the large complex of buildings sits at an elevation of more than 7,000 feet. Agricultural terraces line the surrounding hillsides. *What challenges do you think the Inca faced when building in such a location?*

and bronze for useful objects, they reserved precious metals for statues of gods and goddesses, eating utensils for the nobles, and decoration.

The Inca also mastered the art of weaving, a practice passed down to them from earlier Andean peoples. They raised cotton and sheared the wool from llamas and alpacas to create colorful textiles to be worn as clothing or as adornments, such as belts and bags.

Medical Advances The Inca developed important medical practices, including surgery on the human skull. In such operations, they cleaned the area to be operated on and then gave the patient a drug to make him or her unconscious—procedures similar to the modern use of antiseptics and anesthesia. The Inca also used medical procedures to mummify the dead.

Religion and Ritual The Inca worshipped many gods linked to the forces of nature. People offered food, clothing, and drink to the guardian spirits of the home and the village. Each month had its own festival, from the great ripening and the dance of the young maize to the festival of the water. Festivals were celebrated with ceremonies, sports, and games.

A powerful class of priests served the gods. Chief among the gods was Inti, the sun god. His special attendants, the "Chosen Women," were selected from each region of the empire. During years of training, they studied the mysteries of the religion, learned to prepare ritual food and drink, and made the elaborate wool garments worn by the Sapa Inca and the Coya. After their training, most Chosen Women continued to serve Inti. Others joined the Inca's court or married nobles.

✔ **Checkpoint** How did the Inca excel in the arts and in medicine?

Looking Ahead

At its height, the Inca civilization was a center of learning and political power. But in 1525, the emperor Huayna Capac (WY nuh kah PAHK) died suddenly of illness. Civil war broke out over which of his sons would reign next, weakening the empire at a crucial moment—the eve of the arrival of Spanish invaders.

WITNESS HISTORY VIDEO

Watch *The Mummies of Peru* on the **Witness History Discovery School**™ video program to learn about mummies from long before the time of the Inca.

SECTION **2** Assessment

Progress Monitoring Online
For: Self-quiz with vocabulary practice
Web Code: naa-0621

Terms, People, and Places

1. Place each of the key terms at the beginning of the section into one of the following categories: culture, economy, and technology.

Note Taking

2. **Reading Skill: Contrast** Use your completed chart to answer the Focus Question: What characterized the cultures and civilizations that developed in the Andes?

Comprehension and Critical Thinking

3. **Demonstrate Reasoned Judgment** Why do you think that many separate cultures developed in the Andes before the Inca?
4. **Draw Conclusions** Explain three ways in which you think the Inca system of roads strengthened the empire.
5. **Identify Points of View** From the point of view of the Inca people, what might be some advantages of having an absolute ruler? What might be some disadvantages?

● Writing About History

Quick Write: Gather Details When you write a narrative essay, you often need to gather details about your topic. Suppose you want to write a narrative about the life of the Sapa Inca. Conduct research to find descriptions of the Sapa Inca's life and illustrations of artifacts that related to his rule. You may want to research a particular Sapa Inca, such as Pachacuti.

Empires

What factors allow empires to rise and cause them to fall?

Historically, a key factor in the rise of empires has been success in war. For example, through conquest and alliances, the Inca subdued neighboring groups and established a kingdom based in Cuzco. Leadership, too, is another important factor in empire-building. The Inca used military and diplomatic skills to create an extensive Andean empire. However, controlling a large territory is impossible without an effective system of government. The Inca established a chain of command that reached down to the family level.

Similarly, failures in war, weak leaders, and loss of control of conquered peoples have often caused empires to fall. Civil war among the Inca made them vulnerable to defeat by Spanish invaders. Consider how these other empires rose and fell:

ATAHUALLPA, INCA XIIII.

Atahuallpa, the last Sapa Inca

Han Dynasty

Under the Qin dynasty, China was engulfed in disarray as harsh policies provoked rebellions among the military and peasants. One rebel leader emerged victorious, founding a new dynasty—the Han—in 202 B.C. The first Han emperor set up a government aimed at benefiting the Chinese people, relaxing many strict laws and reducing taxes. He sent officials into every province of the empire to maintain the central government's authority. The Han system of government would last into the 1900s, though the dynasty itself would not. Plagued by peasant rebellions and power struggles, the Han empire split apart. The last Han emperor gave up the throne in A.D. 220.

Roman Empire

The Romans established one of the greatest empires of all time. They possessed strong leadership, an army of disciplined and dedicated soldiers, and a talent for absorbing conquered peoples and turning them into loyal citizens. Their established system of law and government brought security and peace to the Mediterranean region. Yet the mighty Roman empire eventually crumpled under the weight of several forces. Foreign invasions, combined with political, economic, and social problems, dissolved the ties that had held the empire together for more than 400 years.

Ottoman Empire

The Ottoman empire began in the early 1300s as a small Muslim state in far-western Asia, bordering the Byzantine empire. The Ottomans' initial success grew out of their location, which allowed them to plunder wealthy Byzantine cities. For 200 years, strong leaders expanded the empire until it extended from Eastern Europe through Southwest Asia and into North Africa. However, starting in the late 1500s, poor leadership, economic problems, and military unrest, as well as the strengthening of its European enemies, led to a slow Ottoman decline. After limping along for many decades, the empire collapsed completely following World War I.

The powerful Ottoman army

Thinking Critically

1. What factor do you think is most important in causing empires to rise? To fall? Explain.
2. **Connections to Today** For each empire described above, research a political or cultural aspect of the world today that represents the lasting impact of that empire.

SECTION 3

The Haida people believe a raven released the first people from a clam shell.

WITNESS HISTORY 🔊 AUDIO

Birth of Diverse Cultures

❝ For a long time everyone spoke the same language, but suddenly people began to speak in different tongues. Kulsu [the Creator], however, could speak all of the languages, so he called his people together and told them the names of the animals in their own language, taught them to get food, and gave them their laws and rituals. Then he sent each tribe to a different place to live . . . ❞
—Creation myth of the Maidu people of California

Focus Question What factors contributed to the growth of diverse cultures in North America?

Peoples of North America

Objectives

- Understand how groups of people adapted to the desert environment of the Southwest.
- Analyze the evidence from which we have learned about the emergence of culture in eastern North America.
- Examine the cultures that developed in three very different geographic regions.

Terms, People, and Places

Mesa Verde	earthwork
pueblo	Cahokia
Pueblo Bonito	potlatch
kiva	Iroquois League

Note Taking

Reading Skill: Compare and Contrast As you read, outline the experiences and achievements of Native American groups in each culture area discussed. Then compare and contrast the details you have recorded for the various culture areas.

```
I. Southwest
   A. Environment
      1.
      2.
   B. Settlement type
      1.
      2.
```

Hundreds of Native American cultural groups lived in North America before A.D. 1500 and the arrival of Europeans. Based on the environments in which people lived, scholars have categorized them into ten culture areas: Arctic, Subarctic, Northwest Coast, California, Great Basin, Plateau, Southwest, Plains, Southeast, and Northeast. In each area, people adapted to geographic conditions that influenced their ways of life.

Peoples Adapt to the Desert Southwest

For millennia, Native American groups lived by hunting, fishing, and gathering wild plants. After farming spread north from Mesoamerica, many people raised corn and other food crops. Some people farmed so successfully that they built large permanent settlements. Some of the earliest farming cultures arose in what is today the southwestern United States.

The Hohokam Farm in the Desert Perhaps as long ago as 300 B.C., fields of corn, beans, and squash bloomed in the desert of present-day Arizona, near the Salt and Gila rivers. These fields were planted by a people later called the Hohokam, or "Vanished Ones," by their descendants, the Pima and the Papago. To farm in the desert, the Hohokam built a complex irrigation system that included numerous canals. The canals carried river water to fields as far as several miles away. The Hohokam also built temple mounds and ball courts similar in appearance to those of Mesoamerica. Evidence indicates that, for unknown reasons, the Hohokam left their settlements sometime during the A.D. 1400s.

Geography Interactive
For: Audio guided tour
Web Code: nap-0631

Northwest Coast sun mask

Great Serpent Mound

Iroquois baggataway stick
(early lacrosse stick)

Equal-Area Projection

Plains Culture areas
▢ Key archaeological sites
Sources of subsistence, A.D. 1500
🌽 Cultivated plants
🌿 Wild plants
🐟 Fish and shellfish
🦬 Game
🦭 Sea mammals

Native American Culture Groups: Historical Locations

Culture Area	Culture Groups
Arctic	Aleut, Inuit
Subarctic	Beaver, Chipewyan, Cree, Ingalik, Kutchin, Montagnais, Naskapi, Ojibwa, Tanaina
Northwest Coast	Bella Coola, Chinook, Haida, Kwakiutl, Nootka, Tlingit
California	Chumash, Maidu, Miwok, Pomo, Shastan
Great Basin	Paiute, Shoshone, Ute
Plateau	Nez Percé, Spokan, Shuswap
Southwest	Anasazi, Apache, Hohokam, Mojave, Navajo, Papago, Pima, Pueblos (Acoma, Hopi, Laguna, Zuni)
Plains	Arapaho, Blackfoot, Cheyenne, Comanche, Cree, Crow, Hidatsa, Kiowa, Mandan, Omaha, Pawnee, Sioux, Wichita
Southeast	Calusa, Catawba, Cherokee, Chickasaw, Choctaw, Creek, Mississippians, Natchez, Seminole
Northeast	Adena, Algonquin (Delaware, Miami, Mohegan, Ojibwa, Pequot, Potawatomi, Shawnee), Hopewell, Iroquois (Cayuga, Erie, Huron, Mohawk, Onandaga, Oneida, Seneca, Tuscarora), Micmac, Winnebago

Map Skills As Native Americans spread out to populate North America, they developed a wide variety of cultures. In each culture area on the map, peoples shared fairly similar environments and ways of life.

1. **Locate** (a) Plateau culture area (b) Southeast culture area (c) Great Serpent Mound
2. **Place** In which two culture areas could Native Americans hunt sea mammals?
3. **Draw Inferences** Some Native American groups lived in different culture areas at different times. How might sources of subsistence have influenced them to migrate?

The Anasazi Build Cliff Dwellings and Pueblos About A.D. 100, the Anasazi began living in what is today the Four Corners region of Arizona, New Mexico, Colorado, and Utah. Within a few hundred years, they were building villages, some inside caves and some outside.

Between A.D. 1150 and A.D. 1300, the Anasazi built the cliff residences for which they are famous. Using hand-cut stone blocks, they constructed housing <u>complexes</u> on cliffs along the sides of sheer canyon walls. Such cliffs offered protection from raiders. The largest of these cliff dwellings, at **Mesa Verde** (MAY suh VEHR dee) in present-day Colorado, included more than 200 rooms. People climbed ladders to reach their fields on the flatlands above or the canyon floor below.

The Anasazi also built freestanding villages on the ground, which were similar in structure to the cliff dwellings. These communities, which the Spanish later called **pueblos** (PWEB lohs), were made of multi-floor houses that were connected to one another by doorways and ladders.

Remains of **Pueblo Bonito,** the largest Anasazi pueblo, still stand in New Mexico. The huge complex consisted of 800 rooms that could have housed about 3,000 people. Builders used stone and adobe bricks to erect a crescent-shaped compound rising five stories high. In the center of the great complex lay a plaza. There, the Anasazi dug their **kiva** (KEE vuh), a large underground chamber used for religious ceremonies and political meetings. In the kiva, they carved out a small hole in the floor, which represented the place in which the tribe was born. They also painted the walls with geometric designs and scenes of ritual or daily life.

In the late 1200s, a long drought forced the Anasazi to abandon their dwellings. Attacks by Navajos and Apaches—peoples from the north— may have contributed further to their decline. However, the traditions of the Anasazi survived among their numerous groups of descendants. Known collectively as Pueblo Indians, many of these groups continue to live in the southwestern United States today.

 Checkpoint What types of technological advances did early peoples of the Southwest make?

Vocabulary Builder
<u>complex</u>—(KAHM pleks) *n.* a whole composed of various interrelated parts

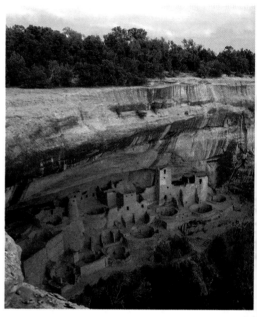

Cliff Palace, the largest dwelling at Mesa Verde, may have housed 250 people.

Cultures Develop in the East

Far to the east of the Anasazi, in the Mississippi and Ohio river valleys, other farming cultures emerged after about 1000 B.C. They, too, left behind impressive constructions from which we can learn a great deal about their lives.

The Adena and Hopewell Build With Earth Both the Adena and the later Hopewell people of the Northeast are known for giant **earthworks** that they built for various purposes by heaping earth in piles and shaping them. Some of the earthworks were large burial mounds, others served as platforms for structures such as temples, and still others served as defensive walls. Mounds were usually cone-shaped, oval, or formed into the shape of an animal. The Adena's Great Serpent Mound in Ohio wriggles and twists in the shape of a snake for almost a quarter of a mile.

Some of the objects found in the Hopewell mounds show that traders extended their influence over a wide area. They acquired goods such as conch shells from the Gulf of Mexico, grizzly bear teeth and obsidian from the Rocky Mountains, and copper from the Great Lakes region. Skilled artisans then hammered and shaped the copper into fine ornaments.

The Mississippians Build Bigger By A.D. 800, these early eastern cultures had disappeared. A new people, whom today we refer to as the Mississippians, gained influence in the Southeast region. As their culture spread, the Mississippians built clusters of earthen mounds and ever larger towns and ceremonial centers.

The greatest Mississippian center, Cahokia in present-day Illinois, housed as many as 20,000 people by about A.D. 1100. Cahokia boasted 120 mounds, atop some of which sat the homes of rulers and nobles. The largest mound probably had a temple on its summit, where priests and rulers offered prayers and sacrifices to the sun.

The Natchez Carry on the Traditions The Mississippians left no written records, and their cities disappeared after Europeans reached the area. Their traditions, however, survived among the Natchez people, who are known for their worship of the sun. They called their ruler, who held absolute power, the Great Sun. He and his family lived on the top of pyramid mounds. Society was divided into castes, the highest group was called the suns.

✓ **Checkpoint** What aspects of cultural life do the earthworks built by the Adena and Hopewell people reveal?

Unique Cultures Develop in Different Geographic Regions

Distinct ways of life developed in each Native American culture area. Here, we examine three cultures areas—the Arctic, the Northwest Coast, and the Eastern Woodlands—in which varied climates and natural environments helped unique cultures develop.

The Inuit Live in a Frozen World In the far northern stretches of Canada, the Inuit (IN oo it; often called the Eskimo) adapted to the harsh climate of the Arctic. By about 2000 B.C., they had settled there, using the resources of the frozen land to survive. Small bands lived by hunting and fishing. Seals and other sea mammals provided them with food, skins for clothing, bones for needles and tools, and oil for cooking. The Inuit paddled kayaks in open waters or used dog sleds to transport goods across the ice. In some areas, the Inuit constructed igloos, or dome-shaped homes made from snow and ice. In others, they built sod dwellings that were partly underground.

Adapting to the Arctic
The Inuit built kayaks with wood or whale bone, over which they stretched oiled animal skins to keep out water. As they paddled through icy waters on the hunt for seals (below right), they wielded harpoons and other weapons and wore snow goggles (below left) to protect their eyes from the glare. *How did the Inuit overcome the challenges of living in the harsh Arctic climate?*

Thriving in a Land of Plenty The peoples of the Northwest Coast lived in an environment far richer in natural resources than the Inuit did. Rivers teemed with salmon, and the Pacific Ocean offered a supply of other fish and sea mammals. Hunters tracked deer, wolves, and bears in the forests. In this land of plenty, people built large permanent villages with homes made of wood. They traded their surplus goods, gaining wealth that was then shared in a ceremony called potlatch. At this ceremony, which is still practiced in Canada and the Northwest coast of the United States today, a person of high rank and wealth distributes lavish gifts to a large number of guests. By accepting the gifts, the guests acknowledge the host's high status.

The Iroquois Join Together On the other side of the continent, the Northeast was home to numerous Native American groups. Many of these spoke the Iroquois (IHR uh kwoy) language, shared similar traditions, and were known collectively as the Iroquois. Typically, the Iroquois cleared land and built villages in the forests. While women farmed, men hunted and frequently fought wars against rival groups.

According to Iroquois tradition, the prophet Dekanawidah (deh kan ah WEE dah) urged these rivals to stop their constant wars. In the late 1500s, he became one of the founders of the unique political system known as the **Iroquois League.** This was an alliance of five Iroquois groups—the Mohawk, Oneida, Onondaga, Cayuga, and Seneca—who were known as the Five Nations. The Iroquois League did not always succeed in keeping the peace. Still, it was the best-organized political group north of Mexico. Member nations governed their own villages but met jointly in a council when they needed to address larger issues. Only men sat on the council, but each clan had a "clan mother" who could name or remove members of the council.

The Iroquois League emerged at the same time that Europeans arrived in the Americas. Just as encounters with Europeans would topple the Aztec and Incan empires, so too would they take a fearful toll on the peoples of North America.

✔ **Checkpoint** How did geography influence the Inuit way of life?

In about 1570, Dekanawidah persuaded warring Iroquois nations to form a confederacy, or an alliance for a common purpose. What benefits do you think a confederacy offered?

Primary Source

❝I, Dekanawidah, and the confederate lords now uproot the tallest pine tree and into the cavity [hole] thereby made we cast all weapons of war. Into the depths of the earth . . . we cast all weapons of strife [conflict]. We bury them from sight forever and plant again the tree. Thus shall all Great Peace be established and hostilities shall no longer be known between the Five Nations but only peace to a united people.❞
—The Constitution of the Five Nations

SECTION 3 Assessment

Progress Monitoring *Online*
For: Self-quiz with vocabulary practice
Web Code: naa-0631

Terms, People, and Places

1. For each term, person, or place listed at the beginning of the section, write a sentence explaining its significance.

Note Taking

2. **Reading Skill: Compare and Contrast** Use your completed outline to answer the Focus Question: What factors contributed to the growth of diverse cultures in North America?

Comprehension and Critical Thinking

3. **Draw Conclusions** What challenges do you think the Anasazi faced when constructing cliff dwellings? Consider location and natural resources.

4. **Categorize** Many of the earthen mounds built in the Southeast are similar in construction. What types of evidence do you think archaeologists looked for to establish the different purposes of these mounds?

5. **Analyze Information** What role do you think language played in enabling the unique political structure of the Iroquois?

● **Writing About History**

Quick Write: Write the Climax A narrative essay should include a climax—that is, the high point of the story that a reader will find most gripping. Suppose you want to write a narrative from the perspective of a member of one of the Native American groups you have read about in this section. Write a climax to the story you would tell of this person's life.

Quick Study Guide

Progress Monitoring *Online*
For: Self-test with vocabulary practice
Web Code: naa-0641

■ Civilizations of Mesoamerica and South America

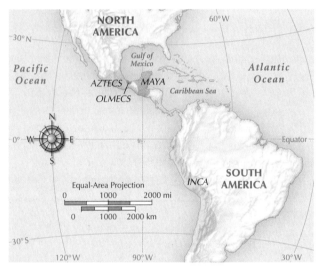

■ Key Sites of the Americas

North America
Mesa Verde—largest Anasazi cliff dwelling
Pueblo Bonito—largest Anasazi pueblo
Great Serpent Mound—large Adena earthwork
Cahokia—largest Mississippian center

Mesoamerica
La Venta, San Lorenzo—major Olmec ceremonial centers
Tikal, Calakmul—largest, most powerful Maya cities
Tenochtitlán—Aztec capital; future site of Mexico City
Teotihuacán—pre-Aztec city of religious importance to the Aztecs

South America
Chavín de Huantar—center of Chavín culture
Moche—center of Moche culture; site of the largest adobe structure in the Americas
Cuzco—capital of Inca empire

■ Cultures of North America

Culture Area	Culture Groups
Arctic	Aleut, Inuit
Subarctic	Beaver, Chipewyan, Cree, Ingalik, Kutchin, Montagnais, Naskapi, Ojibwa, Tanaina
Northwest Coast	Bella Coola, Chinook, Haida, Kwakiutl, Nootka, Tlingit
California	Chumash, Maidu, Miwok, Pomo, Shastan
Great Basin	Paiute, Shoshone, Ute
Plateau	Nez Percé, Spokan, Shuswap
Southwest	Anasazi, Apache, Hohokam, Mojave, Navajo, Papago, Pima, Pueblos
Plains	Arapaho, Blackfoot, Cheyenne, Comanche, Cree, Crow, Hidatsa, Kiowa, Mandan, Omaha, Pawnee, Sioux, Wichita
Southeast	Calusa, Catawba, Cherokee, Chickasaw, Choctaw, Creek, Mississippians, Natchez, Seminole
Northeast	Adena, Algonquin, Hopewell, Iroquois, Micmac, Winnebago

■ The Rise of American Civilizations

1500 B.C.
The Olmecs establish the first American civilization.

900 B.C.
A huge temple complex emerges at Chavín de Huantar in Peru.

300 B.C.
The Maya are building large cities in Central America.

Chapter Events
World Events

1500 B.C.   **1000 B.C.**   **500 B.C.**

1122 B.C.
The Zhou dynasty begins its rule over China.

750 B.C.
Greek city-states such as Athens begin to develop.

200 B.C.
Axum begins to build a large trade network.

Concept Connector

■ Cumulative Review

Record the answers to the questions below on your Concept Connector worksheets. In addition, record information from this chapter about the following concepts:

- People and the Environment: farming methods, the building of Tenochtitlán, geoglyphs, cliff dwellings, earthworks
- Cooperation: Iroquois League
- Empire: Aztec, Inca
- Science: Inca surgery

1. **Political Systems** People in various early civilizations believed in the divine right to rule. Compare the ways that rulers in Egypt, China, and the Inca empire used religion as a basis for their political authority. How did this practice affect culture and economics as well as government?

2. **Geography's Impact** Compare the geographic environments in which civilizations developed in India, Rome, South America, and Mesoamerica. How did natural features such as rivers, seas, mountains, valleys, and rain forests affect different aspects of civilization? Think about the following:
   - trade and economics
   - protection from attack
   - cultural diffusion
   - cooperation

3. **Cooperation** In different civilizations, road systems and trade routes have played various roles in connecting peoples. Some have connected people within a civilization, while others have connected people in different civilizations and geographic regions. What forms of cooperation have been enabled by the use of roads and trade routes? Consider the following peoples in your answer:
   - the Phoenicians
   - the Chinese
   - the Romans
   - the Inca

■ Connections to Today

1. **Migration** Scholars trying to determine when and how the first people migrated to the Americas have not relied on archaeological evidence alone. Scientists have studied the genetic diversity of Native Americans today, which gives clues about how long ago their ancestors arrived in the Americas. Linguists have also studied the diversity of languages that Native Americans speak today to gain similar information about how long people have lived in the Americas. Do you think scholars can use these types of non-archaeological data to determine whether the first people arrived in the Americas by walking over land or traveling by boat? What other types of evidence might be useful to help answer the question?

2. **People and the Environment** When the Aztecs founded Tenochtitlán, they modified the nearby environment in various ways—for example, by building chinampas and canals and filling in parts of the lake to expand the city. The same area is less supportive of a large modern city. In the same spot, more than 18 million people inhabit Mexico City. The surrounding mountains trap pollution from sources such as vehicle exhaust and factory smoke. Thus a cloud of smog hangs permanently over Mexico City. How can people influence the environment in both positive and negative ways? Research the situation in other modern cities, such as Los Angeles and Milan, to help you answer.

Mexico City

Mountains trapping pollution

Smog (pollution)

A.D. 100
The Anasazi settle in the southwestern United States.

A.D. 1100
The Mississippian center of Cahokia thrives.

A.D. 1325
The Aztecs found their capital at Tenochtitlán in Mexico.

A.D. 1438
Pachacuti founds the Inca empire in Peru.

A.D. 1500s
The Iroquois League forms in the eastern United States.

A.D. 500   **A.D. 1000**   **A.D. 1500**

A.D. 622
The Muslim prophet Muhammad leaves Mecca.

A.D. 800
Charlemagne is crowned Holy Roman emperor by Pope Leo III.

A.D. 1556
Akbar begins his rule of Mughal India.

History Interactive
For: Interactive timeline
Web Code: nap-0641

Chapter Assessment

Terms, People, and Places

1. How did the Aztecs build **chinampas?** For what purpose?
2. From whom did the Aztecs collect **tribute?**
3. Describe what you might see on a Maya **stela.**
4. What is **adobe?** What did Moche people build with it?
5. Describe a **quipu.** What do scholars think the Inca may have used quipus for?
6. What was an Inca **ayllu?**
7. How were Anasazi **kivas** constructed? What did each one represent?
8. What is a **potlatch?** In what culture area of North America was it originally practiced?
9. What was the **Iroquois League?** What was its main goal?

Main Ideas

Section 1 (pp. 186–194)
10. In which parts of the Americas did villages first arise? When?
11. Name three advances in learning made by the Maya.
12. Describe the social structure of the Aztec empire.

Section 2 (pp. 195–200)
13. Describe the control the Sapa Inca had over the government and over the Inca people.

Section 3 (pp. 201–205)
14. How were the Anasazi innovative in their building of dwellings?
15. What purposes did the giant earthworks of the Adena and Hopewell people serve?
16. Which people settled in the Arctic region of North America? How did they live?

Chapter Focus Question
17. What circumstances helped the civilizations and diverse cultures of the Americas to develop in ways both common and unique?

Critical Thinking

18. **Geography and History** How do the land-bridge and coastal theories of how people migrated in the Americas differ? How does the time frame of the migration change depending on the theory?
19. **Make Comparisons** How were the farming methods developed by the Maya, the Aztecs, and the Inca different? How were they similar?
20. **Predict Consequences** With the arrival of Europeans in the 1500s, peoples of the Americas would face the threat of conquest by outsiders. Which peoples would you expect to fare the best against attack? Consider location in relation to other groups of people as well as natural features, language, and political organization as you answer.

21. **Synthesize Information** How was the role of trade in Inca society unique as compared to trade in the Maya and Aztec societies? Why?
22. **Analyzing Visuals** This page from an Aztec book shows a symbolic representation of Tenochtitlán. What parts of the image do you think represent Lake Texcoco and the canals the Aztec built? What Aztec legend does the bird in the center of the page represent?

● Writing About History

Writing a Narrative Essay Write a narrative essay telling a story about one of the cultures of the Americas. If you have visited any of these cultures, write the story of your visit, including your impressions. Otherwise, write about the life of a historical individual or a fictional character from the Americas. Consult page SH8 of the Writing Handbook for additional help.

Prewriting
- Choose a culture to write about that you have visited or that interests you most.
- Choose a purpose for your essay. For example, you might want to share your own feelings about an experience or highlight a certain aspect of a culture that you think deserves attention.
- Gather details related to your essay topic.

Drafting
- Identify the climax, or most important part, of your story. Then decide what will happen in the beginning, middle, and end of the essay.
- Write an opening for the essay that will grab a reader's interest.
- Use many details to make the story vivid. Include dialogue when possible to convey your thoughts or those of your character.
- Write a conclusion that summarizes the significance of the experience to you or to the character.

Revising
- Use the guidelines for revising your essay on page SH9 of the Writing Handbook.

Document-Based Assessment

Aztec Training and Education

In Aztec society, a person's place in society was based on rank and family as well as ability. All children received an education that prepared them for a life of hard work. Most men labored in the fields, in trades and crafts, or on public works. Women worked hard in the home and learned the important skill of weaving. The process of educating Aztec youths was complex, as the documents below illustrate.

Document A

"First: thou art to be one who riseth from sleep. One who holdeth vigil through the night. Thou art not to give thyself excessively to sleep, lest . . . thou wilt be named a heavy sleeper . . . a dreamer. . . .

And second, thou art to be prudent in thy travels; peacefully, quietly, tranquilly, deliberately art thou to go. . . .

Third: thou art to speak very slowly, very deliberately. . . .

Fourth: thou art to pretend not to dwell upon that which is done, that which is performed. Especially art thou to . . . forsake evil. . . ."

—A nobleman's advice to his son, from **General History of the Things of New Spain** by Fray Bernardino de Sahagún

Document B

"[A]t fifteen . . . youths might enter either the *calmecac*, a temple or monastery in which they were entrusted to priests, or the school called the *telpochcalli*, 'the house of the young men', which was run by masters chosen from among the experienced warriors. . . . In theory the *calmecac* was kept for the sons and daughters of the dignitaries, but the children of the trading class were also admitted."

—From **Daily Life of the Aztecs** by Jacques Soustelle

Document C

Aztec girls grinding maize and learning to weave, from the Codex Mendoza, a 16th century Aztec book

Document D

"But even those who inherited high rank had to prove themselves and validate their status. Diplomatic skills or prowess on the battlefield could promote upward mobility. But, the close ties of family and lineage—the reality of birthright— were the fundamental cement of Mexica society."

—From **The Aztecs** by Brian M. Fagan

Analyzing Documents

Use your knowledge of history and Documents A, B, C, and D to answer questions 1–4.

1. Document A advises against
   A speaking freely.
   B traveling too often.
   C sleeping too much.
   D doing good.

2. What is the main point of Document B?
   A The Aztecs only educated youths from trading families.
   B Aztec higher education involved training by priests or warriors.
   C *Calmecacs* were temples or monasteries where children of noble and trade families could receive higher education.
   D The Aztecs provided higher education to only the most talented youths.

3. Based on Document D, how might youths who were not of noble birth advance themselves?
   A by marrying into a noble family
   B by training in the best schools
   C by a stroke of good fortune
   D by pursuing a career in trade

4. **Writing Task** Consider the advice of a nobleman in Document A. How might an aspiring Aztec tradesman advise his son or daughter? Use the information from these documents along with what you know from the chapter to answer this question.

Arctic Ocean

North
America

EARLY
MISSISSIPPIAN
CULTURES

ANASAZI
CULTURE

Teotihuacán

Tikal

MAYA
CIVILIZATION

Pacific
Ocean

Atlantic
Ocean

ANDEAN
CULTURES

Tiahuanaco

South
America

SCOTTISH
KINGDOMS

ENGLISH
KINGDOMS

IRISH
KINGDOMS

WALES

Aachen

Europe

CHARLEMAGNE'S
EMPIRE

CHRISTIAN
SPAIN

Rome

Constantinople

BYZANTINE EMPIRE

MUSLIM
STATES

ABBASID CALIPHATE

Baghdad

Jerusalem

GHANA

NUBIAN
STATES

Mecca

Axum

AXUM

Africa

Bantu

Peoples

N

W   E

S

The
WORLD
A.D. 800

210

Turks

Asia

Chang'an
TIBET   TANG   SILLA   JAPAN
   Lhasa   CHINA   Nara

INDIAN
STATES

SOUTHEAST
ASIAN
STATES

Pacific
Ocean

Indian
Ocean

Australia

Scale in Miles
0   1000   2000   3000
Scale in Kilometers
0   1000   2000   3000
Scale at the Equator
Mercator Projection

Geography *Interactive*
For: Audio guided tour
Web Code: nap-2000

UNIT

2

Regional Civilizations

730 B.C.– A.D. 1650

The Rise of Europe
500–1300

Tests of Skill and Courage

❝[A]lmost every fortnight tournaments were held. . . . [O]nce they had reached the field: all [the knights] did was lower their lances. You could see horses galloping on, lances flying into pieces, shields hacked to bits and men falling from saddles. . . . [Y]ou would have heard blows coming from swords, . . . helmets ringing and resounding; some grabbed at bridles to take men prisoner, whilst others, to defend themselves, smote with maces and swords.❞

Tournaments, or mock battles between knights, were often dangerous tests of skill and courage. Listen to the Witness History audio to hear more of this description, which was written in 1226.

◀ A medieval king and his court watch a tournament.

Medieval coat of arms

Chapter Preview

Chapter Focus Question How did feudalism, the manor economy, and the Church shape life in Western Europe as the region slowly developed a new medieval culture?

A Frankish ornament in gold from the early Middle Ages

A guild emblem

Note Taking Study Guide *Online*
For: Note Taking and Concept Connector worksheets
Web Code: nad-0701

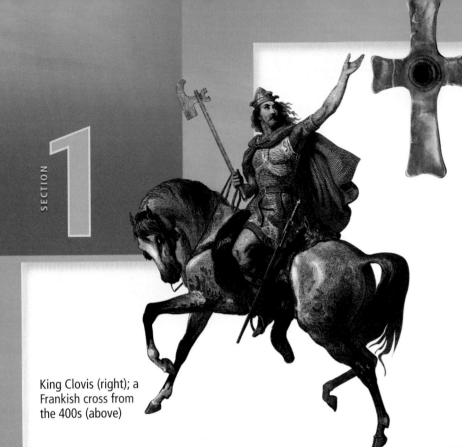

King Clovis (right); a Frankish cross from the 400s (above)

WITNESS HISTORY 🔊 AUDIO

A King Converts to Christianity

In A.D. 496, Clovis, warrior king of the Franks, was engaged in a ferocious battle. According to the *Chronicle of St. Denis,*

66 He looked up to heaven humbly, and spoke thus, 'Most mighty God, whom my queen Clothilde worships and adores with heart and soul, I pledge Thee perpetual service unto Thy faith, if only Thou givest me now the victory over mine enemies.' Instantly . . . his men were filled with burning valor, and a great fear smote his enemies, so that they turned the back and fled. 99

Focus Question How did Germanic tribes divide Western Europe into small kingdoms?

The Early Middle Ages

Objectives

- Describe Western Europe after the collapse of the western Roman empire.
- Describe how Germanic tribes carved Europe into small kingdoms.
- Explain how Charlemagne briefly reunited much of Western Europe and what happened to his empire after his death.

Terms, People, and Places

Clovis	battle of Tours
medieval	Charlemagne
Franks	Magyars
Charles Martel	Vikings

Note Taking

Reading Skill: Identify Main Ideas Keep track of the important characteristics of early medieval Europe in a table. Look for the main idea under each red heading and write it in the second column.

Early Medieval Europe	
Heading	**Main Idea**
Western Europe in Decline	
The Rise of the Germanic Kingdoms	
The Age of Charlemagne	
Europe After Charlemagne	

King **Clovis** won this battle—and many others. The kingdom he established was one of many Germanic kingdoms that replaced the unifying force of the Roman empire in Western Europe.

Western Europe in Decline

At its height, the Roman empire included much of Western Europe. Rome unified the region and spread classical ideas, the Latin language, and Christianity to the tribal peoples of Western Europe. The Germanic peoples who settled in Europe and conquered Rome would later build on these traditions.

After the collapse of Rome, Western Europe entered a period of political, social, and economic decline. From about 500 to 1000, it was politically divided, rural, and largely cut off from advanced civilizations in the Middle East, China, and India. Waves of invaders swept across the region, trade slowed to a trickle, towns emptied, and classical learning virtually ceased. For those reasons, this period in Europe has sometimes been called the Dark Ages.

Today, historians recognize that this period was not "dark." Greco-Roman, Germanic, and Christian traditions slowly blended, creating a new civilization. Much later, this period between ancient times and modern times—roughly from 500 to 1500— would be called the Middle Ages. Its culture would be called **medieval** civilization, from the Latin words for "middle age."

✔ **Checkpoint** Describe Western Europe after the collapse of the western Roman empire.

The Rise of the Germanic Kingdoms

The Germanic tribes that conquered parts of the Roman empire included the Goths, Vandals, Saxons, and Franks. Their culture was very different from that of the Romans. They were mostly farmers and herders, so they had no cities or written laws. Instead, they lived in small communities governed by unwritten customs. Kings were elected by tribal councils. Warriors swore loyalty to the king in exchange for weapons and a share in the plunder taken from conquered people. Between 400 and 700, these Germanic tribes carved Western Europe into small kingdoms.

The Franks Extend Their Power One of these kingdoms was that of the Franks. In 486, Clovis, king of the Franks, conquered the former Roman province of Gaul, which later became the kingdom of France. He ruled his new lands according to Frankish custom but preserved much of the Roman legacy. Clovis took an important step when he converted to Christianity, the religion of his subjects in Gaul. Not only did he earn their support, but he also gained a powerful ally in the pope, leader of the Christian Church of Rome.

A Muslim Empire Threatens Europe As the Franks and other Germanic peoples carved up Europe, a new power was emerging across the Mediterranean. The religion of Islam began in Arabia in the 600s. From there, Muslims, or believers in Islam, created a new civilization and built a huge and expanding empire.

Leaders of the Church and of Christian kingdoms became alarmed when Muslim armies overran Christian lands from Palestine to North Africa to present-day Spain. When a Muslim army crossed into France, **Charles Martel** rallied Frankish warriors. At the **battle of Tours** in 732, Christian warriors triumphed. To them, the victory was a sign that God was on their side. Muslims advanced no farther into Western Europe, although they continued to rule most of what is now Spain. This nearby Muslim presence remained a source of anxiety to many European Christian leaders. In time, however, medieval Europeans would trade with Muslims, whose learning in many areas exceeded their own.

✔ **Checkpoint** How did the Germanic tribes govern their kingdoms?

The Age of Charlemagne

In 768, the grandson of Charles Martel became king of the Franks. He briefly united Western Europe when he built an empire reaching across what is now France, Germany, and part of Italy. Also named Charles, he became known as **Charlemagne** (SHAHR luh mayn), or Charles the Great.

Geography *Interactive*
For: Audio guided tour
Web Code: nap-0711

Empire of Charlemagne, 768–843

- Kingdom of the Franks, 768
- Area conquered by Charlemagne, 768–814
- Division of Charlemagne's empire, (Treaty of Verdun, 843)

Conic Projection
0   100   200 mi
0   100 200 km

Map Skills Charlemagne built an empire in Europe, but his descendants were unable to hold it together.
1. **Locate** (a) the Frankish kingdom in 768 (b) Charlemagne's empire in 814 (c) Tours
2. **Compare** Look at a map of the Roman empire. Compare the location and extent of Charlemagne's empire with that of Rome.
3. **Predicting Consequences** What might be one result of the division of Charlemagne's empire? Explain.

Reading Skill: Identify Main Ideas
Record the most important characteristics of the Age of Charlemagne in a table. You may wish to add these to the table you began in the section opening.

The Age of Charlemagne	
Heading	**Main Idea**
A New Emperor of the Romans	
Creating a Unified Christian Empire	
A Revival of Learning	

Charlemagne spent much of his 46-year reign fighting Muslims in Spain, Saxons in the north, Avars and Slavs in the east, and Lombards in Italy. His conquests reunited much of the old western Roman empire.

A New Emperor of the Romans In 799, Pope Leo III asked Charlemagne for help against rebellious nobles in Rome. The delegation that Charlemagne sent to Rome arrested Leo's opponents. On Christmas Day in the year 800, the pope showed his gratitude by placing a crown on Charlemagne's head and proclaiming him Emperor of the Romans.

This ceremony would have enormous significance. A Christian pope had crowned a Germanic king successor to the Roman emperors. In doing so, Pope Leo III revived the ideal of a united Christian community, which came to be called Christendom. At the same time, he also sowed the seeds for desperate power struggles between future popes and Germanic emperors.

The pope's action also outraged the emperor of the eastern Roman empire in Constantinople. While the western Roman empire had been collapsing, the eastern empire had continued to flourish. The eastern emperor saw himself as the sole Roman ruler. In the long run, the crowning of Charlemagne deepened the split between the eastern and western Christian worlds.

Creating a Unified Christian Empire Charlemagne strove to create a united Christian Europe. Working closely with the Church, he helped spread Christianity to the conquered peoples on the fringes of his empire. Missionaries converted many Saxons and Slavs.

Like other Germanic kings, Charlemagne appointed powerful nobles to rule local regions. To keep control of these provincial rulers, he sent out officials called *missi dominici* (MIH see daw mih NEE chee) to check on roads, listen to grievances, and see that justice was done. Charlemagne instructed the *missi* to "administer the law fully and justly in the case of the holy churches of God and of the poor, of wards and of widows, and of the whole people."

Vocabulary Builder
unify—(YOO nuh fy) *v.* to combine into one

A Revival of Learning Charlemagne regarded education as another way to unify his kingdom. He could read but not write. Still, as a ruler, he saw the need for officials to keep accurate records and write clear reports. Charlemagne set out to revive Latin learning throughout his empire and encouraged the creation of local schools. He also wanted to revive the glory of Rome at his court at Aachen (AH kun). He brought many of the best scholars of Europe to the Palace School there.

✓ **Checkpoint** How did Charlemagne unify Europe?

The Palace School at Aachen

Charlemagne brought a respected scholar, Alcuin (AL kwin) of York, to direct the Palace School. Alcuin created a curriculum that included grammar, rhetoric, logic, arithmetic, geometry, music, and astronomy. Charlemagne, his family, his nobles, and his nobles' sons were all taught there, and it became a center of learning and lively discussion. Alcuin's system would become the educational model for medieval Europe.

Alcuin also hired scholars to copy ancient manuscripts, including the Bible and Latin works of history and science. In this way, the school preserved past knowledge for future generations.

Europe After Charlemagne

After Charlemagne died in 814, his son Louis I took the throne. Later, Louis' sons battled for power. Finally, in 843, Charlemagne's grandsons drew up the Treaty of Verdun, which split the empire into three regions.

Charlemagne's Legacy Although his empire did not remain intact, Charlemagne still left a lasting legacy. He extended Christian civilization into northern Europe and furthered the blending of Germanic, Roman, and Christian traditions. He also set up strong, efficient governments. Later medieval rulers looked to his example when they tried to strengthen their own kingdoms.

New Waves of Invasions Charlemagne's heirs faced new waves of invasions. Despite the victory at Tours, Muslim forces still posed a threat to Christian Europe. In the late 800s, they conquered Sicily, which became a thriving center of Muslim culture. Not until the 900s, when power struggles erupted in the Middle East, did Muslim attacks finally subside.

Geography *Interactive*
For: Audio guided tour
Web Code: nap-0712

Invasions of Europe, 700–1000

Map Skills Between 700 and 1000, Western Europe was battered by invaders.

1. **Locate** (a) France (b) Germany (c) Scandinavia (d) Hungary (e) Muslim-controlled lands

2. **Movement** Describe the invasion routes of the (a) Magyars, (b) Vikings, and (c) Muslims.

3. **Draw Inferences** Note which invaders built settlements. What can you infer about these groups from the fact that they settled in regions they raided?

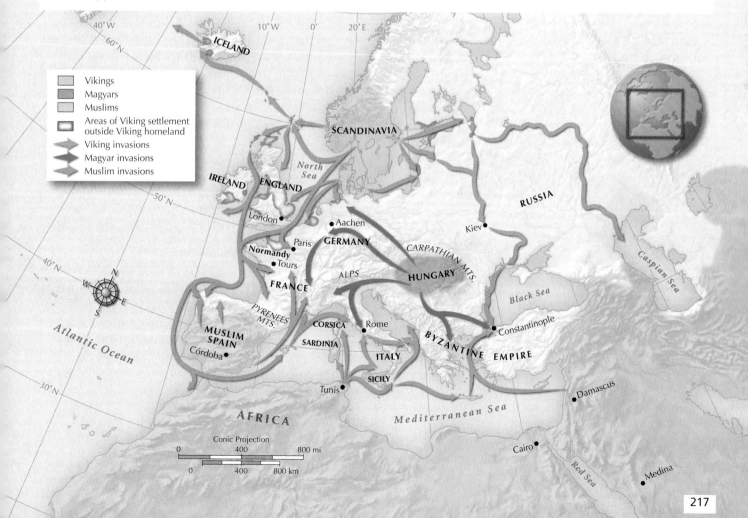

Viking Warship

This painting of a Viking warship with a prow in the shape of a mythical beast was done by an Anglo-Saxon artist around 1025. *What aspect of the ship does the artist emphasize? What does this suggest about the Anglo-Saxon reaction to the Vikings?*

About 900, a new wave of nomadic people, the **Magyars** settled in present-day Hungary. From there, they overran eastern Europe and moved on to plunder Germany, parts of France, and Italy. Finally, after about 50 years, they were pushed back into Hungary.

Raiders From the North The **Vikings** broke the last threads of unity in Charlemagne's empire. At home in Scandinavia—a northern region that now includes Norway, Sweden, and Denmark—the Vikings were independent farmers ruled by land-owning chieftains. They were also expert sailors. Starting in the late 700s, they burst out of Scandinavia, looting and burning communities along the coasts and rivers of Europe.

Viking sailors were not just destructive raiders. They were also traders and explorers who sailed around the Mediterranean Sea and across the Atlantic Ocean. Around the year 1000, they set up a short-lived Viking colony in North America. Vikings opened trade routes that linked northern Europe to Mediterranean lands. They also settled in England, Ireland, northern France, and parts of Russia, where they mixed with the local populations.

✓ **Checkpoint** Describe the invasions of Europe that took place after Charlemagne's death.

SECTION 1
Assessment

Progress Monitoring *Online*
For: Self-quiz with vocabulary practice
Web Code: naa-0711

Terms, People, and Places

1. For each term, person, or place listed at the beginning of the section, write a sentence explaining its significance.

Note Taking

2. **Reading Skill: Identify Main Ideas** Use your completed charts to answer the Focus Question: How did Germanic tribes divide Western Europe into small kingdoms?

Comprehension and Critical Thinking

3. **Recognize Cause and Effect** How did the collapse of the western Roman empire affect Western Europe?

4. **Summarize** How did the Franks create a kingdom in Western Europe, and what external threat did it face?

5. **Analyze Information** What made Charlemagne a successful leader?

6. **Express Problems Clearly** What happened to Charlemagne's empire after he died? Why?

● **Writing About History**

Quick Write: Explore a Topic Choose one person or group discussed in this section and write a series of questions that you could use to write a research report. For example, for the Vikings you could ask the following:

• What were Viking communities in Scandinavia like?

• What kind of community did the Vikings set up in North America?

A monarch knights a young man on the battlefield.

WITNESS HISTORY ◀)) AUDIO

Being Knighted on the Battlefield

A young man of good family has been trained in warfare. He has proven himself in battle, bravely assisting the knight he serves. Now, as another battle looms, his knightly master tells the young squire to kneel. The knight strikes the young man on the shoulder with the flat of his sword or his glove, and says "I make you knight." As his sponsor, the older knight also presents the young man with a sword and spurs. Now the young man is ready to fight for his lord. He has achieved a place of both honor and responsibility in the medieval world: he has become a knight.

Focus Question How did feudalism and the manor economy emerge and shape medieval life?

Feudalism and the Manor Economy

Objectives
- Explain how feudalism shaped medieval society.
- Describe the life of knights and nobles.
- Analyze how the economic system of the manor worked and how it affected peasants and nobles.

Terms, People, and Places

feudalism	tournament
vassal	chivalry
feudal contract	troubadour
fief	manor
knight	serf

Note Taking

Reading Skill: Identify Main Ideas Use a flowchart to keep track of the main ideas of this section. Write the main idea of each red heading in the appropriate box.

Feudalism and the Manor Economy

Feudalism | The World of Knights and Nobles | The Manor

Not all squires were knighted in battle. Others went through elaborate public ceremonies in which their responsibilities were carefully spelled out. Medieval society was a network of mutual obligations. Even kings and nobles exchanged vows of loyalty and service before witnesses. These vows were part of a new political and legal system that governed European life during the Middle Ages.

Feudalism: A Political System

In the face of invasions by Vikings, Muslims, and Magyars, kings and emperors were too weak to maintain law and order. People needed protection for themselves, their homes, and their lands. In response to this basic need for protection, a decentralized political structure evolved, known as feudalism. **Feudalism** was a loosely organized system of rule in which powerful local lords divided their landholdings among lesser lords. In exchange, these lesser lords, or **vassals,** pledged service and loyalty to the greater lord. The way feudalism was put into practice varied from place to place and changed over time.

Mutual Obligations The political and legal relationship between lords and vassals was based on the exchange of land for loyalty and military service. It was established by custom and tradition and by an exchange of pledges known as the **feudal contract.** Under this system, a powerful lord granted his vassal a **fief** (feef), or estate. Fiefs ranged from a few acres to hundreds of square miles. In addition to the land itself, the fief included peasants to work the land, as well as any towns or buildings on it.

As part of this agreement, the lord promised to protect his vassal. In return, the vassal pledged loyalty to his lord. He also agreed to provide the lord with 40 days of military service each year, certain money payments, and advice.

A Structured Society All <u>aristocrats</u> had a place in this structure of power. Below the monarch were powerful lords, such as dukes and counts, who held the largest fiefs. Each of these lords had vassals, and these vassals in turn had their own vassals. In many cases, the same man was both vassal and lord—vassal to a more powerful lord above him and lord to a less powerful vassal below him.

Because vassals often held fiefs from more than one lord, relationships between them grew very complex. A vassal who had pledged loyalty to several lords could have serious problems if his overlords quarreled with each other. What was he to do if both demanded his aid? To solve this problem, a vassal usually had a liege lord to whom he owed his first loyalty.

✔ **Checkpoint**   What was the relationship between lords and vassals?

The World of Knights and Nobles

For medieval nobles, warfare was a way of life. Rival lords battled constantly for power. Many nobles began training in boyhood for a future occupation as a **knight,** or mounted warrior.

Vocabulary Builder
<u>aristocrats</u>—(uh RIS tuh krats) *n.* members of the nobility

● **INFOGRAPHIC**

DEFENDING A CASTLE

Castles were made for defense. They were large complexes where many people and their supplies could hold out for long periods. They had strong, thick stone walls. A drawbridge over the castle moat—a ditch filled with water—could be raised in case of attack.

One way to capture a castle was by siege: the enemy would surround the castle and wait until the defenders' food ran out and they had to surrender. But soldiers could also attack by going over, through, or under the castle's defenses. Some attackers filled in the moat with stones or tunneled under the walls to weaken them until they collapsed. More often, they shot flaming arrows or hurled large stones over the walls. Some tried to go over the walls or to break down the gates.

Motte and Bailey Castle
This early type of castle was developed in the 800s. A keep, or tower, was built on a hill called a motte. A wooden bridge connected the motte to the bailey, a courtyard surrounded by a fence.

Battering Ram
Inside this hut on wheels was a huge log which soldiers used to break down the thick castle gate.

Catapult
A type of catapult called a trebuchet (TREB yoo shet) could hurl stones weighing 600 pounds (270 kilograms) as far as 1,000 feet (300 meters).

Knights and Warfare At the age of seven, a boy slated to become a knight was sent away to the castle of his father's lord. There, he learned to ride and fight. He also learned to keep his armor and weapons in good condition. Training was difficult and discipline was strict. Any laziness was punished with an angry blow or even a severe beating.

With his training finished, the youth was dubbed a knight, often in a public ceremony. His knight master or lord said words like these: "In the name of God, Saint Michael, and Saint George, I dub thee knight; be brave and loyal." Then the young knight took his place beside other warriors.

Knights usually fought on horseback using swords, axes, and lances, which were long poles. They wore armor and carried shields for protection. Other soldiers fought on foot using daggers, spears, crossbows, and longbows. In addition to actual warfare, knights engaged in mock battles called **tournaments.**

Castles and Defense During the early Middle Ages, powerful lords fortified their homes to withstand attack. The strongholds gradually became larger and grander. By the 1100s, monarchs and nobles owned sprawling stone castles with high walls, towers, and drawbridges over wide moats. They were not merely homes for the lords; they were also fortresses. The knights who defended the castle also lived there. In time of war, the peasants in the nearby villages would take refuge within the castle walls. Wars often centered on seizing castles that commanded strategic river crossings, harbors, or mountain passes.

WITNESS HISTORY VIDEO

Watch *The Rise of Feudalism* on the **Witness History Discovery School**™ video program to learn about how the feudal system evolved in medieval Europe.

Discovery SCHOOL

History Interactive
For: An interactive activity
Web Code: nap-0721

Hooks and Ladders
The castle's defenders used poles with hooks to push away attackers' ladders. They also showered the enemy with hot oil and flaming arrows.

Siege Tower
If attackers could span the moat, they would roll this huge tower up to the castle walls. Then they faced hand-to-hand combat at the top.

Thinking Critically
1. **Express Problems Clearly** What were some of the drawbacks of using a castle for defense?
2. **Draw Inferences** What technologies developed in response to castle defenses?

BIOGRAPHY

Eleanor of Aquitaine

Eleanor (1122–1204), daughter of the Duke of Aquitaine, inherited her father's lands when he died in 1137. When she was only 15, she married the heir to the French throne. Eleanor had considerable influence over her husband, King Louis VII, and even accompanied him on the Second Crusade, wearing armor and riding on horseback alongside male crusaders.

When Louis ended his marriage to Eleanor, she regained control of Aquitaine. In 1152, she married another king, Henry II of England, and again became active in politics. In 1173, Eleanor aided several of her sons in an attempt to overthrow Henry. When the revolt failed, Henry had Eleanor imprisoned. After Henry died, her son Richard (known as "the Lion-Heart") became king of England. Richard freed his mother, and she later ruled in his place while he went on a crusade to the Holy Land. **How did Eleanor expand the usual role of medieval women?**

Noblewomen: Restrictions and Power Noblewomen played active roles in this warrior society. While her husband or father was off fighting, the "lady of the manor" took over his duties. She supervised vassals, managed the household, and performed necessary agricultural and medical tasks. Sometimes she might even have to go to war to defend her estate. A few medieval noblewomen took a hand in politics. For example, Eleanor of Aquitaine was a leading force in European politics for more than 50 years.

Women's rights to inheritance were restricted under the feudal system, although women did sometimes inherit fiefs. Land usually passed to the eldest son in a family. A woman frequently received land as part of her dowry, and fierce marriage negotiations swirled around an unmarried or widowed heiress. A widow retained her land.

Like their brothers, the daughters of nobles were sent to friends or relatives for training. Before her parents arranged her marriage, a young woman was expected to know how to spin and weave and how to supervise servants. A few learned to read and write. In her role as wife, a noblewoman was expected to bear many children and be dutiful to her husband.

Chivalry: Romance and Reality In the later Middle Ages, knights adopted a code of conduct called **chivalry.** Chivalry required knights to be brave, loyal, and true to their word. In warfare, they had to fight fairly. For example, a knight agreed not to attack another knight before the opponent had a chance to put on his armor. Warriors also had to treat a captured knight well or even release him if he promised to pay his ransom. Chivalry had limits, though. Its elaborate rules applied to nobles only, not to commoners.

But chivalry also dictated that knights protect the weak, and that included both peasants and noblewomen. In theory, if not always in practice, chivalry placed women on a pedestal. **Troubadours,** or wandering musicians, sang about the brave deeds of knights and their devotion to their lady loves. Their songs became the basis for epic stories and poems. Few real knights could live up to the ideals of chivalry, but they did provide a standard against which a knight's behavior could be measured.

✓ **Checkpoint** How was warfare central to life in the Middle Ages?

The Manor: An Economic System

The heart of the medieval economy was the **manor,** or lord's estate. Most manors included one or more villages and the surrounding lands. Peasants, who made up the majority of the population in medieval society, lived and worked on the manor.

Most peasants on a manor were **serfs,** bound to the land. Serfs were not slaves who could be bought and sold. Still, they were not free. They could not leave the manor without the lord's permission. If the manor was granted to a new lord, the serfs went along with it.

Lords and Peasants: Mutual Obligations

Peasants and their lords were tied together by mutual rights and obligations. Peasants had to work several days a week farming the lord's lands. They also repaired his roads, bridges, and fences. Peasants had to ask the lord's permission to marry. Peasants paid the lord a fee when they inherited their father's acres or when they used the local mill to grind grain. Other payments fell due at Christmas and Easter. Peasants had little opportunity to use money, so they paid with products such as grain, honey, eggs, or chickens.

In return for their labor and other payments, peasants had the right to farm some land for themselves. They were also entitled to their lord's protection from raids or warfare. Although they could not leave the manor freely, they also could not be forced off it. In theory, at least, they were guaranteed food, housing, and land. This system supported the nobility, making feudalism possible.

A Self-Sufficient World

The manor was generally self-sufficient. That is, the peasants who lived there produced almost everything they needed, from food and clothing to simple furniture and tools. Most peasants never ventured more than a few miles from their village. They had no schooling and no knowledge of a larger world outside.

A typical manor included cottages and huts clustered close together in a village. Nearby stood a water mill to grind grain, a church, and the lord's manor house. The fields surrounding the village were divided into narrow strips. Each family had strips of land in different fields so that good land and bad land were shared evenly. Long strips were also easier to plow.

Beyond the fields for growing crops, there were pastures for animals and meadows that provided hay. The forests that lay beyond the cleared land—and all the animals in them—were usually reserved for the use of the lord.

Life on the Manor

The lord of the manor and his family lived in relative luxury. As the illustration below shows, nobles had a variety of foods and were waited on by servants when they dined. Notice the lord's home, or demesne, in the medieval diagram at the right and compare it with the village homes of the peasants who worked his land.

Back-Breaking Labor
These peasants use sickles to harvest grain under the watchful eye—and cane—of the lord's official. A medieval sickle is shown above (right) along with a billhook for maintaining hedges. *What does the illustration suggest about peasant life?*

Peasant Life For most peasants, life was harsh. Men, women, and children worked long hours, from sunup to sundown. During planting season, a man might guide an ox-drawn plow through the fields while his wife walked alongside, urging the ox on with a pointed stick. Children helped in the fields, planting seeds, weeding, and taking care of pigs or sheep. In late winter, when the harvest was gone and new crops had not yet ripened, hunger was common. Disease took a heavy toll, and few peasants lived beyond the age of 35.

The peasant family ate a simple diet of black bread with vegetables such as cabbage, turnips, or onions. They seldom had meat—that was reserved for the lord. Peasants who poached, or illegally killed wild game on their lord's manor, risked harsh punishment. If they lived near a river, peasants might add fish to their diet. At night, the family and their livestock—cows, chickens, pigs, or sheep—slept together in their hut.

Still, peasants found occasions to celebrate, such as marriages and births. Welcome breaks came at Christmas and Easter, when peasants had a week off from work. At these times, people might butcher an animal for a feast. There would also be dancing and rough sports, from wrestling to ball games.

✔ **Checkpoint** How did the manor system work?

SECTION 2 Assessment

Progress Monitoring *Online*
For: Self-quiz with vocabulary practice
Web Code: naa-0721

Terms, People, and Places
1. For each term, person, or place listed at the beginning of the section, write a sentence explaining its significance.

Note Taking
2. **Reading Skill: Identify Main Ideas** Use your completed flowchart to answer the Focus Question: How did feudalism and the manor economy emerge and shape medieval life?

Comprehension and Critical Thinking
3. **Analyze Information** How did a lord benefit from giving his lands away as fiefs?
4. **Make Comparisons** Compare the rights and obligations of noblemen and noblewomen during the Middle Ages.
5. **Draw Conclusions** How did the manor serve the needs of the early Middle Ages?

● **Writing About History**

Quick Write: Develop a Thesis and Choose Supporting Information
Choose a group discussed in this section. Write a sentence expressing your view of this group's place in medieval society. Jot down some information to support your statement. Revise this working thesis as you learn more. For example, you might begin with this thesis:
Peasants did most of the work but derived few benefits from the manor system.

On Pilgrimage

In the Middle Ages, most Western Europeans were devout Christians, and many of them went on pilgrimages to visit holy places. The medieval writer Geoffrey Chaucer noted that, when spring comes,

66 Then people long to go on pilgrimages . . .
In England, down to Canterbury they wend
To seek the holy blissful martyr, quick
To give his help to them when they were sick.99
—Geoffrey Chaucer, *The Canterbury Tales*

Focus Question How did the Church play a vital role in medieval life?

Stained-glass illustration of pilgrims to Canterbury and a pilgrim badge (upper right) showing the saint Thomas Becket

The Medieval Church

Objectives

- Explain how the Church shaped medieval life.
- Understand monastic life and the influence of medieval monks and nuns.
- Analyze how the power of the Church grew during the Middle Ages and how reformers worked for change in the Church.
- Describe the situation of Jews in medieval Europe.

Terms, People, and Places

sacrament	excommunication
Benedictine Rule	interdict
secular	friar
papal supremacy	St. Francis of Assisi
canon law	

Note Taking

Reading Skill: Identify Main Ideas Copy this concept web. As you read, fill in the main idea of each red heading. Add circles to record main ideas for the boldfaced headings.

The Medieval Church

Pilgrimages were only one way that medieval Christians showed their devotion to their faith. The Church and its teachings were central to medieval life. It took centuries for Christian missionaries to spread their faith across Europe. But in time, the Roman Church emerged as the most powerful force in the region. Religion shaped the everyday lives of Christian Europeans, and the Church hierarchy came to exert considerable economic and political power.

The Church Dominates Medieval Life

During the early Middle Ages, the Church's most important achievement was converting the diverse peoples of Western Europe to Christianity. In 597, Pope Gregory I sent St. Augustine to convert the Anglo-Saxons in England. From Britain, later missionaries went back to the continent to spread their faith among Germanic tribes. By the late Middle Ages, Western Europe had become a Christian civilization. Anyone who did not belong to the church community was viewed with suspicion.

The Role of the Parish Priest Christian rituals and faith were part of the fabric of everyday life. In villages, the priest of the parish, or local region, was often the only contact people had with the Church. The priest celebrated the mass and administered the **sacraments,** the sacred rites of the Church. Christians believed that participation in the sacraments would lead them to salvation, or everlasting life with God. Priests also preached the teachings of the Church and explained the Bible, which was in Latin only. They guided people on moral issues and offered assistance to the sick and needy. In the later Middle Ages, some parish priests ran schools.

Geography *Interactive*
For: Audio guided tour
Web Code: nap-0731

Map Skills Missionaries helped spread Christianity throughout medieval Europe.

1. **Locate** (a) Canterbury (b) Rome (c) Cluny (d) Assisi
2. **Region** (a) Name three areas of Europe that became Christian between 476 and 1050. (b) Which areas of Europe came under Muslim control?
3. **Apply Information** (a) How does this map indicate the sequence of events? (b) What can you conclude about the spread of Christianity from this map?

Map legend:
- Mostly Christian, 476
- Mostly Christian, added by 1050
- Muslim, 1050
- ☦ Monastery

The Importance of the Village Church The church was a social center as well as a place of worship because it was often the largest public building in a village. Daily life revolved around the Christian calendar, which included many holidays, such as Easter, and local holy days dedicated to saints. The main events of each person's life took place at the church. Baptism marked entrance into the community, marriages were performed on the church steps, and the dead were buried in the churchyard.

Villages took pride in their church buildings and decorated them with care. In later medieval times, prosperous communities built stone churches rather than wooden ones. Some churches housed relics, which could be possessions or remains of saints. Many people made pilgrimages, or religious journeys, to pray before the relics. The Church required Christians to pay a tithe, or tax equal to a tenth of their income. In the early Middle Ages, the tithe supported the local parish. Later, increasing amounts of money were sent to Rome.

The Rise of Cathedrals Bishops, who supervised parish priests, managed larger churches called cathedrals. By the 1100s, communities used new technology to build huge cathedrals in the ornate, buttressed form known as the Gothic style. These magnificent buildings were a source of pride to the communities that built them. Cities all over Europe competed to build grander, taller cathedrals. Members of the Church contributed money, labor, and skills to help build these monuments glorifying their god.

Church Attitudes Toward Women Church <u>doctrine</u> taught that men and women were equal before God. But on Earth, women were

Vocabulary Builder

<u>doctrine</u>—(DAHK trin) *n.* something taught as the principle of a religion

viewed as weak and easily led into sin. Thus, they needed the guidance of men. At the same time, the Church offered a view of the ideal woman in Mary, whom the Church believed to be the modest and pure mother of Jesus. Many churches were dedicated to the "mother of God" and "queen of heaven." Men and women asked Mary to pray to God on their behalf.

On the one hand, the Church tried to protect women. It set a minimum age for marriage. Church courts could fine men who seriously injured their wives. Yet they often punished women more harshly than men for similar offenses.

✓ **Checkpoint** What role did the Church play in the daily lives of medieval Christians?

Monasteries and Convents

During the early Middle Ages, some men and women withdrew from worldly life to the monastic life. They became monks and nuns. Behind the walls of monasteries and convents, they devoted their entire lives to spiritual goals.

Monastic Life: The Benedictine Rule About 530, a monk named Benedict organized the monastery of Monte Cassino in central Italy. He created rules to regulate monastic life. In time, the **Benedictine Rule** was used by monasteries and convents across Europe.

● **INFOGRAPHIC**

Life in a Monastery

Monasteries were not only places where monks lived and prayed, they were also places of work and study. Many monasteries, or abbeys, housed self-contained communities that grew their own food and made many of the objects they used. Monks worked in the fields, in workshops, and in scriptoria, or writing rooms, where they copied and decorated manuscripts. Music was important to monastic life; and chants marked the canonical hours, or religious divisions, of the day.

▲ The ivory carving above shows monks at work in the scriptorium.

▲ This picture of monks singing is in the center of the letter "C" in an illuminated manuscript.

◄ This church altar painting shows monks harvesting crops.

Thinking Critically
1. **Make a Reasoned Judgment** Which of these activities do you think was most useful to medieval society as a whole? Explain.
2. **Make Comparisons** How were monasteries like manors?

An Educated Woman
Hildegard of Bingen was from a noble family. She founded an abbey, wrote plays, and composed music. ◀)) AUDIO

Under the Benedictine Rule, monks and nuns took three vows. The first was obedience to the abbot or abbess who headed the monastery or convent. The second was poverty, and the third was chastity, or purity. Each day was divided into periods for worship, work, and study. Benedict required monks to work in the fields or at other physical tasks. As part of their labor, monks and nuns cleared and drained land and experimented with crops. Because they developed better agricultural methods, they helped improve the economy of the Middle Ages, which was based on farming.

Service and Scholarship In a world without hospitals or schools, monasteries and convents often provided basic health and educational services. Monks and nuns looked after the poor and sick and set up schools for children. They gave food and lodging to travelers, especially to Christian pilgrims traveling to holy shrines. Some monks and nuns became missionaries.

Monasteries and convents also performed a vital role in keeping learning alive. Their libraries contained Greek and Roman works, which monks and nuns copied as a form of labor. Educated monks and nuns also wrote and taught Latin, which was the language of the church and educated people. In Italy, Abbot Cassiodorus made useful summaries of Greek and Latin works and taught the classics to other monks. In Britain, the Venerable Bede wrote the earliest known history of England.

Opportunities for Women Although women could not become priests, many did enter convents. There, capable women could escape the limits of society. In the 1100s, Abbess Hildegard of Bingen composed religious music and wrote books on many subjects. Because of her mystical visions, popes and rulers sought her advice.

In the later Middle Ages, the Church withdrew rights that nuns had once enjoyed, such as preaching the Gospels, and placed most independent convents under the control of Church officials. It frowned on too much learning for women, preferring them to accept Church authority.

✓ **Checkpoint** Describe monastic life according to Benedictine Rule.

Church Power Grows

In the centuries after the fall of Rome, the Church hierarchy carved out a unique position in Western Europe. It not only controlled the spiritual life of Christians but gradually became the most powerful **secular,** or worldly, force in medieval Europe.

The Church's Role in Society During the Middle Ages, the pope was the spiritual leader of the Western Christian Church, based in Rome. Declaring themselves representatives of God on Earth, medieval popes eventually claimed **papal supremacy,** or authority over all secular rulers, including kings and emperors. The pope headed an army of churchmen who supervised church activities. High clergy, such as bishops and archbishops, were usually nobles. Like other feudal lords, they had their own territories and armies. The pope himself held vast lands in central Italy, later called the Papal States. Some monasteries also held large tracts of land, which gave them considerable economic and political power.

Church officials were closely linked to secular rulers. Churchmen were often highly educated, so feudal rulers appointed them to government positions. In addition, Church officials were often relatives of secular rulers.

Religious Authority and Political Power The medieval Christian Church was dedicated to the worship of God. At the same time, Christians believed that all people were sinners and that many were doomed to eternal suffering. To avoid the tortures of hell, one had to do good works, believe in Christ, and participate in the sacraments. Because the Church administered the sacraments and could deny them as a punishment, it had absolute power in religious matters.

The Church developed its own body of laws, known as **canon law,** as well as its own courts. Canon law, based on religious teachings, governed many aspects of life, including wills, marriages, and morals. Anyone who disobeyed Church law faced a range of penalties. The most severe and terrifying was **excommunication.** Those who were excommunicated could not receive the sacraments or a Christian burial, which condemned them to hell for eternity. A powerful noble who opposed the Church could face the **interdict,** an order excluding an entire town, region, or kingdom from receiving most sacraments and Christian burial. Even the strongest ruler gave in rather than face the interdict, which usually caused revolts by the common people.

A Force for Peace The Church tried to use its great authority to end warfare among nobles. It declared periods of temporary peace known as the Truce of God. It demanded that fighting stop between Friday and Sunday each week and on religious holidays. Such efforts may have contributed to the decline of warfare in Europe during the 1100s.

 Checkpoint How did the Church gain secular power?

Corruption and Reform

The very success of the Church brought problems. As its wealth and power grew, discipline weakened. Pious Christians left their wealth and lands to monasteries and convents, leading some monks and nuns to ignore their vows of poverty. Some clergy lived in luxury. Priests could marry, but some spent more time on family matters than on religious duties, and some even treated the priesthood as a family inheritance. Throughout the Middle Ages, there were calls for reform in the Church.

Two Movements for Reform In the early 900s, Abbot Berno set out to reform his monastery of Cluny in eastern France. First, he revived the Benedictine Rule of obedience, poverty, and chastity. Then, he refused to allow nobles or bishops to interfere in monastery affairs. Instead, Cluny was placed under the direct protection of the pope. Over the next 200 years, many monasteries and convents copied these reforms.

In 1073, Gregory VII, a former monk, became pope and began another push for reform. He wanted to limit secular influence on the Church. Gregory insisted that the Church alone choose Church officials such as bishops. That policy eventually sparked a bitter battle of wills with the German emperor. Gregory also outlawed marriage for priests and prohibited simony (SY muh nee), the selling of Church offices.

New Preaching Orders **Friars,** monks who did not live in isolated monasteries, took a different approach to reform. They traveled around Europe's growing towns, preaching to the poor. The first order of friars, the Franciscans, was founded by a wealthy Italian now known as **St. Francis of Assisi.** Giving up his comfortable life, he devoted himself to preaching

BIOGRAPHY

St. Francis of Assisi
Famous stories about St. Francis of Assisi (1181?–1226) tell of him preaching to the birds and convincing a wolf to stop attacking townspeople if they, in turn, would feed the wolf. St. Francis regarded all nature as the mirror of God, and he called animals his brothers and sisters.

St. Francis came from a wealthy family and had been a fun-loving and worldly young man. Then, in his mid-20s, he heard a voice speak to him while he was praying. He gave up his wealth to "walk in the footsteps," or example, of Jesus. He was soon joined by a small group of followers—the first Franciscan friars—and together they lived a life of service to the poor and the sick. The Church made him a saint in 1228. **What great changes did St. Francis make in his life?**

the Gospels and teaching by his own examples of good works. The Franciscan order preached poverty, humility, and love of God. St. Dominic, a Spanish priest, founded the Dominican order of friars. Dominicans dedicated themselves to teaching official Christian beliefs in order to combat heresies, religious doctrines that differed from church teachings.

Women also supported the reform movement. Some became Dominican nuns and others joined the Poor Clares, linked to the Franciscans. Often these orders welcomed only well-born women whose families gave a dowry, or gift, to the church. Another group, the Beguines, welcomed poor women who could not be accepted by other religious orders.

✓ **Checkpoint** How did monks contribute to the reform of the Church?

Jews in Medieval Europe

In the Middle Ages, Jewish communities existed all across Europe. Jews flourished in present-day Spain, where Muslim rulers were tolerant of both Jews and Christians. Spain became a center of Jewish culture and scholarship, and Jews served as officials in Muslim royal courts. In other parts of Western Europe, Christians and Jews lived side by side in relative peace for centuries. Early German kings gave educated Jews positions at court. Many rulers in northern Europe valued and protected Jewish communities, although they taxed them heavily.

By the late 1000s, Western Europe had become more christianized, and prejudice against Jews increased. When faced with disasters they could not understand, such as illness or famine, Christians often blamed Jews. Jews were not part of the parish structure that regulated Christian lives. Therefore, they had little interaction with the Christians who were suspicious of a culture they did not understand. As the Church grew in power, it issued orders forbidding Jews to own land or practice most occupations. Yet popes and rulers still turned to educated Jews as financial advisers and physicians. In response to growing persecution, thousands of Jews migrated to Eastern Europe. There, rulers welcomed the newcomers' skills and knowledge. Jewish communities thrived in Eastern Europe until modern times.

✓ **Checkpoint** How were Jews treated in medieval Europe?

Preserving Jewish Culture
In spite of living in predominantly Christian areas, Jews celebrated their own religious holidays during the Middle Ages. This 1300s menorah, or Hanukkah lamp, is from France. *Why do you think it might have been difficult for Jews to continue these celebrations?*

Progress Monitoring Online
For: Self-quiz with vocabulary practice
Web Code: naa-0731

 SECTION 3 Assessment

Terms, People, and Places
1. What do the key terms listed at the beginning of this section have in common? Explain.

Note Taking
2. **Reading Skill: Identify Main Ideas** Use your completed concept web to answer the Focus Question: How did the Church play a vital role in medieval life?

Comprehension and Critical Thinking
3. **Synthesize Information** How did monks and nuns contribute to medieval life?
4. **Recognize Cause and Effect** (a) How did the Church increase its secular power? (b) How did riches and power lead to Church abuses and then to reforms?
5. **Draw Conclusions** Why did attitudes toward Jews change in medieval Europe?

● Writing About History

Quick Write: Write an Introduction
Write a working thesis statement about a person or group discussed in this section. Then use a quotation or dramatic event to grab your audience's attention and introduce your thesis. For example, a paper on Abbess Hildegard might begin with her words to a ruler:

"Take care the Highest King does not strike you down because of the blindness that prevents you from governing justly."

A Boy Learns a Trade

In the Middle Ages, boys were apprenticed by legal agreements such as this one:

❝I, Peter Borre, in good faith and without guile, place with you, Peter Feissac, weaver, my son Stephen, for the purpose of learning the trade or craft of weaving, to live at your house, and to do work for you . . . for four continuous years, promising you by this agreement to take care that my son does the said work, . . . will neither steal nor take anything away from you, nor fleen or depart from you for any reason, until he has completed his apprenticeship.❞
—French apprenticeship agreement, 1248

Focus Question How did changes in agriculture and trade lead to the growth of towns and commerce?

A master blacksmith (above) brightens the flame while apprentices (at right) hammer the iron.

Economic Recovery Sparks Change

Objectives

- Summarize how new technologies sparked an agricultural revolution.
- Explain how the revival of trade revolutionized commerce and led to the growth of towns.
- Analyze the rise of the middle class and the role of guilds.
- Describe life in medieval towns and cities.

Terms, People, and Places

charter	middle class
capital	guild
partnership	apprentice
tenant farmer	journeyman

Note Taking

Reading Skill: Identify Main Ideas Outline the main ideas of this section. Use Roman numerals for the main idea of each red heading. Use capital letters for the main ideas of the black headings.

Economic Recovery Sparks Change

I. 1000s—agricultural revolution changed Europe
  A. New technologies allowed farmers
    to grow more crops.
  B.
II.

Like the earlier granting of fiefs, apprenticeship agreements laid out mutual obligations. The French apprenticeship agreement quoted above goes on to say, "And I, the said Peter Feissac, promise you, Peter Borre, that I will teach your son faithfully and will provide food and clothing for him." Enormous changes had to occur in medieval Europe before apprenticeship agreements became commonplace. And these changes began in agriculture.

An Agricultural Revolution

Changes in Europe by 1000 set the foundation for economic prosperity. It began in the countryside, where peasants adopted new farming technologies that made their fields more productive. The result was an agricultural revolution that transformed Europe.

Technology Improves Farming By the 800s, peasants were using iron plows that carved deep into the heavy soil of northern Europe. These plows were an improvement over wooden plows, which were designed for light Mediterranean soils rather than heavier northern soils. Also, a new kind of harness allowed peasants to use horses rather than oxen to pull the plows. Faster-moving horses could plow more land in a day than oxen could, so peasants could enlarge their fields and plant more crops.

Production and Population Grow Other changes brought more land into use. Lords who wanted to boost the incomes of their

Geography Interactive
For: Audio guided tour
Web Code: nap-0741

10°W 60°N 0° 20°W
Bergen
Stockholm
Novgorod
North Sea
Smolensk
To CHINA
50°N
Hamburg Lübeck
Danzig
Kiev
Baltic Sea
Atlantic Ocean
ENGLAND
London
Winchester Bruges
Ypres Ghent
FLANDERS Tournai
Lille
HOLY ROMAN EMPIRE
Caspian Sea
Paris Lagny
Provins
Troyes Bar-sur-Aube
FRANCE
Milan Verona
Lyon Venice
Turin ITALY
NAVARRE Genoa
LEÓN Pisa Florence
León Bayonne Siena
Black Sea
To INDIA
PORTUGAL CASTILE ARAGON Rome
Barcelona
Constantinople
Toledo
Valencia
Córdoba EMPIRE OF THE
ALMOHADS Naples
Cádiz KINGDOM OF SICILY
Adriatic Sea
Tunis
AFRICA
Mediterranean Sea
Tripoli Alexandria

■ Towns holding fairs
○ Major commercial centers
— Major trade routes

Conic Projection
0   200   400 mi
0   200   400 km

◄ French trade fair, fourteenth century

▲ Byzantine earrings, seventh century

Map Skills As trade revived in medieval Europe, trade routes multiplied and many towns hosted trade fairs.

1. **Locate** (a) Constantinople (b) Adriatic Sea (c) Venice (d) Flanders (e) London (f) Baltic Sea
2. **Region** In which areas were there (a) clusters of commercial centers? (b) clusters of trade fairs? (c) many converging trade routes?
3. **Draw Inferences** Why do you think many of these trade routes avoided overland travel and went by sea or river? What does this suggest about travel during this time?

Trade Fairs: Fun and Profit
Before the onset of widespread travel, traders and their customers did business at local trade fairs. These fairs took place each year near navigable rivers or where busy trade routes met. People from the surrounding villages, towns, and castles flocked to the fairs. Peasants traded farm goods and animals and enjoyed the antics of jugglers, acrobats, or even dancing bears. Nobles, wealthy churchmen, and well-off townspeople bought luxury goods such as fine swords, sugar, and silks.

manors had peasants clear forests, drain swamps, and reclaim wasteland for farming and grazing. Peasants also adopted a new way of rotating crops: the three-field system. They planted one field with grain; a second with legumes, such as peas and beans; and the third they left unplanted. The legumes restored fertility to the soil and added protein to the peasants' diet. The new method left only one third of the land unplanted, rather than half. All these improvements allowed farmers to produce more food. With more food available, the population began to grow. Between about 1000 and 1300, the population of Europe almost tripled.

✔ Checkpoint Why did agricultural production improve?

The Revival of Trade and Travel

As Europe's population grew, other changes also took place. In the 1100s, feudal warfare and foreign invasions declined. People felt safer, and began to travel more. The crusaders brought luxury goods back to Europe from the Middle East. Wealthy nobles desired goods that could not be produced on manors. Peasants needed iron for farm tools. Traders began to crisscross Europe to meet the growing demand for goods.

Trade Routes Expand Enterprising traders formed merchant companies that traveled in armed caravans for safety. They followed regular trade routes, many of which had hardly been used for centuries. Along these routes, merchants exchanged local goods for those from remote markets in the Middle East and farther east into Asia.

In Constantinople, merchants bought Chinese silks, Byzantine gold jewelry, and Asian spices. They shipped these goods by sea to Venice, where traders loaded their wares onto pack mules and headed north to Flanders. There, other traders bought the goods at trade fairs and sent them to England and lands along the Baltic Sea. Northern Europeans paid for these goods with products such as honey, furs, cloth, tin, and lead.

In the 1200s, German towns along the Baltic Sea formed the Hanseatic League, an association to protect their trading interests, which dominated trade in Northern Europe for more than 150 years. It took action against robbers and pirates, built lighthouses, and trained ships' pilots.

The Growth of Towns and Cities Many trade fairs closed in the autumn, when the weather made roads impassable. Merchants might wait out the winter near a castle or in a town. These settlements attracted artisans who made goods that merchants could sell. Slowly, these small centers of trade and handicraft became the first medieval cities. Some boasted populations of 10,000, and by the fourteenth century, a few topped 100,000. Europe had not seen towns of this size since Roman times. The richest cities emerged in northern Italy and Flanders—the two ends of the profitable north-south trade route. Both areas were centers of the wool trade and had prosperous textile industries.

To protect their interests, the merchants who set up a new town asked the local lord, or the king himself, for a **charter.** This written document set out the rights and privileges of the town. In return, merchants paid the lord or the king a large sum of money, a yearly fee, or both. Most charters also had a clause, popular with runaway serfs, that declared that anyone who lived in the town for one year and one day was free.

In the late 900s, a monk named Richer set out with a guide from Rheims to Chartres, where he planned to continue his studies. He described the journey:

Primary Source

❝We reached the bridge before the town but could barely see it in the rainy night. I became even more anxious because the bridge had so many holes and large gaps that the citizens of Meaux could hardly cross it in the daytime, much less in the dark—and in a storm! . . .[W]e faced a difficult path over the bridge. As we went, the messenger put his shield over the smaller holes for the horses. He used planks for the larger gaps. At times he would be bending over, now standing up, now running here and there in order to keep the horses calm and safe.❞
—Richer of Rheims 🔊) AUDIO

Why were roads and bridges in such poor condition at this time?

Although charters (below) varied from place to place, they almost always granted townspeople the right to choose their own leaders and control their own affairs. At the left, a town in Flanders receives its charter.

Meanwhile, as Europe's population grew, manors became overcrowded, and lords often allowed peasants to buy their freedom and move to towns.

✔ **Checkpoint**   How and why did medieval towns and cities grow?

A Commercial Revolution

Vocabulary Builder
stimulated—(STIM yuh layt ed) *v.* made more active

As trade revived, the use of money increased. In time, the need for **capital,** or money for investment, <u>stimulated</u> the growth of banking houses. Merchants also extended credit to one another. That is, they arranged to delay payment for goods for a certain set time.

The Beginnings of Modern Business   To meet the needs of the changing economy, Europeans developed new ways of doing business. Groups of merchants joined together in **partnerships.** They pooled their funds to finance a large-scale venture that would have been too costly for any individual trader. This practice made capital more easily available. It also reduced the risk for any one partner because no one had to invest all his or her capital in the company.

Later, merchants developed a system of insurance to help reduce business risks. For a small fee, an underwriter insured the merchant's shipment. If the shipment was lost or destroyed, the underwriter paid the merchant most of its value. If the goods arrived safely, the merchant lost only the insurance payment.

Europeans adopted some practices from the Muslim merchants with whom they traded. These traders had developed methods of using credit rather than cash in their business. European versions included letters of credit and bills of exchange. For example, a merchant would deposit money with a banker in his home city. The banker would issue a bill of exchange, which the merchant could exchange for cash in a distant city. The merchant could thus travel without carrying gold coins, which were easily stolen.

Society Begins to Change These new business practices were part of a commercial revolution that transformed the medieval economy. Slowly, they also reshaped medieval society. For example, the use of money undermined serfdom. Feudal lords needed money to buy fine goods. As a result, many peasants began selling farm products to townspeople and paying rent to their lord in cash rather than in labor. By 1300, most peasants in Western Europe were either **tenant farmers,** who paid rent for their land, or hired farm laborers.

During the Middle Ages, the Church forbade Christians to lend money at interest. As a result, many Jews who were barred from other professions became moneylenders. Although moneylenders played an essential role in the growing medieval economy, their success led to resentment and a rise in anti-Jewish prejudice.

 Checkpoint Describe three changes of the commercial revolution.

The Rise of the Middle Class

In towns, the old social order of nobles, clergy, and peasants gradually changed. By the year 1000, merchants, traders, and artisans formed a new social class. In status, this class ranked between nobles and peasants, so it was called the **middle class.** Nobles and the clergy despised the new middle class. To nobles, towns were a disruptive influence beyond their control. To the clergy, the profits that merchants and bankers made from usury (YOO zhuh ree), or lending money at interest, were immoral.

The Role of Guilds In medieval towns, the middle class gained economic and political power. First, merchants and artisans formed associations known as **guilds.** Merchant guilds appeared first. They dominated town life, passing laws and levying taxes. They also decided whether to spend funds to pave the streets with cobblestones or make other town improvements.

In time, artisans came to resent the powerful merchants. They organized craft guilds. Each guild represented workers in one occupation, such as weavers, bakers, or goldsmiths. In some towns, struggles between craft guilds and the wealthier merchant guilds led to riots.

Guild members cooperated to protect their own economic interests. To prevent competition, they limited guild membership. No one except guild members could work in any trade. Guilds made rules to protect the quality of their goods, regulate hours of labor, and set prices. Guilds also provided social services. They operated schools and hospitals, looked after the needs of their members, and provided support for the widows and orphans of their members.

Becoming a Guild Member Becoming a guild member took many years of hard work. At the age of seven or eight, a child might become an **apprentice,** or trainee, to a guild master. The apprentice usually spent seven years learning the trade. The guild master paid no wages, but was required to give the apprentice food and housing. Few apprentices ever became guild masters unless they were related to one. Most worked for guild members as **journeymen,** or salaried workers. Journeymen often

Medieval Advertising
These guild emblems from 1602 are similar to those used by medieval guilds to represent their crafts. From the top: guild emblems for eyeglass-makers, armorers, barbers, and bakers. *Why do you think the emblems use both pictures and words?*

A Londoner of the 1100s describes a sport enjoyed by youngsters in his city:

Primary Source

66 When the great [swamp] which watereth the walls of the city on the north side, is frozen, many young men play upon the ice . . . some tie bones to their feet and under their heels; and shoving themselves by a little picked staff, do slide as swiftly as a bird flieth in the air. 99
—William Fitz-Stephen

How much time for play do you think young medieval people had? Explain.

The picture below is the earliest known depiction of ice-skating.

accused masters of keeping their wages low so that they could not save enough to open a competing shop.

Women and the Guilds Women worked in dozens of crafts. A woman often engaged in the same trade as her father or husband and might inherit his workshop if he died. Because she knew the craft well, she kept the shop going and sometimes became a guild master herself. Young girls became apprentices in trades such as ribbonmaking and papermaking. Women dominated some trades and even had their own guilds. In Paris, they far outnumbered men in the profitable silk and wool guilds. A third of the guilds in Frankfurt were composed entirely of women.

 Checkpoint Why were guilds important in town life?

Town and City Life

Medieval towns and cities were surrounded by high, protective walls. As a city grew, space within the walls filled to overflowing, and newcomers had to settle in the fields outside the walls. Because of overcrowding, city dwellers added second and third stories to their houses and shops. Therefore, a typical medieval city was a jumble of narrow streets lined with tall houses. Upper floors extended outward over the streets below, making them dim even in daytime. Fire was a constant threat.

In the largest cities, a great cathedral or a splendid guild hall might tower above humbler residences. Almost all cities and towns had a church with a steeple that could be seen for miles. Around the church, people usually lived in neighborhoods with people of similar backgrounds. This meant that guild members, such as butchers, lived in the same area.

During the day, streets echoed with the cries of hawkers selling their wares and porters grumbling under heavy loads. At night, the unlit streets were deserted. Even a rich town had no garbage collection or sewer system. Residents simply flung their wastes into the street. Some larger cities passed laws to promote better sanitary conditions, such as one requiring butchers to dump their garbage on the edge of town. Still, towns remained filthy, smelly, noisy, and crowded—a perfect breeding ground for disease.

Checkpoint What were medieval cities like?

SECTION 4 Assessment

Progress Monitoring Online
For: Self-quiz with vocabulary practice
Web Code: naa-0741

Terms, People, and Places

1. What do many of the key terms listed at the beginning of this section have in common? Explain.

Note Taking

2. **Reading Skill: Identify Main Ideas** Use your completed outline to answer the Focus Question: How did changes in agriculture and trade lead to the growth of towns and commerce?

Comprehension and Critical Thinking

3. **Recognize Cause and Effect** What were two effects of the agricultural revolution of the Middle Ages?

4. **Draw Conclusions** Why was the revival of trade so important?

5. **Summarize** How did the emergence of a middle class affect European life? Explain.

6. **Draw Inferences** What were the advantages and disadvantages of living in a medieval city?

● **Writing About History**

Quick Write: Credit Sources Use a library or the Internet to find three reliable sources of information about a group discussed in this section. Include at least one primary source. Use the guidelines in the Writing Handbook to write bibliography entries for your sources.

The Canterbury Tales
by Geoffrey Chaucer

In *The Canterbury Tales* (1387–1400), Geoffrey Chaucer presents a portrait of medieval English society. The *Tales* are a series of poems that focus on 29 men and women who are on a pilgrimage to the tomb of St. Thomas Becket in Canterbury. To help pass the time, they tell stories to one another. The detailed descriptions of each character provide a sharp look at three classes of society as they were developing in the 1200s and 1300s: nobles, the middle class, and peasants. In the passages below, Chaucer describes a noble knight, a wealthy merchant, and a humble plowman, or farmworker.

Geoffrey Chaucer (1343?–1400)

A knight

There was a Knight, a most distinguished man,
Who from the day on which he first began
To ride abroad had followed chivalry,
Truth, honor, generousness, and courtesy.
He had done nobly in his sovereign's war
And ridden into battle, no man more,
As well in Christian as heathen places,
And ever honored for his noble graces[1]. . . .

There was a Merchant with a forking beard
And motley[2] dress; high on his horse he sat,
Upon his head a Flemish beaver hat
And on his feet daintily buckled boots. . . .
He was expert at currency exchange.
This estimable[3] Merchant so had set
His wits to work, none knew he was in debt,
He was so stately[4] in negotiation,
Loan, bargain, and commercial obligation. . . .

A merchant

There was a Plowman with him there, his brother.
He was an honest worker, good and true,
Living in peace and perfect charity. . . .
For steadily about his work he went
To thrash his corn, to dig or to manure
Or make a ditch; and he would help the poor
For love of Christ and never take a penny
If he could help it, and, as prompt as any,
He paid his tithes in full when they were due. . . .

1. **graces** (GRAYS iz) *n.* decency, thoughtfulness, and manners
2. **motley** (MAHT lee) *adj.* of many colors
3. **estimable** (ES tuh muh bul) *adj.* deserving respect
4. **stately** (STAYT lee) *adj.* dignified

Thinking Critically
1. **Identify Point of View** Which of these characters does Chaucer seem to disapprove of? How can you tell?
2. **Analyze Literature** What qualities do the knight and the plowman have in common? How do they show these qualities?

Quick Study Guide

Progress Monitoring *Online*
For: Self-test with vocabulary practice
Web Code: naa-0751

■ Why Did Europe Decline?

- The western Roman empire collapsed.
- Invaders swept across the region.
- Trade, travel, towns, and learning all decreased.
- Germanic kingdoms carved up a once-unified empire.

■ Key Figures in the Rise of Europe

- Clovis, *King of the Franks, who converted to Christianity*
- Charles Martel, *leader of the Franks at the battle of Tours*
- Charlemagne, *emperor who united much of Western Europe into a Christian kingdom*
- Eleanor of Aquitaine, *politically influential wife of King Louis VII of France and later of King Henry II of England, and mother of King Richard, the Lion-heart*
- Benedict, *monk who instituted the Benedictine Rule for monastic life*
- St. Francis of Assisi, *founder of Franciscan order of friars*

■ Feudalism and the Manor System

FEUDALISM		THE MANOR SYSTEM	
Lord to Vassal ⟷	Vassal to Lord	Lord of Manor to Peasants ⟷	Peasants to Lord
• Fief (land, buildings, workers) • Protection	• Loyalty • Military service • Certain fees • Advice	• Use of land for farming • Protection • Could not be forced off land	• Money or crops as rent • Labor on lord's lands • Certain fees

■ Role of the Church

Daily Life	Economic Power	Political Power
• Mass • Sacraments • Religious calendar • Aid to needy • Moral guidance	• Owned large tracts of land • People willed riches to Church • Agricultural and commercial activity in monasteries	• Papal supremacy • Threat of excommunication, interdict • Raised own armies • Clergy served in governments • Moral authority

■ Rise of Towns and the Middle Class

Agricultural Revolution →	Revival of Trade →	Towns and the Middle Class
• Production increases. • Population grows.	• Warfare decreases. • Travel becomes safer. • Desire for foreign goods increases. • Trade fairs develop. • Towns and cities grow.	• As towns grow, merchants gain power. • Guilds form and become powerful. • Modern business practices develop. • The middle class gains power. • Trade and commerce gain importance.

■ The Rise of Europe

500s
Germanic tribes such as the Franks dominate Western Europe, carving the region into small kingdoms.

732
At the battle of Tours, Christian armies stop the Muslim advance into Europe.

800
Charlemagne is crowned emperor by the pope and begins to unite much of Western Europe into a Christian empire.

Chapter Events
Global Events

500	600	700	800

527
Justinian begins his rule of the Byzantine Empire.

600s
Maya civilization thrives in the Americas.

622
The Muslim prophet Muhammad leaves Mecca, signaling the beginning of the religion of Islam.

Concept Connector

■ Cumulative Review

Record the answers to the questions below on your Concept Connector worksheets. In addition, record information from this chapter about the following concepts:

• **Geography's Impact:** Vikings

1. **Empire** In 800, Pope Leo III crowned Charlemagne king of the Romans. Was Charlemagne's empire really a "Roman" empire, or was it something different? Explain your answer. Think about the following:
   • Size and location
   • Language
   • Religion
   • Education
   • Laws

2. **Trade** Medieval Europe was dominated by feudalism and the manorial system, which held many individuals in agreements of obligation. In this society, who might have become traders and merchants, and how might powerful lords have viewed them?

3. **Political Systems** You read that Shi Huangdi abolished feudalism in China in order to create a strong central government. After reading about feudalism in medieval Europe, do you think that abolishing feudalism was necessary to build a strong empire? Explain your answer.

4. **Economic Systems** In this chapter, you read about the rise of towns and the middle class in medieval Europe. Towns were very different from manorial villages. Townspeople had no lord, could move about freely, and had different economic opportunities. Was the expansion of towns a positive or negative development in Western Europe? Consider the following:
   • effects on the manorial system
   • relationships between townspeople and nobles
   • distribution of wealth
   • role of the Church
   • role of peasants

■ Connections to Today

1. **Cooperation: The European Union** The Romans and Charlemagne attempted to unify Western Europe. Later in the Middle Ages, the Holy Roman Empire and the Church clashed over control of the region. When European nation-states developed, they became economic and military rivals. Now, however, there is an effort to unite Europe through cooperation rather than conquest. The European Union was established in 1993, and a common currency called the euro came into use in 1999. The photo below shows a produce stand in Spain at the time of transition to the euro. Notice that the prices are displayed in both the old Spanish currency and the euro. Research and write a brief report on the European Union and the euro. Discuss their history and how well they have succeeded in unifying Europe.

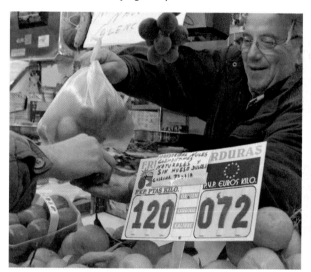

2. **Economic Systems: Banking** You have read that medieval merchants extended credit to one another, and about early forms of letters of credit and bills of exchange. Do research to find out more about these early banking practices. Then investigate how they are used today. Write a brief report comparing these banking practices then and now.

900s	1000s	1200s
Viking raiders plunge much of Europe into disorder, contributing to the emergence of European feudalism.	The European economy begins to recover. The growth of trade and towns are signs of this revival.	The Dominican and Franciscan orders of Christian friars are founded.

History Interactive
For: Interactive timeline
Web Code: nap-0751

900 — 1000 — 1100 — 1200

960	1100s	1230
The Song dynasty is founded in China.	Feudalism develops in Japan.	Sundiata founds the empire of Mali in West Africa.

Chapter Assessment

Terms, People, and Places

Choose the italicized term in parentheses that best completes each sentence.

1. The king of the Franks who conquered Gaul and converted to Christianity was *(Clovis/Charles Martel)*.
2. Scandinavian raiders from the north were *(Magyars/Vikings)*.
3. When a lord inherited a manor, he also gained control of the *(knights/serfs)* who worked on it.
4. The sacred rites of the church are called *(sacraments/canon law)*.
5. Popes claimed *(excommunication/papal supremacy)*, giving them authority over kings and emperors.
6. Monks who traveled around Europe preaching to the poor were called *(friars/secular)*.
7. A *(charter/capital)* set out the rights and privileges of a town.
8. Medieval merchants joined together in *(charters/partnerships)* to reduce financial risk.

Main Ideas

Section 1 (pp. 214–218)
9. How were the Germanic tribes governed?
10. Why did Charlemagne's empire break up after his death?

Section 2 (pp. 219–224)
11. Describe the mutual obligations that emerged under feudalism.
12. How did medieval manors function?

Section 3 (pp. 225–230)
13. What role did the Church play in daily life?
14. How did the Church gain secular power?

Section 4 (pp. 231–237)
15. What were the effects of improvements in agriculture?
16. What led to the growth of towns?
17. What was the commercial revolution?

Chapter Focus Question
18. How did feudalism, the manor economy, and the Church shape life in Western Europe as the region slowly developed a new medieval culture?

Critical Thinking

19. **Recognize Cause and Effect** Why did the collapse of the western Roman empire lead to a new age in Western Europe?
20. **Draw Conclusions** Why was Charlemagne important even though his empire collapsed after his death?
21. **Make Comparisons** Compare and contrast the manor economy with the kind of economy that developed in towns during the commercial revolution.
22. **Synthesize Information** Why was the pope a powerful figure in medieval Europe?
23. **Recognize Cause and Effect** What social changes were caused by the commercial revolution? Explain why.
24. **Predict Consequences** How do you think the existence of a powerful Muslim empire on the fringes of Europe will affect the later Middle Ages? Explain why.

● Writing About History

Writing a Research Report The Middle Ages produced a civilization very different from our own. Write a research report about one aspect of medieval civilization. To choose your topic, focus first on a group that interests you, such as knights, noblewomen, serfs, apprentices, monks, or merchants. Consult the Writing Handbook for additional help.

Prewriting
Go online to **PHSchool.com** and enter **Web Code naa-0752** to read about the groups listed above.

- Choose the group that interests you most and write a series of questions that reflect what you would like to learn about that group.

- Gather more resources and narrow your topic to one or two of the questions you listed.

Drafting
- Develop a working thesis and choose information from your sources to support it.
- Make an outline to organize your report.
- Write an introduction, body, and conclusion. Choose an interesting anecdote or quotation for your introduction or conclusion.

Revising
- Use the guidelines for revising your report on page SH15 of the Writing Handbook.

Document-Based Assessment

The Many Faces of Charlemagne

Medieval documents have provided historians with considerable detailed information about the life and reign of Charlemagne. The author of Document A was Charlemagne's personal biographer, who was a student of Alcuin at the Palace School at Aachen. Document C was written by the Monk of Saint Gall at the request of the royal family about 70 years after Charlemagne's death.

Document A

"Charles spent much time . . . in learning rhetoric [logic] and dialectic, and especially astronomy, from Alcuin. He learnt, too, the art of reckoning [mathematics], and . . . scrutinized most carefully the course of the stars. He tried also to learn to write, and for this purpose used to carry with him . . . tablets and writing-sheets that he might in his spare moments accustom himself to the formation of letters. But he made little advance in this strange task, which was begun too late in life."

—From **The Life of Charlemagne** by Einhard

Document B

◄ This image of Charlemagne was painted by a German artist in the 1500s.

Document C

"Once when he was on a journey Charlemagne came unheralded [unannounced] to a certain town which lies on the seashore in Southern Gaul. While he sat eating his supper incognito [in disguise], a raiding-party of Northmen [Vikings] made a piratical attack on the harbour of this town. As their ships came in sight, some said that they were . . . merchants. . . . Charlemagne in his wisdom knew better. From the build of the ships and their speed through the water he recognized them as enemies rather than merchants. 'Those ships are not loaded with goods,' he said to his men. 'They are loaded with savage enemies.' . . . [His men] rushed off to the ships at full speed, each striving to be the first to reach them. They were not successful. As soon as the Northmen learned that the man whom they were accustomed to call Charles the Hammer was in the neighbourhood, they sailed away at incredible speed."

—From **Charlemagne** by Notker the Stammerer, the Monk of Saint Gall

Document D

This image of Charlemagne on the battlefield was created about 1215. It is at the cathedral in Aachen, Germany, where Charlemagne is buried. ▼

Analyzing Documents

Use your knowledge of Charlemagne and Documents A, B, C, and D to answer questions 1–4.

1. The description of Charlemagne in Document A reveals that he
   A did not care about mathematics.
   B tried hard to educate himself.
   C was a great scholar.
   D was a poor student.

2. Which of the following statements best reflects what the author of Document C wants to convey about Charlemagne?
   A Both his men and his enemies feared him.
   B He was a knowledgeable and powerful military leader.
   C He was wise and willing to take personal risks.
   D He was powerful but had poor judgment.

3. Documents B and C best support the statement that
   A later Europeans admired Charlemagne.
   B Charlemagne was a great king.
   C Charlemagne was admired during his lifetime.
   D all Europeans admire Charlemagne.

4. **Writing Task** Think about the people who created the documents above and their possible motives for portraying Charlemagne. How reliable do you think the documents are? Write about at least two of the documents. Consider which details are probably reliable, how the documents provide insight into Charlemagne's character, and how they might be exaggerations.

Joan of Arc Fights for France

May 5, 1429—The French have been trying to drive the English out of France since 1337. Now a new leader, Joan of Arc, is turning the tide of the Hundred Years' War. She writes a letter to the enemy: "You, men of England, who have no right to be in this Kingdom of France, the King of Heaven entreats and orders you through me, Joan the Maiden, to abandon your fortresses and go back to your own country; or I will make a disturbance such as will be eternally remembered." Listen to the Witness History audio to hear more about the great disturbance she created.

◄ Joan of Arc enters Orleans

Joan of Arc's coat of arms

Chapter Preview

Chapter Focus Question How did changing economic and social conditions, wars, and the growing power of monarchs begin to build the framework for the modern nation-state?

German imperial crown

Medieval inkwell and pen

Note Taking Study Guide *Online*
For: Note Taking and Concept Connector worksheets
Web Code: nad-0801

German imperial crown

A lord pledges fealty to his king.

A Struggle for Royal Authority

Medieval monarchs could not always count on the loyalty of their nobles and churchmen.

❝ **A.D. 1137** King Stephen . . . seized Alexander, bishop of Lincoln, and the Chancellor Roger, his nephew, and threw [them] into prison till they gave up their castles. . . . They had done him homage, and sworn oaths, but they no truth maintained. They were all forsworn, and forgetful of their troth [loyalty]; for every rich man built his castles, which they held against [the king]; and they filled the land full of castles. ❞
—*The Anglo-Saxon Chronicle*

Focus Question How did monarchs in England and France expand royal authority and lay the foundations for united nation-states?

Royal Power Grows

Objectives

- Learn how monarchs gained power over nobles and the Church.
- Describe how William the Conqueror and Henry II strengthened English royal power.
- Analyze the traditions of government that developed under King John and later English monarchs.
- Explain how strong monarchs unified France.

Terms, People, and Places

William the Conqueror	Magna Carta
common law	due process of law
jury	habeas corpus
King John	Parliament
	Louis IX

Note Taking

Reading Skill: Identify Causes Keep track of how royal power increased and decreased by using a cause-effect chart like the one below.

As medieval monarchs struggled to exert royal authority over nobles and churchmen, they slowly built the framework for the European nation-states of today. Nation-states are regions that share a government and that are independent of other states. Each of these nations developed differently, and a monarch's success in establishing power could have consequences for centuries.

Monarchs, Nobles, and the Church

During the early Middle Ages, as you have read, monarchs in Europe stood at the head of society but had limited power. Nobles and the Church had as much power as monarchs. In some cases, they were more powerful than monarchs. Both nobles and the Church had their own courts, collected their own taxes, and fielded their own armies. They jealously guarded their rights and privileges against any effort by monarchs to increase royal authority.

During the High Middle Ages—about 1000 to 1300—the balance of power started to shift. Monarchs used various means to centralize power. They expanded the royal domain and set up systems of royal justice that undermined feudal and Church courts. They organized government bureaucracies, developed tax systems, and built standing armies. Monarchs also strengthened ties with the townspeople of the middle class. Townspeople, in turn, supported royal rulers, who could impose the peace and unity that were needed for successful trade.

✔ **Checkpoint** What groups gained and lost power?

English Kings Strengthen Their Power

During the early Middle Ages, various groups—including Angles, Saxons, and Vikings—invaded and settled England. A feudal structure developed in this diverse society, but English rulers generally kept their kingdoms united. In 1066, however, the Anglo-Saxon king Edward died without an heir. A council of nobles chose Edward's brother-in-law Harold to rule. But William, Duke of Normandy, in France, a tough and ruthless descendant of the Vikings, also claimed the English throne. He was related to King Edward, who, according to William, had promised him the throne. The answer to the rival claims lay on the battlefield.

William of Normandy Conquers England William raised an army and won the backing of the pope. He then sailed across the English Channel to England. At the Battle of Hastings, William and his Norman knights triumphed over Harold. **William the Conqueror,** as he was now called, became king of England on Christmas Day 1066.

Although William's French-speaking nobles dominated England, the country's Anglo-Saxon population survived. Over the next 300 years, there was a gradual blending of Norman French and Anglo-Saxon customs, languages, and traditions.

Expanding Royal Power Now that William had conquered England, he set out to impose his control over the land. Like other feudal monarchs, he granted fiefs to the Church and to his Norman lords, or barons, but he also kept a large amount of land for himself. He monitored who built castles and where. He required every vassal to swear first allegiance to him rather than to any other feudal lord.

To learn about his kingdom, William had a complete census taken in 1086. The result was the *Domesday Book* (pronounced "doomsday"), which listed every castle, field, and pigpen in England. As the title suggests, the survey was as thorough and inevitable as doomsday, believed to be God's final day of judgment that no one could escape. Information in the Domesday Book helped William and later English monarchs build an efficient system of tax collection. William's successors also created the royal exchequer, or treasury, to collect taxes, fees, fines, and other dues.

Developing a Unified Legal System In 1154, an energetic, well-educated king, Henry II, inherited the throne. He broadened the system of royal justice by expanding accepted customs into law. He then sent out traveling justices to enforce these royal laws. The decisions of the royal courts became the foundation of English **common law,** a legal system based on custom and court rulings. Unlike local feudal laws, common law applied to all of England. In time, people brought their disputes to royal courts rather than to those of nobles or the Church. Because royal courts charged fees, the exchequer benefited from the growth of royal justice.

Under Henry II, England also developed an early jury system. When traveling justices visited an area, local officials collected a **jury,** or group of men sworn to speak the truth. These early juries determined which cases should be brought to trial and were the ancestors of today's grand jury. Later, another jury evolved that was composed of 12 neighbors of an accused person. It was the ancestor of today's trial jury.

Conflict With the Church Henry's efforts to extend royal power led to a bitter dispute with the Church over the issue of legal authority.

BIOGRAPHY

William the Conqueror
From the time he became Duke of Normandy at age seven, William the Conqueror's (1028–1087) life and position were in constant danger, mostly from jealous relatives. Four of his guardians were murdered—one in the very room in which William slept.

After William was knighted at the age of 15, he sought the help of his liege lord, Henry I of France, to put down rebellions by his barons. At 20, he led an army to defeat a rebellious cousin. His continuing efforts to gain power included putting pressure on Edward, the English king, to declare him heir to the English throne. **How did William's experience as duke prepare him to be a powerful king of England?**

Henry claimed the right to try clergy in royal courts. Thomas Becket, the archbishop of Canterbury and once a close friend of Henry, fiercely opposed the king on this issue. The conflict simmered for years.

At last, Henry's fury exploded. "What cowards I have brought up in my court," he cried. "Who will rid me of this meddlesome priest?" Four hot-headed knights took Henry at his word. In 1170, they murdered the archbishop in his own cathedral. Henry denied any part in the attack. Still, to make peace with the Church, he eased his attempts to regulate the clergy. Meanwhile, Becket was honored as a martyr and declared a saint. Pilgrims flocked to his tomb at Canterbury, where miracles were said to occur.

 Checkpoint How did William and Henry II increase royal power?

Note Taking

Use a Venn diagram like the one below to show the similar and different ways royal power developed in England and France.

Royal Power

England   France

Evolving Traditions of Government

Later English rulers repeatedly clashed with nobles and the Church as they tried to raise taxes or to impose royal authority over traditional feudal rights. Out of those struggles evolved traditions of government that would have great influence on the modern world.

King John Makes Powerful Enemies A son of Henry II, **King John** was a clever, cruel, and untrustworthy ruler. During his reign, he faced three powerful enemies: King Philip II of France, Pope Innocent III, and his own English nobles. He lost his struggles with each.

Ever since William the Conqueror, Norman rulers of England had held vast lands in France. In 1205, John suffered a setback when he lost a war with Philip II and had to give up lands in Anjou and Normandy.

Next, John battled with Innocent III over selecting a new archbishop of Canterbury. When John rejected the pope's nominee, the pope excommunicated him. Innocent also placed England under the interdict—the papal order that forbade Church services in an entire kingdom. Even the strongest ruler was likely to give in to that pressure. To save himself and his crown, John had to accept England as a fief of the papacy and pay a yearly fee to Rome.

The Magna Carta Finally, John angered his own nobles with oppressive taxes and other abuses of power. In 1215, a group of rebellious barons cornered John and forced him to sign the **Magna Carta,** or great charter. This document contained two very important ideas that would shape English government in the future. First, it asserted that the nobles had certain rights. Over time, these rights were extended to all English citizens. Second, the Magna Carta made it clear that the monarch must obey the law.

Besides protecting their own privileges, the barons included provisions that recognized the legal rights of townspeople and the Church. Two of the most significant were in a clause protecting freemen from arbitrary arrest, imprisonment, and other legal actions, except "by legal judgment of his peers or by the law of the land." This clause formed the basis of the right we know today as **due process of law.**

English nobles presented the Magna Carta to King John at Runnymede, a field along the Thames River. Why did King John agree to the Magna Carta?

Primary Source

❝King John, when he saw that he was deserted by almost all, so that out of his regal superabundance of followers he scarcely retained seven knights, was much alarmed lest the barons would attack his castles and reduce them without difficulty, as they would find no obstacle to their so doing. . . . Accordingly, at the time and place pre-agreed on [Runnymede], the king and nobles . . . began a long discussion about terms of peace and aforesaid liberties. . . . King John, seeing that he was inferior in strength to the barons, without raising any difficulty, granted the underwritten laws and liberties, and confirmed them by his charter.❞
—Roger of Wendover

 AUDIO

Evolution of English Government

1066 **Norman Conquest** William, Duke of Normandy, defeats King Harold of the Anglo-Saxons at Hastings.

1086 *Domesday Book* King William uses this census, or survey of people and property, as a basis for taxation.

1160s–1180s **Common Law** Henry II uses accepted customs to lay the foundation for the English legal system.

1215 **Magna Carta** King John approves this document limiting royal power and extending rights to nobles and freemen.

1295 **Model Parliament** King Edward I expands Parliament to include representatives of common people as well as lords and clergy.

> **Chart Skills** Which of the milestones above increased the power of the monarchy? Which limited the monarch's power? Explain your answers.

Model Parliament

The king presides over nobles and clergy, above. Representatives from towns and counties met separately.

- **A** King Edward I
- **B** Archbishops
- **C** Kings of Scotland and Wales
- **D** Clergy
- **E** Barons (Lords)
- **F** Judges

It is also seen as the basis for the right of **habeas corpus,** the principle that no person can be held in prison without first being charged with a specific crime. Habeas corpus was later clarified and defined in the Petition of Right (1628) and the Habeas Corpus Act (1679).

The king also agreed not to raise new taxes without first consulting his Great Council of lords and clergy. Many centuries later, American colonists would claim that those words meant that any taxation without representation was unjust. In 1215, though, neither the king nor his lords could have imagined such an idea.

The Development of Parliament In keeping with the Magna Carta, English rulers often called on the Great Council for advice. During the 1200s, this council evolved into **Parliament,** which later became England's legislature. As Parliament acquired a larger role in government, it helped unify England.

In 1295, King Edward I summoned Parliament to approve money for his wars in France. "What touches all," he declared, "should be approved by all." He had representatives of the "common people" join with the lords and clergy. The "commons" included two knights from each county and representatives of the towns. Much later, this assembly became known as the Model Parliament because it set up the framework for England's legislature. In time, Parliament developed into a two-house body: the House of Lords with nobles and high clergy and the House of Commons with knights and middle-class citizens. Over the centuries, Parliament gained the crucial "power of the purse": the right to approve any new taxes. With that power, Parliament could insist that the monarch meet its demands before voting for taxes. In this way, it could limit the power of the monarch.

✓ **Checkpoint** How was the power of the English king limited?

Successful Monarchs in France

Unlike William the Conqueror in England, monarchs in France did not rule over a unified kingdom. The successors to Charlemagne had little power over a patchwork of French territories ruled by powerful nobles.

The Capetian Kings In 987, these nobles elected Hugh Capet, the count of Paris, to fill the vacant French throne. They may have chosen him because they thought he was too weak to pose a threat to them. Hugh's own lands around Paris were smaller than those of many of his vassals.

Nevertheless, Hugh and his heirs slowly increased royal power. First, they made the throne hereditary, passing it from father to son. The Capetian dynasty lasted for 300 years, making the kingdom more stable. Next, they added to their lands by playing rival nobles against each other. They also won the support of the Church.

Perhaps most important, the Capetians built an effective bureaucracy. Government officials collected taxes and imposed royal law over the king's lands. By establishing order, they increased their prestige and gained the backing of the new middle class.

Philip Augustus Extends French Power In 1179, Philip II became king of France. Called Philip Augustus, he was a shrewd and able ruler. Instead of appointing nobles to fill government positions, Philip paid middle-class officials who would owe their loyalty to him. He granted charters to many new towns and introduced a new national tax.

Philip also quadrupled royal land holdings. Through trickery, diplomacy, and war, he gained control of English-ruled lands in Normandy, Anjou, and elsewhere. He then began to take over southern France. When he sent his knights to help the pope suppress a heretical group called the Albigensians (al buh JEN see unz) in the south, he was able to add this vast area to his domain. Before his death in 1223, Philip had become the most powerful ruler in Europe.

Vocabulary Builder

<u>domain</u>—(doh MAYN) *n.* territory under one ruler

Geography *Interactive*
For: Audio guided tour
Web Code: nap-0811

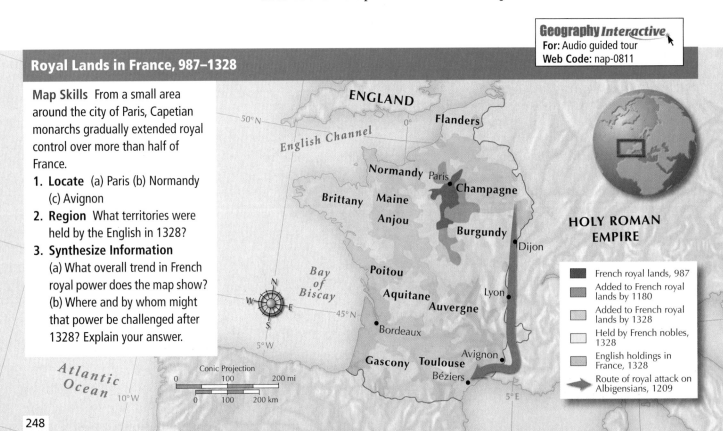

Royal Lands in France, 987–1328

Map Skills From a small area around the city of Paris, Capetian monarchs gradually extended royal control over more than half of France.

1. **Locate** (a) Paris (b) Normandy (c) Avignon
2. **Region** What territories were held by the English in 1328?
3. **Synthesize Information**
   (a) What overall trend in French royal power does the map show?
   (b) Where and by whom might that power be challenged after 1328? Explain your answer.

Legend:
- French royal lands, 987
- Added to French royal lands by 1180
- Added to French royal lands by 1328
- Held by French nobles, 1328
- English holdings in France, 1328
- Route of royal attack on Albigensians, 1209

Louis IX, King and Saint In 1226, Louis IX became King of France. A deeply religious man, Louis persecuted heretics, or those who held beliefs contrary to Church teachings. He also persecuted Jews and led French knights in two Crusades, or wars against Muslims. Within 30 years of his death, the Church declared him a saint.

Louis did much to improve royal government. Like Charlemagne, he sent out roving officials to check on local administrators. He expanded the royal courts, outlawed private wars, and ended serfdom in his personal domain. To ensure justice, he even heard cases himself. His enormous personal prestige helped create a strong national feeling among his subjects. By the time of his death in 1270, France was emerging as an efficient centralized monarchy.

Clashing With the Pope Louis's grandson, Philip IV, ruthlessly extended royal power. To raise cash, he tried to collect new taxes from the clergy. These efforts led to a clash with Pope Boniface VIII. Declaring that "God has set popes over kings and kingdoms," the pope forbade Philip to tax the clergy without papal consent. Philip threatened to arrest any clergy who did not pay. As their quarrel escalated, Philip sent troops to seize Boniface. The pope escaped, but he died soon afterward.

Shortly after, in 1305, a Frenchman was elected pope. Four years later, he moved the papal court to Avignon (ah vee NYOHN), just outside the southern border of France, where French rulers could exercise more control over it. Eventually, this move led to a crisis in the Church when another pope was elected in Rome. The rival popes each claimed to be the true leader of the Church.

Forming the Estates General During this struggle with the pope, Philip rallied French support by setting up the Estates General in 1302. This body had representatives from all three estates, or classes of French society: clergy, nobles, and townspeople. Although later French kings consulted the Estates General, it never gained the power of the purse or otherwise served as a balance to royal power.

✓ **Checkpoint** Describe how two French kings increased royal power.

Louis IX Leads a Crusade
The forces of King Louis IX attack Damietta, a city in Egypt. *What can you tell about medieval weapons and warfare from this painting?*

Assessment

Progress Monitoring *Online*
For: Self-quiz with vocabulary practice
Web Code: naa-0811

Terms, People, and Places

1. What do many of the key terms listed at the beginning of the section have in common? Explain.

Note Taking

2. **Reading Skill: Identify Causes** Use your completed graphic organizers to answer the Focus Question: How did monarchs in England and France expand royal authority and lay the foundations for united nation-states?

Comprehension and Critical Thinking

3. **Analyze Information** How were nobles and the Church obstacles for monarchs who wanted more power?

4. **Summarize** How did William increase royal power in England?

5. **Draw Conclusions** Explain the importance of (a) the Magna Carta and (b) the Model Parliament.

6. **Synthesize Information** Describe the power struggle between French kings and the pope.

● **Writing About History**

Quick Write: Define a Topic Choose a central event or trend from this section. Ask yourself: What happened? When did it begin? What led up to it? What followed? Brainstorm causes and effects. For the growth of royal power in England, you might ask:

- How did William the Conqueror increase royal power?
- How did the nobles react to King John's abuse of power?

Magna Carta

In 1215, a group of barons, or lords, forced King John of England to put his royal seal on the Magna Carta. The barons were tired of the king's military campaigns and heavy taxes. Principles in the Magna Carta shape modern English law and government and influence governments around the world. Below are excerpts from 5 of the 63 articles of this important document.

1. We have also granted to all the freemen of our Kingdom, for us and our heirs, forever, all the underwritten Liberties, to be enjoyed and held by them and their heirs, from us and from our heirs.

12. No scutage [tax] nor aid shall be imposed in our kingdom, unless by the common council of our kingdom; excepting to redeem[1] our person, to make our eldest son a knight, and once to marry our eldest daughter, and not for these, unless a reasonable aid shall be demanded.

14. And also to have the common council of the kingdom, to assess and aid, otherwise than in the three cases aforesaid: and for the assessing of scutages, we will cause to be summoned the Archbishops, Bishops, Abbots, Earls, and great Barons, individually by our letters. And besides, we will cause to be summoned in general by our Sheriffs and Bailiffs[2], all those who hold of us in chief, at a certain day, that is to say at the distance of forty days (before their meeting), at the least, and to a certain place; and in all the letters of summons, we will express the cause of the summons; and the summons being thus made, the business shall proceed on the day appointed, according to the counsel of those who shall be present, although all who have been summoned have not come.

39. No freeman shall be seized, or imprisoned . . . nor will we condemn him, nor will we commit him to prison, excepting by the legal judgment of his peers, or by the laws of the land.

40. To none will we sell, to none will we deny, to none will we delay right of justice.

1. **redeem** (ri DEEM) *v.* to recover ownership of by paying a certain amount of money
2. **bailiff** (BAY lif) *n.* an official in England who collected taxes and acted as magistrate

Thinking Critically

1. **Draw Inferences** Who is not included in the membership of the general council, as described in Article 14? What can you infer from this omission?
2. **Make Generalizations** What do Articles 39 and 40 suggest about abuse of power at this time? Explain your reasoning.

▶ King John approving the Magna Carta at Runnymede, and the Magna Carta itself (above)

SECTION

2

Henry IV
humbling himself
before Pope
Gregory VII

Holy Roman emperor's jewel-
encrusted orb and cross

WITNESS HISTORY 🔊 AUDIO

An Emperor Begs Forgiveness

In 1076 Henry IV, emperor of the vast Holy Roman Empire, knelt in the snow outside an Italian castle. Inside was Pope Gregory VII, who had excommunicated Henry. Gregory described the event in a letter.

❝ Wretchedly with bare feet and clad in wool, [Henry] continued for three days to stand before the gate of the castle. Nor did he desist from imploring with many tears . . . until he had moved all . . . present . . . to such pity and depth of compassion. . . . Finally, won by the persistence of his suit . . . we . . . received him into the favor of communion and into the lap of the Holy Mother Church. ❞

Focus Question How did explosive conflicts between monarchs and popes affect the balance of power in Europe?

The Holy Roman Empire and the Church

Objectives

- Understand why Holy Roman emperors failed to build a unified nation-state in Germany.
- Describe the conflict between Pope Gregory VII and Emperor Henry IV and summarize the struggle to control Italy.
- Analyze how the Church reached the height of its power under Pope Innocent III.

Terms, People, and Places

Holy Roman Empire   lay investiture
Henry IV   Frederick Barbarossa
Pope Gregory VII   Pope Innocent III

Note Taking

Reading Skill: Understand Effects Complete a table to record the actions of Holy Roman emperors and popes and the effects of their actions.

Pope or Emperor	Actions	Effects
Otto I	• Cooperated with Church	• Pope crowned Otto emperor
Gregory VII		

During the early Middle Ages, the Church spread its influence and increased its power across Europe. Meanwhile, monarchs also became more powerful. By 1077, explosive conflicts had arisen between secular rulers and Church officials. The longest and most destructive struggle pitted popes against the rulers of the Holy Roman Empire, who ruled vast lands from Germany to Italy.

The Holy Roman Empire

In the early Middle Ages, Charlemagne brought much of present-day France and Germany under his rule. After his death, the empire dissolved into a number of separate states. In time, the dukes of Saxony extended their power over neighboring German lands. In 936, Duke Otto I of Saxony took the title King of Germany.

Otto I Becomes Emperor Like Charlemagne, Otto I worked closely with the Church. He appointed bishops to top government jobs. He also took an army into Italy to help the pope defeat rebellious Roman nobles. In 962, a grateful pope crowned Otto emperor. Later, Otto's successors took the title Holy Roman emperor—"holy" because they were crowned by the pope, and "Roman" because they saw themselves as heirs to the emperors of ancient Rome.

Emperors Struggle for Control German emperors claimed authority over much of central and eastern Europe as well as parts of France and Italy. In fact, the real rulers of these lands were the emperor's vassals—hundreds of nobles and Church officials. For German emperors, the challenge was to control their vassals. It was a challenge they never met.

Another challenge for the emperors involved the appointment of Church officials. Here, they <u>confronted</u> the power of the popes. Like other monarchs, the Holy Roman emperors often decided who would become bishops and abbots within their realm. At the same time, popes tried to end such interference in the Church from secular rulers.

✓ **Checkpoint** Describe the Holy Roman Empire.

The Feud Between Pope and Emperor

In 1054 **Henry IV** was crowned king of Germany; later he also became Holy Roman emperor. At that time, **Gregory VII** was pope. During their reigns, the conflict between monarchs and the Church erupted.

Gregory VII Causes Controversy Many medieval Europeans admired Pope Gregory VII, who instituted many Church reforms. At the same time, his policies aroused hatred and contempt. Gregory wanted to make the Church independent of secular rulers, so he banned the practice of **lay investiture.** Under this practice, the emperor or another lay person (a person who is not a member of the clergy) "invested," or presented, bishops with the ring and staff that symbolized their office. Only the pope, said Gregory, had the right to appoint and install bishops in office.

Henry IV Responds Pope Gregory's ban brought an angry response from the Holy Roman emperor, Henry IV. He argued that bishops held their lands as royal fiefs. Since he was their overlord, Henry felt entitled to give them the symbols of office. The feud heated up as the two men exchanged insulting letters. Meanwhile, rebellious German princes undermined Henry by supporting the pope.

The Struggle Intensifies In 1076, Gregory excommunicated Henry, freeing his subjects from their allegiance to the emperor. The pope then headed north to crown a new emperor. Faced with revolts, Henry was forced to make peace. In January 1077, he presented himself to the pope as a repentant sinner. Gregory knew that Henry was just trying to save his throne. Still, as a priest, the pope had no choice but to forgive a confessed sinner. He lifted the order of excommunication, and Henry quickly returned to Germany to subdue his rebellious nobles. He also took revenge on Gregory by leading an army to Rome and forcing the pope into exile.

A Compromise: The Concordat of Worms The struggle over investiture dragged on for almost 50 years. Finally, in 1122, both sides accepted a treaty known as the Concordat of Worms (vawrmz). This treaty declared that the Church had the sole power to elect and invest bishops with spiritual authority. The emperor, however, still invested them with fiefs.

✓ **Checkpoint** Describe the feud between the pope and the emperor.

Vocabulary Builder

<u>confronted</u>—(kun FRUNT id) *v.* came face to face with; opposed boldly

Scenes from the Life of Pope Gregory
A medieval drawing shows Henry driving Gregory from Rome (top). Other scenes include Gregory excommunicating Henry (bottom left) and Gregory on his deathbed (bottom right).

The Struggle for Italy

Although the investiture struggle was over, new battles were soon raging between popes and emperors. During the 1100s and 1200s, ambitious German emperors sought to control Italy. As they did so, they came into conflict with popes and with the wealthy cities of northern Italy.

German Emperors Try to Subdue Italy The Holy Roman emperor Frederick I, called Frederick Barbarossa, or "Red Beard," dreamed of building an empire from the Baltic to the Adriatic. For years, he fought to bring the wealthy cities of northern Italy under his control. With equal energy, they resisted. By joining forces with the pope in the Lombard League, they finally managed to defeat Barbarossa's armies.

Barbarossa did succeed, however, in arranging a marriage between his son Henry and Constance, heiress to Sicily and southern Italy. That move entangled German emperors even more deeply in Italian affairs. Barbarossa's grandson, Frederick II, was raised in southern Italy. An able and arrogant leader, he pursued his ambitions in Italy, clashing repeatedly and unsuccessfully with several popes. Like his grandfather, Frederick also tried but failed to subdue the cities of northern Italy.

Effects on Germany and Italy While Frederick II was involved in Italy, German nobles grew more independent. The Holy Roman Empire survived, but remained a patchwork of feudal states. Unlike France and England, Germany would not become a nation-state for another 600 years. Southern Italy and Sicily also faced centuries of upheaval. There, popes turned to the French to overthrow Frederick's heirs. A local uprising against French rule in Sicily led to 200 years of chaos as French and Spanish rivals battled for power. The region that had once been a thriving center of culture was left in ruins.

✔ **Checkpoint** What obstacles did German emperors face in Italy?

Frederick Barbarossa Goes to War
About to embark on a Crusade, Frederick Barbarossa (at left, with red cape over armor) carries an unsheathed sword and an orb with a cross. *How do these two objects symbolize his goals in the Crusade?*

Church Power Reaches Its Height

In the 1200s, the Church reached the peak of its political power. Reforming popes like Gregory VII claimed the right to depose kings and emperors. Gregory's successors greatly expanded papal power.

Papal Supremacy In 1198, the powerful Pope Innocent III took office. As head of the Church, Innocent III claimed supremacy over all other rulers. The pope, he said, stands "between God and man, lower than God but higher than men, who judges all and is judged by no one." Innocent III clashed with all the powerful rulers of his day, and usually won. As you have read, when King John of England dared to appoint an archbishop of Canterbury without the pope's approval, Innocent excommunicated the king and placed his kingdom under interdict. Innocent ordered the same punishment for France when Philip II tried unlawfully to annul, or invalidate, his marriage.

In 1209, Innocent, aided by Philip II, launched a brutal crusade, or holy war, against the Albigensians in southern France. The Albigensians were a religious group regarded as heretics by the Church because they rejected central Catholic beliefs and rituals. Knights from all over western Europe took part. Tens of thousands of people were slaughtered in the Albigensian Crusade.

Innocent strengthened papal power within the Church as well. He extended the Papal States, reformed the Church courts, and changed the way that Church officials were chosen. Finally, he called a council that issued decrees that justified the pope's new power.

Looking Ahead After Innocent's death, popes continued to claim supremacy. During this period, though, the French and English monarchies grew stronger. In 1296, Philip IV of France successfully challenged Pope Boniface VIII on the issue of taxing the clergy. After Philip engineered the election of a French pope, the papacy entered a period of decline.

 Checkpoint How did Innocent III embody the Church's political power?

Saint Francis of Assisi kneels before Pope Innocent III, who approves the rules of the Franciscan order.

SECTION 2 Assessment

Progress Monitoring *Online*
For: Self-quiz with vocabulary practice
Web Code: naa-0821

Terms, People, and Places

1. Place each of the key terms at the beginning of this section into one of the following categories: politics, culture, or geography. Write a sentence for each term explaining your choice.

Note Taking

2. **Reading Skill: Understand Effects** Use your completed table to answer the Focus Question: How did explosive conflicts between monarchs and popes affect the balance of power in Europe?

Comprehension and Critical Thinking

3. **Synthesize Information** Why was the power of German emperors limited?

4. **Determine Relevance** What was the significance of the conflict between Pope Gregory VII and Emperor Henry IV?

5. **Recognize Cause and Effect** How did conflicts between popes and emperors affect Italy?

6. **Analyze Information** How did Pope Innocent III assert the power of the Church?

● **Writing About History**

Quick Write: Narrow Your Topic After exploring a topic, narrow your focus by deciding whether to concentrate on economic, social, political, or cultural elements, or a combination. If your topic is the excommunication of Henry IV, you could choose
• political events leading up to the event
• short-term political effects
• long-term political and social effects
   Choose a topic from the section and list three ways in which you could narrow it for a cause-and-effect essay.

SECTION 3

Crusader knights at the siege of Jerusalem

Crusaders Capture Jerusalem

❝ The Franks entered the city magnificently at the noonday hour. . . . With trumpets sounding and with everything in an uproar, exclaiming, 'Help, God!' they vigorously pushed into the city, and straightaway raised the banner on the top of the wall. All the heathen, completely terrified, changed their boldness to swift flight through the narrow streets of the quarters. . . . Nowhere was there a place where the Saracens could escape the swordsmen. . . . What more shall I tell? Not one of them was allowed to live. ❞
—Fulcher of Chartres

Focus Question How did the Crusades change life in Europe and beyond?

The Crusades and the Wider World

Objectives
- Identify the advanced civilizations that were flourishing in 1050.
- Explain the causes and effects of the Crusades.
- Summarize how Christians in Spain carried out the Reconquista.

Terms, People, and Places

Crusades	Reconquista
Holy Land	Ferdinand and Isabella
Pope Urban II	Inquisition

Note Taking

Reading Skill: Identify Causes and Effects
Track causes of the Crusades in the top ovals and effects in the lower ones of a concept web like this one.

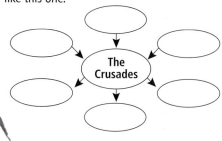

The Crusades

Fulcher of Chartres was just one of thousands of Europeans who took part in a series of wars known as the **Crusades.** In these wars, which began in 1096, Christians battled Muslims for control of lands in the Middle East. As they streamed eastward over the next 200 years, Western Europeans learned that the world was much larger than they had ever dreamed. Their encounters outside Europe would serve to accelerate the pace of change at home.

The World in 1050

In 1050, as Western Europe was just emerging from a period of isolation, many other civilizations were thriving elsewhere. The religion of Islam had given rise to a brilliant civilization that stretched from present-day Spain to India, and Muslim traders and scholars spread goods and ideas even farther.

India was a land of thriving cities where Hindu and Buddhist traditions flourished, and wealthy princes built stunning temples and palaces. In East Asia, under the Tang and Song dynasties, China's culture flourished and influenced neighboring peoples. Meanwhile, the Soninke people of West Africa were building the great trading empire of Ghana.

Across the Atlantic, in Central America, the Maya had cleared rain forests and built cities with towering temples. In the Andes of South America, Native Americans were building a great empire.

The civilizations of the Americas, however, remained apart from the contacts that were taking place among Africans, Europeans, and Asians.

Closer to Western Europe, the Byzantine empire—the former eastern Roman empire—was generally prosperous and united. In the 1050s, the Seljuk Turks invaded the Byzantine empire. The Turks had migrated from Central Asia into the Middle East, where they converted to Islam. By 1071, the Seljuks had overrun most Byzantine lands in Asia Minor (present-day Turkey). The Seljuks also extended their power over the Holy Land, that is, Jerusalem and other places in Palestine where Christians believe Jesus lived and preached. Other Muslim groups had controlled this region in the past, but invasions by the Seljuk Turks threatened the Byzantine empire. The conflict prevented Christian pilgrims from traveling to the Holy Land.

✔ **Checkpoint** What civilizations were flourishing around 1050?

The Crusades

The Byzantine emperor Alexius I urgently asked Pope Urban II for Christian knights to help him fight the Muslim Turks. Although Roman popes and Byzantine emperors were longtime rivals, Urban agreed.

Called to War At the Council of Clermont in 1095, Urban incited bishops and nobles to action. "From Jerusalem and the city of Constantinople comes a grievous report," he began. "An accursed race . . . has violently invaded the lands of those Christians and has depopulated them by pillage and fire." Urban then called for a crusade to free the Holy Land:

> **Primary Source**
>
> 66 Both knights and footmen, both rich and poor . . . [must] strive to help expel [the Seljuks] from our Christian lands before it is too late. . . . Christ commands it. Remission of sins will be granted for those going thither.99
> —Fulcher of Chartres, *Chronicle of the First Crusade*

"God wills it!" roared the assembly. By 1096, thousands of knights were on their way to the Holy Land. As the crusading spirit swept through Western Europe, armies of ordinary men and women inspired by fiery preachers left for the Holy Land, too. Few returned. Religious zeal was not the only factor that motivated the crusaders. Many knights hoped to win wealth and land. Some crusaders sought to escape troubles at home. Others yearned for adventure.

The pope, too, had mixed motives. Urban hoped to increase his power in Europe and perhaps heal the schism, or split, between the Roman and Byzantine churches. In 1054, the two branches of Christianity had divided after disputes over beliefs and authority. Urban also hoped that the Crusades would set Christian knights to fighting Muslims instead of one another.

Fighting a Losing Battle Only the First Crusade came close to achieving its goals. After a long and bloody campaign, Christian knights captured Jerusalem in 1099. They capped their victory with a massacre of Muslim and Jewish residents of the city.

The Crusades continued, off and on, for over 200 years. The crusaders divided their captured lands into four small states, called crusader states. The Muslims repeatedly sought to destroy these Christian states, prompting Europeans to launch new crusades. In 1187, Jerusalem fell to the Muslims.

The Crusades, 1096–1204

Map Skills Urged on by Pope Urban II, thousands of Europeans joined the Crusades to expel Muslims from the Holy Land.

1. **Locate** On the large map, find (a) Holy Roman Empire (b) Rome (c) Jerusalem (d) Acre (e) Constantinople. On the inset map, find (a) Acre (b) Kingdom of Jerusalem.

2. **Movement** What route did English crusaders take to the Holy Land? Why do you think they took that route?

3. **Draw Conclusions** Why was it difficult for Europeans to defend the Crusader states?

COUNTY OF EDESSA
Edessa
Antioch
PRINCIPALITY OF ANTIOCH
Tripoli
COUNTY OF TRIPOLI
Acre
Damascus
Jerusalem
KINGDOM OF JERUSALEM

Miller Projection
0   100   200 mi
0   100   200 km

50°N 10°W
Atlantic Ocean
ENGLAND
POLAND
RUSSIA
HOLY ROMAN EMPIRE
Metz
Regensburg
Vézeley
FRANCE
Clermont
HUNGARY
Venice
Genoa
CROATIA
SERBIA
Marseille
Black Sea
Constantinople
LEÓN
PORTUGAL
CASTILE
Rome
40°N
SELJUK TURKS
KINGDOM OF SICILY
BYZANTINE EMPIRE
Edessa
Antioch
Córdoba
Cyprus
Tripoli
Damascus
Tangier
0°
10°E
Acre
Jerusalem
AFRICA
Crete
Area of inset map
Mediterranean Sea
20°E
30°E
Tripoli
Cairo

Predominantly Muslim lands, 1095
First Crusade, 1096–1099
Second Crusade, 1147–1149
Third Crusade, 1189–1192
Fourth Crusade, 1202–1204

Conic Projection
0   200   400 mi
0   200   400 km

▼ Crusaders load their ships in preparation for sailing to the Holy Land.

By 1187, the Muslim leader Saladin had retaken Jerusalem from the Christian crusaders. King Richard I tried to persuade Saladin to return the city to the Christians. Saladin refused, saying:

Primary Source

❝ To us Jerusalem is as precious . . . as it is to you, because it is the place from where our Prophet [Muhammad] made his journey by night to heaven. . . . Do not dream that we will give it up to you. ❞ 🔊 AUDIO

However, because he recognized how important it was to Christians to be able to visit the sacred sites of their religion, Saladin did reopen Jerusalem to Christian pilgrims. **What does Saladin's response to King Richard's demands show about him?**

The victor was the able Muslim leader Salah al-Din, known to Europeans as Saladin. On the Third Crusade, Europeans failed to retake Jerusalem. After negotiations, though, Saladin did reopen the holy city to Christian pilgrims.

Europeans also mounted crusades against other Muslim lands, especially in North Africa. All ended in defeat. During the Fourth Crusade, the crusaders were diverted from fighting Muslims to fighting other Christians. After helping merchants from the northern Italian city of Venice defeat their Byzantine trade rivals in 1204, crusaders captured and looted Constantinople, the Byzantine capital.

Meanwhile, Muslim armies overran the crusader states. By 1291, they had captured the last Christian outpost, the port city of Acre. As in Jerusalem 200 years earlier, the victors massacred their enemies. This time, the victims were Christians.

✔ **Checkpoint** How successful were the Crusades?

The Impact of the Crusades

The Crusades left a bitter legacy of religious hatred. In the Middle East, both Christians and Muslims committed appalling atrocities in the name of religion. In Europe, crusaders sometimes turned their religious fury against Jews, massacring entire communities.

The crusaders arrived in the Middle East at a time when various Muslim regimes were struggling among themselves for control of the region. These groups rallied together to fight the invaders, and, under Saladin, began to reunify the region from Egypt to Syria.

Though the crusaders failed to keep control of the Holy Land, the Crusades did have significant effects on life in Europe. These wars helped to quicken the pace of changes that were already underway.

European Economies Expand Even before the Crusades, Europeans had developed a taste for luxuries from the Byzantine empire. Returning crusaders brought even more fabrics, spices, and perfumes from the Middle East back to Europe. Trade increased and expanded.

Merchants in Venice and other northern Italian cities had built large fleets to carry crusaders to the Holy Land. Now they used those fleets to carry on trade in such goods as sugar, cotton, and rice with the Middle East.

The Crusades further encouraged the growth of a money economy. To finance a journey to the Holy Land, nobles needed money. They therefore allowed peasants to pay rents in money rather than in grain or labor. Peasants began to sell their goods in towns to earn money, a practice that helped to undermine serfdom.

Effects on Monarchs and the Church The Crusades helped to increase the power of monarchs. These rulers won new rights to collect taxes in order to support the Crusades. Some rulers, such as the French king Louis IX and the English king Richard I, called the Lion-Heart, led Crusades, which added greatly to their prestige.

Enthusiasm for the Crusades brought papal power to its greatest height. This period of enhanced prestige was short-lived, however. As you have read, popes were soon involved in bitter power struggles with monarchs. Also, the Crusades did not end the split between the Roman and Byzantine churches as Pope Urban had hoped. Instead, Byzantine resentment against the West hardened as a result of the Fourth Crusade, during which crusaders had conquered and looted Constantinople.

A Wider Worldview Evolves Contacts with the Muslim world led Christians to realize that millions of people lived in regions they had never even known existed. Soon, a few curious Europeans had left to explore far-off places such as India and China.

In 1271, a young Venetian, Marco Polo, set out for China with his merchant father and uncle. After many years in China, he returned to Venice and wrote a book about the wonders of Chinese civilization. Doubting Europeans wondered if he had really gone to China. To them, his tales of a government-run mail service and black stones (coal) that were burned to heat homes were unbelievable.

The experiences of crusaders and of travelers like Marco Polo expanded European horizons. They brought Europe into a wider world from which it had been cut off since the fall of Rome. In the 1400s, a desire to trade directly with India and China would lead Europeans to a new age of exploration.

✓ **Checkpoint** Summarize the effects of the Crusades.

Prayer beads like these are used by people of many faiths. ▶

● **INFOGRAPHIC**

JERUSALEM

Today Jews, Christians, and Muslims still consider Jerusalem sacred. Despite continued disputes—and violence—over control of the city, pilgrims still visit holy places. Christians come to the Church of the Holy Sepulcher, believed to be the site of Jesus' resurrection. Equally sacred to Muslims is the Dome of the Rock, from which the Prophet Muhammad is believed to have ascended to heaven. And Jewish pilgrims still pray at the Old City's Western Wall, all that remains of the city's ancient temple.

▲ A Muslim woman kneels in prayer (above left); Christian pilgrims carry a cross through the streets (above right).

◀ A Jewish pilgrim prays at the Western Wall.

Medieval map of Jerusalem ▶

Thinking Critically

1. **Analyze Visuals** What do the people in the three photos have in common?
2. **Make Comparisons** How is Jerusalem's situation today similar to its situation at the time of the Crusades?

259

The Reconquista

The crusading spirit continued after the European defeat at Acre, especially in the Iberian peninsula. North African Muslims, called Moors, had conquered most of present-day Spain in the 700s. However, several tiny Christian kingdoms in the north slowly expanded their borders and sought to take over Muslim lands. Their campaign to drive Muslims from the peninsula became known as the **Reconquista,** or "reconquest."

Christians Conquer Spain The first real success of these Christian warriors came in 1085, when they captured the city of Toledo. During the next 200 years, Christian forces pushed slowly and steadily southward. By 1140, the Christian kingdom of Portugal had been established, and by 1300, Christians controlled the entire Iberian Peninsula except for Granada. Muslim influences remained strong, though, and helped shape the arts and literature of Christian Spain. In 1469, the marriage of Ferdinand of Aragon and Isabella of Castile created the unified state called Spain. Using their combined forces, **Ferdinand and Isabella** made a final push against the Muslim stronghold of Granada. In 1492, Granada fell. The Reconquista was complete.

Vocabulary Builder

<u>diverse</u>—(dih VURS) *adj.* varied; different

Spain Expels Non-Christians Ferdinand and Isabella wanted to impose unity on their <u>diverse</u> peoples. Isabella was determined to bring religious as well as political unity to Spain. Under Muslim rule, Spanish Christians, Jews, and Muslims lived in relative peace, allowed to worship as they chose. Isabella ended that tolerance. With the support of the **Inquisition,** a Church court set up to try people accused of heresy, Isabella launched a brutal crusade. Jews and Muslims who had been forced to convert to Christianity could be tried by the Inquisition. If found guilty of practicing their religions, they could be turned over to the secular authorities for punishment. Many who refused to conform to Church teachings were burned at the stake.

The queen achieved religious unity, but at a high price. More than 150,000 people—mostly Muslims and Jews—fled Spain. Many of these exiles were skilled, educated people who had contributed much to Spain's economy and culture.

 Checkpoint What was the Reconquista?

SECTION 3 Assessment

Progress Monitoring *Online*
For: Self-quiz with vocabulary practice
Web Code: naa-0831

Terms, People, and Places

1. For each term, person, or place listed at the beginning of the section, write a sentence explaining its significance.

Note Taking

2. **Reading Skill: Identify Causes and Effects** Use your completed concept web to answer the Focus Question: How did the Crusades change life in Europe and beyond?

Comprehension and Critical Thinking

3. **Draw Conclusions** Why was the invasion of the Byzantine empire by the Turks significant?

4. **Recognize Cause and Effect** Explain three reasons why Europeans joined the Crusades.

5. **Determine Relevance** How did the Crusades accelerate change in Europe?

6. **Demonstrate Reasoned Judgment** Do you think unity in Spain was worth the costs of the Reconquista? Explain.

● Writing About History

Quick Write: Organize Your Essay After defining your topic, use a graphic organizer to organize your information. For example, for the Crusades you might:

- use a flowchart to show events leading up to the First Crusade.
- use a cause-effect chart to show social, economic, and political effects.

Fill in your main ideas for each category in your graphic organizer and use it as a framework for your essay.

Conflict

What issues cause groups of people or countries to come into conflict?

Conflict has existed throughout history, and has often led to violence. It is so common and widespread that historians have used wars as a framework for telling the story of a civilization. For example, the Crusades and the Hundred Years' War are seen as turning points for medieval Europe. Families, religious and ethnic groups, city-states, and nations have all found reason to take up arms against each other. They have fought over power, territory, natural resources, ideas, beliefs, and a host of other issues. Compare the opponents in and the causes of the following major conflicts.

▲ A father and son watch oil fields burning after the Iraqi occupation of Kuwait.

Conflict and Power: The Wars of the Roses

Rival branches of the royal family, the House of Lancaster and the House of York, fought over the English crown starting in 1455. The trouble began when Richard, Duke of York, tried to seize the throne from Henry VI, head of the House of Lancaster. This led to a series of bloody civil wars lasting 30 years, in what became known as the Wars of the Roses. Both leaders and many of their followers died. Power shifted back and forth between the families until Henry Tudor defeated King Richard III, became King Henry VII, and married Elizabeth of York.

Conflict and Territory: The Russo-Japanese War

A clash between two expansion-minded neighbors, Japan and Russia, led to war in the early 1900s. The prize was China's Liaodong Peninsula and its main city, Port Arthur. Japan, an island nation, saw the peninsula as an entryway to the Asian mainland. Russia saw the port as the perfect home for its Pacific fleet. Russia seized the peninsula in 1898. For six years Japan built up its military. In 1904, it attacked the Russian fleet at Port Arthur and then launched a successful invasion. The Russo-Japanese War ended in 1905, with Japan winning the peninsula.

Conflict and Resources: The Persian Gulf War

In August 1990, Iraqi leader Saddam Hussein ordered his army to cross its southwestern border and invade Kuwait. This small Persian Gulf nation has one important resource: oil. Iraq also has oil reserves, but taking over its neighbor and acquiring Kuwait's large petroleum reserves would greatly increase Iraq's power in the Gulf region and the world. That outcome did not materialize. A coalition of anti-Iraq forces, led by the United States, gathered in nearby Saudi Arabia. In early 1991, they began an offensive that shattered Saddam's army and cleared the Iraqis out of Kuwait.

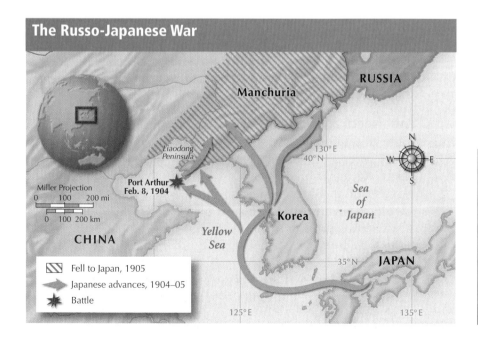

The Russo-Japanese War

RUSSIA

Manchuria

Liaodong Peninsula

130° E
40° N

Port Arthur
Feb. 8, 1904

Miller Projection
0   100   200 mi

0 100 200 km

CHINA

Yellow Sea

Korea

Sea of Japan

35° N

JAPAN

125° E

135° E

Fell to Japan, 1905
Japanese advances, 1904–05
Battle

Thinking Critically

1. **Connect** **(a)** What caused each of the conflicts described above? **(b)** Even though the issues were different, what did the goals and methods of the opponents have in common?
2. Do research to find out more about these and other examples of conflict. Create a chart showing opponents, causes, key events, and results.

Medieval scholars at the University of Paris

Medieval inkwell and pen

Life in a Medieval University

Although some university students were scolded for fooling around rather than studying, this father had the opposite worry:

❝ They tell me that, unlike everyone else, you get out of bed before the first bell sounds in order to study, that you are the first into the classroom and the last to leave it. And that when you get back home you spend the whole day going over what you were taught in your lessons. . . . Many people make themselves permanently ill through excessive study; some of them die, and others . . . waste away day after day. **❞**
—Boncompagno da Signa

Focus Question What achievements in learning, literature, and the arts characterized the High and late Middle Ages?

Learning and Culture Flourish

Objectives

- Explain the emergence of universities and their importance to medieval life.
- Understand how newly translated writings from the past and from other regions influenced medieval thought.
- Describe the literature, architecture, and art of the High and late Middle Ages.

Terms, People, and Places

scholasticism
Thomas Aquinas
vernacular
Dante Alighieri

Geoffrey Chaucer
Gothic style
flying buttresses
illumination

Note Taking

Reading Skill: Recognize Multiple Causes
Keep track of the many causes of the cultural and intellectual flowering of the Middle Ages by completing a flowchart like the one below.

Universities	Scholarship	Literature	The Arts
•	•	•	•
•	•	•	•

↓ ↓ ↓ ↓

Learning and Culture Flourish

In spite of the problems of students studying too much—or sometimes too little—medieval universities brought prestige and profit to the cities in which they were located. Local merchants provided students with housing, food, clothing, and entertainment. But students could also create problems for university communities. The priest Jacques de Vitry complained, "They were always fighting and engaging in scuffles." Who were these students, and why did universities begin to spring up in the 1100s?

Medieval Universities Emerge

By the 1100s, Europe was experiencing dynamic changes. A more reliable food supply and the growth of trade and towns were signs of increased prosperity.

The Need for Educated People Grows As economic and political conditions improved in the High Middle Ages, the need for education expanded. The Church wanted better-educated clergy. Royal rulers also needed literate men for their growing bureaucracies. By acquiring an education, the sons of wealthy townspeople might hope to qualify for high positions in the Church or with royal governments.

By the 1100s, schools had sprung up around the great cathedrals to train the clergy. Some of these cathedral schools evolved into the first universities. They were organized like guilds, with charters to protect the rights of members and established standards for training.

As early as the 900s, the Italian city of Salerno had a respected medical school. Later, Bologna's university—founded in 1158—became famous for legal studies. Paris and Oxford founded their universities in the later 1100s. Soon, other cities rushed to organize universities. Students often traveled from one university to another to study different subjects, seeking food and lodging from whatever patrons they could find to support them.

Student Life University life offered few comforts. A bell wakened students at about 5 A.M. for prayers. Students then attended classes until 10 A.M., when they had their first meal of the day. Afternoon classes continued until 5 P.M. Students usually ate a light supper and then studied until bedtime. Because at first medieval universities did not have permanent buildings, classes were held in rented rooms or in the choir loft of a church. Students sat for hours on hard benches as the teacher dictated and then explained Latin texts. Students were expected to memorize what they heard.

A program of study covered the seven liberal arts: arithmetic, geometry, astronomy, music, grammar, rhetoric, and logic. There were separate programs for the further study of law, medicine, and theology. To show mastery of a subject, students took an oral exam. Earning a degree as a bachelor of arts took between three and six years. Only after several more years of study could a man qualify to become a master of arts and a teacher. Theology was the longest course of study.

Women and Education Women were not allowed to attend universities. And so, for the most part, they were also deprived of the mental stimulation that was an important part of university life. Without a university education, women could not become doctors, lawyers, or church officials.

There were educated women, however. Some girls received good educations in convents, and girls from noble families attended classes at Notre Dame de Paris, located in the French capital. Some nuns became scholars and writers. The writer Christine de Pisan (duh pee ZAHN) examined the issue of women's education. In *The City of Ladies,* she asks Lady Reason whether women are less capable of learning and understanding, as men insist. Lady Reason replies:

Primary Source

 If it were customary to send daughters to school like sons, and if they were then taught the same subjects, they would learn as thoroughly and understand the subtleties of all arts and sciences as well as sons. **99**
—Christine de Pisan

Still, men continued to look on educated women as oddities. Most medieval men felt that women should pursue their "natural" gifts at home—raising children, managing the household, doing needlework—and leave books and writing to men.

✔ **Checkpoint** What was university life like in medieval Europe?

Europeans Acquire "New" Learning

Universities received a further boost from an explosion of knowledge that reached Europe in the High Middle Ages. Many of the "new" ideas had originated in ancient Greece but had been lost to Western Europeans after the fall of Rome.

BIOGRAPHY

Christine de Pisan

Christine de Pisan (1364?–1430?) was more educated than most men of her time. Her father, a physician and astronomer in the French court, saw that she received an excellent education. She spoke French, Italian, and possibly Latin as well.

Christine married at 15. When her husband died 10 years later, she supported herself and her three children by writing. Her first works were poems of lost love dedicated to her husband. Her writing was supported by lords and monarchs.

Because of her desire to comment on social issues, Christine gradually switched her focus from poetry to prose. She described women's place in medieval society and promoted women's rights and accomplishments. **Why do you think Christine began to write about women's issues?**

Medieval Innovation in Europe

Many technological innovations that still affect our daily lives were either invented or adapted by Europeans during the Middle Ages.

The invention of the escapement mechanism allowed a clock to measure hours of equal length regardless of the times of sunrise and sunset. These clocks regulated when church bells rang to mark the divisions of the day. ▼

In the 1200s, the first buttons were used as ornaments and sold by jewelers. Once their practical use was discovered, less expensive buttons allowed garments to have adjustable necklines and detachable sleeves. ▼

The invention of eyeglasses was particularly welcome to medieval monks who copied manuscripts. In fact, a 1313 document attributes this innovation to a Dominican friar from Italy. ▶

A series of innovations ▶ improved medieval farming—and the food supply. The iron plow was more efficient. A new harness allowed a change from oxen to faster horsepower.

Vocabulary Builder

initiated—(ih NISH ee ayt ed) *vt.* started; introduced

Muslim Scholarship Advances Knowledge Muslim scholars had translated the works of Aristotle and other Greek thinkers into Arabic. Their translations and knowledgeable commentaries on these ancient texts spread across the Muslim world. In Muslim Spain, Jewish and Christian scholars translated these works into Latin, the language of Christian European scholars. In the 1100s, when these new translations reached Western Europe, they initiated a revolution in the world of learning.

Christian Scholars Struggle With New Ideas The writings of the ancient Greeks posed a challenge to Christian scholars. Aristotle taught that people should use reason to discover basic truths. Christians, however, accepted many ideas on faith. They believed that the Church was the final authority on all questions. How could they use the logic of Aristotle without undermining their Christian faith?

Some Christian scholars tried to resolve the conflict between faith and reason. Their method, known as **scholasticism,** used reason to support Christian beliefs. Scholastics studied the works of the Muslim philosopher Averroës (uh VEER uh weez) and the Jewish rabbi Maimonides (my MAHN uh deez). These thinkers, too, used logic to resolve the conflict between faith and reason.

The writings of these philosophers influenced the famous scholastic **Thomas Aquinas** (uh KWY nus). In a monumental work, *Summa theologica,* Aquinas concluded that faith and reason exist in harmony. Both lead to the same truth, that God rules over an orderly universe. Aquinas thus brought together Christian faith and classical Greek philosophy.

New Approaches to Science and Mathematics Scientific works, translated from Arabic and Greek, also reached Europe from Spain and the Byzantine empire. Christian scholars studied Hippocrates on medicine and Euclid on geometry, along with works by Arab scientists. They saw, too, how Aristotle had used observation and experimentation to study the physical world. Yet science made little real progress in Europe in the Middle Ages because most scholars still believed that all true knowledge must fit with Church teachings. It would take many centuries before Christian thinkers changed the way they viewed the physical world.

During this period, Europeans adopted Hindu-Arabic numerals, which were much easier to use than the cumbersome system of Roman numerals that had been traditional throughout Europe for centuries. In time, the use of Arabic numerals (as they are commonly called) allowed both scientists and mathematicians to make extraordinary advances in their fields.

✓ **Checkpoint** Describe the new learning of medieval Europe.

Medieval Literature

While Latin remained the written language of scholars and churchmen, new writings began to appear in the **vernacular,** or the everyday languages of ordinary people, such as French, German, and Italian. These writings captured the spirit of the High and late Middle Ages. Medieval literature included epics, or long narrative poems, about knights and chivalry as well as tales of the common people.

Heroic Epics Captivate Across Europe, people began writing down oral traditions in the vernacular. French pilgrims traveling to holy sites loved to hear the *chansons de geste,* or "songs of heroic deeds." The most popular was the *Song of Roland,* written around 1100, which praises the courage of one of Charlemagne's knights. A true chivalric hero, Roland loyally sacrifices his life out of a sense of honor. Spain's great epic, *Poem of the Cid,* tells the story of Rodrigo Díaz de Vivar, a bold and fiery Christian lord who fought both with and against Muslim forces. His nickname, *El Cid,* comes from the Arabic word for "lord."

Dante's *Divine Comedy* "In the middle of the journey of life, I found myself in a dark wood, where the straight way was lost." So begins the *Divine Comedy* written in the early 1300s by the Italian poet **Dante Alighieri** (DAHN tay ah leeg YEH ree). The poem takes the reader on an imaginary journey into hell and purgatory, where souls await forgiveness. Finally, in the third section, Dante describes a vision of heaven.

"Abandon all hope, ye that enter here" is the warning Dante receives as he approaches hell. There, he talks with people from history who tell how they earned a place in hell. Humor, tragedy, and the endless medieval quest for religious understanding are all ingredients in Dante's poem. His journey summarizes Christian ethics, showing how people's actions in life determine their fate in the afterlife.

Near the end of the French epic poem the *Song of Roland,* the great hero, Count Roland, has been wounded in battle. Now he "feels death coming over him." Why does the author include the angels bearing Roland's soul to heaven?

Primary Source

“Count Roland lay stretched out beneath a pine;
He turned his face toward the land of Spain,
Began to remember many things now:
How many lands, brave man, he had conquered;
And he remembered: sweet France, the men of his line,
Remembered Charles, his lord, who fostered him:
Cannot keep, remembering, from weeping, sighing;
But would not be unmindful of himself:
He confesses his sins, prays God for mercy.
Then he held out his right glove to his Lord:
Saint Gabriel took the glove from his hand.
He held his head bowed down upon his arm,
He is gone, his two hands joined, to his end.
Then God sent him his angel Cherubin
And Saint Michael, angel of the sea's Peril;
And with these two there came Saint Gabriel:
They bear Count Roland's soul to Paradise.”

 AUDIO

Chaucer's *Canterbury Tales* In the *Canterbury Tales,* the English writer **Geoffrey Chaucer** describes a band of pilgrims traveling to Saint Thomas Becket's tomb. In brilliant word portraits, he sketches a range of characters, including a knight, a plowman, a merchant, a miller, a monk, and a nun. Each character tells a story to entertain the group. Whether funny, romantic, or bawdy, each tale adds to our picture of medieval life.

✔ **Checkpoint** **Describe three works of medieval literature.**

Architecture and Art

"In the Middle Ages," wrote French author Victor Hugo, "men had no great thought that they did not write down in stone." Those "writings" were the great buildings of the Middle Ages. With riches from trade and commerce, townspeople, nobles, and monarchs indulged in a flurry of building. Their greatest achievements were the towering stone cathedrals that served as symbols of their wealth and religious devotion.

From Romanesque to Gothic In the year 1000, monasteries and towns were building solid stone churches that reflected Roman influences. These Romanesque churches looked like fortresses with thick walls and towers. Typically, the roof of a Romanesque church was a barrel vault, a long tunnel of stone that covered the main part of the structure. It was heavy, supported by massive walls with no windows or only tiny slits of windows for fear of weakening the support for the roof. As a result, the interior of a Romanesque church was dark and gloomy.

About 1140, Abbot Suger wanted to build a new abbey church at St. Denis near Paris. He hoped that it "would shine with wonderful and uninterrupted light." There, builders developed what became known as the **Gothic style** of architecture. Its most important feature was the **flying buttresses,** or stone supports that stood outside the church. These supports allowed builders to construct higher, thinner walls and leave space for large stained-glass windows. Gothic churches soared to incredible heights. Their graceful spires and tall windows carried the eye upward to the heavens. "Since their brilliance lets the splendor of the True Light pass into the church," declared a medieval visitor, "they enlighten those inside."

Making Art in Stone and Glass As churches rose, stonemasons carved sculptures to decorate them both inside and out. In addition to scenes from the Bible and the lives of the saints, sculptors included lifelike forms of plants and animals. They also carved whimsical or frightening images of mythical creatures such as dragons and unicorns.

Stained glass rose window in Notre Dame Cathedral, Paris

At the same time, other skilled craft workers created stained-glass windows that added to the splendor of Gothic churches. These artisans stained small pieces of glass in glowing colors. They then set the pieces in thin lead frames to create pictures depicting the life of Jesus, a biblical event, or other religious themes. These religious pictures helped educate the many people who were unable to read.

Paintings, Manuscripts, and Tapestries Churches also contained religious paintings called altarpieces. The purpose of these paintings, and similar ones that wealthy people had in their homes, was to symbolize religious ideas. In this Gothic style, religious figures were not meant to look like real people in real settings but rather to inspire devotion.

In the 1300s and 1400s, the Gothic style was also applied to the artistic decoration of books, known as **illumination.** Since the early Middle Ages, monks, nuns, and other skilled artisans had illuminated books with intricate designs and miniature paintings of biblical scenes and daily life. They often featured brilliant colors and decorative detail. Artists decorated prayer books known as Books of Hours with depictions of towns and castles, knights and ladies, and peasants in the fields.

Medieval artists also created "paintings" in thread. Stone castles were drafty and cold. Tapestries, or woven wall hangings, were hung in castle rooms and halls to add color and warmth. One of the most famous, the Bayeux Tapestry, is really a huge embroidery 231 feet long. Its 70 scenes depict the Norman Conquest of England, and historians have used it to learn about that event.

✓ Checkpoint Describe the artistic works found in medieval churches.

The Bayeux Tapestry
This section of the famous Bayeux Tapestry shows Harold, who became the last Anglo-Saxon king of England, with his fleet. Harold was killed in the Battle of Hastings in 1066.

SECTION **4** Assessment

Progress Monitoring *Online*
For: Self-quiz with vocabulary practice
Web Code: naa-0841

Terms, People, and Places
1. What do the key terms and people listed at the beginning of the section have in common? Explain.

Note Taking
2. **Reading Skill: Recognize Multiple Causes** Use your completed flowchart to answer the Focus Question: What achievements in learning, literature, and the arts characterized the High and late Middle Ages?

Comprehension and Critical Thinking
3. **Predict Consequences** How might universities that drew students from many lands affect European life in the future? Explain your answer.
4. **Analyze Information** How did new knowledge pose a challenge to Christian scholars?
5. **Synthesize Information** Why were heroic epics in the vernacular popular with medieval Europeans?
6. **Identify Central Issues** How was religion central to the art and architecture of the Middle Ages?

● **Writing About History**
Quick Write: Write a Thesis Statement
Your thesis statement expresses your idea about your topic. It might state the most important cause of an event or that multiple causes were at work, or it might emphasize effects. Refer to your graphic organizer to formulate statements such as:
- Changing economic, political, and social conditions led to the emergence of universities.
- Muslim scholarship had far-reaching effects on European philosophy, science, and mathematics.

The Gothic Cathedral

The Gothic cathedral was the crowning achievement of medieval architecture. Flying buttresses allowed for thinner walls with large windows that flooded the churches with light. Tall spires reached for the heavens and dominated the landscape. European cities competed to build the largest, grandest cathedrals. Notre Dame de Paris, shown here, was begun in 1163. It took artisans almost two centuries to complete it.

▶ **Vaulted Ceilings**
Pointed arches called vaults form a strong skeleton on which the roof material is laid. This view looks up at Notre Dame's vaulted ceiling.

▶ **Gargoyles**
Imaginatively carved figures serve as waterspouts to drain water from the roof. Later, the term *gargoyle* included other grotesque carvings on Gothic churches.

◀ **Flying Buttresses**
These stone arches carry much of the weight of the roof, so thick stone walls are no longer needed.

Thinking Critically
1. **Synthesize Information** How did new technology allow Gothic cathedrals to "soar to the heavens" and be flooded with light?
2. **Draw Conclusions** What does the time and effort required to build Gothic cathedrals reveal about medieval culture?

◄ Lead crosses used in mass graves of plague victims

Stained-glass window depicting fear of the plague, Canterbury Cathedral, England ▼

SECTION 5

WITNESS HISTORY ◀)) AUDIO

The Black Death Approaches

❝We see death coming into our midst like black smoke, a plague which cuts off the young, a rootless phantom which has no mercy or fair countenance. Woe is me. . . . It is an ugly eruption that comes with unseemly haste. It is a grievous ornament that breaks out in a rash. The early ornaments of black death.❞
—Jevan Gethin

The disease called the plague, or the Black Death, reached the British Isles from mainland Europe in 1348, spreading fear and then sickness and death. The Welsh poet who wrote these words died of the plague in 1349.

Focus Question How did the combination of plague, upheaval in the Church, and war affect Europe in the 1300s and 1400s?

A Time of Crisis

Objectives

- Understand how the Black Death caused social and economic decline.
- Describe the problems facing the Church in the late Middle Ages and how the Church reacted.
- Summarize the causes, turning points, and effects of the Hundred Years' War.

Terms, People, and Places

Black Death	schism
epidemic	longbow
inflation	

Note Taking

Reading Skill: Recognize Causes and Effects Keep track of the spread of the Black Death and its effects in a flowchart like this one. Use the middle box to describe what life was like during the plague.

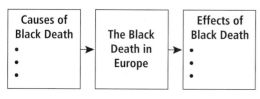

Causes of Black Death		The Black Death in Europe		Effects of Black Death
• • •	→		→	• • •

To Europeans in the mid-1300s, the end of the world seemed to have come. First, widespread crop failures brought famine and starvation. Then, plague and war ravaged populations. Europe eventually recovered from these disasters. Still, the upheavals of the 1300s and 1400s marked the end of the Middle Ages and the beginning of the early modern age.

The Black Death: A Global Epidemic

In the autumn of 1347, a fleet of Genoese trading ships loaded with grain left the Black Sea port of Caffa and set sail for Messina, Sicily. By midvoyage, sailors were falling sick and dying. Soon after the ships tied up at Messina, townspeople, too, began to fall sick and die. Within months, the disease that Europeans called the **Black Death** was raging through Italy. By 1348, it had reached Spain and France. From there, it ravaged the rest of Europe. One in three people died—a death rate worse than in any war in history.

The Plague Spreads from Asia The sickness was bubonic plague, a disease spread by fleas carried by rats. Bubonic plague had broken out before in Europe, Asia, and North Africa but had subsided. One strain, though, had survived in Mongolia. In the 1200s, Mongol armies conquered much of Asia, probably setting off the new **epidemic,** or outbreak of rapid-spreading disease.

WITNESS HISTORY VIDEO

Watch *The Black Death* on the **Discovery School**™ **Witness History** video program to learn about the conditions that helped spread the plague and the effects the disease had on Europe.

In the pre-modern world, rats infested ships, towns, and even the homes of the rich and powerful, so no one took any notice of them. In the early 1300s, rats spread the plague in crowded Chinese cities, which killed about 35 million people there. Fleas jumped from those rats to infest the clothes and packs of traders traveling west. As a result, the disease quickly spread from Asia to the Middle East and then to Europe.

Normal Life Breaks Down In Europe, the plague brought terror and bewilderment, as people had no way to stop the disease. Some people turned to magic and witchcraft for cures. Others plunged into wild pleasures, believing they would soon die anyway. Still others saw the plague as God's punishment. They beat themselves with whips to show that they repented their sins. Normal life broke down as people fled cities or hid in their homes to avoid contracting the plague from neighbors and relatives.

Some Christians blamed Jews for the plague, charging unjustly that they had poisoned the wells to cause the disease. In the resulting hysteria, thousands of Jews were slaughtered.

The Economy Suffers As the plague kept recurring in the late 1300s, the European economy plunged to a low ebb. When workers and employers died, production declined. Survivors demanded higher wages. As the cost of labor soared, **inflation,** or rising prices, broke out too. Landowners and merchants pushed for laws to limit wages. To limit rising costs, landowners converted croplands to land for sheep raising, which required less labor. Villagers forced off the land looked for work in towns. There, guilds limited opportunities for advancement.

Coupled with the fear of the plague, these restrictions sparked explosive revolts. Bitter, angry peasants rampaged in England, France, Germany, and elsewhere. In the cities, artisans fought for more power, usually without success. Revolts erupted on and off through the 1300s and 1400s. The plague had spread both death and social unrest. Western Europe would not fully recover from its effects for more than 100 years.

✔ **Checkpoint** How did the Black Death affect Europe?

Upheaval in the Church

The late Middle Ages brought spiritual crisis, scandal, and division to the Roman Catholic Church. Many priests and monks died during the plague. Their replacements faced challenging questions. Survivors asked, "Why did God spare some and kill others?"

The Church Splits The Church was unable to provide the strong leadership needed in this desperate time. In 1309, Pope Clement V had moved the papal court to Avignon outside the border of southern France. It remained there for about 70 years under French domination. In Avignon, popes reigned over a lavish court. Critics lashed out against the worldly, pleasure-loving papacy, and anticlerical sentiment grew. Within the Church itself, reformers worked for change.

In 1378, reformers elected their own pope to rule from Rome. French cardinals responded by choosing a rival pope. For decades, there was a **schism,** or split, in the Church. During this schism, two and sometimes even three popes claimed to be the true "vicar of Christ."

A procession of the faithful going to Rome to pray for an end to the plague.

A Church council at Constance, Germany, finally ended the crisis in 1417 by removing authority from all three popes and electing a compromise candidate. Pope Martin V returned the papacy to Rome.

Responding to New Heresies As the moral authority of the Church weakened, popular preachers began to call for change. In England, John Wycliffe, an Oxford professor, attacked corruption in Church. Wycliffe insisted that the Bible, not the Church, was the source of Christian truth. His followers began translating the Bible into English so that people could read it themselves rather than rely on the clergy to interpret it. Czech students at Oxford carried Wycliffe's ideas to Bohemia—today's Czech Republic. There, Jan Hus led the call for reforms, supported by his followers, known as Hussites.

The Church responded by persecuting Wycliffe and his followers and suppressing the Hussites. Hus was tried for preaching heresy—ideas contrary to Church teachings. Found guilty, he was burned at the stake in 1415. The ideas of Wycliffe and Hus survived, however. A century later, other reformers took up the same demands.

✓ **Checkpoint** Describe the threats to Church power.

The Hundred Years' War

On top of the disasters of famine, plague, and economic decline came a long, destructive war. Between 1337 and 1453, England and France engaged in a series of conflicts, known as the Hundred Years' War.

French and English Rivalry Grows English rulers had battled for centuries to hold onto the French lands of their Norman ancestors. But French kings were intent on extending their own power in France. When Edward III of England, whose mother had been a French princess, claimed the French crown in 1337, war erupted anew between these rival powers.

Note Taking

Reading Skill: Recognize Causes and Effects Keep track of the Hundred Years' War by completing a flowchart. List causes of the war in the first box, and put effects in the last box. Use the middle box to record major events that occurred during the war.

Causes	Hundred Years' War	Effects
•	•	•
•	•	•
•	•	•

Geography *Interactive*
For: Audio guided tour
Web Code: nap-0851

The Hundred Years' War, 1337–1453

France, 1337
Held by England, 1337
Held by England, 1429
✳ Battle sites
➤ Route of Joan of Arc
— Boundary of France, 1453
○ Site of Joan of Arc's death, 1431

Map Skills The English and French fought for control of France in the Hundred Years' War.
1. **Locate** (a) Normandy (b) Crécy (c) Poitiers (d) Agincourt (e) Calais
2. **Place** (a) What regions of France did England gain between 1337 and 1429? (b) What city in France was still under English control in 1453?
3. **Make Comparisons** (a) How were the boundaries of France different in 1453 than in 1337? (b) How did the Hundred Years' War change Europe?

● **INFOGRAPHIC**

NEW WEAPONS TURN THE TIDE

New military technology not only turned the tide of the Hundred Years' War but also changed warfare itself. Early in the war, English soldiers equipped with a powerful new weapon overpowered their French counterparts. An English archer with a longbow could shoot three arrows in the time it took a French archer with his crossbow to fire just one. Arrows from the powerful six-foot longbow could pierce all but the heaviest armor. The French responded by using cannons, which could smash castle walls. Cannons helped the French capture English-held castles and drive the English from Normandy.

Weapons

Weapons in the medieval painting correspond to those in the photos.

Ⓐ Crossbow

Ⓑ Longbow

Ⓒ Cannon

Thinking Critically

1. **Analyze Visuals** Find the longbows and crossbows in the medieval painting above. Which side seems to be winning? Explain.
2. **Draw Inferences** How might cannons be used in this battle?

England and France were also rivals for control of the English Channel, the waterway between their countries. Each also wanted to control trade in the region. Once fighting started, economic rivalry and a growing sense of national pride made it hard for either side to give up the struggle.

The English Win Early Victories At first, the English won a string of victories—at Crécy in 1346, Poitiers in 1356, and Agincourt in 1415. They owed much of their success to the new **longbow** wielded by English archers. For a time, it looked as though England would bring all of France under its control. Then, in what seemed like a miracle to the French, their fortunes were reversed.

Joan of Arc Fights for France In 1429, a 17-year-old peasant woman, Joan of Arc, appeared at the court of Charles VII, the uncrowned king of France. She told him that God had sent her to save France. Desperate, Charles <u>authorized</u> her to lead an army against the English.

To Charles's amazement, Joan inspired the battered and despairing French troops to fight anew. In one astonishing year, she led the French to several victories and planted the seeds for future triumphs.

Joan paid for success with her life. She was taken captive by allies of the English and turned over to her enemies for trial. To discredit her, the English had Joan tried for witchcraft. She was convicted and burned at the stake. Much later, however, the Church declared her a saint.

The execution of Joan rallied the French, who saw her as a martyr. After Joan's death, the French took the offensive. With a powerful new weapon, the cannon, they attacked English-held castles. By 1453, the English held only the port of Calais in northwestern France.

Impact of the Hundred Years' War The Hundred Years' War set France and England on different paths. The war created a growing sense of national feeling in France and allowed French kings to expand their power. On the other hand, during the war, English rulers turned repeatedly to Parliament for funds, which helped that body win the "power of the purse." Power in English government began to swing towards Parliament. While the loss of French lands shattered English dreams of a continental empire, English rulers turned to new trading ventures overseas.

The Hundred Years' War brought many changes to the late medieval world. Castles and armored knights were doomed to disappear because their defenses could not stand up to the more deadly firepower of the longbow and the cannon. Society was changing. Monarchs needed large armies, not feudal vassals, to fight their wars. More and more, they turned to hired soldiers to do their fighting.

As Europe recovered from the Black Death, the population expanded, and manufacturing grew. These changes led to increased trade. Italian cities flourished as centers of trade and shipping. Europeans borrowed and developed new technologies. This recovery set the stage for further changes during the Renaissance, the Reformation, and the Age of Exploration.

✔ **Checkpoint** Summarize the events of the Hundred Years' War.

Vocabulary Builder

<u>authorized</u>—(AW thur ezd) *vt.* gave official power to

SECTION 5 Assessment

Progress Monitoring *Online*
For: Self-quiz with vocabulary practice
Web Code: naa-0851

Terms, People, and Places

1. For each term, person, or place listed at the beginning of the section, write a sentence explaining its significance.

Note Taking

2. **Reading Skill: Recognize Causes and Effects** Use your completed flowcharts to answer the Focus Question: How did the combination of plague, upheaval in the Church, and war affect Europe in the 1300s and 1400s?

Comprehension and Critical Thinking

3. **Recognize Cause and Effect** What were three effects of the Black Death on late medieval Europe?

4. **Draw Inferences** How did the pope's move to Avignon and the establishment of a rival pope in Rome affect Church authority and power?

5. **Make Comparisons** Compare the effects of the Hundred Years' War on France and on England.

● **Writing About History**

Quick Write: Gather Evidence Gather examples and details to support your thesis. For example, you can support the thesis "Joan of Arc was a cause of French success in the Hundred Years' War" with general facts such as "she led the French to victories and her martyrdom inspired the French soldiers," and so on. Use specific details such as particular battles she led and quotations from soldiers to support your general statements.

THE BLACK DEATH

"Wretched, terrible, destructive year, the remnants of the people alone remain." That description of 1349 was found on a hand-carved sign only months after the bubonic plague reached England. Between 1347 and 1353, the plague, or the Black Death, killed one third of the population of Europe—more than 25 million people.

The plague was caused by bacteria carried by fleas that lived on rats. The epidemic probably originated in China, where infected fleas got into the packs of merchants traveling west. Merchant ships carried the plague from busy Black Sea ports to Sicily. Spreading outward in waves of terror, the Black Death soon ravaged most of Europe.

Flea-covered rats thrived in filthy medieval cities, and the disease spread quickly. Within hours, victims developed egg-sized lumps under their arms. Fever, vomiting, and black spots caused by internal bleeding followed. Once victims started spitting blood, death was certain.

As the disease raced through towns, many people fled to the countryside. Others hid in their homes. The death toll was so high that gravediggers used carts to collect corpses as they walked the streets calling "Bring out your dead!"

So many farm workers died that crops rotted in the fields. Shortages led to demands for higher wages and peasant revolts. Buildings and roads fell to ruin. And survivors lived in fear of the return of the plague, which recurred in waves through the 1600s.

► Outbreaks of the plague continued for centuries. To ward off infections, this doctor from the 1600s wears a leather mask with glass eyes and a long beak filled with herbs and spices.

◄ In crowded medieval cities, houses were close together, and residents threw garbage and human waste into the streets. Rats and fleas were commonplace in the homes of both the rich and the poor.

▼ In the Middle Ages, rats were great travelers. They thrived on ships and moved from port to port—bringing their fleas with them. Fleas that had bitten infected rats then bit people, spreading disease.

Approximate extent of Black Death by:
- 1347
- 1348
- 1349
- 1350
- 1351
- Area relatively unaffected
- → Approximate route of disease

North Sea

Baltic Sea

Atlantic Ocean

EUROPE

Black Sea

ASIA

AFRICA

Mediterranean Sea

Stockholm · Dublin · Lübeck · London · Amsterdam · Cologne · Paris · Kiev · Bordeaux · Venice · Caffa · Avignon · Marseille · Florence · Corsica · Rome · Naples · Constantinople · Sardinia · Lisbon · Messina · Sicily · Athens · Tunis · Crete · Cyprus · Damascus · Tripoli · Alexandria

Conic Projection
0   200   400 mi
0   200   400 km

▲ The plague followed trade routes from Asia to Europe and then spread across the continent. Both cities and rural areas were affected, although a few areas were spared.

▼ As the Black Death took its toll, towns ran out of coffins like the ones shown here. Instead, piles of bodies were buried in huge pits.

▲ Medieval medicine could do little against the plague. This doctor attempts to drain a sore on a woman's neck.

Thinking Critically
1. **Map Skills** (a) Where did the plague first strike in Europe? (b) How long did it take to reach England?
2. **Draw Inferences** Why did the Black Death inspire such fear?
3. **Recognize Cause and Effect** How did the Black Death lead to social disorder?

History Interactive
For: Interactive map, audio, and more
Visit: PHSchool.com
Web Code: nap-0852

275

Quick Study Guide

Progress Monitoring *Online*
For: Self-test with vocabulary practice
Web Code: naa-0861

■ Power Shifts in the High and Late Middle Ages

England	France	Holy Roman Empire
William the Conqueror consolidates royal power, limiting power of lords.	Hugh Capet is elected king by French nobles who feel he is weak.	Otto is crowned Holy Roman emperor, but nobles and Church officials wield power.
Henry II strengthens royal courts, and tries to make clergy accountable to them.	Capetian kings make throne hereditary, take lands from nobles, build a bureaucracy.	Henry IV is excommunicated by Pope Gregory VII, and then forgiven.
King John approves Magna Carta, limiting monarch's power.	Louis IX improves royal government, ends serfdom, creates strong national feeling.	Henry IV forces Pope Gregory VII into exile.
Parliament develops under Edward I.	After Philip IV clashes with Pope Boniface, French monarchs gain more control over popes.	Frederick Barbarossa and Frederick II try to conquer Italy but fail.
During Hundred Years' War, monarchs ask Parliament for funds, increasing Parliament's power.	During Hundred Years' War, English are expelled from most of France, increasing French national feeling.	Holy Roman Empire remains fragmented.

■ Turmoil in Europe

The Crusades—a series of wars, 1096–1204, in which European Christians battled Muslims for control of the Holy Land
The Black Death—an epidemic of the bubonic plague that swept Europe from 1347–1353, killing about one third of the population
The Hundred Years' War—a series of conflicts between England and France from 1337–1453, in which England lost control of most of its territory in France

■ Key Religious Leaders

Pope Gregory VII—banned lay investiture, excommunicated Emperor Henry IV
Pope Innocent III—claimed papal supremacy, helped Church reach height of its power
Pope Urban II—called for the First Crusade
Thomas Becket—Archbishop of Canterbury, opposed Henry II on power of courts to try clergy, murdered by Henry's knights
Thomas Aquinas—scholar who used scholasticism to reconcile faith and reason

■ Key Events of the High and Late Middle Ages

European Events
Global Events

1000

1066
William the Conqueror completes the Norman Conquest of England.

1096
Christians launch the First Crusade.

1100

1215
King John approves the Magna Carta limiting royal power in England.

1200

1000s
The Anasazi build pueblo towns in North America.

1192
Minamoto Yoritomo establishes the Kamakura shogunate in Japan.

Concept Connector

■ Cumulative Review

Record the answers to the questions below on your Concept Connector worksheets.

1. **Conflict** The Crusades were not the first wars between Christians and Muslims. In the 700s, the advance of Muslim armies into Europe was halted at the Battle of Tours. Compare that war with the Crusades. Think about
   - the location
   - the opponents
   - the leaders
   - their goals
   - the results
   - the long-term effects

2. **Democracy** The Magna Carta and the Model Parliament are landmarks in the development of democracy in England. Compare "government by the people" in ancient Greece, ancient Rome, and in England in the 1200s. Think about
   - the role of a monarch, if any
   - the role of a legislature
   - the rights of citizens

3. **Empire** The name of the Holy Roman Empire was supposed to make people think of the greatness and power of the ancient Roman empire. Compare the two. Consider the following:
   - size and location
   - duration
   - how they were governed
   - how well they controlled their people and territory

■ Connections to Today

1. **Conflict: The Holy City of Jerusalem** A battleground since ancient times, the city of Jerusalem is still fought over today. It is a holy city to Jews, Christians, and Muslims, and all three groups have claimed it. Today it is the capital of Israel, the Jewish state, but it is also claimed by the Muslim Palestinians as the capital of the state they hope to establish. Research disputes over Jerusalem since 1948, when the state of Israel was established. Then compare today's disputes to those of the Middle Ages.

2. **Advances in Science: Epidemics** At the time of the Black Death, science provided little insight into the cause, spread, or treatment of disease. Today, in spite of advances in science, the world still suffers from epidemics. In 1918, troop ships carried influenza back and forth between the European battlefields of World War I and the United States. The flu eventually spread worldwide, killing as many as 25 million people. More recently, SARS (severe acute respiratory syndrome) has spread quickly and been carried internationally by airplane travelers. The Chinese officials pictured above are wearing masks to protect themselves from SARS. Research an epidemic that occurred after 1900. Write a brief report comparing its cause, spread, and treatment to those of the Black Death.

History Interactive
For: Interactive timeline
Web Code: nap-0861

1337	1347		1431	1492
The Hundred Years' War between England and France begins.	The Black Death breaks out in Italy.		After leading French troops to victory, Joan of Arc is executed by the English.	King Ferdinand and Queen Isabella complete the Reconquista in Spain.

1300   1400   1500

1300s	1368	1453	1462
The kingdom of Benin is established in West Africa.	The Ming dynasty is established in China.	Ottoman Turks capture Constantinople.	The reign of Ivan the Great begins in Russia.

Chapter Assessment

Terms, People, and Places

Complete each sentence by choosing the correct answer from the list of terms below. You will not use all of the terms.

Frederick Barbarossa	Inquisition
common law	lay investiture
epidemic	schism
habeas corpus	scholasticism
illumination	vernacular

1. _____ is based on custom and court rulings.
2. Pope Gregory banned _____ in order to strengthen the power of the Church.
3. The _____ was part of Queen Isabella's effort to rid Spain of Jews, Muslims, and heretics.
4. _____ used reason to support Christian beliefs.
5. Dante wrote *The Divine Comedy* in the _____ rather than in Latin.
6. The _____ of manuscripts was often done by monks.
7. _____ tried unsuccessfully to conquer Italy.
8. Rival popes caused a _____ in the Church.

Main Ideas

Section 1 (pp. 244–250)
9. How did the monarchs of England and France consolidate their power?

Section 2 (pp. 251–254)
10. Why were the Holy Roman emperors unsuccessful in unifying their empire?

Section 3 (pp. 255–261)
11. How did the Crusades affect the economy and outlook of Europeans?

Section 4 (pp. 262–268)
12. How did changing economic and social conditions lead to the emergence of universities and to new kinds of philosophy and literature?

Section 5 (pp. 269–275)
13. How did war and plague cause major changes in medieval Europe?

Chapter Focus Question
14. How did changing economic and social conditions, wars, and the growing power of monarchs begin to build the framework for the modern nation-state?

Critical Thinking

15. **Predict Consequences** How do you think the lack of a document like the Magna Carta will affect the development of French government?
16. **Demonstrate Reasoned Judgment** Who do you think had a better "case": Gregory VII or Henry IV? Explain and support your position.
17. **Draw Inferences** How did the rise of vernacular literature reflect a change in education and literacy in medieval Europe?
18. **Make Comparisons** How were the Crusades and the Reconquista similar? How were they different?
19. **Analyzing Visuals** Use the medieval illustration of the Model Parliament in Section 1 to explain the relative importance and power of the different groups in English society.
20. **Geography and History** Review the map "Trade in Medieval Europe" in Chapter 7 and the map "Spread of the Black Death" in this chapter. How might trade routes and the spread of the epidemic be linked?

● Writing About History

Writing an Expository Essay: Cause and Effect The High and Late Middle Ages include many important trends and turning points. Write an expository essay analyzing the causes or effects of one of these major events or trends: the Norman Conquest, the Magna Carta, the Reconquista, the preaching of John Wycliffe, the invention of the longbow. Consult page SH10 of the Writing Handbook for additional help.

Prewriting
- Do online or library research to find accounts of each of the topics listed above.
- Choose an event that interests you and brainstorm its causes and effects.
- Define and focus your topic on particular causes or effects. Use a graphic organizer.

Drafting
- Write a thesis statement and choose supporting information.
- Decide how to organize your writing: chronologically, by order of importance, or by categories of causes and effects.
- Write an introduction to present your thesis, a body to support your evidence, and a conclusion.

Revising
- Revise to strengthen your thesis and its supporting evidence. Be sure to use cause-effect transitions.
- Use the guidelines for revising your essay on page SH12 of the Writing Handbook.

Document-Based Assessment

Richard the Lion-heart, King and Crusader

Richard I, king of England from 1189 to 1199, spent only six months in England during his reign. The rest of the time he was at war abroad, most famously as one of the leaders of the Third Crusade. His daring as a warrior gained him the nickname "Lionheart," by which he is still referred to today. On his way home from the Holy Land, Richard was held for ransom by Emperor Henry IV of the Holy Roman Empire. It took his mother, Eleanor of Aquitaine, a year to raise the money to free him.

Document A

"Some . . . advised the king against engaging such a large army, as he then only had around fifty knights with him. Yet their trepidation [fear] only made him more courageous. Putting spur to horse, he charged into the enemy, broke through and scattered their battleline, destroying them. . . . When this was over the king put out an edict by public crier. All the locals who wanted peace could freely come and go, unhindered by his people, and enjoy guaranteed liberty."

—From ***Itinerarium Peregrinorum et Gesta Regis Ricardi,*** eyewitness account of the Third Crusade

Document B

"Yet to the sad 'tis comfort to complain
Friends I have many, and promises abound;
Shame will be theirs; if, for winters twain,
Unransom'd, I still bear a tyrant's chain.
Full well they know, my lords and nobles all . . .
Ne'er did I slight my poorest vassal's call . . .
They know this well who now are rich and strong . . .
That far from them, in hostile bonds I strain."

—poem by King Richard I, written while imprisoned by Holy Roman Emperor Henry IV

Document C

"[King Richard I of England] is one of the most romantic figures of all English history. . . . Richard has become the very epitome [symbol] of chivalry, the knight fighting bravely for his kingdom, his church, and his lady with ax, shield, and horse. . . . That in actual history, [he] does not quite measure up to the standards of his own legend does not dull his allure [appeal]. He was a brilliant military mind and a fearsome general . . . in single combat he was unrivaled in bravery and recklessness. . . . Richard is remembered for his bravado [daring] and cunning—and his extravagance. He is not remembered for his compassion, his tact, or his restraint."

—From ***Warriors of God,*** by James Reston, Jr., 2001

Document D

Richard the Lionheart

Analyzing Documents

Use your knowledge of medieval Europe and the Crusades and Documents A, B, C, and D to answer questions 1–4.

1. According to Document A, Richard I
   A bravely but foolishly rushed at the enemy when he was outnumbered.
   B was a good commander who stayed in the background.
   C was a brave conqueror and town crier.
   D was an impressive warrior and compassionate conqueror.

2. Which of the following statements BEST summarizes Reston's view of Richard the Lion-heart?
   A Although he was a brave warrior, he does not measure up to his own legend.
   B He was compassionate and tactful.
   C He is a truly heroic figure worthy of his reputation.
   D His legend leaves out his good qualities.

3. What do the creators of Documents A and D want to convey about Richard I?
   A his bravery and compassion
   B his bravery and skill as a poet
   C his bravery and skill as a warrior
   D his greatness as a Christian ruler

4. **Writing Task** Which of the documents above are most reliable, and why? How does each one help you understand Richard's character? Write your own description of Richard's character, using at least three of the documents to support your thesis.

9 The Byzantine Empire, Russia, and Eastern Europe

330–1613

Justinian Reforms the Law

At the beginning of his reign, the Byzantine emperor Justinian realized that the laws—inherited from ancient Rome—were long and confusing. He created a commission to collect, organize, and revise them into a body of law called the *Corpus Juris Civilus*, known as Justianian's Code. In the introduction, Justinian explains the basis of the law code:

❝The precepts of the law are these: to live honestly, to injure no one, and to give every man his due. The study of law consists of two branches, law public and law private. The former relates to the welfare of the Roman State; the latter to the advantage of the individual citizen. Of private law then we may say that it is of threefold origin, being collected from the precepts of nature, from those of the law of nations, or from those of the civil law of Rome.**❞**

Listen to the Witness History audio to hear more about Justinian's Code.

◄ **This mosaic from a Byzantine church in Italy shows the emperor Justinian.**

Chapter Preview

Chapter Focus Question How did the Byzantine empire preserve the heritage of Greece and Rome and help to shape the cultures of Russia and Eastern Europe?

Section 1
The Byzantine Empire

Section 2
The Rise of Russia

Section 3
Shaping Eastern Europe

Emperor Constantine I

Gold cross showing the Virgin Mary

Russian necklace

Note Taking Study Guide *Online*
For: Note Taking and Concept Connector worksheets
Web Code: nad-0901

Depiction of the church of the Holy Apostles in Constantinople

Cross and chain

WITNESS HISTORY 🔊 AUDIO

A Sovereign City

In 1203, when the Crusaders arrived at Constantinople, they were amazed by its splendor:

❝ [T]hose who had never seen Constantinople opened wide eyes now; for they could not believe that so rich a city could be in the whole world, when they saw her lofty walls and her stately towers wherewith she was encompassed, and these stately palaces and lofty churches, so many in number as no man might believe who had not seen them, and the length and breadth of this town which was sovereign over all others. ❞
—Villehardouin, a French Crusader

Focus Question What made the Byzantine empire rich and successful for so long, and why did it finally crumble?

The Byzantine Empire

Objectives

- Understand why Constantinople became known as the "New Rome."
- Summarize the ways in which the Byzantine empire flourished under Justinian.
- Analyze how Christianity in the Byzantine empire differed from Christianity in the West.
- Explain why the Byzantine empire collapsed and examine the empire's lasting heritage.

Terms, People, and Places

Constantinople	Theodora
Justinian	patriarch
Justinian's Code	icon
autocrat	Great Schism

Note Taking

Reading Skill: Recognize Sequence Keep track of the sequence of events in the Byzantine empire in a table.

The Byzantine Empire	
330	Constantinople becomes the capital of the eastern Roman empire.

Constantinople sat at a crossroads of land and sea routes, and its great wealth came from trade. In addition to encouraging trade, its leaders constructed strong defenses for their city. As the cities of the western Roman empire crumbled, Constantinople remained secure and prospered. With its high walls and golden domes, it stood as the proud capital of the Byzantine empire.

Constantine Creates a "New Rome"

You have read that as German invaders pounded the Roman empire in the west, the Roman emperor Constantine and his successors shifted their base to the eastern Mediterranean. Constantine rebuilt the Greek city of Byzantium and then renamed it after himself—Constantinople. In 330, he made Constantinople the new capital of the empire. From this "New Rome," roads fanned out to the Balkans, to the Middle East, and to North Africa. In time, the eastern Roman empire became known as the Byzantine empire.

Constantinople Grows The vital center of the empire was Constantinople. The city was located on the shores of the Bosporus, a strait that links the Mediterranean and Black seas. Constantinople had an excellent harbor and was guarded on three sides by water. Emperors after Constantine built an elaborate system of land and sea walls to bolster its defenses.

Equally important, Constantinople commanded key trade routes linking Europe and Asia. For centuries, the city's favorable location made it Europe's busiest marketplace. There, merchants sold silks from China, wheat from Egypt, gems from India, spices from Southeast Asia, and furs from Viking lands in the north.

At the center of the city, Byzantine emperors and empresses lived in glittering splendor. Dressed in luxurious silk, they attended chariot races at the Hippodrome arena. Crowds cheered wildly as rival charioteers careened around and around in their vehicles. The spectacle was another reminder of the city's glorious Roman heritage.

Blending of Cultures After rising to spectacular heights, the Byzantine empire eventually declined to a small area around Constantinople itself. Yet it was still in existence nearly 1,000 years after the fall of the western Roman empire. As the heir to Rome, it promoted a brilliant civilization that blended ancient Greek, Roman, and Christian influences with other traditions of the Mediterranean world.

✓ **Checkpoint** Why did Constantinople become a rich and powerful city?

> Constantine embarked on an ambitious building program to improve his new capital. Byzantium had been a walled city, but the new imperial buildings and growing population required a new set of walls outside the old, tripling the size of the city.
>
> **Primary Source**
>
> 66 [Constantine] enlarged the city formerly called Byzantium, and surrounded it with high walls; likewise he built splendid dwelling houses . . . He erected all the needed edifices [for a great capital]—a hippodrome, fountains, porticoes [covered walkways] and other beautiful adornments. 99
> —Sozomen, Church historian, *circa* 450
>
> 🔊)) AUDIO

Byzantium Flourishes Under Justinian

The Byzantine empire reached its peak under the emperor Justinian, who ruled from 527 to 565. Justinian was determined to revive ancient Rome by recovering lands that had been overrun by invaders. Led by the brilliant general Belisarius, Byzantine armies reconquered North Africa, Italy, and the southern Iberian peninsula. However, the fighting exhausted Justinian's treasury and weakened his defenses in the east. Moreover, the victories were only <u>temporary</u>. Justinian's successors would lose the bitterly contested lands, one after the other.

The Great City Is Rebuilt Justinian left a more lasting monument in the structures of his capital. In 532, riots and a devastating fire swept Constantinople. Many buildings were destroyed and many lives were lost. To restore Roman glory, Justinian launched a program to make Constantinople grander than ever. His great triumph was rebuilding the church of Hagia Sophia (AH yee uh suh FEE uh), which means "Holy Wisdom." Its immense, arching dome improved on earlier Roman buildings. The interior glowed with colored marble and embroidered silk curtains. Seeing this church, the emperor recalled King Solomon's temple in Jerusalem. "Glory to God who has judged me worthy of accomplishing such a work as this!" Justinian exclaimed. "O Solomon, I have surpassed you!"

Justinian's Code Has Far-Reaching Effects Even more important than expanding the empire and rebuilding its capital was Justinian's reform of the law. Early in his reign, he set up a commission to collect, revise, and organize all the laws of ancient Rome. The result was the *Corpus Juris Civilis,* or "Body of Civil Law," popularly known as Justinian's Code. This massive collection included laws passed by Roman assemblies or decreed by Roman emperors, as well as the legal writings of Roman judges and a handbook for students.

Vocabulary Builder

temporary—(TEM puh rehr ee) *adj.* lasting for or relating to a limited time

WITNESS HISTORY VIDEO

Watch *The Byzantine Empire* on the **Witness History Discovery School**™ video program to explore how the Byzantine empire preserved the heritage of ancient Rome and mixed it with the cultures of Asia.

Hagia Sophia

Hagia Sophia, or "Holy Wisdom," stands at a cultural and geographic crossroads. Istanbul—once called Constantinople—is located where Europe meets Asia and Islam meets Christianity. Justinian ordered the construction of Hagia Sophia in 532, after the previous church was destroyed in riots. Since then, the dome has been rebuilt and the building repaired. Despite warfare and invasions, Hagia Sophia has remained intact, a prize for whoever controlled the city. It has served as a cathedral of Eastern Orthodox Christianity, a Roman Christian cathedral, and an Islamic mosque. Since 1935, it has been a museum. The modern interior reflects the Christian and Muslim heritage of the building. Islamic artists avoid using human or animal figures, while Byzantine artists were famous for their mosaics of religious figures, such as the one above.

Round plaques decorated with calligraphy were added between 1847 and 1849. This one shows Muhammad's name.

pendentives

These towers, called minarets, were built after the building became a mosque. Mosque officials, called muezzins, call Muslims to prayer from the minarets.

The dome rises 184 feet from the floor. The architects used a technique that was new in the 500s to support this huge dome. Triangular supports called pendentives were inserted in the corners of the square, which supported the weight of the dome on the square base.

Thinking Critically

1. **Synthesize Information** Explain the significance of Constantinople.
2. **Draw Inferences** Why was Hagia Sophia turned into a museum?

Justinian's Code had an impact far beyond the Byzantine empire. By the 1100s, it had reached Western Europe. There, monarchs modeled their laws on its principles, which helped them to strengthen and centralize their power. Centuries later, the code also guided legal thinkers who began to put together the international law in use today.

Justinian Rules With Absolute Power Justinian used the law to unify the empire under his control. He ruled as an autocrat, or sole ruler with complete authority. The Byzantine emperor also had power over the Church. He was deemed Christ's co-ruler on Earth. As a Byzantine official wrote, "The emperor is equal to all men in the nature of his body, but in the authority of his rank he is similar to God, who rules all." Unlike feudal monarchs in Western Europe, he combined both political power and spiritual authority. His control was aided by his wife, Theodora. A shrewd politician, she served as advisor and co-ruler to Justinian and even pursued her own policies.

Economic and Military Strength Is Second to None The Byzantine empire flourished under a strong central government, which exercised strict control over a prosperous economy. Peasants formed the backbone of the empire, working the land, paying taxes, and providing soldiers for the military. In the cities of the empire, trade and industry flourished. While the economy of Western Europe struggled and use of money declined, the Byzantine empire preserved a healthy money economy. The bezant, the Byzantine gold coin stamped with the emperor's image, circulated from England to China.

At the same time, the Byzantines built one of the strongest military forces in the world. Soldiers, ships, and sailors protected the empire, and fortifications protected its capital. The Byzantines also relied on a secret weapon called Greek fire, a liquid that probably contained petroleum. Thrown toward an enemy, it would ignite on contact, and its fire could not be put out with water. For centuries, Greek fire was an effective and terrifying weapon of the Byzantine navy.

The Empire's Fortunes Change In the centuries after Justinian, the empire faced successive attacks by Persians, Slavs, Vikings, Huns, and Turks. These attacks were largely unsuccessful. The empire thus served as a buffer for Western Europe, especially in preventing the spread of Muslim conquest. Beginning in the 600s and 700s, however, Arab armies gradually gained control of much of the Mediterranean world. Still, Constantinople itself withstood their attack, and the Byzantines held on to their heartland in the Balkans and Asia Minor.

✓ **Checkpoint** Describe Justinian's accomplishments.

Byzantine Christianity

Christianity was as influential in the Byzantine empire as it was in Western Europe. But the way Christianity was practiced differed in the two regions. Over time, these differences became more distinct and caused increasing friction.

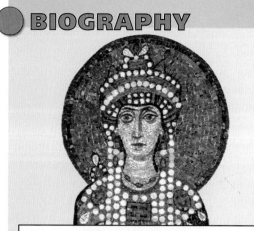

BIOGRAPHY

Empress Theodora
From humble beginnings as the daughter of a bear keeper at Constantinople's Hippodrome, Theodora (497–548) rose to become Justinian's wife, advisor, and co-ruler. A shrewd, tough, and sometimes ruthless politician, Theodora did not hesitate to challenge the emperor and pursue her own policies.

Theodora's most dramatic act came during a revolt in 532. "Emperor, if you wish to flee, well and good; you have the money, the ships are ready, the sea is clear," said Theodora calmly. "But I shall stay," she concluded. "I accept the ancient proverb: Royal purple is the best burial sheet." Theodora's courageous words inspired Justinian to remain in Constantinople and crush the revolt that threatened his power. **How did Theodora contribute to the greatness of the empire?**

Vocabulary Builder
unify—(YOO nuh fy) v. to bring people or things together to form a single unit or entity

Geography *Interactive*
For: Audio guided tour
Web Code: nap-0912

Map Skills The Byzantine empire reached its greatest size by 565. By 1000, it had lost much of its territory to invading armies.

1. **Locate** (a) Constantinople (b) Rome (c) Jerusalem
2. **Describe** Describe the extent of the Byzantine empire in 1020.
3. **Draw Inferences** What does the extent of the empire in 565 suggest about the rule of Justinian?

East and West Differ Since early Christian times, differences had emerged over Church leadership. Although the Byzantine emperor was not a priest, he controlled Church affairs and appointed the **patriarch,** or highest Church official, in Constantinople. Byzantine Christians rejected the pope's claim to authority over all Christians.

Unlike priests in Western Europe, the Byzantine clergy kept their right to marry. Greek, not Latin, was the language of the Byzantine Church. As in the Roman Church, the chief Byzantine holy day was Easter, celebrated as the day Jesus rose from the dead. However, Byzantine Christians placed somewhat less emphasis on Christmas—the celebration of the birth of Jesus—compared to Christians in the West.

The Church Divides During the Middle Ages, the two branches of Christianity drew farther apart. A dispute over the use of **icons,** or holy images, contributed to the split. Many Byzantine Christians used images of Jesus, the Virgin Mary, and the saints in their worship. In the 700s, however, a Byzantine emperor outlawed the veneration of icons, saying it violated God's commandment against worshiping "graven images."

The ban set off violent battles within the empire. From the west, the pope joined in the dispute by condemning the Byzantine emperor. Although a later empress eventually restored the use of icons, the conflict left great resentment against the pope in the Byzantine empire.

In 1054, other controversies provoked a schism, or split, between eastern and western Christianity, known as the **Great Schism.** The Byzantine church became known as the Eastern, or Greek, Orthodox

Church. The western branch became known as the Roman Catholic Church. The pope and the patriarch excommunicated each other. Thereafter, contacts between the two churches were guarded and distant. They treated each other as rivals rather than as branches of the same faith.

✔ **Checkpoint** Why did the Eastern and Western churches differ?

The Empire Suffers Crisis and Collapse

By the time of the schism, the Byzantine empire was in decline. Struggles over succession, court intrigues, and constant wars undermined its strength. As in Western Europe, powerful local lords gained control of large areas. As the empire faltered, its enemies advanced. The Normans conquered southern Italy. Even more serious, the Seljuk Turks advanced across Asia Minor. The Seljuks had been a nomadic people in central Asia. They converted to Islam in their migrations westward.

The Crusades Lead to Plunder In the 1090s, the Byzantine emperor called for Western help to fight the Seljuks, whose attacks blocked the pilgrimage routes to Jerusalem. The result was the First Crusade. During later crusades, however, trade rivalry sparked violence between the Byzantine empire and Venice, a city-state in northern Italy. In 1204, Venetian merchants persuaded knights on the Fourth Crusade to attack Constantinople. For three days, crusaders burned and plundered the city, sending much treasure westward. Western Christians ruled Constantinople for 57 years. Although a Byzantine emperor reclaimed the capital in the 1260s, the empire never recovered. Venetian merchants had gained control of Byzantine trade, draining the wealth of the empire. But there was an even more threatening foe—the increasingly powerful Ottoman Turks, who soon controlled most of Asia Minor and the Balkans.

Constantinople Falls to the Turks In 1453, Ottoman forces surrounded the city of Constantinople. They brought cannons to attack the city's walls. The Byzantine defenders had stretched a huge chain across the harbor to protect against invasion by sea, but the Turks hauled their ships overland and then launched them into the harbor. After a siege lasting two months, the Turks stormed Constantinople's broken walls. It is said that when the last Byzantine emperor was offered safe passage, he replied, "God forbid that I should live an emperor without an empire." He chose instead to die fighting.

Forces led by Ottoman ruler Mehmet II entered the city in triumph. The ancient city was renamed Istanbul and became the capital of the Ottoman empire. Hagia Sophia was turned into an Islamic house of worship, and Istanbul soon emerged as a great center of Muslim culture.

✔ **Checkpoint** How was the Byzantine empire destroyed?

The Byzantine Heritage

Although Byzantine power had faded long before, the fall of Constantinople marked the end of an age. To Europeans, the empire had stood for centuries as the enduring symbol of Roman civilization. Throughout the Middle Ages, Byzantine influence radiated

Turks Take Constantinople
The nineteenth-century painting below shows the Turks entering Constantinople after defeating Byzantine forces.

Byzantine Art
The religious icon above is typical of Byzantine art. Notice that both eyes of each person are shown. An evil person was depicted in profile, with only one eye showing.

across Europe. Even the Ottoman conquerors adapted features of Byzantine government, social life, and architecture.

What was the Byzantine heritage? For 1,000 years, the Byzantines built on the culture of the Hellenistic world. Byzantine civilization blended Christian religious beliefs with Greek science, philosophy, arts, and literature. The Byzantines also extended Roman achievements in engineering and law.

Unique Contributions in the Arts Byzantine artists made unique contributions, especially in religious art and architecture, that influenced Western styles from the Middle Ages to the present. Icons, designed to evoke the presence of God, gave viewers a sense of personal contact with the sacred. Mosaics brought scenes from the Bible to life. In architecture, Byzantine palaces and churches blended Greek, Roman, Persian, and other Middle Eastern styles.

The World of Learning Byzantine scholars preserved the classic works of ancient Greece. In addition, they produced their own great books, especially in the field of history.

Like the Greek historians Herodotus and Thucydides, Byzantine historians were mostly concerned with writing about their own times. Procopius, an advisor to the general Belisarius, chronicled the Byzantine campaign against Persia. In his *Secret History,* Procopius savagely criticized Justinian and Theodora. He called the emperor "both an evil-doer and easily led into evil . . . never of his own accord speaking the truth." Anna Comnena is considered by many scholars to be the Western world's first important female historian. In the *Alexiad,* she analyzed the reign of her father, Emperor Alexius I. Comnena's book portrayed Latin crusaders as greedy barbarians.

As the empire tottered in the 1400s, many Greek scholars left Constantinople to teach at Italian universities. They took valuable Greek manuscripts to the West, along with their knowledge of Greek and Byzantine culture. The work of these scholars contributed to the European cultural flowering that became known as the Renaissance.

 Checkpoint　Describe Byzantine contributions to art and learning.

Progress Monitoring *Online*
For: Self-quiz with vocabulary practice
Web Code: naa-0911

SECTION 1 Assessment

Terms, People, and Places
1. For each term, person, or place listed at the beginning of the section, write a sentence explaining its significance.

Note Taking
2. **Reading Skill: Recognize Sequence** Use your completed table to answer the Focus Question: What made the Byzantine empire rich and successful for so long, and why did it finally crumble?

Comprehension and Critical Thinking
3. **Categorize** Which of Justinian's achievements do you think had the most impact on his empire's greatness? Explain your answer.
4. **Make Comparisons** Compare Byzantine Christianity and Western Christianity at the time of the schism.
5. **Demonstrate Reasoned Judgment** Why was the Byzantine empire so important to Western Europe? Explain.

● **Writing About History**
Quick Write: Gather Information Choose a person you read about in this section, and use at least two reliable library or Internet sources to find out information about him or her. Create a timeline showing the most important events in that person's life. Choose several of those events and ask questions about them, such as the following:
• What led to this event?
• What was the result of this event?

A Russian necklace

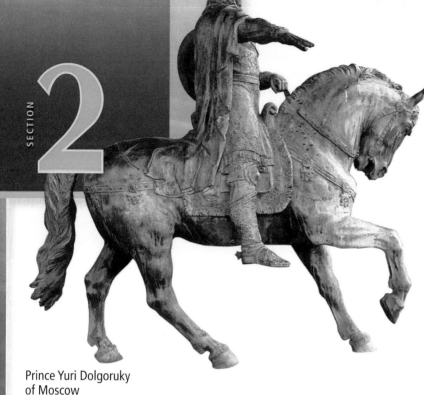

Prince Yuri Dolgoruky
of Moscow

WITNESS HISTORY ◄)) AUDIO

The Third Rome

In Russia, a patriotic monk saw a special meaning in the fall of Constantinople in 1453. Now, he declared, Moscow was the "third Rome," the successor to the Roman and Byzantine empires:

66 [T]he third Rome . . . shines like the sun . . . throughout the whole universe. . . . [T]wo Romes have fallen, and the third one stands, and a fourth one there shall not be. 99
—Philotheos, quoted in *Tsar and People* (Cherniavsky)

Focus Question How did geography and the migrations of different peoples influence the rise of Russia?

The Rise of Russia

Objectives

- Understand how geography influenced the rise of Russia.
- Describe the growth of Kiev.
- Explain how Mongol rule affected Russia.
- Describe how Moscow took the lead in Russia and how its rulers developed authoritarian control.

Terms, People, and Places

steppe	Ivan the Great
Kiev	tsar
Cyrillic	Ivan the Terrible
Golden Horde	

Note Taking

Reading Skill: Recognize Sequence Make a timeline to keep track of the sequence of events in the rise of Russia between the 700s and 1613. The sample below will help you get started. Add events as you read.

Vikings arrive.

700   900   1100   1300   1500   1700

As Western Europe was developing its distinctive medieval civilization, Russian culture took a different path in the east. Connecting Europe and Asia, it became a center of power in its own right. One reason Russia developed differently from Western Europe was its unique geography.

Geography's Influence

Russia lies across the vast Eurasian plain that stretches from Europe to the borders of China. Although mapmakers use the Ural Mountains to mark the boundary between Europe and Asia, these ancient mountains were long ago worn away to wooded hills. They posed no great obstacle to migration.

Three Regions Three broad zones with different climates and resources helped shape early Russian life. The northern forests supplied lumber for building and fuel. Fur-bearing animals attracted hunters, but poor soil and a cold, snowy climate hindered farming. Farmers did settle in a band of fertile land farther south. This second region, which today includes the country of Ukraine, was home to Russia's first civilization.

A third region, the southern **steppe,** is an open, treeless grassland. It offered splendid pasture for the herds and horses of nomadic peoples. With no natural barriers, the steppe was a great highway along which streams of nomads migrated. From Asia, they spread into Europe, settling and conquering new territory.

Rivers Link Russia and Byzantium Russia's network of rivers, running from north to south, provided transportation for both people and goods. They linked early Russians to the advanced Byzantine world in the south. During the early Middle Ages, Russians turned in this direction rather than to Western Europe, which was a fragmented, frontier territory after the fall of the Roman empire.

✓ **Checkpoint** How did geography affect Russian settlement and growth?

Kiev Grows Strong

The city of **Kiev,** the capital of present-day Ukraine, was the center of the first Russian state. Its culture and growth were the result of a mixing of two distinct peoples.

Slavs and Vikings Arrive During Roman times, a group of Slavic people migrated into southern Russia. The Slavs probably came from a region to the northwest, in present-day Poland and Belarus. They had a simple political organization and were organized into clans. They lived in small villages, farming and trading along the rivers that ran between the Baltic and the Black seas.

In the 700s and 800s, Vikings steered their long ships out of Scandinavia. These Vikings, whom the Russians called Varangians, worked their way south along the rivers, trading with and collecting tribute, or forced payment, from the Slavs. They also conducted a thriving trade with Constantinople. Located at the heart of this vital trade network was the city of Kiev.

Russians traditionally date the origins of their country to 862, when Rurik, a prince of a Varangian tribe called the Rus (roos), began his rule of Novgorod in the north. After Rurik's death, Rus lands expanded to include Kiev, which became their capital. The Rus princes lent their name to the growing principality of Russia.

The Byzantines Gain Influence Trade first brought Kiev into the Byzantine orbit. In the 800s, Constantinople sent Christian missionaries to convert the Slavs. About 863, two Greek brothers, Cyril and Methodius, adapted the Greek alphabet so they could translate the Bible into the Slavic tongue. This **Cyrillic** (suh RIL ik) alphabet became the written script that is still used today in Russia, Ukraine, Serbia, and Bulgaria.

In 957, Princess Olga of Kiev converted to Byzantine Christianity. During the reign of her grandson Vladimir, the new religion spread widely. After his own conversion, Vladimir married the sister of a Byzantine emperor. He made Orthodox Christianity the religion of the Rus and began to align his kingdom politically and culturally with the Byzantine empire. Soon, Russians adopted aspects of Byzantine culture, such as art, music, and architecture. Byzantine domes evolved into the onion-shaped domes typical of Russian churches.

Princes Secure Power Kiev gained strength under Vladimir and his son, Yaroslav the Wise. Both won military victories and spread Christianity. Yaroslav set up close ties

Byzantine Missionaries
The icon below shows Cyril and Methodius, Greek missionaries who spread Christianity among the Slavs.

between church and state. Russian rulers, like the Byzantine emperor, eventually controlled the Church, making it dependent on them for support. The Russian Orthodox Church became a pillar of state power.

In addition to giving legal status to the Church, Yaroslav had many religious texts translated into the Slavic language. He made improvements to the city and issued a written law code. However, Kiev declined after his death as rival families battled for the throne.

✓ **Checkpoint**   Why did Kiev become an important city?

The Mongols Rule Russia

In the early 1200s, a young leader united the nomadic Mongols of central Asia. As his mounted bowmen overran lands from China to eastern Europe, he took the title Genghis Khan (GENG is kahn), or "World Emperor."

The Golden Horde Advances Between 1236 and 1241, Batu, the grandson of Genghis, led Mongol armies into Russia. Known as the Golden Horde because of the color of their tents, these invaders looted and burned Kiev and other Russian towns. So many inhabitants were killed, declared a Russian historian, that "no eye remained to weep for the dead." From their capital on the Volga, the Golden Horde ruled Russia for more than 150 years. Areas that were not directly controlled by the Mongols suffered destructive raids from Mongol armies.

Although they were fierce conquerors, the Mongols were generally not meddlesome rulers. Russian princes had to acknowledge the Mongols as their overlords and pay heavy tribute. But as long as the tribute was paid, the Mongols left the Russian princes to rule without much other interference.

The Mongols Exert Influence Historians have long debated how Mongol rule affected Russia. Although the Mongols converted to Islam, they tolerated the Russian Orthodox Church, which grew more powerful during this period. The Mongol conquest also brought peace to the huge swath of land between China and Eastern Europe, and Russian merchants benefited from new trade routes across this region.

In addition, the absolute power of the Mongols served as a model for later Russian rulers. Russian princes developed a strong desire to centralize their own power without interference from nobles, the clergy, or wealthy merchants. Perhaps most important, Mongol rule cut Russia off from contacts with western Europe at a time when Europeans were making rapid advances in the arts and sciences.

✓ **Checkpoint**   Describe Mongol rule of Russia.

Vocabulary Builder

tolerated—(TAHL ur ayt ed) *v.* recognized and did not suppress the different beliefs or practices of other people

St. Basil's Cathedral in Moscow, Russia

Moscow Takes the Lead

During the Mongol period, the princes of Moscow steadily increased their power. Their success was due in part to the city's location near important river trade routes. They also used their positions as tribute collectors for the Mongols to subdue neighboring towns. When the head of the Russian Orthodox Church made Moscow his capital, the city became not just Russia's political center, but its religious center as well.

As Mongol power declined, the princes of Moscow took on a new role as patriotic defenders of Russia against foreign rule. In 1380, they rallied other Russians and defeated the Golden Horde at the battle of Kulikovo (koo lih KOH vuh). Although the Mongols continued their terrifying raids, their strength was much reduced.

The Success of Ivan the Great A driving force behind Moscow's successes was Ivan III, known as **Ivan the Great.** Between 1462 and 1505, he brought much of northern Russia under his rule. He also recovered Russian territory that had fallen into the hands of neighboring Lithuania.

Mongol armor

Geography Interactive
For: Audio guided tour
Web Code: nap-0921

Growth of Russia, 1300–1584

Legend:
- Moscow, about 1300
- Land added, 1300–1462
- Land added, 1462–1533
- Land added, 1533–1584
- Empire of the Golden Horde, 1300
- Battle site

Conic Projection
0 250 500 mi
0 250 500 km

Map Skills Between 1300 and 1584, the lands ruled by Russian princes and tsars grew from a small area around Moscow to a large territory.

1. **Locate** (a) Black Sea (b) Volga River (c) Kiev (d) Moscow (e) Constantinople (f) Kulikovo

2. **Identify** Identify the period when Novgorod came under Moscow's rule.

3. **Apply Information** Locate the natural feature considered the boundary between Europe and Asia. How did this boundary affect the Mongol conquest of Russia?

Ivan built the framework for absolute rule. He tried to limit the power of the *boyars,* or great landowning nobles. After he married a niece of the last Byzantine emperor, Ivan adopted Byzantine court rituals to emphasize Russia's role as the heir to Byzantine power. Like the Byzantine emperors, he used a double-headed eagle as his symbol and sometimes referred to himself as tsar, the Russian word for Caesar. In 1504, a Russian church council echoed Byzantine statements, declaring, "By nature, the tsar is like any other man, but in power and office he is like the highest God."

Ivan the Terrible Establishes Absolute Rule In 1547, Ivan IV, grandson of Ivan the Great, became the first Russian ruler officially crowned tsar. He further centralized royal power by limiting the privileges of the old boyar families and granting land to nobles in exchange for military or other service. At a time when the manor system was fading in Western Europe, Ivan IV introduced new laws that tied Russian serfs to the land.

About 1560, Ivan IV became increasingly unstable. He trusted no one and became subject to violent fits of rage. In a moment of madness, he even killed his own son. He organized the *oprichniki* (ah PREECH nee kee), agents of terror who enforced the tsar's will. Dressed in black robes and mounted on black horses, they slaughtered rebellious boyars and sacked towns where people were suspected of disloyalty. Their saddles were decorated with a dog's head and a broom, symbols of their constant watchfulness to sweep away their master's enemies.

The tsar's awesome power, and the ways he used it, earned him the title Ivan the Terrible. When he died in 1584, he left a land seething with rebellion. But he had introduced Russia to a tradition of extreme absolute power that would shape Russian history well into the twentieth century.

✔ **Checkpoint** How did Ivan III and Ivan IV establish authoritarian power?

BIOGRAPHY

Ivan the Terrible
"I grew up on the throne," explained Ivan the Terrible (1530–1584) of his unhappy childhood. His father, Vasily, died when Ivan was only three years old. Intelligent, well-read, and religious, young Ivan was crowned tsar at age 17.

Although Ivan had long been a harsh ruler, his behavior became increasingly unstable after his wife died. Prone to violence, he crushed any opposition, real or imagined. He had thousands of people in the city of Novgorod killed because he feared a plot against him. Almost every noble family was affected by his murders. "I have surpassed all sinners," he confessed in his will. **How do you think a reign like Ivan's affected Russian life?**

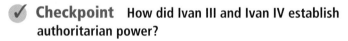

Progress Monitoring *Online*
For: Self-quiz with vocabulary practice
Web Code: naa-0921

Terms, People, and Places

1. Place each of the key terms at the beginning of the section into one of the following categories: government, culture, or geography. Write a sentence for each term explaining your choice.

Note Taking

2. **Reading Skill: Recognize Sequence** Use your completed timeline to answer the Focus Question: How did geography and the migrations of different peoples influence the rise of Russia?

Comprehension and Critical Thinking

3. **Recognize Cause and Effect** How did Russia's geography affect its early history?

4. **Determine Relevance** How important was Byzantine influence on Russia? Explain your answer.

5. **Synthesize Information** How did Mongol rule influence Russia's economy and political structure?

6. **Analyze Information** How did a tradition of absolute rule develop in Russia?

● **Writing About History**

Quick Write: Write a Thesis Statement Use a reliable library or Internet source to list the important events in the life of someone you read about in this section. Describe the personality traits that person displayed in his or her life. Write a thesis statement that presents your conclusion about his or her personality and actions. For example, you might say that Ivan the Terrible was a harsh and unstable ruler.

King Milutin of Serbia

Silver brooch

WITNESS HISTORY 🔊 AUDIO

A Fragmented Region

In 965, Ibrahim-Ibn-Yaqub, a Jewish traveler from Moorish Spain, visited Eastern Europe:

❝ The lands of the Slavs stretch from the Syrian Sea to the Ocean in the north. . . . They comprise numerous tribes, each different from the other. . . . If not for the disharmony amongst them, caused by the multiplication of factions and by their fragmentation into clans, no people could match them for strength. . . . The Slavs wage war with the Byzantines, with the Franks and Langobards, and with other peoples . . . with varying success. ❞

Focus Question How did geography and ethnic diversity contribute to the turmoil of Eastern European history?

Shaping Eastern Europe

Objectives

- Describe how geography influenced the development of Eastern Europe.
- Understand how migrations contributed to cultural diversity in Eastern Europe.
- Learn about three early Eastern European kingdoms.

Terms, People, and Places

Balkan Peninsula   diet
ethnic group   Golden Bull of 1222

Note Taking

Reading Skill: Recognize Multiple Causes As you read, notice the conditions and events that led to the diversity of peoples and cultures in Eastern Europe. Keep track of these causes by filling in a concept web like the one below. Add ovals as needed.

Diversity of Eastern Europe

The history of Eastern Europe has been marked by migration, foreign conquest, war, and revolution. Along with the Slavs described by Ibrahim-Ibn-Yaqub, the region is home to a diverse mix of peoples who have often battled with each other and with foreigners. At the same time, this diverse mix of peoples has greatly enriched the culture of the region.

Geography Shapes Eastern Europe

Eastern Europe has been both a buffer and a crossroads. It is a wide swath of territory lying between German-speaking Central Europe to the west and the largest Slavic nation, Russia, to the east. It reaches from the chilly waters of the Baltic Sea, down across the plains of Poland and Hungary, and then through the mountainous **Balkan Peninsula.** This roughly triangular arm of land, often called simply the Balkans, juts southward into the warm Mediterranean.

Much of the region lies on the great European Plain that links up with the steppes of southern Russia. Its main rivers, such as the Danube and the Vistula (VISH chuh luh), flow either south into the Black Sea or north into the Baltic Sea. Goods and cultural influences traveled along these river routes. As a result, the Balkans in the south felt the impact of the Byzantine empire and, later, the Muslim Ottoman empire. In contrast, northern regions bordering Germany and the Baltic Sea forged closer links to Western Europe. The eastern part of the region felt the strong influence of Russia.

✓ **Checkpoint** How did its rivers affect Eastern Europe?

Migrations Contribute to Diversity

Eastern Europe's geography has contributed to its cultural diversity. The ease of migration through the region encouraged many different peoples to seek new homes there. Some neighboring groups sought to influence or dominate the region. As a result, Eastern Europe now includes a wealth of languages and cultures.

Ethnic Groups Settle in Eastern Europe and the Balkans In the early Middle Ages, the Slavs spread out from a central heartland in Russia. The West Slavs filtered into the present-day Czech and Slovak republics and Poland. The South Slavs occupied the Balkans and became the ancestors of the Serbs, Croats, and Slovenes. The Balkans were peopled by various other ethnic groups as well. (An **ethnic group** is a large group of people who share the same language and cultural heritage.)

Vocabulary Builder

dominate—(DAHM uh nayt) v. to have control, power, or authority over somebody or something

● **INFOGRAPHIC**

Jewish Expulsions

The status of Jews varied greatly in Medieval Europe. Treatment of Jews in different regions and time periods could range from tolerant to oppressive. Restrictions included limits on the types of jobs Jews could hold, curfews, or mandatory special dress or markings. Beginning around the time of the Crusades, Christian Western Europeans began to increase restrictions on Jews. When the Black Death devastated the population in the 1300s, city dwellers often blamed the Jews for causing outbreaks. By 1400, Jews had been expelled from (thrown out of) England and France. By 1500, Spain and Portugal followed suit. The picture to the left shows Jews wearing yellow badges when leaving England. Many Jews settled in more tolerant Muslim regions or Eastern Europe. Those regions benefited from the skills and knowledge the Jews brought with them.

Geography *Interactive*

For: Interactive map and timeline
Web Code: nap-0931

Migration and Expulsions, 500–1650

Thinking Critically
1. **Draw Inferences** Why do you think some Jews migrated voluntarily?
2. **Identify Central Issues** What did Western European leaders hope to achieve by expelling Jews from their lands?

→ Expulsions
→ Migrations

Waves of Asian peoples migrated into Eastern Europe, among them the Huns, Avars, Bulgars, Khazars, and Magyars. Vikings and other Germanic peoples added to the mix.

Christians and Muslims Influence the Region Powerful neighboring states exercised strong cultural and religious influences on Eastern Europe. Byzantine missionaries spread Eastern Orthodox Christianity and Byzantine culture throughout the Balkans. German knights and missionaries from the West brought Roman Catholic Christianity to Poland, Hungary, the Czech area, and the western Balkans. In the 1300s, the Ottomans invaded the Balkans, bringing Islam into pockets of that region.

Jewish Settlers Migrate to Poland In the early Middle Ages, there were thriving Jewish communities in Muslim Spain. Jews had also migrated to Western Europe. Although educated Jews sometimes held important government and scholarly posts, Christians often blamed Jews for hard times and natural disasters. Western European Christians launched brutal attacks on Jewish communities, particularly during the Crusades and the Black Death. Monarchs in England, France, and Spain even expelled Jews from their lands. Faced with persecution or expulsion, many Jews fled east in the late Middle Ages. Eastern Europe became a refuge for many Jewish settlers.

In 1264, Prince Boleslaw of Cracow issued a charter protecting the liberties of Jews, and Polish kings continued a policy of toleration toward Jews for the next 500 years. As a result, Jewish villages sprang up in Poland and other sparsely populated areas of Eastern Europe. Jewish merchants and scholars contributed to the economic and cultural development of Poland during this period.

✓ **Checkpoint** How did three major religions come to Eastern Europe?

Three Early Kingdoms Develop

During the Middle Ages, Eastern Europe included many kingdoms and small states. Sometimes empires absorbed national groups. Alliances or royal marriages might bind others together. A look at the kingdoms of Poland, Hungary, and Serbia will demonstrate these shifting fortunes.

Poland Enjoys Greatness Missionaries brought Roman Catholicism to the West Slavs of Poland in the 900s. Within a century, the first Polish king was crowned. To survive, Poland often had to battle Germans, Russians, and Mongols.

The marriage of Queen Jadwiga (yahd VEE gah) to Duke Wladyslaw Jagiello (vwah DIS wahf yahg YEH loh) of Lithuania in 1386 ushered in Poland's greatest age. Poland-Lithuania was the largest state in Europe, stretching from the Baltic to the Black Sea. Unlike in Russia or most of Western Europe, however, political power in Poland gradually shifted from the monarch to the nobles. They met in a **diet,** or assembly, where

Note Taking

Reading Skill: Recognize Sequence As you read, fill in important events in the history of these countries in a chart like the one below.

Important Events		
Poland	Hungary	Serbia

Duke Jagiello (below) and Queen Jadwiga (right) of Poland

the vote of a single noble could block the passage of a law. This *liberum veto,* or "free veto," made it hard for the government to take decisive action.

Without a strong central government, Poland-Lithuania declined. It enjoyed a final moment of glory in 1683 when the Polish king Jan Sobieski (yahn soh BYEH skee) broke the Ottoman siege of Vienna. In the next century, however, Poland and Lithuania were gobbled up by ambitious neighbors and disappeared from the map.

The Magyars Rule Hungary The Magyars, who had raided Europe from the Asian steppes, eventually settled in Hungary. Like the West Slavs of Poland, they adopted Roman Catholicism. During the Middle Ages, Magyar rulers also controlled present-day Slovakia, Croatia, and parts of Romania. Like King John of England, the Hungarian king was forced to sign a charter recognizing nobles' rights. Known as the **Golden Bull of 1222,** it strictly limited royal power.

The Mongols overran Hungary in 1241, killing as much as half its population. These invaders soon withdrew, so the Mongol invasion did not have the lasting impact on Hungary that it had on Russia. The expansion of the Ottoman Turks, though, ended Hungarian independence in 1526.

The Serbs Establish a Balkan Kingdom Some of the South Slavs who settled the Balkans became the ancestors of the Serbs. Early Serb leaders recognized Byzantine authority, and by the late 800s, most Serbs had accepted Orthodox Christianity. In the late 1100s, they set up their own state, which reached its height in the 1300s under Stefan Dusan (STEH vahn DOO shahn). Dusan also encouraged Byzantine culture, even modeling his law code on that of Justinian.

Dusan's successors lacked his political gifts, however, and Serbia could not withstand the advance of Ottoman Turks. At the battle of Kosovo in 1389, Serbs fought to the death, a memory still honored by their descendants more than 600 years later.

✔ **Checkpoint** How did each kingdom lose its independence?

Stefan Dusan (1308–1355)
As king, Dusan based his law code on the Byzantine example, but he also attacked the empire he admired. He took Albania, Macedonia, and other lands from the Byzantines.

SECTION **3** Assessment

Progress Monitoring Online
For: Self-quiz with vocabulary practice
Web Code: naa-0931

Terms, People, and Places

1. For each term, person, or place listed at the beginning of the section, write a sentence explaining its significance.

Note Taking

2. **Reading Skill: Recognize Multiple Causes** Use your completed concept web to answer the Focus Question: How did geography and ethnic diversity contribute to the turmoil of Eastern European history?

Comprehension and Critical Thinking

3. **Determine Relevance** How did geography affect the development of Eastern Europe?

4. **Identify Central Issues** How did Eastern Europe become home to so many ethnic groups?

5. **Make Comparisons** How were the histories of Poland and Hungary similar? How were they different?

● **Writing About History**

Quick Write: Write an Introduction Research someone you read about in this section, and write a thesis statement expressing an idea about that person's life. Group information that supports your thesis statement into categories, such as actions that show bravery, actions that show religious devotion, or actions that show power. Include specific facts to support these points. Write a paragraph supporting your thesis statement and major points.

Quick Study Guide

Progress Monitoring Online
For: Self-test with vocabulary practice
Web Code: naa-0941

■ Religions in Eastern Europe

Region	Religion
Byzantine empire	Eastern Orthodox Christianity
Russia	Eastern Orthodox Christianity
Poland	Roman Catholicism Many Jewish settlements
Czech area	Roman Catholicism
Hungary	Roman Catholicism
The Balkans	Serbs: Eastern Orthodox Christianity Croats: Roman Catholicism Slovenes: Eastern Orthodox Christianity Bosnians: Islam

■ Key Political Leaders

Byzantine empire
• Constantine established Constantinople (named for himself) as the capital of the eastern Roman empire; converted to Christianity
• Justinian, emperor during the Byzantine empire's golden age

Russia
• Rurik, Rus prince who ruled Novgorod
• Princess Olga of Kiev, converted to Christianity
• Yaroslav the Wise, presided over golden age in Kiev
• Ivan the Great, expanded Russia and centralized power
• Ivan the Terrible, tsar who established absolute power

Eastern Europe
• Queen Jadwiga, queen of Poland, joint ruler of Poland-Lithuania
• Duke Wladislaw Jagiello, Lithuanian duke, joint ruler of Poland-Lithuania
• Stefan Dusan, ruler of Serbia

■ The Byzantine Empire, Eastern Europe, and Russia in 1300

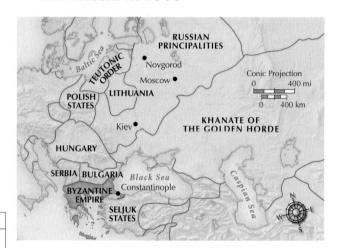

■ Key Events in the Byzantine Empire, Eastern Europe, and Russia

330
Constantinople becomes the capital of the Eastern Roman empire.

527
Justinian begins his rule of the Byzantine empire.

862
Rurik begins his rule of Novgorod, establishing the Rus dynasty.

Chapter Events
Global Events

300   **600**   **900**

622
Muhammad makes a journey, known as the hijra, from Mecca to Yathrib.

800
Pope Leo III crowns Charlemagne emperor of the Romans.

Concept Connector

■ Cumulative Review

Record the answers to the questions below on your Concept Connector worksheets. In addition, record information from this chapter about the following concepts:

- Empires: the Byzantine empire
- Belief Systems: the Great Schism

1. **Cultural Diffusion** Byzantine rulers thought of their empire as the successor to the Roman empire. Like the Romans before them, the Byzantines spread their culture across a wide expanse of Europe. Compare how the two empires spread their cultures. Think about the following:
   - language and learning
   - religion
   - art and architecture
   - political ideas
   - where their culture spread
   - how their culture spread

2. **Geography's Impact** The rivers of Russia and Eastern Europe provided highways for migration, trade, and ideas. Describe two earlier nations or cultures for which rivers were important in the same ways.

3. **Trade** Trade was at the heart of the prosperity and power of Constantinople and the Byzantine empire. In Russia, trade contributed to the rise of Kiev and Moscow. Earlier, trade had been just as important to the ancient Phoenicians. Compare the influence of trade in these three regions. Consider the following:
   - Why did each city or region become a center of trade?
   - Who were its trading partners, and why?
   - What kinds of goods were traded, and why?
   - What effects did trade have on the city or region?

■ Connections to Today

1. **Dictatorship: A Russian Tradition** The Russian tsars established a tradition of absolute dictatorship that continued under Soviet premiers. After the collapse of communism and the breakup of the Soviet Union, Russia set up a democratic government. Today, however, many people fear that Russia is again turning to autocratic rule. Research Soviet rulers such as Joseph Stalin and Nikita Khrushchev and a modern leader such as Vladimir Putin. Compare their rules to those of Ivan the Great and Ivan the Terrible.

2. **Conflict: Balkan Boiling Pot** Throughout the 1990s, violence exploded in the Balkans. In 1992, Eastern Orthodox Serbs, Bosnian Muslims, and Catholic Croats fought a bloody civil war in Bosnia. In 1998, Christian Serbs and Muslims of Albanian heritage clashed in Kosovo. These wars echo ethnic struggles that have gone on for more than 600 years in the Balkans as different ethnic and religious groups have dispersed throughout the region. Even when forced to live together, the different groups have remained independent. Instead of blending together, ethnic and cultural differences in the Balkan region have continued to simmer and occasionally boil over. Research a conflict in the Balkans that occurred after 1900. Describe the conflict and its causes.

History Interactive
For: Interactive timeline
Web Code: nap-0941

| 1236–1241 Mongol armies called the Golden Horde conquer Russia. | 1386 Poland-Lithuania becomes the largest state in Europe. | 1453 Constantinople falls to the Turks. | 1462 Ivan the Great begins his reign in Russia. |

1200   1500

| 1076 Pope Gregory VII excommunicates King Henry IV of Germany. | 1324 Mansa Musa, ruler of Mali, makes a pilgrimage to Mecca. | 1556 Akbar becomes ruler of the Mughal empire in India. |

Chapter Assessment

Terms, People, and Places

Match the following definitions with the terms listed below.

autocrat	Kiev
patriarch	Golden Horde
icon	ethnic group
steppe	Golden Bull of 1222

1. a large group of people who share the same language and cultural heritage
2. open, treeless grassland
3. highest church official in the Eastern Orthodox Church
4. sole ruler with complete authority
5. Mongol armies that invaded Russia
6. charter limiting royal power signed by the Hungarian king
7. holy image of a saint or other religious figure
8. center of the first Russian state

Main Ideas

Section 1 (pp. 282–288)
9. Summarize how the Byzantine empire became rich and successful.
10. Describe the schism between the Orthodox Church and the Church in Rome.

Section 2 (pp. 289–293)
11. How did the Rus, other Viking groups, and the Byzantine empire affect the rise of Kiev?
12. What were the effects of the Mongol rule of Russia?
13. Describe the achievements of Ivan the Great.

Section 3 (pp. 294–297)
14. How did the Balkans become home to such a diverse mix of peoples?
15. How did Poland-Lithuania become the largest state in Europe?

Chapter Focus Question
16. How did the Byzantine empire preserve the heritage of Greece and Rome and help to shape the cultures of Russia and Eastern Europe?

Critical Thinking

17. **Draw Conclusions** The Byzantine empire preserved part of the heritage of the Roman empire. Why was this important?
18. **Synthesize Information** Why was Justinian such a successful ruler?
19. **Analyze Visuals** What aspects of Constantinople appear most prominent in this map? Why does the artist emphasize those?

20. **Test Conclusions** (a) Patriotic Russians called Moscow the third Rome. Why do you think they did so? (b) Do you think Moscow was truly the heir to Rome? Why or why not?
21. **Analyze Information** How did absolute power develop in Russia?
22. **Geography and History** How did the location and geographic features of the Balkans affect its history?
23. **Recognize Cause and Effect** Why did many Jews migrate to Eastern Europe?

● Writing About History

Writing a Biographical Essay Many fascinating people helped shape the fortunes of Russia and the Byzantine Empire. Write a biographical essay about one of the following in which you present a conclusion about the personality, actions, and importance of the person: Justinian, Theodora, Ivan the Great, or Ivan the Terrible. Consult page SH18 of the Writing Handbook for additional help.

Prewriting
- Do online or library research to read accounts of each of the people listed above.
- Choose the person who interests you most and gather information about him or her.

- Make a timeline of important events in the person's life and draw conclusions about his or her personality and importance.

Drafting
- Write a thesis statement that presents your conclusion about the person.
- Write an introduction presenting your thesis statement and two or three major points that support your conclusion.
- Use specific facts to support your main points in the body of your essay, and sum up in your conclusion.

Revising
- Use the guidelines for revising your essay on page SH19 of the Writing Handbook.

Document-Based Assessment

Constantinople: "The Great City"

The Byzantines called Constantinople "The Great City" and "The New Rome." By the time of Constantine, Rome was in steep decline. Byzantium—renamed Constantinople—became the capital of Constantine's empire and a center of governmental, religious, and economic life. The city inspired both praise and condemnation, as the documents below illustrate.

Document A

"The focal point of Constantine's new city was the *Milion,* or the First Milestone. It consisted of four triumphal arches forming a square and supporting a cupola [dome], above which was set the most venerable [revered] Christian relic of all—the True Cross itself, sent back by the Empress Helena from Jerusalem a year or two before. From it all the distances in the Empire were measured; it was, in effect the centre of the world."

—*A Short History of Byzantium*, by John Julius Norwich, 1997

Document B

"The city itself is squalid and fetid and in many places harmed by permanent darkness, for the wealthy overshadow the streets with buildings and leave these dirty, dark places to the poor and to travelers; there murders and robberies and other crimes . . . are committed. . . . In every respect she exceeds moderation; for, just as she surpasses other cities in wealth, so, too, does she surpass them in vice."

—From *Journey of Louis VII to the East (1147)*
by Odo of Deuil, a monk who accompanied the French king
on the Second Crusade

Document C

This nineteenth-century painting shows the Byzantine emperor receiving European troops into Constantinople.

Document D

"It is a busy city, and merchants come to it from every country by sea or land, and there is none like it in the world except Bagdad, the great city of Islam. . . . Wealth like that of Constantinople is not to be found in the whole world. Here also are men learned in all the books of the Greeks, and they eat and drink every man under his vine and his fig tree . . . No Jews live in the city, for they have been placed behind an inlet of the sea. An arm of the sea of Marmora shuts them in on the one side, and they are unable to go out except by way of the sea, when they want to do business with the inhabitants."

—*Itinerary* (1160s), by Benjamin of Tudela,
a Jewish traveler

Analyzing Documents

Use your knowledge of the Byzantine empire, Russia, and Eastern Europe and Documents A, B, C, and D to answer questions 1–4.

1. Constantine's placement of the relic given by Empress Helena, as described in Document A, suggests that the
   A power of the Byzantine empire had shifted to the holy city of Jerusalem.
   B holy city of Jerusalem was still the center of civilization.
   C focus of the Christian world would shift to the East.
   D Byzantine rulers had opposed the crusaders who reclaimed Jerusalem for Christianity.

2. According to Document B, Constantinople's wealth and grandeur
   A helped to eliminate poverty and crime.
   B were the result of highly supervised trading.
   C led to greater literacy and appreciation for the arts.
   D existed side by side with poverty and crime.

3. Document D shows that religious toleration
   A extended to all faiths in ancient Constantinople.
   B was limited in ancient Constantinople.
   C was a founding principle of the city, thanks to Constantine.
   D derived from a strong economic foundation.

4. **Writing Task** Write a letter home from a visitor to ancient Constantinople, describing "the Great City." Use these documents along with information from the chapter in your letter.

10 Muslim Civilizations
622–1629

WITNESS HISTORY AUDIO

Muslims at the Kaaba

In the Arabian town of Mecca, the marketplace echoed with the sounds of buyers and sellers bargaining. One corner, though, was hushed. There, a husky man spoke to a handful of followers:

66 The righteous man is he who believes in God and the Last Day, in the angels and the Book [Scriptures] and the prophets; who, though he loves it dearly, gives away his wealth to kinsfolk, to orphans, to the destitute, to the traveller in need, and to beggars. . . . Such are the true believers. 99
—The Quran

Some bowed their heads, moved by Muhammad's words. Many merchants were infuriated, however. Muhammad's words condemned the many gods that pilgrims came to worship in Mecca. The pilgrim trade would be disrupted, and profits ruined! Muhammad had once been a good merchant himself. They thought he had surely gone mad. Listen to the Witness History audio to hear more about Muhammad.

◄ A modern Muslim pilgrim in Mecca, the holy city of Islam

Mughal emperors Jahangir, Akbar, and Shah Jahan

An astrolabe

Chapter Preview

Chapter Focus Question Who was Muhammad, and how did his teachings lead to the rise and spread of Islam?

The Quran

Note Taking Study Guide *Online*
For: Note Taking and Concept Connector worksheets
Web Code: nad-1001

Muslims at Mount Hira

WITNESS HISTORY ◄)) AUDIO

Messenger of God

During the month of Ramadan, as Muhammad sat meditating in a cave on Mount Hira, an angel in the form of a man came to him. The angel said, "Recite!" Muhammad said, "What shall I recite?" The angel overwhelmed Muhammad in an embrace, and then released him and said again, "Recite!" Muhammad repeated, "What shall I recite?" and again the angel overwhelmed him in an embrace. This happened a third time, after which the angel said, "Recite in the name of your Lord who created—created man from clots of blood." According to Muslim belief, on this and several other occasions, Muhammad heard the angel Gabriel calling him to be the messenger of God.

Focus Question What messages, or teachings, did Muhammad spread through Islam?

Muhammad's name, written in calligraphy

The Rise of Islam

Objectives
- Understand how Muhammad became the prophet of Islam.
- Describe the teachings of Islam.
- Explain how Islam helped shape the way of life of its believers.

Terms, People, and Places

Bedouins	Kaaba
Muhammad	Quran
Mecca	mosque
Yathrib	hajj
hijra	jihad
Medina	Sharia

Note Taking

Reading Skill: Recognize Sequence On a sheet of paper, draw a timeline like the one below and label the main events described in this section.

The religion of Islam, whose followers are called Muslims, emerged in the Arabian Peninsula. This region of southwestern Asia is mostly desert, yet it was home to many Arab tribes in the A.D. 500s. Nomadic herders called **Bedouins** (BED oo inz) moved through the desert to reach seasonal pasturelands for their camels, goats, and sheep. Competition for water and grazing land often led to warfare. Bedouins also traded with settled Arab tribes in oasis towns and protected the caravan trading routes.

Muhammad Becomes a Prophet

Muhammad was born in the oasis town of Mecca around A.D. 570. **Mecca** was a bustling market town at the crossroads of several caravan routes. It was also a thriving pilgrimage center. Many Arabs came to pray at the Kaaba, an ancient temple that housed statues of pagan gods and goddesses. The pilgrims helped make Mecca's merchants wealthy. All weapons had to be laid down near the temple, making Mecca a safe and peaceful place to do business.

Arabia's deserts and trade centers shaped Muhammad's early life. In his youth, he worked as a shepherd among the Bedouins. Later, he led caravans across the desert and became a successful merchant. When he was about 25, Muhammad married Khadija (ka DEE jah), a wealthy widow who ran a prosperous caravan business. Muhammad became known for his honesty in business and was a devoted husband and father.

Muhammad Becomes God's Messenger Muhammad was troubled by the moral ills of Meccan society, especially greed. He often went to a cave in the hills near Mecca to meditate. According to Muslim belief, when he was about 40 years old he heard the voice of the angel Gabriel calling him to be the messenger of God. Muhammad was terrified and puzzled. How could he, an illiterate merchant, become the messenger of God? Khadija encouraged him to accept the call. She became the first convert to the faith called Islam, from the Arabic word that means "to submit to God." Muhammad devoted his life to spreading Islam. He urged Arabs to give up their worship of pagan gods and submit to the one true God. In Arabic, the word for God is *Allah*.

The Hijra: A Turning Point At first, few people listened to Muhammad's teachings. His rejection of traditional Arab gods angered Mecca's merchants, who feared that neglect of their idols would disrupt the pilgrim trade. In 622, faced with the threat of murder, Muhammad and his followers left Mecca for **Yathrib**, a journey known as the **hijra** (hih JY ruh). Later, Yathrib was renamed **Medina**, or "city of the Prophet," and 622 became the first year of the Muslim calendar.

The hijra was a turning point for Islam. In Medina, Muslim converts welcomed Muhammad and agreed to follow his teachings. They became a community of Muslims, or *umma*. Loyalty to the umma was based on Islam instead of old family rivalries. Muhammad created rules that governed and united Muslims and brought peace among the clans of Medina. As his reputation grew, thousands of Arabs adopted Islam. Meanwhile, Meccan leaders grew more hostile toward the Muslims. After Muslims attacked several caravans, the Meccans prepared for war.

After fighting battles with the Meccans, Muhammad triumphantly returned to Mecca in 630. He destroyed the idols in the **Kaaba**, the temple that he believed Abraham had built to worship the one true God. He rededicated the Kaaba to Allah, and it became the most holy place in Islam. For the next two years, Muhammad worked to unite the Arabs under Islam. Muhammad died in 632, but the faith that he proclaimed continued to spread. Today, Islam is one of the world's major religions.

✓ **Checkpoint** How did Muhammad become the prophet of Islam?

The photograph below shows Medina as it appears today. The illustration shows both Medina (left) and Mecca (right) in 1160. *What evidence do you see that Medina is an important pilgrimage site?*

Vocabulary Builder

mediate—(MEE dee ayt) *v.* to act as a go-between

Note Taking

Reading Skill: Identify Main Ideas Copy the web diagram below. As you read, fill in the outer ovals with the teachings of Islam.

Teachings of Islam

Like Judaism and Christianity, Islam is monotheistic, based on belief in one God. The Quran (koo RAHN), the sacred text of Islam, teaches that God is all-powerful and compassionate. It also states that people are responsible for their own actions. Islam does not require priests to mediate between the people and God. Muslims believe that God had sent other prophets, including Abraham, Moses, and Jesus, but that Muhammad was the last and greatest prophet.

Muslims Study the Quran To Muslims, the Quran contains the sacred word of God as revealed to Muhammad. It is the final authority on all matters discussed in the text. The Quran teaches about God's will and provides a guide to life. Its ethical standards emphasize honesty, generosity, and social justice. It sets harsh penalties for crimes such as stealing or murder. According to the Quran, each individual will stand before God on the final judgment day to face either eternal punishment in hell or eternal bliss in paradise.

Muslims believe that the Quran is the direct, unchangeable word of God. Because the meaning and poetic beauty of the Quran reside in its original language, all Muslims, including converts to Islam, learn Arabic. This shared language has helped unite Muslims from many regions throughout the world.

Muslims Follow Duties All observant Muslims perform five basic duties, known as the Five Pillars of Islam. The first is to make a declaration of faith. The second is to pray five times daily. After a ritual washing, Muslims face the holy city of Mecca to pray. Although Muslims may pray anywhere, they often gather in houses of worship called masjids or mosques. A mosque official called a muezzin (myoo EZ in) calls the faithful to prayer.

The third pillar is to give charity to the poor. The fourth is to fast from sunrise to sunset during the holy month of Ramadan—the month in which Muhammad received his first revelations from God. The fifth pillar is to make the hajj, or pilgrimage to Mecca. Pilgrims participate in ceremonies commemorating the actions of Muhammad, Abraham, and Abraham's family. Their simple attire symbolizes the abandonment of the material world for the sake of God.

Another duty is jihad, or struggle in God's service. Jihad is usually a personal duty for Muslims, who focus on overcoming immorality within themselves. At other times, jihad may be interpreted as a holy war to defend Islam and the Muslim community, much like the Crusades to defend Christianity. However, just holy war may be declared only by the community, not by an individual Muslim or small group.

"People of the Book" Muslims, Jews, and Christians worship the same God. The Quran teaches that Islam is God's final and complete revelation, while Hebrew scriptures and the Christian Bible contain portions of earlier revelations. Muslims consider Jews and Christians to be "People of the Book," spiritually superior to polytheistic idol worshipers. Although there have been exceptions, the People of the Book have historically enjoyed religious freedom in many Muslim societies.

✔ **Checkpoint** What are the duties required of Muslims?

THE FIVE PILLARS OF ISLAM

All observant Muslims perform five individual duties, known as the Five Pillars of Islam. These are based on Muhammad's example. The photograph below shows pilgrims praying at the Kaaba, the most important temple of Islam. Whenever Muslims pray, they face the Kaaba, which is located in Mecca. Find Mecca on the map and then read about the Five Pillars of Islam.

1. Declaration of Faith

The Muslim profession of faith is called the *shahada*. It states, "There is no god but God, Muhammad is the messenger of God." Muslims believe that God had sent other prophets, including Abraham, Moses, and Jesus, but that Muhammad was the last and greatest prophet.

2. Daily Prayer

Muslims pray five times each day. After a ritual washing, they face Mecca and perform specific actions as they pray.

3. Alms for the Poor

Muslims care for others by giving charity to the poor. In some Muslim countries, money is collected in the form of a tax called the *zakat*. Other Muslims give individual donations.

4. Fast During Ramadan

Muslims fast from sunrise to sunset during the holy month of Ramadan. The sick and very young children are not required to fast. The children below are celebrating the end of Ramadan.

5. Hajj

Muslims who are physically and financially able must make a pilgrimage to pray at the Kaaba in Mecca at least once. More than two million Muslims visit Mecca each year for this purpose. Pilgrims wear simple garments that erase cultural and class differences so that all stand equal before God.

Miller Projection
0   200   400 mi
0   200 400 km

Muslim lands by 632
Boundary of Byzantine empire
Route of Hijra

BYZANTINE EMPIRE
Syria
Jerusalem
Tigris R.
Euphrates R.
PERSIAN EMPIRE
Arabian Desert
Persian Gulf
Red Sea
Nile R.
Medina
Mount Hira
ARABIAN PENINSULA
Mecca
40° E
Rub Al Khali (Empty Quarter)
20° N
Yemen
50° E
Arabian Sea
Gulf of Aden
10° N

Thinking Critically

1. **Summarize** Describe the Five Pillars of Islam.
2. **Draw Inferences** Why do Muslims perform the Five Pillars?

Islamic Law Court

In this Persian painting, a man and woman seek a decision before a judge. *What does this picture suggest about the rights of Muslim women?*

Vocabulary Builder

<u>affirm</u>—(uh FURM) *v.* to judge as valid

Islam: A Way of Life

Islam is both a religion and a way of life. Its teachings shape the lives of Muslims around the world. Islamic law governs daily life, and Muslim traditions determine ethical behavior and influence family relations.

Sharia—Islamic System of Law Over time, Muslim scholars developed the Sharia, a body of law that includes interpretation of the Quran, examples of behavior from Muhammad's life, and Muslim traditions. Similar to Jewish law, the Sharia regulates moral conduct, family life, business practices, government, and other aspects of individual and community life. It does not separate religion from criminal or civil law, but applies religious principles to all legal situations. Just as the Quran unifies Muslim beliefs, the Sharia unites Muslims under a common legal framework.

Impact of Islam on Women Before Islam, the position of women in Arab society varied. In some communities, women were active in religion, trade, or politics. As in most societies at that time, however, most women had limited rights. Arab women could not inherit property and had to obey a male guardian. Among a few tribes, unwanted daughters were sometimes killed at birth.

Islam extended rights and protection to women by <u>affirming</u> the spiritual equality of all Muslims. The Quran teaches that "Whoever does right, whether male or female, and is a believer, all such will enter the Garden." The Quran prohibited the killing of daughters, granted women an inheritance, and allowed women to reject a marriage offer. Islam also encouraged education for men and women so that all Muslims could study the Quran.

Although spiritually equal under Islam, men and women had different roles and rights. For example, women inherited less than men and had a more difficult time getting a divorce. As Islam spread, Muslims adopted practices of conquered peoples. For example, the practices of veiling upper-class women and secluding them in a separate part of the home were Persian customs. The Quran says that women should dress modestly, which has been interpreted in multiple ways. Still, women's lives varied according to region and class. In rural areas, peasant women often needed to work and did not wear a veil, but took care to dress modestly.

 Checkpoint How did Islam affect Muslim women?

SECTION 1 **Assessment**

Progress Monitoring *Online*
For: Self-quiz with vocabulary practice
Web Code: naa-1011

Terms, People, and Places

1. For each term, person, or place listed at the beginning of the section, write a sentence explaining its significance.

Note Taking

2. **Reading Skill: Recognize Sequence and Identify Main Ideas** Use your completed timeline and web diagram to answer the Focus Question: What messages, or teachings, did Muhammad spread through Islam?

Comprehension and Critical Thinking

3. **Identify Point of View** Why were merchants in Mecca at first opposed to Muhammad's teachings?
4. **Determine Relevance** Why do Muslims consider Mecca sacred?
5. **Recognize Ideologies** How do the Quran and Sharia guide Muslims?
6. **Draw Inferences** Which aspects of Islam would have appealed to the poor, enslaved, and isolated—many of the first Muslim converts? Explain.

● **Writing About History**

Quick Write: Choose a Topic Compare and contrast one tradition of Islam (religious holidays, for example) to a similar tradition within Judaism and/or Christianity. First, choose a topic to compare and contrast. To do so, write a list of the categories from which you can choose a topic to research for both religions. Refer to this list as you collect the facts and details you need to write a compare-and-contrast essay.

The Quran

The Quran, the holy scriptures of Islam, contains 114 *suras*, or chapters, which are divided into verses. Muslims believe that the Quran is the word of God as revealed to Muhammad. They also believe that God instructed Muhammad to arrange the chapters into the order in which they appear. The following excerpts from the Quran tell Muslims how to be righteous and faithful. They also encourage believers to fast and observe the holy month of Ramadan.

Righteousness does not consist in whether you face towards the East or the West. The righteous man is he who believes in God and the Last Day, in the angels and the Book [Scriptures] and the prophets; who, though he loves it dearly, gives away his wealth to kinsfolk, to orphans, to the destitute, to the traveller in need and to beggars, and for the redemption[1] of captives; who attends to his prayers and renders the alms[2] levy; who is true to his promises and steadfast in trial and adversity and in times of war. Such are the true believers; such are the God–fearing.
—The Quran 2:177

Believers, fasting is decreed for you as it was decreed for those before you; perchance you will guard yourselves against evil. Fast a certain number of days, but if any one among you is ill or on a journey, let him fast a similar number of days later; and for those that cannot endure it there is a penance ordained: the feeding of a poor man. He that does good of his own accord shall be well rewarded; but to fast is better for you, if you but knew it.

In the month of Ramadan the [Quran] was revealed, a book of guidance for mankind with proofs of guidance distinguishing right from wrong. Therefore whoever of you is present in that month let him fast. But he who is ill or on a journey shall fast a similar number of days later on.

God desires your well-being, not your discomfort. He desires you to fast the whole month so that you may magnify God and render thanks to Him for giving you His guidance. —The Quran 2:183–185

The wide borders on the pages of this Quran ensure that the reader's fingers will not touch the sacred text.

1. redemption (rih DEMP shun) *n.* freedom from enslavement or captivity by payment of ransom

2. alms (ahmz) *n.* charity given freely to the poor

At the top, the intricate pattern of this Quran illustration echoes the calligraphy at the center, and, below, a young woman reads the Quran.

Thinking Critically

1. **Summarize Information** According to the excerpt above, to whom should righteous people give their wealth?
2. **Analyze Information** In which situation can a righteous person avoid fasting during Ramadan?
3. **Apply Information** How does this passage from the Quran support the Five Pillars of Islam?

309

Muslim soldiers pitching a tent

Nomadic Raids

❝For centuries nomadic Arab tribes had been in the habit of making raids or razzias on other tribes. The usual aim was to drive off the camels or other live-stock of the opponents. The favorite plan was to make a surprise attack with overwhelming force on a small section of the other tribe. In such circumstances it was no disgrace to the persons attacked if they made their escape; and so in many razzias there was little loss of life. . . . From the standpoint of the Mus-lims, the crossing of the straits of Gibraltar in 711 was . . . one more in a series of raiding expeditions which had been pushing ever farther afield. . . . After experiencing one or more such raiding expeditions the inhabitants of the countries traversed usually sur-rendered and became protected allies.❞
—from *The Influence of Islam on Medieval Europe*, by W. Montgomery Watt

Focus Question How did Muhammad's successors extend Muslim rule and spread Islam?

Building a Muslim Empire

Objectives

- Explain how Muslims were able to conquer many lands.
- Identify the divisions that emerged within Islam.
- Describe the rise of the Umayyad and Abbasid dynasties.
- Explain why the Abbasid empire declined.

Terms, People, and Places

Abu Bakr	Umayyads
caliph	Abbasids
Sunni	Baghdad
Shiite	minaret
Sufis	sultan

Note Taking

Reading Skill: Recognize Sequence Copy the timeline below. As you read, fill in the timeline with major events concerning the spread of Islam and the rise and fall of Muslim empires.

711
Arabs reach Spain.

600   800   1000   1200   1400

The death of Muhammad plunged his followers into grief. The Prophet had been a pious man and a powerful leader. No one else had ever been able to unify so many Arab tribes. Could the com-munity of Muslims survive without him?

Early Challenges to Islam

Muslims faced a problem when Muhammad died because he had not named a successor to lead the community. Eventually, they agreed that **Abu Bakr** (uh BOO BAK ur), Muhammad's father-in-law and an early convert to Islam, should be the first **caliph,** or successor to Muhammad. Abu Bakr sternly told the faithful, "If you worship Muhammad, Muhammad is dead. If you worship God, God is alive."

Arabs Unite Under Islam Abu Bakr faced an immediate crisis. The loyalty of some Arab tribal leaders had been dependent on Muhammad's personal command. They refused to follow Abu Bakr and withdrew their loyalty to Islam. After several battles with the wavering tribes, Abu Bakr succeeded in reuniting the Muslims, based on their allegiance to Islam. Once reunited, the Muslims set out on a remarkable series of military campaigns. They began by converting the remaining Arab tribes to Islam, which ended warfare between Arabs and united them under one leader.

Early Victories Under the first four caliphs, the Arab Muslims marched from victory to victory against two great empires on their borders. The Byzantines and Persians had competed with each other over control of Arab lands. Once the Arabs united, they surprised their neighbors, conquering great portions of the Byzantine empire and defeating the Persians entirely. First, they took the Arab provinces of Syria and Palestine from the Byzantines, including the cities of Damascus and Jerusalem. Then, they captured the weakened Persian empire and swept into Byzantine Egypt.

✓ **Checkpoint** How did Muslims overcome early challenges to Islam?

Note Taking

Reading Skill: Compare and Contrast
Copy the Venn diagram below. As you read, fill in the diagram with points on which Sunni and Shiite Muslims agree and differ.

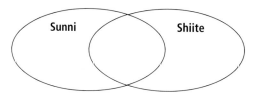

Divisions Emerge Within Islam

When Muhammad died, Muslims disagreed about who should be chosen to be the leader of the community. The split between **Sunni** (SOO nee) and **Shiite** (SHEE yt) Muslims had a profound impact on later Islamic history.

Sunnis and Shiites One group of Muslims felt that Muhammad had designated his son-in-law, Ali, to be his successor. They were called Shiites, after *shi'at Ali*, or followers of Ali. Shiites believe that the true successors to the Prophet are the descendants of Ali and Muhammad's daughter, Fatima. They believe that these descendants, called Imams, are divinely inspired religious leaders, who are empowered to interpret the Quran and the actions of Muhammad. Another group felt that any good Muslim could lead the community, since there could be no prophet after Muhammad. This group soon divided and fought among themselves as well as with others over issues of who could be defined as a "good" Muslim.

The majority of Muslims eventually compromised around the view that the successor to Muhammad should be a pious male Muslim from Muhammad's tribe. This successor is called a caliph and is viewed as a political leader of the religious community, without any divine or prophetic functions. The compromise group, which forms the majority of Muslims in the world today, are known as Sunnis, since they follow the custom of the community, or *sunna*. The Sunni believe that inspiration comes from the example of Muhammad as recorded by his early followers.

The Dome of the Rock
The Dome of the Rock in Jerusalem is the oldest surviving Islamic building. Construction began soon after Muslims captured Jerusalem. According to Muslim teaching, Muhammad ascended to heaven from the rock inside this building. *Why was it important for Muslims to build in Jerusalem?*

311

A Whirling Dervish
Whirling Dervishes are Sufi mystics who dance as a form of prayer.

Like the schism between Roman Catholic and Eastern Orthodox Christians, the division between Sunni and Shiite Muslims has survived to the present day. Members of both branches of Islam believe in the same God, look to the Quran for guidance, and follow the Pillars of Islam. However, Sunnis and Shiites differ in such areas as religious practice, law, and daily life. Today, about 90 percent of Muslims are Sunni. Most Shiites live in Iran, Lebanon, Iraq, and Yemen. The Shiite branch itself has further split into several different subgroups.

Sufis A third tradition in Islam emerged with the **Sufis,** Muslim mystics who sought communion with God through meditation, fasting, and other rituals. Sufis were respected for their piety and some were believed to have miraculous powers.

Like Christian monks and nuns, some Sufis helped spread Islam by traveling, preaching, and being good examples to others. They carried the faith to remote villages, where they blended local traditions and beliefs into Muslim culture.

✓ **Checkpoint**   **Describe differences between Sunni and Shiite Muslims.**

Umayyad Caliphs Build an Empire

After the death of Ali, a powerful Meccan clan set up the **Umayyad** (oo MY ad) caliphate, a dynasty of Sunni caliphs that ruled the Muslim empire until 750. From their capital at Damascus in Syria, they directed the spectacular conquests that extended Arab rule from Spain and Morocco in the west to the Indus River Valley in the east. Their conquests enabled the spread of Islam and created a foundation for the ethnically and religiously diverse civilization that flourished later.

Expanding the Muslim Empire From Egypt, Arab Muslim armies moved west, defeating Byzantine forces across North Africa. In 711, Muslim forces crossed the Strait of Gibraltar and conquered Spain. In 731, a Muslim army moved north into France to settle new areas. There, Frankish forces defeated the Muslims at the battle of Tours. Muslims ruled parts of Spain for centuries, but advanced no farther into Europe. Elsewhere, Muslim forces besieged the Byzantine capital of Constantinople, but failed to take the well-defended city.

Reasons for Muslim Success Several factors can explain the series of Muslim victories. One factor was the weakness of the Byzantine and Persian empires. The longtime rivals had fought each other to exhaustion. Many people also welcomed the Arabs as liberators from harsh Byzantine or Persian rule. Another factor was the Arabs' bold, efficient fighting methods. The Bedouin camel and horse cavalry mounted aggressive and mobile offensives that overwhelmed more traditional armies.

Another important reason for success was the common faith Muhammad had established. Under the first four caliphs, Muslims knitted a patchwork of competing tribes into a unified state. Belief in Islam and the desire to glorify the new religion spurred the Muslim armies to victory.

As the empire expanded, the rulers created an orderly system of administration. Arabic became the language of government, and the empire minted its own coins. In addition, the caliphs supported agricultural policies that helped the empire to prosper.

A Jewish Apothecary
A Jewish apothecary, or pharmacist, dispenses medicine in a Spanish market. *What does this picture tell you about Muslim regions?*

Conquered People Are Treated Fairly The advancing Arabs brought many people under their rule. Muslim leaders imposed a special tax on non-Muslims, but allowed Christians, Jews, and Zoroastrians to practice their own faiths and follow their own laws. Early Umayyads did not attempt to convert these "People of the Book," because the tax supported the Arab troops who settled in conquered areas. As Muslim civilization developed, many Jews and Christians played key roles as officials, doctors, and translators. Muslim leaders wisely prohibited looting and destruction of conquered lands, ensuring continued wealth and prosperity for the empire in the form of tribute and taxes. However, the rulers also urged Arab settlers to stay separate from the native populations, which created an Arab upper class throughout the empire.

In time, many non-Muslims converted to Islam. Some converted to gain political or economic advantages. However, many were drawn to Islam's simple and direct message, and they saw its triumph as a sign of God's favor. Many of the nomadic peoples in North Africa and Central Asia chose Islam immediately. Unlike some religions, Islam had no religious hierarchy or class of priests. In principle, it emphasized the equality of all believers, regardless of race, gender, class, or wealth. In later centuries, Turkish and Mongol converts helped spread Islam far across Asia.

Decline of the Umayyad Caliphate As military victories and negotiation expanded the Muslim empire, the Umayyads faced numerous problems. First, Arabs had to adapt from living in the desert to ruling large cities and huge territories. In many ways, the caliphs ruled like powerful tribal leaders, rather than kings with large bureaucracies. To govern their empire, the Umayyads often relied on local officials. Although they helped govern the empire, non-Arabs often did not have the same privileges that Arabs had, even if they converted to Islam.

While conquests continued, vast wealth flowed into Umayyad hands. When conquests slowed in the 700s, economic tensions increased between wealthy Arabs and those who had less. In addition, more and more resources were used to support the caliphs' luxurious lifestyle. By the eighth century, many Muslims criticized the court at Damascus for abandoning the simple ways of the early caliphs. Shiites considered the Umayyad caliphs to be illegitimate rulers of the Islamic community.

Unrest also grew among non-Arab converts to Islam, who had fewer rights than Arabs.

 Checkpoint What are three reasons for the success of Muslim conquests?

Rise of the Abbasids

Discontented Muslims found a leader in Abu al-Abbas, descended from Muhammad's uncle. With strong support from Shiite and non-Arab Muslims, he captured Damascus in 750. Soon after, he had members of the defeated Umayyad family killed. Only one survived, escaping to Spain. Abu al-Abbas then founded the **Abbasid** (uh BAS id) dynasty, which lasted until 1258.

Changes Under the Abbasids The Abbasid dynasty tried to create an empire based on the equality of all Muslims. The new rulers halted the large military conquests, ending the dominance of the Arab military class. Under the early Abbasids, the empire of the caliphs reached its greatest wealth and power, and Muslim civilization flourished. Under the Abbasids, Islam became a more diverse religion because discrimination against non-Arab Muslims ended. Official policy encouraged conversion to Islam and treated all Muslims equally. The Abbassids created a more sophisticated bureaucracy and encouraged learning.

The Abbasids also moved the capital from Damascus to Baghdad, a small market town on the banks of the Tigris river. This move into Persian territory allowed Persian officials to hold important offices in the caliph's government. It also allowed Persian traditions to influence the development of the caliphate. Although these traditions strongly influenced Arab culture, Islam remained the religion of the empire and Arabic its language. The most important official was known as the vizier, or the head of the bureaucracy, a position that had existed in Persian government.

BIOGRAPHY

Harun al-Rashid

The city of Baghdad reached its peak under the reign of Caliph Harun al-Rashid (763?–809), who ruled from 786 to 809. Both Europeans and his own subjects admired Harun as a model ruler. Many stories and legends recall Harun's wealth, generosity, and support of learning. Poets, physicians, philosophers, and artists all gathered at his court in Baghdad. One story tells how Harun rewarded a favorite poet with a robe of honor, a splendid horse, and 5,000 dirhams—a vast sum of money.

Harun used his generosity to create closer ties with other rulers. He sent the Frankish king Charlemagne several gifts, including a mechanical clock and an elephant. Harun hoped that the Franks would join him in an alliance against the rival Umayyad ruler in Spain.

Despite his lavishness and generosity, Harun amassed a great fortune. At his death, he had millions of dirhams, plus huge stores of jewels and gold. **How did Harun help make Baghdad a major center of Muslim culture?**

Splendors of Baghdad The second Abbasid caliph, al-Mansur, chose **Baghdad** as the site of his new capital. The walls formed a circle, with the caliph's palace in the center. Poets, scholars, philosophers, and entertainers from all over the Muslim world flocked to the Abbasid court. Under the Abbasids, Baghdad exceeded Constantinople in size and wealth. Visitors no doubt felt that Baghdad deserved its title "City of Peace, Gift of God, Paradise on Earth."

The city was beautiful, with many markets, gardens, the palace, and mosques. Domes and **minarets** (min uh RETS), slender towers of the mosques, loomed overhead. Five times each day, muezzins climbed to the tops of the minarets and called the faithful to prayer. Merchants sold goods from Africa, Asia, and Europe. The palace of the caliph bustled with activity.

Muslim Culture in Spain The surviving member of the Umayyad family had fled to Spain and established an independent Muslim state. There, Muslim rulers presided over brilliant courts, where the arts and

Spread of Islam

Map Skills In less than 150 years, Muslim rule spread from Arabia across southwest Asia and North Africa and into Europe.

1. **Locate** (a) Damascus (b) Baghdad (c) Persia (d) Cairo (e) Constantinople (f) Córdoba (g) Tours

2. **Region** During what period did Spain come under Muslim rule?

3. **Apply Information** How might the spread of Islam have contributed to Muslim success in trade?

Geography *Interactive*
For: Interactive map
Web Code: nap-1021

Miller Projection
0   200   400 mi
0   200   400 km

QARAKHANIDS
(922–1211)

Tours
FRANCE
EUROPE
45° N
Danube River
Black Sea
Constantinople
Caspian Sea
Aral Sea
Jaxartes R.
Volga R.
ASIA
Bukhara
Samarkand
Oxus R.

UMAYYADS
(756–1031)
SPAIN
Córdoba
Granada
Strait of Gibraltar
Fez
MOROCCO
IDRISIDS
(789–921)
NORTH AFRICA
Rome
Tunis
Tripoli
Mediterranean Sea
30° E
Alexandria
Cairo
EGYPT
FATIMIDS
(909–1171)
SYRIA
Damascus
Jerusalem
Euphrates R.
Tigris R.
Baghdad
Isfahan
BUYIDS
(932–1055)
PERSIAN EMPIRE
SAMANIDS
(819–999)
SAFFARIDS
(867–1495)
Indus R.
60° E
Persian Gulf
NUBIA
Red Sea
Nile R.
Medina
Mecca
ARABIA
Rub Al Khali
YEMEN
ZAIDI IMAMS
(FROM 860)
AXUM
Gulf of Aden
45° E
15° N
Arabian Sea
Indian Ocean

Muslim lands at death of Muhammad, 632
Lands conquered by Muslims under first four caliphs, 632–661
Lands conquered by Muslims under Umayyad caliphs, 661–750
Muslim world, *circa* 1000
Boundary of Byzantine empire, 632
Abbasid Caliphate at its greatest extent, *circa* 800
FATIMIDS
(909–1171) Muslim dynasties, with dates

◄ The Great Mosque and town of Kairouan, Tunisia

Interior view of the Great Mosque of Córdoba, Spain ►

651
Persian Empire falls to Arabs.

682
Arab armies reach Morocco.

632
Death of Muhammad

732
Franks defeat Muslim forces at the battle of Tours.

750–850
Golden Age of Muslim civilization

circa **1050**
Seljuk Turks begin invasions of Muslim regions.

600   **700**   **800**   **900**   **1000**   **1100**

639–642
Arabs conquer Egypt.

661–750
Umayyad Caliphate

711
Muslims enter Spain.

756–1031
Umayyad Spain

750–1258
Abbasid Caliphate

850
Abbasid empire begins to fragment.

◄ Courtyard of the Umayyad Mosque in Damascus

315

The Great Mosque
The photo above shows the outside of the mosque in Córdoba, Spain. A picture of the inside appears on the previous page. It was built around 785.

learning thrived. In general, they were more tolerant of other religions than were Christian rulers of the time. At centers of learning, such as the city of Córdoba, rulers employed Jewish officials and welcomed Christian scholars to study science and philosophy. Architects built grand buildings, such as the Alhambra, a fortified palace in Granada. Its lovely gardens, reflecting pools, and finely decorated marble columns mark a high point of Muslim civilization in Spain. Muslim rule endured in parts of Spain until 1492.

✓ **Checkpoint**   How did Islam become a more universal faith?

The Muslim Empire Declines

The Abbasids never ruled Spain, and starting about 850, their control over the rest of the Muslim empire fragmented. In Egypt and elsewhere, independent dynasties ruled states that had been part of a unified empire. As the caliph's power faded in some regions, Shiite rulers came to power. Between 900 and 1400, a series of invasions added to the chaos.

Seljuk Turks Take Control   In the 900s, Seljuk Turks migrated into the Middle East from Central Asia. They adopted Islam and built a large empire across the Fertile Crescent. By 1055, a Seljuk **sultan,** or ruler, controlled Baghdad, but he kept the Abbasid caliph as a figurehead. As the Seljuks pushed into Asia Minor, they threatened the Byzantine empire. The conflict prevented Christian pilgrims from traveling to Jerusalem, leading Pope Urban II to call for the First Crusade in 1095.

Mongols Sweep Across Central Asia   In 1216, Genghis Khan led the Mongols out of Central Asia across southwest Asia. Mongol armies returned again and again. In 1258, Hulagu, the grandson of Genghis, burned and looted Baghdad, killing the last Abbasid caliph. Later, the Mongols adopted Islam as they mingled with local inhabitants. In the late 1300s, another Mongol leader, Timur the Lame, or Tamerlane, led his armies into the Middle East. Though he was a Muslim, Tamerlane's ambitions led him to conquer Muslim as well as non-Muslim lands. His armies overran southwest Asia before invading Russia and India.

✓ **Checkpoint**   What caused the Abbassid dynasty to decline?

Progress Monitoring *Online*
For: Self-quiz with vocabulary practice
Web Code: naa-1021

SECTION
2 Assessment

Terms, People, and Places
1. For each term, person, or place listed at the beginning of the section, write a sentence explaining its significance.

Nte Taking

2. **Reading Skill: Recognize Sequence** Use your completed timelines to answer the Focus Question: How did Muhammad's successors extend Muslim rule and spread Islam?

Comprehension and Critical Thinking
3. **Recognize Ideologies** How did the issue of heredity cause the division of Islam into Sunni and Shiite Muslims?
4. **Analyze Information** How did the Umayyads' treatment of non-Muslims and non-Arabs affect their empire?
5. **Recognize Cause and Effect** Why did the empire of the Abbasid caliphs decline and eventually break up?

● **Writing About History**
Quick Write: Explore a Topic Many Bedouins visited Baghdad during the reign of Harun al-Rashid. Write a paragraph through their eyes in which you describe how life in Baghdad differs from nomadic life in the desert. Give details about each point of comparison to make your essay more accessible to readers.

Aristotle educates Muslim scholars (foreground); a Greek medical text translated into Arabic (background)

WITNESS HISTORY 🔊 AUDIO

Inspiration from Aristotle

One night, Caliph al-Mamun had a vivid dream. There in his chambers he came upon a balding, blue-eyed stranger sitting on the low couch.

"Who are you?" the caliph demanded.

"Aristotle," the man replied.

The caliph was delighted. He plied the great Greek philosopher with questions about ethics, reason, and religion. After al-Mamun awoke, his dream inspired him to action. He had scholars collect the great works of the classical world and translate them into Arabic. By 830, the caliph had set up the "House of Wisdom," a library and university in Baghdad. During the Abbasid period, scholars made advances in a variety of fields.

Focus Question What achievements did Muslims make in economics, art, literature, and science?

Muslim Civilization's Golden Age

Objectives

- Describe the role of trade in Muslim civilization.
- Identify the traditions that influenced Muslim art, architecture, and literature.
- Explain the advances Muslims made in centers of learning.

Terms, People, and Places

social mobility	Ibn Khaldun
Firdawsi	al-Khwarizmi
Omar Khayyám	Muhammad al-Razi
calligraphy	Ibn Sina
Ibn Rushd	

Note Taking

Reading Skill: Categorize Copy the chart below. As you read, fill in the categories of the advances made during the golden age of Muslim civilization.

Muslim Achievements	
Economics	
Arts	
Literature	
Philosophy	
Sciences	

Under the Abbasids, Muslim civilization absorbed traditions from many cultures. In the process, a flourishing new civilization arose in cities from Baghdad to Córdoba. It incorporated all the people who lived under Muslim rule, including Jews and Christians. The great works produced by scholars of the Abbasid period shaped Muslim culture and civilization. Through contacts in Spain and Sicily, Christian European scholars began to study Muslim philosophy, art, and science. Muslim scholars also reintroduced knowledge of Greco-Roman civilization to later Europeans.

Social and Economic Advances

Muslim rulers united diverse cultures, including Arab, Persian, Egyptian, African, and European. Later, Mongols, Turks, Indians, and Southeast Asians joined the Muslim community. Muslim civilization absorbed and blended many of their traditions.

Muslims Build an International Trade Network Merchants were honored in Muslim culture, in part because Muhammad had been a merchant. A traditional collection of sayings stated:

Primary Source

66 I commend the merchants to you, for they are the couriers of the horizon and God's trusted servants on Earth. 99
—Sayings of the Prophet

A Muslim Market and Its Wares
At bottom, Muslim merchants sold local goods and goods from distant lands. Persian weavers were known for their beautiful carpets, such as the one shown above.

Between 750 and 1350, merchants built a vast trading network across Muslim lands and beyond. Camel caravans—the "ships of the desert"—crossed the Sahara into West Africa. Muslim, Jewish, and Christian traders traveled the Silk Road toward China and were a vital link in the exchange of goods between East Asia and Europe. Monsoon winds carried Arab ships from East Africa to India and southeast Asia. Some traders made great fortunes.

Trade spread products, technologies, knowledge, and culture. Muslim merchants introduced an Indian number system to the Western world, where they became known as Arabic numerals. Traders also carried sugar from India and papermaking from China, introducing Islam to many new regions. As more people converted and learned Arabic, a common language and religion helped the global exchange grow and thrive.

Extensive trade and a money economy led Muslims to pioneer new business practices. They created partnerships, bought and sold on credit, formed banks to change currency, and invented the ancestors of today's bank checks. The English word *check* comes from the Arabic word *sakk*. Bankers developed a sophisticated system of accounting. They opened branch banks in all major cities, so that a check written in Baghdad might be cashed in Cairo.

Manufactured Goods Are Highly Valued As in medieval Europe, handicraft manufacturing in Muslim cities was typically organized by guilds. The heads of the guilds, chosen by their members, often had the authority to regulate prices, weights and measures, methods of production, and the quality of the product. Most labor was done by wage workers. Muslim artisans produced a wealth of fine goods. Steel swords from Damascus, leather goods from Córdoba, cotton textiles from Egypt, and carpets from Persia were highly valued. Workshops also turned out fine glassware, furniture, and tapestries.

Agriculture Thrives Outside the cities, agriculture flourished across a wide variety of climates and landforms. Both Umayyad and Abbasid rulers took steps to preserve and extend agricultural land. Small farming communities in desert areas faced a constant scarcity of water. To improve farm output, the Abbasids organized massive irrigation projects and drained swamplands between the Tigris and Euphrates rivers. In addition to crops raised for food, farmers cultivated sugar cane, cotton, medicinal herbs, and flowers that were sold in far-off markets. Farmers began to grow crops that came from different regions.

The deserts continued to support nomads who lived by herding. Still, nomads and farmers shared economic ties. Nomads bought dates and grain from settled peoples, while farming populations acquired meat, wool, and hides from the nomads. Pastoral groups also provided pack animals and guides for the caravan trade.

Social Structure and Slavery Muslim society in the eighth and ninth centuries was more open than that of medieval Christian Europe. Muslims enjoyed a certain degree of **social mobility,** the ability to move up in social class. People could improve their social rank through religious, scholarly, or military achievements.

As in many earlier societies, slavery was a common institution in Muslim lands, though Islamic law encouraged the freeing of slaves as an act of charity. Slaves were often from conquered lands because Muslims were not supposed to enslave other Muslims. Some slaves bought their freedom, often with the help of charitable donations or even state funds. However, if non-Muslim slaves converted to Islam, they did not automatically become free. A female slave who bore a child by her Muslim owner gained freedom upon her master's death. Children born of a slave mother and free father were also considered freeborn.

Most slaves worked as household servants, while some were skilled artisans. To help break down the tribal system, Abbasid caliphs also created a class of Turkish slave-soldiers who were loyal only to the caliph. Often educated in Islamic law and government, some of these men rose to high positions in the government, such as vizier. This set the stage for the Turks to become powerful later in the Abbasid era.

 Checkpoint What business practices were pioneered by merchants in Muslim lands?

Muslim Art, Literature, and Architecture

Muslim art and literature reflected the diverse traditions of the various peoples who lived under Muslim rule, including Greeks, Romans, Persians, and Indians. As in Christian Europe and Hindu India, religion shaped the arts and literature of Muslim civilization. The great work of Islamic literature was the Quran itself. Because the Quran strictly banned the worship of idols, Muslim religious leaders forbade artists to portray God or human figures in religious art, giving Islamic art a distinctive style.

Poetry and Tales of Adventure Long before Muhammad, Arabs had a rich tradition of oral poetry. In musical verses, poets chanted the dangers of desert journeys, the joys of battle, or the glories of their clans. Their most important themes—chivalry and the romance of nomadic life—recurred in Arab poetry throughout the centuries. Later Arab poets developed elaborate formal rules for writing poetry and explored both religious and worldly themes. The poems of Rabiah al-Adawiyya expressed Sufi mysticism and encouraged the faithful to worship God selflessly without hope of reward. "If I worship Thee in hope of Paradise / Exclude me from Paradise," she wrote in one prayer poem.

Persians also had a fine poetic tradition. Firdawsi (fur DOW see) wrote in Persian using Arabic script. His masterpiece, the *Shah Namah,* or *Book of Kings,* tells the history of Persia. Omar Khayyám (OH mahr ky AHM), famous in the Muslim world as a scholar and an astronomer, is best known for *The Rubáiyát* (roo by AHT). In this collection of four-line stanzas, Khayyám meditates on fate and the fleeting nature of life:

Primary Source

66 The Moving Finger writes; and having writ,
Moves on; nor all your Piety nor Wit
Shall lure it back to cancel half a line,
Nor all your Tears wash out a word of it. 99
—Omar Khayyám, *The Rubáiyát*

A Hero's Super Powers
The illustration above is from Firdawsi's *Shah Namah,* which tells the story of many Persian heroes—among them, Rustam. Why was Rustam's strength both an advantage and a disadvantage?

Primary Source

66 The tale is told that Rustam had at first
Such strength bestowed by Him who giveth all
That if he walked upon a rock his feet
Would sink therein. Such [power] as that
Proved an abiding trouble, and he prayed
To God in bitterness of soul to [diminish]
His strength that he might walk like other
men. 99
—Firdawsi, *Shah Namah*

BIOGRAPHY

Ibn Rushd (Averroës)

While growing up in Spain, Muslim scholar Ibn Rushd (1126–1198)—known to Europeans as Averroës—was interested in almost every subject and profession. He focused first on medicine and became chief physician to the Muslim ruler in Spain. Later, he studied astronomy and wrote several important books on the subject. Ibn Rushd also studied law, became a famous judge, and wrote a digest of Islamic law.

Ibn Rushd is best known as a philosopher. Muslims, Jews, and Christians alike have studied his commentaries on Aristotle for centuries. For part of his life, however, Ibn Rushd lived in exile outside Spain because some Muslim religious leaders felt that his writings contradicted the teachings of Islam. **What role did Ibn Rushd play in increasing the knowledge of people during the Middle Ages?**

Arab writers also prized the art of storytelling. Along with ancient Arab tales, they gathered and adapted stories from Indian, Persian, Greek, Jewish, Egyptian, and Turkish sources. The best-known collection is *The Thousand and One Nights,* a group of tales narrated by a fictional princess. They include romances, fables, adventures, and humorous anecdotes, many set in Harun al-Rashid's Baghdad. Later versions filtered into Europe, where children heard about "Aladdin and His Magic Lamp" or "Ali Baba and the Forty Thieves."

Religious Buildings Domed mosques and high minarets dominated Muslim cities. Adapted from Byzantine buildings, domes and arches became symbolic of Muslim architecture. For example, the Dome of the Rock in Jerusalem was built around 688. Inside, the walls and ceilings of mosques were decorated with elaborate abstract, geometric patterns. In addition, Muslim artists perfected skills in **calligraphy,** the art of beautiful handwriting. They worked the flowing Arabic script, especially verses from the Quran, into decorations on buildings.

Nonreligious Art Some Muslim artists painted human and animal figures in nonreligious art. Arabic scientific works, including those on the human body, were often lavishly illustrated. Literary works sometimes showed stylized figures. Later Persian, Turkish, and Indian artists excelled at painting miniatures to illustrate books of poems and fables.

✓ **Checkpoint** What elements characterized Muslim art?

Muslims Seek Knowledge

Although Muhammad could neither read nor write, his respect for learning inspired Muslims to make great advances in philosophy, history, mathematics, and the sciences. Both boys and girls received elementary education, which emphasized reading and writing. Muslims needed these skills to study the Quran. Institutions of higher learning included schools for religious instruction and for the study of Islamic law.

Centers of Learning Al-Mamun and later caliphs established Baghdad as the greatest Muslim center of learning. Its libraries attracted well paid and highly respected scholars. Other cities, like Cairo, Córdoba, and Timbuktu were also known as centers of learning. In these places, scholars made advances in philosophy, mathematics, medicine, and other fields. They also preserved the learning of earlier civilizations by translating ancient Persian, Sanskrit, and Greek texts into Arabic.

Philosophy and History Muslim scholars translated the works of the Greek philosophers, as well as many Hindu and Buddhist texts. Scholars tried to harmonize Greek ideas about reason with religious beliefs based on divine revelation. In Córdoba, the philosopher Ibn Rushd—known in Europe as Averroës—put all knowledge except the Quran to the test of reason. His writings on Aristotle were translated into Latin and influenced Christian scholastics in medieval Europe.

Another Arab thinker, **Ibn Khaldun** (IB un kal DOON), set standards for the scientific study of history. He stressed economics and social structure as causes of historical events. He also warned about common causes of error in historical writing, such as bias, exaggeration, and overconfidence in the accuracy of sources. Ibn Khaldun urged historians to trust sources only after a thorough investigation.

Muslim Advances in Astronomy

During the Muslim Golden Age, scientists and mathematicians in Muslim regions made great advances in the field of astronomy. At observatories from Baghdad to Central Asia, astronomers studied eclipses, observed Earth's rotation, and calculated the circumference of Earth to within a few thousand feet. When overland trade along the Silk Road became disrupted in the 1400s, new navigation tools paved the way for seafaring explorers like Christopher Columbus.

A Greek invention, the astrolabe is ▲ a projection of the sky as seen from a specific position on earth. Muslim astronomers added more information to it and made it more accurate.

The quadrant was an early navigation instrument. By measuring the height of a star, sailors could determine their latitude. ▶

◀ An astronomical table

▼ The Jaipur Observatory In Jaipur, India, was built in the 1700s. Astronomers there used Indian scientific knowledge as well as ideas from Muslims.

▲ The picture above shows astronomers at a Turkish observatory with their instruments. What tools are they using?

Thinking Critically

1. **Analyze Information** What evidence do you see that astronomers were respected?
2. **Draw Inferences** What were some benefits of advances in astronomy?

Origin of Arabic Numerals		
Eastern Muslim Regions	Western Muslim Regions	Modern Western
١	١	1
٢	2	2
٣	٣	3
٤	٤	4
٥	٧	5
٦	6	6
٧	١	7
٨	8	8
٩	9	9
٠	٠	0

Arabic numerals originally developed in India and changed as traders introduced them to Muslim lands and, eventually, to Europe.

Mathematics One of the greatest Muslim mathematicians was al-Khwarizmi (al KWAHR iz mee). He pioneered the study of algebra (from the Arabic word *al-jabr*). In the 800s, he wrote a book that was translated into Latin and became a standard mathematics textbook in Europe. Like many scholars of the time, al-Khwarizmi contributed to other fields too. He developed a set of astronomical tables based on Greek and Indian discoveries.

Medicine Building on the knowledge of the ancient Greeks, Muslims made remarkable advances in medicine and public health. Under the caliphs, physicians and pharmacists had to pass a test before they could practice their professions. The government set up hospitals, where injured people could get quick treatment at a facility similar to today's emergency room. Physicians traveled to rural areas to provide healthcare to those who could not get to a city, while others regularly visited jails.

One of the most original medical thinkers was Muhammad al-Razi, head physician at Baghdad's chief hospital. He wrote many books on medicine, including a pioneering study of measles and smallpox. He also challenged accepted medical practices. Treat the mind as well as the body, he advised young doctors. He theorized that if doctors were hopeful with their patients, recovery would be faster.

The famous Persian physician Ibn Sina (IB un SEE nah) was known in Europe as Avicenna. By the age of 16, he was a doctor to the Persian nobility. His great work was the *Canon on Medicine*, a huge encyclopedia of what the Greeks, the Arabs, and he himself had learned about diagnosing and treating diseases. The book includes many prescriptions, made with such ingredients as mercury from Spain, myrrh from East Africa, and camphor from India.

Other Muslim surgeons developed a way to treat cataracts, drawing fluid out of the lenses with a hollow needle. For centuries, surgeons around the world used this method to save patients' eyesight. Arab pharmacists were the first to mix bitter medicines into sweet-tasting syrups and gums. Eventually, European physicians began to attend Muslim universities in Spain. Arabic medical texts were translated into Latin and the works of Avicenna and al-Razi became the standard medical textbooks at European schools for 500 years.

 Checkpoint How did Muslim scholars preserve and build on the learning of earlier civilizations?

SECTION 3 Assessment

Progress Monitoring Online
For: Self-quiz with vocabulary practice
Web Code: naa-1031

Terms, People, and Places

1. For each term, person, or place listed at the beginning of the section, write a sentence explaining its significance.

Note Taking

2. **Reading Skill: Categorize** Use your completed chart to answer the Focus Question: What achievements did Muslims make in economics, art, literature, and science?

Comprehension and Critical Thinking

3. **Summarize** How could slaves gain their freedom in Muslim society?
4. **Recognize Cause and Effect** How did business methods of Muslim merchants encourage trade and industry?
5. **Make Generalizations** What were the central themes of Muslim literature and Arab poetry?
6. **Determine Relevance** How did Ibn Khaldun improve the study and writing of history?

● **Writing About History**

Quick Write: Use Parallel Structure Compare or contrast at least three similarities or differences between Muslim society under the Abbasids and European society in the early Middle Ages. Discuss the points about each subject in the same order. For example, you could contrast the attitude toward merchants first in Muslim society and then in European society. Use similar sentence structures to emphasize the points being compared.

Islamic Art

Most Islamic art shares distinctive characteristics. One reason for this was the prohibition on depicting humans or animals in religious art. As a result, many Muslims use a style known as arabesque, which focuses on floral and geometric shapes. Other artists created an elaborate style of calligraphy, turning the words themselves into works of art.

Flowering Patterns ▶
The arabesque appears in rugs, textiles, and glassware. The arabesque style has religious purposes, among them to show the infinity of God and the unity of Islam. Even the areas that are left empty are carefully planned to project a feeling of weightlessness.

Patterns of Glass and Stone ▼
Many mosques in the Muslim world are decorated with elaborate mosaics—thousands of small pieces of colored glass, ceramic, and stone tiles arranged to create decorative patterns and arabesques. An artist patiently fits the pieces tightly together into a concrete surface, slightly tilting each piece so that it catches the light.

▲ The Art of Beautiful Writing
Calligraphers want to make both words and the writing of them works of art. Like great European artists, gifted calligraphers were honored in Muslim society and have been studied by scholars worldwide. Some of the most elaborate examples, such as the Quran page from the 1700s above, use calligraphy to reinforce the sacred nature of the text. The fifteenth-century inkwell at left shows calligraphic designs worked in metal.

Thinking Critically

1. **Recognize Ideologies** Why did Islam prohibit the depiction of people or animals in religious art?
2. **Determine Relevance** Why would the visual elements of light and space be important artistically for the interior of mosques?

Akbar rides an elephant.

WITNESS HISTORY ◀)) AUDIO

Akbar the Great

Thirteen-year-old Akbar had grown up learning to hunt, run, and fight. Raised in the rugged country of Afghanistan, he never found the time to read and write. Now it was the year 1556, his father was dead, and the boy became *padshah*—"ruler of the empire." Under the guidance of his regent, Akbar immediately began seizing territory lost after his father's death. To seek knowledge, he had books read aloud to him. To promote unity between the Muslims and Hindus in his empire, he married a Hindu princess.

Akbar's father had foretold a bright future for his son, and Akbar fulfilled that prophecy. Many historians view Akbar as the greatest ruler in Indian history.

Focus Question How did Muslim rule affect Indian government and society?

India's Muslim Empires

Objectives

- Describe the impact the Delhi sultanate had on India.
- Explain why Muslim and Hindu traditions clashed and how they blended.
- Summarize the policies of Akbar that strengthened Mughal India.

Terms, People, and Places

sultan	Mughal
Delhi	Akbar
rajah	Nur Jahan
Sikhism	Shah Jahan
Babur	Taj Mahal

Note Taking

Reading Skill: Identify Supporting Details
Copy the outline below. As you read, finish it following the organization in the example.

> I. The Delhi Sultanate
>   A. The Sultan of Delhi Defeats the Hindus
>   1.
>   2.

The arrival of Islam brought changes to India as great as those caused by the Aryan migrations 2,000 years earlier. As Muslims mingled with Indians, each civilization absorbed elements from the other.

The Delhi Sultanate

After the Gupta empire fell in about 550, India again fragmented into many local kingdoms. Rival princes battled for control of the northern plain. Despite power struggles, Indian culture flourished. Hindu and Buddhist rulers spent huge sums to build and decorate magnificent temples. Trade networks linked India to the Middle East, Southeast Asia, and China.

The Sultan of Delhi Defeats the Hindus Although Arabs conquered the Indus Valley in 711, they advanced no farther into the subcontinent. Then around 1000, Muslim Turks and Afghans pushed into India. They were fierce warriors with a tradition of conquest. Sultan Mahmud of Ghazni pillaged much of the north, but he did not settle there. In the late 1100s, though, the **sultan,** or Muslim ruler, of Ghur defeated Hindu armies across the northern plain and made **Delhi** his capital. From there, his successors organized a sultanate, or land ruled by a sultan. The Delhi sultanate, which lasted from 1206 to 1526, marked the start of Muslim rule in northern India.

Why did the Muslim invaders triumph? They won on the battlefield in part because Muslim mounted archers had far greater mobility than Hindu forces, who rode slow-moving war elephants. Also, Hindu princes wasted resources battling one another instead of uniting against a common enemy. In some places, large numbers of Hindus, especially from low castes, converted to Islam. In the Hindu social system, people were born into castes, or social groups, from which they could not change.

Muslim Rule Changes Indian Government and Society Muslim rule brought changes to Indian government and society. Sultans introduced Muslim traditions of government. Many Turks, Persians, and Arabs migrated to India to serve as soldiers or officials. Trade between India and Muslim lands increased. During the Mongol raids of the 1200s, many scholars and adventurers fled from Baghdad to India, bringing Persian and Greek learning. The newcomers helped create a brilliant civilization at Delhi, where Persian art and architecture flourished.

The Sultans Lose Power In 1398, Tamerlane invaded India. He plundered the northern plain and smashed into Delhi. "Not a bird on the wing moved," reported stunned survivors. Thousands of artisans were enslaved to build Tamerlane's capital at Samarkand. Delhi, an empty shell, slowly recovered. The sultans no longer controlled a large empire, however, and northern India again fragmented, this time into rival Hindu and Muslim states.

✔ **Checkpoint** What changes did Muslim rule bring to Indian government and society?

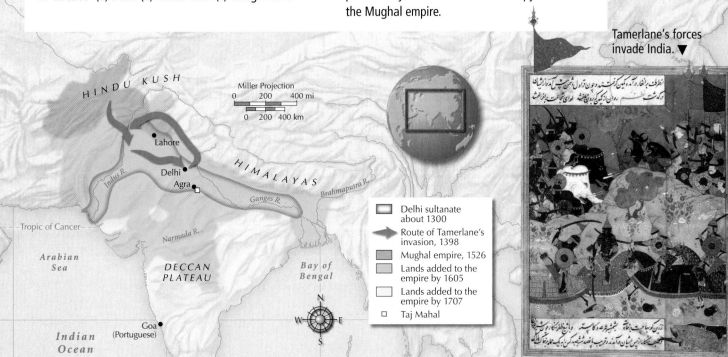

Geography *Interactive*
For: Audio guided tour
Web Code: nap-1041

Delhi Sultanate and Mughal Empire

Map Skills Two Muslim dynasties ruled much of the Indian subcontinent. The Delhi sultanate lasted more than 300 years before the Mughal dynasty replaced it.
1. **Locate** (a) Delhi (b) Hindu Kush (c) Ganges River

2. **Movement** Describe Tamerlane's route into India.
3. **Applying Information** Use the map of Asia in the Atlas and Geography Handbook to identify the present-day countries that now occupy the lands of the Mughal empire.

Tamerlane's forces invade India. ▼

HINDU KUSH

Miller Projection
0   200   400 mi
0   200   400 km

Lahore

Indus R.

Delhi

Agra

HIMALAYAS

Ganges R.

Brahmaputra R.

Tropic of Cancer

Narmada R.

Arabian Sea

DECCAN PLATEAU

Bay of Bengal

Goa
(Portuguese)

Indian Ocean

60°E   75°E   90°E

Delhi sultanate about 1300
Route of Tamerlane's invasion, 1398
Mughal empire, 1526
Lands added to the empire by 1605
Lands added to the empire by 1707
□ Taj Mahal

325

Muslims and Hindus Clash

At its worst, the Muslim conquest of northern India inflicted disaster on Hindus and Buddhists. The widespread destruction of Buddhist monasteries contributed to the drastic decline of Buddhism as a major religion in India. During the most violent onslaughts, many Hindus were killed. Others may have converted to escape death. In time, though, relations became more peaceful.

Vocabulary Builder

onslaught—(AHN slawt) *n.* a vigorous attack

Hindu-Muslim Differences The Muslim advance brought two utterly different religions and cultures face to face. Hinduism was an ancient religion that had evolved over thousands of years. Hindus recognized many sacred texts and prayed before statues representing many gods and goddesses. Islam, by contrast, was a newer faith with a single sacred text. Muslims were devout monotheists who saw the statues and carvings in Hindu temples as false gods.

Hindus accepted differences in caste status and honored Brahmans as a priestly caste. Muslims taught the equality of all believers before God and had no religious hierarchy. Hindus celebrated religious occasions with music and dance, a practice not found in Muslim worship.

A Blending of Cultures Eventually, the Delhi sultans grew more tolerant of their Hindu subjects. Some Muslim scholars argued that behind the many Hindu gods and goddesses was a single god. Hinduism was thus accepted as a monotheistic religion. As a protected subject group, Hindus were allowed to practice their religion as long as they paid a poll tax. Some sultans even left **rajahs,** or local Hindu rulers, in place.

During the Delhi sultanate, a growing number of Hindus converted to Islam. Some lower-caste Hindus preferred Islam because it rejected the caste system. Other converts came from higher castes. They chose to adopt Islam either because they accepted its beliefs or because they served in the Muslim government. Indian merchants were attracted to Islam in part because of the strong trade network across Muslim lands.

During this period, Indian Muslims also absorbed elements of Hindu culture, such as marriage customs and caste ideas. Urdu, a new language, evolved from a blend of Persian, Arabic, and Hindi. Local artisans

A sikh man prays (below left) and a statue of the Hindu god Ganesh (below right)

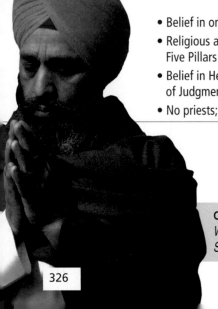

Sikhism: A Blend of Religious Beliefs

Islam	Hinduism
• Belief in one God	• Belief in many gods, all part of Brahman
• Religious and moral duties defined in Five Pillars	• Emphasis on religious and moral duties, or dharma
• Belief in Heaven and Hell, and a Day of Judgment	• Belief in a cycle of birth, death, and rebirth
• No priests; all believers are religious equals	

Sikhism
- Belief in the "Unity of God"
- Belief in reincarnation
- Rejection of caste

Chart Skills This chart shows some teachings of Hinduism, Islam, and Sikhism. *Which teachings of Sikhism are similar to those of Hinduism? Which teachings of Sikhism are similar to those of Islam?*

applied Persian art styles to Indian subjects. Indian music and dance reappeared at the courts of the sultan.

An Indian holy man, Nanak, sought to blend Islamic and Hindu beliefs. He preached "the unity of God, the brotherhood of man, the rejection of caste, and the futility of idol worship." His teachings led to the rise of a new religion, **Sikhism** (SEEK iz um), in northern India. The Sikhs later organized into military forces that clashed with the powerful Mughal rulers of India.

✔ **Checkpoint** How did Muslim and Hindu cultures clash and then blend?

Mughal India

In 1526, Turkish and Mongol armies again poured through mountain passes into India. At their head rode **Babur** (BAH bur), who claimed descent from Genghis Khan and Tamerlane. Babur was a military genius, poet, and author of a detailed book of memoirs.

Babur Founds the Mughal Dynasty Just north of Delhi, Babur met a huge army led by the sultan Ibrahim. "I placed my foot in the stirrup of resolution and my hands on the reins of confidence in God," recalled Babur. His force was small but had cannons, which he put to good use:

Primary Source

66 The sun had mounted spear-high when the onset began, and the battle lasted till midday, when the enemy was completely broken and routed. By the grace and mercy of Almighty God, this difficult affair was made easy to me, and that mighty army . . . was crushed in the dust.99
—Babur, *Memoirs*

In little time, Babur swept away the remnants of the Delhi sultanate and set up the **Mughal** dynasty, which ruled from 1526 to 1857. (*Mughal* is the Persian word for "Mongol.") The map in this section shows you that Babur and his heirs conquered an empire that stretched from the Himalayas to the Deccan Plateau.

Akbar the Great The chief builder of the Mughal empire was Babur's grandson **Akbar.** During his long reign, from 1556 to 1605, he created a strong central government, earning the title Akbar the Great.

Akbar was a leader of unusual abilities. Although a Muslim, he won the support of Hindu subjects through his policy of toleration. He opened government jobs to Hindus of all castes and treated Hindu princes as his partners in ruling the vast empire. Akbar ended the tax on non-Muslims, and he married a Hindu princess.

Akbar could not read or write, but he consulted leaders of many faiths, including Muslims, Hindus, Buddhists, and Christians. Like the early Indian leader Asoka, he hoped to promote religious harmony through tolerance. By recognizing India's diversity, Akbar placed Mughal power on a firm footing.

Akbar strengthened his empire in other ways as well. To improve government, he used paid officials in place of

Akbar (center) with his son, Jahangir, and grandson, Shah Jahan

The Taj Mahal
Shah Jahan began construction on this tomb for his wife in 1632, a year after her death. It took 22,000 workers about 20 years to complete the structure.

Vocabulary Builder
usurp—(yoo SURP) v. to seize and hold by force without legal right

hereditary officeholders. He modernized the army, encouraged international trade, standardized weights and measures, and introduced land reforms.

Akbar's Successors Akbar's son Jahangir (juh HAHN geer) was a weaker ruler than his father. He left most details of government in the hands of his wife, **Nur Jahan.** Fortunately, she was an able leader whose shrewd political judgment was matched only by her love of poetry and royal sports. She was the most powerful woman in Indian history until the twentieth century.

The high point of Mughal literature, art, and architecture came with the reign of **Shah Jahan,** Akbar's grandson. When his wife, Mumtaz Mahal, died at age 39 after having borne 14 children, Shah Jahan was distraught. "Empire has no sweetness," he cried, "life itself has no relish left for me now." He had a stunning tomb built for her, the **Taj Mahal** (tahzh muh HAHL). Designed by a Persian architect, it has spectacular white domes and graceful minarets mirrored in clear blue reflecting pools. Verses from the Quran adorn its walls, and pleasant gardens surround the entire structure. The Taj Mahal stands as perhaps the greatest monument of the Mughal empire.

Shah Jahan planned to build a twin structure to the Taj Mahal as a tomb for himself. However, before he could do so, his son Aurangzeb usurped the throne in 1658. Shah Jahan was kept imprisoned until he died several years later.

 Checkpoint   What policies did Akbar follow to strengthen his empire?

Looking Ahead

In the late 1600s, the emperor Aurangzeb rejected Akbar's tolerant policies and resumed persecution of Hindus. Economic hardships increased under heavy taxes, and discontent sparked revolts against Mughal rule. This climate of discontent helped European traders gain a foothold in the once powerful Mughal empire.

SECTION 4 **Assessment**

Progress Monitoring *Online*
For: Self-quiz with vocabulary practice
Web Code: naa-1041

Terms, People, and Places
1. For each term, person, or place listed at the beginning of the section, write a sentence explaining its significance.

Note Taking
2. **Reading Skill: Identify Supporting Details** Use your completed outline to answer the Focus Question: How did Muslim rule affect Indian government and society?

Comprehension and Critical Thinking
3. **Recognize Cause and Effect** Why were the founders of the Delhi sultanate able to conquer northern India?
4. **Analyze Information** How did relations between Hindus and Muslims evolve over time?
5. **Predict Consequences** Rulers after Akbar rejected the policy of toleration of other religious beliefs. How do you think this rejection of toleration affected relations between Hindus and Muslims?

● **Writing About History**
Quick Write: Add Transition Words Write two paragraphs comparing the major beliefs of Islam and Hinduism. Use comparison or contrast linking words—such as *similarly, in the same way, in contrast,* and *instead*—to connect your ideas as well as to highlight similarities and differences.

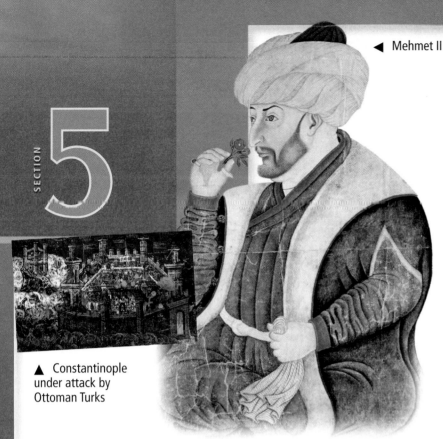

◀ Mehmet II

▲ Constantinople under attack by Ottoman Turks

WITNESS HISTORY ◀)) AUDIO

Constantinople Falls

When Mehmet II became Ottoman sultan in 1451, his goal was to conquer Constantinople, which was all that was left of the once mighty Byzantine empire. The Ottoman fleet was anchored near the city walls. The Byzantines sought help from the pope and European princes as Mehmet's grip tightened. In 1453, Mehmet began a 54-day siege of Constantinople. He used every means to break through the ancient walls of the city, including commissioning a 27-foot cannon hauled overland by oxen. As the walls were bombarded, the defenders quickly repaired them. Time, however, was running out. Constantinople fell to the Ottomans, who made the city their capital.

Focus Question What were the main characteristics of the Ottoman and Safavid empires?

The Ottoman and Safavid Empires

Objectives
- Analyze how the Ottoman empire expanded.
- Describe the characteristics of Ottoman culture.
- Explain how Abbas the Great strengthened the Safavid empire.

Terms, People, and Places

Ottomans	shah
Istanbul	Shah Abbas
Suleiman	Isfahan
janizary	Qajars
Safavid	Tehran

Note Taking

Reading Skill: Synthesize Information Copy this table. As you read, fill in key characteristics of the Ottoman and Safavid empires.

Characteristics	Ottomans	Safavids
Capital		
Dates		
Strongest ruler		
Extent of empire		
Type of Islam		
Relationship with Europe		

While the Mughals ruled India, two other dynasties—the Ottomans and Safavids—dominated the Middle East and parts of Eastern Europe. All three empires owed much of their success to new weapons that changed warfare. Cannons, and later, muskets, gave greater firepower to ordinary foot soldiers, thus reducing the importance of mounted warriors. The new military technology helped the Ottomans and Safavids create strong central governments. As a result, this period from about 1450 to 1650 is sometimes called "the age of gunpowder empires."

The Ottoman Empire Expands

Like the earlier Seljuks, the Ottomans were a Turkish-speaking nomadic people who migrated from Central Asia into northwestern Asia Minor. In the 1300s, they spread across Asia Minor and into Eastern Europe's Balkan Peninsula.

Constantinople Falls to the Ottomans Ottoman expansion threatened the crumbling Byzantine empire. After several failed attempts to capture Constantinople, Mehmet II finally succeeded in 1453. In a surprise move, the Ottomans hauled ships overland and launched them into the harbor outside Constantinople. After a nearly two-month siege, Ottoman cannons finally blasted gaps in the great defensive walls of the city, and it became the new capital of the Ottoman empire. From Constantinople (renamed Istanbul), the Ottoman Turks continued their conquests for the next 200 years.

Suleiman the Magnificent
The picture above shows the sultan Suleiman and his viziers, or advisors.

Vocabulary Builder
<u>edict</u>—(EE dikt) *n.* an order or command having the force of law

Suleiman the Magnificent The Ottoman empire enjoyed a golden age under the sultan Suleiman (soo lay MAHN), who ruled from 1520 to 1566. His people called him "the Lawgiver," while Europeans called him Suleiman the Magnificent. A brilliant general, Suleiman modernized the army and conquered many new lands. He extended Ottoman rule eastward into the Middle East, and also into Kurdistan and Georgia in the Caucasus Mountain region. In the west, Suleiman advanced deeper into Europe through diplomacy and warfare. In 1529, his armies besieged the Austrian city of Vienna, sending fear through Western Europe.

Although they failed to take Vienna, the Ottomans ruled the largest, most powerful empire in both Europe and the Middle East for centuries. At its height, the empire stretched from Hungary to Arabia and Mesopotamia and across North Africa. Suleiman felt justified in claiming to be the rightful heir of the Abbasids and caliph of all Muslims. To the title of "Emperor," he added the symbolic name of "Protector of the Sacred Places" (Mecca and Medina).

 Checkpoint What technology and techniques enabled Suleiman to extend Ottoman rule?

Ottoman Culture

Suleiman was a wise and capable ruler. He strengthened the government of the rapidly growing empire and improved its system of justice. As sultan, Suleiman had absolute power, but he ruled with the help of a grand vizier and a council. A huge bureaucracy supervised the business of government, and the powerful military kept the peace. Ottoman law was based on the Sharia, supplemented by royal <u>edicts</u>. Government officials worked closely with religious scholars who interpreted the law.

Society Is Organized Into Classes Ottoman society was divided into classes, each with its appointed role. At the top were "men of the sword"—soldiers who guarded the sultan and defended the state—and "men of the pen"—scientists, lawyers, judges, and poets. Below them were "men of negotiation," such as merchants, tax collectors, and artisans who carried out trade and production. Finally, there were "men of husbandry," or farmers and herders who produced food for the community.

The Ottomans ruled diverse peoples of many religions. The men of the sword and men of the pen were almost all Muslims, but the other classes included non-Muslims. The people were organized into millets, or religious communities. These included Muslims, Greek Christians, Armenian Christians, and Jews. Each millet had its own leaders who were responsible for education and some legal matters. The Jewish millets included many Jews who had been expelled from Spain in 1492. They brought international banking connections with them, plus a new technology for making cloth that helped the Ottoman empire finance its expansion.

Janizaries—The Elite Force Like earlier Muslim empires, the Ottomans recruited officers for the army and government from among the huge populations of conquered peoples in their empire. The Ottomans levied a "tax" on Christian families in the Balkans, requiring them to turn over their young sons for government service.

The boys were converted to Islam and put into rigorous military training at the palace school. The best soldiers won a prized place in the **janizaries** (JAN ih sehr eez), the elite force of the Ottoman army. The brightest students received special education to become government officials. They might serve as judges, poets, or even grand vizier.

Like the boys, non-Muslim girls from eastern Europe served as slaves in wealthy Muslim households. There, they might be accepted as members of the household. Some of the enslaved girls were freed after the death of their masters.

Literature and the Arts The arts blossomed under Suleiman. Ottoman poets adapted Persian and Arab models to produce works in Turkish. Influenced by Persian artistic styles, Ottoman painters produced detailed miniatures and illuminated manuscripts.

The royal architect Sinan, a janizary military engineer, designed hundreds of mosques and palaces. He compared his most famous building, the Selimiye Mosque at Edirne, to the greatest church of the Byzantine empire. "With God's help and the Sultan's mercy," Sinan wrote, "I have succeeded in building a dome for the mosque which is greater in diameter and higher than that of Hagia Sophia."

Decline of the Ottomans After Suleiman's death in 1566, the Ottoman empire began a slow decline. Suleiman had killed two of his most able sons because he suspected them of treason. His son and successor Selim II left most of the governing to his ministers, and government bureaucracy became corrupt.

By the 1700s, European advances in both commerce and military technology were leaving the Ottomans behind. Russia and other European powers captured Ottoman lands, while local rulers in North Africa and elsewhere broke away from Ottoman control. Able sultans tried to revive Ottoman power with limited success.

✓ **Checkpoint** What were the four divisions of Ottoman society?

An Ottoman soldier on horseback

WITNESS HISTORY VIDEO

Watch *Suleiman the Magnificent* on the **Witness History Discovery School**™ video program to learn more about the golden age of the Ottoman empire.

Discovery
SCHOOL

The Janizary Corps
The soldiers below wear the dress of the sultan's soldiers.

Ottoman and Safavid Empires, 1453–1629

Geography *Interactive*
For: Audio guided tour
Web Code: nap-1051

Map Skills At its greatest extent, the Ottoman empire stretched across three continents. At about the same period, the Safavid empire controlled most of what is today Iran.

1. **Locate** (a) Istanbul (b) Black Sea (c) Isfahan (d) Hungary

2. **Movement** Into what regions did the Ottoman empire expand under Suleiman?

3. **Recognize Point of View** How do you think Russians felt about the expansion of the Ottoman and Safavid empires? Explain.

Ottoman empire, 1453
Lands added, 1453–1520
Lands added under Suleiman, 1520–1566
Safavid empire at death of Shah Abbas the Great, 1629

Miller Projection
0   200   400 mi
0   200   400 km

A Center of Persian Culture Under Shah Abbas, Isfahan flourished. The shah welcomed artists, poets, and scholars to the court. Palace workshops produced magnificent porcelains, clothes, and rugs. Abbas liked to walk the streets of Isfahan in disguise, mingling with the crowds in bazaars. Amid the cries of street vendors and swarms of traders and customers, he asked people about their problems. If he heard stories of corruption, he punished the guilty.

Early 1300s
Ottoman Turks spread into Balkan Peninsula

1453
Constantinople falls to Ottoman Turks

1588–1629
Reign of Shah Abbas

1722
Safavid ruler abdicates

1300   **1400**   **1500**   **1600**   **1700**

1451–1481
Reign of Mehmet II

1520–1566
Reign of Suleiman

1629–1722
Decline of the Safavid empire

1453 Ottoman dates
1722 Safavid dates

332

The Safavid Empire

By the early 1500s, the Safavid (sah FAH vid) dynasty had united an empire in Persia (present-day Iran). Sandwiched between two expansionist powers—Mughal India and the Ottoman empire—the Safavids often engaged in warfare. Religion played a role in the conflict. The Safavids were Shiite Muslims who enforced their beliefs in their empire. The Ottomans were Sunni Muslims who despised the Shiites as heretics.

Abbas the Great The Safavid king was called the shah. The best-known, Shah Abbas the Great, revived the glory of ancient Persia. From 1588 to 1629, he centralized the government and created a powerful military force modeled on the Ottoman janizaries. Abbas used a mixture of force and diplomacy against the Ottomans. He also sought alliances with European states that had reason to fear Ottoman power.

To strengthen the economy, Abbas reduced taxes on farmers and herders and encouraged the growth of industry. Unlike earlier Safavids, Abbas tolerated non-Muslims and valued their economic contributions. He built a new capital at Isfahan (is fah HAHN), which became a center of the international silk trade. Armenians controlled the trade, so Abbas brought thousands of Armenians to Isfahan. He had a settlement built for these Christians just outside the capital, where they governed themselves.

The Safavid Empire Declines Safavid glory slowly faded after the death of Shah Abbas and under continuing pressure from Ottoman armies. Shiite scholars also challenged the authority of the shah by stressing their own authority to interpret law and determine government policy. They encouraged persecution of religious minorities, pushing Sunni Afghans to rebel. The rebels defeated imperial armies, captured Isfahan, and forced the last Safavid ruler to abdicate in 1722.

In the late 1700s, a new dynasty, the Qajars (kuh JAHRZ), won control of Iran. They made Tehran their capital and ruled until 1925. Still, the Safavids left a lasting legacy. They established Shiism firmly in Iran and gave Persians a strong sense of their own identity.

✔ **Checkpoint** How did Shah Abbas revive the glory of ancient Persia?

Vocabulary Builder

sagacious—(suh GAY shus) *adj.* having good judgment

In 1604, a Carmelite missionary visited the Persian court. The monk recorded his observations of Shah Abbas the Great. According to Abbas, how does his style of leadership differ from that of Christian rulers?

Primary Source

66 He is sagacious in mind, likes fame and to be esteemed: he is courteous in dealing with everyone and at the same time very serious. For he will go through the public streets, eat from what they are selling there and ... speak at ease freely with the lower classes ... or will sit down beside this man or that. He says that is how to be a king, and that the king of Spain and other Christians do not get any pleasure out of ruling, because they are obliged to comport themselves with so much pomp and majesty.99

—*A Chronicle of the Carmelites in Persia* ◄))) AUDIO

Progress Monitoring *Online***
For: Self-quiz with vocabulary practice
Web Code: naa-1051

Terms, People, and Places

1. For each term, person, or place listed at the beginning of the section, write a sentence explaining its significance.

Note Taking

2. **Reading Skill: Synthesize Information** Use your completed table to answer the Focus Question: What were the main characteristics of the Ottoman and Safavid empires?

Comprehension and Critical Thinking

3. **Summarize** Describe the extent of the Ottoman empire at its height.
4. **Analyze Information** How did Suleiman govern the Ottoman empire?
5. **Explain** What policies did Abbas the Great use to strengthen the Safavid empire?
6. **Draw Conclusions** Why do you think Ottoman and Safavid rulers allowed some religious toleration?

● Writing About History

Quick Write: Revise Word Choice Compare and contrast Suleiman the Magnificent with Shah Abbas the Great by examining their contributions and the effects they had on their respective empires. As you write, choose specific verbs and adjectives that highlight similarities or differences. For example, *flourished* contrasts with *grew* to emphasize the extent to which a particular culture or location developed.

Chapter 10 Section 5   333

Quick Study Guide

Progress Monitoring *Online*
For: Self-test with vocabulary practice
Web Code: naa-1061

■ Key Muslim Empires

Empire	Muhammad and First Successors (632–661)	Umayyad (661–750) (756–1031 in Spain)	Abbasid (750–1258)	Mughal (1526–1857)	Ottomans (late 1200s–1922)	Safavids (early 1500s–1722)
Key Leader(s)	• Muhammad • Abu Bakr • Umar • Ali	• Mu'awiyah	• Abu al-Abbas • al-Mansur • Harun al-Rashid	• Babur • Akbar • Jahangir • Shah Jahan • Aurangzeb	• Mehmet II • Suleiman • Selim II	• Shah Abbas
Capital	Mecca	Damascus (Córdoba in Spain)	Baghdad	Delhi, Agra	Istanbul	Isfahan

■ Spread of the Arab Empire

Cause and Effect

Long-Term Causes	Immediate Causes
• Weakness of Byzantine and Persian empires • Economic and social changes in Arabia	• Tribes of Arabia unified by Islam around a central message • Wide acceptance of religious message of Islam • Easy acceptance of social ideas of Islam, such as equality among believers

↓

Spread of Islam

↓

Immediate Effects	Long-Term Effects
• Islam spreads from the Atlantic coast to the Indus River valley • Centers of learning flourish in Cairo, Córdoba, and elsewhere	• Muslim civilization emerges • Linking of Europe, Asia, and Africa through Muslim trade network • Arabic becomes shared language of Muslims • Split between Sunnis and Shiites

■ Five Pillars of Islam

- Make the declaration of faith: "There is no god but God, Muhammad is the messenger of God."
- Pray five times per day, facing Mecca.
- Give alms (charity) to the poor.
- Fast from sunrise to sunset during Ramadan.
- Make the hajj, or pilgrimage to Mecca, if physically and financially able.

■ Key Muslim Scholars

- Firdawsi—writer and poet, *Shah Namah (Book of Kings)*
- Omar Khayyám—scholar, astronomer, poet, *The Rubáiyát*
- Ibn Rushd (Averroës)—philosopher, physician, astronomer, judge
- Ibn Khaldun—philosopher and historian
- al-Khwarizmi—mathematician, astronomer, pioneered algebra
- Muhammad al-Razi—physician
- Ibn Sina (Avicenna)—physician, *Canon on Medicine*

■ Key Events of Muslim Civilization

622 Muhammad and his followers journey from Mecca to Medina.

750 Abu al-Abbas establishes the Abbasid dynasty.

900 Arabs complete the conquest of Sicily.

Muslim Events
Global Events

600 — **800** — **1000**

732 Muslims are defeated at the battle of Tours, halting Islam's advance into Western Europe.

802 Jayavarman is crowned god-king of the Khmer empire in Cambodia.

982 Eric the Red establishes the first Viking colonies in Greenland.

Concept Connector

Cumulative Review

Record the answers to the questions below on your Concept Connector worksheets. In addition, record information from this chapter about the following concepts:

- Cultural Diffusion: Spread of Islam
- Empires: Abbasid Empire
- Empires: Mughal Empire

1. **Belief Systems** Muhammad said, "Know ye that every Muslim is a brother to every other Muslim and that ye are now one brotherhood." How might this idea have increased the appeal of Islam to conquered peoples?

2. **Empires** Research the Ottoman sultan Suleiman the Magnificent. Then write a brief essay explaining why Suleiman earned the title "magnificent." Read to learn more about Suleiman's
   - military achievements
   - political changes
   - cultural advancements
   - social changes
   - personal triumphs and tragedies
   - system of janizaries
   - successor

3. **Technology** How did new military technology benefit the Ottoman and Safavid empires? Research to learn more about the following:
   - cannons
   - muskets
   - gunpowder
   - shipbuilding and sailing technology

Connections to Today

1. **Belief Systems** Islam is the religion of nearly one-fifth of the world's population, with millions of Muslims making the hajj, or pilgrimage, to Mecca each year. Research to learn more about the hajj, including when it occurs, the various actions that pilgrims are required to perform, and what those actions symbolize. Include information about what the government of Saudi Arabia does to prepare the city of Mecca for the millions of Muslims who arrive annually to fulfill one of the Pillars of Islam.

2. **Cultural Diffusion** Akbar the Great spoke eloquently about the diversity he found in his land: "O God, in every temple I see people that seek You. In every language I hear spoken, people praise You. If it be a mosque, people murmur the holy prayer. If it be a Christian church, they ring the bell for love of You. . . . It is You whom I seek from temple to temple." Should a nation encourage diversity? Or can lack of unity weaken the fabric of a society? As an American, you live in a highly diverse society. Write a statement in which you identify and explain two advantages and two disadvantages this diversity brings to American society.

History Interactive
For: Interactive timeline
Web Code: nap-1061

1099
Christian crusaders capture Jerusalem from the Muslims.

1206
Muslims set up the Delhi sultanate in northern India.

1453
Mehmet II and the Ottomans capture Constantinople.

1520
Suleiman the Magnificent rules the Ottoman empire.

1588
Shah Abbas the Great begins reign of Safavid empire in Persia.

1200   **1400**   **1600**

1066
William of Normandy defeats Harold at the Battle of Hastings and becomes king of England.

1279
The Mongols gain control of China.

1347
The Black Death devastates Europe.

c. 1503–1506
Leonardo da Vinci paints the *Mona Lisa.*

1558
Elizabeth I becomes queen of England.

Chapter Assessment

Terms, People, and Places

Match the following terms with the definitions listed below.

mosque	rajah
caliph	jihad
calligraphy	minaret
janizary	Sufi
shah	sultan
Quran	Sharia

1. Islamic law
2. successor to Muhammad
3. struggle in God's service
4. Islamic house of worship
5. elite force of the Ottoman army
6. authority or ruler in the Turkish empires
7. art of beautiful handwriting
8. Hindu ruler
9. a Muslim mystic
10. king in Safavid empire

Main Ideas

Section 1 (pages 304–309)
11. What are the Five Pillars of Islam?
12. Who are the "People of the Book," and how did Muslims regard them?

Section 2 (pages 310–316)
13. Who was the first caliph, and how did he reunite the Arabs?
14. How did Muslims treat conquered peoples?

Section 3 (pages 317–323)
15. Describe three business practices introduced by Muslim traders.
16. What medical advances were made by Muslim physicians?

Section 4 (pages 324–328)
17. Why did many Hindus convert to Islam during the Delhi sultanate?
18. How did Akbar's rule affect life in India?

Section 5 (pages 329–333)
19. What were the four social divisions in the Ottoman empire?
20. How did Abbas the Great strengthen the Safavid economy and encourage trade?

Chapter Focus Question
21. Who was Muhammad, and how did his teachings lead to the rise and spread of Islam?

Critical Thinking

22. **Analyze Information** In what ways was traditional Bedouin society different from the society that was formed under Islam?
23. **Draw Conclusions** Muhammad taught that "the ink of the scholar is holier than the blood of the martyr." What do you think he meant? How might this attitude have contributed to the development of Muslim civilization?
24. **Recognize Cause and Effect** Do you think there would have been a split between Sunni and Shiites if Muhammad had designated a successor before he died? Explain.
25. **Geography and History** How do you think the geography of the Middle East might have helped Muslims spread the teachings of Islam throughout the region?
26. **Make Inferences** Do you think Ottoman policies encouraged Christians in the empire to be loyal or disloyal to their Muslim rulers? Explain.
27. **Predict Consequences** How do you think Safavid shahs might have been able to halt or slow the decline of their empire after the reign of Abbas the Great?

● Writing About History

Expository Essay: Compare and Contrast Akbar the Great is considered by historians to be the greatest ruler in Indian history. The reign of his great-grandson Aurangzeb, in contrast, is highly controversial. Although often criticized because of his intolerance toward Hindus, Aurangzeb attempted to eliminate many social evils. Research the two rulers and then write a compare-and-contrast essay on their respective reigns.

Prewriting
• Write a list of the various categories you wish to compare and contrast. Refer to this list as you collect the facts and details you need to write a compare-and-contrast essay.

Drafting
• Discuss the points about each subject in the same order. For example, you could write about Akbar's view toward scholars first, followed by Aurangzeb's view. Use similar sentence structures to emphasize the points being compared.
• Give vivid and descriptive details about each point of comparison to make your essay more accessible to readers.
• Use comparison or contrast linking words—such as *similarly, in the same way, in contrast,* and *instead*—to connect your ideas as well as to highlight similarities and differences.

Revising
• Use the guidelines for revising your essay on page W22 of the Writing Handbook.

Document-Based Assessment

Muslim Trade Networks

In the eighth century A.D., Arab armies spread Islam across North Africa and deep into Asia. Muslim traders advanced in their wake, taking control of established trade routes on both continents. Pilgrims followed these same routes on the annual *hajj* to Mecca, eastward from Africa and westward from Asia. Trade and religion united this vast empire, as the documents below illustrate.

Document A

"Under the Abbasids, the center of the Moslem world was the city of Baghdad (Gift of God), founded by Caliph al-Mansur in 762 on the west bank of the Tigris. . . . The site was not chosen by inadvertence, for the Moslems had taken over the existing long-distance networks that had operated in the East for centuries. . . . if the pilgrimage caravans made only one round trip a year in the prescribed season, it was the traders who, as always, kept the Silk Road active all the year round. By the ninth century, some Arab traders had pushed overland to China."

—From ***The Silk Road*** by Irene M. Franck and David M. Brownstone

Document B

A muezzin calls Muslims to prayer in Urumqi, China.

Document C

"The speed of the Arab conquest of North Africa had been made possible because of the way the Arabs treated the desert as a highway rather than an obstacle. . . . [Control of the Sahara] gave the Arab conquerors immediate control of the inland caravan routes, which had previously been controlled by independent tribal powers . . . These inland routes were put to immediate use by merchants, messengers, military reinforcements and Mecca-bound pilgrims, for they were less dangerous than maritime travel."

—From ***A Traveller's History of North Africa*** by Barnaby Rogerson

Document D

African and Arab Muslims on a merchant ship

Analyzing Documents

Use your knowledge of Muslim civilizations and Documents A, B, C, and D to answer questions 1–4.

1. According to Document A, one reason the Abbasids chose Baghdad as their capital was the city's
   A religious significance to pilgrims.
   B lack of merchants.
   C location near the Silk Road.
   D strategic location for Arab armies.

2. Documents B and D support the statement that
   A All Muslims are Arabs.
   B All Arabs are Muslim.
   C Muslims are ethnically diverse.
   D Muslims only traded over land.

3. According to Document C, the Arabs did not consider the Sahara an obstacle. Why?
   A The Sahara is vast, hot, and dry.
   B The Arabs knew that their enemies would get lost there.
   C The Arabs liked traveling on large, hot highways.
   D The Arabs were used to traveling in the desert.

4. **Writing Task** In what sense did the Muslim trade routes make up a true "network"? Use these documents and information from the chapter to form your answer.

Kingdoms and Trading States of Africa

730 B.C.–A.D. 1591

Merchants at the Royal Court of Benin

By the late 1400s, merchants from Europe arrived at the Royal Court of Benin in West Africa in search of slaves, pepper, stone beads, cloth, and ivory. Such trade brought great wealth and power to the medieval kingdoms of Africa.

The intricate detail on this West African saltcellar reveals the value of the salt it held.

66 After [the king of Benin] had . . . commanded of them the cause of their coming into the country, they answered . . . that they were merchants, traveling into those parts for the commodities of his country for exchange of wares. . . . The king . . . having . . . a certain storehouse . . . of pepper, willed them to look upon the same, and . . . to bring him a sight of such merchandise as they had brought with them. . . . when they were returned and the wares seen, the king grew to this end with the merchants to provide in 30 days the lading of all their ships with pepper. . . . and thereupon sent the country round about to gather pepper. . . . So that within . . . 30 days, they had gathered fourscore tons of pepper. 99

Listen to the Witness History audio to hear more about trade in medieval Africa.

◄ Bronze plaque of Benin warriors in their battle dress

Illustrated Arabic manuscript from the fifteenth century

Chapter Preview

Chapter Focus Question How did trade influence the development of the kingdoms and trading states of Africa?

Shields were used for ceremonial as well as defensive purposes.

Note Taking Study Guide *Online*
For: Note Taking and Concept Connector worksheets
Web Code: nad-1101

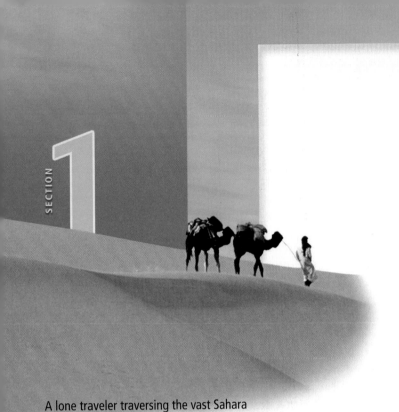

A lone traveler traversing the vast Sahara

Twelfth-century illustration of a traveling caravan

WITNESS HISTORY 🔊 AUDIO

Danger in the Desert

In 1325 a young Moroccan named Ibn Battuta began his pilgrimage to Mecca. This expedition led to a journey throughout Asia and Africa that lasted more than 30 years. Here, Battuta describes the dangers of crossing the Sahara.

66 That desert . . . make[s] sport of him [the traveler] and disorder[s] his mind, so that he loses his way and perishes. For there is no visible road or track . . . nothing but sand blown hither and thither by the wind. You see hills of sand in one place, and afterwards you will see them moved to quite another place. 99

Focus Question How did geography and natural resources affect the development of early societies throughout Africa?

Early Civilizations of Africa

Objectives

- Understand how geography affected migration, cultural development, and trade in Africa.
- Describe the rise and decline of Nubia.
- Explain how outside influences led to change in North Africa.

Terms, People, and Places

Sahara	Bantu
savanna	Nubia
cataract	Meroë
desertification	

Note Taking

Reading Skill: Identify Causes and Effects
As you read this section, make an outline like the one below to keep track of the important effects caused by Africa's geography and natural resources.

> I. The influence of geography
>   A. Geographic patterns
>   1.
>   2.
>   B. Resources spur trade
>   1.
>   2.

The vast and perilous Sahara, the largest desert in the world, is just one geographic feature in the great variety of African landscapes. For thousands of years, the geographic features of this huge continent have played a major role in its development.

The Influence of Geography

Africa is the second largest continent. Its size and location contribute to its wide range of climates, vegetation, and terrains. This variety has greatly influenced the diversity of culture found in Africa.

Geographic Patterns As shown on this section's map, Africa's vegetation regions create wide bands that stretch across the continent. Along the Equator is a band of tropical rain forest. Moving north and south from this band are the continent's largest and most populated regions, the savannas, or grassy plains. Beyond the savannas lie the great African deserts. These vegetation regions affect how people live and how they make a living.

Africa's geographic features also influenced cultural development by acting as barriers or highways to easy movement of people, goods, and ideas. In addition to the deserts and rain forests, Africa's high plateau interior and rivers with cataracts, or waterfalls, hindered easy movement. While on the other hand, the Great Rift Valley served as an interior passageway and the Mediterranean and Red seas provided overseas trade routes to regions in southwest Asia and present-day Europe.

Resources Spur Trade Since ancient times, Africa's mineral wealth has spurred trade across the continent. Salt, gold, iron, and copper were particularly valuable items to early trade and brought great wealth and power to African trading cities. Trade also linked Africa to other continents.

Initially hindered by the vast deserts, early trade greatly expanded with the introduction of a new form of transportation from Asia—the camel. By A.D. 200, these "ships of the desert" had revolutionized trade across the Sahara. Although early traders had made the difficult desert crossing in horse-drawn chariots, camel caravans created new trade networks. Camels could carry heavy loads and plod 20 or 30 miles a day, often without water. The caravans brought great profits to merchants on both sides of the Sahara.

✓ **Checkpoint** What geographic features limited movement in Africa and what made them obstacles?

People and Ideas Migrate

Archaeologists have uncovered evidence that Africa was the home of the earliest ancestors of modern people. In spite of geographic barriers, various members of these groups migrated all over Africa and beyond.

The Sahara Dries Out In Africa, as elsewhere, Paleolithic people developed skills as hunters and food gatherers. By 5500 B.C., Neolithic farmers had learned to cultivate the Nile Valley and to domesticate animals. As farming spread across North Africa, Neolithic villages even appeared in the Sahara, which was then a well-watered area. Ancient rock paintings have been found that show a Sahara that was full of forests and rivers.

About 2500 B.C., a climate change slowly dried out the Sahara. As the land became parched, the desert spread. This process of **desertification** devoured thousands of acres of cropland and pastureland. The Sahara's desertification prompted migration, as people were forced to seek new areas to maintain their ways of life.

The Bantu Migrations Over thousands of years, migrations contributed to the rich diversity of cultures in Africa. Scholars have traced these migrations by studying language patterns. They have learned, for example, that West African farmers and herders migrated to the south and east between about 1000 B.C. and A.D. 1000. Like the Indo-European peoples of Europe and Asia, these West African peoples spoke a variety of languages deriving from a single common language. The root language is called **Bantu,** which gives this movement its name— the Bantu migrations.

As they migrated into southern Africa, the Bantu-speakers spread their skills in farming, ironworking, and domesticating animals. Some existing cultures merged with those of the Bantu-speakers wherever they settled. The influence of the Bantu-speakers is still found in the languages of the region today.

✓ **Checkpoint** How did migration affect the development of African cultures?

The Great Rift Valley
Extending approximately 4,000 miles from Southwest Asia through East Africa, the Great Rift Valley is the longest rift, or deep trench, on Earth's surface. Although many of Africa's highest mountains border the valley, this relatively low and flat corridor was an important passageway for early migrating groups in Africa. *Why do you think the Great Rift Valley would be ideal to travel through?*

Africa's Vegetation

Geography *Interactive*
For: Audio guided tour
Web Code: nap-1111

Map Skills Africa consists of four major vegetation regions. These regions affected where and how people lived.

1. **Locate** (a) the Sahara Desert (b) the Great Rift Valley (c) the Congo River (d) the Mediterranean Sea (e) the Nile River (f) the Red Sea

2. **Movement** Why do you think the Bantu-speakers migrated south in the pattern described instead of north?

3. **Predict Consequences** Using the information provided in the map, predict three areas where you think a trade settlement would most likely develop. Explain your reasoning.

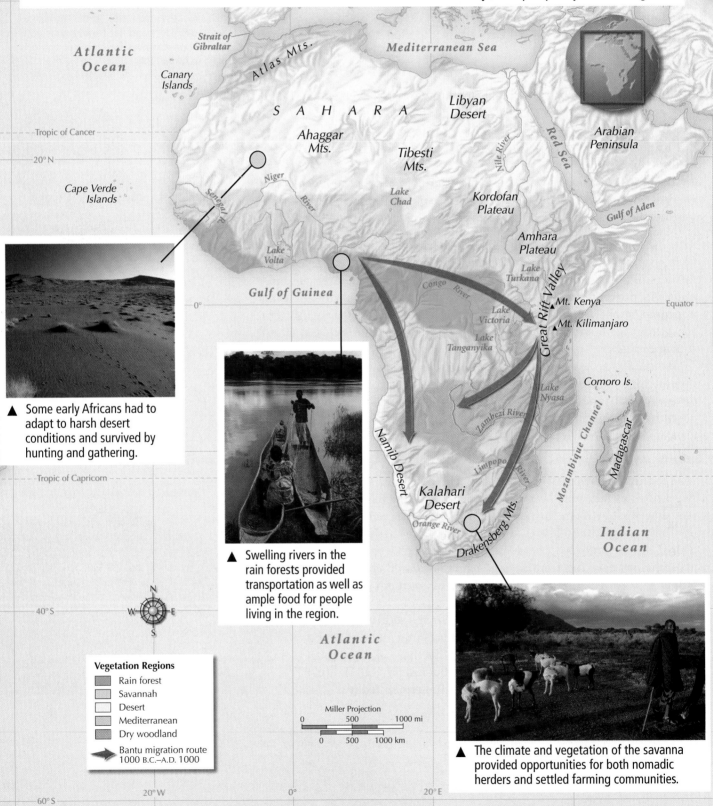

▲ Some early Africans had to adapt to harsh desert conditions and survived by hunting and gathering.

▲ Swelling rivers in the rain forests provided transportation as well as ample food for people living in the region.

▲ The climate and vegetation of the savanna provided opportunities for both nomadic herders and settled farming communities.

Vegetation Regions
- Rain forest
- Savannah
- Desert
- Mediterranean
- Dry woodland
- Bantu migration route 1000 B.C.–A.D. 1000

Miller Projection
0   500   1000 mi
0   500   1000 km

Nubia Flourishes Along the Nile

About 2700 B.C. the great civilization of Egypt was growing along the northern banks of the Nile. At the same time, as shown on the map in the next section, another African civilization was taking shape to the south. On a wide band of fertile land on the upper Nile, the ancient kingdom of **Nubia,** also called Kush, was flourishing in present-day Sudan.

Nubia Rivals Egypt Trade led to contact between Nubia and Egypt. It also led to rivalry as both powers desired to control trade in the region. By 1500 B.C., Nubia was under Egyptian control and remained so for almost 500 years. As a result, Nubians adapted many Egyptian traditions. They modeled palaces and pyramids on Egyptian style and worshiped Egyptian deities.

By 1100 B.C., Egyptian control was declining and Nubia gained its independence. In fact, about 730 B.C., the Nubian king Piankhi (PYAHN kee) actually conquered Egypt. In 670 B.C., however, Nubia was invaded by the Assyrians from Southwest Asia. Unable to match the superior iron weapons of these invaders, the Nubian armies were forced to retreat from Egypt and returned to the south.

Meroë Masters Trade and Iron By 500 B.C., Assyrian invaders had forced Nubian rulers to move their capital from Napata to **Meroë** (MEHR oh ay). Meroë eventually commanded both the Nile's north-south trade route and the east-west trade route from the Red Sea to North Africa. Along this wide trade network, Nubia sent gold, ivory, animal skins, perfumes, and enslaved people to the Mediterranean world and Southwest Asia. Meroë's location was a major reason for its development into a successful center of trade.

Equally important, however, was the region's resources. Meroë was rich in iron ore. Fueled by the region's large quantities of timber, the smelting furnaces of Meroë produced the iron tools and weaponry needed to feed, control, and defend the kingdom. Today, giant heaps of iron waste remain as evidence of ancient Meroë's industry.

Splendor and Decline Although Nubia absorbed much from Egypt, Nubian culture later followed its own course. For example, after gaining independence from Egypt, Nubians worshiped their own gods, including Apedemak, a lion-headed warrior god. At Meroë, artistic styles reflected a greater sense of freedom than did Egyptian styles. Nubians also created their own system of writing, using an alphabet instead of hieroglyphics. Unfortunately, the Nubian alphabet has yet to be deciphered and still remains a mystery.

After the joint reign of King Natakamani and Queen Amanitere in the first century A.D., the splendor of Nubia's golden age dimmed. Finally, about A.D. 350, Nubia was overwhelmed by King Ezana's armies from the kingdom of Axum to its south. Axum would then make its own mark on this region along the Nile.

✔ **Checkpoint** How did conquest affect the development of Nubia?

Cultural Exchange
The Nubian bronze of the Egyptian god Amun (top), was worshipped by some Nubians after they conquered Egypt. The rings with seals (bottom) were found among the funerary treasure of the Meroë queen Amanichaheto. *How do these artifacts illustrate the cultural exchange between Egypt and Nubia?*

Arabic Influences Scholarship
Arabic books with beautifully illustrated title pages such as the one above may have been used by students at early North African universities.

Vocabulary Builder
utilized—(YOOT il yzd) *vt.* put to practical use

Outside Influences Affect North Africa

The Nile was not the only waterway that influenced the development of civilizations in Africa. Early African civilizations also had strong ties to the regions across the Mediterranean and Red seas.

Phoenicians Build Carthage As Nubia was thriving along the Nile, Carthage was rising as a great North African power. Founded by Phoenician traders as a port on the Mediterranean coast, Carthage came to dominate western Mediterranean trade. From 800 B.C. to 146 B.C., it forged an empire that stretched from present-day Tunisia, Algeria, and Morocco to southern Europe. As you have read, however, territorial and trade rivalries between Rome and Carthage eventually led to a series of conflicts called the Punic Wars. At the end of the Third Punic War, the Romans literally burned Carthage to the ground.

Rome Rules North Africa After defeating Carthage, Rome gained control of the narrow strip of North Africa between the Mediterranean coast and the Sahara. There, they built roads, dams, aqueducts, and cities. The Romans developed and <u>utilized</u> North Africa's farmlands as a granary—a region that produces much grain—to feed the Roman empire. North Africa also provided soldiers for the Roman army, including Septimius Severus who would later become an emperor of Rome.

Under Roman rule, Christianity spread to the cities of North Africa. In fact, St. Augustine, the most influential Christian thinker of the late Roman Empire, was born in present-day Algeria. From A.D. 395 to A.D. 430, Augustine was bishop of Hippo, a city located near the ruins of ancient Carthage.

Islam Spreads Into Africa In the 690s, Muslim Arabs conquered and occupied the cities of North Africa. By the early 700s, they had successfully conquered the Berbers, a largely nomadic North African people. Under Arab rule, Islam eventually replaced Christianity as the dominant religion of North Africa, and Arabic replaced Latin as its language. Muslim civilization blossomed in cities such as Cairo, Fez, and Marrakesh, which became famous for their mosques and universities. Over time, Muslim traders from North Africa carried Islam into West Africa.

 Checkpoint How did trade cause change in North Africa?

Progress Monitoring *Online*
For: Self-quiz with vocabulary practice
Web Code: naa-1111

Terms, People, and Places

1. For each term, person, or place listed at the beginning of the section, write a sentence explaining its significance.

Note Taking

2. **Reading Skill: Identify Causes and Effects** Use your completed outline to answer the Focus Question: How did geography and natural resources affect the development of early societies throughout Africa?

Comprehension and Critical Thinking

3. **Recognize Cause and Effect** How did its geography affect movement in Africa?

4. **Determine Relevance** How did the Bantu migrations contribute to Africa's cultural diversity?

5. **Draw Conclusions** Why did the kingdom of Nubia prosper?

6. **Identify Central Issues** What factors motivated outsiders to conquer regions of North Africa?

● **Writing About History**

Quick Write: Understanding Chronology Using the information provided in this section, make a timeline of the events described. Make sure that you place each event in chronological order.

Cultural Diffusion

In what ways have migration and trade affected cultures?

During their migration, Bantu-speaking peoples from West Africa slowly diffused, or spread, their language over much of the African continent. Today, some 85 million Africans speak one of the many Bantu languages. Throughout history, migrants like the Bantu have carried their language, religion, and other cultural traits with them as they traveled. Merchants, too, have introduced their cultures to people along their trade routes. In these ways migration and trade have often influenced existing cultures. Consider the following examples:

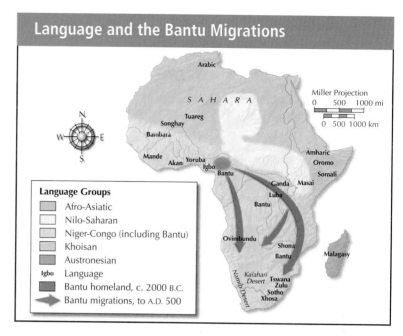

Language and the Bantu Migrations

Language Groups
- Afro-Asiatic
- Nilo-Saharan
- Niger-Congo (including Bantu)
- Khoisan
- Austronesian
- Igbo Language
- Bantu homeland, c. 2000 B.C.
- Bantu migrations, to A.D. 500

Sports

In the years that followed the Meiji Restoration of 1868, the Japanese looked to Western countries for ideas as they set out to modernize their country. One element of Western culture that they adopted was baseball. A young American transplant, who was teaching history at a Tokyo university, introduced the sport to his students in the early 1870s. Another American professor organized the first official baseball game in Japan. Called *yakkyuu*, or "field ball," the game's popularity grew rapidly. In 1936, Japan's first professional league fielded seven teams, and today its twelve teams compete in two leagues.

Former Tokyo Yomiuri Giants star, Hideki Matsui

Religion

Merchants from India carried Buddhism with them as they traveled along the ancient Silk Road. The oasis towns that served as markets and rest stops catered to the needs of those merchants. They allowed merchants to build monasteries, and they welcomed Buddhist monks. Eventually, the oasis dwellers themselves converted to Buddhism. In this way, by A.D. 100, the religion had reached northern China. For more than 500 years, however, Buddhism remained exclusively a religion of merchants and ruling classes. However, it finally gained popular acceptance in part by blending with traditional Chinese beliefs.

Food

The United States has welcomed immigrants from many cultures, which is reflected in the many styles of food that are now considered "American." Take pizza, for example. Brought to the United States by Italian immigrants, pizza has become a standard American food. So has the hamburger, probably introduced by German immigrants. Bagels, first brought to New York City by Jewish immigrants, can be found in most American supermarkets. Today, the taco, a favorite of Mexican immigrants, is readily available throughout the country.

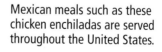
Mexican meals such as these chicken enchiladas are served throughout the United States.

Thinking Critically

1. Cultural diffusion is not usually a complete replacement of one culture with another, but rather a gradual blending of two cultures in which some new traits are adopted and others are not. Explain why you think this is true.
2. **Connections to Today** Using the map above, compare the modern African language groups with the Bantu migration routes. How do the routes of migration explain the language patterns?

Slabs of salt being
readied for market

An intricately detailed saltcellar

WITNESS HISTORY 🔊 AUDIO

The Value of Salt

In 1526, Hassan ibn Muhammad, also known as Leo
Africanus, published an account of his travels through
North and West Africa. Here he describes the value of
goods traded in Gao, a city in the African kingdom of Mali:

66 It is a wonder to see what plenty of merchandise is
daily brought hither, and how costly and sumptuous
[lavish] all things be. Horses bought in Europe for ten
ducats [coins] are here sold again for forty. . . . and
spices are sold at a high rate: but of all other commodities salt is most extremely dear [expensive]. **99**

Focus Question How did the kingdoms of
West Africa develop and prosper?

Kingdoms of West Africa

Objectives

- Understand why gold and salt were important
  in early Africa.
- Describe how the rulers of Ghana, Mali, and
  Songhai built strong kingdoms.
- Summarize how other West African societies
  developed.

Terms, People, and Places

surplus	Mali
commodity	Mansa Musa
Ghana	Songhai
Sundiata	

Note Taking

Reading Skill: Identify Causes and Effects
As you read this section, look for clues that signal
cause and effect. Then use a flowchart like the one
below to record your findings.

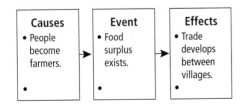

Causes		Event		Effects
• People become farmers.	→	• Food surplus exists.	→	• Trade develops between villages.
•		•		

Trading centers like that of the city of Gao developed over time
throughout Africa as trade extended beyond village borders. Some
of these medieval cities became wealthy international commercial
centers. Between 800 and 1600, several powerful kingdoms won
control of these prosperous cities and their trade.

Trade in the Sahara

Salt was rare in many regions of Africa. It was, however, important to human health. This combination made it highly prized as a
trade item. The earliest development of trade in the region, however, was tied to another important development—agriculture.

Surplus Leads to Trade As the Sahara dried out, some Neolithic
people migrated southward into the savanna, an area of grasslands
that was good for farming. By A.D. 100, settled agricultural villages
were expanding, especially along the Senegal and Niger rivers and
around Lake Chad. This expansion from farming villages to towns
was due, in part, to the development of trade.

Farming villages began to produce a **surplus,** that is, more
than they needed. They began to trade their surplus food for products from other villages. Gradually, a trade network linked the
savanna to forest lands in the south and then funneled goods
across the Sahara to civilizations along the Mediterranean and in
Southwest Asia. From West Africa, caravans crossed the Sahara
carrying leather goods, kola nuts, cotton cloth, and enslaved people. From North Africa, Arab and Berber merchants brought silk,
metal, beads, and horses.

Trading Gold for Salt Two products, gold and salt, dominated the Sahara trade. Gold was widely available in the area of present-day Ghana, Nigeria, and Senegal. It was found in the soil along rivers in various forms, including gold nuggets and dust. Experts today estimate that between A.D. 500–1600 about eight tons of gold were exported annually from West Africa.

In exchange, West Africans traded for an equally important **commodity,** or valuable product—salt. People need salt in their diet, especially in hot, tropical areas, to replace salt lost in perspiration. Salt was also important for its use in food preservation. The Sahara had an abundance of salt. At Taghaza, in the central Sahara, people even built homes out of blocks of salt. But in the savanna, several hundred miles south, salt was scarce. In fact, when caravans reached the kingdom of Ghana, merchants would pay one pound of gold for one pound of salt.

As farming and trade prospered, cities developed on the northern edges of the savanna. Soon strong monarchs arose, gained control of the most profitable trade routes, and built powerful kingdoms.

✓ **Checkpoint** How did farming lead to the development of cities?

Ghana: The Land of Gold

By A.D. 800, the rulers of the Soninke people were able to unite many farming villages and create the kingdom of **Ghana.** (The present-day country of Ghana is not the same as this ancient kingdom. Modern Ghana chose the name to celebrate Africa's rich heritage.) The ancient kingdom of Ghana was located in the fertile, broad "V" made by the Niger and Senegal rivers in present-day Mali. From there, the king controlled gold-salt trade routes across West Africa. The two streams of trade met in the marketplaces of Ghana, where the king collected tolls on all goods entering or leaving his land. So great was the flow of gold that Arab writers called Ghana "the land of gold."

Cities of Splendor The capital of Ghana was Kumbi Saleh, which was made up of two separate walled towns some six miles apart. The first town was dominated by the royal palace, which was surrounded by a complex of domed buildings. Here, in a court noted for its wealth and splendor, the king of Ghana presided over elaborate ceremonies. To his people, he was a godlike figure who <u>administered</u> justice and kept order. In the second town of Kumbi Saleh, prosperous Muslim merchants from north of the Sahara lived in luxurious stone buildings. Lured by the gold wealth of Ghana, these merchants helped make Kumbi Saleh a bustling center of trade.

Vocabulary Builder
<u>administer</u>—(ad MIN is tur) *vt.* to manage or direct

Weights of Gold
In the 1400s, a system of using standardized weights in the form of brass figures, such as the one above, to weigh the gold dust currency was developed in West Africa. The brass figures also served a cultural purpose by representing local proverbs or truisms. The gold dust currency was used to purchase items such as spices similar to those below. *Why do you think having standardized weights was important in trade?*

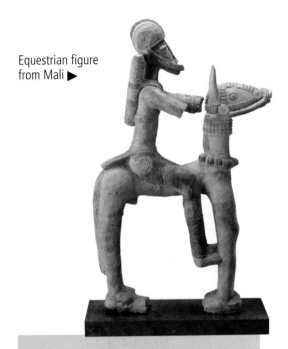

Equestrian figure
from Mali ▶

BIOGRAPHY

Sundiata

Soon after defeating Sumanguru, the ruler who had spared him from execution, Sundiata (?–1255) gained control of Kumbi Saleh, the capital of Ghana. Over the next two decades, Sundiata then proceeded to expand his power and the Mali empire. In addition to his military leadership, he was renowned for his administrative and law-making skills. Even now his leadership is still felt as elements of his legal system still govern the Malinke people today.

Sundiata, whose achievements are legendary, is celebrated as a great hero in West African oral traditions. In fact, West African griots, or storytellers, have passed down the epic of Sundiata from memory for hundreds of years. **Why do you think Sundiata's accomplishments are still celebrated today?**

Vocabulary Builder

tolerance—(TAHL ur uns) *n.* a fair and objective attitude toward opinions and practices which differ from one's own

Influence of Islam Muslim merchants brought their Islamic faith with them to the kingdom of Ghana. The king employed Muslims as counselors and officials, gradually incorporating some of their military technology and ideas about government. Muslims also introduced their written language, coinage, and business methods. Although Islam spread slowly at first, in time, a few city dwellers adopted the religion. However, most of the Soninke people continued to follow their own traditional beliefs.

About 1050, the Almoravids (al muh RAH vuds), pious Muslims of North Africa, launched a campaign to take control of Ghana's trade routes. They eventually overwhelmed Ghana, but were unable to maintain control over their extended empire for long. In time, Ghana was swallowed up by a rising new power, the West African kingdom of Mali.

✔ **Checkpoint** What effect did trade have on the West African kingdom of Ghana?

The Kingdom of Mali

Amid the turmoil of Ghana's collapse, the Mandinka people on the upper Niger suffered a bitter defeat by a rival leader. Their king and all but one of his sons were executed. According to tradition, the survivor was Sundiata, a sickly boy regarded as too weak to be a threat. By 1235, however, Sundiata had crushed his enemies, won control of the gold trade routes, and founded the empire of Mali.

Mansa Musa Rules Mali *Mali* is an Arab version of the Mandinka word that means "where the king dwells." The *mansas*, or kings of Mali, expanded their influence over the gold-mining regions to the south and the salt supplies of Taghaza. Where caravan routes crossed, towns like Timbuktu mushroomed into great trading cities.

The greatest ruler of the kingdom of Mali was Mansa Musa (MAHN sah MOO sah), who came to the throne in about 1312. He expanded Mali's borders westward to the Atlantic Ocean and pushed northward to conquer many cities. During his 25-year reign, Mansa Musa worked to ensure peace and order in his empire. He converted to Islam and based his system of justice on the Quran. However, in order to ensure prosperity and peace in his kingdom, he did not impose Islam on the people, but promoted religious freedom and tolerance.

The Hajj of Mansa Musa In 1324, Mansa Musa fulfilled one of the Five Pillars of Islam by making the hajj, or pilgrimage, to Mecca. Through his pilgrimage, Mansa Musa showed his devotion to Islam. He also forged new diplomatic and economic ties with other Muslim states. In addition, he brought back scholars, architects, and teachers who helped promote Islamic education in Mali. In fact, an Islamic university was built in Timbuktu, which attracted students from far and wide. This movement of wealth, people, and ideas increased Mali's renown.

✔ **Checkpoint** What did Mansa Musa accomplish during his reign over the kingdom of Mali?

Trans-Saharan Trade

People of West Africa traded among themselves for many centuries. By about the 400s, this regional trade system had grown into an extensive trans-Saharan trade system connecting much of Africa. Traveling along these desert routes was long as well as dangerous. It could take over three months to cross the desert. To make the investment worth the trip, large caravans with more than 1,000 camels were assembled. Control of these trade routes led to rivalry and conquest, and over the centuries powerful African kingdoms rose and fell.

The wealth of the Mali empire was renowned as implied by this detail from a 1325 world map depicting Mansa Musa offering gold to a trader. ▼

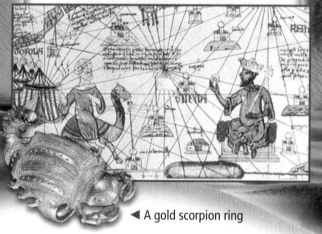

◄ A gold scorpion ring

African Kingdoms and Trading States, 1000 B.C. –A.D. 1600

Geography *Interactive*
For: Interactive map
Web Code: nap-1121

Miller Projection

	Egypt, 712 B.C.–525 B.C.
	Nubia, 1000 B.C.–A.D. 350
	Axum, 300 B.C.–A.D. 600
	Ghana, A.D. 800–A.D. 1050
	Mali, A.D. 1200–A.D. 1450
	Ethiopia, A.D. 1270–A.D. 1550
	Songhai, A.D. 1460–A.D. 1600
—	Major trade routes

A New Empire in Songhai

In the 1400s, disputes over succession weakened Mali. Subject peoples broke away, and the empire shriveled. By the 1460s, the wealthy trading city of Gao (gow) had become the capital of the emerging West African kingdom of **Songhai** (SAWNG hy).

Extending the Empire Songhai developed on the fertile region at the bend of the Niger River in present-day Mali and Niger. Between 1464 and 1492, the soldier-king Sonni Ali built the largest state that had ever existed in West Africa. Sonni Ali brought trade routes and wealthy cities like Timbuktu under his control. Unlike the rulers of Mali, he did not adopt Islam, but instead followed traditional religious beliefs.

Soon after Sonni Ali's death in 1492, however, the emperor Askia Muhammad set up a Muslim dynasty. He further expanded the territory of Songhai and improved the government. To run the empire more efficiently, he set up a bureaucracy with separate departments for farming, the military, and the treasury. Each was supervised by officials appointed by the emperor.

Thinking Critically
1. **Draw Conclusions** Why do you think West and East Africa saw a series of kingdoms develop within the same general areas?
2. **Analyze Information** How was southern Africa connected to the trans-Saharan trade system?

By the 1400s, Timbuktu had become a leading center of learning. The city drew some of the best scholars from all over the Muslim world. In his book, *History and Description of Africa*, Leo Africanus described the intellectual life of the city:

Primary Source

 Here [in Timbuktu] are great store of doctors, judges, priests, and other learned men, that are bountifully maintained at the king's cost and charges. And hither are brought diverse manuscript or written books out of Barbarie [North Africa], which are sold for more money than any other merchandise. 99

How does this description reflect the value of knowledge in Timbuktu?

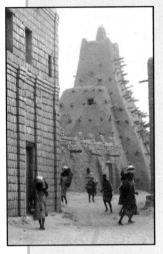

▲ Sankore Mosque, also known as the University of Timbuktu

Like Mansa Musa, Askia Muhammad made a pilgrimage to Mecca that led to stronger ties with the wider Muslim world. Scholars from Muslim lands flocked to Askia Muhammad's court at Gao. In towns and cities across Songhai, he built mosques and opened schools for the study of the Quran.

Armies Invade From the North Although Songhai continued to prosper after Askia Muhammad's death in 1528, disputes over succession led to frequent changes in leadership. In 1549, Askia Daud became emperor, and the empire experienced a period of relative peace. After his death in 1582, succession disputes recurred and led to civil war. At this time of unrest, the sultan of Morocco, Ahmad al-Mansur, sent his armies south to seize the Songhai gold and salt mines. By 1591, these invaders, using gunpowder weapons, conquered the empire.

Like the Almoravids who conquered Ghana, the Moroccans were unable to rule an empire that stretched across the Sahara. Their control over the region weakened, but the glory of Songhai could not be restored.

✓ **Checkpoint** How did Askia Muhammad help shape the empire of Songhai?

Smaller Societies of West Africa

Although smaller than the great kingdoms of Ghana, Mali, and Songhai, other societies flourished in West Africa in the period from 500 to 1500. The kingdom of Benin (beh NEEN) developed in the rain forest, while the fertile northern lands of modern-day Nigeria were home to the Hausa (HOW suh) people. As in the larger kingdoms, farming and trading were also key to the success and prosperity of these societies.

The Forest Kingdom of Benin South of the savanna, Benin rose in the rain forests of the Guinea coast. The forest peoples built farming villages and traded pepper and ivory—and later, slaves—to their neighbors in the savanna.

The rulers of Benin organized their kingdom in the 1300s. Their *oba*, or king, was a political, judicial, and religious leader. Still, much power was spread among other figures, including the queen mother and a council of hereditary chiefs.

A three-mile-long wall surrounded the capital, Benin City. There, a great palace was decorated with elaborate brass plaques and sculptures. According to tradition, artisans from Ife (EE fay), a neighboring forest society, had taught the people of Benin how to cast bronze and brass. Benin sculptors developed their own unique style for representing the human face and form. Their works depicted warriors, queen mothers, and the oba himself. Later they showed helmeted and bearded Portuguese merchants, who began to arrive in growing numbers in the 1500s.

Walled City-States of the Hausa Conflict and invasion were frequent events in West Africa. For protection, the Hausa built walls around their villages. By the 1300s, the Hausa had built a number of independent clay-walled cities. Over time, these cities expanded into thriving

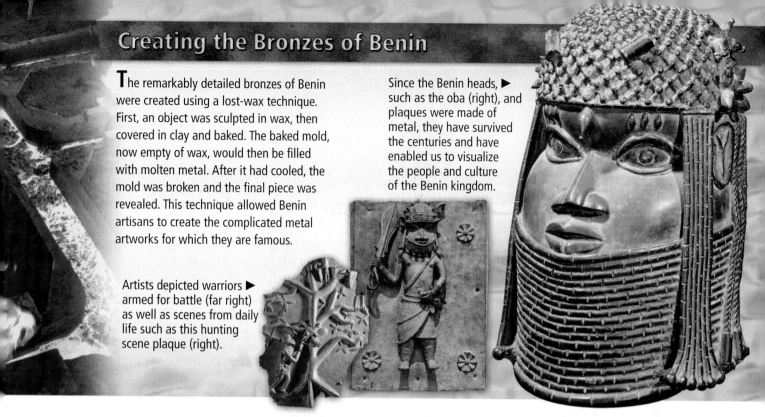

Creating the Bronzes of Benin

The remarkably detailed bronzes of Benin were created using a lost-wax technique. First, an object was sculpted in wax, then covered in clay and baked. The baked mold, now empty of wax, would then be filled with molten metal. After it had cooled, the mold was broken and the final piece was revealed. This technique allowed Benin artisans to create the complicated metal artworks for which they are famous.

Since the Benin heads, ▶ such as the oba (right), and plaques were made of metal, they have survived the centuries and have enabled us to visualize the people and culture of the Benin kingdom.

Artists depicted warriors ▶ armed for battle (far right) as well as scenes from daily life such as this hunting scene plaque (right).

commercial centers where cotton weavers and dyers, leatherworkers, and other artisans produced goods for sale. Merchants traded with Arab and Berber caravans from north of the Sahara. Hausa goods were sold as far away as North Africa and southern Europe.

Kano was the most prosperous Hausa city-state. Its walls, over 12 miles in circumference and up to 50 feet high, protected a population of more than 30,000. Kano's greatest king, Muhammad Rumfa, was a Muslim, as were many of the city's merchants and officials. During his reign, Arabic script influenced the Hausa writing system, and Islamic law greatly influenced government.

Many Hausa rulers were women, such as Amina of the city-state of Zazzau, which is located in present-day Nigeria. In the late 1500s, she conquered Kano and other regions, expanding the boundary of Zaria as far as the Niger River. Under Amina, the Hausa came to dominate many Saharan trade routes.

✔ **Checkpoint** How did other cultures influence the development of Benin and the Hausa city-states?

SECTION 2 Assessment

Progress Monitoring Online
For: Self-quiz with vocabulary practice
Web Code: naa-1121

Terms, People, and Places

1. For each term, person, or place listed at the beginning of the section, write a sentence explaining its significance.

Note Taking

2. **Reading Skill: Identify Causes and Effects** Use your completed flowchart to answer the Focus Question: How did the kingdoms of West Africa develop and prosper?

Comprehension and Critical Thinking

3. **Recognize Cause and Effect** How did the gold-salt trade develop between West Africa and North Africa?

4. **Make Comparisons** How was the reign of Mansa Musa similar to that of Askia Muhammad?

5. **Draw Conclusions** Why do you think the walls surrounding Benin City and the Hausa city-states contributed to their success in trade?

● Writing About History

Quick Write: Gather Details Choose one of the kingdoms from this section and create a list of details about the kingdom in chronological order. Make sure to include how one event led to or was influenced by the subsequent event.

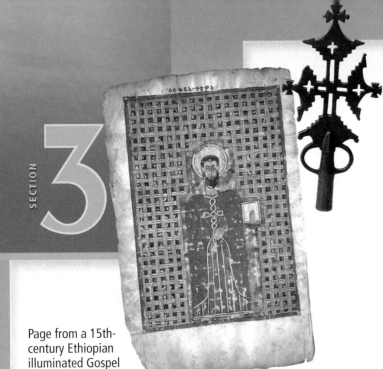

Lalibela processional cross

Page from a 15th-century Ethiopian illuminated Gospel

WITNESS HISTORY ◀)) AUDIO

Divine Intervention

Traditionally, the ancient rulers of Ethiopia commemorated their conquests by having a description of their victories inscribed on stone. In the transcription of his conquest of Nubia, King Ezana acknowledged that his success had divine assistance:

❝ May the Lord of Heaven make my kingdom strong! And as He has this day conquered my enemy for me may He conquer for me wherever I go. . . . I will rule the people with righteousness and justice, and will not oppress them. . . . I have set up this throne by the might of the Lord of Heaven. ❞

Focus Question What influence did religion and trade have on the development of East Africa?

Kingdoms and Trading States of East Africa

Objectives

- Explain how religion influenced the development of Axum and Ethiopia.
- Understand how trade affected the city-states in East Africa.
- Describe the economy of Great Zimbabwe.

Terms, People, and Places

Axum	King Lalibela
Adulis	Swahili
Ethiopia	Great Zimbabwe

Note Taking

Reading Skill: Understand Effects As you read the section, create a flowchart like the one below to keep track of the effects that trade caused on societies in East Africa.

Effects of Trade on East African Societies			
Axum	**Ethiopia**	**Coastal City-States**	**Great Zimbabwe**
• Christianity brought to region	•	• Swahili language developed	•
	•		•

About A.D. 350, King Ezana of Axum conquered and absorbed the ancient Nile kingdom of Nubia. By extending his kingdom into this region, King Ezana increased his control of the Red Sea trade, which led to an extended period of prosperity for the kingdom of Axum.

Axum: Center of Goods and Ideas

Located to the southeast of Nubia, **Axum** extended from the mountains of present-day Ethiopia to the sun-bleached shores of the Red Sea in present-day Eritrea. The peoples of Axum were descended from African farmers and people from the Middle East who brought Jewish traditions through Arabia. This merging of cultures gave rise to a unique written and spoken language, Geez.

Trade Brings Wealth The kingdom of Axum profited from the strategic location of its two main cities, the port of **Adulis** on the Red Sea and the upland capital city of Axum (see the map in the previous section). By A.D. 400, the kingdom commanded a triangular trade network that connected Africa, India, and the Mediterranean world.

A great variety of goods and enslaved people funneled in and out of the markets of these two cities. From the interior of Africa, traders brought ivory, animal hides, and gold to the markets of Axum. Goods from farther south along the African coast came to the harbor of Adulis on the Red Sea. There, the markets offered iron, spices, precious stones, and cotton cloth from India and other lands beyond the Indian Ocean. Ships carried these goods up the Red Sea, where they collected goods from Europe and countries along the Mediterranean.

Axum Converts to Christianity In these great centers of international trade, Greek, Egyptian, Arab, and Jewish merchants mingled with traders from Africa, India, and other regions. As elsewhere, ideas spread along with goods. By the 300s, Christianity had reached the region. After converting to the new religion, King Ezana made Christianity the official religion of Axum. As the religion took hold among the people, older temples were replaced with Christian churches decorated with intricately designed biblical murals and religious images painted on wood panels.

At first, Christianity strengthened the ties between Axum, North Africa, and the Mediterranean world. In the 600s, however, Islam began spreading across North Africa and other regions surrounding Axum. Many African rulers embraced this new faith, creating strong cultural ties across much of the continent. Axum, which remained Christian, was now isolated from its own trade network—by distance from Europe and by religion from many former trading partners. Civil war and economic decline combined to weaken Axum, and the kingdom slowly declined.

✔ **Checkpoint** How did the spread of religion affect the kingdom of Axum?

Ethiopia: A Christian Outpost

Though Axum's political and economic power faded, its cultural and religious influence did not disappear. This legacy survived among the peoples of the interior uplands, in what is today northern Ethiopia. Although Axum's empire was only a portion of the present-day nation, when referring to their kingdom as a whole, the Axumite kings frequently used **Ethiopia,** which was a term the Greeks used for the region.

An Isolated Ethiopia Medieval Ethiopia was protected by rugged mountains, and the descendants of the Axumites were able to maintain their independence for centuries. Their success was due in part to the <u>unifying</u> power of their Christian faith, which gave them a unique sense of identity and helped establish a culture distinct from that of neighboring peoples.

One example of Ethiopia's distinct culture is the unique churches of Lalibela. In the early 1200s, **King Lalibela** came to power in Ethiopia. During his reign, he directed the building of eleven remarkable churches, which were actually carved from ground level downward into the solid rock of the mountains. These amazing structures still exist today and illustrate the architectural and artistic skill of the craftsmen who created them.

Despite their isolation, Ethiopian Christians kept ties with the Holy Land. In fact, some made pilgrimages to Jerusalem. They also were in touch with Christian communities in Egypt. Over time, Ethiopian Christianity absorbed many local customs. Traditional East African music and dance were adapted, and their influence is still felt in Ethiopian church services today. In addition, the services are still conducted in the ancient language of Geez.

Sculpted Churches
Beta Ghiorgis (House of George) is one of the Lalibela solid rock churches created during the thirteenth century. A trench was dug to create a solid block of rock, which was then sculpted and carved into to create the interior and exterior of this cross-shaped church.

Vocabulary Builder
<u>unify</u>—(YOO nuh fy) *vt.* to form into a single unit

Ibn Battuta Witnesses a Unique Trading Tradition

Moroccan *qadi*, or judge, Ibn Battuta (1304–*c*.1368) was born in Tangier to a Berber family of the Muslim faith. After he completed his education at the age of 21, Battuta decided to make the hajj, or Muslim pilgrimage to Mecca. What started as a reasonably challenging trek for the period became one of the great journeys of medieval times. During nearly 30 years of travel, Battuta visited much of Southwest Asia, West Africa, southern Russia, India, and China. Along the way he gained fame and wealth and met kings, sheiks, and holy men—including the Byzantine emperor and the sultan of Delhi—as well as ordinary people. In this excerpt from his book, the *Rihlah*, or *Travels*, Battuta describes the unique trading tradition of Mogadishu.

◄ Ibn Battuta in Egypt

> ❝On leaving Zayla we sailed for fifteen days and came to Maqdashaw [Mogadishu], which is an enormous town. Its inhabitants are merchants.... When a vessel reaches the port, it is met by *sumbuqs*, which are small boats, in each of which are a number of young men, each carrying a covered dish containing food. He presents this to one of the merchants on the ship saying "This is my guest," and all the others do the same. Each merchant on disembarking goes only to the house of the young man who is his host.... The host then sells his goods for him and buys for him, and if anyone buys anything from him at too low a price, or sells to him in the absence of his host, the sale is regarded by them as invalid.❞
>
> —*Ibn Battuta*
> *from the* **Rihlah**

Judaism in Ethiopia The kings of Ethiopia claimed descent from the Israelite king Solomon and the queen of Sheba. This belief was recorded in an ancient Ethiopian book called *The Glory of Kings* and reinforced by the fact that Ethiopians observe some of the Jewish holidays and dietary laws. Some Ethiopians practiced Judaism rather than Christianity. These Ethiopian Jews, the Falasha, lived in the mountains of Ethiopia until the late 1900s, when most evacuated to Israel during a long famine.

✓ **Checkpoint** How did the geographic isolation of medieval Ethiopia shape its culture?

East African City-States

While Axum declined, a string of commercial cities—including Kilwa, Mogadishu, Mombasa, and Sofala—gradually arose along the East African coast. Since ancient times, Phoenician, Greek, Roman, and Indian traders had visited this region. Under the protection of local African rulers, Arab and Persian merchants set up Muslim communities beginning in the 600s. Port cities, as well as offshore islands such as Lamu and Zanzibar were ideally located for trade with Asia. As a result, Asian traders and immigrants from as far away as Indonesia soon added to the rich cultural mix.

Trading Centers Flourish By the 600s, sailors had learned that the annual monsoon winds could carry sailing ships between India and Africa. On the East African coast, rulers took advantage of the opportunities for trade that these winds provided. They welcomed ships from Arabia, Persia, and China. Traders acquired ivory, leopard skins, iron,

Journeys of Ibn Battuta

1325–1327 Journey to Mecca
1327–1330 Sea voyage to East Africa
1330–1333 Journey to South Asia

Sambuq sailing along the East African coast ▶

Thinking Critically

1. **Draw Conclusions** Why do you think the merchants of Mogadishu used this method to conduct business?

2. **Analyze Information** According to Ibn Battuta, regular merchants who traveled to Mogadishu were exempt from this strict trading practice. Why do you think some merchants were allowed this freedom?

copper, and gold from the interior of Africa, as well as from coastal regions. From India, Southeast Asia, and China came cotton cloth, silk, spices, porcelain, glassware, and swords.

Trade was not only beneficial to the merchants; it also helped local rulers build strong, independent city-states. Although they competed for trade, relations between the city-states were generally peaceful. A Muslim visitor described Kilwa, the most successful city-state, as "one of the most beautiful and well-constructed towns in the world." Its royal palace still stands on cliffs that today overlook the ocean. The <u>complex</u> consists of courtyards, terraces, and nearly 100 rooms. Built of coral and cut stone, the structure is evidence of the old city's splendor.

Vocabulary Builder

<u>complex</u>—(KAHM pleks) *n.* a group of connected buildings that form a single whole

Trade Shapes Swahili The successful East African international trade system led to the emergence of a vibrant culture and a new language both known as **Swahili.** By the 1000s, many East African coastal cities had not only grown in wealth but also in size. Traders from the Middle East and Asia began to settle permanently in flourishing trading cities such as Kilwa.

As more settlers arrived, the local East African culture absorbed cultural elements from these new residents. For example, the architecture of private houses and palaces illustrated a blend of East African and Arabic designs that created unique and elegant Swahili buildings and furniture. In addition, over time many Arabic words were absorbed into the local Bantu-based language. In fact, the term *swahili* comes from an Arabic word meaning "of the coast". The language itself was eventually written in Arabic script.

✔ **Checkpoint** How did trade influence the city-states of East Africa?

The Stone Houses of Great Zimbabwe

To the south and inland from the coastal city-states, massive stone ruins sprawl across rocky hilltops near the great bend in the Limpopo River. The looming walls, large palace, and cone-shaped towers were once part of the powerful and prosperous capital of a great inland empire. Today, these impressive ruins are known as **Great Zimbabwe.**

Inland Capital of Trade The word *zimbabwe* comes from a Bantu-based word that means "stone houses." In fact, Great Zimbabwe was built by a succession of Bantu-speaking peoples who settled in the region between 900 and 1500. These newcomers brought iron, mining methods, and improved farming skills. Early settlers raised cattle and built stone enclosures to protect their livestock. In time, these settlers improved their building methods and erected large walls and palaces.

The capital probably reached its height about 1300. By then, it had tapped nearby gold resources and created profitable commercial links with coastal cities such as Sofala. Archaeologists have found beads from India and porcelain from China, showing that Great Zimbabwe was part of a trade network that reached across the Indian Ocean. In addition, they have found artifacts that indicate that Great Zimbabwe had artisans skilled in making jewelry and weaving cotton cloth.

Very little is known about the government in Great Zimbabwe. However, after studying the architecture and artifacts of the ruins, some scholars have suggested that the ruler was a god-king who presided over a large court. Below the king, a central bureaucracy may have ruled an inner ring of provinces, while appointed governors had authority in more distant villages. Although there is much about Great Zimbabwe that remains unknown, as archaeologists continue their research, we are learning more about how the capital and empire developed.

Zimbabwe Falls to Ruins By 1500, Zimbabwe was in decline. Some scholars suggest that the population had grown too great. Civil war and dwindling trade probably contributed as well. By then, Portuguese traders were pushing inland to find the region's source of gold. They failed to discover the gold mines, but their attempts further weakened the small states that formed in the region as Zimbabwe declined.

✔ **Checkpoint** How do the ruins of Great Zimbabwe reflect the capital's former prosperity?

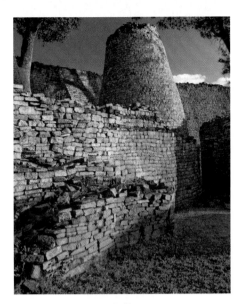

Ruins of Great Zimbabwe
The Great Enclosure, a portion of which is shown here, is one of the two major ruins of Great Zimbabwe. Archaeologists believe the enclosures did not serve any military purpose, but were built to display the ruler's power. However, much about Great Zimbabwe is still being debated.

WITNESS HISTORY VIDEO

Watch *Zimbabwe: Lost City of Africa* on the **Witness History Discovery School**™ video program to see how archaeology has helped unlock the mysteries of this medieval city.

Discovery
SCHOOL

SECTION **3** **Assessment**

Progress Monitoring *Online*
For: Self-quiz with vocabulary practice
Web Code: naa-1131

Terms, People, and Places
1. For each term, person, or place listed at the beginning of the section, write a sentence explaining its significance.

Note Taking
2. **Reading Skill: Understand Effects** Use your completed flowchart to answer the Focus Question: What influence did religion and trade have on the development of East Africa?

Comprehension and Critical Thinking
3. **Synthesize Information** Why did Ethiopia become increasingly isolated from its neighbors over the centuries?
4. **Draw Inferences** Why did the language of Swahili emerge in the East African city-states?
5. **Test Conclusions** What evidence suggests that Great Zimbabwe was a center of trade?

● **Writing About History**
Quick Write: Use Sensory Details Choose one of the locations from this section. Suppose you are a merchant or traveler entering the city for the first time. What sights and sounds do you encounter? Write a letter to your family that describes your experiences from the moment you enter the city until you reach your final destination there.

A Mossi woman from present-day Burkina Faso

Cultural Variety

Ibn Battuta traveled widely throughout Africa and Asia. His travels included more than visits to the capitals and large trading cities. He also visited small African communities where he learned of the great variety of cultures and societies that had developed on the continent.

❝The women [of the Massufa tribe] are shown more respect than the men. The state of affairs amongst these people is indeed extraordinary. . . . no one claims descent from his father, but on the contrary from his mother's brother. A person's heirs are his sister's sons, not his own sons. This is a thing which I have seen nowhere in the world. . . .**❞Focus Question** What factors influenced the development of societies in Africa?

Societies in Medieval Africa

Objectives
- Identify the different ways that the family influenced medieval African cultures.
- Describe the variety of forms of medieval African governments.
- Understand the role of religion and art in medieval societies.

Terms, People, and Places

nuclear family	lineage
patrilineal	consensus
matrilineal	griot

Note Taking

Reading Skill: Recognize Multiple Causes As you read this section, create a concept web like the one below to keep track of the factors that influenced the development of African societies.

Considering Africa's immense size, it is not surprising that Ibn Battuta came across new cultures. Factors such as Africa's varied geography, diverse climates, and later migration and trade played major roles in how early societies developed throughout the continent.

As you have read, throughout the world the Neolithic Revolution led to the beginning of settled farming communities located in areas with fertile soil and proximity to water. These farming settlements grew as surpluses increased, enabling artisans to develop specialized skills.

Advancements in transportation, such as the use of the camel, increased a community's reach beyond its borders, and this exchange allowed villages to grow into towns. Extended trade brought additional wealth, leading to the creation of individual states and kingdoms. Throughout Africa, communities varied in size, environment, and economics. However, each society, including the kingdoms you read about earlier in this chapter, developed around four common elements—family, government, religion, and art.

Family Patterns

In medieval Africa, as elsewhere, the family was the basic unit of society. Patterns of family life varied greatly depending on the culture of the group. In some small societies, for example, the basic family unit was the **nuclear family,** or parents and children living and working together as a unit. In other communities, family units included the extended family—parents, children, and several generations such as grandparents and uncles—who lived and worked close together to ensure the success of the group.

Kinship Family organization varied in other ways. Some families were patrilineal. In these families, important kinship ties such as inheritance were passed through the father's side. Other families, such as the one described by Ibn Battuta, were matrilineal, with inheritance traced through the mother's side. In some cultures, one spouse would move to the other spouse's village and join his or her parents' family.

Matrilineal cultures forged strong ties between brothers and sisters. Brothers were expected to protect their sisters, and sons were expected to help their mother's brothers whenever needed.

Extended Lineages Each family belonged to a lineage, or group of households who claimed a common ancestor. Several lineages formed a clan that traced its descent to an even more remote and often legendary ancestor. Belonging to a particular family, lineage, or clan gave people a sense of community with shared responsibilities to that community.

An individual's place in some medieval African societies was also determined by a system of age grades. An age grade included all girls or boys born in the same year. Each age grade had particular responsibilities and privileges. As they moved up from one age grade to another, children began to take part in village activities, which created social ties beyond the family.

✓ **Checkpoint** How did kinship help identify an individual's place in his or her society?

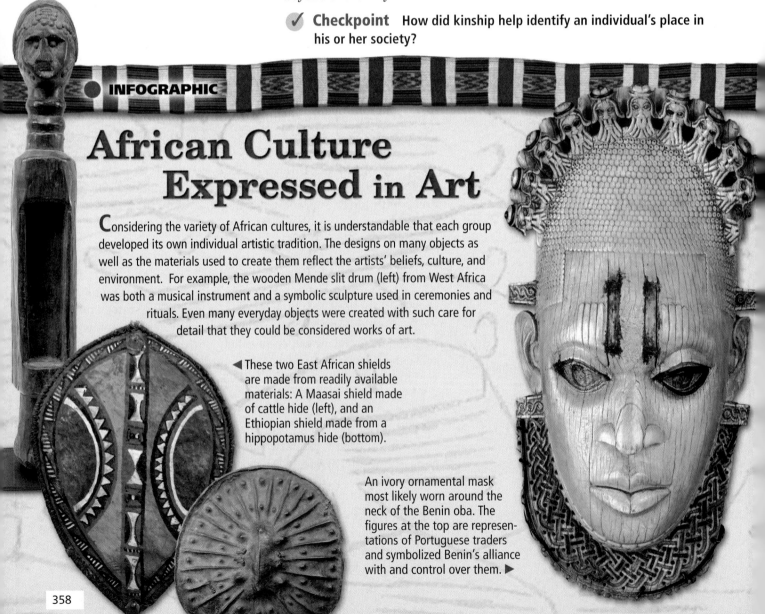

African Culture Expressed in Art

Considering the variety of African cultures, it is understandable that each group developed its own individual artistic tradition. The designs on many objects as well as the materials used to create them reflect the artists' beliefs, culture, and environment. For example, the wooden Mende slit drum (left) from West Africa was both a musical instrument and a symbolic sculpture used in ceremonies and rituals. Even many everyday objects were created with such care for detail that they could be considered works of art.

◄ These two East African shields are made from readily available materials: A Maasai shield made of cattle hide (left), and an Ethiopian shield made from a hippopotamus hide (bottom).

An ivory ornamental mask most likely worn around the neck of the Benin oba. The figures at the top are representations of Portuguese traders and symbolized Benin's alliance with and control over them. ►

Political Patterns

Most medieval African farming peoples lived in tightknit communities and helped one another in tasks such as clearing the land, planting, and harvesting. As communities grew, the need for a form of government arose. Throughout Africa, political patterns varied, depending in part on the size and culture of the community.

Power Sharing Unlike the large kingdoms, smaller medieval African societies were often organized with power shared among a number of people rather than centralized in the hands of a single leader. In some villages, a chief had a good deal of authority, but in many others, elders made the major decisions. In some places, especially in parts of West Africa, women took the dominant role in the marketplace or acted as official peacemakers in the village.

Villages often made decisions by a process known as **consensus,** or general agreement. In open discussions, people whose opinions were valued voiced their views before a final agreement was reached. Because of the experience and wisdom of older men and women, their opinions usually carried the greatest weight.

In villages that were part of a large kingdom such as Songhai, decisions made at a distant court had to be obeyed. These villagers, therefore, had to pay taxes and provide soldiers to the central, and frequently distant, government.

The gold nugget, ▶ shells, and horns on a healer's charm necklace (right) were believed to have magical healing properties.

This West African Dogon ▶ dancer is wearing a grass and shell costume and mask created for the dama funerary ceremony. During the dama, a masked dance is performed symbolizing the end of the mourning period.

▼ The elephant at the base of this West African stool identifies that it was used only by the king of the Asante.

Thinking Critically
1. **Draw Conclusions** How does the Dogon dancer's costume help identify the group's location? Explain.
2. **Synthesize Information** Why do you think symbolism was important in medieval African societies?

Limited Power Another form of government developed when many villages were grouped into districts and provinces that were governed by officials appointed by a king. The kingdom of Kongo, which flourished around A.D. 1500 in central Africa, is an example. There, each village still had its own chief. Taxes were collected through local governors either in goods or in cowrie shells, a common African currency. Unlike rulers of larger West African states who maintained strong standing armies, the kings of Kongo could only call upon men to fight in times of need. In fact, the king was actually chosen by a group of electors and had to govern according to traditional laws. It might seem as though a king wielded absolute power; however, in some societies like the kingdom of Kongo, the monarch's power was somewhat limited.

 Checkpoint How was ruling power shared in some of the smaller African societies?

Religious Beliefs

As you have read, religion played an important role in the development of medieval African societies. Religious beliefs that existed before the arrival of Islam and Christianity were varied and <u>complex</u>. Like the Hindus or ancient Greeks and Romans, some Africans worshiped many gods and goddesses. They identified the forces of nature with divine spirits and tried to influence those forces through rituals and ceremonies.

Many African peoples believed that a single, unknowable supreme being stood above all the other gods and goddesses. This supreme being was the creator and ruler of the universe and was helped by the lesser spirits, who were closer to the people. Some African peoples believed, like the Chinese, that the spirits of their ancestors could help, warn, or punish their descendants on Earth. Just as Christians in medieval Europe called on the saints for help, medieval Africans turned to the spirits of their departed ancestors.

By A.D. 1000, both Christianity and Islam had spread to many regions of Africa. Those who adopted these religions often associated the God of the Christians and Muslims with their traditional supreme being. In this way, Christianity and Islam in Africa absorbed many local practices and beliefs.

 Checkpoint Describe the religious beliefs in medieval Africa.

Traditions in Art and Literature

African artistic traditions extend far back in time to the ancient rock paintings of the Sahara, which were create by about 1000 B.C., and the over 4,000-year-old pyramids of Egypt and Nubia. More recently, but still about 1,000 years ago, the rock churches of Ethiopia and the palace of Great Zimbabwe were built. These accomplishments bear lasting witness to the creative power of these early and medieval civilizations.

Creative Arts African artists worked in many materials including gold, ivory, wood, bronze, and cloth. They created many decorative items such as woven cloth, inscribed jugs and bowls, or jewelry simply for their beauty. Even so, art usually served social and religious purposes as well.

Art strengthened bonds within the community and linked the makers and the users of the work. Patterns used to decorate textiles, baskets,

Vocabulary Builder

<u>complex</u>—(KUM pleks) *adj.* made up of different parts connected in a way that is hard to understand

swords, and other objects had important meanings or special messages that the artisan or owner wanted to convey. Often, they identified an object as the work of a particular clan or the possession of royalty. One example is kente cloth, a traditional West African textile woven of silk and cotton. When it was made in bright gold and blue colors, the symbols of power, only the ruling elite and the wealthy were allowed to wear it.

In medieval Africa, as elsewhere, much art was closely tied to religion. Statues and other objects were used in religious rites and ceremonies. In some rituals, for example, leaders wore elaborately carved masks decorated with cowrie shells or grass. Once the mask was in place, both the wearer and the viewers could feel the presence of the spiritual force it represented.

Literature Early and medieval African societies preserved their histories and values through both written and oral literature. Ancient Egypt, Nubia, and Axum left written records of their past. Later, Arabic provided a common written language in those parts of Africa influenced by Islam. African Muslim scholars gathered in cities such as Timbuktu and Kilwa. Documents in Arabic offer invaluable evidence about the law, religion, and history of the time.

Oral traditions date back many centuries. In West Africa, *griots* (GREE ohz), or professional storytellers recited ancient stories such as the Sundiata epic. The griots preserved both histories and traditional folk tales in the same way that the epics of Homer or Aryan India were passed orally from generation to generation. The histories praised the heroic deeds of famous ancestors or kings. The folk tales, which blended fanciful stories with humor and sophisticated word play, taught important moral lessons. Oral literature, like religion and art, thus encouraged a sense of community and common values within the medieval societies of Africa.

Language of Drums
Not all "oral tradition" is spoken. The talking drums of western and central Africa are used to communicate important information such as messages and announcements as well as traditional texts such as prayers and eulogies for historic individuals. *Why do you think the sound of a drum could be more powerful than the spoken word?*

✔ **Checkpoint** How did African societies preserve their history?

Assessment

Progress Monitoring Online
For: Self-quiz with vocabulary practice
Web Code: naa-1141

Terms, People, and Places

1. For each term, person, or place listed at the beginning of the section, write a sentence explaining its significance.

Note Taking

2. **Reading Skill: Recognize Multiple Causes** Use your completed concept web to answer the Focus Question: What factors influenced the development of societies in Africa?

Comprehension and Critical Thinking

3. **Recognize Cause and Effect** How did an individual's lineage affect his or her life in African societies?

4. **Demonstrate Reasoned Judgment** Do you think consensus is a fair or unfair method of decision making? Explain the reasons for your answer.

5. **Determine Relevance** How was art connected to religion in African cultures?

6. **Identify Central Issues** Why do you think art, literature, and religion inspired a sense of unity within medieval African communities?

● **Writing About History**

Quick Write: Creating Dialogue Select two individuals, such as an elder and a tribal chief or an uncle and nephew, from the topics discussed in this section and create a dialogue between them placing yourself as one of the characters. Make sure that the dialogue generally relates to one of the main subjects of the section such as government or family ties.

Quick Study Guide

Progress Monitoring *Online*
For: Self-test with vocabulary practice
Web Code: naa-1142

■ Major African Kingdoms and Trading States

Kingdom or State	Date	Location	Religion	Economic Base
Egypt	2575 B.C.–1075 B.C.	North Africa	Local religion	Trade
Nubia	1100 B.C.–A.D. 350	Northeast Africa	Local religion	Trade and iron ore
Ghana	800–1050	West Africa	Islam	Gold
Mali	1235–1400s	West Africa	Local religion and Islam	Gold and salt
Songhai	1460–1591	West Africa	Local religion and Islam	Trade
Benin	1300s–1500s	West Africa	Local religion	Pepper, ivory, and slaves
Axum	350–600s	East Africa	Christianity	Trade
Great Zimbabwe	1300s–1500s	East Africa	Unknown	Trade

■ Important Ancient and Medieval African Rulers

Ruler	Kingdom	Accomplishment
Piankhi	Nubia	Conquered Egypt and brought it under Nubian control
Sundiata	Mali	Defeated Sumanguru and founded the empire of Mali
Mansa Musa	Mali	Expanded Mali's borders and based justice system on the Quran
Askia Muhammad	Songhai	Expanded Songhai's territory and improved the government by setting up bureaucracies
Amina	Hausa city-states	Gained control of many Saharan trade routes
King Ezana	Axum	Conquered Nubia and made Christianity the official religion
King Lalibela	Ethiopia	Sponsored the building of the Lalibela churches

■ Key Events in Ancient and Medieval Africa

730 B.C.
Nubia conquers Egypt.

500s B.C.
Meroë becomes Nubian captial and controls North African trade routes.

Chapter Events
Global Events

1000 B.C.　　　　**500 B.C.**　　　　**A.D. 1**

500s B.C.
In India, the sacred Hindu texts are recorded.

460 B.C.
The Age of Pericles begins in Athens.

218 B.C.
Hannibal crosses the Alps to attack Rome during the Second Punic War.

Concept Connector

■ Cumulative Review

Record the answers to the questions below on your Concept Connector worksheets.

1. **Migration** Scholars have studied both the Bantu and Indo-European language families as a means of determining the migration patterns of both groups. Why do you think language is a good indicator of migration patterns? Why do you think tracing migration is important in understanding history? Finally, what other methods might scientists use to understand the movements of populations?

2. **Geography's Impact** As in Africa, the cultures and early history of Eastern Europe were heavily influenced by the region's geography. Compare and contrast the impact geography had on cultural development in Eastern Europe and Africa. For each region, think about the following:
   - geographic passageways and waterways
   - barriers to easy movement and access to new ideas
   - cultural links to other regions

3. **Trade** Many coastal peoples became skilled sailors thanks to their proximity to large bodies of water. Greek, Viking, and East African traders all reached distant lands using their nautical skills and gained access to the goods and ideas of distant cultures. How did this extended travel affect trade in each region? Think about the following:
   - the range of territory visited by each group
   - the type and value of goods available locally and from afar
   - the ease and availability of overland trade routes
   - competition with other groups

■ Connections to Today

1. **People and the Environment: Desertification** Parts of the Sahara were once well-watered areas with rivers that supported forests and grasslands as well as people. Beginning about 2500 B.C. and continuing today, the desert has been gradually spreading. In fact, during the early 1970s a long drought in the Sahel extended the Sahara as much as 60 miles in some areas, and the resulting famine led to the loss of almost 100,000 lives. Desertification is difficult to reverse and is considered not only a major environmental problem in Africa but a serious social and economic problem as well. However, efforts are being made to address the issue. The following African countries are heavily affected by desertification: Burkina Faso, Chad, Gambia, Ghana, Mali, Mauritania, Nigeria, Niger, Senegal, and Sudan. Select one of these nations and then conduct research on how desertification is affecting that country and what the country is doing to address the problem.

2. **Trade: Trade in the 21st Century** As you have read, the extent of medieval African trade was far-reaching. Each region provided commodities to the world that were indigenous and frequently unique to that region. The farther away a trader transported a commodity, the more its value would increase. Considering today's advances in agriculture, manufacturing, and transportation, write a one-page essay on the similarities and differences between medieval trade and trade in the twenty-first century.

History Interactive
For: Interactive timeline
Web Code: nap-1141

A.D. 300s
Axum gains control of an extensive trade network.

A.D. 600s
Islam spreads to North Africa.

A.D. 800s
Kingdom of Ghana controls West African gold-salt trade routes.

A.D. 1200s
Lalibela churches built in Ethiopia.

A.D. 1324
Mansa Musa completes his hajj to Mecca.

A.D. 1500s
The kingdom of Kongo flourishes in central Africa.

500 **1000** **1500**

A.D. 300s
Maya civilization flourishes in Mexico and Central America.

A.D. 668
The Silla dynasty unites Korea.

A.D. 1347
The Black Death begins to ravage Europe.

A.D. 1492
Christopher Columbus sails the Atlantic and reaches the Caribbean.

Chapter Assessment

Terms, People, and Places

Choose the italicized term in parentheses that best completes each sentence.

1. The most populated vegetation region in Africa is the (*Sahara, savanna*).
2. (*Adulis, Axum*) was a prosperous trading port in East Africa.
3. Some medieval African societies made political decisions using a process of (*griot, consensus*).
4. An important (*commodity, surplus*) in medieval African trade was salt.
5. A (*patrilineal, matrilineal*) family passes inheritance through the father's side.
6. (*Bantu, Swahili*) is a root language used by scholars to understand early African migration patterns.
7. (*Mansa Musa, King Lalibela*) based his system of justice on the Quran.
8. The kingdom of (*Ghana, Nubia*) was greatly influenced by its proximity to Egypt.

Main Ideas

Section 1 (pp. 340–345)
9. How did the environment affect the development of societies in Africa?
10. Describe the effects of trade on the cities of North Africa.

Section 2 (pp. 346–351)
11. Summarize how agriculture led to the development of prosperous trading centers.
12. What influence did Islam have on the large kingdoms of West Africa?

Section 3 (pp. 352–356)
13. What factors led to the isolation of Ethiopia from its neighbors?
14. How did trade bring about a blend of cultures in the city-states of East Africa?

Section 4 (pp. 357–361)
15. How did kinship ties influence daily life in medieval Africa?
16. How can artistic traditions identify a community and its environment?

Chapter Focus Question
17. How did trade influence the development of the kingdoms and trading states of Africa?

Critical Thinking

18. **Draw Conclusions** Why do you think the king of Ghana collected tolls on goods entering or leaving his kingdom?
19. **Synthesize Information** What primary factors attracted invaders to the great cities and kingdoms of Africa? Why did these invasions often succeed?
20. **Make Comparisons** Compare and contrast the consequences of adopting a new religion for the kingdoms of Mali and Axum.
21. **Geography and History** How did the geography of Africa affect the value of trade goods?
22. **Make Comparisons** How was the kingdom of Kongo's system of government similar to that of the government of the United States? How was it different?
23. **Distinguish False From Accurate Images** How do trading kingdoms and city-states contradict the misconceptions that many people have of medieval Africa?

● Writing About History

Writing a Narrative Much of African history has been passed down from generation to generation through oral traditions. African oral historians brought the events of the past to life through their engaging and entertaining stories in order to ensure that important people and events were remembered. Write a narrative that could be recounted aloud about a specific event involving one of the following: Saharan trade, Timbuktu, Mansa Musa, King Ezana, Lalibela, Amina. Consult page SH8 of the Writing Handbook for additional help.

Prewriting
- Choose the topic or event that interests you most and take notes about the people and locations involved.

- Collect the facts and details you will need to tell your story, including any historic background your listeners might need to know about the historic event.

Drafting
- Identify the climax of the story and then organize the story in chronological order.
- Make sure to engage your audience with a dramatic opening and include sensory details.
- Write a conclusion that sums up the significance of the event.

Revising
- Use the guidelines for revising your narrative on page SH9 of the Writing Handbook.

Document-Based Assessment

Mansa Musa, King of Mali

From 1312 until 1337, Mansa Musa ruled the West African kingdom of Mali. During his reign, the gold trade in the kingdom expanded as did the amount of territory under Mali's control. The wealth of the kingdom and Mansa Musa's power and generosity became legendary following his pilgrimage to Mecca in 1324. In fact, it is said that he spent so lavishly during his hajj that the value of gold actually fell in Egypt. Mansa Musa's renown spread throughout Africa to Europe and Southwest Asia, as the excerpts and map below demonstrate.

Document A

"We belong to a house which hands on the kinship by inheritance. The king [Abobakar II] who was my predecessor did not believe that it was impossible to discover the furthest limit of the Atlantic Ocean and wished vehemently to do so. . . ."

"Then that Sultan got ready 2,000 ships, 1,000 for himself and the men whom he took with him, and 1,000 for water and provisions. He left me to deputize for him and embarked on the Atlantic Ocean with his men. That was the last we saw of him and all those who were with him, and so, I became king in my own right."

—Mansa Musa, quoted by Ibn Amir Hajib

Document B

"[Mansa Musa] and all those with him . . . were well-dressed, grave, and dignified. He was noble and generous and performed many acts of charity and kindness. He had left his country with 100 loads of gold which he spent during his Pilgrimage on the tribes who lay along his route. . . . As a consequence he needed to borrow money in Egypt and pledged his credit with the merchants at a very high rate of gain so they made 700 dinars profit on 300. Later he paid them back amply. He sent to me 500 mithqals of gold by way of honorarium."

—Ibn Amir Hajib

Document C

Detail of West Africa from a fourteenth-century Spanish world map showing Mansa Musa offering gold to a trader.

Document D

From the beginning of my coming to stay in Egypt I heard talk of the arrival of this sultan Musa on his Pilgrimage. . . . I asked the emir Abu . . . and he told me . . . "When I [the emir] went out to meet him . . . he did me extreme honor and treated me with the greatest courtesy. . . . Then he forwarded to the royal treasury many loads of unworked native gold and other valuables. I tried to persuade him to go up to the Citadel to meet the sultan, but he refused persistently. . . . I realized that the audience was repugnant to him because he would be obliged to kiss the ground and the sultan's hand. . . . so I kept on at him till he agreed.

"[In the sultan's presence Mansa Musa] said 'I make obeisance to God who created me!' then he prostrated himself and went forward to the sultan. The sultan half rose to greet him and sat him by his side."

—Al 'Umari

Analyzing Documents

Use your knowledge of Mansa Musa, the kingdom of Mali, and Documents A, B, C, and D to answer questions 1–4.

1. According to Document A, Mansa Musa became king after his predecessor
   A was killed in a battle.
   B lost favor with religious leaders.
   C left on a sea voyage.
   D was assassinated by an ally of Mansa Musa.

2. The Catalan Atlas, Document C, features Mansa Musa so prominently to
   A provide a reference point for the kingdom of Mali.
   B show that Mansa Musa is the region's monarch.
   C enhance the decorative elements of the map.
   D emphasize the wealth, power, and importance of Mansa Musa.

3. Which qualities of Mansa Musa does Document D show?
   A cruelty and deceit
   B kindness and compassion
   C compassion and generosity
   D generosity and faith

4. **Writing Task** Why is Mansa Musa's rule known as "the Golden Age of Mali"? Use documents from this page along with information from the chapter in your response.

12 The Spread of Civilization in East and Southeast Asia

500–1650

Kublai Khan's Fleet

Although the Mongols dominated much of Asia in the 1200s, they were never able to conquer Japan. Kublai Khan's fleet attempted to invade Japan twice—in 1274 and 1281—but a kamikaze, or "divine wind," helped destroy his fleet both times. Over 700 years later, archaeologists found artifacts and a shipwreck from the Mongol fleet in Imari Bay, Japan. Listen to the Witness History audio to hear more about this exciting discovery.

❝Stepping off the dock into the warm, murky waters of Imari Bay, I swam to the bottom, . . . [and] suddenly I saw the wreck. . . . Clusters of timbers and artifacts suggested that a ship, or ships, had crashed into the shore and been ripped apart. There were bright red leather armor fragments, a pottery bowl decorated with calligraphy, and wood with what seemed like fresh burn marks. My heart started to pound when I swam up to one object and realized it was an intact Mongol helmet.❞
—James P. Delgado, *Archaeology,* January/February 2003

◀ In this illustrated scroll created in the 1290s, the Japanese defeat Kublai Khan's fleet with help from a kamikaze.

Chapter Preview

Chapter Focus Question How did China's culture develop and influence its neighbors in East and Southeast Asia?

Passport, Yuan dynasty

Buddha made of celadon, Korea

Samurai medicine box

Note Taking Study Guide *Online*
For: Note Taking and Concept Connector worksheets
Web Code: nad-1201

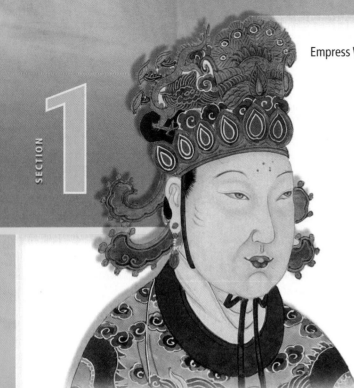

Empress Wu Zhao

WITNESS HISTORY 🔊 AUDIO

The Only Female Emperor in China

Many people in China had reason to distrust Empress Wu Zhao (woo jow). From a lowly place at court, she had risen to a position of influence with the emperor. After his death, she ruthlessly took power into her own hands. She even unseated her own sons from the throne. She declared herself "Son of Heaven," the age-old title of China's emperors. No other woman had ever dared do such a thing!

Focus Question Describe the political, economic, and cultural achievements of the Tang and Song dynasties.

Two Golden Ages of China

Objectives

- Summarize how the Tang dynasty reunified China.
- Explain how the Song dynasty grew rich and powerful despite military setbacks.
- Understand how China created an ordered society.
- Describe the cultural achievements of the Tang and Song dynasties.

Terms, People, and Places

Tang dynasty	Song dynasty
Tang Taizong	gentry
tributary state	dowry
land reform	pagoda

Note Taking

Reading Skill: Compare and Contrast Create a Venn diagram to take notes on the Tang and Song dynasties. Include information that applies to both dynasties where the circles overlap.

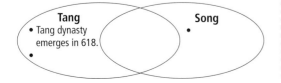

Tang
- Tang dynasty emerges in 618.

Song

In the late 600s, Wu Zhao became the only woman to rule China in her own name. Her strong rule helped guide China through one of its most brilliant periods. At a time when Europe was fragmented into many small feudal kingdoms, two powerful dynasties—the Tang and the Song—restored unity in China.

The Tang Dynasty Reunifies China

After the Han dynasty collapsed in 220, China broke apart and remained divided for nearly 400 years. Yet China escaped the decay that disrupted Western Europe after the fall of Rome. Farm production expanded and technology slowly improved. Buddhism spread, while learning and the arts continued to flourish. Even Chinese cities survived.

Although invaders stormed northern China, they often adopted Chinese civilization rather than demolishing it. Meanwhile, various dynasties rose and fell in the south. During the brief Sui (swee) dynasty (589–618), the emperor Sui Wendi reunited the north and south. But China was not restored to its earlier glory until the emergence of the **Tang dynasty** in 618.

The Tang Build an Empire The first Tang emperor, Li Yuan (lee yoo AHN), was a general under the Sui dynasty. When the Sui began to crumble, Li Yuan's ambitious 16-year-old son, Li Shimin, urged him to lead a revolt. Father and son crushed all rivals and established the Tang dynasty. Eight years later, Li Shimin <u>compelled</u> his aging father to step down and mounted the throne himself, taking the name **Tang Taizong** (ty DZUNG). A brilliant general, government reformer, historian, and master of the calligraphy brush, Tang Taizong would become China's most admired emperor.

Later Tang rulers carried empire-building to new heights, conquering territories deep into Central Asia. Chinese armies forced the neighboring lands of Vietnam, Tibet, and Korea to become **tributary states.** That is, while these states remained self-governing, their rulers had to acknowledge Chinese supremacy and send regular tribute to the Tang emperor. At the same time, students from Korea and Japan traveled to the Tang capital to learn about Chinese government, law, and arts.

The Government and Economy Grow Tang rulers, such as Empress Wu Zhao, helped restore the Han system of uniform government throughout China. They rebuilt the bureaucracy and enlarged the civil service system to recruit talented officials trained in Confucian philosophy. They also set up schools to prepare male students for the exams and developed a flexible new law code.

Tang emperors instituted a system of **land reform** in which they broke up large agricultural holdings and redistributed the land to peasants. This policy strengthened the central government by weakening the power of large landowners. It also increased government revenues, since the peasants who farmed their own land would be able to pay taxes.

The Tang Dynasty Declines Like earlier dynasties, the Tang eventually weakened. Later Tang emperors lost territories in Central Asia to the Arabs. Corruption, high taxes, drought, famine, and rebellions all contributed to the downward swing of the dynastic cycle. In 907, a rebel

Vocabulary Builder

<u>compelled</u>—(kum PELD) *v.* forced to do something

The Tang Dynasty
The Western Market (below left) of the Tang dynasty specialized in foreign goods. Tang Taizong (below right) is considered one of the greatest monarchs in the history of China. *What led to the decline of the Tang Dynasty?*

369

In addition to the advances shown below, the Chinese developed a smallpox vaccine, invented a spinning wheel, and pioneered the use of arches in bridge building. In time, many of these developments traveled westward. Modernized versions of most of these inventions are still widely used today. **How could one of the inventions shown here have aided the spread of Chinese civilization to other lands?**

Gunpowder, 850 ▲
The earliest form of gunpowder was made from a mixture of saltpeter, sulfur, and charcoal, all found in abundance in China. It was first used in fireworks and later in weapons. Song forces were the first to use a cannon (shown above), according to historical records.

◀ **Mechanical Clock, 700s**
The Chinese learned of water-powered clocks from Middle Easterners. Mechanical clocks used a complex series of wheels, shafts, and pins, turning at a steady rate, to tell exact time.

Block Printing, 700s, and ▲ Movable Type, 1040s
Block printing, developed during the Tang dynasty, involved carving a full page of characters onto a wooden block (above). China improved on this printing process during the Song dynasty by inventing movable type, in which precut characters were combined to form a page.

general overthrew the last Tang emperor. This time, however, the chaos following the collapse of a dynasty did not last long.

✔ **Checkpoint**   How did the Tang dynasty reunify China?

The Song Dynasty

In 960, a scholarly general named Zhao Kuangyin reunited much of China and founded the **Song** (sung) **dynasty.** The Song ruled for 319 years, slightly longer than the Tang, but they controlled less territory than the Tang. The Song also faced the constant threat of invaders in the north. In the early 1100s, the battered Song retreated south of the Huang River. There, the southern Song continued to rule for another 150 years. As you will learn, however, in the late 1200s invaders from the north called the Mongols attacked and overthrew the Song.

Despite military setbacks, the Song period was a time of great achievement. China's wealth and culture dominated East Asia even when its armies did not. Under the Song, the Chinese economy expanded because of improved farming methods and open border policy. The latter allowed a new type of faster-growing rice to be imported from Southeast Asia. Farmers were now able to produce two crops a year, one of rice and one of a cash crop to sell. The rise in productivity created surpluses, allowing more people to pursue commerce, learning, or the arts.

Through China's history, a system of canals had been built that encouraged internal trade and transportation. The Grand Canal, completed during the Sui dynasty, linked the Huang River to the Chang River. As a result, food grown in the south could be shipped to the capital in the north. The Grand Canal reached its peak during the Song dynasty, when thousands of tons of grain were shipped to northern China each year.

Under both the Tang and Song, foreign trade flourished. Merchants arrived from India, Persia, and Arabia. Chinese merchants carried goods to Southeast Asia in exchange for spices and special woods. Song porcelain has been found as far away as East Africa. To improve trade, the government issued paper money. China's cities, which had been mainly centers of government, now prospered as centers of trade.

 Checkpoint How was the Song dynasty able to continue its prosperity despite threats from the north?

China's Ordered Society

Under the Tang and Song, China was a well-ordered society. At its head was the emperor, whose court was filled with aristocratic families. The court supervised a huge bureaucracy, from which officials fanned out to every part of China. China's two main social classes were the gentry and the peasantry.

The Gentry Value Education As in previous dynasties, the scholar-official class formed the top stratum of society. Most scholar-officials at court came from the gentry, or wealthy landowning class. They alone could afford to spend years studying the Confucian classics in order to pass the grueling civil service exam. When not in government service, the gentry often served in the provinces as allies of the emperor's officials.

The Song scholar-gentry valued learning more than physical labor. They supported a revival of Confucian thought. New schools of Confucian philosophers emphasized social order based on duty, rank, and proper behavior. Although corruption and greed existed among civil servants, the ideal Confucian official was a wise, virtuous scholar who knew how to ensure harmony in society.

Peasants Work the Land Most Chinese were peasants who worked the land, living on what they produced. Drought and famine were a constant threat, but new tools and crops did improve the lives of many peasants. To add to their income, some families produced handicrafts such as baskets or embroidered items. They carried these products to nearby market towns to sell or trade for salt, tea, or iron tools.

Peasants lived in small, largely self-sufficient villages that managed their own affairs. "Heaven is high," noted one Chinese saying, "and the emperor far away." Peasants relied on one another rather than the government. When disputes arose, a village leader and council of elders put pressure on the parties to resolve the problem. Only if such efforts failed did villagers take their disputes to the emperor's county representative.

In China, even peasants could move up in society through education and government service. If a bright peasant boy received an education and passed the civil service examinations, both he and his family rose in status. Slaves in early China, however, did not have such opportunities. As in many other parts of the world, slavery played a role in early China, though a limited one.

Merchants Have Lowest Status In market towns and cities, some merchants acquired wealth. Still, according to Confucian tradition, merchants had an even lower social status than peasants since their riches came from the labor of others. An ambitious merchant, therefore, might buy land and educate one son to enter the ranks of the scholar-gentry.

Pair of shoes for a woman with bound feet in China

The Confucian attitude toward merchants affected economic policy. Some rulers favored commerce but sought to control it. They often restricted where foreign merchants could live and even limited the activities of private traders. Still, Chinese trade flourished during Song times.

The Status of Women Women had higher status in Tang and early Song times than they did later. Within the home, women were called upon to run family affairs. A man's wife and his mother had great authority, managing servants and family finances. Still, families valued boys more than girls. When a young woman married, she became a part of her husband's family. She could not keep her **dowry,** the payment that a woman brings to a marriage, and could never remarry.

Women's subordinate position was reinforced in late Song times when the custom of foot binding emerged. The custom probably began at the imperial court but later spread to the lower classes. The feet of young girls were bound with long strips of cloth, producing a lily-shaped foot about half the size of a foot that was allowed to grow normally. Tiny feet and a stilted walk became a symbol of nobility and beauty. Foot binding was extremely painful, yet the custom survived. Even peasant parents feared that they could not find a husband for a daughter with large feet.

Not all girls in China had their feet bound. Peasants who needed their daughters to work in the fields did not accept the practice. Yet most women did have to submit to foot binding. Women with bound feet often could not walk without help. Thus, foot binding reinforced the Confucian tradition that women should remain inside the home.

 Checkpoint How did most Chinese people live?

The Tang and Song Develop a Rich Culture

A prosperous economy supported the rich culture of Tang and Song China. Although their splendid royal palaces were long ago destroyed, many paintings, statues, temples, and ceramics have survived.

Artists Paint Harmony Along with poetry, painting and calligraphy were essential skills for the scholar-gentry. In both of these crafts, artists sought balance and harmony through the mastery of simple strokes and lines. The Song period saw the triumph of Chinese landscape painting. Steeped in the Daoist tradition, painters sought to capture the spiritual essence of the natural world. "When you are planning to paint," instructed a Song artist, "you must always create a harmonious relationship between heaven and earth."

Misty mountains and delicate bamboo forests dominated Chinese landscapes. Yet Chinese painters also produced realistic, vivid portraits of emperors or lively scenes of city life.

Architecture and Porcelain Buddhist themes dominated sculpture and influenced Chinese architecture. The Indian stupa evolved into the graceful Chinese **pagoda,** a multistoried temple with eaves that curve up at the corners. Chinese sculptors created striking statues of the Buddha. These statues created such a strong impression that many people today picture the Buddha as a Chinese god rather than an Indian holy man.

A CHINESE HOUSE

Dwellings during the Tang and Song dynasties ranged from caves to round tents to palaces. Ideally, all types of Chinese homes were built facing south so that they received warmth from the sun in the winter. Wealthy families lived in compounds that consisted of groups of buildings separated by a varying number of courtyards as shown in the painting below. Each structure within the compound had a distinct purpose for such things as ancestor worship, a library, or a music hall. Covered walkways, or porticos, joined the buildings. Atop the compound, expensive rooftops made of sloping tiles had terra cotta animals and dragons that adorned the ridges and eaves. Grand gardens with hills, ponds, rare flowers, twisted pine trees, and stones, were an important part of the finest homes. The building and gardens together produced an overall harmonious effect.

◄ The ideal woman during the Tang dynasty was sophisticated and wore head ornaments, combs, and powders. Like this woman, Tang women piled their hair high upon their heads.

Women prepare a feast in this tenth-century painting on silk. This residence is typical of those owned by imperial or wealthy families. ▼

Features of the Home

A Roofs were the most expensive and striking feature of the home. The finest homes had roofs with upturned edges and colorful tiles painted yellow, pale green, or jade green.

B Most houses included enclosed shaded courtyards.

C Each pavilion had a special purpose, whether for banquets or for playing music.

D Trees with gnarled trunks were common adornments for the home.

E Houseguests stayed in rooms located along the outer edge of the compound.

Thinking Critically

1. **Draw Inferences** According to the images shown here, what can you say about the status of women during this time?
2. **Synthesize Information** How does this compound illustrate the belief of the Tang and Song that a harmonious relationship should exist between home and gardens?

Li Bo, Chinese poet

The Chinese perfected techniques in making porcelain, a shiny, hard pottery that was prized as the finest in the world. They developed beautiful glazes to decorate vases, tea services, and other objects that Westerners would later call "chinaware." Artists also produced porcelain figures of camels, elegant court ladies playing polo, and bearded foreigners newly arrived from their travels on the Silk Road.

Chinese Writing Prose and poetry flowed from the brushes of Tang and Song writers. Scholars produced works on philosophy, religion, and history. Short stories that often blended fantasy, romance, and adventure made their first appearance in Chinese literature.

Among the gentry, poetry was the most respected form of Chinese literature. Confucian scholars were expected to master the skills of poetry. We know the names of some 200 major and 400 minor Tang and Song poets. Their works touched on Buddhist and Daoist themes as well as on social issues. Many poems reflected on the shortness of life and the immensity of the universe.

Probably the greatest Tang poet was Li Bo (lee boh). A zestful lover of life and freedom, he moved about from one place to another for most of his life. He wrote some 2,000 poems celebrating harmony with nature or lamenting the passage of time. A popular legend says that Li Bo drowned when he tried to embrace the reflection of the moon in a lake.

More realistic and less romantic were the poems of Li Bo's friend Du Fu. His verses described the horrors of war or condemned the lavishness of the court. A later poet, Li Qingzhao (lee ching jow), described the experience of women left behind when loved ones went off to war. Her poems reflect a time when invasion threatened to bring the brilliant Song dynasty to an end.

 Checkpoint What themes did Tang and Song arts and literature address?

Progress Monitoring *Online*
For: Self-quiz with vocabulary practice
Web Code: naa-1211

SECTION 1 Assessment

Terms, People, and Places

1. For each term, person, or place listed at the beginning of the section, write a sentence explaining its significance.

Note Taking

2. **Reading Skill: Compare and Contrast** Use your completed diagram to answer the Focus Question: Describe the political, economic, and cultural achievements of the Tang and Song dynasties.

Comprehension and Critical Thinking

3. **Draw Conclusions** In what ways did the rise of the Tang dynasty unify and benefit China?

4. **Determine Relevance** What was the significance of the Grand Canal to the Song dynasty?

5. **Recognize Ideologies** (a) Describe the social structure of China under the Tang and Song dynasties. (b) How did the social structure reflect Confucian traditions?

6. **Analyze Information** What ideas and traditions shaped Chinese paintings?

● **Writing About History**
Quick Write: Make a Cause-Effect Tree To make a cause-and-effect tree, choose either the Tang or Song dynasty and write its name in the center of a piece of paper. Above the dynasty's name, write the causes that led to its downfall.

Trade

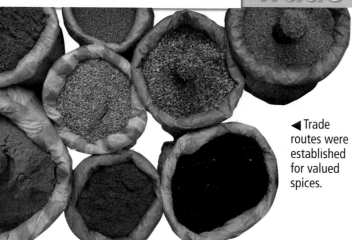

◄ Trade routes were established for valued spices.

What have been the major trade networks in world history?

As trade increased and lands became safe, merchants crossed Asia along the ancient Silk Road. The main trails in this famous network of trade routes ran from China west to the Mediterranean Sea. Connecting routes brought traders from Southeast Asia, India, Persia, Russia, and southern Europe. For more than a thousand years, this network helped shape the tastes and cultures of people over much of Asia and Europe. Other major trade networks around the world had a similar effect. Consider the following examples.

City-to-City Trade

Long before the establishment of the Silk Road, ancient cities traded with one another. A network of overland and water routes connected Bronze Age urban centers such as Mycenae in Greece with Memphis in Egypt, and Ashur in Mesopotamia with Harappa in the Indus Valley. Long-distance trade helped cities obtain resources not available in the local area. Merchants traveled among these ancient cities, carrying copper and tin, stone for making vases, olive oil, grains and other foods, timber, spices, woolen textiles, ivory, and pearls. Meanwhile, the merchants spoke to each other, exchanging ideas about technology, religion, and culture.

Global Trade

Trade involving Europe, Africa, Asia, and the Americas developed between the A.D. 1400s and 1700s. To obtain valued spices such as pepper, nutmeg, and cloves, European powers established routes to the east. Merchants sailed around southernmost Africa and across the Indian Ocean to India, China, and Japan. During the same period, a triangular trade developed in the Atlantic. Europeans traded manufactured goods to Africans for enslaved persons and gold. The enslaved Africans were transported to colonies in the Americas to work on plantations. The sugar, cotton, and tobacco that they produced were shipped to Europe to complete the triangle.

E-Commerce

Toward the end of the twentieth century, a revolutionary kind of trading network took shape. Called electronic commerce, or e-commerce, it combined traditional methods of shipping goods with the efficiency of the Internet. Today, even small businesses can advertise in major markets, show their goods in virtual shops, and sell directly to consumers worldwide. Consumers can also receive some services electronically, such as software updates. E-commerce is also changing the way businesses communicate with each other. More and more companies order supplies and manage transactions via the Internet.

◄ E-commerce has enabled businesses to work more efficiently.

Thinking Critically

1. **(a)** How might a simple trade route grow into a trade network? **(b)** What is revolutionary about the e-commerce trade network?
2. **Connections to Today** Research online to investigate some aspect of global trade today. For example, you might focus on major trade organizations, such as the World Trade Organization, or major trading partners of the United States. Summarize your findings in a brief oral report.

Mongolian archer on horseback

Mongol warrior's boots

WITNESS HISTORY 🔊 AUDIO

Warriors on Horseback

The Mongols were tough warriors who lived in the saddle and were considered the most skilled riders in the world. The Italian traveler Marco Polo described Mongol battle tactics:

66 They keep hovering about the enemy, discharging their arrows first from one side and then from the other. . . . Their horses are so well broken-in to quick changes of movement, that upon the signal given, they instantly turn in any direction, and by these rapid maneuvers many victories have been obtained.99
—Marco Polo, *A Description of the World*

Focus Question What were the effects of the Mongol invasion and the rise of the Ming dynasty on China?

The Mongol and Ming Empires

Objectives
- Summarize how Mongol armies built an empire.
- Describe China under Mongol rule.
- Understand how the Ming restored Chinese rule.
- Explain why the Ming explored the high seas for only a brief period.

Terms, People, and Places

steppe
Genghis Khan
Kublai Khan
Yuan dynasty

Marco Polo
Ming dynasty
Zheng He

Note Taking

Reading Skill: Recognize Sequence Create a timeline like the one below to record important events as you read this section.

Mongols advance into China.

| c. 1200 | 1279 | 1368 | 1405 |

About 1200, the Mongols burst out of Central Asia to conquer an empire stretching across Asia and Europe. In the process, they overran Song China and imposed Mongol rule on its people.

Mongol Armies Build an Empire

The Mongols were a nomadic people who grazed their horses and sheep on the **steppes,** or vast, treeless plains, of Central Asia. Rival Mongol clans spent much of their time warring with one another. In the early 1200s, however, a brilliant Mongol chieftain united these warring tribes. This chieftain took the name **Genghis Khan,** meaning "Universal Ruler." Under his leadership, Mongol forces conquered a vast empire that stretched from the Pacific Ocean to Eastern Europe.

Mongols Invade China Genghis Khan imposed strict military discipline and demanded absolute loyalty. His highly trained, mobile armies had some of the most skilled horsemen in the world. Genghis Khan had a reputation for fierceness. He could order the massacre of an entire city. Yet he also could be generous, rewarding the bravery of a single fighter.

Mongol armies conquered the Asian steppe lands with some ease, but as they turned on China, they encountered the problem of attacking walled cities. Chinese and Turkish military experts taught them to use cannons and other new weapons. The Mongols and Chinese launched missiles against each other from metal tubes filled with gunpowder. This use of cannons in warfare would soon spread westward to Europe.

Genghis Khan did not live to complete the conquest of China. His heirs, however, continued to expand the Mongol empire. For the next 150 years, they <u>dominated</u> much of Asia. Their furious assaults toppled empires and spread destruction from southern Russia through Muslim lands in Southwest Asia to China. Protected by steep mountain ranges, India avoided invasion, but the Mongols arrived in China, devastated the flourishing province of Sichuan (see chwahn), and annihilated its great capital city of Chengdu.

Rulers Establish Order and Peace Once conquest was completed, the Mongols were not oppressive rulers. Often, they allowed conquered people to live much as they had before—as long as they regularly paid tribute to the Mongols.

Genghis Khan had set an example for his successors by ruling conquered lands with toleration and justice. Although the Mongol warrior had no use for city life, he respected scholars, artists, and artisans. He listened to the ideas of Confucians, Buddhists, Christians, Muslims, Jews, and Zoroastrians.

In the 1200s and 1300s, the sons and grandsons of Genghis Khan established peace and order within their domains. Today, many historians refer to this period of order as the *Pax Mongolica*, or Mongol Peace.

Political stability set the stage for economic growth. Under the protection of the Mongols, who now controlled the great Silk Road, trade flourished across Eurasia. According to a contemporary, Mongol rule meant that people "enjoyed such a peace that a man might have journeyed from the land of sunrise to the land of sunset with a golden platter upon his head without suffering the least violence from anyone."

Cultural exchanges increased as foods, tools, inventions, and ideas spread along the protected trade routes. From China, the use of gunpowder moved westward into Europe. Techniques of papermaking also reached parts of Europe, and crops and trees from the Middle East were carried into East Asia.

✔ **Checkpoint** How did the Mongol Empire change once conquest was over?

China Under Mongol Rule

Although Genghis Khan had subdued northern China, the Mongols needed nearly 70 more years to conquer the south. Genghis Khan's grandson, **Kublai Khan** (KOO bly KAHN), finally toppled the last Song emperor in 1279. From his capital at Khanbaliq, present-day Beijing, Kublai Khan ruled all of China as well as Korea and Tibet.

An All-Mongol Government Kublai Khan tried to prevent the Mongols from being absorbed into Chinese civilization as other conquerors of China had been. He decreed that only Mongols could serve in the military. He also reserved the highest government jobs for

Vocabulary Builder

<u>dominated</u>—(DAHM ih nayt id) *v.* ruled or controlled with power

BIOGRAPHY

Genghis Khan
Originally called Temüjin, Genghis Khan (c. 1162–1227) was renowned for being ruthless, determined, and courageous. When Temüjin was nine years old, a rival Mongol clan poisoned his father. At the age of 15, Temüjin was taken prisoner. For the rest of his life, he never forgot the humiliation of being locked in a wooden collar and paraded before his enemies.

When he regained his freedom, Temüjin wandered among drifting clans. He took revenge on the clan that had imprisoned him and in time, became supreme ruler of all the Mongols. Once despised, Genghis Khan would be admired and feared across two continents. **How might Temüjin's experiences have motivated him to unite the Mongol clans?**

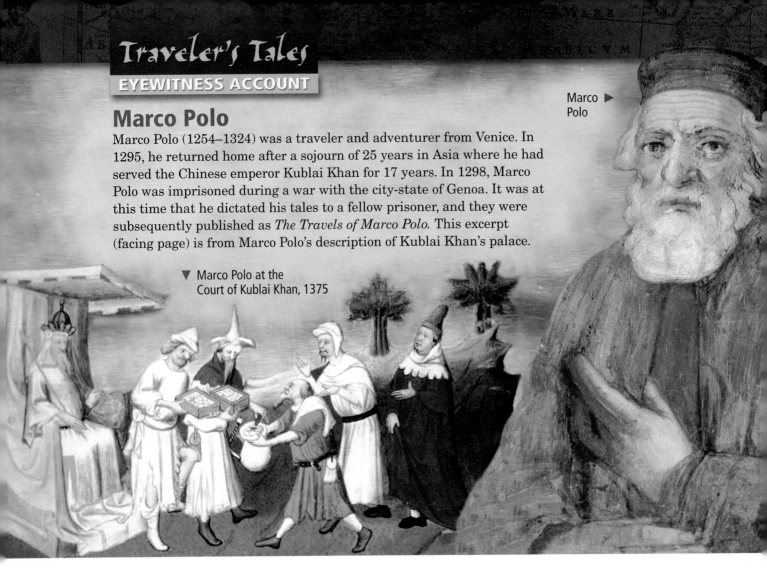

Traveler's Tales
EYEWITNESS ACCOUNT

Marco Polo

Marco Polo (1254–1324) was a traveler and adventurer from Venice. In 1295, he returned home after a sojourn of 25 years in Asia where he had served the Chinese emperor Kublai Khan for 17 years. In 1298, Marco Polo was imprisoned during a war with the city-state of Genoa. It was at this time that he dictated his tales to a fellow prisoner, and they were subsequently published as *The Travels of Marco Polo*. This excerpt (facing page) is from Marco Polo's description of Kublai Khan's palace.

► Marco Polo

▼ Marco Polo at the Court of Kublai Khan, 1375

Mongols or for other non-Chinese officials whom he employed. Still, because there were too few Mongols to control so vast an empire, Kublai allowed Chinese officials to continue to rule in the provinces.

Under Mongol rule, an uneasy mix of Chinese and foreign customs developed. Kublai adopted a Chinese name for his dynasty, the **Yuan** (yoo AHN), and turned Khanbaliq into a Chinese walled city. At the same time, he had Arab architects design his palace, and many rooms reflected Mongol steppe dwellings. Kublai rebuilt and extended the Grand Canal to his new capital, which made the shipment of rice and other goods easier. He also welcomed many foreigners to his court, including the African Muslim world traveler Ibn Battuta.

Marco Polo Writes About China The Italian merchant **Marco Polo** was one of many visitors to China during the Yuan dynasty. Although there is some debate on whether Marco Polo reached China, most historians acknowledge that he did indeed reach Cathay (northern China). In 1271, Polo left Venice with his father and uncle. He crossed Persia and Central Asia to reach China. He then spent 17 years in Kublai's service. Finally, he returned to Venice by sea, visiting Southeast Asia and India along the way.

In his writings, Marco Polo left a vivid account of the wealth and splendor of China. He described the royal palace of Kublai Khan (see Traveler's Tale) and also described China's efficient royal mail system,

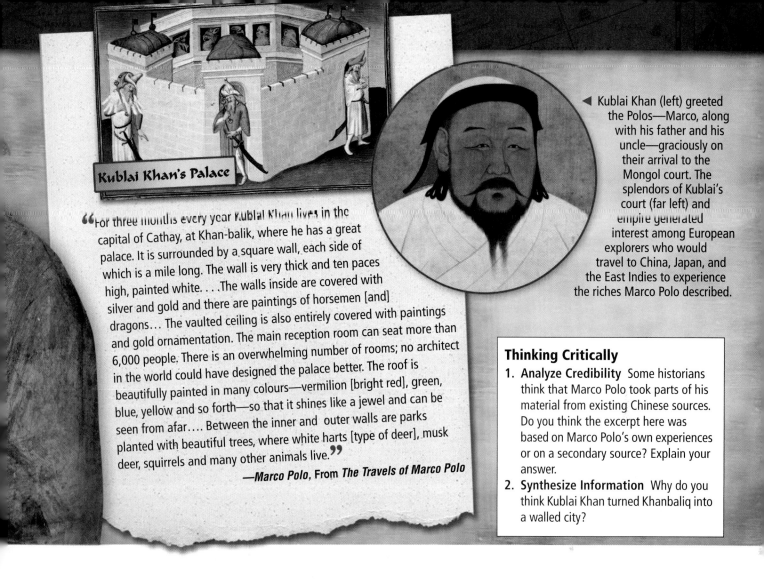

Kublai Khan's Palace

"For three months every year Kublai Khan lives in the capital of Cathay, at Khan-balik, where he has a great palace. It is surrounded by a square wall, each side of which is a mile long. The wall is very thick and ten paces high, painted white. . . .The walls inside are covered with silver and gold and there are paintings of horsemen [and] dragons... The vaulted ceiling is also entirely covered with paintings and gold ornamentation. The main reception room can seat more than 6,000 people. There is an overwhelming number of rooms; no architect in the world could have designed the palace better. The roof is beautifully painted in many colours—vermilion [bright red], green, blue, yellow and so forth—so that it shines like a jewel and can be seen from afar.... Between the inner and outer walls are parks planted with beautiful trees, where white harts [type of deer], musk deer, squirrels and many other animals live."

—Marco Polo, From *The Travels of Marco Polo*

◄ Kublai Khan (left) greeted the Polos—Marco, along with his father and his uncle—graciously on their arrival to the Mongol court. The splendors of Kublai's court (far left) and empire generated interest among European explorers who would travel to China, Japan, and the East Indies to experience the riches Marco Polo described.

Thinking Critically
1. **Analyze Credibility** Some historians think that Marco Polo took parts of his material from existing Chinese sources. Do you think the excerpt here was based on Marco Polo's own experiences or on a secondary source? Explain your answer.
2. **Synthesize Information** Why do you think Kublai Khan turned Khanbaliq into a walled city?

with couriers riding swift ponies along the empire's well-kept roads. Furthermore, he reported that the city of Hangzhou was 10 or 12 times the size of Venice, one of Italy's richest city-states. In the next centuries, Polo's reports sparked European interest in the riches of Asia.

Mongols Continue Outside Contact As long as the Mongol empire prospered, contacts between Europe and Asia continued. The Mongols tolerated a variety of beliefs. The pope sent Christian priests to Beijing, while Muslims set up their own communities in China. Meanwhile, some Chinese products moved toward Europe. They included gunpowder, porcelain, and playing cards.

✓ **Checkpoint** How did Kublai Khan organize Mongol rule in China?

The Ming Restore Chinese Rule

The Yuan dynasty declined after the death of Kublai Khan, which occurred in 1294. Most Chinese despised the foreign Mongol rulers. Confucian scholars retreated into their own world, seeing little to gain from the barbarians. Heavy taxes, corruption, and natural disasters led to frequent uprisings. Finally, Zhu Yuanzhang (dzoo YOO AHND zahng), a peasant leader, forged a rebel army that toppled the Mongols and pushed them back beyond the Great Wall. In 1368, he founded a new Chinese dynasty, which he called the **Ming,** meaning brilliant.

The Mongol Empire

Geography *Interactive*
For: Interactive map
Web Code: nap-1221

Map Skills At its height, the Mongol empire was the largest in the world up to that time.

1. **Locate** (a) Beijing (b) Venice (c) Hangzhou
2. **Region** What happened to the Mongol empire between 1227 and 1294?

3. **Make Comparisons** What countries would Marco Polo pass through if he made his journey today?

Legend:
- Mongol empire at Genghis Khan's death, 1227
- Mongol empire at its greatest extent, 1294
- Boundary of Yuan dynasty of Kublai Khan
- → Route of Marco Polo, 1271–1295

Miller Projection
0 400 800 mi
0 400 800km

◀ An illustration from a fourteenth-century story called *The History of the Mongols*. Mongol troops made a bridge out of boats in order to storm across the Chang River and capture a city controlled by the Song.

A Mongolian passport ▶

◀ Mongol horsemen were known for being fast and furious. They were agile and used such equipment as these stirrups, which allowed them to turn in a wide range of directions while fighting on horseback.

Early Ming rulers sought to reassert Chinese greatness after years of foreign rule. They initially moved the capital to Nanjing, which they felt possessed more characteristics of the Chinese, but eventually moved it back to present-day Beijing. The Ming restored the civil service system, and Confucian learning again became the road to success. The civil service exams became more rigorous than ever. A board of censors watched over the bureaucracy, rooting out corruption and disloyalty.

The Economy Grows Economically, Ming China was immensely productive. The fertile, well-irrigated plains of eastern China supported a population of more than 100 million. In the Chang River valley, peasants produced huge rice crops. Better methods of fertilizing helped to improve farming. Reshaping the landscape helped as well. Some farmers cut horizontal steps called terraces into steep hillsides to gain soil in which to grow crops. In the 1500s, new crops reached China from the Americas, especially corn and sweet potatoes.

Chinese cities, such as Nanjing, were home to many industries, including porcelain, paper, and tools. The Ming repaired the extensive canal system that linked various regions, made trade easier, and allowed cities to grow. New technologies increased output in manufacturing. Better methods of printing, for example, led to the production of a flood of books.

Culture Flourishes Ming China also saw a revival of arts and literature. Ming artists developed their own styles of landscape painting and created brilliant blue and white porcelain. Ming vases were among the most valuable and popular Chinese products exported to the West.

Confucian scholars continued to produce classical poetry. At the same time, new forms of popular literature to be enjoyed by the common people began to emerge. Ming writers composed novels, including *The Water Margin* about an outlaw gang that tries to end injustice by corrupt officials. Ming writers also produced the world's first detective stories.

 Checkpoint How did Ming rulers restore a previous style of Chinese government?

Chinese Fleets Sail the Seas

Early Ming rulers proudly sent Chinese fleets into distant waters to show the glory of their government. The most extraordinary of these overseas ventures were the voyages of the Chinese admiral and diplomat **Zheng He** (jeng he).

Zheng He and His Fleets Starting in 1405, Zheng He commanded the first of seven expeditions. He departed at the head of a fleet of 62 huge ships and over 200 smaller ones, carrying a crew of about 28,000 sailors. The largest ships measured 400 feet long. The goal of each expedition was to promote trade and collect tribute from lesser powers across the western seas.

Between 1405 and 1433, Zheng He explored the coasts of Southeast Asia and India and the entrances to the Red Sea and the Persian Gulf. He also visited many ports in East Africa. In the wake of these expeditions, Chinese merchants settled in Southeast Asia and India and became a permanent presence in their trading centers. Exotic animals, such as giraffes, were imported from foreign lands as well. The voyages also showed local rulers the power and strength of the Chinese empire.

Zheng He set up an engraved stone tablet listing the dates, places, and achievements of his voyages. The tablet proudly proclaimed that the Ming had unified the "seas and continents" even more than the Han and Tang had done. What was the relevance of Zheng He's overseas expeditions?

Primary Source

❝ The countries beyond the horizon and from the ends of the earth have all become subjects. . . . We have traversed immense waterspaces and have beheld in the ocean huge waves like mountains rising sky high, and we have set eyes on barbarian regions far away . . . while our sails loftily unfurled like clouds day and night continued their course, traversing those savage waves as if we were treading on a public thoroughfare.❞

—Zheng He, quoted in *The True Dates of the Chinese Maritime Expeditions in the Early Fifteenth Century* (Duyvendak)

Exploration Ends In 1435, the year Zheng He died, the Ming emperor suddenly banned the building of seagoing ships. Later, ships with more than two masts were forbidden. Zheng He's huge ships were retired and rotted away.

Why did China, with its advanced naval technology, turn its back on overseas exploration? Historians are not sure. Some speculate that the fleets were costly and did not produce profit. Also, Confucian scholars at court had little interest in overseas ventures and commerce. To them, Chinese civilization was the most successful in the world. They wanted to preserve its ancient traditions, which they saw as the source of stability. In fact, such rigid loyalty to tradition would eventually weaken China and once again leave it prey to foreign domination.

Fewer than 60 years after China halted overseas expeditions, the explorer Christopher Columbus would sail west from Spain in search of a sea route to Asia. As you will see, this voyage made Spain a major power and had a dramatic impact on the entire world. We can only wonder how the course of history might have changed if the Chinese had continued the explorations they had begun under the Ming.

✔ **Checkpoint** What occurred in 1435 that changed China's relationship with the rest of the world?

Progress Monitoring *Online*
For: Self-quiz with vocabulary practice
Web Code: naa-1221

SECTION 2 Assessment

Terms, People, and Places

1. For each term, person, or place listed at the beginning of the section, write a sentence explaining its significance.

Note Taking

2. **Reading Skill: Recognize Sequence** Use your completed timeline to answer the Focus Question: What were the effects of the Mongol invasion and the rise of the Ming dynasty on China?

Comprehension and Critical Thinking

3. **Synthesize Information** How did the Mongol conquests promote trade and cultural exchanges?

4. **Recognize Cause and Effect** Describe one effect of each of the following on China: (a) the Mongol invasion (b) the expulsion of the Mongols (c) the rise of the Ming dynasty

5. **Draw Conclusions** How did the Ming emperors try to restore Chinese culture?

● **Writing About History**

Quick Write: Provide Elaboration To illustrate each cause and effect of your essay, you should have supporting details, facts, and examples. List as many specific details as you can about the Mongol invasion of China. Then write a paragraph using the details you listed to explain the effects of the invasion.

Buddha statues
made of celadon

SECTION 3

WITNESS HISTORY ◀)) AUDIO

The Power of Ideas

Buddhism was brought to the Korean peninsula from China in the fourth century. It influenced Korea greatly, and its effects were seen in both culture and politics. Here, a Korean writer discusses Buddhism:

66 If you teach people to rely on this teaching [Buddhism] and practice it, then their minds can be corrected, and their bodies can be cultivated. You can regulate your family, you can govern the state, and you can bring peace to all the world.99
—Gihwa, *The Exposition of the Correct*

Focus Question How are Korea's history and culture linked to those of China and Japan?

Korea and Its Traditions

Objectives
- Describe how geography affected life on the Korean peninsula.
- Understand the influence of China and Buddhism on Korea.
- Explain the major achievements of the Choson dynasty.

Terms, People, and Places

Silla dynasty
Koryo dynasty
celadon
Choson (Yi) dynasty

King Sejong
hangul
literacy rate

Note Taking

Reading Skill: Categorize Draw a concept web like the one shown below. As you read the section, fill in the blank circles with relevant information about Korea. Add more circles as needed.

Korea

As early as Han times, Korea's larger neighbor to the north—China—was an influence. However, although Koreans absorbed many Chinese traditions, they also maintained a separate and distinct culture.

Geography of the Korean Peninsula

Korea is located on a peninsula that juts south from the Asian mainland and points toward Japan. At the northern end of the peninsula, mountains and the Yalu River separate Korea from China.

Living Among Mountains and Seas An early visitor once compared Korea's landscape to "a sea in a heavy gale." Low but steep mountains cover nearly 70 percent of the Korean peninsula. The most important range is the T'aebaek (ta bak). It runs from north to south along the eastern coast, with smaller chains branching off to form hilly areas. Because farming is difficult on the mountains, most people live along the western coastal plains, Korea's major farming region.

Korea has a 5,400-mile coastline with hundreds of good harbors. In addition, the offshore waters feature thousands of islands. Since early times, Koreans have depended upon seafood for most of the protein in their diet. Today, South Korea has one of the largest fishing industries in the world.

Location Affects Korea Korea's location on China's doorstep has played a key role in its development. From its powerful

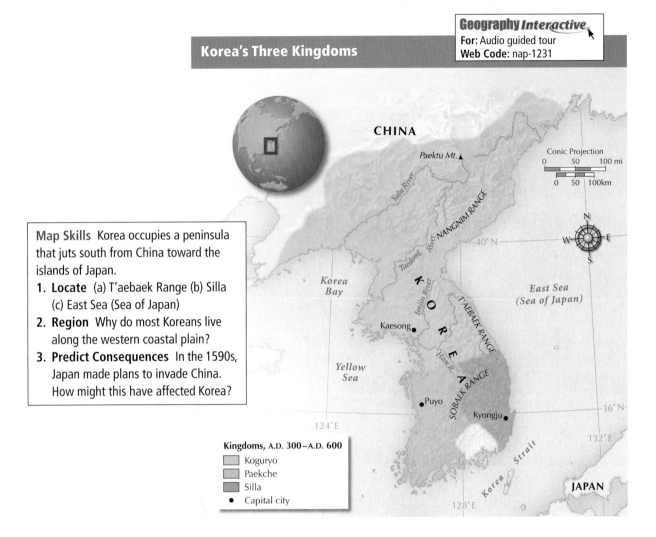

Map Skills Korea occupies a peninsula that juts south from China toward the islands of Japan.

1. **Locate** (a) T'aebaek Range (b) Silla (c) East Sea (Sea of Japan)

2. **Region** Why do most Koreans live along the western coastal plain?

3. **Predict Consequences** In the 1590s, Japan made plans to invade China. How might this have affected Korea?

Kingdoms, A.D. 300–A.D. 600
- Koguryo
- Paekche
- Silla
- ● Capital city

Vocabulary Builder

evolved—(ee VAHLVD) v. developed gradually

mainland neighbor, Korea received many cultural and technological influences. At various times in history, China extended political control over the Korean peninsula. Korea has also served as a cultural bridge linking China and Japan. Koreans have, from early times, adapted and transformed Chinese traditions before passing them on to the Japanese.

The earliest Koreans probably migrated southeastward from Siberia and northern Manchuria during the Stone Age. They evolved their own ways of life before the first wave of Chinese influence reached the peninsula during the Han dynasty. In 108 B.C., the Han emperor, Wudi, invaded Korea and set up a military colony there. From this outpost, Confucian traditions and Chinese ideas about government, as well as Chinese writing and farming methods, spread to Korea.

✔ **Checkpoint** How did the relative location of the Korean peninsula influence the development of Korean civilization?

Development of the Silla and Koryo Dynasties

Between about A.D. 300 and 600, powerful local rulers forged three separate kingdoms: Koguryo in the north, Paekche in the southwest, and Silla in the southeast. Although they shared the same language and cultural background, the three kingdoms often warred with one another or with China. Still, Chinese influences continued to arrive. Missionaries spread Mahayana Buddhism, which took root among the rulers and nobles. Korean monks then traveled to China and India to learn more about Buddhism. They brought home the arts and learning of China.

In 668, with the support of the Tang empress Wu Zhao, the Silla kingdom united the Korean peninsula. From this time until 1910, Korea had only three dynasties. The Silla ruled from 668 to 935, the Koryo ruled from 935 to 1392, and the Choson, or Yi, ruled from 1392 to 1910.

Silla Dynasty Unites Kingdoms Under the Silla dynasty, Korea prospered and the arts flourished. Silla civilization was among the most advanced in the world. Buddhism grew to become a powerful force, and hundreds of Buddhist temples were built. A brisk trade was conducted with China. Chinese culture, written language, and political institutions continued to be extremely important influences on Korea.

Much of this great cultural and technical flowering centered at the Silla capital, Kyongju, which was modeled on the Tang capital at Chang'an. Kyongju was renowned as the "city of gold," where the aristocracy pursued a life of high culture and extravagance. Medicine, astronomy, metal casting, sculpture, and textile manufacturing reached especially high levels.

In 682, the Silla set up a national Confucian academy to train high officials and later instituted a civil-service examination modeled on that of China. But in China, even a peasant could win political influence by passing the exam. In Korea, only aristocrats were permitted to take the test. Eventually, conflicts between peasants and the aristocrats led to the overthrow of the Silla dynasty.

The Koryo Dynasty The Koryo dynasty, from which the modern word Korea is derived, replaced the Silla in 935. A new capital was established at Songak, present day Kaesong.

Confucianism and Buddhism were both influential and widespread during this time. Koreans used woodblock printing from China to produce a flood of Buddhist texts. Later, Korean inventors took the Chinese invention one step further and created movable metal type to print large numbers of books. Koreans also improved on other Chinese inventions. They learned to make porcelain from China, and then perfected the technique for making celadon, or porcelain with an unusual blue-green glaze. Korean celadon vases and jars were prized throughout Asia. In the 1200s, when

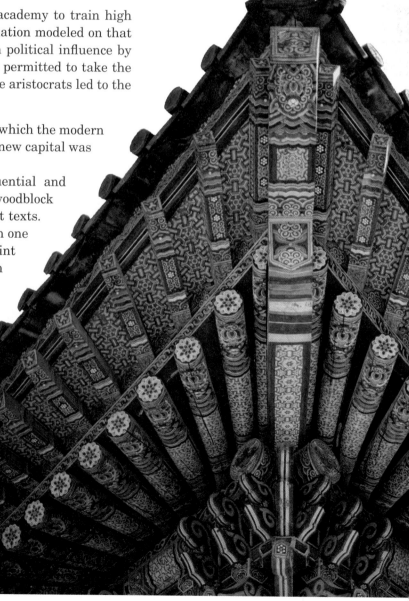

The Pulguksa Temple, completed during the Silla dynasty, is considered to be the most famous Buddhist temple in Korea.

During the Silla dynasty, Buddhism expanded and beautiful temples, such as the Pulguksa Temple shown here, were constructed. This oath is from an early Korean document:

Primary Source

❝Hereafter we will worship the Buddha and revere the clergy. If we break this oath, may heaven strike us dead.❞

Hangul (bottom), the Korean writing system, is fairly simple to learn and was developed to replace the complicated Chinese system (top). Notice that like Chinese, however, hangul is made up of a sequence of symbols that are relatively square-shaped. Hangul is now used for nearly all written communications in both North and South Korea. *Why did Korea want its own system of writing?*

 Chinese characters

▲ Hangul characters

the Mongols overran Korea and destroyed many industries, the secret of making celadon was lost forever.

✔ **Checkpoint**   How did Buddhism influence Korea?

The Choson Dynasty Rules for Over 500 Years

The Mongols first invaded Korea in 1231 and occupied the country from 1259 until the 1350s. When their rule collapsed, the Koryo returned to power. But in 1392, the brilliant Korean general Yi Song-gye (yee sung gyeh) overthrew them and set up the Yi, or **Choson dynasty.** This was the last and longest-lived of Korea's three dynasties. General Yi reduced Buddhist influence and set up a government based upon Confucian principles.

Korea Creates Alphabet   In 1443, Korea's most celebrated ruler, **King Sejong,** decided to replace the complex Chinese system of writing. "The language of this land," he noted, "is different from China's." Sejong had experts develop **hangul,** the Korean phonetic alphabet that uses symbols to represent the sounds of spoken Korean.

Although Confucian scholars and Koreans of the upper classes rejected hangul at the outset, its use quickly spread. Hangul was easier for Koreans to use than the thousands of characters of written Chinese. Its use led to an extremely high **literacy rate,** or percentage of people who can read and write.

Japan Invades   In the 1590s, an ambitious Japanese ruler decided to invade China by way of Korea. Japanese armies landed and for years looted and burned across the peninsula. To stop the invaders at sea, the Korean Admiral Yi Sun-shin, one of Korea's great heroes, used "turtle ships," so named because they were armored and shaped like turtles. The ships were able to sail right into the Japanese fleet. After six years, the Japanese armies withdrew from Korea. As they left, however, they carried off many Korean artisans to introduce their skills to Japan.

✔ **Checkpoint**   How did Korea preserve its own identity under the Choson dynasty?

SECTION 3 Assessment

Progress Monitoring *Online*
For: Self-quiz with vocabulary practice
Web Code: naa-1231

Terms, People, and Places

1. What do each of the key terms listed at the beginning of the section have in common? Explain.

Note Taking

2. **Reading Skill: Categorize** Use your completed concept web to answer the Focus Question: How are Korea's history and culture linked to those of China and Japan?

Comprehension and Critical Thinking

3. **Make Generalizations** Why might Korea's location be considered strategic to other countries?

4. **Synthesize Information** Give two examples of how Koreans adapted or modified Chinese ideas under the Silla or Koryo dynasty.

5. **Analyze Information** Today, Hangul Day is a holiday in South Korea. Why do you think Koreans celebrate the creation of their alphabet?

● **Writing About History**

Quick Write: Create a Flowchart
Organize the information in this chapter by creating a flowchart. The chart should show either the course of Korean unification and the sequence of dynasties or the influences on Korean civilization. Remember that a flowchart connects information to show a relationship between the different pieces of information.

Prince Shotoku depicted on a wall hanging and on a 1000 yen note

WITNESS HISTORY 🔊 AUDIO

The Importance of Harmony

Prince Shotoku of Japan's ruling Yamato clan wanted to create an orderly society. In 604, he outlined ideals of behavior for both the royal court and ordinary people. "Harmony should be valued," he wrote, "and quarrels avoided." Shotoku's words reflected a strong Confucian influence about social order. As he stated:

66 Everyone has his biases, and few men are far-sighted. Therefore some disobey their lords and fathers and keep up feuds with their neighbors. But when the superiors are in harmony with each other and inferiors are friendly, then affairs are discussed quietly and the right view of matters prevails. 99

Focus Question What internal and external factors shaped Japan's civilization, and what characterized Japan's feudal age?

The Emergence of Japan and the Feudal Age

Objectives
- Explain how geography set Japan apart.
- Understand how China influenced Japan, and describe the Heian period.
- Summarize the Japanese feudal system.
- Explain how the Tokugawas united Japan.
- Identify how Zen Buddhism shaped culture in Japan.

Terms, People, and Places

archipelago	kana
tsunami	samurai
Shinto	bushido
selective borrowing	Zen

Note Taking

Reading Skill: Categorize Fill in a table like the one shown below with examples of internal and external factors that shaped Japan's civilization.

Influences on Japan	
Internal Factors	**External Factors**
• geography	•
•	•

Like Korea, Japan felt the powerful influence of Chinese civilization early in its history. At the same time, the Japanese continued to maintain their own distinct culture.

Geography Sets Japan Apart

Japan is located on an **archipelago** (ahr kuh PEL uh goh), or chain of islands, about 100 miles off the Asian mainland and east of the Korean peninsula. Its four main islands are Hokkaido, Honshu, Kyushu, and Shikoku.

Seas Protect Japan Japan is about the size of Montana, but four-fifths of its land are too mountainous to farm. As a result, most people settled in narrow river valleys and along the coastal plains. A mild climate and sufficient rainfall, however, helped Japanese farmers make the most of the limited arable land.

The surrounding seas have both protected and isolated Japan. The country was close enough to the mainland to learn from Korea and China, but too far away for the Chinese to conquer. Japan thus had greater freedom to accept or reject Chinese influences than did other East Asian lands. At times, the Japanese sealed themselves off from foreign influences, choosing to go their own way. The seas that helped Japan preserve its identity also served as

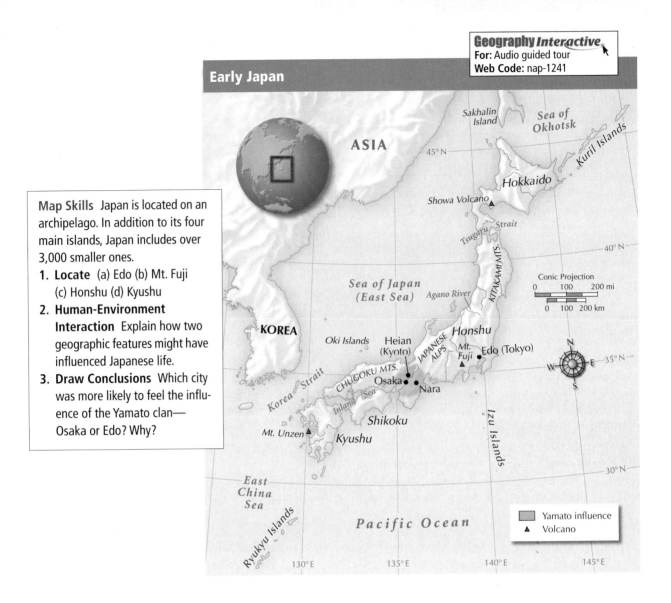

Early Japan

Geography *Interactive*
For: Audio guided tour
Web Code: nap-1241

Map Skills Japan is located on an archipelago. In addition to its four main islands, Japan includes over 3,000 smaller ones.
1. **Locate** (a) Edo (b) Mt. Fuji (c) Honshu (d) Kyushu
2. **Human-Environment Interaction** Explain how two geographic features might have influenced Japanese life.
3. **Draw Conclusions** Which city was more likely to feel the influence of the Yamato clan—Osaka or Edo? Why?

trade routes. The Inland Sea was an especially important link among various Japanese islands. The seas also offered plentiful food resources and the Japanese developed a thriving fishing industry.

Forces of Nature The Japanese came to fear and respect the dramatic forces of nature. Japan lies in a region known as the Ring of Fire, which is made up of a chain of volcanoes that encircle the Pacific Ocean. This region is therefore subject to frequent volcanic activity and earthquakes. Underwater earthquakes can launch killer tidal waves, called **tsunamis,** which sweep over the land without warning, wiping out everything in their path.

✓ **Checkpoint** How did the sea help Japan preserve its identity?

Early Traditions

The people we know today as the Japanese probably migrated from the Asian mainland more than 2,000 years ago. They slowly pushed the earlier inhabitants, the Ainu, onto the northernmost island of Hokkaido.

The Yamato Clan Claims Power Early Japanese society was divided into *uji,* or clans. Each *uji* had its own chief and a special god or goddess who was seen as the clan's original ancestor. Some clan leaders were women, suggesting that women enjoyed a respected position in society.

By about A.D. 500, the Yamato clan came to dominate a corner of Honshu, the largest Japanese island. For the next 1,000 years, the Yamato Plain was the heartland of Japanese government. The Yamato set up Japan's first and only dynasty. They claimed direct descent from the sun goddess, Amaterasu, and chose the rising sun as their symbol. Later Japanese emperors were revered as living gods. While this is no longer the case, the current Japanese emperor still traces his roots to the Yamato clan.

A Religion of Nature Early Japanese clans honored kami, or superior powers that were natural or divine. The worship of the forces of nature became known as **Shinto,** meaning "the way of kami." Although Shinto has not evolved into an international religion like Christianity, Buddhism, or Islam, its traditions survive to the present day in Japan. Hundreds of Shinto shrines dot the Japanese countryside. Though simple in design, they are generally located in beautiful, natural surroundings. Shinto shrines are dedicated to special sites or objects such as mountains or waterfalls, ancient gnarled trees, or even oddly shaped rocks.

The Korean Connection The Japanese language is distantly related to Korean but completely different from Chinese. From early on, Japan and Korea were in continuous contact with each other. Korean artisans and metalworkers settled in Japan, bringing sophisticated skills and technology. Japanese and Korean warriors crossed the sea in both directions to attack each other's strongholds. Some of the leading families at the Yamato court claimed Korean ancestors.

Missionaries from Korea had introduced Buddhism to Japan in the 500s. With it came knowledge of Chinese writing and culture that sparked a sustained period of Japanese interest in Chinese civilization.

✔ **Checkpoint** How did the Yamato clan influence future Japanese government?

Japan Looks to China

In the early 600s, Prince Shotoku of the Yamato clan decided to learn about China directly instead of through Korean sources. He sent young nobles to study in China. Over the next 200 years, many Japanese students, monks, traders, and officials visited the Tang court.

The Japanese Visit China Each visitor to China spent a year or more there—negotiating, trading, but above all studying. The visitors returned to Japan eager to spread Chinese thought, technology, and arts. They also imported Chinese ideas about government. Japanese rulers adopted the title "Heavenly Emperor" and claimed absolute power. They strengthened the central government, set up a bureaucracy, and adopted a law code similar to that of China. Still, the new bureaucracy had little real authority beyond the royal court. Out in the countryside, the old clans remained strong.

In 710, the Japanese emperor built a new capital at Nara, modeled on the Tang capital at Chang'an. There, Japanese nobles spoke Chinese and dressed in Chinese fashion. Their cooks prepared Chinese dishes and served food on Chinese-style pottery. Tea drinking, along with an elaborate tea ceremony, was imported from China. Japanese officials and scholars used Chinese characters to write official histories. Tang music and dances became very popular, as did gardens designed using Chinese influences.

Early Japanese sword and sword guards, both considered to be works of art.

As Buddhism spread, the Japanese adopted pagoda architecture. Buddhist monasteries grew rich and powerful. Confucian ideas and ethics also took root. They included an emphasis on filial piety, the careful management of relationships between superior and inferior, and respect for learning.

Selective Borrowing Preserves Culture In time, the initial enthusiasm for everything Chinese died down. The Japanese kept some Chinese ways but discarded or modified others. This process is known as **selective borrowing.** Japan, for example, never accepted the Chinese civil service examination to choose officials based on merit. Instead, they maintained their tradition of inherited status through family position. Officials were the educated sons of nobles.

By the 800s, as Tang China began to decline, the Japanese court turned away from its model. After absorbing all they could from China, the Japanese spent the next 400 years digesting and modifying these cultural borrowings to produce their own unique civilization. The Japanese asserted their identity by revising the Chinese system of writing and adding **kana,** or phonetic symbols representing syllables. Japanese artists developed their own styles.

✓ **Checkpoint** How did Japan seek out Chinese influences?

The Heian Period

This blending of cultures took place from 794 to 1185. During this time, the imperial capital was in Heian (hay ahn), present-day Kyoto. There, emperors performed traditional religious ceremonies, while wealthy court families like the Fujiwara wielded real power. The Fujiwara married their daughters to the heirs to the throne, thus ensuring their authority.

Women Shape the Court At the Heian court, an elegant and sophisticated culture blossomed. Noblewomen and noblemen lived in a fairy-tale atmosphere of beautiful pavilions, gardens, and lotus pools. Elaborate rules of etiquette governed court ceremony. Courtiers dressed with extraordinary care in delicate, multicolored silk. Draping one's sleeve out a carriage window was a fine art.

Although men at court still studied Chinese, women were forbidden to learn the language. Despite these restrictions, it was Heian women who produced the most important works of Japanese literature of the period.

In the 900s, Sei Shonagon, a lady-in-waiting to the empress during the Heian period, wrote *The Pillow Book*. In a witty series of anecdotes and personal observations, she provides vivid details of court manners, amusements, decor, and dress. In one section, Shonagon discusses the importance of keeping up a good appearance at court:

Primary Source

❝Nothing can be worse than allowing the driver of one's ox-carriage to be poorly dressed. It does not matter too much if the other attendants are shabby, since they can remain at the rear of the carriage; but the drivers are bound to be noticed and, if they are badly turned out, it makes a painful impression.❞
—Sei Shonagon, *The Pillow Book*

Lady Murasaki Writes the World's First Novel The best-known Heian writer was Murasaki Shikibu. Her monumental work, *The Tale of Genji*, was the world's first full-length novel.

The Tale of Genji recounts the adventures and loves of the fictional Prince Genji and his son. In one scene, Genji moves with ease through the festivities at an elaborate "Chinese banquet." After dinner, "under the great cherry tree of the Southern court," the entertainment begins. The main event of the evening is a Chinese poetry contest. Genji and other guests are given a "rhyme word," which they must use to compose a poem in Chinese. Genji's poem is the hit of the banquet.

Elegant though they are, the Heian poems and romances are haunted by a sense of sadness. The writers lament that love does not last and the beauty of the world is soon gone. Perhaps this feeling of melancholy was prophetic. While noble men and women strolled through manicured gardens, clouds of rebellion and civil war were gathering.

✔ **Checkpoint**   **How did women influence culture at the Heian court?**

Warriors Establish Feudalism

Feudal warfare swept Japan in the 1400s. Disorder continued through the following century. Yet, despite the turmoil, a new Japanese culture arose. While the emperor presided over the splendid court at Heian, rival clans battled for control of the countryside. Local warlords and even some Buddhist temples formed armed bands loyal to them rather than to the central government. As these armies struggled for power, Japan evolved a feudal system. As in the feudal world of medieval Europe, a warrior aristocracy dominated Japanese society.

In theory, the emperor stood at the head of Japanese feudal society. In fact, he was a powerless, though revered, figurehead. Real power lay in the hands of the shogun, or supreme military commander. Minamoto Yoritomo was appointed shogun in 1192. He set up the Kamakura shogunate, the first of three military dynasties that would rule Japan for almost 700 years.

The Ways of the Warriors Often the shogun controlled only a small part of Japan. He distributed lands to vassal lords who agreed to support him with their armies in time of need. These great warrior lords were later called daimyo (DY myoh). They, in turn, granted land to lesser warriors called **samurai**, meaning "those who serve." Samurai were the fighting aristocracy of a war-torn land.

Like medieval Christian knights in Europe, samurai were heavily armed and trained in the skills of fighting. They also developed their own code of values. Known as **bushido**, or the "way of the warrior," the code emphasized honor, bravery, and absolute loyalty to one's lord.

Noblewomen Lose Ground At first, some noblewomen in Japanese feudal society trained in the military arts. A few even became legendary warriors. At times, some noblewomen supervised their family's estates.

As the age of the samurai progressed, however, the position of women declined steadily. When feudal warfare increased, inheritance was limited to sons. Unlike the European ideal of chivalry, the samurai code did not set women on a pedestal. The wife of a warrior had to accept the same hardships as her husband and owed the same loyalty to his overlord.

BIOGRAPHY

Murasaki Shikibu
"If only you were a boy, how happy I would be!" said Murasaki Shikibu's father. Although he was praising her intelligence, he was also revealing how Japan valued men over women. Growing up, Murasaki Shikibu (978[?]–1014[?]) studied with her brother. This fact was probably kept secret, because learning by girls was considered improper.

After the death of her husband, she went to the imperial court as a lady-in-waiting. There, as Lady Murasaki, she penned the world's first full-length novel, *The Tale of Genji*, a story of the Heian age that has been celebrated for more than a thousand years. **What personal qualities can you infer that Lady Murasaki possessed?**

WITNESS HISTORY VIDEO

Watch *The Samurai of Japan* on the **Witness History Discovery School**™ video program to learn about the samurai.

DISCOVERY
SCHOOL

Peasants, Artisans, and Merchants Far below the samurai in the social hierarchy were the peasants, artisans, and merchants. Peasants, who made up 75 percent of the population, formed the backbone of feudal society in Japan. Peasant families cultivated rice and other crops on the estates of samurai. Some peasants also served as foot soldiers in feudal wars. On rare occasions, an able peasant soldier might rise through the ranks to become a samurai himself.

Artisans, such as armorers and swordmakers, provided necessary goods for the samurai class. Merchants had the lowest rank in Japanese feudal society. However, as you will see, their status gradually improved.

Japan Holds Off Mongols During the feudal age, most fighting took place between rival warlords, but the Mongol conquest of China and Korea also threatened Japan. When the Japanese refused to accept Mongol rule, Kublai Khan launched an invasion from Korea in 1274. A fleet carrying 30,000 troops arrived, but shortly afterwards a typhoon wrecked many Mongol ships and drove the invaders back to the mainland.

In 1281, the Mongols landed an even larger invasion force, but again a typhoon destroyed much of the Mongol fleet. The Japanese credited their miraculous delivery to the kamikaze (kah muh KAH zee), or divine winds. The Mongol failure reinforced the Japanese sense that they were a people set apart who enjoyed the special protection of the gods.

✔ **Checkpoint** What was bushido and why was it important?

The Tokugawas Unite Japan

The Kamakura shogunate crumbled in the aftermath of the Mongol invasions. A new dynasty took power in 1338, but the level of warfare increased after 1450. To defend their castles, daimyo gave arms to peasants as well as to samurai, which led to even more ruthless fighting. A popular saying of the time declared, "The warrior does not care if he's called a dog or beast. The main thing is winning."

Gradually, several powerful warriors united large parts of Japan. By 1590, the brilliant general Toyotomi Hideyoshi (hee day YOH shee), a commoner by birth, had brought most of Japan under his control. He then tried, but failed, to conquer Korea and China. In 1600, the daimyo Tokugawa Ieyasu (toh koo gah wah ee AY ah soo) defeated his rivals to become master of Japan. Three years later, he was named shogun. The Tokugawa shogunate would go on to rule Japan until 1868.

Central Government Imposed The Tokugawa shoguns were determined to end feudal warfare. They maintained the outward forms of feudal

Feudal Society in Japan

Emperor
Held highest rank in society but had no political power

Shogun
Actual ruler

Daimyo
Large landowners

Samurai
Warriors loyal to daimyo

Peasants
Three-fourths of the population

Merchants
Lowest status but gradually gained influence

Artisans
Made swords and armor for the samurai class

Chart Skills The organizational chart above illustrates the social levels of feudal society in Japan. *According to the chart, who occupied the lowest position? How does the chart show this?*

CODE OF THE SAMURAI

"If you think of saving your life," it was said, "you had better not go to war at all." The true samurai was supposed to have no fear of death. Samurai prepared for hardship by going hungry or walking barefoot in the snow. For a samurai, it was said, "when his stomach is empty, it is a disgrace to feel hungry." A samurai who betrayed the code of bushido was expected to commit seppuku, or ritual suicide, rather than live without honor. Bushido covered nearly every aspect of a samurai's life, including how to walk, bow, and hold chopsticks. It was also important for a warrior to balance his life by engaging in such activities as writing poetry, painting, or reading Japanese literature. In the 1400s, samurai warlord Hojo Soun advised his samurai followers, "Hold literary skills in your left hand, martial skills in your right."

► A Japanese family emblem

▼ Two samurai warriors duel in this woodblock print. The samurai wore colorful, patterned pants and robes under their armor. As weapons and armor progressed throughout the centuries, the sword and spear replaced the bow and arrows of the early samurai.

◄ Samurai warriors wore helmets with horns or antlers and fierce-looking masks to scare off the enemy. Their body armor was made of metal or leather scales that were tied together with string.

Thinking Critically

1. **Draw Conclusions** What might be the advantages and disadvantages of the type of armor used by a samurai?
2. **Synthesize Information** How did the rules that governed the samurai affect their way of life?

society but imposed central government control on all Japan. For this reason, their system of government is called centralized feudalism.

The Tokugawas created a unified, orderly society. To control the daimyo, they required these great lords to live in the shogun's capital at Edo (present-day Tokyo) every other year. A daimyo's wife and children had to remain in Edo full time, giving the shogun a powerful check on the entire family. The shogun also forbade daimyo to repair their castles or marry without permission.

Zen Gardening

Zen beliefs shaped Japanese culture in many ways. At Zen monasteries, upper-class men learned to express devotion to nature in such activities as landscape gardening. *How did Zen gardening reflect Zen values?*

New laws fixed the old social order rigidly in place and upheld a strict moral code. Only samurai were allowed to serve in the military or hold government jobs. They were expected to follow the traditions of bushido. Peasants had to remain on the land. People in lower classes were forbidden to wear luxuries such as silk clothing.

The Economy Booms While the shoguns tried to hold back social change, the Japanese economy grew by leaps and bounds. With peace restored to the countryside, agriculture improved and expanded. New seeds, tools, and the use of fertilizer led to a greater output of crops.

Food surpluses supported rapid population growth. Towns sprang up on the lands around the castles of daimyo. Edo grew into a booming city, where artisans and merchants flocked to supply the needs of the daimyo and their families.

Trade flourished within Japan. New roads linked castle towns and Edo. Each year, daimyo and their servants traveled to and from the capital, creating a demand for food and services along the route. In the cities, a wealthy merchant class emerged. In accordance with Confucian tradition, merchants had low social status. Japanese merchants, however, were able to gain influence by lending money to daimyo and samurai. Sometimes, merchants further improved their social position by arranging to marry their daughters into the samurai class.

 Checkpoint How did the Tokugawas set up centralized feudalism?

Zen Buddhism Shapes Culture

During Japan's feudal age, a Buddhist sect from China won widespread acceptance among samurai. Known in Japan as **Zen,** it emphasized self-reliance, meditation, and devotion to duty.

Zen had seemingly contradictory traditions. Zen monks were great scholars, yet they valued the uncluttered mind and <u>stressed</u> the importance of reaching a moment of "non-knowing." Zen stressed compassion for all, yet samurai fought to kill. In Zen monasteries, monks sought to experience absolute freedom, yet rigid rules were in place.

Vocabulary Builder

<u>stressed</u>—(stresd) *vt.* emphasized

Zen Buddhists believed that people could seek enlightenment through meditation and through the precise performance of everyday tasks. For example, the elaborate rituals of the tea ceremony reflected Zen values of peace, simplicity, and love of beauty. Zen reverence for nature also influenced the development of fine landscape paintings.

 Checkpoint How was Zen Buddhism similar to bushido?

Artistic Traditions Change

Cities such as Edo and Osaka were home to an explosion in the arts and theater. At stylish entertainment quarters, sophisticated nobles mixed with the urban middle class. Urban culture emphasized luxuries and pleasures and differed greatly from the feudal culture that had dominated Japan for centuries.

New Drama Develops In the 1300s, feudal culture had produced Noh plays performed on a square, wooden stage without scenery. Men wore elegant carved masks while a chorus chanted important lines to musical accompaniment. The action was slow, and each movement had a special meaning. Many Noh plays presented Zen Buddhist themes, emphasizing the need to renounce selfish desires. Others recounted fairy tales or the struggles between powerful feudal lords.

In the 1600s, towns gave rise to a popular new form of drama called Kabuki. Kabuki was influenced by Noh plays, but it was less refined and included comedy or melodrama. Puppet plays, known as bunraku, were also enormously popular in towns. A narrator told a story while handlers silently manipulated near-life-sized puppets. Bunraku plays catered to popular middle-class tastes.

Painting and Printmaking Japanese paintings often reflected the influence of Chinese landscape paintings, yet Japanese artists developed their own styles. On magnificent scrolls, painters boldly recreated historical events, such as the Mongol invasions.

In the 1600s, the vigorous urban culture produced a flood of colorful woodblock prints to satisfy middle-class tastes. Some woodblock artists produced humorous prints. Their fresh colors and simple lines give us a strong sense of the pleasures of town life in Japan.

 Checkpoint What new art forms catered to the growing middle class?

Progress Monitoring Online
For: Self-quiz with vocabulary practice
Web Code: naa-1241

Terms, People, and Places

1. For each term, person, or place listed at the beginning of the section, write a sentence explaining its significance.

Note Taking

2. **Reading Skill: Categorize** Use your completed table to answer the Focus Question: What internal and external factors shaped Japan's civilization, and what characterized Japan's feudal age?

Comprehension and Critical Thinking

3. **Make Comparisons** How was the Japanese development of kana similar to the Korean development of hangul?

4. **Analyze Information** How did the Japanese preserve their own identity and culture?

5. **Recognize Causes and Effects** Describe three results of the centralized feudalism imposed by the Tokugawas.

● Writing About History

Quick Write: Write a Thesis Statement and Introduction Review this section by thinking about cause and effect relationships in Japanese history. Write a thesis statement and introductory paragraph for an essay that discusses a cause and effect in ancient Japan. Remember that an introduction should map out what the essay will discuss.

Kabuki Theater

An *onnagata*, or actor who plays the part of a woman ▼

Kabuki is one of the most popular styles of traditional Japanese theater. Kabuki emerged in towns in the early 1600s and was less refined than the Noh plays that had previously been performed for feudal audiences. While actors in Noh plays use slow movements to tell a story, Kabuki actors often use lively and exaggerated movements. Although a woman named Okuni was credited with creating Kabuki, women have been banned from playing Kabuki roles for most of the theater's 400-year history.

▼ The first Kabuki plays were staged in a dry riverbed in Kyoto and featured female casts and dancing. A 1629 edict barred women from acting in Kabuki plays. With women banned from Kabuki, men known as *onnagata* played female roles. The *onnagata* achieved their impersonations with the help of elaborate costumes and make-up. Today, Kabuki artists perform a repertoire of about 300 plays involving everything from tragedies to light family comedies.

As Kabuki developed, ▶ various acting styles emerged. One of the best known was the *aragoto* or "rough business" style, which emphasized aggressiveness and masculinity. Actors employing this style would often strike an exaggerated pose known as a *mie*, which involved crossing the eyes and making a dramatic face.

Thinking Critically

1. **Make Comparisons** How did Kabuki differ from the Noh plays that had preceded it?
2. **Draw Inferences** How is Kabuki different from a typical play you might see in your community?

Burmese statue of
King Anawrahta

WITNESS HISTORY 🔊 AUDIO

Buddhism in Burma

According to the chronicles of early Burma (modern Myanmar), King Anawrahta converted to Theravada Buddhism due to the influence of a monk named Shin Arahan.

66 'Preach [to] me somewhat—yea, but a little—of the Law preached by the Lord, the Master!' And Shin Arahan preached the Law, beginning with the things not to be neglected. . . . Then the king's heart was full of faith, steadfast, and immovable; faith sank into him as oil filtered a hundred times soaks into cotton.99
—*The Glass Palace Chronicle of the Kings of Burma*

Focus Question How was Southeast Asia affected by the cultures of both China and India?

Diverse Cultures of Southeast Asia

Objectives
• Describe the geography of Southeast Asia.
• Understand the impact of India on the history of Southeast Asia.
• Summarize the characteristics of the new kingdoms and empires in Southeast Asia.
• Explain the emergence of Vietnam.

Terms, People, and Places
matrilineal
stupa
paddy

Note Taking

Reading Skill: Summarize As you read the section, prepare an outline like the one below to summarize the diverse characteristics of Southeast Asia.

> I. Geography of Southeast Asia
>   A. Location
>   1. Mainland set apart by mountains and plateaus
>   2.
>   B. Trade routes in the southern seas

Buddhism was one of many exports from India that had a profound effect on the peoples of Southeast Asia. Located between China and India, the region known today as Southeast Asia was strongly influenced by both of these powerful neighbors. Even so, the distinct cultures of Southeast Asia retained their own unique identities.

Geography of Southeast Asia

Southeast Asia is made up of two major regions. The first, mainland Southeast Asia, includes several peninsulas that jut south between India and China. Today, this region is home to Myanmar, Thailand, Cambodia, Laos, Vietnam, and part of Malaysia. The second region, island Southeast Asia, consists of more than 20,000 islands scattered between the Indian Ocean and the South China Sea. It includes the present-day nations of Indonesia, Singapore, Brunei (broo NY), and the Philippines.

Separated by Mountains The mainland is separated from the rest of Asia by mountains and high plateaus. Still, traders and invaders did push overland into the region. Mountains also separate the four main river valleys of Southeast Asia—the Irrawaddy (ihr uh WAH dee), Chao Phraya (chow PRY uh), Mekong, and Red. These river valleys were home to early civilizations.

Empires and Kingdoms of Southeast Asia

Geography *Interactive*

For: Audio guided tour
Web Code: nap-1251

Map Skills The region we call Southeast Asia consists of both a mainland area and thousands of islands. It was home to numerous ancient and diverse cultures.

1. **Locate** (a) Pagan kingdom (b) Angkor Wat (c) Strait of Malacca
2. **Movement** From which direction did the Mongol invasion take place?
3. **Recognize Sequence** During which centuries were these empires and kingdoms most likely to have come into contact with one another?

Legend:
- Pagan kingdom, A.D. 1044–A.D. 1287
- Khmer empire, A.D. 800–A.D. 1350
- Srivijaya empire, A.D. 600s–A.D. 1200s
- Vietnam kingdom, A.D. 939–A.D. 1883
- Mongol invasion, A.D. 1287

Miller Projection
0   300   600 mi
0   300   600km

Island Southeast Asia has long been of strategic importance. All seaborne trade between China and India had to pass through either the Malacca or Sunda straits. Whoever commanded these straits controlled rich trade routes.

Trade Routes in the Southern Seas The monsoons, or seasonal winds, shaped trading patterns in the southern seas. Ships traveled northeast in summer and southwest in winter. Between seasons, while waiting for the winds to shift, merchants harbored their vessels in Southeast Asian ports, which became important centers of trade and culture. Soon, an international trade network linked India, Southeast Asia, and China to East Africa and the Middle East. Originally, the key product of Southeast Asia was spices, and only a fraction of those traded in the region made their way to the markets in Europe.

Early Traditions The peoples of Southeast Asia developed their own cultures before Indian or Chinese influences shaped the region. At Bang Chiang in Thailand, archaeologists have found jars and bronze bracelets at least 5,000 years old. This evidence is challenging old theories about when civilization began in the region.

Over the centuries, diverse ethnic groups speaking many languages settled in Southeast Asia. Living in isolated villages, they followed their own religious and cultural patterns. Many societies were built around the nuclear family rather than the extended families of India and China.

Women had greater equality in Southeast Asia than elsewhere in Asia. Female merchants took part in the spice trade, gaining fame for their skill in bargaining, finance, and languages. In some port cities, they gained enough wealth and influence to become rulers. Matrilineal descent, or inheritance through the mother, was an accepted custom in Southeast Asia. Women also had some freedom in choosing or divorcing their marriage partners. Even after Indian and Chinese influences arrived, women retained their traditional rights.

 Checkpoint How did geography make Southeast Asia strategically important?

Indian Culture Spreads to Southeast Asia

Indian merchants and Hindu priests filtered into Southeast Asia, slowly spreading their culture. Later, Buddhist monks and scholars introduced Theravada beliefs. Following the path of trade and religion came the influence of writing, law, government, art, architecture, and farming.

Indian Influence Reaches Its Peak In the early centuries A.D., Indian traders settled in Southeast Asian port cities in growing numbers. They gave presents to local rulers and married into influential families. Trade brought prosperity as merchants exchanged products such as cotton cloth, jewels, and perfume for raw materials such as timber, spices, and gold.

In time, local Indian families exercised considerable power. Also, people from Southeast Asia visited India as pilgrims or students. As these contacts increased, Indian beliefs and ideas won widespread acceptance. Indian influence reached its peak between 500 and 1000.

Indians Bring Islam Long after Hinduism and Buddhism took root in Southeast Asia, Indians carried a third religion, Islam, into the region. By the 1200s, Muslims ruled northern India. From there, traders spread Islamic beliefs and Muslim culture throughout the islands of Indonesia and as far east as the Philippines. Today, Indonesia has the largest Muslim population of any nation in the world. Arab merchants, too, spread the new faith. The prevalence of Islam in lands surrounding the Indian Ocean contributed to the growth of a stable, thriving trade network.

The Shwezigon Pagoda
King Anawrahta made the Pagan kingdom a Buddhist center and had many stupas and pagodas built. Shown here are the elaborate interior columns at the famous Shwezigon Pagoda. *What does this pagoda suggest about the importance of Buddhism?*

 Checkpoint What changes occurred as India increased contact with Southeast Asia?

New Kingdoms and Empires Emerge

The blend of Indian influences with local cultures in time produced a series of kingdoms and empires in Southeast Asia. Some of these would rival those of India.

Angkor Wat

Angkor was the capital of the Khmer empire for more than 500 years. Built during this time were many impressive complexes of buildings. The most famous is Angkor Wat (above right), which still stands today in Cambodia. Inside, the temple walls are covered with detailed bas-relief carvings (above). *What does Angkor Wat reveal about the strength of the Khmer empire?*

The Pagan Kingdom Arises The kingdom of Pagan (puh GAHN) arose in the fertile rice-growing Irrawaddy Valley in present-day Myanmar. In 1044, King Anawrahta (an ow RAHT uh) united the region. He is credited with bringing Buddhism to the Burman people. Buddhism had reached nearby cultures long before, but Anawrahta made Pagan a major Buddhist center. He filled his capital city with magnificent **stupas,** or dome-shaped shrines, at about the same time that people in medieval Europe were beginning to build Gothic cathedrals.

Pagan flourished for some 200 years after Anawrahta's death, but fell in 1287 to conquering Mongols. When the Burmans finally threw off foreign rule, they looked back with pride to the great days of Pagan.

The Khmer Empire Indian influences also helped shape the Khmer (kuh MEHR) empire, which reached its peak between 800 and 1350. Its greatest rulers controlled much of present-day Cambodia, Thailand, and Malaysia. The Khmer people adapted Indian writing, mathematics, architecture, and art. Khmer rulers became pious Hindus. Like the princes and emperors of India, they saw themselves as god-kings. Most ordinary people, however, preferred Buddhism.

In the 1100s, King Suryavarman II (sur yuh VAHR mun) built the great temple complex at Angkor Wat. The ruins that survive today, though overgrown with jungle and pocked by the bullets of recent wars, are among the most impressive in the world. Hundreds of carved figures tell Hindu myths and glorify the king. Although the images of Vishnu, Shiva, and the Buddha reflect strong Indian influence, the style is uniquely Khmer.

Srivijaya Empire Flourishes In Indonesia, the trading empire of Srivijaya (sree wih JAW yuh) flourished from the 600s to the 1200s. Srivijaya controlled the Strait of Malacca, which was vital to shipping. Both Hinduism and Buddhism reached this island empire. As elsewhere in Southeast Asia, however, the local people often blended Indian beliefs into their own forms of worship based on nature spirits.

Later, Islam spread to Sumatra, Java, and other islands. Local rulers adopted the new religion, which cemented commercial links with other Muslim trading centers around the Indian Ocean.

✓ **Checkpoint** How did India influence the Pagan kingdom and the Khmer and Srivijaya empires?

Vietnam Emerges

In most of Southeast Asia, Indian influence outweighed Chinese influence. Indian traditions spread mostly through trade rather than conquest. China, however, sent military forces to conquer the neighboring state of Annam (now the northern part of Vietnam). The heart of northern Vietnam was the Red River delta, around present-day Hanoi. There, the river irrigated fertile rice **paddies,** or fields, which provided food for a growing population.

Chinese Domination In 111 B.C., Han armies conquered the region, and China remained in control for the next 1,000 years. During that time, the Vietnamese absorbed Confucian ideas. They adopted the Chinese civil service system and built a government bureaucracy similar to that found in China. Vietnamese nobles adopted the custom of speaking and writing the Chinese language. Unlike the rest of Southeast Asia, where Theravada Buddhism had the strongest <u>impact</u>, Vietnam adopted Mahayana beliefs from China. Daoism also helped shape Vietnamese society.

The Vietnamese Preserve Their Identity Despite these powerful Chinese influences, the Vietnamese preserved a strong sense of their separate identity. In A.D. 39, two noble sisters, Trung Trac and Trung Nhi, led an uprising that briefly drove the Chinese occupiers from the land. They tried to restore a simpler form of government based on ancient Vietnamese traditions. To this day, the Trung sisters are remembered as great martyrs and heroes. Finally in 939, as the Tang dynasty collapsed in China, Vietnam was able to break free from China. Thereafter, the Vietnamese turned back repeated Chinese efforts to re-conquer their land, but they still remained a tributary state of China for years to come.

✓ **Checkpoint** How did China influence Vietnam?

Vocabulary Builder
<u>impact</u>—(IM pakt) *n.* effect

SECTION 5 **Assessment**

Progress Monitoring *Online*
For: Self-quiz with vocabulary practice
Web Code: naa-1251

Terms, People, and Places
1. For each term, person, or place listed at the beginning of the section, write a sentence explaining its significance.

Note Taking
2. **Reading Skill: Summarize** Use your completed outline to answer the Focus Question: How was Southeast Asia affected by the cultures of both China and India?

Comprehension and Critical Thinking
3. **Analyze Information** How did geography make Southeast Asia of strategic importance?
4. **Make Comparisons** How did the spread of Indian influence differ from the spread of Chinese influence in Southeast Asia?
5. **Identify Central Issues** How did Vietnam retain its own identity despite adapting much of China's culture?

● **Writing About History**
Quick Write: Gather Evidence to Support Thesis Statement Write a thesis statement on the impact of India on Southeast Asia. Review the section and list facts that support the thesis statement.

Quick Study Guide

Progress Monitoring Online
For: Self-test with vocabulary practice
Web Code: naa-1261

■ Cultural Achievements of the Tang and Song Dynasties

- *Calligraphy* Artists sought balance and harmony through the mastery of simple strokes and lines.
- *Chinese landscape painting* Painters sought to capture the spiritual essence of nature.
- *Porcelain* The Chinese perfected skills in making porcelain that would be prized around the world.
- *Architecture* Pagodas, influenced by Indian Buddhism, graced the landscape.
- *Literature* Writers created short stories and thousands of poems.

■ The Mongol and Ming Empires

c.1200: Mongols unite warring tribes and begin conquering China.	Genghis Khan builds the Mongol empire by taking land from Russia to China.	1279: Kublai Khan topples last Song emperor.
Kublai Khan expands the empire to its largest size. Mongols attempt to run the empire without the Chinese, with some success.	1368: Chinese peasant leader pushes out Mongols and founds the Ming dynasty.	Ming rule reasserts a Chinese government. The economy booms during a period of cultural flowering and overseas exploration.

■ China's Influence on Its Neighbors

Korea — Chinese Influence

Language
- Writing
- Histories and poems
- Woodblock printing

Government
- United with help of Tang China
- Confucian principles of government
- Restricted role of women
- Civil service examinations

Belief systems
- Buddhism
- Confucian emphasis on family

Arts
- Landscape paintings
- Porcelain

Japan — Chinese Influence

Language
- Chinese spoken in the capital
- Official histories written in Chinese

Government
- Code of laws
- Absolute authority of emperor
- Strong central government
- Civil service

Belief systems
- Buddhism
- Confucianism

Arts
- Tang music, dance, and gardens
- Tea ceremony
- Architecture of the capital
- Pagoda architecture

■ Events From 500–1650

500s	618	668	794	960
Buddhism is introduced to Japan.	The Tang dynasty begins in China.	Silla rulers unite Korea.	The Japanese royal court moves to Heian.	The Song dynasty is founded in China.

Chapter Events
Global Events

500   **700**   **900**

527	800
Justinian becomes ruler of the Byzantine empire.	Charlemagne is crowned emperor by the pope.

Concept Connector

Cumulative Review

Record the answers to the questions below on your Concept Connector worksheets. In addition, record information from this chapter about the following concepts:

- Technology: printing press
- Technology: gunpowder
- Empires: Mongol
- Empires: Ming
- Trade: Chinese trade in southern China and up coast
- Belief Systems: Shinto

1. **Empire** The Roman empire and the Tang dynasty each established a system of government to rule over their lands. What do the two empires and their governments have in common? How are they different? Think about the following:
   - the importance of law
   - government officials
   - economic reforms
   - challenges

2. **Geography's Impact** A nation's geography can determine its culture and even its government. Geography shaped how Japanese people lived, much as it determined how Mesopotamians lived between the Tigris and Euphrates rivers. Describe the impact of geography in Japan and in Mesopotamia. Think about the following:
   - ways of living
   - natural disasters
   - trade

3. **Cultural Diffusion** China had an enormous influence on all of East Asia. Many people who spread Chinese culture were Buddhist missionaries. Hundreds of years earlier, Christian missionaries worked to spread Christianity throughout the Roman empire. How did new ideas and aspects of culture spread in both regions as a result? Think about the following:
   - what was shared in addition to religion
   - acceptance of new ideas
   - reaction to missionaries

Connections to Today

1. **Economics: Rapid Growth in China** During the Ming dynasty, China's economy grew rapidly. Agriculture, trade, and manufacturing created much wealth. Today, China is going through another economic boom. Find articles about China in newspapers or news magazines. Gather statistics that demonstrate how China's economy is expanding. Write a paragraph about China's economy.

2. **Government: A Peninsula Divided** Korean unity lasted almost 1,300 years. But today, the Korean peninsula is again divided into hostile camps. While North Korea is a communist country, South Korea is a democracy. Both North and South Korea want to reunify Korea. Both have massed soldiers and equipment along the border between them. The United States is South Korea's most powerful ally. North Korea maintains close ties to Communist China and has worked to develop nuclear weapons. As a result, Korea is one of the world's hot spots. The Korean War was fought there (1950–1953), and there is a fear that the troubled Korean Peninsula may be the site of more bloodshed. How is today's division of Korea different from that of the early kingdoms?

1279
The Mongol conquest of China is completed.

1392
The Choson dynasty begins its 518-year reign in Korea.

1603
Tokugawa Ieyasu becomes shogun of Japan.

1100   **1300**   **1500**   **1700**

1300s
The kingdom of Benin is established in West Africa.

1492
Christopher Columbus voyages from Spain to the Americas.

History Interactive
For: Interactive timeline
Web Code: nap-1201

403

Chapter Assessment

Terms, People, and Places

Match the following terms with the definitions below. You will not use all the terms.

literacy rate	stupa
land reform	Marco Polo
hangul	Kublai Khan
archipelago	pagoda
samurai	matrilineal

1. dome-shaped shrine
2. percentage of people who can read or write
3. the Mongol leader who unseated the last Song emperor
4. chain of islands
5. breakup of large agricultural holdings for redistribution among peasants
6. alphabet that uses symbols to represent the sounds of spoken Korean
7. multistoried Buddhist temple with its origins in India
8. member of the warrior class in Japanese feudal society

Main Ideas

Section 1 (pp. 368–375)
9. How did Tang rulers carry empire building to new heights?

Section 2 (pp. 376–382)
10. What impact did Mongol rule have on Asia?

Section 3 (pp. 383–386)
11. Describe the location of Korea in relation to China and Japan.

Section 4 (pp. 387–396)
12. How has Japan's island geography affected its history?
13. How did life in Japan change under the Tokugawas?

Section 5 (pp. 397–401)
14. Identify two early traditions of people in Southeast Asia.

Chapter Focus Question
15. How did China's culture develop and influence its neighbors in East and Southeast Asia?

Critical Thinking

16. **Draw Conclusions** How might a map of China before the Tang dynasty differ from a map of China afterward? Give two examples.
17. **Synthesize Information** How was the Mongol period both destructive and constructive?
18. **Analyze Information** (a) Describe the Japanese practice of selective borrowing. (b) What are some of the benefits and disadvantages of borrowing from other cultures?
19. **Geography and History** In what ways are the geographies of Japan and Korea similar? What similar effects has geography had on these nations?
20. **Make Comparisons** How were the kingdoms and empires in Southeast Asia similar and different?
21. **Analyzing Visuals** Ming dynasty artisans created a unique form of blue and white porcelain, as shown here. How does this vase build on earlier Chinese achievements?

● Writing About History

Writing an Expository Essay The regions of East and Southeast Asia were influenced by neighboring countries such as China and India. Write an expository essay to compare and contrast the ways China influenced Korea and Japan. Consult page SH10 of the Writing Handbook for additional help.

Prewriting
- Draw a Venn diagram to compare and contrast the cultures of Korea and Japan as influenced by China. Remember to list common factors in the shared center of the diagram.

Drafting
- Now that you have identified points of comparison and contrast, decide how you want to present the details. Would it make more sense to use subject-by-subject organization or point-by-point organization?
- Write a thesis statement and an attention-grabbing introduction.
- Provide elaboration to fully develop your points of comparison and contrast.

Revising
- Use the guidelines for revising your report on page SH12 of the Writing Handbook.

Document-Based Assessment

Shinto: "The Way of the Spirits"

Shinto originated in prehistoric times. At the heart of Shinto is the belief in spirit beings that govern the natural world. Many shrines and festivals are dedicated to these kami. Over the centuries, Confucianism, Daoism, and especially Buddhism, influenced Shinto. The native religion absorbed elements of these foreign religions, while remaining uniquely Japanese, as the documents here illustrate.

Document A

▼ People walk through a wooden torii, or tall shrine gate, in front of the Meiji Shinto Shrine, Japan.

Document B

"At this time the heavenly deities, all with one command, said to the two deities Izanagi-nö-mikötö and Izanami- nö-mikötö: 'Complete and solidify this drifting land!'

Giving them the Heavenly Jeweled Spear, they entrusted the mission to them. Thereupon, the two deities stood on the Heavenly Floating Bridge and, lowering the jeweled spear, stirred with it. They stirred the brine with a churning-churning sound; and when they lifted up [the spear] again, the brine dripping down from the tip of the spear piled up and became an island. This was the island Onögörö."

—From ***Kojiki***, an ancient Shinto text

Document C

"Speaking in general, it may be said that kami signifies, in the first place, the deities of heaven and earth that appear in the ancient records and also the kami spirits of the shrines where they are worshipped. . . . It also includes such objects as birds, beasts, trees, plants, seas, mountains, and so forth. In ancient usage, anything whatsoever which was outside the ordinary, which possessed superior power, or which was awe-inspiring was called kami. . . . It is needless to say that among human beings who are called kami the successive generations of sacred emperors are all included."

—Motoori Norinaga (1730–1801), a great Japanese scholar

Document D

"The Japanese pray to kami (deities) for longevity, health, wealth, fame, and all other world benefits, while they turn to *hotoke* (Buddha) for their personal religious salvation."

—Luis de Almeida, a Portuguese Jesuit visitor, 1565

Analyzing Documents

Use your knowledge of Shinto and Documents A, B, C, and D to answer the questions below.

1. The people in Document A are most likely visiting the shrine to
   A attend a funeral.
   B visit relatives.
   C pray to the kami and worship.
   D for good karma.

2. What does the legend in Document B describe?
   A the creation of Japan
   B the creation of the Japanese people
   C the gift of rice from the kami to the Japanese people
   D the gift of fire from the kami to the Japanese people

3. According to Document C, the emperors of Japan are
   A spirits of the shrines.
   B objects in nature.
   C kami.
   D deities of heaven and earth.

4. In what ways is Shinto a unique religion? Use these documents along with information from the chapter in your answer. (Hint: You may compare Shinto to a religion with which you are familiar.)

THE WORLD
in 1700

Possessions and Trading Posts

- England
- France
- Netherlands
- Spain
- Portugal
- Other states

TLINGIT

North America

PUEBLOS

NEW FRANCE

ENGLISH COLONIES

NEW SPAIN

Atlantic Ocean

Pacific Ocean

GUIANA

South America

PERU

BRAZIL

N

NORWAY-DENMARK

SWEDEN

NETHERLANDS

POLAND

ENGLAND

Europe

FRANCE

AUSTRIA

PORTUGAL SPAIN

OTTOMAN EMPIRE

Gorée
Cacheu

BORNU

DARFUR

FUNJ

HAUSA STATES

ETHIOPIA

ASANTE

Accra

BENIN

Elmina

São Tomé

Africa

RWANDA

BURUNDI

KONGO

ANGOLA

MOZAMBIQUE

Sofala

Cape Town

RUSSIAN EMPIRE

Asia

CHINESE
EMPIRE

PERSIAN
EMPIRE

Deshima   JAPAN

*Pacific
Ocean*

MUGHAL
EMPIRE   BURMA
    Bombay   Macao
Goa   PHILIPPINE
    Madras   ISLANDS
        SIAM
Cochin   Pondicherry   ANNAM
    CEYLON

*Indian
Ocean*

DUTCH EAST INDIES
            PORTUGUESE
            TIMOR

Bourbon

Australia

Mercator Projection
0   1,000   2,000 miles
0   1,000   2,000 kilometers
Scale at the Equator

Geography *Interactive*
For: Audio guided tour
Web Code: nap-3000

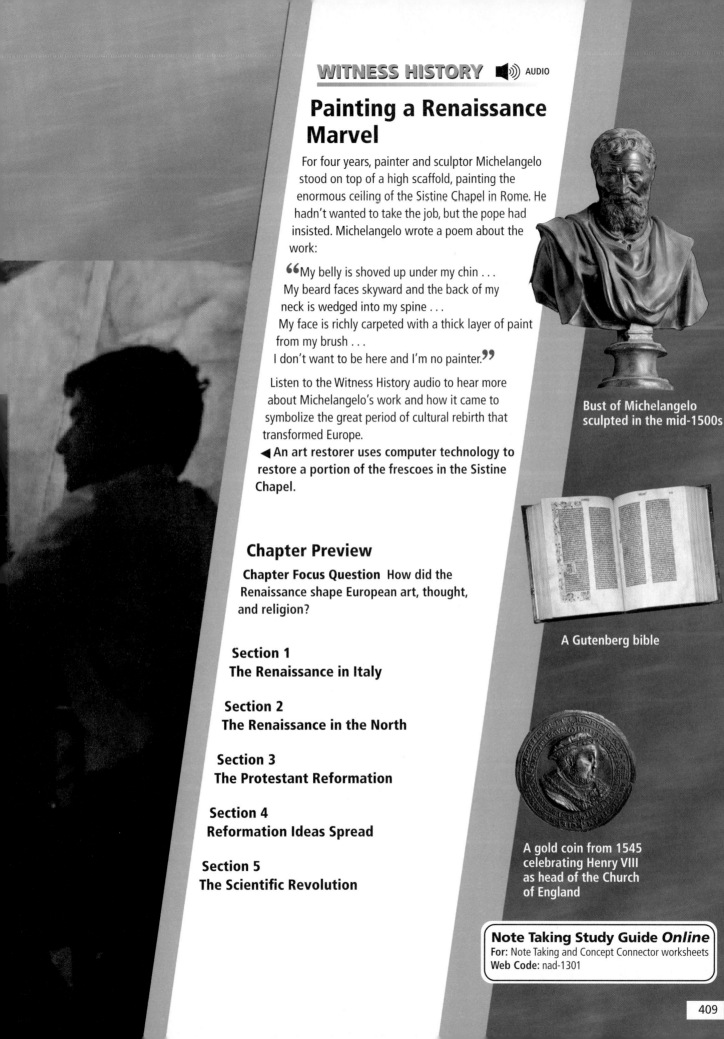

Painting a Renaissance Marvel

For four years, painter and sculptor Michelangelo stood on top of a high scaffold, painting the enormous ceiling of the Sistine Chapel in Rome. He hadn't wanted to take the job, but the pope had insisted. Michelangelo wrote a poem about the work:

66 My belly is shoved up under my chin . . .
My beard faces skyward and the back of my neck is wedged into my spine . . .
My face is richly carpeted with a thick layer of paint from my brush . . .
I don't want to be here and I'm no painter. **99**

Listen to the Witness History audio to hear more about Michelangelo's work and how it came to symbolize the great period of cultural rebirth that transformed Europe.

◀ An art restorer uses computer technology to restore a portion of the frescoes in the Sistine Chapel.

Bust of Michelangelo sculpted in the mid-1500s

A Gutenberg bible

Chapter Preview

Chapter Focus Question How did the Renaissance shape European art, thought, and religion?

Section 1
The Renaissance in Italy

Section 2
The Renaissance in the North

Section 3
The Protestant Reformation

Section 4
Reformation Ideas Spread

Section 5
The Scientific Revolution

A gold coin from 1545 celebrating Henry VIII as head of the Church of England

Note Taking Study Guide *Online*
For: Note Taking and Concept Connector worksheets
Web Code: nad-1301

Vasari designed the Uffizi Gallery in Florence, which houses his self-portrait.

A detail from the Uffizi

WITNESS HISTORY 🔊 AUDIO

An Artist Becomes a Biographer

In 1546, a young artist named Giorgio Vasari dined at the Cardinal's residence in Rome. The conversation turned to the amazing artistic achievement of Renaissance Italy. Vasari decided to record a tribute to all the important Italian artists who had contributed to this remarkably creative time period. Four years later, Vasari published his book *Lives of the Most Eminent Painters, Sculptors, and Architects.* A true "Renaissance man"— he was an able painter and architect as well as a writer—Vasari also became a biographer and historian of his era.

Focus Question What were the ideals of the Renaissance, and how did Italian artists and writers reflect these ideals?

The Renaissance in Italy

Objectives

- Describe the characteristics of the Renaissance and understand why it began in Italy.
- Identify Renaissance artists and explain how new ideas affected the arts of the period.
- Understand how writers of the time addressed Renaissance themes.

Terms, People, and Places

humanism	Leonardo
humanities	Michelangelo
Petrarch	Raphael
Florence	Baldassare Castiglione
patron	Niccolò Machiavelli
perspective	

N̲o̲te Taking

Reading Skill: Identify Main Ideas As you read, create an outline like the one below to record main ideas about the Italian Renaissance.

    I. What was the Renaissance?
    A. A changing worldview
       1.
       2.
    B. A spirit of adventure

A new age had dawned in Western Europe, given expression by remarkable artists and thinkers. Europeans called this age the Renaissance, meaning "rebirth." It began in the 1300s and reached its peak around 1500. The Renaissance marked the transition from medieval times to the early modern world.

What Was the Renaissance?

The Renaissance was a time of creativity and great change in many areas—political, social, economic, and cultural. It marked a slow shift from an agricultural to an urban society, in which trade assumed greater importance than in the past. It was also a time when creative thinking and new technology let people <u>comprehend</u> and describe their world more accurately.

A New Worldview Evolves During the Renaissance, creative minds set out to transform their own age. Their era, they felt, was a time of rebirth after what they saw as the disorder and disunity of the medieval world.

Renaissance thinkers had a reawakened interest in the classical learning of Greece and Rome, which medieval scholars had preserved. They continued to use Latin as the language of the Church as well as for scholarship. Yet they produced new attitudes toward culture and learning. Medieval scholars had focused more on religious beliefs and spirituality. In contrast, Renaissance thinkers explored the richness and variety of human experience in the here and now. At the same time, society placed a new emphasis on individual achievement. Indeed, the Renaissance ideal was a person with talents in many fields.

A Spirit of Adventure The Renaissance supported a spirit of adventure and a wide-ranging curiosity that led people to explore new worlds or to reexamine old ones. Navigators who sailed across the ocean, scientists who looked at the universe in new ways, and writers and artists who experimented with new forms and techniques all shared that spirit. In part, that spirit of adventure came from a new view of man himself. As Italian thinker Pico della Mirandola asserted in 1486: "To [man] it is granted to have whatever he chooses, to be whatever he wills."

Expressing Humanism At the heart of the Italian Renaissance was an intellectual movement known as humanism. Humanists studied the classical culture of Greece and Rome, but used that study to increase their understanding of their own times. Though most humanists were pious Christians, they focused on worldly subjects rather than on the religious issues that had occupied medieval thinkers. Humanists believed that education should stimulate the individual's creative powers. They emphasized the humanities—subjects such as grammar, rhetoric (the study of using language effectively), poetry, and history—that had been taught in ancient Greek and Roman schools.

Francesco Petrarch (PEE trahrk), a Florentine who lived in the 1300s, was an early Renaissance humanist, poet, and scholar. He assembled a library of Greek and Roman manuscripts in monasteries and churches. In later years his efforts and those of others encouraged by his example enabled the works of Cicero, Homer, and Virgil to again become known to Western Europeans.

 Checkpoint What were the main characteristics of the Renaissance?

Italy: Cradle of the Renaissance

The Renaissance began in Italy. Over the next hundred years it spread to the rest of Europe, eventually transforming the entire Western world. Italy was the birthplace of the Renaissance for several reasons.

Italy's History and Geography Renaissance thinkers had a new interest in ancient Rome. Since Italy had been the center of the Roman empire, it was a logical place for this reawakening to <u>emerge</u>. Architectural remains, statues, and coins were all available for people to study. Rome was also the seat of the Roman Catholic Church, an important patron of the arts. As the center of Catholicism, Rome also served as an inspiration for religious themes used by artists and writers.

Italy's location encouraged trade with well-developed markets on the eastern Mediterranean and in northern Africa, as well as in northern Europe. Ships carrying a great variety of goods docked at Italy's many ports. Extensive banking, manufacturing, and merchant networks developed to support trade. While trade declined throughout most of Europe during the Middle Ages, it remained strong in Italy. Trade provided the wealth that fueled Italy's Renaissance. Trade routes also carried new ideas, important in shaping the Renaissance.

Michelangelo's _David_
Michelangelo sculpted his masterpiece _David_ out of a block of marble left over from another sculpture. Completed in 1504, the statue was commissioned to express the power and strength of Florence.

Vocabulary Builder

comprehend—(kahm pree HEND) _v._ understand; take in
emerge—(ee MURJ) _v._ develop; rise from; become known

Italian Bankers
An illuminated manuscript from the late 1400s depicts a typical scene in an Italian banking house. *How is the wealth of the banker shown in this image?*

Italy's Vibrant City-States Unlike the kingdoms of most of the rest of Europe, Italy was divided into many small city-states. Each Italian city-state was controlled by a powerful family and dominated by a wealthy and powerful merchant class. These merchant families exerted both political and economic leadership, and their interest in art and emphasis on personal achievement helped to shape the Italian Renaissance.

The Medici (MED uh chee) family of **Florence,** for example, ranked among the richest merchants and bankers in Europe. Cosimo de' Medici gained control of the Florentine government in 1434, and the family continued as uncrowned rulers of the city for many years. Cosimo's grandson Lorenzo, known as "the Magnificent," represented the Renaissance ideal. A clever politician, he held Florence together during difficult times in the late 1400s. He was also a generous **patron,** or financial supporter, of the arts. At Lorenzo's invitation, poets and philosophers frequently visited the Medici palace. Artists learned their craft by sketching ancient Roman statues displayed in the Medici gardens.

The Medicis' great wealth and influence transformed Florence. Perhaps more than any other city, it came to symbolize the energy and brilliance of the Italian Renaissance. Like the ancient city of Athens, it produced a dazzling number of gifted poets, artists, architects, scholars, and scientists in a relatively short span of time.

 Checkpoint Why was Italy a favorable setting for the Renaissance?

Renaissance Art Flowers

The Renaissance attained its most glorious expression in its paintings, sculpture, and architecture. Wealthy patrons, popes, and princes played a major role in this artistic flowering. Ordinary people—who were beginning to appreciate human experiences not related to the Church—also played a role.

Reflecting Humanist Thought Renaissance art reflected the ideas of humanism. Like artists of the Middle Ages, Renaissance artists portrayed religious themes. However, they often set religious figures such as Jesus and Mary against classical Greek or Roman backgrounds. Painters also produced portraits of well-known figures of the day, reflecting the humanist interest in individual achievement. Renaissance artists studied ancient Greek and Roman works and revived many classical forms. The sculptor Donatello, for example, created a life-size statue of a soldier on horseback. It was the first such figure done since ancient times.

Using New Artistic Techniques Roman art had been very realistic, but in medieval times art became much more stylized. Renaissance painters returned to the realism of classical times by developing new techniques for representing both humans and landscapes. In particular, the rules of **perspective** allowed Renaissance artists to create realistic art. By making distant objects smaller than those close to the viewer, artists could paint scenes that appeared three-dimensional.

Geography *Interactive*
For: Audio guided tour
Web Code: nap-1311

Legend:
- Duchy of Milan
- Republic of Genoa
- Republic of Florence
- Papal States
- Republic of Venice
- Kingdoms under Spanish sovereignty
- Other city-states
- Boundary of Holy Roman Empire
- Major sea route
- ◉ Banking center

Map Skills The states and kingdoms of Italy lay at the center of Europe's sea trade.

1. **Locate** (a) Florence (b) Palermo (c) Crete
2. **Identify** Which republic controlled Crete? Which kingdom controlled Sicily?
3. **Apply Information** Why were so many banking centers located in Italy?

Other techniques enabled Renaissance artists to give their work energy and realism. Renaissance painters used shading to make objects look round and real, and new oil paints to reflect light. Painters and sculptors also studied human anatomy and drew from observing live models. As a result, they were able to portray the human body much more accurately than medieval artists had done.

Architecture: A "Social Art" Architecture was transformed in Renaissance Italy. Architect Leon Alberti described architecture as a "social art," meant to blend beauty with utility and improvement of society. Architects rejected the Gothic style of the late Middle Ages as disorderly. Instead, they adopted the columns, arches, and domes that had been favored by the Greeks and Romans. For the cathedral in Florence, Filippo Brunelleschi (broo nay LAYS kee) created a majestic dome, which he modeled on the dome of the Pantheon in Rome. Like other Renaissance artists, Brunelleschi was multitalented. He studied art and sculpture with Donatello and was an accomplished engineer, inventing many of the machines used to construct his dome.

Leonardo da Vinci Artist Leonardo da Vinci (duh VIN chee) (1452–1519) had an endless curiosity that fed a genius for invention. He made sketches of nature and of models in his studio, and dissected corpses to learn how bones and muscles work. As a result, Leonardo's paintings grip people with their realism. The *Mona Lisa* is a portrait of a woman whose mysterious smile has baffled viewers for centuries. *The Last Supper*, showing Jesus and his apostles on the night before the crucifixion, is both a moving religious painting and a masterpiece of perspective. Because Leonardo experimented with a new type of paint, much of *The Last Supper* decayed over the years. However, it has recently been restored.

Leonardo thought of himself as an artist. Yet his talents and accomplishments ranged over many areas, including botany, anatomy, optics, music, architecture, and engineering. He made sketches for flying machines and undersea boats centuries before the first airplane or submarine was actually built. Though most of his paintings are lost today, his many notebooks survive as a testament to his genius and creativity.

Michelangelo Artist Michelangelo Buonarroti (1475–1564), like Leonardo, had many talents—he was a sculptor, engineer, painter, architect, and poet. Michelangelo has been called a "melancholy genius" because his work reflects his many life-long spiritual and artistic struggles. In his twenties, he created marble masterpieces such as *David* and the

● **INFOGRAPHIC**

The Discovery of Perspective

Before the 1400s, artists did not know how to create perspective, or the technique of showing distant objects on flat surfaces the way the eye actually sees them. The discovery of perspective revolutionized art. Using simple geometry, Renaissance artists could for the first time reproduce what their eyes actually saw.

Brunelleschi is credited with inventing perspective. His many studies (left) helped him design Florence's Duomo, completed in 1436. At 185 feet (56 m) high, it was the largest domed structure built since A.D. 125. ▶

Artist Leon Alberti refined Brunelleschi's ideas. ▶
He wrote books explaining the rules of perspective, and developed the "perspective net" (right).
To show perspective, the artist looks over an eyepiece and through the net at a model (far right).
Then he reproduces the outlines of the model on paper with grids corresponding to those on the net.

Pietà. The *Pietà* captures the sorrow of the Biblical Mary as she cradles her dead son Jesus on her knees. Michelangelo's heroic statue of *David,* the Biblical shepherd who killed the giant Goliath, recalls the harmony and grace of ancient Greek tradition.

One of Michelangelo's greatest projects was painting a series of huge murals to decorate the ceiling of the Sistine Chapel in Rome. The enormous task, which took four years to complete and left the artist partially crippled, depicted the biblical history of the world from the Creation to the Flood. Michelangelo was also a talented architect. His most famous design was for the dome of St. Peter's Cathedral in Rome. It served as a model for many later structures, including the United States Capitol building in Washington, D.C.

Raphael A few years younger than Michelangelo, Raphael (rah fah EL) (1483–1520) was widely admired both for his artistic talent and "his sweet and gracious nature." Raphael studied the works of the great masters but developed his own style of painting that blended Christian and classical styles. He is probably best known for his tender portrayals of the Madonna, the mother of Jesus. In *The School of Athens,* Raphael pictured an imaginary gathering of great thinkers and scientists, including Plato, Aristotle, Socrates, and the Arab philosopher Averroës. With typical Renaissance self-confidence, Raphael included the faces of Michelangelo, Leonardo—and himself.

✓ **Checkpoint** How were Renaissance ideals reflected in the arts?

History Interactive,
For: Interactive *The Last Supper*
Web Code: nap-1312

Leonardo eagerly explored perspective in his mural *The Last Supper.* He uses converging lines, like those shown below, to create a vanishing point. This vanishing point draws the viewer's eye to the space above Jesus, and gives the painting the illusion of space and depth. ▶

Thinking Critically
1. **Apply Information** Why was the invention of perspective necessary for artists to achieve realism in painting?
2. **Analyze Visuals** What other techniques bring the eye to the central figure of Jesus in *The Last Supper*?

In the mid-1500s, Giorgio Vasari wrote a biography of Leonardo da Vinci, whose self-portrait is shown here. Why is Leonardo da Vinci described today as an ideal "Renaissance man"?

Primary Source

❝Sometimes, in supernatural fashion, beauty, grace, and talent are united beyond measure in one single person. . . . This was seen by all mankind in Leonardo da Vinci . . . so great was his genius, and such its growth, that to whatever difficulties he turned his mind, he solved them with ease. In him was great bodily strength . . . with a spirit and courage ever royal and magnanimous; and the fame of his name so increased, that not only in his lifetime was he held in esteem, but his reputation became even greater among posterity after his death.❞ AUDIO

Writing for a New Society

Italian writers reflected the trademark Renaissance curiosity and interest in the humanities. Humanists and historians wrote works of philosophy and scholarship. Other writers developed a literature of guidebooks to help ambitious men and women who wanted to achieve success in the Renaissance world.

Castiglione's Ideal Courtier The most widely read of these handbooks was *The Book of the Courtier*. Its author, Baldassare Castiglione (kahs teel YOH nay), describes the manners, skills, learning, and virtues that a member of the court should have. Castiglione's ideal courtier was a well-educated, well-mannered aristocrat who mastered many fields, from poetry to music to sports.

Castiglione's ideal differed for men and women. The ideal man, he wrote, is athletic but not overactive. He is good at games, but not a gambler. He plays a musical instrument and knows literature and history but is not arrogant. The ideal woman offers a balance to men. She is graceful and kind, lively but reserved. She is beautiful, "for outer beauty," wrote Castiglione, "is the true sign of inner goodness."

Machiavelli's Successful Prince Niccolò Machiavelli (mahk ee uh VEL ee) wrote a guide for rulers on how to gain and maintain power. Unlike ancient writers such as Plato, Machiavelli did not discuss leadership in terms of high ideals. Instead, his book *The Prince* looked at real rulers in an age of ruthless power politics. Machiavelli stressed that the end justifies the means. He urged rulers to use whatever methods were necessary to achieve their goals.

Machiavelli saw himself as an enemy of oppression and corruption, but critics attacked his cynical advice. (In fact, the term "Machiavellian" came to refer to the use of deceit in politics.) Later students of government, however, argued that Machiavelli provided a realistic look at politics. His work continues to spark debate because it raises important ethical questions about the nature of government and the use of power.

✓ **Checkpoint**   How did Renaissance writings express realism?

Progress Monitoring *Online*
For: Self-quiz with vocabulary practice
Web Code: naa-1311

SECTION 1
Assessment

Terms, People, and Places

1. For each term, person, or place listed at the beginning of the section, write a sentence explaining its significance.

Note Taking

2. **Reading Skill: Identify Main Ideas** Use your completed outline to answer the Focus Question: What were the ideals of the Renaissance, and how did Italian artists and writers reflect these ideals?

Comprehension and Critical Thinking

3. **Make Generalizations** How was the Renaissance worldview different from that of the Middle Ages?

4. **Summarize** In what ways did Italian city-states encourage the Renaissance?

5. **Synthesize Information** How did humanism influence Renaissance painting and sculpture?

6. **Recognize Ideologies** Why were nature and human nature important to Renaissance artists and writers?

● **Writing About History**

Quick Write: Generate Arguments Consider the following thesis statement for a persuasive essay: Renaissance Italy produced some of the greatest writers and thinkers that the world has ever known. Next, generate a number of arguments that support that thesis. Rank your arguments in order of importance.

The Prince by Niccolò Machiavelli

Florentine Niccolò Machiavelli (1469–1527) served in the government as a diplomat for fourteen years before becoming a full-time writer and scholar. In 1513, he used his experience in politics and his studies of ancient Roman history to write a book called *The Prince*. In this book, Machiavelli combined his personal experience of politics with his knowledge of the past to offer a guide to rulers on how to gain and maintain power.

Here the question arises: is it better to be loved than feared, or vice versa? I don't doubt that every prince would like to be both; but since it is hard to accommodate these qualities, if you have to make a choice, to be feared is much safer than to be loved. For it is a good general rule about men, that they are ungrateful, fickle[1], liars and deceivers, fearful of danger and greedy for gain. While you serve their welfare, they are all yours, offering their blood, their belongings, their lives, and their children's lives, as we noted above—so long as the danger is remote. But when the danger is close at hand, they turn against you. Then, any prince who has relied on their words and has made no other preparations will come to grief; because friendships that are bought at a price, and not with greatness and nobility of soul, may be paid for but they are not acquired, and they cannot be used in time of need. People are less concerned with offending a man who makes himself loved than one who makes himself feared: the reason is that love is a link of obligation which men, because they are rotten, will break any time they think doing so serves their advantage; but fear involves dread of punishment, from which they can never escape.

Still, a prince should make himself feared in such a way that, even if he gets no love, he gets no hate either; because it is perfectly possible to be feared and not hated, and this will be the result if only the prince will keep his hands off the property of his subjects or citizens, and off their women. When he does have to shed blood, he should be sure to have a strong justification and manifest[2] cause; but above all, he should not confiscate[3] people's property, because men are quicker to forget the death of a father than the loss of a patrimony[4]. Besides, pretexts[5] for confiscation are always plentiful; it never fails that a prince who starts living by plunder can find reasons to rob someone else. . . .Returning to the question of being feared or loved, I conclude that since men love at their own inclination but can be made to fear at the inclination of the prince, a shrewd prince will lay his foundations on what is under his own control, not on what is controlled by others.

A portrait of Niccolò Machiavelli painted in the late 1500s

WITNESS HISTORY VIDEO

Watch *Machiavelli's The Prince* to explore the world of an important "Renaissance man" on the **Witness History Discovery School**™ video program.

Discovery SCHOOL

Thinking Critically

1. **Summarize Information** Why does Machiavelli believe that it is better for a prince to be feared than to be loved?

2. **Make Comparisons** Reread the section of the text titled Castiglione's Ideal Courtier. Is Machiavelli's description of an ideal prince consistent with that of Castiglione's courtier? Why or why not?

1. **fickle** (FIK ul) *adj.* changeable
2. **manifest** (MAN uh fest) *adj.* clear; plain to see
3. **confiscate** (KAHN fis kayt) *v.* to seize or take

4. **patrimony** (PA truh moh nee) *n.* property or inheritance
5. **pretexts** (PREE teksts) *n.* excuses; false reasons

A modern artist depicts Gutenberg and his printing press; at top right is a Bible Gutenberg printed *circa* 1455.

WITNESS HISTORY 🔊 AUDIO

An Expanding World

❝ All the world is full of knowing men, of most learned schoolmasters, and vast libraries; and it appears to me as a truth, that neither in Plato's time, nor Cicero's . . . there was ever such conveniency for studying, as we see at this day there is. ❞
—François Rabelais, 1532

Scholars and artists throughout northern Europe in the 1500s lived in an exciting time. The newly invented printing press made the world seem smaller. All over Europe, the world of knowledge was expanding in ways that would have been unthinkable in medieval times.

Focus Question How did the Renaissance develop in northern Europe?

The Renaissance in the North

Objectives
- Explain how the printing revolution shaped European society.
- Describe the themes that northern European artists, humanists, and writers explored.

Terms, People, and Places

Johann Gutenberg
Flanders
Albrecht Dürer
engraving
vernacular

Erasmus
Thomas More
utopian
Shakespeare

N**ote** Taking

Reading Strategy: Identify Main Ideas Keep track of the main ideas of the section by creating a chart like the one below. Add boxes to complete the chart.

Renaissance in the North		
Printing Revolution	Artists and Writers	Humanists

As the Renaissance began to flower in Italy, northern Europe was still recovering from the ravages of the Black Death. But by the 1400s, the cities of the north began to enjoy the economic growth—and the wealth—needed to develop their own Renaissance.

The Printing Revolution

An astounding invention aided the spread of the Renaissance. In about 1455, **Johann Gutenberg** (GOOT un burg) of Mainz, Germany, printed the first complete edition of the Bible using a printing press with movable type. A printing revolution had begun that would transform Europe. Before the printing press, there were only a few thousand books in all of Europe. These books had been slowly copied out by hand. By 1500, according to some estimates, 15 to 20 million volumes had been produced on printing presses.

The printing revolution brought immense changes. Printed books were cheaper and easier to produce than hand-copied works. With books more readily available, more people learned to read. Readers gained access to a broad range of knowledge, from medicine and law to mining. As printing presses were established in Italy and other parts of Europe, printed books exposed educated Europeans to new ideas and new places.

✔ **Checkpoint** What was the impact of the printing press?

Northern Renaissance Artists

The northern Renaissance began in the <u>prosperous</u> cities of Flanders, a region that included parts of present-day northern France, Belgium, and the Netherlands. Flanders was a thriving center of trade for northern Europe. From Flanders, the Renaissance spread to Spain, France, Germany, and England.

Flemish Painters In the 1400s, Jan van Eyck was one of the most important Flemish painters. Van Eyck's portrayals of townspeople as well as religious scenes abound in rich, realistic details. In the 1500s, Flemish painter Pieter Bruegel (BROY gul) used vibrant colors to portray lively scenes of peasant life, earning him the nickname "Peasant Bruegel." Bruegel also addressed religious and classical themes, but he set them against a background of common people.

In the 1600s, Peter Paul Rubens blended the realistic tradition of Flemish painters like Bruegel with the classical themes and artistic freedom of the Italian Renaissance. As a scholar and humanist, Rubens had a wide knowledge of mythology, the Bible, and classical history. Many of his enormous paintings portray these themes.

Dürer: "Leonardo of the North" German painter Albrecht Dürer (DYOOR ur) was one of the first northern artists to be profoundly affected by Renaissance Italy. In 1494, he traveled to Italy to study the Italian masters. He soon became a pioneer in spreading Renaissance ideas to northern Europe. At the same time, his own methods influenced artists in Italy. Because of his wide-ranging interests, which extended far beyond art, he is sometimes called the "Leonardo of the North."

Dürer's important innovation was to apply the painting techniques he had learned in Italy to engraving. In engraving, an artist etches a design on a metal plate with acid. The artist then uses the plate to make prints. Dürer had studied engraving in his goldsmith father's workshop and perfected the technique. Many of Dürer's engravings and paintings portray religious upheaval, one of the northern Renaissance's most powerful themes.

✓ **Checkpoint** What themes did northern Renaissance artists explore?

Northern Humanists and Writers

Northern European humanists and writers also helped spread Renaissance ideas. Humanist scholars stressed education and classical learning, hoping to bring about religious and moral reform. Though humanist scholars wrote mainly in Latin, other writers began writing in the vernacular, or everyday language of ordinary people. This appealed to a new, middle class audience who lived in northern towns and cities.

Erasmus: Making Humanism Popular The Dutch priest and humanist Desiderius Erasmus (ih RAZ mus), born in 1466, was one of the most important scholars of the age. He wrote texts on a number of subjects and used his knowledge of classical languages to produce a new Greek edition of the Bible.

Vocabulary Builder
prosperous—(PRAHS pur us) *adj.*
successful; wealthy

Dürer, Artist and Gentleman
In Germany artists were viewed merely as skilled craftsmen, prompting Dürer to comment that "[In Italy] I am a gentleman, at home I am a parasite." He worked hard to change that view, learning languages and court manners to promote himself. Dürer painted this self-portrait in 1498 when he was 26 years old. *Judging from the painting, how did Dürer view his own importance?*

Realism in Northern European Art

Northern European artists eagerly pursued realism in their art. The new technique of oil painting allowed them to produce strong colors and a hard surface that could survive the centuries. They also used oils to achieve depth and to create realistic details. Artists placed a new emphasis on nature, recording in their art what they actually saw. Landscapes became a major theme, not just the backdrop to human activities.

▲ Pieter Bruegel the Elder is best known for his scenes of daily life. In *Winter Landscape With Skaters and a Bird Trap*, every detail—from the bare trees to the people walking on ice—conveys the white and frozen reality of northern Europe in winter.

Erasmus helped spread Renaissance humanism to a wider public. He called for a translation of the Bible into the vernacular. He scorned those who "... don't want the holy scriptures to be read in translation by the unlearned ... as if the chief strength of the Christian religion lay in people's ignorance of it. ..." To Erasmus, an individual's chief duties were to be open-minded and to show good will toward others. As a priest, he was disturbed by corruption in the Church and called for reform.

Sir Thomas More's Ideal Society Erasmus's friend, the English humanist Sir Thomas More, also pressed for social reform. In *Utopia,* More describes an ideal society in which men and women live in peace and harmony. No one is idle, all are educated, and justice is used to end crime rather than to eliminate the criminal. Today, the word **utopian** has come to describe any ideal society often with the implication that such a society is ultimately impractical.

Rabelais's Comic Masterpiece The French humanist François Rabelais (rab uh LAY) had a varied career as a monk, physician, Greek scholar, and author. In *Gargantua and Pantagruel,* he chronicles the adventures of two gentle giants. On the surface, the novel is a comic tale of travel and war. But Rabelais uses his characters to offer opinions on religion, education, and other serious subjects. Like More and Erasmus, Rabelais was deeply religious, but had doubts about the organized church.

Shakespeare Writes for All Time The towering figure of Renaissance literature was the English poet and playwright William Shakespeare. Between 1590 and 1613, he wrote 37 plays that are still performed around the world. Fellow playwright and poet Ben Jonson correctly predicted at the time that Shakespeare "... was not of an age, but for all time."

Oils made from linseed, walnuts, or poppies were mixed with colored pigments to make oil paint. Oil paints have two qualities that allow them to achieve realism— they can blend together, thus creating more realistic colors, and they reflect light, adding depth and glow.

▲ Jan van Eyck refined and spread the technique of oil painting. In *Portrait of Giovanni Arnolfini and His Wife*, van Eyck layered oil paints to create the shimmering fabrics the couple wore.

▲ Albrecht Dürer kept extensive notebooks on nature. He used his avid curiosity and his keen powers of observation to paint amazingly realistic pictures of plants and animals.

Thinking Critically

1. **Analyze Images** What realistic details appear in van Eyck's painting?
2. **Compare and Contrast** Compare these paintings with the Cranach woodcut in Section 3. How do the artists' intentions differ?

Shakespeare's genius was in expressing universal themes in everyday, realistic settings. His work explores Renaissance ideals such as the complexity of the individual and the importance of the classics. At the same time, his characters speak in language that common people can understand and appreciate. Shakespeare's love of words also vastly enriched the English language. More than 1,700 words appeared for the first time in his works.

✓ **Checkpoint** What Renaissance ideas did Shakespeare's work address?

SECTION 2 Assessment

Progress Monitoring *Online*
For: Self-quiz with vocabulary practice
Web Code: naa-1321

Terms, People, and Places

1. What do the key people listed at the beginning of the section have in common? Explain.

Note Taking

2. **Reading Skill: Identify Main Ideas** Use your completed chart to answer the Focus Question: How did the Renaissance develop in northern Europe?

Comprehension and Critical Thinking

3. **Predict Consequences** What impact would the printing press have on religious reform movements of the 1500s?
4. **Analyze Information** How did northern Renaissance artists blend Italian Renaissance ideas with their own?
5. **Identify Point of View** How did Erasmus's training as a priest sharpen his critique of the Church?
6. **Synthesize Information** What factors encouraged the use of the vernacular in literature in Renaissance society?

● Writing About History

Quick Write: Generate Arguments List a number of arguments that could be used to oppose your thesis in a persuasive essay. For example, reread the thesis statement in the Section 1 Quick Write. Then use the information from Section 2 to generate arguments opposing your thesis. Be sure to cite important northern European artists and technological developments. Organizing your arguments into a pro-and-con chart can be helpful.

Shakespeare's Globe Theatre

In his play *As You Like It,* William Shakespeare wrote that "all the world's a stage." When it came to showcasing his own work, however, the playwright chose the Globe Theatre. In 1599, when the English people were increasingly eager for plays and other sorts of entertainment, Shakespeare and his company of actors built the Globe on the south bank of London's Thames River. The three-story, open-air theater could seat 3,000 people and had a stage more than 40 feet wide. Shakespeare wrote many of his plays—including *Hamlet, Macbeth,* and *Othello*—specifically to be performed at the Globe Theatre. Twenty of Shakespeare's plays were performed there during his lifetime. During a performance of his play *Henry VII* in 1613, onstage cannon fire ignited the theater's thatched roof and destroyed the building.

▲ William Shakespeare

The 1997 reconstruction of the Globe Theatre (below) is faithful to the original. Wealthy theatergoers in the seventeenth century sat in galleries along the theater's walls. Poorer people bought cheap seats on the ground in front of the stage.

The center of the theater was open to the sky. Because the theater had no interior lights, plays were performed in the afternoon to let in as much light as possible.

The theater's round shape meant that the audience surrounded the stage on three sides. The stage was not curtained off, further drawing the audience into the action. ▶

Thinking Critically

1. **Draw Inferences** What are the advantages and disadvantages of staging productions in an open-air theater like the Globe?
2. **Synthesize Information** What about Shakespeare's plays drew people from all social classes to the theater?

Luther is shown tacking his 95 Theses to a church door in Wittenberg. At top right is a print block from a printing press.

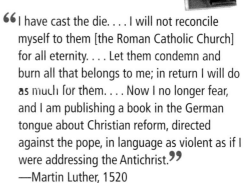

WITNESS HISTORY 🔊 AUDIO

A Monk Rebels

❝I have cast the die. . . . I will not reconcile myself to them [the Roman Catholic Church] for all eternity. . . . Let them condemn and burn all that belongs to me; in return I will do as much for them. . . . Now I no longer fear, and I am publishing a book in the German tongue about Christian reform, directed against the pope, in language as violent as if I were addressing the Antichrist.❞
—Martin Luther, 1520

Focus Question How did revolts against the Roman Catholic Church affect northern European society?

The Protestant Reformation

Objectives
- Summarize the factors that encouraged the Protestant Reformation.
- Analyze Martin Luther's role in shaping the Protestant Reformation.
- Explain the teachings and impact of John Calvin.

Terms, People, and Places

indulgences	John Calvin
Martin Luther	predestination
Wittenberg	Geneva
Charles V	theocracy
diet	

Note Taking

Reading Skill: Identify Main Ideas Use a concept web like the one below to record main ideas about the Reformation. Add circles as necessary.

In the 1500s, the Renaissance in northern Europe sparked a religious upheaval that affected Christians at all levels of society. Northern European calls for church reform eventually unleashed forces that would shatter Christian unity. This movement is known as the Protestant Reformation.

Background to the Reformation

Many northern Europeans faced a great deal of uncertainty in their lives. As in Renaissance Italy, most people were poor and life could be violent. Fixed medieval economies were giving way to more uncertain urban, market-based economies, and wealth was distributed unequally. Renaissance humanist ideas found fertile ground in this uncertain society. Spread by the printing press, humanist ideas such as a return to classical education and an emphasis on social reform quickly took root. Many people looked for ways to shape a society that made more sense to them. Increasingly, they used humanist ideas to question a central force in their lives—the Church.

Church Abuses Beginning in the late Middle Ages, the Church had become increasingly caught up in worldly affairs. Popes competed with Italian princes for political power. They fought long wars to protect the Papal States against invasions by secular rulers. They plotted against powerful monarchs who tried to seize control of the Church within their lands. The Church also fought to expand its own interests.

Analyzing Art

Protestant Art German artist Lucas Cranach the Elder expressed his views of Protestantism (left panel) and Catholicism (right panel) in this woodcut made in 1545. He wrote that the work was meant to show the difference between the "true religion" and the "false idolatrous teaching."

A Angels float peacefully in the sky above Luther.

B A preaching Martin Luther is shown as having a direct connection to God above.

C A Catholic clergyman sells indulgences.

D The pope counts bags of money.

1. According to Cranach, which of the religions shown is the "true religion"?
2. Find another detail in the painting that expresses the artist's opinion.

Like other Renaissance rulers, popes led lavish lives, supported the arts, and hired artists to beautify churches. To finance such projects, the Church increased fees for services such as marriages and baptisms. Some clergy also sold **indulgences.** According to Church teaching, an indulgence was a lessening of the time a soul would have to spend in purgatory, a place where souls too impure to enter heaven atoned for sins committed during their lifetimes. In the Middle Ages, the Church had granted indulgences only for good deeds. By the late 1400s, however, indulgences could be bought with money.

Many Christians protested such practices, especially in northern Europe. Christian humanists such as Erasmus urged a return to the simple ways of the early Christian church. They stressed Bible study and rejected what they saw as the worldliness of the Church.

Early Revolts Against the Church Long before the Protestant Reformation, a few thinkers protested against the Church more strongly. In England in the 1300s, John Wycliffe launched a systematic attack against the Church, using sermons and writings to call for change. After his death, his followers met secretly to keep alive the movement he started. Jan Hus, born about 40 years after Wycliffe in what is now the Czech Republic, led a reform movement for which he was executed.

✓ **Checkpoint** What factors set the stage for the Protestant Reformation?

Martin Luther: Catalyst of Change

In 1517, protests against Church abuses erupted into a full-scale revolt. The man who triggered the revolt was a German monk and professor of theology named **Martin Luther.**

As a young man, Luther prayed and fasted and tried to lead a holy life. He once remarked that "... if ever a monk got into heaven by monkery, so should I also have gotten there." Still, he found himself growing disillusioned with what he saw as Church corruption and worldliness. At last, an incident in the town of Wittenberg prompted him to take action.

Writing the 95 Theses In 1517, a priest named Johann Tetzel set up a pulpit on the outskirts of Wittenberg, in Germany. He offered indulgences to any Christian who contributed money for the rebuilding of the Cathedral of St. Peter in Rome. Tetzel claimed that purchase of these indulgences would assure entry into heaven not only for the purchasers but for their dead relatives as well.

To Luther, Tetzel's actions were the final outrage, because they meant that poor peasants could not get into heaven. He drew up 95 Theses, or arguments, against indulgences. Among other things, he argued that indulgences had no basis in the Bible, that the pope had no authority to release souls from purgatory, and that Christians could be saved only through faith. In accordance with the custom of the time, he may have posted his list on the door of Wittenberg's All Saints Church.

Igniting a Firestorm Almost overnight, copies of Luther's 95 Theses were printed and distributed across Europe, where they stirred furious debate. The Church called on Luther to recant, or give up his views. Luther refused. Instead, he developed even more <u>radical</u> new <u>doctrines</u>. Before long, he was urging Christians to reject the authority of Rome. He wrote that the Church could only be reformed by secular, or non-Church, authorities.

In 1521, Pope Leo X excommunicated Luther. Later that year, the new Holy Roman emperor, Charles V, summoned Luther to the diet at the city of Worms. The word diet, or assembly of German princes, comes from a Middle English word meaning "a day for a meeting." Luther went, expecting to defend his writings. Instead, the emperor simply ordered him to give them up. Luther again refused to recant.

Charles declared Luther an outlaw, making it a crime for anyone in the empire to give him food or shelter. Still, Luther had many powerful supporters and thousands hailed him as a hero. They accepted his teachings and, following his lead, renounced the authority of the pope.

Vocabulary Builder
<u>radical</u>—(RAD ih kul) *adj.* extreme; calling for change
<u>doctrine</u>—(DAHK trin) *n.* practice; teaching

BIOGRAPHY

Martin Luther
"I am rough, boisterous, stormy, and altogether warlike," concluded Martin Luther (1483–1546). Luther's strong personality allowed him to take on the powerful Catholic Church. As a monk, Luther closely studied the Bible and came to believe that only its words—and not the pope or the Catholic Church—should dictate a person's actions.

When he appeared at the Diet of Worms, Luther (right) was 37 years old. Though depressed and fearful about the confrontation, he is said to have affirmed, "Here I stand, I cannot do otherwise." When he refused to retract his statements, an order was given to destroy his books. Yet his influence grew, leading to a deep division within Christianity and the founding of a new church that took his name. **Why did Luther refuse to retract his statements?**

Comparing Catholicism, Lutheranism, and Calvinism

	Catholicism	Lutheranism	Calvinism
Salvation	Salvation is achieved through faith and good works.	Salvation is achieved through faith.	God alone predetermines who will be saved.
Sacraments	Priests perform seven sacraments, or rituals—baptism, confirmation, marriage, ordination, communion, anointing the sick, and repentance.	Accepts some of the sacraments, but rejects others because rituals cannot erase sin —only God can.	Accepts some of the sacraments, but rejects others because rituals cannot erase sin—only God can.
Head of Church	Pope	Elected councils	Council of elders
Importance of the Bible	Bible is one source of truth; Church tradition is another.	Bible alone is source of truth.	Bible alone is source of truth.
How Belief Is Revealed	Priests interpret the Bible and Church teachings for the people.	People read and interpret the Bible for themselves.	People read and interpret the Bible for themselves.

Chart Skills *Who was the head of the Lutheran church? Why was this an important difference from the organization of the Catholic Church?*

Luther's Teachings At the heart of Luther's teachings were several beliefs, shown in the chart at left. All Christians, he said, have equal access to God through faith and the Bible. Like Erasmus and other humanist scholars, Luther wanted ordinary people to be able to read and study the Bible, so he translated parts of it into German. He also wanted every town to have a school so that all children could learn to read the Bible. Luther wanted to change other church practices. He banned indulgences, confession, pilgrimages, and prayers to saints. He simplified the elaborate ritual of the mass and instead emphasized the sermon. And he permitted the clergy to marry.

Luther's Ideas Spread The new printing presses spread Luther's writings throughout Germany and Scandinavia, prompting him to declare that "Printing was God's highest act of grace." Fiery preachers denounced Church abuses. By 1530, the Lutherans were using a new name, Protestant, for those who "protested" papal authority.

Many clergy saw Luther's reforms as the answer to Church corruption. A number of German princes, however, embraced Lutheran beliefs for more selfish reasons. Some saw Lutheranism as a way to throw off the rule of both the Church and the Holy Roman emperor. Others welcomed a chance to seize Church property in their territories, and use it for their own purposes. Still other Germans supported Luther because of feelings of national loyalty. They were tired of German money going to support churches and clergy in Italy.

The Peasants' Revolt Many peasants also took up Luther's banner. They hoped to gain his support for social and economic change. In 1524, a Peasants' Revolt erupted across Germany. The rebels called for an end to serfdom and demanded other changes in their harsh lives. However, Luther strongly favored social order and respect for political authority. As the Peasants' Revolt grew more violent, Luther denounced it. With his support, nobles suppressed the rebellion, killing tens of thousands of people and leaving thousands more homeless.

The Peace of Augsburg During the 1530s and 1540s, Charles V tried to force Lutheran princes back into the Catholic Church, but with little success. Finally, after a number of brief wars, Charles and the princes reached a settlement. The Peace of Augsburg, signed in 1555, allowed each prince to decide which religion—Catholic or Lutheran—would be followed in his lands. Most northern German states chose Lutheranism. The southern German states remained largely Catholic.

 Checkpoint How did Luther's teachings affect people and society in northern Europe?

Switzerland's Reformation

Swiss reformers also challenged the Catholic Church. Ulrich Zwingli, a priest and an admirer of Erasmus, lived in the Swiss city of Zurich. Like Luther, he stressed the importance of the Bible and rejected elaborate church rituals. Many of his ideas were adopted by Zurich's city council. The other reformer was **John Calvin,** who would profoundly affect the direction of the Reformation.

Calvin was born in France and trained as a priest and lawyer. In 1536, he published a widely-read book that set forth his religious beliefs and explained how to organize and run a Protestant church. Calvin shared many of Luther's beliefs. But he put forth a number of ideas of his own. He preached **predestination,** the idea that God had long ago determined who would gain salvation. To Calvinists, the world was divided into two kinds of people—saints and sinners. Calvinists tried to live like saints, believing that only those who were saved could live truly Christian lives.

In 1541, Protestants in the Swiss city-state of **Geneva** asked Calvin to lead their community. Calvin set up a **theocracy,** or government run by church leaders. Calvin's followers in Geneva came to see themselves as a new "chosen people" entrusted by God to build a truly Christian society. Calvinists stressed hard work, discipline, thrift, honesty, and morality. Citizens faced fines or other harsher punishments for offenses such as fighting, swearing, laughing in church, or dancing. To many Protestants, Calvinist Geneva seemed like a model community.

Reformers from all over Europe visited Geneva and then returned home to spread Calvin's ideas. By the late 1500s, Calvinism had taken root in Germany, France, the Netherlands, England, and Scotland. This new challenge to the Roman Catholic Church set off bloody wars of religion across Europe. In Germany, Catholics and Lutherans opposed Calvinists. In France, wars raged between French Calvinists and Catholics. Calvinists in the Netherlands avoided persecution by preaching in the remote countryside. In England, some Calvinists sailed to the Americas in the early 1600s to escape persecution at home. In Scotland, a Calvinist preacher named John Knox led a religious rebellion, overthrowing the Catholic queen.

✔ **Checkpoint** How were Calvin's ideas put into practice?

A Calvinist Church, 1564
The Calvinist belief in simplicity is reflected in the design of this church. No images other than scriptures and coats of arms decorate the church, and the preacher's pulpit is the center of focus.

SECTION 3 Assessment

Progress Monitoring *Online*
For: Self-quiz with vocabulary practice
Web Code: naa-1331

Terms, People, and Places

1. For each term, person, or place listed at the beginning of the section, write a sentence explaining its significance.

Note Taking

2. **Reading Skill: Identify Main Ideas** Use your completed concept web to answer the Focus Question: How did revolts against the Roman Catholic Church affect northern European society?

Comprehension and Critical Thinking

3. **Synthesize Information** Why did the sale of indulgences become a critical issue during the Renaissance but not during the Middle Ages?

4. **Compare Points of View** How did Luther's ideas differ from those expressed by the Catholic Church?

5. **Draw Inferences** How might Luther have felt about the Calvinist theocracy in Geneva?

● Writing About History

Quick Write: Choose Strongest Argument Consider this thesis statement: The Reformation was the most important event in European history. List possible arguments for a persuasive essay that supports this thesis. Review each one and choose the strongest. Make sure that factual points in the text support your argument.

Painter Hans Holbein shows Henry VIII as a commanding and regal king. A gold medal (top right) celebrates King Henry as the head of the Church of England.

A King Speaks Out

Henry VIII, the Catholic king of England, was deeply disturbed by Luther's teachings. In 1521 he wrote to the pope to express his displeasure.

❝ . . . we believe that no duty is more incumbent on a Catholic sovereign than to preserve and increase the Catholic faith . . . so when we learned that the pest of Martin Luther's heresy had appeared in Germany and was raging everywhere . . . we bent all our thoughts and energies on uprooting [those heresies] in every possible way. . . . ❞

Just a few years later, Henry would break with the Catholic Church and set England on the path to becoming a Protestant country.

Focus Question How did the Reformation bring about two different religious paths in Europe?

Reformation Ideas Spread

Objectives

- Describe the new ideas that Protestant sects embraced.
- Understand why England formed a new church.
- Analyze how the Catholic Church reformed itself.
- Explain why many groups faced persecution during the Reformation.

Terms, People, and Places

sect	compromise
Henry VIII	Council of Trent
Mary Tudor	Ignatius of Loyola
Thomas Cranmer	Teresa of Avila
Elizabeth	ghetto
canonize	

Note Taking

Reading Skill: Identify Main Ideas As you read about the spread of the Protestant Reformation, record the main ideas in a flowchart like this one below. Add more boxes as necessary.

Protestant sects explode throughout Europe.

Throughout Europe, Catholic monarchs and the Catholic Church fought back against the Protestant challenge by taking steps to reform the Church and to restore its spiritual leadership of the Christian world. Still, Protestant ideas continued to spread.

An Explosion of Protestant Sects

As the Reformation continued, hundreds of new Protestant **sects,** or religious groups that had broken away from an established church, sprang up. Many of these followed variations on the teachings of Luther, Calvin, and Zwingli. Some sects, however, had ideas that were even more radical—such as rejecting infant baptism. Infants, they argued, are too young to understand what it means to accept the Christian faith. They became known as Anabaptists.

A few Anabaptist sects sought radical social change as well. Some wanted to abolish private property. Others sought to speed up the coming of God's day of judgment by violent means. When radical Anabaptists took over the city of Munster in Germany, even Luther advised his supporters to join Catholics in suppressing the threat to the traditional order. Most Anabaptists, however, were peaceful. They called for religious toleration and separation of church and state. Despite harsh persecution, these groups influenced Protestant thinking in many countries. Today, the Baptists, Mennonites, and Amish all trace their religious ancestry to the Anabaptists.

✓ **Checkpoint** Who were the Anabaptists?

The English Reformation

In England, religious leaders like John Wycliffe had called for Church reform as early as the 1300s. By the 1520s, some English clergy were exploring Protestant ideas. The break with the Catholic Church, however, was the work not of religious leaders but of King Henry VIII.

Henry VIII Seeks an Annulment At first, Henry VIII stood firmly against the Protestant revolt. The pope even awarded him the title "Defender of the Faith" for a pamphlet that he wrote denouncing Luther.

In 1527, however, an issue arose that set Henry at odds with the Church. After 18 years of marriage, Henry and his Spanish wife, Catherine of Aragon, had only one surviving child, Mary Tudor. Henry felt that England's stability depended on his having a male heir. He had already fallen in love with a young noblewoman named Anne Boleyn, who served the Queen. He hoped that if he married her she would bear him a son. Because Catholic law does not permit divorce, he asked the pope to annul, or cancel, his marriage. Popes had annulled royal marriages before. But this pope refused. He did not want to offend the Holy Roman emperor Charles V, Catherine's nephew.

Breaking With the Church Henry was furious. Spurred on by his advisors, many of whom leaned toward Protestantism, he decided to take over the English church. Guided by his chancellor Thomas Cromwell, he had Parliament pass a series of laws. They took the English church from the pope's control and placed it under Henry's rule. At the same time, Henry appointed Thomas Cranmer archbishop of the new church. Cranmer annulled the king's marriage, and in 1533 Henry married Anne Boleyn. Soon, Anne gave birth to a daughter, Elizabeth.

In 1534, Parliament passed the Act of Supremacy, making Henry "the only supreme head on Earth of the Church of England." Many loyal Catholics refused to accept the Act of Supremacy and were executed for treason. Among them was the great English humanist Sir Thomas More, who served in Henry's government but tried to resign in protest. More was later canonized, or recognized as a saint, by the Catholic Church.

Strengthening the Church of England Between 1536 and 1540, royal officials investigated Catholic convents and monasteries. Claiming that they were centers of immorality, Henry ordered them closed. He then confiscated, or seized, their lands and wealth. Henry shrewdly granted some of these lands to nobles and other high-ranking citizens. He thus secured their support for the Anglican Church, as the new Church of England was called. Despite these actions, Henry was not a religious radical. He rejected most Protestant doctrines. Aside from breaking away from Rome and allowing use of the English Bible, he kept most Catholic forms of worship.

Religious Turmoil When Henry died in 1547, he had only one surviving son—despite having married six times. Nine-year-old Edward VI inherited the throne. The young king and his advisors were devout Protestants and took steps to make England a truly Protestant country. Under Edward, Parliament passed new laws bringing Protestant reforms to England. Thomas Cranmer drew up the Protestant *Book of Common Prayer,* which became required reading in all of the country's church services. Though it outlined a moderate form of Protestant service, it sparked uprisings. These uprisings were harshly suppressed.

BIOGRAPHY

Elizabeth I

The life of Elizabeth I (1533–1603) did not start favorably. When she was only two years old her mother, Anne Boleyn, was beheaded so that her father, Henry VIII, could remarry. The young princess grew up in isolation. Still, Henry VIII was affectionate to his daughter and saw to it that she received a rigorous education. Even as a teenager she was well-respected for her sharp mind, fluency in languages, and understanding of philosophy and theology.

Under the reign of her half-sister Mary Tudor, Elizabeth became both a rallying symbol for Protestants and a target for Catholics. Though arrested and imprisoned, she survived her sister to become queen of England at age 25. The well-loved Elizabeth used her talents to unify England, expand its international power, and encourage a period of great artistic flowering. **Why do you think the period under Elizabeth's reign is now called the Elizabethan Age?**

When Edward died in his teens, his half-sister Mary Tudor became queen. She was determined to return England to the Catholic faith. Under Queen Mary hundreds of English Protestants, including Archbishop Cranmer, were burned at the stake for heresy.

The Elizabethan Settlement On Mary's death in 1558, the throne passed to 25-year-old Elizabeth, the daughter of Henry VIII and Anne Boleyn. For years, Elizabeth had survived court intrigues, including the religious swings under Edward and Mary. As queen, Elizabeth had to determine the future of the Church of England. Moving cautiously at first, she slowly enforced a series of reforms that over time came to be called the Elizabethan settlement.

The queen's policies were a **compromise,** or acceptable middle ground, between Protestant and Catholic practices. The Church of England preserved much Catholic ritual, and it kept the hierarchy of bishops and archbishops. Unlike Henry, the queen did not call herself "supreme head" of the church, but she reaffirmed that the monarch was the "supreme governor" over spiritual matters in England. At the same time, Elizabeth restored a version of the *Book of Common Prayer,* accepted moderate Protestant doctrine, and allowed English to replace Latin in church services. Her sensible compromises, which satisfied most Catholics and Protestants, largely ended decades of religious turmoil.

During a long reign, Elizabeth used all her skills to restore unity to England. Even while keeping many Catholic traditions, she made England a firmly Protestant nation. After her death, England faced new religious storms. But it escaped the endless religious wars that tore apart France and many other European states during the 1500s.

✓ **Checkpoint** Why was the Church of England established?

Major Events of the English Reformation

1521 Henry VIII writes to the pope to condemn Luther's teachings.

1529 Parliament begins passing laws to make Henry VIII head of the church in England.

1533 Henry VIII divorces Catherine of Aragon and marries Anne Boleyn.

1534 Parliament passes the Act of Supremacy.

King Henry the eyght.

The Catholic Reformation

As the Protestant Reformation swept across northern Europe, a vigorous reform movement took hold within the Catholic Church. Led by Pope Paul III, it is known as the Catholic Reformation, or the Counter-Reformation. During the 1530s and 1540s, the pope set out to revive the moral authority of the Church and roll back the Protestant tide. He also appointed reformers to end corruption within the papacy itself. They and their successors led the Catholic Reformation for the rest of the century.

Council of Trent To establish the direction that reform should take, the pope called the Council of Trent in 1545. Led by Italian cardinal Carlo Borromeo, the council met off and on for almost 20 years. The council reaffirmed the traditional Catholic views that Protestants had challenged. It declared that salvation comes through faith and good works. According to the council, the Bible, while a major source of religious truth, is not the only source. The council also took steps to end abuses in the Church. It provided stiff penalties for worldliness and corruption among the clergy. It also established schools to create a better-educated clergy who could challenge Protestant teachings.

Empowering the Inquisition Pope Paul strengthened the Inquisition to fight Protestantism. As you have read, the Inquisition was a Church court set up during the Middle Ages. The Inquisition used secret testimony, torture, and execution to root out heresy. It also prepared the *Index of Forbidden Books*, a list of works considered too immoral or irreligious for Catholics to read. The list included books by Luther and Calvin, as well as earlier works by Petrarch and other humanists.

1547 Henry VIII dies; his son Edward VI becomes king and begins making Protestant reforms.

1553 Edward VI dies; Mary Tudor ▶ becomes queen and restores Catholic doctrines.

1558 Mary Tudor dies; Elizabeth I becomes queen and unifies England with the Elizabethan Settlement.

Analyze Information
Because of Henry VIII's determination to obtain a divorce, Catholic England had become a solidly Protestant nation by 1600. *How long did it take Henry VIII to become head of the Church of England?*

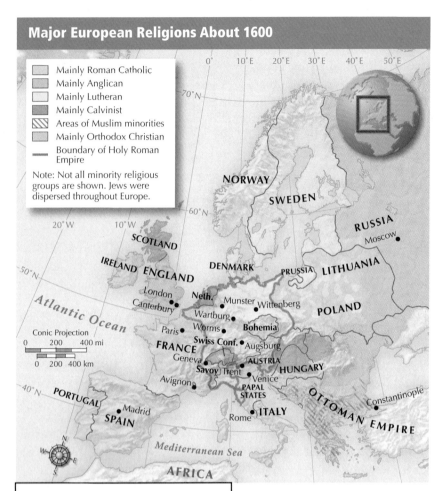

Mainly Roman Catholic
Mainly Anglican
Mainly Lutheran
Mainly Calvinist
Areas of Muslim minorities
Mainly Orthodox Christian
Boundary of Holy Roman Empire

Note: Not all minority religious groups are shown. Jews were dispersed throughout Europe.

Map Skills By 1600, the spread of Protestantism had transformed Catholic Europe.

1. **Locate** (a) London (b) Wittenberg (c) Rome
2. **Identify** Identify the religion practiced in each of the locations above.
3. **Understand Main Ideas** Explain why most people in each region were practicing that religion by 1600.

Geography *Interactive*
For: Audio guided tour
Web Code: nap-1341

Vocabulary Builder
rigorous—(RIG ur us) *adj.* strict; thorough

Founding the Jesuits In 1540, the pope recognized a new religious order, the Society of Jesus, or Jesuits. The order was founded by Ignatius of Loyola, a Spanish knight raised in the crusading tradition. After his leg was shattered in battle, he found comfort reading about saints who had overcome mental and physical torture. Vowing to become a "soldier of God," Ignatius drew up a strict program for the Jesuits. It included spiritual and moral discipline, rigorous religious training, and absolute obedience to the Church. Led by Ignatius, the Jesuits embarked on a crusade to defend and spread the Catholic faith worldwide.

To further the Catholic cause, Jesuits became advisors to Catholic rulers, helping them combat heresy in their lands. They set up schools that taught humanist and Catholic beliefs and enforced discipline and obedience. Daring Jesuits slipped into Protestant lands in disguise to minister to Catholics. Jesuit missionaries spread their Catholic faith to distant lands, including Asia, Africa, and the Americas.

Teresa of Avila As the Catholic Reformation spread, many Catholics experienced renewed feelings of intense faith. Teresa of Avila symbolized this renewal. Born into a wealthy Spanish family, Teresa entered a convent in her youth. Finding convent routine not strict enough, she established her own order of nuns. They lived in isolation, eating and sleeping very little and dedicating themselves to prayer and meditation.

Impressed by her spiritual life, her superiors in the Church asked Teresa to reorganize and reform Spanish convents and monasteries. Teresa was widely honored for her work, and after her death the Church canonized her. Her spiritual writings rank among the most important Christian texts of her time, and are still widely read today.

Legacy of the Catholic Reformation By 1600, the majority of Europeans remained Catholic. Tireless Catholic reformers, like Francis de Sales in France, had succeeded in bringing back Protestant converts. Moreover, renewed piety found expression in literature and art. Across Catholic Europe, charity flourished and church abuses were reduced.

Still, Protestantism had gained a major foothold on the continent. The Reformation and the Catholic Reformation stirred up intense feeling and debate. Religious conflict played into heated disagreements about government, which would erupt into war throughout much of Europe. At the end, Europe would remain—and still remains today—divided by differing interpretations of Christianity.

✓ **Checkpoint** What was the outcome of the Catholic Reformation?

Widespread Persecution

During this period of heightened religious passion, persecution was widespread. Both Catholics and Protestants fostered intolerance and persecuted radical sects like the Anabaptists, people they thought were witches, and Jews.

Conducting Witch Hunts Between 1450 and 1750, tens of thousands of women and men died as victims of witch hunts. Those accused of being witches, or agents of the devil, were usually women. Most victims of the witch hunts died in the German states, Switzerland, and France, all centers of religious conflict. When the wars of religion came to an end, the persecution of witches also declined.

Scholars have offered various reasons for this persecution, but most agree that it had to do with people's twin beliefs in Christianity and magic. Most people believed that among them were witches who practiced magical deeds, often with the aid of the devil. Thus witches were seen as anti-Christian. Because witches often behaved in non-traditional ways, many people accused of witchcraft were often social outcasts, such as beggars. Midwives and herbalists were also targeted.

Persecuting Jews For many Jews in Italy, the early Renaissance had been a time of relative prosperity. While Spain had expelled its Jews in 1492, Italy allowed them to remain. Still, pressure remained strong on Jews to convert. In 1516, Venice ordered Jews to live in a separate quarter of the city called the **ghetto.** Other Italian cities soon followed.

During the Reformation, restrictions on Jews increased. At first, Luther hoped that Jews would be converted to his teachings. When they did not convert, he called for them to be expelled from Christian lands and for their synagogues to be burned. In time, some German princes did expel Jews. In the 1550s, Pope Paul IV placed added restrictions on Jews. Even Emperor Charles V, who supported toleration of Jews in the Holy Roman Empire, banned them from Spanish territories and new American colonies. From the early 1500s on, many Jews migrated to the Mediterranean parts of the Ottoman Empire and to the Netherlands.

✓ **Checkpoint** Why were Jews and other people persecuted?

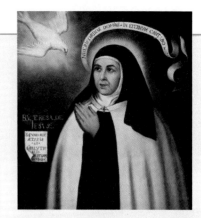

Teresa of Avila wrote a book in 1610 describing her work with reforming Catholic convents and monasteries.

Primary Source

❝At about this time there came to my notice the harm and havoc that were being wrought in France by these Lutherans and the way in which their unhappy sect was increasing. . . . I wept before the Lord and entreated Him to remedy this great evil. I felt that I would have laid down a thousand lives to save a single one of all the souls that were being lost there. And, seeing that I was a woman, and a sinner . . . I determined to do the little that was in me. . . .❞

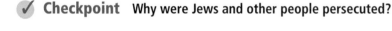

SECTION 4 **Assessment**

Progress Monitoring *Online*
For: Self-quiz with vocabulary practice
Web Code: naa-1341

Terms, People, and Places

1. Place each of the key terms at the beginning of this section into one of the following categories: politics, culture, economy, or geography. Write a sentence for each term explaining your choice.

Note Taking

2. **Reading Skill: Identify Main Ideas** Use your completed flowchart to answer the Focus Question: How did the Reformation bring about two different religious paths in Europe?

Comprehension and Critical Thinking

3. **Identify Point of View** Why were the Anabaptists considered to be radical?
4. **Understand Sequence** How did reforms cause England to become a Protestant country?
5. **Recognize Ideologies** Why might the Catholic Church have found the ideas of Ignatius to be particularly relevant to the Catholic Reformation?
6. **Make Comparisons** Why did witch hunting decline with the end of the religious wars, while persecution of Jews did not?

● **Writing About History**

Quick Write: Decide on an Organizational Strategy Write a thesis statement for a persuasive essay about the spread of the Reformation. List your supporting arguments, from strongest to weakest. Then make an outline that shows where your arguments will appear and how they relate to your thesis statement. You may want to save your strongest argument for the last paragraph of body text before your conclusion.

WITNESS HISTORY 🔊 AUDIO

Mountains on the Moon

In 1609, Italian astronomer Galileo Galilei heard of a new Dutch invention, the telescope. It was designed to help people see distant enemy ships. Galileo was interested for another reason—he wondered what would happen if he trained a telescope on the night sky. So he built his own telescope for this purpose. When he pointed it at the sky, he was amazed. The new telescope allowed him to see mountains on the moon, fiery spots on the sun, and four moons circling the planet Jupiter. "I did discover many particulars in Heaven that had been unseen and unheard of until this our age," he later wrote.

Focus Question How did discoveries in science lead to a new way of thinking for Europeans?

An 1800s artist imagines Galileo at work, peering into the sky. Galileo's telescope is shown at top right.

The Scientific Revolution

Objectives

- Explain how new discoveries in astronomy changed the way people viewed the universe.
- Understand the new scientific method and how it developed.
- Analyze the contributions that Newton and other scientists made to the Scientific Revolution.

Terms, People, and Places

Nicolaus Copernicus	scientific method
heliocentric	hypothesis
Tycho Brahe	Robert Boyle
Johannes Kepler	Isaac Newton
Galileo	gravity
Francis Bacon	calculus
René Descartes	

Note Taking

Reading Skills: Identify Main Ideas Use a table like the one below to record information about important people of the Scientific Revolution.

Thinkers of the Scientific Revolution	
Nicolaus Copernicus	Developed sun-centered universe theory

The Renaissance and the Reformation facilitated the breakdown of the medieval worldview. In the mid-1500s, a profound shift in scientific thinking brought about the final break with Europe's medieval past. Called the Scientific Revolution, this movement pointed toward a future shaped by a new way of thinking about the physical universe. At the heart of the Scientific Revolution was the assumption that mathematical laws governed nature and the universe. The physical world, therefore, could be known, managed, and shaped by people.

Changing Views of the Universe

Until the mid-1500s, Europeans' view of the universe was shaped by the theories of the ancient writers Ptolemy and Aristotle. More than 1,000 years before the Renaissance, they had taught that Earth was the center of the universe. Not only did this view seem to agree with common sense, it was accepted by the Church. In the 1500s and 1600s, however, people began to question this view.

Copernicus Challenges Ancient Astronomy In 1543, Polish scholar **Nicolaus Copernicus** (koh PUR nih kus) published *On the Revolutions of the Heavenly Spheres*. In it, he proposed a **heliocentric,** or sun-centered, model of the universe. The sun, he said, stands at the center of the universe. Earth is just one of several planets that revolve around the sun.

Most experts rejected this revolutionary theory. In Europe at the time, all scientific knowledge and many religious teachings were based on the arguments developed by classical thinkers. If Ptolemy's reasoning about the planets was wrong, people believed, then the whole system of human knowledge might be called into question. But in the late 1500s, the Danish astronomer **Tycho Brahe** (TEE koh BRAH uh) provided evidence that supported Copernicus's theory. Brahe set up an astronomical observatory. Every night for years, he carefully observed the sky, accumulating data about the movement of the heavenly bodies.

After Brahe's death, his assistant, the brilliant German astronomer and mathematician **Johannes Kepler,** used Brahe's data to calculate the orbits of the planets revolving around the sun. His calculations supported Copernicus's heliocentric view. At the same time, however, they showed that each planet does not move in a perfect circle, as both Ptolemy and Copernicus believed, but in an oval-shaped orbit called an ellipse.

Galileo's "Heresies" Scientists from many different lands built on the foundations laid by Copernicus and Kepler. In Italy, **Galileo** Galilei assembled an astronomical telescope. As you have read, he observed that the four moons of Jupiter move slowly around that planet—exactly, he realized, the way Copernicus said that Earth moves around the sun.

Galileo's discoveries caused an uproar. Other scholars attacked him because his observations <u>contradicted</u> ancient views about the world. The Church condemned him because his ideas challenged the Christian teaching that the heavens were fixed in position to Earth, and perfect.

In 1633, Galileo was tried before the Inquisition, and for the rest of his life he was kept under house arrest. Threatened with death unless he withdrew his "heresies," Galileo agreed to state publicly in court that Earth stands motionless at the center of the universe. Legend has it that as he left the court he muttered, "And yet it moves."

✓ **Checkpoint**   Why was Copernicus's theory seen as radical?

A New Scientific Method

Despite the opposition of the Church, by the early 1600s a new approach to science had emerged, based upon observation and experimentation. During the Renaissance, the works of the ancient Greek <u>philosopher</u> Plato were rediscovered. Plato taught that man should look beyond simple appearances to learn nature's truths. He believed that mathematics, one of the greatest human achievements, was the key to learning these truths. His teachings were rediscovered by Renaissance scientists and helped shape people's view of the physical world.

Views of the Moon
Galileo sketched the views of the moon he saw through his telescope in 1609 (left). Pictures of the moon taken through a modern telescope (right) look remarkably similar.

Vocabulary Builder
<u>contradict</u>—(kahn truh DIKT) *v.* to go against

Vocabulary Builder
<u>philosopher</u>—(fih LAHS uh fur) *n.* a person who is an expert in the study of knowledge

Bacon and Descartes: Revolutionary Thinkers The new scientific method was really a revolution in thought. Two giants of this revolution were the Englishman **Francis Bacon** and the Frenchman **René Descartes** (day KAHRT). Each devoted himself to understanding how truth is determined. Both Bacon and Descartes, writing in the early 1600s, rejected Aristotle's scientific assumptions. They also challenged the scholarly traditions of the medieval universities that sought to make the physical world fit in with the teachings of the Church. Both argued that truth is not known at the beginning of inquiry but at the end, after a long process of investigation.

Bacon and Descartes differed in their methods, however. Bacon stressed experimentation and observation. He wanted science to make life better for people by leading to practical technologies. Descartes emphasized human reasoning as the best road to understanding. In his *Discourse on Method* (1637), he explains how he decided to discard all traditional authorities and search for provable knowledge. Left only with doubt, he concluded that doubt was the only thing he could not question, and that in order to doubt he had to exist as a rational, thinking being. Therefore he made his famous statement, "I think, therefore I am."

A Step-by-Step Process Over time, a step-by-step process of discovery evolved that became known as the **scientific method**. The scientific method required scientists to collect and accurately measure data. To explain the data, scientists used reasoning to propose a logical **hypothesis,** or possible explanation. They then tested the hypothesis with further observation or experimentation. Mathematical calculations were used to convert the observations and experiments into scientific laws. After reaching a conclusion, scientists repeated their work at least once—and usually many times—to confirm and refine their hypotheses or formulate better ones.

Diagram Skills The scientific method, still used today, is based on careful observation and measurement of data. *Why is Step 7 an important part of the process?*

✔ **Checkpoint** How did Bacon and Descartes each approach the new scientific method?

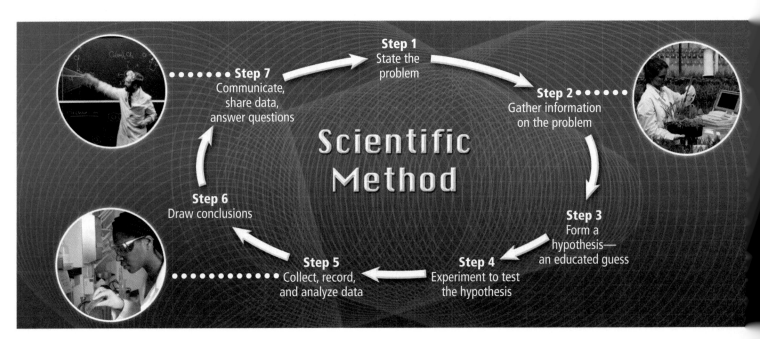

Scientific Method

Step 1
State the problem

Step 2 • • • • • •
Gather information on the problem

Step 3
Form a hypothesis— an educated guess

Step 4
Experiment to test the hypothesis

Step 5
Collect, record, and analyze data

Step 6
Draw conclusions

Step 7
Communicate, share data, answer questions

Breakthroughs in Medicine and Chemistry

The 1500s and 1600s saw dramatic changes in many branches of science, especially medicine and chemistry. The rapid changes in science and technology that began in this period still continue to this day.

Exploring the Human Body Medieval physicians relied on the works of the ancient physician Galen. Galen, however, had made many errors, in part because he had limited knowledge of human anatomy. During the Renaissance, physicians made new efforts to study the human body. In 1543, Andreas Vesalius (vuh SAY lee us) published *On the Structure of the Human Body,* the first accurate and detailed study of human anatomy. Vesalius used whatever means he could to increase his knowledge of anatomy. He used friendships with people of influence to get invitations to autopsies. He also autopsied bodies that he himself obtained—counting on friends in the local government to look the other way.

In the early 1540s, French physician Ambroise Paré (pa RAY) developed a new and more effective ointment for preventing infection. He also developed new surgical techniques, introduced the use of artificial limbs, and invented several scientific instruments. Then in the early 1600s, William Harvey, an English scholar, described the circulation of the blood for the first time. He showed how the heart serves as a pump to force blood through veins and arteries. Later in the century, the Dutch inventor Anton van Leeuwenhoek (LAY wun hohk) perfected the microscope and became the first human to see cells and microorganisms. These pioneering scientists opened the way for further discoveries.

Human Anatomy
Renaissance artists and scientists, determined to learn how things really worked, studied nature with great curiosity. In the 1400s, Leonardo drew the muscles of the human arm with amazing accuracy (right). Renaissance doctors learned much about human anatomy from dissections (left). *How does this painting from the 1500s reflect the advances in scientific thinking?*

An English poet wrote the following as an epitaph for Newton's gravestone. What does it suggest about how people of the time viewed Newton's importance?

Primary Source

❝Nature and Nature's Laws lay hid in night,
    God said, Let Newton be! and all was light.❞
—Alexander Pope, *Epitaphs*

Transforming Chemistry The branch of science now called chemistry was in medieval times called alchemy. Alchemists believed that any substance could be transformed into any other substance, and many of them tried unsuccessfully to turn ordinary metals into gold. With the advances of the Scientific Revolution, the experiments of alchemists were abandoned. However, some of their practices—especially the manipulation of metals and acids—set the stage for modern chemistry.

In the 1600s, English chemist **Robert Boyle** refined the alchemists' view of chemicals as basic building blocks. He explained all matter as being composed of tiny particles that behave in knowable ways. Boyle distinguished between individual elements and chemical compounds, and explained the effect of temperature and pressure on gases. Boyle's work opened the way to modern chemical analysis of the composition of matter.

✔ **Checkpoint** How did Boyle transform the science of chemistry?

Isaac Newton Links the Sciences

As a student in England, Isaac Newton devoured the works of the leading scientists of his day. By age 24, he had formed a brilliant theory to explain why the planets moved as they did. According to one story, Newton saw an apple fall from a tree. He wondered whether the force that pulled that apple to Earth might not also control the movements of the planets. In the next 20 years, Newton perfected his theory. Using mathematics, he showed that a single force keeps the planets in their orbits around the sun. He called this force gravity.

In 1687, Newton published a book explaining the law of gravity and other workings of the universe. Nature, argued Newton, follows uniform laws. All motion in the universe can be measured and described mathematically. To many, Newton's work seemed to link the sciences just as gravity itself bound the universe together.

For more than 200 years, Newton's laws held fast. In the early 1900s, startling new theories of the universe called some of his ideas into question. Yet his laws of motion and mechanics continue to have many practical uses. For example, calculus—a branch of mathematics partially developed by Newton and used to explain his laws—is still applied today.

✔ **Checkpoint** How did Newton use observations of nature to explain the movements of the planets?

 SECTION 5 Assessment

Progress Monitoring *Online*
For: Self-quiz with vocabulary practice
Web Code: naa-1351

Terms, People, and Places

1. What do all of the key people listed at the beginning of this section have in common? Explain.

Note Taking

2. **Reading Skill: Identify Main Ideas** Use your completed table to answer the Focus Question: How did discoveries in science lead to a new way of thinking for Europeans?

Comprehension and Critical Thinking

3. **Recognize Ideologies** Why did the theories of Copernicus and Galileo threaten the views of the Church?

4. **Make Generalizations** In what ways did the scientific method differ from earlier approaches to learning?

5. **Recognize Cause and Effect** What impact did Renaissance ideas have on medicine?

6. **Synthesize Information** How did Newton use the ideas of Plato?

● **Writing About History**

Quick Write: Write a Conclusion Write a conclusion to a persuasive essay about the Scientific Revolution. Your conclusion should restate a thesis statement, supported by one or two strong arguments. You may want to end your essay with a quotation. For example, you could use the Pope quotation to support a thesis that Newton's ideas were the most important of the Scientific Revolution.

Science and Technology

How has science changed people's lives throughout history?

Copernicus played a critical role in the Scientific Revolution. His heliocentric theory, supported by the work of Kepler, Galileo, and other scientists, undermined the existing worldview of the Church and of most European scholars. It helped lead to a whole new approach to science, based on observation and experimentation. Despite its revolutionary nature, Copernicus's theory did not directly change people's lives. Yet many of the scientific observations and experiments that followed had important practical effects, as the following medical examples reveal.

▲ The drawing on the right reflects Ptolemy's Earth-centered view of the universe. Copernicus's sun-centered universe is shown at left.

Organ Transplantation

An organ transplant is the transfer of a living body organ to an ill person in order to restore that person's health. Dr. Joseph Murray performed the first transplant in 1954 when he transferred a kidney from one twin to the other. Since then, the success rate for transplants has grown steadily, thanks to new techniques and new drugs that keep the body from rejecting a donated organ. During 2003, surgeons transplanted more than 25,000 organs, including hearts, lungs, livers, and kidneys.

Vaccination

You probably received your first vaccination as an infant. Vaccination, also called immunization, introduces killed or altered bacteria or viruses into the body. This triggers the body's immune system, enabling it to defend against the disease. In the 1790s, Edward Jenner launched the scientific study of immunization when he discovered a vaccine against smallpox, a disease that had plagued humankind since ancient times. By 1980, vaccination had finally rid the world of smallpox.

Microscope

Anton van Leeuwenhoek had a hobby. In his spare time, he liked to grind lenses and use them to observe worlds formerly hidden from sight. In 1684, using his simple microscope, he became the first person to describe red blood cells accurately. In modern times, the microscope has served as a vital tool for saving lives. Doctors use it to identify the bacteria and other germs causing an illness. Based on their findings, they can tailor their treatment to fight the patient's specific disease.

▲ A greatly enlarged image of tiny bacteria

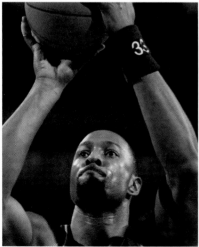

▲ Alonzo Mourning plays in his first basketball game after receiving a kidney transplant.

▲ This French illustration shows Edward Jenner administering a vaccine.

Thinking Critically

1. How did the Scientific Revolution pave the way for the medical successes described above? How have those successes changed people's lives?

2. **Connections to Today** Do research to find out more about these and other examples of scientific break-throughs. Choose one breakthrough and write a press release announcing it to the world.

Quick Study Guide

Progress Monitoring *Online*
For: Self-test with vocabulary practice
Web Code: naa-1361

■ Major Themes of the Renaissance

- Importance of classical learning
- Emphasis on the individual
- Adventurous spirit and willingness to experiment
- Focus on realism in art and literature
- Questioning of traditional religious ideas

■ Important Figures of the Scientific Revolution

Person	Achievement	Date
Nicolaus Copernicus	Developed the sun-centered model of the universe	1543
Tycho Brahe and Johannes Kepler	Built astronomical observatory to calculate the planetal orbits; supported Copernicus's views	Late 1500s
Galileo Galilei	Developed telescope to view the planets and confirmed Copernicus's theory	1600
Francis Bacon	Called for new scientific method	Early 1600s
René Descartes	Developed new philosophy of human reasoning	Early 1600s
Isaac Newton	Developed laws of gravity and motion; invented calculus	Late 1600s
Robert Boyle	Identified basic building blocks of matter, opening the way for modern chemistry	Late 1600s

■ Causes and Effects of the Protestant Reformation

Cause and Effect	
Long-Term Causes	**Immediate Causes**
• Roman Catholic Church becomes more worldly. • Humanists urge a return to simple religion. • Shift to more uncertain, urban-based economies causes people to look for society that makes more sense to them. • Monarchs and other leaders question the pope's authority and wealth.	• Johann Tetzel sells indulgences in Wittenberg. • Martin Luther posts 95 Theses. • Luther translates the Bible into German. • The printing press spreads reform ideas. • Calvin and other reformers preach against Roman Catholic traditions.

↓

The Protestant Reformation	

↓

Immediate Effects	**Long-Term Effects**
• Peasants' Revolt • Catholic Reformation • Strengthening of the Inquisition • Luther's calls for Jewish expulsion result in Jewish migration to Eastern Europe	• Religious wars in Europe • Founding of Lutheran, Calvinist, Anglican, Presbyterian, and other Protestant churches • Weakening of Holy Roman Empire • Increased anti-Semitism

■ Key Events of the Renaissance and the Reformation

1300s
The Renaissance begins in the city-states of Italy.

1434
The Medici family gains control of Florence's government.

Chapter Events
World Events

1300 **1350** **1400**

1324
Mansa Musa makes hajj.

1368
The Ming dynasty is founded in China.

1450
The kingdom of Songhai emerges in West Africa.

Concept Connector

■ Cumulative Review

Use your Concept Connector worksheets and the text to help answer these questions. In addition, record information from this chapter about the following concepts.

1. **Cultural Diffusion** During the Middle Ages, many European peoples were cut off from each other as trade broke down and disease ravaged populations. With the Renaissance, renewed trade and increased curiosity about the world led to great cultural diffusion. For example, art techniques developed in Italy spread to northern Europe, and vice versa. Compare the cultural diffusion of the Renaissance to the spread of Islam from about 750 to 1200. Consider:
   - cultural achievements
   - trading centers
   - economic growth
   - religious expression

2. **Science** Many people disputed Copernicus's heliocentric view of the universe, because it challenged the belief of the Earth-centered universe that both made sense to them and was taught to them by the Church. Compare the reaction of people to Copernicus's ideas with the reaction of people to the ideas of Isaac Newton. Why were Newton's theories not seen as controversial?

3. **Cultural Diffusion** The European Renaissance ushered in a period of great cultural achievements that would eventually influence people far beyond Europe. Compare the achievements of Europe during the Renaissance with achievements of the Tang and Song dynasties of China. Consider the following: architecture, print technology, literature, and painting.

■ Connections to Today

1. **Technology: The Communications Revolution** During the Renaissance, new technology like the printing press revolutionized life. Consider the various impacts that the printing press had during the Renaissance, In areas ranging from literacy to religion. Then choose a modern technology that has had a comparable effect. Write two paragraphs explaining why the technology you chose is as important in terms of its impact today as the printing press was in Renaissance times.

2. **Science: Controversial Debates** When Galileo invented his telescope and used it to observe the universe, he opened up a firestorm of debate. Galileo's discoveries challenged traditional views and led people to question many of the things that they had held as firm beliefs. Since Galileo's time, scientific theories have continued to spark furious debate. Think of a recent debate caused by a scientific theory, the use of a medical procedure, or the development of a new technology. Identify both sides of the debate, and then list arguments for each.

History Interactive
For: Interactive timeline
Web Code: nap-1361

1456
The Gutenberg printing press produces the first printed Bible.

1512
Michelangelo completes the Sistine Chapel frescoes.

1517
Martin Luther posts his 95 Theses.

1534
English Parliament passes the Act of Supremacy.

1633
Galileo is tried before the Inquisition for his theories.

King Henry the eyght.

1500 **1550** **1600**

1453
Constantinople falls to the Ottoman Turks.

1492
Christopher Columbus reaches the Caribbean islands.

1532
Spanish forces defeat the Incan empire of South America.

1620
Pilgrims found the Plymouth Colony in Massachusetts.

Chapter Assessment

Terms, People, and Places

Complete each sentence by choosing the correct answer from the list of terms below. You will not use all of the terms.

patron	indulgence	ghetto
humanism	predestination	heliocentric
vernacular	compromise	hypothesis
utopian		

1. Lorenzo de' Medici was a _____ of the Florentine arts.
2. Rabelais and Shakespeare wrote in the _____ to appeal to the common people.
3. Calvin's belief in _____ set him apart from Catholics.
4. Elizabeth's sensible _____ helped keep England unified in the face of religious conflict.
5. Copernicus's _____ theory of the universe challenged the accepted teachings of the Church.

Main Ideas

Section 1 (pp. 410–417)
6. How did the new Renaissance worldview shape the work of Italian Renaissance artists and writers?

Section 2 (pp. 418–422)
7. What was the role of the printing press in spreading Renaissance ideas?
8. How did northern European artists and writers apply Renaissance ideas in their work?

Section 3 (pp. 423–427)
9. How did the Renaissance open the door to the Protestant Reformation?

Section 4 (pp. 428–433)
10. Why did the Church respond with its Catholic Reformation?

Section 5 (pp. 434–439)
11. How were the scientists of the Scientific Revolution influenced by Renaissance ideas?

Chapter Focus Question
12. How did the Renaissance shape European art, thought, and religion?

Critical Thinking

13. **Geography and History** How did Italy's geography encourage the spread of the Renaissance?
14. **Analyze Information** In what ways was the Renaissance a break with medieval times? In what ways was it a continuation of medieval times?
15. **Predict Consequences** Under what circumstances are religious beliefs likely to inspire anger or violence?
16. **Analyze Visuals** What Renaissance theme does the bas-relief below express?

17. **Test Conclusions** The Renaissance and Scientific Revolution are often described as eras of human progress. Evaluate whether this is an accurate description.
18. **Recognize Cause and Effect** Why did England escape the kinds of religious wars that tore apart other European nations?
19. **Synthesize Information** An English author wrote, "The preaching of sermons is speaking to a few of mankind, but printing books is talking to the whole world." How does this statement suggest a relationship between two of the key events discussed in this chapter?

● Writing About History

Writing a Persuasive Essay European history from 1300 to the 1600s was a time of great change, discovery, and religious upheaval. Write a persuasive essay that presents your position on either the Renaissance, the Reformation, or the Scientific Revolution. Consult page SH16 of the Writing Handbook for additional help.

Prewriting
• Choose a topic and decide what your main position will be.

• Think of arguments that both support and oppose your position, and answer them.
• Gather evidence that supports your position.

Drafting
• State your position in a thesis statement.
• Organize your arguments into a draft outline.
• Write the introduction, body text, and closing arguments. Be sure to support your arguments with a variety of points, including facts, comparisons, and statistics.

Revising
• Use the guidelines for revising your report on page SH17 of the Writing Handbook.

Document-Based Assessment

The Impact of the Printing Press

In a time when new ideas and discoveries were commonplace, the invention of the printing press was no less than astonishing in its impact. Documents A, B, and D describe the spread of printing during the Renaissance. Document C, written by a historian in the 1500s, describes its impact at the time.

Document A

"In 1455 all Europe's printed books could have been carried in a single wagon. Fifty years later, the titles ran to tens of thousands, the individual volumes to millions. Today, books pour off presses at the rate of 10,000 million *a year*. That's some 50 million tons of paper. Add in 8,000 to 9,000 daily newspapers, and the Sundays, and the magazines, and the figure rises to 130 million tons . . . It would make a pile 700 meters [2,297 feet] high—four times the height of the Great Pyramid."

—From ***Gutenberg: How One Man Remade the World with Words*** by John Man

Document B

"Printing spread from Mainz to Strasbourg (1458), Cologne (1465), Augsburg (1468), Nuremberg (1470), Leipzig (1481), and Vienna (1482). German printers, or their pupils, introduced the 'divine' art to Italy in 1467, Switzerland and Bohemia in 1468, France and the Netherlands in 1470, Spain, England, Hungary, and Poland between 1474 and 1476, Denmark and Sweden in 1482–1483. By 1500 the presses had issued about six million books in approximately forty thousand editions, more books, probably, than had been produced in western Europe since the fall of Rome . . . Now individuals could afford to own books, where before they had normally been owned almost exclusively by institutions—monasteries, cathedral chapters, and colleges."

—From ***The Foundation of Early Modern Europe, 1460–1559*** by Eugene F. Rice, Jr.

Document C

"As if to offer proof that God has chosen us to accomplish a special mission, there was invented in our land a marvelous new and subtle art, the art of printing. This opened German eyes even as it is now bringing enlightenment to other countries. Each man became eager for knowledge, not without feeling a sense of amazement at his former blindness."

—From ***Address to the Estates of the Empire*** by Johann Sleidan

Document D

The Spread of Printing in Renaissance Europe

Analyzing Documents

Use your knowledge of the Renaissance and Documents A, B, C, and D to answer questions 1–4.

1. According to Document B, the increased supply and lower cost of books had what effect?
   A More people became teachers.
   B More people became printers.
   C More people bought books.
   D More people bought printing presses.

2. What information about printing can be found only on Document D?
   A specific dates when printing presses were introduced
   B areas where the concentration of printing presses was densest
   C numbers of printing presses introduced into selected cities
   D countries where printing presses were introduced

3. What does German historian Sleidan, in Document C, imply is the *most important* role of the printing press?
   A spreading the Protestant religion
   B teaching German history to other countries
   C making books cheaper
   D giving Germans more knowledge

4. **Writing Task** How did the invention of the printing press affect the spread of the Reformation? Use specific evidence from the documents above, along with information from this chapter, to support your answer.

14

The Beginnings of Our Global Age: Europe, Africa, and Asia

1415–1796

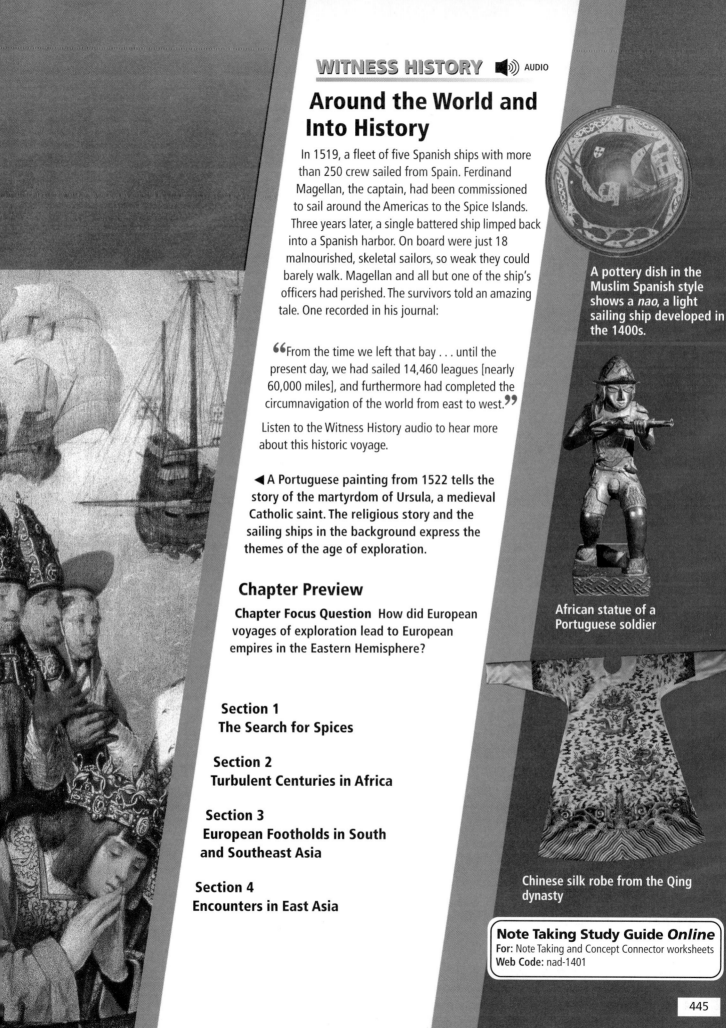

Around the World and Into History

In 1519, a fleet of five Spanish ships with more than 250 crew sailed from Spain. Ferdinand Magellan, the captain, had been commissioned to sail around the Americas to the Spice Islands. Three years later, a single battered ship limped back into a Spanish harbor. On board were just 18 malnourished, skeletal sailors, so weak they could barely walk. Magellan and all but one of the ship's officers had perished. The survivors told an amazing tale. One recorded in his journal:

66 From the time we left that bay . . . until the present day, we had sailed 14,460 leagues [nearly 60,000 miles], and furthermore had completed the circumnavigation of the world from east to west.**99**

Listen to the Witness History audio to hear more about this historic voyage.

◀ A Portuguese painting from 1522 tells the story of the martyrdom of Ursula, a medieval Catholic saint. The religious story and the sailing ships in the background express the themes of the age of exploration.

A pottery dish in the Muslim Spanish style shows a *nao*, a light sailing ship developed in the 1400s.

African statue of a Portuguese soldier

Chinese silk robe from the Qing dynasty

Chapter Preview

Chapter Focus Question How did European voyages of exploration lead to European empires in the Eastern Hemisphere?

Section 1
The Search for Spices

Section 2
Turbulent Centuries in Africa

Section 3
European Footholds in South and Southeast Asia

Section 4
Encounters in East Asia

Note Taking Study Guide *Online*
For: Note Taking and Concept Connector worksheets
Web Code: nad-1401

A French traveler in the 1400s illustrated workers harvesting pepper in southern India; a clove plant is shown at left.

WITNESS HISTORY 🔊 AUDIO

The Search Is On

Cinnamon, pepper, nutmeg, cloves . . . these and other spices were a vital part of the world economy in the 1400s. Because the spice trade was controlled by Arab merchants and traders, Europeans didn't know how to get the spices they desperately wanted. Even when Europeans learned that spice plants could be obtained in Asia, they didn't have a hope of growing them in Europe. As an Indonesian ruler boasted to a European trader,

❝ You may be able to take our plants, but you will never be able to take our rain.❞

Europeans knew that the only way they could take control of the spice trade would be to establish sea routes to Asia—at any cost.

Focus Question How did the search for spices lead to global exploration?

The Search for Spices

Objectives
- Understand European motivations for exploring the seas.
- Analyze early Portuguese and Spanish explorations.
- Describe European searches for a direct route to Asia.

Terms, People, and Places

Moluccas
Prince Henry
cartographer
Vasco da Gama
Christopher Columbus

Line of Demarcation
Treaty of Tordesillas
Ferdinand Magellan
circumnavigate

Note Taking

Reading Skill: Identify Causes and Effects
Examine the text for clues that signal cause and effect. Then use a flowchart like this one to record major causes and effects of European exploration.

Throughout history, groups of people—from the ancient Greeks to Muslim Arabs and the Vikings of Scandinavia—had explored the seas, trading and migrating over long distances. The European sailors of the 1400s began a dramatic new period of exploration.

Motivations for Exploring the Seas

Europeans traded with Asians long before the Renaissance. The Crusades introduced Europeans to many luxury goods from Asia, carried on complex overland routes through the Mongol empire of the 1200s and 1300s. The Black Death and the breakup of the Mongol empire disrupted that trade. By the 1400s, though, Europe's population was growing, along with its demand for trade goods. The most valued items were spices, used to preserve food, add flavor to meat, and make medicines and perfumes. The chief source of spices was the **Moluccas,** an island chain in present-day Indonesia, which Europeans then called the Spice Islands.

In the 1400s, Arab and Italian merchants controlled most trade between Asia and Europe. Muslim traders brought prized goods to eastern Mediterranean ports, and Italian traders carried them to European markets. Europeans outside Italy knew that it would be more profitable to gain direct access to Asia. They were also driven by Renaissance curiosity to seek new lands.

 Checkpoint What factors encouraged European exploration?

Early Voyages of European Exploration, 1487–1609

Map Skills Spain, England, France, and the Netherlands quickly followed Portugal's lead in exploring the world by ship.

1. **Locate** (a) West Indies (b) East Indies (c) Line of Demarcation (d) Strait of Magellan

2. **Describe** Describe the route of Columbus.

3. **Draw Inferences** Why do you think explorers from different countries followed similar routes?

Explorers for Portugal
- - - ▸ Dias, 1487–1488
———▸ Da Gama, 1497–1499

Explorers for Spain
- - - ▸ Columbus, 1492–1493
———▸ Balboa, 1510–1513
· · · · · ▸ Magellan and Elcano, 1519–1522

Explorers for England
———▸ Cabot, 1497

Explorers for France
———▸ Cartier, 1534–1535

Explorers for the Netherlands
———▸ Hudson, 1609

Portugal Sails East

Prince Henry led the way in sponsoring exploration for Portugal, a small nation next to Spain. First, Prince Henry's navigators discovered and claimed the Madeira and Azores islands to the west and southwest of Portugal. By 1415, Portugal had expanded into Muslim North Africa, seizing the port of Ceuta (SYOO tah) on the North African coast.

Mapping the African Coast Prince Henry saw great promise in Africa. The Portuguese could convert the Africans—who practiced either Islam or tribal religions—to Christianity. He also believed that in Africa he would find the sources of riches the Muslim traders controlled.

Finally, Prince Henry hoped to find an easier way to reach Asia, which meant going around Africa. The Portuguese felt that with their expert knowledge and technology, they could accomplish this feat. At Sagres, in southern Portugal, Henry gathered scientists, **cartographers,** or mapmakers, and other experts. They redesigned ships, prepared maps, and trained captains and crews for long voyages. Henry's ships then slowly worked their way south to explore the western coast of Africa.

Henry died in 1460, but the Portuguese continued their quest. In 1488, Bartholomeu Dias rounded the southern tip of Africa. Despite the turbulent seas around it, the tip became known as the Cape of Good Hope because it opened the way for a sea route to Asia.

Seeking India In 1497, Portuguese navigator **Vasco da Gama** followed in Dias's footsteps, leading four ships around the Cape of Good Hope. Da Gama, however, had plans to go farther. After a ten-month voyage, da Gama reached the great spice port of Calicut on the west coast of India. On the long voyage home, the Portuguese lost half their ships, and many sailors died of hunger, thirst, and scurvy, a disease caused by a lack of vitamin C in the diet.

Despite the hard journey, the venture proved highly profitable. In India, da Gama had acquired a cargo of spices that he sold at an enormous profit. He quickly outfitted a new fleet, seeking greater profits. In 1502, he forced a treaty on the ruler of Calicut. Da Gama then left Portuguese merchants there whose job was to buy spices when prices were low and store them until the next fleet could return. Soon, the Portuguese had seized key ports around the Indian Ocean, creating a vast trading empire. Da Gama's voyages confirmed Portugal's status as a world power.

✔ **Checkpoint**   How did Portuguese exploration lead to the creation of a trading empire?

INFOGRAPHIC
NAVIGATING THE WORLD

In the 1400s, European knowledge of the world—and how to navigate it—greatly expanded. Geographers gave navigators more accurate maps, and shipmakers built ships more suitable for crossing the ocean. Navigators began to use existing instruments like the compass and astrolabe in new ways. With each voyage, they added to their knowledge, resulting in even better maps and improved technology.

The portolan map ▶
Navigators used portolan maps with magnetic compasses. The lines on the portolan map radiated out from compass points, showing navigators how to find their way to key ports.

A better compass ▲
The Chinese had used the compass for centuries, but the magnetic compass did not become a customary navigational tool until the 1400s. The magnetic compass uses an iron needle, magnetized by a mineral called lodestone, that aligns with Earth's north-south poles. Navigators used it to find their bearings and chart courses.

Columbus Sails West

News of Portugal's successes spurred other people to look for a sea route to Asia. An Italian navigator from Genoa, named **Christopher Columbus**, wanted to reach the East Indies—a group of islands in Southeast Asia, today part of Indonesia—by sailing west across the Atlantic. Like most educated Europeans, Columbus knew that Earth was a sphere. A few weeks sailing west, he reasoned, would bring a ship to eastern Asia. His plan made sense, but Columbus greatly underestimated Earth's size. And he had no idea that two continents lay in his path.

Reaching Faraway Lands Portugal refused to sponsor him, but Columbus persuaded Ferdinand and Isabella of Spain to finance his voyage. To increase their <u>authority</u>, the Spanish rulers had taken radical measures, including expelling Jews from Spain. They hoped their actions would strengthen Catholicism. However, the loss of some of Spain's most affluent and cultured people weakened the nation. The rulers hoped Columbus's voyage would bring wealth and prestige.

Vocabulary Builder

<u>authority</u>—(uh THAWR uh tee) *n.* the power to give commands and enforce obedience

◀ **A more accurate world map**
In the 1400s, world maps showed Europe accurately (far left) but the rest of the world as one giant landmass. By 1560, the geographer Abraham Ortelius had produced a map (left) that showed all of the continents with accurate shapes.

▼ **A faster ship**
The light, fast caravel was developed in the 1400s. Unlike most heavy European ships, it was easily maneuvered along coasts and could travel long distances.

◀ **A new use for an old tool**
Astronomers had used astrolabes in ancient times. Renaissance sailors found them useful for navigation. Navigators looked through the astrolabe at the sun or a star, and determined its angle using the degrees marked on the instrument. The angle of the sun or star helped them to determine their ships' latitude as well as the local time.

Thinking Critically
1. **Synthesize Information** Why would a portolan map be inappropriate as a resource for a geography class?
2. **Draw Inferences** What limitations did the astrolabe have that the magnetic compass did not?

Henry the Navigator

All of the European explorers owed a debt to Prince Henry (1394–1460), whose Christian faith, curiousity, and national pride ushered in the great age of European exploration. The English nicknamed Henry "the Navigator." Yet Henry himself, who sponsored and encouraged navigators, geographers, and merchants, never traveled the seas. Henry's work required financial risks, and his enthusiasm motivated his navigators to take great personal risks. Henry also inspired generations of later explorers. **What characteristics does the artist ascribe to Henry (center figure in black)?**

On August 3, 1492, Columbus sailed west with three small ships, the *Niña*, the *Pinta*, and the *Santa María*. Although the expedition encountered good weather and a favorable wind, no land came into sight for many weeks. Provisions ran low, and the crew became anxious. Finally, on October 12, land was spotted.

Columbus spent several months cruising the islands of the Caribbean. Because he thought he had reached the Indies, he called the people of the region "Indians." In 1493, he returned to Spain to a hero's welcome. In three later voyages, Columbus remained convinced that he had reached the coast of East Asia. Before long, though, other Europeans realized that Columbus had found a route to previously unknown continents.

Dividing the Globe in Half In 1493 Ferdinand and Isabella appealed to the Spanish-born Pope Alexander VI to support their claim to the lands of the new world. The pope set a **Line of Demarcation,** dividing the non-European world into two zones. Spain had trading and exploration rights in any lands west of the line. Portugal had the same rights east of the line. The specific terms of the Line of Demarcation were agreed to in the **Treaty of Tordesillas,** signed between the two countries in 1494. The actual line was unclear, because geography at the time was imprecise. However, the treaty made it obvious to both Spain and Portugal—and to other European nations, eager to defy what they saw as Spain and Portugal's arrogance—that they needed to build their own empires quickly.

Naming the Western Hemisphere An Italian sea captain named Amerigo Vespucci wrote a journal describing his voyage to Brazil. In 1507, a German cartographer named Martin Waldseemüller used Vespucci's descriptions of his voyage to publish a map of the region, which he labeled "America." Over time, the term "Americas" came to be used for both continents of the Western Hemisphere. The islands Columbus had explored in the Caribbean became known as the West Indies.

 Checkpoint How did Columbus influence the Treaty of Tordesillas?

The Search for a Direct Route Continues

Though Europeans had claimed vast new territories, they had not yet found a direct route to Asia. The English, Dutch, and French explored the coast of North America unsuccessfully for a "northwest passage," or a route from the Atlantic Ocean to the Pacific through the Arctic islands. Meanwhile, in 1513 the Spanish adventurer Vasco Núñez de Balboa, helped by local Indians, hacked a passage westward through the tropical forests of Panama. From a ridge on the west coast, he gazed at a huge body of water. The body of water that he named the South Sea was in fact the Pacific Ocean.

On September 20, 1519, a minor Portuguese nobleman named **Ferdinand Magellan** set out from Spain with five ships to find a way to reach the Pacific. Magellan's ships sailed south and west, through storms and calms and tropical heat. At last, his fleet reached the coast of South America. Carefully, they explored each bay, hoping to find one that would lead to the Pacific. In November 1520, Magellan's ships entered a bay at the southern tip of South America. Amid brutal storms, rushing tides, and unpredictable winds, Magellan found a passage that later became known as the Strait of Magellan. The ships emerged into Balboa's South Sea. Magellan renamed the sea the Pacific, from the Latin word meaning *peaceful*.

Their mission accomplished, most of the crew wanted to return to Spain the way they had come. Magellan, however, insisted that they push on across the Pacific to the East Indies. Magellan underestimated the size of the Pacific. Three more weeks, he thought, would bring them to the Spice Islands. Magellan was wrong. For nearly four months, the ships plowed across the uncharted ocean. Finally, in March 1521, the fleet reached the Philippines, where Magellan was killed. On September 8, 1522, nearly three years after setting out, the survivors— one ship and 18 sailors—reached Spain. The survivors had been the first people to **circumnavigate,** or sail around, the world. Antonio Pigafetta, one of the few survivors of the expedition, observed: "I believe of a certainty that no one will ever again make such a voyage."

✓ **Checkpoint**   What was the significance of Balboa's discovery?

SECTION 1

Assessment

Progress Monitoring *Online*
For: Self-quiz with vocabulary practice
Web Code: naa-1411

Terms, People, and Places

1. For each term, person, or place listed at the beginning of the section, write a sentence explaining its significance.

Note Taking

2. **Reading Skill: Identify Causes and Effects** Use your completed flowchart to answer the Focus Question: How did the search for spices lead to global exploration?

Comprehension and Critical Thinking

3. **Recognize Cause and Effect** How did the Renaissance motivate European explorers?

4. **Recognize Ideologies** How did Prince Henry's Christian faith shape his role as a sponsor of exploration?

5. **Identify Alternatives** If Columbus had understood the real geography of the world, would he still have made his voyage? Why or why not?

6. **Predict Consequences** What effect might Magellan's circumnavigation of the world have on English, Dutch, and French explorers?

● **Writing About History**

Quick Write: Gather Information Choose one of the following people from this section for a biographical essay: Prince Henry, Christopher Columbus, or Ferdinand Magellan. Gather information about the person you chose. Note events that were both directly and indirectly influenced by this person.

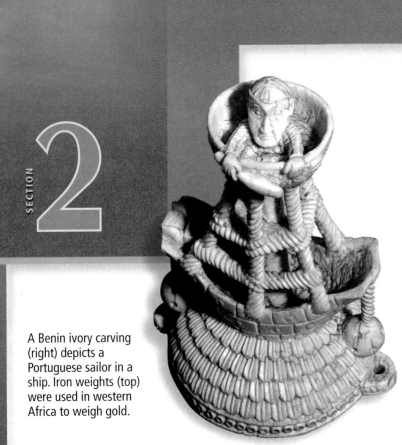

A Benin ivory carving (right) depicts a Portuguese sailor in a ship. Iron weights (top) were used in western Africa to weigh gold.

SECTION 2

WITNESS HISTORY ◀ᵈ)) AUDIO

Great Seabirds Arrive

A Portuguese captain named Alvise Cadamosto reached West Africa in the mid-1400s. He described the reaction of the West Africans to the sight of his ship:

66 It is said that the first time they saw sails . . . they believed they were great seabirds with white wings, which were flying and had come from some strange place. . . . Some thought the ships were fishes, others that they were ghosts that went by night, at which they were terrified. **99**

—Alvise Cadamosto, 1455

Focus Question What effects did European exploration have on the people of Africa?

Turbulent Centuries in Africa

Objectives
- Describe how the Portuguese established footholds on Africa's coasts.
- Analyze how European actions affected the slave trade and the rise of African states.
- Explain how the European presence in Africa expanded.

Terms, People, and Places

Mombasa	Osei Tutu
Malindi	monopoly
plantation	Oyo empire
Affonso I	Cape Town
missionary	Boers
Asante kingdom	

Note Taking

Reading Skill: Identify Effects As you read, record effects of European exploration in Africa in a chart like the one below.

Effects of European Exploration		
European Footholds	Slave Trade	New African States

European encounters with Africa had occurred for hundreds of years. Yet the European explorers who arrived in the 1400s brought great and unforeseen changes to Africa's peoples and cultures.

Portugal Gains Footholds

As you have read, the Portuguese who explored Africa's coasts in the 1400s were looking for a sea route to Asia that bypassed the Mediterranean. They also wanted to buy goods directly from their source, rather than trading through Arab middlemen.

The Portuguese began carrying out their strategy in West Africa, building small forts to collect food and water and to repair their ships. They also established trading posts to trade muskets, tools, and cloth for gold, ivory, hides, and slaves. These were not colonies peopled by settlers. Instead, the Portuguese left just enough men and firepower to defend their forts.

From West Africa, the Portuguese sailed around the continent. They continued to establish forts and trading posts, but they also attacked existing East African coastal cities such as **Mombasa** and **Malindi,** which were hubs of international trade. With cannons blazing, they expelled the Arabs who controlled the East African trade network and took over this thriving commerce for themselves. Each conquest added to their growing trade empire.

Over the next two centuries, some Portuguese explorers managed to reach parts of present-day Congo, Zambia, and Zimbabwe, establishing limited trade. In general, however, the Portuguese did not venture far from the coasts. They knew little about Africa's interior, and they lacked accurate maps or other resources to help them explore there. Furthermore, Africans in the interior, who wanted to control the gold trade, resisted such exploration. As a result of all these factors, when the Portuguese empire declined in the 1600s, the Portuguese did not leave a strong legacy in Africa.

✔ **Checkpoint** Why did the Portuguese establish a presence mainly along the African coast?

The African Slave Trade Explodes

In the 1500s and 1600s, Europeans began to view slaves as the most important item of African trade. Slavery had existed in Africa, as elsewhere around the world, since ancient times. Egyptians, Greeks, Romans, Persians, Indians, and Aztecs often enslaved defeated foes. The English word *slave* comes from the large number of Slavs taken from southern Russia to work as unpaid laborers in Roman times.

The Arab empire also used slave labor, often African captives. In the Middle East, enslaved Africans worked on farming estates or large-scale irrigation projects. Others became artisans, soldiers, or merchants. Some rose to prominence in the Muslim world even though they were slaves.

A Valuable Commodity
Since ancient times, gold was a valuable trade good in western Africa. Beginning in the 1500s, it became an important part of the slave trade. Europeans melted down African gold jewelry like the pieces above to make gold coins.

Europeans Enter the Slave Trade Portuguese traders quickly joined the profitable slave trade, followed by other European traders. Europeans bought large numbers of slaves to perform labor on their **plantations**—large estates run by an owner or an owner's overseer—in the Americas and elsewhere. Europeans also bought slaves as exotic servants for rich households. By the 1500s, European participation had encouraged a much broader Atlantic slave trade.

Europeans seldom went into Africa's interior to take part in slave raids. Instead, they relied on African rulers and traders to seize captives in the interior and bring them to coastal trading posts and forts. There, the captives were exchanged for textiles, metalwork, rum, tobacco, weapons, and gunpowder. Over the next 300 years, the slave trade grew into a huge and profitable business to fill the need for cheap labor. Each year, traders shipped tens of thousands of enslaved Africans across the Atlantic to work on sugar, rice, tobacco, and other plantations in the Americas. These slaves were considered to be property, and they had no hope of bettering their situations.

A Portuguese observer described the first ship of African slaves arriving in Portugal in 1444 from West Africa. Judging from the writer's words, what was his opinion of what he saw?

Primary Source

❝Some kept their heads low and their faces bathed in tears, looking at each other . . . others struck themselves in the face and threw themselves to the ground; and others sang sad songs—although we did not understand their words, the sound told of their great sorrow. . . . The mothers threw themselves flat on the ground. They were beaten but they refused to give up their children.❞
—From *Chronicle of the Discovery and Conquest of Guinea*

 AUDIO

African Leaders Resist Some African leaders tried to slow down or stop the transatlantic slave trade. But in the end, the system that supported the trade was simply too strong for them. An early voice raised against the slave trade was that of Affonso I, ruler of Kongo in west-central Africa. As a young man, Affonso had been tutored by Portuguese missionaries, who hoped to convert Africans to Christianity.

Major African States About 1700

Major African States About 1700

- ▨ Major slave trading region
- — African state about 1700
- • City

Miller Projection
0 500 1000 mi
0 500 1000 km

Map Skills By about 1700, many of Africa's states and kingdoms were involved in the slave trade.

1. **Locate** (a) Malindi (b) Kongo (c) Asante (d) Bornu
2. **Describe** Which states were part of a major slave trading region?
3. **Synthesize Information** In general, where were most slave trading regions located? Explain.

Geography *Interactive*
For: Audio guided tour
Web Code: nap-1421

Vocabulary Builder
dominate—(DAHM uh nayt) *v.* to rule or control by superior power

Vocabulary Builder
unified—(YOO nuh fyd) *v.* combined into one

After becoming king in 1505, he called on the Portuguese to help him develop Kongo as a modern Christian state. But he became alarmed as more and more Portuguese came to Kongo each year to buy slaves. Affonso wanted to maintain contact with Europe but end the slave trade. His appeal failed, and the slave trade continued.

In the late 1700s, another African ruler tried to halt the slave trade in his lands. He was the almany (from the Arabic words meaning "religious leader") of Futa Toro, in present-day Senegal. Since the 1500s, French sea captains had bought slaves from African traders in Futa Toro. In 1788, the almany forbade anyone to transport slaves through Futa Toro for sale abroad. However, the inland slave traders simply worked out a new route to the coast. Sailing to this new market, the French captains easily purchased the slaves that the almany had prevented them from buying in Futa Toro.

✔ **Checkpoint** How did the African slave trade expand?

New African States Arise

The slave trade had major effects on African states in the 1600s and 1700s. In West Africa, for example, the loss of countless numbers of young women and men resulted in some small states disappearing forever. At the same time, there arose new states whose way of life depended on the slave trade. The rulers of these powerful new states waged war against other Africans to dominate the slave trade.

The Asante Kingdom The Asante kingdom (uh SAHN teh) emerged in the area occupied by present-day Ghana. In the late 1600s, an able military leader, Osei Tutu, won control of the trading city of Kumasi. From there, he conquered neighboring peoples and unified the Asante kingdom. The Asante faced a great challenge in the Denkyera, a powerful neighboring enemy kingdom. Osei Tutu realized that in order to withstand the Denkyera, the people of his kingdom needed to be firmly united. To do this, he claimed that his right to rule came from heaven, and that people in the kingdom were linked by spiritual bonds. This strategy paid off when the Asante defeated the Denkyera in the late 1600s.

Under Osei Tutu, government officials, chosen by merit rather than by birth, supervised an efficient bureaucracy. They managed the royal monopolies on gold mining and the slave trade. A monopoly is the exclusive control of a business or industry. The Asante traded with Europeans on the coast, exchanging gold and slaves for firearms. They also played rival Europeans against one another to protect themselves. In this way, they built a wealthy, powerful state.

The Oyo Empire The Oyo empire arose from successive waves of settlement by the Yoruba people of present-day Nigeria. It began as a relatively small forest kingdom. Beginning in the late 1600s, however, its leaders used wealth from the slave trade to build up an impressive army. The Oyo empire used the army to conquer the neighboring kingdom of Dahomey. At the same time, it continued to gain wealth by trading with European merchants at the port city of Porto-Novo.

✔ **Checkpoint** What caused some African states to grow?

The European Presence Expands

Following the Portuguese example, by the 1600s several European powers had established forts along the western coast of Africa. As Portuguese power declined in the region, British, Dutch, and French traders took over their forts. Unlike the Portuguese, they established permanent footholds throughout the continent.

In 1652, Dutch immigrants arrived at the southern tip of the continent. They built **Cape Town,** the first permanent European settlement, to supply ships sailing to or from the East Indies. Dutch farmers, called **Boers,** settled around Cape Town. Over time, they ousted, enslaved, or killed the people who lived there. The Boers held a Calvinist belief that they were the elect, or chosen, of God. They looked on Africans as inferiors and did not respect their claims to their own land. In the 1700s, Boer herders and ivory hunters began to push north from the Cape Colony. Their migrations would eventually lead to battle with several African groups.

By the mid-1600s, the British and French had both reached present-day Senegal. The French established a fort in the region around 1700. In the late 1700s, stories about British explorers' search for the source of the Nile River sparked an interest in Africa among Europeans, especially the French and British. In 1788, the British established the African Association, an organization that sponsored explorers to Africa. Over the next century, European exploration of Africa would explode.

✔ **Checkpoint** How did the European presence in Africa expand?

Elmina Castle
European traders called the places where they held and traded slaves "castles." Built by the Portuguese in 1482, Elmina Castle in present-day Ghana was used as a base for trading slaves, gold, and imported European products.

SECTION
2 Assessment

Progress Monitoring *Online*
For: Self-quiz with vocabulary practice
Web Code: naa-1421

Terms, People, and Places

1. What do many of the key terms and people listed at the beginning of the section have in common? Explain.

Note Taking

2. **Reading Skill: Identify Effects** Use your completed chart to answer the Focus Question: What effects did European exploration have on the people of Africa?

Comprehension and Critical Thinking

3. **Determine Relevance** How did the Portuguese strategy of building forts instead of permanent colonies affect Portugal's history in Africa?

4. **Recognize Cause and Effect** How did Europeans change the nature of African slavery?

5. **Analyze Information** Why did the Asante and Oyo need to trade with Europeans to maintain power?

6. **Predict Consequences** Would the Europeans have taken the same course in Africa if the people there had been Christian like themselves?

● **Writing About History**

Quick Write: Write a Thesis Statement Write a thesis statement that will support a biographical essay about either Osei Tutu or Affonso I. Remember that the facts and events you cite in your essay should support your thesis statement. For example, the following thesis statement is not supported by the facts in the text: Affonso I was instrumental in slowing the slave trade in Africa.

King Affonso I:
Letter to King John III of Portugal

In 1490, the Portuguese converted the son of a Kongo king to Christianity and then helped him take his father's throne. The new king, born Nzinga Mbemba, was renamed Affonso. King Affonso soon realized that his relationship with Portugal had extremely negative consequences, as can be seen from his letter to King John III of Portugal in 1526. In this letter, the king of Kongo appeals to the king of Portugal to end the slave trade.

▲ A Congolese brass and wood crucifix dating from the 1500s blends Christian and traditional African symbols.

Sir, Your Highness of Portugal should know how our Kingdom is being lost in so many ways. This is caused by the excessive freedom given by your officials to the men and merchants who are allowed to come to this Kingdom to set up shops with goods and many things which have been prohibited by us. Many of our vassals, whom we had in obedience, do not comply[1] because they have the things in greater abundance than we ourselves. It was with these things that we had them content and subjected under our jurisdiction[2], so it is doing a great harm not only to the service of God, but to the security and peace of our Kingdoms and State as well.

And we cannot reckon how great the damage is, since the mentioned merchants are taking every day our natives, sons of the land and the sons of our noblemen and vassals and our relatives. The thieves and men of bad conscience grab them wishing to have the things and wares of this Kingdom which they are ambitious of; they grab them and get them to be sold. And so great, Sir, is the corruption and licentiousness[3] that our country is being completely depopulated, and your Highness should not agree with this nor accept it as in your service. And to avoid it we need from those your Kingdoms no more than some priests and a few people to teach in schools, and no other goods except wine and flour for the holy sacrament.

That is why we beg of Your Highness to help and assist us in this matter, commanding your factors[4] that they should not send here either merchants or wares, because it is our will that in these kingdoms there should not be any trade of slaves nor outlet for them. Concerning what is referred to above, again we beg of Your Highness to agree with it otherwise we cannot remedy such an obvious damage.

▲ King John III of Portugal

Thinking Critically
1. **Identify Causes** What does King Affonso believe has caused his vassals to become disobedient?
2. **Analyze Information** What specifically does King Affonso say he still needs from the Portuguese?

---

1. comply (kum PLY) *v.* agree to a request
2. jurisdiction (joor is DIK shun) *n.* area of authority or power
3. licentiousness (ly SEN shus nis) *n.* lack of morality
4. factors (FAK turs) *n.* agents

Commander Afonso de Albuquerque (right); a Portuguese rifle (top)

WITNESS HISTORY 🔊 AUDIO

Gunfire Over Malacca

In 1511, a Portuguese fleet commanded by Afonso de Albuquerque (AL buh kur kee) dropped anchor off Malacca, a rich Islamic trading port that controlled the sea route linking India, Southeast Asia, and China. The fleet remained at anchor for several weeks before opening fire. According to a Malaysian account:

> 66 The cannon balls came like rain. And the noise of the cannon was as the noise of thunder in the heavens and the flashes of fire of their guns were like flashes of lightning in the sky: and the noise of their matchlocks [guns] was like that of groundnuts [peanuts] popping in the frying pan. 99
> —From the *Malay Annals*

Focus Question How did European nations build empires in South and Southeast Asia?

European Footholds in South and Southeast Asia

Objectives
- Summarize how Portugal built a trading empire in South and Southeast Asia.
- Analyze the rise of Dutch and Spanish dominance in the region.
- Understand how the decline of Mughal India affected European traders in the region.

Terms, People, and Places

Afonso de Albuquerque
Mughal empire
Goa
Malacca
outpost

Dutch East India Company
sovereign
Philippines
sepoys

Note Taking

Reading Skill: Identify Causes and Effects As you read this section, fill in a chart like the one below with the causes and effects of European exploration in South and Southeast Asia.

Portugal	Netherlands	Spain	Britain
•	•	•	•
•	•	•	•

Portugal was the first European power to gain a foothold in Asia. The Portuguese ships were small in size and number, but the firepower of their shipboard cannons was unmatched. In time, this superior firepower helped them win control of the rich Indian Ocean spice trade and build a trading empire in Asia.

Portugal Builds an Eastern Empire

After Vasco da Gama's voyage, the Portuguese, under **Afonso de Albuquerque's** command, burst into the Indian Ocean. By that time, Muslim rulers, originally from central Asia, had established the **Mughal empire** throughout much of India. The southern regions of India, however, were still controlled by a patchwork of local princes. The Portuguese won these princes to their side with promises of aid against other Europeans. With these southern footholds, Albuquerque and the Portuguese hoped to end Muslim power and turn the Indian Ocean into a "Portuguese lake."

A Rim of Trading Outposts In 1510, the Portuguese seized the island of **Goa** off the coast of India, making it their major military and commercial base. Albuquerque burned coastal towns and crushed Arab fleets at sea. The Portuguese took the East Indies port of **Malacca** in 1511, massacring the city's Muslims.

In less than 50 years, the Portuguese had built a trading empire with military and merchant **outposts**, or distant areas under their control, rimming the southern seas. They used the cities they had seized on the east coast of Africa to resupply and repair their ships. For most of the 1500s, Portugal controlled the spice trade between Europe and Asia.

A Limited Impact Despite their sea power, the Portuguese lacked resources and faced too much resistance to make great inroads into the region. They made harsher efforts to convert local people to Christianity than they had in Africa, attacking Muslims and destroying Hindu temples. Still, by 1600 the Portuguese had converted fewer than a million people to Christianity. The conversion rate was especially low among Asian Muslims.

✓ **Checkpoint** How did the Portuguese control the spice trade?

Rise of the Dutch

The Dutch were the first Europeans to challenge Portuguese domination of Asian trade. The land we know today as the Netherlands included a group of provinces and prosperous trading cities on the North Sea. In the early 1500s it was part of the Holy Roman Empire, but later the Protestant northern provinces won independence. The independent Netherlands entered vigorously into competition for overseas influence.

Building a Mighty Sea Power In 1599, a Dutch fleet returned to Amsterdam from Asia after more than a year's absence. It carried a cargo of pepper, cloves, and other spices. The success of this voyage led to a frenzy of overseas activity. Soon Dutch warships and trading vessels had made the Netherlands a leader of European commerce. Dutch power set up colonies and trading posts around the world. With their strategic settlement at Cape Town, the Netherlands had a secure foothold in the region.

A Powerful Dutch Company In 1602, a group of wealthy Dutch merchants formed the **Dutch East India Company.** From the beginning, this company had an unusual amount of power. Unlike Portuguese and Spanish traders, whose expeditions, were tightly controlled by government, the Dutch East India Company had full **sovereign** powers. With its power to build armies, wage war, negotiate peace treaties, and govern overseas territory, it came to dominate the region.

Vocabulary Builder

strategic—(struh TEE jik) *adj.* important to carrying out a plan of action

Different Perspectives

A European artist (right) shows the king of Sri Lanka and a Dutch explorer meeting as equals. In the Indian painting to the left, Europeans are shown as vassals bringing gifts to India's ruler. *How did European and Asian artists bring their own perspectives to early encounters?*

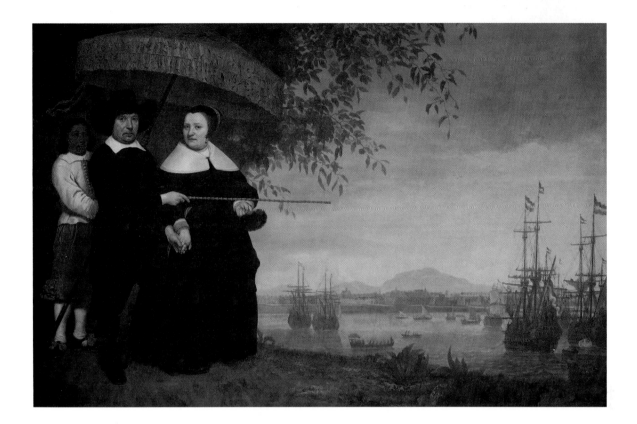

Asserting Dutch Dominance In 1641, the Dutch captured Malacca from the Portuguese and opened trade with China. Soon they were able to enforce a monopoly in the Spice Islands, controlling shipments to Europe as well as much of the trade within Southeast Asia. Like the Portuguese, the Dutch used military force to further their trading goals. Yet they forged closer ties with local rulers than the Portuguese had. Many Dutch merchants married Asian women.

In the 1700s, the growing power of England and France contributed to the decline of the Dutch trading empire in the East. Still, the Dutch maintained an empire in Indonesia until the 1900s.

 Checkpoint How did the Dutch build up a strong presence in Southeast Asia?

Symbols of the Dutch Empire
The Dutch painting *Jacob Mathieusen and His Wife* (c. 1650) shows a senior official in the Dutch East India Company overlooking the Dutch fleet in Batavia, Indonesia. A slave holds a parasol, an Asian symbol of power. *How can you tell that the artist was European?*

Spain Seizes the Philippines

While the Portuguese and Dutch set up bases on the fringes of Asia, Spain took over the **Philippines.** Magellan had claimed the archipelago for Spain in 1521. Within about 50 years, Spain had conquered and colonized the islands, renaming them for the Spanish king Philip II. Unlike most other peoples of Southeast Asia, the Filipinos were not united. As a result, they could be conquered more easily.

In the spirit of the Catholic Reformation, Spanish priests set out to convert the Filipino people to Christianity. Later, missionaries from the Philippines tried to spread Catholic teachings in China and Japan.

The Philippines became a key link in Spain's overseas trading empire. The Spanish shipped silver mined in Mexico and Peru across the Pacific to the Philippines. From there, they used the silver to buy goods in China. In this way, large quantities of American silver flowed into the economies of East Asian nations.

 Checkpoint Why was Spain able to conquer the Philippines easily?

An Indian Sepoy
An Indian officer in the British army poses with his wife in this Indian painting dating from the 1700s.

Mughal India and European Traders

For two centuries, the Mughal empire had enjoyed a period of peace, strength, and prosperity. European merchants were dazzled by India's splendid Mughal court and its many luxury goods.

A Center of Valuable Trade Mughal India was the center of the valuable spice trade. It was also the world leader in textile manufacturing, exporting large quantities of silk and cotton cloth. The Mughal empire was larger, richer, and more powerful than any kingdom in Europe. When Europeans sought trading rights, Mughal emperors saw no threat in granting them. The Portuguese—and later the Dutch, English, and French—thus were permitted to build forts and warehouses in Indian coastal towns.

A Great Empire Shatters Over time, the Mughal empire weakened. Conflicts between Hindu and Muslim princes rekindled. Years of civil war drained Mughal resources. Rulers then increased taxes, sparking rebellions. Corruption became widespread, and the central government collapsed. As Mughal power faltered, French and English traders fought for power. Like the Dutch, both the British and the French had established East India companies. These companies made alliances with local officials and independent rajahs, or local chiefs. Each company organized its own army of sepoys, or Indian troops.

By the mid-1700s, the British and the French had become locked in a bitter struggle for global power. The fighting involved both nations' lands in Asia and the Americas. In India, the British East India Company used an army of British troops and sepoys to drive out the French. The company then forced the Mughal emperor to recognize its right to collect taxes in the northeast. By the late 1700s, it had used its great wealth to dominate most of India.

 Checkpoint How did Britain gain control of India?

SECTION 3 Assessment

Progress Monitoring Online
For: Self-quiz with vocabulary practice
Web Code: naa-1431

Terms, People, and Places

1. For each term, person, or place listed at the beginning of the section, write a sentence explaining its significance.

Note Taking

2. **Reading Skill: Identify Causes and Effects** Use your completed flowchart to answer the Focus Question: How did European nations build empires in South and Southeast Asia?

Comprehension and Critical Thinking

3. **Draw Inferences** You read that the Portuguese did not attempt to conquer inland territory. What does that tell you about their assessment of the inland empires?

4. **Analyze Information** Why did the leaders of the Netherlands give so much power to the Dutch East India Company?

5. **Identify Central Issues** What about the location of the Philippines made it a valuable asset for Spain?

6. **Identify Assumptions** The Mughal empire gave trading rights to several European countries. What assumptions about the power of those countries does this show?

● **Writing About History**

Quick Write: Present Evidence to Support a Thesis Write a biographical essay about Afonso de Albuquerque. First, think of a thesis statement that describes the main points you want to make. Then write the main body text, referring frequently to your thesis statement. The details in a biographical essay should directly support your main point. For example, if your thesis is that Albuquerque was a violent man, you would include details about his takeover of Malacca.

A Chinese watercolor portrays Matteo Ricci with European objects, including a model of the universe. A geography book that Ricci translated into Chinese is shown at the top.

WITNESS HISTORY ◀)) AUDIO

A Jesuit in China

In 1583, a young Jesuit priest arrived in China. He had studied Chinese and immediately impressed Chinese rulers with his fluency as well as his knowledge of European science. Matteo Ricci recognized that the Chinese would not accept a European religion "unless it be seasoned with an intellectual flavoring." In his nearly 30 years in China, Ricci translated five European books into Chinese. Ricci adopted Chinese dress and established friendships with Confucian scholars. When he died in 1610 at age 58, he was buried near the emperor. Much of Europe's knowledge about China came from Ricci's writings.

Focus Question How were European encounters in East Asia shaped by the worldviews of both Europeans and Asians?

Encounters in East Asia

Objectives

- Describe European contacts with Ming China.
- Understand the Manchu conquest and its impact on European trade.
- Analyze the factors that led Korea to isolate itself from other nations.
- Summarize Japan's attitudes toward foreign trade and how they changed over time.

Terms, People, and Places

Macao	Qing
Guangzhou	Qianlong
Matteo Ricci	Lord Macartney
Manchus	Nagasaki

Note Taking

Reading Skill: Understand Effects Fill in a chart like the one below with effects of European contacts in East Asia.

Portuguese ships first reached China from their base in Malacca in 1514. To the Chinese, the Portuguese, like other foreigners, were barbarians. Europeans, by contrast, wrote enthusiastically about China. In 1590, a visitor described Chinese artisans "cleverly making devices out of gold, silver and other metals," and wrote with approval: "They daily publish huge multitudes of books."

European Contact With Ming China

European interest in China and other parts of East Asia continued to grow. The Ming, however, had no interest in Europe—since, as a Ming document proclaimed, "our empire owns the world."

The Ming Limit Trade The Portuguese wanted Chinese silks and porcelains, but had little to offer in exchange. European textiles and metalwork were inferior to Chinese products. The Chinese therefore demanded payment in gold or silver. The Ming eventually allowed the Portuguese a trading post at Macao near Canton, present-day Guangzhou (GWAHNG joh). Later, they let Dutch, English, and other Europeans trade with Chinese merchants. Foreigners could trade only at Canton under the supervision of imperial officials. When each year's trading season ended, they had to sail away.

Seeking Converts Portuguese missionaries arrived in China along with the traders. In later years the Jesuits—from Spain, Italy, and Portugal—arrived. Most Jesuits had a broad knowledge of many subjects, and the Chinese welcomed the chance to learn about Renaissance Europe from these scholars. The brilliant Jesuit priest Matteo Ricci (mah TAY oh REE chee) made a particularly strong impression on the Chinese. Still, Ricci and other priests had little success spreading their religious beliefs in China. They did, however, become important sources of information for Europeans who knew little about China.

✔ **Checkpoint** Why did Ming China demand that Europeans pay for goods with gold or silver?

Vocabulary Builder

imperial—(im PIHR ee ul) *adj.* relating to an emperor or empire

The Manchu Conquest

By the early 1600s, the aging Ming dynasty was decaying. Revolts erupted, and Manchu invaders from the north pushed through the Great Wall. The Manchus ruled a region in the northeast, Manchuria, that had long been influenced by Chinese civilization. In 1644, victorious Manchu armies seized Beijing and made it their capital.

● **INFOGRAPHIC**

TRADE AMONG EUROPE, AFRICA, AND ASIA

Merchants and traders followed on the heels of the European explorers, establishing trading posts and ports throughout the Eastern Hemisphere. Within a few years, European ships carrying valuable goods were criss-crossing the waters of Europe, Africa, and Asia.

Africa
Divers in the 1990s exploring a European shipwreck off the southwestern coast of England found these African objects. Dating from the 1600s, the objects point to a thriving trade relationship between Africa and Europe at the time.

Miller Projection
0   1,000 miles

0   1,000 kilometers
Scale at the Equator

Founding the Qing Dynasty The Manchus set up a new dynasty called the **Qing** (ching). The Manchus won the support of Chinese scholar-officials because they adopted the Confucian system of government. For each top government position, the Qing chose two people, one Manchu and one Chinese. Local government remained in the hands of the Chinese, but Manchu troops stationed across the empire ensured loyalty.

Two rulers oversaw the most brilliant age of the Qing. Kangxi (kahng shee), who ruled from 1661 to 1722, was an able administrator and military leader. He extended Chinese power into Central Asia and promoted Chinese culture. Kangxi's grandson **Qianlong** (chyahn lung) had an equally successful reign from 1736 to 1796. He expanded China's borders to rule the largest area in the nation's history. Qianlong retired after 60 years because he did not want to rule longer than his grandfather had.

Spreading Peace and Prosperity The Chinese economy expanded under both emperors. New crops from the Americas, such as potatoes and corn, had been introduced into China. These crops boosted farm output, which in turn contributed to a population boom. China's population rose from 140 million in 1740 to over 300 million by 1800. The silk, cotton, and porcelain industries expanded. Internal trade grew, as did the demand for Chinese goods from all over the world.

WITNESS HISTORY VIDEO

Watch *Manchu China and the West* on the **Witness History Discovery School**™ video program to learn more about the interactions between two very different cultures.

Discovery SCHOOL

India
Indians turned cotton into clothes, wall hangings (left), and household goods. Though cotton had been grown in India, Egypt, and China since ancient times, it was not known to most Europeans until the 1600s.

China
The Chinese prized silk, using it to make elaborate clothes like the imperial robe below. Europeans eagerly became involved in the silk trade in the 1600s.

Japan
Japanese blue-and-white porcelain, like this dish made in the 1600s, was prized by Europeans. Later Dutch pottery known as delftware was an imitation of this Japanese style.

The Spice Islands
Cloves and other spices originated in the Moluccas, later called the Spice Islands. Asians used such spices for centuries before Europeans began to import them.

History *Interactive*
For: Interactive trade routes
Web Code: nap-1431

Thinking Critically
1. **Analyze Information** Which European country most likely monopolized the Indian cotton trade?
2. **Make Predictions** What impact would important goods like cotton have on European struggles for power in the Americas?

Ports controlled by
● England ● Netherlands ● Spain
● France ○ Portugal — Trade routes

Emperor Qianlong wrote a letter to King George III denying Britain's request for more trading rights and permanent ambassadors. How does Emperor Qianlong's language express his view that China is superior to Britain?

Primary Source

 As to your entreaty to send one of your nationals . . . to my Celestial Court, this request is contrary to all usage of my dynasty and cannot possibly be entertained. . . .

I have but one aim in view, namely, to maintain a perfect governance and to fulfill the duties of the State: strange and costly objects do not interest me. . . . Our dynasty's majestic virtue has penetrated unto every country under Heaven, and Kings of all nations have offered their costly tribute by land and sea. As your Ambassador can see for himself, we possess all things. I set no value on objects strange or ingenious, and have no use for your country's manufactures. **"**

Rejecting Contact With Europeans The Qing maintained the Ming policy of restricting foreign traders. Still, Europeans kept pressing to expand trade to cities other than Guangzhou. In 1793, **Lord Macartney** arrived in China at the head of a British diplomatic mission. He brought samples of British-made goods to show the Chinese the advantages of trade with Westerners. The Chinese, who looked on the goods as rather crude products, thought they were gifts offered as tribute to the emperor.

Further misunderstandings followed. Macartney insisted on an audience with the emperor. The Chinese told Macartney he would have to perform the traditional kowtow, touching his head to the ground to show respect to the emperor. Macartney refused. He also offended the Chinese by speaking of the natural superiority of the English. The negotiations faltered.

At the time, Qianlong's attitude seemed justified by China's successes. After all, he already ruled the world's greatest empire. Why should he negotiate with a nation as distant as Britain? In the long run, however, his policy proved disastrous. In the 1800s, China would learn that its policy of ignoring Westerners and their technology would have undesired consequences.

✔ **Checkpoint** How did the Qing respond to Britain's diplomatic mission?

Korea Chooses Isolation

Before the 1500s, Korean traders had far-reaching contacts across East Asia. A Korean map from the 1300s accurately outlines lands from Japan to the Mediterranean. Koreans probably acquired this knowledge from Arab traders who came to Korea.

In 1592, and again in 1597, the Japanese invaded Korea. The Japanese were driven out in 1598, but the invasions proved disastrous for Korea. Villages were burned to the ground, famine and disease became widespread, and the population decreased. Then, in 1636, before the country was fully recovered, the Manchus invaded Korea. When the Manchus set up the Qing dynasty in China, Korea became a tributary state. It was run by its own government but forced to acknowledge China's supremacy.

Devastated by the two invasions, Korean rulers adopted a policy of isolation, excluding foreigners except the Chinese and a few Japanese. When European sailors were shipwrecked on Korean shores, they were imprisoned and held as spies. Although Korea had few contacts with much of the world for almost 250 years, Koreans on tribute missions brought back maps as well as books on scientific discoveries. This was also a great age for Korean arts and literature.

✔ **Checkpoint** Why did Korea become isolated?

Foreign Traders in Japan

Unlike the Chinese or Koreans, the Japanese at first welcomed Westerners. In 1543, the Portuguese reached Japan, followed by the Spanish, Dutch, and English. They arrived at a turbulent time, when Japanese daimyo were struggling for power. The daimyo quickly adopted Western firearms which may have helped the Tokugawa shoguns centralize power and impose order.

Jesuits, such as the Spanish priest Francis Xavier, found the Japanese curious about Christianity. A growing number of Japanese adopted the new faith. The Japanese also welcomed the printing press the Jesuits brought. The Tokugawa shoguns, however, grew increasingly hostile toward foreigners. After learning that Spain had seized the Philippines, they may have seen the newcomers as threats. They also worried that Japanese Christians—who may have numbered as many as 300,000—owed their <u>allegiance</u> to the pope, rather than to Japanese leaders. In response, the Tokugawas expelled foreign missionaries. They brutally persecuted Japanese Christians, killing many thousands of people.

By 1638, the Tokugawas had turned against European traders as well. Japan barred all European merchants and forbade Japanese to travel abroad. To further their isolation, they outlawed the building of large ships, thereby ending foreign trade. In order to keep informed about world events, they permitted just one or two Dutch ships each year to trade at a small island in **Nagasaki** harbor.

Japan remained isolated for more than 200 years. Art and literature flourished, and internal trade boomed. Cities grew in size and importance, and some merchant families gained wealth and status. By the early 1700s, Edo (present-day Tokyo) had a million inhabitants, more than either London or Paris.

✓ Checkpoint   Why did the Tokugawas turn against Europeans?

Bringing Trade and Christianity
This 1600s decorative screen shows Japanese people meeting a Portuguese ship carrying European goods and missionaries. *Did the presence of missionaries help or hurt European-Japanese trade relations?*

Vocabulary Builder
<u>allegiance</u>—(uh LEE juns) *n.* loyalty or devotion to a cause or person

SECTION 4 Assessment

Progress Monitoring *Online*
For: Self-quiz with vocabulary practice
Web Code: naa-1441

Terms, People, and Places
1. Place each of the key terms, people, or places listed at the beginning of the section into one of the following categories: politics, culture, government, or geography. Write a sentence for each term explaining your choice.

Note Taking
2. **Reading Skill: Understand Effects** Use your completed chart to answer the Focus Question: How were European encounters in East Asia shaped by the worldviews of both Europeans and Asians?

Comprehension and Critical Thinking
3. **Analyze Credibility** Reread the quotation from the Ming document on page 461. Do you think its characterization of China is credible? Explain.
4. **Draw Inferences** What do Qing China's trade policies with Europeans in the 1700s tell you about the state of the Qing economy?
5. **Make Comparisons** Why did both Japan and Korea respond to increased foreign contact by going into isolation?
6. **Synthesize Information** Why did Japan allow limited contact with the Dutch, but not with the Spanish or Portuguese?

● **Writing About History**
Quick Write: Write a Conclusion Write a sentence to conclude a biographical essay about Matteo Ricci. Read the information about Ricci in this section. Then construct a broad summary sentence that covers the main point you want to make about his life. For example, if your thesis is that Ricci believed Chinese culture to be superior to European culture, you would include that point in your summary sentence.

Quick Study Guide

Progress Monitoring *Online*
For: Self-test with vocabulary practice
Web Code: naa-1451

■ Causes of European Exploration

- Desire for Asian luxury goods such as spices, gold, and silks
- Motivation to spread Christianity
- Strategic need to gain more direct access to trade
- Desire to gain glory for country
- Renaissance curiosity to explore new lands
- Competition with other European countries

■ European Footholds in the Eastern Hemisphere

Country	Date	Foothold	Reason for Interest
Portugal	1502	Calicut, India	Spices
Portugal	1510	Goa, India	Military and commercial base
Portugal	1511	Malacca, Southeast Asia	Center of sea trade
Spain	1521	The Philippines	Center of sea trade
Portugal	1589	Mombasa, East Africa	Hub of international trade
Netherlands	1652	Cape Town, southern Africa	Strategic port for repairing and resupplying ships
Great Britain	1757	Northeastern India	Spices, trade goods

■ Important European Explorers

Explorer	Accomplishment
Vasco da Gama (Portugal)	Sailed around Cape of Good Hope; established ports on Indian Ocean
Christopher Columbus (Spain)	Sailed west across Atlantic Ocean to Caribbean
Vasco Núñez de Balboa (Spain)	Crossed Panama, reaching Pacific Ocean
Ferdinand Magellan (Spain)	Circumnavigated the globe

■ Major Asian Dynasties and Empires

Ruler	Location	Description	European Contact
Mughal empire	India	Major trading empire	After two centuries of peace and prosperity, civil war between Muslim and Hindu princes weakened empire; European powers took control in 1700s
Ming dynasty	China	Prosperous dynasty that had sponsored overseas exploration	Allowed some trade with Europeans and sought out European learning; revolts in the 1600s led to overthrow by the Manchus
Qing dynasty	China	Powerful dynasty that expanded Chinaís borders and promoted Chinese culture	Increasingly restricted European trading rights
Choson dynasty	Korea	Chinese-influenced Confucian state	Had few contacts with the outside world except for China and Japan
Tokugawa shogunate	Japan	Powerful warrior kingdom	Welcomed Europeans at first but then expelled missionaries and most traders

■ Europe, Africa, and Asia 1415–1796

1492
Christopher Columbus reaches the Caribbean.

1498
Portuguese explorer Vasco da Gama rounds Africa and reaches India.

1522
Magellan's expedition circumnavigates the globe.

Chapter Events Global Events	**1450**	**1500**	**1550**

1453
The Ottoman Turks take Constantinople, ending the Byzantine empire.

1500
The kingdom of Kongo thrives in Africa.

1556
Akbar begins the Mughal reign in India.

Concept Connector

■ Cumulative Review

Record the answers to the questions below on your Concept Connector worksheets. In addition, record information from this chapter about the following concepts:

- Technology: the compass
- Trade: Dutch trading empire; Indian trade in Southeast Asia
- Cultural Diffusion: Indian influence on Southeast Asia

1. **Empire** With the founding of the Qing empire, the Manchus established one of China's most successful dynasties. One reason for the Manchus' success was their adoption of Chinese customs and inclusion of Chinese in their government structure. The Yuan dynasty, established by the Mongols, was another foreign-ruled Chinese dynasty. Compare the Qing and the Yuan dynasties. Consider the following:
   - culture and language
   - approaches to trade
   - involvement of Chinese in the government

2. **Conflict** As the French and British began to establish global empires in the 1600s and 1700s, they frequently came into conflict. This was not the first time that these two nations had opposed each other. List other examples of French-British conflict from European history. Consider the factors that seem to have made them historic enemies.

3. **Trade** In the 1500s and 1600s, Europeans took different approaches to establishing trade in the Eastern Hemisphere. In some regions, Europeans established posts and took over cities without regard to the people who lived there. In other regions, Europeans worked hard to establish legitimate trade relations. Compare these two approaches, using specific examples from the text. Think about the following:
   - the region's geography and European knowledge of it
   - the government of the people in the region
   - European perceptions of the people and their religion
   - the technological achievements of the people

■ Connections to Today

1. **Trade: The Dutch Trading Empire** In the 1500s, the Dutch began establishing an overseas trade empire in Southeast Asia, using the tools of sea power and monopolistic trade policies. Today, the Dutch are not known for their sea power or overseas domination, yet the strong economy of the Netherlands still depends heavily on trade. Research Dutch trade, including its global rank in exports, the number and types of companies owned by the Dutch in the United States, and the role of multinational companies in the economy of the Netherlands. Write two paragraphs summarizing the importance of trade to the Netherlands today.

2. **Technology: The Compass** European exploration would not have been possible without the compass. The compass allowed navigators to find direction accurately, rather than relying on the sun, stars, and moon. Consider the events and discoveries that the compass made possible. Then think of recent technological inventions that have had profound impacts on the world today. Which technology do you consider to be equivalent in its impact to the compass? Why?

1602 The Dutch establish the Dutch East India Company.

1641 The Dutch take Malacca from the Portuguese.

1736 China's emperor Qianlong begins his reign.

History Interactive
For: Interactive timeline
Web Code: nap-1451

1600   **1650**   **1700**   **1750**

1603 The Tokugawas come to power in Japan.

1642 The English Civil War begins.

1756 The Seven Years' War breaks out between Britain and France.

Chapter Assessment

Terms, People, and Places

1. Define **cartographer.** How did Prince Henry encourage the work of cartographers?
2. Write a sentence or two that shows why scurvy was a problem for sailors who **circumnavigated** the globe.
3. What was the role of European **plantations** in the growth of slavery?
4. Define **outpost.** Why were European outposts important in the development of overseas empires?
5. Why did European trading companies organize armies of **sepoys** in India?
6. How did the Asante kingdom use **monopolies** to keep its power?

Main Ideas

Section 1 (pp. 446–451)
7. How did European interest in the spice trade lead to the discovery of new routes and lands?

Section 2 (pp. 452–456)
8. How did new sea routes lead to an expanded European presence in Africa?
9. What legacy did the Portuguese leave in Africa?

Section 3 (pp. 457–460)
10. How did Portugal gain dominance of the spice trade?
11. How did the Dutch use their foothold in Cape Town to develop an overseas trade empire?
12. What effect did European trade have on the Mughal empire?

Section 4 (pp. 461–465)
13. Summarize European attempts to establish trade and missions in East Asia.
14. Why were East Asians generally resistant to European trade and ideas?

Chapter Focus Question
15. How did European voyages of exploration lead to European empires in the Eastern Hemisphere?

Critical Thinking

16. **Predict Consequences** What might have happened if Asian explorers, rather than Europeans, had first reached the Americas?
17. **Geography and History** How did Japan's geography allow the Tokugawas to maintain a long period of isolation?
18. **Draw Conclusions** Did missionaries hurt or help European attempts to establish trade in Asia? Explain your answer.
19. **Analyze Visuals** The woodcut below was made in 1555 by a Swedish geographer. What does it tell you about European knowledge of the world before the age of exploration?

20. **Recognize Cause and Effect** How did competition among European countries affect overseas exploration and conquest?

● Writing About History

Writing a Biographical Essay Many great Europeans, Africans, and Asians shaped the history of our global age. Write about one of the following important people in a biographical essay: Ferdinand Magellan, Affonso I, Afonso de Albuquerque, Emperor Qianlong, or Matteo Ricci. Consult page SH18 of the Writing Handbook for additional help.

Prewriting
• Choose the person who interests you the most. Take notes about this person and his role in shaping the age of global exploration.

• Draw conclusions about the person you have chosen. Think about how you can turn these conclusions into main points for your essay.

Drafting
• Write an introduction and a thesis statement. Your thesis statement should summarize the main point you want to make about the person you chose.
• Write the body text, introducing details and evidence that support your thesis statement. Then write a conclusion.

Revising
• Use the guidelines for revising your essay on page SH19 of the Writing Handbook.

Document-Based Assessment

Why Did Europeans Explore the Seas?

In the 1400s, Europeans began to embark on long and dangerous voyages to unknown destinations. Why did this age of exploration begin? In Documents A and B, a contemporary observer and a modern day historian describe the impetus behind these early expeditions.

Document A

"The discovery of the new Western World followed, as an incidental consequence, from the long struggle of the nations of Europe for commercial supremacy and control of the traffic with the East. In all these dreams of the politicians and merchants, sailors and geographers, who pushed back the limits of the unknown world, there is the same glitter of gold and precious stones, the same odour of far-fetched spices."

—Sir Walter Raleigh, 1509

Document B

"The starting point for the European expansion out of the Mediterranean and the Atlantic continental shelf had nothing to do with, say, religion or the rise of capitalism—but it had a great deal to do with pepper. . . . . [Pepper] comprised more than half of all the spice imports into Italy over a period of more than a century. No other single spice came within one-tenth of the value of pepper. . . . However, since about 1470 the Turks had been impeding the overland trade routes east from the Mediterranean. As a result the great Portuguese, Italian, and Spanish explorers all sailed west or south in order to reach the Orient. The Americas were discovered as a by-product in the search for pepper."

—From ***Seeds of Change*** by Henry Hobhouse

This page from a sixteenth-century book about navigation depicts England's Queen Elizabeth in the ship at the right. ▶

Document C

◀ This fifteenth-century painting depicts Henry the Navigator, standing at right in round black hat. A Portuguese prince, Henry did much to advance maritime exploration and the fields of navigation and cartography.

Document D

Analyzing Documents

Use your knowledge of European exploration and Documents A, B, C, and D to answer questions 1–4.

1. Documents A and B both make the point that the discovery of new lands was motivated by
   A religious fanaticism.
   B adventurous dreams.
   C wanting to make money.
   D Renaissance ideals.

2. What motivation for exploration is implied in Document C?
   A the search for spices
   B the desire to please king or country
   C the desire to spread Christianity
   D both B and C

3. What does Document D suggest about how European monarchs viewed exploration?
   A They saw it as vitally important to their nations.
   B They viewed exploration as interesting but unnecessary.
   C They saw it as important but not worth spending money on.
   D They had no opinion about exploration.

4. **Writing Task** Using information from the chapter, assess the various motivations for exploration. Are there any that are not shown in these documents? Choose the motivation you think was the most compelling for Europeans. Use specific evidence from the chapter and documents to support your argument.

15

The Beginnings of Our Global Age: Europe and the Americas

1492–1750

A Heavenly City

By the 1400s, the Aztec city of Tenochtitlán was one of the largest and most well-planned cities in the world. Aztec wealth had provided clean streets, beautiful gardens, and overflowing storehouses. An Aztec poem written in the early 1500s expressed the writer's pride in the great city:

66 Proudly stands the city of Mexico— Tenochtitlán.
Here no one fears to die in war . . .
Keep this in mind, oh princes . . .
Who could attack Tenochtitlán?
Who could shake the foundation of heaven? **99**

Just a few years after this poem was written, Tenochtitlán would fall to an unknown invader from far away. Listen to the Witness History audio to hear more about the end of the Aztec empire.

◄ Contemporary Mexican artist Diego Rivera depicts the Totonacs, Indians who were conquered by the Aztecs and later joined the Spanish.

Aztec feather shield made during the time of Moctezuma

Chapter Preview

Chapter Focus Question How did European colonization of the Americas shape global economies and societies?

Portuguese colonial carving made from brazilwood

Canadian powder horn showing fur trading routes

Note Taking Study Guide *Online*
For: Note Taking and Concept Connector worksheets
Web Code: nad-1501

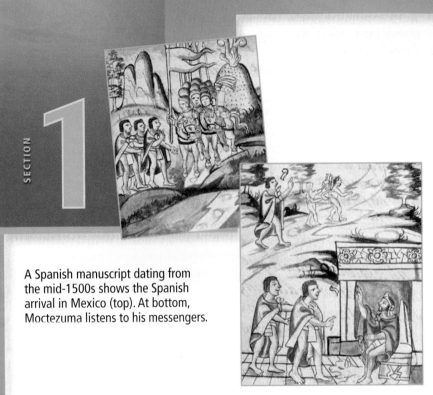

A Spanish manuscript dating from the mid-1500s shows the Spanish arrival in Mexico (top). At bottom, Moctezuma listens to his messengers.

WITNESS HISTORY ◀⑴ AUDIO

Moctezuma Hears Strange News

In 1519, the Aztec ruler Moctezuma heard an astounding report from his messengers. They described unusual people who had just arrived in the region—people with white skin and yellow hair, clad completely in iron, who rode "deer" as tall as a house and had dogs with burning yellow eyes. According to a Spanish translation of native accounts, "When Moctezuma heard this, he was filled with terror. It was as if his heart grew faint, as it shrank; he was overcome by despair."

Focus Question How did a small number of Spanish conquistadors conquer huge Native American empires?

Conquest in the Americas

Objectives
- Analyze the results of the first encounters between the Spanish and Native Americans.
- Explain how Cortés and Pizarro gained control of the Aztec and Incan empires.
- Understand the short-term and long-term effects of the Spanish on the peoples of the Americas.

Terms, People, and Places

conquistador
immunity
Hernán Cortés
Tenochtitlán
Malinche

alliance
Moctezuma
Francisco Pizarro
civil war

N̲o̲te Taking

Reading Skill: Recognize Sequence Keep track of the sequence of events that led to European empires in the Americas by completing a chart like the one below.

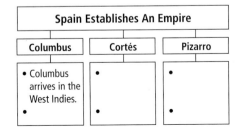

In 1492, explorer Christopher Columbus landed in the Caribbean islands that are now called the West Indies. The wave of exploration he spurred in the Americas would have drastic, far-reaching consequences for the people who already lived there.

First Encounters in the Americas

Columbus's first meeting with Native Americans began a cycle of encounter, conquest, and death that would be repeated throughout the Western Hemisphere.

Meeting the Taínos When Columbus first arrived in the West Indies, he encountered the Taíno (TY noh) people. The Taínos lived in villages and grew corn, yams, and cotton, which they wove into cloth. They were friendly and open toward the Spanish. Columbus noted that they were "generous with what they have, to such a degree as no one would believe but he who had seen it."

Despite the friendly reception, relations soon soured. The Taínos offended the Spanish when out of ignorance they failed to pay proper respect to Christian symbols. Columbus's actions showed that he felt himself superior to the Taínos and could therefore decide their fate. He claimed their land for Spain, and then took several Taínos as prisoners to take back to the Spanish king.

Columbus's encounter was repeated by a wave of Spanish conquistadors (kahn KEES tuh dawrz), or conquerors, who soon arrived in the Americas. They first settled on the islands of Hispaniola (now the Dominican Republic and Haiti), Cuba, and Puerto Rico.

Throughout the region, the conquistadors seized the Native Americans' gold ornaments and then made them pan for more gold. At the same time, the Spanish forced the Native Americans to convert to Christianity.

Guns, Horses, and Disease Although Spanish conquistadors only numbered in the hundreds as compared to millions of Native Americans, they had many advantages. Their guns and cannons were superior to the Native Americans' arrows and spears, and European metal armor provided them with better protection. They also had horses, which not only were useful in battle and in carrying supplies, but also frightened the Native Americans, who had never seen a horse.

Most importantly, an invisible invader—disease—helped the conquistadors take control of the Taínos and other Native Americans. Europeans unknowingly carried diseases such as smallpox, measles, and influenza to which Native Americans had no immunity, or resistance. These diseases spread rapidly and wiped out village after village. As a result, the Native American population of the Caribbean islands declined by as much as 90 percent in the 1500s. Millions of Native Americans died from disease as Europeans made their way inland.

 Checkpoint How did Spanish conquistadors treat the Taínos?

Cortés Conquers Mexico

From the Caribbean, Spanish explorers probed the coasts of the Americas. They spread stories of empires rich in gold, but they also told of fierce fighting people. Attracted by the promise of riches as well as by religious zeal, a flood of adventurers soon followed.

Cortés Advances on the Aztecs Among the earliest conquistadors was Hernán Cortés. Cortés, a landowner in Cuba, heard of Spanish expeditions that had been repelled by Indians. He believed that he could succeed where none had before. In 1519, he landed on the coast of Mexico with about 600 men, 16 horses, and a few cannons. He began an inland trek toward Tenochtitlán (teh nawch tee TLAHN), the capital of the Aztec empire. A young Indian woman named Malinche (mah LEEN chay), called Doña Marina by the Spanish, served as his translator and advisor. Malinche knew both the Maya and Aztec languages, and she learned Spanish quickly.

Malinche told Cortés that the Aztecs had gained power by conquering other groups of people. The Aztecs sacrificed thousands of their captives to the Aztec gods each year. Many conquered peoples hated their Aztec overlords, so Malinche helped Cortés arrange alliances with them. They agreed to help Cortés fight the Aztecs.

Moctezuma Faces a Dilemma Meanwhile, messengers brought word about the Spanish to the Aztec emperor Moctezuma (mahk tih ZOO muh). Terrified, he wondered if the leader of the pale-skinned, bearded strangers might be Quetzalcoatl (ket sahl koh AHT el), an Aztec god-king who had long ago vowed to return from the east. Because Moctezuma did not know for sure if Cortés was a god, he did not know how to respond to the news. He sent gifts of turquoise, feathers, and other goods with religious importance, but urged the strangers not to continue to Tenochtitlán.

Cortés, however, had no intention of turning back. He was not interested in the Aztec religious objects, but was extremely interested in the gold and silver ornaments that Moctezuma began sending him.

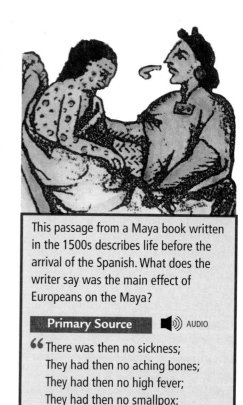

This passage from a Maya book written in the 1500s describes life before the arrival of the Spanish. What does the writer say was the main effect of Europeans on the Maya?

Primary Source 🔊 AUDIO

❝ There was then no sickness;
They had then no aching bones;
They had then no high fever;
They had then no smallpox;
They had then no burning chest. . .
At that time the course of humanity was orderly.
The foreigners made it otherwise when they arrived here. ❞

Malinche Shapes History
Malinche's parents sold her as a slave when she was a child, believing that she was born under an unlucky star. Despite her unfortunate beginning, she left a major mark on the history of the Americas.

Díaz Sets the Record Straight

Bernal Díaz del Castillo was a Spanish soldier who came to Cuba in 1514. In 1519, he accompanied Hernán Cortés on his conquest of the Aztecs. More than 40 years later, Díaz wrote his *True History* because he felt other accounts of the conquest—written by historians who had not been there—were inaccurate. He insisted that as an eyewitness of events he was a better historical source. For example, Díaz was there when Moctezuma took Cortés to the top of the great temple to look at Tenochtitlán, his magnificent capital city on the lake.

Vocabulary Builder

compel—(kum PEL) *v.* to force

Cortés became more determined than ever to reach Tenochtitlán. Fighting and negotiating by turns, Cortés led his forces inland toward the capital. At last, the Spanish arrived in Tenochtitlán, where they were dazzled by the grandeur of the city.

Tenochtitlán Falls to the Spanish Moctezuma welcomed Cortés to his capital. However, relations between the Aztecs and Spaniards soon grew strained. The Spanish scorned the Aztecs' religion and sought to convert them to Christianity. At the same time, as they remained in the city, they saw more of the Aztec treasure. They decided to imprison Moctezuma so they could gain control of the Aztecs and their riches.

Cortés compelled Moctezuma to sign over his land and treasure to the Spanish. In the meantime, a new force of Spanish conquistadors had arrived on the coast to challenge Cortés. In the confusion that followed—with various groups of Spanish, Aztecs, and Native Americans all fighting for control—the Aztecs drove the Spanish from the city. More than half of the Spanish were killed in the fighting, as was Moctezuma.

Cortés retreated to plan an assault. In 1521, in a brutal struggle, Cortés and his Indian allies captured and demolished Tenochtitlán. The Spanish later built Mexico City on the ruins of Tenochtitlán. As in the Caribbean, disease had aided their cause. Smallpox had spread among the Aztecs from the 1519 encounter, decimating the population.

✓ **Checkpoint** What impact did the Aztecs' religious beliefs have on Cortés's approach to Tenochtitlán?

66 When we saw so all those cities and villages built in the water, and other great towns on dry land, and that straight and level causeway leading toward [Tenochtitlán], we were astounded. These great towns and [pyramids] and buildings rising from the water, all made of stone, seemed like an enchanted vision… Indeed, some of our soldiers asked whether it was not all a dream…. It was all so wonderful that I do not know how to describe this first glimpse of things never heard of, seen or dreamed of before. 99

66 We turned back to the great market and the swarm of people buying and selling. The mere murmur of their voices was loud enough to be heard more than three miles away. Some of our soldiers who had been in many parts of the world, in Constantinople, in Rome, and all over Italy, said that they had never seen a market so well laid out, so large, so orderly, and so filled with people. 99

— Bernal Díaz del Castillo
from *The True History of the Conquest of New Spain*

Hernán Cortés ▶

Thinking Critically

1. **Draw Inferences** Why do you think Díaz included the opinions of "some of our soldiers"?
2. **Make a Reasoned Judgment** Do you agree with Díaz that the best historical accounts are written by people who participated in or witnessed the events? Explain your answer.

Pizarro Takes Peru

Cortés's success inspired other adventurers, among them Spaniard Francisco Pizarro (pee SAHR oh). Pizarro was interested in Peru's Inca empire, which was reputed to have even more riches than the Aztecs. Pizarro arrived in Peru in 1532, just after the Incan ruler Atahualpa (ah tah WAHL puh) had won the throne from his brother in a bloody **civil war.** A civil war is fought between groups of people in the same nation.

Pizarro's secretary described Atahualpa as

Primary Source

66 a man of thirty years, good-looking and poised, somewhat stout, with a wide, handsome, and ferocious face, and the eyes flaming with blood . . . 99
—Francisco de Xerez

Atahualpa refused to become a Spanish vassal or convert to Christianity. In response, Pizarro, aided by Indian allies, captured him and slaughtered thousands of Inca. The Spanish demanded a huge ransom for the ruler. The Inca paid it, but the Spanish killed Atahualpa anyway.

Despite continuing resistance, Pizarro and his followers overran the Incan heartland. He had superior weapons, and the Inca were weakened by European diseases. From Peru, Spanish forces surged across Ecuador and Chile. Before long, Spain had added much of South America to its growing empire. Pizarro himself was killed by a rival Spanish faction a few years after he established the city of Lima.

✓ **Checkpoint** What factors encouraged Spanish success in Peru?

Effects of the Spanish Conquistadors

The Spanish conquistadors accomplished a major victory in the Americas. Within a few decades, a few hundred European soldiers—helped by superior weapons, horses, and especially disease—had conquered millions of Native Americans. The Spanish had seized huge quantities of valuable goods. And they had used Native American labor to establish silver mines in Peru and Mexico to finance their new empire. In the 1500s and early 1600s, treasure fleets sailed each year to Spain or the Spanish Philippines loaded with gold and silver. With this wealth, Spain became Europe's greatest power.

The effect on Native Americans, however, was quite different. Some Native Americans believed that the disasters they suffered marked the world's end. As tens of thousands of Indians died, some of the bewildered and demoralized survivors felt that their gods were less powerful than the god of their conquerors. They therefore stopped resisting. Many Native Americans converted to Christianity in the hopes that their suffering would end.

Yet many Indians continued to resist the Spanish in any way they could. For centuries, the Maya fought Spanish rule in Mexico and Central America. Long after the death of Atahualpa, revolts erupted among the Inca. And throughout the Americas, Indians resisted European influences by preserving aspects of their own culture, including language, religious traditions, and clothing. In time, Native American culture came to influence the culture of Latin America.

The early encounters between the Spanish conquistadors and Native Americans had long-lasting impacts that reached far beyond these two groups. By establishing an empire in the Americas, Spain dramatically changed the pattern of global encounter set in motion with the first European exploration of Africa. For the first time, much of the world was now connected by sea routes, on which traveled ships carrying goods, people, and ideas.

✓ **Checkpoint** In what ways did Native Americans resist Europeans?

Sunken Treasure
Spanish ships sunk in the waters off Cuba's coast hundreds of years ago still yield gold and silver treasure to divers today. A craftsman of mixed Spanish and Native American ancestry made these ceremonial weapons in 1631.

Progress Monitoring Online
For: Self-quiz with vocabulary practice
Web Code: naa-1511

Terms, People, and Places

1. What do each of the key terms listed at the beginning of the section have in common? Explain.

Note Taking

2. **Reading Skill: Recognize Sequence** Use your completed chart to answer the Focus Question: How did a small number of Spanish conquistadors conquer huge Native American empires?

Comprehension and Critical Thinking

3. **Determine Relevance** Which factor was the most important in aiding Spanish success in the Americas?

4. **Summarize Information** How did Cortés gain control of Tenochtitlán?

5. **Recognize Cause and Effect** How did the Incan civil war affect the Spanish outcome in Peru?

6. **Identify Alternatives** How might the history of Europeans in the Americas have been different if the Indians had not been killed by European diseases?

● Writing About History

Quick Write: List Things to Compare
When you write an expository essay comparing and contrasting two things, you first need to decide which things are useful to compare. List several people, places, or activities from this section to compare. The things you choose should be appropriate for comparison. For example, comparing Malinche and Columbus would not make sense because their roles and purposes were so different from one another.

A 1584 drawing of slaves laboring at the Potosí silver mine, Bolivia

WITNESS HISTORY 🔊 AUDIO

A Missionary Protests

66 Everything that has happened since the marvellous discovery of the Americas . . . seems to overshadow all the deeds of famous men past, no matter how heroic, and to silence all talk of other wonders of the world. Prominent amid the aspects of this story which have caught the imagination are the massacres of innocent peoples. . . . 99
—Friar Bartolomé de Las Casas, 1542

Focus Question How did Spain and Portugal build colonies in the Americas?

Spanish and Portuguese Colonies in the Americas

Objectives

- Explain how Spain ruled its empire in the Americas.
- Analyze the major features of Spanish colonial society and culture.
- Describe how Portugal and other European nations challenged Spanish power.

Terms, People, and Places

viceroy	creole
encomienda	mestizo
Bartolomé de Las Casas	mulatto
peon	privateer
peninsulare	

Note Taking

Reading Skill: Recognize Sequence Use a flowchart like this one to keep track of the steps the Spanish took to establish an overseas empire. Add boxes as necessary.

A flood of Spanish settlers and missionaries followed the conquistadors to Spain's new empire. Wherever they went they established colonies, claiming the land and its people for their king and Church. When there was resistance, the newcomers imposed their will by force. Over time, however, a new culture emerged that reflected European, Native American, and African traditions.

Ruling the Spanish Empire

By the mid-1500s, Spain claimed a vast empire stretching from California to South America. In time, it divided these lands into four provinces, including New Spain (Mexico) and Peru.

Governing the Provinces Spain was determined to maintain strict control over its empire. To achieve this goal, the king set up the Council of the Indies to pass laws for the colonies. He also appointed **viceroys,** or representatives who ruled in his name, in each province. Lesser officials and audiencias (ow dee EN see ahs), or advisory councils of Spanish settlers, helped the viceroy rule. The Council of the Indies in Spain closely monitored these colonial officials to make sure they did not assume too much authority.

Spreading Christianity To Spain, winning souls for Christianity was as important as gaining land. The Catholic Church worked with the government to convert Native Americans to Christianity.

Cultural Blending
Encounters with Native Americans, or stories about such encounters, influenced Spanish and Portuguese artists. This painting dating from the early 1500s places a Biblical story—the adoration of the Magi—in the Americas, with Native American figures.

Vocabulary Builder

drastic—(DRAS tik) *adj.* severe; having a strong effect

Church leaders often served as royal officials and helped to regulate the activities of Spanish settlers. As Spain's American empire expanded, Church authority expanded along with it.

Franciscans, Jesuits, and other missionaries baptized thousands of Native Americans. They built mission churches and worked to turn new converts into loyal subjects of the Catholic king of Spain. They also introduced European clothing, the Spanish language, and new crafts such as carpentry and locksmithing. Where they could, the Spanish missionaries forcibly imposed European culture over Native American culture.

Controlling Trade To make the empire profitable, Spain closely controlled its economic activities, especially trade. The most valuable resources shipped from Spanish America to Spain were silver and gold. Colonists could export raw materials only to Spain and could buy only Spanish manufactured goods. Laws forbade colonists from trading with other European nations or even with other Spanish colonies.

When sugar cane was introduced into the West Indies and elsewhere, it quickly became a profitable resource. The cane was refined into sugar, molasses, and rum. Sugar cane, however, had to be grown on plantations, large estates run by an owner or the owner's overseer. And plantations needed large numbers of workers to be profitable.

Encomienda—A System of Forced Labor At first, Spanish monarchs granted the conquistadors **encomiendas** (en koh mee EN dahs), the right to demand labor or tribute from Native Americans in a particular area. The conquistadors used this system to force Native Americans to work under the most brutal conditions. Those who resisted were hunted down and killed. Disease, starvation, and cruel treatment caused drastic declines in the Native American population.

The encomienda system was used in the mines as well as on plantations. By the 1540s, tons of silver from the Potosí region of Peru and Bolivia filled Spanish treasure ships. Year after year, thousands of Native Americans were forced to extract the rich ore from dangerous shafts deep inside the Andes Mountains. As thousands of Indians died from the terrible conditions, they were replaced by thousands more.

A Spanish Priest Speaks Out A few bold priests, like **Bartolomé de Las Casas** (bahr toh loh MAY deh lahs KAHS ahs), condemned the evils of the encomienda system. In vivid reports to Spain, Las Casas detailed the horrors that Spanish rule had brought to Native Americans and pleaded with the king to end the abuse.

Prodded by Las Casas, Spain passed the New Laws of the Indies in 1542. The laws forbade enslavement and abuse of Native Americans, but Spain was too far away to enforce them. Many Native Americans were forced to become **peons,** workers forced to labor for a landlord in order to pay off a debt. Landlords advanced them food, tools, or seeds, creating debts that workers could never pay off in their lifetime.

Bringing Workers From Africa To fill the labor shortage, Las Casas urged colonists to import workers from Africa. He believed that Africans were immune to tropical diseases and had skills in farming, mining, and metalworking. Las Casas later regretted that advice because it furthered the brutal African slave trade.

The Spanish began bringing Africans to the Americas as slave laborers by the 1530s. As demand for sugar products skyrocketed, the settlers imported millions of Africans as slaves. They were forced to work as field hands, miners, or servants in the houses of wealthy landowners. Others became skilled artists and artisans. Within a few generations, Africans and their American-born descendants greatly outnumbered European settlers throughout the Americas. In the cities, some enslaved Africans earned enough money to buy their freedom. Others resisted slavery by rebelling or running away.

✔ **Checkpoint** What was the encomienda system?

Colonial Society and Culture

In Spanish America, the mix of diverse peoples gave rise to a new social structure. The blending of Native American, African, and European peoples and traditions resulted in a culture distinct to the Americas.

Cultural Blending Although Spanish culture was dominant in the cities, the blending of diverse traditions changed people's lives throughout the Americas. Settlers learned Native American styles of building, ate foods native to the Americas, and traveled in Indian-style canoes. Indian artistic styles influenced the newcomers. At the same time, Europeans taught their religion to Native Americans. They also introduced animals, especially the horse, thereby transforming the lives of many Native Americans. Africans contributed to this cultural mix with their farming methods, cooking styles, and crops. African drama, dance, and song heightened Christian services. In Cuba, Haiti, and elsewhere, Africans forged new religions that blended African and Christian beliefs.

A Spanish Cathedral
A group of Tzotzil Maya women gather in front of the Cathedral of San Cristóbal in Chiapas, Mexico. The church was originally built in 1528. *How can you tell that the church is a vital part of life in the town?*

479

A Changing Population

The population of Spanish America changed dramatically within a century, as the two circle graphs illustrate. Artist Miguel Cabrera showed this diversity in a 1700s painting of a single family made up of a Spanish father, a Native American mother, and a mestizo daughter.

Population of Spanish America

1570
- Black, mulatto, and mestizo 2.5%
- White 1.3%
- Native American 96.2%

1650
- White 6.3%
- Black 6.9%
- Mulatto and mestizo 5.7%
- Native American 81.1%

SOURCE: *Spain and Portugal in the New World*, Lyle N. McAlister

Chart Skills Study the circle graphs. *By what percentage did the black, mulatto, and mestizo population increase from 1570 to 1650?*

A Layered Society Spanish colonial society was made up of distinct social classes. At the top were **peninsulares** (peh neen soo LAH rayz), people born in Spain. (The term *peninsular* referred to the Iberian Peninsula, on which Spain is located.) Peninsulares filled the highest positions in both colonial governments and the Catholic Church. Next came **creoles,** American-born descendants of Spanish settlers. Creoles owned most of the plantations, ranches, and mines.

Lower social groups reflected the mixing of populations. They included **mestizos,** people of Native American and European descent, and **mulattoes,** people of African and European descent. Native Americans and people of African descent formed the lowest social classes.

Lively Towns and Cities Spanish settlers generally lived in towns and cities. The population of Mexico City grew so quickly that by 1550 it was the largest Spanish-speaking city in the world. Colonial cities were centers of government, commerce, and European culture. Around the central plaza, or square, stood government buildings and a Spanish-style church. Broad avenues and public monuments symbolized European power and wealth. Cities were also centers of intellectual and cultural life. Architecture and painting, as well as poetry and the exchange of ideas, flourished in Spanish cities in the Americas.

Emphasizing Education To meet the Church's need for educated priests, the colonies built universities. The University of Mexico was established as early as 1551. A dozen Spanish American universities were already educating young men long before Harvard was founded in 1636 as the first college in the 13 English colonies.

Women wishing an education might enter a convent. One such woman was Sor Juana Inés de la Cruz (sawr HWAN uh ee NES deh lah krooz). Refused admission to the University of Mexico because she was female, Juana entered a convent at around the age of 18. There, she devoted herself to study and the writing of poetry. She earned a reputation as one of the greatest poets ever to write in the Spanish language.

✓ **Checkpoint** What was the role of the Church in colonial education?

Note Taking

Compare and Contrast Complete a Venn diagram like this one to compare and contrast the Spanish and Portuguese empires in the Americas.

Spanish empire · Portuguese empire

The Portuguese Colony in Brazil

Λ large area of South America remained outside the Spanish empire. By the Treaty of Tordesillas in 1494, Portugal claimed its empire in the east, Brazil.

Settling Brazil As in the Spanish empire, the Native Americans who lived in Brazil—the Tupian Indians—had been largely wiped out by disease. In the 1530s, Portugal began to issue grants of land to Portuguese nobles, who agreed to develop the land and share profits with the crown. Landowners sent settlers to build towns, plantations, and churches.

Unlike Spain's American colonies, Brazil offered no instant wealth from silver or gold. However, early settlers cut and exported brazilwood. The Portuguese named the colony after this wood, which was used to produce a valuable dye. Soon they turned to plantation agriculture and raising cattle. Like the Spanish, the Portuguese forced Indians and Africans to clear land for plantations. As many as four million Africans were sent to Brazil. As in Spanish America, a new culture emerged in Brazil that blended European, Native American, and African elements.

Challenging Portugal and Spain In the 1500s, the wealth of the Americas helped make Spain the most powerful country in Europe, with Portugal not far behind. The jealous English and Dutch shared the resentment that French king Francis I felt when he declared, "I should like to see Adam's will, wherein he divided the Earth between Spain and Portugal."

To get around those countries' strict control over colonial trade, smugglers traded illegally with Portuguese and Spanish colonists. In the Caribbean and elsewhere, Dutch, English, and French pirates preyed on treasure ships from the Americas. Some pirates, called *privateers,* even operated with the approval of European governments. Other European explorers continued to sail the coasts of the Americas, hunting for gold and other treasure, as well as a northwest passage to Asia.

✓ **Checkpoint** What was Brazil's economy based on?

Smuggling Brazilwood
A panel carved from brazilwood in the 1550s shows French privateers illegally cutting Portuguese brazilwood and storing it on their boats.

SECTION 2 Assessment

Progress Monitoring *Online*
For: Self-quiz with vocabulary practice
Web Code: naa-1521

Terms, People, and Places

1. Place each of the key terms at the beginning of the section into one of the following categories: culture, government, or economics. Write a sentence for each term explaining your choice.

Note Taking

2. **Reading Skill: Recognize Sequence** Use your completed flowchart and Venn diagram to answer the Focus Question: How did Spain and Portugal build colonies in the Americas?

Comprehension and Critical Thinking

3. **Identify Alternatives** How might the Spanish have solved the problem of finding a dependable labor supply without the use of slavery?

4. **Analyze Information** How did the mix of peoples in Spanish America result in a new social structure?

5. **Make Comparisons** In what ways were the Spanish and Portuguese empires in the Americas similar? In what ways were they different?

6. **Draw Inferences** Why did some European monarchs support the illegal activities of privateers?

● **Writing About History**

Quick Write: Make a Venn Diagram When you write an essay comparing and contrasting two things, you first need to make clear how they are similar and different. A graphic organizer can help you outline similarities and differences. Choose two people, places, or events from the section. Then create a Venn diagram that you can use to compare and contrast them. Refer to the Venn diagram at the beginning of the section as an example.

A statue of Samuel de Champlain holding up an astrolabe overlooks the Ottawa River in Canada (right). Champlain's astrolabe appears above.

A Piece of the Past

In 1867, a Canadian farmer of English descent was cutting logs on his property with his fourteen-year-old son. As they used their oxen to pull away a large log, a piece of turf came up to reveal a round, yellow object. The elaborately engraved object they found, dated 1603, was an astrolabe that had belonged to French explorer Samuel de Champlain. This astrolabe was a piece of the story of the European exploration of Canada and the French-British rivalry that followed.

Focus Question How did European struggles for power shape the North American continent?

Struggle for North America

Objectives
- Explain why the colony of New France grew slowly.
- Analyze the establishment and growth of the 13 English colonies.
- Understand why Europeans competed for power in North America and how their struggle affected Native Americans.

Terms, People, and Places

New France
revenue
Pilgrims
compact
French and Indian War
Treaty of Paris

Note Taking

Reading Skill: Recognize Sequence Create a timeline like the one below to record the sequence of important events in the struggle for North America.

Cartier explores
eastern Canada.

|———————|———————|———————|———————|
1534   1607

In the 1600s, France, the Netherlands, England, and Sweden joined Spain in settling North America. North America did not yield vast treasure or offer a water passage to Asia, as they had hoped. Before long, though, the English and French were turning large profits. By 1700, France and England controlled large parts of North America. Their colonies differed from each other and from those of Spanish America in terms of language, government, resources, and society.

Building New France

By the early 1500s, French fishing ships were crossing the Atlantic each year to harvest rich catches of cod off Newfoundland, Canada. Within a hundred years, the French had occupied nearly half of North America.

Explorers and Missionaries French claims in Canada—which the French called **New France**—quietly grew while French rulers were distracted by wars at home in Europe. In 1534, Jacques Cartier (zhahk kahr tee AY) began exploring the coastline of eastern Canada, eventually discovering the St. Lawrence River. Traveling inland on the river, he claimed much of present-day eastern Canada for France. Jesuits and other missionaries soon followed the explorers. They advanced into the wilderness, trying with little success to convert the Native Americans they met to Christianity.

Furs, Trapping, and Fishing French explorers and fur traders gradually traveled inland with the help of Native American allies, who sought support against rival Native American groups. Eventually, France's American empire reached from Quebec to the Great Lakes and down the Mississippi River to Louisiana and the Gulf of Mexico.

The population of New France, however, grew slowly. The first permanent French settlement was not established until 1608, when Samuel de Champlain established a colony in Quebec. Wealthy landlords bought huge tracts, or areas of land, along the St. Lawrence River. They sought settlers to farm the land, but the harsh Canadian climate, with its long winters, attracted few French peasants.

Many who went to New France soon abandoned farming in favor of the more profitable fur trapping and trading. They faced a hard life in the wilderness, but the soaring European demand for fur ensured good prices. Fishing was another industry that supported settlers, who exported cod and other fish to Europe.

BIOGRAPHY

Jacques Cartier

In 1534, Jacques Cartier (1491–1557) sailed to North America on behalf of France. His commission was to find spices, gold, and a passage to Asia. Cartier found none of these things, despite several attempts, and ended his career in relative obscurity.

During his own lifetime, no one guessed the impact that Cartier's voyages would have. In his thousand-mile trek into Canada's interior, he staked France's later claim to a huge amount of North American territory. His legacy also lives on in the Canadian place names he coined such as the St. Lawrence River and the name Canada—derived from an Iroquois word meaning "village" or "settlement." **Why were Cartier's discoveries undervalued at the time?**

An Empire Slowly Expands In the late 1600s, the French king Louis XIV set out to strengthen royal power and boost **revenues,** or income, from taxes from his overseas empire. He appointed officials to oversee economic activities in New France. He also sent soldiers and more settlers—including women—to North America. Louis, however, who was Catholic, prohibited Protestants from settling in New France. By the early 1700s, French forts, missions, and trading posts stretched from Quebec to Louisiana, and the population was growing. Yet the population of New France remained small compared to that of the 13 English colonies that were expanding along the Atlantic coast.

 Checkpoint Why did French settlers abandon farming in favor of fur trapping and trading?

The 13 English Colonies

In 1497, a Venetian navigator known by the English name John Cabot found rich fishing grounds off Newfoundland, which he claimed for England. Later English navigators continued to search for a northwest passage to Asia, with no success. In the 1600s, England concentrated on establishing colonies along the Atlantic seaboard—the coast of the present-day eastern United States.

Establishing the First Colonies The English built their first permanent colony at Jamestown, Virginia, in 1607. Although the colony was meant to bring wealth and profit, in the early years of the colony many settlers died of starvation and disease. The rest survived with the help of friendly Native Americans. The colony finally made headway when the settlers started to grow and export tobacco, a plant that had been cultivated by Native Americans for thousands of years.

In 1620, another group of English settlers landed at Plymouth, Massachusetts. They were **Pilgrims,** or English Protestants who rejected the Church of England. They sought religious freedom rather than commercial profit. Before coming ashore, they signed the Mayflower Compact, in which they set out guidelines for governing their North American colony. A **compact** is an agreement among people. Today, we see this document as an important early step toward self-government.

Many Pilgrims died in the early years of the Plymouth colony. Local Native Americans, however, taught them to grow corn and helped them survive in the new land. Soon, a new wave of English Protestant immigrants arrived to establish the Massachusetts Bay Colony.

The English Colonies Grow In the 1600s and 1700s, the English established a total of 13 colonies. Some, like Virginia and New York, were commercial ventures, organized for profit. Others, like Massachusetts, Pennsylvania, and Maryland, were set up as havens for persecuted religious groups. Still others, like Georgia and South Carolina, were gifts from English kings to loyal supporters.

Settlers in all of the colonies spent the early years just struggling to survive. They quickly abandoned dreams of finding riches like the Spanish gold and silver. However, over time they learned to create wealth by using the resources native to their surroundings. In New England, prosperous fishing, timber, and shipbuilding industries grew. In the middle colonies, farmers grew huge quantities of grain on the abundant land. In the South, colonists found that cash crops such as rice and tobacco grew well in the warm climate. They therefore developed a plantation economy to grow these crops. As in New Spain, the colonists imported African slaves to clear land and work the plantations. In several colonies, especially in the South, enslaved Africans and their descendants would eventually outnumber people of European descent.

Governing the Colonies Like the rulers of Spain and France, English monarchs asserted control over their American colonies. They appointed royal governors to oversee colonial affairs and had Parliament pass laws to regulate colonial trade. Yet, compared with settlers in the Spanish and French colonies, English colonists enjoyed a large degree of self-government. Each colony had its own representative assembly, elected by propertied men, that advised the governor and made decisions on local issues.

The tradition of consulting representative assemblies grew out of the English experience. Beginning in the 1200s, Parliament had begun to play an important role in English affairs. Slowly, too, English citizens had gained certain legal and political rights. England's American colonists expected to enjoy the same rights. When colonists later protested British policies in North America, they viewed themselves as "freeborn Englishmen" who were defending their traditional rights.

✔ Checkpoint For what reasons were the 13 English colonies established?

A Fanciful View
An English play promised that "... gold is more plentiful there [Virginia] than copper is with us.... and as for rubies and diamonds, they go forth on holy days and gather them by the seashore." *Does this photo of the recreation of the Jamestown colony support the playwright's views?*

Geography *Interactive*
For: Audio guided tour
Web Code: nap 1531

INUIT
KUTCHIN
KASKA
INUIT
NORTH AMERICA
TLINGIT
CREE
OJIBWA
Canada
40°N
UTE
NOMADIC PLAINS CULTURES
SIOUX
NOMADIC HUNTERS
PUEBLO
COMANCHE
APACHE
WOODLAND CULTURES
English Colonies
Pacific Ocean
20°N

Viceroyalty of New Spain

Equal-Area Projection
0   500   1000 mi
0   500   1000 km

▲ A Chippewa beadwork bag reflects the influence of the French nuns who taught the Native Americans how to embroider.

▼ Europeans used American gold and silver to make dishes like this Portuguese platter dating from the 1500s.

Atlantic Ocean

Guiana
CARIBANA
MANOA
SHUAR
NOMADIC HUNTERS
ARUAC
SOUTH AMERICA
GÊ
GUARANI
Brazil

Viceroyalty of Peru

0°

N W E S

40°S

140°W   120°W

NOMADIC HUNTERS

60°W   40°W

England
France
Spain
Portugal
Netherlands
UTE Native culture

▼ A coat of arms from the time the Dutch briefly controlled the colony of New Netherland (New York) shows the importance of the beaver to the colony's trade.

New Encounters
As Europeans explored the Americas, claiming lands for their monarchs, they encountered diverse groups of Native Americans who already lived there. Europeans and Native Americans both relied on the resources of the land they inhabited. Though the groups often clashed, they influenced each other in many ways.

▲ English settlers made chests like this one out of native American oak, using traditional English patterns.

Map Skills Within a hundred years or so, European exploration of the Americas had led to huge land claims by various countries.
1. **Locate** (a) Brazil (b) English colonies (c) Peru (d) New Spain
2. **Describe** What geographical factor do all of the European land claims share? Why is this so?
3. **Draw Conclusions** Why do you think the boundaries of the European land claims end as illustrated on the map?

Struggling for Power

By the 1600s, Spain, France, England, and the Netherlands all had colonies in North America. They began to fight—both in the colonies and around the world—to protect and expand their interests.

Competing for Colonies By the late 1600s, French claims included present-day Canada as well as much of the present-day central United States. The Spanish had moved north, making claims to present-day Texas and Florida. Meanwhile, the English and Dutch maintained colonies along the East Coast. Native Americans throughout the colonies entered the conflict, hoping to play the Europeans against one another. Competition was also fierce in the Caribbean, as European nations fought to acquire the profitable sugar-producing colonies. By the 1700s, the French and English Caribbean islands, worked by enslaved Africans, had surpassed the whole of North America in exports to Europe.

Bitter Rivalry Turns to War During the 1700s, Britain and France emerged as powerful rivals. They clashed in Europe, North America, Africa, and Asia. In North America, war between the two powers erupted in 1754. Called the **French and Indian War,** it raged until 1763. It also turned into a worldwide struggle known as the Seven Years' War, which spread to Europe in 1756 and then to India and Africa.

During the war, British soldiers and colonial troops launched a series of campaigns against the French in Canada and on the Ohio frontier. At first, France won several victories. Then, in 1759, British troops launched an attack on Quebec, the capital of New France. The British scaled steep cliffs along the river and captured the city. Although the war dragged on until 1763, the British had <u>prevailed</u> in Canada.

The 1763 **Treaty of Paris** officially ended the worldwide war and ensured British dominance in North America. France was forced to cede Canada and its lands east of the Mississippi River to Britain. It handed the Louisiana Territory over to Spain. However, France regained the rich sugar-producing islands in the Caribbean and the slave-trading outposts in Africa that the British had seized during the war.

✓ **Checkpoint** Why was the French and Indian War fought?

Progress Monitoring *Online*
For: Self-quiz with vocabulary practice
Web Code: naa-1531

Vocabulary Builder

<u>prevail</u>—(pree VAYL) *v.* to succeed; to triumph

Living Languages

A sign in British Columbia—written in both English and the local Indian language—shows how Native American influence lingers long after the Americas became British.

SECTION 3 Assessment

Terms, People, and Places

1. For each term, person, or place listed at the beginning of the section, write a sentence explaining its significance.

Note Taking

2. **Reading Skill: Recognize Sequence** Use your completed timeline to answer the Focus Question: How did European struggles for power shape the North American continent?

Comprehension and Critical Thinking

3. **Make Comparisons** Why did New France grow slowly compared with Spanish and English colonies?

4. **Identify Central Issues** Why did the English colonies have a large degree of self-government?

5. **Make Generalizations** How did Britain come to dominate North America?

6. **Draw Inferences** Why did Native American groups side with European powers rather than join together to oppose them?

● Writing About History

Quick Write: Write a Thesis Statement
Once you have chosen the things you will compare and contrast in your essay, you must write a thesis statement. Your thesis statement should address clearly how the things you are comparing relate similarly or differently to your topic. For example, your thesis statement might focus on how the French and the English took different paths in establishing colonies in the Americas.

This portrait of Olaudah
Equiano dates from the 1780s.
The iron shackles shown at the
right were used to bind slaves
during the slave trade.

WITNESS HISTORY 🔊 AUDIO

Forced Into Slavery

❝The first object which saluted my eyes when I
arrived on the coast was the sea, and a slave ship
which was then riding at anchor and waiting for its
cargo. These filled me with astonishment, which
was soon converted into terror when I was carried
on board.❞

So wrote Olaudah Equiano. In the 1750s, when he was
11 years old, Equiano was seized from his Nigerian
village by slave traders. He was then transported as
human cargo from West Africa to the Americas.

Focus Question How did the Atlantic slave trade
shape the lives and economies of Africans and
Europeans?

The Atlantic Slave Trade

Objectives

- Explain how triangular trade worked.
- Understand the nature of the Middle Passage
  and describe its effects.
- Analyze the impact of the Atlantic slave trade.

Terms, People, and Places

Olaudah Equiano   Middle Passage
triangular trade   mutiny

Note Taking

Reading Skill: Recognize Sequence Use a
flowchart like the one below to record the events
that led to millions of Africans being shipped to the
Americas.

Triangular trade intensifies.

Vocabulary Builder

commodity—(kuh MAHD uh tee) *n.*
anything bought and sold

Enslaved Africans like Olaudah Equiano formed part of an international trade network that arose during the 1500s. The Spanish
were the first major European partners in the slave trade, buying
slaves to labor in Spain's South American empire. As other European powers established colonies in the Americas, the slave trade—
and with it the entire international trade network—intensified.

Triangular Trade Across the Atlantic

The Atlantic slave trade formed one part of a three-legged international trade network known as **triangular trade.** This was a
triangle-shaped series of Atlantic trade routes linking Europe,
Africa, and the Americas.

Shipping People and Goods Triangular trade worked in the
following way. On the first leg, merchant ships brought European
goods—including guns, cloth, and cash—to Africa. In Africa, the
merchants traded these goods for slaves. On the second leg, known
as the **Middle Passage,** the slaves were transported to the Americas. There, the enslaved Africans were exchanged for sugar,
molasses, and other products manufactured at plantations owned
by Europeans.

On the final leg, merchants carried sugar, molasses, cotton, and
other American goods such as furs, salt fish, and rum made from
molasses. These goods were shipped to Europe, where they were
traded at a profit for the European commodities that merchants
needed to return to Africa.

WITNESS HISTORY VIDEO

Watch *The Atlantic Slave Trade* on the **Witness History Discovery School**™ video program to experience the Middle Passage.

Discovery
SCHOOL

Industries and Cities Thrive Triangular trade was immensely profitable for many people. Merchants grew wealthy. Even though there were risks such as losing ships at sea, the money to be made from valuable cargoes usually outweighed the risks. Certain industries that supported trade thrived. For example, a shipbuilding industry in New England grew to support the shipping industry. Other colonial industries, such as fishing, raising tobacco, and processing sugar, became hugely successful.

Thriving trade led to successful port cities. European cities such as Nantes, France, and Bristol, England, grew prosperous because of triangular trade. In North America, even newly settled towns such as Salem, Massachusetts, and Newport, Rhode Island, quickly grew into thriving cities. Even though few slaves were imported directly to the northern cities, the success of the port cities there was made possible by the Atlantic slave trade.

✔ **Checkpoint** How did triangular trade affect colonial economies?

● **INFOGRAPHIC**

The Middle Passage:
A Forced Journey

The Middle Passage was a crucial part of triangular trade (inset map). Most slaves did not tell about their passage—many died, and those who survived faced lives of bondage in the Americas. But some Europeans recorded their impressions about the slave trade. And a few remarkable slaves learned to read and write, making their stories part of history.

A historic drawing shows how slaves were packed into tiny spaces in the ship's hold. ▼

History Interactive
For: Interactive triangular trade
Web Code: nap-1541

A slave "castle" in Ghana ▼

❝When we arrived at the castle, I saw [my kidnapper] take a gun, a piece of cloth, and some lead [to trade] for me… when a vessel arrived to conduct us away to the ship, there was nothing to be heard but the rattling of chains, smacking of whips, and the groans and cries of our fellow-men…. And when we found ourselves at last taken away, death was more preferable than life.❞

—*Nigerian slave Ottobah Cugoano, 1787*

488

Horrors of the Middle Passage

To merchants, the Middle Passage was just one leg of triangular trade. For enslaved Africans, the Middle Passage was a horror.

The Trek to the Ships The terrible journey began before the slave ships set sail. Most Africans were taken from inland villages. After they were enslaved, they were forced to march to coastal ports. Men, women, and children were bound with ropes and chains, often to one another, and forced to walk distances as long as a thousand miles. They might be forced to carry heavy loads, and often the men's necks were encircled with thick iron bands.

Many captives died along the way. Others tried to escape, and were often quickly recaptured and brutally punished. Those who survived the march were <u>restrained</u> in coastal holding pens and warehouses in slave shipping ports such as Elmina, Ghana, or Gorée, Senegal. They were held there until European traders arrived by ship.

Vocabulary Builder

<u>restrain</u>—(rih STRAYN) *v.* to keep under control; to keep from action

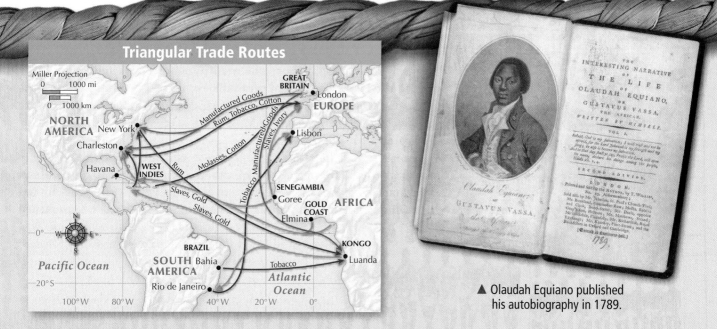

Triangular Trade Routes

Miller Projection

NORTH AMERICA — New York, Charleston, Havana, WEST INDIES

GREAT BRITAIN — London, EUROPE, Lisbon

Manufactured Goods; Rum, Tobacco, Cotton; Slaves, Ivory; Molasses, Cotton; Tobacco Manufactured Goods; Rum; Slaves, Gold; Slaves, Gold

SENEGAMBIA — Goree, GOLD COAST — Elmina, AFRICA, KONGO — Luanda

BRAZIL, SOUTH AMERICA — Bahia, Rio de Janeiro, Tobacco

Pacific Ocean

Atlantic Ocean

▲ Olaudah Equiano published his autobiography in 1789.

> "This work is so hard that any slave, newly put to it, in the course of a month becomes so weak that often he is totally unfit for labour. If he falls back behind the rest, the driver keeps forcing him up with the whip."
>
> —Ashton Warner, early 1800s

An 1823 painting shows slaves ▶ laboring on the island of Antigua.

Thinking Critically

1. **Map Skills** What were slaves exchanged for in the West Indies?
2. **Draw Inferences** Why are there so few first-person slave narratives?

SLAVERY ADVERTISEMENT.

Just Imported in the ship GRANBY, JOSEPH BLEWER Master,

Seventy *Gold-Coast* SLAVES

of various ages, and both sexes,

To be sold on board said ship at Mr. Plumsted's wharf, by

WILLING and MORRIS,

And a part of them are intended to be sent in a few days to Dock Creek, there to be sold, by Mr. Thomas Mudock for cash or country produce.

William Cowper wrote the following poem in the 1700s. How does he use irony to express his disapproval of the slave trade?

Primary Source

❝ I own I am shocked at the purchase of slaves,
And fear those who buy them and sell them are knaves;
What I hear of their hardships, their tortures and groans,
Is almost enough to draw pity from stones.
I pity them greatly, but I must be mum,
For how could we do without sugar and rum? ❞

Aboard the "Floating Coffins" Once purchased, Africans were packed below the decks of slave ships, usually in chains. Hundreds of men, women, and children were crammed into a single vessel for voyages that lasted from three weeks to three months. The ships faced many perils, including storms at sea, raids by pirate ships, and **mutinies,** or revolts, by the captives.

Disease was the biggest threat to the lives of the captives and the profit of the merchants. Of the slaves who died, most died of dysentery. Many died of smallpox. Many others died from apparently no disease at all. Whatever the cause, slave ships became "floating coffins" on which up to half the Africans on board died from disease or brutal mistreatment.

Some enslaved Africans resisted, and others tried to seize control of the ship and return to Africa. Suicide, however, was more common than mutiny. Many Africans believed that in death they would be returned to their home countries. So they hanged themselves, starved themselves, or leapt overboard.

✔ **Checkpoint** How did enslaved Africans resist captivity?

Impact of the Atlantic Slave Trade

The slave trade brought enormous wealth to merchants and traders, and provided the labor that helped profitable colonial economies grow. Yet the impact on Africans was devastating. African states and societies were torn apart. The lives of individual Africans were either cut short or forever brutalized.

Historians still debate the number of Africans who were directly involved in the Atlantic slave trade. In the 1500s, they estimate about 2,000 enslaved Africans were sent to the Americas each year. In the 1780s, when the slave trade was at its peak, that number approached 80,000 a year. By the mid-1800s, when the overseas slave trade was finally stopped, an estimated 11 million enslaved Africans had reached the Americas. Another 2 million probably died under the brutal conditions of the Middle Passage between Africa and the Americas.

✔ **Checkpoint** How did the slave trade affect Africans?

SECTION 4 **Assessment**

Progress Monitoring *Online*
For: Self-quiz with vocabulary practice
Web Code: naa-1541

Terms, People, and Places

1. What do each of the key terms and people listed at the beginning of the section have in common? Explain.

Note Taking

2. **Reading Skill: Recognize Sequence** Use your completed flowchart to answer the Focus Question: How did the Atlantic slave trade shape the lives and economies of Africans and Europeans?

Comprehension and Critical Thinking

3. **Synthesize Information** What role did each of the following play in triangular trade: a New England merchant, an African slave, and a Southern plantation owner?

4. **Recognize Assumptions** What European assumptions about Africans does the Atlantic slave trade show?

5. **Predict Consequences** Would the growth of the American colonies have been different if there had been no Atlantic slave trade? Explain.

● **Writing About History**

Quick Write: Gather Evidence to Support a Thesis Statement Once you have written your thesis statement, gather specific evidence—facts and quotes—that support it. For example, assume for this section that your thesis statement concludes that the African slave trade was the most influential event of the age of exploration. Gather specific evidence from the section that supports this statement.

A trading post in the West Indies thrives in the mid-1500s; a powder horn is inscribed with North American fur trading routes.

SECTION 5

Uniting the World

❝The discovery of America, and that of a passage to the East Indies by the Cape of Good Hope, are the two greatest and most important events recorded in the history of mankind. By uniting, in some measure, the most distant parts of the world, by enabling them to relieve one another's wants, to increase one another's enjoyments, and to encourage one another's industry, their general tendency would seem to be beneficial.❞
—Adam Smith, *The Wealth of Nations,* 1776

Focus Question How did the voyages of European explorers lead to new economic systems in Europe and its colonies?

Effects of Global Contact

Objectives
- Explain how European exploration led to the Columbian Exchange.
- Analyze the commercial revolution.
- Understand the impact that mercantilism had on European and colonial economies.

Terms, People, and Places

Columbian Exchange   entrepreneur
inflation   mercantilism
price revolution   tariff
capitalism

Note Taking

Reading Skill: Recognize Sequence Create a flowchart like the one below to keep track of the events that resulted from global exchange in the 1500s and 1600s.

The voyages of exploration in the 1500s and 1600s marked the beginning of what would become European domination of the globe. By the 1700s, European exploration had brought major changes to the people of Europe, Asia, Africa, and the Americas.

The Columbian Exchange

When Columbus returned to Spain in March 1493, he brought with him plants and animals that he had found in the Americas. Later that year, Columbus returned to the Americas with some 1,200 settlers and a collection of European animals and plants. In this way, Columbus began a vast global exchange that would profoundly affect the world. Because this exchange began with Columbus, we call it the **Columbian Exchange.**

New Foods and Animals In the Americas, Europeans found a variety of foods that were new to them, including tomatoes, pumpkins, peppers. They eagerly transported these to Europe. Two of these new foods, corn and potatoes, became important foods in the Old World. Easy to grow and store, potatoes helped feed Europe's rapidly growing population. Corn spread all across Europe and to Africa and Asia, becoming one of the world's most important cereal crops.

Europeans also carried a wide variety of plants and animals to the Americas, including wheat and grapes from Europe and bananas and sugar cane from Africa and Asia. Cattle, pigs, goats, and chickens, unknown before the European encounter, joined the Native American diet. Horses and donkeys transported people and goods quickly. Horses also provided the nomadic peoples of western North America with a new, more effective way to hunt buffalo.

The Spanish brought horses to the Americas by ship (below). A Spanish saying went "After God, we owe the victory to the horses." Horses also dramatically affected Native American life. An artist painted this scene of Plains Indians in 1830. *How does the artist show the importance of the horse to Native American life and culture?*

Vocabulary Builder

dispersal—(dih SPUR sul) *n.* scattering; spreading of

The Global Population Explodes The transfer of food crops from continent to continent took time. By the 1700s, however, corn, potatoes, manioc, beans, and tomatoes were contributing to population growth around the world. While other factors help account for the population explosion that began at this time, the dispersal of new food crops from the Americas was certainly a key cause.

The Columbian Exchange also sparked the migration of millions of people. Each year shiploads of European settlers sailed to the Americas, lured by the promise of a new life in a land of opportunities. Europeans also settled on the fringes of Africa and Asia, places made known to them because of exploration. In addition, as you have read, the Atlantic slave trade forcibly brought millions of Africans to the Americas.

In some parts of the world, populations declined as a result of increased global contact. The transfer of European diseases, such as smallpox and measles, decimated many Native American populations. Other populations were wiped out as a result of conflicts.

✓ **Checkpoint** Why did the global population explode?

A Commercial Revolution

The opening of direct links with Asia, Africa, and the Americas had far-reaching economic consequences for Europeans and their colonies.

The Price Revolution Strikes In the 1500s, prices began to rise in many parts of Europe. At the same time, there was much more money in circulation. A rise in prices that is linked to a sharp increase in the amount of money available is called **inflation.** The period in European history when inflation rose rapidly is known as the **price revolution.** Inflation was fueled by the enormous amount of silver and gold flowing into Europe from the Americas by the mid-1500s.

Capitalism Emerges Expanded trade, an increased money supply, and the push for overseas empires spurred the growth of European **capitalism,** or an economic system in which most businesses are owned privately. **Entrepreneurs,** or people who take on financial risk to make profits, were key to the success of capitalism. Entrepreneurs organized, managed, and assumed the risks of doing business. They hired workers and paid for raw materials, transport, and other costs of production.

As trade increased, entrepreneurs sought to expand into overseas ventures. Capitalists, because of their resources, were more willing to take risks. Thus, the price revolution of the early modern age gave a boost to capitalism. Entrepreneurs and capitalists made up a new business class devoted to the goal of making profits. Together, they helped change local European economies into an international trading system.

Exploring New Business Methods Early European capitalists discovered new ways to create wealth. From the Arabs, they adapted methods of bookkeeping to show profits and losses from their ventures. During the late Middle Ages, as you have read, banks increased in importance, allowing wealthy merchants to lend money at interest. Joint stock companies, also developed in late medieval times, grew in importance. They allowed people to pool large amounts of capital needed for overseas ventures. Individuals who invested in these companies could join in any profits that the company made. If the company lost money, individuals would only lose their initial investments.

Note Taking

Recognize Sequence Use a flowchart like this one to keep track of the sequence of events that led to new global economic systems.

TULIPMANIA
The Boom of the 1630s

In the 1630s, frenzy over a single good—the tulip—took hold in the Netherlands. People made and lost fortunes as the price of tulips rose from a handful of change to over a million dollars, only to abruptly crash. At the height of the mania, it was actually cheaper to purchase a painting of tulips by a Dutch master than to buy one tulip bulb.

Prices in Holland, 1630s

150 guilders	Average annual income
5,000 guilders	Price for a still-life painting of tulips by a Dutch master
10,000 guilders	Cost of a luxurious Amsterdam estate house

(Note: 100 guilders = approx. $12,500 in U.S. dollars today)

▲ Joannes Busschaert painted *Still Life of Tulips, Roses, Fruit, and Shells* in the early 1600s. A tulip bulb with its flower is shown at right.

Price of a Single Tulip Bulb

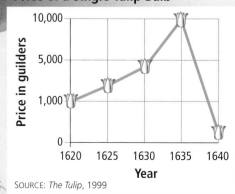

SOURCE: *The Tulip*, 1999

Who Loses in a Trade War?

In the 1990s, a trade war over bananas broke out between the United States and the European Union. The European Union wanted to buy bananas from small banana growers in its former colonies in Africa and the Caribbean. The United States, wanting to assist large South and Central American banana growers, responded by heavily taxing common European imports. In 2001, an agreement was reached that ended the trade war. **Critical Thinking** *In a trade war, who are the winners and losers?*

Everyone Wins

"The discrimination of the current illegal system is eliminated because all applicants will be treated equally and each applicant gains market access in the same proportion . . . . Dole believes that this system will benefit those banana exporters that invest in the jobs, people, countries and infrastructure that it takes to grow markets, open trade and compete. . . ."

—Dole Food Company press release, 2001

The Less Powerful Lose

"St. Lucia continues to be concerned that the thrust towards allowing market forces to totally determine the scope, structure and outcomes of economic activity, is not being counterbalanced by mechanisms to fairly distribute welfare gains and to protect the more vulnerable, small states like Saint Lucia, from the consequences of market failure. . . ."

—Earl Huntley, ambassador of Saint Lucia, in a statement to the UN, 2001

Bypassing the Guilds The growing demand for goods led merchants to find ways to increase production. Traditionally, guilds controlled the manufacture of goods. But guild masters often ran small-scale businesses without the capital to produce for large markets. They also had strict rules regulating quality, prices, and working conditions.

Enterprising capitalists devised a way to bypass the guilds called the "putting-out" system. It was first used to produce textiles but later spread to other industries. Under this system, for example, a merchant capitalist distributed raw wool to peasant cottages. Cottagers spun the wool into thread and then wove it into cloth. Merchants bought the wool cloth from the peasants and sent it to the city for finishing and dyeing. Finally, the merchants sold the finished product for a profit.

The "putting-out" system, also known by the term "cottage industry," separated capital and labor for the first time. In the 1700s, this system would lead to the capitalist-owned factories of the Industrial Revolution.

✓ **Checkpoint** How did the "putting-out" system work?

Mercantilism Arises

European monarchs enjoyed the benefits of the commercial revolution. In the fierce competition for trade and empire, they adopted a new economic policy, known as **mercantilism,** aimed at strengthening their national economies. Mercantilists believed that a nation's real wealth was measured in its gold and silver treasure. To build its supply of gold and silver, they said, a nation must export more goods than it imported.

The Role of Colonies To mercantilists, overseas colonies existed for the benefit of the parent country. They provided resources and raw materials not available in Europe. In turn, they enriched a parent country by serving as a market for its manufactured goods. To achieve these goals, European powers passed strict laws regulating trade with their colonies. Colonists could not set up their own industries to manufacture goods. They were also forbidden to buy goods from a foreign country. In addition, only ships from the parent country or the colonies themselves could be used to send goods in or out of the colonies.

Increasing National Wealth Mercantilists urged rulers to adopt policies that they believed would increase national wealth and government revenues. To boost production, governments exploited mineral and timber resources, built roads, and backed new industries. They imposed national currencies and established standard weights and measures.

Governments also sold monopolies to large producers in certain industries as well as to big overseas trading companies. Finally, they imposed **tariffs,** or taxes on imported goods. Tariffs were designed to protect local industries from foreign competition by increasing the price of imported goods. All of these measures led to the rise of national economies, in which national governments had a lot of control over their economies. However, modern economists debate whether mercantilist measures actually made nations wealthier.

Impact on European Society By the 1700s, European societies were still divided into distinct social classes. Merchants who invested in overseas ventures acquired wealth, while the price revolution hurt nobles, whose wealth was in land. Economic changes took generations, even centuries, to be felt by the majority of Europeans, who were still peasants. The merchants and skilled workers of Europe's growing cities thrived. Middle-class families enjoyed a comfortable life. In contrast, hired laborers and those who served the middle and upper classes often lived in crowded quarters on the edge of poverty.

✔ **Checkpoint** How did economic changes affect different Europeans?

A Dutch Merchant Family
Dutch artist Adriaen van Ostade painted this scene of a Dutch family in the mid-1600s. With the Netherlands' trading wealth, even middle-class families could afford fine clothes, luxury goods, and paintings.

Progress Monitoring Online
For: Self-quiz with vocabulary practice
Web Code: naa-1551

SECTION 5 Assessment

Terms, People, and Places
1. For each term, person, or place listed at the beginning of the section, write a sentence explaining its significance.

Note Taking
2. **Reading Skill: Recognize Sequence** Use your completed flowcharts to answer the Focus Question: How did the voyages of European explorers lead to new economic systems in Europe and its colonies?

Comprehension and Critical Thinking
3. **Identify Point of View** How might a Native American assess the impact—both positive and negative—of the Columbian Exchange?
4. **Draw Inferences** What characteristics must a society have in order for capitalism to be possible?
5. **Identify Assumptions** What basic assumption did mercantilists hold about their colonies?
6. **Synthesize Information** Why did the economic changes of the time have little impact on many Europeans?

● **Writing About History**
Quick Write: Write the Body and Conclusion The body of a compare-and-contrast essay should include specific evidence to support your thesis. Suppose that you are comparing the effects of global contact on European merchants and European peasants. Find evidence in this section that you can use to make this comparison.

Transforming the World:
The Columbian Exchange

Christopher Columbus's landing in the Americas in 1492, and his later voyages, revolutionized the world. European ships—heading both to and from the Americas—carried animals, food plants, and diseases that transformed lives and ways of life around the world. Hundreds of years after the Columbian Exchange began, the patterns of people's lives still reflect the influence of those early European voyages of exploration.

NORTH AMERICA

Atlantic Ocean

SOUTH AMERICA

Barley, a grain cultivated by the ancient Egyptians, is widely used in the Americas to feed livestock. ▼

From the Western Hemisphere
Corn
Potatoes
Sweet potatoes
Beans
Peanuts
Squash
Pumpkins
Chili peppers
Turkeys
Pineapples
Tomatoes
Cocoa
Cassava/Manioc
Silver
Quinine
Sunflowers

Originally from India, chickens and their eggs shaped diets worldwide—adding nutrition that boosted population growth. ▼

A Cuban man plows a field with oxen, work animals brought to the Americas from Africa and Asia. ▼

GOAT

▲ Native to Asia, goats provide milk and wool to people throughout both hemispheres.

An African woman ► harvests corn, one of the world's most widely grown food plants.

Dr. McMUNN'S
Kinate of QUININE and Cinchonine
IN FLUID FORM AND ALWAYS READY FOR USE.

EUROPE

The bark of a South American ▲ tree yields quinine, a medicine used to treat malaria. Quinine has benefited millions of people in the southern Eastern Hemisphere who are at high risk for malaria.

AFRICA

From the Eastern Hemisphere

Wheat
Sugar
Bananas
Rice
Oats
Barley
Rye
Grapes
Coffee
Horses
Pigs
Cows, Oxen
Goats
Chickens
Smallpox
Typhus

Silver and gold for coins like these were minted in the Americas. Shipped across the ocean, they brought wealth and power to European nations. ▼

◄ Peanuts have become an important staple crop in western Africa, where they add protein to soups and stews or are pressed into cooking oil.

▲ Sunflowers, native to the American Great Plains, thrive in chilly northern Europe and Asia. Ukraine, Russia, and China press sunflower seeds for cooking oil.

Thinking Critically
1. **Analyze Visuals** Explain the importance of one Western Hemisphere item to a person in the Eastern Hemisphere.
2. **Draw Inferences** Choose an item from one of the lists. Explain how the history of the hemisphere it traveled to might be different if the Columbian Exchange had not happened.

497

Quick Study Guide

Progress Monitoring *Online*
For: Self-test with vocabulary practice
Web Code: naa-1561

■ Key Elements of Europe's Commercial Revolution

- **Columbian Exchange** Foods, ideas, and technologies are exchanged between the hemispheres, resulting in population growth.
- **Inflation** Rising prices occur along with an increase in the money supply.
- **Price Revolution** Rising prices are coupled with inflation.
- **Capitalism** People invest money to make a profit.
- **Mercantilism** European countries adopt mercantilist policies—such as establishing colonies, increasing exports, and limiting imports—to compete for trade and empire.

■ Triangular Trade Routes

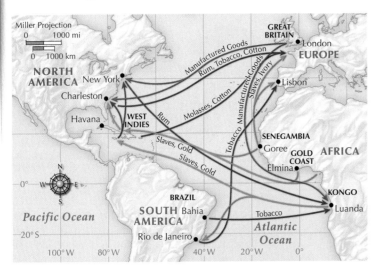

■ Major European Settlements/Colonies in the Americas

Date	Region Settled	Country	Purpose
1520s	Mexico	Spain	Find gold
1530s	Peru	Spain	Find gold
1530s	Brazil	Portugal	Establish settlements and plantations
Early 1500s	New France (eastern Canada)	France	Take part in fur trade and fishing
Early 1600s	13 colonies (present-day eastern United States)	England	Various reasons including establishing settlements and escaping religious persecution

■ The Native American Population Declines

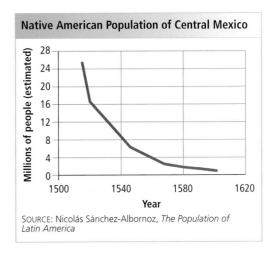

Native American Population of Central Mexico

SOURCE: Nicolás Sánchez-Albornoz, *The Population of Latin America*

■ Europe and the Americas, 1492–1750

1492 Columbus lands in the Americas.

1521 Cortés completes conquest of the Aztecs.

1530s Cartier explores the St. Lawrence River, claiming eastern Canada for France.

1607 British colonists found Jamestown, Virginia.

Chapter Events
Global Events

1500 **1550** **1600**

1498 Portuguese explorer da Gama rounds Africa and reaches India.

1526 The Mughal dynasty is founded in India.

Concept Connector

Cumulative Review

Record the answers to the questions below on your Concept Connector worksheets. In addition, record information from this chapter about the following concept:

• Genocide: Native Americans

1. **Empire** Compare the establishment of the Spanish empire in the Americas with the establishment of the Roman empire. How were they similar and different? Think about the role of
   • imperialism
   • technology
   • disease
   • methods of rule
   • religion

2. **Trade** The slave trade reached its height after the age of exploration, when overseas colonies established by Europeans required huge numbers of laborers to grow cash crops. However, the slave trade had existed long before this time period. Think about the early slave trade that occurred in ancient Egypt, Greece, and Rome, as well as in the Muslim world. Compare those examples with the Atlantic slave trade of the 1700s and 1800s.

3. **Economic Systems** In the 1700s, European nations adopted the economic policy of mercantilism in order to gain wealth and build empires. Mercantilism depended heavily on the establishment of overseas colonies. How did mercantilism differ from the manorialism practiced in medieval times? Consider the following:
   • the roles of colonists and serfs
   • the purposes of self-sufficiency and profit-making
   • the global impact

Connections to Today

1. **Cultural Diffusion** During the Columbian Exchange, people were exposed to goods, ideas, and diseases that changed their lives forever. Many of these exchanges were positive, such as the introduction of the horse to the Americas. Some were negative, such as the introduction of European diseases to the Americas. Think about similar exchanges that have happened in recent times. Research and write about a positive exchange and a negative exchange. To direct your research, consider topics such as disease, new technology, the introduction of fish or animals into non-native regions, and the availability of new foods.

2. **Trade** Throughout history, people and governments have worked to establish profitable trade methods. Some very successful trade methods have had terrible consequences for other people. Consider how Europe's commercial revolution was achieved in large part because of the Atlantic slave trade. Then think about trade practices today that, though profitable, might hurt some people. Write two to three paragraphs describing the pros and cons of modern trade practices. Consider the following:
   • trade pacts like NAFTA
   • voluntary labeling of products such as Fair Trade
   • practices such as child labor

1619
First cargo of African slaves arrives in Virginia.

1750s
Olaudah Equiano writes a book about his experiences during the Atlantic slave trade.

1763
The Treaty of Paris is signed, ending the French and Indian War.

1650   1700   1750

1630s
Japan bars foreign merchants from the country.

1687
Englishman Isaac Newton publishes his book explaining the laws of gravity.

1735
The reign of Chinese emperor Qianlong begins.

History Interactive
For: Interactive timeline
Web Code: nap-1561

Chapter Assessment

Terms, People, and Places

Match the following terms with the definitions listed below.

immunity	inflation
revenue	encomienda
privateer	mutiny

1. the right to demand labor from Native Americans
2. income from taxes
3. rise in prices linked to an increase in the money supply
4. pirate operating under government approval
5. resistance to disease
6. revolt

Main Ideas

Section 1 (pp. 472–476)
7. How did the explorations of conquistadors such as Hernán Cortés and Francisco Pizarro contribute to the Spanish empire in the Americas?
8. What effect did European exploration have on Native American populations?

Section 2 (pp. 477–481)
9. How did Spain structure its American empire?
10. Write a sentence or two explaining the role of each of the following in Spanish colonial society: peon, peninsulare, creole, mulatto, and mestizo.

Section 3 (pp. 482–486)
11. Why did the Pilgrims make a compact when they arrived in North America?
12. What was the result of the British and French struggle in North America?

Section 4 (pp. 487–490)
13. How did triangular trade affect Africans?
14. How did the slave trade benefit Europeans?

Section 5 (pp. 491–497)
15. What impact did American gold and silver have on European economies?
16. How did the policy of mercantilism affect global economies?

Chapter Focus Question
17. How did European colonization of the Americas shape global economies and societies?

Critical Thinking

18. **Compare Points of View** You read that many Native Americans saw the Spanish takeover as a sign that their gods were less powerful than those of the Spanish. How did the Spanish likely interpret their victory?
19. **Predict Consequences** How would society in the United States today be affected if mysterious diseases wiped out 90 percent or more of the population?
20. **Analyzing Visuals** The painting below, titled *First Landing of Columbus*, was painted in 1803. Consider what you have learned in this chapter. Do you think this painting accurately shows that event? Explain your answer.

● Writing About History

Writing a Compare and Contrast Essay The European nations that settled the Americas all wanted wealth and empire—but went about getting them in different ways. Write a compare and contrast essay that discusses two of the European powers involved in settling the Americas. Consult page SH10 of the Writing Handbook for additional help.

Prewriting
- Choose a topic that lends itself to comparison and contrast. Possibilities include important leaders, economic goals, interactions with Native Americans, or religious goals.
- Create graphic organizers, such as tables or Venn diagrams, to help you see similarities and differences.

Drafting
- Write an introduction and a thesis statement. Your thesis statement should summarize the main points you want to make about the things you are comparing.
- Write the body text, introducing details and evidence that support your thesis statement. Organize your text by subject or by point. Then write a conclusion.

Revising
- Use the guidelines for revising your essay on page SH12 of the Writing Handbook.

Document-Based Assessment

The Impact of Piracy

In 1580, Admiral Francis Drake returned to England after circumnavigating the globe. A delighted Queen Elizabeth I knighted the commander when she visited his ship, the *Golden Hind*, in 1581. The British queen had good reason to be grateful. Drake's voyage brought huge revenues to the royal treasury and dealt a blow to her enemy, King Philip II of Spain. The documents below give different views of Drake's activities.

Document A

"Passing the Straits of Magellan, untraversed as yet by any Englishman, [Drake] swept the unguarded coast of [Chile] and Peru, loaded his bark with the gold-dust and silver-ingots of Potosí, and with the pearls, emeralds, and diamonds which formed the cargo of the great galleon that sailed once a year from Lima to Cadiz. With spoils of above half-a-million in value the daring adventurer steered undauntedly for the Moluccas, rounded the Cape of Good Hope, and after completing the circuit of the globe dropped anchor again in Plymouth harbour. . . . The welcome he received from Elizabeth on his return was accepted by Philip as an outrage which could only be expiated [atoned for] by war. . . . She met a request for Drake's surrender by knighting the freebooter, and by wearing in her crown the jewels he had offered her as a present."

—From *A Short History of the English People* by J.R. Green

Document B

"[The Ambassador urged his king] . . . that no foreign ship be spared, in . . . the . . . Indies, but that every one should be sent to the bottom, and not a soul on board of them allowed to live. This will be the only way to prevent the English and French from going to these parts to plunder, for at present there is hardly an Englishman who is not talking of undertaking the voyage, so encouraged are they by Drake's return."

—Don Bernardino de Mendoza,
Philip II's ambassador to London, around 1580

Document C

"To Lima we came the 13th of February; and, being entered the haven, we found there about twelve sail of ships lying fast moored at an anchor, having all their sails carried on shore; for the masters and merchants were here most secure, having never been assaulted by enemies, and at this time feared the approach of none such as we were. Our general rifled these ships, and found in one of them a chest full of reals of plate, and good store of silks and linen cloth. . . . In which ship he had news of another ship called the *Cacafuego*, which was gone toward Payta, and that the same ship was laden with treasure. Whereupon we stayed no longer here, but cutting all the cables of the ships in the haven, we let them drive whither they would, either to sea or to the shore; and with all speed we followed the *Cacafuego* which was gone toward Payta. . . ."

—From *Sir Francis Drake's Famous Voyage Round the World, 1580* by Francis Pretty

Document D

Analyzing Documents

Use your knowledge of American colonial history and Documents A, B, C, and D to answer questions 1–4.

1. According to Document A, Drake's exploits in Chile and Peru
   A were not commercially successful.
   B were done impulsively, without Queen Elizabeth's consent or approval.
   C gave King Philip II a reason to start a war against England.
   D met with outrage and anger from Queen Elizabeth and the English-speaking world.

2. According to Document B, what was Don Bernardino de Mendoza's main concern regarding Drake?
   A that Drake would return to the West Indies soon
   B that other seamen would copy Drake's exploits
   C that Spanish seamen would join future Drake expeditions
   D that other nations would join with England against Spain

3. Document D shows Queen Elizabeth I with Francis Drake. Which of the other documents does this one support?
   A Document A
   B Document B
   C Document C
   D Documents A, B, and C

4. **Writing Task** Write a news article about Drake's exploits that might have appeared in a Spanish newspaper around 1580. Use the documents along with information from the chapter to support your article.

A Child Becomes King

In 1643, the five-year-old heir to the French crown, Louis XIV, made his first public appearance. The tiny monarch climbed the throne and sat for hours as officials conducted the ceremony announcing the new reign. Louis XIV had been orphaned as a baby, and was a sickly, shy child. As a child, he would often bring a cat to government councils, stroking the fur as he sat in silence. Despite this quiet beginning, Louis XIV proved to be a strong, able ruler who came to symbolize the period of absolute monarchy we now call the "Age of Absolutism." Listen to the Witness History audio to hear more about this powerful king.

◄ **Louis XIV receives foreign ambassadors at his Versailles court in 1678.**

Chapter Preview

Chapter Focus Question What events led to the rise of absolute monarchies and the development of centralized nation-states in Europe?

A French bishop's official seal

Oliver Cromwell's battle helmet

Carpentry tool owned by Peter the Great

Note Taking Study Guide *Online*
For: Note Taking and Concept Connector worksheets
Web Code: nad-1601

Philip II wears royal dress. In the background, his Armada heads to England.

A late 1500s Spanish coin commemorates Philip's rule.

WITNESS HISTORY 🔊 AUDIO

A Working Monarch

"It is best to keep an eye on everything," Philip II of Spain often said—and he meant it. As king of the most powerful nation in Europe, he gave little time to pleasure. Instead, he plowed through a mountain of paperwork each day, making notes on even the most trivial matters. But Philip's determination to "keep an eye on everything" extended far beyond trivia. It helped him build Spain into a strong centralized state. By the late 1500s, he had concentrated all power in his own hands. Over the next 200 years, other European monarchs would pursue similar goals.

Focus Question How did Philip II extend Spain's power and help establish a golden age?

Spanish Power Grows

Objectives
- Describe the empire that Charles V inherited.
- Analyze how Spanish power increased under Philip II.
- Explain how the arts flourished during Spain's golden age.

Terms, People, and Places

Hapsburg empire	divine right
Charles V	armada
Philip II	El Greco
absolute monarch	Miguel de Cervantes

Note Taking

Reading Skill: Identify Main Ideas and Supporting Details As you read about how Philip II extended Spanish power, create an outline to record details that support the main ideas in this section. This example will help you get started.

> I. Charles V Inherits Two Crowns
>   A. Ruling the Hapsburg Empire
>   1. Spain
>   2. Holy Roman Empire and Netherlands
>   B. Charles V abdicates

By the 1500s, Spain had shaken off its feudal past and emerged as the first modern European power. Queen Isabella and King Ferdinand had unified the country, enforced religious unity, and commanded the Spanish conquest of the Americas.

Charles V Inherits Two Crowns

In 1516, Ferdinand and Isabella's grandson, Charles I, became king of Spain, and thereby ruler of the Spanish colonies in the Americas as well.

Ruling the Hapsburg Empire When his other grandfather died in 1519, Charles I also became heir to the sprawling Hapsburg empire, which included the Holy Roman Empire and the Netherlands. As ruler of this empire, Charles took the name Charles V. Historians now usually refer to him by this title.

Ruling two empires involved Charles in constant warfare. As a devout Catholic, he fought to suppress Protestantism in the German states. After years of religious conflict, however, Charles was forced to allow the German princes to choose their own religion.

Charles also faced the Muslim Ottoman empire, which was based in Turkey but stretched across the Balkans. Under Suleiman, Ottoman forces advanced across central Europe to the walls surrounding Vienna, Austria. Although Austria held firm during the siege, the Ottomans occupied much of Hungary following their crushing victory at the Battle of Mohács. Ottoman naval forces also continued to challenge Spanish power in the Mediterranean.

The Wars of Philip II, 1571–1588

Geography *Interactive*
For: Audio guided tour
Web Code: nap-1611

Map Skills Phillip II waged war to increase Spanish power and defend Roman Catholicism.

1. **Locate** (a) Spain (b) Madrid (c) Ottoman Empire (d) Strait of Lepanto (e) Netherlands (f) English Channel.
2. **Region** Which battles shown on the map took place in a territory ruled directly by Spain?
3. **Analyzing Information** Why do you think Spain joined Venice and other Italian states in defending the Strait of Lepanto?

Charles V Abdicates The Hapsburg empire proved to be too scattered and <u>cumbersome</u> for any one person to rule effectively. Exhausted and disillusioned, Charles V gave up his titles and entered a monastery in 1556. He divided his empire, leaving the Hapsburg lands in central Europe to his brother Ferdinand, who became Holy Roman emperor. He gave Spain, the Netherlands, some southern Italian states, and Spain's overseas empire to his 29-year-old son Philip, who became Philip II.

 Checkpoint Why did Charles V divide the Hapsburg Empire?

Philip II Solidifies Power

During his 42-year reign, Philip II expanded Spanish influence, strengthened the Catholic Church, and made his own power absolute. Thanks in part to silver from Spanish colonies in the Americas, he made Spain the foremost power in Europe.

Centralizing Power Like his father, Philip II was hard working, devout, and ambitious. Unlike many other monarchs, Philip devoted most of his time to government work. He seldom hunted, never jousted, and lived as simply as a monk. The King's isolated, somber palace outside Madrid, known as the Escorial (es kohr YAHL), reflected his character. It served as a church, a residence, and a tomb for the royal family.

Vocabulary Builder

<u>cumbersome</u>—(KUM bur sum) *adj.* hard to handle because of size, weight, or many parts

PHILIP II AND THE RISE OF SPAIN

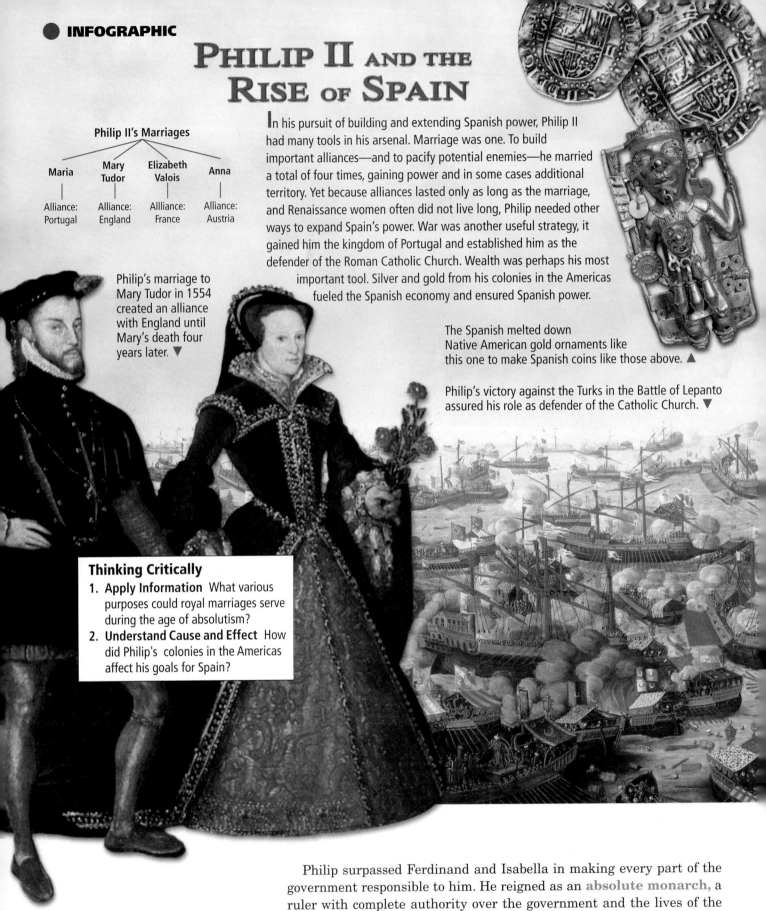

In his pursuit of building and extending Spanish power, Philip II had many tools in his arsenal. Marriage was one. To build important alliances—and to pacify potential enemies—he married a total of four times, gaining power and in some cases additional territory. Yet because alliances lasted only as long as the marriage, and Renaissance women often did not live long, Philip needed other ways to expand Spain's power. War was another useful strategy, it gained him the kingdom of Portugal and established him as the defender of the Roman Catholic Church. Wealth was perhaps his most important tool. Silver and gold from his colonies in the Americas fueled the Spanish economy and ensured Spanish power.

Philip II's Marriages

- Maria — Alliance: Portugal
- Mary Tudor — Alliance: England
- Elizabeth Valois — Alliance: France
- Anna — Alliance: Austria

Philip's marriage to Mary Tudor in 1554 created an alliance with England until Mary's death four years later. ▼

The Spanish melted down Native American gold ornaments like this one to make Spanish coins like those above. ▲

Philip's victory against the Turks in the Battle of Lepanto assured his role as defender of the Catholic Church. ▼

Thinking Critically

1. **Apply Information** What various purposes could royal marriages serve during the age of absolutism?
2. **Understand Cause and Effect** How did Philip's colonies in the Americas affect his goals for Spain?

Philip surpassed Ferdinand and Isabella in making every part of the government responsible to him. He reigned as an **absolute monarch,** a ruler with complete authority over the government and the lives of the people. Like other European rulers, Philip asserted that he ruled by **divine right.** That is, he believed that his authority to rule came directly from God. Philip therefore saw himself as the guardian of the Roman Catholic Church. The great undertaking of his life was to defend the Catholic Reformation and turn back the rising Protestant tide in Europe. Within his empire, Philip enforced religious unity, turning the Inquisition against Protestants and other people thought to be heretics.

Battles in the Mediterranean and the Netherlands Philip fought many wars as he attempted to advance Spanish Catholic power. In the Mediterranean, the Ottoman empire continued to pose a threat to European control of the region. At the Battle of Lepanto in 1571, Spain and its Italian allies soundly defeated an Ottoman fleet off the coast of Greece. Although the Ottoman Empire would remain a major power in the Mediterranean region for three more centuries, Christians still hailed the battle as a great victory and a demonstration of Spain's power.

During the last half of his reign, Philip battled rebels in the Netherlands. At the time, the region included 17 provinces that are today Belgium, the Netherlands, and Luxembourg. It was the richest part of Philip's empire. Protestants in the region resisted Philip's efforts to crush their faith. Protestants and Catholics alike opposed high taxes and autocratic Spanish rule, which threatened local traditions of self-government.

In the 1560s, riots against the Inquisition sparked a general uprising in the Netherlands. Savage fighting raged for decades. In 1581, the northern, largely Protestant provinces declared their independence from Spain and became known as the Dutch Netherlands. They did not gain official recognition, however, until 1648. The southern, mostly Catholic provinces of the Netherlands remained part of the Spanish Empire.

The Armada Sails Against England By the 1580s, Philip saw England's Queen Elizabeth I as his chief Protestant enemy. First secretly, then openly, Elizabeth had supported the Dutch against Spain. She encouraged English captains such as Francis Drake, known as sea dogs, to plunder Spanish treasure ships and loot Spanish cities in the Americas. To Philip's dismay, Elizabeth made the pirate Drake a knight.

To end English attacks and subdue the Dutch, Philip prepared a huge **armada,** or fleet, to carry a Spanish invasion force to England. In 1588, the Spanish Armada sailed with more than 130 ships, 20,000 men, and 2,400 pieces of artillery. The Spanish were confident of victory. "When we meet the English," predicted one Spanish commander, "God will surely arrange matters so that we can grapple and board them, either by sending some strange freak of weather or, more likely, just by depriving the English of their wits."

This prediction did not come to pass. In the English Channel, lumbering Spanish ships were outmaneuvered by the lighter, faster English ships. Strong winds favored the English, scattering the Armada. After further disasters at sea, the tattered remnants limped home in defeat.

An Empire Declines The defeat of the Armada marked the beginning of the end of Spanish power. Throughout the 1600s, Spain's strength and prosperity decreased. One reason for this decline was that Philip II's successors ruled far less ably than he had.

Spain Loses Territory
The Treaty of Munster, signed in 1648, recognized the independence of the Netherlands' Protestant provinces.

Economic problems were also to blame. Costly overseas wars drained wealth out of Spain almost as fast as it came in. Treasure from the Americas led Spain to neglect farming and commerce. The government heavily taxed the small middle class, weakening a group that in other European nations supported royal power. The expulsion of Muslims and Jews from Spain deprived the economy of many skilled artisans and merchants. Finally, the influx of American gold and silver led to soaring inflation.

As Spain's power dwindled in the 1600s and 1700s, Dutch, English, and French fleets challenged—and eventually surpassed—Spanish power both in Europe and around the world.

✓ **Checkpoint**   What were Philip II's motivations for waging war?

Spain's Golden Age

The century from 1550 to 1650 is often referred to as Spain's *Siglo de Oro* (SEEG loh day OHR oh), or "golden century," for the brilliance of its arts and literature. Philip II was an enthusiastic patron of the arts and also founded academies of science and mathematics.

Among the famous painters of this period was a man called El Greco, meaning "the Greek." Though not Spanish by birth, El Greco is considered to be a master of Spanish painting. Born on the Greek island of Crete, El Greco had studied in Italy before settling in Spain. He produced haunting religious pictures and striking portraits of Spanish nobles. El Greco's use of vibrant colors influenced the work of Diego Velázquez (vuh LAHS kes), court painter to King Philip IV. Velázquez is perhaps best known for his vivid portraits of Spanish royalty.

Spain's golden century produced several outstanding writers. Lope de Vega (LOH pay duh VAY guh), a peasant by birth, wrote more than 1,500 plays, including witty comedies and action-packed romances. Miguel de Cervantes (sur VAN teez) was the most important writer of Spain's golden age. His *Don Quixote*, which pokes fun at medieval tales of chivalry, is considered to be Europe's first modern novel. Although *Don Quixote* mocks the traditions of Spain's feudal past, Cervantes depicts with affection both the foolish but heroic idealism of Don Quixote and the unromantic, earthy realism of his sidekick, Sancho Panza.

✓ **Checkpoint**   What was the *Siglo de Oro*?

View of Toledo
El Greco's painting shows the Spanish city of Toledo, where he lived for 40 years. This is El Greco's only landscape painting. *How does El Greco express religious themes in this painting?*

Progress Monitoring *Online*
For: Self-quiz with vocabulary practice
Web Code: naa-1611

SECTION 1 Assessment

Terms, People, and Places

1. For each term, person, or place listed at the beginning of the section, write a sentence explaining its significance.

Note Taking

2. **Reading Skill: Identify Main Ideas and Supporting Details** Use your completed outline to answer the Focus Question: How did Philip II extend Spain's power and help establish a golden age?

Comprehension and Critical Thinking

3. **Compare and Contrast** How were Charles V and Philip II alike and different in their goals of ensuring absolute power and strengthening Catholicism?

4. **Synthesize Information** Why did Spanish power and prosperity decline?

5. **Summarize** Why is the period from 1550 to 1650 considered Spain's golden age?

● **Writing About History**

Quick Write: Generate Arguments Choose a topic from this section that could be the subject of a persuasive essay—for example, whether England was really a threat to Spain. Then write two thesis statements, one arguing each side of your topic. Make sure that the arguments clearly explain opposite or differing opinions on the topic.

Don Quixote by Miguel de Cervantes

Although the age of chivalry had long passed, stories about knights-errant were still popular in the early 1600s. The heroes of these stories were brave knights who traveled far and wide performing noble deeds. Miguel de Cervantes's novel *Don Quixote* satirizes such romances. His hero, the elderly Don Quixote, has read too many tales of chivalry. Imagining himself a knight-errant, he sets out across the Spanish countryside with his practical servant, Sancho Panza. In this famous excerpt, Don Quixote's noble motives give dignity to his foolish battle with the windmills.

▲ Miguel de Cervantes

▼ An illustration from *Don Quixote* shows Sancho Panza shouting after his master, who is battling windmills.

Just then they came in sight of thirty or forty windmills that rise from that plain, and no sooner did Don Quixote see them than he said to his squire: "Fortune is guiding our affairs better than we ourselves could have wished. Do you see over yonder, friend Sancho, thirty or forty hulking giants? I intend to do battle with them and slay them. With the spoils we shall begin to be rich, for this is a righteous war. . . ."

"What giants?" asked Sancho Panza.

"Those you see over there," replied his master, "with the long arms; some of them have them well-nigh[1] two leagues in length."

"Take care, sir," cried Sancho. "Those over there are not giants but windmills, and those things that seem to be armed are their sails, which when they are whirled around by the wind turn the millstone."

"It is clear," replied Don Quixote, "that you are not experienced in adventures. Those are giants, and if you are afraid, turn aside and pray whilst I enter into fierce and unequal battle with them."

Uttering these words, he clapped spurs to Rozinante, his steed, without heeding the cries of his squire, Sancho, who warned him that he was not going to attack giants, but windmills. But so convinced was he that they were giants that he neither heard his squire's shouts nor did he notice what they were, though he was very near them. Instead, he rushed on, shouting in a loud voice: "Fly not, cowards and vile caitliffs[2]; one knight alone attacks you!" At that moment a slight breeze arose and the great sails began to move. . . .

He ran his lance into the sail, but the wind twisted it with such violence that it shivered the lance in pieces and dragged both rider and horse after it, rolling them over and over on the ground, sorely damaged.

1. **well-nigh** (wel ny) *adv.* nearly
2. **caitliff** (KAYT lif) *n.* cowardly person

Thinking Critically

1. **Synthesize Information** What values of chivalry motivate Don Quixote's attack on the windmills?
2. **Analyze Literature** How does Cervantes show both sides of Don Quixote—the noble and the foolish—in this excerpt?

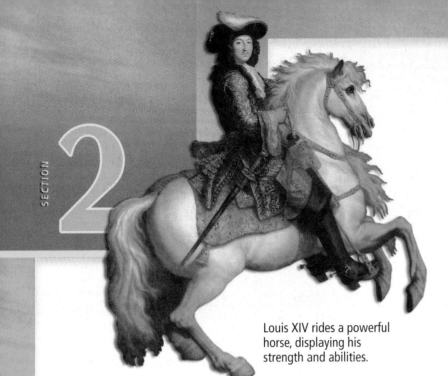

Louis XIV rides a powerful horse, displaying his strength and abilities.

A delicate, beaded shoe from Louis's era

WITNESS HISTORY 🔊 AUDIO

Life at Versailles

At Versailles, the palace court of Louis XIV, life revolved around the king. Nobles waited days or weeks for the honor of attending the king while he dressed or bathed. Every evening the king was at the center of a lavish entertainment, followed by a supper of dozens of rich dishes. The elaborate and extravagant rituals that governed life at court masked a very serious purpose—they were a way for Louis XIV to control every aspect of court life and ensure his absolute authority.

Focus Question How did France become the leading power of Europe under the absolute rule of Louis XIV?

France Under Louis XIV

Objectives
- Understand how Henry IV rebuilt France after the wars of religion.
- Explain how Louis XIV became an absolute monarch.
- Describe how Versailles was a symbol of royal power.
- Identify Louis XIV's successes and failures.

Terms, People, and Places

Huguenots	intendant
Henry IV	Jean-Baptiste Colbert
Edict of Nantes	Versailles
Cardinal Richelieu	*levée*
Louis XIV	balance of power

Note Taking

Reading Skill: Identify Supporting Details As you read about the rule of Louis XIV and how he strengthened the monarchy, use a concept web like the one below to record details that support the main ideas in this section. Add as many circles as you need.

In the last half of the fifteenth century, France enjoyed a period of peace. After driving out the English, the French kings were able to solidify their power within their own realm. But in the 1500s, rivalry with Charles V of Spain and then religious conflict plunged the kingdom into turmoil.

Henry IV Restores Order

In the late 1500s France was torn apart by turbulent wars of religion. A century later, France was a strong, unified nation-state ruled by the most powerful monarch in Europe.

Religious Strife From the 1560s to the 1590s, religious wars between the Catholic majority and French Protestants, called **Huguenots** (HYOO guh nahts), tore France apart. Leaders on both sides used the strife to further their own ambitions.

The worst incident began on St. Bartholomew's Day (a Catholic holiday), August 24, 1572. While Huguenot and Catholic nobles were gathered for a royal wedding, a plot by Catholic royals led to the massacre of 3,000 Huguenots. In the next few days, thousands more were slaughtered. For many, the St. Bartholomew's Day Massacre symbolized the complete breakdown of order in France.

Bringing Peace to a Shattered Land In 1589, a Huguenot prince inherited the French throne as **Henry IV.** For four years Henry fought against fierce Catholic opposition to gain control of France. Finally, to end the conflict, he converted to Catholicism. "Paris is well worth a Mass," he is supposed to have said. To protect Protestants, however, in 1598 he issued the **Edict of Nantes** granting the Huguenots religious toleration and other freedoms.

Henry IV then set out to repair France. His goal, he said, was not the victory of one sect over another, but "a chicken in every pot"—a good Sunday dinner for every peasant. Under Henry, the government reached into every area of French life. Royal officials administered justice, improved roads, built bridges, and revived agriculture. By building the royal bureaucracy and reducing the influence of nobles, Henry IV laid the foundations on which future French monarchs would build absolute power.

Cardinal Richelieu Strengthens Royal Authority When Henry IV was killed by an assassin in 1610, his nine-year-old son, Louis XIII, inherited the throne. For a time, nobles reasserted their power. Then, in 1624, Louis appointed Cardinal Richelieu (ree shul YOO) as his chief minister. This cunning, capable leader devoted the next 18 years to strengthening the central government.

Richelieu sought to destroy the power of the Huguenots and nobles—two groups that did not bow to royal authority. Although he allowed the Huguenots to practice their religion, he smashed their walled cities and outlawed their armies. Likewise, he defeated the private armies of the nobles and destroyed their fortified castles. While reducing their independence, Richelieu tied the nobles to the king by giving them high posts at court or in the royal army.

Richelieu also handpicked his able successor, Cardinal Mazarin (ma za RAN). When five-year-old Louis XIV inherited the throne in 1643, the year after Richelieu's death, Mazarin was in place to serve as chief minister. Like Richelieu, Mazarin worked tirelessly to extend royal power.

 Checkpoint What rights did the Edict of Nantes extend to Huguenots?

An Absolute Monarch Rises

Soon after Louis XIV became king, disorder again swept France. In an uprising called the *Fronde*, nobles, merchants, peasants, and the urban poor each rebelled in order to protest royal power or preserve their own. On one occasion, rioters drove the boy king from his palace. It was an experience Louis would never forget. When Mazarin died in 1661, the 23-year-old Louis resolved to take complete control over the government himself. "I have been pleased to entrust the government of my affairs to the late Cardinal," he declared. "It is now time that I govern them myself."

"I Am the State" Like his great-grandfather Philip II of Spain, Louis XIV firmly believed in his divine right to rule. He took the sun as the symbol of his absolute power. Just as the sun stands at the center of the solar system, he argued, so the Sun King stands at the center of the nation. Louis is often quoted as saying, *"L'état, c'est moi"* (lay TAH seh MWAH), which in English translates as "I am the state."

During his reign, Louis did not once call a meeting of the Estates General, the medieval council made up of representatives of all French social classes. In fact, the Estates General did not meet between 1614 and 1789. Thus, the Estates General played no role in checking royal power.

BIOGRAPHY

Cardinal Richelieu
Armand Richelieu's (1585–1642) parents expected great things from him. They even invited the king of France to attend Armand's christening, promising that someday he would be a leader of France.

The young boy also aspired to greatness as he was growing up. At first, he received training to become a disciplined and authoritative military officer. Then, at his family's request, he switched direction. At age 17, he began training to become a bishop in the Catholic Church. The path was different but the purpose was the same: to become a leader and to serve the monarch.

Over the next 40 years, Armand Richelieu rose to the highest levels of authority in both religious and political circles. He became the true power behind the throne of King Louis XIII. **What characteristics of Richelieu does the artist portray in this painting?**

Louis XIV Strengthens Royal Power Louis spent many hours each day attending to government affairs. To strengthen the state, he followed the policies of Richelieu. He expanded the bureaucracy and appointed **intendants,** royal officials who collected taxes, recruited soldiers, and carried out his policies in the provinces. These and other government jobs often went to wealthy middle-class men. In this way Louis cemented his ties with the middle class, thus checking the power of the nobles and the Church. The king also built the French army into the strongest in Europe. The state paid, fed, trained, and supplied up to 300,000 soldiers. Louis used this highly disciplined army to enforce his policies at home and abroad.

Colbert Builds France's Finances Louis's brilliant finance minister, **Jean-Baptiste Colbert** (kohl behr), imposed mercantilist policies to bolster the economy. He had new lands cleared for farming, encouraged mining and other basic industries, and built up luxury trades such as lacemaking. To protect French manufacturers, Colbert put high tariffs on imported goods. He also fostered overseas colonies, such as New France in North America, and regulated trade with the colonies to enrich the royal treasury. Colbert's policies helped make France the wealthiest state in Europe. Yet not even the financial genius of Colbert could produce enough income to support the huge costs of Louis's court and his many foreign wars.

 Checkpoint Why did Louis XIV choose the sun as his symbol?

Versailles: Symbol of Royal Power

In the countryside near Paris, Louis XIV turned a royal hunting lodge into the immense palace of **Versailles** (ver SY). He spared no expense to make it the most magnificent building in Europe. Its halls and salons displayed the finest paintings and statues, and they glittered with chandeliers and mirrors. In the royal gardens, millions of flowers, trees, and fountains were set out in precise geometric patterns. Versailles became the perfect symbol of the Sun King's wealth and power. As both the king's home and the seat of government, it housed nobles, officials, and servants.

Conducting Court Ceremonies Louis XIV perfected elaborate ceremonies that emphasized his own importance. Each day began in the king's bedroom with a major ritual known as the *levée* (luh VAY), or rising. High-ranking nobles competed for the honor of holding the royal washbasin or handing the king his diamond-buckled shoes. At night, the ceremony was repeated in reverse. Wives of nobles vied to attend upon women of the royal family.

Rituals such as the *levée* served a serious purpose. French nobles were descendants of the feudal lords who held power in medieval times. At liberty on their estates, these nobles were a threat to the power of the monarchy. By luring nobles to Versailles, Louis turned them into courtiers angling for privileges rather than rival warriors battling for power. His tactic worked because he carefully protected their prestige and left them exempt from paying taxes.

The Sun King developed his philosophy of absolutism with the help of a brilliant bishop named Jacques Bénigne Bossuet (1627–1704). In his writings, Bossuet argued that the Bible shows that a monarch rules by the will of God. Therefore, opposition to the monarch is a sin. Bossuet also believed that, although the monarch should rule absolutely, it was God's will that he or she act only in the best interest of the nation. **According to Bossuet, what is the role of a king?**

Primary Source

❝The royal power is absolute. . . . The prince need render account of his acts to no one. . . . Without this absolute authority [he] could neither do good nor repress evil. It is necessary that his power be such that no one can hope to escape him. . . . The prince . . . is not regarded as a private person: he is a public personage, all the state is in him; the will of all the people is included in his. As all perfection and all strength are united in God, so all the power of individuals is united in the person of the prince.❞
—Bishop Jacques Bénigne Bossuet, "Politics Drawn from the Very Words of Scripture," 1679

Separate Classes
LIFE IN FRANCE IN THE 1600S

It is no surprise that the life of Louis XIV is central to French history. Historians and social observers wrote volumes about this larger-than-life king, and buildings like Versailles survive as testaments to his legacy. Yet the vast majority of French people were not nobles, and never set foot in Versailles. They performed various jobs, from artisan, to soldier, to merchant. Rather than fancy balls, they enjoyed street plays and cockfights. Many were peasants, living hard and simple lives in the countryside. All of these people paid heavy taxes that supported the nobles' lavish lifestyles.

▲ A noblewoman is dressed in the romantic style of the time. French monarchs used Versailles' Hall of Mirrors, in the background above, for political and social ceremonies. In the foreground is a richly embroidered bag that a noble may have owned.

Women in the lower classes, like the woman below, might have been field workers, street vendors, or maids for noble families. In the background, French villagers tend livestock and wash clothes. ▼

"In France, nine-tenths of the people die of hunger, one-tenth of indigestion."

—Italian ambassador to Louis's court

Thinking Critically
1. **Draw Inferences** Read the quotation. Judging from the quotation, what is the speaker's view of the differences between nobles and commoners?
2. **Draw Conclusions** Why are the lives of nobles and royalty better documented than those of commoners?

513

Patronizing the Arts The king and his court supported a "splendid century" of the arts. The age of Louis XIV came to be known as the classical age of French drama. In painting, music, architecture, and decorative arts, French styles became the model for all Europe. A new form of dance drama, ballet, gained its first great popularity at the French court. As a leading patron of culture, Louis sponsored the French Academies, which set high standards for both the arts and the sciences.

✓ **Checkpoint** How did Louis XIV secure support from the nobility?

A Strong State Declines

Louis XIV ruled France for 72 years—far longer than any other monarch. At the end of Louis's reign, France was the strongest state in Europe. However, some of Louis's decisions eventually caused France's prosperity to erode.

Waging Costly Wars Louis XIV poured vast resources into wars meant to expand French borders. However, rival rulers joined forces to check these ambitions. Led by the Dutch or the English, these alliances fought to maintain the **balance of power.** The goal was to maintain a distribution of military and economic power among European nations to prevent any one country from dominating the region.

In 1700, Louis's grandson Philip V inherited the throne of Spain. To maintain the balance of power, neighboring nations led by England fought to prevent the union of France and Spain. The War of the Spanish Succession dragged on until 1713, when an exhausted France signed the Treaty of Utrecht (YOO trekt). Philip remained on the Spanish throne, but France agreed never to unite the two crowns.

Persecuting Huguenots Louis saw France's Protestant minority as a threat to religious and political unity. In 1685, he revoked the Edict of Nantes. More than 100,000 Huguenots fled France, settling mainly in England, the Netherlands, Germany, Poland, and the Americas. The Huguenots had been among the hardest working and most prosperous of Louis's subjects. Their loss was a serious blow to the French economy, just as the expulsion of Spanish Muslims and Jews had hurt Spain.

✓ **Checkpoint** How did Louis's actions weaken France's economy?

Vocabulary Builder

erode—(ee ROHD) v. wear away or disintegrate

SECTION **2** Assessment

Progress Monitoring *Online*
For: Self-quiz with vocabulary practice
Web Code: naa-1621

Terms, People, and Places
1. What do each of the key terms, people, and places listed at the beginning of the section have in common? Explain.

Note Taking

2. **Reading Skill: Identify Supporting Details** Use your completed concept web to answer the Focus Question: How did France become the leading power of Europe under the absolute rule of Louis XIV?

Comprehension and Critical Thinking
3. **Draw Inferences** How did Henry IV's conversion to Catholicism help France unite?
4. **Identify Central Issues** What was the purpose of Louis XIV's extravagant palace and daily rituals?
5. **Recognize Ideologies** Why did other European nations form alliances to oppose France's plans to expand?

● **Writing About History**

Quick Write: Support Opinions With Evidence Choose a topic from the section, such as whether or not you think Louis XIV's reign was good for France. Make a list of evidence from the text that supports your opinion.

514   The Age of Absolutism

Political Systems

How have societies chosen to govern themselves?

A society is a complex network of relationships among individuals and groups whose goals may clash. To avoid chaos, societies create governments to make decisions in the common interest. They also create governments to defend themselves from attack. Throughout history those governments, or political systems, have taken many forms, depending on historical circumstances. The ancient Greeks designated three types of government: rule by one (monarchy, autocracy); rule by the few (aristocracy, oligarchy); and rule by the many (democracy). Consider the following historical examples:

▲ A present-day artist recreates a meeting of the Roman Senate.

► An Egyptian pharaoh

Rule by One

1. The ancient Egyptians needed an efficient government to manage activities related to the annual flooding of the Nile. At the head of the government stood an absolute monarch, the pharaoh. The pharaoh relied on his vizier, or chief minister, to handle the country's affairs. The vizier directed a large government bureaucracy. Most Egyptians had no say in how they were governed.

2. As chairman of the Communist Party, Mao Zedong ruled China from 1949 until his death in 1976. In reality, he stood above the party as an autocrat with dictatorial powers. At will, he purged party members and military leaders who crossed him. Through the party, he maintained tight control over the government, economy, and most other aspects of Chinese society.

Rule by the Few

1. Ancient Sparta, a military society, had two kings, a council of elders, and a group of officials who ran the day-to-day affairs. They were all members of the aristocracy, Sparta's governing class of nobles and soldiers. For the Greeks, *aristocracy* meant government by those best suited to rule. Unlike neighboring Athens, Sparta never experienced tyranny.

2. After the fall of the Roman Empire, the political system known as feudalism arose in Europe. In this system, the power lay with a military elite. The Greeks might have preferred to call it an *oligarchy*—government based on private interests rather than the interests of the whole society. Nobles traded land and labor for political and military service. Warfare dominated people's lives.

▼ A black South African votes in his country's first open election since the end of apartheid.

Rule by the Many

1. In 1789, the French Revolution abolished the monarchy and established a republic. This democracy, however, was unstable. France went through periods of empire, republic, and monarchy until the constitution of 1958 established the Fifth Republic. Today the government has a two-house parliament and a strong president who is directly elected. All citizens 18 and older, except for certain criminals, can vote.

2. In 1961, South Africa left the British Commonwealth to become an independent republic. The movement to end apartheid, or racial separation, resulted in a new constitution in 1997. All citizens over age 18 can vote to elect members to a two-house Parliament. The lower house then elects a president as the nation's head of state and chief executive.

Thinking Critically

1. **Connect** (a) Which of these three forms of government strikes you as the fairest? Why? (b) Which do you think is most capable of defending a society from attack? Why?
2. Conduct Internet or library research to find out more about these and other examples of political systems. Write a paragraph expressing your thoughts about one political system.

A portrait of King James of England painted around 1619 gives no hint of the monarch's frequent clashes with Parliament.

WITNESS HISTORY 🔊 AUDIO

Charting a Collision Course

In 1603 James I, a monarch with strong ideas about his role, took the English throne. In 1610 the king made a speech to Parliament that would have quite the opposite effect of what he intended:

❝ The state of Monarchy is the supremest thing upon earth; for kings are not only God's lieutenants upon earth and sit upon God's throne, but even by God himself they are called gods. . . . Kings are justly called gods for that they exercise a manner or resemblance of Divine power upon earth. . . . And to the King is due both the affection of the soul and the service of the body of his subjects. . . . ❞
—James I

Focus Question How did the British Parliament assert its rights against royal claims to absolute power in the 1600s?

Parliament Triumphs in England

Objectives
- Describe the Tudor monarchs' relations with Parliament.
- Analyze how clashes between the Stuarts and Parliament ushered in a century of revolution.
- Understand how the English Civil War and the development of the Commonwealth led to the Glorious Revolution.
- Explain the development of English constitutional government.

Terms, People, and Places

James I	limited monarchy
dissenter	constitutional
Puritans	government
Charles I	cabinet
Oliver Cromwell	oligarchy
English Bill of Rights	

Note Taking

Reading Skill: Identify Supporting Details As you read the section, use a flowchart to record details about the evolution of the English Parliament. One has been started for you.

> Tudors consult with and control Parliament.

⬇   ⬇   ⬇

In the 1600s, while Louis XIV perfected royal absolutism in France, political power in England took a different path. Despite attempts by English monarchs to increase royal authority, Parliament steadily expanded its own influence.

The Tudors Work With Parliament

From 1485 to 1603, England was ruled by Tudor monarchs. Although the Tudors believed in divine right, they shrewdly recognized the value of good relations with Parliament. As you have read, when Henry VIII broke with the Roman Catholic Church, he turned to Parliament to legalize his actions. Parliament approved the Act of Supremacy, making the monarch head of the Church of England.

A constant need for money also led Henry to consult Parliament frequently. Although he had inherited a bulging treasury, he quickly used up his funds fighting overseas wars. To levy new taxes, the king had to seek the approval of Parliament. Members of Parliament tended to vote as Henry's agents instructed. Still, they became accustomed to being consulted on important matters.

When Elizabeth I gained the throne, she too both consulted and controlled Parliament. Her advisors conveyed the queen's wishes to Parliament and forbade discussion of certain subjects, such as foreign policy or the queen's marriage. Her skill in handling Parliament helped make "Good Queen Bess" a popular and successful ruler.

✔ **Checkpoint** Why did Henry VIII work with Parliament?

A Century of Revolution Begins

Elizabeth died childless in 1603. Her heir was her relative James Stuart, the ruling king of Scotland. The Stuarts were neither as popular as the Tudors nor as skillful in dealing with Parliament. They also inherited problems that Henry and Elizabeth had long <u>suppressed</u>. The result was a "century of revolution" that pitted the Stuart monarchs against Parliament.

The Stuarts Issue a Challenge The first Stuart monarch, James I, had agreed to rule according to English laws and customs. Soon, however, he was lecturing Parliament about divine right. "I will not be content that my power be disputed upon," he declared. Leaders in the House of Commons fiercely resisted the king's claim to absolute power.

James repeatedly clashed with Parliament over money and foreign policy. He needed funds to finance his lavish court and wage wars. When members wanted to discuss foreign policy before voting funds, James dissolved Parliament and collected taxes on his own.

James also clashed with dissenters, Protestants who differed with the Church of England. One group, called Puritans, sought to "purify" the church of Catholic practices. Puritans called for simpler services and a more democratic church without bishops. James rejected their demands, vowing to "harry them out of this land or else do worse."

Parliament Responds In 1625, Charles I inherited the throne. Like his father, Charles behaved like an absolute monarch. He imprisoned his foes without trial and squeezed the nation for money. By 1628, however, his need to raise taxes forced Charles to summon Parliament. Before voting any funds, Parliament insisted that Charles sign the Petition of Right. This document prohibited the king from raising taxes without Parliament's consent or from jailing anyone without legal justification.

Charles did sign the Petition, but he then dissolved Parliament in 1629. For 11 years, he ignored the Petition and ruled the nation without Parliament. During that time, he created bitter enemies, especially among Puritans. His Archbishop of Canterbury, William Laud, tried to force all clergy to follow strict Anglican rules, dismissing or imprisoning dissenters. Many people felt that the archbishop was trying to revive Catholic practices.

In 1637, Charles and Laud tried to impose the Anglican prayer book on Scotland. The Calvinist Scots revolted. To get funds to suppress the Scottish rebellion, Charles once again had to summon Parliament in 1640. When it met, however, Parliament launched its own revolt.

The Long Parliament Begins The 1640 Parliament became known as the Long Parliament because it lasted on and off until 1653. Its actions triggered the greatest political revolution in English history. In a mounting struggle with Charles I, Parliament tried and executed his chief ministers, including Archbishop Laud. It called for the abolition of bishops and declared that the Parliament could not be dissolved without its own consent.

Vocabulary Builder

<u>suppressed</u>—(suh PRESD) *v.* kept from being revealed; put down by force

---

A Voice for Absolutism

In 1651, two years after the English Civil War ended, English political philosopher Thomas Hobbes published *Leviathan*. In this book, he explained why he favored an absolute monarchy. How might people who supported Parliament over the monarch have argued against Hobbes's view?

Primary Source

❝ During the time men live without a common power to keep them all in awe, they are in that condition which is called war. . . . In such condition, there is no place for industry. . . . no arts; no letters; no society; and, which is worst of all, continual fear and danger of violent death. And the life of man [is] solitary, poor, nasty, brutish, and short.❞
—Thomas Hobbes, *Leviathan*   AUDIO

ENGLAND DIVIDED:
PARLIAMENT AND THE MONARCHY FIGHT FOR POWER

1485–1603
The Tudors rule England.
The Tudor monarchs, especially Henry VIII and Elizabeth I, ❶ control Parliament tactfully, recognizing and respecting its role in government.

1603–1625
Stuart king James I rules.
James I becomes king and immediately clashes with Parliament. In 1621, James scolds Parliament for usurping royal power, and Parliament responds with a declaration of its own rights. In the last Parliament of his reign, the aging James gives in to Parliament.

1625–1649
Stuart king Charles I rules.
Charles dissolves Parliament when it tries to expand powers to deal with an economic crisis. The Parliament of 1628 produces the Petition of Right, and later Parliaments ❷ clash with Charles over what they charge are violations of the document. Charles dissolves Parliament again.

1640–1653
The Long Parliament meets.
Faced with economic problems and invasions by Scotland, Charles is forced to call Parliament. The Long Parliament, as it became known, works to steadily expand its powers. Eventually Charles strikes back, adopting the motto "Give Caesar his Due."

Charles lashed back. In 1642, he led troops into the House of Commons to arrest its most radical leaders. They escaped through a back door and soon raised their own army. The clash now moved to the battlefield.

✔ **Checkpoint**   What was the Petition of Right?

Fighting a Civil War

The civil war that followed lasted from 1642 to 1651. Like the *Fronde* that occurred about the same time in France, the English Civil War posed a major challenge to absolutism. But while the forces of royal power won in France, in England the forces of revolution triumphed.

Cavaliers and Roundheads At first, the odds seemed to favor the supporters of Charles I, called Cavaliers. Many Cavaliers were wealthy nobles, proud of their plumed hats and fashionably long hair. Well trained in dueling and warfare, the Cavaliers expected a quick victory. But their foes proved to be tough fighters with the courage of their convictions. The forces of Parliament were composed of country gentry, town-dwelling manufacturers, and Puritan clergy. They were called Roundheads because their hair was cut close around their heads.

The Roundheads found a leader of genius in Oliver Cromwell. A Puritan member of the lesser gentry, Cromwell proved himself to be a skilled general. He organized a "New Model Army" for Parliament, made up of officers selected for skill rather than social class, into a disciplined fighting force.

Warrant to Execute King Charles the First. AD 1648.

1642–1649
The English Civil War rages.
War breaks out ③ between Parliament's Roundheads (right) and Charles I's Cavaliers (left). The parliamentary forces, led by Oliver Cromwell, eventually win. In 1649, Charles is executed. ④

1649–1660
The English Commonwealth begins and ends.
Abolishing the monarchy and House of Lords, Parliament rules as a commonwealth with Cromwell as leader. ⑤ Problems plague the nation, and the Commonwealth falls apart upon Cromwell's death in 1658. Groups in favor of monarchy begin to gain power.

1660–1685
The monarchy is restored.
Charles II works with Parliament to repair the shattered nation, but clashes with Parliament when he works to restore Catholicism. In 1678, Charles dissolves Parliament and builds the monarchy's power. His successor, James II, continues to push for Catholic power, and incites a backlash. James II flees England in 1688.

1688
The Glorious Revolution assures Parliament's power.
William and Mary become England's monarchs ⑥ with Parliament's blessing—provided that they agree to very limited powers under Parliament's domination.

Thinking Critically
1. **Recognize Point of View** What does Charles I's usage of the phrase "Give Caesar his Due" tell you about his view of royal power?
2. **Recognize Ideologies** How did the religious beliefs of key people on this timeline shape political outcomes?

XXVIII. WILLIAM the THIRD and MARY the SECOND, from 1688 to 1702.
⑥

WILLIAM the hero, with MARIA mild,
(He James's nephew, she his eldest child)
Fix'd freedom and the church, reform'd the coin;
Oppos'd the French, and settled Brunswick's line.

Cromwell's army defeated the Cavaliers in a series of decisive battles. By 1647, the king was in the hands of parliamentary forces.

A King Is Executed Eventually, Parliament set up a court to put the king on trial. It condemned him to death as "a tyrant, traitor, murderer, and public enemy." On a cold January day in 1649, Charles I stood on a scaffold surrounded by his foes. "I am a martyr of the people," he declared. Showing no fear, the king told the executioner that he himself would give the sign for him to strike. After a brief prayer, Charles knelt and placed his neck on the block. On the agreed signal, the executioner severed the king's neck with a single stroke.

The execution sent shock waves throughout Europe. In the past, a king had occasionally been assassinated or killed in battle. But for the first time, a ruling monarch had been tried and executed by his own people. The parliamentary forces had sent a clear message that, in England, no ruler could claim absolute power and ignore the rule of law.

✓ **Checkpoint** What was the result of the English Civil War?

Cromwell and the Commonwealth

After the execution of Charles I, the House of Commons abolished the monarchy, the House of Lords, and the established Church of England. It declared England a republic, known as the Commonwealth, under the leadership of Oliver Cromwell.

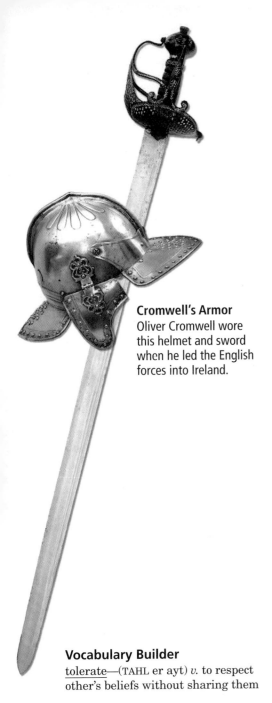

Cromwell's Armor
Oliver Cromwell wore this helmet and sword when he led the English forces into Ireland.

Vocabulary Builder

tolerate—(TAHL er ayt) v. to respect other's beliefs without sharing them

Challenging the Commonwealth The new government faced many threats. Supporters of Charles II, the uncrowned heir to the throne, attacked England by way of Ireland and Scotland. Cromwell led forces into Ireland and brutally crushed the uprising. He then took harsh measures against the Irish Catholic majority that are still vividly remembered in that nation today. In 1652, Parliament passed a law exiling most Catholics to barren land in the west of Ireland. Any Catholic found disobeying this order could be killed on sight.

Squabbles also splintered forces within the Commonwealth. One group, called Levellers, thought that poor men should have as much say in government as the gentry, lawyers, and other leading citizens. "The poorest he that is in England hath a life to live as the greatest he," wrote one Leveller. In addition, female Levellers asserted their right to petition Parliament. These ideas horrified the gentry, who dominated Parliament. Cromwell suppressed the Levellers, as well as more radical groups who threatened ownership of private property. In 1653, as the challenges to order grew, Cromwell took the title Lord Protector. From then on, he ruled as a virtual dictator through the army.

Puritans: A Sobering Influence Under the Commonwealth, Puritans—with their goal of rooting out godlessness—gained a new voice in society. The English Civil War thus ushered in a social revolution as well as a political one.

Parliament enacted a series of laws designed to make sure that Sunday was set aside for religious observance. Anyone over the age of 14 who was caught "profaning the Lord's Day" could be fined. To the Puritans, theaters were frivolous. So, like John Calvin in Geneva, Cromwell closed all theaters. Puritans also frowned on taverns, gambling, and dancing.

Puritans felt that every Christian, rich and poor, must be able to read the Bible. To spread religious knowledge, they encouraged education for all people. By mid-century, families from all classes were sending their children to school, girls as well as boys. Puritans also pushed for changes in marriage to ensure greater fidelity. In addition to marriages based on business interests, they encouraged marriages based on love. Still, as in the past, women were seen mainly as caretakers of the family, subordinate to men.

Although Cromwell did not <u>tolerate</u> open worship by Roman Catholics, he believed in religious freedom for other Protestant groups. He even welcomed Jews back to England after more than 350 years of exile.

The Commonwealth Ends Oliver Cromwell died in 1658. Soon after, the Puritans lost their grip on England. Many people were tired of military rule and strict Puritan ways. In 1660, a newly elected Parliament invited Charles II to return to England from exile.

England's "kingless decade" ended with the Restoration, or return of the monarchy. Yet Puritan ideas about morality, equality, government, and education endured. In the following century, these ideas would play an important role in shaping the future of Britain's colonies in the Americas.

✓ **Checkpoint** What was the Commonwealth?

From Restoration to Glorious Revolution

In late May 1660, cheering crowds welcomed Charles II back to London. John Evelyn, a supporter and diarist whose writings are an important source of information about English political and social history, wrote:

" This day came in his Majesties Charles the Second to London after a sad, and long Exile . . . with a Triumph of above 20,000 horse and [soldiers], brandishing their swords, and shouting with unexpressible joy; the [ways strewn] with flowers, the bells ringing, the streetes hung with [tapestry]. "
—John Evelyn, *Diary*

Charles II With his charm and flashing wit, young Charles II was a popular ruler. He reopened theaters and taverns and presided over a lively court in the manner of Louis XIV. Charles reestablished the Church of England but encouraged toleration of other Protestants such as Presbyterians, Quakers, and Baptists.

Although Charles accepted the Petition of Right, he shared his father's belief in absolute monarchy and secretly had Catholic sympathies. Still, he shrewdly avoided his father's mistakes in dealing with Parliament.

James II is Forced to Flee Charles's brother, James II, inherited the throne in 1685. Unlike Charles, James practiced his Catholic faith openly. He angered his subjects by suspending laws on a whim and appointing Catholics to high office. Many English Protestants feared that James would restore the Roman Catholic Church.

In 1688, alarmed parliamentary leaders invited James's Protestant daughter, Mary, and her Dutch Protestant husband, William III of Orange, to become rulers of England. When William and Mary landed with their army late in 1688, James II fled to France. This bloodless overthrow of the king became known as the Glorious Revolution.

The English Bill of Rights Before they could be crowned, William and Mary had to accept several acts passed by Parliament in 1689 that became known as the **English Bill of Rights.** The Bill of Rights ensured the superiority of Parliament over the monarchy. It required the monarch to summon Parliament regularly and gave the House of Commons the "power of the purse," or control over spending. A king or queen could no longer interfere in parliamentary debates or suspend laws. The Bill of Rights also barred any Roman Catholic from sitting on the throne.

The Bill of Rights also restated the traditional rights of English citizens, such as trial by jury. It abolished excessive fines and cruel or unjust punishment. It affirmed the principle of *habeas corpus*. That is, no person could be held in prison without first being charged with a specific crime.

In addition, a separate Toleration Act, also of 1689, granted limited religious freedom to Puritans, Quakers, and other dissenters. Still, only members of the Church of England could hold public office. And Catholics were allowed no religious freedom.

Puritan girls spent hours working on embroidered samplers like this one. Such work was considered part of their education. ▼

Our Puritan Heritage

Decades before the Puritans gained power in England, Puritans living in the Massachusetts Bay colony worked to put into action their own ideas about religion and government. The Puritans knew that to assure survival of their beliefs and culture, they would have to educate their children to read and write. As soon as they were able, the Puritans began to set up schools, starting with the Boston Latin School in 1635 and then Harvard College (below) in 1636.

Eventually, the colonies became the United States. Over time, the rest of the country adopted the Puritan tradition of establishing public schools to help train children to become good citizens of their community. A literate, well-informed citizenry has continued to be a major aim of American schools to this day. **What other institutions help to train American children to be good citizens?**

A Limited Monarchy The Glorious Revolution created not a democracy, but a type of government called **limited monarchy,** in which a constitution or legislative body limits the monarch's powers. English rulers still had much power, but they had to obey the law and govern in partnership with Parliament. In the age of absolute monarchy elsewhere in Europe, the limited monarchy in England was quite radical.

The Glorious Revolution also greatly influenced important political thinkers of the time, such as John Locke. Locke's ideas were later used by leaders of the American Revolution as the basis for their struggle, and are found in documents such as the Declaration of Independence.

 Checkpoint What was the Glorious Revolution?

Constitutional Government Evolves

In the century following the Glorious Revolution, three new political institutions arose in Britain: political parties, the cabinet, and the office of prime minister. The appearance of these institutions was part of the evolution of Britain's **constitutional government**—that is, a government whose power is defined and limited by law.

Political Parties Emerge In the late 1600s, political parties emerged in England as a powerful force in politics. At first, there were just two political parties—Tories and Whigs. Tories were generally aristocrats who sought to preserve older traditions. They supported broad royal powers and a dominant Anglican Church. Whigs backed the policies of the Glorious Revolution. They were more likely to reflect urban business interests, support religious toleration, and favor Parliament over the crown.

The Cabinet System The cabinet, another new feature of government, evolved in the 1700s after the British throne passed to a German prince. George I spoke no English and relied on the leaders in Parliament to help him rule. Under George I and his German-born son George II, a handful of parliamentary advisors set policy. They came to be referred to as the cabinet because of the small room, or "cabinet," where they met. In time, the cabinet gained official status.

The Prime Minister Leads the Cabinet Over time, the head of the cabinet came to be known as the prime minister. This person was always the leader of the majority party in the House of Commons. Eventually, the prime minister became the chief official of the British government. From 1721 to 1742, the able Whig leader Robert Walpole molded the cabinet into a unified body by requiring all members to agree on major issues.

Influence of the Glorious Revolution

Outcome in England

English Bill of Rights	Writings of John Locke	Constitutional Government
• People elect representatives to Parliament, which is supreme over monarch. • All citizens have natural rights.	• People have natural rights such as life, liberty, and property. • There is a social contract between people and government.	• Government is limited and defined by law. • Political parties, the cabinet, and the office of prime minister arise.

Impact on the United States

Colonists believed that they too had rights, including the right to elect people to represent them.	Locke's ideas shaped the American Revolution and the writing of the Declaration of Independence and the Constitution.	The new American nation formed a constitutional government with two parties and a cabinet; the American system included even more provisions for the separation of powers.

Chart Skills A common protest during the American Revolution was "no taxation without representation." *Which English outcome of the Glorious Revolution influenced that idea?*

Although the title was not yet in use, Walpole is often called Britain's first prime minister. In time, the power of the prime minister would exceed that of the monarch. Other countries later adopted and adapted the cabinet system, including the United States.

✓ **Checkpoint** What three political institutions contributed to the evolution of Britain's constitutional government?

A Society Still Ruled by the Few

The decades that Walpole headed the cabinet were a time of peace and prosperity. But even as Parliament and the cabinet assumed new powers, British government was far from democratic. Rather, it was an oligarchy—a government in which the ruling power belongs to a few people.

In Britain, landowning aristocrats were believed to be the "natural" ruling class. The highest nobles held seats in the House of Lords. Other wealthy landowners and rich business leaders in the cities controlled elections to the House of Commons. The right to vote was limited to a relatively few male property owners.

Most Britons had neither the wealth nor the privileges of the upper class and lived very differently, making a meager living from the land. In the 1700s, even that poor existence was threatened. Wealthy landowners, attempting to increase agricultural production, bought up farms and took over common lands, evicting tenant farmers and small landowners. Because they controlled Parliament, they easily passed laws ensuring that their actions were legal. As a result many landless families drifted into towns, where they faced a harsh existence.

However, a relatively strong middle class—including merchants, craftspeople, and manufacturers—was growing. These prosperous and often wealthy people controlled affairs in the towns and cities. Some improved their social standing by marrying into the landed gentry. The middle class also produced talented inventors and entrepreneurs who would soon help usher in the Industrial Revolution.

✓ **Checkpoint** How did British society remain divided?

SECTION 3 Assessment

Progress Monitoring Online
For: Self-quiz with vocabulary practice
Web Code: naa-1631

Terms, People, and Places

1. Place each of the key terms at the beginning of the section into one of the following categories: politics, culture, or government. Write a sentence for each explaining your choice.

Note Taking

2. **Reading Skill: Identify Supporting Details** Use your completed flowchart to answer the Focus Question: How did the British Parliament assert its rights against royal claims to absolute power in the 1600s?

Comprehension and Critical Thinking

3. **Contrast** How did the Stuarts differ from the Tudors in their approach to Parliament?

4. **Identify Central Issues** In less than 100 years, England changed from a monarchy to a commonwealth and back to a monarchy. What central issue caused this political upheaval?

5. **Draw Conclusions** What were two results of the Glorious Revolution?

6. **Summarize** How did constitutional government evolve in England in the 1700s?

● **Writing About History**

Quick Write: Answer Opposing Arguments To write a strong persuasive essay you need to address arguments that could be raised to refute your own position. Choose a topic from this section—for example, whether Parliament had the right to replace James II—and list the arguments for and against your position.

The English Bill of Rights

When the Catholic James II was forced from the English throne in 1688, Parliament offered the crown to his Protestant daughter Mary and her husband, William of Orange. But Parliament insisted that William and Mary submit to a Bill of Rights. This document, reflecting the long-standing struggle between monarch and Parliament, sums up the powers that Parliament had been seeking since the Petition of Right in 1628. This document ensured the superiority of Parliament over the monarchy and spelled out basic rights.

An engraving made in 1689 shows the new English rulers, William and Mary.

The original English Bill of Rights, now more than 300 years old, is carefully preserved in a museum in London, England.

Whereas, the late King James II ... did endeavor to subvert[1] and extirpate[2] the Protestant religion and the laws and liberties of this kingdom ... and whereas the said late King James II having abdicated the government, and the throne being vacant ... the said lords [Parliament] ... being now assembled in a full and free representative [body] of this nation ... do in the first place ... declare:

1. That the pretended power of suspending of laws or the execution of laws by regal authority without consent of Parliament is illegal. ...

4. That levying money for or to the use of the crown by pretense of prerogative[3] without grant of Parliament ... is illegal;

5. That it is the right of the subjects to petition the king, and all commitments and prosecutions for such petitioning are illegal.

6. That ... raising or keeping a standing army within the kingdom in time of peace, unless it be with consent of Parliament, is against law. ...

8. That election of members of Parliament ought to be free. ...

9. That the freedom of speech and debates or proceedings in Parliament ought not to be challenged or questioned in any court or place out of Parliament. ...

10. That excessive bail ought not to be required, nor excessive fines imposed, nor cruel and unusual punishments inflicted. ...

13. And that, for redress of all grievances and for the amending, strengthening, and preserving of the laws, Parliaments ought to be held frequently. ...

Thinking Critically

1. **Synthesize Information** What is the meaning of item 6, and why do you think it was included in the Bill of Rights?
2. **Draw Inferences** Why do you think the members of Parliament included item 9? Why do you think this item might have been important?

1. **subvert** (sub VURT) *v.* to destroy, overthrow, or undermine
2. **extirpate** (EKS tur payt) *v.* to eliminate
3. **prerogative** (pree RAHG uh tiv) *n.* a right

Flemish artist Pieter Snayers painted several battles during the Thirty Years' War, including this one fought near Prague in 1620.

This silver flask held musket powder in the Thirty Years' War.

WITNESS HISTORY 🔊 AUDIO

War Rages in Germany

The conflict known as the Thirty Years' War ravaged the German states of central Europe for much of the first half of the seventeenth century. A German family Bible contained this entry describing the war's end:

> 66 They say that the terrible war is now over. But there is still no sign of a peace. Everywhere there is envy, hatred, and greed: that's what the war has taught us. . . . We live like animals, eating bark and grass. No one could have imagined that anything like this would happen to us. Many people say that there is no God. 99

Focus Question How did the two great empires of Austria and Prussia emerge from the Thirty Years' War and subsequent events?

Rise of Austria and Prussia

Objectives
- Outline causes and results of the Thirty Years' War.
- Understand how Austria and Prussia emerged as great powers.
- Describe how European nations tried to maintain a balance of power.

Terms, People, and Places

elector	War of the Austrian
Ferdinand	Succession
mercenary	Prussia
depopulation	Frederick William I
Peace of Westphalia	Frederick II
Maria Theresa	

Note Taking

Reading Skill: Identify Supporting Details As you read this section, use a table like the one below to record details about the emergence of Austria and Prussia as European powers.

Rise of Austria	Rise of Prussia
• Austrian ruler keeps title of Holy Roman Emperor.	• Hohenzollern rulers take over German states.
•	•

The Thirty Years' War took a terrible toll on the people of the German states. Finally, two great German-speaking powers, Austria and Prussia, rose out of the ashes. Like Louis XIV in France, their rulers perfected skills as absolute monarchs.

The Thirty Years' War Ravages Europe

By early modern times, as the French philosopher Voltaire later observed, the Holy Roman Empire was neither holy, nor Roman, nor an empire. Instead, by the seventeenth century it had become a patchwork of several hundred small, separate states. In theory, these states were ruled by the Holy Roman emperor, who was chosen by seven leading German princes called **electors.** In practice, the emperor had little power over the many rival princes. This power vacuum contributed to the outbreak of the Thirty Years' War. Religion further divided the German states. The north had become largely Protestant, while the south remained Catholic.

A Brutal War Begins The Thirty Years' War was actually a series of wars. It began in Bohemia, the present-day Czech Republic. **Ferdinand,** the Catholic Hapsburg king of Bohemia, sought to suppress Protestants and to assert royal power over nobles. In May 1618, a few rebellious Protestant noblemen tossed two royal officials out of a castle window in Prague. This act, known as the Defenestration of Prague, sparked a general revolt, which Ferdinand moved to suppress. As both sides sought allies, what began as a local conflict widened into a general European war.

Europe After the Thirty Years' War (1648)

Controlled by
Spanish Hapsburgs

Controlled by
Austrian Hapsburgs

Italian city-states

Controlled by Prussian
Hohenzollerns

Boundary of Holy
Roman Empire

10°W   0°   NORWAY   10°E   SWEDEN   20°E   RUSSIA

SCOTLAND

North Sea

DENMARK   *Baltic Sea*   PRUSSIA   POLAND

IRELAND   ENGLAND   Dutch Neth.   BRANDENBURG

50°N   London   Berlin   Silesia

Spanish Neth.   WESTPHALIA   SAXONY   Prague   Bohemia   TRANSYLVANIA

Atlantic Ocean   Paris   Alsace   Vienna

Lorraine   BAVARIA   AUSTRIA   HUNGARY

Conic Projection

0   200   400 mi

0   200   400 km

FRANCE   SWISS FED.   OTTOMAN EMPIRE   *Black Sea*

Milan

Papal States

40°N   PORTUGAL   Corsica   Rome

Madrid   Naples

SPAIN   Sardinia

N   *Mediterranean Sea*   Sicily

W   E

S

Map Skills After the Thirty Years' War, the Peace of Westphalia redrew the map of Europe.

1. **Locate** (a) Poland (b) Sweden (c) Spanish Netherlands (d) Westphalia
2. **Regions** (a) Who controlled Bohemia in 1648? (b) What lands did the Spanish Hapsburgs control?
3. **Drawing Conclusions** How can you tell from the maps that the Holy Roman Empire was not a strong, unified state?

European Nation-States, 1700

60°N   10°W   0°   SWEDEN   20°E

Stockholm   Moscow

North Sea   *Baltic Sea*   RUSSIA

ENGLAND   10°E   PRUSSIA   Warsaw   *Dnieper R.*

50°N   Berlin   POLAND

London   *Rhine R.*   Prague   *Vistula R.*

Atlantic Ocean   Paris   Vienna

AUSTRIA   *Black Sea*

Conic Projection

0   200   400 mi

0   200   400 km

FRANCE   ALPS   *Danube R.*

PYRENEES MTS.

40°N   Rome

Madrid

SPAIN

Mediterranean Sea

Major European monarchy

The following year, Ferdinand was elected Holy Roman Emperor. With the support of Spain, Poland, and other Catholic states, he tried to roll back the Reformation by force. In the early stages of the war, he defeated the Bohemians (who had rebelled when he became emperor) and their Protestant allies. Alarmed, Protestant powers like the Netherlands and Sweden sent troops into Germany. Before long, political motives outweighed religious issues. Catholic and Protestant rulers shifted alliances to suit their own interests. At one point, Catholic France joined Lutheran Sweden against the Catholic Hapsburgs.

A Terrible Loss of Life The fighting took a terrible toll. Roving armies of **mercenaries,** or soldiers for hire, burned villages, destroyed crops, and killed without mercy. Murder and torture were followed by famine and disease. Wolves, not seen in settled areas since the Middle Ages, stalked the deserted streets of once-bustling villages. The war led to a severe **depopulation,** or reduction in population. Exact statistics do not exist, but historians estimate that as many as one third of the people in the German states may have died as a result of the war.

Peace at Last Finally, in 1648, the exhausted combatants accepted a series of treaties, known as the **Peace of Westphalia.** Because so many powers had been involved in the conflict, the treaties aspired both to bring about a general European peace and to settle other international problems. Among the combatants France emerged a clear winner, gaining territory on both its Spanish and German frontiers. The Hapsburgs were not so fortunate. They had to accept the almost total independence of all the princes of the Holy Roman Empire. In addition, the Netherlands and the Swiss Federation (present-day Switzerland) won recognition as independent states.

Vocabulary Builder
aspired—(uh SPY urd) *v.* aimed; sought

The Thirty Years' War left German lands divided into more than 360 separate states—"one for every day of the year." These states still acknowledged the rule of the Holy Roman emperor. Yet each state had its own government, currency, church, armed forces, and foreign policy. The German states, potentially the most powerful nation in Europe if they could be unified, thus remained fragmented for another 223 years.

✓ **Checkpoint** What were some effects of the Peace of Westphalia?

Hapsburg Austria Changes its Focus

Though weakened by war, the Hapsburgs still wanted to create a strong united state. They kept the title "Holy Roman emperor," but focused their attention on expanding their own lands. To Austria, they would soon add Bohemia, Hungary, and, later, parts of Poland and some Italian states.

Challenges to Unity Uniting these lands proved difficult. Not only were they divided by geography, they included a number of diverse peoples and cultures as well. By the 1700s, the Hapsburg Empire included Germans, Magyars, Slavs, and others. In many parts of the empire, people had their own languages, laws, political assemblies, and customs.

The Hapsburgs did exert some control over these diverse peoples. They sent German-speaking officials to Bohemia and Hungary and settled Austrians on lands they had seized in these provinces. They also put down revolts in Bohemia and Hungary. Still, the Hapsburgs never developed a centralized governmental system like that of France.

Maria Theresa

When Maria Theresa (1717–1780) became Hapsburg empress at the age of 23, her chances of remaining in power seemed very slim. She later said, "I found myself all at once without money, without troops, and without advice." A decade after her crowning she wrote, "I do not think anyone would deny that history hardly knows of a crowned head who started his rule under circumstances more grievous than those attending my accession."

But the determined empress survived. She appointed superb advisors and was able to maintain control of her empire. During her 40-year reign, Vienna became a center for music and the arts.

Maria Theresa had one thing in common with most women of her day—being a mother. She gave birth to a total of 16 children—11 girls and 5 boys. Among them were future emperors Joseph II and Leopold II and Queen Marie Antoinette of France. **What traits did Maria Theresa need to stay in power?**

A Woman Emperor Takes the Throne In the early 1700s, a new challenge threatened Hapsburg Austria. Emperor Charles VI had no male heir. His daughter, Maria Theresa, was intelligent and capable, but no woman had yet ruled Hapsburg lands in her own name. Charles persuaded other European rulers to recognize his daughter's right to succeed him. When he died, however, many ignored their pledge.

The War of the Austrian Succession Shortly after Charles's death in 1740, Frederick II of Prussia seized the rich Hapsburg province of Silesia. This action sparked the eight-year War of the Austrian Succession. Maria Theresa set off for Hungary to appeal for military help from her Hungarian subjects. The Hungarians were ordinarily unfriendly to the Hapsburgs. But she made a dramatic plea before an assembly of Hungarian nobles. According to one account, the nobles rose to their feet and shouted, "Our lives and blood for your Majesty!" She eventually got further help from Britain and Russia, who did not want Prussia to upset the balance of power by gaining new lands.

Maria Theresa never succeeded in forcing Frederick out of Silesia. Still, she did preserve her empire and win the support of most of her people. Equally important, she strengthened Hapsburg power by reorganizing the bureaucracy and improving tax collection. She even forced nobles and clergy to pay taxes and tried to ease the burden of taxes and labor services on peasants. As you will read, her son and successor, Joseph II, later extended many of her reforms.

✓ **Checkpoint** What caused the War of the Austrian Succession?

Hohenzollern Prussia

While Austria was molding a strong Catholic state, a region called Prussia emerged as a new Protestant power. In the 1600s, the Hohenzollern (HOH un tsahl urn) family ruled scattered lands across north Germany. In the century following the Peace of Westphalia, ambitious Hohenzollern rulers united their holdings, creating Prussia.

Creating a Bureaucracy Hohenzollerns rulers set up an efficient central bureaucracy. Frederick William I was a Prussian ruler who came to power upon the death of his father in 1713. He cleverly gained the loyalty of the Prussian nobles, called *Junkers* (YOON kerz), by giving them positions in the army and government. His tactic reduced the nobles' independence and increased his own control. Frederick also placed great emphasis on military values and forged one of the best-trained armies in Europe. One Prussian military leader boasted, "Prussia is not a state which possesses an army, but an army which possesses a state." By 1740, Prussia was strong enough to challenge its rival Austria.

A Crown Prince Learns the Art of War Frederick William made sure that, from an early age, his son Frederick was trained in the art of war. He wrote,

Primary Source

 His tutor must take the greatest pains to imbue my son with a sincere love for the soldier's profession and to impress upon him that nothing else in the world can confer upon a prince such fame and honor as the sword. **"**

In fact, young Frederick II preferred playing the flute and writing poetry. His father despised these pursuits and treated the young prince so badly that he tried to flee the country. Discovering these plans, Frederick William put his son in solitary confinement. Then he forced the 18-year-old prince to watch as the friend who had helped him was beheaded.

Frederick's harsh military training had an effect. After becoming king in 1740, Frederick II lost no time in using his army. As you have read, he boldly seized Silesia from Austria, sparking the War of the Austrian Succession. In several later wars, Frederick continued to brilliantly use his disciplined army, forcing all to recognize Prussia as a great power. His exploits earned him the name Frederick the Great.

 Checkpoint How did Frederick William increase his power?

The Rivalry of Great Powers

By 1750, the great European powers included Austria, Prussia, France, Britain, and Russia. These nations formed various alliances to maintain the balance of power. Though nations sometimes switched partners, two basic rivalries persisted. Prussia battled Austria for control of the German states, while Britain and France competed to develop their overseas empires.

On occasion, these rivalries resulted in worldwide conflict. The Seven Years' War, which lasted from 1756 until 1763, was fought on four continents. Prussia, Austria, Russia, France, and Britain battled in Europe. Britain and France also fought in India and Africa. In North America, where the conflict is known as the French and Indian War, Native American groups took sides with the French or the British. The Treaty of Paris ending these wars gave Britain a huge empire, thus changing Europe's balance of power for the next hundred years.

 Checkpoint What were the two main rivalries after 1750?

Petitioning a King
Frederick the Great, strolling in his gardens, receives a petition from a common person. *What characteristics of Frederick does the artist hint at in the painting?*

SECTION 4 Assessment

Progress Monitoring *Online*
For: Self-quiz with vocabulary practice
Web Code: naa-1641

Terms, People, and Places

1. For each term, person, or place listed at the beginning of the section, write a sentence explaining its significance.

Note Taking

2. **Reading Skill: Identify Supporting Details** Use your completed table to answer the Focus Question: How did the two great empires of Austria and Prussia emerge from the Thirty Years' War and subsequent events?

Comprehension and Critical Thinking

3. **Recognize Cause and Effect** What impact did the Thirty Years' War have on the German states?

4. **Compare** What two major powers emerged in Europe at the end of the Thirty Years' War? How were the goals of these two nations similar?

5. **Make Generalizations** How did European nations maintain a balance of power?

● **Writing About History**

Quick Write: Write a Thesis Statement Select a topic from the section that you might use as the subject of a persuasive essay—for example, whether Austria or Prussia was more successful at developing a strong nation-state. Then write a thesis statement that summarizes your opinion on this topic.

The palace (left) of Catherine the Great (far left) reflects both European and traditional Russian architectural styles.

WITNESS HISTORY 🔊 AUDIO

A Foreign Princess Takes the Throne

For twenty years, the German princess Catherine lived at the Russian court, enduring an unhappy marriage to the Russian heir apparent, who was widely considered to be insane. She filled her time reading, studying French philosophy, building alliances behind the scenes, and biding her time. When her husband became emperor in 1762, she called on her allies to act. Within a few months he had been deposed and Catherine proclaimed empress of Russia. Like Peter the Great before her, Catherine would rule with intelligence, a firm hand, and a mind set on modernization.

Focus Question How did Peter the Great and Catherine the Great strengthen Russia and expand its territory?

Absolute Monarchy in Russia

Objectives

- Explain how Peter the Great tried to make Russia into a modern state.
- Identify the steps Peter took to expand Russia's borders.
- Describe how Catherine the Great strengthened Russia.

Terms, People, and Places

Peter the Great	warm-water port
westernization	St. Petersburg
autocratic	Catherine the Great
boyar	partition

Note Taking

Reading Skill: Identify Main Ideas As you read this section, make a Venn diagram like the one below to compare events in the reigns of Peter the Great and Catherine the Great.

Peter
- Visited European countries
-

Adopted Western ideas

Catherine
- Established port on Black Sea
-

In the early 1600s, Russia was still a medieval state, untouched by the Renaissance or Reformation and largely isolated from Western Europe. As you have read, the "Time of Troubles" had plunged the country into a period of disorder and foreign invasions. The reign of the first Romanov tsar in 1613 restored a measure of order. Not until the end of the century, however, did a tsar emerge who was strong enough to regain the absolute power of earlier tsars. Peter the Great, as he came to be called, used his power to put Russia on the road to becoming a great modern power.

Peter the Great Modernizes Russia

Peter, just 10 years old when he took the throne in 1682, did not take control of the government until 1689. Although he was not well educated, the young tsar was immensely curious. He spent hours in the "German quarter," the Moscow neighborhood where many Dutch, Scottish, English, and other foreign artisans and soldiers lived. There, he heard of the new technology that was helping Western European monarchs forge powerful empires.

Journey to the West In 1697, Peter set out to learn about Western ways for himself. He spent hours walking the streets of European cities, noting the manners and homes of the people. He visited factories and art galleries, learned anatomy from a doctor, and even had a dentist teach him how to pull teeth. In England, Peter was impressed by Parliament. "It is good," he said, "to hear subjects speaking truthfully and openly to their king."

Peter brought to Russia a group of technical experts, teachers, and soldiers he had recruited in Europe. He then embarked on a policy of **westernization,** that is, the adoption of Western ideas, technology, and culture. But persuading fellow Russians to change their way of life proved difficult. To impose his will, Peter became the most **autocratic** of Europe's absolute monarchs, meaning that he ruled with unlimited authority.

Controlling the Church and the Nobles Peter pursued several related goals. He wanted to strengthen the military, expand Russian borders, and centralize royal power. To achieve his ends, he brought all Russian institutions under his control, including the Russian Orthodox Church. He also forced the haughty **boyars,** or landowning nobles, to serve the state in civilian or military positions.

Some changes had a symbolic meaning. For example, after returning from the West, Peter <u>stipulated</u> that boyars shave their beards. He also forced them to replace their old-fashioned robes with Western-style clothes. To end the practice of secluding upper-class women in separate quarters, he held grand parties at which women and men were expected to dance together. Russian nobles opposed this radical mixing of the sexes in public, but they had to comply.

Peter knew that nobles would serve the state only if their own interests were protected. Therefore, he passed laws ensuring that nobles retained control over their lands, including the serfs on those lands. In doing so, Peter strengthened serfdom. Under his rule serfdom spread in Russia, long after it had died out in Western Europe. Further, he forced some serfs to become soldiers or to work as laborers on roads, canals, and other government projects.

Modernizing With Force Using autocratic methods, Peter pushed through social and economic reforms. He imported Western technology, improved education, simplified the Russian alphabet, and set up academies for the study of mathematics, science, and engineering. To pay for his sweeping reforms, Peter adopted mercantilist policies, such as encouraging exports. He improved waterways and canals, developed mining and textile manufacturing, and backed new trading companies.

Peter had no mercy for any who resisted the new order. When elite palace guards revolted, he had more than 1,000 of the rebels tortured and executed. Then, as an example of his power, he left their rotting corpses outside the palace walls for months.

✔ **Checkpoint** What rewards and punishments did Peter use to solidify his control over the nobles?

Peter Expands Russia's Borders

From his earliest days as tsar, Peter worked to build Russia's military power. He created the largest standing army in Europe, built a world-class navy from scratch, and set out to extend Russian borders to the west and south.

Seeking a Warm-Water Port Russian seaports, located along the Arctic Ocean, were frozen over during the winter. To increase Russia's ability to trade with the West, Peter desperately wanted a **warm-water port**—one that would be free of ice all year round.

Vocabulary Builder

<u>stipulated</u>—(STIP yuh layt ed) *v.* made a specific demand

A Russian cartoon shows Peter the Great personally cutting off the beard of a boyar.

The nearest warm-water coast was located along the Black Sea. To gain control of this territory, Peter had to push through the powerful Ottoman Empire. In the end, Peter was unable to defeat the Ottomans and gain his warm-water port, but the later Russian monarch Catherine the Great would achieve that goal before the century ended.

The Great Northern War In 1700, Peter began a long war against the kingdom of Sweden, which at the time, dominated the Baltic region. Early on, Russia suffered humiliating defeats. A Swedish force of only 8,000 men

● **INFOGRAPHIC**

Peter the Great and His Navy

As a sixteen-year-old boy, Peter found the hull of an old European sailing vessel in a storehouse. He restored the boat and taught himself to sail it on the lakes and rivers near Moscow. The find sparked a lifelong love for all things having to do with sailing. As tsar, Peter traveled to Europe to learn everything he could about shipbuilding. Armed with this knowledge, he created a European-style navy, thus turning Russia into a leading world power. In later years, Peter named the boat he had restored "the grandfather of the Russian navy." On his fifty-first birthday he sailed it into St. Petersburg harbor to meet its "grandchildren," Peter's navy.

A woodcut dating from the 1800s shows Peter, disguised as a ship's carpenter, learning from Dutch shipbuilders in the late 1600s. Peter's own carpentry tool and drawing are shown at bottom.

◀ A modern painter shows Peter as a common shipbuilder in the Netherlands.

A Russian artist who was a contemporary of Peter's shows St. Petersburg's harbor, filled with the ships that Peter had built. ▼

Russia's Navy Grows

(Line graph: "Number of vessels" on the y-axis marked 0, 400, 800, 1200; "Year" on the x-axis marked 1705, 1714, 1725, showing a rising curve.)

Thinking Critically

1. **Draw Inferences** Peter's motto was "I am a student and I seek teachers." How do you think this motto relates to his practice of passing himself off as a common man while studying in Europe?
2. **Make Comparisons** How did the absolute monarchies of Peter the Great and Louis XIV differ in terms of each monarch's dealings with common people?

defeated a Russian army five times its size. Undaunted, Peter rebuilt his army, modeling it after European armies. Finally, in 1709, he defeated the Swedes and won territory along the Baltic Sea.

Building St. Petersburg On this land won from Sweden, Peter built a magnificent new capital city, St. Petersburg. Seeking to open a "window on the West," he located the city on the Baltic coast along the swampy shores of the Neva River. He forced tens of thousands of serfs to drain the swamps. Many thousands died, but Peter's plan for the city succeeded. He then invited Italian architects and artisans to design great palaces in Western style. Peter even planned the city's parks and boulevards himself. Just as Versailles became a monument to French absolutism, St. Petersburg became a great symbol of Peter's effort to forge a modern Russia.

Blazing Trails to the Pacific Russian traders and raiders also crossed the plains and rivers of Siberia, forging new trails westward. Under Peter, Russia signed a treaty with Qing China that defined their common border in the east. The treaty recognized Russia's right to lands north of Manchuria.

In the early 1700s, Peter hired the Danish navigator Vitus Bering to explore what became known as the Bering Strait between Siberia and Alaska (see map on the next page). After Peter's death, Russian traders built outposts in Alaska and northern California. Few Russians moved east of the Ural Mountains at this time, but the expansion made Russia the largest country in the world. It still is today, nearly 300 years later.

Peter the Great's Legacy When Peter died in 1725, he left a mixed legacy. He had expanded Russian territory, gained ports on the Baltic Sea, and created a mighty army. He had also ended Russia's long period of isolation. From the 1700s on, Russia would be increasingly involved in the affairs of Western Europe. Yet many of Peter's ambitious reforms died with him. Nobles, for example, soon ignored his policy of service to the state.

Like earlier tsars, Peter the Great had used terror to enforce his absolute power. His policies contributed to the growth of serfdom, which served only to widen the gap between Russia and the West that Peter had sought to narrow.

✔ **Checkpoint** What impact did Peter's defeat of Sweden have on Russia's expansion?

Catherine the Great Follows Peter's Lead

Peter died without an heir and without naming a successor. This set off a power struggle within the Romanov family, from whom all the tsars had come since the early 1600s. Under a series of ineffective rulers, Russian nobles reasserted their independence. Then, a new monarch took the reins of power firmly in hand. She became known to history as Catherine the Great.

WITNESS HISTORY VIDEO

Watch *Peter the Great* on the **Witness History Discovery School**™ video program to learn more about this larger-than-life tsar.

Discovery SCHOOL

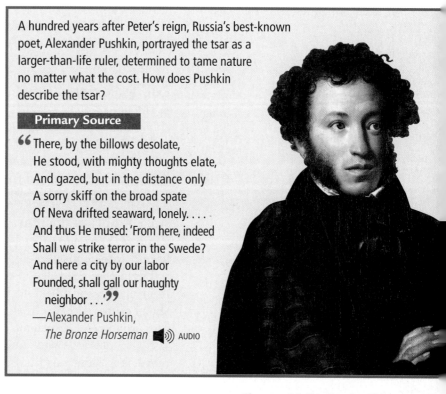

A hundred years after Peter's reign, Russia's best-known poet, Alexander Pushkin, portrayed the tsar as a larger-than-life ruler, determined to tame nature no matter what the cost. How does Pushkin describe the tsar?

Primary Source

❝ There, by the billows desolate,
He stood, with mighty thoughts elate,
And gazed, but in the distance only
A sorry skiff on the broad spate
Of Neva drifted seaward, lonely. . . .
And thus He mused: 'From here, indeed
Shall we strike terror in the Swede?
And here a city by our labor
Founded, shall gall our haughty
neighbor . . .' ❞
—Alexander Pushkin,
The Bronze Horseman 🔊)) AUDIO

Expansion of Russia, 1689–1796

Geography *Interactive*
For: Interactive Russia map
Web Code: nap-1651

Map Legend:
- Russia, 1689
- Land added by Peter the Great by 1725
- Land added by Catherine the Great by 1796
- Austria, 1796
- Prussia, 1796
- Trade routes
- Bering's exploration route, 1725–1729

Conic Projection

0   500   1000 mi
0   500   1000 km

Map Skills During the 1600s and 1700s, Russia expanded its power and influence both eastward and westward to become the largest nation in the world.

1. **Locate** (a) Sweden (b) Baltic Sea (c) St. Petersburg (d) Black Sea (e) Siberia (f) Bering Sea
2. **Place** Why were ports on the Black Sea more appealing to Russia than those on the Baltic?
3. **Predict Consequences** How might this map look different if Peter the Great had not developed a modern navy?

Rise to Power A German princess by birth, Catherine came to Russia at the age of 15 to wed the heir to the Russian throne. She learned Russian, embraced the Russian Orthodox faith, and won the loyalty of the people. In 1762, a group of Russian army officers loyal to her deposed and murdered her mentally unstable husband, Tsar Peter III. Whether or not Catherine was involved in the assassination is uncertain. In any case, with the support of the military, she ascended the Russian throne.

An Enlightened Ruler Catherine proved to be an efficient, energetic empress. She reorganized the provincial government, codified laws, and began state-sponsored education for both boys and girls.

Like Peter the Great, Catherine embraced Western ideas and worked to bring Russia fully into European cultural and political life. At court, she encouraged French language and customs, wrote histories and plays, and organized performances. As you will read in the next chapter, she was also a serious student of the French thinkers who led the intellectual movement known as the Enlightenment.

A Ruthless Absolute Monarch Catherine was also an absolute monarch, like other European rulers of the time, and often she was among the most ruthless. She granted a charter to the boyars outlining important rights, such as exemption from taxes. She also allowed them to increase their stranglehold on the peasants. When peasants rebelled against the harsh burdens of serfdom, Catherine took firm action to repress them. As a result, conditions grew worse for Russian peasants. Under Catherine, even more peasants were forced into serfdom.

Like Peter the Great, Catherine was determined to expand Russia's borders. Waging the Russo-Turkish war against the Ottoman Empire gained her a warm-water port on the Black Sea in 1774. She also took steps to seize territory from neighboring Poland.

The Partitions of Poland In the 1770s, Catherine, King Frederick II of Prussia, and Emperor Joseph II of Austria hungrily eyed Poland. As you have read, the Polish-Lithuanian Commonwealth had once been a great European power. However, its rulers were unable to centralize their power or diminish the influence of the Polish nobility. The divided Polish government was ill-prepared to stand up to the increasing might of its neighbors, Russia, Prussia, and Austria.

To avoid fighting one another, the three monarchs agreed in 1772 to partition, or divide up, Poland. Catherine took part of eastern Poland, where many Russians and Ukrainians lived. Frederick and Joseph took control of Polish territory in the west. Poland was further partitioned in 1793. Then in 1795, Austria, Prussia, and Russia each took their final slices and the independent country of Poland vanished from the map. Not until 1919 would a free Polish state reappear.

 Checkpoint How were Catherine's goals similar to those of Peter?

Looking Ahead

By the mid-1700s, absolute monarchs ruled four of the five leading countries in Europe. Britain, with its strong Parliament, was the only exception. As these five nations competed with one another, they often ended up fighting to maintain a balance of power. At the same time, new ideas were in the air. Radical changes would soon shatter the French monarchy, upset the balance of power, and revolutionize European societies.

SECTION 5 Assessment

Progress Monitoring Online
For: Self-quiz with vocabulary practice
Web Code: naa-1651

Terms, People, and Places

1. For each term, person, or place listed in the beginning of the section, write a sentence explaining its significance.

Note Taking

2. **Reading Skill: Identify Main Ideas** Use your completed Venn diagram to answer the Focus Question: How did Peter the Great and Catherine the Great strengthen Russia and expand its territory?

Comprehension and Critical Thinking

3. **Identify Central Issues** What were three goals of Peter the Great and what was one step that he undertook to achieve each goal?

4. **Analyze Information** Why was obtaining a warm-water port a major priority for Peter?

5. **Compare Points of View** How did Peter and Catherine envision Russia's future?

● **Writing About History**

Quick Write: Write the Text Body Choose a topic from the section on which you might write a persuasive essay—for example: Was Peter the Great really "great"? Write the body of your text, using a list of points you have made to guide you. Remember to open and close the body of the text with particularly strong arguments.

Quick Study Guide

Progress Monitoring *Online*
For: Self-test with vocabulary practice
Web Code: naa-1652

■ Key Rulers

Spain: Charles V (Charles I of Spain); Philip II
France: Henry IV; Louis XIV
Britain: Henry VIII; Elizabeth I; James I; Charles I; Oliver
Cromwell; Charles II; James II; William and Mary
Austria: Ferdinand; Charles VI; Maria Theresa
Prussia: Frederick William; Frederick the Great
Russia: Peter the Great; Catherine the Great

■ Key Events

- **Battle of Lepanto, 1571**—Spain and allies against
Ottoman Empire
- **Netherlands rebellions, 1560s–1580s**—political and
religious revolts against Spain
- **Spanish Armada attacks England, 1588**
- **St. Bartholomew's Day Massacre, 1572**—slaughter
of French Huguenots
- **Thirty Years' War, 1618–1648**
- **English Civil War, 1642–1648**
- **The *Fronde*, 1648–1653**—uprising of various groups
in France
- **Glorious Revolution, 1688**—bloodless change of
monarchs in England
- **War of the Spanish Succession, 1700–1713**
- **Great Northern War, 1700–1721**—Russia and allies
against Sweden
- **War of the Austrian Succession, 1740–1748**
- **Seven Years' War, 1756–1763**
- **Russo-Turkish War, 1768–1774**—Russia against the
Ottoman Empire
- **Partitions of Poland, 1772, 1793, 1795**

■ Partitions of Poland, 1701–1795

■ Key Events in the Age of Absolutism

Chapter Events Global Events	**1550**	**1600**	**1650**

1556
Philip II
becomes king
of Spain.

1618
The Thirty
Years' War
begins.

1642
The English
Civil War
begins.

1556
Akbar the Great
becomes emperor
of Mughal India.

1607
British
colonists found
Jamestown.

Concept | Connector

■ Cumulative Review

Record the answers to the questions below in your Concept Connector worksheets.

1. **Revolution** In England, the Glorious Revolution of 1688 was celebrated as a bloodless transfer of power—ordained by the people embodied by the Parliament—from one ruler to another. This was a radical event for its time, because the transfer of power had never been accomplished by Parliament in this way before, nor with so little violence. Read about how power was transferred from one English ruler to another between 1377 and 1688 and create an annotated timeline of these events. Think about the following:
   * the cause of each transfer of power
   * the fate of each ruler
   * the level of conflict related to each transfer of power

2. **Political Systems** Compare the absolute monarchy in France under Louis XIV to imperial rule in ancient Rome. How were these two systems similar, and how were they different? Create a chart to compare and contrast the two systems in the following categories. Consider the following aspects:
   * theoretical basis
   * ruler's level of power
   * symbols
   * status of democratic institutions

3. **Democracy** The Magna Carta of 1215 was a landmark legal development because it limited the power of the English monarch and protected some civil rights. Read about the rights and protections it granted as well as the limits it established on the monarchy. Compare these with the rights and protections ensured by the English Bill of Rights of 1688. Write one or two paragraphs that summarize how the later document increased democracy in England from what it was under Magna Carta and further limited the powers of the monarchy.

■ Connections to Today

1. **Conflict** The Age of Absolutism was also an "age of religious conflicts." Many of these conflicts, primarily between Catholics and Protestants, were long lasting and extremely violent. Several caused major wars. Find and read a newspaper or Internet article about a country or region where religious conflict is still a concern today—for example, Bosnia, India, Iraq, Israel, or Northern Ireland. Write a two- or three-paragraph summary of what you learn.

2. **Democracy** The English Bill of Rights is one of the source documents for ideas included in the American Declaration of Independence and the United States Constitution. Review the excerpt from the English Bill of Rights on page 524. Write a three-paragraph essay that summarizes how aspects of the English Bill of Rights are still present in American ideas of democracy today.

| 1697 Peter the Great of Russia tours Europe. | 1707 The Act of Union unites England and Scotland. | 1715 King Louis XIV of France dies. | | 1795 Russia, Prussia, and Austria divide up Poland. |

1700   **1750**   **1800**

History Interactive
For: Interactive timeline
Web Code: nap-1652

| 1680s The Asante kingdom is organized in West Africa. | 1736 Qianlong begins reign as emperor of China. | 1754 The French and Indian War erupts in North America. | 1793 The emperor of China rejects British trade. |

Chapter Assessment

Terms, People, and Places

Complete each sentence by choosing the correct answer from the list of terms below. You will not use all the terms.

absolute monarch	constitutional monarchy
divine right	limited monarchy
balance of power	oligarchy
westernization	partition
habeas corpus	

1. After the Glorious Revolution, several new institutions marked the transition of England's government to a _____.
2. The theory of _____ states that monarchs rule by the will of God.
3. The English Bill of Rights sets out the principle of _____.
4. Peter the Great pursued a policy of _____ to make Russia more modern.
5. The _____ of Poland occurred in the 1700s when the rulers of Austria, Russia, and Prussia agreed to split that country among themselves.
6. In this period, nearly every major European nation was ruled by a(n) _____.

Main Ideas

Section 1 (pp. 504–509)
7. How did resources from the Spanish colonies in the Americas contribute to the decline of Spain?
8. What was the Spanish Armada?

Section 2 (pp. 510–515)
9. What were two symbols of the reign of Louis XIV and what was their significance?

Section 3 (pp. 516–524)
10. (a) What were the immediate causes of the English Civil War? (b) What were some important results?
11. How did the Glorious Revolution limit royal power in England?

Section 4 (pp. 525–529)
12. What events led to the start of the Thirty Years' War?

Section 5 (pp. 530–535)
13. What reforms did Peter the Great carry out?
14. What was one long-term goal of the Russian monarchs and how was it finally achieved?

Chapter Focus Question
15. What events led to the rise of absolute monarchies and the development of centralized nation-states in Europe?

Critical Thinking

16. **Draw Conclusions** Based on the material in the chapter, how effective do you think the policy of maintaining a balance of power was among European nations?
17. **Analyze Information** Explain what Louis XIV meant when he said, "I am the state."
18. **Test Conclusions** Based on what you have learned about the Glorious Revolution, do you think the name for that event is accurate? Why or why not?
19. **Compare** Compare the goals and policies of Peter the Great with those of one of the following monarchs: (a) Louis XIV (b) Frederick II (c) Maria Theresa.
20. **Synthesize Information** What was the historical significance of the execution of Charles I of England?
21. **Understand Effects** What was the general impact of the Thirty Years' War on Europe?

● Writing About History

Writing a Persuasive Essay During the Age of Absolutism, strong monarchs created centralized nation-states whose governments they ruled with complete authority. Write a persuasive essay in which you argue a position on one aspect of this age. Consider topics such as: Was absolute monarchy an effective system? Was the divine right of kings a valid basis for rule? Consult page SH16 of the Writing Handbook for additional help.

Prewriting
• Choose a listed topic or another one that interests you, one that provokes an argument and has at least two sides. Then choose a side of the argument.
• Collect evidence, using a graphic organizer to list points on both sides of the issue.

• Research Internet or print sources to find materials that analyze your position from both sides. Take notes on relevant details, events, and people.

Drafting
• Clearly state the position that you will argue in a thesis statement. Use the rest of your introduction to provide readers necessary context about the issue.
• Make an outline to organize your argument and supporting details. Then choose information from your research that supports each part of your outline.

Revising
• Use the guidelines for revising your essay on page SH17 of the Writing Handbook.

Document-Based Assessment

The Rise of Parliament

The struggle between English monarchs and Parliament raged through the seventeenth century, and was fought on battlefields and legal fronts. The documents below illustrate the points of view of a monarch, Parliament, and a well-known philosopher.

Document A

"THE KINGS THEREAFTER in Scotland were before any estates or ranks of men within the same, before any Parliaments were holden or laws made; and by them was the land distributed (which at first was wholly theirs), states erected and decerned, and forms of government devised and established. And it follows of necessity that the Kings were the authors and makers of the laws and not the laws of the Kings."

—From *True Law of Free Monarchies,* 1598

Document B

"The Petition exhibited to his Majesty by the lords Spiritual and Temporal, and Commons, in this present Parliament assembled, concerning divers Rights and Liberties of the Subjects, with the King's Majesty's royal answer thereunto in full Parliament. . . . Your subjects have inherited this freedom, that they should not be compelled to contribute to any tax, tallage, aid, or other like charge not set by common consent, in parliament. . . . No man, of what estate or condition that he be, should be put out of his land or tenements, nor taken, nor imprisoned, nor disinherited nor put to death without being brought to answer by due process of law."

—From *The Petition of Right, 1628*

Document C

"Men, being, as has been said, by nature all free, equal, and independent, no one can be . . . subjected to the political power of another without his own consent. The only way whereby anyone divests himself of his natural liberty, and puts on the bonds of civil society is by agreeing with other men to join and unite into a community. . . .

It is evident, that *absolute monarchy,* which by some men is counted the only government in the world, is indeed *inconsistent with civil society.*"

—From *Two Treatises on Government* by John Locke, 1690.

Document D

A mid-1600s engraving depicts Charles I as a political and religious martyr.

Analyzing Documents

Use your knowledge of the age of absolutism and Documents A, B, C, and D to answer questions 1–4.

1. What is the main point of Document A?
   A Kings are subject only to laws of parliament.
   B Kings make laws but are not subject to them.
   C Kings no longer have the power of life and death over subjects.
   D Parliament now has the power of life and death over subjects.

2. Document B is a declaration of whose rights?
   A the king's rights
   B Parliament's rights
   C subjects' rights
   D the landed aristocracy's rights

3. Document C
   A supports Document A.
   B supports Document B.
   C supports both Document A and Document B.
   D supports Document A and Document D.

4. **Writing Task** Would you describe the rise of Parliament in England as an evolution or a revolution? Use documents from this page along with information from the chapter in your response.

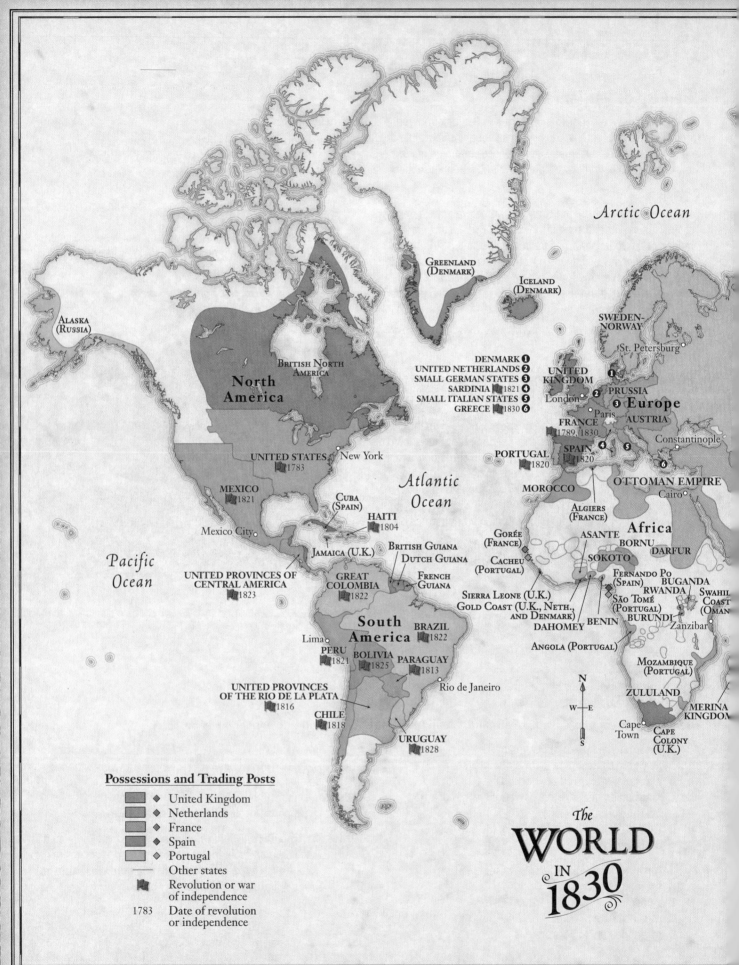

The WORLD IN 1830

Arctic Ocean

GREENLAND (DENMARK)

ICELAND (DENMARK)

ALASKA (RUSSIA)

BRITISH NORTH AMERICA

North America

SWEDEN-NORWAY

St. Petersburg

DENMARK ❶
UNITED NETHERLANDS ❷
SMALL GERMAN STATES ❸
SARDINIA 1821 ❹
SMALL ITALIAN STATES ❺
GREECE 1830 ❻

UNITED KINGDOM

London

PRUSSIA

❸ **Europe**

AUSTRIA

Paris

FRANCE 1789, 1830

Constantinople

UNITED STATES 1783

New York

Atlantic Ocean

PORTUGAL 1820

SPAIN 1820

OTTOMAN EMPIRE

Cairo

MEXICO 1821

MOROCCO

ALGIERS (FRANCE)

Africa

Mexico City

CUBA (Spain)

HAITI 1804

JAMAICA (U.K.)

BRITISH GUIANA
DUTCH GUIANA

FRENCH GUIANA

GORÉE (FRANCE)

CACHEU (PORTUGAL)

ASANTE

BORNU

DARFUR

SOKOTO

FERNANDO PO (SPAIN)

BUGANDA

RWANDA

SWAHIL COAST (OMAN)

Pacific Ocean

UNITED PROVINCES OF CENTRAL AMERICA 1823

GREAT COLOMBIA 1822

South America

SIERRA LEONE (U.K.)
GOLD COAST (U.K., NETH., AND DENMARK)

DAHOMEY

BENIN

São Tomé (PORTUGAL)

BURUNDI

Zanzibar

Lima

PERU 1821

BOLIVIA 1825

BRAZIL 1822

PARAGUAY 1813

ANGOLA (PORTUGAL)

MOZAMBIQUE (PORTUGAL)

UNITED PROVINCES OF THE RIO DE LA PLATA 1816

Rio de Janeiro

ZULULAND

CHILE 1818

URUGUAY 1828

N

W—E

S

Cape Town

CAPE COLONY (U.K.)

MERINA KINGDOM

Possessions and Trading Posts

◆ United Kingdom
◆ Netherlands
◆ France
◆ Spain
◆ Portugal

— Other states

Revolution or war of independence

1783 Date of revolution or independence

RUSSIAN EMPIRE

Asia

CENTRAL
ASIAN
STATES

PERSIA   SIKH
          KINGDOM   NEPAL
AFGHAN-   BHUTAN
ISTAN   Delhi

CHINA   Beijing   KOREA   JAPAN
                    (CHINA)   Edo (Tokyo)
                    DESHIMA (NETHERLANDS)

OMAN   INDIA   BURMA   MACAO (PORTUGAL)   Pacific
Bombay (U.K.)   Calcutta   Ocean
GOA   SOUTHEAST ASIAN STATES
(PORTUGAL) Bangkok SIAM
PONDICHERRY   MALAY   PHILIPPINES
(FRANCE)   STATES   (SPAIN)
CEYLON (U.K.)

TENASSERIM (U.K.)   SINGAPORE (U.K.)

Indian   DUTCH EAST INDIES
Ocean   Batavia

           PORTUGUESE TIMOR

MAURITIUS (U.K.)
RÉUNION (FRANCE)

           Australia

WESTERN AUSTRALIA   NEW SOUTH WALES
(U.K.)   (U.K.)
                            Sydney

     TASMANIA (U.K.)

MERCATOR PROJECTION
SCALE IN MILES
0   1000   2000   3000

0   1000   2000   3000
SCALE IN KILOMETERS
SCALE AT THE EQUATOR

Geography *Interactive*
For: Audio guided tour
Web Code: nap-4000

17

The Enlightenment and the American Revolution

1700–1800

Pens to Inspire Revolution

Enlightenment thinker Denis Diderot compiled a controversial 28-volume work called the *Encyclopedia,* which was published between 1751 and 1772. This work was a forum for Enlightenment thinkers such as Montesquieu, Rousseau, and Voltaire. These thinkers believed that with the power of reason, they could fix the problems of society. Although the *Encyclopedia* was banned in many places and censored in others, it would prove to be a major factor in the years of revolutions to come. It contains the passage below on freedom. Listen to the Witness History audio to hear more about this work.

66No man has received from nature the right to give orders to others. Freedom is a gift from heaven, and every individual of the same species has the right to enjoy it as soon as he is in enjoyment of his reason.99
—Denis Diderot

Denis Diderot bust

Rococo fan

◀ Madame Geoffrin (far right in blue), in her famous salon where Enlightenment thinkers gathered to share ideas.

Chapter Preview

Chapter Focus Question How did Enlightenment thinkers inspire revolutionaries to push for radical changes in government and society?

British tax stamp used in the American colonies

Section 1
Philosophy in the Age of Reason

Section 2
Enlightenment Ideas Spread

Section 3
Birth of the American Republic

Note Taking Study Guide *Online*
For: Note Taking and Concept Connector worksheets
Web Code: nad-1701

Jean-Jacques Rousseau
and quill pen

Rousseau Stirs Things Up

In Jean-Jacques Rousseau's most important work, *The Social Contract,* he argued that in order to be free, people should do what is best for their community. Rousseau had many supporters who were inspired by his passionate writings. European monarchs, on the other hand, were angry that Rousseau was questioning authority. As a result, Rousseau worried about persecution for much of his life. The "chains" below represent the social institutions that confined society.

❝ Man is born free, and everywhere he is in chains. ❞
—Rousseau, *The Social Contract*

Focus Question What effects did Enlightenment philosophers have on government and society?

Philosophy in the Age of Reason

Objectives

- Explain how science led to the Enlightenment.
- Compare the ideas of Hobbes and Locke.
- Identify the beliefs and contributions of the *philosophes.*
- Summarize how economic thinking changed during this time.

Terms, People, and Places

natural law	Montesquieu
Thomas Hobbes	Voltaire
John Locke	Diderot
social contract	Rousseau
natural right	laissez faire
philosophe	Adam Smith

Note Taking

Reading Skill: Summarize Draw a table like the one shown here. As you read the section, summarize each thinker's works and ideas.

Thinkers' Works and Ideas	
Hobbes	*Leviathan,* social contract
Locke	
Montesquieu	

By the early 1700s, European thinkers felt that nothing was beyond the reach of the human mind. Through the use of reason, insisted these thinkers, people and governments could solve every social, political, and economic problem. In essence, these writers, scholars, and philosophers felt they could change the world.

Scientific Revolution Sparks the Enlightenment

The Scientific Revolution of the 1500s and 1600s had transformed the way people in Europe looked at the world. In the 1700s, other scientists expanded European knowledge. For example, Edward Jenner developed a vaccine against smallpox, a disease whose path of death spanned the centuries.

Scientific successes convinced educated Europeans of the power of human reason. **Natural law,** or rules discoverable by reason, govern scientific forces such as gravity and magnetism. Why not, then, use natural law to better understand social, economic, and political problems? Using the methods of the new science, reformers thus set out to study human behavior and solve the problems of society. In this way, the Scientific Revolution led to another revolution in thinking, known as the Enlightenment. Immanuel Kant, a German philosopher best known for his work *The Critique of Pure Reason,* was one of the first to describe this era with the word "Enlightenment." Despite Kant's skepticism about the power of reason, he was enthusiastic about the Enlightenment and believed, like many European philosophers, that natural law could help explain aspects of humanity.

✓ **Checkpoint** What convinced educated Europeans to accept the power of reason?

Hobbes and Locke Have Conflicting Views

Thomas Hobbes and John Locke, two seventeenth-century English thinkers, set forth ideas that were to become key to the Enlightenment. Both men lived through the upheavals of the English Civil War. Yet they came to very different conclusions about human nature and the role of government.

Hobbes Believes in Powerful Government
Thomas Hobbes outlined his ideas in a work titled *Leviathan*. In it, he argued that people were naturally cruel, greedy, and selfish. If not strictly controlled, they would fight, rob, and oppress one another. Life in the "state of nature"—without laws or other control—would be "solitary, poor, nasty, brutish, and short."

To escape that "brutish" life, said Hobbes, people entered into a social contract, an agreement by which they gave up their freedom for an organized society. Hobbes believed that only a powerful government could ensure an orderly society. For him, such a government was an absolute monarchy, which could impose order and compel obedience.

Locke Advocates Natural Rights
John Locke had a more optimistic view of human nature. He thought people were basically reasonable and moral. Further, they had certain natural rights, or rights that belonged to all humans from birth. These included the right to life, liberty, and property.

In *Two Treatises of Government,* Locke argued that people formed governments to protect their natural rights. The best kind of government, he said, had limited power and was accepted by all citizens. Thus, unlike Hobbes, Locke rejected absolute monarchy. England during this time experienced a shift in political power known as the Glorious Revolution. James II, an unpopular absolute monarch, left the throne and fled England in 1688. Locke later wrote that he thought James II deserved to be dethroned for violating the rights of the English.

Locke proposed a radical idea about this time. A government, he said, has an obligation to the people it governs. If a government fails its obligations or violates people's natural rights, the people have the right to overthrow that government. Locke's idea would one day influence leaders of the American Revolution, such as Benjamin Franklin, Thomas Jefferson, and James Madison. Locke's idea of the right of revolution would also echo across Europe and Latin America in the centuries that followed.

✓ **Checkpoint** How did Hobbes and Locke differ in their views on the role of government?

Hobbes Writes the *Leviathan*
The title page from *Leviathan* (1651) by Hobbes demonstrates his belief in a powerful ruler. The monarch here represents the Leviathan who rises above all of society.

The *Philosophes*

In the 1700s, there was a flowering of Enlightenment thought. This was when a group of Enlightenment thinkers in France applied the methods of science to understand and improve society. They believed that the use of reason could lead to reforms of government, law, and society. These thinkers were called *philosophes* (fee loh ZOHFS), which means "philosophers." Their ideas soon spread beyond France and even beyond Europe.

Voltaire

François-Marie Arouet, known as Voltaire (1694–1778), was an impassioned poet, historian, essayist, and philosopher who wrote with cutting sarcasm and sharp wit. Voltaire was sent to the Bastille prison twice due to his criticism of French authorities and was eventually banned from Paris. When he was able to return to France, he wrote about political and religious freedom. Voltaire spent his life fighting enemies of freedom, such as ignorance, superstition, and intolerance. **What did Voltaire attack in his writings?**

Montesquieu

Born to wealth, Charles Louis de Secondat (1689–1755) inherited the title Baron de Montesquieu from his uncle. Like many other reformers, he did not let his privileged status keep him from becoming a voice for democracy. His first book titled *Persian Letters* ridiculed the French government and social classes. In his work published in 1748, *The Spirit of the Laws,* he advanced the idea of separation of powers—a foundation of modern democracy. **What did Montesquieu think was necessary to protect liberty?**

Montesquieu Advances the Idea of Separation of Powers An early and influential thinker was Baron de **Montesquieu** (MAHN tus kyoo). Montesquieu studied the governments of Europe, from Italy to England. He read about ancient and medieval Europe, and learned about Chinese and Native American cultures. His sharp criticism of absolute monarchy would open doors for later debate.

In 1748, Montesquieu published *The Spirit of the Laws*, in which he discussed governments throughout history. Montesquieu felt that the best way to protect liberty was to divide the various functions and powers of government among three branches: the legislative, executive, and judicial. He also felt that each branch of government should be able to serve as a check on the other two, an idea that we call checks and balances. Montesquieu's beliefs would soon profoundly affect the Framers of the United States Constitution.

Voltaire Defends Freedom of Thought Probably the most famous of the *philosophes* was François-Marie Arouet, who took the name **Voltaire.** "My trade," said Voltaire, "is to say what I think," and he did so throughout his long, controversial life. Voltaire used biting wit as a weapon to expose the abuses of his day. He targeted corrupt officials and idle aristocrats. With his pen, he battled inequality, injustice, and superstition. He detested the slave trade and deplored religious prejudice.

Voltaire's outspoken attacks offended both the French government and the Catholic Church. He was imprisoned and forced into exile. Even as he saw his books outlawed and even burned, he continued to defend the principle of freedom of speech.

Diderot Edits the *Encyclopedia* Denis **Diderot** (DEE duh roh) worked for years to produce a 28-volume set of books called the *Encyclopedia*. As the editor, Diderot did more than just compile articles.

His purpose was "to change the general way of thinking" by explaining ideas on topics such as government, philosophy, and religion. Diderot's *Encyclopedia* included articles by leading thinkers of the day, including Montesquieu and Voltaire. In these articles, the *philosophes* denounced slavery, praised freedom of expression, and urged education for all. They attacked divine-right theory and traditional religions. Critics raised an outcry. The French government argued that the *Encyclopedia* was an attack on public morals, and the pope threatened to excommunicate Roman Catholics who bought or read the volumes.

Despite these and other efforts to ban the *Encyclopedia,* more than 4,000 copies were printed between 1751 and 1789. When translated into other languages, the *Encyclopedia* helped spread Enlightenment ideas throughout Europe and across the Atlantic Ocean to the Americas.

Rousseau Promotes *The Social Contract* Jean-Jacques Rousseau (roo SOH), believed that people in their natural state were basically good. This natural innocence, he felt, was corrupted by the evils of society, especially the unequal distribution of property. Many reformers and revolutionaries later adopted this view. Among them were Thomas Paine and Marquis de Lafayette, who were leading figures of the American and French Revolutions.

In 1762, Rousseau set forth his ideas about government and society in *The Social Contract.* Rousseau felt that society placed too many limitations on people's behavior. He believed that some controls were necessary, but that they should be minimal. Additionally, only governments that had been freely elected should impose these controls.

Rousseau put his faith in the "general will," or the best conscience of the people. The good of the community as a whole, he said, should be placed above individual interests. Rousseau has influenced political and social thinkers for more than 200 years. Woven through his work is a hatred of all forms of political and economic oppression. His bold ideas would help fan the flames of revolt in years to come.

Women Challenge the *Philosophes* The Enlightenment slogan "free and equal" did not apply to women. Though the *philosophes* said women had natural rights, their rights were limited to the areas of home and family.

By the mid- to late-1700s, a small but growing number of women protested this view. Germaine de Staël in France and Catharine Macaulay and Mary Wollstonecraft in Britain argued that women were being excluded from the social contract itself. Their arguments, however, were ridiculed and often sharply condemned.

Wollstonecraft was a well-known British social critic. She accepted that a woman's first duty was to be a good mother but felt that a woman should be able to decide what was in her own interest without depending on her husband. In 1792, Wollstonecraft published *A Vindication of the Rights of Woman.* In it, she called for equal education for girls and boys. Only education, she argued, could give women the tools they needed to participate equally with men in public life.

✔ **Checkpoint** What topics were addressed by the *philosophes* in their *Encyclopedia* articles?

Vocabulary Builder

philosophy—(fih LAHS uh fee) *n.* love of, or the search for, wisdom or knowledge

Heated Debate
Rousseau (left) and Voltaire (right) are pictured here in the midst of an argument. Even though the *philosophes* were reform-minded, they disagreed about some issues. *Compare the beliefs of Rousseau and Voltaire.*

New Economic Thinking

French thinkers known as physiocrats focused on economic reforms. Like the *philosophes,* physiocrats based their thinking on natural laws. The physiocrats claimed that their rational economic system was based on the natural laws of economics.

Laissez Faire Replaces Mercantilism Physiocrats rejected mercantilism, which required government regulation of the economy to achieve a favorable balance of trade. Instead, they urged a policy of **laissez faire** (les ay FEHR), allowing business to operate with little or no government interference. Physiocrats also supported free trade and opposed tariffs.

Smith Argues for a Free Market Scottish economist **Adam Smith** greatly admired the physiocrats. In his influential work *The Wealth of Nations,* he argued that the free market should be allowed to regulate business activity. Smith tried to show how manufacturing, trade, wages, profits, and economic growth were all linked to the market forces of supply and demand. Wherever there was a demand for goods or services, he said, suppliers would seek to meet that demand in order to gain profits. Smith was a strong supporter of laissez faire. However, he felt that government had a duty to protect society, administer justice, and provide public works. Adam Smith's ideas would help to shape productive economies in the 1800s and 1900s.

✓ **Checkpoint** Why did Smith support laissez faire?

Investors in Paris, France, 1720

SECTION 1
Assessment

Progress Monitoring *Online*
For: Self-quiz with vocabulary practice
Web Code: naa-1711

Terms, People, and Places

1. For each term, person, or place listed at the beginning of the section, write a sentence explaining its significance.

Note Taking

2. **Reading Skill: Summarize** Use your completed tables to answer the Focus Question: What effects did Enlightenment philosophers have on government and society?

Comprehension and Critical Thinking

3. **Summarize** How did the achievements of the Scientific Revolution contribute to the Enlightenment?

4. **Recognize Cause and Effect** What did the *philosophes* do to better understand and improve society?

5. **Synthesize Information** Explain the connection between the policy of laissez faire and natural economic laws.

● Writing About History

Quick Write: Explore a Topic On some essay tests, you may have a choice of topic. You should choose one that you feel most knowledgeable about. Choose from the following, and draft a single sentence that identifies the main idea:
(a) social contracts (b) freedom of speech (c) women in the mid-1700s

John Locke:
Two Treatises of Government

English philosopher John Locke (1632–1704) published *Two Treatises of Government* in 1690. Locke believed that all people had the same natural rights of life, liberty, and property. In this essay, Locke states that the primary purpose of government is to protect these natural rights. He also states that governments hold their power only with the consent of the people. Locke's ideas greatly influenced revolutions in America and France.

John Locke and a book of his writings

But though men, when they enter into society give up the equality, liberty, and executive power they had in the state of Nature into the hands of society . . . the power of the society or legislative constituted by them can never be supposed to extend farther than the common good. . . . Whoever has the legislative or supreme power of any commonwealth, is bound to govern by established standing laws, promulgated[1] and known to the people, and not by extemporary[2] decrees, by indifferent and upright judges, who are to decide controversies by those laws; and to employ the force of the community at home only in the execution of such laws, or abroad to prevent or redress foreign injuries and secure the community from inroads[3] and invasion. And all this to be directed to no other end but the peace, safety, and public good of the people. . . .

The reason why men enter into society is the preservation of their property; and the end while they choose and authorize a legislative is that there may be laws made, and rules set, as guards and fences to the properties of all the society, . . .

Whensoever, therefore, the legislative [power] shall transgress[4] this fundamental rule of society, and either by ambition, fear, folly, or corruption, endeavor to grasp themselves, or put into the hands of any other, an absolute power over the lives, liberties, and estates of the people, by this breach of trust they forfeit the power the people had put into their hands for quite contrary ends, and it devolves[5] to the people; who have a right to resume their original liberty, and by the establishment of a new legislative (such as they shall think fit), provide for their own safety and security. . . .

1. promulgated (PRAHM ul gayt id) *vt.* published or made known.

2. extemporary (ek STEM puh rehr ee) *adj.* without any preparation.

3. inroads (IN rohdz) *n.* advances at the expense of someone.

4. transgress (trans GRES) *vt.* go beyond; break.

5. devolves (dih VAHLVZ) *vt.* passes.

Thinking Critically

1. **Draw Inferences** According to Locke, how should a land be governed? Why do you think this is the case?

2. **Identify Central Issues** What does Locke say can happen if a government fails to protect the rights of its people?

Mozart and a sheet of his music

WITNESS HISTORY 🔊 AUDIO

Mozart, the Musical Genius

As a young boy, Wolfgang Amadeus Mozart astonished royalty with his musical talent. Although his life was relatively short, he composed more than 600 pieces of music. Many pieces embraced the spirit of the Enlightenment.

66 Few have captured the spirit of the Enlightenment, its intellectual and social agenda, as has Mozart in his opera, *The Magic Flute,* . . . [It] is a series of variations on the triumph of light over darkness, of sun over moon, of day over night, of reason, tolerance, and love over passion, hate, and revenge. 99
—Isaac Kramnick, historian

Focus Question As Enlightenment ideas spread across Europe, what cultural and political changes took place?

Enlightenment Ideas Spread

Objectives

- Identify the roles that censorship and salons played in the spread of new ideas.
- Describe how the Enlightenment affected the arts and literature.
- Understand how *philosophes* influenced enlightened despots.
- Explain why Enlightenment ideas were slow to reach most Europeans.

Terms, People, and Places

censorship
salons
baroque
rococo

enlightened despot
Frederick the Great
Catherine the Great
Joseph II

Note Taking

Reading Skill: Categorize On a sheet of paper, draw a concept web to help you record information from this section.

Salons · Spread of Enlightenment Ideas

Paris, France, the heart of the Enlightenment, drew many intellectuals and others eager to debate new ideas. Reforms proposed one evening became the talk of the town the next day. Enlightenment ideas flowed from France, across Europe, and beyond. Everywhere, thinkers examined traditional beliefs and customs in the light of reason and found them flawed. Even some absolute monarchs experimented with Enlightenment ideas, although they drew back when changes threatened the established way of doing things.

New Ideas Challenge Society

Enlightenment ideas spread quickly through many levels of society. Educated people all over Europe eagerly read not only Diderot's *Encyclopedia* but also the small, inexpensive pamphlets that printers churned out on a broad range of issues. More and more, people saw that reform was necessary in order to achieve a just society.

During the Middle Ages, most Europeans had accepted without question a society based on divine-right rule, a strict class system, and a belief in heavenly reward for earthly suffering. In the Age of Reason, such ideas seemed unscientific and irrational. A just society, Enlightenment thinkers taught, should ensure social justice and happiness in this world. Not everyone agreed with this idea of replacing the values that existed, however.

Writers Face Censorship Most, but not all, government and church authorities felt they had a sacred duty to defend the old order. They believed that God had set up the old order. To protect against the attacks of the Enlightenment, they waged a war of **censorship,** or restricting access to ideas and information. They banned and burned books and imprisoned writers.

To avoid censorship, *philosophes* and writers like Montesquieu and Voltaire sometimes disguised their ideas in works of fiction. In the *Persian Letters,* Montesquieu used two fictional Persian travelers, named Usbek and Rica, to mock French society. The hero of Voltaire's satirical novel *Candide,* published in 1759, travels across Europe and even to the Americas and the Middle East in search of "the best of all possible worlds." Voltaire slyly uses the tale to expose the corruption and hypocrisy of European society.

Ideas Spread in Salons New literature, the arts, science, and philosophy were regular topics of discussion in **salons,** or informal social gatherings at which writers, artists, *philosophes,* and others exchanged ideas. The salon originated in the 1600s, when a group of noblewomen in Paris began inviting a few friends to their homes for poetry readings. By the 1700s, some middle-class women began holding salons. Here middle-class citizens could meet with the nobility on an equal footing to discuss and spread Enlightenment ideas.

Madame Geoffrin (zhoh FRAN) ran one of the most respected salons. In her home on the Rue St. Honoré (roo sant ahn ur AY), she brought together the brightest and most talented people of her day. The young musical genius Wolfgang Amadeus Mozart played for her guests, and Diderot was a regular at her weekly dinners for philosophers and poets.

✓ **Checkpoint** What did those opposed to Enlightenment ideas do to stop the spread of information?

Arts and Literature Reflect New Ideas

In the 1600s and 1700s, the arts <u>evolved</u> to meet changing tastes. As in earlier periods, artists and composers had to please their patrons, the men and women who commissioned works from them or gave them jobs.

From Grandeur to Charm In the age of Louis XIV, courtly art and architecture were either in the Greek and Roman tradition or in a grand, ornate style known as **baroque.** Baroque paintings were huge, colorful, and full of excitement. They glorified historic battles or the lives of saints. Such works matched the grandeur of European courts at that time.

Louis XV and his court led a much less formal lifestyle than Louis XIV. Architects and designers reflected this change by developing the **rococo** style. Rococo art moved away from religion and, unlike the heavy splendor of the baroque, was lighter, elegant, and charming. Rococo art in salons was believed to encourage the imagination. Furniture and tapestries featured delicate shells and flowers, and more pastel colors were used. Portrait painters showed noble subjects in charming rural settings, surrounded by happy servants and pets. Although this style was criticized by the *philosophes* for its superficiality, it had a vast audience in the upper class and with the growing middle class as well.

Satire by Swift
Jonathan Swift published the satirical *Gulliver's Travels* in 1726. Here, an illustration from the book depicts a bound Gulliver and the Lilliputians, who are six-inch-tall, bloodthirsty characters. Although *Gulliver's Travels* satirizes political life in eighteenth-century England, it is still a classic today. *Why did writers hide their feelings about society?*

Vocabulary Builder
evolved—(ee VAHLVD) *v.* developed gradually over time

The Enlightenment Inspires Composers The new Enlightenment ideals led composers and musicians to develop new forms of music. There was a transition in music, as well as art, from the baroque style to rococo. An elegant style of music known as "classical" followed. Ballets and opera—plays set to music—were performed at royal courts, and opera houses sprang up from Italy to England. Before this era, only the social elite could afford to commission musicians to play for them. In the early to mid-1700s, however, the growing middle class could afford to pay for concerts to be performed publicly.

Among the towering musical figures of the era was Johann Sebastian Bach. A devout German Lutheran, Bach wrote beautiful religious works for organ and choirs. He also wrote sonatas for violin and harpsichord. Another German-born composer, George Frideric Handel, spent much of his life in England. There, he wrote *Water Music* and other pieces for King George I, as well as more than 30 operas. His most celebrated work, the *Messiah,* combines instruments and voices and is often performed at Christmas and Easter.

Composer Franz Joseph Haydn was one of the most important figures in the development of classical music. He helped develop forms for the string quartet and the symphony. Haydn had a close friendship with another famous composer, Wolfgang Amadeus Mozart. Mozart was a child prodigy who gained instant celebrity status as a composer and performer. His brilliant operas, graceful symphonies, and moving religious music helped define the new style of composition. Although he died in poverty at age 35, he produced an enormous amount of music during his lifetime. Mozart's musical legacy thrives today.

Composers adopted the graceful rococo style in their works of music. They wrote pieces for an instrument called the harpsichord (above) that reflected this new style. ◀🔊 AUDIO

● **INFOGRAPHIC**

ROCOCO REACTION

In the eighteenth century, France experienced an aesthetic shift in art, clothing, music, and architecture. Curving lines, pastel colors, elegant music, and paintings depicting delightful love scenes replaced the formal lines and dark colors of the baroque style. The rise of this new style, referred to as rococo, reflected changes in French society that were brought about by the Enlightenment. As the French elite became more involved in the salons of the day (numbering about 800 in Paris), they competed with each other for the most fashionable home in which to host their intellectual discussions.

The Novel Takes Shape By the 1700s, literature developed new forms and a wider audience. Middle-class readers, for example, liked stories about their own times told in straightforward prose. One result was an outpouring of novels, or long works of prose fiction. English novelists wrote many popular stories. Daniel Defoe wrote *Robinson Crusoe,* an exciting tale about a sailor shipwrecked on a tropical island. This novel is still well known today. In a novel called *Pamela,* Samuel Richardson used a series of letters to tell a story about a servant girl. This technique was adopted by other authors of the period.

✔ **Checkpoint** How did the arts and literature change as Enlightenment ideas spread?

Enlightened Despots Embrace New Ideas

The courts of Europe became enlivened as *philosophes* tried to persuade rulers to adopt their ideas. The *philosophes* hoped to convince the ruling classes that reform was necessary. Some monarchs did accept Enlightenment ideas. Others still practiced absolutism, a political doctrine in which a monarch had seemingly unlimited power. Those that did accept these new ideas became **enlightened despots,** or absolute rulers who used their power to bring about political and social change.

Frederick II Attempts Reform Frederick II, known as **Frederick the Great,** exerted extremely tight control over his subjects during his reign as king of Prussia from 1740 to 1786. Still, he saw himself as the "first servant of the state," with a duty to work for the common good.

Ornate Artifacts
In the examples of the rococo style shown here, notice the elegance of the delicate lace and floral patterns, as well as the charming paintings depicting the pleasures of everyday life.

Thinking Critically
1. **Make Generalizations** Based on what you see in the collection of images here, describe what you think it would have been like to live during this time period.
2. **Draw Inferences** Why might the *philosophes* have disliked the rococo style?

Geography *Interactive*
For: Audio guided tour
Web Code: nap-1721

Frederick the Great

Emperor Joseph II

Catherine the Great

Map Skills Although the center of the Enlightenment was in France, the ideas of reform spread to the rulers of Austria, Prussia, and Russia.

1. **Locate** (a) Paris (b) Prussia (c) Austria
2. **Location** Which enlightened despot ruled farthest from Paris?
3. **Draw Conclusions** According to the map, what regions of Europe were affected by enlightened despots?

Frederick openly praised Voltaire's work and invited several of the French intellectuals of the age to Prussia. Some of his first acts as king were to reduce the use of torture and allow a free press. Most of Frederick's reforms were directed at making the Prussian government more efficient. To do this, he reorganized the government's civil service and simplified laws. Frederick also tolerated religious differences, welcoming victims of religious persecution. "In my kingdom," he said, "everyone can go to heaven in his own fashion." His religious tolerance and also his disdain for torture showed Frederick's genuine belief in enlightened reform. In the end, however, Frederick desired a stronger monarchy and more power for himself.

Catherine the Great Studies *Philosophes'* Works

Catherine II, or **Catherine the Great,** empress of Russia, read the works of the *philosophes* and exchanged letters with Voltaire and Diderot. She praised Voltaire as someone who had "fought the united enemies of humankind: superstition, fanaticism, ignorance, trickery." Catherine believed in the Enlightenment ideas of equality and liberty.

Catherine, who became empress in 1762, toyed with implementing Enlightenment ideas. Early in her reign, she made some limited reforms in law and government. Catherine abolished torture and established religious tolerance in her lands. She granted nobles a charter of rights and criticized the institution of serfdom. Still, like Frederick in Prussia, Catherine did not intend to give up power. In the end, her main political contribution to Russia proved to be an expanded empire.

Joseph II Continues Reform In Austria, Hapsburg empress Maria Theresa ruled as an absolute monarch. Although she did not push for reforms, she is considered to be an enlightened despot by some historians because she worked to improve peasants' way of life. The most radical of the enlightened despots was her son and successor, Joseph II. Joseph was an eager student of the Enlightenment, and he traveled in disguise among his subjects to learn of their problems.

Joseph continued the work of Maria Theresa, who had begun to modernize Austria's government. Despite opposition, Joseph supported religious equality for Protestants and Jews in his Catholic empire. He ended censorship by allowing a free press and attempted to bring the Catholic Church under royal control. He sold the property of many monasteries that were not involved in education or care of the sick and used the proceeds to support those that were. Joseph even abolished serfdom. Like many of his other reforms, however, this measure was canceled after his death.

 Checkpoint Why were the *philosophes* interested in sharing their beliefs with European rulers?

Lives of the Majority Change Slowly

Most Europeans were untouched by either courtly or middle-class culture. They remained what they had always been—peasants living in small rural villages. Echoes of serfdom still remained throughout Europe despite advances in Western Europe. Their culture, based on centuries-old traditions, changed slowly.

By the late 1700s, however, radical ideas about equality and social justice finally seeped into peasant villages. While some peasants eagerly sought to topple the old order, others resisted efforts to bring about change. In the 1800s, war and political upheaval, as well as changing economic conditions, would transform peasant life in Europe.

 Checkpoint During this time, why did change occur slowly for most Europeans?

Progress Monitoring Online
For: Self-quiz with vocabulary practice
Web Code: naa-1721

Terms, People, and Places

1. For each term, person, or place listed at the beginning of the section, write a sentence explaining its significance.

Note Taking

2. **Reading Skill: Categorize** Use your completed concept webs to answer the Focus Question: As Enlightenment ideas spread across Europe, what cultural and political changes took place?

Comprehension and Critical Thinking

3. **Draw Conclusions** How did ideas of a "just society" change during the Age of Reason?

4. **Summarize** Explain the differences between baroque and rococo, and how these styles were reflected in art.

5. **Analyze Information** What did Frederick the Great mean when he said, "In my kingdom, everyone can go to heaven in his own fashion"?

6. **Predict Consequences** What actions might peasants take as they learn more about ideas such as equality?

● **Writing About History**
Quick Write: Narrowing Your Response In the essay prompt below, identify and list the key words. Then write a brief outline of the main ideas to help you form the best response. In your own words, explain what is being asked of you in the instructions.

- Think of the various effects of the Enlightenment. Identify which effect you think most contributed to society, both short-term and long-term. Explain your response.

Note Taking

Reading Skill: Summarize Fill in a concept web like the one below with information about the enlightened despots and their contributions.

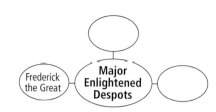

View of La Scala in
Milan, mid-1800s ▼

Opera

Operas originated in Florence, Italy, in the seventeenth century. First called *drama per musica*, or drama through music, these musical performances typically involve large casts and elaborate sets and costumes. When Italian operas were performed in France, they emphasized glory and love, and included ballet and lavish stage settings to please the French court. Handel, Mozart, Verdi, Wagner, and Puccini composed some of the world's most famous operas. 🔊 AUDIO

◄ Empress Maria Theresa of Austria, whose country ruled Italy by the early 1700s, founded Milan's La Scala (background image), one of Europe's oldest and most celebrated opera houses. Built in 1776, this opera house still showcases the great operas of the nineteenth century, including composer Giuseppe Verdi's masterpieces, *Aida* and *La Traviata*. Verdi's first opera, *Oberto*, was performed at La Scala, and he was the beloved house composer for many years. After years of care and renovation, the interior of La Scala retains its elegance as operatic performances continue to entertain audiences today.

◄ The "Three Tenors" (from left), Placido Domingo, José Carreras, and Luciano Pavarotti, are some of the best-known opera singers of the modern era. In the hierarchy of the opera stage, the tenor is the highest male voice and usually plays the part of the hero. The female lead is typically sung by a soprano, which is the highest female voice. Singers in the lower ranges (mezzo-soprano and alto for women, baritone and bass for men) generally play villainous or comic roles.

Thinking Critically

1. **Draw Inferences** How do you think composing an opera is different from composing a symphony?
2. **Determine Relevance** Why did operas appeal to composers and musicians during the Enlightenment?

Thomas Paine

Paine's *Common Sense*

Early in 1776, English colonists in North America eagerly read the newly published *Common Sense,* by Thomas Paine. This pamphlet called on them to declare their independence from Britain and echoed the themes of the Enlightenment.

66 'Tis repugnant to reason, to the universal order of things, to all examples from former ages, to suppose that this Continent can long remain subject to any external power.99
—Thomas Paine, *Common Sense*

Focus Question How did ideas of the Enlightenment lead to the independence and founding of the United States of America?

Birth of the American Republic

Objectives

- Describe characteristics of Britain and the 13 English colonies in the mid-1700s.
- Outline the events that led to the American Revolution.
- Summarize the events and significance of the American Revolution.
- Analyze how the new Constitution reflected the ideas of the Enlightenment.

Terms, People, and Places

George III	Yorktown, Virginia
Stamp Act	Treaty of Paris
George Washington	James Madison
Thomas Jefferson	Benjamin Franklin
popular sovereignty	federal republic

Note Taking

Reading Skill: Recognize Sequence As you read, complete a timeline like the one below with important dates that led up to the formation of the United States government.

French and Indian War ends.

1763

On the eve of the American Revolution, Britain was a formidable foe whose power stretched throughout the world. In addition, an ambitious new ruler sought to expand the powers of the monarchy.

Britain Becomes a Global Power

There are several key reasons for Britain's rise to global prominence:

- Location placed England in a position to control trade. In the 1500s and 1600s, English merchants sent ships across the world's oceans and planted outposts in the West Indies, North America, and India. From these tiny settlements, England would build a global empire.
- England offered a climate favorable to business and commerce and put fewer restrictions on trade than some of its neighbors.
- In the 1700s, Britain was generally on the winning side in European conflicts. With the Treaty of Utrecht, France gave Nova Scotia and Newfoundland to Britain. In 1763, the end of the French and Indian War and the Seven Years' War brought Britain all of French Canada. The British also monopolized the slave trade in Spanish America, which brought enormous wealth to British merchants.
- England's territory expanded closer to home as well. In 1707, England and Wales were united with Scotland to become the United Kingdom of Great Britain. Free trade with Scotland created a larger market for farmers and manufacturers. Ireland had come under English control during the 1600s. It was formally united with Great Britain in 1801.

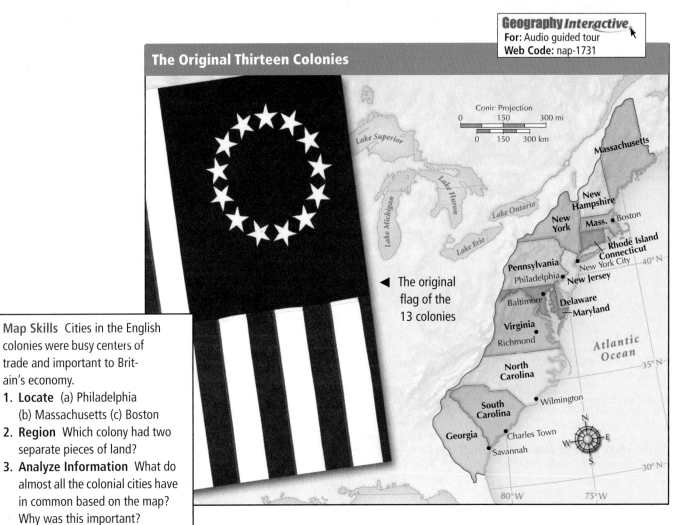

The Original Thirteen Colonies

Geography *Interactive*
For: Audio guided tour
Web Code: nap-1731

◀ The original flag of the 13 colonies

Map Skills Cities in the English colonies were busy centers of trade and important to Britain's economy.

1. **Locate** (a) Philadelphia (b) Massachusetts (c) Boston
2. **Region** Which colony had two separate pieces of land?
3. **Analyze Information** What do almost all the colonial cities have in common based on the map? Why was this important?

Vocabulary Builder

<u>assert</u>—(uh SURT) *vt.* to insist on being recognized

In 1760, George III began a 60-year reign. Unlike his father and grandfather, the new king was born in England. He spoke English and loved Britain. But George was eager to recover the powers the crown had lost. Following his mother's advice, "George, be a king!" he set out to reassert royal power. He wanted to end Whig domination, choose his own ministers, dissolve the cabinet system, and make Parliament follow his will. Gradually, George found seats in Parliament for "the king's friends." Then, with their help, he began to <u>assert</u> his leadership. Many of his policies, however, would prove disastrous.

✔ **Checkpoint** What led to Britain's rise to global prominence in the mid-1700s?

The 13 Colonies in the Mid-1700s

By 1750, a string of 13 prosperous colonies stretched along the eastern coast of North America. They were part of Britain's growing empire. Colonial cities such as Boston, New York, and Philadelphia were busy commercial centers that linked North America to the West Indies, Africa, and Europe. Colonial shipyards produced many vessels for this trade.

Britain applied mercantilist policies to its colonies in an attempt to strengthen its own economy by exporting more than it imported. To this end, in the 1600s, Parliament had passed the Navigation Acts to regulate colonial trade and manufacturing. For the most part, however, these acts were not rigorously enforced. Therefore, activities like smuggling were common and not considered crimes by the colonists.

By the mid-1700s, the colonies were home to diverse religious and ethnic groups. Social distinctions were more blurred than in Europe, although wealthy landowners and merchants dominated government and society. In politics, as in much else, there was a good deal of free discussion. Colonists felt entitled to the rights of English citizens, and their colonial assemblies exercised much control over local affairs. Many also had an increasing sense of their own destiny separate from Britain.

✓ **Checkpoint** In what ways were the colonies already developing independence from Britain?

Colonists Express Discontent

The Seven Years' War and the French and Indian War in North America had drained the British treasury. King George III and his advisors thought that the colonists should help pay for these wars. To increase taxes paid by colonists, Parliament passed the Sugar Act in 1764, which imposed import taxes, and the Stamp Act in 1765, which imposed taxes on items such as newspapers and pamphlets. "No taxation without representation," the colonists protested. They believed that because they had no representatives in Parliament, they should not be taxed. Parliament repealed the Stamp Act in 1766, but then passed a Declaratory Act that said it had complete authority over the colonists.

Drafting the Declaration
Benjamin Franklin, John Adams, and Thomas Jefferson (from left to right)

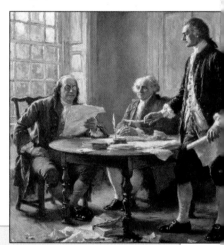

Colonists Rebel Against Britain A series of violent clashes intensified the colonists' anger. In March 1770, British soldiers in Boston opened fire on a crowd that was pelting them with stones and snowballs. Colonists called the death of five protesters the Boston Massacre. Then in December 1773, a handful of colonists hurled a cargo of recently arrived British tea into the harbor to protest a tax on tea. The incident became known as the Boston Tea Party. When Parliament passed harsh laws to punish Massachusetts for the destruction of the tea, other colonies rallied to oppose the British response.

As tensions increased, fighting spread. Finally, representatives from each colony gathered in Philadelphia and met in a Continental Congress to decide what action to take. Among the participants were the radical yet fair-minded Massachusetts lawyer John Adams, who had defended the British soldiers involved in the Boston Massacre in their trial; Virginia planter and soldier George Washington; and political and social leaders from all 13 colonies.

Colonists Declare Independence In April 1775, the ongoing tension between the colonists and the British exploded into war in Lexington and Concord, Massachusetts. This war is known as the Revolutionary War, or the American Revolution. The Congress met soon after and set up a Continental Army, with George Washington in command. Although many battles ended in British victories, the colonists were determined to fight at any cost. In 1776, the

The Declaration of Independence stands as one of the most important documents in all of history. It still serves as inspiration for people around the world. Where did some of the ideas of the Declaration originate?

Primary Source

❝We hold these truths to be self-evident, that all men are created equal, that they are endowed by their Creator with certain unalienable Rights, that among these are Life, Liberty and the pursuit of Happiness. That to secure these rights, Governments are instituted among Men, deriving their just powers from the consent of the governed; That whenever any Form of Government becomes destructive of these ends it is the Right of the People to alter or to abolish it, and to institute new Government, laying its foundation on such principles and organizing its powers in such form, as to them shall seem most likely to effect their Safety and Happiness.❞
—*Declaration of Independence,* July 4, 1776 ◀)) AUDIO

George Washington

When George Washington (1732–1799) was chosen to lead the American army, the British thought he would be a failure. Washington indeed faced many challenges, including an army that did not have weapons, uniforms, or bedding. He struggled to incorporate order and discipline and to instill pride and loyalty in his soldiers. Washington persevered to American victory. His success as a leader continued when he became the nation's first President. **How did Washington hold the army together through difficult times?**

James Madison

James Madison (1751–1836) arrived at the Constitutional Convention in Philadelphia in May 1787 with his thick notebooks on history and government. Madison chose a seat in front of the president's chair and kept detailed notes of the debates. Madison was greatly respected and quickly became the Convention's floor leader. His notebooks remained unpublished for more than 50 years, but they are now our main source of information about the birth of the Constitution. **What did the Framers of the Constitution have in common?**

Benjamin Franklin

Benjamin Franklin (1706–1790) was a philosopher, scientist, publisher, legislator, and diplomat. Sent by Congress to France in 1776 to seek financial and military support for the war, he soon became popular in France because of his intellect and wit. Those who admired America's goal of attaining freedom also admired Franklin. When Franklin returned to America after nine years, he served as a delegate to the Constitutional Convention as the eldest of the delegates. **Why was Franklin admired in France?**

Second Continental Congress took a momentous step, voting to declare independence from Britain. Thomas Jefferson of Virginia was the principal author of the Declaration of Independence, a document that reflects John Locke's ideas of the government's obligation to protect the people's natural rights to "life, liberty, and property."

The Declaration included another of Locke's ideas: people had the right "to alter or to abolish" unjust governments—a right to revolt. The principle of popular sovereignty, which states that all government power comes from the people, is also an important point in the Declaration. Jefferson carefully detailed the colonists' grievances against Britain. Because the king had trampled colonists' natural rights, he argued, the colonists had the right to rebel and set up a new government that would protect them. Aware of the risks involved, on July 4, 1776, American leaders adopted the Declaration, pledging "our lives, our fortunes, and our sacred honor" to creating and protecting the new United States of America.

✓ **Checkpoint** What Enlightenment ideas are reflected in the Declaration of Independence?

The American Revolution Continues

At first, the American cause looked bleak. The British had a large number of trained soldiers, a huge fleet, and greater resources. About one third of the American colonists were Loyalists, or those who supported Britain. Many others refused to fight for either side. The Americans lacked military resources, had little money to pay soldiers, and did not have a strategic plan.

Still, colonists had some advantages. One was the geography of the diverse continent. Since colonists were fighting on their own soil, they were familiar with its thick woods and inadequate roads. Other advantages were their strong leader, George Washington, and their fierce determination to fight for their ideals of liberty.

To counteract these advantages, the British worked to create alliances within the colonies. A number of Native American groups sided with the British, while others saw potential advantages in supporting the colonists' cause. Additionally, the British offered freedom to any enslaved people who were willing to fight the colonists.

France Provides Support The first turning point in the war came in 1777, when the Americans triumphed over the British at the Battle of Saratoga. This victory persuaded France to join the Americans against its old rival, Britain. The alliance brought the Americans desperately needed supplies, trained soldiers, and French warships. Spurred by the French example, the Netherlands and Spain added their support.

Hard times continued, however. In the brutal winter of 1777–1778, Continental troops at Valley Forge suffered from cold, hunger, and disease. Throughout this crisis and others, Washington was patient, courageous, and determined. He held the ragged army together.

WITNESS HISTORY VIDEO

Watch *The Enlightenment and the American Revolution* on the **Witness History Discovery School**™ video program to learn more about the American Revolution.

Fearless Leader
George Washington directs his troops on the battlefield. *What traits did Washington possess that helped lead Americans to victory?*

The Roots of American Democracy

The Framers of the United States Constitution were well educated and widely read. They were familiar with governments of ancient Greece and Rome and those of contemporary Great Britain and Europe. Political writings such as Montesquieu's *The Spirit of the Laws*, Rousseau's *Social Contract*, and Locke's *Two Treatises of Government* contained principles that greatly influenced the Framers in the development of the Constitution. Centuries later, these fundamental democratic principles of American government—popular sovereignty, limited government, separation of powers, and checks and balances—are still in place. The diagram here shows checks and balances, one of Montesquieu's ideas, which ensures that one branch does not accumulate too much power.

Congress may impeach judges; Senate may reject appointment of judges.

Judicial Branch

Courts may declare acts of Congress unconstitutional.

Legislative Branch

Checks and Balances

Courts may declare executive actions unconstitutional.

President appoints judges.

President may veto legislation.

Executive Branch

Congress may impeach the President and may override veto; Senate approves or rejects treaties and appointments.

History *Interactive*
For: Interactive diagram
Web Code: nap-1732

Thinking Critically
1. **Draw Conclusions** What additional ideas might the Framers have learned from the political writings of the Enlightenment thinkers?
2. **Summarize** Explain how the basic principle of checks and balances works.

Treaty of Paris Ends the War In 1781, the French fleet blockaded the Chesapeake Bay, which enabled Washington to force the surrender of a British army at **Yorktown, Virginia.** With that defeat, the British war effort crumbled. Two years later, American, British, and French diplomats signed the **Treaty of Paris,** ending the war. In that treaty, Britain recognized the independence of the United States of America. The Americans' victory can be attributed to their resilient dedication to attaining independence.

 Checkpoint What advantages did the colonists have in battling Britain for their independence?

A New Constitution

The Articles of Confederation was the nation's first constitution. It proved to be too weak to rule the new United States effectively. To address this problem, the nation's leaders gathered once more in Philadelphia. Among them were George Washington, **James Madison,** and **Benjamin Franklin.**

During the hot summer of 1787, they met in secret to redraft the articles of the new constitution. The result was a document that established a government run by the people, for the people.

Enlightenment Ideas Have Great Impact
The Framers of the Constitution had studied history and absorbed the ideas of Locke, Montesquieu, and Rousseau. They saw government in terms of a social contract into which "We the People of the United States" entered. They provided not only for an elective legislature but also for an elected president rather than a hereditary monarch. For the first President, voters would choose George Washington.

The Constitution created a *federal republic,* with power divided between the federal, or national, government and the states. A central feature of the new federal government was the separation of powers among the legislative, executive, and judicial branches, an idea borrowed directly from Montesquieu. Within that structure, each branch of government was provided with checks and balances on the other branches.

The Bill of Rights, the first ten amendments to the Constitution, was important to the passage of the Constitution. It recognized the idea that people had basic rights that the government must protect, such as freedom of religion, speech, and the press. The Bill of Rights, like the Constitution, put the *philosophes'* Enlightenment ideas into practice. In 1789, the Constitution became the supreme law of the land, which means it became the nation's fundamental law. This remarkable document has endured for more than 200 years.

Symbol of Freedom
The Constitution of the United States created the most progressive government of its day. From the start, the new republic was a symbol of freedom to European countries and reformers in Latin America. Its constitution would be copied or adapted by many lands throughout the world. The Enlightenment ideals that had inspired American colonists brought changes in Europe too. In 1789, a revolution in France toppled the monarchy in the name of liberty and equality. Before long, other Europeans would take up the cry for freedom as well.

✓ **Checkpoint** Explain the influence of Enlightenment ideas on the United States Constitution and Bill of Rights.

The U.S. Bill of Rights

1st: Guarantees freedom of religion, speech, press, assembly, and petition

2nd: Right to bear arms

3rd: Prohibits quartering of troops in private homes

4th: Protects from unreasonable searches and seizures

5th: No punishment without due process of law

6th: Right to a speedy and public trial in the state where the offense was committed

7th: Right to jury trial for civil cases if over $20

8th: Prohibits excessive bail and cruel and unusual punishments

9th: Civil rights are not restricted to those specified by these amendments.

10th: Powers not granted to the national government belong to the states and to the people.

Chart Skills The first ten amendments to the United States Constitution are known as the Bill of Rights. *What is the significance of the 10th Amendment?*

SECTION

3 Assessment

Progress Monitoring *Online*
For: Self-quiz with vocabulary practice
Web Code: naa-1731

Terms, People, and Places
1. For each term, person, or place listed at the beginning of the section, write a sentence explaining its significance.

Note Taking
2. **Reading Skill: Recognize Sequence** Use your completed timeline to answer the Focus Question: How did ideas of the Enlightenment lead to the independence and founding of the United States of America?

Comprehension and Critical Thinking
3. **Make Generalizations** Describe society and politics in the 13 English colonies during the mid-1700s.
4. **Express Problems Clearly** Explain why conflict between the colonists and Britain increased after 1763.
5. **Identify Point of View** What reasons might a Loyalist have for opposing the American Revolution?
6. **Determine Relevance** Give two examples of why the Bill of Rights is important to you.

● Writing About History
Quick Write: Providing Elaboration To prove that you fully understand a subject, you need to include specific details. You should use facts, dates, names, examples, explanations, or quotes to support your answer. Write a paragraph to describe the events that led to the American Revolution. Then read through your response and add specific details where you can.

SPREADING THE WORD OF REVOLUTION

While Enlightenment thinkers had a profound impact on the leaders of the American Revolution, newspapers made a great impact on the colonists. Colonists depended on newspapers for information about the war and the economy. News about the war was the first great news event to report in America. Would the colonists be free? Or would English control continue? As demand increased, newspapers began publishing several times a week instead of weekly. The number of newspapers increased from 29 to 48 from 1770 to 1775. During this time, the American newspaper changed from a weak form of communication to a propaganda machine that included controversial political cartoons and essays.

Trouble for newspapers came in 1765 when the British government passed the Stamp Act. Newspapers were forced to pay the tax imposed by the Stamp Act or face heavy penalties. Colonists already felt they had no representation so they became even more discontented. Many newspapers strongly opposed the Stamp Act and showed their resentment in their pages with cartoons, editorial content, and typographical devices. The *Maryland Gazette*, for example, set a skull and crossbones on its front page where the tax stamp belonged (facing page). Others ceased publication. The strength of the press was evident when the British government was forced to repeal the Stamp Act. Newspapers had voiced protest effectively and would continue to be a powerful medium of communication for years to come.

◀ Engraving by Paul Revere of the 1770 Boston Massacre. Revere exaggerated the event to incite anger among the colonists against the British.

▼ Engraving of the Battle of Lexington, the first battle of the American Revolution. Demand for exciting news of the war led to the creation of more newspapers.

The *Maryland Gazette*, October 10, 1765

The MARYLAND GAZETTE, EXPIRING:

In Hopes of a Resurrection to LIFE again.

The first political cartoon (left) in an American newspaper was created by Benjamin Franklin and appeared in 1754. The Sons of Liberty, an organization that loudly opposed the Stamp Act, used newspapers (above) to increase colonial participation.

JOIN, or DIE.

1789 French Revolution begins.

1775 American Revolution begins.

1821 Mexico gains independence from Spain.

1791 Haitian revolt against France begins.

1821 Peru declares independence from Spain.

1819 Colombia achieves independence from Spain.

1825 Bolivia achieves independence from Spain.

1822 Brazil proclaims independence from Portugal.

1811 Paraguay proclaims independence from Spain.

1818 Chile declares independence from Spain.

An Era of Revolutions

As word of revolution spread throughout the colonies, the news also spread throughout the world. The American Revolution had a great impact on other parts of the world because it established the first government with all powers based on the consent of its people. Americans' attainment of freedom inspired revolts in France, in Hispaniola (present-day Haiti), and throughout Latin America as shown on this map.

History *Interactive*

For: Interactive map, audio, and more
Visit: PHSchool.com
Web Code: nap-1733

Thinking Critically

1. **Recognize Propaganda** Explain how the front page of the *Maryland Gazette* was used as a propaganda tool.
2. **Make Comparisons** How does the newspaper affect people's perceptions today?

Quick Study Guide

Progress Monitoring *Online*
For: Self-test with vocabulary practice
Web Code: naa-1741

■ Enlightenment Thinkers

- **Thomas Hobbes:** social contract in which people give power to the government for an organized society
- **John Locke:** natural rights—life, liberty, and property
- **Baron de Montesquieu:** separation of powers; checks and balances
- **Voltaire:** battled corruption, injustice, and inequality; defended freedom of speech
- **Denis Diderot:** *Encyclopedia*
- **Jean-Jacques Rousseau:** social contract in which people follow the "general will" for true liberty
- **Adam Smith:** free market; laissez faire

■ Enlightenment Ideas Influence Democracy

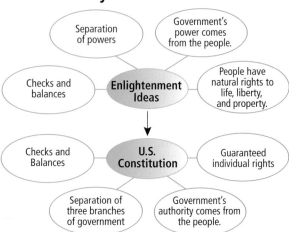

■ American Declaration of Independence: Main Ideas

Declaration of Independence: Main Ideas
• All men are created equal and have natural rights to life, liberty, and the pursuit of happiness.
• It is the government's obligation to protect these rights.
• If a government fails to protect these rights, the people can revolt and set up a new government.

■ The U.S. Bill of Rights

The U.S. Bill of Rights
1st: Guarantees freedom of religion, speech, press, assembly, and petition
2nd: Right to bear arms
3rd: Prohibits quartering of troops in private homes
4th: Protects from unreasonable searches and seizures
5th: No punishment without due process of law
6th: Right to a speedy and public trial in the state where the offense was committed
7th: Right to jury trial for civil cases if over $20
8th: Prohibits excessive bail and cruel and unusual punishments
9th: Civil rights are not restricted to those specified by these amendments.
10th: Powers not granted to the national government belong to the states and to the people.

■ Key Events
From 1700–1789

1700s
France sees flowering of Enlightenment thought.

1721
Johann Sebastian Bach publishes his Brandenburg Concertos.

1740
Frederick II begins his reign in Prussia.

Chapter Events
Global Events

1720

1730

1740

1735
China's Emperor Qianlong begins his long reign.

Concept Connector

■ Cumulative Review

Record the answers to the questions below on your Concept Connector worksheets. In addition, record information from this chapter about the following concepts:

- Political Systems: federal government
- Democracy: The American Declaration of Independence

1. **Cooperation** Throughout time, people have used cooperation to reach common goals. As you have read in this chapter, colonists in America joined together to fight for their independence from Britain and were ultimately successful. Without cooperation, change would be difficult to achieve. Think of another time in history when groups of people cooperated for a mutual benefit. How might the outcome have changed had they not cooperated? Read to learn more about the:
   - development of trade routes in medieval Europe
   - Glorious Revolution

2. **Conflict** There are many different causes for the conflicts that have occurred throughout history. There have been conflicts about religion, land, and power, for example. The Thirty Years War in the early 1600s had both religious and political causes. Compare the American Revolution to the Thirty Years' War. How were they similar and different? Think about the:
   - cause(s) of conflict
   - scope of conflict
   - groups involved
   - goals or strategic plans
   - results

3. **Culture** Enlightenment thinkers found inspiration not only in the cultures of other lands, but also in the cultures of other times. The relatively new science of archaeology gave thinkers more access to the knowledge of past civilizations. During the early 1700s, archaeologists discovered the ruins of the ancient Roman cities of Herculaneum and Pompeii, buried under volcanic debris for many centuries. How do you think Enlightenment thinkers may have benefited from this discovery?

■ Connections To Today

1. **Democracy: Still Strong Today** As you have read, the Framers of the United States Constitution were inspired by Montesquieu, Rousseau, and Locke. Democratic revolutions around the world were inspired by the same Enlightenment ideas that had inspired American colonists. Even today, nations seeking a model for democratic government often turn to the Constitution of the United States. Research and write a newspaper article about one of these nations.

2. **Culture: Modern Salons** Salons provided a way for people to gather and share ideas, especially during the Enlightenment. Today, we know that many people do this without ever meeting in person—through the Internet. People are able to join chat rooms and newsgroups to share their thoughts. Many discussions on the Internet lack the serious-minded tone of a salon conversation and the benefit of face-to-face conversation. The Internet does, however, provide a sense of community, where people can gather to discuss ideas, even if it is a "virtual" living room. Compare salons of the Enlightenment and Internet chat rooms. Explain which you think is the better forum for sharing ideas, and why.

1751	1759	1762	1776
Diderot publishes *Encyclopedia*.	**Voltaire publishes *Candide*.**	**Rousseau publishes *The Social Contract*.**	**American leaders sign the Declaration of Independence.**

1750 — **1760** — **1770** — **1780**

1754	1763	1789
French and Indian War begins.	**Treaty of Paris gives Britain control of Canada.**	**The French Revolution begins.**

History *Interactive*

For: Interactive timeline
Web Code: nap-1701

Chapter Assessment

Terms, People, and Places

Complete each sentence by choosing the correct answer from the list of terms below. You will not use all of the terms.

natural rights	Montesquieu
John Locke	federal republic
laissez faire	Yorktown, Virginia
rococo	Frederick the Great
baroque	Treaty of Paris
Joseph II	Rousseau

1. In a _____, power is divided between the federal government and the states.
2. _____ advanced the idea of separation of powers.
3. The _____ style influenced by the Enlightenment was personal, elegant, and charming.
4. The enlightened despot who ended censorship was _____.
5. The American Revolution ended when George Washington forced the surrender of the British at _____.
6. _____ believed in _____, which are the rights to life, liberty, and property.

Main Ideas

Section 1 (pp. 544–549)
7. What idea did John Locke advocate for the role of a government?
8. Explain the economic policy of laissez faire.

Section 2 (pp. 550–556)
9. How did the Enlightenment affect some rulers in Europe, and what are these rulers known as?

Section 3 (pp. 557–565)
10. How did taxation create tensions between the American colonies and the British government?

11. How does the Bill of Rights reflect a key Enlightenment idea?

Chapter Focus Question
12. How did Enlightenment thinkers inspire revolutionaries to push for radical changes in government and society?

Critical Thinking

13. **Synthesize Information** Choose one *philosophe* from this chapter and describe how he or she might respond to a human rights issue that has been in the news recently.
14. **Predict Consequences** Given the impact the Enlightenment thinkers had on the American Revolution, what can you predict will happen in other areas of the world? Explain why you predicted what you did.
15. **Analyzing Visuals** Identify the style of this painting and describe its characteristics.

16. **Make Comparisons** Compare Britain and the 13 colonies in the mid-1700s.
17. **Analyze Information** What ideas about government do you think English settlers brought with them to the Americas?

● Writing About History

Writing for Assessment Select either a philosopher from the Enlightenment or an important figure from the American Revolution. Explain how his or her actions, beliefs, and/or works contributed to improving society. Provide specific examples.

Prewriting
• Consider what you know about the people in this chapter and choose one who interests you.
• Develop a focus or main idea. Write a single sentence identifying the main idea you will develop.
• As you prepare to write your essay, make sure you understand the instructions. Circle verbs, nouns, or important phrases in the question.

Drafting
• Develop a thesis statement that identifies the focus of your essay.
• Make an outline for your essay and fill in facts and examples.
• Write an introduction to explain your thesis, a body to provide evidence for your thesis, and a conclusion.

Revising
• Even though time is limited on essay tests, you should still leave time to check your writing for accuracy and clarity.
• Use the guidelines for revising your essay on page SH22 of the Writing Handbook.

Document-Based Assessment

Enlightenment Thought

Enlightenment thinkers believed in the possibility of social, political, and economic change. Often critical of society during this time, they were driven by the power of human reason and progress.

Document A

"Common sense is not so common."

—From **Philosophical Dictionary** by Voltaire

Document B

"A prince ought not to deem it beneath his dignity to state that he considers it his duty not to dictate anything to his subjects in religious matters, but to leave them complete freedom."

—From **What Is Enlightenment?** by Immanuel Kant

Document C

"A strange consequence that necessarily follows from the use of torture is that the innocent person is placed in a condition worse than that of the guilty, for if both are tortured, the circumstances are all against the former. Either he confesses the crime and is condemned, or he is declared innocent and has suffered a punishment he did not deserve."

—From **On Crimes and Punishments** by Marchese di Beccaria

Document D

Diderot and Catherine the Great

Document E

Selected Enlightenment Thinkers			
Thinker	Lifespan	Nationality	Key Work
Jean DíAlembert	1717–1783	French	*Encyclopedia*
Jeremy Bentham	1748–1832	English	*The Principles of Morals and Legislation*
Cesare Beccaria	1738–1794	Italian	*Crimes and Punishment*
Denis Diderot	1713–1784	French	*Encyclopedia*
David Hume	1711–1776	Scottish	*Treatise of Human Nature*
Immanuel Kant	1724–1804	E. Prussian	*Critique of Pure Reason*
John Locke	1632–1704	English	*Essay Concerning Human Understanding*
Charles Montesquieu	1689–1755	French	*The Spirit of the Laws*
Jean-Jacques Rousseau	1712–1778	French	*The Social Contract*
Adam Smith	1723–1790	English	*The Wealth of Nations*
Voltaire	1694–1778	French	*Philosophical Dictionary*

Analyzing Documents

Use your knowledge of the Enlightenment and Documents A, B, C, D, and E to answer the questions below.

1. Kant believes in _____ based on Document B.
   A freedom of religion
   B freedom of speech
   C the government making a religious choice for its people
   D dignity

2. In Document C, the author condemned
   A capital punishment.
   B religion of any kind.
   C torture.
   D the Inquisition.

3. Catherine the Great and Diderot pictured in Document D are most likely
   A sharing war stories.
   B sharing Enlightenment ideas.
   C planning the American Revolution.
   D discussing population growth in France.

4. **Writing Task** Which of the above documents do you think best exemplifies the spirit of the Enlightenment? Why? Use your knowledge of the Enlightenment and specific information from the documents to support your opinion.

The Loss of Blood Begins

On July 14, 1789, after a daylong hunting expedition, King Louis XVI returned to his palace in Versailles. Hours earlier, armed Parisians had attacked the Bastille. They had cut the chains of the prison drawbridge, crushing a member of the crowd, and poured into the courtyard. Chaos ensued as shots rang out, blood was spattered, and heads were paraded down the streets on spikes. When Louis heard the news, he exclaimed, "Then it's a revolt?" "No, sire," replied the duke bearing the news, "it's a revolution!" The French Revolution had begun. Listen to the Witness History audio to hear more about the fall of the Bastille.

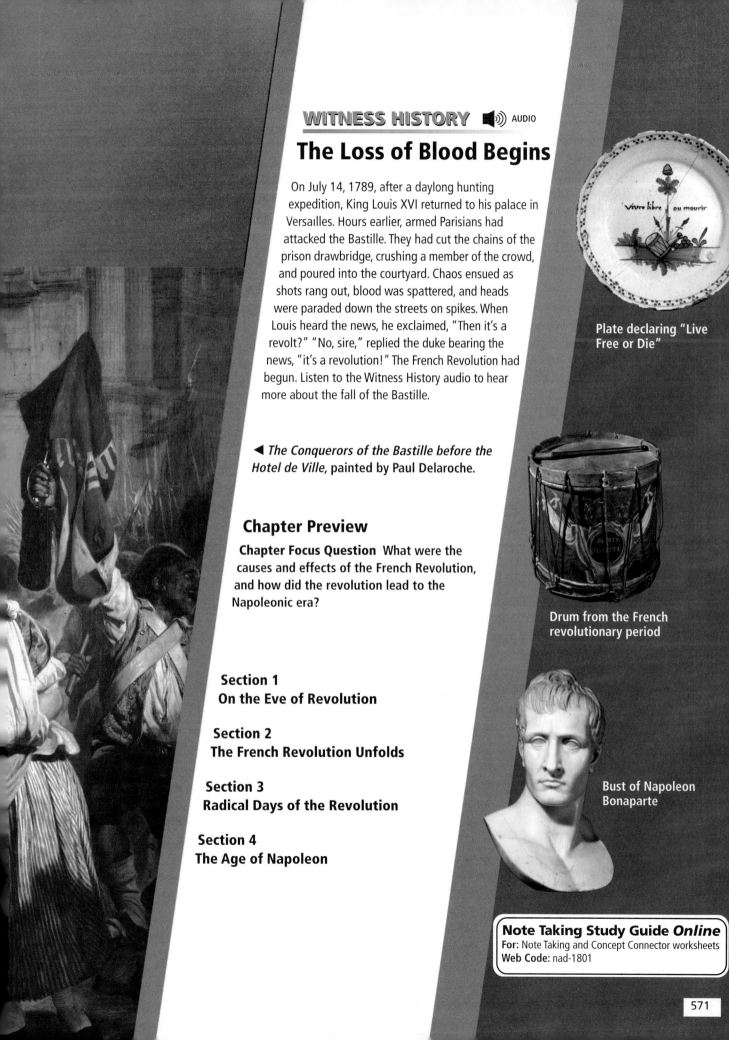

Plate declaring "Live Free or Die"

◀ *The Conquerors of the Bastille before the Hotel de Ville,* painted by Paul Delaroche.

Chapter Preview

Chapter Focus Question What were the causes and effects of the French Revolution, and how did the revolution lead to the Napoleonic era?

Drum from the French revolutionary period

Section 1
On the Eve of Revolution

Section 2
The French Revolution Unfolds

Section 3
Radical Days of the Revolution

Bust of Napoleon Bonaparte

Section 4
The Age of Napoleon

Note Taking Study Guide *Online*
For: Note Taking and Concept Connector worksheets
Web Code: nad-1801

Camille Desmoulins and
French Revolution banner

LIBERTÉ ÉGALITÉ

WITNESS HISTORY 🔊 AUDIO

Inciting Revolution

Camille Desmoulins was a French revolutionary leader and journalist who wrote pamphlets and journals to express his views on the revolution. He also spoke to Parisian crowds and his stirring speeches in 1789 were a cause of the storming of the Bastille prison on July 14, 1789. This excerpt is from one of his speeches, "Better to Die than not Live Free":

> **❝** In a democracy, tho the people may be deceived, yet they at least love virtue. It is merit which they believe they put in power as substitutes for the rascals who are the very essence of monarchies. The vices, concealments, and crimes which are the diseases of republics are the very health and existence of monarchies. **❞**

Focus Question What led to the storming of the Bastille, and therefore, to the start of the French Revolution?

On the Eve of Revolution

Objectives
- Describe the social divisions of France's old order.
- List reasons for France's economic troubles in 1789.
- Explain why Louis XVI called the Estates-General and summarize what resulted.
- Understand why Parisians stormed the Bastille.

Terms, People, and Places

ancien régime	Jacques Necker
estate	Estates-General
bourgeoisie	cahier
deficit spending	Tennis Court Oath
Louis XVI	Bastille

Note Taking

Reading Skill: Recognize Multiple Causes
Create a chart to identify causes of the French Revolution. Add as many boxes as you need.

Causes of the French Revolution

Inequalities among classes

On April 28, 1789, unrest exploded at a Paris wallpaper factory. A rumor had spread that the factory owner was planning to cut wages even though bread prices were soaring. Enraged workers vandalized the owner's home.

Riots like these did not worry most nobles. They knew that France faced a severe economic crisis but thought financial reforms would ease the problem. The nobles were wrong. The crisis went deeper than government finances. Reform would not be enough. By July, the hungry, unemployed, and poorly paid people of Paris had taken up arms. Their actions would push events further and faster than anyone could have foreseen.

French Society Divided

In 1789, France, like the rest of Europe, still clung to an outdated social system that had emerged in the Middle Ages. Under this **ancien régime,** or old order, everyone in France was divided into one of three social classes, or **estates.** The First Estate was made up of the clergy; the Second Estate was made up of the nobility; and the Third Estate comprised the vast majority of the population.

The Clergy Enjoy Wealth During the Middle Ages, the Church had exerted great influence throughout Christian Europe. In 1789, the French clergy still enjoyed enormous wealth and privilege. The Church owned about 10 percent of the land, collected tithes, and paid no direct taxes to the state. High Church leaders such as bishops and abbots were usually nobles who lived very well. Parish priests, however, often came from humble origins and might be as poor as their peasant congregations.

The First Estate did provide some social services. Nuns, monks, and priests ran schools, hospitals, and orphanages. But during the Enlightenment, *philosophes* targeted the Church for reform. They criticized the idleness of some clergy, the Church's interference in politics, and its intolerance of dissent. In response, many clergy condemned the Enlightenment for undermining religion and moral order.

Nobles Hold Top Government Jobs The Second Estate was the titled nobility of French society. In the Middle Ages, noble knights had defended the land. In the 1600s, Richelieu and Louis XIV had crushed the nobles' military power but had given them other rights—under strict royal control. Those rights included top jobs in government, the army, the courts, and the Church.

At Versailles, ambitious nobles competed for royal appointments while idle courtiers enjoyed endless entertainments. Many nobles, however, lived far from the center of power. Though they owned land, they received little financial income. As a result, they felt the pinch of trying to maintain their status in a period of rising prices.

Many nobles hated absolutism and resented the royal bureaucracy that employed middle-class men in positions that once had been reserved for them. They feared losing their traditional privileges, especially their freedom from paying taxes.

Third Estate Is Vastly Diverse The Third Estate was the most diverse social class. At the top sat the bourgeoisie (boor zhwah ZEE), or middle class. The bourgeoisie included prosperous bankers, merchants, and manufacturers, as well as lawyers, doctors, journalists, and professors. The bulk of the Third Estate, however, consisted of rural peasants.

REVEIL DU TIERS ETAT

Analyzing Political Cartoons

The Old Regime This cartoon represents the social order in France before the French Revolution. While a member of the Third Estate is beginning to express anger and rise up, a nobleman representing the Second Estate and a priest, representing the First Estate, recoil in surprise and fear.

1. How does the cartoonist portray the Third Estate? Explain why.
2. What were the differences among the social classes in pre-revolutionary France?

Some were prosperous landowners who hired laborers to work for them. Others were tenant farmers or day laborers.

The poorest members of the Third Estate were <u>urban</u> workers. They included apprentices, journeymen, and others who worked in industries such as printing or cloth making. Many women and men earned a meager living as servants, stable hands, construction workers, or street sellers of everything from food to pots and pans. A large number of the urban poor were unemployed. To survive, some turned to begging or crime.

From rich to poor, members of the Third Estate resented the privileges enjoyed by their social "betters." Wealthy bourgeois families in the Third Estate could buy political office and even titles, but the best jobs were still reserved for nobles. Urban workers earned miserable wages. Even the smallest rise in the price of bread, their main food, brought the threat of greater hunger or even starvation.

Because of traditional privileges, the First and Second Estates paid almost no taxes. Peasants were burdened by taxes on everything from land to soap to salt. Though they were technically free, many owed fees and services that dated back to medieval times, such as the corvée (kawr VAY), which was unpaid labor to repair roads and bridges. Peasants were

● **INFOGRAPHIC**

What Is the Third Estate?

❝1. What is the Third Estate? *Everything.*
   2. What has it been until now in the political order? *Nothing.*
   3. What does it want to be? *Something.*❞
   —Abbé Emmanuel Sieyès

Sieyès, a clergyman before the revolution, captured the spirit of the Third Estate with these words in a pamphlet published in January 1789. The vast Third Estate—peasants, dentists, laborers, and more—comprising more than 95 percent of France, was ready to fight for equality.

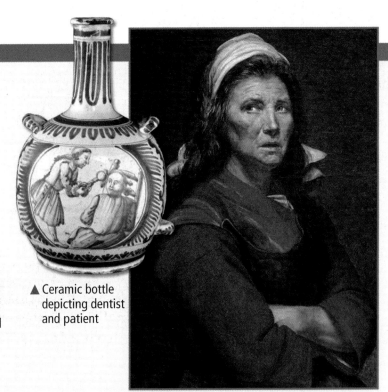

▲ Ceramic bottle depicting dentist and patient

▲ *Woman of the French Revolution*, painting of a peasant woman by Jacques-Louis David

▼ Eighteenth-century French street traders

Thinking Critically

1. **Identify Point of View** According to the quote by Sieyès, why was the Third Estate ready to revolt?
2. **Make Generalizations** Why did Sieyès say the Third Estate was "nothing"?

also incensed when nobles, hurt by rising prices, tried to reimpose old manor dues.

In towns and cities, Enlightenment ideas led people to question the inequalities of the old regime. Why, people demanded, should the first two estates have such great privileges at the expense of the majority? Throughout France, the Third Estate called for the privileged classes to pay their share.

✓ **Checkpoint** What was the social structure of the old regime in France?

Financial Troubles

Economic woes in France added to the social unrest and heightened tensions. One of the causes of the economic troubles was a mushrooming financial crisis that was due in part to years of **deficit spending.** This occurs when a government spends more money than it takes in.

National Debt Soars Louis XIV had left France deeply in debt. The Seven Years' War and the American Revolution strained the treasury even further. Costs generally had risen in the 1700s, and the lavish court soaked up millions. To bridge the gap between income and expenses, the government borrowed more and more money. By 1789, half of the government's income from taxes went to paying the interest on this enormous debt. Also, in the late 1780s, bad harvests sent food prices soaring and brought hunger to poorer peasants and city dwellers.

To solve the financial crisis, the government would have to increase taxes, reduce expenses, or both. However, the nobles and clergy fiercely resisted any attempt to end their exemption from taxes.

Economic Reform Fails The heirs of Louis XIV were not the right men to solve the economic crisis that afflicted France. Louis XV, who ruled from 1715 to 1774, pursued pleasure before serious business and ran up more debts. **Louis XVI** was well-meaning but weak and indecisive. He did, however, wisely choose **Jacques Necker,** a financial expert, as an advisor. Necker urged the king to reduce extravagant court spending, reform government, and abolish burdensome tariffs on internal trade. When Necker proposed taxing the First and Second Estates, however, the nobles and high clergy forced the king to dismiss him.

As the crisis deepened, the pressure for reform mounted. The wealthy and powerful classes demanded, however, that the king summon the **Estates-General,** the legislative body consisting of representatives of the three estates, before making any changes. A French king had not called the Estates-General for 175 years, fearing that nobles would use it to recover the feudal powers they had lost under absolute rule. To reform-minded nobles, the Estates-General seemed to offer a chance of carrying out changes like those that had come with the Glorious Revolution in England. They hoped that they could bring the absolute monarch under the control of the nobles and guarantee their own privileges.

✓ **Checkpoint** What economic troubles did France face in 1789, and how did they lead to further unrest?

Poorer peasants and city dwellers in France were faced with great hunger as bad harvests sent food prices soaring. People began to riot to demand bread. In the countryside, peasants began to attack the manor houses of the nobles. Arthur Young, an English visitor to France, witnessed these riots and disturbances. Why did the poor attack the nobles' homes?

Primary Source

66 Everything conspires to render the present period in France critical: the [lack] of bread is terrible: accounts arrive every moment from the provinces of riots and disturbances, and calling in the military, to preserve the peace of the markets. 99
—Arthur Young, *Travels in France During the Years 1787–1789*

Louis XVI Calls the Estates-General

As 1788 came to a close, France tottered on the verge of bankruptcy. Bread riots were spreading, and nobles, fearful of taxes, were denouncing royal tyranny. A baffled Louis XVI finally summoned the Estates-General to meet at Versailles the following year.

Estates Prepare Grievance Notebooks

In preparation, Louis had all three estates prepare **cahiers** (kah YAYZ), or notebooks, listing their grievances. Many cahiers called for reforms such as fairer taxes, freedom of the press, or regular meetings of the Estates-General. In one town, shoemakers denounced regulations that made leather so expensive they could not afford to make shoes. Servant girls in the city of Toulouse demanded the right to leave service when they wanted and that "after a girl has served her master for many years, she receive some reward for her service."

The cahiers testified to boiling class resentments. One called tax collectors "bloodsuckers of the nation who drink the tears of the unfortunate from goblets of gold." Another one of the cahiers condemned the courts of nobles as "vampires pumping the last drop of blood" from the people. Another complained that "20 million must live on half the wealth of France while the clergy . . . devour the other half."

Delegates Take the Tennis Court Oath

Delegates to the Estates-General from the Third Estate were elected, though only propertied men could vote. Thus, the delegates were mostly lawyers, middle-class officials, and writers. They were familiar with the writings of Voltaire, Rousseau, and other *philosophes*. They went to Versailles not only to solve the financial crisis but also to insist on reform.

The Estates-General convened in May 1789. From the start, the delegates were deadlocked over the issue of voting. Traditionally, each estate had met and voted separately. Each group had one vote. Under this system, the First and Second Estates always outvoted the Third Estate two to one. This time, the Third Estate wanted all three estates to meet in a single body, with votes counted "by head."

After weeks of stalemate, delegates of the Third Estate took a daring step. In June 1789, claiming to represent the people of France, they declared themselves to be the National Assembly. A few days later, the National Assembly found its meeting hall locked and guarded. Fearing that the king planned to dismiss them, the delegates moved to a nearby indoor tennis court. As curious spectators looked on, the delegates took their famous **Tennis Court Oath**. They swore "never to separate

The Oath Is Taken
Delegates of the Third Estate declare themselves to be the National Assembly, representing the people of France. They take the Tennis Court Oath (bottom), vowing to create a constitution. The National Assembly later issues the assignat (top) as currency to help pay the government's debts. *What was the significance of the Tennis Court Oath?*

and to meet wherever the circumstances might require until we have established a sound and just constitution."

When reform-minded clergy and nobles joined the Assembly, Louis XVI grudgingly accepted it. But royal troops gathered around Paris, and rumors spread that the king planned to dissolve the Assembly.

 Checkpoint What actions did delegates of the Third Estate take when the Estates-General met in 1789?

Parisians Storm the Bastille

On July 14, 1789, the city of Paris seized the spotlight from the National Assembly meeting in Versailles. The streets buzzed with rumors that royal troops were going to occupy the capital. More than 800 Parisians assembled outside the Bastille, a grim medieval fortress used as a prison for political and other prisoners. The crowd demanded weapons and gunpowder believed to be stored there.

The commander of the Bastille refused to open the gates and opened fire on the crowd. In the battle that followed, many people were killed. Finally, the enraged mob broke through the defenses. They killed the commander and five guards and released the handful of prisoners who were being held there, but found no weapons.

The Bastille was a symbol to the people of France representing years of abuse by the monarchy. The storming of and subsequent fall of the Bastille was a wake-up call to Louis XVI. Unlike any other riot or short-lived protest, this event posed a challenge to the sheer existence of the regime. Since 1880, the French have celebrated Bastille Day annually as their national independence day.

 Checkpoint What was the significance of the storming of the Bastille?

Parisians storm the Bastille on July 14, 1789.

SECTION **1** Assessment

Progress Monitoring *Online*
For: Self-quiz with vocabulary practice
Web Code: naa-1811

Terms, People, and Places

1. What do many of the key terms, people, and places listed at the beginning of the section have in common? Explain.

Note Taking

2. **Reading Skill: Recognize Multiple Causes** Use your completed chart to answer the Focus Question: What led to the storming of the Bastille, and therefore, to the start of the French Revolution?

Comprehension and Critical Thinking

3. **Compare Point of View** How did the views of society differ between the nobles and peasants in 1789 France?

4. **Identify Point of View** Suppose that you are Jacques Necker. Write a paragraph that explains how your economic reform program will benefit France.

5. **Express Problems Clearly** What issues arose when Louis XVI called the Estates-General in 1789?

● **Writing About History**

Quick Write: Make a Cause-and-Effect Organizer Choose a specific event from this section and write it in the center of a piece of paper. List causes above it and effects below it. This will give you the details to include in your cause-and-effect essay. You may need to do additional research to gather more details.

Women march
to the palace.

Parisian Women Storm Versailles

On October 5, 1789, anger turned to action as thousands of women marched from Paris to Versailles. They wanted the king to stop ignoring their suffering. They also wanted the queen. French women were particularly angry with the Austrian-born queen, Marie Antoinette. They could not feed their children, yet she lived extravagantly. The women yelled as they looked for her in the palace:

66 Death to the Austrian! We'll wring her neck! We'll tear her heart out! 99
—mob of women at Versailles, October 6, 1789

Focus Question What political and social reforms did the National Assembly institute in the first stage of the French Revolution?

The French Revolution Unfolds

Objectives
- Explain how the political crisis of 1789 led to popular revolts.
- Summarize the moderate reforms enacted by the National Assembly in August 1789.
- Identify additional actions taken by the National Assembly as it pressed onward.
- Analyze why there was a mixed reaction around Europe to the events unfolding in France.

Terms, People, and Places

faction	émigré
Marquis de Lafayette	sans-culotte
Olympe de Gouges	republic
Marie Antoinette	Jacobins

Note Taking

Reading Skill: Identify Supporting Details As you read this section, prepare an outline like the one shown below. Remember to use numbers for supporting details.

> I. Political crisis leads to revolt
>   A. The Great Fear
>   1. Inflamed by famine and rumors
>   2.
>   B.

Excitement, wonder, and fear engulfed France as the revolution unfolded at home and spread abroad. Historians divide this revolutionary era into different phases. The moderate phase of the National Assembly (1789–1791) turned France into a constitutional monarchy. A radical phase (1792–1794) of escalating violence led to the end of the monarchy and a Reign of Terror. There followed a period of reaction against extremism, known as the Directory (1795–1799). Finally, the Age of Napoleon (1799–1815) consolidated many revolutionary changes. In this section, you will read about the moderate phase of the French Revolution.

Political Crisis Leads to Revolt

The political crisis of 1789 coincided with the worst famine in memory. Starving peasants roamed the countryside or flocked to towns, where they swelled the ranks of the unemployed. As grain prices soared, even people with jobs had to spend as much as 80 percent of their income on bread.

Rumors Create the "Great Fear" In such desperate times, rumors ran wild and set off what was later called the "Great Fear." Tales of attacks on villages and towns spread panic. Other rumors asserted that government troops were seizing peasant crops.

Inflamed by famine and fear, peasants unleashed their fury on nobles who were trying to reimpose medieval dues. Defiant peasants set fire to old manor records and stole grain from storehouses. The attacks died down after a period of time, but they clearly demonstrated peasant anger with an unjust regime.

Paris Commune Comes to Power Paris, too, was in turmoil. As the capital and chief city of France, it was the revolutionary center. A variety of **factions,** or dissenting groups of people, competed to gain power. Moderates looked to the **Marquis de Lafayette,** the aristocratic "hero of two worlds" who fought alongside George Washington in the American Revolution. Lafayette headed the National Guard, a largely middle-class militia organized in response to the arrival of royal troops in Paris. The Guard was the first group to don the tricolor—a red, white, and blue badge that was eventually adopted as the national flag of France.

A more radical group, the Paris Commune, replaced the royalist government of the city. It could mobilize whole neighborhoods for protests or violent action to further the revolution. Newspapers and political clubs— many even more radical than the Commune—blossomed everywhere. Some demanded an end to the monarchy and spread scandalous stories about the royal family and members of the court.

 Checkpoint What caused French peasants to revolt against nobles?

The National Assembly Acts

Peasant uprisings and the storming of the Bastille stampeded the National Assembly into action. On August 4, in a combative all-night meeting, nobles in the National Assembly voted to end their own privileges. They agreed to give up their old manorial dues, exclusive hunting rights, special legal status, and exemption from taxes.

Special Privilege Ends "Feudalism is abolished," announced the proud and weary delegates at 2 A.M. As the president of the Assembly later observed, "We may view this moment as the dawn of a new revolution, when all the burdens weighing on the people were abolished, and France was truly reborn."

Were nobles sacrificing much with their votes on the night of August 4? Both contemporary observers and modern historians note that the nobles gave up nothing that they had not already lost. Nevertheless, in the months ahead, the National Assembly turned the reforms of August 4 into law, meeting a key Enlightenment goal— the equality of all male citizens before the law.

Declaration of the Rights of Man In late August, as a first step toward writing a constitution, the Assembly issued the Declaration of the Rights of Man and the Citizen. The document was modeled in part on the American Declaration of Independence, written 13 years earlier. All men, the French declaration announced, were "born and remain free and equal in rights." They enjoyed natural rights to "liberty, property, security, and resistance to oppression." Like the writings of Locke and the *philosophes,* the constitution insisted that governments exist to protect the natural rights of citizens.

The declaration further <u>proclaimed</u> that all male citizens were equal before the law. Every Frenchman had an equal right to hold public office "with no distinction other than that of their virtues and talents." In addition, the declaration asserted freedom of religion and called for taxes to

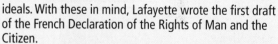

French Reaction to the American Revolution

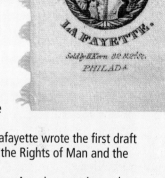

The Marquis de Lafayette (honored on ribbon at right) and Thomas Paine were leading figures in both the American and French revolutions. Lafayette, a French nobleman and military commander, helped the Americans defeat the British at Yorktown. He admired the American Declaration of Independence and American democratic ideals. With these in mind, Lafayette wrote the first draft of the French Declaration of the Rights of Man and the Citizen.

Thomas Paine was a famous American patriot and writer whose ideas in *Common Sense* had a great influence on the American Revolution. During the French Revolution, Paine moved to France. There, he defended the ideals of the revolution and was elected to serve in the revolutionary government.

Identify Central Issues How did the American Revolution influence the French Revolution?

Vocabulary Builder

proclaimed—(proh KLAYMD) *vt.* announced officially

be levied according to ability to pay. Its principles were captured in the enduring slogan of the French Revolution, "Liberty, Equality, Fraternity."

Many women were disappointed that the Declaration of the Rights of Man did not grant equal citizenship to them. In 1791, **Olympe de Gouges** (oh LAMP duh GOOZH), a journalist, demanded equal rights in her Declaration of the Rights of Woman and the Female Citizen. "Woman is born free," she proclaimed, "and her rights are the same as those of man." Therefore, Gouges reasoned, "all citizens, be they men or women, being equal in the state's eyes, must be equally eligible for all public offices, positions, and jobs." Later in the revolution, women met resistance for expressing their views in public, and many, including Gouges, were imprisoned and executed.

The Declaration of the Rights of Man met resistance as well. Uncertain and hesitant, Louis XVI did not want to accept the reforms of the National Assembly. Nobles continued to enjoy gala banquets while people were starving. By autumn, anger again turned to action.

Women March on Versailles On October 5, about six thousand women marched 13 miles in the pouring rain from Paris to Versailles. "Bread!" they shouted. They demanded to see the king.

Much of the crowd's anger was directed at the Austrian-born queen, **Marie Antoinette** (daughter of Maria Theresa and brother of Joseph II). The queen lived a life of great pleasure and extravagance, and this led to further public unrest. Although compassionate to the poor, her small acts went largely unnoticed because her lifestyle overshadowed them. She was against reforms and bored with the French court. She often retreated to the Petit Trianon, a small chateau on the palace grounds at Versailles where she lived her own life of amusement.

The women refused to leave Versailles until the king met their most important demand—to return to Paris. Not too happily, the king agreed. The next morning, the crowd, with the king and his family in tow, set out for the city. At the head of the procession rode women perched on the barrels of seized cannons. They told bewildered spectators that they were bringing Louis XVI, Marie Antoinette, and their son back to Paris. "Now

Playing Dress-Up

Marie Antoinette spent millions on her clothing and jewels and set fashion trends throughout France and Europe. This painting (top) was painted by her friend and portraitist, Elisabeth Vigée-Lebrun. Queens traditionally did not own property, but Marie Antoinette had her own small royal mansion and amusement village, or hamlet (bottom), where she played as milkmaid and shepherdess. *Why did the French common people resent Marie Antoinette?*

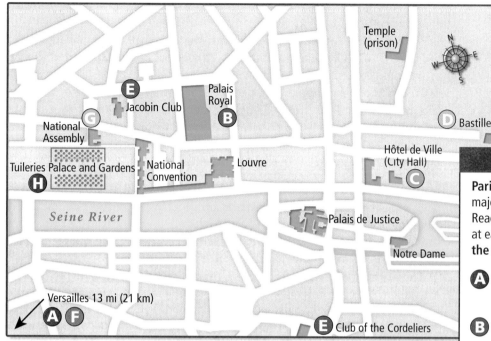

Analyzing Visuals

Paris in Revolution This map shows major landmarks of the French Revolution. Read below about the events that occurred at each landmark. **Why was Paris the revolutionary center in France?**

A **June 5, 1789** Delegates of the Third Estate take the Tennis Court Oath in Versailles.

B **July 12, 1789** Desmoulins incites a crowd at the Palais Royal, a famous meeting place.

C **July 14, 1789** Crowd meets at City Hall, the traditional protest place, before storming the Bastille.

D **July 14, 1789** Parisians storm the Bastille.

E **Oct. 1789** Political clubs (Cordeliers and Jacobins) established in Paris.

F **Oct. 5, 1789** Women march from Paris to Versailles.

G **Sept. 3, 1791** National Assembly produces the Constitution of 1791.

H **Aug. 10, 1792** Mob invades the Tuileries palace after meeting at City Hall.

we won't have to go so far when we want to see our king," they sang. Crowds along the way cheered the king, who now wore the tricolor. In Paris, the royal family moved into the Tuileries (TWEE luh reez) palace. For the next three years, Louis was a virtual prisoner.

✓ **Checkpoint** How did the National Assembly react to peasant uprisings?

The National Assembly Presses Onward

The National Assembly soon followed the king to Paris. Its largely bourgeois members worked to draft a constitution and to solve the continuing financial crisis. To pay off the huge government debt—much of it owed to the bourgeoisie—the Assembly voted to take over and sell Church lands.

The Church Is Placed Under State Control In an even more radical move, the National Assembly put the French Catholic Church under state control. Under the Civil Constitution of the Clergy, issued in 1790, bishops and priests became elected, salaried officials. The Civil Constitution ended papal authority over the French Church and dissolved convents and monasteries.

Reaction was swift and angry. Many bishops and priests refused to accept the Civil Constitution. The pope condemned it. Large numbers of French peasants, who were conservative concerning religion, also rejected the changes. When the government punished clergy who refused to support the Civil Constitution, a huge gulf opened between revolutionaries in Paris and the peasantry in the provinces.

The Constitution of 1791 Establishes a New Government The National Assembly completed its main task by producing a constitution. The Constitution of 1791 set up a limited monarchy in place of the absolute monarchy that had ruled France for centuries. A new Legislative Assembly had the power to make laws, collect taxes, and decide on issues of war and peace. Lawmakers would be elected by tax-paying male citizens over age 25.

To make government more efficient, the constitution replaced the old provinces with 83 departments of roughly equal size. It abolished the old provincial courts, and it reformed laws.

To moderate reformers, the Constitution of 1791 seemed to complete the revolution. Reflecting Enlightenment goals, it ensured equality before the law for all male citizens and ended Church interference in government. At the same time, it put power in the hands of men with the means and leisure to serve in government.

Louis's Escape Fails Meanwhile, Marie Antoinette and others had been urging the king to escape their humiliating situation. Louis finally gave in. One night in June 1791, a coach rolled north from Paris toward the border. Inside sat the king disguised as a servant, the queen dressed as a governess, and the royal children.

The attempted escape failed. In a town along the way, Louis's disguise was uncovered by someone who held up a piece of currency with the king's face on it. A company of soldiers escorted the royal family back to Paris, as onlooking crowds hurled insults at the king. To many, Louis's dash to the border showed that he was a traitor to the revolution.

✔ **Checkpoint** What were the provisions of the Constitution of 1791?

Radicals Take Over

Events in France stirred debate all over Europe. Supporters of the Enlightenment applauded the reforms of the National Assembly. They saw the French experiment as the dawn of a new age for justice and equality. European rulers and nobles, however, denounced the French Revolution.

Rulers Fear Spread of Revolution European rulers increased border patrols to stop the spread of the "French plague." Fueling those fears were the horror stories that were told by émigrés (EM ih grayz)—nobles, clergy, and others who had fled France and its revolutionary forces. Émigrés reported attacks on their privileges, their property, their religion, and even their lives. Even "enlightened" rulers turned against France. Catherine the Great of Russia burned Voltaire's letters and locked up her critics.

Edmund Burke, a British writer and statesman who earlier had defended the American Revolution, bitterly condemned revolutionaries in Paris. He predicted all too accurately that the revolution would become more violent. "Plots and assassinations," he wrote, "will be anticipated by preventive murder and preventive confiscation." Burke warned: "When ancient opinions and rules of life are taken away . . . we have no compass to govern us."

Threats Come From Abroad The failed escape of Louis XVI brought further hostile rumblings from abroad. In August 1791, the king of Prussia and the

Analyzing Political Cartoons

The French Plague European rulers, nobles, and clergy (such as, from left, Catherine the Great of Russia, the Pope, Emperor Leopold II of Prussia, and George III of England) feared the revolution in France would spread to their countries. Many émigrés fueled the flames with their tales of attacks by the revolutionary government.

1. Why were European rulers against revolutionary ideas coming into their countries?
2. How does the cartoonist portray the "plague?"

emperor of Austria—who was Marie Antoinette's brother—issued the Declaration of Pilnitz. In this document, the two monarchs threatened to intervene to protect the French monarchy. The declaration may have been mostly a bluff, but revolutionaries in France took the threat seriously and prepared for war. The revolution was about to enter a new, more radical phase of change and conflict.

Radicals Fight for Power and Declare War In October 1791, the newly elected Legislative Assembly took office. Faced with crises at home and abroad, it survived for less than a year. Economic problems fed renewed turmoil. Assignats (AS ig nats), the revolutionary currency, dropped in value, causing prices to rise rapidly. Uncertainty about prices led to hoarding and caused additional food shortages.

In Paris and other cities, working-class men and women, called **sans-culottes** (sanz koo LAHTS), pushed the revolution into more radical action. They were called sans-culottes, which means "without breeches," because they wore long trousers instead of the fancy knee breeches that upper-class men wore. By 1791, many sans-culottes demanded a **republic,** or government ruled by elected representatives instead of a monarch.

Within the Legislative Assembly, several hostile factions competed for power. The sans-culottes found support among radicals in the Legislative Assembly, especially the Jacobins. A revolutionary political club, the **Jacobins** were mostly middle-class lawyers or intellectuals. They used pamphleteers and sympathetic newspaper editors to advance the republican cause. Opposing the radicals were moderate reformers and political officials who wanted no more reforms at all.

The National Assembly Declares War on Tyranny The radicals soon held the upper hand in the Legislative Assembly. In April 1792, the war of words between French revolutionaries and European monarchs moved onto the battlefield. Eager to spread the revolution and destroy tyranny abroad, the Legislative Assembly declared war first on Austria and then on Prussia, Britain, and other states. The great powers expected to win an easy victory against France, a land divided by revolution. In fact, however, the fighting that began in 1792 lasted on and off until 1815.

Sans-culotte, 1792

✔ **Checkpoint** How did the rest of Europe react to the French Revolution?

SECTION 2 **Assessment**

Progress Monitoring Online
For: Self-quiz with vocabulary practice
Web Code: naa-1821

Terms, People, and Places

1. For each term, person, or place listed at the beginning of the section, write a sentence explaining its significance.

Note Taking

2. **Reading Skill: Identify Supporting Details** Use your completed outline to answer the Focus Question: What political and social reforms did the National Assembly institute in the first stage of the French Revolution?

Comprehension and Critical Thinking

3. **Make Comparisons** How was the French Declaration of the Rights of Man and the Citizen similar to the American Declaration of Independence?

4. **Summarize** What did the Constitution of 1791 do, and how did it reflect Enlightenment ideas?

5. **Draw Inferences** Describe what happened to France's constitutional monarchy because of the French Revolution.

● **Writing About History**

Quick Write: Create a Flowchart As you prepare to write a cause-and-effect essay, you need to decide how to organize it. To do this, create a flowchart that shows the effects of the French Revolution on other countries. Do you want to write about the events in chronological order? By the importance of each event?

Declaration of the Rights of Man and the Citizen

Painting of the declaration

The National Assembly issued this document in 1789 after having overthrown the established government in the early stages of the French Revolution. The document was modeled in part on the English Bill of Rights and on the American Declaration of Independence. The basic principles of the French declaration were those that inspired the revolution, such as the freedom and equality of all male citizens before the law. The Articles below identify additional principles.

Therefore the National Assembly recognizes and proclaims, in the presence and under the auspices[1] of the Supreme Being, the following rights of man and of the citizen:

1. Men are born and remain free and equal in rights. Social distinctions may be founded only upon the general good.
2. The aim of all political association is the preservation of the natural and imprescriptible[2] rights of man. These rights are liberty, property, security, and resistance to oppression. . . .
4. Liberty consists in the freedom to do everything which injures no one else. . . .
5. Law can only prohibit such actions as are hurtful to society. . . .
6. Law is the expression of the general will. Every citizen has a right to participate personally, or through his representative, in its formation. It must be the same for all, whether it protects or punishes. All citizens, being equal in the eyes of the law, are equally eligible to all dignities and to all public positions and occupations, according to their abilities, and without distinction except that of their virtues and talents.
7. No person shall be accused, arrested, or imprisoned except in the cases and according to the forms prescribed by law. . . .
11. The free communication of ideas and opinions is one of the most precious of the rights of man. Every citizen may, accordingly, speak, write, and print with freedom. . . .
13. A common contribution is essential for the maintenance of the public [military] forces and for the cost of administration. This should be equitably distributed among all the citizens in proportion to their means.

Thinking Critically

1. **Summarize** Summarize article 6. Why is this article especially significant?
2. **Identify Central Issues** What central idea does this declaration share with the American Declaration of Independence?

1. **auspices** (AWS puh siz) *n.* approval and support
2. **imprescriptible** (im prih SKRIP tuh bul) *adj.* that which cannot be rightfully taken away

Marie Antoinette transported by cart to the guillotine

WITNESS HISTORY 🔊 AUDIO

The Engine of Terror

A new execution device called the guillotine was introduced during this phase of the revolution. With its large, diagonal blade that came crashing down from a great height, it cut off heads swiftly and accurately. Thousands of people were sent to the guillotine and executed without trial. In his novel *A Tale of Two Cities*, Charles Dickens describes daily life during the Reign of Terror:

66 Along the Paris streets, the death-carts rumble, hollow and harsh. Six tumbrils [carts that carried condemned persons to the guillotine] carry the day's wine to La Guillotine. 99

Focus Question What events occurred during the radical phase of the French Revolution?

Radical Days of the Revolution

Objectives
- Understand how and why radicals abolished the monarchy.
- Explain why the Committee of Public Safety was created and why the Reign of Terror resulted.
- Summarize how the excesses of the Convention led to the formation of the Directory.
- Analyze how the French people were affected by the changes brought about by the revolution.

Terms, People, and Places

suffrage
Robespierre
Reign of Terror
guillotine

Napoleon
nationalism
Marseilles

Note Taking

Reading Skill: Recognize Sequence Make a timeline like the one shown here. Add dates and important events as you read this section.

Aug. 1792
Mob invades
royal palace.

| Sept. | Jan. | July |
| 1792 | 1793 | 1794 |

In 1793, the revolution entered a radical phase. For a year, France experienced one of the bloodiest regimes in its long history as determined leaders sought to extend and preserve the revolution.

The Monarchy Is Abolished

As the revolution continued, dismal news about the war abroad heightened tensions. Well-trained Prussian forces were cutting down raw French recruits. In addition, royalist officers were deserting the French army, joining émigrés and others hoping to restore the king's power.

Tensions Lead to Violence Battle disasters quickly inflamed revolutionaries who thought the king was in league with the enemies. On August 10, 1792, a crowd of Parisians stormed the royal palace of the Tuileries and slaughtered the king's guards. The royal family fled to the Legislative Assembly, escaping before the mob arrived.

A month later, citizens attacked prisons that held nobles and priests accused of political offenses. About 1,200 prisoners were killed; among them were many ordinary criminals. Historians disagree about the people who carried out the "September massacres." Some call them bloodthirsty mobs. Others describe them as patriots defending France from its enemies. In fact, most were ordinary citizens fired to fury by real and imagined grievances.

Radicals Take Control and Execute the King Backed by Paris crowds, radicals then took control of the Assembly. Radicals

Vocabulary Builder

radical—(RAD ih kul) *adj.* extreme; departure from the usual or traditional

called for the election of a new legislative body called the National Convention. **Suffrage,** the right to vote, was to be extended to all male citizens, not just to property owners.

The Convention that met in September 1792 was a more <u>radical</u> body than earlier assemblies. It voted to abolish the monarchy and establish a republic—the French Republic. Deputies then drew up a new constitution for France. The Jacobins, who controlled the Convention, set out to erase all traces of the old order. They seized lands of nobles and abolished titles of nobility.

During the early months of the Republic, the Convention also put Louis XVI on trial as a traitor to France. The king was convicted by a single vote and sentenced to death. On a foggy morning in January 1793, Louis mounted a scaffold in a public square in Paris. He started to speak, "Frenchmen, I die innocent. I pardon the authors of my death. I pray God that the blood about to be spilt will never fall upon the head of France. . . ." Then a roll of drums drowned out his words. Moments later, the king was beheaded. The executioner lifted the king's head by its hair and held it before the crowd.

In October, Marie Antoinette was also executed. The popular press celebrated her death. The queen, however, showed great dignity as she went to her death.

 Checkpoint   What occurred after radicals took control of the Assembly?

■ COMPARING VIEWPOINTS

On the Execution of a King

On January 21, 1793, King Louis XVI of France was executed by order of the National Convention. Reaction to this event was both loud and varied throughout Europe. The excerpts below present two different views on this event. **Critical Thinking** *Which of the two viewpoints makes a better case for or against the execution of King Louis XVI? Cite examples from both statements to support your argument.*

For the Execution

The crimes of Louis XVI are unhappily all too real; they are consistent; they are notorious. Do we even have to ask the question of whether a nation has the right to judge, and execute, its highest ranking public official . . . when, to more securely plot against the nation, he concealed himself behind a mask of hypocrisy? Or when, instead of using the authority confided to him to protect his countrymen, he used it to oppress them? Or when he turned the laws into an instrument of violence to crush the supporters of the Revolution? Or when he robbed the citizens of their gold in order to subsidize their foes, and robbed them of their subsistence in order to feed the barbarian hordes who came to slaughter them? Or when he created monopolies in order to create famine by drying up the sources of abundance so that the people might die in misery and hunger? . . .

—Jean-Paul Marat

Against the Execution

The Republican tyrants of France have now carried their bloody purposes to the uttermost diabolical stretch of savage cruelty. They have murdered their King without even the shadow of justice, and of course they cannot expect friendship nor intercourse with any civilized part of the world. The vengeance of Europe will now rapidly fall on them; and, in process of time, make them the veriest wretches on the face of the earth. The name of Frenchman will be considered as the appellation of savage, and their presence shunned as a poison, deadly destructive to the peace and happiness of Mankind. It appears evident, that the majority of the National Convention, and the Executive Government of that truly despotic country, are comprised of the most execrable villains upon the face of the earth. . . .

—*London Times,* January 25, 1793

Terror and Danger Grip France

By early 1793, danger threatened France on all sides. The country was at war with much of Europe, including Britain, the Netherlands, Spain, and Prussia. In the Vendée (vahn DAY) region of France, royalists and priests led peasants in rebellion against the government. In Paris, the sans-culottes demanded relief from food shortages and inflation. The Convention itself was bitterly divided between Jacobins and a rival group, the Girondins.

The Convention Creates a New Committee To deal with the threats to France, the Convention created the Committee of Public Safety. The 12-member committee had almost absolute power as it battled to save the revolution. The Committee prepared France for all-out war, issuing a *levée en masse,* or mass levy (tax) that required all citizens to contribute to the war effort. In addition, the 12 members of the Committee were in charge of trials and executions.

Spurred by revolutionary fervor, French recruits marched off to defend the republic. Young officers developed effective new tactics to win battles with masses of ill-trained but patriotic forces. Soon, French armies overran the Netherlands. They later invaded Italy. At home, they crushed peasant revolts. European monarchs shuddered as the revolutionaries carried "freedom fever" into conquered lands.

Robespierre "the Incorruptible" At home, the government battled counterrevolutionaries under the guiding hand of Maximilien Robespierre (ROHBZ pyehr). Robespierre, a shrewd lawyer and politician, quickly rose to the leadership of the Committee of Public Safety. Among Jacobins, his selfless dedication to the revolution earned him the nickname "the incorruptible." The enemies of Robespierre called him a tyrant.

Robespierre had embraced Rousseau's idea of the general will as the source of all legitimate law. He promoted religious toleration and wanted to abolish slavery. Though cold and humorless, he was popular with the sans-culottes, who hated the old regime as much as he did. He believed that France could achieve a "republic of virtue" only through the use of terror, which he coolly defined as nothing more than "prompt, severe, inflexible justice." "Liberty cannot be secured," Robespierre cried, "unless criminals lose their heads."

The Guillotine Defines the Reign of Terror Robespierre was one of the chief architects of the **Reign of Terror,** which lasted from September 1793 to July 1794. Revolutionary courts conducted hasty trials. Spectators greeted death sentences with cries of "Hail the Republic!" or "Death to the traitors!"

In a speech given on February 5, 1794, Robespierre explained why the terror was necessary to achieve the goals of the revolution:

Primary Source

66 It is necessary to stifle the domestic and foreign enemies of the Republic or perish with them. . . . The first maxim of our politics ought to be to lead the people by means of reason and the enemies of the people by terror. . . . If the basis of popular government in time of peace is virtue, the basis of popular government in time of revolution is both virtue and terror. 99

—Maximilien Robespierre, quoted in *Pageant of Europe* (Stearns)

BIOGRAPHY

Robespierre

Maximilien Robespierre (1758–1794) did not have an easy childhood. His mother died when he was only 6 years old. Two years later, his father abandoned him and his three siblings. The children's aunts and grandfather then raised them. Because of this, Robespierre assumed responsibilities at an early age. Eventually, he went to study law at the University of Paris. His performance was so noteworthy that he was chosen to deliver a speech to Louis XVI on the occasion of the king's coronation. But young Robespierre was snubbed. After listening to the address in a pouring rainstorm, the king and queen left without acknowledging Robespierre in any way. Years later, in 1789, Robespierre was elected to the Estates-General, where his career as a revolutionary began. **How do you think Robespierre's early life might have influenced his political ideas?**

Suspect were those who resisted the revolution. About 300,000 were arrested during the Reign of Terror. Seventeen thousand were executed. Many were victims of mistaken identity or were falsely accused by their neighbors. Many more were packed into hideous prisons, where deaths from disease were common.

The engine of the Terror was the **guillotine** (GIL uh teen). Its fast-falling blade extinguished life instantly. A member of the legislature, Dr. Joseph Guillotin (gee oh TAN), had introduced it as a more humane method of beheading than the uncertain ax. But the guillotine quickly became a symbol of horror.

Within a year, the Terror consumed those who initiated it. Weary of bloodshed and fearing for their own lives, members of the Convention turned on the Committee of Public Safety. On the night of July 27, 1794, Robespierre was arrested. The next day he was executed. After the heads of Robespierre and other radicals fell, executions slowed dramatically.

✔ **Checkpoint** Why did Robespierre think the Terror was necessary to achieve the goals of the revolution?

The Revolution Enters Its Third Stage

In reaction to the Terror, the revolution entered a third stage. Moving away from the excesses of the Convention, moderates produced another constitution, the third since 1789. The Constitution of 1795 set up a five-

● **INFOGRAPHIC**

THE REIGN OF TERROR

From autumn 1793 to midsummer 1794, the revolution in France was overshadowed by a time of terror as the Committee of Public Safety rounded up "suspected persons" all over France. Only about 15 percent of those sentenced to death by guillotine (model at left) were of the nobility and clergy. Most were artisans and peasants of the Third Estate. Prisons in Paris—which included places such as former mansions and palaces, religious premises, and colleges—became more and more crowded as the number of suspects increased. Once sentenced to death, the condemned might travel an hour to the guillotine by cart as onlookers threw mud at them.

Thieves stole ▲ items such as silver as émigrés fled the country due to the Terror.

◀ Interrogation of aristocratic prisoners at L'Abbaye prison man Directory and a two-house legislature elected by male citizens of property. The middle class and professional people of the bourgeoisie were the dominant force during this stage of the French Revolution. The Directory held power from 1795 to 1799.

Weak but dictatorial, the Directory faced growing discontent. Peace was made with Prussia and Spain, but war with Austria and Great Britain continued. Corrupt leaders lined their own pockets but failed to solve pressing problems. When rising bread prices stirred hungry sans-culottes to riot, the Directory quickly suppressed them. Another threat to the Directory was the revival of royalist feeling. Many émigrés were returning to France, and devout Catholics, who resented measures that had been taken against the Church, were welcoming them. In the election of 1797, supporters of a constitutional monarchy won the majority of seats in the legislature.

As chaos threatened, politicians turned to **Napoleon** Bonaparte, a popular military hero who had won a series of brilliant victories against the Austrians in Italy. The politicians planned to use him to advance their own goals. To their dismay, however, before long Napoleon would outwit them all to become ruler of France.

✓ **Checkpoint** What changes occurred after the Reign of Terror came to an end?

History Interactive

For: Interactive French Revolution
Web Code: nap-1821

◀ People never knew if friends or family might appear on a list of guillotine victims. There is some debate on the humaneness of death by guillotine. Some authorities claim that even after the head has been severed, the victim could remain conscious for up to 30 seconds.

Georges Danton, ▶ a Revolutionary leader, challenged the Terror and was guillotined.

◀ This engraving depicts Robespierre's execution by guillotine. His was not the last. "Twenty minutes later, [those condemned for the day] were in front of the scaffold…. Pale, tense, shivering… several of them lowered their heads or shut their eyes…. The third [victim] was…the Princess of Monaco…. On the platform, her youthful beauty shone in the dazzling July light." The executioners then tossed the bodies and heads into large baskets near the scaffold.

Thinking Critically
1. **Identify Point of View** What were the goals of the Committee of Public Safety?
2. **Predict Consequences** How do you think life in France changed after the Terror came to an end?

French Nationalism
"La Marseillaise" (top) and a revolutionary-period drum (bottom) helped rally the French people.

Revolution Brings Change

By 1799, the 10-year-old French Revolution had dramatically changed France. It had dislodged the old social order, overthrown the monarchy, and brought the Church under state control.

New symbols such as the red "liberty caps" and the tricolor confirmed the liberty and equality of all male citizens. The new title "citizen" applied to people of all social classes. All other titles were eliminated. Before he was executed, Louis XVI was called Citizen Capet, from the name of the dynasty that had ruled France in the Middle Ages. Elaborate fashions and powdered wigs gave way to the practical clothes and simple haircuts of the sans-culottes.

Nationalism Spreads Revolution and war gave the French people a strong sense of national identity. In earlier times, people had felt loyalty to local authorities. As monarchs centralized power, loyalty shifted to the king or queen. Now, the government rallied sons and daughters of the revolution to defend the nation itself. Nationalism, a strong feeling of pride in and devotion to one's country, spread throughout France. The French people attended civic festivals that celebrated the nation and the revolution. A variety of dances and songs on themes of the revolution became immensely popular.

By 1793, France was a nation in arms. From the port city of Marseilles (mahr say), troops marched to a rousing new song. It urged the "children of the fatherland" to march against the "bloody banner of tyranny." This song, "La Marseillaise" (mahr say ez), would later become the French national anthem.

Revolutionaries Push For Social Reform Revolutionaries pushed for social reform and religious toleration. They set up state schools to replace religious ones and organized systems to help the poor, old soldiers, and war widows. With a major slave revolt raging in the colony of St. Domingue (Haiti), the government also abolished slavery in France's Caribbean colonies.

✔ **Checkpoint** What changes occurred in France because of the French Revolution?

Progress Monitoring *Online*
For: Self-quiz with vocabulary practice
Web Code: naa-1831

SECTION 3 **Assessment**

Terms, People, and Places

1. Place each of the key terms at the beginning of the section into one of the following categories: politics, culture, geography, or technology. Write a sentence for each term explaining your choice.

Note Taking

2. **Reading Skill: Recognize Sequence** Use your completed timeline to answer the Focus Question: What events occurred during the radical phase of the French Revolution?

Comprehension and Critical Thinking

3. **Summarize** Summarize the goals and actions of the Jacobins.
4. **Identify Central Issues** Why was the Committee of Public Safety created?
5. **Recognize Cause and Effect** How did the Reign of Terror cause the National Convention to be replaced by the Directory?
6. **Predict Consequences** How do you think French nationalism affected the war between France and the powers of Europe?

● Writing About History

Quick Write: Provide Elaboration To illustrate each cause and effect of your essay, you should have supporting details, facts, and examples. Choose one of the events below and list as many specific details as possible. Then write a paragraph using the details you listed to explain what caused the event.
• Reign of Terror
• Execution of King Louis XVI
• Creation of the Committee of Public Safety

Art of Revolution

Revolutions have visual chronicles as well as written ones, and in the days before photography, these depictions were often rendered with paint. The French artist Jacques-Louis David (ZHAHK loo EE dah VEED) and the Spanish artist Francisco Goya both portrayed aspects of revolution on canvas, but they had differing viewpoints. David supported the early French Revolution and embraced the revolutionary spirit in his work. Goya, however, was a realist who showed human suffering and the horrors of war in his paintings.

▲ *Napoleon Crossing Mont Saint Bernard,* **Jacques-Louis David, 1801**
Imprisoned after moderates turned against the Reign of Terror, David barely escaped with his life. When Napoleon rose to power, David deftly switched his political allegiance to the new Emperor of France and became one of Bonaparte's chief portraitists. Notice the names carved into the rocks. David included these names of great past rulers to show Napoleon's level of greatness. David's depictions of Napoleon helped cement him as a strong and heroic leader.

▲ *The Third of May, 1808,* **Francisco José de Goya y Lucientes, 1814**
One of the consequences of the French Revolution and Napoleon's rise was that France soon found itself at war with the rest of Europe. Francisco Goya saw firsthand the impact of these wars. Born in northern Spain, he rose to become the official painter of the Spanish court. When Napoleon invaded Spain and deposed its king, Goya chronicled the horrors of the resulting guerrilla warfare.

> **Thinking Critically**
> 1. **Compare Points of View** What elements in each painting express the viewpoint of the artist? How are the elements different?
> 2. **Recognize Ideologies** How do you think the ideology of the French Revolution led to the scene Goya portrays here?

SECTION 4

Unfinished portrait of Napoleon by Jacques-Louis David and Napoleon's signature

 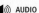
Enter Napoleon Bonaparte

After the execution of King Louis XVI, France entered a state of confusion and chaos without a single leader. Meanwhile, Napoleon Bonaparte, a brilliant and ambitious captain in the French army, was rapidly rising in the military ranks. Soon enough, Napoleon would come to rule almost all of Europe. One of his earliest victories in Lodi, Italy, convinced him that he was only just beginning his successful rise to power:

66 From that moment, I foresaw what I might be. Already I felt the earth flee from beneath me, as if I were being carried into the sky. 99
—Napoleon Bonaparte

Focus Question Explain Napoleon's rise to power in Europe, his subsequent defeat, and how the outcome still affects Europe today.

The Age of Napoleon

Objectives

- Understand Napoleon's rise to power and why the French strongly supported him.
- Explain how Napoleon built an empire and what challenges the empire faced.
- Analyze the events that led to Napoleon's downfall.
- Outline how the Congress of Vienna tried to create a lasting peace.

Terms, People, and Places

plebiscite	scorched-earth policy
Napoleonic Code	abdicate
annex	Congress of Vienna
Continental System	legitimacy
guerrilla warfare	Concert of Europe

Note Taking

Reading Skill: Identify Main Ideas As you read the section, use a flowchart to list the important events that led from Napoleon's rise to power to his defeat. Add boxes as you need them.

Napoleon quickly advances through military ranks.

From 1799 to 1815, Napoleon Bonaparte would dominate France and Europe. A hero to some, an evil force to others, he gave his name to the final phase of the revolution—the Age of Napoleon.

Napoleon Rises to Power

Napoleon was born in Corsica, a French-ruled island in the Mediterranean. At age nine, he was sent to France to be trained for a military career. When the revolution broke out, he was an ambitious 20-year-old lieutenant, eager to make a name for himself.

Napoleon favored the Jacobins and republican rule. However, he found the conflicting ideas and personalities of the French Revolution confusing. He wrote to his brother in 1793: "Since one must take sides, one might as well choose the side that is victorious, the side which devastates, loots, and burns. Considering the alternative, it is better to eat than be eaten."

Victories Cloud Losses During the turmoil of the revolution, Napoleon rose quickly in the army. In December 1793, he drove British forces out of the French port of Toulon (too LOHN). He then went on to win several dazzling victories against the Austrians, capturing most of northern Italy and forcing the Hapsburg emperor to make peace. Hoping to disrupt British trade with India, he led an expedition to Egypt in 1798. The Egyptian campaign proved to be a disaster, but Napoleon managed to hide stories of the worst losses from his admirers in France. He did so by establishing a network of spies and censoring the press.

Success fueled Napoleon's ambition. By 1799, he moved from victorious general to political leader. That year, he helped overthrow the weak Directory and set up a three-man governing board known as the Consulate. Another constitution was drawn up, but Napoleon soon took the title First Consul. In 1802, he had himself named consul for life.

Napoleon Crowns Himself Emperor Two years later, Napoleon had acquired enough power to assume the title Emperor of the French. He invited the pope to preside over his coronation in Paris. During the ceremony, however, Napoleon took the crown from the pope's hands and placed it on his own head. By this action, Napoleon meant to show that he owed his throne to no one but himself.

At each step on his rise to power, Napoleon had held a plebiscite (PLEB uh syt), or popular vote by ballot. Each time, the French strongly supported him. As you will read, although the people theoretically had a say in government through their votes, Napoleon still held absolute power. This is sometimes called democratic despotism. To understand why people supported him, we must look at his policies.

✓ **Checkpoint** How did Napoleon rise to power so quickly in France?

Napoleon Reforms France

During the Consulate and empire, Napoleon consolidated his power by strengthening the central government. Order, security, and efficiency replaced liberty, equality, and fraternity as the slogans of the new regime.

To restore economic prosperity, Napoleon controlled prices, encouraged new industry, and built roads and canals. He set up a system of public schools under strict government control to ensure well-trained officials and military officers. At the same time, Napoleon backed off from some of the revolution's social reforms. He made peace with the Catholic Church in the Concordat of 1801. The Concordat kept the Church under state control but recognized religious freedom for Catholics. Revolutionaries who opposed the Church denounced the agreement, but Catholics welcomed it.

Napoleon won support across class lines. He encouraged émigrés to return, provided they take an oath of loyalty. Peasants were relieved when he recognized their right to lands they had bought from the Church and nobles during the revolution. The middle class, who had benefited most from the revolution, approved of Napoleon's economic reforms and the restoration of order after years of chaos. Napoleon also opened jobs to all, based on talent, a popular policy among those who remembered the old aristocratic monopoly of power.

Among Napoleon's most lasting reforms was a new code of laws, popularly called the **Napoleonic Code.** It embodied Enlightenment principles such as the equality of all citizens before the law, religious toleration, and the abolition of feudalism.

The Egyptian Campaign
The Battle of the Pyramids, July 21, 1798, painted by Louis-Francois Lejeune. *How did Napoleon hide the fact that the Egyptian campaign was a disaster?*

But the Napoleonic Code undid some reforms of the French Revolution. Women, for example, lost most of their newly gained rights and could not exercise the rights of citizenship. Male heads of households regained complete authority over their wives and children. Again, Napoleon valued order and authority over individual rights.

 Checkpoint What reforms did Napoleon introduce during his rise to power?

Napoleon Builds an Empire

From 1804 to 1812, Napoleon furthered his reputation on the battlefield. He successfully battled the combined forces of the greatest European powers. He took great risks and even suffered huge losses. "I grew up on the field of battle," he once said, "and a man such as I am cares little for the life of a million men." By 1812, his Grand Empire reached its greatest extent.

As a military leader, Napoleon valued rapid movements and made effective use of his large armies. He developed a new plan for each battle so opposing generals could never <u>anticipate</u> what he would do next. His enemies paid tribute to his leadership. Napoleon's presence on the battlefield, said one, was "worth 40,000 troops."

The Map of Europe Is Redrawn As Napoleon created a vast French empire, he redrew the map of Europe. He annexed, or incorporated into his empire, the Netherlands, Belgium, and parts of Italy and Germany. He also abolished the tottering Holy Roman Empire and created a 38-member Confederation of the Rhine under French protection. He cut Prussian territory in half, turning part of old Poland into the Grand Duchy of Warsaw.

Napoleon controlled much of Europe through forceful diplomacy. One tactic was placing friends and relatives on the thrones of Europe. For example, after unseating the king of Spain, he placed his own brother, Joseph Bonaparte, on the throne. He also forced alliances on European powers from Madrid to Moscow. At various times, the rulers of Austria, Prussia, and Russia reluctantly signed treaties with the "Corsican ogre," as the monarchs he overthrew called him.

In France, Napoleon's successes boosted the spirit of nationalism. Great victory parades filled the streets of Paris with cheering crowds. The people celebrated the glory and grandeur that Napoleon had gained for France.

Napoleon Strikes Britain Britain alone, of all the major European powers, remained outside Napoleon's European empire. With only a small army, Britain relied on its sea power to stop Napoleon's drive to rule the continent. In 1805, Napoleon prepared to invade England. But at the Battle of Trafalgar, fought off the southwest coast of Spain, British Admiral Horatio Nelson smashed the French fleet.

With an invasion ruled out, Napoleon struck at Britain's lifeblood, its commerce. He waged economic warfare through the Continental System, which closed European ports to British goods. Britain responded with its own blockade of European ports. A blockade involves shutting off ports to keep people or supplies from moving in or out. During their long struggle, both Britain and France seized neutral ships suspected of trading with the other side. British attacks on American ships sparked anger in the United States and eventually triggered the War of 1812.

Vocabulary Builder

anticipate—(an TIS uh payt) *vt.* to foresee or expect

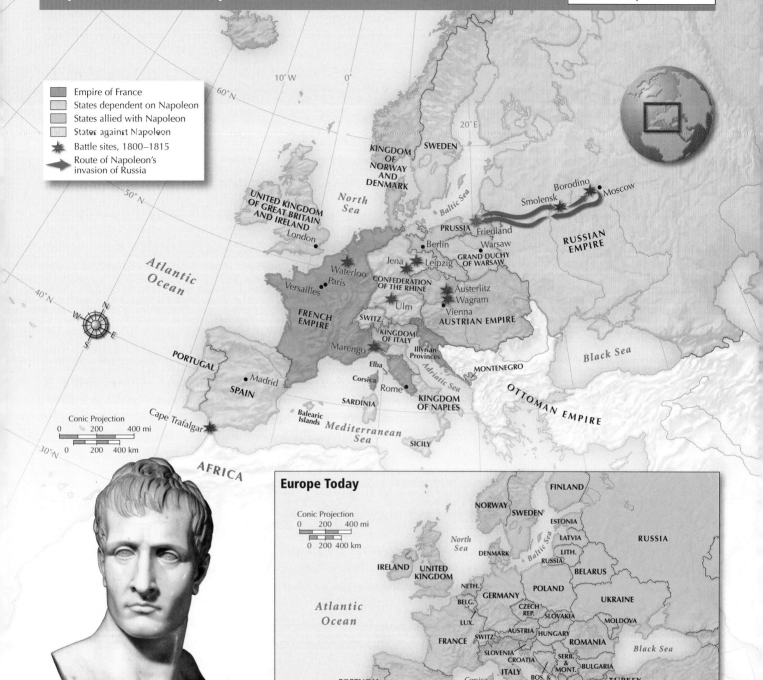

Napoleon's Power in Europe, 1812

Geography *Interactive*
For: Audio guided tour
Web Code: nap-1841

Legend:
- Empire of France
- States dependent on Napoleon
- States allied with Napoleon
- States against Napoleon
- ★ Battle sites, 1800–1815
- ➤ Route of Napoleon's invasion of Russia

Labels on main map:
Atlantic Ocean · North Sea · Baltic Sea · KINGDOM OF NORWAY AND DENMARK · SWEDEN · UNITED KINGDOM OF GREAT BRITAIN AND IRELAND · London · PRUSSIA · Berlin · Friedland · Warsaw · GRAND DUCHY OF WARSAW · RUSSIAN EMPIRE · Smolensk · Borodino · Moscow · Jena · Leipzig · Waterloo · Paris · Versailles · CONFEDERATION OF THE RHINE · Austerlitz · Wagram · Ulm · Vienna · AUSTRIAN EMPIRE · FRENCH EMPIRE · SWITZ. · KINGDOM OF ITALY · Marengo · Illyrian Provinces · Adriatic Sea · MONTENEGRO · Black Sea · OTTOMAN EMPIRE · PORTUGAL · Madrid · SPAIN · Elba · Corsica · Rome · KINGDOM OF NAPLES · SARDINIA · Balearic Islands · Mediterranean Sea · SICILY · Cape Trafalgar · AFRICA

Conic Projection
0 200 400 mi
0 200 400 km

Europe Today

Labels: FINLAND · NORWAY · SWEDEN · ESTONIA · LATVIA · RUSSIA · LITH. · DENMARK · RUSSIA · BELARUS · IRELAND · UNITED KINGDOM · NETH. · BELG. · GERMANY · POLAND · UKRAINE · LUX. · CZECH REP. · SLOVAKIA · MOLDOVA · FRANCE · SWITZ. · AUSTRIA · HUNGARY · ROMANIA · SLOVENIA · CROATIA · SERB. & MONT. · BULGARIA · TURKEY · PORTUGAL · SPAIN · ITALY · BOS. & HERZ. · MACEDONIA · GREECE · ALBANIA · Corsica · Sardinia · Balearic Is. · Mediterranean Sea · Sicily · Crete · CYPRUS · MALTA · Atlantic Ocean · North Sea · Baltic Sea · Black Sea

Conic Projection
0 200 400 mi
0 200 400 km

Bust of Napoleon Bonaparte

Map Skills Napoleon's empire reached its greatest extent in 1812. Most of the countries in Europe today have different names and borders.

1. **Locate:** (a) French empire, (b) Russian empire, (c) Germany
2. **Region** Locate the Confederation of the Rhine. What is this area called today?
3. **Make Comparisons** Compare Europe of Napoleon's empire to Europe of today on the maps above. How has Europe changed?

In the end, Napoleon's Continental System failed to bring Britain to its knees. Although British exports declined, Britain's powerful navy kept vital trade routes open to the Americas and India. Meanwhile, trade restrictions created a scarcity of goods in Europe, sent prices soaring, and intensified resentment against French power.

French armies under Napoleon spread ideas of the revolution across Europe. They backed liberal reforms in the lands they conquered. In some places, they helped install revolutionary governments that abolished titles of nobility, ended Church privileges, opened careers to men of talent, and ended serfdom and manorial dues. The Napoleonic Code, too, influenced countries in continental Europe and Latin America.

✔ **Checkpoint** **How did Napoleon come to dominate most of Europe by 1812?**

Napoleon's Empire Faces Challenges

In 1812, Napoleon continued his pursuit of world domination and invaded Russia. This campaign began a chain of events that eventually led to his downfall. Napoleon's final defeat brought an end to the era of the French Revolution.

Nationalism Works Against Napoleon Napoleon's successes contained seeds of defeat. Although nationalism spurred French armies to success, it worked against them too. Many Europeans who had welcomed the ideas of the French Revolution nevertheless saw Napoleon and his armies as foreign oppressors. They resented the Continental System and Napoleon's effort to impose French culture on them.

From Rome to Madrid to the Netherlands, nationalism unleashed revolts against France. In the German states, leaders encouraged national loyalty among German-speaking people to counter French influence.

Spain and Austria Battle the French Resistance to foreign rule bled French-occupying forces dry in Spain. Napoleon introduced reforms that sought to undermine the Spanish Catholic Church. But many Spaniards remained loyal to their former king and devoted to the Church. When the Spanish resisted the invaders, well-armed French forces responded with

As shown in this painting, the Russian winter took its toll on Napoleon's army. Philippe Paul de Ségur, an aide to Napoleon, describes the grim scene as the remnants of the Grand Army returned home. **What were the effects of this disaster in Russia?**

Primary Source

❝ In Napoleon's wake [was] a mob of tattered ghosts draped in . . . odd pieces of carpet, or greatcoats burned full of holes, their feet wrapped in all sorts of rags. . . . [We] stared in horror as those skeletons of soldiers went by, their gaunt, gray faces covered with disfiguring beards, without weapons . . . with lowered heads, eyes on the ground, in absolute silence.❞
—*Memoirs of Philippe Paul de Ségur*

brutal repression. Far from crushing resistance, however, the French response further inflamed Spanish nationalism. Efforts to drive out the French intensified.

Spanish patriots conducted a campaign of **guerrilla warfare,** or hit-and-run raids, against the French. (In Spanish, *guerrilla* means "little war.") Small bands of guerrillas ambushed French supply trains or troops before retreating into the countryside. These attacks kept large numbers of French soldiers tied down in Spain when Napoleon needed them elsewhere.

Spanish resistance encouraged Austria to resume hostilities against the French. In 1805, at the Battle of Austerlitz, Napoleon had won a crushing victory against an Austro-Russian army of superior numbers. Now, in 1809, the Austrians sought revenge. But once again, Napoleon triumphed—this time at the Battle of Wagram. By the peace agreement that followed, Austria surrendered lands populated by more than three million subjects.

The Russian Winter Stops the Grand Army Tsar Alexander I of Russia was once an ally of Napoleon. The tsar and Napoleon planned to divide Europe if Alexander helped Napoleon in his Continental System. Many countries objected to this system, and Russia became unhappy with the economic effects of the system as well. Yet another cause for concern was that Napoleon had enlarged the Grand Duchy of Warsaw that bordered Russia on the west. These and other issues led the tsar to withdraw his support from the Continental System. Napoleon responded to the tsar's action by assembling an army with soldiers from 20 nations, known as the Grand Army.

In 1812, with about 600,000 soldiers and 50,000 horses, Napoleon invaded Russia. To avoid battles with Napoleon, the Russians retreated eastward, burning crops and villages as they went. This **scorched-earth policy** left the French hungry and cold as winter came. Napoleon entered Moscow in September. He realized, though, that he would not be able to feed and supply his army through the long Russian winter. In October, he turned homeward.

The 1,000-mile retreat from Moscow turned into a desperate battle for survival. Russian attacks and the brutal Russian winter took a terrible toll. Fewer than 20,000 soldiers of the once-proud Grand Army survived. Many died. Others deserted. French general Michel Ney sadly concluded: "General Famine and General Winter, rather than Russian bullets, have conquered the Grand Army." Napoleon rushed to Paris to raise a new force to defend France. His reputation for success had been shattered.

✔ **Checkpoint** What challenges threatened Napoleon's empire and what led to the disaster in Russia?

Napoleon Falls From Power
A defeated Napoleon after his abdication on April 6, 1814, in a painting by Paul Delaroche

WITNESS HISTORY VIDEO

Watch *Napoleon's Lost Army* on the **Witness History Discovery School**™ video program to learn about Napoleon's invasion of Russia in 1812.

Napoleon Falls From Power

The disaster in Russia brought a new alliance of Russia, Britain, Austria, and Prussia against a weakened France. In 1813, they defeated Napoleon in the Battle of the Nations at Leipzig.

Napoleon Abdicates Briefly The next year, Napoleon **abdicated,** or stepped down from power. The victors exiled him to Elba, an island in the Mediterranean. They then recognized Louis XVIII, brother of Louis XVI, as king of France.

The restoration of Louis XVIII did not go smoothly. He agreed to accept the Napoleonic Code and honor the land settlements made during the revolution. However, many émigrés rushed back to France bent on revenge. An economic depression and the fear of a return to the old regime helped rekindle loyalty to Napoleon.

As the victorious allies gathered in Vienna for a general peace conference, Napoleon escaped his island exile and returned to France. Soldiers flocked to his banner. As citizens cheered Napoleon's advance, Louis XVIII fled. In March 1815, Napoleon entered Paris in triumph.

Crushed at the Battle of Waterloo Napoleon's triumph was short-lived. His star soared for only 100 days, while the allies reassembled their forces. On June 18, 1815, the opposing armies met near the town of Waterloo in Belgium. British forces under the Duke of Wellington and a Prussian army commanded by General Blücher crushed the French in an agonizing day-long battle. Once again, Napoleon was forced to abdicate and to go into exile on St. Helena, a lonely island in the South Atlantic. This time, he would not return.

Napoleon's Legacy Napoleon died in 1821, but his legend lived on in France and around the world. His contemporaries as well as historians today have long debated his legacy. Was he "the revolution on horseback," as he claimed? Or was he a traitor to the revolution?

No one, however, questions Napoleon's impact on France and on Europe. The Napoleonic Code consolidated many changes of the revolution. The France of Napoleon was a centralized state with a constitution. Elections were held with expanded, though limited, suffrage. Many more citizens had rights to property and access to education than under the old regime. Still, French citizens lost many rights promised so fervently by republicans during the Convention.

On the world stage, Napoleon's conquests spread the ideas of the revolution. He failed to make Europe into a French empire. Instead, he sparked nationalist feelings across Europe. The abolition of the Holy Roman Empire would eventually help in creating a new Germany. Napoleon's impact also reached across the

BIOGRAPHY

Prince Clemens von Metternich

As Austria's foreign minister, Metternich (1773–1859) used a variety of means to achieve his goals. In 1809, when Napoleon seemed vulnerable, Metternich favored war against France. In 1810, after France had crushed Austria, he supported alliance with France. When the French army was in desperate retreat from Russia, Metternich became the "prime minister of the coalition" that defeated Napoleon. At the Congress of Vienna, Metternich helped create a new European order and made sure that Austria had a key role in it. He would skillfully defend that new order for more than 30 years. **Why did Metternich's policies toward France change?**

Europe After the Congress of Vienna, 1815

Geography *Interactive*
For: Audio guided tour
Web Code: nap 1842

Map Skills At the Congress of Vienna, European leaders redrew the map of Europe in order to contain France and keep a balance of power.

1. **Locate** (a) German Confederation, (b) Netherlands, (c) Vienna
2. **Region** Name three states that were in the German Confederation.
3. **Recognize Cause and Effect** Why did the Congress enlarge some of the countries around France?

Boundary of the German Confederation

Quadruple Alliance, 1815
- Great Britain
- Prussia
- Austrian Empire
- Russian Empire

Atlantic. In 1803, his decision to sell France's vast Louisiana Territory to the American government doubled the size of the United States and ushered in an age of American expansion.

✔ **Checkpoint** How did Napoleon impact Europe and the rest of the world?

Leaders Meet at the Congress of Vienna

After Waterloo, diplomats and heads of state again sat down at the **Congress of Vienna.** They faced the monumental task of restoring stability and order in Europe after years of war. The Congress met for 10 months, from September 1814 to June 1815. It was a brilliant gathering of European leaders. Diplomats and royalty dined and danced, attended concerts and ballets, and enjoyed parties arranged by their host, Emperor Francis I of Austria. The work fell to Prince Clemens von Metternich of Austria, Tsar Alexander I of Russia, and Lord Robert Castlereagh of Britain. Defeated France was represented by Prince Charles Maurice de Talleyrand.

Congress Strives For Peace The chief goal of the Vienna decision makers was to create a lasting peace by establishing a balance of power and protecting the system of monarchy. Each of the leaders also pursued his own goals. Metternich, the dominant figure at the Congress, wanted to restore things the way they were in 1792. Alexander I urged a "holy alliance" of Christian monarchs to suppress future revolutions. Lord Castlereagh was determined to prevent a revival of French military power. The aged diplomat Talleyrand shrewdly played the other leaders against one another so France would be accepted as an equal partner.

The peacemakers also redrew the map of Europe. To contain French ambitions, they ringed France with strong countries. In the north, they added Belgium and Luxembourg to Holland to create the kingdom of the Netherlands. To prevent French expansion eastward, they gave Prussia lands along the Rhine River. They also allowed Austria to reassert control over northern Italy.

To turn back the clock to 1792, the architects of the peace promoted the principle of legitimacy, restoring hereditary monarchies that the French Revolution or Napoleon had unseated. Even before the Congress began, they had put Louis XVIII on the French throne. Later, they restored "legitimate" monarchs in Portugal, Spain, and the Italian states.

Congress Fails to See Traps Ahead To protect the new order, Austria, Russia, Prussia, and Great Britain extended their wartime alliance into the postwar era. In the Quadruple Alliance, the four nations pledged to act together to maintain the balance of power and to suppress revolutionary uprisings, especially in France. Another result of the Congress was a system known as the Concert of Europe, in which the powers met periodically to discuss any problems affecting the peace of Europe.

The Vienna statesmen achieved their immediate goals in creating a lasting peace. Their decisions influenced European politics for the next 100 years. Europe would not see war on a Napoleonic scale until 1914. They failed, however, to foresee how powerful new forces such as nationalism would shake the foundations of Europe and Latin America in the next decades.

 Checkpoint Explain the chief goal and outcome of the Congress of Vienna.

Portrait of Louis XVIII

SECTION 4 Assessment

Progress Monitoring *Online*
For: Self-quiz with vocabulary practice
Web Code: naa-1841

Terms, People, and Places

1. For each term, person, or place listed at the beginning of the section, write a sentence explaining its significance.

Note Taking

2. **Reading Skill: Identify Main Ideas** Use your completed flowchart to answer the Focus Question: Explain Napoleon's rise to power in Europe, his subsequent defeat, and how the outcome still affects Europe today.

Comprehension and Critical Thinking

3. **Demonstrate Reasoned Judgment** If you were a French voter in 1803, how would you have voted on the plebiscite to make Napoleon emperor? Explain.

4. **Synthesize Information** Describe the resistance Napoleon encountered as countries grew to resent him.

5. **Make Comparisons** How does the peacekeeping solution adopted by the Congress of Vienna compare to today's peacekeeping missions?

● **Writing About History**

Quick Write: Clarify When you write a rough draft of a cause-and-effect essay, you should highlight the causes and effects. Use two highlighters, one to show causes, and the other to show effects. Eliminate causes or effects that do not support your main point, and add transitional phrases as needed. Write a paragraph about Napoleon's downfall. Highlight the causes and effects to evaluate the effectiveness of your paragraph.

Geography's Impact

How have geographic factors affected the course of history?

Geography played a critical role in Napoleon's disastrous invasion of Russia in 1812. Russia's severe winter weather helped destroy his Grand Army. In this way, geography affected the course of history by helping end Napoleon's quest to control all of Europe. Geography has also had more subtle—but still powerful—effects on history. The first civilizations arose in river valleys, where rich soil helped farmers feed growing populations. Humans continue to settle near rivers and along coastlines to have access to food, transportation, and trade. Consider the additional examples below that show the role of geography in history.

Silk was traded between China and Europe.

German soldiers in Russia, World War II

Landforms and Defense

People throughout history have taken advantage of local landforms to defend themselves. For example, settlements located on high ground made enemies' attacks more difficult as they had to climb as they fought. It also made it easier to spy an enemy. With this type of defense in mind, Greeks built the Acropolis of Athens on a steep hill thousands of years ago. *Acropolis* means "city at the top." In Paris, France, the founders used a different approach. They built their town on an island in the middle of the Seine River. Medieval castles often reflected all these strategies: positioned on a hill, beside a river, and encircled by a moat.

Resources and Trade Routes

Ancient overland trade routes were really just beaten paths. Merchants traveled far and wide for resources that were not available at home. Towns grew up along the trade routes to serve the merchants' needs for food and shelter. A famous trade route named the Silk Road was a set of caravan trails that led from China all the way to the Mediterranean Sea. Europeans willingly paid great sums for silk, porcelain, and other products that only China, with its particular set of resources, could provide.

Climate and Military Outcomes

Napoleon could rightfully blame his defeat on Russia's harsh climate. But he was not the only general who has cursed the forces of nature. Throughout history, climate has affected the outcome of military campaigns. It has helped turn back invaders or otherwise brought misery to foreign armies. In the late 1200s, Japan twice avoided becoming a province of Mongol China because a typhoon destroyed the invading Mongol fleet. The Japanese refer to this climatic savior as *kamikaze,* or "divine wind." In 1941, Hitler moved to take over the Soviet Union. Hitler's forces, much like Napoleon's, were not prepared for Russia's harsh winter. Thousands of Germans froze to death.

The Acropolis, built on a hill for defense

Thinking Critically

1. How have landforms and climate affected where people live? Explain your answer.

2. **Connections to Today** Research online to find information on the tsunami that occurred in South Asia in 2004. Summarize the impact of geography.

Quick Study Guide

Progress Monitoring *Online*
For: Self-test with vocabulary practice
Web Code: naa-1851

■ What Inspired the French Revolution?

- **Social:** Enlightenment ideas such as equality and justice
- **Political:** Ideas from the American Revolution
- **Economic:** Inequalities among classes; unrest due to extravagant monarchy

■ Reforms of the National Assembly

Political
• Proclaimed all male citizens equal before the law.
• Limited the power of the monarchy.
• Established the Legislative Assembly to make laws.
• Granted all tax-paying male citizens the right to elect members of the Legislative Assembly.

Social and Economic
• Abolished special privileges of the nobility.
• Announced an end to feudalism.
• Called for taxes to be levied according to ability to pay.
• Abolished guilds and forbade labor unions.
• Compensated nobles for lands seized by peasants.

Religious
• Declared freedom of religion.
• Took over and sold Church lands.
• Placed the French Catholic Church under control of the state.
• Provided that bishops and priests be elected and receive government salaries.

■ Causes and Effects of the French Revolution

Cause and Effect	
Long-Term Causes	**Immediate Causes**
• Corrupt and inconsistent leadership • Prosperous members of Third Estate resent privileges of First and Second Estates. • Spread of Enlightenment ideas	• Huge government debt • Poor harvests and rising price of bread • Failure of Louis XVI to accept financial reforms • Formation of National Assembly • Storming of Bastille

↓

The French Revolution

↓

Immediate Effects	Long-Term Effects
• Declaration of the Rights of Man and the Citizen adopted. • France adopts its first written constitution. • Revolutionary France fights coalition of European powers. • Monarchy abolished; execution of king and queen. • Reign of Terror	• Napoleon gains power. • Napoleonic Code established. • French public schools set up. • French conquests spread nationalism. • Congress of Vienna convenes to restore stability to Europe. • Revolutions occur elsewhere in Europe and in Latin America.

Connections to Today
• French law reflects Napoleonic Code. • France eventually became a democratic republic.

■ Key Events From 1789–1815

1789
Parisians storm the Bastille on July 14, starting the French Revolution.

1793
Radicals execute the king and queen, which leads to the Reign of Terror.

1799
Napoleon overthrows the Directory.

Chapter Events
Global Events

1790   **1795**   **1800**

1789
The United States Constitution is ratified.

1793
China rejects British trade offer.

Concept Connector

■ Cumulative Review

Record the answers to the questions below on your Concept Connector worksheets. In addition, record information from this chapter about the following concepts:

• Cooperation: Coalitions against Napoleon

1. **Democracy** The First and Second Estates had power and wealth at the expense of the Third Estate. These class differences in France caused revolt and revolution, as you have learned in this chapter. Thus began the fight for democracy as members of the Third Estate demanded equal say in government. Compare the Assembly's Declaration of the Rights of Man and the Citizen to the American Declaration of Independence. What principles of democracy are included in both documents? Consider these influencing factors:
    • the early governments in Greece and Rome
    • England's political system
    • Enlightenment thinkers

2. **Nationalism** The French Revolution brought about waves of nationalism that spread throughout France. Under Napoleon, nationalism spurred French armies to success. The tricolor flag, the song *La Marseillaise,* and the words Liberty, Equality, and Fraternity all helped unite the French people in a cause to defend their nation. What spurred nationalism in the American Revolution? Think about the following:
    • symbols
    • common goals

3. **Revolution** In the French Revolution, the Third Estate revolted to topple the Old Regime. The Protestant Reformation caused a similar upheaval when peasants revolted for an end to serfdom. Research the Peasants' Revolt that erupted in Germany in 1524. How does it compare to the French Revolution? Think about the following:
    • causes
    • effects
    • goals

■ Connections To Today

1. **Geography's Impact: Wars in the Middle East**
    Geography played an important role in Napoleon's defeat in Russia. Napoleon's Grand Army, once nearly 500,000 soldiers strong, shrank to about 20,000 due to the brutal Russian winter. Research newspaper and magazine articles to find how geography has impacted wars in the Middle East. Compile your research and write a script for your local newscast. Consider the following:
    • location
    • landforms
    • climate

    Burning oil pipeline, September 14, 2004, caused by sabotage in the Middle East

2. **Cooperation: United Nations** Diplomats and heads of states from the powers that defeated Napoleon—Austria, Russia, Prussia, and Great Britain—gathered at the Congress of Vienna in 1814. Their main goal was to restore peace after the French Revolution and Napoleonic era. Today, U.N. peacekeeping operations take place around the globe with the same goal of keeping or restoring peace. Research to find more information on the Congress of Vienna and U.N. peacekeeping operations. Draw a table to write facts about each in individual columns. Think about the following:
    • history and purpose of the organizations
    • definitions of "peacekeeping"

| 1804 Napoleon crowns himself emperor of France. | | 1812 Napoleon invades Russia. | 1814 Congress of Vienna meets. | 1815 Napoleon is defeated at Waterloo. |

1805 — **1810** — **1815**

| 1804 Haiti declares independence from France. | | 1812 The United States declares war on Britain. | |

History Interactive
For: Interactive timeline
Web Code: nap-1801

Chapter Assessment

Terms, People, and Places

Match the following terms with the definitions below.

sans-culotte	Olympe de Gouges
bourgeoisie	plebiscite
Napoleonic Code	deficit spending
abdicate	Maximilien Robespierre
Estates-General	nationalism

1. a meeting of the representatives of the three estates
2. situation in which a government spends more money than it takes in
3. strong feeling of devotion to one's country
4. the middle class
5. journalist who demanded equal rights for women
6. leader of the Committee of Public Safety
7. ballot in which voters have a direct say on an issue
8. working-class men and women in France; means "without breeches"
9. law code that embodied Enlightenment principles such as equality
10. step down from power

Main Ideas

Section 1 (pp. 572–577)
11. What caused discontent in the old French regime?
12. When the Estates-General convened in May 1789, what actions did members of the Third Estate take and why?

Section 2 (pp. 578–584)
13. Describe one reform that the National Assembly enacted through each of the following documents: **(a)** the Declaration of the Rights of Man and the Citizen, **(b)** the Civil Constitution of the Clergy, **(c)** the Constitution of 1791.

Section 3 (pp. 585–591)
14. What was the Reign of Terror?

Section 4 (pp. 592–601)
15. List the reforms that Napoleon made as leader of France.
16. How did the Congress of Vienna try to restore the balance of power in Europe?

Chapter Focus Question
17. What were the causes and effects of the French Revolution, and how did the revolution lead to the Napoleonic era?

Critical Thinking

18. **Draw Conclusions** What impact did Enlightenment ideas have on the French Revolution?
19. **Recognize Cause and Effect** Explain the events that led to the end of the monarchy.
20. **Geography and History** How did the geography of the Russian empire work against Napoleon's Grand Army?
21. **Analyzing Cartoons** In the cartoon shown here, the figure on the left represents the British, and the other figure represents Napoleon. What are the figures carving, and why?

● Writing About History

Expository Essay: Cause and Effect There were many key events in the French Revolution and Napoleonic era that affected France and the rest of the world. Write an essay that explains the causes of one of the following events and discuss what resulted: Parisians storming the Bastille; Women marching on Versailles; Napoleon crowning himself emperor of the French. Consult page SH10 of the Writing Handbook for additional help.

Prewriting
• Consider what you know about these events and choose one that you think best shows cause and effect.

• Take time to research facts, descriptions, and examples, to clearly illustrate the causes and effects in your essay.

Drafting
• Choose one of the following to organize the causes and effects in your essay: show the chronological order of events, or order the events from the least important to the most important.
• As you draft your essay, illustrate each cause and effect with supporting facts and details.

Revising
• Review your entire draft to ensure you show a clear relationship between the causes and effects.
• Analyze each paragraph to check that you have provided a thorough set of facts and details.

Document-Based Assessment

Storming the Bastille

One of the most famous and dramatic moments of the French Revolution was the storming of the Bastille. This prison fortress with 90-foot-high walls symbolized the injustices of absolute monarchy. The following documents describe the event from different viewpoints.

Document A

"Shouts of 'Give us the Bastille' were heard, and nine hundred had pressed into the undefended outer courtyard, becoming angrier by the minute. . . . At about half past three in the afternoon the crowd was reinforced by companies of *gardes françaises* [French guards] and by defecting soldiers, including a number who were veterans of the American campaign. Two in particular, Second-Lieutenant Jacob Elie, the standard-bearer of the Infantry of the Queen, and Pierre-Augustin Hulin, the director of the Queen's laundry, were crucial in turning the incoherent assault into an organized siege."

—From ***Citizens: A Chronicle of the French Revolution,*** (1989) by Simon Schama

Document B

"How much the greatest event it is that ever happened in the world! and how much the best!"

—**Letter, July 30, 1789,** by Charles James Fox (1749–1806), British politician, on the fall of the Bastille

Document C

"The mob came closer and the governor declared his willingness to capitulate [give up]. . . The streets and houses, even the roofs were filled with people abusing and cursing me. Daggers, bayonets, pistols were constantly pointed at me. I did not know how I would be killed but was sure my last hour had come. Those who had no arms were throwing stones at me, the women wrenched their teeth and threatened me with their fists. Two soldiers behind me had already been killed by the furious mob and I am convinced I could not have reached City Hall had not one officer . . . escorted me."

—**"Reports of the Taking of the Bastille, July 14, 1789, by One of Its Defenders"** (1834) by Ludwig von der Fluhe (Swiss officer)

Document D

Demolition of the Bastille, 1789

Analyzing Documents

Use your knowledge of the storming of the Bastille and Documents A, B, C, and D to answer questions 1–4.

1. In Document B, Charles James Fox was mostly likely enthusiastic about the fall of the Bastille because
   A he had a personal grudge against prison guards.
   B the people stood up to authority.
   C he supported King Louis XVI.
   D he was anxious to see what the people of France would do next.

2. Which document attempts to give an objective view of the storming of the Bastille?
   A Document B
   B Document A
   C Document C
   D Document D

3. In Document C, which words best indicate which side the author is on?
   A the governor declared his willingness to capitulate
   B daggers, bayonets, pistols
   C even the roofs were filled with people
   D furious mob

4. **Writing Task** Compare the four documents. Which lasting document best conveys the significance of the event? Use your knowledge of this event and specific evidence from the documents to support your opinion.

19

The Industrial Revolution Begins

1750–1850

A Different Kind of Revolution

While the American Revolution and the French Revolution were being fought in the late 1700s, another kind of revolution took hold in Britain. Though not political, this revolution—known as the Industrial Revolution—brought about just as many changes to society. Paul Johnson, historian, describes this time period as "the age, above all in history, of matchless opportunities for penniless men with powerful brains and imaginations." Listen to the Witness History audio to hear more about the start of the Industrial Revolution.

Train ticket, 1830

◀ On September 27, 1825, the Stockton and Darlington Railway in England became the world's first steam railway to offer passenger and freight service.

James Watt

Chapter Preview

Chapter Focus Question What technological, social, economic, and cultural changes occurred as the Industrial Revolution took hold?

Section 1
Dawn of the Industrial Age

Section 2
Britain Leads the Way

Section 3
Social Impact of the Industrial Revolution

Section 4
New Ways of Thinking

Socialist leaflet

Note Taking Study Guide _Online_
For: Note Taking and Concept Connector worksheets
Web Code: nad-1901

Matthew
Boulton

WITNESS HISTORY 🔊 AUDIO

From Hand Power to Steam Power

For centuries, people used their own energy to provide the power for their work. While the idea of using steam power came about in the seventeenth century, it was not until engineer James Watt improved the steam engine that it could be applied to machinery. His financial partner Matthew Boulton, a successful manufacturer, proclaimed:

66 I have at my disposal what the whole world demands, something which will uplift civilization more than ever by relieving man of all undignified drudgery. I have *steam power*.**99**

Focus Question What events helped bring about the Industrial Revolution?

Dawn of the Industrial Age

Objectives
- Analyze why life changed as industry spread.
- Summarize how an agricultural revolution led to the growth of industry.
- Outline the new technologies that helped trigger the Industrial Revolution.

Terms, People, and Places

anesthetic
enclosure
James Watt
smelt

Note Taking

Reading Skill: Recognize Multiple Causes
Several key events led to the Industrial Revolution. As you read the section, create a flowchart of these causes. Add categories as needed.

For thousands of years following the rise of civilization, most people lived and worked in small farming villages. However, a chain of events set in motion in the mid-1700s changed that way of life for all time. Today, we call this period of change the Industrial Revolution.

The Industrial Revolution started in Britain. The economic changes that Britain experienced affected people's lives as much as previous political changes and revolutions had. In contrast with most political revolutions, it was neither sudden nor swift. Instead, it was a long, slow, uneven process in which production shifted from simple hand tools to complex machines. From its beginnings in Britain, the Industrial Revolution has spread to the rest of Europe, North America, and around the globe.

Life Changes as Industry Spreads

In 1750, most people worked the land, using handmade tools. They lived in simple cottages lit by firelight and candles. They made their own clothing and grew their own food. In nearby towns, they might exchange goods at a weekly outdoor market.

Like their ancestors, these people knew little of the world that existed beyond their village. The few who left home traveled only as far as their feet or a horse-drawn cart could take them. Those bold adventurers who dared to cross the seas were at the mercy of the winds and tides.

With the onset of the Industrial Revolution, the rural way of life began to disappear. By the 1850s, many country villages had grown into industrial towns and cities. Those who lived there were able to buy clothing and food that someone else produced.

Industrial age travelers moved rapidly between countries and conti nents by train or steamship. Urgent messages flew along telegraph wires. New inventions and scientific "firsts" poured out each year. Between 1830 and 1855, for example, an American dentist first used an anesthetic, or drug that prevents pain during surgery; an American inventor patented the first sewing machine; a French physicist measured the speed of light; and a Hungarian doctor introduced antiseptic methods to reduce the risk of women dying in childbirth.

Still more stunning changes occurred in the next century, which cre ated our familiar world of skyscraper cities and carefully tended suburbs. How and why did these great changes occur? Historians point to a series of interrelated causes that helped trigger the industrialization of the West. The "West" referred originally to the industrialized countries in Europe but today includes many more.

 Checkpoint Why was the Industrial Revolution a turning point in world history?

Agriculture Spurs Industry

Oddly enough, the Industrial Revolution was made possible in part by a change in the farming fields of Western Europe. From the first agricultural revolution some 11,000 years ago, when people learned to farm and domesticate animals, until about 300 years ago, farming had remained pretty much the same. Then, a second agricultural revolution took place that greatly improved the qual ity and quantity of farm products.

Farming Methods Improve The Dutch led the way in this new agricultural revolution. They built earthen walls known as dikes to reclaim land from the sea. They also combined smaller fields into larger ones to make better use of the land and used fertilizer from livestock to renew the soil.

In the 1700s, British farmers expanded on Dutch agricultural exper iments. Educated farmers exchanged news of experiments through farm journals. Some farmers mixed different kinds of soils to get higher crop yields. Others tried out new methods of crop rotation. Lord Charles Townshend urged farmers to grow turnips, which restored exhausted soil. Jethro Tull invented a new mechanical device, the seed drill, to aid farmers. It deposited seeds in rows rather than scattering them wastefully over the land.

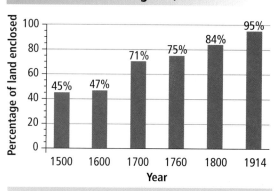

Land Enclosures in England, 1500–1914

Graph Skills According to the graph, between which years was the largest percentage of land enclosed? What was the result of these land enclosures?

SOURCE: *Oxford Atlas of World History*, 1999

Jethro Tull's seed drill

Enclosure Increases Output but Causes Migration Meanwhile, rich landowners pushed ahead with **enclosure,** the process of taking over and consolidating land formerly shared by peasant farmers. In the 1500s, landowners had enclosed land to gain more pastures for sheep to increase wool output. By the 1700s, they wanted to create larger fields that could be cultivated more efficiently. The British Parliament facilitated enclosures through legislation.

As millions of acres were enclosed, farm output rose. Profits also rose because large fields needed fewer workers. But such progress had a large human cost. Many farm laborers were thrown out of work, and small farmers were forced off their land because they could not compete with large landholders. Villages shrank as cottagers left in search of work. In time, jobless farm workers migrated to towns and cities. There, they formed a growing labor force that would soon tend the machines of the Industrial Revolution.

Vocabulary Builder

statistics—(stuh TIS tiks) *pl.n.* data that are gathered and tabulated to present information

Population Multiplies The agricultural revolution contributed to a rapid growth of population. Precise population statistics for the 1700s are rare, but those that do exist are striking. Britain's population, for example, soared from about 5 million in 1700 to almost 9 million in 1800. The population of Europe as a whole shot up from roughly 120 million to about 180 million during the same period. Such growth had never before been seen.

Why did this population increase occur? First, the agricultural revolution reduced the risk of death from famine because it created a surplus of food. Since people ate better, they were healthier. Also, better hygiene and sanitation, along with improved medical care, further slowed deaths from disease.

✔ **Checkpoint** How did an agricultural revolution contribute to population growth?

BIOGRAPHY

James Watt

How did a clever Scottish engineer become the "Father of the Industrial Revolution"? After repairing a Newcomen steam engine, James Watt (1736–1819) became fascinated with the idea of improving the device. Within a few months, he knew he had a product that would sell. Still, Watt lacked the money needed to produce and market it.

Fortunately, he was able to form a partnership with the shrewd manufacturer Matthew Boulton. They then founded Soho Engineering Works in Birmingham, England, to manufacture steam engines. Watt's version of the steam engine shown here had a separate condensing chamber and was patented in 1769. Eventually, a measure of mechanical and electrical power, the watt, would be named for James Watt. **How might the Industrial Revolution have been different if Watt had not found a business partner?**

New Technology Becomes Key

Another factor that helped trigger the Industrial Revolution was the development of new technology. Aided by new sources of energy and new materials, these new technologies enabled business owners to change the ways work was done.

An Energy Revolution During the 1700s, people began to harness new sources of energy. One vital power source was coal, used to develop the steam engine. In 1712, British inventor Thomas Newcomen had developed a steam engine powered by coal to pump water out of mines. Scottish engineer James Watt looked at Newcomen's invention in 1764 and set out to make improvements on the engine in order to make it more efficient. Watt's engine, after several years of work, would become a key power source of the Industrial Revolution. The steam engine opened the door not only to operating machinery but eventually to powering locomotives and steamships.

The Quality of Iron Improves Coal was also a vital source of fuel in the production of iron, a material needed for the construction of machines and steam engines. The Darby family of Coalbrookdale pioneered new methods of producing iron. In 1709, Abraham Darby used coal instead of charcoal to smelt iron, or separate iron from its ore.

Darby's experiments led him to produce less expensive and better-quality iron, which was used to produce parts for the steam engines. Both his son and grandson continued to improve on his methods. In fact, Abraham Darby III built the world's first iron bridge. In the decades that followed, high-quality iron was used more and more widely, especially after the world turned to building railroads.

Abraham Darby III completed the world's first iron bridge in 1779. The bridge still stands today.

✔ **Checkpoint** What new technologies helped trigger the Industrial Revolution?

SECTION 1 Assessment

Progress Monitoring *Online*
For: Self-quiz with vocabulary practice
Web Code: naa-1911

Terms, People, and Places

1. For each term, person, or place listed at the beginning of the section, write a sentence explaining its significance.

Note Taking

2. **Reading Skill: Recognize Multiple Causes** Use your completed flowchart to answer the Focus Question: What events helped bring about the Industrial Revolution?

Comprehension and Critical Thinking

3. **Recognize Cause and Effect** What were the immediate and long-term effects of the agricultural revolution that occurred in the 1700s?

4. **Predict Consequences** How do you think population growth contributed to the Industrial Revolution?

5. **Summarize** Explain how new sources of energy, specifically coal, contributed to the Industrial Revolution.

● Writing About History

Quick Write: Give Background To explain a historical process, you should first orient the reader to time and place. Ask yourself when and where the process occurred. Practice by explaining in one or two sentences how an agricultural revolution led to the Industrial Revolution.

Early train ticket

Train passengers in Britain

Riding the Railway

One of the most important developments of the Industrial Revolution was the creation of a countrywide railway network. The world's first major rail line went from Liverpool to Manchester in England. Fanny Kemble, the most famous actress of the day, was one of the first passengers:

66 We were introduced to the little engine which was to drag us along the rails. . . This snorting little animal, . . . started at about ten miles an hour. . . . You can't imagine how strange it seemed to be journeying on thus, without any visible cause of progress other than the magical machine . . . 99

Focus Question What key factors allowed Britain to lead the way in the Industrial Revolution?

Britain Leads the Way

Objectives
• Understand why Britain was the starting point for the Industrial Revolution.
• Describe the changes that transformed the textile industry.
• Explain the significance of the transportation revolution.

Terms, People, and Places

capital	Eli Whitney
enterprise	turnpike
entrepreneur	Liverpool
putting-out system	Manchester

Note Taking

Reading Skill: Identify Causes and Effects Fill in the circles of a concept web like the one below with the key factors that helped Britain take an early lead in industrialization. In a separate concept web, fill in the effects of Britain's early lead.

When agricultural practices changed in the eighteenth century, more food was able to be produced, which in turn fueled population growth in Britain. The agricultural changes also left many farmers homeless and jobless. These two factors led to a population boom in the cities as people migrated from rural England into towns and cities. This population increase, in turn, created a ready supply of labor to mine the coal, build the factories, and run the machines. The start of the Industrial Revolution in Britain can be attributed to many factors. Population growth was just one of them.

Why Britain?

What characteristics of eighteenth-century Britain made it ripe for industrialization? Historians cite several reasons for Britain's lead.

Natural Resources Abound Britain had the advantage of plentiful natural resources such as natural ports and navigable rivers. Rivers supplied water power and allowed for the construction of canals. These canals increased accessibility for trade and were instrumental in bringing goods to market. In addition, Britain was able to establish communications and transport relatively cheaply due to its easy accessibility to the sea from all points. Britain's plentiful supply of coal was fundamental to its industrialization and was used to power steam engines. Vast supplies of iron were available to be used to build the new machines.

The Effects of Demand and Capital In thc 1700s, Britain had plenty of skilled mechanics who were eager to meet the growing demand for new, practical inventions. This ready workforce, along with the population explosion, boosted demand for goods. In order to increase the production of goods to meet the demand, however, another key ingredient was needed. Money was necessary to start businesses.

From the mid-1600s to 1700s, trade from a growing overseas empire helped the British economy prosper. Beginning with the slave trade, the business class accumulated capital, or money used to invest in enterprises. An enterprise is a business organization in an area such as shipping, mining, railroads, or factories. Many businessmen were ready to risk their capital in new ventures due to the healthy economy.

In addition to the advantages already cited, Britain had a stable government that supported economic growth. While other countries in Europe faced river tolls and other barriers, Britain did not. The government built a strong navy that protected its empire, shipping, and overseas trade. Although the upper class tended to look down on business people, it did not reject the wealth produced by the new entrepreneurs. These entrepreneurs were those who managed and assumed the financial risks of starting new businesses.

✔ **Checkpoint** What conditions in Britain paved the way for the Industrial Revolution?

Shuttle used to speed up weaving process

Geography *Interactive*
For: Audio guided tour
Web Code: nap-1921

Resources and Industries in England, 1750

Map Skills Plentiful supplies of coal, advancements in the textile industry, iron smelting, and the manufacturing of iron goods contributed to Britain's position as the world's leading industrial nation in the late eighteenth century.

1. **Locate** (a) London (b) Manchester (c) Thames River
2. **Region** Identify the centers of woolen industry in England.
3. **Draw Inferences** What were the industrial advantages of the rivers during this time?

Legend:
- Coalfield
- Navigable river
- Copper mining and smelting
- Iron extraction and smelting
- Linen cloth
- Metalware and cutlery
- Shipbuilding
- Tin mining and smelting
- Woolen cloth

These textile machines were constructed to increase cotton production. The flying shuttle sped up weaving, while the spinning jenny and the water frame increased the speed of spinning thread. How did these inventions change the textile industry?

◀ John Kay's flying shuttle, 1733 ▶

◀ James Hargreaves' spinning jenny, 1764

Richard Arkwright's water frame, 1769 ▶

The Textile Industry Advances

The Industrial Revolution first took hold in Britain's largest industry—textiles. In the 1600s, cotton cloth imported from India had become popular. British merchants tried to organize a cotton cloth industry at home. They developed the **putting-out system,** also known as cottage industry, in which raw cotton was distributed to peasant families who spun it into thread and then wove the thread into cloth in their own homes. Skilled artisans in the towns then finished and dyed the cloth.

Inventions Speed Production Under the putting-out system, production was slow. As the demand for cloth grew, inventors came up with a string of remarkable devices that revolutionized the British textile industry. For example, John Kay's flying shuttle enabled weavers to work so fast that they soon outpaced spinners. James Hargreaves solved that problem by producing the spinning jenny in 1764, which spun many threads at the same time. A few years later, in 1769, Richard Arkwright patented the water frame, which was a spinning machine that could be powered by water.

Meanwhile, in America, these faster spinning and weaving machines presented a challenge—how to produce enough cotton to keep up with England. Raw cotton grown in the South had to be cleaned of dirt and seeds by hand, a time-consuming task. To solve this, **Eli Whitney** invented a machine called the cotton gin that separated the seeds from the raw cotton at a fast rate. He finished the cotton gin in 1793, and cotton production increased exponentially.

Factories Are Born in Britain The new machines doomed the putting-out system. They were too large and expensive to be operated at home. Instead, manufacturers built long sheds to house the machines. At first, they located the sheds near rapidly moving streams, harnessing the water power to run the machines. Later, machines were powered by steam engines.

Spinners and weavers now came each day to work in these first factories, which brought together workers and machines to produce large quantities of goods. Early observers were awed at the size and output of these establishments. One onlooker noted: "The same [amount] of labor is now performed in one of these structures which formerly occupied the industry of an entire district."

 Checkpoint What led to the advancement of the British textile industry?

The Transportation Revolution

As production increased, entrepreneurs needed faster and cheaper methods of moving goods from place to place. Some capitalists invested in **turnpikes,** private roads built by entrepreneurs who charged travelers a toll, or fee, to use them. Goods traveled faster as a result, and turnpikes soon linked every part of Britain. Other entrepreneurs had canals dug to connect rivers together or to connect inland towns with coastal ports. Engineers also built stronger bridges and upgraded harbors to help the expanding overseas trade.

Canals Boom During the late 1700s and early 1800s, factories needed an efficient, inexpensive way to receive coal and raw materials and then to ship finished goods to market. In 1763, when the Bridgewater canal opened, it not only made a profit from tolls, but it cut in half the price of coal in Manchester. The success of this canal set off a canal-building frenzy. Entrepreneurs formed companies to construct canals for profit. Not all the canals that were built had enough traffic to support them, however, and bankruptcy often resulted. Then, beginning in the 1830s, canals lost their importance as steam locomotives made railroads the new preferred form of transportation.

Welcome the Steam Locomotive It was the invention of the steam locomotive that made the growth of railroads possible. In the early 1800s, pioneers like George Stephenson developed steam-powered locomotives to pull carriages along iron rails. The railroad did not have to follow the course of a river. This meant that tracks could go places where rivers did not, allowing factory owners and merchants to ship goods swiftly and cheaply over land. The world's first major rail line, from Liverpool to Manchester, opened in England in 1830. In the following decades, railroad travel became faster and railroad building boomed. By 1870, rail lines crisscrossed Britain, Europe, and North America.

Vocabulary Builder

decades—(DEK aydz) *n.* ten-year periods

One Thing Leads to Another As the Industrial Revolution got under way, it triggered a chain reaction. Once inventors developed machines that could produce large quantities of goods more efficiently, prices fell. Lower prices made goods more affordable and thus created more consumers who further fed the demand for goods. This new cycle caused a wave of economic and social changes that dramatically affected the way people lived.

 Checkpoint Why was the development of railroads important to industrialization?

Progress Monitoring *Online*
For: Self-quiz with vocabulary practice
Web Code: naa-1921

Terms, People, and Places

1. For each term, person, or place listed at the beginning of the section, write a sentence explaining its significance.

Note Taking

2. **Reading Skill: Identify Causes and Effects** Use your completed concept webs to answer the Focus Question: What key factors allowed Britain to lead the way in the Industrial Revolution?

Comprehension and Critical Thinking

3. **Analyze Information** Explain how each of the following helped contribute to demand for consumer goods in Britain: **(a)** population explosion, **(b)** general economic prosperity.
4. **Determine Relevance** What was the significance of new machines to the textile industry?
5. **Summarize** Explain how advances in transportation contributed to Britain's global trade.

● **Writing About History**

Quick Write: Create a Flowchart Flowcharts are useful tools to help you write an explanatory essay. Create a flowchart to show the changes that occurred in the textile industry. Be sure that the sequence of events is clear.

Monmouth
Street, London

WITNESS HISTORY 🔊 AUDIO

Stench and Sickness

As more and more people moved to the cities to work, they had little choice about where to live. There was no public water supply, waste lined the unpaved streets, and disease spread rapidly in these unsanitary conditions. Dr. Southwood-Smith worked in two districts of London and wrote:

66 Uncovered sewers, stagnant ditches and ponds, gutters always full of putrefying matter . . . It is not possible for any language to convey an adequate conception of the poisonous condition in which large portions of both these districts always remain, . . . from the masses of putrefying matter which are allowed to accumulate. 99

Focus Question What were the social effects of the Industrial Revolution?

Social Impact of the Industrial Revolution

Objectives
- Explain what caused urbanization and what life was like in the new industrial cities.
- Compare and contrast the industrial working class and the new middle class.
- Understand how the factory system and mines changed the way people worked.
- Analyze the benefits and challenges of industrialization.

Terms, People, and Places

urbanization
tenement
labor union

Note Taking

Reading Skill: Understand Effects As you read the section, complete a table that lists benefits and challenges of industrialization.

Industrialization	
Benefits	**Challenges**
• Created jobs	• Crowded cities
•	•

The Industrial Revolution brought great riches to most of the entrepreneurs who helped set it in motion. For the millions of workers who crowded into the new factories, however, the industrial age brought poverty and harsh living conditions.

In time, reforms would curb many of the worst abuses of the early industrial age in Europe and the Americas. As standards of living increased, people at all levels of society would benefit from industrialization. Until then, working people would suffer with dangerous working conditions; unsafe, unsanitary, and overcrowded housing; and unrelenting poverty.

People Move to New Industrial Cities

The Industrial Revolution brought rapid **urbanization,** or the movement of people to cities. Changes in farming, soaring population growth, and an ever-increasing demand for workers led masses of people to migrate from farms to cities. Almost overnight, small towns around coal or iron mines mushroomed into cities. Other cities grew up around the factories that entrepreneurs built in once-quiet market towns.

The British market town of Manchester numbered 17,000 people in the 1750s. Within a few years, it exploded into a center of the textile industry. Its population soared to 40,000 by 1780 and 70,000 by 1801. Visitors described the "cloud of coal vapor" that polluted

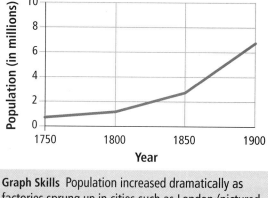

Population Growth in London, c. 1750–1900

Population (in millions) vs *Year*

Graph Skills Population increased dramatically as factories sprung up in cities such as London (pictured here). How many more people were in London in 1900 than in 1750 according to the line graph?

SOURCE: *International Historical Statistics, Europe 1750–1993,* 1998

the air, the pounding noise of steam engines, and the filthy stench of its river. This growth of industry and rapid population growth dramatically changed the location and distribution of two resources—labor and people.

✔ **Checkpoint** What led to the massive migration of people from farms to cities?

New Social Classes Emerge

The Industrial Revolution created a new middle class along with the working class. Those in the middle class owned and operated the new factories, mines, and railroads, among other industries. Their lifestyle was much more comfortable than that of the industrial working class.

When farm families moved to the new industrial cities, they became workers in mines or factories. Many felt lost and bewildered. They faced tough working conditions in uncomfortable environments. In time, though, factory and mine workers developed their own sense of community despite the terrible working conditions.

The Industrial Middle Class Those who benefited most from the Industrial Revolution were the entrepreneurs who set it in motion. The Industrial Revolution created this new middle class, or bourgeoisie (boor zhwah ZEE), whose members came from a variety of backgrounds. Some were merchants who invested their growing profits in factories. Others were inventors or skilled artisans who developed new technologies. Some rose from "rags to riches," a pattern that the age greatly admired.

Middle-class families lived in well-furnished, spacious homes on paved streets and had a ready supply of water. They wore fancy clothing and ate well. The new middle class took pride in their hard work and their determination to "get ahead." Only a few had sympathy for the poor. Women of the middle class did not leave the home to work but instead focused their energy on raising their children. This contrasted with the wealthy, who had maidservants to look after their children, and the working class, whose children were a part of the workforce.

The Industrial Working Class While the wealthy and the middle class lived in pleasant neighborhoods, vast numbers of poor struggled to survive in foul-smelling slums. They packed into tiny rooms in **tenements,** or multistory buildings divided into apartments. These tenements had no running water, only community pumps. There was no sewage or sanitation system, so wastes and garbage rotted in the streets. Sewage was also dumped into rivers, which created an overwhelming stench and <u>contaminated</u> drinking water. This led to the spread of diseases such as cholera.

Workers Stage Futile Protests Although **labor unions,** or workers' organizations, were illegal at this time, secret unions did exist among frustrated British workers. They wished to initiate worker reforms, such as increases in pay, but had no political power to effect change. Sometimes their frustration led to violence. The first instances of industrial riots occurred in England from 1811 to 1813. Groups of textile workers known as the Luddites (LUD yts) resisted the labor-saving machines that were costing them their jobs. Some of them smashed textile machines with sledgehammers and burned factories. They usually wore masks and operated at night. There was widespread support among the working class for these Luddite groups.

Workers Find Comfort in Religion Many working-class people found comfort in a religious movement called Methodism. This movement was influenced by the Industrial Revolution as people moved to cities and lost connections with their old churches. John Wesley had founded the Methodist movement in the mid-1700s. Wesley <u>stressed</u> the need for a personal sense of faith. He encouraged his followers to improve themselves by adopting sober, moral ways.

Methodist meetings featured hymns and sermons promising forgiveness of sin and a better life to come. Methodist preachers took this message of salvation into the slums. There, they tried to rekindle hope among the working poor. They set up Sunday schools where followers not only studied the Bible but also learned to read and write. Methodists helped channel workers' anger away from revolution and toward reform.

 Checkpoint How did members of the working class react to their new experiences in industrial cities?

Life in the Factories and Mines

The heart of the new industrial city was the factory. There, the technology of the machine age and the rapid pace of industrialization imposed a harsh new way of life on workers.

Factory Workers Face Harsh Conditions Working in a factory system differed greatly from working on a farm. In rural villages, people worked hard, but their work varied according to the season. Life was also hard for poor rural workers who were part of the putting-out system, but at least they worked at their own pace. In the grim factories of industrial towns, workers faced a rigid schedule set by the factory whistle.

Vocabulary Builder

<u>contaminated</u>—(kun TAM uh nayt id) *adj.* unclean and impure; polluted

Vocabulary Builder

<u>stressed</u>—(stresd) *vt.* emphasized

WITNESS HISTORY VIDEO

Watch *In Old New York* on the **Witness History Discovery School**™ video program to learn about life during the Industrial Age.

DISCOVERY SCHOOL

Working hours were long, with shifts lasting from 12 to 16 hours, six or seven days a week. Workers could only take breaks when the factory owners gave permission. Exhausted workers suffered accidents from machines that had no safety devices. They might lose a finger, a limb, or even their lives. In textile mills, workers constantly breathed air filled with lint, which damaged their lungs. Those workers who became sick or injured lost their jobs.

The majority of early factory workers were women rather than men. Employers often preferred to hire women workers because they thought women could adapt more easily to machines and were easier to manage. In addition, employers generally paid women half what they paid men.

Factory work created a double burden for women. Their new jobs took them out of their homes for 12 hours or more a day. They then returned to their tenements, which might consist of one damp room with a single bed. They had to feed and clothe their families, clean, and cope with such problems as sickness and injury.

Miners Face Worse Conditions The Industrial Revolution increased the demand for iron and coal, which in turn increased the need for miners. Although miners were paid more, working conditions in the mines were even worse than in the factories. They worked in darkness, and the coal dust destroyed their lungs. There were always the dangers of explosions, flooding, and collapsing tunnels. Women and children carted heavy loads of coal, sometimes on all fours in low passages. They also climbed ladders carrying heavy baskets of coal several times a day.

Children Have Dangerous Jobs Factories and mines also hired many boys and girls. These children often started working at age seven or eight, a few as young as five. Nimble-fingered and quick-moving, they changed spools in the hot and humid textile mills where sometimes they could not see because of all the dust. They also crawled under machinery to repair broken threads in the mills. Conditions were even worse for children who worked in the mines. Some sat all day in the dark, opening

Even children as young as five years old worked in the mines. James Kay-Shuttleworth worked as a physician among the different classes of the Industrial Revolution in Manchester. His profession allowed him to see the working conditions of poor in the cities. How was work in factories and mines different from work on the farm?

Primary Source

66 Whilst the engine runs, people must work—men, women, and children are yoked together with iron and steam. The animal machine is chained fast to the iron machine, which knows no suffering and weariness.99
—James Kay-Shuttleworth, 1832

and closing air vents. Others hauled coal carts in the extreme heat. Because children had helped with work on the farm, parents accepted the idea of child labor. The wages the children earned were needed to keep their families from starving.

Child labor reform laws called "factory acts" were passed in the early 1800s. These laws were passed to reduce a child's workday to twelve hours and also to remove children under the age of eight or nine from the cotton mills. Because the laws were generally not enforced, British lawmakers formed teams of inspectors to ensure that factories and mines obeyed the laws in the 1830s and 1840s. More laws were then passed to shorten the workday for women and require that child workers be educated.

✔ **Checkpoint** How did the Industrial Revolution affect the lives of men, women, and children?

Families could afford to take trips to such places as the zoo as wages increased.

The Results of Industrialization

Since the 1800s, people have debated whether the Industrial Revolution was a blessing or a curse. The early industrial age brought terrible hardships. In time, however, reformers pressed for laws to improve working conditions. Labor unions won the right to bargain with employers for better wages, hours, and working conditions. Eventually working-class men gained the right to vote, which gave them political power.

Despite the social problems created by the Industrial Revolution—low pay, dismal living conditions—the Industrial Age did have some positive effects. As demand for mass-produced goods grew, new factories opened, which in turn created more jobs. Wages rose so that workers had enough left after paying rent and buying food to buy a newspaper or visit a music hall. As the cost of railroad travel fell, people could visit family in other towns. Horizons widened and opportunities increased.

✔ **Checkpoint** Why was the Industrial Revolution seen as both a blessing and a curse?

Progress Monitoring *Online*
For: Self-quiz with vocabulary practice
Web Code: naa-1931

SECTION 3 Assessment

Terms, People, and Places

1. What do each of the key terms listed at the beginning of the section have in common? Explain.

Note Taking

2. **Reading Skill: Understand Effects** Use your completed table to answer the Focus Question: What were the social effects of the Industrial Revolution?

Comprehension and Critical Thinking

3. **Analyze Information** How did the Industrial Revolution affect (a) cities and (b) population distribution?

4. **Synthesize Information** Explain how the Industrial Revolution changed the living conditions for both the middle class and the working class.

5. **Demonstrate Reasoned Judgment** Do you think increases in wages justify harsh working conditions? Why or why not?

● **Writing About History**

Quick Write: Gather Details When writing an explanatory essay, you should include facts, examples, and descriptions that help explain your topic. Make a list of details to help explain what life was like when people moved from rural areas to the new industrial cities.

Friedrich Engels: *The Condition of the Working Class in England in 1844*

In *The Condition of the Working Class in England in 1844*, Friedrich Engels recorded his observations of the wretched living conditions in poor areas of nineteenth-century England. In this excerpt, Engels describes working-class districts in Manchester. He depicts the misery and filth typical of the living areas of industrial workers.

Friedrich Engels, 1845

The houses are packed very closely together and since the bank of the river is very steep it is possible to see a part of every house. All of them have been blackened by soot, all of them are crumbling with age and all have broken window-panes and window-frames. In the background there are old factory buildings which look like barracks. On the opposite, low-lying bank of the river, one sees a long row of houses and factories. The second house is a roofless ruin, filled with refuse, and the third is built in such a low situation that the ground floor is uninhabitable and has neither doors nor windows. In the background one sees the paupers'[1] cemetery, and the stations of the railways to Liverpool and Leeds. . . .

The recently constructed extension of the Leeds railway which crosses the Irk at this point has swept away some of these courts and alleys, but it has thrown open to public gaze some of the others. So it comes about that there is to be found immediately under the railway bridge a court which is even filthier and more revolting than all the others. This is simply because it was formerly so hidden and secluded that it could only be reached with considerable difficulty [but is now exposed to the human eye]. I thought I knew this district well, but even I would never have found it had not the railway viaduct [elevated roadway] made a breach[2] in the slums at this point. One walks along a very rough path on the river bank, in between clothesposts and washing lines, to reach a chaotic group of little, one-storied, one-roomed cabins. Most of them have earth floors, and working, living and sleeping all take place in the one room. In such a hole, barely six feet long and five feet wide, I saw two beds—and what beds and bedding!—which filled the room, except for the fireplace and the doorstep. Several of these huts, as far as I could see, were completely empty, although the door was open and the inhabitants were leaning against the door posts. In front of the doors filth and garbage abounded. I could not see the pavement, but from time to time I felt it was there because my feet scraped it. . . .

1. **pauper** (PAW pur) *n.* poor person
2. **breach** (breech) *n.* break

Thinking Critically
1. **Draw Inferences** (a) How did the development of the railways affect the working-class districts? (b) How does Engels feel about the living conditions he observes?
2. **Make Generalizations** What seems to be Engels' general attitude toward the Industrial Revolution?

Workers on break, London

The Struggle of the Working Class

Karl Marx and Friedrich Engels give their view on how the Industrial Revolution affected workers:

❝ Owing to the extensive use of machinery and to division of labor, the work of the proletarians has lost all individual character, and, consequently, all charm for the workman. He becomes [a limb] of the machine, and it is only the most simple, most monotonous, and most easily acquired knack, that is required of him....❞

—From *The Communist Manifesto*

Focus Question What new ideas about economics and society were fostered as a result of the Industrial Revolution?

New Ways of Thinking

Objectives

- Understand laissez-faire economics and the beliefs of those who supported it.
- Describe the doctrine of utilitarianism.
- Summarize the theories of socialism.
- Explain Marx's views of the working class and the response to Marxism.

Terms, People, and Places

Thomas Malthus	Robert Owen
Jeremy Bentham	Karl Marx
utilitarianism	communism
socialism	proletariat
means of production	social democracy

Note Taking

Reading Skill: Identify Main Ideas Write an outline like the one here to show the new economic and social theories.

> I. Laissez-faire economics
>   A. Adam Smith and free enterprise
>   1.
>   2.
> II. Malthus on population
>   A.

Everywhere in Britain, British economist Thomas Malthus saw the effects of the population explosion—crowded slums, hungry families, unemployment, and widespread misery. After careful study, in 1798 he published *An Essay on the Principle of Population*. He concluded that poverty was unavoidable because the population was increasing faster than the food supply. Malthus wrote: "The power of population is [far] greater than the power of the Earth to produce subsistence for man."

Malthus was one of many thinkers who tried to understand the staggering changes taking place in the early Industrial Age. As heirs to the Enlightenment, these thinkers looked for natural laws that governed the world of business and economics.

Laissez-Faire Economics

During the Enlightenment, physiocrats argued that natural laws should be allowed to operate without interference. As part of this philosophy, they believed that government should not interfere in the free operation of the economy. In the early 1800s, middle-class business leaders embraced this laissez-faire, or "hands-off," approach.

As you have learned, the main proponent of laissez-faire economics was Adam Smith, author of bestseller *The Wealth of Nations*. Smith asserted that a free market—the unregulated exchange of goods and services—would come to help everyone, not just the rich. The free market, Smith said, would produce more goods at lower prices, making them affordable to everyone. A growing economy would also encourage capitalists to reinvest profits in new ventures. Supporters of this free-enterprise capitalism pointed to the successes of the Industrial Age, in which government had played no part.

Malthus Holds Bleak View Also a laissez-faire economist, Thomas Malthus predicted that population would outpace the food supply. The only checks on population growth, he said, were nature's "natural" methods of war, disease, and famine. As long as population kept increasing, he went on, the poor would suffer. He thus urged families to have fewer children and discouraged charitable handouts and vaccinations.

During the early 1800s, many people accepted Malthus's bleak view as the factory system changed people's lifestyles for the worse. His view was proved wrong, however. Although the population boom did continue, the food supply grew even faster. As the century progressed, living conditions for the Western world slowly improved—and then people began having fewer children. By the 1900s, population growth was no longer a problem in the West, but it did continue to afflict many nations elsewhere.

Ricardo Shares View Another influential British laissez-faire economist, David Ricardo, dedicated himself to economic studies after reading Smith's *The Wealth of Nations*. Like Malthus, Ricardo did not hold out hope for the working class to escape poverty. Because of such gloomy predictions, economics became known as the "dismal science." In his "Iron Law of Wages," Ricardo pointed out that wage increases were futile because increases would only cover the cost of necessities. This was because when wages were high, families often had more children instead of raising the family's current standard of living.

Both Malthus and Ricardo opposed any government help for the poor. In their view, the best cure for poverty was not government relief but the unrestricted "laws of the free market." They felt that individuals should be left to improve their lot through thrift, hard work, and limiting the size of their families.

✓ **Checkpoint** Explain the response to laissez-faire economics during the nineteenth century.

Population Theory
Thomas Malthus believed poor families should have fewer children to preserve the food supply. *What were the advantages of families with many children?*

Utilitarians For Limited Government

Other thinkers sought to modify laissez-faire doctrines to justify some government intervention. By 1800, British philosopher and economist Jeremy Bentham was advocating utilitarianism, or the idea that the goal of society should be "the greatest happiness for the greatest number" of its citizens. To Bentham, all laws or actions should be judged by their "utility." In other words, did they provide more pleasure or happiness than pain? Bentham strongly supported individual freedom, which he believed guaranteed happiness. Still, he saw the need for government to become involved under certain circumstances.

Bentham's ideas influenced the British philosopher and economist John Stuart Mill. Although he believed strongly in individual freedom, Mill wanted the government to step in to improve the hard lives of the working class. "The only purpose for which power can be rightfully exercised over any member of a civilized community, against his will," Mill wrote, "is to prevent harm to others." Therefore, while middle-class business and factory owners were entitled to increase their own happiness, the government should prevent them from doing so in a manner that would harm workers.

Mill further called for giving the vote to workers and women. These groups could then use their political power to win reforms. Most middle-class people rejected Mill's ideas. Only in the later 1800s were his views

"The population... is crowded into one dense mass of cottages. ...This is an atmosphere loaded with the exhalation of a large manufacturing city."
—J.P. Kay

Owen's Utopia

The poverty and filth of the Industrial Age did not sit well with Robert Owen, a British social reformer. Like other Utopians, he believed there was a way he could change society for the better. To prove his point, he set up his cotton mill in New Lanark, Scotland, as a model village. He insisted that the conditions in which people lived shaped their character. Owen reduced working hours, built homes for workers, started a school for children, and opened a company store where workers could buy food and clothes. He showed that an employer could offer decent living and working conditions and still run a profitable business. Between 1815 and 1825, about 20,000 people visited New Lanark to study Owen's reforms. The complex eventually fell into decline but visitors can still wander the village today.

▲ The Industrial Age brought harsh living conditions and poverty as people crowded into cities.

Thinking Critically

1. **Make Generalizations** Based on the images, how did life for children at New Lanark differ from those who lived in industrial cities?
2. **Recognize Ideologies** Do you think Utopianism was an effective solution for the challenges of the Industrial Age? Why or why not?

"...[I have never seen] so much order, good government, tranquility, and rational happiness prevail."
—Visitor to New Lanark

▲ Children attended geography classes and dance lessons at the school in New Lanark.

History Interactive,
For: Interactive Village
Web Code: nap-1941

624

slowly accepted. Today's democratic governments, however, have absorbed many ideas from Mill and the other utilitarians.

 Checkpoint What did John Stuart Mill see as the proper role of government?

Socialist Thought Emerges

While the champions of laissez-faire economics praised individual rights, other thinkers focused on the good of society in general. They condemned the evils of industrial capitalism, which they believed had created a gulf between rich and poor. To end poverty and injustice, they offered a radical solution—socialism. Under socialism, the people as a whole rather than private individuals would own and operate the means of production—the farms, factories, railways, and other large businesses that produced and distributed goods. Socialism grew out of the Enlightenment faith in progress, its belief in the basic goodness of human nature, and its concern for social justice.

Are Utopians Dreamers? A number of early socialists established communities in which all work was shared and all property was owned in common. When there was no difference between rich and poor, they said, fighting between people would disappear. These early socialists were called Utopians. The name implied that they were impractical dreamers. The Utopian Robert Owen set up a model community in New Lanark, Scotland, to put his own ideas into practice.

Owen Establishes a Utopia A poor Welsh boy, Owen became a successful mill owner. Unlike most industrialists at the time, he refused to use child labor. He campaigned vigorously for laws that limited child labor and encouraged the organization of labor unions.

 Checkpoint What did early socialists believe?

Karl Marx Explains Class Struggles

In the 1840s, Karl Marx, a German philosopher, condemned the ideas of the Utopians as unrealistic idealism. He <u>formulated</u> a new theory, "scientific socialism," which he claimed was based on a scientific study of history. He teamed up with another German socialist, Friedrich Engels, whose father owned a textile factory in England.

Marx and Engels wrote a pamphlet, *The Communist Manifesto*, which they published in 1848. "A spectre [ghost] is haunting Europe," it began, "the spectre of communism." Communism is a form of socialism advocated by Marx, in which an inevitable struggle between social classes would lead to the creation of a classless society where all means of production would be owned by the community.

In *The Communist Manifesto*, Marx theorized that economics was the driving force in history. He argued that there was "the history of class struggles" between the "haves" and the "have-nots." The "haves" had always owned the means of production and thus controlled society and all its wealth. In industrialized Europe, Marx said, the "haves" were the bourgeoisie. The "have-nots" were the proletariat, or working class.

According to Marx, the modern class struggle pitted the bourgeoisie against the proletariat. In the end, he predicted, the proletariat would be

Vocabulary Builder

formulated—(FAWR myoo layt id) *vt.* devised or developed, as in a theory or plan triumphant. Workers would then take control of the means of production and set up a classless, communist society. Such a society would mark the end of the struggles people had endured throughout history, because wealth and power would be equally shared. Marx despised capitalism. He believed it created prosperity for only a few and poverty for many. He called for an international struggle to bring about its downfall. "Workers of all countries," he urged, "unite!"

 Checkpoint What did Marx predict was the future of the proletariat?

Marxism in the Future

At first, Marxism gained popularity with many people around the world. Leaders of a number of reform movements adopted the idea that power should be held by workers rather than by business owners. Marx's ideas, however, would never be practiced exactly as he imagined.

Marxism Briefly Flourishes In the 1860s, Germany adapted Marx's beliefs to form a social democracy, a political ideology in which there is a gradual transition from capitalism to socialism instead of a sudden violent overthrow of the system. In the late 1800s, Russian socialists embraced Marxism, and the Russian Revolution of 1917 set up a communist-inspired government. For much of the 1900s, revolutionaries around the world would adapt Marxist ideas to their own situations and needs. Independence leaders in Asia, Latin America, and Africa would turn to Marxism.

Marxism Loses Appeal As time passed, however, the failures of Marxist governments would illustrate the flaws in Marx's arguments. He predicted that workers would unite across national borders to wage class warfare. Instead, nationalism won out over working-class loyalty. In general, people felt stronger ties to their own countries than to the international communist movement. By the end of the twentieth century, few nations remained with communist governments, while nearly every economy included elements of free-market capitalism.

 Checkpoint How accurate did Marx's predictions about social classes prove to be?

Workers of the World
An 1895 leaflet urges that "Workers of the World Unite," the slogan of the socialist movement of Marx (above) and Engels.

SECTION 4 **Assessment**

Progress Monitoring *Online*
For: Self-quiz with vocabulary practice
Web Code: naa-1941

Terms, People, and Places
1. For each term, person, or place listed at the beginning of the section, write a sentence explaining its significance.

Note Taking

2. **Reading Skill: Identify Main Ideas** Use your completed outline to answer the Focus Question: What new ideas about economics and society were fostered as a result of the Industrial Revolution?

Comprehension and Critical Thinking
3. **Identify Points of View** What were the views of laissez-faire economists (a) Adam Smith, (b) Thomas Malthus, and (c) David Ricardo?
4. **Compare Points of View** Contrast the approaches of utilitarians and socialists to solving economic problems.
5. **Synthesize Information** How might workplace reforms have altered Marxist predictions of world revolution?

● **Writing About History**
Quick Write: Write a Thesis Statement As in other types of essays, it is important to clearly state your thesis, or main idea, when writing an explanatory essay. Write a thesis statement followed by a short paragraph on one of the theories discussed in this section.

Economic Systems

What types of economic systems have societies used to produce and distribute goods and services?

When Adam Smith wrote *The Wealth of Nations* in 1776, traditional agriculture formed the heart of nearly all world economies. In the 1800s, industry began to dominate, especially in Europe and the United States. Industrialists wanted to control their own businesses. Using Smith's laissez-faire ideas, they pushed for free markets and an end to government interference. The resulting market economy is one of the basic economic systems in the modern world. Other systems followed. These systems can be differentiated by those who make the following key economic decisions: (1) What will be produced? (2) How will it be produced? (3) To whom will the product be distributed?

Brazilian market economy

Market Economy

In a market economy, the key economic decisions emerge from the interaction of buyers and sellers in a market. A market allows individuals to exchange, or trade, things. The market economy is also called the free market, the free enterprise system, or capitalism. One key element of this economic system is supply and demand. Producers make, or supply, only what consumers want, or demand. Another element is self-interest, where producers and consumers consider only their own personal gain when making decisions. A third element is competition. Here, producers compete for consumers' money by lowering prices or introducing new products.

Centrally Planned Economy

In a centrally planned economy, the central government, rather than individual producers and consumers in markets, makes the key economic decisions. The centrally planned economy is also called a command economy, a socialist economy, or communism. In a typical communist country, the government sets goals for production and manages nearly all aspects of production and distribution. Everything in a command economy is produced according to a rigid plan. This discourages new ideas and new products that could stimulate economic growth. The result is often poor quality goods, serious shortages, and falling production.

Mixed Economy

A mixed economy is one that has both free enterprise and socialist characteristics. Economic equality, socialists argue, is possible only if the public—in the form of the government—controls the centers of economic power. Although socialist nations may be democracies, socialism requires a high degree of central planning to achieve economic equality. In mixed economies, government plays a significant role in making the key economic decisions. In modern times, the number of mixed economies has grown. Market systems have benefited from some government intervention, and centrally planned systems have benefited from some free enterprise.

Thinking Critically

1. (a) What legitimate role might government have in what is otherwise a market economy? (b) Why might a centrally planned economy begin encouraging some free enterprise?
2. **Connections to Today** Locate a newspaper article about China's economy. Write a one-paragraph summary of the article and try to relate the content of the article to the information about economic systems described above.

A Cuban government poster seeks to inspire productivity.

Quick Study Guide

Progress Monitoring *Online*
For: Self-test with vocabulary practice
Web Code: naa-1951

■ New Inventions and Ideas

Inventors and Thinkers	Inventions and Ideas
Jethro Tull	Seed drill
Thomas Newcomen	Steam engine
James Watt	Improved steam engine
John Kay	Flying shuttle
James Hargreaves	Spinning jenny
Richard Arkwright	Water frame
Eli Whitney	Cotton gin
George Stephenson	Steam-powered locomotive
John Wesley	Methodism
Adam Smith	Laissez-faire economics
Thomas Malthus	Population growth could outpace food supply.
Jeremy Bentham	Utilitarianism
Robert Owen	Utopian communities
Karl Marx	Communism, Marxism

■ Effects of the Industrial Revolution

Industrial Revolution
• Population growth • Rural to urban migration • Growth of cities
• Poor working conditions in factories • Low wages • Overcrowding in cities
• Laissez-faire economics • Utilitarianism • Socialism • Marxism

■ Why Britain Industrialized First

Industrial Revolution in Britain
Plentiful natural resources
Ready workforce
Prosperous economy
Availability of capital and demand
Stable government

■ Responses to the Industrial Revolution

- Bentham/Mill: utilitarianism
- Socialism
- Owen: utopianism
- Marx/Engels: communism

■ Events From 1750–1850

Early Industrial Revolution Events
Global Events

1760s
Watt improves the steam engine.

1764
The spinning jenny is invented.

1750

1775

1762
Catherine the Great comes to power in Russia.

1770
Cook claims Australia for Britain.

1788
Futa Toro outlaws slave trade.

Concept Connector

Cumulative Review

Record the answers to the questions below on your Concept Connector worksheets. In addition, record information from this chapter about the following concepts:

- Economic Systems: market economy
- Economic Systems: centrally planned economy
- Economic Systems: mixed economy

1. **Economic Systems** What is socialism? Compare socialism to mercantilism, another economic system. Research to learn how they are similar and different. Think about these factors:
   - who supported each system
   - main theories
   - existence today

2. **Technology** Once James Watt made improvements to Thomas Newcomen's steam engine, it became a key power source of the Industrial Revolution. Research to learn why steam power made such an impact and then compare it to the impact of the printing press. Think about the following:
   - who benefited from the use of the invention
   - what preceded the invention
   - why the invention was so important

3. **Trade** The development of the railway network in the 1800s led to increased trade as people and goods were able to travel faster and farther. Research the Silk Road, the ancient trade route that started in China and stretched to Asia Minor and India. How was railroad travel of the Industrial Revolution both similar to and different from travel on the Silk Road? Think about the following:
   - speed of transport
   - multiple uses
   - advantages and disadvantages

Connections To Today

1. **Migration: Twentieth Century Global Migrations**
   During the Industrial Revolution, rural workers migrated to urban areas to live and work. Today, people still migrate in various parts of the world. Do online and library research to find information on rural-to-urban migration in a country located in Asia or Africa. Write a brief newspaper article in which you compare the experiences of those who migrated then and now.

Strawberry pickers at work, South Africa

2. **People and the Environment: Population Growth**
   The population growth that occurred during the Industrial Revolution often created filth and unsanitary conditions as people crowded into tenements. The growth also caused an increase in the demand for products, which led to the opening of more factories. Do online and library research to find the history of population growth in the town or state in which you live. What are the patterns and results?

1800	1807	1830	1848	
Owen begins social reforms at New Lanark.	Fulton develops the first successful steamboat, the *Clermont*.	The Liverpool-Manchester Railroad opens.	Marx and Engels publish *The Communist Manifesto*.	**History Interactive** For: Interactive timeline Web Code: nap-1901

1800

1825

1850

1804	1814	1819	1848
Napoleon becomes the emperor of France.	Congress of Vienna meets to restore stability in Europe.	Bolívar captures Bogotá.	Revolutions sweep Europe.

Chapter Assessment

Terms, People, and Places

Complete each sentence by choosing the correct answer from the list of terms below. You will not use all of the terms.

smelt	James Watt
urbanization	Manchester
Thomas Malthus	tenement
proletariat	socialism
enterprise	utilitarianism

1. _____ predicted that population would outpace the food supply.
2. A member of the _____ most likely lived in a small, crowded building called a _____.
3. Investors in Britain were ready to risk their capital to invest in _____.
4. Those who advocated _____ believed that the goal of society was to bring about the greatest happiness for the greatest number.
5. To _____ involves separating iron from its ore.
6. _____ improved the efficiency and design of Newcomen's steam engine.

Main Ideas

Section 1 (pp. 608–611)
7. How did the enclosure movement affect farmers?
8. Identify three causes of the population explosion that occurred in the 1700s.

Section 2 (pp. 612–615)
9. Describe four factors that helped bring about the Industrial Revolution in England.

10. How did the Industrial Revolution transform the textile industry?

Section 3 (pp. 616–621)
11. (a) What were the main characteristics of factory work? (b) What challenges did factory work create for women?

Section 4 (pp. 622–627)
12. List the government reforms sought by John Stuart Mill.
13. (a) Describe Karl Marx's view of history. (b) How have events challenged that view?

Chapter Focus Question
14. What technological, social, economic, and cultural changes occurred as the Industrial Revolution took hold?

Critical Thinking

15. **Synthesize Information** What were the impacts of each of the following technologies: (a) steam power, (b) improved methods for smelting iron, (c) railroad?
16. **Geography and History** Explain the link between Britain's natural resources and its rise as an industrial nation.
17. **Analyze Information** Describe how the Industrial Revolution affected each of the following: (a) size of population, (b) cities, (c) working and living conditions, (d) women and children.
18. **Predict Consequences** If more people had supported utilitarianism, how do you think it would have influenced society?
19. **Recognize Ideologies** Explain the major differences between Adam Smith's free market ideas and Karl Marx's socialist ideas.

● Writing About History

Expository: Explanatory Essay During the late 1700s, the Industrial Revolution began to transform Britain. An agricultural revolution triggered a chain of events, and Britain sped ahead of the rest of the world to become the first industrial nation. But why is the Industrial Revolution considered to be a "revolution"? Write an explanatory essay to answer this question.

Prewriting
• Ask yourself what you need to know in order to write an effective explanation. Think about what you already know about revolutions.
• Do research to gather facts, descriptions, examples, and other details to clearly illustrate your point.

Drafting
• Create a Venn diagram to compare aspects of the Industrial Revolution to another revolution you have learned about, such as the American Revolution or the French Revolution.
• Write a thesis statement once you have a focus for your essay. Begin your introduction with an interesting lead-in to get your reader's attention.
• Be sure to include comparisons, analogies, and facts in your essay to support your explanation.

Revising
• Use the guidelines for revising your essay on page SH12 of the Writing Handbook.

Document-Based Assessment

New Economic and Social Theories

Various thinkers of the day attempted to understand and interpret the dramatic changes brought about by the Industrial Revolution. They responded with a wide range of explanations and solutions, as the documents below illustrate.

Document A

"As every individual, therefore, endeavours as much as he can both to employ his capital in the support of domestic industry, and so to direct that industry that its produce may be of the greatest value; every individual necessarily labours to render the annual revenue of the society as great as he can. . . . By preferring the support of domestic to that of foreign industry, he intends only his own security; and by directing that industry in such a manner as its produce may be of the greatest value, he intends only his own gain, and he is in this, as in many other cases, led by an invisible hand to promote an end which was no part of his intention. . . . every individual it is evident, can, in his local situation, judge much better than any statesman or lawgiver can do for him."

—From ***The Wealth of Nations*** by Adam Smith, 1776

Document B

"In those characters which now exhibit crime, the fault is obviously not in the individual, but the defects proceed from the system in which the individual was trained. Withdraw those circumstances which tend to create crime in the human character, and crime will not be created. Replace them with such as are calculated to form habits of order, regularity, temperance, industry; and these qualities will be formed. . . . Proceed systematically on principles of undeviating persevering kindness, yet retaining and using, with the least possible severity, the means of restraining crime from immediately injuring society, and by degrees even the crimes now existing in adults will also gradually disappear. . . ."

—From ***A New View of Society*** by Robert Owen, 1816

Document C
New Lanark Mills, Scotland

Document D

" . . . the power of population is indefinitely greater than the power in the earth to produce subsistence for man. Population, when unchecked, increased in a geometrical ratio. Subsistence increases only in an arithmetical ratio. A slight acquaintance with numbers will show the immensity of the first power in comparison of the second. . . . No fancied equality, no agrarian regulations in their utmost extent, could remove the pressure of it even for a single century. And it appears, therefore, to be decisive against the possible existence of a society, all the members of which should live in ease, happiness, and comparative leisure; and feel no anxiety about providing the means of subsistence for themselves and families. Consequently, if the premises are just, the argument is conclusive against the perfectibility of the mass of mankind."

—From ***An Essay on the Principle of Population 1798*** by Thomas Malthus

Analyzing Documents

Use your knowledge of the new economic and social theories and Documents A, B, C, and D to answer the questions below.

1. According to Adam Smith in Document A, individuals promote the good of society because of
    A high ideals.
    B self-interest.
    C government pressure.
    D religion.

2. How did Robert Owen explain the fact that some people become criminals?
    A the invisible hand of fate
    B struggles between the ruling class and the oppressed
    C the influence of problems in society
    D the power of population over production

3. Thomas Malthus argued that a society where all individuals enjoy happiness, comfort, and pleasure is
    A only possible with increased agricultural output.
    B impossible because of the base nature of human greed.
    C impossible because of the pressures of population.
    D possible when people are treated decently and fairly.

4. **Writing Task** Suppose you were working in Britain in the year 1840. Which of the above economic philosophies would you support? Remember to identify your occupation and social class. Use your knowledge of the Industrial Revolution and the documents above to support your opinion.

20 Revolutions in Europe and Latin America

1790–1848

◀ Bolívar fights Spanish troops in his endeavor to free South America.

Freedom From Tyranny

Several revolutions erupted in Europe between 1815 and 1829, and the spread of revolutionary Ideals would Ignite new uprisings in 1830 and 1848. Also occurring during this time were the wars of independence in Latin America. These revolts began in the late 1700s and early 1800s and were inspired by the success of the American Revolution and the ideals of the French Revolution. Simón Bolívar was one of the great heroes in the fight for independence in Spanish South America. He helped win independence for Bolivia, Colombia, Ecuador, Peru, and Venezuela. Listen to the Witness History audio to learn more about revolutions in Europe and Latin America.

❝A state too extensive in itself, or by virtue of its dependencies, ultimately falls into decay; its free government is transformed into a tyranny; it disregards the principles which it should preserve, and finally degenerates into despotism. The distinguishing characteristic of small republics is stability. . . .❞
—Simón Bolívar

Simón Bolívar's crown

French tricolor flag

Chapter Preview

Chapter Focus Question How did revolutionary ideals in Europe and Latin America ignite uprisings in the first half of the nineteenth century?

José de San Martín

Section 1
An Age of Ideologies

Section 2
Revolutions of 1830 and 1848

Section 3
Revolts in Latin America

Note Taking Study Guide *Online*
For: Note Taking and Concept Connector worksheets
Web Code: nad-2001

Hungarian revolutionary
Lajos Kossuth

WITNESS HISTORY 🔊 AUDIO

A "Revolutionary Seed"

Prince Clemens von Metternich warned that a seed had been planted in Europe that threatened Europe's monarchs and undermined its basic social values. This seed was nourished with the ideas spread by the French Revolution and Napoleon Bonaparte.

> ❝Passions are let loose . . . to overthrow everything that society respects as the basis of its existence: religion, public morality, laws, customs, rights, and duties, all are attacked, confounded [defeated], overthrown, or called in question.❞

Focus Question What events proved that Metternich was correct in his fears?

An Age of Ideologies

Objectives

- Understand the goals of the conservatives.
- Explain how liberals and nationalists challenged the old order.
- Summarize the early challenges to the old order in Europe.

Terms, People, and Places

ideology
universal manhood suffrage
autonomy

Note Taking

Reading Skill: Identify Main Ideas As you read the section, fill in a table like the one below with main ideas about conservatism, liberalism, and nationalism.

Conservatism	Liberalism	Nationalism
•	•	•
•	•	•

At the Congress of Vienna, the powers of Europe tried to uproot the "revolutionary seed" and suppress nationalist fervor. Others, however, challenged the order imposed in 1815. The clash of people with opposing ideologies, or systems of thought and belief, plunged Europe into more than 30 years of turmoil.

Conservatives Prefer the Old Order

The Congress of Vienna was a victory for the conservative forces, which included monarchs and their officials, noble landowners, and church leaders. Conservatives agreed to work together—in an agreement called the Concert of Europe—to support the political and social order that had existed before Napoleon and the French Revolution. Conservative ideas also appealed to peasants, who wanted to preserve traditional ways.

Conservatives of the early 1800s wanted to return to the way things had been before 1789. After all, they had benefited under the old order. They wanted to restore royal families to the thrones they had lost when Napoleon swept across Europe. They supported a social hierarchy in which lower classes respected and obeyed their social superiors. Conservatives also backed an established church—Catholic in Austria and southern Europe, Protestant in northern Europe, and Eastern Orthodox in eastern Europe.

Conservatives believed that talk about natural rights and constitutional government could lead only to chaos, as in France in 1789. If change had to come, they argued, it must come slowly. Conservatives felt that they benefited all people by defending peace and stability. Conservative leaders like Metternich sought to suppress revolutionary ideas. Metternich urged monarchs to oppose freedom of the press, crush protests in their own countries, and send troops to douse the flames of rebellion in neighboring lands.

 Checkpoint What was the goal of the conservatives in the Concert of Europe?

Liberals and Nationalists Seek Change

Inspired by the Enlightenment and the French Revolution, liberals and nationalists challenged the conservatives at every turn. Liberalism and nationalism ignited a number of revolts against established rule.

Liberals Promise Freedom Because liberals spoke mostly for the bourgeoisie, or middle class, their ideas are sometimes called "bourgeois liberalism." Liberals included business owners, bankers, and lawyers, as well as politicians, newspaper editors, writers, and others who helped to shape public opinion.

Liberals wanted governments to be based on written constitutions and separation of powers. Liberals spoke out against divine-right monarchy, the old aristocracy, and established churches. They defended the natural rights of individuals to liberty, equality, and property. They called for rulers elected by the people and responsible to them. Thus, most liberals favored a republican form of government over a monarchy, or at least wanted the monarch to be limited by a constitution.

The liberals of the early 1800s saw the role of government as limited to protecting basic rights such as freedom of thought, speech, and religion. They believed that only male property owners or others with a financial stake in society should have the right to vote. Only later in the century did liberals support the principle of **universal manhood suffrage,** giving all adult men the right to vote.

Liberals also strongly supported the laissez-faire economics of Adam Smith and David Ricardo. They saw the free market as an opportunity for capitalist entrepreneurs to succeed. As capitalists (and often employers), liberals had different goals from those of workers laboring in factories, mines, and other enterprises of the early Industrial Revolution.

Nationalists Strive for Unity For centuries, European rulers had gained or lost lands through wars, marriages, and treaties. They exchanged territories and the people in them like pieces in a game. As a result, by 1815 Europe had several empires that included many nationalities. The Austrian, Russian, and Ottoman empires, for example, each included diverse peoples.

Analyzing Political Cartoons

Conflicting Ideologies This cartoon shows Prince Metternich standing resolute against the angry crowd behind him who are pushing for reform. Metternich represented the conservative order and opposed revolutionary ideals such as freedom and progress.
1. How does the cartoonist portray those in the crowd? What does the crowd support?
2. What did Metternich do to suppress revolutionary ideas?

635

In the 1800s, national groups who shared a common heritage set out to win their own states. Within the diverse Austrian empire, for example, various nationalist leaders tried to unite and win independence for each particular group. Nationalism gave people with a common heritage a sense of identity and the goal of creating their own homeland. At the same time, however, nationalism often bred intolerance and led to persecution of other ethnic or national groups.

✓ **Checkpoint** How did the liberalism of the early 1800s reflect Enlightenment ideals?

Central Europe Challenges the Old Order

Spurred by the ideas of liberalism and nationalism, revolutionaries fought against the old order. During the early 1800s, rebellions erupted in the Balkan Peninsula and elsewhere along the southern fringe of Europe. The Balkans, in southeastern Europe, were inhabited by people of various religions and ethnic groups. These peoples had lived under Ottoman rule for more than 300 years.

Serbia Seeks Independence The first Balkan people to revolt were the Serbs. From 1804 to 1813, the Serb leader Karageorge (ka rah JAWR juh) led a guerrilla war against the Ottomans. The intense struggle was unsuccessful, but it fostered a sense of Serbian identity. A revival of Serbian literature and culture added to the sense of nationhood.

In 1815, Milos Obrenovic (oh BRAY noh vich) led the Serbs in a second, more successful rebellion. One reason for the success was that Obrenovic turned to Russia for assistance. Like the Serbs, the Russian people were Slavic in language and Christian Orthodox in religion. By 1830, Russian support helped the Serbs win **autonomy,** or self-rule, within the

Serbs in Battle
Serb leader Karageorge (below left) leads the Serbs against the Ottomans at the Battle of Misar during the first Serbian rebellion. *(a) Why would this battle and others like it help lead to a sense of Serbian national identity? (b) Why was this sense of nationalism important for the Serbs?*

Ottoman empire. The Ottoman sultan later agreed to formal independence. In the future, Russia would continue to defend Serbian interests and affect events in the Balkans.

Greece Revolts to End Ottoman Rule In 1821, the Greeks revolted, seeking to end centuries of Ottoman rule. At first, the Greeks were badly divided. But years of suffering in long, bloody wars of independence helped shape a national identity. Leaders of the rebellion justified their struggle as "a national war, a holy war, a war the object of which is to reconquer the rights of individual liberty." The Greeks had the support of romantic writers such as English poet Lord Byron, who went to Greece to aid the fight for independence.

Admirers of Greece in Europe backed the Greek rebels. In the late 1820s, Britain, France, and Russia forced the Ottomans to grant independence to some Greek provinces. By 1830, Greece was independent. The European powers, however, pressured the Greeks to accept a German king, a move meant to show that they did not support the nationalism that brought about the revolution.

More Challenges Erupt Several other challenges to the Vienna peace settlement erupted in the 1820s. Revolts occurred along the southern fringe of Europe. In Spain, Portugal, and various states in the Italian peninsula, rebels struggled to gain constitutional governments.

Metternich urged conservative rulers to act decisively and crush the dangerous uprisings. In response, a French army marched over the Pyrenees to suppress a revolt in Spain. Austrian forces crossed the Alps to smash rebellious outbreaks in Italy.

Troops dampened the fires of liberalism and nationalism, but could not smother them. In the next decades, sparks would flare anew. Added to liberal and nationalist demands were the goals of the new industrial working class. By the mid-1800s, social reformers and <u>agitators</u> were urging workers to support socialism or other ways of reorganizing property ownership.

✓ **Checkpoint** Why would a monarch order his army to suppress an uprising in another country?

Note Taking

Reading Skill: Identify Supporting Details As you read, fill in a table like the one below with supporting details about revolts in Serbia, Greece, and other countries during the early 1800s.

Serbia	Greece	Other Revolts
•	•	•
•	•	•

Vocabulary Builder

agitator—(AJ ih tayt ur) *n.* someone who attempts to arouse feeling for or against something, especially a political cause

SECTION 1 **Assessment**

Progress Monitoring *Online*
For: Self-quiz with vocabulary practice
Web Code: naa-2011

Terms, People, and Places

1. For each term, person, or place listed at the beginning of the section, write a sentence explaining its significance.

Note Taking

2. **Reading Skill: Identify Main Ideas** Use your completed charts to answer the Focus Question: What events proved that Metternich was correct in his fears?

Comprehension and Critical Thinking

3. **Identify Point of View** What were the goals of conservative leaders?
4. **Compare Points of View** (a) How did the political goals of liberals differ from those of conservatives? (b) How did nationalists threaten the borders set up by European monarchs?
5. **Recognize Cause and Effect** (a) Why did the Serbs and Greeks revolt? (b) Why were there uprisings in Spain, Portugal, and the Italian states?

● **Writing About History**

Quick Write: Choose a Topic To write an effective persuasive essay, you should begin with a clearly stated opinion or argument on an issue that has more than one side. Look back over Section 1, jotting down issues that have two or more sides. Then choose an issue and write a well-constructed sentence that states your opinion or argument against it.

Alexis de Tocqueville

French tricolor flag

WITNESS HISTORY 🔊 AUDIO

More Revolution in the Wind

Alexis de Tocqueville was a liberal French leader who closely observed the widespread support for revolutionary ideas. He knew that the revolutions of the 1820s were not over.

❝We are sleeping on a volcano . . . Do you not see that the Earth trembles anew? A wind of revolution blows, the storm is on the horizon.❞
—Alexis de Tocqueville

Focus Question What were the causes and effects of the revolutions in Europe in 1830 and 1848?

Revolutions of 1830 and 1848

Objectives
- Describe how French rebels won some reforms in 1830.
- Analyze how the spirit of reform spread in 1830.
- Explain the revolutions that surged through France and throughout the rest of Europe in 1848.

Terms, People, and Places

radicals
Louis Philippe
recession
Napoleon III
Louis Kossuth

Note Taking

Reading Skill: Identify Main Ideas As you read the section, fill in a table like the one below with a country, date, and a main idea about the revolutions of 1830 and 1848. Add rows as needed.

Revolutions of 1830 and 1848		
France	1830	Radicals force king to abdicate.

The quick suppression of liberal and nationalist uprisings in the 1820s did not end Europe's age of revolutions. In 1830 and 1848, Europeans saw street protests explode into full-scale revolts. As in 1789, the upheavals began in Paris and radiated out across the continent.

French Rebels Win in 1830

When the Congress of Vienna restored Louis XVIII to the French throne, he wisely issued a constitution, the Charter of French Liberties. It created a two-house legislature and allowed limited freedom of the press. Still, the king retained much power.

Citizens Lead the July Revolution When Louis XVIII died in 1824, his younger brother, Charles X, inherited the throne. Charles, a strong believer in absolutism, rejected the very idea of the charter. In July 1830, he suspended the legislature, limited the right to vote, and restricted the press.

Liberals and **radicals**—those who favor extreme change—responded forcefully to the king's challenge. In Paris, angry citizens threw up barricades across the narrow streets. From behind them, they fired on the soldiers and pelted them with stones and roof tiles. Within days, rebels controlled Paris. The revolutionary tricolor flew from the towers of Notre Dame cathedral. A frightened Charles X abdicated and fled to England.

The "Citizen King" Rules France With the king gone, radicals wanted to set up a republic. Moderate liberals, however, insisted on a constitutional monarchy and chose **Louis Philippe** as king. Louis Philippe was a cousin of Charles X and in his youth had supported the revolution of 1789.

The French called Louis Philippe the "citizen king" because he owed his throne to the people. Louis got along well with the liberal bourgeoisie. He dressed like them in a frock coat and top hat. Sometimes he strolled the streets, shaking hands with well-wishers. Liberal politicians filled his government.

Under Louis Philippe, the upper bourgeoisie prospered. Louis extended suffrage, but only to France's wealthier citizens. The vast majority of the people still could not vote. The king's other policies also favored the middle class at the expense of the workers.

 Checkpoint What actions did Charles X take in 1830, and how did French rebels respond?

The Spirit of Reform Spreads

The revolts in Paris inspired the outbreak of uprisings elsewhere in Europe. As Metternich said, "When France sneezes, Europe catches cold." Most of the uprisings were suppressed by military force. But some rebels did win changes. Even when they failed, revolutions frightened rulers badly enough to encourage reform.

Belgium Wins Independence The one notable success in 1830 took place in Belgium. In 1815, the Congress of Vienna had united the Austrian Netherlands (present-day Belgium) and the Kingdom of Holland under the Dutch king. The Congress had wanted to create a strong barrier to help prevent French expansion in the future.

The Belgians resented the new arrangement. They and the Dutch had different languages. The Belgians were Catholic, while the Dutch were Protestant. The Belgian economy was based on manufacturing; the Dutch, on trade.

In 1830, news of the Paris uprising ignited a revolutionary spark in Belgium. Students and workers threw up barricades in Brussels, the

To the Barricades!

In 1830 and again in 1848, French rebels erected barricades in the streets using mattresses, wagons, furniture, and whatever else they could find that might offer protection during the fighting with government soldiers. *How does Hugo describe the barricades in his famous novel* Les Misérables?

Primary Source

❝You saw there, in a chaos full of despair, rafters from roofs, patches from garrets with their wall paper, window sashes with all their glass planted in the rubbish, awaiting artillery, chimneys torn down, wardrobes, tables, benches, a howling topsy-turvy, . . . which contain at once fury and nothingness.❞
—Victor Hugo

WITNESS HISTORY VIDEO

Watch *Revolutionary France:* Les Misérables on the **Witness History Discovery School**™ video program to learn more about the 1830 revolution in France.

capital. Britain and France believed that they would benefit from the separation of Belgium and Holland and supported Belgian demands for independence. As a result, in 1831, Belgium became an independent state with a liberal constitution.

Rebels Fail in Poland Nationalists in Poland also staged an uprising in 1830. But, unlike the Belgians, the Poles failed to win independence for their country.

In the late 1700s, Russia, Austria, and Prussia had divided up Poland. Poles had hoped that the Congress of Vienna would restore their homeland in 1815. Instead, the great powers handed most of Poland to Russia.

In 1830, Polish students, army officers, and landowners rose in revolt. The rebels failed to gain widespread support, however, and were brutally crushed by Russian forces. Some survivors fled to Western Europe and the United States, where they kept alive the dream of freedom.

✔ **Checkpoint** How did the Belgian and Polish revolutions in 1830 end differently?

The French Revolt Again in 1848

In the 1840s, discontent began to grow in France once again. Radicals formed secret societies to work for a French republic. Utopian socialists called for an end to private ownership of property. Even liberals denounced Louis Philippe's government for corruption and called for expanded suffrage.

Near the end of the decade, discontent was heightened by a **recession,** or period of reduced economic activity. Factories shut down and people lost their jobs. Poor harvests caused bread prices to rise. Newspapers blamed government officials for some of the problems. With conditions much like those in 1789, Paris was again ripe for revolution.

Vocabulary Builder

denounce—(dee NOWNS) *vt.* to express harsh criticism of something or somebody, usually in public

● **INFOGRAPHIC**

1848: The Year of Hope and Despair

Revolution in Europe spread like wildfire in the days and months of 1848. Although an outbreak in January occurred in Italy, France's successful February Revolution was the spark for other revolts throughout Europe. As shown on the map here, revolutions were not confined to one city or country. They engulfed the continent of Europe and numbered almost fifty in the first four months of the year alone. Despite the failures of the revolutions, Europe was transformed as governments and the rising middle class began to cooperate with one another.

Gained independence, 1830–1831
Repression of revolutions in 1848
Revolutions of 1848

Turmoil Spreads During "February Days" In February 1848, when the government took steps to silence critics and prevent public meetings, angry crowds took to the streets. During the "February Days," overturned carts, paving stones, and toppled trees again blocked the streets of Paris. Church bells rang alarms, while women and men on the barricades sang the revolutionary anthem "La Marseillaise." A number of demonstrators clashed with royal troops and were killed.

As the turmoil spread, Louis Philippe abdicated. A group of liberal, radical, and socialist leaders proclaimed the Second Republic. (The First Republic had lasted from 1792 until 1804, when Napoleon became emperor.)

From the start, deep differences divided the new government. Middle-class liberals wanted moderate political reforms. Socialists wanted far-reaching social and economic change and forced the government to set up national workshops to provide jobs for the unemployed.

The Working Class Loses Out During "June Days" By June, however, upper- and middle-class interests had won control of the government. They saw the national workshops as a waste of money and shut them down.

Furious, workers again took to the streets of Paris. This time, however, bourgeois liberals turned violently against the protesters. Peasants, who feared that socialists might take their land, also attacked the rioting workers. At least 1,500 people were killed before the government crushed the rebellion.

The fighting of the "June Days" left a bitter legacy. The middle class both feared and distrusted the socialists, while the working class harbored a deep hatred for the bourgeoisie.

A New Napoleon Comes to Power By the end of 1848, the National Assembly, now dominated by members who wanted to restore order,

JUNE

"June Days" in France again saw Paris streets crowded with angry protestors when the workshops for the unemployed were closed. Before this worker revolt ended, about 1,500 died in the first two days, while as many as 3,000 more were executed for their participation in the uprising.

FEBRUARY

Opposition grew as Louis Philippe refused to listen to the middle class, workers, or peasants. In February, crowds revolted in the streets. As the turmoil of the "February Days" spread, Louis Philippe abdicated and a group of liberal, radical, and socialist leaders proclaimed the Second Republic.

MARCH

News of France's successful February revolution spread throughout the German states. In March, demonstrations broke out in the streets of Berlin, and the king agreed to an all-German constitution. When troops randomly fired two shots into the crowd, the demonstrations turned into eight hours of bitter violence.

Thinking Critically
1. **Make Comparisons** How were the "February Days" and the "June Days" similar and different?
2. **Recognize Ideologies** What ideals survived despite how quickly most rebellions throughout Europe were crushed?

Cause and Effect

Long-Term Causes

- Spread of Enlightenment ideas
- Growth of nationalism and liberalism
- Poverty caused by the Industrial Revolution

Immediate Causes

- Uprisings in Paris
- Economic recession
- Poor harvests
- Corrupt governments

The Revolutions of 1848

Immediate Effects

- A new republic in France
- Fall of Metternich
- Promises of reform in Austria, Italy, and Prussia

Long-Term Effects

- A new empire in France
- Successes for liberalism, nationalism, and socialism
- Germany and Italy united
- Labor unions
- Increased voting rights for men

Connections to Today

- Ongoing efforts to ensure basic rights for all citizens
- Ongoing efforts to ensure limited government and popular sovereignty worldwide

Analyze Cause and Effect The revolutions of 1848 were the result of new ways of thinking and hard times for workers. *Could one of these factors by itself have caused such widespread rebellion? Why or Why not?*

Italian revolutionary flag

issued a constitution for the Second Republic. It created a strong president and a one-house legislature. But it also gave the vote to all adult men, the widest suffrage in the world at the time. Nine million Frenchmen now could vote, compared with only 200,000 who had that right before.

When elections for president were held, the overwhelming winner was Louis Napoleon, nephew of Napoleon Bonaparte. The "new" Napoleon attracted the working classes by presenting himself as a man who cared about social issues such as poverty. At the same time, his famous name, linked with order and past French glory, helped him with conservatives.

Once in office, Louis Napoleon used his position as a stepping-stone to greater power. By 1852, he had proclaimed himself emperor, taking the title **Napoleon III.** Thus ended the short-lived Second Republic.

Like his celebrated uncle, Napoleon III used a plebiscite to win public approval for his seizure of power. A stunning 90 percent of voters supported his move to set up the Second Empire. Many thought that a monarchy was more stable than a republic or hoped that Napoleon III would restore the glory days of Napoleon Bonaparte.

Napoleon III, like Louis Philippe, ruled at a time of rapid economic growth. For the bourgeoisie, the early days of the Second Empire brought prosperity and contentment. In time, however, Napoleon III would embark on foreign adventures that would bring down his empire and end French leadership in Europe.

 Checkpoint How did the French revolutions of 1830 and 1848 differ?

Revolution Surges Through Europe

In 1848, revolts in Paris again unleashed a tidal wave of revolution across Europe. For opponents of the old order, it was a time of such hope that they called it the "springtime of the peoples." Although events in France touched off the revolts, grievances had been piling up for years. Middle-class liberals wanted a greater share of political power for themselves, as well as protections for the basic rights of all male citizens. Workers demanded relief from the miseries of the Industrial Revolution. And nationalists of all classes ached to throw off foreign rule.

Change in the Austrian Empire In the Austrian empire, revolts broke out in the major cities. Even though Metternich censored the press, books were smuggled to universities throughout the empire. Students demanded change. When workers joined the students on the streets of Vienna, Metternich resigned and fled in disguise.

Revolution continued to spread. In Budapest, Hungarian nationalists led by journalist **Louis Kossuth** demanded an independent government, an end to serfdom, and a written constitution to protect basic rights. In Prague, the Czechs made similar demands. Overwhelmed by events, the Austrian government agreed to the reforms. The gains were temporary, however.

Austrian troops soon regained control of Vienna and Prague and smashed the rebels in Budapest.

Revolts in Italy Uprisings also erupted in the Italian states. Nationalists wanted to end Hapsburg domination and set up a constitutional government. From Venice in the north to Naples in the south, Italians set up independent republics. Revolutionaries even expelled the pope from Rome and installed a nationalist government. Before long, the forces of reaction surged back here, too. Austrian troops ousted the new governments in northern Italy. A French army restored the pope to power in Rome. In Naples, local rulers canceled the reforms they had reluctantly accepted.

Rebellion in the German States In the German states, university students demanded national unity and liberal reforms. Economic hard times and a potato famine brought peasants and workers into the struggle. In Prussia, liberals forced King Frederick William IV to agree to a constitution written by an elected assembly. Within a year, though, he dissolved the assembly.

Throughout 1848, delegates from German states met in the Frankfurt Assembly. Divisions soon <u>emerged</u> over whether Germany should be a republic or a monarchy and whether to include Austria in a united German state. Finally, the assembly offered Prussia's Frederick William IV the crown of a united Germany. To their dismay, the conservative king rejected the offer because it came not from the German princes but from the people—"from the gutter," as he described it.

By 1850, rebellion faded, ending the age of liberal revolution that had begun in 1789. Why did the uprisings fail? The rulers' use of military force was just one reason. Another was that revolutionaries did not have mass support, and in many instances, constitutions that represented their principles were withdrawn or replaced. In the decades ahead, liberalism, nationalism, and socialism would win successes not through revolution, but through political activity.

✔ **Checkpoint** What was the outcome of most of the revolutions outside France in 1848?

Analyzing Political Cartoons

A Year of Revolution This English cartoonist comments on the revolutions of 1848 and the reaction of European rulers. Based on the cartoon,
1. What ideal led to the revolutions of 1848?
2. How did the revolutions affect Europe's monarchs?

Vocabulary Builder

<u>emerge</u>—(ee MURJ) *v.* to arise, appear, or come out of

---

Progress Monitoring *Online*
For: Self-quiz with vocabulary practice
Web Code: naa-2021

SECTION 2 **Assessment**

Terms, People, and Places
1. For each term, person, or place listed at the beginning of the section, write a sentence explaining its significance.

Note Taking
2. **Reading Skill: Identify Causes and Effects** Use your completed chart to answer the Focus Question: What were the causes and effects of revolutions in Europe in 1830 and 1848?

Comprehension and Critical Thinking
3. **Draw Conclusions** What were the conditions under which the people of France lived that led to revolution rather than peace?
4. **Analyze Information** (a) Where did revolution spread in 1830? (b) Were these revolutions successful? Explain.
5. **Make Generalizations** Why did most of the revolutions of 1848 fail to achieve their goals?

● **Writing About History**

Quick Write: Gather and Organize Evidence In order to write a well-organized persuasive essay, you need to gather evidence to support your position. Gather evidence from the section to support an essay on whether workers were justified in taking to the streets in 1830 and 1848. Then create a chart that lists both sides of the issue.

Revolution

Fighting at the Hôtel de Ville, July 28, 1830

Why have political revolutions occurred?

The wave of revolution that swept Europe in the early 1800s mainly involved a clash between liberal and conservative political ideas. Conservatives wanted to ensure stability and preserve their own power and wealth by restoring traditional social and political structures. Liberals wanted more power for the people in the form of written constitutions and republican governments. Liberal ideas also crossed the Atlantic to Latin America, where they fueled revolutionary movements for independence. Consider these other examples of political revolutions.

Glorious Revolution

For centuries, England's kings struggled with Parliament for power. The Revolution of 1688 resolved this long-standing dispute in favor of Parliament. King James II wanted to restore Roman Catholicism, but Parliament supported the Church of England. When the queen gave birth to a boy, members of Parliament feared that it was the start of a Catholic monarchy. They invited James's daughter Mary and her husband, William III of Orange, to rule England, and James II fled the country. Parliament emerged with increased powers. The revolution was called "glorious" because it was bloodless.

Meiji Restoration

Military dictators known as shoguns governed Japan for some 600 years, well into the 1800s. Emperors ruled in name only during this time. By the mid-1800s, industrialization and the growth of trade had created new groups of wealthy Japanese who challenged the traditional class structure. In addition, Western powers threatened Japan's self-imposed isolation from outside "barbarians." In 1858, the shogun—against the emperor's wishes—gave in to American demands and signed a treaty giving the United States trading rights. The resulting anti-foreign uprising swept the shogun from power in 1868 and restored direct rule to the emperor, in what is called the Meiji Restoration.

Islamic Revolution

In 1953, the United States helped restore the shah of Iran, Muhammad Reza Pahlavi, to the ruling position that he had lost during World War II. In the next 25 years, as an American ally in the Cold War, the shah increased his power. Favoring Western culture, he modernized Iran and tried to undercut the power of the Muslim clergy, who held fast to traditional religious ways. Meanwhile, the shah's secret police tortured and executed many of his critics. Widespread discontent led to huge anti-shah and anti-Western demonstrations, eventually causing the shah to flee. An exiled Muslim religious leader, the Ayatollah Ruhollah Khomeini, returned to Iran. In 1979, he and his supporters proclaimed Iran an Islamic republic.

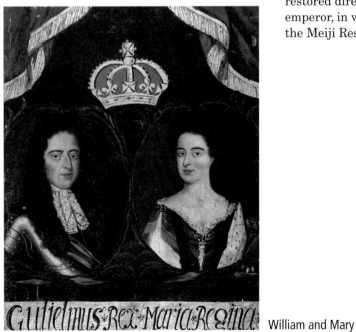

William and Mary

Thinking Critically

1. Identify the revolution, or huge political change, that took place in each of the examples presented above. What factors led to the revolution in each case?

2. **Connection to Today** Research online to find a news article on a recent revolution. Summarize the article in one or two paragraphs.

Simón Bolívar

Crown awarded to Bolívar

WITNESS HISTORY 🔊 AUDIO

A Revolutionary Is Born

Like many wealthy Latin Americans, young Simón Bolívar was sent to Europe to complete his education. In Europe he became a strong admirer of the ideals of the Enlightenment and the French Revolution. One day while speaking with his Italian tutor about freedom and individual rights, he fell on his knees and swore an oath:

❝ I swear before God and by my honor never to allow my hands to be idle nor my soul to rest until I have broken the chains that bind us to Spain. ❞

Focus Question Who were the key revolutionaries that led the movements for independence in Latin America, and what were their accomplishments?

Revolts in Latin America

Objectives

- Explain the causes of discontent in Latin America.
- Describe Haiti's fight for freedom.
- Summarize the revolts in Mexico and Central America.
- Understand how revolutions ignited South America.

Terms, People, and Places

peninsulare	Toussaint L'Ouverture
creole	Father Miguel Hidalgo
mestizo	Father José Morelos
mulatto	José de San Martín
Simón Bolívar	Dom Pedro

Note Taking

Reading Skill: Identify Main Ideas As you read the section, fill in a table like the one below with a country, a date, and a main idea about revolts in Latin America. Add rows as needed.

Revolts in Latin America		
Haiti	1791	Toussaint L'Ouverture

Liberal ideas were spreading to Latin America with explosive results. From Mexico to the tip of South America, revolutionary movements arose to overthrow the reigning European powers. By 1825, most of Latin America was freed from colonial rule.

Discontent Fans the Fires

By the late 1700s, the revolutionary fever that gripped Western Europe had spread to Latin America. There, discontent was rooted in the social, racial, and political system that had emerged during 300 years of Spanish rule.

Social and Ethnic Structures Cause Resentment Spanish-born **peninsulares,** members of the highest social class, dominated Latin American political and social life. Only they could hold top jobs in government and the Church. Many **creoles**—the European-descended Latin Americans who owned the haciendas, ranches, and mines—bitterly resented their second-class status. Merchants fretted under mercantilist policies that tied the colonies to Spain.

Meanwhile, a growing population of **mestizos,** people of Native American and European descent, and **mulattoes,** people of African and European descent, were angry at being denied the status, wealth, and power that were available to whites. Native Americans suffered economic misery under the Spanish, who had conquered the lands of their ancestors. In the Caribbean region and parts of South America, masses of enslaved Africans who worked on plantations longed for freedom.

Portrait of Joseph Bonaparte,
King of Spain, 1808

The Enlightenment Inspires Latin Americans In the 1700s, educated creoles read the works of Enlightenment thinkers. They watched colonists in North America throw off British rule. Translations of the Declaration of Independence and the Constitution of the United States circulated among the creole elite.

During the French Revolution, young creoles like Simón Bolívar (boh LEE vahr) traveled in Europe and were inspired by the ideals of "liberty, equality, and fraternity." Yet despite their admiration for Enlightenment ideas and revolutions in other lands, most creoles were reluctant to act.

Napoleon Invades Spain The spark that finally ignited widespread rebellion in Latin America was Napoleon's invasion of Spain in 1808. Napoleon ousted the Spanish king and placed his brother Joseph on the Spanish throne. In Latin America, leaders saw Spain's weakness as an opportunity to reject foreign domination and demand independence from colonial rule.

 Checkpoint Where did creoles get many of their revolutionary ideas?

Slaves Win Freedom for Haiti

Even before Spanish colonists hoisted the flag of freedom, revolution had erupted in a French-ruled colony on the island of Hispaniola. In Haiti, as the island is now called, French planters owned very profitable sugar plantations worked by nearly a half million enslaved Africans. Sugar plantations were labor-intensive. The slaves were overworked and underfed.

Toussaint L'Ouverture Leads a Slave Revolt Embittered by suffering and inspired by the talk of liberty and equality, the island's slaves rose up in revolt in 1791. The rebels were fortunate to find an intelligent and skillful leader in Toussaint L'Ouverture (too SAN loo vehr TOOR), a self-educated former slave. Although untrained, Toussaint was a brilliant general and inspiring commander.

Toussaint's army of former slaves faced many enemies. Some mulattoes joined French planters against the rebels. France, Spain, and Britain all sent armies against them. The fighting took more lives than any other revolution in the Americas. But by 1798, the rebels had achieved their goal: slavery was abolished, and Toussaint's forces controlled most of the island.

Haiti Wins Independence In 1802, Napoleon Bonaparte sent a large army to reconquer the former colony. Toussaint urged his countrymen to take up arms once again to resist the invaders. In April 1802 the French agreed to a truce, but then they captured Toussaint and carried him in chains to France. He died there in a cold mountain prison a year later.

The struggle for freedom continued, however, and late in 1803, with yellow fever destroying their army, the French surrendered. In January 1804, the island declared itself an independent country under the name Haiti. In the following years, rival Haitian leaders fought for power. Finally, in 1820, Haiti became a republic.

 Checkpoint How were slaves instrumental in achieving Haiti's independence?

Mexico and Central America Revolt

The slave revolt in Haiti frightened creoles in Spanish America. Although they wanted power themselves, most had no desire for economic or social changes that might threaten their way of life. In 1810, however, a creole priest in Mexico, **Father Miguel Hidalgo** (hee DAL goh), raised his voice for freedom.

Father Hidalgo Cries Out for Freedom Father Hidalgo presided over the poor rural parish of Dolores. On September 15, 1810, he rang the church bells summoning the people to prayer. When they gathered, he startled them with an urgent appeal, "My children, will you be free?" Father Hidalgo's speech became known as "el Grito de Dolores"—the cry of Dolores. It called Mexicans to fight for independence.

A ragged army of poor mestizos and Native Americans rallied to Father Hidalgo and marched to the outskirts of Mexico City. At first, some creoles supported the revolt. However, they soon rejected Hidalgo's call for an end to slavery and his plea for reforms to improve conditions for Native Americans. They felt that these policies would cost them power.

After some early successes, the rebels faced growing opposition. Less than a year after he issued the "Grito," Hidalgo was captured and executed, and his followers scattered.

José Morelos Continues the Fight Another priest picked up the banner of revolution. **Father José Morelos** was a mestizo who called for wide-ranging social and political reform. He wanted to improve

Liberty!
Toussaint L'Ouverture and his army of former slaves battle for independence from France and an end to slavery. Although Toussaint achieved his goal of ending slavery, Haiti (see inset) did not become independent until after his death. *Why do you think Toussaint and his army were willing to risk death to achieve their goals?*

conditions for the majority of Mexicans, abolish slavery, and give the vote to all men. For four years, Morelos led rebel forces before he, too, was captured and shot in 1815.

Spanish forces, backed by conservative creoles, hunted down the surviving guerrillas. They had almost succeeded in ending the rebel movement when events in Spain had unexpected effects.

Mexico Wins Independence In Spain in 1820, liberals forced the king to issue a constitution. This move alarmed Agustín de Iturbide (ee toor BEE day), a conservative creole in Mexico. He feared that the new Spanish government might impose liberal reforms on the colonies as well.

Iturbide had spent years fighting Mexican revolutionaries. Suddenly, in 1821, he reached out to them. Backed by creoles, mestizos, and Native Americans, he overthrew the Spanish viceroy. Mexico was independent at last. Iturbide took the title Emperor Agustín I. Soon, however, liberal Mexicans toppled the would-be monarch and set up the Republic of Mexico.

New Republics Emerge in Central America Spanish-ruled lands in Central America declared independence in the early 1820s. Iturbide tried to add these areas to his Mexican empire. After his overthrow, local leaders set up a republic called the United Provinces of Central America. The union soon fragmented into the separate republics of Guatemala, Nicaragua, Honduras, El Salvador, and Costa Rica.

 Checkpoint How did events in Spain affect the fight for Mexican independence?

Revolution Ignites South America

In South America, Native Americans had rebelled against Spanish rule as early as the 1700s, though with limited results. It was not until the 1800s that discontent among the creoles sparked a widespread drive for independence.

Bolívar Begins the Fight In the early 1800s, discontent spread across South America. Educated creoles like Simón Bolívar admired the French and American revolutions. They dreamed of winning their own independence from Spain.

In 1808, when Napoleon Bonaparte occupied Spain, Bolívar and his friends saw the occupation as a signal to act. In 1810, Bolívar led an uprising that established a republic in his native Venezuela. Bolívar's new republic was quickly toppled by conservative forces, however. For years, civil war raged in Venezuela. The revolutionaries suffered many setbacks. Twice Bolívar was forced into exile on the island of Haiti.

Then, Bolívar conceived a daring plan. He would march his army across the Andes and attack the Spanish at Bogotá, the capital of the viceroyalty of New Granada (present-day Colombia). First, he cemented an alliance with the hard-riding llaneros, or Venezuelan cowboys. Then, in a grueling campaign, he led an army through swampy lowlands and over the snowcapped Andes. Finally, in August 1819, he swooped down to take Bogotá from the surprised Spanish.

Other victories followed. By 1821, Bolívar had succeeded in freeing Caracas, Venezuela. "The Liberator," as he was now called, then moved south into Ecuador, Peru, and Bolivia. There, he joined forces with another great leader, José de San Martín.

LATIN AMERICAN INDEPENDENCE

LATIN AMERICA, 1844

☐ Independent nations with dates of independence

*United Provinces of Central America had dissolved by 1844.

**Gran Colombia had dissolved by 1830.

Once Toussaint L'Ouverture, who was born a slave, was legally freed, he devoted himself to freeing slaves in St-Domingue (now Haiti), which led to Haiti's independence.

Because Father Miguel Hidalgo rang the church bells calling people to revolt against the Spanish, his name became the symbol of Mexican independence.

José de San Martín fought against Napoleon's army for years before helping Bolívar liberate Argentina, Chile, and Peru.

Simón Bolívar freed Venezuela, Colombia, Panama, Ecuador, Peru, and Bolivia from Spanish rule.

UNITED STATES

Atlantic Ocean

MEXICO 1821

Gulf of Mexico

Mexico City ⊛

Bahamas (Br.)

Cuba (Sp.)

DOMINICAN REPUBLIC 1844

Jamaica (Br.)

HAITI 1804

Puerto Rico (Sp.)

British Honduras (Br.)

Caribbean Sea

UNITED PROVINCES OF CENTRAL AMERICA*

GUATEMALA 1838
EL SALVADOR 1838
HONDURAS 1838
NICARAGUA 1838
COSTA RICA 1838

Mosquito Coast (Br.)

Panama (PART OF COLOMBIA)

Trinidad (Br.)

British Guiana (Br.)

Dutch Guiana (Neth.)

French Guiana (Fr.)

Caracas ⊛

VENEZUELA 1830

COLOMBIA 1819
Bogotá ⊛

GRAN COLOMBIA**

Quito ⊛

ECUADOR 1822

EQUAL AREA PROJECTION
SCALE IN MILES
0   500   1000

0   500   1000
SCALE IN KILOMETERS

Pacific Ocean

Lima ⊛

PERU 1824

BRAZIL 1822

Atlantic Ocean

La Paz ⊛

BOLIVIA 1825

PARAGUAY 1811

Rio de Janeiro ⊛

⊛ Asunción

CHILE 1818
Santiago

ARGENTINE CONFEDERATION 1816

URUGUAY 1828

Buenos Aires ⊛   ⊛ Montevideo

PATAGONIA

Falkland Islands (Br.)
(Argentine 1820–1833)

40°N
20°N
Equator
20°S
40°S
60°W
80°W

LATIN AMERICA ABOUT 1790

New Spain

UNITED STATES

Bahamas (Br.)

Cuba   Hispaniola

Mexico City ⊛

British Honduras (Br.)

Mosquito Coast (Br.)

West Indies

Guianas

New Granada

Bogotá ⊛

EQUAL AREA PROJECTION
SCALE IN MILES
0   2000

0   2000
SCALE IN KILOMETERS

Lima ⊛

Brazil

Peru

La Plata

Rio de Janeiro ⊛

⊛ Buenos Aires

☐ British
☐ Dutch
☐ French
☐ Portuguese
☐ Spanish

Geography *Interactive*

For: Interactive maps and biographies
Web Code: nap-2031

Thinking Critically

1. **Synthesize Information** Why did so many Latin American nations gain independence by 1830?
2. **Recognize Cause and Effect** What influenced the leaders of Latin American independence?

Dom Pedro, Emperor of Brazil

San Martín Joins the Fight Like Bolívar, San Martín was a creole. He was born in Argentina but went to Europe for military training. In 1816, this gifted general helped Argentina win freedom from Spain. He then joined the independence struggle in other areas. He, too, led an army across the Andes, from Argentina into Chile. He defeated the Spanish in Chile before moving into Peru to strike further blows against colonial rule. San Martín turned his command over to Bolívar in 1822, allowing Bolívar's forces to win the final victories against Spain.

Freedom Leads to Power Struggles The wars of independence ended by 1824. Bolívar then worked tirelessly to unite the lands he had liberated into a single nation, called Gran Colombia. Bitter rivalries, however, made that dream impossible. Before long, Gran Colombia split into four independent countries: Colombia, Panama, Venezuela, and Ecuador.

Bolívar faced another disappointment as power struggles among rival leaders triggered destructive civil wars. Before his death in 1830, a discouraged Bolívar wrote, "We have achieved our independence at the expense of everything else." Contrary to his dreams, South America's common people had simply changed one set of masters for another.

Vocabulary Builder

proclaim—(proh KLAYM) *vt.* to announce publicly or formally

Brazil Gains Independence When Napoleon's armies conquered Portugal, the Portuguese royal family fled to Brazil. When the king returned to Portugal, he left his son **Dom Pedro** to rule Brazil. "If Brazil demands independence," the king advised Pedro, "proclaim it yourself and put the crown on your own head."

In 1822, Pedro followed his father's advice. A revolution had brought new leaders to Portugal who planned to abolish reforms and demanded that Dom Pedro return. Dom Pedro refused to leave Brazil. Instead, he became emperor of an independent Brazil. He accepted a constitution that provided for freedom of the press, freedom of religion, and an elected legislature. Brazil remained a monarchy until 1889, when social and political turmoil led it to become a republic.

 Checkpoint How were the goals of the South American revolutions different from their results?

Progress Monitoring Online
For: Self-quiz with vocabulary practice
Web Code: naa-2031

SECTION 3 Assessment

Terms, People, and Places

1. What do many of the key terms listed at the beginning of the section have in common? Explain.

Note Taking

2. **Reading Skill: Identify Supporting Details** Use your completed chart to answer the Focus Question: Who were the key revolutionaries that led the movements for independence in Latin America, and what were their accomplishments?

Comprehension and Critical Thinking

3. **Draw Conclusions** How did social structure contribute to discontent in Latin America?

4. **Analyze Information** (a) What was the first step on Haiti's road to independence? (b) Why did creoles refuse to support Hidalgo or Morelos?

5. **Identify Central Issues** Why did Bolívar admire the American and French revolutions?

● **Writing About History**

Quick Write: Use Effective Language Most effective persuasive essays contain memorable and convincing details and vivid, persuasive language. Suppose you were one of the revolutionary leaders mentioned in the section. Write notes for a speech in which you persuade others to join your cause. Include at least three compelling reasons why people should follow you.

Simón Bolívar: *Address to the Congress of Venezuela*

Encouraged by the revolutions in British North America and France, colonists in Spanish South America soon began to create a force for independence. Simón Bolívar was one of the leaders of this movement. The excerpt below is from Bolívar's Address to the Second National Congress of Venezuela, given in 1819. In this speech, Bolívar offers advice on what type of government to set up in Venezuela.

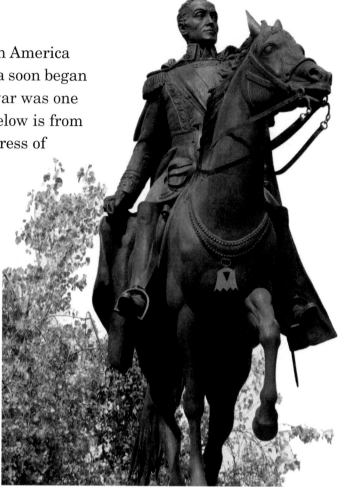

Statue of Bolívar as the Liberator, Mexico City

Subject to the threefold yoke of ignorance, tyranny, and vice, the American people have been unable to acquire knowledge, power, or [civic] virtue. The lessons we received and the models we studied, as pupils of such pernicious[1] teachers, were most destructive. . . .

If a people, perverted by their training, succeed in achieving their liberty, they will soon lose it, for it would be of no avail to endeavor to explain to them that happiness consists in the practice of virtue; that the rule of law is more powerful than the rule of tyrants, because, as the laws are more inflexible everyone should submit to their beneficent austerity; that proper morals, and not force, are the bases of law; and that to practice justice is to practice liberty.

Therefore, Legislators, your work is so much the more arduous[2], inasmuch as you have to reeducate men who have been corrupted by erroneous[3] illusions and false incentives[4]. Liberty, says Rousseau, is a succulent[5] morsel, but one difficult to digest. . . .

Legislators, meditate well before you choose. Forget not that you are to lay the political foundation for a newly born nation which can rise to the heights of greatness that Nature has marked out for it if you but proportion this foundation in keeping with the high plane that it aspires to attain. Unless your choice is based upon the peculiar . . . experience of Venezuelan people—a factor that should guide you in determining the nature and form of government you are about to adopt for the well-being of the people . . . the result of our reforms will again be slavery.

1. **pernicious** (pur NISH us) *adj.* harmful, injurious
2. **arduous** (AHR joo us) *adj.* difficult
3. **erroneous** (eh ROH nee us) *adj.* mistaken, wrong
4. **incentive** (in SEN tiv) *n.* reason for doing something
5. **succulent** (SUK yoo lunt) *adj.* juicy, tasty

Thinking Critically
1. **Analyze Literature** How did Bolívar feel the people of Latin America were prepared for new government?
2. **Draw Inferences** Do you think Bolívar was practical or idealistic? Use examples from the excerpt to defend your opinion.

Quick Study Guide

Progress Monitoring *Online*
For: Self-test with vocabulary practice
Web Code: naa-2041

■ Revolutions in Europe

Successful	Unsuccessful
Serbia (autonomy 1830)	Poland (1830)
Greece (1830)	Austria (1848)
Belgium (1830)	Italy (1848)
	Germany (1848)

■ Events in France

July 1830	1840	February 1848
• Rebels take control of Paris. • Constitutional monarchy proclaimed. • Louis Philippe becomes king.	• Recession heightens discontent.	• Rebels take to the streets. • Second Republic is proclaimed. • Louis Philippe abdicates.

June 1848	1850	1852
• Bourgeois liberals crush workers' rebellion.	• Louis Napoleon is voted president of the Second Republic.	• Louis Napoleon becomes emperor of the Second Empire.

■ Independence Movements in Latin America

Cause and Effect

Long-Term Causes	Immediate Causes
• European domination • Spread of Enlightenment ideas • American and French Revolutions • Growth of nationalism	• Social injustices • Revolutionary leaders emerge. • Napoleon invades Spain.

Independence Movements

Immediate Effects	Long-Term Effects
• Toussaint L'Ouverture leads slave revolt in Haiti. • Bolívar, San Martin, and others lead successful revolts. • Colonial rule ends in much of Latin America.	• Numerous independent nations in Latin America • Continuing efforts to achieve stable democratic governments and to gain economic independence

■ Age of Revolution

Chapter Events

1804	1810	1819	1821
Haiti declares independence from France.	Father Miguel Hidalgo urges Mexicans to fight for independence from Spain.	Simón Bolívar seizes Bogotá from the Spanish.	Simón Bolívar liberates Caracas, Venezuela.

Chapter Events
Global Events

1800	**1810**	**1820**

1803	1814	1819	1823
United States buys Louisiana from France.	Napoleon is banished to Elba.	The United States acquires Spanish Florida.	U.S. President James Monroe issues the Monroe Doctrine.

Concept Connector

Cumulative Review

Record the answers to the questions below on your Concept Connector worksheets. In addition, record information from this chapter about the following concepts:

- Conflict: European revolutionaries in 1830 and 1848
- Revolution: Latin American revolutions against European rulers

1. **Empire** Colonists in Latin America in the early 1800s had much in common with colonists in North America in the mid-1700s. In each case, the colonies were part of an empire whose capital was thousands of miles away. How did the empires use their colonies for their own gain? What did the colonists have in common? Think about the following:
   - nationalism
   - the role of geography in empires
   - economic exploitation by empires

2. **Nationalism** How was Latin American nationalism in the early 1800s similar to, or different from, French nationalism in 1789? Think about the following:
   - leaders of each revolution
   - targets of each revolution

3. **Democracy** After the American Revolution, a new nation was formed under a written constitution. This did not happen in Latin America. How were the results of the American Revolution different from the revolutions in Latin America? Think about the following:
   - groups that had power afterwards
   - the relationship between land ownership and power

Connections to Today

1. **Independence: Mexican Independence Day** Today, the people of Mexico remember Father Hidalgo's speech as "el Grito de Dolores." Every September 15, the anniversary of the speech, the president of Mexico rings a bell—suggestive of the church bell in Dolores. The president then honors the Grito de Dolores by repeating the speech. The next day, September 16, marks the anniversary of the beginning of the fight against the Spanish. It is celebrated as Mexican Independence Day, a national holiday. Schools and businesses shut down, and people throw huge parties. Fireworks light the night sky. Why is the ringing of bells an important custom of Mexican Independence Day?

2. **Conflict: Chechnya and Russia** There are many struggles for independence in the world today. Certain Basques in Spain, Tibetans in China, and Chechens in Russia are all seeking their independence. In some cases, such as in Chechnya, revolutionaries resort to terrorism to fight for their goals. Conduct research and write a one-page report about Chechnya and why its revolutionaries seek independence from Russia.

1830
French revolutionaries battle the king's troops in the streets of Paris.

HISTOIRE D'UN
GAMIN DE PARIS
Par J. LERMINA.

1848
Revolutions break out across much of Europe.

History Interactive
For: Interactive timeline
Web Code: nap-2001

1830

1840

1839
China and Britain clash in the Opium War.

1850

1850
Taiping Rebellion begins in China.

Chapter Assessment

Terms, People, and Places

Match the following terms with the definitions below.

creole	*peninsulare*
autonomy	ideology
Louis Philippe	mestizo
recession	José de San Martín

1. system of thought and belief
2. self-rule
3. person in Spain's colonies in the Americas who was an American-born descendant of Spanish settlers
4. period of reduced economic activity
5. person in Spain's colonies in the Americas who was of Native American and European descent
6. known as the "citizen king"
7. fought for freedom in South America
8. member of the highest class in Spain's colonies in the Americas

Main Ideas

Section 1 (pp. 634–637)
9. In the early 1800s, what were the main goals of (a) conservatives, (b) liberals, and (c) nationalists?

Section 2 (pp. 638–644)
10. What were the causes of the French revolution of 1830?
11. Describe the outcomes of the 1848 rebellions in Europe.

Section 3 (pp. 645–651)
12. (a) How did Mexico gain independence from Spain? (b) How did Mexico's independence change the lives of its people?
13. Why is Simón Bolívar known as "The Liberator"?

Chapter Focus Question
14. How did revolutionary ideals in Europe and Latin America ignite uprisings in the first half of the nineteenth century?

Critical Thinking

15. **Recognize Cause and Effect** How did the clash of conservatism, liberalism, and nationalism contribute to unrest in Europe in the 1800s?
16. **Draw Conclusions** Why do you think liberals of the early 1800s supported limited voting rights?
17. **Synthesize Information** In the 1820s, Britain, France, and Russia supported the Greek struggle for independence. (a) Why did these European powers support the Greeks? (b) Did the European powers usually respond to revolution in this way? Explain.
18. **Analyze Information** You have read Metternich's comment: "When France sneezes, Europe catches cold." (a) What did he mean by these words? (b) Was Metternich correct?
19. **Geography and History** Review the map in Section 3. How does the map show that Bolívar failed to achieve one of his dreams?
20. **Analyzing Visuals** The scene below is part of a famous mural by José Clemente Orozco. How do you think Orozco feels about Father Hidalgo?

21. **Geography and History** (a) How did climatic conditions help Haitians defeat the French? (b) Do you think the distance between Europe and Latin America affected the Latin American wars for independence? Explain.

● Writing About History

Writing a Persuasive Essay The early 1800s were a time of revolution across Europe. Liberals and nationalists attempted to organize revolts that might overthrow Europe's colonial rule. Write a persuasive essay that a liberal or nationalist might have published in a local newspaper in an attempt to persuade people to join a revolution.

Prewriting
- Take notes about the ideas that motivated revolutionaries in the early 1800s.
- Generate arguments that a liberal or nationalist might make.

Drafting
- Using a convincing thesis, or main argument, make an outline that organizes the essay.
- Write an attention-grabbing introduction, a body, and a conclusion.
- Open and close with your strongest argument.

Revising
- Make sure your arguments are logical and clearly explained. Provide additional evidence where needed.
- Use the guidelines for revising your report on page SH17 of the Writing Handbook.

Document-Based Assessment

The Revolutions of 1848: The Aftermath

The revolutions of 1848 began spontaneously in February 1848 on the streets of Paris. Reformers won short-lived success with the abdication of Louis Philippe. Uprisings spread across Europe to Austria, Hungary, Germany, and Italy, among others. These rebellions were quelled in short order, as the documents below illustrate, but some reverberations were more lasting.

Document A

"[O]n June 23rd, 1848 . . . the proletarians of Paris were defeated, decimated [killed off so that a large part of the population was removed], crushed with such an effect that even now they have not yet recovered from the blow. And immediately, all over Europe, the new and old Conservatives and Counter-Revolutionists raised their heads with an effrontery [boldness] that showed how well they understood the importance of the event. The Press was everywhere attacked, the rights of meeting and association were interfered with, every little event in every small provincial town was taken profit of to disarm the people to declare a state of siege, to drill the troops in the new maneuvers and artifices [clever tricks] that Cavaignac [French general known for his harsh treatment of Parisian rebels] had taught them."

—From ***The Paris Rising—Frankfort Assembly***
by Frederich Engels (February, 1852)

Document B

"[German] factory workers failed to win any lasting class advantages in 1848–1849 . . . Many artisans exerted themselves for the revolution; in October 1849 the magazine of the cigar workers estimated that three hundred in this industry alone had been forced to flee to Switzerland. . . . For German democrats—whether workers or from the middle class—the revolution left little immediate consolation. In a few states democrats retained large representation in the parliaments, but reactionary changes in the suffrage systems soon ended that. . . . But the long-range results of the revolution were not altogether negative. To be sure, those who worked for democracy after 1849 knew better than to try to create a republic. They also knew the futility of resorting to revolutionary violence. But their effort did not cease."

—From ***The Democratic Movement in Germany, 1789–1914***
by John L. Snell

Document C

Metternich Flees Austria

Document D

"The rising of 1848 was a spontaneous expression of national feeling but completely uncoordinated and therefore defeated in detail. After it, once more patrolled by Austria, Italy sank back into inaction. . . . From the wreck of Italian political institutions in 1849 there was only one survival, the constitution granted by [King] Charles Albert in Piedmont [kingdom in northwestern Italy]. It provided for a Premier or President of the Council, who, like the Senate, was nominated by the King, and a Chamber of Deputies numbering two hundred and four, elected on a narrow franchise [vote]."

—From ***The Evolution of Modern Italy***
by Arthur James Whyte

Analyzing Documents

Use your knowledge of the revolutions of 1848 and Documents A, B, C, and D to answer questions 1–4.

1. Which words describe the attitude of the author of Document A toward the counter-revolutionaries?
   A admiration and pride
   B understanding and sympathy
   C hatred and disapproval
   D respect and sympathy

2. According to Document B, what strategies did the democrats of Germany follow after the revolution was put down?
   A revolutionary plots
   B voter-registration drives
   C underground efforts
   D parliamentary politics

3. In Document C, Prince Clemens von Metternich is
   A proud to resign.
   B continuing Austrian governance.
   C expressing nationalism.
   D unpopular and defeated.

4. **Writing Task** Describe the aftermath of the revolutions of 1848. If you had lived in 1849, would you have seen causes for optimism or pessimism? How would your answer be different from the viewpoint of the twenty-first century?

Migration

What factors cause large groups of people to move from one place to another?

In the 1800s, famine drove more than a million Irish to leave their homeland. In later years, millions more Europeans would migrate to North and South America, mainly seeking economic opportunity. Like most emigrants, they left behind their homes and cultures for a future that was uncertain at best. What drives people to take such a bold step? Motivators include poverty and unemployment, civil unrest, and natural disasters such as famine and drought. These "push factors" sometimes, but not always, combine with a common "pull factor": the promise of a better life in the new location. Consider the following causes and historical examples of migration:

◄ Migration of refugees during the 1947 partition of India and Pakistan.

Aggression

Migration played a major role in the fall of the Roman empire. It all started with the Mongols, aggressive warriors from central Asia, who attacked the Huns in the A.D. 200s. Over time, the Huns migrated westward. They pushed the Goths, a Germanic group, out of the Russian steppe and toward Roman lands. The Goths, in turn, displaced another Germanic people, the Vandals. This chain reaction or "bumper car" migration continued, sending wave after wave of invaders into the western Roman empire, which eventually collapsed.

Forced Migration

European traders imposed the forced migration of some 12 million enslaved Africans from the 1500s to the 1800s. More than a million Africans died during the brutal passage across the Atlantic to the Americas. Another involuntary migration took place in the Soviet Union during the 1930s. Joseph Stalin sent millions of peasants and political opponents to forced-labor camps in Siberia and other remote areas. Many of them died or were killed in the camps.

Persecution

In 1948, the British granted India independence, splitting it along religious lines into India (Hindu) and Pakistan (Muslim). Hundreds of thousands died in the violence that followed. More than 7 million Muslims fled from India to Pakistan to escape persecution. More than 7 million Hindus and Sikhs migrated in the opposite direction for the same reason.

▼ Immigrants arriving in New York City.

Thinking Critically

1. (a) What were some possible "pull" factors for Irish emigrants? (b) How do the "push" and "pull" factors for voluntary migration differ from those for involuntary migration?

2. **Connections to Today** Use news sources to read about an example of recent migration. Write a one paragraph summary of the migration including explanations of push and/ or pull factors influencing the migration.

Nationalism

How have people used nationalism as a basis for their actions?

Starting in the late 1700s, a spirit of nationalism swept across Europe and the Americas. Nationalism is a powerful force characterized by strong feelings of pride in and devotion to one's nation. It gives people a sense of identity beyond their family and local area. Nationalism can compel people to fight to establish their own nation, through revolution. It can move people to volunteer to defend their country from outside attack. It can even cause people to attack another country in order to acquire more territory for the homeland. Consider the following examples:

Three Sarajevan girls run through "Sniper Alley" in Sarajevo.

Revolution

The American Revolution may have been the first major eruption of nationalism. Americans sought liberty and equality. This search, prevented by Britain's efforts to maintain control, helped unify the diverse American colonies. Americans already spoke the same language and followed the same basic religion. Faced with Britain's tyranny, nationalist feelings arose in the form of patriotism. Those feelings gained full expression in the Declaration of Independence of July 4, 1776.

Defense

In June 1940, the British expected an invasion. Their nation stood alone against the German military machine, which was ready to strike as soon as Britain's defenses weakened. They never weakened. Prime Minister Winston Churchill set the tone when he urged the nation to stand up to Hitler. The British responded with courage and devotion to the cause of freedom. Despite a bombing blitz that devastated London, British morale remained high, and Hitler gave up his plans.

Aggression

Yugoslavia has been an ethnic powder keg since its creation in 1918. Nationalist tensions broke up this federation of six republics after the fall of communism. Four republics declared their independence, but the republic of Serbia aggressively tried to keep the nation together. It supported Serbian nationalists in civil wars and used "ethnic cleansing" to clear regions of non-Serbs in hopes of absorbing those regions into a "Greater Serbia." Intervention by NATO finally ended this practice and restored an uneasy peace in 1999.

Queen Elizabeth and King George VI of Great Britain visit a London neighborhood that had been bombed by Germany in 1941.

Thinking Critically

1. **(a)** Is nationalism a positive force? Explain your answer. **(b)** What event or events in recent years brought out nationalistic feelings among Americans? Why?
2. **Connections to Today** Do library research to identify an example of nationalism today.

Technology

How has technology changed the way people live and work?

The British colonized India to extract its natural resources and to sell British-made products. To serve these ends, Britain made sure that the Suez Canal, its shipping "lifeline" to India, remained open. Britain also built a massive railway system to carry finished goods into India and raw materials out. The introduction of railway technology changed India and encouraged a spirit of nationalism. As the following examples demonstrate, advances in transportation technology always have the potential of changing society.

Container Ships

By the early 1900s, diesel ships replaced the sailing and steam-powered ships that had carried British goods to India years before. Some shippers had begun putting cargo in sealed, standard-sized containers for easier handling. By the 1960s, specially designed container ships could transport hundreds of the locked and sealed cargo boxes. Shippers developed automated equipment to unload and store the containers quickly. These containers fit perfectly onto truck trailers and railroad flatcars. The new technology greatly increased the efficiency of shipping goods, while reducing the cost.

Automobiles

Like the first machine-powered ships, the earliest automobiles ran on steam power. That changed, however, after the invention of the internal-combustion gasoline engine in 1878. Until the early 1900s, cars served mainly as recreational vehicles for the rich. Then Henry Ford mass produced his inexpensive Model T. By 1930, more than 25 million cars were on the road in the United States alone. The rise of the automobile changed industrialized societies. Networks of roads and highways grew. Suburbs blossomed. More people traveled than ever before.

Airplanes

Decades after the Wright brothers made their first successful flight in 1903, only the most adventurous people traveled by air. In 1940, airliners began to have pressurized cabins that allowed them to fly above turbulence. Other technological innovations, including radar, made airplanes safer. By 1960, more Americans traveled from city to city on planes than on trains and buses, and air travel had replaced ships as the leading way to cross the Atlantic. Today, airlines throughout the world carry millions of passengers each year.

Freight Transport
Billion tkm*

	Road	Rail	Sea
European Union	1,516	358	1,254
United States	1,534	2,183	414
Japan	313	22	244
China	597	1,362	NA
Russia	22	1,434	93

* Tons per kilometer
NA Not available
SOURCE: EUROPA Statistical Pocketbook Online, 2004

Thinking Critically

1. How did each of these transportation technologies affect people's lives?
2. **Connections to Today** Learn more about a present-day advance in transportation technology. Write a summary of how this innovation may change the way people live or work.

Dictatorship

▲ Julius Caesar on a Roman coin, c. 44 B.C.

◄ Francisco Franco in 1948

How have dictators assumed and maintained power?

One easy way to compare forms of government is to divide them into two categories: democracies and dictatorships. In democracies the people tell the leaders what to do, and in dictatorships the leaders tell the people what to do. Not all dictators are fascist, like Mussolini was. However, Mussolini, like Stalin and Hitler, was a classic dictator. Each took all political power for himself and used brutal police or military forces to maintain that power. None was held responsible to the will of the people. Consider these other examples of dictators, ancient and modern:

Julius Caesar, Ancient Rome

During the Roman Republic, the Roman Senate would appoint a dictator to serve as Rome's top official in times of civil strife. Dictators had broad powers, but usually served for only six months. Some Roman rulers, including Julius Caesar, found the law too restrictive. In 49 B.C., Caesar and his army crossed the Rubicon River and marched on Rome. As a result of the civil war that followed, Caesar took control of Rome and declared himself dictator. By 44 B.C., he had gained enough power to have himself made dictator for life. He had also gained enemies in the Senate, many of whom joined in a successful scheme to assassinate him.

Francisco Franco, Spain

Civil war raged in Spain during the 1930s. Loyalists fought to preserve Spain's republican government. They fought against the conservative Nationalists, who were made up largely of military groups, led by General Francisco Franco.

During the war, Franco accepted military help from Hitler and Mussolini. After his victory, Franco created a dictatorship based on fascism. One of his first actions was to kill or imprison thousands of former Loyalists. He remained in power into the 1970s by limiting dissent and by satisfying the varied factions on whom he relied for support.

Fidel Castro, Cuba

In 1952, an army revolt brought Fulgencio Batista to power in Cuba. Batista promised to end government corruption. Instead, he looted the treasury, threw his opponents in jail, and stifled the press. In 1956, Fidel Castro and a small group of rebels began a guerrilla war against the Batista regime. In 1959, Batista fled and Castro took control. However, Castro did not restore political and civil rights, as he had promised. Instead, he began a communist dictatorship. His regime killed political opponents and jailed anyone suspected of disloyalty. The Soviet Union supported Castro by giving Cuba economic and military aid.

◄ Fidel Castro visiting a school in 1961

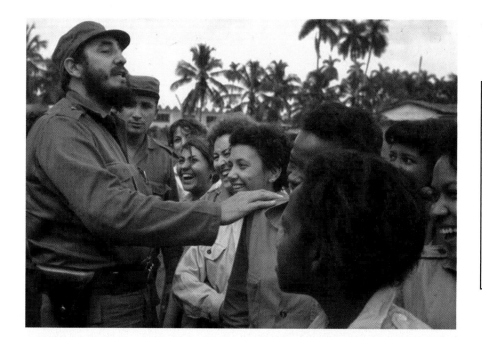

Thinking Critically

1. Why is it difficult for political opponents to succeed against a dictator?
2. **Connect to Today** Do research at a local library or on the Internet to find out more about these and other dictators. Write a biographical sketch of a fictional modern-day dictator. Give your leader characteristics of several real dictators.

Genocide

What factors have led groups of people or governments to commit genocide?

After learning the extent of the Jewish Holocaust in World War II, British Prime Minster Winston Churchill called genocide "a crime that has no name." As a result of the Nuremberg trials in which Nazi officials were tried for "crimes against humanity," the United Nations drew up a treaty defining and criminalizing genocide. Genocide is any act committed with the idea of destroying an entire national, ethnic, racial or religious group. The Holocaust is perhaps the most well-known case of genocide, but consider these other examples from the twentieth century:

▲ Skulls of victims of the Cambodian Khmer Rouge

▲ Jewish survivor of Ebensee concentration camp

Armenia

In 1915, as World War I raged, the government of the Ottoman empire ordered the systematic extermination of most of the male Armenian population and the forced deportation of Armenian women, children, and elderly. By the end of the brutal deportation, up to 1.5 million Ottoman Armenians had been exterminated.

Several German military leaders who later became Nazis were stationed in the Ottoman empire during World War I, and may have applied what they observed there to their persecution of Jewish people during World War II.

Cambodia

In 1975, after years of civil war, Pol Pot, leader of the Khmer Rouge, came to power in Cambodia, a Southeast Asian country. Pol Pot attempted to transform Cambodia into a communist agricultural society by exterminating the country's professional and educated middle class. Over the course of four years of Khmer Rouge rule, between one and two million people were massacred or worked to death through forced labor.

▶ Jean Paul Akayesu, a local government official, being tried by a UN court for ordering mass killings in Rwanda.

Rwanda

In the African nation of Rwanda, the Tutsi and Hutu groups share the same language and other cultural characteristics. But social, political, and economic factors divide them. In 1994, the Hutu-led government called on military personnel to eliminate members of the Tutsi political opposition. The hatred and violence spread quickly. Soon Hutu civilians were murdering their Tutsi neighbors. In 100 days, more than 800,000 Tutsis were slaughtered.

Armenian Genocide in the Ottoman Empire

Black Sea

Istanbul (Constantinople)

OTTOMAN EMPIRE

Tigris R.

Euphrates R.

35°N

Cyprus

Tripoli

Mediterranean Sea

Conic Projection
0   200   400 mi
0   200   400 km

● Centers of deportation and massacre

➡ Principal routes of deportation

Thinking Critically

1. How was the role of government similar in the Holocaust and in the genocides described above?
2. Conduct research at your school or local library to find out more about these and other examples of genocide. Write a brief essay about what happened and why.

Cooperation

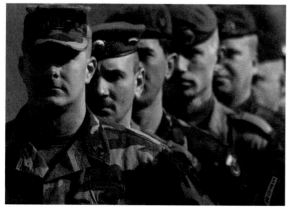

These soldiers, from five different nations, were all part of a NATO-led peacekeeping force in Bosnia in 1999.

In what ways have groups or countries cooperated over time?

Throughout history, people have worked together to achieve their goals, knowing that there is "strength in numbers." For example, prehistoric humans cooperated in hunting for food. Later, countries worked together as allies to defend themselves from threats or to attack other countries. Today, military alliances still exist, but countries also cooperate to improve trade and to resolve problems that affect the entire world. Consider the following examples of cooperation:

Military

After World War II, facing the threat of attack by the Soviet Union, 12 nations from North America and Europe formed a defensive alliance called the North Atlantic Treaty Organization (NATO). Led by the United States, NATO played a vital role in winning the Cold War. Today, 26 NATO members contribute to the group's collective security.

Economic

The goal of expanding trade has continued to lead to international alliances. The European Union (EU), established in 1993, focuses on economic cooperation among its 25 members. Another regional trading group, the North American Free Trade Agreement (NAFTA), started in 1994. NAFTA's free trade zone includes the United States, Canada, and Mexico.

World Issues

Today, the issue of climate change has led to cooperation among nations and the people of the world. In 2005, the Kyoto Accords went into effect. This treaty is an attempt to limit the global emissions of greenhouse gases, such as carbon dioxide. Many scientists believe that these gases contribute to climate change, which could damage the environment.

The European Union

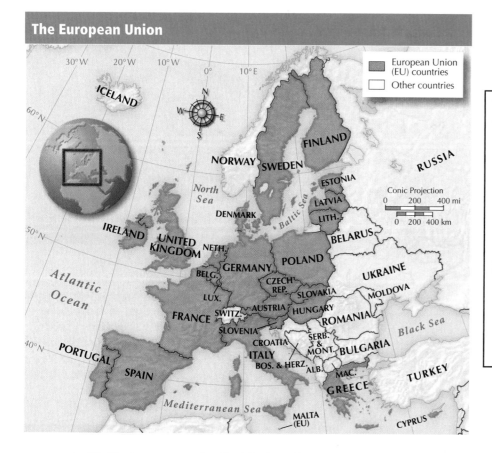

Thinking Critically

1. Markets are often limited to a single country because of legal barriers and fees collected at borders. When nations join the European Union (EU), barriers and fees no longer limit trade across borders. Based on the map, how has the EU changed the physical extent of markets in member countries?

2. **Connections to Today** Research these or other examples of international cooperation to find out more about them. Write an editorial supporting or opposing economic or military agreements among nations.

Democracy

How has the practice of democracy developed over time?

The American Revolution led to the establishment of a nation based on the principle of democracy, or rule by the people. Later democratic revolutions in Latin America, Africa, and Asia looked back to the birth of the United States for inspiration. Even today, developing nations around the world seeking a model for democratic government often turn to the Constitution of the United States. Yet democracy developed before 1776 and before the Enlightenment ideals that so deeply influenced the American framers. Much of that early development took place in England, although history's first democracies developed in the city-states of ancient Greece.

▲ Ancient Greek orator Demosthenes gives a speech to a crowd of Athenians.

Athenian Democracy

Athens had a direct democracy. That is, all citizens—a male minority that excluded women, people not from Athens, and slaves—could take part in ruling the city-state. This new form of government was partly a reaction to earlier rule by tyrants. The men of Athens rejected submitting to a powerful central authority. Athenian democracy upheld the ideals of liberty and equality. The citizens of Athens safeguarded free speech. They believed that all citizens must be equal before the law.

▼ In the annual open-air assembly in Appenzell, Switzerland, citizens vote directly on major issues.

Magna Carta

During the Middle Ages in Europe, democracy did not exist. However, in England the king was forced to accept limits on his rule. He agreed to consult the most powerful groups in the realm before making important decisions, such as raising taxes. The Magna Carta was one of the first documents to set limits on a king's power. This agreement between King John of England and his barons, crafted in 1215, established the rights of barons. It also emphasized that the law applied to everyone, including the king.

English Bill of Rights

In 1689, one year after England's Glorious Revolution, Parliament passed a Bill of Rights. This bill restated existing laws and made it clear that the monarch must follow them. It declared that the ruler had to seek the consent of Parliament, which represented propertied English males, before taking certain actions. It also affirmed several rights of the people, including the right to petition the monarch, freedom of speech in Parliament, and freedom from excessive bail, excessive fines, and cruel punishments.

Thinking Critically

1. What motivated people in the examples above to seek democracy?
2. **Connections to Today** Using reliable online or library sources, research a recent struggle for democracy in a country such as Ukraine or Myanmar. How do recent events compare to the ones mentioned on this page?

People and the Environment

▲ A Haitian man burns trees to clear land for farming. Haiti, once heavily forested, has only about 1% forest cover today.

What impact have people had on the environment?

People have been changing the environment from the time they first made stone axes. As populations grew, so did their environmental impact. With the inventions of the Industrial Revolution, people's ability to alter the environment increased dramatically. Technological improvements in one field boosted improvements in other fields, increasing the overall impact of all technologies on the environment. This pattern continues today. Consider the human impact on land, water, and air through the following examples:

Land

Small populations of prehistoric hunter-gatherers had little long-term impact on their environment. The gradual shift to agriculture, however, put new stresses on the land. The more stable food supply supported higher populations, which required more food. Slash-and-burn techniques of clearing land eliminated forests in some areas. Waters from irrigation deposited salt on the soil, destroying soil fertility. In modern times overfarming, overgrazing, and other agricultural practices have encouraged large-scale soil erosion, in which winds carry valuable topsoil away. Today, wind erosion in China and West Africa is expanding deserts and stealing soils needed for food production.

Water

Through the ages, people have used rivers not just for drinking water and transportation but also as sewers. Waste creates unsanitary conditions for people downriver and eventually pollutes the ocean. People have also dammed rivers for flood control, hydropower, and irrigation. Farmers in Central Asia have taken so much water out of two rivers that they have turned a huge inland sea into a salty lake. The Aral Sea, once the fourth-largest body of inland water in the world, has shrunk by more than half in the last 50 years. With less river water draining into the sea, the region's wetlands are drying up, deserts are forming, and plant and animal life are disappearing.

Air

Air pollution is nothing new. In 1661, an English writer complained about the filthy smoke "belching forth" from coal fires. He said that the inhabitants of London "breathe nothing but an impure and thick Mist." Later, the popularity of coal-fired steam engines brought still more air pollution. By the mid-1900s, however, automobile exhaust had replaced coal smoke as the leading source of air pollution in many cities. London, Tokyo, Los Angeles, and Mexico City experienced a new phenomenon: poisonous smog. Today, government-imposed pollution standards have begun to clean the air in many cities, but few city dwellers anywhere would describe their air as fresh or pure.

◀ Bangladeshi children wade through unsanitary flood waters to access clean water from a pump.

Thinking Critically

1. Are negative impacts on the environment inevitable as countries industrialize? Explain your answer.
2. **Connections to Today** Research a developing country—such as Brazil, China, or Thailand—that is struggling with environmental issues. Explain the issues and their impact as well as how the country is meeting its environmental challenges.

Contents

Spanish doubloons

Lithuanian woman, 1991

The Concept Connector Handbooks provide you with reference information that will make it easier for you to compare key concepts and events across time and place.

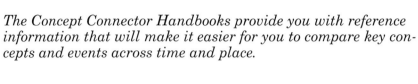

▩ Atlas and Geography Handbook

▩ History Handbook

Ancient Egypt

Egypt

Mediterranean Sea

Nile Delta

Giza

Memphis

Libyan Desert

Nile River

Thebes

Red Sea

Miller Projection

0   200 mi

0   200 km

Nubian Desert

Great Wall of China

Detail of the Bayeux Tapestry

Atlas and Geography

What Is Geography?

Geography is the study of Earth's features, including its people, their surroundings, and the resources available to them. By describing the human environment in different times and places, geographers have added to our knowledge of world history. Often geographers must draw conclusions from limited evidence. For example, studies might turn up common artistic styles or religious rituals in two widely separated groups of people. A geographer might conclude that the groups traded with each other and, in the process, developed shared cultural traits. Geographers use their favorite tool, the map, to show the results of their observations.

Landforms and Water Bodies

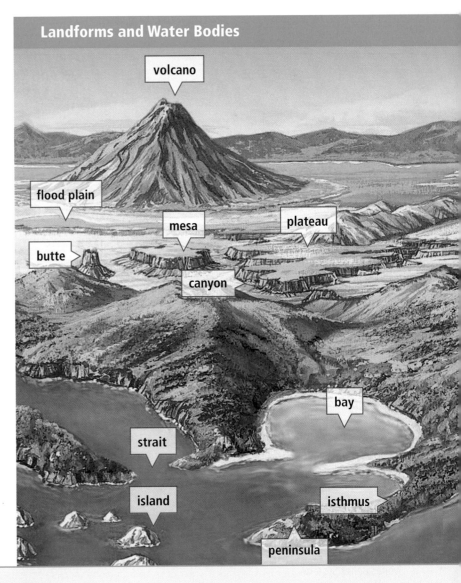

Glossary of Geographic Terms

basin
an area that is lower than surrounding land areas; some basins are filled with water

bay
a part of a larger body of water that extends into the land

butte
a small, high, flat-topped landform with cliff-like sides

canyon
a deep, narrow valley with steep sides; often has a stream flowing through it

cataract
a large waterfall or steep rapids

delta
a plain at the mouth of a river, often triangular in shape, formed when sediment is deposited by flowing water

flood plain
a broad plain on either side of a river, formed when sediment settles during floods

glacier
a huge, slow-moving mass of snow and ice

hill
an area that rises above surrounding land and has a rounded top; lower and usually less steep than a mountain

island
an area of land completely surrounded by water

isthmus
a narrow strip of land that connects two larger areas of land

mesa
a high, flat-topped landform with cliff-like sides; larger than a butte

mountain

mountain pass

glacier

basin

cataract

hill

tributary

valley

plain

delta

river mouth

mountain
 a landform that rises steeply at least 2,000 feet (610 m) above surrounding land; usually wide at the bottom and rising to a narrow peak or ridge

mountain pass
 a gap between mountains

peninsula
 an area of land almost completely surrounded by water and connected to the mainland by an isthmus

plain
 a large area of flat or gently rolling land

plateau
 a large, flat area that rises above the surrounding land; at least one side has a steep slope

river mouth
 the point where a river enters a lake or sea

strait
 a narrow stretch of water that connects two larger bodies of water

tributary
 a river or stream that flows into a larger river

valley
 a low stretch of land between mountains or hills; land that is drained by a river

volcano
 an opening in the Earth's surface through which molten rock, ashes, and gases from the Earth's interior escape

Atlas and Geography

The World: Political

Alaska
(United States)

CANADA

NORTH
AMERICA

UNITED STATES

Atlantic
Ocean

Hawaii
(United States)   Tropic of Cancer

MEXICO   see inset below

Pacific
Ocean

Galápagos   French Guiana
Islands   COLOMBIA   (France)
(Ecuador)   SURINAME
                 ECUADOR
                                             BRAZIL
American Samoa   PERU   SOUTH
(United States)   AMERICA
                                             BOLIVIA
SAMOA

                 French Polynesia   PARAGUAY
                 (France)   Equator

TONGA   Pitcairn Islands   CHILE
                 (Great Britain)   ARGENTINA
                                                          URUGUAY

Southern Ocean
                 Tropic of Capricorn

Inset map

Gulf of Mexico   UNITED
                        STATES   B A H A M A S

Tropic of Cancer

MEXICO   Turks and
                                        Caicos Islands
                            CUBA   (U.K.)   St. Martin (St. Maarten)
                                        U.S. Virgin British Virgin (France & Neth. Antilles)
                                        Islands   Islands   Anguilla ANTIGUA AND
                                        (U.S.)   (U.K.)   (U.K.)   BARBUDA
        Cayman Islands   HAITI
        (U.K.)   Puerto Rico ST. KITTS Montserrat (U.K.)
                         JAMAICA   (U.S.)   AND NEVIS   Guadeloupe (France)
BELIZE   DOMINICAN   DOMINICA
                               REPUBLIC
GUATEMALA   Martinique (France)
        HONDURAS   Caribbean Sea   ST. LUCIA   BARBADOS

EL SALVADOR   ST. VINCENT AND THE GRENADINES GRENADA
        NICARAGUA   Conic Projection
                        0   200   400 miles   Aruba (Neth.) Netherlands TRINIDAD
                                                               Antilles   AND TOBAGO
                        0   200   400 kilometers   (Neth.)

COSTA RICA   Lake
                        PANAMA   COLOMBIA Maracaibo VENEZUELA

Pacific   SOUTH AMERICA   GUYANA
Ocean

World Map

20°W | 0° | 20°E | 40°E | 60°E | 80°E | 100°E | 120°E | 140°E | 160°E

Greenland (Denmark)

Arctic Ocean

Arctic Circle

ICELAND

inset below

80°N

RUSSIA

60°N

EUROPE

ASIA

KAZAKHSTAN

GEORGIA

AZER.

ARMENIA

UZBEK.

TURKMEN.

KYRGYZSTAN

TAJIKZSTAN

MONGOLIA

NORTH KOREA

SOUTH KOREA

JAPAN

40°N

MOROCCO

ALGERIA

LIBYA

ISRAEL

JORDAN

EGYPT

KUWAIT

IRAQ

IRAN AFGHAN.

BAHRAIN PAKISTAN

QATAR

SAUDI ARABIA

U.A.E.

OMAN

CHINA

NEPAL BHUTAN

INDIA

BANGLADESH

MYANMAR (BURMA)

LAOS

THAILAND VIETNAM

CAMBODIA

Pacific Ocean

TAIWAN (Claimed by China)

20°N

AFRICA

CHAD

SUDAN

CEN. AFR. REP.

CAMEROON

ERITREA

DJIBOUTI

YEMEN

ETHIOPIA

SOMALIA

SRI LANKA

MALDIVES

PHILIPPINES

MARSHALL ISLANDS

KIRIBATI

e inset below

GABON

DEM. REP. OF CONGO

CONGO

UGANDA

KENYA

RWANDA

BURUNDI

TANZANIA

SEYCHELLES

BRUNEI

MALAYSIA

SINGAPORE

INDONESIA

TIMOR-LESTE

FEDERATED STATES OF MICRONESIA

PAPUA NEW GUINEA

NAURU

SOLOMON ISLANDS TUVALU

0°

Atlantic Ocean

ANGOLA

MALAWI

ZAMBIA

COMOROS

MOZAMBIQUE

MADAGASCAR

Indian Ocean

OCEANIA

VANUATU

FIJI ISLANDS

ZIMBABWE

BOTSWANA

NAMIBIA

SWAZILAND

SOUTH AFRICA LESOTHO

MAURITIUS

AUSTRALIA

New Caledonia (France)

20°S

N

W E

S

NEW ZEALAND

40°S

Robinson Projection

0 | 1000 | 2000 miles

0 | 1000 | 2000 kilometers

20°W | 0° | 20°E | 40°E | 60°E | 80°E | 100°E | 120°E | 140°E | 160°E

Southern Ocean

ANTARCTICA

West Africa inset

20°W | 20°N

Western Sahara (Morocco)

ALGERIA

MAURITANIA

N

W E

S

MALI

NIGER

SENEGAL

GAMBIA

GUINEA-BISSAU

GUINEA

10°N

BURKINA FASO

BENIN

SIERRA LEONE

IVORY COAST

TOGO

GHANA

NIGERIA

Atlantic Ocean

LIBERIA

Azimuthal Equidistant Projection

0 | 200 | 400 miles

0 | 200 | 400 kilometers

Gulf of Guinea

EQUATORIAL GUINEA

0°

Europe inset

20°W | 10°W

60°N

SWEDEN

FINLAND

NORWAY

N

W E

S

Conic Projection

0 | 200 | 400 miles

0 | 200 | 400 kilometers

50°N | 70°N

Barents Sea

IRELAND

UNITED KINGDOM

North Sea

DENMARK

ESTONIA

LATVIA

LITHUANIA

RUSSIA

BELARUS

RUSSIA

NETHERLANDS

Baltic Sea

Atlantic Ocean

Bay of Biscay

GERMANY

BELGIUM LUX.

POLAND

UKRAINE

FRANCE

LIECH.

SWITZ.

CZECH REP.

SLOVAKIA

AUSTRIA

HUNGARY

SLOVENIA

CROATIA

ROMANIA

MOLDOVA

PORTUGAL

SPAIN

ANDORRA

MONACO ITALY

SAN MARINO

Corsica (France)

BOS. AND HERZ.

SERBIA AND MONT.

BULGARIA

Black Sea

40°N

Gibraltar (U.K.)

Ceuta (Spain)

Melilla (Spain)

Balearic Isands (Spain)

Sardinia (Italy)

VATICAN CITY

ALBANIA

MAC.

GREECE

TURKEY

CYPRUS

SYRIA

LEBANON

MOROCCO

ALGERIA

TUNISIA

MALTA

Sicily (Italy)

Crete (Greece)

Mediterranean Sea

10°E | 30°E

Atlas and Geography

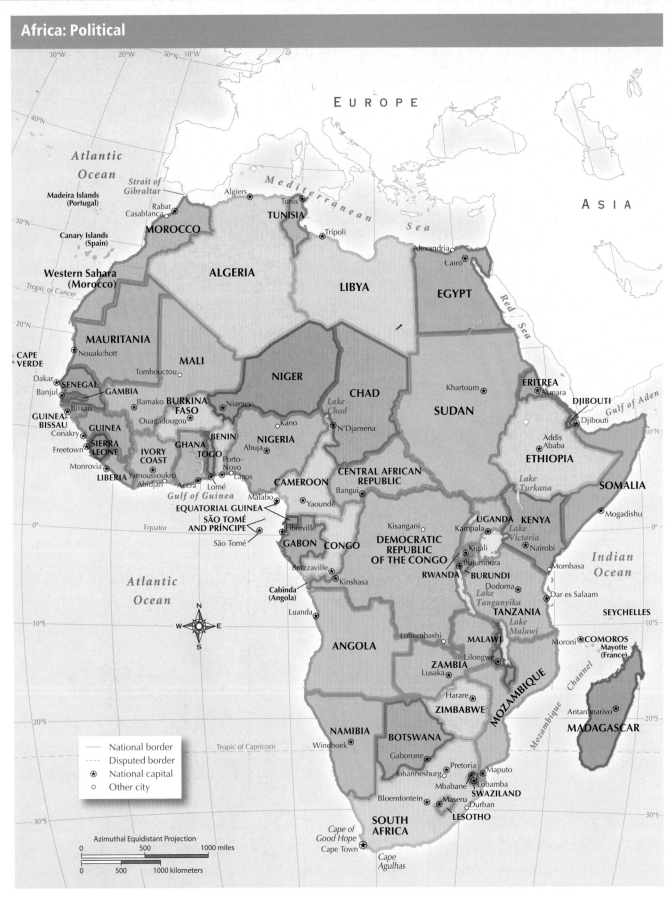

EUROPE

ASIA

Atlantic Ocean

Strait of Gibraltar

Madeira Islands (Portugal)

Mediterranean Sea

Rabat
Casablanca
Algiers
Tunis
TUNISIA
Tripoli

Canary Islands (Spain)
MOROCCO

Alexandria
Cairo

Tropic of Cancer

Western Sahara (Morocco)

ALGERIA

LIBYA

EGYPT

Red Sea

CAPE VERDE

Nouakchott

MAURITANIA

MALI

Tombouctou

NIGER

CHAD

Khartoum

ERITREA
Asmara

DJIBOUTI
Djibouti

Gulf of Aden

Dakar
SENEGAL
Banjul **GAMBIA**
Bissau
GUINEA-BISSAU
Conakry **GUINEA**
Freetown **SIERRA LEONE**
Monrovia
LIBERIA

Bamako
BURKINA FASO
Ouagadougou
GHANA
IVORY COAST
Yamoussoukro
Abidjan
Accra

Niamey
BENIN
TOGO
Lomé
Porto-Novo

Kano
NIGERIA
Abuja
Lagos

N'Djamena
Lake Chad

CAMEROON
Yaoundé

CENTRAL AFRICAN REPUBLIC
Bangui

SUDAN

Addis Ababa
ETHIOPIA

Lake Turkana

SOMALIA
Mogadishu

Gulf of Guinea
Malabo
EQUATORIAL GUINEA
SÃO TOMÉ AND PRÍNCIPE
São Tomé

Equator

Libreville
GABON
CONGO
Brazzaville
Kinshasa

Kisangani
DEMOCRATIC REPUBLIC OF THE CONGO
Kigali
RWANDA
Bujumbura
BURUNDI

UGANDA
Kampala
Lake Victoria
KENYA
Nairobi

Indian Ocean

Mombasa

Atlantic Ocean

Cabinda (Angola)
Luanda

ANGOLA

Lubumbashi

Dodoma
Lake Tanganyika
TANZANIA
Lake Malawi
Dar es Salaam

SEYCHELLES

MALAWI
Lilongwe
ZAMBIA
Lusaka

Moroni **COMOROS**
Mayotte (France)

Harare
ZIMBABWE

MOZAMBIQUE

Mozambique Channel

Antananarivo

MADAGASCAR

Tropic of Capricorn

NAMIBIA
Windhoek

BOTSWANA
Gaborone

Pretoria
Johannesburg
Maputo
Mbabane Lobamba
SWAZILAND

Bloemfontein
Maseru
LESOTHO
Durban

Cape of Good Hope
Cape Town
SOUTH AFRICA
Cape Agulhas

Legend:
— National border
--- Disputed border
⊛ National capital
○ Other city

Azimuthal Equidistant Projection
0   500   1000 miles
0   500   1000 kilometers

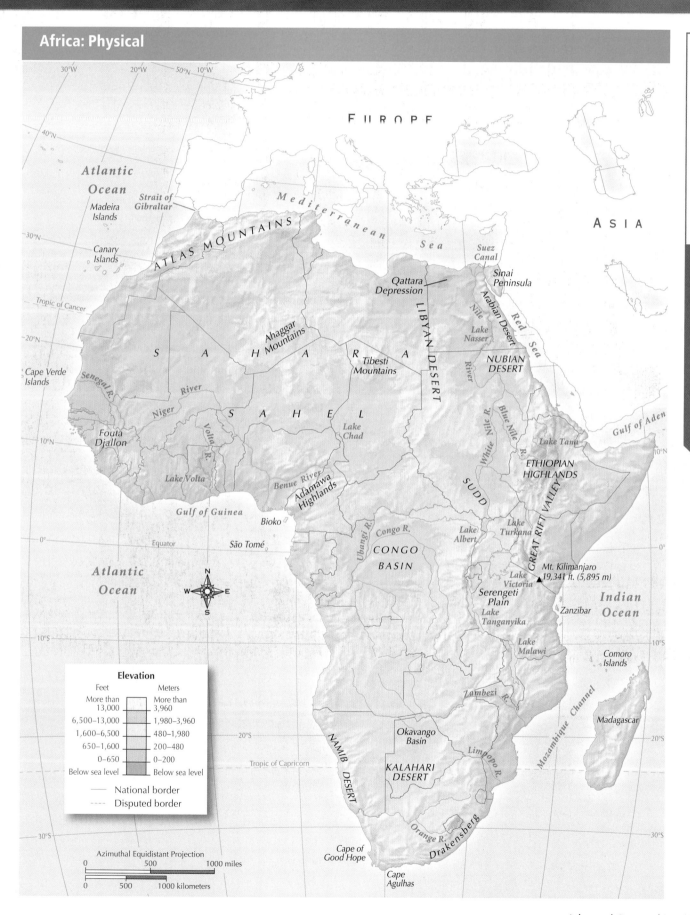

EUROPE

Atlantic
Ocean

Madeira
Islands

Canary
Islands

Cape Verde
Islands

Mediterranean Sea

ASIA

Strait of
Gibraltar

ATLAS MOUNTAINS

Tropic of Cancer

Suez
Canal

Sinai
Peninsula

Qattara
Depression

Nile

Red Sea

Arabian Desert

Gulf of Aden

LIBYAN DESERT

Lake
Nasser

NUBIAN
DESERT

S A H A R A

Ahaggar
Mountains

Tibesti
Mountains

River

Senegal R.

Niger River

S A H E L

Lake
Chad

White Nile R.

Blue Nile R.

Lake Tana

Fouta
Djallon

Volta R.

Lake Volta

ETHIOPIAN
HIGHLANDS

Benue River

Adamawa
Highlands

SUDD

Gulf of Guinea

Bioko

Ubangi R.

Congo R.

CONGO
BASIN

Lake
Albert

Lake
Turkana

GREAT RIFT VALLEY

São Tomé

Equator

Atlantic
Ocean

N
W   E
S

Lake
Victoria

Serengeti
Plain

Lake
Tanganyika

Mt. Kilimanjaro
19,341 ft. (5,895 m)

Zanzibar

Indian
Ocean

Lake
Malawi

Comoro
Islands

Mozambique Channel

Madagascar

Zambezi R.

Elevation

Feet	Meters
More than 13,000	More than 3,960
6,500–13,000	1,980–3,960
1,600–6,500	480–1,980
650–1,600	200–480
0–650	0–200
Below sea level	Below sea level

——— National border
- - - - Disputed border

NAMIB DESERT

Okavango
Basin

KALAHARI
DESERT

Limpopo R.

Tropic of Capricorn

Orange R.

Drakensberg

Cape of
Good Hope

Cape
Agulhas

Azimuthal Equidistant Projection

0   500   1000 miles

0   500   1000 kilometers

Atlas and Geography

Asia: Political

Asia: Physical

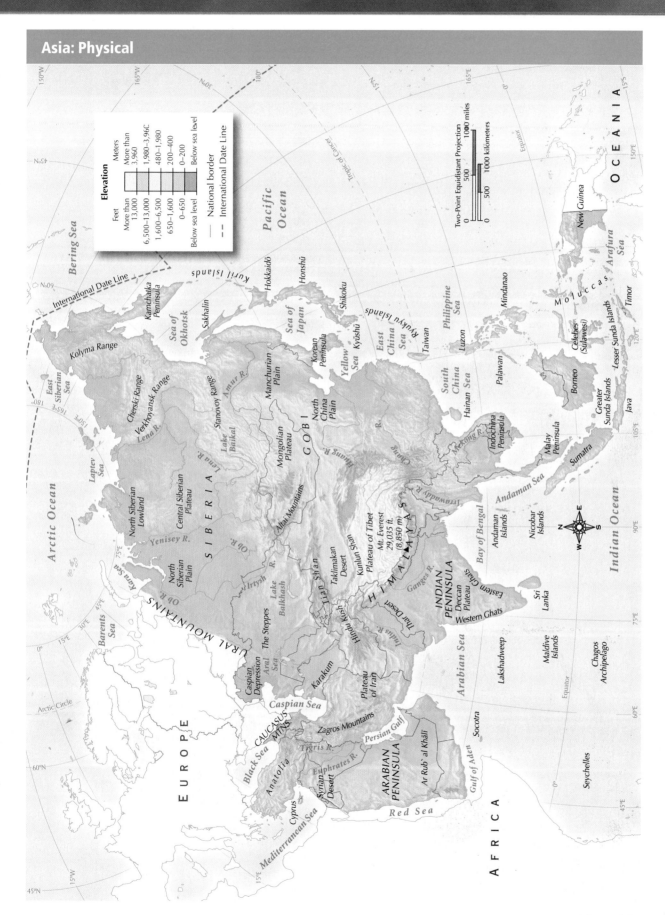

Elevation

Feet	Meters
More than 13,000	More than 3,960
6,500–13,000	1,980–3,96C
1,600–6,500	480–1,980
650–1,600	200–400
0–650	0–200
Below sea level	Below sea level

— National border
-- International Date Line

Two-Point Equidistant Projection

0   500   1000 miles

0   500   1000 kilometers

Atlas and Geography

Europe: Political

National border
National capital
Other city

Europe: Physical

URAL MOUNTAINS

Ural R.

Kama R.

Pechora R.

Caspian Sea

Volga R.

Caspian Depression

CAUCASUS MTS.

Mt. Elbrus
18,510 ft. (5,642 m)

Volga Upland

Don R.

N. Dvina R.

White Sea

Kola Peninsula

Barents Sea

Lake Onega

Lake Ladoga

Central Russian Upland

Sea of Azov

Black Sea

N O R T H   E U R O P E A N   P L A I N

Dnieper R.

Dniester R.

Bosporus

Sea of Marmara

Dardanelles

Gulf of Finland

Carpathian Mountains

Danube R.

Balkan Mountains

Vistula R.

Great Hungarian Plain

Transylvanian Alps

BALKAN PENINSULA

Pindus Mts.

Aegean Sea

Crete

Gulf of Bothnia

SCANDINAVIAN PENINSULA

Kjölen Mountains

Gotland

Baltic Sea

Lake Vänern

Lake Vättern

Sjælland

Oder R.

Elbe R.

Dinaric Alps

Adriatic Sea

ITALIAN PENINSULA

Apennines

Ionian Sea

Maltese Isands

Sicily

Tyrrhenian Sea

Sardinia

Corsica

Jutland

North Sea

Rhine R.

Danube R.

A L P S

Mt. Blanc
15,775 ft.
(4,808 m)

Po R.

Mediterranean Sea

ARCTIC OCEAN

Norwegian Sea

Arctic Circle

Jan Mayen

Faeroe Islands

Shetland Islands

Great Britain

Thames R.

English Channel

Seine R.

Loire R.

Lake Geneva

Massif Central

Garonne R.

Pyrenees

Balearic Isands

British Isles

Ireland

Bay of Biscay

Ebro R.

Meseta

Douro R.

Tagus R.

IBERIAN PENINSULA

Guadalquivir R.

Strait of Gibraltar

AFRICA

Iceland

Denmark Strait

ATLANTIC OCEAN

ASIA

Elevation

Feet	Meters
More than 13,000	More than 3,960
6,500–13,000	1,980–3,960
1,600–6,500	480–1,980
650–1,600	200–400
0–650	0–200
Below sea level	Below sea level

— National border

Lambert Conformal Conic

0   200   400 miles

0   200   400 kilometers

Atlas and Geography

National border

- - - International Date Line

⊛ National capital

◦ Other city

Lambert Azimuthal Equal-Area Projection

0   1000   2000 miles

0   1000   2000 kilometers

North and South America: Physical

Bering Strait

Ellesmere Island

International Date Line

Mt. McKinley (Denali) 20,320 ft. (6,194 m)

Beaufort Sea

Greenland

Bering Sea

Victoria Island

Baffin Bay

Alaska Range

Mackenzie R.

Great Bear Lake

Baffin Island

Davis Strait

Arctic Circle

Aleutian Islands

Gulf of Alaska

Yukon R.

Great Slave Lake

Hudson Bay

Labrador Sea

ROCKY MOUNTAINS

CANADIAN SHIELD

Island of Newfoundland

Lake Winnipeg

Great Lakes

St. Lawrence R.

Cascades

Missouri R.

GREAT PLAINS

Atlantic Ocean

Great Salt Lake

Sierra Nevada

Colorado R.

Mississippi R.

Ohio R.

APPALACHIAN MTS.

Rio Grande

Gulf of California

Baja California

Sierra Madre Occidental

Sierra Madre Oriental

Gulf of Mexico

Tropic of Cancer

Cuba

Hispaniola

Yucatán Peninsula

Jamaica

Greater Antilles

Lesser Antilles

Caribbean Sea

Pacific Ocean

Isthmus of Panama

Llanos

Orinoco R.

Guiana Highlands

Galápagos Islands

Equator

AMAZON BASIN

Amazon R.

ANDES MOUNTAINS

Lake Titicaca

São Francisco R.

Brazilian Highlands

Gran Chaco

Paraguay R.

Paraná R.

Tropic of Capricorn

Aconcagua 22,834 ft. (6,960 m)

Pampas

Rio de la Plata

Atlantic Ocean

Patagonia

Falkland Islands

Tierra del Fuego

Cape Horn

Elevation

Feet	Meters
More than 13,000	More than 3,960
6,500–13,000	1,980–3,960
1,600–6,500	480–1,980
650–1,600	200–400
0–650	0–200
Below sea level	Below sea level

—— National border

- - - International Date Line

Lambert Azimuthal Equal-Area Projection

0   1000   2000 miles

0   1000   2000 kilometers

180° 165°W 150°W 135°W 120°W 105°W 90°W 75°W 60°W 45°W 30°W 15°W 0°

45°N 30°N 15°N 0° 15°S 30°S 45°S 60°N

Australia, New Zealand, and Oceania: Political-Physical

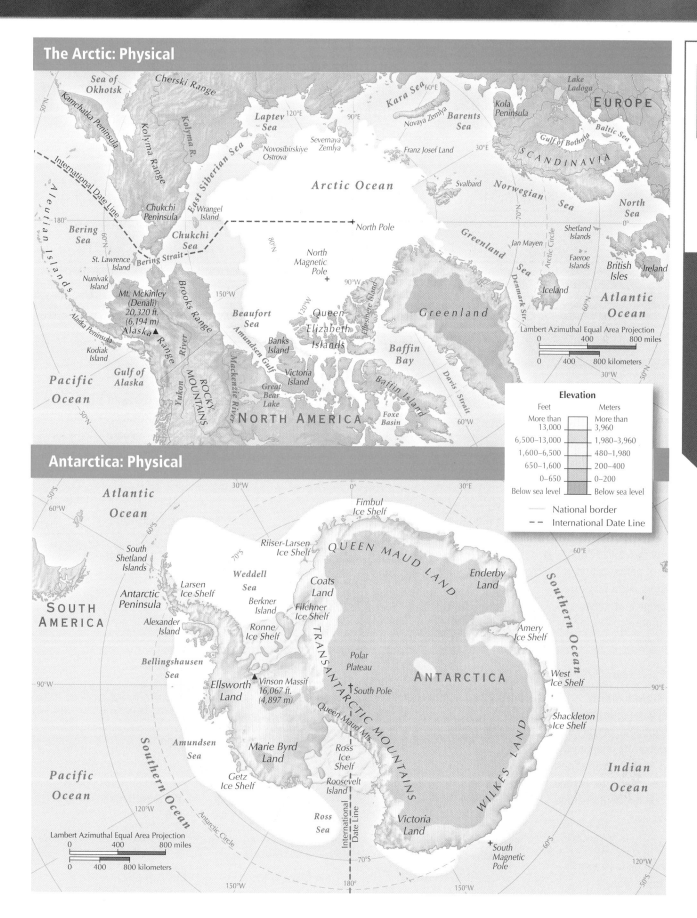

The Arctic: Physical

Sea of Okhotsk · Cherski Range · Kara Sea · 60°E · Lake Ladoga · EUROPE

Kamchatka Peninsula · Kolyma Range · Kolyma R. · Laptev Sea · 120°E · 90°E · Novaya Zemlya · Barents Sea · Kola Peninsula · Baltic Sea

Novosibirskiye Ostrova · Severnaya Zemlya · 30°E · Franz Josef Land · SCANDINAVIA · Gulf of Bothnia

East Siberian Sea · Arctic Ocean · Svalbard · Norwegian Sea · North Sea

International Date Line · 180° · Chukchi Peninsula · Wrangel Island · North Pole · 0° · Greenland Sea · Arctic Circle · Shetland Islands

Aleutian Islands · Bering Sea · 60°N · Chukchi Sea · 80°N · North Magnetic Pole · Jan Mayen · Faeroe Islands · British Isles · Ireland

St. Lawrence Island · Bering Strait · 90°W · Iceland · Denmark Str. · Atlantic Ocean

Nunivak Island · 150°W · Beaufort Sea · 120°W · Queen Elizabeth Islands · Greenland · 60°N

Mt. McKinley (Denali) 20,320 ft. (6,194 m) · Alaska ▲ · Brooks Range · Amundsen Gulf · Banks Island · Baffin Bay · 30°W

Alaska Peninsula · Alaska Range · Yukon River · Mackenzie River · Victoria Island · Baffin Island · Davis Strait

Kodiak Island · Gulf of Alaska · ROCKY MOUNTAINS · Great Bear Lake · Foxe Basin · 60°W

Pacific Ocean · 50°N · NORTH AMERICA

Lambert Azimuthal Equal Area Projection
0 · 400 · 800 miles
0 · 400 · 800 kilometers

Antarctica: Physical

Atlantic Ocean · 30°W · Fimbul Ice Shelf · 0° · 30°E

60°W · Riiser-Larsen Ice Shelf · QUEEN MAUD LAND · Enderby Land · 60°E

South Shetland Islands · 70°S · Weddell Sea · Coats Land · Southern Ocean

Antarctic Peninsula · Larsen Ice Shelf · Berkner Island · Filchner Ice Shelf · Amery Ice Shelf

Alexander Island · Ronne Ice Shelf · Polar Plateau · ANTARCTICA · West Ice Shelf

Bellingshausen Sea · Ellsworth Land · ▲ Vinson Massif 16,067 ft. (4,897 m) · TRANSANTARCTIC MOUNTAINS · † South Pole · 90°E

90°W · Amundsen Sea · Marie Byrd Land · Queen Maud Mts. · Ross Ice Shelf · Shackleton Ice Shelf

Pacific Ocean · Getz Ice Shelf · Roosevelt Island · Victoria Land · WILKES LAND · Indian Ocean

120°W · Southern Ocean · Antarctic Circle · Ross Sea · International Date Line · South Magnetic Pole · 60°S

150°W · 180° · 150°W · 70°S · 120°W

Lambert Azimuthal Equal Area Projection
0 · 400 · 800 miles
0 · 400 · 800 kilometers

Elevation

Feet	Meters
More than 13,000	More than 3,960
6,500–13,000	1,980–3,960
1,600–6,500	480–1,980
650–1,600	200–400
0–650	0–200
Below sea level	Below sea level

—— National border
- - - International Date Line

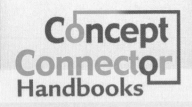

History

Historians study how people lived in the past. They might examine their tools, weapons, jewelry, and building sites, but they rely mainly on written records. For this reason, we say that history began when writing began.

History is a changing story. A historian living at the time of an event may write what seems like a valid description, but a historian writing 100 years later may describe the same event another way entirely. This is because different generations have different perspectives on, or ways of looking at, history. In addition, as time passes, new evidence may appear to alter the interpretation of an event.

Major Eras in World History

Historians attempt to make sense of vast stretches of history by dividing them into periods. This periodization makes it easier to discuss a group of events by relating them to a broader theme.

History and Prehistory

You might think of history as everything that has ever happened. For historians, however, history began around 5,000 years ago with the appearance of writing in two civilizations—Sumer and Egypt. Everything before that is prehistory.

Prehistory   **3000 B.C.**   **History**

Writing systems appear in Sumer (above) and in Egypt *c.* 3000 B.C.*

* The *c.* before the date is Latin for *circa*, meaning "around" or "approximately."

Technology Periodization
This model of periodization divides history according to the technology that drove economic progress.

| Stone Age 2 million B.C. – 3000 B.C. | | | Iron Age 1200 B.C. – A.D.1000 |

| 2 million B.C. | 10,000 B.C. | 5000 B.C. | B.C./A.D. |

Agricultural Age 9000 B.C. – A.D.1800   Bronze Age 3300 B.C. – 700 B.C.

Western Periodization
This model of periodization reflects a European perspective. Classical generally refers to the Greek and Roman civilizations. Middle Ages refers to Europe between the fall of Rome and the Renaissance.

Ancient World 4000 B.C. – 1000 B.C.

| 2 million B.C. | 10,000 B.C. | 5000 B.C. | B.C./A.D. |

Classical Period 1000 B.C. – A.D. 400

Global Periodization
This model of periodization reflects a more global perspective.

Classical Era 1000 B.C. – 400 B.C.   Spread of Monotheism A.D. 1 – 750

| 2 million B.C. | 10,000 B.C. | 5000 B.C. | B.C./A.D. |

Ancient Civilizations 4000 B.C. – 1000 B.C.   Great Empires 400 B.C. – A.D.400

Your textbook is divided this way, into units. Each unit deals with a period, or era, in world history. There are endless ways to categorize the past, depending on one's point of view. The time-lines below show three different examples of periodization.

Decades, Centuries, and Millenniums

Most nations today use a standard calendar that dates events from the believed birth of Jesus. For dates preceding his birth, this calendar uses the abbreviation B.C. ("before Christ"). For dates after his birth, it uses A.D. (anno Domini, Latin for "in the year of our Lord"). An alternative version of this calendar uses the abbreviations B.C.E. and C.E., meaning "Before the Common Era" and "Common Era."

| B.C. | 1 B.C./A.D. 1 | A.D. 100 | A.D. 200 | A.D. 300 | A.D. 400 |

Decade = 10 Years

Century = 100 Years
10 Centuries = 1000 years = 1 millennium
What we call the "Third Century" is the 200s, just as the "Twentieth Century" is the 1900s.

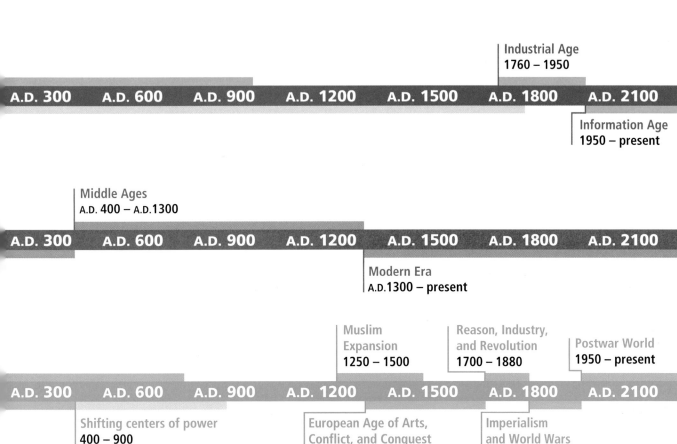

Industrial Age
1760 – 1950

| A.D. 300 | A.D. 600 | A.D. 900 | A.D. 1200 | A.D. 1500 | A.D. 1800 | A.D. 2100 |

Information Age
1950 – present

Middle Ages
A.D. 400 – A.D.1300

| A.D. 300 | A.D. 600 | A.D. 900 | A.D. 1200 | A.D. 1500 | A.D. 1800 | A.D. 2100 |

Modern Era
A.D.1300 – present

Muslim Expansion
1250 – 1500

Reason, Industry, and Revolution
1700 – 1880

Postwar World
1950 – present

| A.D. 300 | A.D. 600 | A.D. 900 | A.D. 1200 | A.D. 1500 | A.D. 1800 | A.D. 2100 |

Shifting centers of power
400 – 900

European Age of Arts, Conflict, and Conquest
1350 – 1700

Imperialism and World Wars
1880 – 1950

History

World Regional Timelines

Africa

Menes unites Egypt
3100 B.C.

Bantu migrations begin
2000 B.C.

Romans destroy Carthage
146 B.C.

Islam spreads to North Africa
A.D. 600s

Ghana controls trans-Saharan gold-salt trade
A.D. 800s

5000 B.C. | 3000 B.C. | B.C./A.D. | A.D. 300 | A.D. 600 | A.D. 900

Great Pyramid and Sphinx at Giza, in Egypt
2550 B.C.

Ironworking flourishes at Meroë, on the Nile River
500 B.C.

Axum converts to Christianity
A.D. 350

East Africa trading cities prosper
A.D. 1000

Europe

Rise of Greek city-states
700s B.C.

5000 B.C. | 3000 B.C. | B.C./A.D. | A.D. 300 | A.D. 600 | A.D. 900

Western Roman empire falls
A.D. 476

Asia

Sumerian city-states thrive
3200 B.C.

Persian empire created
539 B.C.

Buddhism introduced to Japan
500s

5000 B.C. | 3000 B.C. | B.C./A.D. | A.D. 300 | A.D. 600 | A.D. 900

Indus Valley civilization develops
2500 B.C.

Gupta Golden Age begins in India
A.D. 320

Muhammad's Hijira from Mecca to Medina
622

The Americas

Cultivation of maize and cotton
3200 B.C.

Hopewell culture flourishes
A.D. 200s

Mississippian civilization thrives
800s

5000 B.C. | 3000 B.C. | B.C./A.D. | A.D. 300 | A.D. 600 | A.D. 900

Rise of Olmec civilization
1400 B.C.

Height of Maya civilization
500s

Turning point: a decisive moment in world history that triggers a major social, political, economic, or cultural transformation.

World Population Growth

Graph Skills As the graph shows, the world's population gradually rose over many centuries, until it shot up suddenly, starting in the 1700s. Improvements in agriculture, greater control of disease, and the shift from manual labor to machines all helped to increase the population.

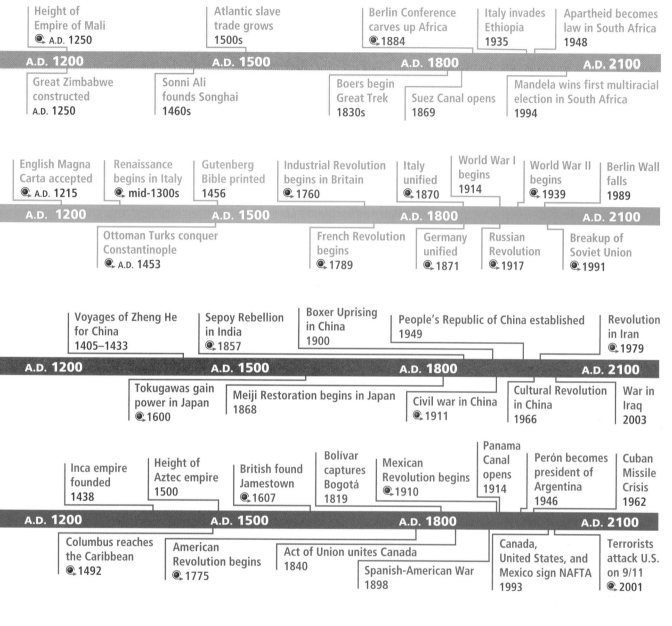

Height of
Empire of Mali
A.D. 1250

Atlantic slave
trade grows
1500s

Berlin Conference
carves up Africa
1884

Italy invades
Ethiopia
1935

Apartheid becomes
law in South Africa
1948

A.D. 1200 — **A.D. 1500** — **A.D. 1800** — **A.D. 2100**

Great Zimbabwe
constructed
A.D. 1250

Sonni Ali
founds Songhai
1460s

Boers begin
Great Trek
1830s

Suez Canal opens
1869

Mandela wins first multiracial
election in South Africa
1994

English Magna
Carta accepted
A.D. 1215

Renaissance
begins in Italy
mid-1300s

Gutenberg
Bible printed
1456

Industrial Revolution
begins in Britain
1760

Italy
unified
1870

World War
I
begins
1914

World War II
begins
1939

Berlin Wall
falls
1989

A.D. 1200 — **A.D. 1500** — **A.D. 1800** — **A.D. 2100**

Ottoman Turks conquer
Constantinople
A.D. 1453

French Revolution
begins
1789

Germany
unified
1871

Russian
Revolution
1917

Breakup of
Soviet Union
1991

Voyages of Zheng He
for China
1405–1433

Sepoy Rebellion
in India
1857

Boxer Uprising
in China
1900

People's Republic of China established
1949

Revolution
in Iran
1979

A.D. 1200 — **A.D. 1500** — **A.D. 1800** — **A.D. 2100**

Tokugawas gain
power in Japan
1600

Meiji Restoration begins in Japan
1868

Civil war in China
1911

Cultural Revolution
in China
1966

War in
Iraq
2003

Inca empire
founded
1438

Height of
Aztec empire
1500

British found
Jamestown
1607

Bolívar
captures
Bogotá
1819

Mexican
Revolution begins
1910

Panama
Canal
opens
1914

Perón becomes
president of
Argentina
1946

Cuban
Missile
Crisis
1962

A.D. 1200 — **A.D. 1500** — **A.D. 1800** — **A.D. 2100**

Columbus reaches
the Caribbean
1492

American
Revolution begins
1775

Act of Union unites Canada
1840

Spanish-American War
1898

Canada,
United States, and
Mexico sign NAFTA
1993

Terrorists
attack U.S.
on 9/11
2001

The Parthenon, Athens, Greece

History

Imperialism, Colonialism, Nationalism, and Revolution

Imperialism	Colonialism
A policy of pursuing, often through conquest, the economic and political domination of another state.	A policy of politically dominating a dependent territory or people.

↓ ↓

Nationalism
A strong feeling of pride in, or devotion to, one's nation.

↓

Revolution
The overthrow of a government from within.

Conquest and Empire

An empire is a group of states or territories controlled by one ruler. Empires often form in a haphazard way. For example, a small state with a strong army successfully defends itself against one neighboring state after another and incorporates their lands. Or at some point, an able ruler aggressively seeks more territory. Over time, the state expands into an empire. A strong military and able leadership are two factors that go into creating an empire. However, successful empires also must develop a government system that can maintain control of conquered peoples.

Selected Empires in World History

Conquests	Time Span	Location
Roman	509 B.C.–A.D. 180	Mediterranean region, Western Europe, Britain
Arab Muslim	A.D. 624–750	Southwest Asia, North Africa, Spain
Mongol	1206–1294	China, Central Asia, Eastern Europe
Ottoman	1299–1566	Southwest Asia, North Africa, Balkans, Eastern Europe
Spanish	1492–1560	Mexico, Central America, South America, Cuba, Florida

First Landing of Columbus by Frederick Kemmelmeyer

Major Conflicts in World History

This table shows selected major wars and conquests. Hundreds of other conflicts, large and small, have occurred throughout history. The cause of a conflict may be as simple as "I want what you have." For example, the basic need for food—and the land to grow it on—has been a prime cause of war. But most of the time, the reasons for wars are more complex. They can involve intertwining economic, political, religious, and cultural forces.

A sans-culotte figure from the French Revolutionary period

Selected Conflicts in World History

Conflict	Time Span	Location	Combatants
Persian Wars	499–448 B.C.	Greece	Greeks vs. Persians
Peloponnesian War	431–404 B.C.	Greece	Athens vs. Sparta
Punic Wars	264–146 B.C.	Mediterranean region	Rome vs. Carthage
Crusades	A.D. 1096–1291	Southwest Asia	Christians vs. Muslims
Hundred Years' War	1337–1443	France	England vs. France
Wars of King Philip II	1571–1588	Europe	Spain vs. Dutch Netherlands; Spain vs. England
Thirty Years' War	1618–1648	Central Europe (German states)	Holy Roman Empire, Spain, Poland, and others vs. Netherlands, Sweden, France, and others
English Civil War	1642–1649	England	Parliament (Roundheads) vs. Charles I and supporters (Cavaliers)
Seven Years' War (includes French and Indian War)	1756–1763	Europe; North America; India	Austria, Russia, and France vs. Prussia and Britain; Britain and its American colonies vs. France and its Native American allies; Britain vs. France
American Revolution	1775–1783	North America	Britain vs. its American colonies
French Revolution	1789–1799	France	Reformers (mainly middle class and peasants) vs. Louis XVI and supporters (mainly nobles and clergy)
Napoleonic Wars (end of the French Revolution)	1799–1815	Europe	France vs. combined European powers
Latin American Wars of Independence	1802–1824	Latin America	Colonies in Latin America vs. France and Spain
American Civil War	1860–1865	United States	North (Unionists) vs. South (Secessionists)
World War I	1914–1918	Europe (mainly France and Russia)	Allied powers vs. Central powers
World War II	1939–1945	North Africa, Europe, East Asia, Pacific Islands	Allies vs. Axis powers
Korean War	1950–1953	Korea	North Korea and China vs. South Korea and United States
Vietnam War	1959–1975	Vietnam	North Vietnam vs. South Vietnam and the United States

Regional Organizations

Through treaties, nations with common regional interests often work together to improve themselves politically, economically, and socially.

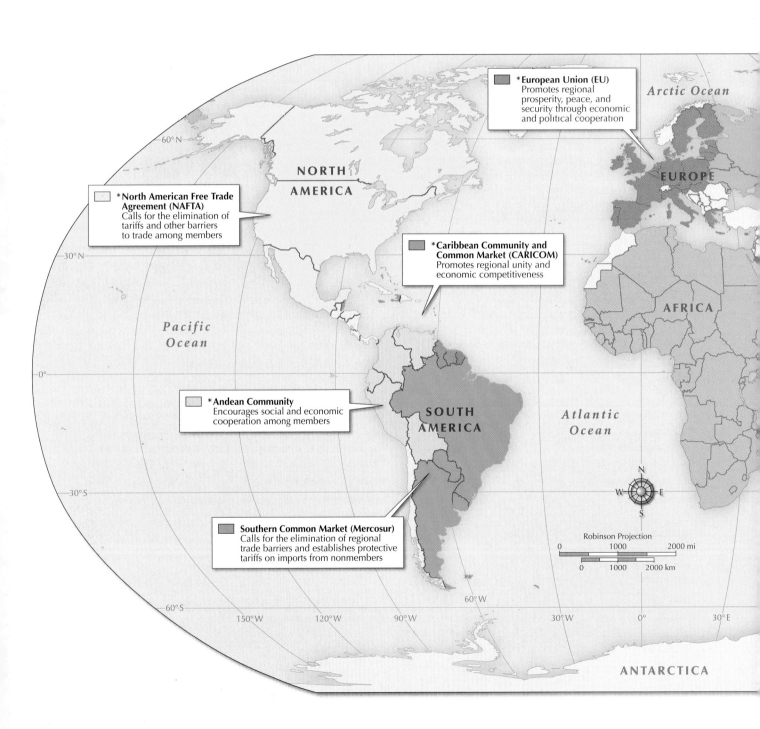

*European Union (EU)
Promotes regional prosperity, peace, and security through economic and political cooperation

*North American Free Trade Agreement (NAFTA)
Calls for the elimination of tariffs and other barriers to trade among members

*Caribbean Community and Common Market (CARICOM)
Promotes regional unity and economic competitiveness

*Andean Community
Encourages social and economic cooperation among members

Southern Common Market (Mercosur)
Calls for the elimination of regional trade barriers and establishes protective tariffs on imports from nonmembers

NORTH AMERICA

SOUTH AMERICA

EUROPE

AFRICA

Arctic Ocean

Pacific Ocean

Atlantic Ocean

ANTARCTICA

Robinson Projection
0   1000   2000 mi
0   1000   2000 km

Commonwealth of Independent States (CIS)
Encourages regional economic cooperation and the coordination of foreign and immigration policies

ASIA

***South Asian Association for Regional Cooperation (SAARC)**
Provides a platform for working together to accelerate economic and social development

Gulf Cooperation Council (GCC)
Promotes regional unity through coordination of economic and defense policies

Pacific Ocean

Indian Ocean

AUSTRALIA

African Union (formerly Organization of African Unity)
Promotes unity, democracy, and economic development among member states

***Association of Southeast Asian Nations (ASEAN)**
Seeks to advance economic cooperation, trade, and joint research and to promote peace and security in the region

0° E   90° E   120° E   150° E

*Free trade zone

International Organizations

These organizations promote cooperation across regions:

- Arab League
- International Monetary Fund (IMF)
- North Atlantic Treaty Organization (NATO)
- Organization for Economic Cooperation and Development (OECD)
- Organization of American States (OAS)
- Organization of Petroleum Exporting Countries (OPEC)
- United Nations (UN)
- World Trade Organization (WTO)

The United Nations

Of all the organizations in the world, the UN stands out as the main coordinator of international activities. With the support of its 191 member nations, the UN plays a vital, ongoing role in keeping the peace, fighting disease, promoting economic development, and providing humanitarian aid.

International aid poured into Indonesia following the December 2004 tsunami. Here an American navy pilot delivers supplies from the United States Agency for International Development (USAID), an independent federal agency.

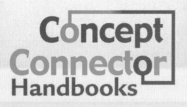

Economics

Three Key Economic Questions		
What goods and services should be produced?	**How should goods and services be produced?**	**Who consumes the goods and services?**
How much of our resources should we devote to national defense, education, public health, or consumer goods? Which consumer goods should we produce?	Should we produce food on large corporate farms or on small family farms? Should we produce electricity with oil, nuclear power, coal, or solar power?	How do goods and services get distributed? The question of who gets to consume which goods and services lies at the very heart of the differences between economic systems. Each society answers the question of distribution based on its combination of social values and goals.

In 1923, due to the collapse of German currency, it was cheaper to paper a wall with Deutsche marks than it was to buy wallpaper.

In every society throughout history, people have had access to resources, such as water, fertile land, and human labor. Yet everywhere in the world, people's resources are limited. Economics is the study of how people choose to use their limited resources to meet their wants and needs.

Until modern times, people focused largely on resources related to agriculture. They farmed the land to produce food, mainly for their own consumption. This traditional way of meeting basic needs still defines some economies today. However, modern societies have also developed other economic systems to deal with the complexities of expanding trade and industrialization. An economic system is the method used by a society to produce and distribute goods and services.

Basic Economic Questions

Through its economic system, society answers three key questions. How a society answers these questions depends on how much it values different economic goals. Four different economic systems have developed in response to these three questions.

Economic Goals	
Economic efficiency	Making the most of resources
Economic freedom	Freedom from government intervention in the production and distribution of goods and services
Economic security and predictability	Assurance that goods and services will be available, payments will be made on time, and a safety net will protect individuals in times of economic disaster
Economic equity	Fair distribution of wealth
Economic growth and innovation	Innovation leads to economic growth, and economic growth leads to a higher standard of living.
Other goals	Societies pursue additional goals, such as environmental protection.

Modern Economic Systems

A society's economic system reflects how that society answers the three key economic questions. Different systems produce different results in terms of productivity, the welfare of workers, and consumer choice. This table provides information about the main economic systems in the world today.

A Grameen Bank officer meets with loan recipients in India.

Modern Economic Systems

	Description	Origin	Location Today
Traditional	People make economic decisions based on custom or habit. They produce what they have always produced and just as much as they need, using long-established methods.	Accompanied the rise of agriculture and home crafts	Mainly in rural areas within developing nations
Market (Capitalist, Free-Enterprise)	Economic decisions are made in the marketplace through interactions between buyers and sellers according to the laws of supply and demand. Individual capitalists own the means of production. Government regulates some economic activities and provides such "public goods" as education.	Capitalism has existed since the earliest buying and selling of goods in a market. The market economic system developed in response to Adam Smith's ideas and the shift from agriculture to industry in the 1800s.	Canada, Germany, Japan, United States, and a handful of other nations
Centrally Planned (Command, Socialist, Communist)	Central government planners make most economic decisions for the people. In theory, the workers own the means of production. In practice, the government does. Some private enterprise, but government dominates.	In the 1800s, criticism of capitalism by Karl Marx and others led to calls for distributing wealth according to need. After the 1917 Russian Revolution, the Soviet Union developed the first command economy.	Communist countries, including China, Cuba, North Korea, and Vietnam
Mixed (Social Democratic, Liberal Socialist)	A mix of socialism and free enterprise in which the government plays a significant role in making economic decisions.	The Great Depression of the 1930s ended laissez-faire capitalism in most countries. People insisted that government take a stronger role in fixing economic problems. The fall of communism in Eastern Europe in the 1990s ended central planning in most countries. People insisted on freer markets.	Most nations, including Brazil, France, India, Italy, Poland, Russia, Sweden, and the United Kingdom

Major Trade Organizations

This map shows the major regional trade associations in the world today. In addition, 147 countries belong to the World Trade Organization (WTO). The WTO works to encourage trade by reducing tariffs, promoting international agreements, and mediating trade disputes among member nations.

This illustration represents the cooperation among nations involved in NAFTA.

NORTH AMERICA

NAFTA

Pacific Ocean

CARICOM

CACM

Mercosur

SOUTH AMERICA

60° N

30° N

0°

150° W   120° W   90° W   60° W

- Association of Southeast Asian Nations (ASEAN)
- Caribbean Community and Common Market (CARICOM)
- Central American Common Market (CACM)
- Economic Community of West African States (ECOWAS)
- European Union (EU)
- North American Free Trade Agreement (NAFTA)
- Organization of Petroleum Exporting Countries (OPEC)
- Southern African Development Community (SADC)
- Southern Common Market (Mercosur)

Glossary of Economic Terms

barter
the direct exchange of one set of goods or services for another

budget
a plan for income and spending

capital
any human-made resource that is used to create other goods or services

communism
a political system characterized by a centrally planned economy with all economic and political power resting in the hands of the central government

currency
coins and paper bills used as money

depression
a recession that is especially long and severe

developed nation
industrialized country with a higher average level of material well-being

developing nation
country with limited industrialization and a lower average level of material well-being

economic system
the method used by a society to produce and distribute goods and services

entrepreneur
ambitious leader who combines land, labor, and capital to create and market new goods or services

export
a good that is sent to another country for sale

free enterprise
an economic system that permits the conduct of business with minimal government intervention

goods
physical objects such as clothes or shoes

import
a good that is brought in from another country for sale

industrialization
the extensive organization of an economy for the purpose of manufacturing

inflation

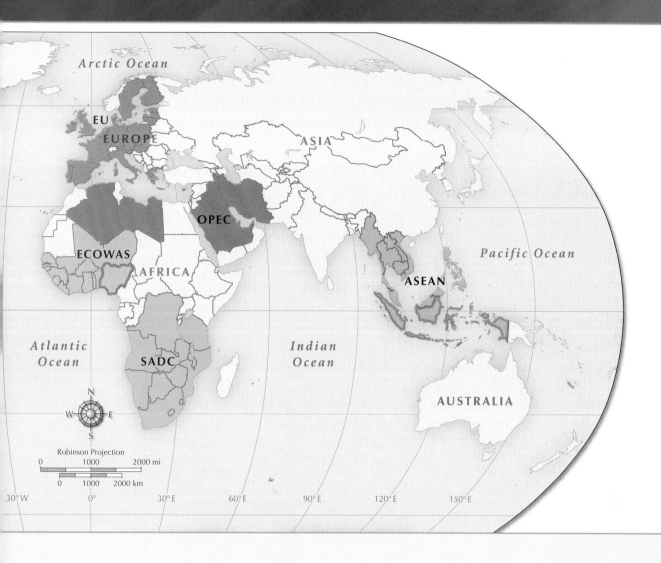

a general increase in prices

law of demand
economic law that states that consumers buy more of a good when its price decreases and less when its price increases

law of supply
tendency of suppliers to offer more of a good at a higher price

market
an arrangement that allows buyers and sellers to exchange things

market economy
economic system in which decisions on production and consumption of goods and services are based on voluntary exchange in markets

mixed economy
economic system that combines tradition and the free market with limited government involvement

opportunity cost
the most desirable alternative given up as the result of a decision

recession
a prolonged economic contraction

scarcity
limited quantities of resources to meet unlimited wants

socialism
a social and political philosophy based on the belief that democratic means should be used to evenly distribute wealth throughout a society.

tariff
a tax on imported goods

tax
a required payment to a government

traditional economy
economic system that relies on habit, custom, or ritual to decide questions of production and consumption of goods and services

welfare
government aid to the poor

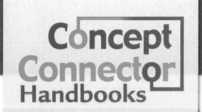

Science and Technology

Science is knowledge systematically acquired through observation, experimentation, and theoretical explanation. Technology is the practical application of science. Science and technology are often paired, and for good reason. They work together, each one promoting progress in the other field. Inventors use the latest science to develop cutting-edge technology that, in turn, helps scientists gather new information. That new information often leads to further advances in technology.

▲ Egyptian A-frame and plumb line

■ Key Developments in Science and Technology

Coin showing Alexander the Great ▶

Science and Technology

| Copper tools and ornaments 10,000 B.C. | Light wooden plow 4000 B.C. | Kiln-fired bricks, pots 3500 B.C. | | Irrigation 2400 B.C. | Iron weapons 1400 B.C. |

10,000 B.C. **5000 B.C.** **B.C.** **A.D.**

| Widespread domestication of plants and animals 9000–6000 B.C. | Bronze objects 4500 B.C. | Dam 4000 B.C. | Pyramids 2800 B.C. | Plumbing, water pipes, sewer drains 2700 B.C. | Coins 600 B.C. |

Greek symbol of peace, now a symbol of medicine ▶

Hippocrates, father of medicine, born 460 B.C.

Medicine

10,000 B.C. **5000 B.C.** **B.C.** **A.D.**

Greek physician Galen born A.D. 130

Egyptian cursive writing on papyrus ▼

Communication

| | | Pictographs 3500 B.C. | Writing 3200 B.C. | Alphabet 1700 B.C. | Paper A.D. 105 |

10,000 B.C. **5000 B.C.** **B.C.** **A.D.**

Papyrus 2800 B.C.

Transportation

| | Ancient dugout canoe c. 6000 B.C. | Wheeled cart from Sumer c. 3500 B.C. | Roman chariot c. A.D. 1 |

10,000 B.C. **5000 B.C.** **B.C.** **A.D.**

Portuguese square-sailed ship ▶

Square-sailed ships 3000 B.C.

◀ Italian compass

▼ Seed drill

Gunpowder *c.* A.D. 900	Magnetic compass *c.* 1100		Glass lens *c.* 1300		Compound microscope 1590		Lightning rod 1752	Power loom 1785

A.D. 1100   **A.D. 1300**   **A.D. 1500**   **A.D. 1700** →

Magnifying glass 1250   Mechanical clock *c.* 1400   Newton formulates Law of gravitation 1687   Steam engine 1769

Bald's *Leechbook* *c.* 900

Early vaccination ▶

William Harvey's *Circulation of the Blood* 1628   Smallpox vaccine 1796

A.D. 1100   **A.D. 1300**   **1500**   **A.D. 1700** →

Gutenberg Bible ▶

Printing press using moveable type *c.* 1450

A.D. 1100   **A.D. 1300**   **A.D. 1500**   **A.D. 1700** →

◀ Model of a caravel

Viking ship 800s   Stagecoach 1500s   Hot-air balloon 1783

A.D. 1100   **A.D. 1300**   **A.D. 1500**   **A.D. 1700** →

Caravel 1200s

Science and Technology

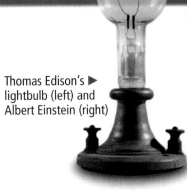

Thomas Edison's ► lightbulb (left) and Albert Einstein (right)

Science and Technology

| | Electric motor 1821 | | Theory of evolution 1849 | | Incandescent lamp 1879 | | Quantum theory 1900 | Frozen food 1924 |

A.D. 1800   **A.D. 1850**   **A.D. 1900**

| Canning of food 1809 | | Mechanical reaper 1843 | | Special Theory of Relativity 1905 | Plastics 1909 | Liquid fuel rocket 1926 |

Medicine

| | Anesthesia 1842 | Pasteurization of milk 1865 | Antiseptic surgery 1867 | Diphtheria antitoxin 1891 | Typhus vaccine 1909 |

A.D. 1800   **A.D. 1850**   **A.D. 1900**

| Government focus on improving hygiene and public sanitation 1850–1950 | Genetics; laws of heredity 1866 | Rabies vaccine 1885 | X-ray 1895 | Penicillin, first antibiotic 1928 |

Communication

| Telegraph 1837 | | Radio 1895 |

A.D. 1800   **A.D. 1850**   **A.D. 1900**

◄ Early telephone

| Telephone 1846 | Electronic television 1927 |

Transportation

| Steam locomotive 1825 | Biplane 1903 |

A.D. 1800   **A.D.1850**   **A.D. 1900**

| Steamboat 1807 | Automobile c. 1860–1890 |

Daimler motor car ►

▲ DNA sequence

◀ Sign for fallout shelter

CAPACITY 1730

FALLOUT SHELTER

Nuclear reactor
1942

Laser
1960

A.D. 1950

A.D. 2000

A.D. 2050

Apollo moon
landing
1969

Cloning of a mammal
1996

Polio vaccine
1952

Human heart
transplant
1967

Smallpox eradicated
worldwide
1979

A.D. 1950

A.D. 2000

A.D. 2050

Founding of World
Health Organization
1948

DNA
structure
1953

Measles
vaccine
1963

Chicken pox
vaccine
1974

Electronic computer
1944

Portable typewriter
1950

Personal digital assistant
2000

A.D. 1950

A.D. 2000

A.D. 2050

Transistor
1948

Color television
1960s

◀ The Earth
from space

Space shuttle
1981

A.D. 1950

A.D. 2000

A.D. 2050

First commercial jet airliner
1949

Queen Mary 2 ocean liner
2005

◀ Jet airplanes

Concept Connector Handbooks

Government and Civics

The main purpose of government is to create and enforce a society's public policies. Public policies cover such matters as defense, crime, taxation, and much more. Governments must have power in order to make and carry out public policies. Every government has and exercises three basic kinds of power: legislative, executive, and judicial. Legislative refers to the power to make laws. Executive refers to the power to enforce laws. Judicial refers to the power to interpret laws. These powers of government are often outlined in a nation's constitution, or body of fundamental laws. Different forms of government exercise their powers in different ways.

Forms of Government

Political scientists classify governments in order to help them describe, compare, and analyze different forms. Three particularly helpful classifications involve determining (1) the geographic distribution of governmental power within the state, (2) the relationship between the legislative and executive branches of the government, and (3) who can participate in the government. As the chart shows, modern forms of government vary widely.

Presidential elections in Ukraine, 2004

Forms of Government

Country	Where is the power?		What is the relationship between the legislative and executive branches?		Who can participate?	
	Unitary: All powers held by the government belong to a single, central agency.	**Federal:** The powers of government are divided between a central government and several regional governments.	**Parliamentary:** The executive branch is made up of the prime minister, or premier, and that official's cabinet. The prime minister and cabinet are members of the legislative branch, or parliament.	**Presidential:** The executive and legislative branches of government are separate, independent of each other, and coequal.	**Democracy:** Supreme political authority rests with the people, who choose a small group of individuals to act as their representatives to carry out the day-to-day conduct of government.	**Dictatorship:** The government is not accountable to the people for its policies or for how they are carried out. Those who rule do not represent or consider the will of the people.
Botswana	✓		✓		✓	
Brazil		✓		✓	✓	
Costa Rica	✓		✓		✓	
Cuba	✓		✓			✓
France	✓			✓	✓	
India		✓	✓		✓	
Syria	✓			✓		✓
United States		✓		✓	✓	

Federal vs. Unitary Government

Today, about two dozen nations, including the United States, have a federal system of government. In this kind of system, two levels of government—central and state—divide power between them. In the unitary system, which is more common by far, all powers belong to the central government. One disadvantage of a federal system is its inefficiency. People must obey two sets of laws, which may overlap or even conflict. In a unitary system, one government governs all the people directly, even though it may yield certain powers to the states. On the other hand, a federal system allows for checks on the power of the central government and for some diversity of laws in regions with a distinctive culture, history, or language.

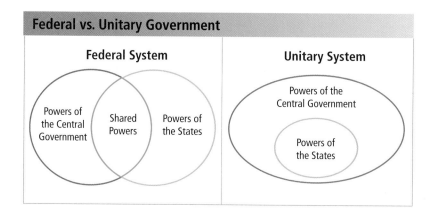

Federal vs. Unitary Government

Federal System

Powers of the Central Government | Shared Powers | Powers of the States

Unitary System

Powers of the Central Government

Powers of the States

Presidential and Parliamentary Governments

The Presidential Relationship Voters elect the legislature and the chief executive, who is part of the executive branch. The legislative and executive branches are independent and coequal.

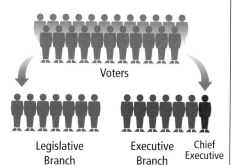

Voters

Legislative Branch

Executive Branch

Chief Executive

The Parliamentary Relationship Voters elect the legislature. The chief executive is drawn from the legislature.

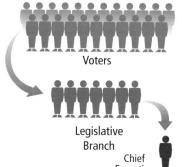

Voters

Legislative Branch

Chief Executive

Basic Concepts of Democracy

1. **A recognition of the fundamental worth and dignity of every person.** At various times, the welfare of one or a few individuals is subordinate to the interests of the many in a democracy. For example, a democratic society may force people to pay a tax or obey traffic signals.

2. **A respect for the equality of all persons.** The democratic concept of equality insists that all people are entitled to equality of opportunity and equality before the law—not necessarily equal distribution of wealth.

3. **A faith in the majority rule and an insistence upon minority rights.** In a democracy, the will of the people and not the dictate of the ruling few determine public policy. Unchecked, however, a majority could destroy its opposition and, in the process, destroy democracy. Thus, democracy insists upon majority rule restrained by minority rights.

4. **An acceptance of the necessity of compromise.** In a democracy, public decision making must be largely a matter of give-and-take among the various competing interests. People must compromise to find the position most acceptable to the largest number. Compromise is the process of blending and adjusting competing views and interests.

5. **An insistence upon the widest possible degree of individual freedom.** In a democracy, each individual must be as free to do as he or she pleases as far as the freedom of all will allow. Oliver Wendell Holmes once had this to say about the relative nature of each individual's rights: "The right to swing my fist ends where the other man's nose begins."

Government and Civics

Louis XIV of France

Catherine the Great of Russia

Forms of Dictatorship

Typically militaristic in character, an authoritarian or dictatorial regime usually acquires political power by force and may turn to foreign aggression to enhance its military strength and prestige. Authoritarianism has taken several related forms throughout history.

Absolutism A system in which the ruler holds complete authority over the government and the lives of the people. Some absolute monarchs ruled according to the principle of divine right. Modern forms of absolutism include military dictatorships that try to control every element of people's lives (see Totalitarianism).

Despotism Absolute rule with no constitutional restraints. The term *despot* was an honorable title in ancient times. Later, absolute monarchs who favored reforms became known as enlightened despots. Today, despot refers to a brutal and oppressive ruler.

Autocracy The concentration of power in one individual or group that uses force to maintain absolute control and smother any political opposition.

Mehmed II of the Ottoman Empire

Glossary of Political Terms

bureaucracy
a large, complex administrative structure that handles the everyday business of government

citizen
a member of a state or nation who is entitled to full civil rights

civil service
those civilian employees who perform the administrative work of government

compromise
an adjustment of opposing principles or systems by modifying some aspect of each

constitution
the body of fundamental laws setting out the principles, structures, and processes of a government

foreign policy
everything a nation's government says and does in world affairs

immigrant
a person legally admitted as a permanent resident of a country

jury
a legally chosen group of persons who hear evidence and decide questions of fact in a court case

nation
a group of people who share the same way of life and live in the same area and under the same central government

Totalitarianism   A form of absolutism in which the government sweeps away existing political institutions and exerts complete control over nearly every aspect of the society. In this system, a supreme leader often becomes the sole source of society's rules.

Communism   An ideology that, in theory, calls for ownership of all land and other productive property by the workers. In practice, a system of repressive, single-party government that completely controls its citizens' lives and stifles all opposition.

Fascism   A form of government that seeks to renew society by demanding citizens' complete devotion to the state. Often led by a dictator who strictly controls industry and labor, denies freedom and individual rights, and uses police and the military to silence opposition.

Adolf Hitler of Germany

Concept Connector   Government and Civics

Mural of Saddam Hussein

Mao Zedong's Little Red Book

politics
the activities of those who run or seek to run a government

rule of law
idea that all citizens, including government officials, are subject to the law

sovereign
having supreme power within its own territory

state
a group of people living in a defined territory who have a government with the power to make and enforce law without the consent of any higher authority

suffrage
the right to vote

tax
a charge levied by government on persons or property to meet public needs

treaty
a formal agreement between two or more sovereign states

Culture

Culture is a way of life, or a set of values and behaviors, that people in a society learn, share, and pass on from generation to generation. Culture mainly involves what people think, what they do, and what they create. It consists of such elements as language, religion, art, social organization, and technology. Cultures can change over time. Some elements are forgotten, and others are improved or replaced. Still others are picked up from outside cultures. This spread of ideas, customs, and technologies from one culture to another is known as cultural diffusion. Historically, cultures have spread mainly through trade, migration, and conquest.

World Languages

Language is a part of culture. Yet it is also the main tool by which people transmit their culture. Many thousands of languages have arisen since humans first began to communicate. Some 6,800 of those languages still survive. Related languages can be grouped into language families.

Principal Languages of the World	
Language	**Speakers* (in millions)**
Mandarin (Chinese)	873
Spanish	322
English	309
Hindi	180
Portuguese	177
Bengali	171
Russian	145
Japanese	122
German	95
Wu (Chinese)	77
* estimated number for whom this is their first language	

Sign in a Native American language and English (above); fragment of a Dead Sea scroll, written in ancient Hebrew (below)

Major Belief Systems

Most of the world's major belief systems have existed for more than 2,000 years. Today, if the world included only 1,000 people, 330 of them would be Christian, 215 would be Muslim, 149 would be Hindu, 140 would follow no religion, 59 would be Buddhist, 37 would follow Chinese traditional religions, and 41 would hold primal-indigenous beliefs.

Major World Religions/Belief Systems

	Leading Figure; Dates	Key Beliefs	Writings	Number of Followers
Buddhism	Siddhartha Gautama (the Buddha); late sixth to fourth century B.C.	No gods, but buddhas, or "enlightened ones" exist; reincarnation (cycle of birth, death, and rebirth); the Four Noble Truths: (1) suffering is a part of life; (2) selfish desire leads to suffering; (3) desire can be overcome; (4) the Eightfold Path leads away from desire, toward release from the cycle of birth, death, and rebirth	*Tripitaka (The Three Baskets)*; the sutras; the tantras	373 million
Chinese Traditional Religions (blend of Buddhism, Confucianism, and Daoism)	Blending began in the A.D. 900s	Reincarnation (from Buddhism); virtuous way of life (from Confucianism); acting in harmony with nature and avoiding aggressive action (from Daoism)	*Dao de Jing (The Way of Power)*; *Zhuangzi* (named after the greatest interpreter of Daoism); (see also Buddhism and Confucianism)	398 million
Christianity	Jesus of Nazareth; early first century A.D.	One God; to save humans, God sent Jesus, who suffered, died, and rose from the dead; the Trinity: three figures (God the Father, God the Son, and God the Holy Spirit) united as one; love God above all else	The Bible: the Old Testament (Hebrew Bible) and the New Testament; various creeds and statements of faith	2.07 billion
Confucianism	Confucius; around 500 B.C.	No gods; not an organized religion, but a system of moral conduct based on the teachings of Confucius; kindness, love, and respect lead to a virtuous way of life	The *Lun yü (Analects)*; the *Wu-ching (Five Classics)*; the *Ssu Shu (Four Books)*	6.43 million (mainly in Korea)
Hinduism	No founder or central institution; around 1500 B.C.	Brahman, the ultimate God, is the source of all existence; many lesser gods, the main ones being Vishnu and Siva; reincarnation; law of karma (actions in one life affect next life); ahimsa (principle of noninjury or nonviolence)	The Vedas, sutras, epics, and puranas	837 million
Islam	Muhammad; early A.D. 600s	One God, Allah; Five Pillars, or duties: (1) profession of faith; (2) prayer; (3) charity; (4) fasting; (5) pilgrimage to Mecca in Saudi Arabia	Quran	1.25 billion
Judaism	Abraham; around 2000 B.C.	One God; God made a covenant, or pact, with Abraham and the Jewish people that if they obey God's commands, God will make Israel a great nation; actions are more important than beliefs	The Torah (the "Law"), the Nevi'im (the "Prophets"), and the Ketuvim (the "Writings"); oral tradition, written as the Talmud	14.6 million
primal-indigenous (includes tribal religions, animism, shamanism, and paganism)	Such religions have existed since prehistoric times	May be a high god; nature spirits (powerful life forces inhabiting the elements of nature); communication with spirits through prayers and offerings ensures the support of the spirits	none	238 million
Shinto	No founder; well established by the A.D. 500s	Many gods; Kami (superior, mystical, or divine powers) are the sources of human life; main deity is sun goddess Amaterasu O-mikami; each person is worthy of respect; truthfulness and purification (physical and spiritual) bring the blessings of the kami	No central sacred scripture; chief books: *Kojiki (Records of Ancient Matters)* and *Nihon shoki (Chronicles of Japan)*	2.68 million
Sikhism (combines elements of Hinduism and Islam)	Nanak; around A.D. 1500	One God; reincarnation; meditation can release one from the cycle of reincarnation; law of karma; all humans are equal	*Adi Granth (First Book)*	24.3 million

Culture

The Arts

The arts tell much about a culture. Ancient civilizations produced artists only after they were capable of generating an agricultural surplus. Some people could then be spared from the fields to devote themselves to other pursuits, including the arts. Works of art, from paintings and sculptures to music, dance, and writing, reflect the culture in which the artist lived. Notice the variations among the arts presented in these pictures. Think about what each picture says about the culture that produced it.

Romantic poet, writer, and artist William Blake's *Songs of Innocence*, 1789 ▼

▲ Neoclassical bust of Napoleon by Antonio Canova, *c.* 1802

Major Art Movements

classicism
Greek and Roman art; emphasis on harmony, proportion, balance, and simplicity

byzantine
500s–1400s, Europe, Russia

Romanesque
late eleventh century, Europe

Gothic
1100s–1400s, Europe; cathedral architecture and religious art

Renaissance
c. 1400–1600, Europe; Leonardo, Michelangelo, Raphael

mannerism
c. 1520–1600, Europe; Parmigianino

baroque
seventeenth and early eighteenth centuries, Europe; Bernini, Caravaggio, Rubens

rococo
eighteenth century, Europe; Fragonard

neoclassicism
late eighteenth and early nineteenth centuries, Europe; revival of ancient Greek and Roman art; David, Canova

romanticism
late eighteenth to mid-nineteenth century, Europe, United States; Delacroix, Géricault, Turner, Blake, Hudson River school

Barbizon School
c. 1840–1870, France; landscapes; Rousseau, Corot, Millet

realism
nineteenth century, Europe and United States; Daumier, Courbet, Eakins

impressionism
late nineteenth century, France and United States; Monet, Renoir, Cassatt

pointillism
1880s, France; Seurat, Signac

Costume from Georg Friedrich Handel's baroque opera *Agrippina*, 1709 (right) ▶

Pointillist painting by Georges Seurat, *Porte-en-Bessin*, 1888 (far right) ▶

Poster for ▶
Émile Zola's
realist novel
La Terre, 1887

▲ Self-portrait by
German expressionist
Käthe Kollwitz, 1920

◀ Bronze sculpture by Italian
futurist Umberto Boccioni,
*Unique Forms of Continuity
in Space*, 1913

postimpressionism
late nineteenth century, France;
Cézanne, Van Gogh, Gauguin

art nouveau
late nineteenth century, Europe;
decorative arts

cubism
early twentieth century, Europe;
Picasso, Braque

fauvism
c. 1905–1908, France; pure, bold
colors applied in a spontaneous
manner; Matisse

expressionism
c. 1905–1925, northern Europe;
Rouault, Kokoschka, Schiele

futurism
c. 1909–1919, Italy; Boccioni

constructivism
c. 1915, Russia; abstract style using
non-traditional materials;
Rodchenko, Tatlin, Gabo, Pevsner

dadaism
c. 1915–1923, France; rejected
accepted aesthetic standards;
Duchamp

surrealism
1920s–1930s, Europe; Magritte, Dalí,
Miró, Ernst, de Chirico

art deco
1920s–1930s; decorative arts characterized by sleek lines and slender
forms

abstract expressionism
1940s, New York City; Pollock,
de Kooning, Motherwell, Kline

minimalism
late 1950s, United States; Judd,
Martin, Kelly

color field painting
1950s, United States; Newman,
Rothko, Frankenthaler

pop art
1950s, United States; Warhol,
Lichtenstein, Oldenburg

conceptual art
1960s and 1970s, interna-
tional; questioned the definition of "art"

Sculpture for a park in Minneapolis
by pop artist Claes Oldenburg,
Spoonbridge and Cherry, 1988 ▼

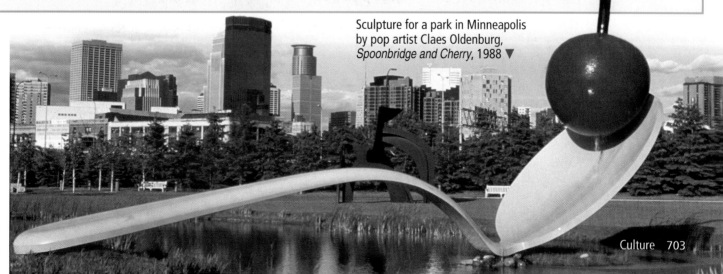

A

Abbasids dynasty that ruled in Bagdad from 750–1258 (p. 314)

Abbasids dinastía que gobernó Bagdad durante los años 750–1258

abdicate to give up or step down from power (p. 598)

abdicar renunciar de un puesto de poder

absolute monarch ruler with complete authority over the government and lives of the people he or she governs (p. 506)

monarca absoluto gobernante que tiene autoridad absoluta sobre la administración y la vida de los que están bajo su mando

acculturation the blending of two or more cultures (p. 74)

aculturación mezcla de dos o más culturas

acropolis highest and most fortified point within a Greek city-state (p. 119)

acrópolis el punto más alto y fortificado de una ciudad-estado griega

acupuncture medical treatment, originated in ancient China, in which needles are inserted into the skin at specific points to relieve pain or treat various illnesses (p. 106)

acupuntura tratamiento médico, originario de China, por el que se introducen agujas en la piel en puntos específicos para aliviar el dolor o como tratamiento de diversas enfermedades

adobe a mixture of clay and plant fibers that becomes hard as it dries in the sun and that can be used for building (p. 196)

adobe mezcla de arcilla y fibras vegetales que se endurece al secarse al sol y se puede usar en la construcción

Adulis strategic trading port of the kingdom of Axum (p. 352)

Adulis puerto comercial estratégico del reino de Axum

ahimsa Hindu belief in nonviolence and reverence for all life (p. 77)

ahimsa creencia hindú en la no violencia y en el respeto a todas las formas de vida

Alexandria an ancient Hellenistic city in Egypt (p. 140)

Alejandría antigua ciudad helenista en Egipto

alliance formal agreement between two or more nations or powers to cooperate and come to one another's defense (pp. 126, 473)

alianza acuerdo formal de cooperación y defensa mutua entre dos o más naciones o potencias

alphabet writing system in which each symbol represents a single basic sound (p. 43)

alfabeto sistema de escritura en el que cada símbolo representa un único sonido

ancien régime old order; system of government in pre-revolution France (p. 572)

ancien regime antiguo orden; sistema de gobierno en la Francia prerevolucionaria

anesthetic drug that prevents pain during surgery (p. 609)

anestesia fármaco que suprime el dolor durante la cirugía

animism the belief that spirits and forces live within animals, objects, or dreams (p. 13)

animismo creencia de que los espíritus y fuerzas pueden vivir en animales, objetos o sueños

annex add a territory to an existing state or country (p. 594)

anexar agregar un territorio a un estado o país existente

anthropology the study of the origins and development of people and their societies (p. 5)

antropología estudio del origen y desarrollo de los pueblos y sus sociedades

anti-Semitism prejudice against Jews (p. 230)

antisemitismo prejuicio contra los judíos

apostle leader or teacher of a new faith or movement (p. 168)

apóstol líder o maestro de una nueva fe o movimiento

apprentice a young person learning a trade from a master (p. 235)

aprendiz persona joven que aprendía un oficio de un maestro

aqueduct in ancient Rome, underground or bridgelike stone structure that carried water from the hills into the cities (p. 164)

acueducto en la antigua Roma, estructura parecida a un puente que llevaba agua desde las colinas hasta las ciudades

archaeology the study of people and cultures through their material remains (p. 5)

arqueología estudio de pueblos y culturas antiguas por medio de sus restos materiales

archipelago chain of islands (p. 387)

archipiélago cadena de islas

aristocracy government headed by a privileged minority or upper class (p. 120)

aristocracia gobierno encabezado por una minoría privilegiada o de clase alta

armada fleet of ships (p. 507)

armada flota de barcos

artifact an object made by human beings (p. 4)
artefacto objeto hecho por seres humanos
artisan a skilled craftsperson (p. 20)
artesano trabajador cualificado que hace objetos a mano
Asante kingdom kingdom that emerged in the 1700s in present-day Ghana and was active in the slave trade (p. 454)
reino Asante reino que surgió en el siglo XVIII en el actual Ghana y que tenía comercio de esclavos
assassination murder of a public figure, usually for political reasons (p. 139)
asesinato acto de dar muerte a una figura pública, generalmente por razones políticas
assimilate absorb or adopt another culture (p. 139)
asimilar absorber o adoptar otra cultura
Athens a city-state in ancient Greece (p. 121)
Atenas ciudad-estado en la antigua Grecia
atman in Hindu belief, a person's essential self (p. 77)
atman según la creencia hindú, el ser esencial de una persona
autocrat ruler who has complete authority (p. 285)
autócrata gobernante que tiene autoridad total
autocratic having unlimited power (p. 531)
autocrático que tiene poder ilimitado
autonomy self-rule (p. 636)
autonomía autogobierno
Axum trading center, and powerful ancient kingdom in northern present-day Ethiopia (p. 352)
Axum ciudad capital, centro de comercio y poderoso antiguo reino del norte de la presente Etiopía
ayllu in the Inca empire, a close-knit village (p. 198)
ayllu en el imperio Inca, aldea muy unida

B

Baghdad capital city of present-day Iraq; capital of the Muslim empire during Islam's golden age (p. 314)
Bagdad capital del actual Iraq; capital del imperio musulmán durante la época dorada del islam
balance of power distribution of military and economic power that prevents any one nation from becoming too strong (p. 514)
equilibrio de poder distribución del poder militar y económico que evita que una nación se vuelva demasiado fuerte

Balkan Peninsula triangular arm of land that juts from southeastern Europe into the Mediterranean (p. 294)
Península Balcánica extensión triangular de tierra que sobresale del sudeste de Europa hasta el Mediterráneo
Bantu root language of West Africa on which some early African migration patterns are based (p. 341)
Bantú lengua madre del África occidental en la que están basados algunos patrones migratorios africanos
baroque ornate style of art and architecture popular in the 1600s and 1700s (p. 551)
barroco estilo artístico y arquitectónico elaborado que se dio en los siglos XVII y XVIII
barter economy economic system in which one set of goods or services is exchanged for another (p. 42)
economía de trueque sistema económico en el que se utiliza el intercambio de mercancías o servicios
Bastille fortress in Paris used as a prison; French Revolution began when Parisians stormed it in 1789 (p. 577)
Bastilla fortificación en París usada como prisión; la Revolución Francesa empezó cuando los parisinos la asaltaron en 1789
Battle of Tours battle in 732 in which the Christian Franks led by Charles Martel defeated Muslim armies and stopped the Muslim advance into Europe (pp. 215, 312)
Batalla de Tours batalla en 732 en la que los francos cristianos liderados por Charles Martel derrotaron al ejército musulmán y detuvieron el avance árabe en Europa
Bedouin a desert-dwelling Arab nomad (p. 304)
Beduino nómada árabe que vive en el desierto
Benedictine Rule rules drawn up in 530 by Benedict, a monk, regulating monastic life. The Rule emphasizes obedience, poverty, and chastity and divides the day into periods of worship, work, and study. (p. 227)
Regla Benedictina en 530, reglas establecidas por Benedicto, un monje, para regular la vida monástica. La Regla enfatizaba la obediencia, pobreza y castidad, y divide el día en períodos de adoración, trabajo y estudio.
bishop high-ranking Church official with authority over a local area, or diocese (p. 171)
Obispo funcionario eclesiástico de alto nivel con autoridad sobre un área local o diócesis

Black Death an epidemic of the bubonic plague that ravaged Europe in the 1300s (p. 269)

Peste Negra epidemia de la peste bubónica que arrasó Europa en el siglo XIV

Boers Dutch people who settled in Cape Town, Africa, and eventually migrated inland (p. 455)

Boers holandeses establecidos en Ciudad del Cabo, África, que con el tiempo emigraron hacia el interior

bourgeoisie the middle class (p. 573)

burguesía clase media

boyar landowning noble in Russia under the tsars (p. 531)

boyar noble ruso que poseía tierras en la época de los zares (p. 531)

brahman in the belief system established in Aryan India, the single spiritual power that resides in all things (p. 73)

brahman en el sistema de creencias establecido en la India aria, el único poder espiritual que reside en todas las cosas

bureaucracy system of government that includes different job functions and levels of authority (p. 45)

burocracia sistema de gobierno que incluye diferentes trabajos y niveles de autoridad

bushido code of conduct for samurai during the feudal period in Japan (p. 391)

bushido código de conducta de los samuráis durante el período feudal japonés

C

cabinet parliamentary advisors to the king who originally met in a small room, or "cabinet" (p. 522)

gabinete miembros del parlamento consejeros del rey que originalmente se reunían en un pequeño cuarto o "gabinete"

cahier notebook used during the French Revolution to record grievances (p. 576)

memorándum cuaderno usado durante la Revolución Francesa para anotar los agravios

Cahokia in Illinois, the largest earthwork of the Mississippian culture, *c.* A.D. 700 (p. 204)

Cahokia en Illinois, el mayor terraplén de la cultura de los mississippianos, construido alrededor del 700 D.C.

calculus a branch of mathematics in which calculations are made using special symbolic notations; developed by Isaac Newton (p. 438)

cálculo rama de las matemáticas en la que los cálculos se hacen con notaciones simbólicas especiales; fue desarrollado por Isaac Newton

caliph successor to Muhammad as political and religious leader of the Muslims (p. 310)

califa sucesor de Mahoma como líder religiosoy político de los musulmanes

calligraphy the art of producing beautiful handwriting (pp. 100, 320)

caligrafía arte de producir una bella escritura a mano

canon law body of laws of a church (p. 229)

ley canónica serie de leyes de una iglesia

canonize recognize a person as a saint (p. 429)

canonizar reconocer a una persona como santo

Cape Town seaport city and legislative capital of South Africa; first Dutch colony in Africa (p. 455)

Ciudad del Cabo ciudad portuaria y capital legislativa de Sudáfrica; fue la primera colonia holandesa en África

capital money or wealth used to invest in business or enterprise (pp. 234, 613)

capital dinero o bienes que se usan para invertir en negocios o empresas

capitalism economic system in which the means of production are privately owned and operated for profit (p. 493)

capitalismo sistema económico por el que los medios de producción son propiedad privada y se administran para obtener beneficios

cartographer mapmaker (p. 447)

cartógrafo persona que hace mapas

caste in traditional Indian society, an unchangeable social group into which a person is born (p. 78)

casta grupo social en la sociedad tradicional de India, en el que una persona nace y del que no se puede cambiar

Çatalhüyük one of the world's first villages, established in modern-day Turkey around 7000 B.C. (p. 14)

Çatalhüyük una de las primeras aldeas del mundo establecida en la Turquía actual alrededor del 7000 A.C.

cataract waterfall (pp. 45, 340)

catarata cascada, caída de agua

celadon porcelain made in Korea with an unusual blue-green glaze (p. 385)

celadon porcelana hecha en Korea con brillo azulverdoso poco común

censorship restriction on access to ideas and information (p. 551)

censura restricción en el acceso a ideas o información

census population count (p. 159)
  censo recuento de la población
character written symbol in writing systems such as that of the Chinese (p. 100)
  carácter símbolo escrito en los sistemas de escritura como en el chino
charter in the Middle Ages, a written document that set out the rights and privileges of a town (p. 233)
  fuero en la Edad Media, documento escrito que establecía los derechos y privilegios de un pueblo
Chavín a culture that thrived in the Andean region from about 900 B.C. to 200 B.C. (p. 195)
  chavín cultura que tuvo su apogeo en la región andina, desde alrededor de 900 A.C. a 200 A.C.
chinampas in the Aztec empire, artificial islands used to cultivate crops and made of mud piled atop reed mats that were anchored to the lakebed with willow trees (p. 192)
  chinampas en el imperio azteca, islas artificiales que se usaban para la agricultura y que estaban hechas de barro apilado sobre esteras de junco ancladas al fondo del lago con ramas de sauce
chivalry code of conduct for knights during the Middle Ages (p. 222)
  caballería código de conducta para los caballeros durante la Edad Media
Choson dynasty Korean dynasty that ruled from 1392 to 1910, the longest-lived of Korea's three dynasties (p. 386)
  dinastía Choson dinastía coreana que gobernó desde 1392 a 1910, la que más duró de las tres dinastías coreanas
circumnavigate to travel completely around the world (p. 451)
  circunnavegar viajar alrededor del mundo
citizen a native or resident of a town or city (p. 119)
  ciudadano nativo o residente de un pueblo o ciudad
city-state a political unit that includes a city and its surrounding lands and villages (p. 23)
  ciudad estado unidad polítca compuesta por una diudad y las tierras que la rodean
civil law branch of law that deals with private rights and matters (p. 37)
  derecho civil cuerpo legal que trata de los derechos y asuntos privados de los individuos
civil servant government official (p. 104)
  funcionario público oficial del gobierno
civil war war fought between two groups of people in the same nation (p. 475)

guerra civil guerra en la que luchan dos grupos de personas de una misma nación
civilization a complex, highly organized social order (p. 19)
  civilización orden social complejo y altamente organizado
clan group of families with a common ancestor (p. 94)
  clan grupo de familias con un antepasado en común
clergy the body of people who conduct Christian services (p. 171)
  clero grupo de gente que oficia en los servicios religiosos cristianos
codify to arrange or set down in writing (p. 37)
  codificar organizar o establecer por escrito
colony territory settled and ruled by people from another land (p. 43)
  colonia territorio poblado y gobernado por personas de otro lugar
Columbian Exchange the global exchange of goods, ideas, plants and animals, and disease that began with Columbus' exploration of the Americas (p. 491)
  Intercambio colombino intercambio global de bienes, ideas, plantas, animales y enfermedades que comenzaron con la exploración de las Américas por parte de Colón
comedy in ancient Greece, play that mocked people or social customs (p. 135)
  comedia en la antigua Grecia, obra de teatro donde se hacía burla de personas o costumbres
commodity valuable product (p. 347)
  mercancía producto valioso
common law a legal system based on custom and court rulings (p. 245)
  derecho consuetudinario sistema legal basado en la costumbre y en las sentencias de los tribunales
communism form of socialism advocated by Karl Marx; according to Marx, class struggle was inevitable and would lead to the creation of a classless society in which all wealth and property would be owned by the community as a whole (p. 625)
  comunismo forma de socialismo defendido por Karl Marx; según Marx, la lucha de clases era inevitable y llevaría a la creación de una sociedad sin clases en la que toda la riqueza y la propiedad pertenecería a la comunidad como un todo
compact an agreement among people (p. 484)
  pacto acuerdo

compromise an agreement in which each side makes concessions; an acceptable middle ground (p. 430)

compromiso acuerdo en el que cada parte hace concesiones; un término medio aceptable

Concert of Europe a system in which Austria, Russia, Prussia, and Great Britain met periodically to discuss any problems affecting the peace in Europe; resulted from the post-Napoleon era Quadruple Alliance (p. 600)

Concierto de Europa sistema por el cual Austria, Rusia, Prusia y Gran Bretaña se reunían periódicamente para discutir cualquier problema que afectara a la paz en Europa; resultado de la Cuádruple Alianza de la era postnapoleónica

Congress of Vienna assembly of European leaders that met after the Napoleonic era to piece Europe back together; met from September 1814 to June 1815 (p. 599)

Congreso de Viena asamblea de líderes europeos que se reunió después de la era napoleónica para reconstruir Europa; se reunieron desde septiembre de 1814 a junio de 1815

conquistador Spanish explorers who claimed lands in the Americas for Spain in the 1500s and 1600s (p. 472)

conquistador los exploradores españoles que apropiaron tierras en América para España en los siglos XVI y XVII

consensus general agreement (p. 359)

consenso acuerdo general

Constantinople the capital of the eastern Roman empire; capital of the Byzantine and Ottoman empires, now called Istanbul (pp. 174, 282)

Constantinopla capital del Imperio Romano Oriental; capital de los imperios bizantino y otomano, en la actualidad llamada Estambul

constitutional government government whose power is defined and limited by law (p. 522)

gobierno constitucional gobierno cuyo poder está definido y limitado por las leyes

consul in ancient Rome, official from the patrician class who supervised the government and commanded the armies (p. 152)

cónsul funcionario de la clase patricia que en la Roma antigua supervisaba el gobierno y dirigía los ejércitos

Continental System blockade designed by Napoleon to hurt Britain economically by closing European ports to British goods; ultimately unsuccessful (p. 594)

sistema continental bloqueo diseñado por Napoleón para dañar a Gran Bretaña económicamente que consistía en cerrar los puertos europeos a los productos británicos; con el tiempo no tuvo éxito

Council of Trent a group of Catholic leaders that met between 1545 and 1563 to respond to Protestant challenges and direct the future of the Catholic Church (p. 431)

Concilio de Trento grupo de líderes católicos que se reunieron entre 1545 y 1563 para tratar los retos protestantes y liderar el futuro de la Iglesia Católica

covenant a binding agreement; specifically, in the Jewish tradition, the binding agreement God made with Abraham (p. 58)

convenio acuerdo vinculante; específicamente, en la tradición judía, el acuerdo vinculante hecho entre Dios y Abraham

creole person in Spain's colonies in the Americas who was an American-born descendent of Spanish settlers (pp. 480, 645)

criollo descendiente de colonos españolas nacido en las colonias españolas de América

criminal law branch of law that deals with offenses against others (p. 37)

derecho penal rama de la ley que se ocupa de los delitos contra otros

Crusades a series of wars from the 1000s through 1200s in which European Christians tried to win control of the Holy Land from Muslims (p. 255)

Cruzadas serie de guerras entre el siglo XI y el siglo XIII en las que los cristianos europeos intentaron ganar el control sobre los musulmanes de la Tierra Santa

cultural diffusion the spread of ideas, customs, and technologies from one people to another (p. 23)

difusión cultural divulgación de ideas, costumbres y tecnología de un pueblo a otro

culture the way of life of a society, which is handed down from one generation to the next by learning and experience (p. 5)

cultura forma de vida de una sociedad que se pasa de una generación a la siguiente mediante el aprendizaje y la experiencia

cuneiform in the ancient Middle East, a system of writing that used wedge-shaped marks (p. 33)

cuneiforme en el antiguo Oriente Medio, sistema de escritura cuyos caracteres tenían forma de cuña

ENGLISH/SPANISH GLOSSARY

Cuzco capital city of the Inca empire (p. 197)
  Cuzco capital del imperio Inca
Cyrillic relating to the Slavic alphabet derived from the Greek and traditionally attributed to St. Cyril; in modified form still used in modern Slavic languages (p. 290)
  cirílico relativo al alfabeto eslavo, derivado del griego y tradicionalmente atribuido a San Cirilo; todavía en uso, de forma modificada, en las lenguas eslavas modernas

D

decimal system system of numbers based on 10 (p. 88)
  sistema de decimal sistema numérico basado en el número 10
decipher to figure out the meaning of (p. 55)
  descrifrar descubrir el significado de algo
deficit spending situation in which a government spends more money than it takes in (p. 575)
  gasto deficitario situación en la que un gobierno gasta más de lo que recauda
Delhi the third-largest city in India; capital of medieval India (p. 324)
  Delhi tercera ciudad más grande de India; capital de la India medieval
delta triangular area of marshland formed by deposits of silt at the mouth of some rivers (p. 45)
  delta área triangular de tierra pantanosa que se forma con los depósitos de limo en la desembocadùra de algunos ríos
democracy government in which the people hold ruling power (p. 121)
  democracia forma de gobierno en el que la soberanía reside en el pueblo
depopulation reduction in the number of people in an area (p. 527)
  despoblación reducción del número de la población en una zona
desertification process by which fertile or semi-desert land becomes desert (p. 341)
  desertización proceso por el que la tierra fértil o semifértil se convierte en desierto
dharma in Hindu belief, a person's religious and moral duties (p. 77)
  dharma según la creencia hindú, las obligaciones morales y religiosas de un individuo
Diaspora the spreading of the Jews beyond their historic homeland (p. 60)

Diáspora diseminación de los judíos más allá de su patria histórica
dictator ruler who has complete control over a government; in ancient Rome, a leader appointed to rule for six months in times of emergency (p. 152)
  dictador dirigente con control absolute sobre el gobierno; en la antigua Roma, líder designado para gobernar durante seis meses en casos de emergencia
diet assembly or legislature (pp. 296, 425)
  dieta asamblea o cuerpo legislativo
direct democracy system of government in which citizens participate directly in the day-to-day affairs of government rather than through elected representatives (p. 126)
  democracia directa sistema de gobierno en el que los ciudadanos participan directamente en lugar de hacerlo a través de representantes electos en los asuntos diarios del gobierno
dissent ideas that oppose those of the government (p. 84)
  disentir ideas que se oponen a las del gobierno
dissenter Protestant whose views and opinions differed from those of the Church of England (p. 517)
  disidente protestante cuyos puntos de vista y opiniones diferían de los de la Iglesia de Inglaterra
divine right belief that a ruler's authority comes directly from God (p. 506)
  derecho divino creencia de que la autoridad de un gobernante proviene directamente de Dios
domesticate to tame animals and adapt crops so they are best suited to use by humans (p. 13)
  domesticar domar animales y adaptar plantas con el propósito de adecuarlos para el uso humano
dowry in some societies, payment a bride's family makes to the bridegroom and his family; payment a woman brings to a marriage (pp. 89, 372)
  dote en algunas sociedades, pago de la familia de la novia al novio y a su familia; pago que una mujer proporciona a sumatrimonio
due process of law the requirement that the government act fairly and in accordance with established rules in all that it does (p. 246)
  garantías procesales debidas requisito para que el gobierno actúe justamente y en concordancia con las normas establecidas en todo lo que hace

Dutch East India Company a trading company established by the Netherlands in 1602 to protect and expand its trade in Asia (p. 458)

Compañía Holandesa de las Indias Orientales compañía de comercio establecida por Holanda en 1602 para proteger y aumentar su comercio con Asia

dynastic cycle rise and fall of Chinese dynasties according to the Mandate of Heaven (p. 95)

ciclo dínastico florecimiento y caída de las dinastías chinas de acuerdo con el Mandato del Cielo

dynasty ruling family (p. 45)

dinastía familia gobernante

E

earthwork an embankment or other construction made of earth (p. 203)

terraplén muro de contención u otra construcción hecha de tierra

Edict of Nantes law issued by French king Henry IV in 1598 giving more religious freedom to French Protestants (p. 510)

Edicto de Nantes ley promulgada por el rey francés Enrique IV en 1598 por la que se concedía mayor libertad religiosa a los protestantes frances (p. 510)

Eightfold Path as taught by the Buddha, the path one must follow to achieve nirvana (p. 80)

Óctuple Sendero como enseñó Buda, el camino que debe seguir todo individuo para conseguir el nirvana

elector one of seven German princes who would choose the Holy Roman emperor (p. 525)

elector uno de los siete príncipes germanos que elegían al emperador del Sacro Romano

émigré person who flees his or her country for political reasons (p. 582)

exiliado persona que deja su país por razones políticas

empire a group of states or territories controlled by one ruler (p. 23)

imperio grupo de estados o territorios controlados por un gobernante

enclosure the process of taking over and consolidating land formerly shared by peasant farmers (p. 610)

cercamiento proceso de consolidar y apropiarse de una tierra que anteriormente compartían campesinos

encomienda right the Spanish government granted to its American colonists to demand labor or tribute from Native Americans (p. 478)

encomienda derecho a exigir tributo o trabajo a los natives americanos, que el gobierno español otorgó a sus colonos en América

engineering application of science and mathematics to develop useful structures and machines (p. 164)

ingeniería aplicación de las ciencias y matemáticas al desarrollo do máquinas y estructuras útiles

English Bill of Rights series of acts passed by the English Parliament in 1689 that limited the rights of the monarchy and ensured the superiority of Parliament (p. 521)

Declaración de derechos de los ingleses serie de leyes aprobadas por el parlamento inglés en 1689 que limitaba los derechos de la monarquía y establecía la primacía del parlamento

engraving art form in which an artist etches a design on a metal plate with acid and then uses the plate to make multiple prints (p. 419)

grabado forma de arte en la que un artista graba un diseño con ácido en una placa de metal y después la usa para producir múltiples impresiones

enlightened despot absolute ruler who used his or her power to bring about political and social change (p. 553)

déspota ilustrado gobernante absoluto que usa su poder para precipitar cambios políticos y sociales

enterprise a business organization in such areas as shipping, mining, railroads, or factories (p. 613)

empresa entidad empresarial en áreas como transportes, minería, ferrocariles o fábricas

entrepreneur person who assumes financial risk in the hope of making a profit (pp. 493, 613)

empresario persona que asume riesgos financieros con la esperanza de obtener beneficios

Epic of Gilgamesh Mesopotamian narrative poem that was first told in Sumer (p. 30)

El poema de Gilgamesh poema narrativo de Mesopotamia que se contó por primera vez en Sumeria

epidemic outbreak of a rapidly spreading disease (p. 269)

epidemia brote de una enfermedad que se extiende rápidamente

estate social class (p. 572)

estado clase social

Estates-General legislative body made up of representatives of the three estates in pre-revolutionary France (p. 575)

Estados Generales cuerpo legislativo formado por representantes de los tres estados en la Francia prerevolucionaria

ethics moral standards of behavior (p. 60)

ética estándar moral de conducta

Ethiopia ancient Greek term for Axumite kingdom; present-day country in East Africa (p. 353)

Etiopía antiguo término griego para el reino de Axumite; también es un país actual del este de África

ethnic group large group of people who share the same language and cultural heritage (p. 295)

étnico grupo grande de personas que comparten el idioma y la herencia cultural

Etruscans a people who inhabited early Italy (p. 151)

estrucos pueblo que habitaba principalmente al norte the Roma

excommunication exclusion from the Roman Catholic Church as a penalty for refusing to obey Church law (p. 229)

excomunión exclusión de la Iglesia Católica Romana como castigo por rehusar obedecer la ley de la Iglesia

expansionism policy of increasing the amount of territory a government holds (p. 104)

expansionismo política de aumentar el territorio que posee un gobierno

F

faction dissenting group of people (p. 579)

facción grupo de disidentes

federal republic government in which power is divided between the national, or federal, government and the states (p. 563)

república federal gobierno en el que el poder se divide entre el gobierno nacional o federal y los estados

Fertile Crescent region of the Middle East in which civilizations first arose (p. 30)

Medialuna Fértil región de Oriente Medio en la cual surgieron las primeras civilizaciones

feudal contract exchange of pledges between lords and vassals (p. 219)

contrato feudal intercambio de garantías entre los señores y los vasallos

feudalism loosely organized system of government in which local lords governed their own lands but owed military service and other support to a greater lord (pp. 95, 219)

feudalismo sistema de gobierno poco organizado en el que los señores goberna ban sus propias tierras, pero debían servicio militar y otras formas de apoyo a un superior

fief in medieval Europe, an estate granted by a lord to a vassal in exchange for service and loyalty (p. 219)

estado feudal durante la Edad Media, terreno que un señor cedía a un vasallo a cambio de servicio y lealtad

filial piety respect for parents (p. 97)

piedad filial respeto hacia los padres

Flanders a region that included parts of present-day northern France, Belgium, and the Netherlands; was an important industrial and financial center of northern Europe during the Middle Ages and Renaissance (p. 419)

Flandes región que incluye partes de los actuales norte de Francia, Bélgica y Holanda; fue un importante centro industrial y financiero del norte de Europa durante la Edad Media y el Renacimiento

Florence a city in the Tuscany region of northern Italy that was the center of the Italian Renaissance (p. 412)

Florencia ciudad de la región de Toscana en el norte de Italia que fue el centro del Renacimiento italiano

flying buttresses stone supports on the outside of a building that allowed builders to construct higher, thinner walls that contained large stained-glass windows (p. 266)

contrafuertes flotantes soportes de piedra en la parte exterior de un edificio que permitía a los constructores construir paredes más finas y más altas que contenían ventanas con vidrieras

Four Noble Truths as taught by the Buddha, the four basic beliefs that form the foundation of Buddhism (p. 80)

Cuatro Verdades Nobles como enseñó Buda, las cuatro creencias básicas que forman la base del budismo

Franks a Germanic tribe that conquered present-day France and neighboring lands in the 400s (p. 215)

francos tribu germánica que conquistó la actual Francia y las tierras colindantes en el siglo V

French and Indian War war between Britain and France in the Americas that happened from 1754 to 1763; it was part of a global war called the Seven Years' War (p. 486)

Guerra franco-india guerra entre Gran Bretaña y Francia en América, que duró desde 1754 a 1763; fue parte de una guerra global que se conoció como la Guerra de los Siete Años

fresco colorful painting completed on wet plaster (p. 115)

fresco pintura colorida realizada sobre una pared de yeso húmedo

friar a medieval European monk who traveled from place to place preaching to the poor (p. 229)

fraile monje de la Europa medieval que viajaba de un lugar a otro predicando a los pobres

G

Geneva Swiss city-state which became a Calvinist theocracy in the 1500s; today a major city in Switzerland (p. 427)

Ginebra ciudad estado suiza que se convirtió en una teocracia calvinista en el siglo XVI; en la actualidad es una de las principales ciudades de Suiza

gentry wealthy, landowning class (p. 371)

alta burguesía clase social rica, dueña de tierras

Ghana early West African trading kingdom located in parts of present-day Mauritania and Mali (p. 347)

Ghana antiguo reino comerciante de África occidental ubicado en partes de la actual Mauritania y Mali

ghetto separate section of a city where members of a minority group are forced to live (p. 433)

gueto área separada de una ciudad donde se fuerza a vivir a los miembros de una minoría

Goa a state in western India; formerly a coastal city that was made the base of Portugal's Indian trade (p. 457)

Goa estado en el oeste de India; antiguamente una ciudad costera que se convirtió en la base del comercio en la India de Portugal

golden age period of great cultural achievement (p. 86)

edad de oro período de grandes logros culturales

Golden Bull of 1222 charter that strictly limited royal power in Hungary (p. 297)

Bula de Oro de 1222 carta constitucional que limitaba rigurosamente el poder de la realeza en Hungría

Golden Horde the Mongol armies that invaded Europe in 1237 and ruled Russia for over two centuries (p. 291)

Horda Dorada los ejércitos mongoles que invadieron Europa en 1237 y que gobernaron Rusia durante más de dos siglos

Gothic style type of European architecture that developed in the Middle Ages, characterized by flying buttresses, ribbed vaulting, thin walls, and high roofs (p. 266)

estilo gótico tipo de arquitectura europea que se desarrolló en la Edad Media caracterizada por contrafuertes flotantes, bóvedas estriadas, paredes finas y techos altos

gravity force that pulls objects in Earth's sphere to the center of Earth (p. 438)

gravedad fuerza que atrae los objetos dentro de la esfera terrestre al centro de la Tierra

Great Schism the official split between the Roman Catholic and Byzantine churches that occurred in 1054 (p. 286)

Gran Cisma división oficial entre las iglesias católica romana y bizantina ocurrida en 1054

Great Zimbabwe powerful East African medieval trade center and city-state located in southeastern present-day Zimbabwe (p. 356)

Gran Zimbabwe poderoso centro de comercio medieval de África oriental y ciudad estado ubicada en el sureste del actual Zimbabwe

griot professional storyteller in early West Africa (p. 361)

griot antiguo narrador de historias profesional en África occidental

Guangzhou a coastal city in southeastern China, also known as Canton (p. 461)

Guangzhou ciudad costera del sudeste de China, también conocida como Cantón

guerrilla warfare fighting carried on through hit-and-run raids (p. 597)

guerra de guerrillas lucha que se caracteriza por rápidos ataques y retiradas

guild in the Middle Ages, an association of merchants or artisans who cooperated to uphold standards of their trade and to protect their economic interests (p. 235)

gremio en la Edad Media, asociación de mercaderes o artesanos que cooperaban para mantener los valores de sus oficios y para proteger sus intereses económicos

guillotine device used during the Reign of Terror to execute thousands by beheading (p. 588)

guillotina aparato usado durante el Reinado del Terror para decapitar a miles de personas

H

habeas corpus principle that a person cannot be held in prison without first being charged with a specific crime (p. 247)

habeus corpus principio por el que no puede encarcelarse a una persona sin haber sido antes acusada formalmente de un delito específico

hajj one of the Five Pillars of Islam, the pilgrimage to Mecca that all Muslims are expected to make at least once in their lifetime (p. 306)

hayyi uno de los Cinco Pilares del Islam, la peregrinación a la Meca que se espera hagan todos los musulmanes por lo menos una vez en la vida

hangul alphabet that uses symbols to represent the sounds of spoken Korean (p. 386)

hangul alfabeto que usa símbolos para representar gráficamente los sonidos del idioma coreano

Hapsburg empire Central European empire that lasted from the 1400s to the 1900s and at its height included the lands of the Holy Roman Empire and the Netherlands (p. 504)

Imperio Habsburgo imperio centroeuropeo que duró desde el siglo XV hasta el siglo XX, y que en su plenitud abarcó los territorios del Sacro Imperio Romano y Holanda

Harappa large ancient city of the Indus civilization, located in present-day Pakistan (p. 70)

Harappa antigua gran ciudad de la civilización del Indo, ubicada en el presente Pakistán

heliocentric based on the belief that the sun is the center of the universe (pp. 142, 434)

heliocéntrico sistema basado en la creencia de que el Sol es el centro del universo

heresy religious belief that is contrary to the official teachings of a church (p. 171)

herejía creencia religiosa contraria a las enseñanzas oficiales de la iglesia

hierarchy system of ranking groups (p. 32)

jerarquía sistema que clasifica a las personas de una sociedad

hieroglyphics system of writing in which pictures called hieroglyphs represent objects, concepts, or sounds (p. 54)

jeroglíficos sistema de escritura cuyos dibujos, llamados jeroglíficos, representan objetos, conceptos o sonidos

hijra Muhammad's journey from Mecca to Medina in 622 (p. 305)

héjira trayecto de Mahoma de la Meca a Medina en el año 622

historian a person who studies how people lived in the past (p. 4)

historiador persona que estudia el modo de vida de la gente en el pasado

Holy Land Jerusalem and other places in Palestine where Christians believe Jesus had lived and preached (p. 256)

Tierra Santa Jerusalem y otros lugares en Palestina donde los cristianos creen que Jesús vivió y predicó

Holy Roman Empire empire of west central Europe from 962 to 1806, comprising present-day Germany and neighboring lands (p. 251)

Sacro Imperio Romano imperio de la Europa central occidental desde 962 a 1806, que comprendía la actual Alemania y las tierras aledañas

Huari a culture that thrived in the Andean region from about A.D. 600–A.D. 1000 (p. 196)

huari cultura que tuvo su apogeo en la región andina desde alrededor de 600 D.C. a 1000 D.C.

Huguenots French Protestants of the 1500s and 1600s (p. 510)

Hugonotes protestantes franceses de los siglos XVI y XVII

humanism an intellectual movement at the heart of the Renaissance that focused on education and the classics (p. 411)

humanismo movimiento intelectual durante el auge del Renacimiento que se centraba en la educación y los clásicos

humanities study of subjects such as grammar, rhetoric, poetry, and history, that were taught in ancient Greece and Rome (p. 411)

humanidades estudio de asignaturas como la gramática, la retórica, poesía e historia que se enseñaban en las antiguas Grecia y Roma

Huns a nomadic people of central Asia (p. 175)

hunos pueblo nómada del centro de Asia

hypothesis an unproved theory accepted for the purposes of explaining certain facts or to provide a basis for further investigation (p. 436)

hipótesis teoría sin probar aceptada con el propósito de explicar determinados hechos o de proveer una base para una investigación posterior más profunda

I

icon holy image of Christ, the Virgin Mary, or a saint venerated in the Eastern Orthodox Church (p. 286)

ENGLISH/SPANISH GLOSSARY

ícono imagen sagrada de Cristo, la Vírgen María o de un santo venerado por la iglesia ortodoxa oriental

illumination the artistic decoration of books and manuscripts (p. 267)

iluminación decoración artística de libros y manuscritos

immunity natural protection, resistance (p. 473)

inmunidad protección natural, resistencia

imperialism domination by one country of the political, economic, or cultural life of another country or region (p. 156)

imperialismo dominio por parte de un país de la vida política, económica o cultural de otro país o región

indulgence in the Roman Catholic Church, pardon for sins committed during a person's lifetime (p. 424)

indulgencia perdón por los pecados cometidos en vida concedido por la Iglesia Católica Romana

inflation economic cycle that involves a rapid rise in prices linked to a sharp increase in the amount of money available (pp. 174, 270, 492)

inflación ciclo económico caracterizado por un rápida subida de los precios ligada a un aumento rápido del dinero disponible

Inquisition a Church court set up to try people accused of heresy (p. 260)

Inquisición tribunal de la Iglesia establecido para juzgar a la gente acusada de herejía

intendant official appointed by French king Louis XIV to govern the provinces, collect taxes, and recruit soldiers (p. 512)

intendente oficial publico nombrado por el rey francés Luis XIV para gobernar las provincias, recaudar impuestos y reclutar soldados

interdict in the Roman Catholic Church, excommunication of an entire region, town, or kingdom (p. 229)

interdicto en la Iglesia Católica Romana, excomunión de una región, pueblo o reino

Inti the Inca sun god (p. 199)

Inti dios sol inca

Iroquois League political alliance of five Iroquois groups, known as the Five Nations, in the late 1500s (p. 205)

Liga de los iroqueses alianza política de cinco grupos iroqueses, conocida como las Cinco Naciones, de finales del siglo XVI

Isfahan capital of Safavid empire during the 1600s; located in present-day Iran (p. 333)

Isfahan capital del imperio safavid durante el siglo XVII, situada en actual Irán

Istanbul capital of the Ottoman empire; located in the northwest of present-day Turkey; formerly Constantinople (p. 329)

Estambul capital del imperio otomano; situada en el noroeste de la actual Turquía; anteriormente llamada Constantinopla

J

Jacobin member of a radical political club during the French Revolution (p. 583)

jacobino miembro de un club político radical durante la Revolución Francesa

janizary elite force of the Ottoman army (p. 331)

jenízaro fuerza de élitedel ejército otomano

Jericho the world's first village, established in the modern-day West Bank between 10,000 and 9000 B.C. (p. 14)

Jericó la primera aldea del mundo establecidas en la actual Cisjordania entre alrededor del año 10,000 y 9000 A.C.

jihad in Islam, an effort in God's service (p. 306)

yihad en el Islam, un esfuerzo al servicio de Dios

joint family family organization in which several generations share a common dwelling (p. 89)

familia extendida organización familiar en la que varias generaciones comparten una vivienda

journeyman a salaried worker employed by a guild master (p. 235)

oficial trabajador asalariado empleado por el maestro del gremio

jury legal group of people sworn to make a decision in a legal case (pp. 126, 245)

jurado grupo de personas que han prestado juramento para tomar una decisión en un caso legal

Justinian's Code collection of Roman laws organized by the Byzantine emperor Justinian and later serving as a model for the Catholic Church and medieval monarchs (p. 283)

Código Justiniano recopilación de leyes romanas organizada por el emperador bizantino Justiniano y que luego sirvió como modelo para la iglesia católica y los monarcas medievales

K

Kaaba the most sacred temple of islam, located at Mecca (p. 305)

Kaaba el templo más sagrado del islam, ubicado en La Meca

kana in the Japanese writing system, phonetic symbols representing syllables (p. 390)
kana en el sistema japonés de escritura, símbolos fonéticos que representan sílabas

karma in Hindu belief, all the actions that affect a person's fate in the next life (p. 77)
karma según la creencia hindú, todas las acciones que afectan el destino de una persona en su próxima vida

Kiev capital of medieval Russia and of present-day Ukraine (p. 290)
Kiev capital de la Rusia medieval y de la actual Ucrania

kiva large underground chamber that the Anasazi used for religious ceremonies and political meetings (p. 203)
kiva gran sala subterránea que usaban los anazasi para ceremonias religiosas y reuniones políticas

knight a European noble who served as a mounted warrior (p. 220)
caballero noble europeo que servía como guerrero montado

Knossos an ancient Minoan city on the island of Crete (p. 114)
Cnosos antigua ciudad minoica en la isla de Creta

Koryo dynasty Korean dynasty that ruled from 935 to 1392 (p. 385)
dinastía Koryo dinastía coreana que gobernó desde 935 a 1392

L

labor union workers' organization (p. 618)
sindicato organización de trabajadores

laissez faire policy allowing business to operate with little or no government interference (p. 548)
laissez faire política que permite a los negocios y empresas operar con poca o ninguna interferencia del gobierno

land reform breakup of large agricultural holdings for redistribution among peasants (p. 369)
reforma agraria división de grandes propiedades dedicadas a la agricultura para distribuirlas entre los campesinos

latifundia huge estates bought up by newly wealthy Roman citizens (p. 157)
latifundios grandes propiedades adquiridas por los ciudadanos romanos que se habían vuelto ricos recientemente

lay investiture appointment of bishops by anyone who is not a member of the clergy (p. 252)
investidura nombramiento de obispos por cualquiera que no sea miembro del clero

legion basic unit of the ancient Roman army, made up of about 5,000 soldiers (p. 154)
legión unidad básica del ejército de la antigua Roma, que consistía de unos 5,000 soldados

legislature lawmaking body (p. 122)
asamblea legislativa cuerpo encargado de promover y promulgar las leyes

legitimacy principle by which monarchies that had been unseated by the French Revolution or Napoleon were restored (p. 600)
legitimidad principio por el que las monarquías que habían sido derrocadas por la Revolución Francesa o por Napoleón fueron restituidas

levée morning ritual during which nobles would wait upon French king Louis XIV (p. 512)
recepción matutina ritual de la mañana en el que los nobles atendían al rey Luis XIV

limited monarchy government in which a constitution or legislative body limits the monarch's powers (p. 522)
monarquía limitada gobierno en el que la constitución o el cuerpo legislativo limitan los poderes de la monarquía

Line of Demarcation line set by the Treaty of Tordesillas dividing the non-European world into two zones, one controlled by Spain and the other by Portugal (p. 450)
Línea de demarcación línea establecida por el Tratado de Tordesillas que dividía el mundo fuera de Europa en dos zonas: una controlada por España y otra por Portugal

lineage group claiming a common ancestor (p. 358)
linaje grupo que reivindica un antepasado en común

literacy rate percentage of people who can read and write (p. 386)
tasa de alfabetización porcentaje de personas que pueden leer y escribir

Liverpool city and one of the largest ports in England; first major rail line linked Liverpool to Manchester in 1830 (p. 615)
Liverpool ciudad y uno de los puertos más grandes de Inglaterra; línea importante de ferrocarril unió Liverpool con Manchester en 1830

loess fine windblown yellow soil (p. 93)
loes tierra fina y amarilla que se llava el viento

logic rational thinking (p. 130)
lógica pensamiento racional

longbow six-foot-long bow that could rapidly fire arrows with enough force to pierce most armor (p. 272)

arco largo arco de seis pies de largo que podía disparar rápidamente flechas con suficiente fuerza como para agujerear una armadura

M

Macao region of southeastern China made up of a peninsula and two islands, a Portuguese territory from the mid-1800s to 1999 (p. 461)

Macao región al sudeste de China formada por una península y dos islas; fue territorio portugués desde mediados del siglo XIX a 1999

Magna Carta the Great Charter approved by King John of England in 1215; it limited royal power and established certain rights of English freemen (p. 246)

Carta Magna carta constitucional aprobada por el Rey Juan de Inglaterra en 1215; limitaba el poder real y establecía ciertos derechos de los ingleses libres

Magyars an ethnic group centered in present-day Hungary (p. 218)

magiar grupo étnico establecido en la actual Hungría

maize corn (p. 187)

maíz elote

Malacca a state and coastal city in SW Malaysia, was an early center of the spice trade (p. 457)

Malacca estado y ciudad costera en el sudoeste de Malasia; fue uno de los primeros centros del comercio de especias

Mali medieval West African trading empire located in present-day Mali (p. 348)

Mali imperio comerciante de África occidental medieval ubicado en el actual Mali

Malindi a coastal town in SE Kenya (p. 452)

Malindi pueblo costero al sudeste de Kenia

Manchester city in England; one of the leading industrial areas; example of an Industrial Revolution city; first major rail line linked Manchester to Liverpool in 1830 (p. 615)

Manchester ciudad de Inglaterra; una de las principales áreas industriales; ejemplo de ciudad de la Revolución Industrial; la primera línea importante de ferrocarril unió Manchester con Liverpool en 1830

Manchus people originally from Manchuria, north of China, who conquered the Ming dynasty and ruled China as the Qing dynasty from the mid-1600s to the early 1900s (p. 462)

manchus personas originalmente de Manchuria, al norte de China, que derrotaron a la dinastía Ming y gobernaron como la dinastía Chin desde mediados del siglo XVII a principios del siglo XX

manor during the Middle Ages in Europe, a lord's estate which included one or more villages and the surrounding lands (p. 222)

señorío durante la Edad Media en Europa, propiedad de un señor que incluía uno o más pueblos y sus terrenos adyacentes

Marseilles French port city; troops marched to a patriotic song as they marched from this city, the song eventually became the French national anthem (p. 590)

Marsella ciudad portuaria francesa; las tropas que marcharon al ritmo de una canción patriótica desde esta ciudad inspiraron el himno nacional francés

martyr person who suffers or dies for his or her beliefs (p. 170)

mártir persona que sufre o muere por sus creencias

matrilineal term for a family organization in which kinship ties are traced through the mother (pp. 358, 399)

matrilineal organización familiar en la que los lazos de parentesco se siguen a través de la madre

means of production farms, factories, railways, and other large businesses that produce and distribute goods (p. 625)

medios de producción granjas, fábricas, ferrocarriles y otros grandes negocios que producen y distribuyen mercancías

Mecca a city in western Saudi Arabia; birthplace of the prophet Muhammad and most holy city for Islamic people (p. 304)

Meca ciudad en el oeste de Arabia Saudita; lugar de nacimiento del profeta Mahoma y ciudad sagrada para los creyentes islámicos

medieval referring to the Middle Ages in Europe or the period of history between ancient and modern times (p. 214)

medieval se refiere a la Edad Media en Europa, es decir, el período de la historia entre la edad antigua y la edad moderna

Medina a city in western Saudi Arabia; a city where Muhammad preached (p. 305)

Medina ciudad en el oeste de Arabia Saudita; ciudad donde predicó Mahoma

mercantilism policy by which a nation sought to export more than it imported in order to build its supply of gold and silver (p. 494)

mercantilismo política por la que una nación trataba de exportar más de lo que importaba para aumentar sus reservas de o ro y plata

mercenary soldier serving in a foreign army for pay (pp. 177, 527)

mercenario soldado que sirve en un ejército extranjero a cambio de dinero

Meroë capital of the ancient kingdom of Nubia (p. 343)

Meroë capital del antiguo reino de Nubia

Mesa Verde the largest complex of Anasazi cliff-dwellings in the United States Southwest, built between about A.D. 1150 and A.D. 1300 (p. 203)

Mesa Verde el mayor complejo de viviendas anazasi construidas en acantilados en el sudoeste de Estados Unidos, entre alrededor de 1150 D.C. y 1300 D.C.

Mesoamerica region of North America, including Mexico and Central America, in which civilizations with common cultural features developed before Europeans entered the continent (p. 186)

Mesoamérica región de América del Norte, que incluye a México y América Central, en la cual se desarrollaron, antes de la llegada de los europeos al continente, civilizaciones con características culturales similares

Mesopotamia region within the Fertile Crescent that lies between the Tigris and Euphrates rivers (p. 30)

Mesopotamia región del Creciente Fértil que se encuentra entre los ríos Tigris y Éufrates

messiah savior sent by God (p. 167)

mésias salvador enviado por Dios

mestizo person in Spain's colonies in the Americas who was of Native American and European descent (pp. 480, 645)

mestizo persona de las colonias españolas de América descendiente de nativos y europeos

middle class a group of people, including merchants, traders, and artisans, whose rank was between nobles and peasants (p. 235)

clase media grupo de personas, incluyendo mercaderes, comerciantes y artesanos, cuyo rango estaba entre los nobles y los campesinos

Middle Passage the leg of the triangular trade route on which slaves were transported from Africa to the Americas (p. 487)

Travesía Intermedia parte de la ruta del comercio triangular en la que los esclavos eran transportados desde África a las Américas

minaret slender tower of a mosque, from which Muslims are called to prayer (p, 314)

minarete torre esbelta de una mezquita desde la que se convoca a los musulmanes a la oración

Ming dynasty Chinese dynasty in which Chinese rule was restored; held power from 1368 to 1644 (p. 379)

dinastia Ming dinastia china en la que se restauro el gobierno chino; se mantuvo en el poder desde a 1644

missionary someone sent to do religious work in a territory or foreign country (pp. 85, 453)

misioneros personas enviadas para hacer trabajos religiosos en un territorio u otro país

Moche a culture that thrived in the Andean region from about 400 B.C. to A.D. 600 (p. 196)

moche cultura preincaica que tuvo su apogeo en la región andina, desde alrededor de 400 A.C. a 600 D.C.

Mohenjo-Daro ancient city of the Indus civilization, located in present-day Pakistan (p. 70)

Mohenjo-Daro antigua ciudad de la civilización del Indo, ubicada en el presente Pakistán

moksha in Hindu belief, the ultimate goal of existence, which is to achieve union with brahman (p. 77)

moksha según la creencia hindú, el objetivo final de la existencia, que es llegar a la unión con el brahman

Moluccas a group of islands in eastern Indonesia; was the center of the spice trade in the 1500s and 1600s (p. 446)

Molucas grupo de islas en el este de Indonesia; fue el centro del comercio de especias en los siglos XVI y XVII

Mombasa a city in southeastern Kenya, located on a small coastal island (p. 452)

Mombasa ciudad al sudeste de Kenia, localizada en una pequeña isla costera

monarchy government in which a king or queen exercises central power (p. 120)

monarquía gobierno en el que el poder reside en el rey o la reina

money economy economic system in which goods or services are paid for through the exchange of a token of an agreed value (p. 42)

economía de dinero sistema económico en el que las mercancías y los servicios se pagan mediante el intercambio de una moneda con un valor establecido

monopoly complete control of a product or business by one person or group (pp. 103, 454)

monopolio control total de un producto o negocio por una persona o grupo

monotheistic believing in one God (p. 57)
monoteísta creencia en un solo Dios

monsoon seasonal wind that regularly blows from a certain direction for part of the year (p. 69)
monzón viento estacional que regularmente sopla desde una dirección específica durante una parte del año

mosaic picture made from chips of colored stone or glass (p. 162)
mosaico imagen hecha con pedazos de piedras o vidrios de colores

mosque Muslim house of worship; (p. 306)
mezquita templo musulmán

Mughal Muslim dynasty that ruled much of present-day India from 1526 to 1857 (p. 327)
Mughal dinastía musulmana que gobernó gran parte de la India actual de 1526 a 1857

Mughal empire Muslim empire that ruled most of northern India from the mid-1500s to the mid-1700s; also known as the Mogul or Mongol empire (p. 457)
imperio Mughal imperio musulmán que gobernó la mayor parte del norte de India desde mediados del siglo XVI a mediados del siglo XVIII; también se conoce como imperio Mogul o Mongol

mulatto in Spain's colonies in the Americas, person who was of African and European descent (pp. 480, 645)
mulato en las colonias españolas de América descendiente de africanos y europeos

mummification the preservation of dead bodies by embalming and wrapping them in cloth (p. 53)
momificación práctica de preservar los cuerpos de los muertos embalsamándolos y envolviéndolos en vendas

mutiny revolt, especially of soldiers or sailors against their officers (p. 490)
motín revuelta, especialmente de soldados y marineros contra sus oficiales

mystic person who devotes his or her life to seeking direct communion with divine forces (p. 73)
místico persona que dedica su vida a buscar la comunión directa con las fuerzas divinas

N

Nagasaki a coastal city in southern Japan on the island of Kyushu; city in Japan where the second atomic bomb was dropped in August, 1945 (p. 465)

Nagasaki ciudad costera en el sur de Japón en la isla de Kyushu; ciudad de Japón donde fue lanzada la segunda bomba atómica en agosto de 1945

Napoleonic Code body of French civil laws introduced in 1804; served as model for many nations' civil codes (p. 593)
Código Napoleónico cuerpo de las leyes civiles francesas presentadas en 1804, que sirvieron como modelo para los códigos civiles de muchos países

nationalism a strong feeling of pride in and devotion to one's country (p. 590)
nacionalismo fuerte sentimiento de orgullo y devoción hacia el país propio

natural law rules of conduct discoverable by reason (p. 544)
leyes naturales normas de conducta que se pueden descubrir mediante la razón

natural right right that belongs to all humans from birth, such as life, liberty, and property (p. 545)
derecho natural derecho que pertenece a todos los humanos desde el nacimiento: vida, libertad y propiedad

Nazca a culture that thrived in the Andean region from about 200 B.C. to A.D. 600 (p. 196)
Nazca cultura que tuvo su apogeo en la región andina desde alrededor de 200 A.C. a 600 D.C.

Neolithic Period the final era of prehistory, which began about 9000 B.C.; also called the New Stone Age (p. 11)
período Neolítico era final de la prehistoria que empezó hacia el 9000 A.C.; también llamado Nueva Edad de Piedra

Neolithic Revolution the period of time during which the introduction of agriculture led people to transition from nomadic to settled life (p. 13)
revolución neolítica período durante el cual el comienzo de la agricultura llevó a la gente a la transición de la vida nómada a la vida sedentaria

New France French possessions in present-day Canada from the 1500s to 1763 (p. 482)
Nueva Francia posesiones francesas en el actual Canadá desde el siglo XVI a 1763

New Stone Age the final era of prehistory, which began about 9000 B.C.; also called the Neolithic Period (p. 11)
Nueva Edad de Piedra era final de la prehistoria que empezó aproximadamente hacia el 9000 A.C.; también llamado período Neolítico

nirvana in Buddhist belief, union with the universe and release from the cycle of rebirth (p. 80)

nirvana en el budismo, unión con el universo y liberación del ciclo de la reencarnación

nomad a person who moves from place to place in search of food (p. 11)

nómada persona que se traslada de un lugar a otro en busca de alimentos

Nubia ancient kingdom in northeastern Africa, also called Kush (p. 343)

Nubia antiguo reino del noreste africano, también llamado Kush

nuclear family family unit consisting of parents and children (p. 357)

familia nuclear unidad familiar que consta de los padres y sus hijos

O

Old Stone Age the era of prehistory that lasted from 2 million B.C. to about 9000 B.C. (p. 11)

Antigua Edad de Piedra era de la prehistoria que duró desde aproximadamente 2 millones de años A.C. hasta el 9000 A.C.; también llamado período Paleolítico

Olduvai Gorge a gorge in Tanzania in which many hominid remains have been found (p. 8)

desfiladero Olduvai desfiladero en Tanzania donde se han encontrado muchos restos de homínidos

oligarchy government in which ruling power belongs to a few people (pp. 120, 523)

oligarquía gobierno en el que el poder está en manos de unas pocas personas

Olmecs the earliest American civilization, located along the Gulf Coast of Mexico from about 1500 B.C. to 400 B.C. (p. 188)

olmecas la primera civilización americana, ubicada a lo largo de la costa del Golfo de México, desde alrededor de 1500 A.C. a 400 A.C.

oracle bone in Shang China, animal bone or turtle shell used by priests to predict the future (p. 100)

hueso de oráculo en la China Shang, hueso de animal o caparazón de tortuga usado por los sacerdotes para predecir el futuro

Ottomans Turkish-speaking nomadic people who migrated from Central Asia into northwestern Asia Minor (p. 329)

otomanos grupo nómada de habla turca que emigró de Asia Central al noroeste de Asia Menor

ostracism practice used in ancient Greece to banish or send away a public figure who threatened democracy (p. 126)

ostracismo en la antigua Grecia, el acto de desterrar o enviar lejos a una figura pública que amenazaba la democracia

outpost a distant military station or a remote settlement (p. 458)

fuerte fronterizo estación militar distante o asentamiento lejano

Oyo empire Yoruba empire that arose in the 1600s in present-day Nigeria and dominated its neighbors for a hundred years (p. 455)

imperio Oyo el imperio Yoruba que surgió en el siglo XVII en la actual Nigeria y dominó a sus vecinos durante cien años

P

paddy rice field (p. 401)

arrozal campo de arroz

pagoda multistoried Buddhist temple with eaves that curve up at the corners (p. 372)

pagoda templo budista de varios pisos con aleros que se curvan en las esquinas

Paleolithic Period the era of prehistory that lasted from at least 2 million B.C. to about 9000 B.C.; also called the Old Stone Age (p. 11)

período Paleolítico era de la prehistoria que duró desde aproximadamente 2 millones de años A.C. hasta el 9000 A.C.; también llamado la Antigua Edad de Piedra

papal supremacy the claim of medieval popes that they had authority over all secular rulers (p. 228)

supremacía papal demanda de los papas medievales de que ellos tenían autoridad sobre todos los gobernantes laicos

Parthenon the chief temple of the Greek goddess Athena on the Acropolis in Athens, Greece (p. 132)

Partenón el principal templo de la diosa griega Atena, situado en la Acrópolis de Atenas en Grecia

papyrus plant used to make a paper-like writing material in ancient Egypt (p. 54)

papiro planta usada por los antiguos egipcios para hacer un material de escritura parecido al papel

Parliament the legislature of England, and later of Great Britain (p. 247)

Parlamento asamblea legislativa de Inglaterra, y más tarde de Gran Bretaña

partition a division into pieces (p. 535)
  partición división en partes

partnership a group of merchants who joined together to finance a large-scale venture that would have been too costly for any individual trader (p. 234)
  asociación grupo de mercaderes que se unen para financiar una empresa más grande que hubiera sido demasiado costosa para un solo comerciante

patriarch in the Roman and Byzantine empires, highest church official in a major city (pp. 171, 286)
  patriarca en el Imperio Romano y imperio bizantino, el funcionario de rango más alto en la iglesia de una ciudad importante

patriarchal relating to a society in which men hold the greatest legal and moral authority (p. 59)
  patriarcal relacionado con una sociedad en la que los hombres tienen la autoridad legal y moral

patrician in ancient Rome, member of the landholding upper class (p. 152)
  patricio miembro de la clase alta terrateniente en la antigua Roma

patrilineal term for a family organization in which kinship ties are traced through the father (p. 358)
  patrilineal organización familiar en la que los lazos de parentesco se siguen a través del padre

patron a person who provides financial support for the arts (p. 412)
  mecenas persona que proporciona apoyo financiero a la cultura y las artes

Peace of Westphalia series of treaties that ended the Thirty Years' War (p. 527)
  Paz de Westfalia serie de tratados por los que se puso fin a la Guerra de los Treinta Años

peninsulare member of the highest class in Spain's colonies in the Americas (pp. 480, 645)
  peninsular miembro de la clase más alta en las colonias españolas de América

peon worker forced to labor for a landlord in order to pay off a debt (p. 478)
  peón trabajador forzado a trabajar para un terrateniente para pagar una deuda

perspective artistic technique used to give paintings and drawings a three-dimensional effect (p. 412)
  perspectiva técnica artística usada para lograr el efecto de tercera dimensión en dibujos y pinturas

phalanx in ancient Greece, a massive tactical formation of heavily armed foot soldiers (p. 120)

falange en la antigua Grecia, sólida formación táctica de soldados a pie fuertemente armados

pharaoh title of the rulers of ancient Egypt (p. 45)
  faraón título de los gobernantes del antiguo Egipto

Philippines a country in southeastern Asia made up of several thousand islands (p. 459)
  Filipinas país al sudeste de Asia formado por varios miles de islas

philosophe French for "philosopher"; French thinker who desired reform in society during the Enlightenment (p. 546)
  philosophe palabra francesa que significa "filósofo"; pensador francés que abogaba por reformas en la sociedad durante la Ilustración

philosopher someone who seeks to understand and explain life; a person who studies philosophy (p. 130)
  filósofo persona que trata de comprender y explicar la vida; persona que estudia la filosofía

philosophy system of ideas (p. 97)
  filosofía sistema de ideas

pictograph a simple drawing that looks like the object it represents (p. 22)
  pictografía dibujo sencillo que se parece al objeto que representa (also called pictograms)

Pilgrims English Protestants who rejected the Church of England (p. 484)
  peregrinos protestantes ingleses que rechazaron la Iglesia de Inglaterra

plantation large estate run by an owner or overseer and worked by laborers who live there (p. 453)
  plantación gran propiedad administrada por un dueño o capataz y cultivada por trabajadores que viven en ella

plateau raised area of level land (p. 69)
  meseta área elevada de tierra plana

plebeian in ancient Rome, member of the lower class, including farmers, merchants, artisans, and traders (p. 152)
  plebeyo en la antigua Roma, miembro de clase baja, que incluía granjeros, mercaderes, artesanos y comerciantes

plebiscite ballot in which voters have a direct say on an issue (p. 593)
  plebiscito votación en la que los votantes expresan su opinión sobre un tema en particular

polis city-state in ancient Greece (p. 118)
  polis ciudad-estado de la antigua Grecia

polytheistic believing in many gods (p. 20)
  politeísta creencia en muchos dioses

ENGLISH/SPANISH GLOSSARY

pope head of the Roman Catholic Church; in ancient Rome, bishop of Rome who claimed authority over all other bishops (p. 171)

papa cabeza de la iglesia Católica Romana; obispo de Roma que afirmaba tener autoridad sobre los otros obispos

popular sovereignty basic principle of the American system of government which asserts that the people are the source of any and all governmental power, and government can exist only with the consent of the governed (p. 560)

soberanía popular principio básico del sistema de gobierno estadounidense en el que se determina que el pueblo es la fuente de todo poder gubernamental, y que el gobierno sólo puede existir con el consentimiento de los gobernados

potlatch among Native American groups of the Northwest Coast, ceremonial gift-giving by people of high rank and wealth (p. 205)

potlatch entre los grupos indígenas de la costa noroeste, ceremonia en que la gente de alto rango o riqueza hacía regalos

predestination Calvinist belief that God long ago determined who would gain salvation (p. 427)

predestinación creencia calvinista de que Dios decidió hace mucho tiempo quién conseguiría la salvación

prehistory the period of time before writing was invented (p. 4)

prehistoria período anterior a la invención de los sistemas de escritura

price revolution period in European history when inflation rose rapidly (p. 492)

revolución del precio período en la historia de Europa en que la inflación aumentó rápidamente

privateer privately owned ship commissioned by a government to attack and capture enemy ships, especially merchant's ships (p. 481)

corsario barco privado comisionado por un gobierno para atacar y capturar barcos enemigos, especialmentelos barcos mercantes

proletariat working class (p. 625)

proletariado clase trabajadora

prophet spiritual leader who interprets God's will (p. 60)

profeta líder espiritual a quien se le atribuye la interpretación de la voluntad de Dios

Prussia a strong military state in central Europe that emerged in the late 1600s (p. 528)

Prusia estado centroeuropeo militarmente poderoso que emergió a finales del siglo XVII

pueblo Native American village of the United States Southwest (p. 203)

pueblo poblado indígena del sudoeste de Estados Unidos

Pueblo Bonito the largest Anasazi pueblo, built in New Mexico in the A.D. 900s (p. 203)

Pueblo Bonito el mayor poblado anazasi, construido en Nuevo México en el siglo X D.C.

Puritans members of an English Protestant group who wanted to "purify" the Church of England by making it more simple and more morally strict (p. 517)

puritanos miembros de un grupo de protestantes ingleses que querían "purificar" la Iglesia de Inglaterra, haciéndola más sencilla y moralmente más estricta

putting-out system a system developed in the 18th century in which tasks were distributed to individuals who completed the work in their own homes; also known as cottage industry (p. 614)

sistema de trabajo a domicilio sistema desarrolla do en el siglo XVIII en el que las tareas se distribúan a individuos quienes completaban el trabajo en sus hogares; tambien se conoce como industria familiar

Q

Qajars members of the dynasty that ruled present-day Iran from the late 1700s until 1925 (p. 333)

Qajars miembros de la dinastía que gobernó la zona del actual Irán desde fines del siglo XVIII hasta 1925

Qing dynasty dynasty established by the Manchus in the mid 1600s and lasted until the early 1900s; China's last dynasty (p. 463)

dinastía Chin dinastía establecida por los manchus a mediados del siglo XVII que duró hasta principios del siglo XX; fue la última dinastía china

Quran the holy book of Islam (p. 306)

Corán el libro sagrado del islam

quipu knotted strings used by Inca officials for record-keeping (p. 197)

quipu cuerdas con nudos que usaban los incas como llevar registros

R

radicals those who favor extreme changes (p. 638)

radicales persona que quiere hacer cambios extremos

rajah in ancient India, the elected warrior chief of an Aryan tribe (pp. 72, 326)

rajah jefe guerrero electo de una tribu aria en la antigua India

recession period of reduced economic activity (p. 640)

recesión periodo de reducción de la actividad económica

Reconquista during the 1400s, the campaign by European Christians to drive the Muslims from present-day Spain (p. 260)

Reconquista durante el siglo XV, campaña por parte de cristianos europeos para expulsar a los musulmanes de la actual España

Reign of Terror time period during the French Revolution from September 1793 to July 1794 when people in France were arrested for not supporting the revolution and many were executed (p. 587)

Reinado del terror período durante la Revolución Francesa desde septiembre de 1793 a julio de 1794, en el que la gente en Francia era arresta da por no apoyar la revolución; mucha gente fue ejecutada

reincarnation in Hindu belief, the rebirth of the soul in another bodily form (p. 77)

reencarnación según la creencia hindú, renacimiento del alma en otra forma corporal

republic system of government in which officials are chosen by the people (pp. 151, 583)

república sistema de gobierno en el que los gobernantes son elegidos por el pueblo

revenue money taken in through taxes (p. 483)

rentas públicas dinero que se recauda por impuestos

rhetoric art of skillful speaking (p. 130)

retórica arte de hablar con habilidad

rococo personal, elegant style of art and architecture made popular during the mid-1700s that featured designs with the shapes of leaves, shells, and flowers (p. 551)

rococó estilo de arte y arquitectura elegante y personal que se hizo popular a mediados del siglo XVIII y que incluía diseños con formas de hojas, conchas y flores

Rosetta Stone stone monument that includes the same passage carved in hieroglyphics, demotic script, and Greek and that was used to decipher the meanings of many hieroglyphs (p. 55)

piedra de Rosetta piedra arquitectónica que incluye el mismo pasaje esculpido con caracteres jeroglíficos, demóticos y en escritura griega que se usó para descifrar el significado de muchos jeroglíficos

S

Sabbath a holy day for rest and worship (p. 60)

sabbat día sagrado para descansar y rendir culto

sacrament sacred ritual of the Roman Catholic Church (p. 225)

sacramento ritual sagrado de la Iglesia Católica Romana

Safavid Shiite Muslim empire that ruled much of present-day Iran from the1500s into the 1700s (p. 333)

Safávida imperio musulmán chiíta que gobernó la mayor parte del actual Irán desde el siglo XVI hasta el siglo XVIII

Sahara largest desert in the world, covering almost all of North Africa (p. 340)

Sahara desierto más grande del mundo que cubre casi todo el norte de África

salon informal social gathering at which writers, artists, *philosophes,* and others exchanged ideas (p. 551)

salón reuniones sociales informales en las que escritores, artistas, filósofos y otros intercambiaban ideas

samurai member of the warrior class in Japanese feudal society (p. 391)

samurai miembro de la clase guerrera en la sociedad japonesa feudal

sans-culotte working-class man or woman who made the French Revolution more radical; called such because he or she wore long trousers instead of the fancy knee breeches that the upper class wore (p. 583)

sans-culotte hombre o mujer de la clase obrera que hicieron la Revolución Francesa más radical; llamados así porque llevaban pantalones largos a la rodilla como los que llevaba en vez de los pantalones ajustados la clase altas a la rodilla como los que llevaba la clase alta

Sapa Inca the title of the Inca emperor (p. 197)

Sapa Inca título del emperador inca

satirize make fun of (p. 162)

satirizar burlarse de algo

savanna grassy plain with irregular patterns of rainfall (p. 340)

sabana planicie con pastizales cuyo régimen de lluvias es irregular

schism permanent division in a church (p. 270)
cisma división permanente de una iglesia

scholasticism in medieval Europe, the school of thought that used logic and reason to support Christian belief (p. 264)
escolástica en la Edad Media europea, escuela de pensamiento que usaba la lógica y el razonamiento para apoyar las creencias cristianas

scientific method careful, step-by-step process used to confirm findings and to prove or disprove a hypothesis (p. 436)
método científico proceso cuidadoso y de varios pasos que se usa para confirmar descubrimientos y para aprobar o desaprobar una hipótesis

scorched-earth policy military tactic in which soldiers destroy everything in their path to hurt the enemy (p. 597)
política de tierra quemada táctica militar en la que los soldados destruyen todo lo que tienen a su paso para perjudicar al enemigo

scribe in ancient civilizations, a person specially trained to read, write, and keep records (p. 22)
escriba en las civilizaciones antiguas, persona especialmente educada para leer, escribir y mantener registros

sect a subgroup of a major religious group (pp. 82, 428)
secta subgrupo de un grupo religioso importante

secular having to do with worldly, rather than religious, matters; nonreligious (p. 228)
secular que tiene que ver más con asuntos mundanos que religiosos; no religioso

selective borrowing adopting or adapting some cultural traits but discarding others (p. 390)
préstamo selectivo adoptar o adaptar algunos rasgos culturales y descartar otros

sepoy Indian soldier who served in an army set-up by the French or English trading companies (p. 460)
sepoy soldado indio que sirvió en un ejército establecido por las compañías de comercio francesas o inglesas

serf in medieval Europe, a peasant bound to the lord's land (p. 222)
siervo en la Europa medieval, campesino vinculado a las tierras del señor

shah king (p. 333)
sha rey

Sharia body of Islamic law that includes interpretation of the Quran and applies Islamic principles to everyday life (p. 308)

Sharía ley canónica del islam que incluye la interpretación del Corán y que aplica los principios islámicos a la vida diaria

Shiite a member of one of the two major Muslim sects; believe that the descendents of Muhammad's daughter and son-in-law, Ali, are the true Muslim leaders (p. 311)
chiíta miembro de una de las dos sectas musulmanas principales; creedor de que los descendientes de la hija y el yerno de Mahoma, Alí, son los verdaderos líderes musulmanes

Shinto principal religion in Japan that emphasizes the worship of nature (p. 389)
Shinto principal religión de Japón que enfatiza la adoración a la naturaleza

shogun in Japanese feudal society, supreme military commander, who held more power than the emperor (p. 391)
shogún en la sociedad feudal japonesa, jefe military supremo con más poder que el emperador

shrine altar, chapel, or other sacred place (p. 114)
santuario altar, capilla u otro lugar sagrado

Sikhism religion founded by Nanak that blended Islamic and Hindu beliefs (p. 327)
sikhismo religión fundada por Nanak que incorpora creencias islámicas e hindúes

Silla dynasty Korean dynasty that ruled from 668 to 935 (p. 385)
dinastía Silla dinastía coreana que gobernó desde 668 a 935

smelt melt in order to get the pure metal away from its waste matter (p. 611)
refinar fundir mineral para separar el mineral puro de las impurezas

social contract an agreement by which people gave up their freedom to a powerful government in order to avoid chaos (p. 545)
contrato social acuerdo mediante el cual el pueblo cede sus libertades a un gobierno poderoso para evitar el caos

social democracy political ideology in which there is a gradual transition from capitalism to socialism instead of a sudden violent overthrow of the system (p. 626)
democracia social ideología política en la que hay una transición gradual del capitalismo al socialismo en vez de un derrocamiento violento del sistema

social mobility the ability to move in social class (p. 318)
movilidad social la capacidad de cambiar de clase social

socialism system in which the people as a whole rather than private individuals own all property and operate all businesses (p. 625)

socialismo sistema en el que el pueblo como un todo, en vez de los individuos, son dueños de todas la propiedades y manejan todos los negocios

Song dynasty Chinese dynasty from 960 to 1279; known for its artistic achievements (p. 370)

dinastía Song dinastía china desde 960 a 1279; conocida por sus grandes logros artísticos

Songhai medieval West African kingdom located in present-day Mali, Niger and Nigeria (p. 349)

Songhai reino medieval de África occidental ubicado en el presente Mali, Níger y Nigeria

sovereign having full, independent power (p. 458)

soberano tener poder pleno e independiente

Sparta city-state in ancient Greece (p. 120)

Esparta antigua ciudad-estado en Grecia

St. Petersburg capital city and major port that Peter the Great established in 1703 (p. 532)

San Petersburgo ciudad y capital con un puerto importante, establecida en 1703 por Pedro el Grande

Stamp Act law passed in 1765 by the British Parliament that imposed taxes on items such as newspapers and pamphlets in the American colonies; repealed in 1766 (p. 559)

Ley del Timbre ley promulgada en 1765 por el Parlamento Británico que imponía gravá menes a artículos como diarios y panfletos en las colonias americanas; revocada en 1766

stela in the ancient world, a tall, commemorative monument that was often decorated (p. 190)

estela en el mundo antiguo, gran monumento monolítico conmemorativo que comúnmente estaba decorado

steppe sparse, dry, treeless grassland (pp. 19, 289, 376)

estepa tierra de pastos escasos y secos sin árboles

stipend a fixed salary given to public office holders (p. 126)

estipendio salario fijo de los funcionarios públicos

strait narrow water passage (p. 116)

estrecho paso angosto de agua

stupa large domelike Buddhist shrine (p. 400)

stupa gran altar budista en forma de cúpula

subcontinent large landmass that juts out from a continent (p. 68)

subcontinente gran masa de tierra que sobresale de un continente

suffrage right to vote (p. 586)

sufragio derecho al voto

Sufis Muslim mystics who seek communion with God through meditation, fasting, and other rituals (p. 312)

sufis místicos musulmanes que buscan la comunión con dios mediante la meditación, el ayuno y otros rituals

sultan Muslim ruler (pp. 316, 324)

sultán gobernante musulmán

Sumer site of the world's first civilization, located in southeastern Mesopotamia (p. 30)

Sumeria lugar de la primera civilización del mundo, ubicada en el sureste de Mesopotamia

Sunni a member of one of the largest Muslim sects; Sunnis believe that inspiration came from the example of Muhammad as recorded by his early followers (p. 311)

sunita miembro de una de las dos sectas musulmanas principales; los sunitas creen que la inspiración proviene del ejemplo de Mahoma según fue registrada por sus primeros seguidores

surplus an amount that is more than needed; excess (pp. 17, 346)

excedente cantidad de algo superior a lo que se necesita; exceso

Swahili an East African culture that emerged about 1000 A.D.; also a Bantu-based language, blending Arabic words and written in Arabic script (p. 355)

swahili cultura del este de África que emergió alrededor del año 1000 D.C.; también un idioma basado en el Bantú, que mezcla palabras árabes y usa la escritura árabe

T

Taj Mahal a tomb built by Shah Jahan for his wife (p. 328)

Taj Mahal tumba construida por Shah Jahan para su esposa; considerado como uno de los monumentos más importantes del imperio mughal

Tang dynasty Chinese dynasty from 618 to 907 (p. 368)

dinastía Tang dinastía china desde 618 a 907

tariff tax on imported goods (p. 495)

tasa impuesto a mercancías importadas

technology the skills and tools people use to meet their basic needs (p. 8)

tecnología herramientas y destrezas que usan las personas para satisfacer sus necesidades básicas

Tehran capital of the Qajar dynasty and present-day Iran (p. 333)

ENGLISH/SPANISH GLOSSARY

Teherán capital de la dinastía Qajar y del actual Irán

tenant farmer someone who would pay rent to a lord to farm part of the lord's land (p. 235)

agricultor arrendatario alguien que paga un alquiler a un señor para poder cultivar la tierra de éste

tenement multistory building divided into crowded apartments (p. 618)

apartamento de vecindad edificio de varios pisos dividido en apartamentos donde vive mucha gente

Tennis Court Oath famous oath made on a tennis court by members of the Third Estate in France (p. 576)

Juramento del juego de pelota famoso juramento hecho en una cancha de frontón por los miembros del Tercer Estado en Francia

Tenochtitlán capital city of the Aztec empire, on which modern-day Mexico City was built (pp. 192, 473)

Tenochtitlán capital del imperio azteca, sobre la cual se construyó la actual Ciudad de México

Teotihuacán city that dominated the Valley of Mexico from about A.D. 200 to A.D. 750 and that influenced the culture of later Mesoamerican peoples (p. 193)

Teotihuacán ciudad que dominó el Valle de México desde alrededor de 200 D.C. a 750 D.C., y que influyó en la cultura de los pueblos mesoamericanos posteriores

theocracy government run by religious leaders (p. 427)

teocracia gobierno administrado por líderes religiosos

Tiahuanaco a culture that thrived in the Andean region from about A.D. 200–A.D. 1000 (p. 196)

tiahuanaco cultura preincaica que tuvo su apogeo en la región andina desde alrededor de 200 D.C. a 1000 D.C.

Torah the most sacred text of the Hebrew Bible, including its first five books (p. 57)

Tora el texto más sagrado de la Biblia judía que incluye sus cinco primeros libros

tournament a mock battle in which knights would compete against one another to display their fighting skills (p. 221)

torneo batalla simulada en la que los caballeros competían entre ellos para lucir sus destrezas de lucha

traditional economies economies that rely on habit, custom, or ritual and tend not to change over time (p. 17)

economía de subsistencia economía basada en hábitos, costumbres o rituales y que no suele cambiar con el paso del tiempo

traditional economy a type of economy that relies on habit, custom, or ritual and tends not to change over time (p. 17)

economía tradicional tipo de economía que depende de los hábitos, costumbres, rituales o tendencias y que no suele cambiar a lo largo del tiempo

tragedy in ancient Greece, a play about human suffering often ending in disaster (p. 134)

tragedia en la antigua Grecia, obra teatral que trataba del sufrimiento humano y que a menudo terminaba con un desastre

Treaty of Paris treaty of 1763 that ended the Seven Years' War and resulted in British dominance of the Americas (p. 486)

Tratado de París en 1763, tratado que terminó con la Guerra de los Siete Años y resultó en el dominio británico de las Américas

Treaty of Paris peace treaty made final in 1783 that ended the American Revolution (p. 562)

Tratado de París tratado de paz de 1783 que dio final a la Revolución Americana

Treaty of Tordesillas treaty signed between Spain and Portugal in 1494 which divided the non-European world between them (p. 450)

Tratado de Tordesillas tratado firmado por España y Portugal en 1494 por el que se dividían entre ellos el mundo fuera de Europa

triangular trade colonial trade routes among Europe and its colonies, the West Indies, and Africa in which goods were exchanged for slaves (p. 487)

comercio triangular ruta colonial de comercio entre Europa y sus colonias en las Indias Occidentales y África, en donde las mercancías se cambiaban por esclavos

tribunes in ancient Rome, official who was elected by the plebeians to protect their interests (p. 152)

tribuno en la antigua Roma, funcionario elegido por los plebeyos para proteger sus intereses

tributary state independent state that has to acknowledge the supremacy of another state and pay tribute to its ruler (p. 369)

estado tributario estado independiente que debe reconocer la supremacía de otro estado y pagar tributo a su gobernante

tribute payment that conquered peoples may be forced to pay their conquerors (p. 193)

tributo pago que los conquistadores podían obligar a pagar a los pueblos conquistados

Trojan War in Greek epic poems and myths, a ten-year war between Mycenae and the city of Troy in Asia Minor (p. 116)

Guerra de Troya en los mitos y poemas griegos, guerra de diez años de duración entre Micenas y la ciudad de Troya situada en Asia Menor

troubadour a wandering poet or singer of medieval Europe (p. 222)

trovador poeta o cantante itinerante de la Europa medieval

tsar title of the ruler of the Russian empire (p. 293)

zar título del regente del imperio ruso

tsunami very large, damaging wave caused by an earthquake or very strong wind (p. 388)

tsunami ola enorme y destructiva causada por un terremoto o vientos muy fuertes

turnpike private road built by entrepreneurs who charged a toll to travelers who used it (p. 614)

autopista de peaje carretera construida con capital privado; el dueño de la carretera cobra una tarifa a los viajeros por usarla

tyrant in ancient Greece, ruler who gained power by force (p. 122)

tirano en la antigua Grecia, gobernante que llegó al poder por medio de la fuerza

U

Umayyads members of the Sunni dynasty of caliphs that ruled a Muslim empire from 661 to 750 (p. 312)

omeyas miembros de la dinastía Sunita de califas que gobernó un imperio musulmán de 661 a 750

universal manhood suffrage right of all adult men to vote (p. 635)

sufragio universal masculino derecho de todos los hombres adultos a votar

urbanization movement of people from rural areas to cities (p. 616)

urbanización movimiento de personas de las áreas rurales a las ciudades

utilitarianism idea that the goal of society should be to bring about the greatest happiness for the greatest number of people (p. 623)

utilitarismo idea de que el objetivo de la sociedad debería ser lograr la mayor felicidad para el mayor número de personas

utopian idealistic or visionary, usually used to describe a perfect society (p. 420)

utópico idealista o visionario, normalmente se usa para describir una sociedad perfecta

V

Valley of Mexico valley in Mexico in which the numerous Mesoamerican civilizations, including the Aztecs, arose (p. 192)

Valle de México valle en México en el cual se desarrollaron numerosas civilizaciones mesoamericanas, incluyendo los aztecas

vassal in medieval Europe, a lord who was granted land in exchange for service and loyalty to a greater lord (p. 219)

vasallo durante la Edad Media, señor a quien se le cedía un terreno a cambio de servicio y lealtad al señor más importante

Vedas a collection of prayers, hymns, and other religious teachings developed in ancient India beginning around 1500 B.C. (p. 72)

Vedas con onjunto de oraciones, himnos y otras enseñanzas religiosas desarrolladas en la antigua India a partir de alrededor del siglo XVI a. de C.

veneration special regard (p. 71)

veneración estima especial

vernacular everyday language of ordinary people (pp. 265, 419)

vernáculo lenguaje diario de la gente corriente

Versailles royal French residence and seat of government established by King Louis XIV (p. 512)

Versalles residencia de la realeza francesa y sede de gobierno establecidos por el rey Luis XIV

veto block a government action (p. 152)

veto bloquear una acción del gobierno

viceroy representative who ruled one of Spain's provinces in the Americas in the king's name; one who governed in India in the name of the British monarch (p. 477)

virrey representante que regía una de las provincias de España en las Américas en nombre del rey; quien gobernaba en India en nombre del monarca británico

Vikings Scandinavian peoples whose sailors raided Europe from the 700s through the 1100s (p. 218)

vikingo pueblo escandinavo cuyos marineros asaltaron Europa durante los siglos VIII al XII

vizier chief minister who supervised the business of government in ancient Egypt (p. 45)

ENGLISH/SPANISH GLOSSARY

visir ministro principal que supervisaba los asuntos de gobierno en el antiguo Egipto

W

War of the Austrian Succession series of wars in which various European nations competed for power in Central Europe after the death of Hapsburg emperor Charles VI (p. 528)

Guerra de Sucesión Austriaca serie de guerras en las que diversos países europeos lucharon por la hegemonía en centroeuropa después de la muerte de Carlos IV, emperador Habsburgo

warlord local military ruler (p. 105)

jefe militar cabeza de un ejército local

warm-water port port that is free of ice year-round (p. 532)

puerto de aguas templadas puerto en el que sus aguas nunca se congelan a lo largo del año

westernization adoption of western ideas, technology, and culture (p. 531)

occidentalización adopción de ideas, tecnología y cultura occidentales

Wittenberg a city in northern Germany, where Luther drew up his 95 theses (p. 425)

Wittenberg ciudad al norte de Alemania donde Lutero redactó sus 95 tesis

Y

Yathrib final destination of Muhammad's hijra and the home of the first community of Muslims; later renamed Medina; located in the northwest of present-day Saudi Arabia (p. 305)

Yathrib destino final de la hégira de Mahoma y hogar de la primera comunidad de musulmanes; posteriormente rebautizada como Medina; ubicada en el noroeste de la actual Arabia Saudita

Yorktown, Virginia location where the British army surrendered in the American Revolution (p. 562)

Yorktown, Virginia lugar donde el ejército británico se rindió en la Revolución Americana

Yuan dynasty Chinese dynasty ruled by the Mongols from 1279 to 1368; best known ruler was Kublai Khan (p. 378)

dinastía Yuan dinastía china gobernada por los mongoles desde 1279 a 1368; su gobernante más conocido fue Kublai Khan

Z

Zen the practice of meditation; a school of Buddhism in Japan (p. 394)

zen práctica de meditación; escuela del budismo en Japón

ziggurat in ancient Mesopotamia, a large, stepped platform thought to have been topped by a temple dedicated to a city's chief god or goddess (p. 32)

zigurat templo piramidal de la antigua Mesopotamia dedicado al dios o diosa principal de una ciudad

INDEX

Italicized letters after page numbers refer to the following: *c* = chart; *g* = graph; *m* = map; *p* = picture; *q* = primary source.

Aachen   **archipelago**

INDEX

INDEX

INDEX

INDEX

INDEX

Staff Credits

The people who make up the **World History © 07** team—representing design services, editorial, editorial services, educational technology, marketing, market research, photo research and art development, production services, publishing processes, and rights & permissions—are listed below. Bold type denotes core team members.

Marla Abramson, Leann Davis Alspaugh, Stephanie Bradley, **Peter Brooks,** Kerry Lyn Buckley, Kerry Cashman, Todd Christy, Lori-Anne Cohen, Laura Edgerton Riser, Tom Ferreira, Lara Fox, Ellen Welch Granter, **Diane Grossman, Mary Ann Gundersen,** Mary Hanisco, Salena Hastings, Lance Hatch, Katharine Ingram, Tim Jones, Judie Jozokos, Lynne Kalkanajian, Courtney Lane, Ruth Lopriore, **Grace Massey, Constance J. McCarty,** Mark O'Malley, **Deborah Nicholls,** Jen Paley, Jonathan Penyack, **Gabriela Perez-Fiato,** Judi Pinkham, Marcy Rose, Rashid Ross, Robyn Salbo, **Colleen Searson,** Greg Slook, Laurel Smith, **Lisa Smith-Ruvalcaba,** Kara Stokes, **Sarah Yezzi**

Additional Credits

Paul Astwood, Gaylord Brynolfson, Sandra M. Graff, Lynette Haggard, John Judge, Kevin Keane, Beth Kun, Susan Nimmo, Kim Schmidt, Jan Shapiro, Ted Smykal, Erin Sunderland, Paula Wehde

Vendor

Pronk & Associates Inc.

Maps

XNR Productions, Inc.: **SH25, SH27, SH28, SH29,** 10, 18, 31, 37, 40–41, 45, 47, 63, 69, 74–75, 81, 85, 93, 103, 105, 119, 125, 127, 138, 151, 156, 164, 169, 174, 178–179, 181, 187, 189, 196, 202, 206, 210–211, 215, 217, 222, 226, 232, 248, 257, 261, 271, 275, 286, 292, 295, 298, 307, 315, 325, 332, 341, 342, 345, 349, 355, 380, 384, 388, 398, 406–407, 413, 432, 443, 447, 454, 462–463, 475, 485, 489, 496–497, 498, 505, 526, 532, 536, 540–541, 554, 558, 565, 595, 599, 613, 640, 647, 649, 665, 668–669, 670, 671, 672, 673, 674, 675, 676, 677, 678, 679, 686–687, 690–691

Illustrations

Kerry Cashman **SH13, SH26, SH39,** 6–7, 10, 12, 21, 24–25, 34, 39, 42, 47, 49, 52, 54, 58, 62–63, 77, 79, 87, 95, 97, 99, 104–105, 127, 132–133, 140–141, 143, 144–145, 163, 172, 174–175, 180, 180–181, 192, 206–207, 227, 232, 234, 238–239, 247, 259, 264, 272, 274–275, 276–277, 284, 295, 298–299, 307, 321, 323, 334–335, 349, 351, 354–355, 358–359, 362–363, 370, 373, 378–379, 380, 390, 393, 396, 402–403, 414–415, 420–421, 430–431, 436, 437, 440–441, 448–449, 462–463, 466–467, 474–475, 480, 488–489, 496–497, 498–499, 506, 509, 513, 518–519, 534, 536–537, 552, 558, 562, 564–565, 566–567, 574, 581, 588–589, 602–603, 614, 624, 628–629, 640–641, 649, 652–653, 666–667, 680–681, 681, 682–683, 692–693, 694–695, 697, 698–699; Ellen Welch Granter **SH2, SH3, SH4, SH9, SH10, SH12, SH13, SH15, SH16, SH17, SH21, SH30, SH41;** Kevin Jones Associates 12, 14, 21, 33, 39, 49, 52, 179, 204, 220–221, 582, **614, 635;** Jen Paley **SH5, SH20, SH23, SH37,** 4, 5, 8, 11, 17, 20, 22, 24, 30, 33, 36, 44, 49, 50, 54, 57, 59, 62, 68, 76, 84, 92, 101, 108, 114, 118, 119, 124, 130, 137, 144, 150, 155, 159, 161, 166, 171, 173, 175, 180, 186, 188, 195, 201, 202, 206, 214, 216, 219, 225, 231, 238, 244, 246, 247, 251, 255, 262, 269, 271, 276, 282, 289, 294, 296, 298, 304, 306, 307, 310, 311, 317, 322, 324, 326, 329, 334, 340, 346, 352, 357, 362, 368, 376, 383, 387, 397, 402, 410, 418, 423, 426, 428, 434, 440, 446, 452, 457, 461, 466, 472, 477, 480, 482, 487, 491, 493, 496, 497, 498, 504, 506, 510, 516, 522, 525, 530, 534, 544, 550, 554, 555, 557, 563, 566, 569, 572, 578, 585, 592, 602, 608, 609, 612, 616, 617, 622, 628, 634, 637, 638, 642, 645, 652, 682, 684, 685, 688, 689, 696, 697, 700, 701; Ted Smykal **SH4, SH6, SH7, SH8, SH9, SH10, SH11, SH14, SH15, SH16, SH17, SH18, SH19, SH21,** 33, 493, 554

Photos

Cover and Title Page

Copyright © 2005 by Kimbell Art Museum, Fort Worth, TX

Front End-Paper

EP: B, Corbis; T, Corbis; TM, V&A Museum/Art Resource; M, Boyd Norton/Evergreen Photo Alliance; BM, Royalty-Free/Corbis.

Table of Contents

v, Kenneth Garrett/National Geographic Image Collection; **vi,** T, Alan Hills and Barbara Winter (c) The British Museum; B, ACE STOCK LIMITED/Alamy; **vii,** Alison Wright/The Image Works; **viii–ix,** Musee de la Tapisserie, Bayeux, France/Bridgeman Art Library; **ix,** Giraudon/Art Resource, NY; **x,** T, Victoria & Albert Museum, London/Art Resource, NY; B, Victoria & Albert Museum, London/Art Resource, NY; **xi,** R, akg-images; B, Science Museum/SSPL; **xii,** Mary Evans Picture Library; **xiii,** Corbis; **xiv,** Kapoor Baldev/Sygma/Corbis; **xv,** Gordon Wiltsie; **xvi,** L, © Wanda Beaver; R, © Photos by Eric L. Johnson/Courtesy of the Museum of World War II, Natick MA; **xvii,** Chris Howes/Wild Places Photography/Alamy **xix,** The Art Archive/British Museum; **xxi,** Robertstock; **xxiv,** Bildarchiv Preussischer Kulturbesitz/Art Resource, NY; **xxvi,** Library of Congress; **xx,** R, akg-images; L, Corbis; **xvi,** Background, Time Life Pictures/Getty Images; **xxii,** British Museum/HIP/The Image Works; **xxiii,** L, Panorama Stock; R, Harvard-Yenching Library, Harvard University

Frontmatter

xxix, Time Life Pictures/Getty Images

Skills Handbook

SH1, © Jose Luis Pelaez, Inc.;/CORBIS; **2SH,** © IT Stock Free/AGE Fotostock; **SH3,** © Ed Bock/CORBIS; **6SH,** © Bananastock/PictureQuest; **13SH,** Public Record Office/HIP/The Image Works; **SH22,** Arthur Tilley/Getty Images; **24SH,** © Roger Wood/CORBIS; **SH31,** Keystone/Getty Images; **32SH,** North Wind Picture Archives; **SH33,** © Arcadio/Cartoonists & Writers Syndicate; **SH35,** The Science Museum/Science & Society Picture Library; **38SH,** Bettman/CORBIS; The Granger Collection, New York; **40SH,** © Charles Gupton/CORBIS

Chapter One

2–3, Time Life Pictures/Getty Images; **3,** T, Corbis; M, Michael Holford; B, Reunion des Musees Nationaux/Art Resource; **4,** L, Kenneth Garrett/National Geographic Image Collection; R, Gallo Images/Corbis; **5,** The Granger Collection; **6–7,** Kenneth Garrett/National Geographic Image Collection; **7,** TL, Peabody Museum, Harvard University; BL, Michael P. Fogden/Bruce Coleman Inc.; R, Roger M. Richards; **8,** Robert F. Sisson/National Geographic; **9,** Institute of Human Origins; **10,** Stone/Getty Images, Inc.; **11,** Michael Holford; **12,** TL, Dorling Kindersley; M, Peter Bostrom/Lithic Casting Lab; R, Topham/The Image Works; BL, Dorling Kindersley; Background, Gregg Anderson; **13,** Reunion des Musees Nationaux/Art Resource; **16,** TR, Sisse Brimberg/National Geographic Society; L, J. M. Labat/Photo Researchers; MR, © Photo RMN - © Loïc Hamon/Art Resource; BM, E.R. Degginer/Color-Pic; BR, Dorling Kindersley; BL, Grant Heilman Photography; **17,** Reunion des Musees Nationaux/Art Resource, NY; **21,** B, © Juan Silva/Getty Images; T, Robert Cortwright/Bridge Ink; **23,** Alinari/Art Resource, NY; **24,** Gallo Images/Corbis, © Peter Bostrom; **25,** L, Michael Holford; R, Corbis; **26,** T, © Rothco Cartoons; B, Time Life Pictures/Getty Images; **27,** © Peter Brown

Chapter Two

28–29, Background, © Corbis. All Rights Reserved; **29,** T, The Granger Collection, New York; D, Staatliche Sammlung Ägyptischer Kunst Munich/Dagli Orti/The Art Archive; M, © The Trustees of The British Museum; **30,** T, Bettman/Corbis; B, © The Trustees of The British Museum; **32,** Paul Holzer/Dorling Kindersley; **33,** TR, Réunion des Musées Nationaux/Art Resource, NY; TL, Réunion des Musées Nationaux/Art Resource, NY; M, The Bridgeman Art Library International Ltd; B, © Robert Frerck/Odyssey Productions, Inc.; **34,** T, © Roger Ressmeyer/CORBIS; B, © P-JS/GRANT HEILMAN PHOTOGRAPHY, INC.; **35,** T, Ronald Sheridan @ Ancient Art & Architecture Collection Ltd; B, Courtesy of Thom Kapheim and Bolchazy-Carducci Publishers; **36,** T, Louvre/Reunion des Musees Nationaux; Background, The Art Archive/Musée du Louvre Paris/Dagli Orti; **37,** Erich Lessing/Art Resource, NY; **38,** © Topham/The Image Works; **39,** TR, CM Dixon/HIP/The Image Works; BL, Erich Lessing /Art Resource, NY ; BR, Erich Lessing /Art Resource, NY; **42,** BR, © Michael Holford Photographs; TR, The Granger Collection, New York; M, The British Museum/Dorling Kindersley; BL, Alan Hills and Barbara Winter (c) The British Museum; TL, Ian O'Leary/Dorling Kindersley; **43,** Ronald Sheridan/Ancient Art & Architecture Collection Ltd; **44,** Werner Forman/Art Resource, NY; **45,** © Corbis; All rights reserved; **47,** Andrea Jemolo/AKG Images; **48,** Dagli Orti/Egyptian Museum Cairo/Picture Desk, Inc./Kobal Collection; **49,** The Granger Collection, New York; **50,** L, Reunion des Musees Nationaux; Alistair Duncan/Dorling Kindersley Media Library; **51,** © The British Museum/HIP; **52,** TL, Art Resource/Musee du Louvre; BL, Library of Congress; Inset, ML, Peter Hayman/The British Museum/Dorling Kindersley; Inset, R, Peter Hayman/The British Museum/Dorling Kindersley; Inset, L, Peter Hayman/The British Museum/Dorling Kindersley; Inset, MR, Peter Hayman/The British Museum/Dorling Kindersley; Background, Randy Faris/Corbis; T, The Art Archive/Egyptian Museum Cairo/Dagli Orti; **53,** © Roger Wood/CORBIS; **54,** L, Werner Forman/AKG Images; M, © Michael Holford; R, The Image Works; **55,** T, The Art Archive/Dagli Orti; Kenneth Garrett/National Geographic Image Collection; **56,** TL, Archivo

Iconografico, S.A/Corbis; TR, Staatliche Sammlung Ägyptischer Kunst Munich/Dagli Orti/The Art Archive; B, Giraudon/Art Resource; **57,** Moses with the Tablets of the Law (mural), English School, (20th century)/West London Synagogue, London, UK/Bridgeman Art Library; **58,** Inset, R, The Granger Collection, New York; Inset, L, Photo, The Israel Museum, Jerusalem; Background, The Granger Collection, New York; L, Nathan Benn/Corbis; R, Richard T. Nowitz/Corbis; **61,** T, Copyright of the Biblioteca Palatina, Parma; Image taken from the facsimile of the Parma Psalter, Facsimile Editions, London; B, Peter Hvizdak/The Image Works; **62,** Michael S. Yamashita/Corbis; **63,** T, Reunion des Musees Nationaux; B, Asian Art & Archaeology, Inc/Corbis; **64,** © Corbis, All Rights Reserved; **65,** B, Erich Lessing/Art Resource NY; T, Zen Radovan/Land of the Bible Photo Archive

Chapter Three
66–67, Eddie Gerald; **67,** By permission of the British Library; Or;11515f.11v Qin Shi Huang; B, Kamat's Potpourri; M, The Metropolitan Museum of Art, Gift of R. H. Ellsworth Ltd;, in honor of Susan Dilon, 1987 (1987.80.1); Photograph by Bruch White; Photograph © 1994 The Metropolitan Museum of Art; **68,** TL, Scala/Art Resource, NY; R, Ancient Art & Architecture/DanitaDelimont.com; **70,** Bryn Campbell/The Observer/Getty Images; **71,** BL, Copyright J. M. Kenoyer, Courtesy Dept; of Archaeology and Museums, Govt; of Pakistan; L, The Art Archive; R, CM Dixon/HIP/The Image Works; **73,** L, Angelo Hornak/CORBIS; R, Photo by Ling Long/Imaginechina; **75,** B, V & A Images/Victoria and Albert Museum; T, Bildarchiv Preussischer Kulturbesitz/Art Resource, NY; **76,** R, Mark Downey/Lucid Images; L, Robert Maass/CORBIS; **77,** Background, Sheldan Collins/CORBIS; T, Lindsay Hebberd/CORBIS; M, Angelo Hornak/CORBIS; BR, The Metropolitan Museum of Art, Gift of R. H. Ellsworth Ltd;, in honor of Susan Dilon, 1987 (1987.80.1); Photograph by Bruch White; Photograph © 1994 The Metropolitan Museum of Art; **79,** BL, Alan King/Alamy; BR, Chris Lisle/Alamy; T, The Art Archive/Jobon Rendaiji Temple Kyoto/Laurie Platt Winfrey; **81,** © Tibor Hirsch/Photo Researchers, Inc.; **82,** Profimedia;CZ s.r.o./Alamy; **83,** TL, IML Image Group Ltd/Alamy; B, The National Trust Photolibrary/Alamy; TR, The Art Archive/British Library; **84,** Kamat's Potpourri; **87,** Background, © Karen Kasmauski/Corbis; **88,** H. Hansum/Bucknell University; TL, akg-images/Jean-Louis Nou; B, Lindsay Hebberd/CORBIS; TM, The Trustees of

The British Museum; TR, Dinodia/Omni-Photo Communications; **90,** AP/Wide World Photo; **91,** T, Hulton Archive/Getty Images; B, SUDHARAK OLWE/DINODIA PHOTO LIBRARY; Inset, Borromeo/Art Resource, NY; **92,** The Granger Collection, New York; **94,** B, © Asian Art & Archaeology, Inc.;/CORBIS; T, © Asian Art & Archaeology, Inc.;/CORBIS; **95,** Giraudon/Art Resource, NY; **97,** The Granger Collection, New York; **98,** Réunion des Musées Nationaux/Art Resource, NY; **99,** BL, ANT PHOTO LIBRARY/NHPA; Background, TL, BR, Copyright The British Museum; TM, The Trustees of The British Museum; TR, Museum of Fine Arts, Boston, Massachusetts, USA/Bridgeman Art Library International; BM, Maryann Frazier/Photo Researchers Inc.; **100,** T, By permission of the British Library; Or.8212/480–484 paper fragments from Loulan; B, Ashmolean Museum, University of Oxford, UK/Bridgeman Art Library; **101,** L, By permission of the British Library; Or.11515f.11v Qin Shi Huang; R, By permission of the British Library; **102,** The Art Archive/Bibliothèque Nationale Paris; **103,** Free Agents Limited/CORBIS; **104,** Inset, Bildarchiv Preussischer Kulturbesitz/Art Resource, NY; **104–105,** © ArtWolfe/Getty Images; **105,** Inset, The Minneapolis Institute of Arts, The John R; Van Derlip Trust Fund; **106,** TEK Image/Photo Researchers, Inc.; **107,** V & A Images, The Victoria & Albert Museum; **108,** L, © Charles & Josette Lenars/CORBIS; R, Werner Forman/Art Resource, NY; **109,** Bettmann/CORBIS; **110,** Photri Microstock; **111,** Dorling Kindersley/Ashmolean Museum, Oxford

Chapter Four
112–113, © Erich Lessing/Art Resource; **112–113,** akg-images/Erich Lessing; **113,** B, © Alinari Archives/CORBIS; T, © Alinari/Art Resource; M, Copyright of Christie's Images Inc., 2004; **114,** Scala/Art Resource, NY; **115,** T, Nimatallah/Art Resource, NY; B, Pearson Education US ELT; **116,** Erich Lessing/Art Resource, NY; **117,** Kevin Fleming/CORBIS; **118,** L, akg-images; R, Copyright of Christie's Images Inc., 2004; **119,** Elio Ciol/CORBIS; **120,** BL, Réunion des Musées Nationaux/Art Resource, NY; **121,** TR, ACE STOCK LIMITED/Alamy; **122,** Bildarchiv Preussischer Kulturbesitz/Art Resource, NY; **123,** Steve Vidler/SuperStock; **124,** Louvre, Paris, France, Lauros/Giraudon/Bridgeman Art Library; **125,** Scala/Art Resource, NY; **127,** Background, Ancient Art and Architecture Collection Ltd;/Bridgeman Art Library; M, © 2004 AAAC/Topham/The Image Works; L, © Gianni Dagli Orti/CORBIS; TR, akg-images/John Hios; MR, akg-

images/John Hios; **128,** Bildarchiv Preussischer Kulturbesitz/Art Resource, NY; **129,** © The British Museum/Heritage-Images; **130,** Alinari/Art Resource, NY; **131,** The Metropolitan Museum of Art, Catharine Lorillard Wolfe Collection, Wolfe Fund, 1931 (31.45); Photograph © 1995 The Metropolitan Museum of Art; **132,** BL, SuperStock Inc.;/SuperStock; TL, Erich Lessing/Art Resource, NY; R, The Metropolitan Museum of Art, Fletcher Fund, 1931 (31.11.10); Photograph © 1999 The Metropolitan Museum of Art; **132–33,** © Neil Setchfield/Lonely Planet Images; **133,** R, © Carl & Ann Purcell/Corbis; L, © Dorling Kindersley; **134,** T, Erich Lessing/Art Resource, NY; BL, © Ruggero Vanni/CORBIS; BR, © Archivo Iconografico, S.A./CORBIS; **135,** Nimatallah/Art Resource, NY; **136,** © Alinari/Art Resource, **137,** Robert Frerck, Odyssey Productions, Chicago; **138,** T, Archeological Museum, Istanbul, Turkey/Hirmer Fotoarchiv, Munich Germany; **139,** Bildarchiv Preussischer Kulturbesitz/Art Resource, NY; **140,** Inset, The Granger Collection, New York; Background, © Archivo Iconografico, S.A./CORBIS; **141,** L, The Art Archive/National Archaeological Museum Athens/Dagli Orti; M, SSPL/The Image Works; R, Time Life Pictures/Getty Images; **142,** Comstock/SuperStock; **143,** TL, © Egypt Exploration Society; TR, © Thierry Orban/CORBIS SYGMA; B, © Hubert Stadler/CORBIS; **144,** Louvre/Reunion des Musees Nationaux; **145,** R, Michael Ventura; L, Archeological Museum, Istanbul, Turkey/Hirmer Fotoarchiv, Munich Germany; **146,** Elio Ciol/CORBIS; **147,** Scala/Art Resource, NY

Chapter Five
148–149, The Art Archive/Villa of the Mysteries Pompeii/Dagli Orti (A); **149,** T, Bildarchiv Preussischer Kulturbesitz/Art Resource, NY; M, Archivo Iconografico, S.A./CORBIS; B, The Art Archive/Archaeological Museum Spalato/Dagli Orti; **150,** The Art Archive/Musée du Louvre Paris/Dagli Orti; **151,** The Art Archive/Galleria di Storia ed Arte Udine/Dagli Orti; **154,** Réunion des Musées Nationaux/Art Resource, NY; **155,** L, The Art Archive/Archaeological Museum Venice/Dagli Orti (A); R, Mimmo Jodice/CORBIS; **156,** © Gianni Dagli Orti/CORBIS; **157,** Background, The Trustees of British Museum; Inset, Scala/Art Resource, NY; **158,** The Art Archive/Dagli Orti; **160,** Archivo Iconografico, S.A./CORBIS; **161,** Mary Evans Picture Library; **162,** Topham/The Image Works; **163,** BR, Topham/The Image Works; M, Erich Lessing/Art Resource, NY; TR, The Brigdeman Art Library; Inset,B, Erich Lessing/Art Resource, NY; BL, The Art

Archive/Dagli Orti; **164,** Danilo Donadoni/Bruce Coleman Inc.; **166,** L, Scala/Art Resource, NY; R, Erich Lessing/Art Resource, NY; **167,** B, Nathan Benn/CORBIS; T, The Brigeman Art Library; **168,** Mary Evans Picture Library; **170,** Archivo Iconografico, S.A./CORBIS; **172,** The British Library/HIP/The Image Works; **173,** L, The Granger Collection, New York; R, Kunstmuseum, Bern, Switzerland/Bridgeman Art Library; **174,** Scala/Art Resource, NY; **174–175,** © Historical Picture Archive/CORBIS; **175,** L, The Art Archive/Pinacoteca Comunale Fermo Ascoli Piceno/Dagli Orti; R, The Art Archive/Archaeological Museum Spalato/Dagli Orti (A); **176,** © Bryan Reinhart/Masterfile; **179,** Gift of Stephen V. Grancsay, 1942; (42.50.1) Photograph 1982 The Metropolitan Museum of Art; **180,** R, © Gianni Dagli Orti/CORBIS; L, Kamat's Potpourri; **181,** T, Scala/Art Resource, NY; B, Photograph by Jorge Pérez de Lara; **182,** The Art Archive/Villa of the Mysteries Pompeii/Dagli Orti; **183,** Bildarchiv Preussischer Kulturbesitz/Art Resource, NY

Chapter Six
184–185, Charles & Josette Lenars/CORBIS; **185,** MR, Photograph by Jorge Pérez de Lara; T, Werner Forman/Topham/The Image Works; M, The Art Archive/Archaeological Museum Lima/Mireille Vautier; B, Canadian Museum of Civilization, artifact no; IV-C-869, image no; D2003-14624; **186,** L, John Bigelow Taylor/Art Resource, NY; R, LIMA-PERU; **187,** The Art Archive/Archaeological Museum Lima/Mireille Vautier; **188,** Danny Lehman/CORBIS; **189,** T, Richard A. Cooke/CORBIS; B, Werner Forman/Topham/The Image Works; **190,;** **191,** B, Danny Lehman/CORBIS; TL, akg-images/Francois Guénet; BR, Macduff Everton/CORBIS; TR, Werner Forman/Topham/The Image Works; M, Peter Arnold, Inc.;/Alamy; ML, Paul Almasy/CORBIS; **192,** B, © Dorling Kindersley; T, The Granger Collection, NY; **193,** R, Prisma/ANCIENT ART & ARCHITECTURE COLLECTION LTD; L, The Art Archive/Archaeological Museum Teotihuacan Mexico/Dagli Orti; **195,** L, The Art Archive/Archaeological Museum Lima/Dagli Orti; R, Werner Forman/Topham/The Image Works; **196,** R, Jacob Halaska/Index Stock Imagery; L, The Art Archive/Archaeological Museum Lima/Dagli Orti; **197,** The Granger Collection, New York; **198,** Alison Wright/The Image Works; **200,** T, Bildarchiv Preussischer Kulturbesitz/Art Resource, NY; B, The Art Archive/British Library; **201,;** **202,** TR, Richard A. Cooke/CORBIS; BR, Canadian Museum of Civilization, artifact no; III-I-553, image no; S97-17382; L, The Granger Collection,

New York; **203,** George H. Huey/COR-BIS; **204,** Canadian Museum of Civilization, artifact no; IV-C-869, image no. D2003-14624; **206,** L, The Art Archive/Museum of Mankind London/Eileen Tweedy; R, © Royalty-Free/Corbis; **207,** © Gianni Dagli Orti/CORBIS; **208,** T, Bodleian Library, University of Oxford; B, Charles & Josette Lenars/CORBIS, **209,** The Ann Ronan Picture Library/Heritage-Images

Chapter Seven
212–213, Bodleian Library; **213,** T, British Library; M, Snark/Art Resource, NY; B, Scala/Art Resource; **214,** L, Bettmann/Corbis; R, Reunion des Musee Nationaux/Art Resource/NY; **216,** Reunion des Musee Nationaux/Art Resource/NY; **218,** The British Library/Topham-HIP/The Image Works; **219,** Archivo Iconografico, S.A./CORBIS; **222,** Topham/The Image Works; **223,** T, North Wind Picture Archive; B, © The British Library/HIP/The Image Works; **224,** T, © The British Library/HIP/The Image Works; B, Dorling Kindersley; **225,** L, © Archivo Iconografico, S.A./CORBIS; R, HIP/Art Resource, NY; **227,** R, Kunsthistorisches Museum, Vienna, Austria/www;bridgeman;co;uk; M, Erich Lessing/Art Resource, NY; L, Lambeth Palace Library, London, UK/www;bridgeman;co;uk; **228,** Scala/Art Resource, NY; **229,** Louvre, Paris, France/www;bridgeman;co;uk; **230,** Musee du judaisme/RMN/Art Resource, NY; **231,** L, British Library/The Art Archive; R, British Library/The Art Archive; **232,** R, Michael Holford; L, Erich Lessing/Art Resource; **233,** The Pierpont Morgan Library, New York, NY,/Art Resource; **234,** L, Biblioteque Royale Belgium; R, Bridgeman Art Library; **235,** Scala/Art Resource; Scala/Art Resource; Scala/Art Resource; PRS Archive; **237,** T, The British Library/The Image Works; M, Superstock; B, The British Library/The Image Works; **239,** B, Michael Holford; T, AP/Wide World Photos; **240,** Bodleian Library; **241,** R, D;Y;/Art Resource; L, © Ali Meyer/CORBIS

Chapter Eight
242, TR, ENA/Popperfoto/Robertstock/Retrofile; **242–243,** © Gianni Dagli Orti/CORBIS; **243,** T, The Art Archive/Musée Municipal Vaucouleurs/Dagli Orti; BR, Inset, Dorling Kindersley Media Library/York Archaeological Trust for Excavation and Research Ltd; M, akg-images; BR, Background, Dorling Kindersley Media Library; **244,** L, The Art Archive/Archives Nationales Paris/JFB; R, akg-images; **245,** © Franz-Marc Frei/CORBIS; **247,** The Royal Collection © 2000 Her Majesty

Queen Elizabeth II; **249,** © Corbis; All Rights Reserved; **250,** T, Dept; of the Environment, London, UK/The Bridgeman Art Library; B, The Granger Collection, New York; **251,** L, SEF/Art Resource, NY; R, Erich Lessing/Art Resource, NY; **252,** Foto Marburg/Art Resource, NY; **253,** © The British Library/HIP/The Image Works; **254,** The Art Archive/San Francesco Assisi/Dagli Orti; M, Scala/Art Resource, NY; **257,** Bibliotheque des Arts Decoratifs, Paris, France/www;bridgeman;co;uk; **258,** The Art Archive/Galleria degli Uffizi Florence/Dagli Orti; **259,** TM, © Reuters/CORBIS; TL, © David Turnley/CORBIS; BR, The Art Archive/University Library Coimbra/Dagli Orti; Background, Amos Zezmer/Omni-Photo Communications, Inc.; TR, Ellen Howdon (c) Dorling Kindersley, Courtesy of Glasgow Museum; **261,** © SAUSSIER-VAN DER STOCKT/GAMMA; **262,** L, © Corbis; All Rights Reserved; R, Background, Dorling Kindersley Media Library; TR, Inset, Dorling Kindersley Media Library/York Archaeological Trust for Excavation and Research Ltd; **263,** © The British Library/HIP/The Image Works; **264,** TR, Peter Anderson (c) Dorling Kindersley, Courtesy of Saxon Village Crafts, Battle, East Sussex; B, The Pierpont Morgan Library/Art Resource New York; M, © Araldo de Luca/CORBIS; L, © Dave G; Houser/CORBIS; **266,** B, Giraudon/Art Resource, NY; **266–267,** Musee de la Tapisserie, Bayeux, France/www;bridgeman;co;uk; **268,** Background, Dorling Kindersley; TR, Vanni/Art Resource, NY; MR, © Corbis; All Rights Reserved; Inset, Neil Lukas © Dorling Kindersley; **269,** T, © Science Museum, London/Topham-HIP/The Image Works; B, © Topham/The Image Works; M, © Science Museum, London/Topham-HIP/The Image Works; **270,** Musee Conde, Chantilly, France/www;bridgeman;co;uk; **272,** Background, Snark/Art Resource, NY; TR, Geoff Dann © Dorling Kindersley; TL, Geoff Dann © Dorling Kindersley; BR, © The Board of Trustees of the Armouries/HIP/The Image Works; **274,** B, Frank Greenaway © Dorling Kindersley; Inset, Dorling Kindersley; T, © Bettmann/CORBIS; BL, © Stock Montage/SuperStock; **275,** R, Bibliotheque Royale de Belgique, Brussels, Belgium/www;bridgeman;co;uk; L, The Granger Collection; **276,** © The Board of Trustees of the ARmouries/HIP?The Image Works; **277,** R, Reuters/CORBI; B, © Topham/The Image Works; **278,** BR, The Art Archive/Galleria degli Uffizi Florence/Dagli Orti; **279,** © Gianni Dagli Orti/CORBIS

Chapter Nine
280–281, Scala/Art Resource, NY;

281, T, N; Carter/North Wind Picture Archives; B, Kremlin Museums, Moscow, Russia/Bridgeman Art Library International; M, Werner Forman/Art Resource, NY; **282,** L, The Granger Collection, New York; R, Werner Forman/Art Resource, NY; **284,** Inset, Michele Burgess/Index Stock; Background, Robert Frerck, Odyssey Productions, Chicago; **285,** San Vitale, Ravenna, Italy/Bridgeman Art Library; **287,** Visual Arts Library (London)/Alamy; **288,** Giraudon/Art Resource, NY; **289,** L, DK Images; R, Kremlin Museums, Moscow, Russia/Bridgeman Art Library International; **290,** Museum of History of Sofia, Bulgaria/Archives Charmet/Bridgeman Art Library International; **291,** Doug Page/Index Stock; **292,** Andy Crawford © Dorling Kindersley, Courtesy of the History Museum, Moscow; **293,** Tretyakov Gallery, Moscow, Russia/Bridgeman Art Library International; **294,** L, Erich Lessing/Art Resource, NY; R, The Art Archive/Historical Museum of Republic of Crimea Simferopol/Dagli Orti (A); **295,** Bibliothèque royale de Belgique; **296,** L, Zamek Krolewski W Warszawie/From the Collection of the Royal Castle in Warsaw; R, Zamek Krolewski W Warszawie/From the Collection of the Royal Castle in Warsaw; **297,** Erich Lessing/Art Resource, NY; **298,** Scala/Art Resource, NY; **299,** T, AP Photo/Elvis Barukcic; B, akg-images; **300,** T, Scala/Art Resource, NY; B, Visual Arts Library (London)/Alamy; **301,** PRISMA/Ancient Art & Architecture Collection

Chapter Ten
302–303, © ABBAS/MAGNUM PHOTOS; **303,** T, The Trustees of the Chester Beatty Library, Dublin/Bridgeman Art Library; M, The Granger Collection, New York; B, Laurence Pordes © Dorling Kindersley, Courtesy of the British Library; **304,** R, ArkReligion.com; L, Peter Sanders Photography; **305,** Background, Kurt Stier/CORBIS; Inset, Fitzwilliam Museum, University of Cambridge, UK/Bridgeman Art Library; **307,** TR, Reuters/CORBIS; ML, Prisma ANCIENT ART & ARCHITECTURE COLLECTION LTD; MR, AP/Wide World Photo; B, Trip/Alamy; TL, Steven Rubin/The Image Works; **308,** Bibliotheque Nationale de France; **309,** TR, COPYRIGHT © THE BRIDGEMAN ART LIBRARY; BR, 2005 Richard l'Anson/Lonely Planet Images; L, Laurence Pordes © Dorling Kindersley, Courtesy of the British Library; **310,** Monasterio de El Escorial/Index/Bridgeman Art Library; **311,** Gary Cross (© Dorling Kindersley; **312,** Expuesto - Nicolas Randall/Alamy; **313,** The Granger Collection, New York; **314,** Snark/Art Resource, NY; **315,** BR, José Fuste

Raga/zefa/CORBIS; T, Roger Wood/CORBIS; BL, Photographer's Choice/Getty Images; **316,** Peter M; Wilson/CORBIS; **317,** Background, Werner Forman/Art Resource, NY; Inset, Topkapi Palace Museum, Istanbul, Turkey/Bridgeman Art Library; **318,** B, Werner Forman/TopFoto/The Image Works; T, Peter Harholdt/CORBIS; **319,** Royal Asiatic Society, London, UK/Bridgeman Art Library; **320,** Ancient Art & Architecture Collection; **321,** ML, B.N.F./CORBIS SYGMA; B, The Image Bank/Getty Images; TR, The Granger Collection, New York; MR, University Library, Istanbul, Turkey/Bridgeman Art Library; TL, © The British Museum/HIP/The Image Works; Background, By permission of the British Library; **323,** BR, Corbis; Background, Charles & Josette Lenars/CORBIS; ML, Victoria & Albert Museum, London/Art Resource, NY; TL, Archivo Iconografico, S.A./CORBIS; **324,** Time Life Pictures/Getty Images; **325,** The Art Archive/Victoria and Albert Museum London/Eileen Tweedy; **326,** R, Burstein Collection/CORBIS; L, Annie Griffiths Belt/CORBIS; **327,** The Trustees of the Chester Beatty Library, Dublin/Bridgeman Art Library; **328,** Taxi/Getty Images; **329,** R, Topkapi Palace Museum, Istanbul, Turkey, Giraudon/Bridgeman Art Library; L, The Art Archive/Moldovita Monastery Romania/Dagli Orti; **330,** Ancient Art & Architecture Collection; **331,** T, Topkapi Palace Museum, Istanbul, Turkey/Bridgeman Art Library; B, Private Collection, Archives Charmet/Bridgeman Art Library; **332,** Nat & Yanna Brandt/Photo Researchers, Inc.; **334,** Snark/Art Resource, NY; **335,** Time Life Pictures/Getty Images; **336,** The Trustees of the Chester Beatty Library, Dublin/Bridgeman Art Library; **337,** L, Private Collection/Bridgeman Art Library; R, rochaphoto/Alamy

Chapter Eleven
338–339, © Dirk Bakker; **339,** T, The Metropolitan Museum of Art, Gift of Paul and Ruth W; Tishman, 1991 (1991.435ab); Photograph © 1992 The Metropolitan Museum of Art; M, Los Angeles County Museum of Art, The Nasli M; Heeramaneck Collection, gift of Joan Palevsky; B, Hamill Gallery of African Art, Boston, MA; **340,** L, GoodShoot/CORBIS; R, Bibliotheque Nationale, Paris, France/Bridgeman Art Library; **341,** Images of Africa Photobank/Alamy; **342,** R, A van Zandbergen/Afripics.com; M, Christopher and Sally Gable © Dorling Kindersley; L, © Michele Westmorland/Corbis; **343,** B, Bildarchiv Preussischer Kulturbesitz/Art Resource, NY; T, The British Museum © Dorling Kindersley; **344,** Los Angeles County Museum of Art,

The Nasli M; Heeramaneck Collection, gift of Joan Palevsky; **345,** L, REU TERS/Kimimasa Mayama; R, Getty Images; **346,** L, Nik Wheeler/CORBIS; R, The Metropolitan Museum of Art, Gift of Paul and Ruth W; Tishman, 1991 (1991.435ab); Photograph © 1992 The Metropolitan Museum of Art; **347,** T, Werner Forman/Art Resource, NY; B, Masterfile; **348,** Photograph by Frank Khoury National Museum of African Art Smithsonian Institution; **349,** Inset, T, The Granger Collection, New York; Background, Topham/The Image Works; Inset, B, African Private Collection/Boltin Picture Library/Bridgeman Art Library; **350,** ML, Betty Press - Woodfin Camp; **351,** R, National Museum Lagos, Nigeria/Held Collection/Bridgeman Library International; M, akg-images; L, Werner Forman/CORBIS; Background, Annebicque Bernard/CORBIS SYGMA; **352,** R, The Metropolitan Museum of Art, Purchase, Elaine Rosenberg Gift and funds from various donors, 1998 (1998.37); Photograph © 2001 The Metropolitan Museum of Art; L, The Metropolitan Museum of Art, Rogers Fund, 1998 (1998.66); Photograph © 1998 The Metropolitan Museum of Art; **353,** Mike Andrews/Ancient Art & Architecture Collection; **354,** akg-images; **354–355,** Boyd Norton/Evergreen Photo Alliance; **356,** Chris Howes/Wild Places Photography/Alamy; **357,** Hans Zimmermann/DAS FOTOARCHIV; **358,** R, The British Museum; TL, Hamill Gallery of African Art, Boston, MA; M, Hamill Gallery of African Art, Boston, MA; BL, Hamill Gallery of African Art, Boston, MA; **358–359,** Background,T, Seattle Art Museum/CORBIS; Background, B, Hamill Gallery of African Art, Boston, MA; **359,** R, Glen Allison/Mira.com; BL, Hamill Gallery of African Art, Boston, MA; TL, Ellen Howdon/Dorling Kindersley © St Mungo, Glasgow Museums; **361,** Brian Seed 2005; **362,** B, Bibliotheque Nationale, Paris, France/Bridgeman Art Library; T, The British Museum © Dorling Kindersley; **363,** B, Werner Forman/Art Resource, NY; T, The Metropolitan Museum of Art, Rogers fund, 1998 (1998.66); Photograph © 1998 The Metropolitan Museum of Art; **364,** Hans Zimmermann/DAS FOTOARCHIV; **365,** The Granger Collection, New York

Chapter Twelve
366–367, AAAC/Topham/The Image Works; **367,** B, Sekai Bunka/AAA; T, © Nigel Tudor; M, Rick Browne/Photo Researchers, Inc.; **368,** The Art Archive/British Library; **369,** R, The Granger Collection, New York; Background, Panorama Stock; **370,** R, Panorama Stock; BL, Science Museum/Michael Holford; TL, Panorama Stock;

372, © Norma Joseph/Robert Harding World Imagery; **373,** T, Bildarchiv Preussischer Kulturbesitz / Art Resource, NY; Background, The Metropolitan Museum of Art, Ex. Coll.: C.C. Wang Family, Promised Gift of the Oscar L. Tang Family (L.1997.24.2) Photograph courtesy of the Metropolitan Museum of Art. Photograph ©1997 The Metropolitan Museum of Art; **374,** The Art Archive/British Library; **375,** T, © Jeremy Horner/CORBIS; B, Jack Kurtz/The Image Works; **376,** L, Victoria and Albert Museum, London, Great Britain/Art Resource, NY; R, Dorling Kindersley; **377,** The Granger Collection; New York; **378,** Background, © SuperStock; **378–379,** The Art Archive/Palazzo Farnese Caprarola/Dagli Orti; **379,** L, Bridgeman Art Library; R, National Palace Museum, Taipei, Taiwan, Republic of China; **380,** R, Panorama Stock; M, Nigel Tudor; L, Werner Forman/Art Resource, NY; **382,** ChinaStock Photo Library; **383,** Inset, Rick Browne/Photo Researchers, Inc.; Background, Rick Browne/Photo Researchers, Inc.; **385,** © Archivo Iconografico, S.A./CORBIS; **386,** B, © Alon Reininger/Contact Press Images; T, LIU JIN/AFP/Getty Images; **387,** B, © Prentice Hall; T, Erich Lessing/Art Resource, NY; **389,** The Art Archive; **390,** Musee des Beaux-Arts, Angers, France/Bridgeman Art Library; **391,** Mary Evans Picture Library; **393,** Background, RMN/Art Resource; L, V & A Museum/Art Resource; **394,** Catherine Karnow/Corbis; **396,** T, © Asian Art & Archaeology, Inc.;/CORBIS; M, British Library, London, UK/Bridgeman Art Library; B, © C; Jopp/Robert Harding World Imagery; **397,** © Eric Trachtenberg; **399,** © Massimo Listri/CORBIS; **400,** Background, Digital Vision/Getty Images; Inset, Frank Carter/Lonely Planet Images; **402,** © Ali Meyer/CORBIS; **403,** L, Victoria and Albert Museum, London, Great Britain/Art Resource, NY; R, The Art Archive; **404,** R, akg-images; The Granger Collection, New York; **405,** Peter Wilson © Dorling Kindersley

Chapter Thirteen
408–409, © Vittoriano Rastelli/CORBIS; **409,** T, Arte & Immagini srl/Corbis; M, The Pierpont Morgan Library/Art Resource, NY; B, HIP/Art Resource, NY; **410,** L, Scala/Art Resource, NY; R, Ashley Simmons/Alamy Images; **411,** The Bridgeman Art Library/Getty Images; **412,** 4 week minimum turnaround time; **414,** M, Dorling Kindersley; R, Private Collection/Bridgeman Art Library; L, Scala/Art Resource, NY; **414–415,** The Image Bank/Getty Images; **415,** R, Mary Evans Picture Library; L, Dorling Kindersley; **416,** Mary Evans Picture Library; **417,**

Archivo Iconografico, S;A/Corbis; **418,** L, Mary Evans Picture Library; R, The Pierpont Morgan Library/Art Resource, NY; **419,** Archivo Iconografico, S.A./Corbis; **420,** Scala/Art Resource, NY; **421,** TR, Dorling Kindersley; M, Erich Lessing/Art Resource, NY; L, Erich Lessing/Art Resource, NY; BR, Susannah Price/Dorling Kindersley; **422,** T, Mary Evans Picture Library; B, Andrea Pistolesi/Getty Images, Inc.; M, Dorling Kindersley; R, Dorling Kindersley; **423,** L, AAAC/Topham/The Image Works; R, Dorling Kindersley; **424,** Bildarchiv Preussischer Kulturbesitz/Art Resource, NY; **425,** © The Corcoran Gallery of Art/CORBIS; **427,** Erich Lessing/Art Resource, NY; **428,** L, National Trust Photographic Library/Derrick E; Witty/The Image Works; R, HIP/Art Resource, NY; **429,** Fine Art Photographic Library/Corbis; **430,** Inset, The Granger Collection; **430–431,** Background, © Michael Busselle/CORBIS; **431,** L, Mary Evans Picture Library; R, The Granger Collection; **433,** Erich Lessing/Art Resource, NY; **434,** L, The Granger Collection, New York; R, Gustavo Tomsich/Corbis; **435,** L, The Granger Collection; R, © Reuters/CORBIS; **436,** R, Maximilian Stock Ltd;/Photo Researchers, Inc.; TL, Kevin Fleming/Corbis; BL, Royalty-Free/Corbis; **437,** R, AAAC/Topham/The Image Works; L, Glasgow University Library, Scotland/Bridgeman Art Library; **439,** TR, Victoria & Albert Museum, London/Art Resource, NY; MR, SciMAT/Photo Researchers, Inc.; BR, Mary Evans Picture Library/Photo Researchers, Inc.; BL, Sam Forencich/NBAE via Getty Images; TL, Victoria & Albert Museum, London/Art Resource, NY; **440,** Scala/Art Resource, NY; **441,** T, FRANK & EARNEST, © Thaves/Dist; by Newspaper Enterprise Association, Inc.; The Pierpont Morgan Library/Art Resource, NY; The Granger Collection; **442,** T, Scala/Art Resource, NY; B, © Vittoriano Rastelli/CORBIS

Chapter Fourteen
444–445, Instituto Portugues de Museus; **445,** T, V & A Museum/Art Resource; B, © Christie's Images/CORBIS; **446,** R, Bridgeman Art Library; L, Ann Ronan Picture Library/The Image Works; **448,** L, The Granger Collection; R, National Maritime Museum; **448–449,** Museu de Marinha; The Granger Collection; **449,** TL, Antiquarian Images; TR, Michael Holford; M, HIP/Scala/Art Resource; **450,** Preussischer Kulturbesitz/Art Resource, NY; **452,** L, Topham/The Image Works; R, Museum of African Art/Smithsonian Institution; **453,** Michael Holford; **455,** Werner Forman/Art Resource; **456,** B, The Art Archive/Museo de Arte Antiga Lisgon/Dagli Orti; T, Metropolitan Museum of Art, Gift of Ernest Anspach, 1999 (199.295.4) Photograph

(c) 2002 Metropolitan Museum of Art; **457,** R, Rainer Daehnhardt/Portuguese Academy of Antique Arms; British Library; **458,** R, Maritime Museum of Rotterdam; L, Royal Collection (c) 2005, Her Majesty Queen Elizabeth II; **459,** Rijksmuseum Amsterdam; **460,** British Library; **461,** L, The Ricci Institute, University of San Francisco; R, Vatican Library; **462,** The British Museum/The Image Works; **463,** M, © Christie's Images/CORBIS; L, The Granger Collection; R, British Museum/HIP/The Image Works; **464,** Cleveland Museum of Art; **465,** Michael Holford; **466,** L, The British Museum/The Image Works; R, HIP/Scala/Art Resource; **467,** Cleveland Museum of Art; **468,** T, The Granger Collection; B, Instituto Portugues de Museus; **469,** T, Giraudon/Art Resource; B, Granger Collection

Chapter Fifteen
470–471, Schalkwijk/Art Resource, NY; **471,** T, Erich Lessing/Art Resource, NY; Musee Departemental des Antiquites, Rouen, France/Bridgeman Art Library; B, © Canadian Museum of Civilization, catalogue no; D-1511, image no; S90-1861; **472,** Biblioteca Medicea-Laurenziana/Florence Bridgeman Art Library; **473,** T, The Granger Collection; B, Biblioteque Nationale de France; **474,** Inset, akg-images; **474–475,** Background, Corbis; **475,** Frank Nowikowski; **476,** Ira Block; **477,** Hispanic Society of New York; **478,** Divisao de Documentacao Fotografica-Instituto Portugues De Museus; **479,** Dan Lehmann/Corbis; **480,** Joseph Martin/AKG Images; **481,** Musee Departemental des Antiquites, Rouen, France/Bridgeman Art Library; **482,** R, © Lee Snider/Photo Images/CORBIS; L, (c) Canadian Museum of Civilization, catalogue # 989.56.1, photo Merle Toole, #S90-640; **483,** Corbis; **484,** Michael Schwarz/Image Works; **485,** TR, National Museum of Natural History/Smithsonian Institution; BL, Art Resource; TL, Victoria & Albert Museum, London/Art Resource, NY; BR, New York Historical Society; **486,** Gunter Marx; **487,** L, Royal Albert Museum/Bridgeman Art Library; R, Chicago Historical Society; **488,** B, Ariadne Van Zandbergen/Lonely Planet Images; T, Corbis; **488–489,** Background, Corbis; © Royalty-Free/Corbis; **489,** T, British Library; B, British Library; **490,** Bettmann/Corbis; **491,** R, The Art Archive; L, (c) Canadian Museum of Civilization, catalogue no; D-1511, image no; S90-1861; **492,** R, Francis C; Mayer/Corbis; L, Bancroft Library/UC-Berkeley; **493,** Background, © Darrell Gulin/CORBIS; R, RF/Corbis; M, Corbis, **494,** R, Robert Harding Image Library; L, Journal-Courier/Steve Warmowski/The

Image Works; **495,** Erich Lessing/Art Resource; **496,** M, Julie Habel/Corbis; BL, © Ed Quinn/CORBIS; R, © PoodlesRock/CORBIS; TL, © Carlos Goldin/CORBIS; **497,** BL, Kim Blaxland/Getty Images; MR, Ira Block; TL, Corbis; BR, Ron Giling/Peter Arnold Inc.; TR, © Liba Taylor/CORBIS; **498,** © Steve Vidler/eStock Photo; **499,** TR, Levine/Roberts, BR, Lisa Knouse Braiman/Business Week; L, Stock Montage; **500,** R, National Gallery of Art; L, Schalkwijk/Art Resource, NY; **501,** Mary Evans Picture Library

Chapter Sixteen
502–503, Erich Lessing/Art Resource, NY; **503,** B, Museums On Line; M, Dorling Kindersley; T, Erich Lessing/Art Resource; **504,** L, Bettmann/Corbis; Background, L, Bettmann/Corbis; R, Archivo Iconographica, S.A./Corbis; **506,** L, Bridgeman Art Library; MR, British Library/Bridgeman Art Library; Background, The National Maritime Museum; TR, Archivo Iconographica, S.A./Corbis; TL, Archivo Iconographica, S.A./Corbis; **507,** Bridgeman Art Library; **508,** Bridgeman Art Library; **509,** T, Art Resource; B, Mary Evans Picture Library; **510,** L, Versailles, châteaus de Versailles et de Trianon/RMN/Art Resource; R, Bata Shoe Museum; **511,** © National Gallery Collection; By kind permission of the Trustees of the National Gallery, London/CORBIS; **513,** Background, T, Superstock; Background, B, RMN/Art Resource; TL, Art Resource; BR, Topham/The Image Works; MR, Victoria & Albert Museum/Art Resource; **515,** TR, Historical Picture Archive/Corbis; TL, Prisma/Ancient Art and Architecture Collection; B, Bettmann/Corbis; **516,** Art Resource; **517,** Archivo Iconographico S.A./Corbis; **518,** TR, The Granger Collection; BR, British Museum/HIP/The Image Works; L, Fine Art Photographic Library/Corbis; **519,** TR, Bridgeman Art Library; L, Mary Evans Picture Library; B, The Granger Collection; **520,** Background, HIP/The Image Works; Inset, Dorling Kindersley; **521,** B, The Granger Collection; T, Atwater Kent Museum/Bridgeman Art Library; **524,** B, The Parliamentary Archives; T, Corbis; **525,** L, Erich Lessing/Art Resource; R, Royal Armouries; **528,** Archivo Iconographica, S.A./Corbis; **529,** Mary Evans Picture Library; **530,** R, Corbis; L, Corbis; **531,** The Granger Collection; **533,** Corbis; **534,** BL, The Granger Collection; Inset, C, Museums On Line; Background, B, Sovfoto; TR, akg-images; **536,** R, Mary Evans Picture Library; L, Royal Armouries; **537,** T, The Granger Collection; B, Bata Shoe Museum; **538,** Archivo Iconographica, S.A./Corbis; **539,** Bridgeman Art Library

Chapter Seventeen
542–543, Réunion des Musées Nationaux/Art Resource, NY; **543,** T, Réunion des Musées Nationaux/Art Resource, NY; M, Bridgeman Art Library; B, The Granger Collection; **544,** Background, © Archivo Iconografico, S.A./Corbis; Inset, Dorling Kindersley; **545,** The Granger Collection; **546,** R, Château de Versailles, France, Lauros/Giraudon/Bridgeman Art Library; L, Réunion des Musées Nationaux/Art Resource, NY; **547,** L, The Granger Collection; R, Royalty-Free/Corbis; **548,** © Archivo Iconografico, S.A./Corbis; **549,** T, The Granger Collection; B, © Archivo Iconografico, S.A./Corbis; **550,** Inset, Bettmann/Corbis; Background, Bildarchiv der Osterreichische Nationalbibliothek; **551,** The Granger Collection; **552,** L, Victoria & Albert Museum/Art Resource; **552–553,** Bridgeman Art Library; Background, T, Russ Lappa; Background, B, Russ Lappa; **553,** Inset, L, John Heseltine/Corbis; Inset, M, Francis G; Mayer/Corbis; R, Dorling Kindersley; **554,** L, Kurpfalzisches Museum, Heidelberg, Germany/The Bridgeman Art Library; R, Museum of Tropinin and His Contemporaries, Moscow, Russia/Bridgeman Art Library; M, © Archivo Iconografico, S.A./Corbis; **556,** Background, © Archivo Iconografico, S.A./Corbis; TL, Zuma/Corbis; BL, Reuters/Corbis; **557,** L, The Granger Collection; R, The Granger Collection; **558,** Joe Sohm/Chromosohm/VOA; **559,** SuperStock, Inc.; **560,** L, National Portrait Gallery, Smithsonian Institution/Art Resource, NY; M, Art Resource; R, © The Corcoran Gallery of Art/CORBIS; **561,** Bridgeman Art Library; **562,** Background, The Granger Collection; **564,** Inset, Bettmann/Corbis; **564–565,** Bettmann/Corbis; **565,** Inset, L, Bettmann/Corbis; Inset, R, Hulton/Getty Images, Inc.; Background, T, Library of Congress; **566,** The Granger Collection; **567,** T, Steve Artley; B, British Library, London, UK/Bridgeman Art Library; **568,** R, Christie's Images/Corbis; L, The Granger Collection; **569,** Corbis

Chapter Eighteen
570–571, Giraudon/Art Resource, NY; **571,** T, Musee de L'Histoire Vivante, Montreuil, France, Archives Charmet/Bridgeman Art Library; M, Erich Lessing/Art Resource, NY; B, Scala/Art Resource, NY; **572,** T, Erich Lessing/Art Resource, NY; B, The Granger Collection, NY; **573,** Snark/Art Resource, NY; **574,** TR, Giraudon/Art Resource, NY; B, Musee de la Ville de Paris, Musee Carnavalet, Paris, France, Archives Charmet/Bridgeman Art Library; TL, Musee du Ranquet,

Clermont-Ferrand, France/Giraudon/Bridgeman Art Library; **575,** Musee Carnavalet, Paris, France, Lauros/Giraudon/Bridgeman Art Library; **576,** Background, Chateau de Versailles, France/Bridgeman Art Library; Inset, Giraudon/Art Resource, NY; **577,** Réunion des Musées Nationaux/Art Resource, NY; **578,** Réunion des Musées Nationaux/Art Resource, NY; **579,** (c) Judith Miller/Dorling Kindersley/Bill & Myrtle Aquilino; **580,** Background, Chateau de Versailles, France, Giraudon/Bridgeman Art Library; Inset, AKG Images; **583,** Giraudon/Art Resource, NY; **584,** Musee de la Ville de Paris, Musee Carnavalet, Paris, France, Giraudon/Bridgeman Art Library; **585,** The Art Archive/Bibliothèque des Arts Décoratifs Paris/Dagli Orti; **586,** Leonard de Selva/CORBIS; **587,** Giraudon/Art Resource, NY; **588,** L, Musee de la Ville de Paris, Musee Carnavalet, Paris, France, Giraudon/Bridgeman Art Library; R, The Art Archive/Musée Carnavalet Paris/Dagli Orti; M, Hulton Archive/Getty Images; **589,** TL, Hulton-Deutsch Collection/Corbis; BL, Musee de la Revolution Francaise, Vizille, France/Bridgeman Art Library; R, Max Alexander/Dorling Kindersley Media Library; **590,** T, British Library, London, UK/Bridgeman Art Library; B, Erich Lessing/Art Resource, NY; **591,** T, Réunion des Musées Nationaux/Art Resource, NY; B, Erich Lessing/Art Resource, NY; **592,** T, Scala/Art Resource, NY; B, Private Collection/Bridgeman Art Library; **593,** Giraudon/Art Resource, NY; **595,** Scala/Art Resource, NY; **596,** Musee des Beaux-Arts, Rouen, France Lauros/Giraudon/Bridgeman Art Library; **597,** Giraudon/Art Resource, NY; **598,** Bibliotheque Nationale, Paris, France, Archives Charmet/Bridgeman Art Library; **600,** Giraudon/Art Resource, NY; **601,** B, Anders Blomqvist/Lonely Planet Images; TL, Christie's Images/CORBIS; TR, © Sovfoto/Eastfoto; **602,** Cleveland Museum of Art; **603,** B, Private Collection/Bridgeman Art Library; T, © Riyadh Biji/Reuters/Corbis; **604,** R, The Fotomas Index; L, Giraudon/Art Resource, NY; **605,** Giraudon/Art Resource, NY

Chapter Nineteen
606–607, © NRM/Pictorial Collection/SSPL/The Image Works; **607,** T, National Railway Museum/Science and Society Picture Library; M, Bettman/CORBIS; B, Austrian Archives/CORBIS; **608,** NRM/SSPL/The Image Works; **609,** Time Life Pictures/Getty Images; **610,** Inset, Bettman/CORBIS; B, The Granger Collection, New York; **611,** photolibrary; **612,** L, Fine Art Photographic Library, London/Art Resource, NY; R, National Railway Museum/Sci-

ence and Society Picture Library; **613,** Science Museum/SSPL; **616,** Mary Evans Picture Library; **617,** Hulton Archive/Getty Images; **619,** T, Mary Evans Picture Library; B, Manchester Archives and Local Studies; **620,** Museum of London; **621,** Hulton-Deutsch Collection/CORBIS; **622,** Hulton-Deutsch Collection/CORBIS; **623,** B, The Granger Collection, New York; T, Fine Art Photographic Library/Art Resource, NY; **624,** L, Topham/The Image Works; R, The Stapleton Collection/Bridgeman Art Library; **626,** B, Austrian Archives/CORBIS; T, The Granger Collection, New York; **627,** T, J; Halaska/Photo Researchers, Inc.; B, Courtesy Judi Pinkham; **628,** L, akg-images; R, Mary Evans Picture Library; **629,** T, Peter Titmuss/Alamy; B, The Art Archive/Museo Historico Nacional Buenos Aires/Dagli Orti; **630,** NRM/Pictorial Collection/SSPL/The Image Works; **631,** Image Select/Art Resource, NY

Chapter Twenty
632–633, The Art Archive/Simon Bolivar Amphitheatre Mexico/Dagli Orti; **633,** T, Coleccion Museo Nacional de Columbia, Bogota; M, Musee des Tissus de Lyon/Pierre Verrier/Museum-Images 2003; BR, The Granger Collection, New York; **634,** Hadtorteneti Muzeum, Budapest, Hungary/Archives Charmet/Bridgeman Art Library International; **636,** R, Igor Ursic/Chancery of HRH Crown Prince Alexander/The Royal Palace in Belgrade; L, Igor Ursic/Chancery of HRH Crown Prince Alexander/The Royal Palace in Belgrade; **638,** R, Musée des Tissus de Lyon/Pierre Verrier/Museum-Images 2003; L, North Wind Picture Archive; **639,** Musee de la Ville de Paris, Musee Carnavalet, Paris, France, Lauros/Giraudon/Bridgeman Art Library; **640,** ullstein bild/The Granger Collection, New York; **641,** L, Private Collection, Archives Charmet/Bridgeman Art Library; M, ullstein bild/The Granger Collection, New York; R, Louvre, Paris, France/Bridgeman Art Library International; Background, ullstein bild/The Granger Collection, New York; **642,** Scala/Art Resource, NY; **643,** The Granger Collection, New York; **644,** B, HIP/Art Resource, NY; T, Musee du Petit Palais, Paris, France/Bridgeman Art Library International; **645,** L, The Art Archive/Museo Nacional Bogota/Dagli Orti; R, Coleccion Museo Nacional de Columbia, Bogota; **646,** Chateau de Versailles, France/Bridgeman Art Library International; **647,** Bettmann/CORBIS; **649,** TM, Bettmann/CORBIS; TL, The Granger Collection, New York; B, The Granger Collection, New York; TR, The Art Archive/Archaeological and Ethnological Museum

Quito Ecuador/Dagli Orti; **650,** The Art Archive/Miramare Museum Trieste/Dagli Orti (A); **651,** North Wind Picture Archives; **652,** North Wind Picture Archives; **653,** T, Reuters/Corbis; M, The Art Archive/Bibliothéque des Art Décoratifs Paris/Marc Charmet; B, Popular Book Co; Ltd; **654,** T, age fotostock/SuperStock; B, The Art Archive/Simon Bolivar; **655,** akg-images

Concept Connectors and Handbooks
664–665, Musée de la Tapisserie, Bayeux, France/www.bridgeman.co.uk; **664,** T, Archivo Iconographica, S.A./Corbis; BL, © Pascal Le Segretain/CORBIS SYGMA; **665,** Free Agents Limited/CORBIS; **680,** © Robert Frerck/Odyssey Productions, Inc.; **683,** Anders Blomqvist/Lonely Planet Images; **684,** T, Istituto Mazziniano/Museo Risorgimento, Genova; B, National Gallery of Art; **685,** Giraudon/Art Resource, NY; **687,** AP/Wide World Photos; **688,** Corbis; **689,** Rafiqur Rahman/Reuters America LLC; **690,** Lisa Knouse Braiman/Business Week; **692,** TL, The Granger Collection, NY; TR, A; Eaton/Ancient Art & Architecture Collection; MR, Comstock/SuperStock; ML, © Michael Holford; B, V&A Museum/Art Resource; **693,** TL, National Maritime Museum; TR, Time Life Pictures/Getty Images; MR, Mary Evans Picture Library/Photo Researchers, Inc.; ML, The Pierpont Morgan Library/Art Resource, NY; B, Museu de Marinha; **694,** TL, © Michael Holford; TR, Alfred Eisenstaedt/Time & Life Pictures/Getty Images; M, The Art Archive/Dagli Orti (A); B, © ScienceMuseum, London/HIP/The Image Works; **695,** T, Photo Researchers, Inc.; M, Getty Images; BR, ESA/Corbis; BL, Chris Sorensen Photography; **696,** © James Hill; **698,** TL, Versailles, châteaux de Versailles et de Trianon/RMN/Art Resource; BL, Giraudon/Art Resource, NY; R, Museum of Tropinin and His Contemporaries, Moscow, Russia/Bridgeman Art Library; **699,** TR, © Corbis; BL, © Dave Bartruff/CORBIS; BR, Peter Jordan/Network; **700,** T, Gunter Marx; B, The Granger Collection, New York; **702,** TL, Scala/Art Resource, NY; TR, © Fitzwilliam Museum, University of Cambridge, UK; BL, © Archivo Iconografico, S.A./CORBIS; BR, Erich Lessing/Art Resource, NY; **703,** TL, Art Resource/The Museum of Modern Art; TM, Copyright ARS, NY;/Art Resource, NY; TR, © Historical Picture Archive/CORBIS; B, ©, Jeff Greenberg/eStockPhoto

Text
Grateful acknowledgment is made to the following for copyrighted material:

ACT, Inc.
Excerpt from "Writing Test Scores" from www.act.org. Copyright © 2005 by Act, Inc. All rights reserved.

Anglo-Norman Text Society c/o Birkbeck College
Excerpt from "Test of Skill and Courage" from History of William Marshall, Volume I - Text & Translation (11. 1-10031) edited by A.J. Holden, with English translation by S. Gregory and historical notes by D. Crouch. © Anglo-Norman Text Society 2002. All rights reserved.

BBCi c/o BBC News Online
Excerpt "Black Death (Poem: "We see death coming…")" by Dr. Mike Ibeji from www.bbc.co.uk. British Broadcasting Corporation © 2002-2005.

The College Board
Excerpt from "Scoring Guide" from www.collegeboard.com. Copyright © 2005 collegeboard.com. All rights reserved.

Columbia University Press
Excerpts from Poem: "3 ("Refrain from exalting the worthy…")", "The Unitary Principle: Reciprocity of Humanity: 43." and "Government by Personal Virtue: 97." from Sources Of Chinese Tradition, Volume I compiled by WM. Theodore de Bary, et. al. Copyright © 1960 Columbia University Press. All rights reserved.

Doubleday A division of Random House, Inc.
Excerpt from "Ja Nus Hons Pris" by Richard the 1st of England from Warriors Of God, Richard The Lionheart And Saladin In The Third Crusade by James Reston, Jr. Copyright © 2001 by James Reston, Jr. All rights reserved.

The Free Press, A Division of Simon & Schuster, Inc.
Excerpts from "The Republic" by Plato from Greek Philosophy: Thales To Aristotle, Second Edition, Revised and Expanded edited by Reginald E. Allen. Copyright © 1966, 1985 by Reginald E. Allen. All rights reserved.

Gulliver Books, An Imprint of Harcourt, Inc.
Poem: "My belly is shoved up under my chin…" by Michelangelo from Living History: Italian Renaissance edited by John D. Clare. Text copyright © 1995, 1994 by John D. Clare. All rights reserved.

Harcourt, Inc.
Excerpt from "Julius Caesar: Act III" by William Shakespeare from Shakespeare: The Complete Works by G. B. Harrison, copyright © 1968 by Harcourt, Inc. and renewed 1980 by G. B. Harrison.

Henry Holt and Company, Inc.
Excerpt from "Aeneid" by Virgil (Publius Vergilius Maro) from The Classical Roman Reader, New Encounters With Ancient Rome edited by Kenneth J. Atchity. Copyright © 1997 by Kenneth J. Atchity. All rights reserved.

Houghton Mifflin Company
Poems: "Proudly stands the city of Mexico-Tenochtitlan…" and "There was then no sickness…" from Stolen Continents: The "New World" Through Indian Eyes by Ronald Wright. Copyright © 1992 by Ronald Wright.

Indiana University Press
Song: "Our homes and humble dwellings…" from The Mexican Corrido as a Source for Interpretive Study of Modern Mexico (1870–1950) by Merle E. Simmons. Copyright © 1957 by Merle E. Simmons.

Alfred A. Knopf, Inc., An imprint of Random House, Inc.
Excerpt from "Book Twenty: The Ranging of Powers" from The Iliad by Homer, translated by Robert Fitzgerald. Copyright © 1974 by Robert Fitzgerald. Excerpt from "Column VI" from Gilgamesh translated from the Sin-leqi-unninni version by John Gardner and John Maier, et. al. Copyright © 1984 by Estate of John Gardner and by John Maier. All rights reserved under International and Pan-American Copyright Conventions.

Oxford University Press, Inc.
Poem: "This is the common good, for the polis and the whole demos…" by Tyrtaeus of Sparta from Ancient Greece: A Political, Social, And Cultural History edited by Sarah B. Pomeroy, et. al. Copyright © 1999 by Oxford University Press, Inc. Excerpts from "The Sign of the Covenant, Genesis, Chapter 17, Verses 4-8", "The Ten Commandments, Exodus, Chapter 20, Verses 2–3", "The Divine Shepherd, Psalm 23, Verses 1–5", "The Beatitudes, Chapter 5, Verses 5–9" and "The Gift of Love, Chapter 13, Verses 1–13" from The Holy Bible With The Apocrypha, Revised Standard Version, published by Oxford University Press, Inc. Revised Standard Version of the Bible, Old Testament Section, Copyright 1952; New Testament Section, First Edition, Copyright 1946; Second Edition © 1971 by Division of the Christian Education of the National Council of the Churches of Christ in the United States of America. Copyright © 2002 by Oxford University Press, Inc. All rights reserved.

Penguin Books, Ltd.
Excerpts from "Prologue" from The Canterbury Tales by Geoffrey Chaucer, translated into Modern English by Nevill Coghill. Copyright © 1951 by Nevill Coghill. Copyright © Nevill Coghill, 1958, 1960, 1975, 1977. Excerpts from "2:177" and excerpt "96.1" from The Koran, With A Parallel Arabic Text translated with Notes by N.J. Dawood. Copyright © N.J. Dawood, 1956, 1959, 1966, 1968, 1974, 1990, 1993, 1994, 1995, 1998, 2000. All rights reserved. The moral right of the translator has been asserted.

The University of Chicago Press
Excerpt from "Antigone" by Sophocles from Greek Tragedies, Volume I edited by David Grene and R. Lattimore. Copyright © 1954 by The University of Chicago Press. Excerpts from "The Edicts of Asoka" from The Edicts Of Asoka by N.A. Nikam and Richard McKeon. © 1959 by The University of Chicago. Excerpt from "57.1, The Descent of the First Generations" from The Mahabharata, 1: The Book Of The Beginning translated and edited by J.A.B. van Buitenen. © 1973 by The University of Chicago. All rights reserved.

University of California Press, Inc.
Excerpt from "The Bronze Horseman" by Alexander Pushkin, translated by Waclaw Lednicki from Waclaw Lednicki, Pushkin's Bronze Horseman (Berkeley, CA: University of California Press, 1955).

The Arthur Waley Estate
Excerpts "Book II: 2., 13. and 17" from The Analects Of Confucius by Confucious, translated and annotated by Arthur Waley. First Vintage Books Edition, August 1989. All rights reserved under International and Pan-American Copyright Conventions.

Warner/Chappell Music, Inc., A Division of Warner Brothers Music
Excerpt from "Brother Can You Spare a Dime?" lyrics by E.Y. Harburg & Jay Gorney. Copyright Warner Bros., Inc

W. W. Norton & Company, Inc.
Excerpt from "On Cruelty and Clemency: Whether It Is Better to Be Loved or Feared" by Niccolo Machiavelli from The Prince: A Norton Critical Edition, Second Edition translated by Robert M. Adams. Translation copyright © 1992, 1977 by W.W. Norton & Company, Inc. Excerpt from "176." from The Song of Roland, translated by Frederick Goldin. Copyright © 1978 by W.W. Norton & Company, Inc. All rights reserved.

Note: Every effort has been made to locate the copyright owner of material reprinted in this book. Omissions brought to our attention will be corrected in subsequent editions.

Connect to history

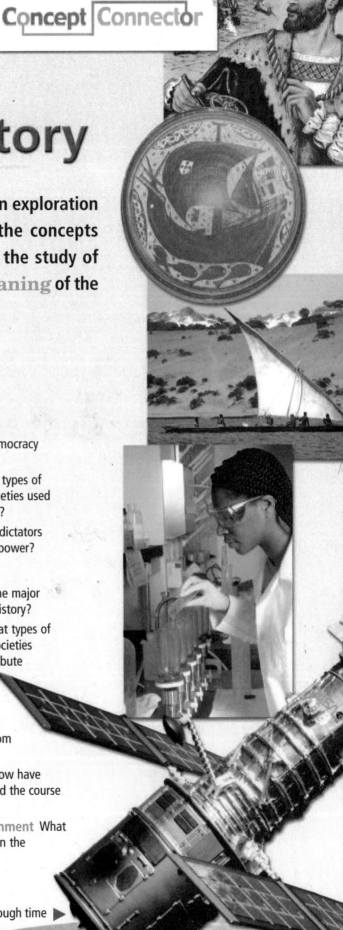

History is more than a chronology of facts. It is an exploration of big ideas across time and place. Using the concepts below will help you understand and enjoy the study of history by connecting with the drama and meaning of the human experience.

Explore these concepts to make valuable connections to history.

History

Empire What factors allow empires to rise and cause them to fall?

Cooperation In what ways have groups or countries cooperated over time?

Conflict What issues cause peoples or countries to come into conflict?

Revolution Why have political revolutions occurred?

Nationalism How have people used nationalism as a basis for their actions?

Genocide What factors have led peoples or governments to commit genocide?

Culture

Cultural Diffusion In what ways have migration and trade affected cultures?

Belief Systems What major belief systems have emerged over time?

Science & Technology

Science How has science changed people's lives throughout history?

Technology How has technology affected human development?

Government

Democracy How has democracy developed over time?

Political Systems What types of political systems have societies used to govern and create laws?

Dictatorship How have dictators assumed and maintained power?

Economics

Trade What have been the major trade networks in world history?

Economic Systems What types of economic systems have societies used to produce and distribute goods and services?

Geography

Migration Why do large groups of people move from one place to another?

Geography's Impact How have geographic factors affected the course of history?

People and the Environment What impact have people had on the environment?

Science and technology through time ▶